ISSN 0732-1864

ℝ

Volume 80

Nineteenth-Century Literature Criticism

Topics Volume

Excerpts from Criticism of Various
Topics in Nineteenth-Century Literature,
including Literary and Critical Movements,
Prominent Themes and Genres, Anniversary
Celebrations, and Surveys of National Literatures

Suzanne Dewsbury
Editor

GALE GROUP

Detroit
San Francisco
London
Boston
Woodbridge, CT

This book is printed on acid-free paper that meets the minimum requirements of American National Standard for Information Sciences—Permanence Paper for Printed Library Materials, ANSI Z39.48-1984.

Library of Congress Catalog Card Number 84-643008
ISBN 0-7876-3151-5
ISSN 0732-1864
Printed in the United States of America

10 9 8 7 6 5 4 3 2 1

Contents

Preface vii

Acknowledgments xi

Preface

Since its inception in 1981, *Nineteenth-Century Literature Criticism* has been a valuable resource for students and librarians seeking critical commentary on writers of this transitional period in world history. Designated an "Outstanding Reference Source" by the American Library Association with the publication of its first volume, *NCLC* has since been purchased by over 6,000 school, public, and university libraries. The series has covered more than 300 authors representing 29 nationalities and over 17,000 titles. No other reference source has surveyed the critical reaction to nineteenth-century authors and literature as thoroughly as *NCLC*.

Scope of the Series

NCLC is designed to introduce students and advanced readers to the authors of the nineteenth century, and to the most significant interpretations of these authors' works. The great poets, novelists, short story writers, playwrights, and philosophers of this period are frequently studied in high school and college literature courses. By organizing and reprinting commentary written on these authors, *NCLC* helps students develop valuable insight into literary history, promotes a better understanding of the texts, and sparks ideas for papers and assignments. Each entry in *NCLC* presents a comprehensive survey of an author's career or an individual work of literature and provides the user with a multiplicity of interpretations and assessments. Such variety allows students to pursue their own interests; furthermore, it fosters an awareness that literature is dynamic and responsive to many different opinions.

Every fourth volume of *NCLC* is devoted to literary topics that cannot be covered under the author approach used in the rest of the series. Such topics include literary movements, prominent themes in nineteenth-century literature, literary reaction to political and historical events, significant eras in literary history, prominent literary anniversaries, and the literatures of cultures that are often overlooked by English-speaking readers.

NCLC continues the survey of criticism of world literature begun by Gale's *Contemporary Literary Criticism (CLC)* and *Twentieth-Century Literary Criticism (TCLC)*, both of which excerpt and reprint commentary on authors of the twentieth century. For additional information about *TCLC, CLC,* and Gale's other criticism series, users should consult the Guide to Gale Literary Criticism Series preceding the title page in this volume.

Coverage

Each volume of *NCLC* is carefully compiled to present:

- criticism of authors, or literary topics, representing a variety of genres and nationalities
- both major and lesser-known writers and literary works of the period
- 4-8 authors or 4-6 topics per volume
- individual entries that survey critical response to an author's work or a topic in literary history, including early criticism to reflect initial reactions, later criticism to represent any rise or decline in reputation, and current retrospective analyses.

Organization

An author entry consists of the following elements: author heading, biographical and critical introduction, list of principal works, excerpts of criticism (each preceded by a bibliographic citation and an annotation), and a bibliography of further reading.

- The **Author Heading** consists of the name under which the author most commonly wrote, followed by birth and death dates. If an author wrote consistently under a pseudonym, the pseudonym will be listed in the author heading and the real name given in parentheses on the first line of the biographical and critical introduction. Also located at the beginning of the introduction to the author entry are any name variations under which an author wrote, including transliterated forms for an author whose language uses a nonroman alphabet.

- The **Biographical and Critical Introduction** outlines the author's life and career, as well as the critical issues surrounding his or her work. References are provided to past volumes of *NCLC* in which further information about the author may be found.

- Most *NCLC* entries include a **Portrait** of the author. Many entries also contain reproductions of materials pertinent to an author's career, including manuscript pages, title pages, dust jackets, letters, and drawings, as well as photographs of important people, places, and events in an author's life.

- The list of **Principal Works** is chronological by date of first publication and identifies the genre of each work. In the case of foreign authors with both foreign-language publications and English translations, the English-language version is given in brackets. Unless otherwise indicated, dramas are dated by first performance, not first publication.

- **Criticism** in each author entry is arranged chronologically to provide a perspective on changes in critical evaluation over the years. All titles of works by the author featured in the entry are printed in boldface type to enable the user to easily locate discussion of particular works. Also for purposes of easier identification, the critic's name and the publication date of the essay are given at the beginning of each piece of criticism. Unsigned criticism is preceded by the title of the journal in which it appeared. Publication information (such as publisher names and book prices) and some parenthetical numerical references (such as page and line references to specific editions of works) have been deleted at the editors' discretion to provide smoother reading of the text. Footnotes that appear with previously published pieces of criticism are reprinted at the end of each essay or excerpt. In the case of excerpted criticism, only those footnotes that pertain to the excerpted text are included.

- A complete **Bibliographic Citation** provides original publication information for each piece of criticism.

- Critical excerpts are prefaced by **Annotations** providing the reader with a summary of the critical intent of the piece. Also included, when appropriate, is information about the critic's reputation, individual approach to literary criticism, and particular expertise in an author's works, as well as information about the relative importance of the critical excerpt. In some cases, the annotations cross-reference excerpts by critics who discuss each other's commentary.

- An annotated list of **Further Reading** appearing at the end of each entry suggests secondary sources on the author. In some cases it includes essays for which the editors could not obtain reprint rights.

Cumulative Indexes

- Each volume of *NCLC* contains a cumulative **Author Index** listing all authors who have appeared in Gale's Literary Criticism Series, along with cross-references to such biographical series as *Contemporary Authors* and *Dictionary of Literary Biography*. Useful for locating authors within the various series, this index is particularly valuable for those authors who are identified with a certain period but who, because of their death dates, are placed in another, or for those authors whose careers span two periods. For example, Fyodor Dostoevsky is found in *NCLC*, yet Leo Tolstoy, another major nineteenth-century Russian novelist, is found in *TCLC* because he died after 1899.

- Each *NCLC* volume includes a cumulative **Nationality Index** which lists all authors who have appeared in *NCLC*, arranged alphabetically under their respective nationalities.

- Each new volume in Gale's Literary Criticism Series includes a cumulative **Topic Index**, which lists all literary topics treated in *NCLC, TCLC, LC 1400-1800*, and the *CLC* Yearbook.

- Each new volume of *NCLC*, with the exception of the Topics volumes, contains a **Title Index** listing the titles of all literary works discussed in the volume. In response to numerous suggestions from librarians, Gale has also produced a **Special Paperbound Edition** of the *NCLC* title index. This annual cumulation lists all titles discussed in the series since its inception. Additional copies of the index are available on request. Librarians and patrons have welcomed this separate index: it saves shelf space, is easy to use, and is recyclable upon receipt of the following year's cumulation. Titles discussed in the Topics volume entries are not included in the *NCLC* cumulative index.

Citing *Nineteenth-Century Literature Criticism*

When writing papers, students who quote directly from any volume in Gale's Literary Criticism Series may use the following general forms to footnote reprinted criticism. The first example pertains to material drawn from periodicals, the second to material reprinted from books:

[1]Kim McQuaid, "William Apes, Pequot: An Indian Reformer in the Jackson Era," *The New England Quarterly*, 50 (December 1977), 605-25; excerpted and reprinted in *Nineteenth-Century Literature Criticism*, Vol. 73, ed. Janet Witalec (Farmington Hills, Mich.: The Gale Group, 1999), pp. 3-4.

[2]Richard Harter Fogle, *The Imagery of Keats and Shelley: A Comparative Study* (Archon Books, 1949); excerpted and reprinted in *Nineteenth-Century Literary Criticism*, Vol. 73, ed. Janet Witalec (Farmington Hills, Mich.: The Gale Group, 1999), pp. 157-69.

Suggestions Are Welcome

In response to suggestions, several features have been added to *NCLC* since the series began, including annotations to excerpted criticism, a cumulative index to authors in all Gale literary criticism series, entries devoted to criticism on a single work by a major author, more illustrations, and a title index listing all literary works discussed in the series.

Readers who wish to suggest authors, single works, or topics to appear in future volumes, or who have other suggestions, are cordially invited to write: The Editors, *Nineteenth-Century Literature Criticism*, The Gale Group, 27500 Drake Rd., Farmington Hills, MI 48331-3535; call toll-free at 1-800-347-GALE.

Acknowledgments

The editors wish to thank the copyright holders of the excerpted criticism included in this volume and the permissions managers of many book and magazine publishing companies for assisting us in securing reproduction rights. We are also grateful to the staffs of the Detroit Public Library, the Library of Congress, the University of Detroit Mercy Library, Wayne State University Purdy/Kresge Library Complex, and the University of Michigan Libraries for making their resources available to us. Following is a list of the copyright holders who have granted us permission to reproduce material in this volume of *NCLC*. Every effort has been made to trace copyright, but if omissions have been made, please let us know.

COPYRIGHTED EXCERPTS IN *NCLC*, VOLUME 80, WERE REPRODUCED FROM THE FOLLOWING PERIODICALS:

American Quarterly, v. XXXVIII, Fall, 1976. Copyright 1976, American Studies Association. Reproduced by permission of The Johns Hopkins University Press.—*Éire-Ireland*, v. XV, Summer, 1980; v. XVII, Spring, 1982. Copyright © 1980, 1982 Irish American Cultural Institute. Both reproduced by permission of the publisher.—*The French Review*, v. LVI, May, 1983. Copyright 1983 by the American Association of Teachers of French. Reproduced by permission.—*The Irish Monthly*, v. LVIII, July, 1930 for "Two Forgotten Irish Novelists" by Louis Lachal, S. J.—*The Markham Review*, v. 8, Fall, 1978. © Wagner College 1978. Reproduced by permission.—*Nineteenth-Century Fiction*, v. 37, June, 1982 for "What is 'Sensational' about the 'Sensation Novel'?" by Patrick Brantlinger. © 1982 by the Regents of the University of California. Reproduced by permission of the publisher and the author.—*The Quarterly Journal of Speech*, v. 58, October, 1972 for "Plays, Well-Constructed and Well-Made" by Patti P. Gillespie. Copyright © 1974 by the Speech Communication Association. Used by permission of the National Communication Association and the author.—*Research Studies*, v. 40, September, 1972 for "'A Thirst for Empire': The Indian Captivity Narrative as Propaganda" by Richard VanDerBeets. Reproduced by permission of the author.—*Victorian Studies*, v. XIX, March, 1976. © The Trustees of Indiana University 1976. Reproduced by permission of the Trustees of Indiana University.—*The Wordsworth Circle*, v. X, Autumn, 1979. © 1979 Marilyn Gaull. Reproduced by permission of the editor.

COPYRIGHTED EXCERPTS IN *NCLC*, VOLUME 80, WERE REPRODUCED FROM THE FOLLOWING BOOKS:

Altick, Richard D. From *Deadly Encounters: Two Victorian Sensations*. University of Pennsylvania Press, 1986. Copyright © 1986 by the University of Pennsylvania Press. All rights reserved. Reproduced by permission of the author.—Burnham, Michelle. From *Captivity & Sentiment: Cultural Exchange in American Literature, 1682-1861*. University Press of New England, 1997. © 1997 by the Trustees of Dartmouth College. All rights reserved. Reproduced by permission of the University Press of New England.—Castiglia, Christopher. From *Bound and Determined: Captivity, Culture-Crossing, and White Womanhood from Mary Rowlandson to Patty Hearst*. The University of Chicago Press, 1996. © 1996 by The University of Chicago. All rights reserved. Reproduced by permission of the publisher and the author.—Cronin, John. From *Gerald Griffin (1803-1840): A Critical Biography*. Cambridge University Press, 1978. © Cambridge University Press 1978. Reproduced by permission of Cambridge University Press and the author.—Dunne, Tom. From "Fiction as 'The Best History of Nations': Lady Morgan's Irish Novels" in *The Writer*

to *Narratives of North American Indian Captivity: A Selective Bibliography*. By Alden T. Vaughan. Garland Publishing, Inc., 1983. © 1983 Alden T. Vaughan. All rights reserved. Reproduced by permission.

PHOTOGRAPHS AND ILLUSTRATIONS APPEARING IN *NCLC*, VOLUME 80, WERE RECEIVED FROM THE FOLLOWING SOURCES:

A title page for *Plot and Passion* by Tom Taylor, 1853, photograph. The Department of Rare Books and Special Collections, The University of Michigan Library. Reproduced by permission.—A title page for *Richelieu; or, The Conspiracy: A Play in Five Acts* by Edward Bulwer-Lytton, London, Published by Saunders and Otley, 1889, photograph. The Department of Rare Books and Special Collections, The University of Michigan Library. Reproduced by permission.—Carleton, William, photograph. Sean Sexton; Sean Sexton Collection/Corbis. Reproduced by permission.—Charles Reade, photograph of a painting by Charles Mercier. By courtesy of the National Portrait Gallery, London. Reproduced by permission.—Collins, William Wilkie, photograph. The Library of Congress.—Rowson, Susanna, engraving. Archive Photos, Inc. Reproduced by permission.—Sharp, Joseph Henry, illustrator. From a cover of *The Last of the Mohicans*, by James Fenimore Cooper. Bantam Books, 1989. Reproduced by permission of Bantam Books, a division of Bantam Doubleday Dell Publishing Group, Inc.

The Irish Novel

INTRODUCTION

The nineteenth-century Irish novelist wrote during a time of tremendous political, religious, and class tension, and all these matters found their way into the Irish novel. Shortly after an unsuccessful 1798 rebellion aimed at eliminating English rule in Ireland, the Act of Union (1800) yoked together the Irish and English parliaments, although Catholics were denied representation in this newly-joined government body until 1829. Ireland's nineteenth-century population was divided into two primary classes: the land owning, Protestant class with strong ties to England, and the peasant, Catholic class with deep Gaelic roots. Irish novelists, beginning with Maria Edgeworth (1768-1849) in 1800, rose out of and wrote about these two Irish classes. Edgeworth and her predecessors all attempted in some way to define, describe, illuminate, or explain Irish character, a national identity, contemporary socio-political issues, and Irish history, and more often than not their writing was targeted at a largely English audience. Critics such as J. C. Beckett and Thomas Flanagan note that the Irish novel was weakened by the conflict within Irish novelists who were attempting to make their writing appealing and interesting to English tastes and at the same time to avoid undercutting or betraying their country's national identity and values or their own sense of "Irishness."

With the publication of *Castle Rackrent* in 1800, Maria Edgeworth was the first Irish author to write, in English, a novel focusing on Irish characters and Irish themes. Born into the land-owning class and educated in England, Edgeworth at age 15 returned to Ireland and helped her father run their family estate. Like many critics, O. Elizabeth McWhorter Harden praises Edgeworth's powers of observation and her careful depiction of "provincial life and manners." Harden goes on to observe that in *Castle Rackrent,* Edgeworth presents an example for later writers to follow in her "respectful" representation of the Irish peasantry. According to Harden, *Castle Rackrent* is also the first "saga" novel, in that it follows the history of one family through several generations. In addition to these developments in content and form, *Castle Rackrent* is the first novel in which the point of view is that of a detached, minor character, told in the first person. While Harden praises this point of view in *Castle Rackrent,* critics such as William Howard argue that the novel's narrator is so extreme in his loyalty to the Rackrent family and that his personal eccentricities are such that

his ability to serve as a "regional spokesman" is impaired. Howard contends that in this novel, Edgeworth's own upper class life and values were too far removed from that of the narrator for Edgeworth to successfully represent his social and racial biases. Howard argues that in Edgeworth's later novel, *Ormond* (1814), Edgeworth chooses a more appropriate narrative point of view and that in this novel, the gulf between Edgeworth's own views and those of the native Irish are revealed.

While Sydney Owenson, later Lady Morgan (1776-1859), was not born with the privileges of Edgeworth, as the daughter of an Irish actor and a Protestant English mother she had access to the upper echelons of Irish society. Of one of her most popular novels, *The Wild Irish Girl* (1806), J. C. Beckett comments that the English audience who made the novel so popular "was even more ignorant of the realities of Irish rural life than the author herself." Despite such criticisms, critics such as Colin B. Atkinson and Jo Atkinson observe that Morgan's novels emphasize sympathy and reconciliation between England and Ireland, Protestant and Catholic. In fact, Atkinson and Atkinson demonstrate, all Morgan's Irish novels feature the union of a Protestant with a Catholic. Similarly, Tom Dunne argues that while Morgan's novels are chastised for their frivolity and flamboyance, the author realistically depicts the conflict between two competing interpretations of Irish history and character.

Unlike Edgeworth and Morgan, Charles Lever (1806-72) gained little popularity with Irish audiences. He was born and raised in Ireland to English parents, and his writings are primarily concerned with the gentry. Lewis Melville observes that while English audiences viewed novels such as *The Confessions of Harry Lorrequer* (1839) and *Charles O'Malley, the Irish Dragoon* (1840) as humorous depictions of fun-loving Irishmen, Irish readers felt that Lever caricatured his countrymen and perpetuated cultural stereotypes.

Although Edgeworth and Morgan arguably presented fairer characterizations of the middle and lower Irish classes than did Lever, they nevertheless were in a position of observing these classes from the outside. In discussing Edgeworth's *Ormond,* William Howard observes that during the nineteenth century, the prevalent Romantic belief was that human nature was best understood and observed in the life and character of society's lower classes. While this presented a difficulty for Edgeworth and Morgan, novelists such as John

Banim (1798-1842) and Michael Banim (1796-1874), Gerald Griffin (1803-40), and William Carleton (1794-1869) had an advantage.

The Banim brothers were sons of a middle class farmer and shopkeeper, and they intimately knew and understood the difficulties faced by the Irish peasantry. Louis Lachal argues that in the novels that formed the *Tales by the O'Hara Family* series, the Banims portray the negative characteristics of the peasantry—including ignorance, poverty, and cruelty—as the result of the persecution, both religious and political, that this class had suffered for so many years at the hands of English Protestants. Lachal also demonstrates that the Banim brothers attempted to present the more noble and generous characteristics of the Irish peasantry as well.

Like the Banims, Gerald Griffin was born into a middle-class Catholic family, his father being a brewer in Limerick. Horatio Sheafe Krans characterizes Griffin's depiction of the rural middle class Irish life in novels such as *The Collegians* (1829) and *The Rivals* (1829) as "sober, decorous, prudent, domestic." Krans also observes that like the Banims' writings, Griffin's works reflect his strong Catholic sympathies. Likewise, John Cronin finds in Griffin's work a vigorous interest in and sympathy for the deplorable conditions suffered by the Irish peasantry. Cronin maintains that even though Griffin's work is flawed by melodrama, sometimes in the form of absurd plot construction, novels such as *The Rivals* and *Tracy's Ambition* (1829) demonstrate Griffin's power to realistically portray rural Irish life and its implicit religious and class conflict. Additionally, Cronin argues that Griffin's portrayal of the Irish peasantry is a bit more soft and gentle than that of the Banim brothers.

The Irish novelist to rise from the depths of the country's lowest class, William Carleton was the son of Irish-speaking peasant tenants. Like Griffin, he gleaned an education from rural "hedge-schools," and the proper education of peasants became a theme in his writings. Benedict Kiely reviews the critical comparison of Carleton to Sir Walter Scott, commenting that in Scott's outsider view of the peasantry, the Scottish author was often "altruistic or antiquarian" in his portrayal, compared to Carleton who was so intimately knowledgeable about the lives and struggles of the peasantry. John Kelly surveys Carleton's treatment of the problems of the Irish peasantry, noting that in novels such as *Art Maguire* (1845), *Valentine M'Clutchy* (1845), *The Black Prophet* (1847), and *The Emigrants of Ahadarra* (1848), Carleton examines such issues as alcoholism, Protestant bigotry, famine and the problem of absentee landlords, and the flight of the Irish from their homeland. Kelly studies the influence of Ireland's cultural conflicts and political and religious strife on Carleton's writings. In discussing Carleton's later conversion to Protestantism, Kelly finds evidence in *The*

Black Prophet that speaks to Carleton's growing interest in Protestant theology. Despite some critical backlash regarding Carleton's conversion, many modern critics agree that Carleton remains one of the greatest of the Irish fiction writers not only of the nineteenth-century, but of all of Ireland's history.

REPRESENTATIVE NOVELS

John Banim
 The Boyne Water 1826
 The Last Baron of Crana 1826
 The Conformists 1829
 The Nowlans 1826

Michael Banim
 Crohoore of the Bill-Hook 1825
 The Croppy 1828

John and Michael Banim
 Tales by the O'Hara Family (three series) 1825, 1826, 1829

William Carleton
 Fardorougha the Miser 1839
 Art Maguire 1845
 Parra Sastha 1845
 Rody the Rover 1845
 Valentine M'Clutchy 1845
 The Black Prophet 1847
 The Emigrants of Ahadarra 1848
 The Tithe Proctor 1849

Maria Edgworth
 Castle Rackrent 1800
 Ennui 1809
 The Absentee 1812
 Ormond 1814

Gerald Griffin
 The Collegians 1829
 The Rivals 1829
 Tracy's Ambition 1829
 The Invasion 1832

Sheridan Le Fanu
 The Cock and Anchor 1845
 Torlough O'Brien 1847

Charles Lever
 The Confessions of Harry Lorrequer 1839
 Charles O'Malley, The Irish Dragoon 1840
 Jack Hinton, the Guardsman 1842
 The Martins of Cro'Martin 1847

Sydney Owenson, Lady Morgan
 The Wild Irish Girl 1806

O'Donnell. A National Tale 1814
Florence Macarthy. An Irish Tale 1818
The O'Briens and the O'Flahertys. A National Tale
1827

OVERVIEWS

Maurice Harmon (essay date 1967)

SOURCE: "Irish Literature, 1800-1890: Introduction," in *Modern Irish Literature 1800-1967,* Dufour Editions, 1967, pp. 11-14.

[*In the following essay, Harmon offers an outline of nineteenth-century Irish literature, noting the ways in which the novels of the time period reflected the socio-political structure of the country.*]

Irish writing in this period can be divided into three main categories—novels, poetry and scholarship. Little of what was produced is of interest to the critic; it appeals mainly to the literary and cultural historian. Yet, no student of Irish Literature since 1890 can ignore the nineteenth century background. The writers of the Literary Rivival (1890-1920) were frequently anxious to discover whatever was usable in their literary past and their creation of a distinctive and valuable literature was made possible in large measure by the weaknesses and strength of what their predecessors had written.

The literature of 1800-1890 was bound up with the question of national identity, which included issues of culture, race, religion and politics. Unlike their European and British counterparts, the novelists tried to find social identity through nationality, race and religion; they generally ignored issues of social choice and personal morality. The poets were even more attached to nationalistic interests and the folklorists, editors and scholars, whose work runs all through the period, hoped to create a sense of national identity by revealing the nature of the cultural heritage.

Their country was divided into two main classes; the Anglo-Irish were the owners of the land, Protestant, English-speaking, and drawn to English literature, history and culture; the 'native' Irish were peasants, Catholic, Gaelic-speaking, and drawn to Gaelic traditions and loyalties. But beneath this general division lay a chaos of classes, creeds, aspirations and loyalties. Not unexpectedly the novelists sought to define their contemporary society by relating it to the past from which so much of their political and social life had come. Their explanatory impulses were further determined by their self-consciousness in relation to England. Knowing how remote Irish life was to England, they felt obliged to interpret it, to inform about it, to act as advocates on its behalf, and were defensive about their own particular knowledge of it. This propagandistic aim seriously undermined the artistic merit of their novels. Yet our understanding of nineteenth century Ireland would be incomplete without their fictional re-creation of its complex and stratified culture.

Two of these novelists deserve special consideration. Maria Edgeworth wrote with considerable skill of her own Anglo-Irish landlord class. Her four Irish novels study its fortunes in a perceptive manner. *Castle Rackrent,* in particular, judges their lack of responsibility and their abuse of power. The book is memorable as an indictment of a class and as a finely wrought novel. William Carleton, the other major fiction writer of the period, wrote with authority and intimacy of peasant life. A peasant by birth, the son of Gaelic-speaking parents, he had wide experience of his own class. He was taught by hedge schoolmasters, travelled the countryside as a poor scholar, went to Lough Derg as a pilgrim, tried for the priesthood, and joined a secret, extremist society. His *Traits and Stories of the Irish Peasantry* deals with the realities of peasant life with unequalled vividness and feeling.

The poets were also conscious of national needs. Writing sometimes for *The Nation,* a newspaper devoted specifically to the creation of a national consciousness, they sought to awaken the spirit of Irish nationality in all sections of the country. On the whole, their work has little literary merit, except for an occasional poem or ballad that anthologies retain. But they did make people conscious of the cultural and historical past and, in their search for a distinctive native manner, tried to escape the stress patterns of English poetry by imitating the rhythms of native music, poetry and speech. Yeats rightly singled out Davis, Mangan and Ferguson as part of a poetic tradition to which he also belonged. Thomas Davis was the intellectual leader of the poets of the 1848 period, as Yeats was of the later Revival. He was deeply involved with nationalistic issues and his poetry suffered as a result, but he did exemplify the moral value of a cultural consciousness. James Clarence Mangan was not usually dominated by patriotic motives. Helped by prose translations from the Gaelic by the scholars O'Donovan, O'Curry and Petrie he wrote a number of fine lyrics. He is the best poet of his period. Samuel Ferguson, a scholar and poet, whose work carries the literary movement forward to the early days of the Revival, was the first to make poetic use of the old legends and stories, setting thereby an example not lost upon his successors.

The work of the many scholars, editors, translators, collectors and folklorists is of importance not only in the development of Irish scholarship but in the establishment of a national literary tradition. Without them it is unlikely that modern Irish literature could have built up its vital relationships with native folklore and culture, with Gaelic literature of the seventeenth and eighteenth century, and with the great heritage of epic, saga, legend, mythology, history and poetry of Celtic and medieval Ireland. They provided source material and imaginative stimulus for poets, dramatists and novelists and generated an interest in the native heritage in those directly responsible for the creation of the Revival. Standish O'Grady, Douglas Hyde, Lady Gregory and W.B. Yeats were profoundly influenced by their work and were in turn collectors and interpreters of the heritage.

The publication of Standish O'Grady's *History of Ireland: Heroic Period* (1878) might well be taken as the starting point of the Revival. Frequently acclaimed by its leaders as the father of the new movement, O'Grady gave imaginative intensity to Irish history and legend. Going beyond the orthodox scholarship of his predecessors, he identified with the epic heroes and sought to reconstruct the life of the past. Close to his work in importance was that of Douglas Hyde and of George Sigerson. Their collections of Gaelic poetry in English translation made frequent use of Gaelic metrical forms—internal rhyme, alliteration, consonance, assonance and syllabic verse. Hyde, in particular, with his scheme of parallel versions of the same poems, was the first to show the value of Irish peasant speech, using it in both his poetic translations and prose commentaries. Together with Lady Gregory in her germinal *Gods and Fighting Men* and *Cuchulain of Muirthemne,* Hyde made possible the effective use of the native idiom in drama, poetry and prose. Yeats's debt to the scholars and collectors is too immense to be summed up here. Significantly, he began his career with critical assessments of Carleton, *The Nation* poets, Ferguson, and with gleanings from what previous folklorists had gathered. His interest and indebtedness to the whole range of nineteenth century literary output and to what he found there of ancient and medieval Ireland would in themselves justify one's interest in this period.

Thomas Flanagan (essay date 1987)

SOURCE: "The Nature of the Irish Novel," in *Family Chronicles: Maria Edgeworth's* Castle Rackrent, ed. by Cóilín Owens, Wolfhound Press, 1987, pp. 41-51.

[*In the following essay, Flanagan argues that nineteenth-century Irish novels were all written, to some degree, with a propagandist goal of explaining or defending Ireland or the Irish character to an English audience; Flanagan contends that this was the weakest feature of the Irish novel.*]

Nineteenth-century Ireland[1] was a land splintered by divided loyalties and ancient hatreds. Sir Walter Scott, visiting the country in 1825, noted with some contempt: "Their factions have been so long envenomed, and they have such narrow ground to do their battle in, that they are like men fighting with daggers in a hogshead."[2] Much later Yeats, writing as an Irishman and in bitterness, would make the same point:

> Out of Ireland have we come.
> Great hatred, little room,
> Maimed us at the start.
> I carry from my mother's womb
> A fanatic heart.[3]

One is tempted to seize upon these quotations as epigraphs to a study of Irish fiction, for most Irish novels accept as given the condition to which they point. The English novelist was concerned with social choice and personal morality, which are the great issues of European fiction. But to the Irish novelist these were subordinated to questions of race, creed, and nationality—questions which tend of their nature to limit the range and power of fiction. Yet for the Irishman these were the crucial points by which he was given social identity.

If the social pattern was much more various than is generally supposed, the popular notion of a dual society, the masters and the ruled, has a large measure of truth. On one side stood "native" Ireland. It had become a nation of peasants, fiercely Catholic, indifferent or hostile to statute law, Gaelic-speaking or at least heavily influenced by the traditions of Gaelic society, nourished by dark and sanguinary resentments and aspirations. On the other side stood the nation of the Anglo-Irish, land-owning, Protestant, and, of course, English-speaking. Though this nation aspired, intermittently, to political independence, in point of fact, its culture and its modes of thought were indisputably English.

The Irish novelists, being men of their generation, realized that the two nations were yoked in a common fate, that despite all hatreds and blood-letting they would have to endure each other. And yet, when all the fair words had been spoken, each writer would find himself pledged to his own people. Maria Edgeworth might reach gropingly, in her last novels, to Gaelic Ireland, but she remained a lady of the Big Houses, anxious for peace, but for peace upon the terms imposed by the Big Houses. And Gerald Griffin, for all the liberality of his sentiments, was haunted by his vision of that older Ireland which existed before the Big Houses, and which remained incarnate in the shattered Norman keeps of the Geraldines. Each novelist was forced to pose to himself the question of what Ireland was and of what it meant to be an Irishman. From tensions of this kind the Irish novels derive their strength.

The Irish novelist, like any writer, was quarrelling with himself and with his culture. A special and distinguishing circumstance obtained, however. The quarrel was addressed, in the first instance, not to his own people but to strangers, and it was usually couched in the language of explanation. That is to say, most of the Irish novels were addressed to an English audience, and most of them offered to explain and interpret the sister kingdom. The supposed "editor" of the history of *Castle Rackrent* places his story "before the English reader as a specimen of manners and characters, which are perhaps unknown in England. Indeed the domestic habits of no nation in Europe were less known to the English than those of their sister country, till within these few years."[4] Nor is this novel an exception; of the fiction which we shall be considering, only the early stories of William Carleton were written directly for an Irish audience. And Carleton's stories, when collected and published as a book, were preceded by a note in which the author acknowledged the English reading public as his probable audience.[5]

This circumstance had a decisive effect upon the aims and purposes of the Irish novel. Numberless prefaces, forewords, and introductions make the same tedious avowal of intentions. Ireland, so much statements may be summarized, is for the first time to be represented "as it really is," and in a spirit free of religious and political rancour. Lady Morgan, an inveterate offender in this regard, tells us in the preface to *O'Donnel* that her tale is devoted to "the purposes of conciliation, and to incorporate the leaven of favourable opinion with that heavy mass of bitter prejudice, which writers, both grave and trifling, have delighted to raise against my country."[6] She assures us in the preface to *Florence Macarthy* that her aim throughout her career has been "to sketch the brilliant aspect of a people struggling with adversity, and by the delineation of national virtues, to excite sympathy, and awaken justice."[7] Griffin and Carleton, better and less didactic writers, make similar avowals. And since Richard Lovell Edgeworth, who supplied the introductions to his daughter's novels, was a professional moralist, his remarks may be entrusted to the reader's imagination.

The "editor" of *Castle Rackrent* spoke sober truth: the English reader knew less of Ireland than he did of most European countries. What little he did know was unpleasant. Some hideous insurrection would remind him of its existence, or a reckless Ascendancy duellist would cause a day's gossip. The Act of Union, however, made Ireland a matter of direction concern, and the English public was soon burdened with the rumours of agrarian outrage and armed conspiracies which had hitherto been swallowed by the silences of Dublin Castle. Then, in the eighteen twenties, the mass agitation for the removal of the Penal Laws gave evidence of what was to become a recurrent problem: Ireland's ability to provoke a parliamentary crisis.

There was a general desire for information about Ireland, and an interest in the nature of Irish society.

Novels were then considered proper vehicles of such information, and writers rushed into print with accounts of "Ireland today." Orange novelists like the aptly named George Brittaine came forward with sombre chronicles of brutish priest-ridden peasants held in check by a devout garrison of British Christians. Catholic writers like John Banim replied in kind. And liberal Protestants attempted a judicious adjustment of the two extreme positions—a task which was to find more favour in English than in Hibernian eyes. The atmosphere was charged with political passions, and every Irish writer, no matter how far removed he may have been from such concerns, knew that his picture of Ireland would be scanned for its political overtones.

Nor was Catholic Emancipation the only issue which could enmesh the novelist in controversy. The peasant question, the questions of land and of absenteeism are all represented in the novels of the period. All of these, however, came to be overshadowed, in the final decade of the half century, by the single issue of the repeal of the Act of Union, which would mean, of course, the restoration of Irish nationality. The Edgeworths were supporters of the Union, although Richard Lovell, for reasons peculiar to his temperament, had cast his vote against it in the Irish Parliament. And Ireland's claim to nationhood is the chief theme in Lady Morgan's fiction. The issue became one of wide public concern, however, only with the revival of O'Connell's agitation and with the founding of *The Nation* in 1842.

Thus the Irish novel, in one of its aspects, can be termed a kind of advocacy before the bar of English public opinion. In plot and in characterization it often served the interests of special pleading. Maria Edgeworth's scrupulous landlords, venal agents, and irresponsible peasants, like John Banim's oppressed and unwilling rebels and conspirators, are too carefully posed for the vindication of a thesis to constitute a representation of Ireland "as it really was." This propagandistic bent of the Irish novel is its weakest point. That it performed successfully the services of propaganda is doubtful. Very likely the contrasting and conflicting images of Ireland cancelled each other out. The major writers, however much they may have differed, saw Irish experience as being essentially tragic, and this is the one view which English readers were not prepared to accept. The reading public much preferred the Ireland of Charles Lever—an enchanting and dowdy land of *dolce far niente,* in which dashing dragoons and impoverished fox hunters held genial sway over a mob of feckless rustics.

Irish novels were invariably reviewed by British journals on the assumption that they had been written to please English taste or to shape English opinion. John Wilson Croker's slashing attacks upon Lady Morgan in the pages of *The Quarterly Review* were inspired by his fear of the damage which her novels might do to the high-Tory position which claimed his own slippery allegiance. Similarly it was to England that the Irish writer looked for critical judgment.

In only a few instances, such as Carleton's remarks upon the novels of Banim and Lever, Thomas Davis's review of Carleton's own work, or an occasional article in *The Dublin University Magazine,* is criticism from contemporary Irish sources relevant or important.

The dependence of Irish writers on an English audience did not seem at all exceptionable. London, after all, was indisputably the intellectual and literary capital of the British Isles. The problem, rather, is to define the sense in which their work may properly be called Irish. This problem, which is enmeshed in old and barren controversies and clouded over by doctrinaire political and cultural assumptions, inevitably confronts the student of the literature of nineteenth-century Ireland.

Irishmen, to be sure, had made generous contributions to the literature of the two preceding centuries—Swift, Congreve, Farquhar, Sheridan, Goldsmith, and Burke were all Irish. Except for Swift, however, who in this as in all things is a law unto himself, the fact of Irish birth is irrelevant to their accomplishments. Children of the English garrison, they took quick and natural root in English soil. The attempts which have been made to trace out an "Ango-Irish"—let alone a "Celtic"—strain in their writings are quite unconvincing.[8] Goldsmith's friends, it is true, made a standing joke of his Irish background, and his transformation of a Roscommon village into "sweet Auburn" presents us with a literary oddity. And Burke, who was descended from one of the old Norman families and whose mother was a Roman Catholic, possessed a familiarity with Irish affairs which was to stand him in good stead. But Sheridan's Irish birth we are likely to remember only because of his name and because he was in the habit of tossing a stage-Irishman into his plays. As for Congreve—we accept the fact with mild incredulity. The same might be said of the century's only Irish novelist, Henry Brooke, the author of *The Fool of Quality* (1765-70).

There did exist in the eighteenth century a literature which was indisputably Irish—the poetry of the Gaelic hedge writers, who had inherited the traditions of Gaelic letters as fully as had Goldsmith those of English poetry. This literature was "hidden"—to employ Daniel Corkery's evocative phrase—but it was not unknown. Goldsmith himself glimpsed Turlough O'Carolan, "the last of the bards," and recorded his impressions in a brief essay.[9] It was a dying tradition, however, and might have perished without record had it not been for the retentive memory of the peasantry and the devoted labours of a few amateurs from within the garrison itself. But the development of an interest among members of the Ascendancy in the literature of the older

Ireland is discussed at greater length in Chapter Eight, and need not be anticipated here. It will suffice, for the moment, to realize that high walls of language and caste separated the two cultures of eighteenth-century Ireland. Nor were these the only barriers. Brian Merriman's brilliant poem, *The Midnight Court,* is remarkable as much for the sophistication as for the antiquity of its traditional form.[10]

A single incident may bring the issue close to our own subject. In 1805 Arthur O'Neill, old and blind, sat dictating the story of his life to a clerk named Tom Hughes, who served the M'Cracken family of Belfast. O'Neill was one of the last of the race of Irish harpers, and his attachments were to that aristocratic world of the Gael which had almost vanished.

"When dinner was announced," he says, speaking of an assemblage some sixty years before, "very near a hundred of the O's and Macs took their seats. My poor self being blind, I did what blind men generally do, I groped a vacancy near the foot of the table. Such a noise arose of cutting, carving, roaring, laughing, shaking hands, and such language as generally occurs between friends, who only see each other once a year. While dinner was going on, I was hobnobbed by nearly every gentleman present. When Lord Kenmare hobnobbed me, he was pleased to say, 'O'Neill, you should be at the head of the table, as your ancestors were the original Milesians of this kingdom.' "[11]

Behind the darkened eyes of Art O'Neill, an old man talking out his life to a clerk of the family upon whose charity he depended, the Gaelic world lived and glowed in the bright colours of heraldry. This is not surprising, for in his youth he had had another patron—Murtough Oge O'Sullivan, the half-legendary swordsman of Fontenoy and the Kerry coast. And he had crossed the sea in 1745 to play at Holyrood before Charles Edward Stuart, the "saviour and deliverer" of the Munster poets. Indeed, it has been supposed that he was present when the Irish lords met to decide whether they would risk one last throw of the dice on the Jacobite cause.[12]

O'Neill, who like all the Gaelic artists was proud to the point of snobbishness, naturally sought out the hospitality of those few titled O's and Macs who had survived the penal legislation, but he could be sure of a welcome in many a Protestant Big House. In this fashion, amicably but with little real understanding on either side, the two cultures touched one another. One such Big House is of particular interest to us. "Always," O'Neill says, "on my return from the Granard Balls, I stopped at Counsellor Edgeworth's of Edgeworthstown, where I was well received."[13] In this house . . . the first and perhaps the finest of Irish narratives was written.

The "Granard Balls," which in fact were harp competitions, were held for three years running, beginning in 1781. When Lady Morgan was writing *The Wild Irish Girl,* she gathered a certain amount of information concerning the famous harpers, which she incorporated in the footnotes of that curious novel. Richard Lovell Edgeworth read the novel when it appeared in 1806, and it stirred a dim and inaccurate memory. "I believe that some of the harpers you mention were at the Harpers' Prize Ball at Granard in 1782 or 1783. One female harper, of the name of Bridget, obtained the second prize; Fallon carried off the first. I think I have heard the double-headed man."[14]

In Lady Morgan's misty imagination the harpers and bards trailed clouds of Ossianic grandeur—an attitude which Edgeworth would have called damned folly. Edgeworth was a generous man, in his brisk, hard-tempered fashion, and Art O'Neill was surely received with kindness. But O'Neill was one in an endless stream of mendicants who came to the gates of the Big House at Edgeworthstown—harpers, pipers, pilgrims, prophecymen, fiddlers. This stream troubled Edgeworth's orderly mind and stirred his conscience, but it never touched his imagination. But then neither did O'Neill truly see "the Counsellor," as he calls Edgeworth, since every gentleman must have a title, and "the Major" or "his Reverence" or "his Lordship" did not apply.

Between these two men of the eighteenth century—the friend of Murtough Oge O'Sullivan and the friend of Erasmus Darwin—there could be no communication. Maria Edgeworth shared, in part, her father's impatience with the world which Art O'Neill represented. In the pages of *The Absentee* she deals satirically with life at Kilpatrick House, which was everything that Art O'Neill expected a Big House to be—festive, improvident, and swarming with retainers and "follyers." But if she knew little of his Ireland and cared less, she understood the moral life of her own caste with an artist's piercing, intuitive understanding. Out of her knowledge she created *Castle Rackrent.*

With this novel a tradition begins, for it is the first fictional narrative of Irish life to be written in the English language. The writers who followed Maria Edgeworth display an equal concern with the Irish scene. Are their novels to be called Irish or English or, by way of ambiguous compromise, Anglo-Irish?

Douglas Hyde dismisses them in magisterial fashion from his *Literary History of Ireland,* telling us that he has "abstained altogether from any analysis or even mention of the work of Anglicised Irishmen of the last two centuries. Their books, as those of Farquhar, of Swift, of Goldsmith, of Burke, find, and have always found, their true and natural place in every history of *English* literature that has been written, whether by Englishmen themselves or by foreigners."[15] And it is true that the nineteenth-century Irish writers have found a place in English literature, but whether, like Farquhar and Goldsmith, they have found their true and natural place is another matter. In most such histories they are to be found huddled together, a worried Hibernian band, with Marryat and Surtees pressing them hard from one side and "The Imitators of Scott" from the other.

Hyde is perfectly justified in excluding them from his own work, for he is writing the history of "the literature produced by the Irish-speaking Irish." But his statement remains somewhat disingenuous, for the point upon which he insisted throughout his distinguished career was that only the literature of the "Irish-speaking Irish" was truly Irish. To the Gaelic enthusiasts of Hyde's generation Ireland's English-language literature was in every way deplorable. It was committed to the representation of Irish life in alien and unassimilable forms, and it had resigned itself to a humiliatingly "colonial" status. In its attempts to "explain" and to "show" Ireland, it was inevitably defensive in tone and attitude.

The argument rested upon false assumptions, for a culture must be judged by what it is and does, not by what it *should* be doing. If Irish culture is to be defined by the Gaelic language, we must conclude that when the last of the hedge poets died, Ireland ceased to have a culture. Long before the Church and O'Connell cast the heavy weight of their authority on the side of English, and long before famine and emigration had thinned the ranks of Irish-speakers, it had become clear that such literary and intellectual life as Ireland possessed would find expression in English.

There is no strong reason why we should not join Professor Corkery in calling this literature Anglo-Irish. And there remains considerable point to the questions which he addresses to it:

> The answer to the question: Is there an Anglo-Irish literature? must depend on what regard we have for what Synge spoke of as collaboration—without, perhaps, taking very great trouble to explore his own thought. The people among whom the writer lives, what is their part in the work he produces? Is the writer in the people's voice? Has there ever been, can there be, a distinctive literature that is not a national literature? A national literature is written primarily for its own people: every new book in it—no matter what its theme—foreign or native—is referable to their life, and its literary traits to the traits already established in its literature. The nation's own critical opinion of it is the warrant of life or death for it. Can Anglo-Irish, then, be a distinctive literature if it is not a national literature? And if it has not primarily been written for Ireland, if it be impossible to refer it to Irish life for its elucidation, for its continued existence or non-existence be independent of Irish opinion—can it be a national literature?[16]

Professor Corkery, as the reader may have inferred, is an extreme cultural nationalist, and is happiest when a work of art is Gaelic, patriotic, Catholic, and puritanical (though the latter two terms are, in the Irish context, interchangeable). Fortunately, the brilliant accomplishments of modern Irish writers have not depended for a warrant of life or death upon the official opinion of the Republic of Ireland. The warrant for the continued existence of Yeats and Joyce and Synge is in the keeping of the republic of letters, which is at once more just and more generous.

Corkery, has, however, defined somewhat inadvertently the anomalous status of the Irish literature of the nineteenth and twentieth centuries. It is a literature which has never been able to depend for its existence on Irish opinion; only rarely has it been written primarily for its own people; more rarely still has it drawn upon "traits" established in the literature. And yet it is a literature rooted in Irish life and experience, a literature which often forces us to turn for elucidation to the thought and culture of Ireland.

Whether a body of literature which must be defined in these terms may properly be called national, whether it should be spoken of as Irish or as Anglo-Irish or as Colonial are questions which might be set forth at greater length, but not, I think, with much profit. Speaking of "that literature which had no existence until towards the end of the eighteenth century," Corkery says: "In our youth and even later it used always to be spoken of as Irish literature: and this custom old-fashioned folk have not yet given up: to them, Thomas Moore's *Melodies* are still Irish Melodies."[17] I have chosen to follow the practice of these old-fashioned folk. For one thing, they seem to have an old-fashioned preference for accuracy: *Irish Melodies* is the title which Moore, however mistakenly, gave to his work. It is also true that the word "Anglo-Irish" has slippery political and social connotations. If Maria Edgeworth belonged by class and allegiance to the Anglo-Irish, Gerald Griffin most certainly did not.

The novels of nineteenth-century Ireland were always spoken of as Irish, and we may accept the term with a full and clear understanding of what it meant. To be sure, we must also bear in mind implications which were not then clear. We have a deeper sense now of the interdependence of language and culture. We can appreciate that much which was rich and various, much which was uniquely Irish perished when Gaelic fell into disuse. O'Connell, in a remark which the Gaelic League would later make notorious, said that "although the Irish language is connected with many recollections that twine round the hearts of Irishmen, yet the superior utility of the English tongue, as the medium of all modern communications, is so great that I can witness without a sigh the gradual disuse of Irish."[18] We may agree with the judgement and

yet wonder if he realized how final a sentence he was passing on much that he cherished.

We must also bear in mind the validity of certain of Corkery's strictures. A literature which seeks to vindicate and justify the culture from which it draws its being labours under a heavy burden. (Although one which announces truculently that its heroism, suffering, and ineffable purity place it beyond the need of vindication bears a much heavier one.) When these have been taken into proper account, however, and when the limitations and particular merits of each novelist have been recognised, it becomes clear that the major Irish novelists were engaged upon a subtle and profound study of a complicated and self-contradictory society.

Notes

[1] From *The Irish Novelists: 1800-1850* (New York: Columbia U P, 1959), chapter 3, 35-46. Reprinted with the permission of the author and Columbia University Press.

[2] John Gibson Lockhart, *Life of Sir Walter Scott, Bart,* 2nd ed. 12 vols. (Edinburgh, 1839) 8:25.

[3] "Remorse for Intemperate Speech," *Collected Poems of William Butler Yeats* (New York: Macmillan, 1976) 249.

[4] *Castle Rackrent* 96-97.

[5] David J. O'Donoghue, preface, First Series of William Carleton, *Traits and Stories of the Irish Peasantry,* 4 vols. (Dublin, 1886) 1:xxiv-xxvi.

[6] Lady Morgan, *O'Donnel: A National Tale,* 3 vols. (London, 1814) 1:x.

[7] Lady Morgan, *Florence Macarthy: An Irish Tale,* 4 vols. (London, 1863) 1:vi.

[8] See, for example, William O'Brien, *Edmund Burke as an Irishman* (Dublin: Gill, 1924).

[9] Oliver Goldsmith, "Carolan," *Miscellaneous Writings,* ed. John Prior, 4 vols. (New York, 1850) 4:208-10.

[10] It has been put into admirable English verse: *The Midnight Court: A Rhythmical Bacchanalia from the Irish of Bryan Merryman,* tr. Frank O'Connor (Dublin: Fridberg, 1945).

[11] "The Memoir of Arthur O'Neill" was first published in full by Charlotte Milligan Fox, *Annals of the Irish Harpers* (London: Smith, Elder, 1911) 137-87. Samuel Ferguson had drawn upon material from the manuscript in preparing the notes to

the 1840 edition of Bunting's *Ancient Musick of Ireland.* The passage quoted appears in *Annals* 147.

[12] *Annals* 146n.

[13] *Annals* 178.

[14] *Lady Morgan's Memoirs: Autobiography, Diaries, and Correspondence,* ed. W. Hepworth Dixon, 2nd ed., 2 vols. (London, 1863) 2:293.

[15] Hyde, *A Literary History of Ireland* (New York: Scribner's, 1899) ix.

[16] Daniel Corkery, *Synge and Anglo-Irish Literature* (Dublin & Cork: Cork U P) 2.

[17] Corkery 2.

[18] W. J. O'Neill Daunt, *Personal Recollections of Daniel O'Connell,* 2 vols. (London: Chapman, 1848) 1:15.

PRINCIPAL FIGURES

Hugh Alexander Law (essay date 1926)

SOURCE: "Early Nineteenth Century Novelists," in *Anglo-Irish Literature,* 1926, pp. 171-200.

[*In the following essay, Law surveys the novels written by the most prominent nineteenth-century Irish authors and comments on the strengths and weaknesses of these authors' major works.*]

Poetry—there can be no doubt about it—even minor poetry, wears far better than any but the greatest prose; and of all forms of prose-writing none, as is natural enough, is so affected by changing fashions as is the work of the novelist. One can still get a deal of pleasure from the verses of quite minor bards of the eighteenth and early nineteenth centuries. But of the far more numerous prose-writings of that period few survive. How many portly histories, how many sermons full of learned quotations from Greek and Latin authors and bound in solid calf, have mouldered to dust or are to be found thrown contemptuously into the sixpenny boxes of the second-hand booksellers! Old letters and diaries, indeed—the uncared for fruit of leisure hours—retain their interest, revealing as they do, and that in exact proportion as they are the less studied, the intimate thoughts and doings of our forefathers. But of all the novels that so delighted Miss Lydia Languish and her successors does a poor dozen remain readable at this day? Lady Mary Wortley Montague once declared "This Richardson is a strange

fellow. I heartily despise him, and eagerly read him, nay, sob over his works in the most scandalous manner." Modern novel-readers are little likely to follow Lady Mary in either respect, for the simple reason that not one in a thousand has ever read a line of *Clarissa Harlowe, Pamela* or *Sir Charles Grandison,* notwithstanding that Dr. Johnson declared *Clarissa* to be "the first book in the world for its knowledge of the human heart."

These remarks are perhaps not altogether impertinent to the consideration of the next group of Anglo-Irish writers, the novelists of the first half of the nineteenth century. Of these Maria Edgeworth is, perhaps deservedly, the most esteemed. Like her English and Scottish rivals, Jane Austen and Susan Ferrier, she has plenty of quiet humour, and, when content to observe rather than moralise, a real gift for characterisation. Mr. Yeats has gone so far as to call her, writing (it is true) some years ago, "the one serious novelist coming from the upper classes in Ireland, and the most finished and famous produced by any class there." Both parts of the verdict might perhaps be the subject of appeal; but as a first hand and an agreeable witness of the ways of a vanished society, Miss Edgeworth can be studied to great advantage. Sir Walter Scott's tribute (in the postscript to the first edition of *Waverley*) has often been quoted:—

> It has been my object to describe those persons, not by caricatured and exaggerated use of the national dialect, but by their habits, manners and feelings; so as in some distant degree to emulate the admirable Irish portraits drawn by Miss Edgeworth; so different from the "Teagues" and "dear joys," who so long, with the most perfect family resemblance to each other, occupied the drama and the novel.

To suggest a rivalry with Scott, even on Scott's own generous testimony, would be a poor service to Maria Edgeworth. It is enough for her fame that she was the first considerable writer frankly to take the manners of the Irish countryside as the theme of a novel.

Her father, Richard Lovell Edgeworth, of an old family settled at Edgeworthstown in County Longford, was a man of much force of character and of decidedly individual opinions. He differed from the patriot party in the Irish Parliament, in believing a Union to be for the advantage of Ireland; yet refused all ministerial solicitations, and voted against Castlereagh's Bill, for the eccentric reason that he took the majority of his countrymen to be averse from it. Moreover, in the management of his estate, he followed the unheard-of course of making no distinction between Catholic and Protestant tenants. During his lifetime he was his daughter's constant literary critic, and to his interference is commonly attributed the didactic trend of much of her work.[1]

Maria Edgeworth was fifteen years of age when the family came to reside permanently at Edgeworthstown, "too old," it has been well remarked, "for the unembarrassed friendship with all neighbours, rich and poor, that is the priceless heritage of Irish country life."

It was some compensation for this loss that from the first her father, who always refused to allow agents or bailiffs to stand between him and his tenants, made her his lieutenant in the ordering of his estate. Thus she gained a firsthand knowledge of the economy of the countryside and of the virtues and failings, the feelings, opinions, habits and wants of its inhabitants to an extent not often granted to a daughter of the Big House. In each of her Irish novels, the Land Question, in one form or another, is the main subject of the piece; nor will anyone who can remember the Ireland even of the later eighteen-seventies blame her for making so much turn on the character of landowners and their agents. Her second great interest (which, also, she owed to her father, a disciple of Rousseau) lay in the principles of education, understanding by that term not merely formal instruction, but also and chiefly the ordering of mind and character. Of Miss Edgeworth, in her character of instructor of youth, Mr. Ruskin has declared: "There's no one whose every page is so full and so delightful; no one who brings you into the company of pleasanter or wiser people; no one who tells you more truly how to do right."

Castle Rackrent, the first of Miss Edgeworth's Irish stories, was published in 1800. It is in effect a not unkindly satire upon the vices and follies of a certain kind of landowner which, though the authoress insists she is dealing with a bygone phase of manners, not only existed plentifully in her own day, but for many a day to come. Here, as elsewhere in her novels the principal personages are types rather than individuals. Thus we have Sir Patrick the inventor of raspberry whiskey, Sir Murtagh the great lawyer, "with a lawsuit for every letter of the alphabet," Sir Kit the rake and spend-thrift, and Sir Condy, a good, easy man who "could never be brought to hear of business, but still put it off, saying, 'settle it anyhow,' or 'bid 'em call again to-morrow, or speak to me about it some other time.' " The fortunes of the house are recounted by Old Thady, steward to the three last baronets, and father to Attorney Jason Quirk, whom the follies of its owners and his own cunning are presently to establish in possession of the Rackrent estate. A short quotation or two will give some notion of his method of narration. Poor Sir Condy, Thady's own favourite, has come to the end of his tether. His lady's dowry is spent, and things are at such a pass that there is not even turf to be had for love or money. The inevitable Jason relieves the present distress, getting Sir Condy of course tighter into his clutches. But the money thus obtained is soon dispersed in election expenses and fine living in Dublin. After a series of domestic

quarrels, Lady Rackrent goes back to her own people; and Jason Quirk forecloses on his mortgage.

"The very next day, being too proud, as he said to me, to stay an hour longer in a house that did not belong to him," Sir Condy moves into the small house just vacated by Jason. "And the next morning it came into my head to go, unknown to anybody, with my master's compliments, round to many of the gentlemen's houses, whom he and my lady used to visit, and people that I knew were his great friends and would go to Cork to serve him any day in the year, and I made bold to try to borrow a trifle of cash from them. They all treated me very civil for the most part, and asked a great many questions very kind about my lady and Sir Condy, and all the family, and were greatly surprised to hear from me that Castle Rackrent was sold and my master at the Lodge for his health; and they all pitied him greatly, and he had their good wishes, if that would do, but money was a thing they unfortunately had not any of them at this time to spare. I had my journey for my pains, and I, not used to walking, nor supple as formerly, was greatly tired, but had the satisfaction of telling my master, when I got to the Lodge, all the civil things said by high and low."

Thus we come to the last scene in this tragi-comedy. Deserted by wife and boon-companions, Sir Condy consoles himself with the thought that his humbler neighbours must still have a great respect for him and the family. Therefore he sets his mind on seeing his own funeral before he dies. A mock wake is arranged.

"And there was a great throng of people, men, women and childer, and there being only two rooms at the Lodge, except what was locked up full of Jason's furniture and things, the house was soon as full as it could hold, and the heat, and smoke, and noise wonderful great; and standing amongst them that were near the bed, but not thinking at all of the dead, I was startled by my master's voice from under the great coats that had been thrown all on top, and I went close, no one noticing. 'Thady,' says he, 'I've had enough of this; I'm smothering, and can't hear a word of all they're saying of the deceased.' 'God bless you, and be still and quiet,' says I, 'a bit longer, for my shister's afraid of ghosts and would die on the spot with fright, was she to see you come to life all of a sudden this way without the least preparation.' So he lays him still, though well-nigh stifled, and I made all haste to tell the secret of the joke, whispering to one and t'other, and there was a great surprise, but not so great as we had laid out it would. 'And aren't we to have the pipes and tobacco, after coming so far to-night?' said some; but they were all well enough pleased when his honour got up to drink with them, and sent for more spirits from a shebean-house, where they very civilly let him have it upon credit. So the night passed off very merrily, but to my mind Sir Condy was rather upon the sad order in the midst of it all, not finding there had been such a great talk about himself after his death as he had always expected to hear."

A few days later Sir Condy is waked in earnest. "He had," ends Thady, "but a very poor funeral after all."

Never again, though a careful and industrious writer, was Miss Edgeworth to write anything so good as this first of her Irish books. The remainder of them appeared at fairly long intervals during the next seventeen years—*The Essay on Irish Bulls* (a collaboration with her father) in 1802, *Ennui* in 1809, *The Absentee* in 1812, *Ormond* in 1817. Thereafter she appears to have renounced Irish themes. Like most of her class at that time she hated and feared O'Connell and, doubtless even more than most of her fellows, sorrowed over the estrangement effected by the Catholic Relief and Repeal agitations between that class and the mass of the people. This is not to say that she dismissed Ireland from her thoughts. Much the greater part of her adult life was spent at Edgeworthstown; and in the crisis of the Great Famine she wrote to the Prime Minister, Lord John Russell, proposing certain measures of relief, which he refused to entertain. Her last book, *Orlandino* (1847), was written in furtherance of Father Mathew's temperance movement.

Of *Ennui* and *The Absentee* all that need be said here is that they are variations upon themes very dear to the heart of the Edgeworths—the duties of landowners and the ruin in which both they and their people are involved when they desert their country homes for life in more fashionable centres. In each the hero is a young man, Irish born but English bred, who returns to his country after long absence and finds happiness in coming to see that "if it was in the power of any man to serve the country which gave him bread, he ought to sacrifice every inferior consideration and to reside where he could be most useful."

In *Ennui* we catch a glimpse of the events of '98, of which Miss Edgeworth had had personal experience in her youth; in *The Absentee*, of Dublin after the Union, of which her description differs considerably from the accounts more commonly received. In both books she turns her knowledge of estate management to excellent account; and if both are somewhat affected as works of art by that love of "triste utilité" which Madame de Stael found in her work, they are at least the more valuable as historical documents. The worst that can be said of them is that, anyone not interested in the Land Question (and who has not been in Ireland, down to our own day?) will hardly find the tales particularly enthralling, and that her chief characters are usually dull dogs. Yet the puppets have a curious trick of suddenly coming to life, as when Lady Clonbrony in *The Absentee* after being proof against the most urgent considerations of duty and self interest, is suddenly

reconciled to life in Ireland by the prospect of getting rid of "the yellow damask furniture" at Clonbrony Castle.

> "Oh, return, let us return home!" cried Miss Nugent with a voice of great emotion. "Return, let us return home! My beloved aunt, speak to us; say that you will grant our request." She knelt beside Lord Colambre as she spoke. Is it possible to resist that voice—that look? thought Lord Colambre.
>
> "If anybody knew," said Lady Clonbrony, "if anybody could conceive how I detest the sight, the thoughts of that yellow damask furniture in the drawing-room at Clonbrony Castle—" . . .
>
> "The furniture in this house—" said Miss Nugent, looking round.
>
> "Would do a great deal towards it, I declare," cried Lady Clonbrony, "that never struck me before, Grace, I protest; and what would not suit, one might sell or exchange here. It would be a great amusement to me, and I should like to set the fashion of something better in that country. And I declare now, I should like to see those poor people, and the Widow O'Neill. I do assure you, I think I was happier at home; only that one gets—I don't know how—a notion that one's nobody out of Lon'on. But after all, there's many drawbacks in Lon'on, and many of the people are very impertinent, I'll allow; and, if there's a woman I could hate, it is Mrs. Dareville; and if I was leaving Lon'on, I should not regret Lady Langdale neither; and Lady St. James is as cold as a stone. . . . . Eh—let me see; Dublin—the winter, Merrion Square new furnished; and the summer, Clonbrony Castle—"

Perhaps it is partly contrast with the stilted style of most of the dialogue that makes this irresistible. But, anyhow, there's no denying it is very human comedy.

In *Ormond* again, while Sir Ulick O'Shane seems to exist only in order that the author may paint in darker colours than before the miseries of a man who neglects duty and forfeits his honour in pursuit of a seat in Parliament and government favour, we have in his cousin, "King Corny," a lively, sympathetic and convincing portrait of one of those landowners of the old stock who, notwithstanding their faults and failings, were deservedly beloved by the people round them. Excellent too are some of the quite minor characters. Take, for example, Mrs. McCrule. Ormond is anxious to get a small friend into a charitable institution. The boy is a Catholic, and the worthy Mrs. McCrule, "foreseeing that Ireland would be ruined if little Tommy should prove the successful candidate," comes to remonstrate with Ormond and Lady Annaly.

> "And there's no telling or conceiving," pursued Mrs. McCrule, "how in the hands of a certain party, you

know, ma'am, anything now, even the least and most innocent child (not that I take it upon me to say that this child is so very innocent, though, to be sure, he is very little)—but innocent or not, there is positively nothing, Lady Annaly, ma'am, which a certain party, certain evil-disposed persons, cannot turn to their purposes."

"I cannot contradict that—I wish I could," said Lady Annaly.

"But I see your ladyship and Miss Annaly do not consider this matter as seriously as I could wish. 'Tis an infatuation," said Mrs. McCrule, uttering a sigh, almost a groan for her ladyship's and her daughter's infatuation. "But if people, ladies especially, knew half as much as I have learned, since I married Mr. McCrule, of the real state of Ireland; or if they had but half a quarter as many means as I have of obtaining information, Mr. McCrule being one of his Majesty's very active justices of the peace, riding about, and up and down, ma'am, scouring the country, sir, you know, and having informers, high and low, bringing us every sort of intelligence; I say, my dear Lady Annaly, ma'am, you would, if you only heard a hundredth part of what I heard daily, tremble—your ladyship would tremble from morning till night."

Mrs. McCrule's portrait must surely have been drawn from a living model. Vivid sketches of the sort are not rare in Miss Edgeworth's novels; but it might be argued with a good deal of force that she is really at her best, not in the works designed for publication, but in her private letters. Here, free from the responsibility of pointing a moral, she is all compact of shrewdly humorous observation. What, for instance, could be more entertaining than the description she gives, in a letter dated March 8, 1834, of a recent visit to County Galway? Or where, within its limits, is there a better picture of the West of Ireland before the Famine had made light hearts heavy and quenched the fire on so many hearthstones of gentle and simple? Some change there had been, indeed, since the late owner of Ballynahinch, Dick Martin—"Hair-trigger Dick," from the fighting of innumerable duels, "Humanity Martin" as author of the first Act for the prevention of cruelty to animals—ruled the trackless wilds of Connemara. Power now was something short of absolute. But the traditional feeling lingered, as we can see from Miss Edgeworth's portrait of Mary Martin, the only child of the house, with her prodigious acquirements—"she has more knowledge of books, both scientific and learned, than any female creature I ever saw or heard of at her age"—and prodigious pride.

"One morning we went with Miss Martin to see the fine green Connemara marble-quarries. Several of the common people gathered round while we were looking at the huge blocks; these people Miss Martin called

her *tail.* Sir Culling wished to obtain an answer to a question from some of the people, which he desired Miss Martin to ask for him, being conscious that in his English tone it would be unintelligible. When the question had been put and answered, Sir Culling objected: 'But Miss Martin you did not put the question exactly as I desired you to state it.' 'No,' said she, with colour raised and head thrown back, 'no, because I knew how to put it so that my people could understand it. *Je sais mon métier de reine.*' "

Poor young Queen! But a few years were to pass before her pride was to be sadly humbled, the Martins to go down, like so many more of the old gentry, in a gallant struggle to feed "their people," and she herself to die in poverty and exile.

Mr. Stephen Gwynn, in a delightful volume of essays entitled, *Irish Books and Irish People,* seems to deny to Charles Lever that personal observation of contemporary manners with which he justly credits Maria Edgeworth. It is, of course true that the best known of Lever's books, *The Confessions of Harry Lorrequer,* and *Charles O'Malley the Irish Dragoon,* treat of a time either preceding or immediately following his birth in 1806; but a like criticism might be made of *Ormond,* whose visit to Paris is indicated as occurring "during the latter years of Louis the Fifteenth." So far as his campaigning tales are concerned, Lever certainly did not lack first-hand authorities; for, when he wrote, many of those who had served in the French war were still alive—notably his friend, William Hamilton Maxwell, author of *Stories of Waterloo,* and of *Wild Sports of the West,* the latter still interesting as a highly coloured but probably not inaccurate picture of County Galway during the first quarter of the nineteenth century. Moreover, among Lever's acquaintances were certainly many survivors of the old duelling, hard-drinking squires, and some who had personal experience of the later years of Grattan's Parliament.

> I was living, he says in the preface to a new edition of *Harry Lorrequer,* in a very secluded spot when I formed the idea of jotting down these stories, many of them heard in boyhood, others constructed out of real incidents that had occurred to my friends in travel, and some again—as the adventures of Trevanion and the French duellist for example— actual facts well known to many who had formed part of the army of occupation in France. To give what consistency I might to a mass of incongruous adventure, to such a variety of strange situations befalling one individual, I was obliged to imagine a character, which probably my experiences—and they were not very mature at the time—assured me as being perfectly possible; one of a strong will and a certain energy, rarely persistent in purpose and perpetually the sport of accident, with a hearty enjoyment of the pleasure of the hour, and a very reckless indifference to the price to be paid for it. If I looked out on my acquaintances, I believed I

saw many of the traits I was bent on depicting, and for others I am half afraid I had only to take a peep into myself.

The confession, as he calls it, gives the just measure of Lever's attainments. No one need go to him for that subtle analysis of character and motive, for those probings into the sub-conscious mind, which are the chief stock-in-trade of the moderns. But for romantic adventure, gaiety and good stories Lever is hard to beat.

He is continually accused of caricaturing his country-men. It might be sufficient to ask, in reply, as Mr. Birrell asks in the course of an essay on Carlyle: "When will mankind learn that literature is one thing and sworn testimony another?" The question is even more apposite to a novelist than to a historian and moralist. No doubt, he consistently heightens his effects; but it would be rash to assert that life in early nineteenth century Ireland did not afford ample warrant for the most extravagant of the tales. There is as much drinking and duelling, hard riding and hard living in Barrington as in Lever; and Barrington at least professes to be relating facts. Nay, if John Eglinton is to be believed, it was the old Gaelic bards who "gave Ireland for its ideal the jolly fellow, subsequently incarnated in the works of Lever and Lover." Dr. Barret, Frank Webber, Major Monsoon and a host of others were all drawn from life; and Lever was himself the hero of several of the pranks which he attributes to Webber during his Trinity College days—such as those recorded in the fourteenth and seventeenth chapters of *Charles O'Malley*. Moreover there is force in the contention which he once urged, that what was extravagant in his writing was itself exaggerated in popular belief by association with the drawings of Hablot Browne, as anyone can see for himself who will make the experiment of reading the books without looking at "Phiz's clever but grotesque "illustrations."

No sane creature can ever have supposed Ireland to be inhabited exclusively by fox-hunting gentlemen and their retainers, dashing dragoons, comic aldermen, flirtatious damsels, and devil-may-care stable-boys. Certainly no one in Ireland was misled; and if our neighbours chose to confuse literature and sworn testimony it is difficult to see why, at this time of day, we should be greatly concerned with their mistake. Lever himself was perfectly aware that there were graver sides to Irish life, as the tone of his later books sufficiently proves. Perhaps his worst fault, as an Irish novelist, is that amazing ignorance of the teaching and practice of the Catholic Church which leads him to perpetrate such absurdities and errors of taste as the story of Mickey Free's interview with Father Roach.

While mainly concerned with the gentry—as were nearly all contemporary novelists—Lever shows himself by many little touches, to be lacking neither in sympathy for nor understanding of the mass of the people. In his young days, before he abandoned the practice of medicine for literature, he had done noble work among the fever-stricken people of County Clare; and in one of his later prefaces he speaks with feeling and reverence of the courage, patience and unselfishness displayed by the poor. No doubt there was then as always a "hidden Ireland" of which he knew, and could know, nothing. But, for all his obvious limitations, Lever's epitaph might well be found in the concluding sentences of his last book:—

> "Isn't it Irish?—Irish the whole of it."
> "So they said down there, and stranger than all, they seemed rather proud of it."

What Maria Edgeworth and Charles Lever did for the gentry, Griffin did for the middling classes, and the two Banims and William Carleton for the peasantry.

The lives and literary aims and achievements of Lever and Griffin are strangely dissimilar. Though born within three years of each other, one had already renounced authorship when the other published the first of his many books. Just about the time that Lever was carelessly throwing together the *Confessions of Harry Lorrequer* for the *Dublin Magazine*—with "no thought of future authorship of any kind; far less any idea of abandoning his profession as a physician for the precarious livelihood of the pen"—Griffin, having joined the Christian Brothers, was writing from a monastery in Cork:—

"I have since been enlightening the craniums of wondering Paddies in this quarter, who learn from me, with profound amazement and profit, that o-x spells ox; that the top of the map is the north, and the bottom the south, with various other 'branches'; as also that they ought to be good boys and do as they are bid, and say their prayers every morning and evening, etc.; and yet it seems curious even to myself that I feel a great deal happier in the practice of this daily routine than I did while I was moving about your great city, absorbed in the modest project of rivaling Shakespeare and throwing Scott into the shade."

Nevertheless, as the last words humorously suggest, it was Griffin who, in youth, had cherished the more formidable ambitions. Born in the city of Limerick in 1803, he betook himself to London in his twentieth year, having in his pocket the MS. of three or four tragedies and in his heart "the project of reforming the London Theatre." His plays unfortunately did not find favour with the managers; and Griffin was compelled, like Goldsmith before him, to drudge for the booksellers and the press. He suffered greatly during this time from ill-health and penury, both of which afflictions (again like Goldsmith) he bore with courage, piety and good humour. At the end of a three years' struggle, having won what he called "half a name," mainly as a writer of Irish tales, he came home to Ireland. *Hollantide* and *Tales of the Munster Festivals* appeared, soon after, in 1827; *The Collegians,* in 1829; then some books of less interest, among them, a historical novel, *The Duke of Monmouth* marked like everything of Griffin's by dramatic power and poetical feeling.

The Collegians—strangely misnamed since it nowhere treats of college life—is the first and most famous of Irish romantic novels. "The tale," says Mr. Stephen Gwynn, "was suggested by a murder which excited all Ireland. A young southern squire carried off a girl with some money, and procured her death by drowning. He was arrested at his mother's house, and a terrible scene took place, terribly rendered in the book. Griffin, of course, changes the motive; the girl is carried off, not for money but for love, and she is sacrificed to make way for a stronger passion. Eily O'Connor, the victim, is a pretty and pathetic figure; the hero-villain Hardress Cregan, and the mother who indirectly causes the crime are effective, though melodramatic; but the actual murderer, Danny-the-Lord, Hardress Cregan's familiar, is worthy of Scott or Hugo."

The stage still exercised its fascination over him. He wrote every passage "as if it belonged to actual drama," believing as he told his brother that "the talent required for both kinds of writing was very similar, that is to say, that to be successful as a novel-writer one should have a great deal of dramatic talent. He used to point out the best novels as containing a large proportion of dialogue, and requiring very little aid from narrative, and the most impressive scenes in them as highly dramatic in character." He longed to see Edmund Kean in the part of Hardress Cregan.

It is curious to reflect that, though Griffin's desire to see his creations appear in living presence upon the stage was never gratified during his lifetime, the rejected play of *Gisippus* was produced with much success just after his death, and that under the title of "The Colleen Bawn," his novel, dramatised by Dion Boucicault, still maintains its hold upon a third generation of Irish playgoers.

The contrast between the literary fortunes of Griffin and Lever has already been suggested: not less dissimilar were their literary methods. There is the making of a score of romantic dramas in every one of Lever's earlier books, but in not one of them is there a semblance of dramatic unity. Equally remote does Griffin seem from Miss Edgeworth; yet these two are nearer together in their conceptions of novel-writing than at first appears. Even more than she, Griffin was perpetually haunted by the conviction—for which there is perhaps more to be said than modern writers will allow—that the marriage of art and morality is sacred.

"Isn't it extraordinary how impossible it is to write a perfect novel," he said to his brother, when discussing *The Collegians,* "one that should be read with deep interest and yet be perfect as a moral tale. . . . . Look at these two characters of Kyrle Daly and Hardress Cregan, for example. Kyrle Daly, full of high principle, prudent, amiable and affectionate; not wanting in spirit, nor free from passion, but keeping his passions under control, thoughtful, kindhearted and charitable; a character in every way deserving of our esteem. Hardress Cregan, his mother's proud pet, nursed in the very lap of passion, and ruined by indulgence—not without good feelings, but for ever abusing them; having a full sense of justice and honour, but shrinking like a craven from their dictates; following pleasure headlong, and eventually led into crimes of the blackest dye by total absence of self-control. Take Kyrle Daly's character in what way you will, it is infinitely preferable; yet I will venture to say, nine out of ten who read this book will prefer Hardress Cregan, just because he is a fellow of high mettle with a dash of talent about him."

Scruples of this sort grew upon him, until he finally renounced all literary ambition and was admitted a postulant of the Christian Brothers. Two years later he died at the age of 37, having previously burned the manuscript of his unpublished works and having endeavoured to buy up and suppress such as had already appeared. In *Eileen Aroon* and the *Sister of Charity* he had sung the praises of Truth and of Renunciation. No change of mind, but only deepened conviction, is shown in the noble words in which he speaks of his entry into the religious life.

"I have entered this house at the gracious call of God, to die to the world and to live to Him: all is to be changed; all my own pursuits henceforward to be laid aside, and those only embraced which He points out to me. Give me Grace, O my God, to close my mind against all that has been, or may be, in which Thou hast no part; that it be not like a roofless building, where all kinds of birds, clean and unclean, fly in and out without hindrance; but, like an enclosed tabernacle, devoted solely to Thy use and to Thy love."

In his early essays in story-telling Griffin followed in the track of John and Michael Banim, whose *Tales of the O'Hara Family* had appeared in 1825 and 1826. John, the younger of the two brothers, was the author also of *Damon and Pythias,* a tragedy, and of a volume of essays, *Revelations of the Dead;* Michael who long survived him, of *Father Connell, Clough Fion, The Croppy, The Town of the Cascades,* and other tales. With the exception of the book first mentioned, all these are now nearly forgotten, and all seem to be out of print.

To the success that attended the *O'Hara Family* may perhaps be attributed the vogue which now sprang up in short stories and sketches dealing with various aspects of Irish peasant life. Hitherto Anglo-Irish writers had rarely so much as recognised the existence of their poorer fellow countrymen, unless in so far as these were in direct contact with the gentry as tenants or dependents. Yet all the time the peasants were living their own lives and handing down from parent to child a traditional learning, inexpressibly rich in romantic incident and in humorous, racy and poetic diction. From now on, however, this newly-discovered vein was continuously developed, until at one time it threatened to become—not perhaps altogether fortunately, since it takes all sorts to make even a small island—almost the sole theme of our novelists and playwrights.

The new spirit, whether in fiction, archæology, or historical research, found a ready welcome in the pages of the *Dublin Penny Journal* and *Irish Penny Journal,* two excellent magazines edited by Dr. George Petrie, which had among their contributors the Banims, Crofton Croker, Mrs. Hall, D'Alton, Furlong and William Carleton. Of these Carleton was certainly the most notable. Sir Charles Gavan Duffy calls him "an Irish peasant lifting a head like Slieve Donard over his contemporaries." But this noble metaphor, if taken too literally, may be a little misleading. Carleton's works lack the unity of a single, majestic mountain. It would be more exact, though infinitely less picturesque, to say that they resemble a chain of hills among which the traveller wanders, exhilarated and depressed by turns, eager but footsore, compelled to leap from tussock to tussock over intervening pools of black bogwater, immersed in quagmires, torn by briars, wounded by stones, losing his way in mists, always cheated till nightfall of the ultimate eminence which constantly recedes as he approaches—and yet rewarded, now and again, by some happy prospect of far-flung countryside, by friendly greetings of men and women at work on the little stone-walled fields and by the welcome of the little wayside houses.

Many of Carleton's books, more particularly those of his later days, are all but unreadable—slovenly, sentimental, tedious. *Traits and Stories of the Irish Peasantry, Fardorougha, The Emigrants of Ahadarra,* and *The Black Prophet* contain by common consent his best work. The Traits and Stories are intimate, pathetic, above all humorous; though the humour is worn out by repetition, the pathos somewhat too obvious, and the intimacy broken by the asides in which Carleton expounds, presumably for the benefit of English readers, the follies, foibles, vices and superstitions of the Irish peasant. By these stories he must certainly have done more than Lever, who never professed, as did Carleton, to be writing nothing but "truthful fiction," to create, or at least to perpetuate, the tradition of the Stage Irishman. His tailor who is forever complaining that he is "blue-mowlded for want of a batin" is the very archetype of that objectionable character; and though the

jest is well enough and the story short, the one is as threadbare as the schoolmaster's breeches before the other is brought to an end. Again while *Phelim O'Toole's Courtship* is richly humorous (more particularly in the opening pages) could anything be better calculated to bring the Irish people into contempt than the scene at the Holy Well, with its mingling of piety with superstition, cursing, and drunkenness and its grotesque invocations of imaginary saints? Even more irritating to the ordinary reader of to-day is Carleton's much too evident desire to play the part of a self-appointed censor of manners. He is not content to let the story carry its own moral, but is for ever pushing himself forward to inveigh against idleness or intemperance or superstition or faction fighting or Ribbonism.

Fardorougha is a great novel, perhaps the greatest thing that Carleton did; and contains besides, in the miser's wife a most touching and lovely memorial of the virtues of a simple, pious, and lovable peasant-woman. But of all his numerous stories perhaps the most generally pleasing is *The Poor Scholar,* a tale included in the second series of *Traits and Stories*. It has its over-sentimental passages, its *longeurs,* its strained coincidences, its lapses into propagandist debate; but the abiding effect of the book is one of real beauty and intimate truth. There are few more affecting pages in any literature than those which tell of Jimmy McEvoy's departure from his northern home after the parish priest has coaxed the congregation into finding the money required for the boy who is going to seek his schooling in far-off Munster, his adventures on the way, his misery at the school, and, most tenderly told of all, his return, now that he is a priest, to the home where his mother has so long awaited him.

In the *Black Prophet,* a book of amazing though unequal power, we have a picture of famine days, painted as it could only be by one who had himself experienced that which he describes. This story was published in 1846; *The Emigrants of Ahadarra* in 1847. Thereafter, though he wrote much more before his death in 1869, there is nothing that seems to call for particular mention.

During his long life (he was born in 1794 near Clogher in the county Tyrone) he aimed at furnishing his countrymen "with such a pleasant encyclopædia of social duty—now lit up with their mirth, and again made tender with their sorrow, as will force them to look upon him as a benefactor." He said again of himself: "I have written many works on Irish life, and up to the present day the man has never lived who could lay his finger on any passage of my writings, and say, 'That is false.' " But, as Mr. Darrell Figgis remarks in his introduction to a selection from the *Stories:*—"Truth is something more than a verbal or factual accuracy, and it is never his accuracy that is in question. In reading through the mass of his 'many works on Irish life,' the bewilderment lies, not in any falsity (his knowledge was too intimate for that) but in the changing standpoints from which he told his truth, in his progress round the many possible standpoints, and the curious aspect the standpoint of to-day suddenly came to wear when viewed from the standpoint of to-morrow."

Carleton was singularly unfortunate in his environment. Only in the year preceding that of his birth had the worst provisions of that Penal Code been repealed which Burke described in a classic phrase as "a complete system full of coherence and consistency, well digested and composed in all its parts . . . as well fitted for the oppression, impoverishment and degradation of a people, and the debasement in them of human nature itself, as ever proceeded from the perverted ingenuity of man."

Before he died Catholic Emancipation was all but complete, in so far as legislation could complete it; but though the fetters had been removed, the marks of them were still stamped upon the minds of the people, and on none more ineffaceably than on William Carleton's. For all his vigorous talents, he was curiously lacking in independence and easily took on the colours of those about him. All through his work, one sees the half-educated peasant of the Penal days, distracted between his own instincts and the conventions imposed upon him, and struggling to express his thoughts in a language still alien to the life he is trying to portray. Yet, with all his faults and limitations, Carleton remains a great, if not altogether a lovable, figure. "Born and bred among the people—full of their animal vehemence—skilled in their sports—as credulous and headlong in boyhood, and as fitful and varied in manhood as the wildest—he had felt with them, and must ever sympathise with them. Endowed with the highest dramatic genius, he has represented their love and generosity, their wrath and their negligence, their crimes and their virtues, as a hearty peasant—not a note-taking critic. . . . . Come what change there may over Ireland, in these *Tales and Sketches* the peasantry of the past hundred years can be for ever lived with."[2]

Notes

[1] See, however, on this point, and generally, the admirable Introduction contributed by Sir Malcolm Seton to the *Selections from Maria Edgeworth,* published by the Talbot Press.

[2] Thomas Davis: Essay on *Habits and Characters of the Peasantry.*

Stephen Gwynn (essay date 1936)

SOURCE: "Miss Edgeworth's Successors," in *Irish Literature and Drama in the English Language: A Short History,* Thomas Nelson and Sons, 1936, pp. 61-79.

[*In the following essay, Gwynn reviews the works of upper and lower class authors considered to be "native" Irish.*]

Before steam transport, Edinburgh and Dublin were a longer journey from London than New York is to-day, and were naturally much more distinct in character than they became when the distance could be covered in a day. Yet the cultivated, well-to-do class in both capitals belonged to the same social order, and members of it, when they wrote, wrote in the main for London readers. Miss Edgeworth was born into this class, Moore was admitted to it, and they were published in London.

But inevitably in cities so distant, each centre had its own fugitive literature addressed to its local public— its own journals and magazines. These swarmed in Dublin, as indeed they still do; and through the medium of these, Irish works of a very different type from that represented by Moore and Miss Edgeworth began to get a hearing.

Something similar could be seen in Edinburgh; Hogg, the Ettrick shepherd, was a pillar of *Blackwood's Magazine.* But Hogg, peasant though he was, continued the tradition of a literature to which peasant and noble had contributed for five hundred years, and which in his lifetime had been carried to its supreme height by an Ayrshire ploughman. The men who in Ireland were the counterparts of Hogg or of Hogg's contemporary (and Barrie's forerunner) John Galt, had no such literary tradition. The literature of the Gaelic people was in its own language. If Irish peasants were represented speaking English, they must be represented speaking ignorantly. But Scott's Lowlanders, or Galt's, speak the distinct and cultivated tongue of which Burns was the supreme master.

Ireland's native writers of last century knew English in one sense perfectly, just as Burns did. But it was not in their blood and bones. Burns is not only one of the greatest lyric poets, but also among the most technically accomplished; yet if Burns had left only what he wrote in standard English, his name would hardly have survived. His native tongue was Scots. Language is not merely a mechanical instrument of expressing disembodied thoughts; it has infinite colours and tones, and the perception of them is acquired by heredity. The Irishmen who wrote then of Ireland had to write of it in a language which certainly was not yet the language of their parent stock. Three names stand out— Carleton, Banim, and Griffin; and of these the most important and most significant is William Carleton, for he came not only of native Irish race, but of Irish-speaking peasants. The name is the anglicized form of O'Carolan. His mother was a Kelly.

He was born in 1794, on the borders of Tyrone and Monaghan, in a district where the most distressing features of Irish life were savagely accentuated; for here the divisions of race and religion were not merely between the landlord class and the tenantry. The soil was not only owned by Protestants but in part occupied by them; and the peasantry were divided into two camps, each having its own oath-bound association, ready to administer its own conception of justice. Faction fighting was rampant everywhere in the Ireland of that day; but here, in Ulster and the part of Ulster where numbers were most evenly balanced, it took on the character of a smouldering guerilla war between Orangemen and Ribbonmen.

William Carleton was the youngest child by five years—in a family of fourteen children. His father was, by the standard of his times, a moderately well-to-do farmer; he spoke English as fluently as he spoke Irish, and he had, what is still to be met with among peasant "shanachys," a marvellous verbal memory. "As a narrator of old tales, legends, and historical anecdotes," his son writes, he was "unrivalled, and his stock of them inexhaustible. What rendered this of such peculiar advantage to me as a literary man was that I heard them as often, if not oftener, in the Irish language as in the English; a circumstance which enabled me to transfer the genius, the idiomatic peculiarity and conversational spirit of the one language into the other, precisely as the people themselves do in their dialogues, whenever the heart or the imagination happens to be moved by the darker or the better passions."

That sentence, from the unfinished autobiography which was the last of Carleton's writings, seems of capital importance. Carleton attempted instinctively what Synge, nearly a century later, was to do by study with a finished literary art; he tried to bring from one language into the other the form and colour of the Irish mind. The content of that mind, Irish feeling and Irish thought, Ireland's sense of her own past and hopes for her future could be expressed, and were expressed, in English far better by other pens than Carleton's. Neither Irish history nor Irish legend took hold on him; his interest was only in the life that lay about him, that he had taken part in with lusty vigour, and that could be turned to picturesque and popular account.

But music moved him, and his mother, who spoke Irish more easily than English, came of a family who had composed, he says, "several fine old Irish songs and airs, some in praise of a patron or a friend and others to celebrate rustic beauties."

Carleton showed exceptional quickness as a scholar, though schooling was hard to come by, and he had practically no access to books. But his parents gave him every chance they could, and set him apart for learning—to make a priest. But the vocation was lacking, and if one can accept his own account, the scholar, although always dressed in black, and regarded as "the

young priest," led the countryside in athletics—leaping, weight-throwing, and dancing, to the general admiration. Upon one thing, however, he was resolute: he would not be a spade labourer; and until he was well over twenty he lived on his relations and his friends, evidently thinking it not only right but natural that his ambition should be assisted. This help was given him, as his own account makes clear, by people little better off than himself. That they gave it, and that he not only took it, but in his old age told gladly how gladly he took it, is a significant fact in the study of Irish literature.

Gaelic Ireland, for good or for bad, was a country in which unusual privileges and prestige attached to literature and to learning—to the historian and to the poet. In the seventeenth century all this system of culture was finally broken up: a few scholars gathered up the records of it. Throughout the eighteenth century, Gaelic Ireland was a country of unlettered peasants who nevertheless preserved the desire for letters. No more public provision was made for their schools than for their worship; priest and schoolmaster alike were outside the law, and the priest indeed actually under its ban. The Irish knew as well as any other people the worth of education; and their devotion to their religion was traditional. No one could become a priest without an education costing years of study; and it became a matter of piety throughout the whole community to assist any lad who would take on him the heavy task of qualifying for priesthood. Such charity would carry its own blessing, so a devout people believed. But there was also, I think, the feeling (perhaps subconscious) that every member of the beaten-down people who attained to education raised the people with him. At all events William Carleton clearly thought that his pursuit of learning and his endeavour to rise out of "slavery" deserved support none the less, though he was not going to be a priest.

The best known among his *Traits and Stories of the Irish Peasantry* is "The Poor Scholar," which, apart from its merit as literature, is a capital document on the surprising system by which boys from the poorer parts of Ireland set out to the richer land of Munster, where farmers could keep a schoolmaster among them able to teach the classics. The poor scholar got his board and lodging free in one of the farmhouses, helping the children of the house with their lessons. Money to pay the school fees and expenses of his journey was subscribed by the people of his parish—Protestant neighbours often adding their contribution. Carleton describes the whole with great fire and full knowledge, for he himself set out as a poor scholar, though before he had gone far on his journey his heart failed him and he came home.

But such learning as he got, he got in similar schools—and he learnt to read and write Latin fluently; and when he began to support himself, it was by teaching. His sketches of the Irish schoolmaster—they recur in several of his stories—show the class as pretentious and pedantic, talking an English stuffed with long words. In the eighteenth century their predecessors, probably no better instructed in the classics or mathematics, were, as has been shown, masters of the Irish tongue, transmitters of a formed Gaelic style. Those of Carleton's day, like Carleton himself, in most cases, might know Irish, but regarded English as the language of culture and used it as a matter of self-respect. In Scotland, the equivalents for them and their pupils had in the first place in their ears the traditional literature of their original Lowland tongue, its lyrics and ballads; but more than that, they had as the very foundation of all instruction, the Bible translated into English at the moment when English genius reached its highest literary expression. Carleton cannot properly be called a self-educated man; he was given, and he grasped at, all the education that could have fitted him for the priesthood; but in the craft of literary expression he was without that subconscious preparation which comes of a man's familiarity with masterpieces in the language that he is to use. A Bible Christian has a formidable advantage when it comes to expressing either his thoughts or his feelings; and Carleton, though as his writings show he was truly educated in the teaching of Christianity, never got the cadences of the English Bible into his ear or on his tongue.—One strange thing about him is that though no one has expressed more perfectly the simple religious feeling of Catholic Ireland, his own fidelity was most dubious. After a series of makeshift scrapings through stray teaching jobs, he succeeded in getting work in Dublin, as a clerk in the office of the Sunday School Society. This was about 1825, in the year when O'Connell's agitation was at its height, and opponents of Catholic emancipation were busy as proselytizers.

The Sunday School Society was not the most active form of this, but some clergymen conducted a vigorous pamphleteering campaign, and the *Christian Examiner* was their organ. Carleton, now turned of thirty and married, was anxious to earn money; he had already tried his hand at essay writing; but the Reverend Cæsar Otway (himself a writer who is still readable) suggested that he should supply studies of Irish peasant life, to illustrate its superstitions. His first published work was a description of the pilgrimage to Lough Derg in County Donegal and the two days of fasting and other mortifications. Naturally, under these conditions, it was not written in a tone to please Catholics.

For the *Christian Examiner* Carleton continued to write from 1828 to 1831, and in the two last of these years also for the *National Magazine,* said to have been started by students of Trinity College. In 1830 he published—in Dublin—his first book: *Traits and Stories of the Irish Peasantry.* A second volume with the same title followed it in 1833, and contained "The Poor Scholar" and "Tubber Derg," which are generally counted his best work. Yet the longer story (making a full volume) of "Fardorogha the Miser" has much more remarkable power. This appeared first in the *Dublin University Magazine,* to which, from its foundation in 1833 Carleton was a frequent contributor, until 1842, when Lever became its editor. In the latter year *The Nation* newspaper was founded as the organ of Young Ireland; and this is a landmark in the history both of Irish literature and Irish politics.

Carleton was then close on fifty. His popularity was established not only in Ireland, but in England; yet Catholic and Nationalist Ireland looked askance at him, by reason of his contributions to the *Christian Examiner,* which with all their unwelcome criticism of the priesthood had been reissued in a volume as *Tales of Irish Life.* From 1842 onwards his friendship with the group whose organ was *The Nation* produced a marked change in the bent of his work, and his power of denunciation was now expended on bad landlords and agents. "Valentine McClutchy," a savagely propagandist story of this kind, had a great vogue; but the most popular by far of all his works was the novel *Willy Reilly,* published in 1850.

He lived on, still writing, till 1868. But essentially, as a writer, he belongs to the period before the Famine of 1846-48. His reputation was then fully made, as indeed is proved by the public movement to secure him a pension in 1847. This list of signatories to a memorial presented to the Lord-Lieutenant was headed by the Lord Chancellor and the Duke of Leinster; it included the Provost of Trinity College, the Catholic Archbishop of Dublin, and from Ulster Dr. Montgomery and Dr. Cooke, the two foremost Presbyterian divines. Noblemen, great names in the Orange order, figured along with Smith O'Brien and Gavan Duffy, both of whom were shortly to be on trial for high treason; and the pension of £200 was granted by Lord John Russell's government. But the most significant name of all was Maria Edgeworth, who wrote—not for publication, but for Carleton's eye—her admiration for "works which give with such masterly strokes and in such strong and vivid colour the pictures of our country's manners, her virtues and her vices, without ministering to party prejudice or exciting dangerous passions."

She wrote this after "Valentine McClutchy" had appeared. But then Miss Edgeworth herself had not been sparing in her censure of the Irish land system; and she was too reasonable a woman not to take it as right that Carleton should throughout be for the tenant as against the landlord and the agent and the process server. She counted it for virtue to him, doubtless, that he denounced most vigorously the Ribbon lodges, and gave a picture of the way in which one villain could twist to his own personal ends a league formed to protect—or to revenge—the whole body.

The most notable thing about Carleton is that one feels him to be writing for Ireland, not for England. He is telling stories of his own people to a different class of Irishmen. Yet, even so, he feels it necessary to explain, as Maria Edgeworth did not explain in *Castle Rackrent*. What is worse, however, just because he feels himself to be addressing the class who have his people in their power, he is deplorably prone to harangue—especially on the Land Laws. "The Poor Scholar" is spoilt by the digression which describes how an absentee landlord was induced to look into his agent's doings. This change of heart is the poor scholar's work, but we lose sight of the poor scholar for much too long. In "Tubber Derg" such digressions have more justification, since the whole is the history of a decent farmer family driven out to beg on the roads; a case only too common.

Readers of Carleton should remember that the long Napoleonic wars sent the price of food up prodigiously, and consequently Irish landlords could and did raise the rents, and raise their own scale of living. Then came depression after the war; but the Irish population had so multiplied that applicants swarmed for every farm. The margin was too narrow, and in 1822 famine came with a severity that is only not remembered because, a generation later, a greater scourge destroyed not thousands, but hundreds of thousands, leaving a land drained of its vitality. The Ireland which Carleton described was the Ireland of his youth—overcrowded, miserably poor, yet full of lusty life.

A novelist seeking for striking incident naturally dwelt on its lawlessness. Murder for revenge is a recurring incident in all these stories; so are frauds and injustices that breed murder. Where people had nothing to eat but potatoes and milk, and whisky cost three-halfpence a glass (provided it paid no duty), poteen making was a great industry—often also a desperate resource for earning the rent. Secret alliances for this fitted in easily with the secret societies; and gangs used to defying the law were ready aids for abduction, a practice introduced by the landlord class and adopted by the poor. Duelling does not come into tales of the peasantry, but faction fighting supplies even darker colour.

Add to these the emotions of a race accustomed to give every feeling full vent in words, or wailings, or shouts of delight or despair and defiance—the strong impulses of a religion, cherished under every difficulty, yet mixed with many superstitious beliefs—and you have the ingredients that Carleton and his rivals worked with. But none of them came as he did from the very soil, out of the most typical peasantry.

For the tenderness of his work one would turn above all to "The Poor Scholar" and to the last passage in "Tubber Derg." But nothing stands out with such original force as the study of the peasant miser in "Fardorogha," which, if the writer's art had matched his power of conception, might rank with Turgeniev's "King Lear of the Steppes." And in that same story the character of the miser's wife deserves to be noted for its portraiture of what is best in the Christian religion as expressed through the person of a Catholic Irish peasant woman.

But the art is at every point sadly to seek. Carleton never filled a really large canvas; and even in his short tales he is always redundant. He encumbers the essential utterance with a burden of superfluous words. He was, more is the pity, a thoroughly uneducated writer. He had a strong power for visual imagery; when he describes a landscape, it is clearly present to the mind's eye; and he had a natural feeling for the rhythmic beauty of words. Many an ear has been haunted by the opening of his poem, "Sir Turlogh's Bride":

> "The bride she bound her golden hair,
>   Killeevy, oh, Killeevy."

But the effect is frittered away through a tedious procession of long stanzas. A few lines may be quoted also (from a poem published in *The Christian Examiner*) to illustrate the two-handed talent of this natural-born but untaught writer:

> "As the white low mist the meadows kissed
>   In the summer twilight's glow,
> And the otter splashed and the wild duck
>   dashed
>   In the sedgy lake below,
> 'Twas sweet to hear the silver bell
>   For the flocks on high Dunroe:
> From the rail's hoarse throat the ceaseless
>   note
>   Would flit, now far, now nigh,
> And the quavering hum of the snipe would
>   come
>   Quick shooting from the sky."

Certainly the man who wrote these lines knew his countryside among the hills and little loughs of the Ulster border, and felt it in his heart.

The other novelists need less attention. John and Michael Banim were sons of a well-to-do shopkeeper in Kilkenny who dealt in sporting guns and fishing tackle. John Banim, born in 1798, was writing romances and verses from his childhood, and as a boy in his teens saw and adored Tom Moore, acting in the Kilkenny Theatre. No wonder he adored, since "Anacreon Moore" called him "a brother poet," and gave him a season-ticket for the plays. At fifteen he decided to be an artist, studied for two years in the Academy attached to the Royal Dublin Society, and at eighteen set up as a teacher of drawing in Kilkenny. Then, after a passionate and tragic love idyll, he gave up art and decided to try his fortune in Dublin as an author. Finding poor sustenance there, he pushed across to London with a poem, "Ossian's Paradise," for which a publisher surprisingly was found. Less surprisingly, the publisher went bankrupt. But Banim, not discouraged, wrote a play, *Damon and Pythias,* and Macready as Damon with Charles Kemble as Pythias brought it out at Covent Garden. With the money so gotten he went back to Kilkenny, paid his debts, and discussed with his elder brother Michael the possibility of tales illustrating Irish life. So began the project of *Tales of the O'Hara Family*— a joint work. It began in 1823, before Carleton had published anything.

John Banim went back to London, bringing a wife; and in London he met another Irish adventurer, carrying as his equipment a blank verse tragedy. This was Gerald Griffin, son of a moderately well-to-do business man in Limerick, who after failure in business was left with enough means to buy a pleasant house on the tidal Shannon. Here again was a precocious talent, and the lad was barely nineteen when he set out for London, without friends or resources—except some aid from his elder brother, then settled as a doctor near Adare.

Without Banim's help, Griffin must have gone under, but thanks to it and to his own energy he made shift with some miserable hack work at translating, and a job as reporter in Parliament—meanwhile hawking about his finished tragedy, *Aguire,* and completing another, *Gisippus*—which was in fact acted by Macready, but not until after its author's death. His stay in London lasted from 1823 to 1827, when his brother persuaded him to return to County Limerick. Nothing that he wrote in this period has importance; but within that time his friend's success had opened a door. "Nobody knew anything of Banim till he published his 'O'Hara' tales, which are becoming more and more popular every day," Griffin wrote. The second series, published in 1826, was equally popular, and it is memorable that Banim sought to assist the younger man by asking him to contribute as one of the imaginary O'Hara family. Griffin did not accept, but followed on the same track with *Tales of the Munster Festivals,* which appeared in 1828 while he stayed with his brother at Pallas Kenry. In these surroundings he began his full-length novel, *The Collegians*—which was written under the encouragement due to the reception of his Munster tales. Finished hastily in London, it appeared in 1829, and in the next year he returned to the pleasant surroundings of his brother's home.

Banim, less fortunate, though perhaps more successful, had no such refuge open to him; he had a wife and children, and must live where he could best earn in the only way at his command. Even this was rendered impossible by failing health, and in 1829 he was ordered to France. By 1830, in his thirty-second year, he wrote of himself as "a paralysed man walking with much difficulty," and two years later he was forced to appeal for public help. He claimed for himself that at twenty-five he was "known at least as a national novelist, even though of a humble order," and that since then he had written twenty successful novels and five successful dramas."

Help came: in 1835, when he and his wife, also an invalid, returned to Ireland, a benefit performance was given for them at the Theatre Royal in Dublin, and at Kilkenny the novelist was welcomed with an address from the citizens; further, a pension of £150 a year helped through the remaining years of his crippled existence till it ended in 1842. Till the last, he and his brother contrived to issue in collaboration *Tales of the O'Hara Family*.

Gerald Griffin had died in 1840; but had gradually ceased to write or at least to publish, from a growing sense that desire for literary fame was not compatible with a truly religious life, for after a period of scepticism he had returned with fervour to his Catholic faith, and finally, in 1838, decided to enter a monastic life, but not one of contemplation. He joined the lay order of Christian Brothers founded for the purpose of educating the children of the poor. After two years' happy service with them, he caught typhus fever and died within a few days.

During this period of his life he abstained altogether from writing, and before he entered upon it, made a general destruction of his manuscripts. The best known of all his work, the song "Eileen Aroon," was recovered from some scraps overlooked. Oddly enough, however, he left the drama *Gisippus* in his brother's care, and it was performed at Drury Lane in February 1842, with great applause, Macready and Helen Faucit playing the chief parts.

It is clear that of these men the Banims were the pioneers, and both they and Griffin anticipated Carleton. The idea of producing from Irish sources of inspiration something like what Scott had drawn from Scotland, was John Banim's; but his brother Michael actually wrote *Crohoore of the Billhook,* much the most powerful of the "O'Hara" tales. Still, when the professional man of letters died, the home-keeping brother wrote no more, but settled down to be postmaster at Kilkenny. All the work of the Banims and all that of Gerald Griffin lies before the literary movement connected with *The Nation;* and the Ireland of which they wrote had not been swept by the famine.

But the writers of *The Nation* accepted *The Collegians* as the outstanding Irish novel. Its life was prolonged at least till the close of the century by Dion Bouccicault's dramatized version, *The Colleen Bawn.* To-day it is not easily read; certain scenes have force (recalling the Brontës), but it degenerates constantly into hysterical violence; and for the most part Griffin is describing the manners of people among whom he had not lived— the Irish landlord class. Eily O'Connor, the lovely daughter of the ropemaker at Garryowen, is a living and most pathetic figure; but the peasant characters are drawn with exaggeration, except one who plays a very small part, Myles na Coppaleen, the pony dealer from Killarney. But if none of Griffin's prose wears well, nearly all the songs scattered through this book in profusion are full of life, merry or mournful.

Broadly speaking, in these novelists of purely Irish stock we get the picture of a country where transitions are violent, and contrast savagely accumulated: where life is held cheap, yet where affections are of passionate intensity; where the tragic and the ludicrous jostle each other. Yet the darker strain predominates: whether in "The Poor Scholar" or "Fardorogha," in *Crohoore of the Billhook,* or in *The Collegians,* there is far more to shock and terrify than to amuse—though in all these books humour is present, almost as an obligatory element. That is Ireland of the days before the famine, seen through Irish eyes; and it cannot be said that the English public was indifferent to the merits of the picture. All these men were praised—Banim and Carleton were pensioned—by Englishmen in power. Yet what they offered was not what England wanted from an Irish novelist. England wanted to be made to laugh. It got what it wanted from a very similar picture, presented, but with a very different emphasis, in the work of these men's contemporary Charles Lever, who throughout the whole Victorian period passed as the representative Irish novelist.

Charles Lever was Irish only as Swift was; that is to say, he was born and bred in Ireland, but born of English parents. His father was a building contractor, who by government influence got the contract for the Dublin Custom House—a very noble piece of work to be connected with. Charles, his second son, was born in 1806, and was going joyously through Trinity while Griffin and Banim were struggling and starving in London. His elder brother took orders, and was curate at Portumna on Lough Derg, where Charles spent many vacations, and so drew his impressions of Irish country life outside Dublin from the country of the Galway Blazers. He was a handsome highspirited youth with a passion for practical joking, and lived gloriously and uproariously in college as a medical student. Having got his qualification, he was prompted by the spirit of adventure to go out as surgeon on an emigrant ship bound for Quebec, and spent the summer of 1829 in wanderings, even among the Indian tribes. According to his own story, he was adopted into a tribe and had to escape by stealth. After his return, he spent a period at the University of Gottingen, and explored Germany

before he returned to Dublin to walk the hospitals, and establish a social club in rivalry of the German *Bundesschaft.* At this time he began contributing to the local magazines.

In 1832, when cholera broke out, the young doctor was sent down to cope with it in West Clare, and had his headquarters in Kilrush, where there was a kind of informal club in which he heard a vast deal of anecdote of Irish life west of the Shannon. Here also he met extreme typical examples of the Irish parish priest, as seen in general society.

From Clare his profession took him to the most opposite part of Ireland; for he became dispensary doctor in Portstewart, on the borders of Derry and Antrim, some ten miles from the Giant's Causeway. Here the people to whom he must minister were Ulster Protestants, speaking with a Scottish accent and in a Scottish dialect. Living near by was W. H. Maxwell, a sporting clergyman, whose duties in County Mayo were largely left to a curate and the two made friends. Maxwell had already written *Captain Blake of the Rifles.* The young doctor was noted for his talk; a shy child, son of the rector of Portstewart, who generally fled before visitors, used to creep into the room when he heard that Dr. Lever was there, telling story after story. Presently the friendship with Maxwell led to a visit to Maxwell's parish in County Mayo, and each man encouraged the other. Maxwell began to write his *Wild Sports of the West;* Lever began to send to the *Dublin University Magazine* a loosely connected string of stories, which had for their title, "The Confessions of Harry Lorrequer."

This magazine had been started in 1833 by six Trinity College men, one of whom was Isaac Butt; and Butt was editor when the first number of "Lorrequer" appeared in February 1837.

Gerald Griffin's career was finished; Banim was broken in health; but Carleton, in the height of his powers, was at the same time contributing to this Dublin equivalent of *Blackwood.* Lever, still anonymous, began to find "Harry Lorrequer" much talked of; also, he began to feel life at Portstewart tedious. In 1837 he took the step of transferring himself with his wife and children to Brussels, where he could count on backing from Sir Hamilton Seymour, who had been Castlereagh's private secretary, and was then Minister at Brussels. And since the Minister long afterwards described Charles Lever as "one of the most agreeable among the four or five most agreeable men he ever fell in with," and wondered whether he did not "shine even more in conversation than in writing," it is certain that this young Irish doctor had, socially speaking, a brilliant life in Brussels.

Meanwhile "Lorrequer" went on, not planned as a continuous story, but simply as a number of scenes in the life of an exuberant young English subaltern, whose regimental duty had brought him to Ireland, and who had been captured by the humours and adventures of that country. It did not even appear regularly, and the last instalment was published early in 1840. But the same number announced that in the next would be found the beginning of "Charles O'Malley, the Irish Dragoon," by "Harry Lorrequer," who was now recognized as indispensable to the magazine. Not the diversions of a soldier in peace time but war was now the theme; and the Peninsular campaign, on which Lever had embarked his hero, offered splendid material. He carried the same rattling spirits into serious narrative as into broad farce, and his popularity was established while he was still anonymous. The author's name was not disclosed until "Jack Hinton" was finished, and by this time, in 1842, Lever had given up medicine and accepted a handsome income as editor of *The Dublin University Magazine.* A fine old house at Templeogue, five miles from the centre of Dublin, and facing across the little river Dodder to the mountains, now became his home. Here he lived with the profuse hospitality which was the Irish characteristic that most appealed to him; and as his books multiplied, he came to be considered as the one Irish novelist, for no other writer on Irish subjects approached his popularity outside Ireland.

It would be absurd to say that he did not know Ireland; born and bred in Dublin, married to an Irish wife, he had spent several years as a doctor in typical Irish countrysides; and his novels are there to witness that he delighted in Ireland, as many an Englishman, made Irish by adoption, has done since. It is even true that he identified himself with Ireland—naturally enough, with one section of it, the landowning class. He accepted the Irish reverence and affection for "the old stock," and one may even say that for him it added to their picturesqueness if the stock was Catholic. If he made no very clear distinction between Gael and Norman, that is natural, because for him the extreme characteristic expression of Irish life was to be found in Connaught, and few people remember that Burke or Blake, for instance, is a Norman-English name. In fact, for Charles Lever, Irish history began with Grattan's Parliament, and like many another good Unionist he kept all his respect for those who opposed the Union, and had a fine contempt for its bribed supporters. None the less, he was by all his instincts for the English connection, and instinctively regarded those of the Catholic Irish who were not peasants as vulgar persons seeking to push their way into civilized society.

Lever had left his editorship before the famine; he only remained three years in Dublin. During that time his own work did not change its character. But it was not possible for any intelligent man to know Ireland before the famine and after it without showing the mark of those years. Between 1842 and 1845 Ireland was heading for a calamity as great as ever fell on any country, and it struck both the main classes, landlord and tenant, with ruinous force. Lever's later work has value to-day only because of his sympathy with a landlord class that had been splendid in prodigality, and went down into picturesque ruin.

PEASANT AND MIDDLE CLASS IRISH NOVELISTS

Horatio Sheafe Krans (essay date 1903)

SOURCE: "The Novelists of the Peasantry," in *Irish Life in Irish Fiction,* Columbia University Press, 1903, pp. 120-96.

[*In the following essay, Krans examines the lives and works of novelists born in Ireland and raised as Catholics, discussing in particular how these novelists portrayed the lives and character of the Irish peasant and middle classes.*]

At the close of the first quarter of the nineteenth century a group of young writers began to appear whose works were more national and more worthy of being considered as an elucidation of Irish life and the character of the race than those of any previous novelist, except perhaps Miss Edgeworth. This is the group of novelists of the peasantry. They were all of Celtic stock, and bred in the Catholic faith. At this time O'Connell's agitation had awakened the Irish Catholics, and there is doubtless a connection between this little outburst of literary energy and the repeal of Catholic disabilities.

There is a strong contrast between the careers of these novelists of the peasantry and the gentry novelists. Lady Morgan in her theatrical and literary Bohemia or in Belgravia, Maxwell and his sporting life, Lever's high-living and gay company, the comfortable lives of Miss Edgeworth, the Crokers and Mrs. Hall, and Lover drolling it in the drawing-rooms of Dublin or London, make a series of pictures quite different from that of John Banim's harassed, hand-to-mouth existence, Griffin's fight for bread and fame, and the necessitous career of Carleton, struggling for education and a livelihood. With the novelists of the peasantry the devil-may-care temper that gave the novels of the gentry their characteristic tone no longer rules. They cannot take hold of life in the same free, off-hand manner.

John Banim, the first of the group, was born in 1798, the year of the Rebellion, and the same in which Croker and Carleton first saw the light, in Kilkenny, where his father—a bit of old Ireland in his testy temper, his warm heart, and his love of a social glass—was engaged in the double occupation of farmer and shopkeeper, in the latter capacity a dealer in the necessaries of a sportsman's and angler's outfit. His father was of the "strong farmer" class, that is, somewhere between the thriving peasant and the gentleman farmer. He kept a pair of blood-horses, and in Banim's boyhood (though reverses soon came) was in easy circumstances. John's formal education began under an eccentric pedagogue, who, by a weakness for drink and other foibles, could rival the hedge-schoolmasters of Carleton's tales; it was continued at a preparatory school at Kilkenny, and ended there with his fifteenth year. In the same year he left home for Dublin to study drawing, returning two years later to support himself in a school position as drawing-master. He shortly formed a romantic and unfortunate attachment for one of his pupils. He was not thought eligible by the young lady's father, his suit was scornfully rejected, and all communication forbidden between the lovers. Under the agitation of the separation the delicate, high-strung girl became ill and died. Banim, intensely emotional by nature, abandoned himself to the tide of grief. Exposure to bad weather at the time of the funeral and after, when he wandered for days careless and scarce conscious of his whereabouts, together with the agony of his sorrow, resulted in a collapse of body and mind from which it took months to recover; this planted the seeds of a disorder that eventually brought him to his death. On his partial recovery he resolved to give up art for literature, went to Dublin, and half starved there for two years. But in spite of struggles the Dublin experiment ended prosperously. He wrote a tragedy, *Damon and Pythias,* that was accepted by Macready and put upon the stage at Covent Garden with triumphant success. This was in 1821. A visit home followed the success of the tragedy, during which he married and planned a fresh literary campaign. London was thought a better field than Dublin for his talents, and in 1822, with a few pounds in his pocket and accompanied by his young wife, he entered upon the struggle of life there without a single friend or even an introductory letter.

The illness of his wife after their arrival in London soon exhausted their slender store, and necessity drove Banim to continued literary labor beyond his strength. At this time, when circumstances called for all his health and energy, anxiety and excessive toil induced a terrible illness, a return of the racking pains that had tortured him for months after the death of his first love. From this to the end of his life Banim fought his battle with a broken sword. He worked on with set teeth, besieged and prostrated by illness after illness. He scarce wrote three pages of his stories, he tells his brother, free from "wringing, burning, agonizing pain." The story of his life from his arrival in London to his death is a story of toil, disappointment, and disaster, with painful illness as an almost constant attendant. When only thirty-one years old, his health was so feeble that change of air and scene was declared to be his only hope. In 1829 he left London for Boulogne-sur-Mer. There he was stricken with paralysis of the lower limbs.

When in 1832 cholera was epidemic in Boulogne, the paralyzed man was attacked by it, recovered, relapsed, and again fought his way back to life. This left him ever after weak and shattered in body, and for a time in mind. At last, baffled and broken, he owned himself defeated in the struggle, and wrote for help to his literary friends. And this prostration came just as fame and fortune began to smile upon him. The three series of the *O'Hara Tales* (1825, 1826, 1829), written by him and his brother Michael in collaboration, had been entirely successful, and his novel *The Boyne Water* (1825) had been well received. But at the moment when the road for the first time seemed smooth before him, his literary work was done. The appeal to his brethren of the pen had not been in vain. Subscriptions from literary men, a benefit performance in Dublin, a purse from his fellow-citizens of Kilkenny, and other generous gifts kept him beyond want for the rest of his life. In 1835 he returned to Kilkenny to die. His brother Michael, who met him in Dublin to take him home, was shocked at the ravages that disease and wasting toil had wrought, and describes him—he was then in his thirty-seventh year—as "a meagre, attenuated, almost white-haired old man." After seven more painful years John Banim died at Kilkenny in 1842.

Michael Banim, John's eldest brother, who has appeared in the background of this sketch, was born at Kilkenny in 1796. His education was the same as John's, except that for a time he took up the study of law, only to abandon it shortly, however, because of a reverse of fortune that befell his father. With the self-sacrifice that marked all his relations with father and brother, he devoted himself to unravelling the tangled threads of his father's business. In 1825 he wrote, at John's suggestion, a tale for *The Tales of the O'Hara Family.* This was *Crohoore of the Bill-hook,* one of the most popular of the series, and he continued throughout his brother's literary life to publish jointly with him. After a series of ups and downs of fortune, he died, an old man of seventy-eight, in 1874.

The first of John Banim's novels, considered in their historical sequence, is *The Boyne Water,* a novel after the manner of Scott, in which the thread of a double love story is followed through numberless thrilling adventures, with the siege of Londonderry, the battle of the Boyne, and the siege of Limerick as the great features. The story opens before the outbreak of hostilities between James and William. Parties of Protestant gentry, wrathful and dismayed, dining together in Dublin, tap their swords significantly, and denounce Tyrconnel's policy that is sweeping Protestants from the army, civic offices, the bench, and the bar, and striving to substitute a Catholic for a Protestant ascendency. Frantic parsons declaim against open mass-houses where before there was godly silence, against tolerated priests, Papist prelates at court, and the imminence of universal Popery. All hands contemplate with well-grounded terror the spectacle of the English ascendency for the moment abolished, the native Irish restored to their rights and ready to retaliate upon those who had trampled upon them since Cromwell's time. The love plot turns on a typical dilemma growing out of the conditions of the day, when religious and political feeling ran high, and the nation arrayed itself, Protestant against Catholic, in opposing ranks. There are twin heroes and heroines. Evelyn, a young Protestant gentleman, becomes engaged to Eva M'Donnell, a young Catholic lady. The young lady's brother, Edmund M'Donnell, engages himself to Evelyn's sister. The double marriage is being celebrated when, in the midst of the ceremony, a messenger bursts in with the announcement, "William the Deliverer has landed." In the excitement of the moment the ceremony is suspended; the parsons and priests, who were officiating together at the mixed wedding, break out in fierce recriminations; the parties to the wedding are drawn into the angry altercation. The Protestant sister leaves the Catholic lover's arms for the protection of her brother, and in like manner the Catholic sister takes her place by her brother's side. M'Donnell hastens to join James's army; the Protestant brother and sister make the best of their way to Londonderry, the Protestant refuge in the north. This flight gives occasion for a picture of the country at this critical moment. The roads are astir with Protestants, gentle and simple, hastening to the northern towns where the Williamites were to stand at bay, and passing these are parties of Catholics hurrying in an opposite direction.

The interest in the book as a love story soon fades away, and attention is centred upon battles and sieges and the historical personages that appear upon the stage. The whole story of the long siege of Derry is told from the time King James and his army sat down before the closed gates to the day the English ship broke the boom across the river, and the besiegers were forced sullenly to withdraw. The horrors of the siege are not spared. The Protestants are even reduced to feed upon carrion, and die in the streets of hunger and the fever that comes of it. The Rev. George Walker, the soul of the fighting men of the city, is always well to the front. Clad in his clericals, armed, and with a military sash, he now leads a sally from the walls, now prays for victory in the churches.

The battle scenes at the Boyne are designed to be the feature of the book. All through them there are interesting glimpses of the oddly sorted companions in arms that made up the army of James—the ragged, wild Irish regiments, in motley uniforms, bare-legged, and armed with rusty pikes and firelocks, in strange contrast to the bright chivalry of their French allies. The careful descriptions of the battleground are the result of a tour made by Banim especially to familiarize himself with its topography. The figure of William on his white horse, stern, silent, and in person commanding

and inspiring his troops, is contrasted with that of the incapable James, in the churchyard on Dunore hill, lending a willing ear to the French officer who counsels flight for France, while Sarsfeld vainly urges his majesty to head in person a last charge, and strike with his own arm for his triple crown.

The chief incidents of *The Last Baron of Crana* (1826) fall in the years just following the events of *The Boyne Water*. The novel is both an illustration of the working of the penal laws upon the Catholics within their jurisdiction and a picture of the life of a class of Catholics who lived in open defiance of them. With the first chapter the story plunges into the midst of the battle of Aughrim. Sir Redmund O'Burke, an officer in James's army, is prompted by a soldier's admiration of courage to save the life of Captain Pendergast of William's army from the swords of James's troopers. The tide of the battle then sweeps the two apart, to meet again as William's army wins the day. Sir Redmund lies mortally wounded, and with his last breath asks Pendergast to protect his young son who has survived the battle. In obedience to the dying request, Pendergast finds O'Burke's son, and takes him to his home in the north. With the youth go a priest, his tutor, and a faithful Catholic retainer. *En route* to the north they stop in Dublin. As in *The Boyne Water,* so here the political temper of the time is reflected in the sentiments voiced at gatherings of Protestant gentlemen where Pendergast is a guest. He, with three Catholics now dependent on him for protection, listens eagerly to hear the feeling of the victors regarding the fate of the Catholics. Every voice is raised against the treaty of Limerick as a measure of unmerited leniency toward the vanquished and of ungrateful injustice to the supporters of King William.

In due time, the persecuting laws are passed against the Catholics, and Pendergast must either keep O'Burke uneducated and forbid him the ministrations of his church, or break the law of the land that made education for a Catholic illegal and forbade a Catholic priest to exercise his functions. He chooses the latter course, and breaks the laws for his young friend's sake. O'Burke is daily tutored by the priest, and in a hut a little removed from the house the mass is regularly celebrated. Moved by a private spite an enemy, who knows of these proceedings, swears out a warrant against O'Burke, the priest, and the faithful retainer of O'Burke, who is a Catholic, and whom Pendergast has made his gamekeeper, and also against some Catholic gentlemen who happen at the time to be Pendergast's guests. The officer of the law visits the house, and orders the household before him. First laying down five pounds, he demands O'Burke's sleek hunter, for by law a Protestant could always claim the horses of a Catholic by paying five pounds a head, and on the same basis takes the handsome coach-horses of Pendergast's guests. He then demands the discharge of Pendergast's gamekeeper, who, as a Catholic, illegally held the position. All the Catholics are then fined in accordance with another statute which provided that all good men must attend Sabbath services of the Established Church once a week, on penalty of a fine for each absence. The suspects are asked how often they have attended public worship in a church of the established form. All answer, "Never." Accordingly the fine is reckoned from the time of the passing of the statute six years back up to date. The bailiff pays his respects last to the priest. When the latter finds himself discovered, knowing death to be the penalty of exercising his office, he fells the bailiff with a swinging blow, dashes through the window, and escapes.

Such is the illustration in this fiction of the penal laws at work upon those within their jurisdiction. The career of the last Baron of Crana, the personage who gives the book its name, represents the career of many Catholics, some of the better sort, who defied the laws and warred against them.

At the close of the civil war, the young Baron of Crana knows that his estates will be confiscated, on the ground of his having held a commission in James's army. In reckless defiance of a condition of things in which he and his Catholic brethren are so outrageously treated he joins a band of Rapparees, and becomes their leader. The Rapparees, so called from their carrying raparies or half-pikes, were wild bands of plunderers, originally recruited from the Catholics who had fought for King James, and who, after the termination of hostilities, continued to exist as freebooters and gentlemen of the road. To them it was a virtue to break the laws, and rob and plunder the officers of a usurping king, the persecutor of them and their faith. It was their delight to rob the rich Sassenachs, and to empty the money-bags of tithe-proctors and tax gatherers as they returned from their rounds laden with King William's dues. The Rapparees, generally speaking recruited from the lower ranks of society, had also a scattering of ruined Catholic gentlemen—some even of the Baron of Crana's pretensions—who took refuge among them, preferring, for one reason or another, the life of outlaws at home to military service in the armies of France or Spain. The leaders of these bands sometimes rivalled Robin Hood in daring, courage, and generosity, and, like him, were the darlings of the poor, whom they disdained to molest. It was as a leader of these bands that the last Baron of Crana, ruined by his devotion to the cause of James, unsettled by the wars, without home or occupation, wound up his career.

In *The Conformists* (1829) Banim again illustrates the practical working of the penal laws. Hugh Darcy, a Catholic country gentleman, is confronted with the problem of educating his two sons in the face of the laws against Catholic education. Tutors fear prosecution, and will not risk teaching the boys, so Mr. Darcy resolves to make a shift to teach them himself. But he loves his ease, soon tires of racking his brains over rusty Latin and forgotten mathematics, and relinquishes the effort, to spend the evenings more comfortably over the bottle. Making the care of the estate his excuse, he leaves the education of the boys in their mother's hands. A Catholic neighbor, who can find no one to teach his daughters, begs Mrs. Darcy, as a special kindness, to allow them to share with the boys the advantages of her instruction. The request granted, two bright young ladies become the fellow-students of her sons, and this situation leads to a collision with the penal laws.

Dan, the younger son, clever with rod and gun but a dunce at his books, is ashamed to display his backwardness before the young ladies, and to make up for lost time betakes himself surreptitiously to a hedge-schoolmaster who, hounded out of his profession by the penal laws, earned his bread as a laborer upon a neighboring farm. This man, overcoming his fears, consents to help Dan out, and, in a lonely spot, screened by a hedge, they daily toil with book and slate. But the plan ends in disaster. The officers of the law get wind of the illegal education, and one fine day a bailiff bursts rudely upon the studious seclusion of the pair. The hedge-schoolmaster gives leg-bail and escapes, but young Dan is dragged off to jail to expiate his crime.

The incident that concludes this story shows the operation of one of the most outrageous and intolerable provisions of the code—that which makes the son of a Catholic who conforms the legal heir to his father's estate. On the son's turning Protestant, not only does he become legal heir, but the father is not allowed, from the moment the son reads his recantation, to sell or mortgage any part of his property. Here the law is brought into operation in this way. Dan has become engaged. An ingenious conspiracy of his enemies forces him to believe that father and mother, brother and mistress have combined against him in an unnatural plot involving the breaking of his engagement and the marriage of his brother to his lady. Dan determines to take his revenge with a weapon as cruel and unnatural as those his family are turning, he believes, against himself. The penal law above referred to is ready to his hand. He resolves to turn Protestant, and thus revenge himself at once upon father, brother, and mistress, by securing the whole patrimony to himself. The story is no less successful as an illustration of the working of the penal law from the fact that Dan finds he has wronged his family in suspecting them, becomes reconciled to them, and marries the lady of his choice.

The Irish novels are one more witness to the purity of the Catholic priesthood in Ireland. The priest unfaithful to his vows is a figure almost unknown to them. *The Nowlans* (1826) is the only one of these stories in which the breaking of a priest's vows for the love of a woman is the central situation.

John Nowlan, the hero of *The Nowlans,* is a handsome, intelligent young peasant, with all the peasant's dower of impulse and passion. Set apart for the priesthood, he has completed his education in the three R's, some Greek and Latin, and plenty of theology. Mr. Long, a wealthy country gentleman, taking a fancy to young Nowlan, domesticates him in the "big house," where he becomes tutor in the classics to Miss Letty Adams, Mr. Long's pretty niece.

The expected happens; the ardent young peasant finds himself inextricably in love with the inexperienced girl who returns his passion. The young man vainly tries to tear himself away from temptation. His resistance is weakened by doubts concerning the faith and practice of his own church. Protestants, seeking to convert him, bring batteries of arguments to bear against his creed. They assail, too, and with special effect at this critical moment, the Roman rule of celibacy as unnatural, and praise marriage as the grand condition of virtuous happiness. The Established Church clergyman, whom Nowlan has come to know, a young man just married and living in blameless happiness with his lovely wife, is to Nowlan the tempting image of a bliss within his own reach if he will but yield to argument. In the ferment of such thoughts and temptations, he and Letty, forgetting all that opposes their love, give themselves up to it completely. Nowlan's vows are broken, and the young pair flee to Dublin to live a life of poverty and struggle until Letty's death in child-bed. At last Nowlan, chastened by repentance, returns to follow the profession which sin and misfortune had interrupted. Thus the only one of these novels that has for its main situation the temptation and sin of a priest, ends in repentance, and a reconciliation between the erring priest and his church.

In *The Peep o' Day, or John Doe* (1825) John Banim has written a story of one of the secret societies—the Shanavests, so called from the part of dress by which the members chose to be distinguished. Their object is here the lowering of rack-rents and tithes. By anonymous letters they proscribe rents and tithe-rates, and where their demands are disregarded inflict summary and dire punishment. They attend to other matters also. In one instance a Shanavest letter commands a Catholic lawyer to plead gratis for all defenders in the tithe-proctor's court; in another the priest finds a Shanavest notice nailed to his door demanding the reduction of Christmas and Easter dues, the reduction of marriage fees to two shillings per pair, and of christening fees to ten pence per head.

The leader of the Shanavests of this tale is the son of a once prosperous farmer. His father was ruined and his sister robbed of her good name by a villanous middleman. To revenge his father and sister he joins the illegal association of which he eventually becomes the leader, bringing his vengeance to a full accomplishment at the story's end, by having the middleman shot and his body tossed into the flames of his own house, which the Shanavests had fired.

Michael Banim's *Crohoore of the Bill-Hook* (1825) is also a story of the secret societies. The Whiteboys are "up." A black-hearted tithe-proctor has aroused their ire and receives a midnight visit. He is dragged from his bed, and buried alive up to the neck. One of the band with a pruning knife in his hand then steps up and after an address delivered in a tone of savage mockery slices the ears from the victim's head. The victim is then made to swear, on the book, that he will abandon forever his unpopular profession. This done, the troop, with a wild "hurrah" that testifies their triumph, withdraw.

The action of *Crohoore* is placed in the period when the peasants labored under the cruel code, then almost in full operation. While deprecating the violence of the Whiteboys, the story aims to make clear the grievances from which the Whiteboy movement arose, and to disabuse Englishmen of the idea that the Whiteboy disturbances were groundless outbreaks of savagery and malice. The peasantry are presented in their poverty and ignorance, neglected, galled, and hard-driven by middlemen and tithe-proctors who squeezed the very marrow from their bones. Under maddening hardships it is seen how natural, almost inevitable, it was that they should blindly seek redress and wreak vengeance in the only way open to them.

In *The Croppy* (1828), by Michael Banim, the scene is the County Wexford; the time, the eve of and during the Rebellion of '98. The novel is a love story moving through a series of historic and semi-historic incidents representing the life men lived in those days of suspense and danger. The novel takes its title from a word applied to the rebels by their enemies as a term of contempt. The rebels affected a fashion of close-cut polls in imitation of the French Republicans. This way of wearing the hair was considered a badge of disaffection, and the crop-head rebel was dubbed the "croppy." *The Croppy* introduces the two parties who were to be antagonists in the impending struggle—the Catholic peasantry, mostly identified with the United Irishmen, the society planning the Rebellion which was to free Ireland from English rule, and the Orangemen, the loyalists and conspiracy hunters, bent on preventing an outbreak or suppressing one if it should occur.

The meetings of the United Irishmen of the early part of the story reflect the attitude of the peasantry of the south toward the Rebellion. An emissary of the United Irishmen comes down from the north to see how matters stand in the County Wexford on the eve of the rising. In a smithy he meets a parochial committee of the society—decent men, snug farmers and small tradesmen they seem—to canvass the situation. He asks if, in their operations, they have proceeded in the spirit of the oath of membership by which they swore to make the society a brotherhood of Irishmen of every religious persuasion. The frank replies told the familiar tale, that generous patriots groaned to hear, of a great movement inspired by the ideal of a happy freedom for a United Ireland, gone wrong, and sunk to the level of a bitter sectarian struggle rooted in old hate, fear, and religious bigotry.

The Croppy gives a sample, too, of the outrages of the Orange yeomanry that marked the attempts to quell the growing disaffection. These deeds convinced the Catholics that the Orangemen were conspiring to exterminate them, and precipitated the Rebellion. This is the kind of thing that was happening all over the country. A United Irishman blacksmith had been making pikes for the use of the rebels, and the pike-heads were concealed beneath the anvil in the shop. Some informer revealed the fact to the yeomanry. The man's son rushes into the smithy with the news that the yeomanry are at his heels to search for concealed weapons. Messengers at once post off to warn neighbors similarly involved. The smith, as the guilty man, hastens from the shop to conceal himself, thinking his wife and children will be unharmed. The yeomanry clatter up to the door; find the bird flown; seize the son and some of the neighbors who are suspected; burn the smithy, and try to turn their captives into informers by torture. Some are fastened to trees and flogged within an inch of their lives. The smith's son is strung up to the limb of a tree and lowered, to try if they can wring from the convulsed lips and bewildered senses of the boy confessions regarding the conspiracy and the hiding-place of his father. The boy, still keeping silence, is again strung up, and again lowered to gasp out a false story, that can do his friends no harm, and may do good, to the effect that the Catholics were about to sweep down on the Orangemen ten thousand strong. This assertion fell in with the belief held by the Orangemen (corresponding to the Catholic fear of them) that their enemies were planning a massacre. Hence operations stop at once; the lad is left to expire in the arms of his parents; there is a rush for the horses, and the Orange cavalry gallop to quarters to prepare for the descent of the ten thousand.

The difficulties of the country gentry who sought to remain neutral during the Rebellion are illustrated in the dilemma of the Sir Thomas Hartley of the story. He is one of those whose sympathies had gone with the United Irishmen up to the time their proceedings changed from open remonstrance to secret conspirarcy; but he shrank from rebellion, and refused to wade through blood to freedom. He detested the bigotry of the Orangemen, however, and actively opposed their pitch-cappings, scourgings, half-hangings and whole-hangings of peasants on the mere suspicion of rebellion. As a result of his conduct the Orangemen marked

him for an enemy and a traitor, and the rebellious peasantry believed they had in him a secret champion of their conspiracy. Of one side of this understanding he is made well aware at the very outbreak of the Rebellion, when, sitting at home, he is startled one day by a tremendous shout, like the clamor of a thousand throats. Looking from his window he sees, swarming on his lawn, a motley multitude composed of the Catholic peasantry of the whole neighborhood, armed with rusty guns, bludgeons, scythes, and formidable pikes. The peasantry are "up" and the Rebellion has begun. A spokesman steps before the mob and informs Sir Thomas that he, the "barrow-knight," has been chosen to take command of the troops of the Union drawn up before him, and that they are ready to follow him to the world's end. On his declining the honor, and declaring he will have no hand in the Rebellion, the threatening shouts of the wild crowd bear in upon him the perils of the trimmer's position:—

> "What's the rason you have for skulkin' back, Sir Thomas?"
>
> "You're afeared, Sir Thomas, an' the curse o' Cromwell on all cowards. But ar'n't you afeared iv *us*? Ar'n't you afeared we'd drag you down from that windee, an' make you march wid us, or die by us?"
>
> "Oncet more, an' for the last time, Sir Thomas, will you be one among us or an inemy agin us?"
>
> "Smash the duour!"

Sir Thomas, by good fortune, is able to escape rebel violence, but only to be caught on the other horn of the dilemma. The Orangemen, regarding his inactivity as disloyalty, pack the jury, try him, and condemn him to death as a traitor.

The scenes from the heart of the Rebellion make a vivid picture of the state of the County Wexford—the roads astir with the rebels in disorderly mobs, burning houses and piking the enemies they could lay hands on, while the Orangemen retaliated by bayoneting or shooting every timid straggler in a peasant's coat who had not turned out with the main body. The rebel army, officers and men, becomes familiarly known. The scene upon the hill of Ballyorvil, where the rebels are preparing for the attack on Enniscorthy, is curious to the last degree in the glimpses given of the grotesque appearance and doings of the "throops of the Union." In the front of this body were collected all who bore firearms, some few shouldering muskets, and the rest clutching guns of every kind and calibre, plundered from the villages they passed through on their way, wrested from parties of defeated Orangemen, or dragged from places of concealment to grace the long-expected day. Ammunition was scarce, and carried for the most part in bits of paper thrust inaccessibly into the depths of their pockets. Behind the "gunsmen" rose groves of long pikes roughly fashioned from the anvil, rude, black weapons, but serviceable, and fit instruments in this civil strife where the pomp and circumstance of war found no place. This army was clad as strangely as it was armed. Uniforms there were none. Some had pouches or cross-belts wrested from the soldiers, but most were dressed in their usual costumes, except that many doffed coats, stockings, and brogues to go into action in the broiling summer weather as cool and light as possible. The leaders, mostly farmers and small tradesmen, with a few priests, among them the burly figure of the Father Rourke of history, later hung upon Wexford bridge, were out in front of their commands. They were clad like the rank and file, except perhaps for a green hatband or some badge of green fastened upon them. These officers, with difficulty raising their tones of command above the general clamor, in which the shrill cries of women and children who had accompanied the men bore no inconsiderable part, were busied in pushing, pulling, coaxing, and cursing their unruly throngs into some sort of disposition for march and battle.

From the hill of Ballyorvil the story follows the rebel forces as they sweep pell-mell, with undisciplined courage into Enniscorthy; to their camp on Vinegar Hill, with particular attention to the slaughter *ad libitum* of cattle to appease their hunger, and Orangemen to satisfy their revenge; thence to Wexford, and to the capture of Ross, and the retreat therefrom, with which the novel as a story of the Rebellion concludes.

The preoccupation of the Banims with the past and present fortunes of their co-religionists, and their strong Catholic sympathies, are written all over their work, which is largely concerned with the pressure of the penal laws upon the Catholics, with the lives and ministrations of the priests of their church, and in general with the Catholic peasantry. Gerald Griffin, a friend of Banim's, who brought out a collection of Irish stories shortly after the publication of the second series of *O'Hara* tales, was, like Banim, a Catholic, wrote with strong Catholic sympathies, and kept before his eyes a declared purpose of faithfully presenting in his stories his Catholic countrymen and their religion. A Catholic spirit, if not always apparent upon the surface of his work, still breathes through it all.

Griffin came of a middle-class Catholic family. His father was a brewer in the city of Limerick, where Gerald was born in 1803. In 1810 the family left Limerick to reside in the country, at first at Fairy Lawn (near Loughill on the Shannon), then at Adare, and later at Pallas Kenry. Like Carleton and the Banims he received an imperfect education, intrusted to the care of whatever tutors or masters happened to be at hand, among them a preceptor who maintained in his methods

some of the oddities of the hedge-school "philomaths." Memories of this man and of the school he kept in the little thatched Catholic chapel are preserved in the schoolroom scene of Griffin's *The Rivals* (1830). Gerald's boyhood and youth seem a record of almost unbroken happiness. He spent his time in hunting, or in boating and fishing upon the Shannon, or in rambles about the country. His taste for the romantic past delighted in the antiquarian remains in which the neighborhood was rich. The noble assemblage of ecclesiastical ruins within the demesne of the Earl of Dunraven, which adjoined the town of Adare, especially appealed to his reverent and pious nature, and doubtless helped to strengthen that interest in his country's past which eventually found expression in his historical novel *The Invasion* (1832). The scenes and experiences of this happy boyhood and youth were the stuff of which his prose and poetry were made. In those days he gleaned from the remote and quiet neighborhoods in which he lived, or which he visited, their legends, traditions, and folk-tales, and came by the knowledge of peasant life and character which he afterward worked into his fiction.

With his twentieth year this life of happy pastimes and pastoral calm, so gracefully reflected in many wistful retrospects of his poetry, came to an end. A love for literature, which had been his from childhood, developed into an overwhelming passion for literary fame, and in 1823, extravagantly hopeful of quick success, he left home for London to live by his pen in the city wilderness. A letter to his parents, written after two years of life in London, tells of his early plans:—

> "I cannot with my present experience conceive anything more comical than my own views and measures at the time. A young gentleman totally unknown, even to a single family in London, coming into town with a few pounds in one pocket and a brace of tragedies in another, supposing that one will set him up before the others are exhausted, is not a very novel, but a very laughable delusion."

A cherished ambition of succeeding by his own unaided efforts, an extreme sensitiveness that made him unwilling to put himself under obligations to those upon whom he felt he had no claim, threw him back upon his own resources and made it difficult for the one friend of earlier days whom he found in London, Banim, or for chance friends or acquaintances, no matter how kindly intentioned, to render him any assistance.

Disappointment and delay, of course, attended his efforts to get his plays upon the stage. His purse empty, reduced to desperate straits, he turned to hack work of any and every kind. In spite of wasting and continuous labor he could scarce keep soul and body together. He lived in wretched lodgings in poverty as extreme as ever a Grub Street penny-a-liner survived, going sometimes for days without food, and toiling all the while at a pace beyond human nature to endure. Pride forbade him to own himself vanquished. "That horrid word 'failure,' " he wrote to his brother; "no, death first." And this was no vain boast, for at times the grim alternative to which he alludes was not far from its accomplishment.

The story of his first two years is distressing and painful to read. But after that prospects brightened. He obtained by slow degrees a footing as a magazine writer. In 1827 he made a decided hit with *Holland Tide* (1826), a series of tales of Irish life that completely established his character with the periodicals, and seemed to promise much for the future. Early in 1827 he returned to live with his brother at Pallas Kenry, where he wrote *Tales of the Munster Festivals* (1827), which more than sustained the reputation made by *Holland Tide. The Collegians* (1829) crowned his two preceding successes. To Griffin, however, the game had not been worth the candle. He had, to use his own phrase, "won half a name," but at the expense of a constitution sapped and shattered by severe trials and wasting toil.

The rest of the story may be briefly told. He lived mostly at home in Pallas Kenry with his brothers, for a time continuing his literary work. Always of a religious nature, religion gradually filled more and more of his feeling and thought, and he resolved to take up a religious vocation. In 1838 he joined the Christian Brothers, a Roman Catholic lay order who gave themselves to the education of the children of the poor. With them he lived and worked until his death of a fever in 1840.

In his survey of Irish life, Griffin attends to the life of the peasantry and to the life of his own order—the rural middle class; the gentry are occasionally introduced; the nobility are scarcely heard of.

Three of the *Tales of the Munster Festivals,* "Card-Drawing," "The Hand and the Word," and "The Aylmers of Bally-Aylmer," deal with life on the southwest coast of Ireland. In the first two of these the fisher-folk appear. They are seen occupied as was their daily wont—they talk Irish, hunt seals, go to sea in canoes to fish, lade the turf-boats, till their gardens, eat potatoes and oaten bread, exercise themselves in offices of kindness toward strangers, and obey their priests in all reasonable matters. They are seen also, under the spur of dark passion, acting out, now and again, the tragedies that broke upon the peaceful regularity of their lives. The tales of the fisher-folk gain wonderfully in effect from the romantic setting of giddy precipice and perilous sea before which the little dramas are enacted. Griffin knew this coast well, felt its wild charm, and makes the reader feel it. The outlook of these stories is upon the stupendous cliffs and crags for which the coast is famous, upon vistas of bizarre and fantastic grandeur—insular columns and pinnacles, amphitheatres, and arches, deep caverns, and grottos worn from the solid rock, and, girdling all, the board Atlantic tossing its bright green waves against the rocky walls, or heaving sullenly at their feet. The scenes from this wild coast are introduced not merely for their picturesqueness, but are used to bring together in a single impression the fearful in landscape and the dangerous and desperate in human passion, so that moral and physical gulfs and precipices combine to produce situations of poignant terror. The scene in "The Hand and the Word," in which Pennie's happy lover, struggling for his life with a jealous rival, is hurled from a beetling crag into the sea hundreds of feet below, is an instance of this. A situation in "Card-Drawing" is another instance. Kinchela, tortured by the guilt of a murder, the responsibility for which he has fastened upon his rival, is being lowered by a rope from the cliff-top. Suspended in mid-air between the cliff-top and the sea, he hears a strand of the rope snap just above him and beyond his reach. In an agony of terror he holds the incident for the threat of an angry God against his murderous and unrepentant soul.

In "The Aylmers of Bally-Aylmer" the gentry of the coast of Kerry are in the foreground. The story is laid in the eighteenth century. The country about the home of the Aylmers is a wild district of mountain and bog, doomed by nature to poverty, far removed from any considerable centre of civilization, and traversed by few regular roads. The state of society in this section, to judge from the story, was much like that which subsisted in the Highlands of Scotland in the early part of the eighteenth century. Smuggling was the lucrative trade, and practised by all classes, gentlemen and peasants, Catholics and Protestants alike. To be known to meddle in the "running trade" brought no opprobrium upon the character of a gentleman. In the deep natural harbors among the mountains privateers found their shelter. All classes united in a conspiracy to baffle the officers of the revenue, and informers found themselves in such danger that their trade was almost abandoned. Gentlemen brought in oceans of Burgundy and brandy, never destined to pass through the hands of an exciseman, which they got in exchange for sheepskins and other commodities.

Griffin alone of the novelists touches upon one odd and incongruous element of Irish life—that of the Palatines, or "Palentins," as the peasantry called them. They were German emigrants brought over by a few great landlords assisted by a grant from the Irish Parliament. This was early in the eighteenth century, when English commercial legislation adverse to Irish interests had resulted in poverty, famine, and an almost total depopulation of districts in the south and west. With the hope of reviving agriculture at a time when the penal laws were driving native energy to the continent, these Palatines were brought over. They were a part of the tide of German emigration that set toward the American colonies at the same period. The "Limerick Dutchman" and the "Pennsylvania Dutch" are of one stock. As they appear in Griffin's story of "Suil Dhuv, or The Coiner" they are peaceful and inoffensive in their habits; in religion Protestants, adhering to one or another non-Conformist type of worship; and possessed of the thrift and industry which those who brought them over thought might be edifying to the shiftless and go-easy ways of the Catholic peasantry.

"Suil Dhuv, or the Coiner" acquaints the reader with the footing upon which these foreigners stood with the native peasantry among whom they had dropped, as it were from the clouds. A difference in religion, habits, and disposition, and the partiality shown by the lords of the soil to their new protégés in granting them long leases and other favors, are seen to result in a deep-rooted hatred between Palatine and native. The natives, generous and open-handed to a fault, had an inexpressible contempt for the unremitting exertion in acquiring and the caution in distributing money of these foreign interlopers whose "heart was in a trifle," and whose cold-blooded prudence never gave the rein to genial or convivial impulse. They hated also their dry Puritanical exactness in religious matters, and, indeed, had little in common with them beyond the religious bigotry and national prejudice that moved each to return heartily the evil feelings of the other.

In the fat Palatine parson of the story, some of the traits that aroused the contemptuous aversion of the Catholic peasantry crop out. When he speaks, it is in a strong German accent, strangely mingled with the broad drawling patois of the natives, and in a dry formal phraseology of religious cant. He has the true Evangelical appetite and solicitude as to the quantity and quality of his food and drink, which Thackeray and other satirists of the brethren have made the target of their shafts. And his portrait includes also greed for gold as a feature, a weakness comically illustrated by the purchase of a brass ingot believed by him to be pure gold. He obtained it by imposing, as he thought, upon what he mistook for the extreme simplicity of the peasant who offered it to him. The peasant turned out to be a clever rascal, whose plausible story and simple countenance enabled him to palm off his wares on unsuspecting strangers.

In "The Half Sir," "The Barber of Bantry," "Tracy's Ambition," and *The Collegians,* middle-class life has a prominent place. In "The Half Sir" it is the hero's social position as one of this class that gives the story its coloring, and the plot its direction. This hero is a young man of low origin who has inherited a fortune. This fortune and his education have raised a barrier between him and the class to which he belonged. His sympathies lead him to seek the society of rank and position. Here he finds himself snubbed right and left.

His misery over the slights and cold shoulders to which he has exposed himself are surrounded with an atmosphere of tragic gloom quite out of keeping with the weakness of the situation. Weary of slights and snubs, the hero abjures high society, and settles down as a misanthropic member of the middle class. As such he has his differences from the nobility and gentry. Sporting tastes are wanting; he can stay away from hunts, horse-races, or cock-fights without compunction. Sociable and convivial tastes are also undeveloped; he never gives dinners, dances, or parties, and shows no zeal to make himself and his friends drunk at every opportunity. His benefactions do not stream from the heart in the bursts of impulsive generosity that delight both the giver and the humble recipient of bounty. The poor man can scarcely be grateful to so cold and phlegmatic a benefactor.

The "half quality" of whom this hero is a type were not in high favor with the peasantry. A peasant of this tale has referred contemptuously to the hero as a "half sir," and is asked what he means by the expression. He makes himself clear. The "half sir," he says, is—

> "A sort of small gentleman, that way: the singlings[1] of a gentleman, as it were. A made man—not a born gentleman. Not great, all out, nor poor, that way entirely. Betuxt and betune, as you may say. Neither good potale, nor yet strong whiskey. Neither beef nor vale. . . . A man that wouldn't go to a hunt, nor a race-course, nor a cock-fight, nor a hurlenmatch, nor a dance, nor a fencen-bout, nor any one born thing. Sure that's no gentleman! A man that gives no parties nor was ever known yet to be drunk in his own house. O poh!—A man that was never seen to put his hand in his pocket of a frosty mornen and say to a poor man, 'Hoy, hoy! my good fellow, here's a tinpenny for you, and get a drap o' something warm and comfortable agen the day.' A man that was never by any mains *overtaken in liquor* himself, nor the cause of anybody else being so, either. Sure such a man as that has no heart!"

Mr. Edmund Moynahan and his family in *The Barber of Bantry* are distinctly middle class, though eventually Moynahan forfeits his standing. Unhappily drawn into the bacchanalian whirl of the gentry, he loses his habitual sobriety, and becomes a "sitter-up-o'-nights" and bottle companion to his genteel, bibulous neighbors, drowning integrity and respectability in claret and whiskey punch. But before his fall he was an exemplary member of his class. He rose and retired early. The dawn saw him watching his laborers in the field or on the road, and till sunset he was occupied in business, or in advising and assisting his tenants. His wife was a stirring, competent woman. She knew *Buchanan's Domestic Medicine* from cover to cover; superintended the dairy or the flaxdressers at work in the barn; knit stockings, and nursed the sick tenantry. Dancing, riding, flirting, dinner-giving, and the like she left to the gentry. In the Moynahan establishment, economy and industry went hand in hand. Nor were the Moynahans without their pleasures. In the evening there was reading aloud, while Mr. Moynahan dozed; Mrs. Moynahan knit or played with the children; and occasionally there came a chance visitor to be entertained with temperate cheer. They were pious people, too; they fasted on fast days and kept holy days holy; they were edified by the unadorned exhortation of the parish priest; in short, they lived at peace with themselves, the world, and heaven.

Mr. Moynahan was no convivialist; he prided himself upon the *wholesomeness* of his fare, and frowned upon the wild and extravagant follies of the gentry, eschewing the luxury and profusion he could not afford. The duelling habits of the gentry were to him bloodthirsty and barbarous. Horse-races, hunts, and cock-fights were not his passions. Like the "half sir," he was neither sporting man nor convivialist.

Mr. Moyanahan was tax-collector for his district, and in this vocation also failed to conform naturally to the standards of the gentry. When he began to assess taxes, he shocked his genteel acquaintances by a very ungenteel disposition to do so in proportion to real values and according to law. The code of the gentry expected a tax-collector to make his own fortune as fast as possible, and to let his friends off easily. Moynahan seemed indisposed to follow the customary procedure; he showed a very ungenteel squeamishness in cheating the King's exchequer for his own good and the good of his friends. On his visits to them in a professional capacity he was surprised at receiving assurances that they had no windows, no hearths, no carriages, horses, nor cows; in a word, that the wealth they were wont on all other occasions to display with pride had suddenly and mysteriously dwindled to nothing. If he shook his head and suggested the propriety of a personal inspection, he was answered by a polite reminder that to do so would be a reflection upon their veracity. He was then invited to dine and spend the night with them, and loaded with attentions. A company of taxable gentlemen were there to meet him. The conversation did not fail to bring out the course of his predecessors in office; they had pursued a certain line of conduct; he surely would not make himself singular. Each member of the company had some little thing he might want. One was anxious to supply his cellar, another his table, a hundred his pantry. All hands looked forward to his visit, and assured him that every house in the country had a convivial board, a comfortable chamber, and a blazing fire for the tax-gatherer. Of course, so much kindness and generosity overcame the ungenteel scruples of the good-natured man; the least the tax-collector could do for his friends was to write down fifty, or less, where a hundred should stand. The middle-class conscience at last conformed to the standard of the gentry.

The Daly family in *The Collegians* have many traits in common with the middle-class people just referred to. There is the same homeliness, the same happy, if somewhat insipid, domesticity. They have the tendency, present also in the others, to moralize every incident that comes within reach. And they share also with the others the pietistic sentiment (very different from the heart-felt religion of the peasantry) that does duty as a sanction for the little prudences and decorums demanded by their circumstances and position.

The middle class, as Griffin portrays it, differs from the nobility and gentry in the lack of the dash and go, the frankness and high spirit, the sporting and convivial tastes, the recklessness, and wild wit and gayety. It wants also the primitive force, the depth, the fervor, the homely but subtle and searching humor of peasant life. It is more sober and subdued in tone and temper, more decorous. It is prudent, takes thought for the morrow, is domestic, moral, conscientious, and pious, with conventionality, tameness, timidity, and insipidity for its unpleasant features.

William Carleton, the last and greatest of this group, and the greatest of these Irish novelists, was born in Prillisk, County Tyrone, in 1798. His father was a peasant tenant, and William passed his youth among scenes precisely similar to those he describes in his stories. Both father and mother were peasants of the finest type. They seem to have summed up in themselves the best traits, the accomplishments, and the knowledge of their class, and to have possessed in a high degree the domestic virtues which are the glory of the humbler Irish. Of his parents Carleton says:—

> "My father indeed was a very humble man, but on account of his unaffected piety and stainless integrity of principle, he was held in high esteem by all who knew him, no matter of what rank they might be. . . . My father possessed a memory not merely great or surprising, but absolutely astonishing. As a narrator of old tales, legends, and historical anecdotes he was unrivalled, and his stock of them inexhaustible. He spoke the Irish and the English languages with equal fluency. With all kinds of charms, old ranns, or poems, old prophecies, religious superstitions, tales of pilgrims, miracles and pilgrimages, anecdotes of blessed priests and friars, revelations from ghosts and fairies, he was thoroughly well acquainted. I have never heard since, during a tolerably large intercourse with Irish society, both educated and uneducated—with the antiquary, the scholar, or the humble *senachie*—any single legend, tradition, or usage, that, so far as I can recollect, was perfectly new to me, or unheard before in some similar or cognate guise.

> "My mother possessed the sweetest and most exquisite of human voices. In her early life, I had often been told, by those who had heard her sing,

that any previous intimation of her attendance at a dance, wake, or other festive occasion, was sure to attract crowds of persons, many from a distance of several miles, in order to hear from her lips the touching old airs of the country. No sooner was it known that she would attend any such meeting, than the news of it spread through the neighborhood like wild-fire, and the people flocked from all parts to hear her, just as the fashionable world does now, when the name of some eminent songstress is announced in the papers—with this difference, that upon such occasions, the voice of the one falls only on the cultivated *ear,* whilst that of the latter falls deep upon the untutored heart. She was not so well acquainted with the English tongue as my father, although she spoke it with sufficient ease for all the purposes of life; and for this reason among others she always gave the Irish versions of the songs in question rather than the English ones."[2]

Carleton's education was of the humblest description. As his father removed from one small farm to another, from townland to townland, Carleton attended the hedge-schools wherever he happened to be. Government, in its endeavor to crush out Catholic education, had only surrounded it, as it had the Catholic priesthood, with a halo; and Carleton shared in the strange enthusiasm for Greek and Latin, and "the larnin'" in general, that was not uncommon among ditchers and ploughboys. Carleton sat under a series of hedge-schoolmasters, and knew by experience both the harmlessly eccentric, and cruel and violent variety; a niece of his died of an inflammation that resulted from the master's plucking her ear with such violence as to bring on inflammation of some of the internal tendons. Carleton also picked up here and there some smattering of higher learning as opportunity offered.

In his fifteenth year he started for Munster in search of education as a poor scholar. The plan was not carried out, however, and he was soon home again, devoting himself assiduously to the enjoyment of fairs and markets, wakes, weddings, christenings, and merrymakings. For some two or three years he remained at home, and was distinguished as a dancer and athlete of local celebrity, and a prominent figure at all festivities. As a true peasant, too,—we have his own word for it,—he was an adept at dressing and swinging the "sprig of shillelagh." He enjoyed also a great reputation for his supposed learning, among his own family more especially, which led them to destine him for the priesthood.

When about nineteen he left home again, this time on a pilgrimage. His father had often told him the stories that centred about St. Patrick's Purgatory on the little island in Lough Derg. To this romantic spot Carleton went as one of the stream of pilgrims. What he saw there affected him unfavorably, set him thinking on religious questions, and was the occasion of his later change of faith, for the became a Protestant, though in later years he returned, in sympathy at least, to the religion of his fathers.

An epoch in Carleton's life was made by his chancing upon a copy of *Gil Blas.* A longing to see the world consumed him, and he left home a third time, making his way to Dublin, where for years he had a hard struggle with poverty; indeed, all through his life the wolf was never far from the door. In Dublin he fell in with Cæsar Otway, a Protestant controversialist and proselytizer, who, though of a harsh and unamiable character, stood Carleton's friend, and gave him his start in literature by getting him to write his account of his Lough Derg pilgrimage (from a Protestant controversialist point of view) in *The Lough Derg Pilgrim,* later included in the *Traits and Stories.*

From this time on his life was uneventful. He married the daughter of a schoolmaster, and taught for a while, but eventually supported himself entirely by his pen. When about thirty years old he published the *Traits and Stories of the Irish Peasantry* (1830), which established his reputation. Then came *Fardarougha the Miser* (1839), and *Valentine M'Clutchy* (1847).

The Young Ireland movement was at this time in full swing. Carleton did not escape from its influence, and contributed to *The National Library* the short novels *Paddy Go-Easy* (1845), *Rody the Rover* (1845), and *Art Maguire* (1847), all designed to correct peasant weaknesses and follies—intemperance, bad farming and housekeeping, and secret societies. On Banim's death, he applied, without success, for the pension the government had given his fellow-novelist. Had he obtained it, he would have been freed from the hack work that may have had something to do with the decline of his genius. Carleton died in Dublin in 1869, at the age of seventy.

Carleton's work, unique in many ways, is especially so for the light it throws upon the strange system of peasant education that prevailed in the days of his youth. "The Hedge School" and "Going to Maynooth," two tales from the *Traits and Stories,* give a most full and faithful account of the hedge-schoolmaster—that quaint and curious product of the laws against Catholic education,—of his school, his methods of instruction, his pupils, and his status in rural social life. The fact that the hedge-schoolmaster and the hedge-school have passed away forever under the stress of social changes gives these stories a strong interest as social documents.

The hedge-schoolmasters were a class of men so called because, when the penal laws were in operation and to teach publicly in a schoolhouse was impossible, they would settle on some green spot behind a hedge, where the sons of the farmers from the country round flocked to them, in spite of spies and statutes, to learn whatever they could teach. Even after the abolition of the penal laws against Catholic education the same customs for a long time prevailed in neighborhoods where from poverty or other reasons there was no schoolhouse.

These masters, as Carleton presents them, were for the most part originals, eccentric to the last degree. They combined a real enthusiasm for learning with a deal of ludicrous pedantry. Learning was scarce in the country, and any one having the character of it excited in the peasantry a profound reverence that kept the pride of these gentlemen at the full stretch of inflation. In their deportment they were consequential and dictatorial, with the airs of superiority that resulted from a sense of their own knowledge and a pitying contempt for the dark ignorance of those around them. In the effort to preserve their professional dignity, they intrenched themselves behind a great solemnity of manner, which the irrepressible humor of their country was continually attacking and breaking through. A curious custom that prevailed among them, in accordance with which a hedge-schoolmaster established himself by driving away those less qualified and usurping their place, made acuteness and quickness as essential to them as learning. If a schoolmaster desired to settle in a town which already possessed a teacher, the proper method of procedure was to challenge him to a public debate upon the chapel green or some convenient place. The peasants always witnessed these debates with the keenest relish, and encouraged them as tending to maintain a high standard in the profession. In such contests the victory was to the ready-witted, and once a master was defeated—"sacked" or "made a hare of" were the Irish expressions—the reverence of the country-side was gone from him and forthwith transferred to the person of the victor. It was not expected of the hedge-schoolmaster to instruct in morality or religion; that was the priest's business, and, indeed, these men were far from exemplary in manners and morals. An inordinate love of whiskey, odd as it may appear, was often a recommendation in a teacher, and one which, to do them justice, few were without. This is illustrated in "The Hedge-School." An Irish peasant is asked why he sent his child to Mat Meegan, a master notoriously addicted to liquor, rather than to Mr. Frazer, a man of sober habits who taught in the same neighborhood:—

" 'Why do I send them to Mat Meegan, is it?' he replied—'and do you think, sir,' said he, 'that I'd send them to that dry-headed dunce, Mr. Frazher, with his black coat upon him, and his caroline hat, and him wouldn't take a glass of poteen wanst in seven years? Mat, sir, likes it, and teaches the boys ten times betther whin he's dhrunk nor whin he's sober; and you'll never find a good tacher, sir, but's fond of it. As for Mat, when he's *half gone,* I'd turn him agin the country for deepness in larning; for it's then he rhymes it out of him, that it would do one good to hear him.'

" 'So,' said I, 'you think that a love of drinking poteen is a sign of talent in a schoolmaster?'

" 'Ay, or in any man else, sir,' he replied. 'Look at tradesmen, and 'tis always the cleverest that you'll find fond of the dhrink! If you had hard Mat and Frazher, the other evening, at it—what a hare Mat made of him! but he was just in proper tune for it, being, at the time, purty well I thank you, and did not lave him a leg to stand upon. He took him in Euclid's Ailments and Logicals, and proved in Frazher's teeth, that the candlestick before them was the church-steeple, and Frazher himself the person; and so sign was on it, the other couldn't disprove it, but had to give in.' "

The schoolroom scenes in "The Hedge-School" are wonderful in dialogue and as genre pictures, and impress the reader with a sense of reality as vivid as the printed page can convey. One or two extracts from the story will illustrate this, the first a passage describing the scholars. Surrounding a large turf fire in the centre of the schoolhouse floor is a circle of urchins—

"Sitting on the bare earth, stones, and hassocks, and exhibiting a series of speckled shins, all radiating towards the fire like sausages on a *Poloni* dish. There they are—wedged as close as they can sit; one with half a thigh off his breeches, another with half an arm off his tattered coat—a third without breeches at all, wearing as a substitute a piece of his mother's old petticoat pinned about his loins—a fourth, no coat—a fifth, with a cap on him, because he has got a scald, from having sat under the juice of fresh hung bacon—a sixth with a black eye—a seventh two rags about his heels to keep his kibes clean—an eighth crying to get home, because he has got a headache, though it may be as well to hint, that there is a drag-hunt to start from beside his father's in the course of the day. In this ring, with his legs stretched in a most lordly manner, sits, upon a deal chair, Mat himself, with his hat on, basking in the enjoyment of unlimited authority. His dress consists of a black coat, considerably in want of repair, transferred to his shoulders through the means of a clothes-broker in the county-town; a white cravat, round a large stuffing, having that part which comes in contact with the chin somewhat streaked with brown—a black waistcoat, with one or two 'tooth-an'-egg' metal buttons sewed on where the original had fallen off—black corduroy inexpressibles, twice dyed, and sheep's-gray stockings. In his hand is a large, broad ruler, the emblem of his power, the woeful instrument of executive justice and the signal of terror to all within his jurisdiction. In a corner below is a pile of turf, where, on entering, every boy throws his two sods, with a *hitch* from under his left arm. He then comes up to the master, catches his forelock with finger and thumb, and bobs down his head, by way of making him a bow, and goes to his seat. Along the walls on the ground is a series of round stones, some of them capped with a straw collar or hassock, on which the boys sit; others have bosses, and many of them hobs—a light but compact kind of boggy substance found in the mountains. On these several of them sit; the greater number of them, however, have no seats whatever, but squat themselves down, without compunction, on the hard floor. . . . Near the master himself are the larger boys, from twenty-two to fifteen—shaggy-headed slips, with loose-breasted shirts lying open about their bare chests; ragged colts, with white, dry, bristling beards upon them, that never knew a razor; strong stockings on their legs; heavy brogues, with broad, nail-paved soles; and breeches open at the knees."

In "The Poor Scholar" Carleton presents a social type as distinctly the product of the penal laws as the hedge-schoolmaster. The so-called "poor scholars" were recruited from the poorest of the peasantry in districts where next to no Catholic education could be had, where the stirring lad might contrive to learn reading and writing, but scarcely more.

It was the highest ambition of the Irish peasant to make a priest of his boy, as it was of the Scotch peasant to see his son a minister of the Kirk. If a boy showed a love for "the larnin'," was eager to pursue it, and generally clever and promising, his father was apt to destine him for the priesthood. A subscription raised among the neighbors solved the question of ways and means. Thus provided with a small sum to start him, the poor scholar made for the south—for Munster, the paradise of hedge-schoolmasters and the goal for poor scholars. The sketch of Jemmy M'Evoy, the poor scholar of Carleton's tale, will bring out the general character and experiences of the class.

Jemmy M'Evoy is the son of a poor man who tills a "spot" of barren farmland. For all their drudgery from morning to night and from year's end to year's end, the family can scarce keep body and soul together. Jemmy resolves to raise his old father from distress, or die in the struggle. He plans to start for Munster as a poor scholar to educate himself for the priesthood, and swears he will never return until he can come back "a priest an' a gintleman." To further the plan, the support of the parish priest is enlisted. He puts the case before his congregation, and asks from them, as was customary, a generous subscription to start the poor scholar to Munster to make himself "a priest an' a gintleman." A good collection comes in; his funds are sewed in the lining of his coat; and the bundle is over his shoulder. Then follows the parting with mother and father and brothers and sisters—an uproar of grief, last embraces, and benedictions mingled with the bursts of lamentation; then the open road for the south; kind entertainment by the way, and no pay accepted from the poor scholar; Munster at last; a hedge-school receives him, and the first step is taken toward making himself "a priest an' a gintleman." The poor scholar, quick and industrious as he is, serves as the butt of the

master's gibes and insult, and the victim of his brutal temper. As a climax to his trials he catches a contagious fever that is raging. The master then promptly turns him out upon the road. Having pulled through the fever, steady in the purpose to make himself a priest and relieve the destitution of his family, he returns to the hedge-school to brave again the tyrannies of the master. The poor scholar's trials end happily, however. The story of the master's barbarity gets abroad, and brings him kind friends who send him to a good school. In due time he is ordained; returns to his home in the north; is received by his own with open arms and pious jubilations, and is "a priest an' a gintleman" at last.

In *Valentine M'Clutchy* (a powerful book, despite its grossly partisan spirit) Carleton gives a detailed study of the character and career of an Irish land agent or middleman of the worst type, of Orange bigotry at work, and of the so-called New Reformation movement in its attempts at the conversion of Papists.

There are middlemen, or land agents, everywhere, but political and social conditions gave Ireland a type of its own. The course of Irish history had made most of its landlords Protestants. The position of an Irish Protestant landlord living in the midst of a degraded population, differing from him in race and religion, had but little attraction, and hence the landlord was apt to live abroad, especially if he possessed English as well as Irish estates, as many Irish landlords did. The system of middlemen was the necessary result of this absenteeism. The landlord, disliking the trouble and difficulty of collecting rents from a number of small tenants, abdicated his active functions, and let his land for a long term, and, generally speaking, at a moderate rent, to a large tenant, or middleman, who took upon himself the whole practical management of the estate, raised the rent of the landlord, and over and above this made a profit for himself by subletting. Sometimes the head tenant followed the example of his landlord, and, abandoning all serious industry, left the care of the property to his subtenant, and in turn became an absentee. He, perhaps, sublet his tenancy again at an increased rent, and the process continued until there might be a half-dozen persons between the landlord and the cultivator of the soil. The fact that many of the landlords were almost perpetual absentees, together with the fact that many of the Irish land agents were magistrates as well, gave Irish middlemen almost unlimited power for tyranny and oppression, and made them the pest of Irish society.

Valentine M'Clutchy, who gives this book its name, has worked himself up from processserver to bailiff, from bailiff to constable, from constable to under-agent, or practical manager of the estate, and thence to chief agent or middleman. This last position he obtained by displacing the good agent who preceded him. The young absentee lord, who spent his time in fashionable dissipations in England, was, between his betting books, his yacht, and his mistress, always in desperate financial straits. M'Clutchy contrived to convince his lordship that the old agent was too soft and humane. He would handle the estate, he assured the young lord, less tenderly, and bring in a larger return. So the estate changed hands, and M'Clutchy became head agent. Once in the position, it is his principle to make the interest of landlord and tenant subservient to his own. To put this principle into practice he strengthens his arm to the utmost. As middleman he has all the power of a landlord. He next aims for the magistracy. A bribe sets him upon the bench; and the powers of the landlord for good or ill are backed by the arm of the law.

He now goes to work in the most approved style of bad agent. The schools, which the good agent, his predecessor, had patronized, are opposed on the ground that they make the peasant independent and politically unmanageable. With apparent good nature he allows the tenants to fall into arrears with their rent; in reality he is lax that he may get a lever to force stiff-necked peasants into compliance with his dictation at election time on penalty of immediate eviction. He tricks them by defective leases. They have trusted his verbal promises only to find them brazenly forgotten, or denied at convenience. They have known him to secrete papers in the thatch eaves of their cabins—forged proofs of treasonable plots of which they are innocent. They have seen his drunken, profligate son outrage their feelings in times of deep distress by making the tenure of house and home conditional upon a daughter's or sister's dishonor. The tenants have come to fear his power and his craft, and to recognize as well the business capacity that guides his cruelty and rapacity.

Though M'Clutchy has the peasantry under his heel, is on the road to wealth, and commands a kind of consideration in the country as a stirring man of business and a strong ally of the government, all does not run smooth. The temper of the peasantry becomes ferocious. A coward as well as a tyrant, he fears for his life, and to make himself secure in his tyranny determines to raise an Orange Yeomanry Cavalry corps. A petition to the government for its incorporation being granted, he organizes the corps, captains it himself, and makes it the instrument of his outrages and the support of his personal and official tyrannies.

This is the one of the Irish novels that, in following the career of M'Clutchy as a zealous Orangeman, master of an Orange lodge, and captain of a corps of Orange cavalry, best succeeds in putting the reader on intimate terms with the Orangemen in general, their place in the Irish life of the first decade of the nineteenth century, their prejudices, feelings, aims, and manners.

The Orangemen took their name, of course, from William of Orange, who was regarded as the champion of Irish Protestantism. In its origin Orangeism was an outgrowth of the feuds between the lower ranks of Papists and Protestants in the north—at first only the Protestant side of a party fight. Subsequently, when there was imminent danger of a French invasion, the gentlemen of the Ascendency, who had hitherto held aloof from the society, placed themselves at the head of their Protestant tenantry, and began organizing the Orangemen into lodges. The country gentlemen who identified themselves with the Orangemen were almost all bigots, frantically opposed to admitting Catholics to Parliament, or to any concession of Catholic relief, and red-hot champions of the existing constitution of church and state. The society, under their control, became a political association, in recognized alliance with the government, against Catholic disaffection, and every kind of rebel, Protestant or Catholic. A desire on the part of the Orangemen to enroll themselves into cavalry and infantry corps for the defence of the Protestant constitution was regarded with favor by the government, and members recruited from the Orange lodges were incorporated as Yeomanry Corps. A book of rules and regulations circulated among the members of the society, showed that it aimed at high moral excellence. Every Orangeman was expected, it was said, to have a sincere love for his Maker, to be an enemy to brutality, and to promote the honor of King and country and the principles of Protestant Ascendency. He was expected to refrain from cursing and intemperance, and to combat, so far as was in his power, the forces of atheism and anarchy.

Carleton's satire turns upon the discrepancy between the high-flown professions and the actual practice of the Orangemen. He describes the meeting of the lodge of which M'Clutchy is the master. The lodge room is reeking with the fumes of hot punch and tobacco. A mixed company is assembled—Orange blacksmiths, butchers, bakers, and candlestick makers, pious, punch-loving Dissenters, grand jurors, hard-drinking squires, all more or less boisterously drunk, singing party songs, quarrelling, and now and again pausing to drink in due form the loyal toast to "the glorious, pious, and immortal memory of the great and good King William, who saved us from Popery, brass money, and wooden shoes," or its complement, "To hell with the Pope." From such meetings as these the yeomanry not infrequently sallied, when sufficiently drunk, to ride through the streets, firing about at random, singing, and shouting "Any money for the face of a papist," "To hell with the Pope," "Ram down the Catholics," and the like. Or sometimes they might pay a visit to an inoffensive Catholic family—to satisfy a private grudge perhaps—on the pretext of searching for concealed weapons, routing the household out of bed, turning the house upside down, insulting the women folk, and terrifying all hands with the possibility of they knew not what drunken violence. Or, again, they might ride to the house of the priest, startling the good man from his rest by firing volleys over his house-top (if their aim was steady enough to clear it) to the tune of "Croppies Lie Down." But this was only boisterous "funning." Their real service was in riding with M'Clutchy to dispossess poor, rack-rented tenants, who, perhaps, had so good a "back" in the country that for a few bailiffs to evict, without an armed force, was out of the question. The fate of M'Clutchy in this novel was not infrequently the fate of men of his class. The bad middleman, unjust magistrate, and violent Orangeman was found dead one morning, shot through the heart by a peasant whom he had wronged.

Carleton throws a flood of light on the secret societies, which, Catholic or Protestant, and under different names, were so startling a feature of Irish life. In most of his tales and novels he relies for a strong element of interest upon these societies and their operations. There is a romantic appeal in the mystery that hangs over their nocturnal meetings, and the desperate deeds in which discovery means death to the perpetrator, and success means death or violence to the victim.

Rody the Rover is devoted exclusively to this subject. Carleton was at one time himself a Ribbonman, and, so far at least as the operation and effects of Ribbonism are concerned, knew whereof he spoke. According to the theory of this story Ribbonism originated with a set of bold, shrewd rascals who, ready to stake their lives for the chance of gain, and pretending to be friends of the peasantry and champions of their religion, banded them together and incited them to violence. Then the originators of the society, who were in the secret of the movements of the lodges all over the country, would repair at their convenience to Dublin Castle, represent themselves as in a position to make valuable disclosures as to the plans of the disaffected peasantry, provided they were substantially remunerated for the danger they ran as informers.

Rody, the central figure of the story, is an emissary of the instigators of the movement, and his procedure is meant to illustrate the methods of effecting its organization. The field of operations is a little village. Here a young stranger one fine day makes his appearance. He gives himself out a fugitive from justice. In a scrimmage between Catholics and Orangemen he laid an Orangeman low, he says, and the man, to get him in trouble, refused to recover. This of course opens all hearts and homes to him. Tom M'Mahon, an unsuspecting young peasant, takes Rody—for so is the stranger called—to his own home. Plausible, shrewd, and daring, Rody insinuates himself into M'Mahon's friendship, and finally tells him, in awful secrecy, that he wishes to make him a member of a widespread conspiracy for the liberation of their country and religion. He professes himself unable to reveal the leaders of the conspiracy, but darkly hints that O'Connell and other patriots and Catholic champions are behind the

movement, though their safety and policy compel them to denounce the society publicly. M'Mahon takes these overtures in good faith, and, after binding himself by an oath never to reveal the person who has made the communication to him, the Ribbon oath itself is administered. Having taken the oath he is straightway made an Article Bearer (one entitled to administer the oath to others), and empowered to enroll and captain fifty of the boys of the neighborhood. The story proceeds to show the difficulties Tom M'Mahon found in controlling his men after he had called this organization, with its possibilities for evil, into existence. He is honest and humane, but soon the control of the men gets into other hands. Instead of aiming, vaguely perhaps, at generous religious and patriotic ends, the Ribbonmen, now led by the base and ignorant, make their society subserve plans of private spite, and are ready to rush into acts of violence at the dictates of headlong impulses and base passions. Soon the whole character of the neighborhood changes. The midnight meetings, and the whiskey-drinking that went with them, broke up habits of regular industry. Peace was gone; dark passions awoke and ruled, with bloodshed, riot, and conflagration as the order of the day and night, while soldiers, posses of sheriffs, and peelers were ever tramping the country-side.

The ending of the story emphasizes the thought of the whole book. Tom M'Mahon, though generous and honest, is accused of a murder which he did his best to prevent his brother Ribbonmen from committing. Rody is instrumental in fastening the responsibility of the crime upon him. M'Mahon, though innocent, is executed. The instigators of all the trouble, who are back of Rody, turn informers and are handsomely rewarded by the government, a reward by which Rody also profits in his degree. Thus, in Carleton's view, in the matter of Ribbonism, the peasantry are blind and silly dupes in the hands of rapacious and designing monsters, who play the part of double-faced traitors, stir up disaffection only to betray it to the government, and grow fat upon the proceeds. *Rody the Rover* is said to have produced a deep impression among the peasantry. Carleton himself claimed it resulted in the disbandment of six hundred Ribbon lodges. True as Carleton's picture is of the effects of Ribbonism, and useful and convincing as was its lesson to the people of the futility of accomplishing their ends by the operation of secret societies that defied the law, its theory of the origin of Ribbonism is baseless. The origin of the society is wrapped in a cloud of mystery and uncertainty which investigation has not yet dispelled.

In *The Black Prophet,* Carleton writes the story of one of the famines that from time to time desolated Ireland, and made fearful pages in the annals of the most distressful country that ever yet was seen. Before a background of dreadful and harrowing scenes from the famine of 1817 is unfolded a tale of crime and guilt in itself sufficient to shadow the story with gloom. Carleton was a young man at the time when the action of this story is supposed to have occurred, and images of the suffering of those days seem to have been branded upon his memory, as upon the memory of the people in general, in letters of fire. Of this and other famines the potato, that dangerous and demoralizing esculent, Raleigh's fatal gift, was the more immediate cause. It was the staple, almost the only food of the people, and a failure of the crop meant starvation.

In *The Black Prophet* the approach of this famine of 1817, and the succeeding stages in its progress, are presented in special instances of tragic distress. It opens with descriptions of the natural phenomena that foretold the coming calamity—the heavy canopy of low, dull clouds that emptied themselves in ceaseless rain upon the land; the fields that should have waved with ripe grain covered only with thin, backward crops; lowlands ravaged by flood; the corn prostrate under layers of mud and gravel, and all autumn's bounty destroyed by the wet and sunless days that spoke ominously of imminent dearth and destitution. The famine comes in course, and with it the pestilence; and the progress of the two is followed as they sweep over the land, leaving terror and desolation in their train. The kitchens, well-stocked in happier times, are now unfurnished. The family groups are sickly, woe-worn, marked by the look of care and depression which bad and insufficient food impressed upon the countenance. Harrowing pictures, sparing no physical horror, are given of the afflicted people. Every face has the look of painful abstraction, telling plainly of the sleepless solicitation of hunger that mingles itself with every thought and act. All who come upon the scene of the story bear in some form the sorrowful impress of the fatal visitation that ravaged the land. Garments hang loose about wasted persons; the eyes move with a dull and languid motion; the parchment skin clings to the sharp protruding bones.

It was typhus that went with the famine of 1817, a trying disease both to sufferers and to those who tend them—slow in coming, long to stay, and attended by a train of tedious and lingering miseries that were increased a hundred-fold by destitution and want. All the feelings of family affection, almost morbidly intense among the lower Irish, were allowed, while the disease ran its course, full and painful time to be racked to the limit of human suffering.

The misery had many aspects. Everywhere were reminders of the gloomy triumph famine and pestilence were achieving over the country. The roads were black with funerals, and chapel bells busy ringing dead men's knells. Numberless fever-stricken mendicants died in the temporary sheds erected for them by the roadsides. Families hitherto respectable and independent cast aside shame and pride, and in the frightful struggle between life and death went about soliciting alms with the clamor and importunity of professional beggars, or, goaded by the cravings of hunger, fought like vultures for the dole of charity at the soup shops, or other public depots of relief where rations of bread and meal were dispensed. Not the least of the trials of the afflicted people was the sight of the bursting granaries of snug farmers and miserly meal-mongers who found their profit in selling little doles of meal at famine prices; or the sight of lines of heavily laden provision carts on their way to neighboring harbors for exportation, meeting or mingling with the funerals that were continually passing along the highways. Hunger breaks through stone walls, and, as might be expected at such a time, the restraints that normally protect property were disregarded. Starving multitudes in the ravening madness of famine broke into and pillaged granaries and mills, or attacked the cruel misers, who, forced to distribute provisions on pain of death, at last became charitable with a bad grace. Provision carts also were intercepted by starving hordes who helped themselves to the contents, gobbling up the raw meal like famished maniacs, or staggering home to their families with bundles of the precious spoil.

The Black Prophet is a lookout upon a land laboring under a grievous affliction, where suffering, sorrow, and death prevailed. But now and again the horrors of famine are transfigured by the light of love they kindle, by the profound sympathies, the heroic self-sacrifice, the beautiful spirit of piety and lowly resignation that are awakened. This terrible calamity even wears at moments the expression of benevolence, as when it drives black passions from the hearts of the peasants, and wipes out hates and feuds to make of old enemies kind friends ready with help and pity. And there are lovely and memorable characters whose personalities remain as old acquaintances after the incidents of the story are forgotten—old men and women with the rugged and primitive grandeur of Old Testament people; Mave Sullivan, a character sweet and sound, made all of gentleness, firmness, purity, and love; and Sally M'Gowan, irresistibly interesting in the fierce untamed beauty of a mixed nature, swept by the tides of impulse to evil or good.

The Black Prophet is a book which no one can read with indifference. It is written from the heart of the author saddened by the spectacle of the terrible affliction upon his countrymen. Its pictures are dreadful as a new *Inferno*. The atmosphere of this story of suffering and crime is one of deadening gloom, and it haunts the mind at last with a general sense of the appalling disasters to which man, body and spirit, is exposed.

Notes

[1] "Singlings" are the first runnings of spirits in the process of distillation.

[2] O'Donoghue's *Life of Carleton,* Vol. I, pp. 5-7.

Louis Lachal (essay date 1930)

SOURCE: "Two Forgotten Irish Novelists," in *The Irish Monthly,* Vol. LVIII, No. 685, July, 1930, pp. 338-349.

[*In the following essay, Lachal studies the works of John and Michael Banim, arguing that the Banim brothers, unlike their aristocratic predecessor Maria Edgeworth, were able to truly appreciate the drastic changes that needed to be made to improve the lives of most Irish people.*]

The work of the "O'Hara Family" has been to a great extent forgotten. It is regrettable, for John and Michael Banim, who wrote under this *nom-de-plume,* did much for Ireland. They may be called the first national novelists. They were great admirers of Scott, and had the ambition to do for Ireland what Scott did for his country by his tales.

Maria Edgeworth, of course, proceded them, but can she be called a national novelist in any full sense? True she came of an old County Longford family, and most of her long life was spent in Ireland. She came to know the Irish peasantry well, but, unfortunately, from outside. She also knew well the country life of the nobility and the gentry. There is, however, a great defect in her work. Though sympathising deeply with Ireland, she was unable to understand that radical changes were needful if the grievances that weighed upon the country were to be removed. The Banims had not this defect. Moreover, they knew the peasantry well and with an intimate knowledge.

Born in Kilkenny in the last decade of the 18th century, Michael and John Banim were the eldest children of a middle-class shopkeeper. Michael was the senior by some two years. When old enough they were sent to Dr. McGrath's School, well known in Ireland at the time. John's was a precocious genius, and even in his school-days he had literary ambitions. Stories are told of a romance and some poems which he wrote even at this early period. However, art was the attraction when school-days were over, and he went to Dublin to study it.

When his course in Dublin was finished, the young artist opened a small art school in Kilkenny. Soon after he fell deeply in love with one of his pupils, a girl of only seventeen. Her parents did not approve, and she was sent to another part of the country. But they had not reckoned on the strength of the attachment. The result was tragic for both lovers. Consumption hurried the young girl to the grave, and Banim, in the excess of his grief, developed spinal disease, which attacked him continually until he became permanently paralysed about twelve years later.

A year or two more and we find John Banim in London striving to make good as a writer. His first big work, *The Celt's Paradise,* a lengthy poem, brought him the acquaintance of literary men. Richard Lalor Shiel and Sir Walter Scott were pleased with the work. Soon after he produced *Damon and Pythias,* a tragedy in verse, which deservedly gained much praise.

It may be interesting to mention another Irish writer here, Gerald Griffin. He, too, was in London at the time, and fortune was dealing badly with him. He and Banim came together, and Banim proved a friend in need. "What would I have done had I not found Banim?" he wrote. This kindness speaks well for John Banim, for his own fortunes were often low enough, as will be seen.

Meanwhile the elder brother had begun to study law. After a year or two, however, a serious reverse in his father's business interrupted him, and "with a self-sacrifice for which his whole life was remarkable, Michael Banim gave up his cherished design and quietly stepped back into what he considered the path of duty. He took up the tangled threads of business, applied his whole energy and perseverance to the task, and at length had the satisfaction of unravelling the complication and replacing his parents in comfort both material and mental."

When, in 1822, John returned to visit the old home, the great work of the Banims really began. In the course of one of their rambles John broached a plan to write a series of national tales representing the Irish people truly to the English public. Michael, with immediate enthusiasm, sketched the outlines of a suitable story. At John's suggestion he wrote it himself, and it duly appeared as *Crohoore of the Bill-hook* in the first edition of the *Tales by the O'Hara Family,* and was immediately popular.

John returned to London, and the writing began in real earnest. The manuscripts passed to and fro between them, each helping the other. Thus Barnes O'Hara to Abel, or John to Michael, wrote: "Whenever you see, or rather feel, an opening, write over a sentence or phrase in your own idiom, or add a touch of your humour, or substitute yours for mine." And again he writes: "In your criticism be very blunt and plain—but short—a hint is enough on any point, because we understand each other so perfectly." He does not fear hard knocks: "The more severe, the more friendly you will be," or "I hope your favourable thoughts of the 3rd volume are not kindly meant as a salve to make up for your previous hard knocks."

Great care, too, was taken in the setting of the scenes, Michael especially making careful examination of the districts where they were laid. So intimately are the brothers bound up in their work that it is often difficult to ascertain the authorship of individual tales from internal evidence alone. It is estimated that of the twenty-five tales Michael wrote thirteen.

The Banims, in general, gave a true picture of the Irish character, with its bright and dark sides. They, unlike Lover or Lever, were in sympathy with and understood the heart of the people. They showed the Irish, not as the strange, grotesque caricatures so often portrayed in fiction, but as men of noble impulses and generous traits. They saw another side, too. Though the Irishman could be sympathetic, kind, and forgiving, he could become stern, bitter, revengeful.

Ignorance, poverty, and cruelty are shown to exist among the peasantry. But these things have their cause. They are the natural result of religious persecution and political oppression. Later Michael Banim wrote: "It was the object of the authors, while admitting certain and continued lawlessness, to show that causes existed consequently creating the lawlessness. Through the medium of fiction this purpose was constantly kept in view."

The first series of the *O'Hara Tales* appeared in 1825. They were immediately popular. We have already mentioned *Crohoore of the Bill-hook*. There were also *The Fetches* and *John Doe or the Peep o' Day* by John Banim. From then on the *Tales* appeared frequently.

Crohoore of the Bill-hook illustrates well the plan of the authors. Its action lies in one of the darkest periods of Irish history, when the peasantry, crushed under the tithe-proctor, middle-man, and penal laws, retorted by the savage outrages of the secret societies. One of these societies, the "Whiteboys," is largely dealt with in the book. Michael Banim does not justify outrage, but explains it by a picture of the causes from which it came.

Banim's indictment of the tithe-proctor, personified in the person of Peery Clancy, reveals as loathsome a character as it seems possible to imagine. This villain had become rich from squeezing "from the very, very poorest their last acid shilling: they were his best profit, his fat of the land, his milk and honey." Such was the immediate cause that drove the peasant to Whiteboyism. There were other causes, too. Banim thus expresses them: "First of all, there was, doubtless, a religious frenzy to urge them on. They saw their creed denounced, their form of worship under heavy penalties, interdicted . . ." and the peasant came to hate the opposite creed "because it was the privileged one; because his own was persecuted; because he attributed to its spirit the civil excommunication against him and his priests, and even the petty and gratuitous annoyances he suffered from its lowest professors. And in such a state of feeling he found himself, while already ground down by unnatural rackrents, compelled to contribute to the support, in splendour and superiority, of that very rival Church— in fact, to pay to its ministers the hard-earned pittance he could not afford his own. This view of his situation first made the Irish peasant a Whiteboy."

The Fetches, by John Banim, is of a quite different type. It has no particular historical background and its chief interest centres round the Fetch superstition that is found or that used be found in some parts of Ireland. "Of some persons appointed to die, a double or a counterpart becomes visible before his or her death at a time or place where the original could not by possibility appear," is an explanation of it.

Henry Tresham "was the slave of a gloomy mind" and he infects his beloved with his own mental disease. The tale is well told and with power. It leads surely to the terrible end of the two lovers.

Among the best known of the other novels of John Banim, *The Nowlans, The Boyne Water, The Conformists, The Last Baron of Crana,* may be cited. *The Boyne Water* is probably his greatest work. The novel is closely modelled on Scott, and scene after scene of the long drama of the Williamite wars passes before the reader. Great historical figures move across the stage. The rival kings and the principal generals are vividly presented. The characters include Sarsfield, Galloping Hogan the Rapparee, Carolan the bard, and many others. The story is well told, while the politics and great questions of the day are thrashed out in its conversations. John Banim shows in this tale as elsewhere his keen eye for natural beauty, and the wild scenery of the Antrim coast is fully described as also the scenes through which Sarsfield passed on his famous ride. The book ends with the treaty of Limerick.

In preparation for this great work John Banim showed extraordinary care. These lines are from a letter to Michael. "I will visit every necessary spot in the north and south; Derry, Lough Neagh, from that down to the Boyne; and then Limerick once more," and later, "I traced on the spot the localities connected with the last siege of Limerick."

This accuracy of setting is noticeable in all their work. Many of the stories are laid in the Kilkenny district with which, of course, the brothers were very familiar. When it became necessary to examine any other part of Ireland, usually Michael did so, sent his information along to John or used it in the revision of manuscript. Among the best of Michael's works may be mentioned, besides *Crohoore, Father Connell* and *The Town of the Cascades*. A volume of stories published under the title of *The Bit o' Writing* has also been very popular. *Father Connell* was the last joint work of the brothers, and *The Town of the Cascades* the last of the *Tales*. It was published after a long interval in 1864.

John Banim's life, as has been already hinted, was a hard one. In spite of all endeavours to shake off financial troubles, he was for a long time unsuccessful. Sickness, too, preyed upon him, until no three pages were written without "wringing, agonising pain." A health trip to the Continent did him little good. He returned to Kilkenny and his last years were spent in "Windgap Cottage" there, a cripple, for paralysis had completely deprived him of the use of his legs, a Government pension supplied his wants and those of his small family, a wife and daughter. Death came after the tranquil happiness of his last years, in 1842.

Michael, too, had his share of sorrow. In 1841, less than a year after his marriage, a merchant failed him and he lost almost all his fortune. Following that a severe illness sapped his vitality and he was never again a strong man. He lived on as postmaster at Kilkenny until a few years before his death in 1873.

The Banims had much in common, though Michael did not possess the poetic vein of his brother. The touch of John was lighter and more delicate, more artistic, more literary. His work rings truer. Though both at times tend to be melodramatic, Michael is the more frequent offender. Moreover, the use of the deus ex machina is more frequent in Michael's work. However, more on these defects later.

Both were strong in description, though John had probably a deeper appreciation of and more perfect expression of natural beauty and grandeur. Michael's more homely genius was at its best when describing the peasants and their pastimes. His native heath, Kilkenny and its surroundings, is the familiar background of his pages and he describes at times with rare charm. Kilkenny's river, the "silver-winding Nore," the ways of whose trout he knew well, gleams in his pages with fresh beauty in such a work as *The Mayor of Windgap.*

Take this scene from John's pages, "The earth, wherever it was seen bare, appeared dry and crumbling into dust; the rocks and stones were partially bleached white, or their few patches of moss burnt black or deep red. Up the valley, as far as my eye could travel, and at last over the broad bosom of the distant hill, which seemed torn and indented with the headlong torrent it had once pored down, far and uniform on every side a vertical July sun was shining." *[The Fetches].* Does not the writer paint with life-like accuracy, the picture he saw when he looked up the long, lonely valley, parched by the summer's sun?

John Banim's work is often gloomy and tragic. His brightness is not as spontaneous as Michael's. This dark note is probably due to a great extent, to the worry that lay heavy on his mind and the sickness that tortured his body. But this did not diminish the vigour and great realistic power of his work. One might cite as examples the description of the battle of Aughrim which begins *The Last Baron of Crana,* or the vigour that runs through the many scenes of his great novel, *The Boyne Water.*

Before turning again to his brother, the poems of John Banim deserve mention. The best known, *Aileen* and *Soggarth Aroon,* show how he could excel in gentler subjects.

Michael Banim's disposition and genius was more humane and more bright. It has been written of him that "his peculiar kindness of manner won the confidence of the peasantry and enabled him to gain that deep insight into their daily lives which he afterwards reproduced in his life-like portraits of character." He found happiness in studying the lives of those around him and in the beautiful scenery of his own county. The peasants opened their cottage doors to him and he was a welcome guest at their festivities and dances. He could sympathise with age: "And ould age brings the snowy head—spring comes to the fields and to the trees, and the flowers to the fields after the winter passes; but there is no spring for the ould man; none in this world at laste; if he hopes for the spring time, his hope must be fixed on heaven." *[The Mayor of Windgap].* And many a time he had listened to and laughed at the "ould woman's gaddin' tongue: ould women, we all know, must get nothing at all to tell, if you'd have the hearth swept." *[The Mayor of Windgap].* Much of the local colour for the tales was supplied by him. John had lost touch to a certain extent with the peasant classes of his own land or never had the natural charm and kindness which enabled Michael to win their hearts and get to know them intimately. Thus the opening chapters of *Peter of the Castle,* which give a detailed account of country match-making and marriage festivities of the time, were supplied by Michael. He supplied, too, the description of the pattern, a sort of country holiday scene which takes up the first few chapters of *John Doc or the Peep o' Day.*

The following is a description or extracts from a description of a scene he knew surpassingly well. How keenly and how good-humouredly he observed! "A fair-day is a day of great bustle and excitement in the city of Kilkenny. Being chiefly a mart for black cattle and pigs, the streets are invaded at an early hour, and the ears of the quiet, snoring citizens outraged by the unusual noise of lowing cows and bullocks trotting or rushing along under peaceful chamber windows, by the shouting of their drivers, and the clattering of alpeens on their backbones and horns."

He turns in another direction where "disposed on unpainted deal doors (which had been taken off their hinges for the purpose), or planks, there was gingerbread and all such humble confectionery; the coarsest fruits in season; white and yellow cheese, and wooden trenchers and noggins and the et ceteras of the turner's ware picturesquely thrown together. The proprietors of these commodities might be seen, early in the morning, running in breathless haste to secure good and safe spots for opening their sales. And while they clattered along in by no means silent emulation, or contested with each other the right to a favourite stand; while the cattle bellowed and the sheep bleated, and the horses neighed, and the headstrong pigs ran through their grunting gamut, and the surrounding rush and roar of a thronging multitude was heard over all—startling, as we have before said, was the commencement of a fair-day to the tranquil and by no means commercial or bustling citizens of Kilkenny."

And a page further on: "We might . . . pass a good hour in the now mid-day bustle and uproar of the fair. We might pause to admire the more than Ciceronian art of the buyer and the seller of 'a slip of a pig'; the half-proffered earnest-money, technically slapped down on the open palm of the vendor; his demur, the seemingly determined turn-off of the purchaser, and the affected carelessness of the other, who, meantime, watches shrewdly every movement of his man; the expected return; the splitting of the differ; and, last, at the final close, one protesting he gave too much, the other swearing he sold too cheap; but both sensible that the unconscious grunter had been obtained exactly at his fair value. . . . We might even peep into the regular shops along the main street, and witness, in one or all, the self-flattering praises of the dealers on their goods, and the suspicious and heretic looks of the country-buyers, certain, in exaggerated mistrust, that, along with hearing naught but misstatement, they can purchase at five times less than what they are asked. An hour, did we say?—alas! the whole day—or else our memory is treacherous, or our tastes altered—might be well spent in the ever-changing varieties of the fair. We regret that now, when we have not rehearsed the hundredth part of its novelties, pleasures, and incidents, we are no longer free to indulge our teeming garrulity: but the story to which we have yoked ourselves requires our immediate attention."

Power too, is in the writings of Michael Banim and he handles tragedy well, but with him the brighter side of the story is never long absent. In the *Mayor of Windgap* Gerald Kennedy, the hero, is urged on, in his ignorance, to the murder of his own father. The interest becomes intense, rising to the climax, a cry from the young man's heart:

"O my God! he continued, flinging himself upon his knees, straining his eyes and stretching his arms upwards, while the tone of his voice was fervent and ringing—Almighty eye of the Universe! behold before Thee, an erring and an humbled being! Accept Omnipotent the gratitude of a stricken bursting heart, which gives Thee praise and adoration, because that of parents' blood, or of the blood of any of Thy creatures, I am guiltless—guiltless—guiltless!"

The reader will admit that Banim achieves great strength and power. But he will notice too that there are faults.

Is he not stilted and rhetorical, in such a phrase as "Almighty eye of the Universe." This tendency will be noted throughout the Banim's works.

One might also dwell on the introduction of the deus-ex-machina, the creation of doubles, the weakness of the denouement, other artificial properties of the conventional novel.

There is a more serious artistic defect to lay at the door of Michael Banim. One is usually satisfied in John's tales by the fulfilment of dramatic justice, by the giving of reality to the plot. Not so with his brother. Michael Banim is obsessed by the idea of the happy ending. This glaring example is from *Father Connell:* The grim details of what the reader is convinced is the murder of an old servant have been related. This weak paragraph ends the chapter. "Dead, however, she was not, but on the contrary quite alive and up, to receive her little fortune, and enjoy it in a quiet relief from worldly care and labour." Several other examples, just as weak, could be pointed out.

Or one could dwell on the lapses of Michael Banim into melodrama, particularly in one or two of the short stories, published in the volume called *A Bit of Writin'*. This is a collection of tales, several of which are splendidly told. It is probably better, however, to pass on to a short study of the most pleasing of the *Tales by the O'Hara Family, Father Connell,* the last joint work of the brothers, which Michael wrote at John's suggestion.

The scene is Kilkenny, and the hero strictly modelled, as is said in the preface on their beloved parish priest. His character, one of the noblest in fiction, is that of an ideal shepherd, kind, simple, generous, lovable, yet fierce and untiring in the protection of his flock. There are grim and terrible scenes in the story. There is, moreover, a severe indictment of abuses. We may study the author roused by the rapacity of the absentee landlords and their neglect of their tenants. The one he speaks of "resided in nabob style in another country."

In his despatches to his agents his constant cry was, like the gnome, for "more, more," and in the highly civilised land in which he sojourned, desperate and unteachable savages he called those from whom he drew his ample income, never admitting meanwhile, that the merciless exactions inflicted on his wretched tenantry, by his agents, to meet the insatiable craving for "more, more" had made these deserted people poor beyond endurance; and necessarily reckless and fierce towards all whom they considered as the causes of their oppression."

But for the most part, the tale is brightened by kindliness and a humour, so pleasant, so homely, so kind that one comes to love the author so revealed.

The character sketches also are considered masterly. Besides the priest and his protégé, Neddy Fennell, there is his redoubtable housekeeper, Mrs. Molloy. "Mrs. Molloy was a peculiarity in her way; tall, coarsely-featured, pock-marked, and with an authoritative something like a beard, curling on her doubled chin; and almost fat in person and in limbs. Her bearing was lofty, her look arbitrary, if not severe . . . Let it be added that her voice was the contrary of what Shakespeare calls: 'an excellent thing in woman,' and that her master was not a little afraid of its not infrequent exercise." Then there are Costigan, the murderer and robber, Mary Cooney and her mother the potato-beggar, the bullying, good-natured McNeary, and many more.

Father Connell naturally invites comparison with such novels as *The Vicar of Wakefield* or *My New Curate.* It was more in common with the second. Canon Sheehan shows that deep knowledge of the peasantry that Michael Banim had. His old parish priest had the same gentle, homely kindness of Father Connell. But *My New Curate* is nearly a century later than *Father Connell,* and things have changed. The peasants are more prosperous, more sure of themselves in Canon Sheehan's novel. But the two old priests, simple in their piety and gentle in their kindness, both like Goldsmith's vicar, "Lovers of happy human faces," are the same in spirit.

Michael Banim, as one would guess from his writings, was the best of brothers. In John's days of adversity, he earnestly besought him to return to Kilkenny and share his home. "You speak a good deal too much about what you think you owe me," he write. "As you are my brother, never allude to it again. My creed on this subject is that one brother should not want while the other can supply him." Unambitious and modest, he stepped into the background and left to his brother much of the praise he might rightly have claimed.

Finally, Michael Banim was a militant Catholic and a patriotic Irishman. He threw himself into the struggle for Catholic Emancipation. Later, movements for the economic and educational uplift of his country, found in him a strong supporter.

An edition of the works of the Banims in 10 volumes, including a life of John Banim, was published in New York in 1896.

Benedict Kiely (essay date 1948)

SOURCE: "Book the Sixth: The Story-Teller," in *Poor Scholar: A Study of the Works and Days of William Carleton (1794-1869),* Sheed and Ward, 1948, pp. 177-95.

[*In the following essay, Kiely assesses William Carleton's place in Irish literary history and explores how Carleton* *turned away from topics pertinent to the Irish peasantry in the writing of his later years.*]

ONE

1

He is among the greatest, possibly the greatest writer of fiction that Ireland has given to the English language. He wrote good stories and he wrote very inferior stories; he wrote well and he wrote at times with an excruciating badness; he wrote always with a certain spontaneous outpouring of things seen and heard and vividly remembered, with little evidence that he had ever given more than a moment of his mind to models or forms or the practices of other writers. He would have gladly thought that he had done for Ireland what Walter Scott had done for Scotland, allowed himself to be flattered by the facial resemblance that in his early days he bore to the estimable author of *Waverley,* was possibly quite complimented when Daniel O'Connell referred to him as the Walter Scott of Ireland. But the wide humanity of Scott that could raise common beggars to the high dignity of kings had nevertheless to approach the beggar from the outside, at times with a fatal altruism, at times with a fatal antiquarianism. Carleton was in his high moments neither altruist nor antiquary; he was himself one of the beggars, speaking and moving and laughing and weeping with an intimacy that began in the soul. His great admiration for Scott dragged him at times away from that inner place where he was strong, to creaking efforts to emulate that great power of bringing the past back, giving movement and voices to the mighty dead. If Walter Scott had made Rob Roy MacGregor the hero of a great story there was nothing in the wide world to prevent William Carleton making a hero of Redmond Count O'Hanlon, the rapparee who had in his time in the mountains of Southern Ulster taken to himself the titles of Protector of the rights and properties of his benefactors and contributors, and chief Ranger of the mountains, surveyor-general of all the high roads of Ireland, or lord-examiner of all passengers. Wordsworth, out of his abysmal respectability, had written a "noble ballad" with a first verse saying that Robin Hood was a famous man and the English ballad-singer's joy, but that Scotland had a thief as good and boasted her brave Rob Roy. Augustin Thierry in his *Norman Conquest* had "taken great pains to show us the significance of the careers of the men whom Robin Hood, whether he be a real or imaginary outlaw, typifies."

Ireland was as rich in rapparees and robbers as in persons of the Romish religion. Redmond Count O'Hanlon, the greatest of all Irish rapparees, had ridden and robbed and lived gallantly in the mountains to the East of Carleton's country. In his youth Carleton had read "with more avidity than its literary merits warranted, a curious little chap-book, written by one J. Cosgrave, and sold no doubt extensively to the Irish peasantry at fairs and markets." It was called: "The Lives and Actions of the Most Notorious Irish Highwaymen, Tories, and Rapparees; from Redmond O'Hanlon to Cahier na Gappul; To which is added the Goldfinder or the History of Manus Maconiel." With this anti-quarian detail at his hand, with a dozen folk-tales in his head, with the full authority of Thierry, Wordsworth and Walter Scott, he still failed miserably to draw back out of the mists the great figure of Galloping O'Hanlon.[1] Admiration for Scott could make him attempt at least twice to echo the Jeanie Deans theme, once in the story of Ellen Duncan and once in one of his early tales; could make him write enthusiastically: "The hand of the mighty wizard has given to immortality an humble woman for refusing to swear a lie—for performing a journey to London in order to save a sister's life." But the mightiest wizardry of the mighty wizard necessitated a reverence for the past, even a devotion to the oddities of the past, neither of which William Carleton ever possessed. In an unpublished sketch[2] he satirised antiquarianism and made the anti-quarian say: "I thought I did not properly belong to the present time, wherein I felt myself as if by accident only, and the impression was strong upon me that I was nothing more or less than a living antique."

Not only by choice but by the limitations of education and imagination William Carleton belonged to his own time with a completeness that swept him along in the current of contemporary life, identifying his work with the bright days and equally with the black skies of the world in which he lived, identifying his own character in a remarkably intimate way with the characters to whom he gave new and lasting life. The people who tragically kept calling him an Irish Burns writing in prose were awkwardly expressing at least a part of the truth. For Burns was and is not only a popular poet but a legendary figure in the part of Ireland from which William Carleton came. The echoes of the ploughman's songs and poems came across the sea to the ears of the young Irishman growing up into a closer contact with literary things. Like Burns he had learned a great deal from poor men and women, and a little, very little, from the pages of books. Carlyle writing of Burns could, with little alteration, have been writing of Carleton: "What warm, all-comprehending fellow-feeling; what trustful, boundless love; what generous exaggeration of the object loved! His rustic friend, his nut-brown maiden, are no longer mean and homely, but a hero and a queen whom he prizes as the paragons of Earth. The rough scenes of Scottish life, not seen by him in any Arcadian illusion, but in the rude contradiction, in the smoke and soil of a too harsh reality, are still lovely to him: Poverty is indeed his companion, but Love also, and Courage; the simple feelings, the worth, the nobleness, that dwell under the straw roof, are dear

and venerable to his heart: and thus over the lowest provinces of man's existence he pours the glory of his own soul; and they rise, in shadow and sunshine, soft-ened and brightened into a beauty which other eyes discern not in the highest."

2

A lot from men and women; a little, very little, from books; a little also from the contacts that life brought him with men of his own time who were also busy in the writing of books. Writing with his sight failing and old age creeping on he told a friend that the autobiog-raphy would certainly be an important work for in it he meant to include a general history of Irish literature "its origin, its progress, its decline, and its natural and progressive extension." Ireland could point with pride, he said, only to three names: the name of Gerald Grif-fin, the name of John Banim, and, "do not accuse me of vanity", the name of William Carleton. No one could with justice accuse him of unreasoning vanity; but the sweeping nature of that statement might raise doubts as to whether he had the balance or the equipment necessary for a survey of the origin, development, decline and revival of Irish literature. Anyway death cut across the splendid plans for an important work, left the autobiography not a history of literature, but, much more appropriately, a testimony to the days of boyhood and youth, when he had grown up so close to the people that in his old age he was able to write with a touch of prophecy of days to come: "Banim and Griffin are gone, and I will soon follow them—*ultimus Romanorum,* and after that will come a lull, an obscu-rity of perhaps half a century, when a new condition of civil society and a new phase of manners and habits among the people—for this is a *transition* state—may introduce new fields and new tastes for other writers."

When the new revival came, not half a century but about thirty years later, it came as the prelude not only to transition but to transition in revolution. Its great writers were working harder than ever in the quarry that William Carleton had opened, rediscovering also the merits of Carleton. For the songs and stories he had heard from his parents and the language in which he had heard them became a strange, rejuvenating force to Irishmen writing in English; an explosive, inspira-tional force to Irishmen experimenting in politics. The tattered people that he had seen in glory and in agony were winning the hearts of young women and young poets from the big families, and the greatest of all Irish poets was trying his hardest to tell the world that his country was Kiltartan Cross and his country-men Kiltartan's poor. With Lever in Florence, gath-ering material for his stories in a life of perpetual banqueting that cost him about £1,200 a year, that new ruthlessly-Irish Ireland could have had little notable sympathy. Lever, defending himself against charges of extravagance, pointed out that his expenditure was not a luxury but a necessity, that it fed his lamp which otherwise would have died into darkness, that his banquets and receptions were really his opportunities for studying characters and picking up a thousand invaluable details. "You can't keep drawing wine off the cask perpetually, and putting nothing in; and this is my way of replenishing it." But, looking back at Lever, the new Ireland would naturally prefer him filling his cask with yellow whisky or black porter, than with the red and white wines of continental places, would prefer him when he wrote that to the shrewd observer of human nature the book of the human heart was nowhere opened as in Ireland. "Where do passions, feelings, prejudices, lie so much on the surface? And where is the mystery that wraps the anomalous condition of human nature more worthy of study? Where, amid poverty and hardship, are such happiness and contentment to be met—natural and ever ready courtesy—the kind and polite attention, the free hospitality, as in the Irish peasant? Where is self most forgotten in all this wide and weary world? We answer fearlessly, in the cabin of the poor Irishman. We have travelled in most countries of the old continent, and much of the new, and we know of nothing either for qualities of heart or head, to call their equal."[3]

Not at all averse to thinking that it possessed almost everything a little better than everybody else, the new Ireland could return with pleasure to that line of talk. It could remember, too, in Carleton's favour that, in spite of the large number of people that at one time or another he had rubbed the wrong way, he had known the inside of the Irishman's cabin and the inside of his heart in a way always impossible to Lever, impossible even to John Banim or Michael Banim or Gerald Griffin. He had taken social customs, some peculiar to Ireland of his time, more of them existing practically unchanged in the opening years of a new century, and written great stories around them. He had seen the tragedy of famine, the beginning of mass-emigration, and had written great novels, with black backgrounds of hunger and perpetually moving backgrounds of exodus and abandonment. He had looked back at a highwayman who was a national hero and gathered together in a little book some of the daring galloping stories of the great O'Hanlon. He had heard a popular ballad that was almost a national institution and written around it the most popular of all his novels, telling the story of Willy Reilly and Helen Folliard and her father, the squire, and beauty and adventure, and elopement and banishment, and true love in the end triumphant. In a dozen places he had analysed, not without wisdom, the ills of the Ireland of his time, and had suggested remedies for those ills.

In spite of the contradictions in his own soul, in spite of the terror of his time, he was the greatest laugher his country produced, until James Joyce, seeking in exile a refuge from contradiction, looking back at one great Dublin day that comprehended all time and hinted at eternity, heard the randy laughter of the streets and the pubs, saw the dark figure and the divided soul of Stephen Dedalus. With Carleton as with Joyce Ireland joined in the laughter, knowing it genuinely for the native laughter, but always resenting the recording of hollow unhumorous echoes that every Irishman had been trying hard to forget. Phil Purcell's pigs, tall and loose and with unusually long legs, no flesh, short ears as if they had been cropped for sedition, long faces of a highly intellectual cast, an activity that surpassed greyhounds and beagles, were undeniably funny. But Irish readers following their uproariously devastating career on English farms could feel uneasily that the character of Phil and the waywardness of his pigs revealed to the world something about Ireland that was not in the least humorous, something unkempt and lawless and uncouth. Phelim O'Toole was Carleton's most laughable creation; but when Phelim's fond mother, looking at her son with the eyes of love, said: "Doesn't he become the pock-marks well, the crathur," and his father, looking at Phelim with the eyes of pride and hope for the half-acre, said, "Doesn't the droop in his eye set him off all to pieces," they had innocently hinted at an abyss of pain and pathetic deformity that made all laughter as thin as froth from broken water. To be able to convey in that way the delicate fragility of human joy, always transient, frequently depending for its existence on the human power for unconscious self-deception, may be just one of the faculties of a comprehensive, creative spirit. But in Carleton's Ireland it made pitifully obvious the fact that all joy was only a little, brief light against wide, overshadowing gloom, that all dancing was over the grave or under the gallows. Never forgetful of the method of the old story-teller he pulled his chair to the corner of the fire, told his listeners tales that were humorous or sad or terrible. But he never equalled the story-teller by the hearth in the ability to make his listeners forget that outside the closed door there was rain and the buffeting wind and the black night.

TWO

1

Moore died in 1852, fading quietly out of life like the last liquid linked sweetness of one of the melodies that interpreted his own rose-coloured Ireland, his own rose-coloured world. John Hogan, the poverty-stricken sculptor whose genius preserved for ever several of the great figures of that time, had once submitted a model for the design of a Moore statue; and when, with Hogan in the grave, Carleton was appealing for help for the sculptor's widow and orphans, he wrote in the *Irish Quarterly Review* a tribute not only to Hogan but to the poet. "I have had the honour and pleasure," he wrote, "of knowing the great poet personally—well and closely did I study his features. I have heard him sing his own songs accompanied by himself on the piano; and at the conclusion of each song there was uniformly an upturning of the eyes, which flashed and sparkled with such a radiance of inspiration as I never witnessed before nor ever expect to witness again. Whether John Hogan ever saw Thomas Moore or not I cannot say—but this I can say, that the model which he conceived and executed for his monument would have given Moore to the world in the very fervour of inspiration with which he usually concluded his own songs." As it happened Hogan's model was not accepted, and at the corner of College Street in the City of Dublin a statue was erected, to be abused by Carleton as "one of the vilest jobs that ever disgraced the country, such a stupid abomination as has made the whole kingdom blush with indignation and shame." The unfortunate statue, carved comically enough by a man called Moore, became later, because of the proximity of a public lavatory, the subject of popular jokes on the dead poet who had sung of friendship and sweet Avoca and the meeting of the waters. The popular jokes swept upwards from Dublin ground-currents to touch the surface again in the meditations of Leopold Bloom; and changed times were causing men to think that Tom Moore had exactly the site and the statue he deserved. But across the best part of a century it is refreshing and illuminating to consider the days when the poet and the sculptor and the story-teller came into association and knew each other for remarkable men.

Moore brought with him to the grave, or left after him in some of his poems, the ineffectual ardour of the time when Robert Emmett had plotted and dreamed and cried out that no man should write his epitaph until Ireland was a nation. The men of Young Ireland, remembering Tone and Emmett and in their turn to influence young men in the future, had been broken and scattered by the law to the new, distant lands in which a large proportion of the Irish people were seeking refuge from poverty and hunger. Irish politics had drifted into the doldrums; and when a modern Irishman looks around for a convenient historic precedent for political corruption, he thinks of Sadleir and Keogh and the "Pope's Brass Band", and the decadent characters of that time. In 1855 Charles Gavan Duffy who sat in parliament for New Ross wrote a retiring address to his constituents, and by implication to the people of Ireland, and sailed round the world to make a great success of himself far away in Australia. He had determined to retire "from all share and responsibility in the public affairs of Ireland" until better times returned; and, while a captious person might have justifiably argued that the way to bring about the return of better times was not by retiring to Australia, he did undeniably give solid reasons for refusing any longer to expend energy and breath as a member of the Irish Parliamentary Party.

He pointed out that the Irish popular party was reduced to an ineffective handful, deserted even by those who had created it, opposed by many members of the Catholic hierarchy. In public life shameless profligacy was openly defended and applauded; and the party that had commenced its life with fifty members had lost forty of the fifty to the ranks of its opponents, and in general there was "no more hope for the Irish cause than for the corpse on the dissecting-table". The Catholic Archbishop of Dublin "who was foremost and loudest to pronounce for the principle of independent opposition, lends all the weight of his authority to its opponents." The majority of the Irish bishops had followed his example and the few popular patriots left uncorrupted had been "disparaged from popular hustings, and in pastoral letters, for no sin that I know of but because we will not sell ourselves to the enemies of our country." The public action of the priesthood had been deliberately fettered and "the boldest of the patriot priests had been banished from public life, and remain banished." Sadleir and Keogh had made their own party within the party, winning popularity for themselves by violent opposition to the Ecclesiastical Titles Bill and by such noisy defence of all causes Catholic that they earned from the public that ironic title of Pope's Brass Band. Irish political life no longer offered any hope to an honest man. "Quitting public life," wrote Duffy, "I will quit, at the same time, my native country. I cannot look on in dumb inaction at her ruin. I cannot sit down under the system of corruption and terrorism established among us."

Corruption and terrorism in political life. A people bled white by famine and emigration. The good and great, dead or banished or going out to give themselves to the making of young nations because their own, ancient, broken nation would not have them. The corpse on the dissecting table. Dumb inaction. Griffin and Banim dead and William Carleton left—*ultimus Romanorum*. It was a poor land for a man in the end of his days. It was a poor land for ending old things or beginning new things. William Carleton knew that; growing old and gathering around him dreams and memories. John Henry Newman was to make that discovery, reading out in a hall to a Dublin audience the "cloistral, silverveined" sentences that made up the lectures on university education. Caught awkwardly between the wishes of the hierarchy and the talents of revolutionary young men that he would gladly have had lecturing in his new university, Newman was to wish with all his heart that he had never seen Ireland. But Newman could recross the sea to England, could console himself anyway with his sense of high spiritual mission, with the feeling that "all who take part with the Apostle, are on the winning side."

William Carleton thought of following into exile the two beloved daughters who had gone across the sea to Canada. But all around the world from Australia came a letter from Gavan Duffy, the great cry of heart speaking to heart across unknown lands and illimitable oceans, the cry of Ireland in exile calling to Ireland, the testimony of one man for another that stands as high as a mountain above all the carping and criticism of lesser men. "Do not dream of Canada, my friend; an oak of the forest will not bear transplanting. Even a shrub like myself does not take kindly all at once to the new climate and soil. I never for a moment regretted having left Ireland where Judge Keogh and Archbishop Cullen predominate; but the slopes of Howth, the hills of Wicklow, and the friends of manhood are things not to be matched in this golden land." Far away in Australia the Irish emigrant was making himself at home, preserving the rural life that his counterpart had willingly abandoned when he walked across the boundaries of the great American cities. Duffy told Carleton that he would enjoy most of all in Australia the reincarnation of the Irish farmhouse "with all the rude plenty of thirty years ago revived" as Carleton and Duffy remembered it in Monaghan and Tyrone. "But it would need the author of the *Traits and Stories* to describe the strange hybrid, an Australian-Irish farmer with the keenness and vigour of a new country infused into his body. I am just returned from my election, where they fought for me like lions in the name of the poor old country; and to do them justice, Protestants as well as Catholics. We have bigots here, but the love of country is a stronger passion than bigotry in the heart of the exile."[4]

At home or abroad that love of country could be an emptiness in the heart, an unforgettable torment in the bones. And why, in God's name, should men remember with such torturing sentiment a land that had given them nothing but hunger? Walking by the round waters of Dublin Bay, as lonely as Ossian the poet after the passing of the Fenians, William Carleton was at liberty to speculate on that mystery. North of him, and lying in dark blue laziness across the light blue water was the hill of Howth. South of him and sharp against the sky were the two conical mountains across the county-border in Wicklow, differing in colour and character from the round Dublin hills circling lazily above the city. Duffy in Australia could close his eyes and see those hills and long for them with the passion of the exile. Carleton in Dublin could see them dimly through ageing eyes, could remember Duffy, and dream of his daughters in Canada, and dream of men and women and places that had been, and because of him would be for ever.

2

He could dream of his father's stories and his mother's songs, knowing with satisfaction in his own age that he had taken up the business of story-telling where his father had left off, had spoken in a different language to a different, wider world. In naming the novel *The Red-Haired Man's Wife,* that was not published until after his death, he was remembering his mother's

William Carleton

sweetest song, the song she sang with reluctance in an English translation because the new words quarrelled with the old music. But strangely enough the shapeless, wandering novel that he wrote under that name had no word in it of the song as Blind Raftery, the Connaught poet, had written it, as James Stephens, poet and friend of the fairies, was to hear it in the opening years of a new century when he, with others, was eagerly listening to and drawing inspiration from voices speaking out of buried decades. Douglas Hyde, whom James Stephens called the fairy godfather of the new Ireland, followed in the counties across the Shannon the footsteps of Antony Raftery, gathered together all his Gaelic songs with their faint echoes of the classical Gaelic tradition and their tattered scraps from Greece and Rome hanging crazily around a body of pure poetry. He collected also the stories behind the songs: the story of Mary Hynes whose beauty broke men's hearts and in the end broke her own; and the beauty of the song the blind poet made of Mary Hynes has haunted Irish poets for fifty years.[5] The story of the tailor who jettisoned the grace of God and trampled on the laws of men for the sake of the red-haired man's wife had all the elements of high romance. Carleton must have heard it, or heard some altered version of it; for the song itself passing from lip to lip had one version in Connaught and another in Ulster. But the novel for which he borrowed the name of the song swung pitifully between the promising adventures of a lout who strolled from market to market jilting all the girls of the country, and the Victorian approaches of his brother to the heart of a young lady who bore as much resemblance to the red-haired man's wife as an aged nun to Cleopatra. The young fellow even took it upon him to assist the young lady and her sister to an improved knowledge of the civilised language of the French nation. For their benefit he read and translated the novels of Erckmann-Chatrian—"which just then were beginning to attract considerable notice from the reading public on account of the very interesting record which they gave of peasant life in Alsace and the vivid pictures of scenery in that and other departments not generally visited by travellers."

All that was very nice, but it indicated terribly two pitiful things: not only was Carleton's creative power gone, but he was trying so hard to be educated that when—almost certainly—a great story, raw and bleeding with life, was under his hand, he turned from it to write of the polite life in which he was never naturally at home. That tendency was never quite absent from his work, except in its highest moments. It is in most of those hideous early tales that he wrote for Caesar Otway, in the abomination of "Father Butler," in "The Brothers." It is as unpleasantly unreal as a defensive complex always is, for the young man from the cabins whose way of life had changed when he walked up to Dublin and became a writer, was defending himself in the worst possible way against the superiority of people born in high houses. At moments that complex evidenced itself in an effort to interpret ways of life about which he knew little or nothing. Almost every novelist has at some time or other made that mistake. But when he tried to interpret his own people and at the same time to be superior to his own people, when he tried to see them as a gentleman on horseback going the road past a boon of labouring men would see them, he was making a mistake more serious than the mistake of a novelist trying to do something outside his ability.

For some reason peculiar to the period in which it was written *Jane Sinclair* was a very popular novel. The alternative title was *The Fawn of Springvale,* and Jane was the fawn, and the fawn fell in love, was elegantly deserted, went pathetically mad, and died in a decline. The opening description of Springvale was idyllic, possibly too idyllic for hungry Ireland, certainly too idyllic to act as a background for the villainy of the black prophet or the flirtations of Phelim O'Toole. So when Carleton peopled that lovely valley he introduced characters that possibly never had their like on sea or land. The first incident of the story sent Jane's pet dove floating wounded on the water in danger of death by drowning. William Sinclair, brother to the devoted fawn, looks with fraternal regret at the vanishing bird and says: "Indeed, my dear Jane, I never regretted my ignorance of swimming so much as I do this moment.

The truth is, I cannot swim a stroke, otherwise I would save poor little Ariel for your sake." The father of the fawn, who was a minister, always at hand with spiritual consolation, says: "Don't take it so much to heart, my dear child. Grief, girl, ought *not* to be so violent for the death of a favourite bird."

Written as burlesque it would have been admirable. But for some reason, hidden deep in his own soul or in the circumstances of his life or the persuasions of his wife, Carleton did not intend it as burlesque. He was every bit as serious about the moral meaning of the character of Sir Thomas Gourlay, the central figure in the long boredom of the novel that was first called *Red Hall* and was later reprinted as *The Black Baronet.* His object in writing this novel was "to exhibit in contrast, three of the most powerful passions that can agitate the human heart: love, ambition, and revenge." Displaying the horror of the heart gripped by the claws of ambition Sir Thomas soliloquises in the style of tenth-rate tragedy: "Well, well, I believe every man has an ambition for something. Mine is to see my daughter a countess, that she may trample with velvet slippers on the necks of those who would trample on hers if she were beneath them." A harmless ambition, worthy of comic opera any day in the year, but a little more than ludicrous when placed in contrast with the gloom and villainy and clanking of chains in lunatic asylums with which Carleton surrounded it. Nor was it worthy of the comparison made by some literary friend who pointed out to Carleton that Massinger had treated a similar subject in *A New Way to Pay Old Debts;* nor was it really necessary for Carleton to state that when he wrote *Red Hall* he hadn't read a line of Massinger or even seen Sir Giles on the stage.

The stories of love-demented Jane and ambition-demented Sir Thomas may in their actual incidents have had some basis in fact. Of the latter he pointed out that "the incidents seem to be extraordinary and startling but they are true"; and, although when writing *Jane Sinclair* he visited Grangegorman Asylum looking for copy and found "to the honour of the sex" that no woman within those walls had gone mad for love, still the incidents in the fawn's tragedy are so insignificant that they might as well have happened as not have happened. He used the copy gathered then in Grangegorman when he coloured the story of the black baronet with interiors from a lunatic asylum, and in that curious way he linked up the black unreality of one novel with the white unreality of the other. For the incidents may have been based on fact, but the characters were unreal, their souls and the words in which they expressed their souls were unreal. Lucy Gourlay, the persecuted daughter of ambitious Sir Thomas, said to her lover: "I know you may probably feel that this avowal ought to be expressed with more hesitation, veiled over by the hypocrisy of language, disguised by the hackneyed forms of mere sentiment, uttered like the assertion of a coquette, and degraded by that tampering with truth which makes the heart lie unto itself." What Lucy meant to say was that she loved him, and being a man of great perseverance and penetration he eventually found it out. There were novels in which language like that was the vernacular. But it did not belong in the work of a man who had once seen the red-cheeked farmer's daughter smile at Denis O'Shaughnessy, heard her coaxing voice telling him to take the kiss and spare the King's English.

3

More unreal even than the sesquipedalianism that returned to him—not as matter for mockery but as a medium of expression—in his lesser works and in his later days, was his moral purpose. A literary lady in present-day Ireland said somewhere, very foolishly, that Carleton had no moral purpose; a statement difficult to reconcile with any wide reading of Carleton's writings. If by "moral purpose" is meant the intention to effect some general good by his writings then *Valentine McClutchy* and the tract about Art Maguire, the drunkard, and the skit about Paddy-Go-Easy and his wife, Nancy, are very definite evidence of effective moral purpose. They were effective even when offensive because they dealt with evident, practical things as tangible as the handle of a spade, something he could feel and judge with the cunning ability of the peasant. But beyond those tangible, visible realities, there was a world where moral purpose took his characters by the throat and deliberately strangled them. Something between moral purpose and malnutrition had set him prostituting his creative power for the benefit of Caesar Otway. Moral purpose brought forth Jane Sinclair and Sir Thomas Gourlay, one meant to be an angel and the other meant to be a monster, but both undeniably born dead. Moral purpose meant in the end that his genius dried up like water running into sand when in *The Double Prophecy* he sent Maria Brindsley to work diligently with her needle in a dressmaker's shop in Armagh City, her virtue fortified with whalebone stiff enough to resist the assaults of all the officers in the British army.

From this arid rigidity there was only one escape, only one gateway opening out into the green meadows, sending the man back along melodious, blossoming paths to find the boy who had died somewhere in the hard streets of Dublin, or in that hellhole of a cellar in Dirty Lane, or had been crushed to death by the burdens of life or the spectacle of the devastation of his people. Writing down the story of his youth he was doing naturally the thing that he did best of all: remembering and recording, until even the most trivial events became as full of moment as a major war, until the most insignificant people walked the sunlit earth with the stature and stride of demigods. He was at school again: in Jack Stuart's barn with Mrs. Dumont,

and the thunders of revolution in France and Bonaparte's men on all the roads of Europe were echoes faint and far away; or in a hole in a clay-bank with Pat Frayne, at the death-bed of the tradition of Gaelic learning. Once again he was stealing Jack Stuart's apples, suffering from Jack Stuart's protective devices and becoming as a consequence the hero of all the boys of the neighbourhood. He was following the beautiful Anne Duffy from the place where Mass was said at the Forth, past Ned McKeown's crossroads where men argued about Bonaparte in two languages, down the hilly road to the village of Augher; and all the time the boy had, unknown to himself, been mapping out a path for the lazy, good-natured feet of Paddy-Go-Easy following Nancy from Mass and market. He was a candidate for the priesthood taking the long, hard road to Munster, torn one way by love of learning and another by love of home, until sleeping in a midland inn a bull roared in his dreams and decided the battle in his erratic soul.

Once again he was stretching his long legs along the road the pilgrims went to the holy island, not knowing then that one day he would find himself writing with a disapproving superiority of the people and forgetting the whole purpose of pilgrimage. Or he was trying his strength in Clogher Mill, or leaping the water at Clogher Karry, or watching the dancing of Buckramback, or hearing the fiddling of Mickey McRory, or turning the pages of Gil Blas and seeing a new world, coloured like the rainbow, opening out before him. His tragedy and the tragedy of his people was that the road he followed out of the valley did not lead to the end of the rainbow, did not lead him at all into a coloured land, but led instead past wayside gibbets and decaying bodies to the high stifling streets. There, appropriately enough, the best story that he had ever started to write ended abruptly.

Maybe that abrupt ending was the best thing that could have happened to that particular story. He had interesting things to tell about even in that latter portion of his life when all events were the writing of books and the reading of books, the meeting of people who read or wrote or published books. He could have written of his relations with Caesar Otway, although short of tearing his own soul into fragments it is doubtful if he could have made that business any clearer than it already was from external evidence. He could have given his final judgment of the men of Young Ireland, of Mangan alone of the men of that time comparable to him for tattered, wayward genius, of Duffy over the sea and Davis in an untimely grave, and John Mitchel shouting defiance of the British Empire in every land where he made his stay. He could have written of the future as he saw it in William Allingham, who sent to Carleton some of his budding verses on the subject of frost and skating before daylight, and who hoped to see the verses published in the *Dublin University Magazine*. "As to

Poetry," wrote Allingham, "you ask me would I be content to herd with nameless creatures in an obscure corner of some periodical? I answer—certainly not." Or he could have spoken of the passing time as it showed itself in John Banim who had written to him as to "an honourable Irishman, as well as a fellow-labourer in the unkindly soil of literature."

He had carried his story far enough to include his visit to Charles Robert Maturin, and he was possibly remembering that visit and his readings of Maturin's novels and stories when in later years he wrote the weird historical romance called *The Black Spectre* and sub-titled *The Evil Eye.* For that not very successful effort in the macabre was as near as Carleton ever got to the world of Mrs. Radcliffe. Maturin belonged to that world, not only because of the romance *Melmoth the Wanderer,* praised highly both by Scott and Byron, but by the eccentricities of his own existence, down to such a detail as the red wafer pasted on his brow when writing, to warn his family that he was creating and was not to be disturbed.[6] Carleton, fresh from the country, was admitted to the presence of this extraordinary creature in his house in York Street, found him dressed in a very slovenly manner, slippered feet, a loose cravat about his neck, a brown outside coat much too wide and too large, a tendency to become abstracted in the middle of a conversation, to raise an open hand and cry: "Hush! I have an image." The comment of the man who learned to be a writer but never forgot to be a sensible countryman was: "After having left him, I would, had I possessed the experience which I do now, have pronounced him to be as vain a creature as ever lived."

4

But there were other meetings that went unrecorded because the story ended when it did, other portraits in miniature that were never painted permanently for the benefit of times to come. There was his meeting in London with Thackeray whom he admired more than any other contemporary writer. (On his deathbed he re-read *The Newcomes.*) Thackeray, in his turn, had admiration for the *Traits and Stories,* thinking Carleton pre-eminent above all the novelists of the time in masterly knowledge of the human heart and in the expression of its emotions. To John McKibbin of Belfast Carleton delivered his opinions on Dickens and Thackeray, opinions possibly influenced by the memory of a pleasant meeting with one and something that looked not unlike avoidance of a meeting on the part of the other: "Thackeray is your great man in drawing the upper English. I spent an endeared day with him. He knows Ireland very well in an English way. He was pleased to tell me quite sincerely that in point of graphic delineation of life I was all their master. Dickens is fertile, varied, and most ingenious, but all is caricature. There does not appear a genuine, fine,

sensible Englishman in all his works. His women are dolls and make-weights. The character of Pickwick is a compound of Uncle Toby and the Vicar of Wakefield."[7]

In London he called also on Leigh Hunt and had apparently another endeared day. The only record of the visit that remains is in a letter written by Hunt some time later: "I shall be most happy to see you, if you can come again. It will give me an opportunity of thanking you in person (strange motive to gratitude!) for having fairly torn me to pieces in sympathy with your poor miser Fardorougha—a thing which I had never contemplated as possible with a hater of miserliness, though I now see very well why it is quite so, and upon absolute brotherly grounds."

To another friend Carleton once sent a copy of the *Nation* newspaper pointing out that it contained week after week what was "probably the ablest and profoundest criticism of the day." One critique to which he directed particular attention was written by a young lady, acquainted with all languages and all literatures, and all history, ancient and modern. Reasonably enough on that evidence he referred to her as "the most extraordinary prodigy of a female that this country, or perhaps any other, has ever produced." The young lady was to live to be a very good friend to Carleton, writing to him that a mind like his should not deliberately kill itself "by conjuring up imaginary gloom." His name, she said, was made; his reputation assured; he had a pension of two hundred pounds a year as well as a fine and clever family. He should go to Paris, chase gloom by a change of scene, take his daughters with him, make himself happy. "God and the world have done more for you than for millions—one gave you genius, the other gave you fame; and if you want lessons of noble feelings, of lofty, elevated, pure, unworldly sentiment, go to your own books for them." Only close friendship could sermon him in that accurate, incisive way without the certainty of permanent offence, and that woman lived on to talk tenderly of the novelist, William Carleton, to the poet, William Yeats. She signed her letter with the pen-name under which she found her place in the procession of Irish patriotic writers: "Speranza"; and the woman who was to become the wife of William Wilde and the mother of Oscar Wilde certainly needed all the spirit that her name indicated.

There were so many places, so many people that his autobiography could have pictured had he, the story-teller, lived to write to the end the story of his own life. According to O'Donoghue he even neglected to include in the account of the early part of his life how he had written a letter in Latin to the commander of a British regiment asking admission into the ranks, and how the surprised officer had gently dissuaded him from hiding his classical talents under a red coat. The incident interestingly links him, the first novelist to write in English of the Irish people, with the randy story of one of the last great poets to write in Gaelic for the Irish people: with Red Owen O'Sullivan, Owen of the sweet mouth, the schoolmaster and spalpeen from the Kerry mountains, running from hunger and his own reputation and the mothers of his unlawful children into the army and navy of the English king. The man from Tyrone had, as far as we know, only hunger and poverty in pursuit, for his manly pride in being a lad with the girls had, apparently, nothing of the Munsterman's thoroughness. Another anecdote that he left unrecorded described how, searching for employment, he made his way into the shop of a bird-stuffer; and when the bird-stuffer, instinctively doubting the applicant's abilities, asked him how he stuffed birds, the reply—strong with all the sense of Ulster, Catholic and Protestant, Orange and Green—was that he stuffed birds with potatoes and meal.

The precedent of his omissions is as good an excuse as any for the use of selection and a mean in a study of the life that he lived. For he had himself the sense of the significance of the half-dozen great events in the life of every man. When he ended his autobiography he was describing how he had gone to teach school in the town of Carlow, bringing his young wife with him to poor lodgings that consisted of one small room about fourteen feet by ten. The coals supplied in the lodgings were "of that vile and unhealthy description to be found in some of the coal-mines which lie between the counties of Carlow and Kilkenny." The proportion of sulphur in the coals was very high and every morning the cream of sulphur lay so white and thick under the door that they could scrape it up with a knife. "In fact the place was not habitable; not only we ourselves, but our children, became ill, and I found that to live there was only another word for death."

That was the last sentence on the unfinished manuscript of the autobiography to which he had planned to devote his old age. With the pen poised in his hand he must have seen the ominous second meaning of those last nine words; "to live there was only another word for death." He had written down in great detail the golden record of the boyhood and youth that had made him, in much less detail the record of the early trials that had almost broken him. There was still a great story to tell of meeting notable people and writing notable books, a great estimate to make of the past and present and future of Irish literature in relation to the Irish people. Those nine words may have warned him that his own story and the story of his people must return to horror, to the land in which to live was only another word for death.

For he was the story-teller talking of fun and coloured movement not in a contented house where all men were happy, but in a wakehouse where all the noise and merriment was a mask or an antidote for mourning. Inevitably there would be at moments a lull in the fun, a break in the story, a silence with eyes turning to the door of the room where the body lay under-board, with waxen hands and face, and the brown shroud, and the soul gone out from suffering into unfathomable mystery.

Notes

[1] Francis Carlin, an Irish poet who died recently in the U.S.A., wrote his great *Ballad of Douglas Bridge* in praise of O'Hanlon's men; and Philip Rooney has written around O'Hanlon a fine story: *North Road.*

[2] O'Donoghue, vol. ii.

[3] *Dublin University Magazine,* vol. xiv, p. 98.

[4] O'Donoghue, vol. ii.

[5] Yeats and Stephens tried to echo it in English. Padraic Fallon has recently succeeded where they failed.

[6] Maturin was the uncle of Oscar Wilde's mother; and Oscar Wilde, in his exile in France, called himself, after a Christian martyr and a Maturin book, Sebastian Melmoth.

[7] O'Donoghue, vol. ii.

John Cronin (essay date 1978)

SOURCE: "Regional Writer, Historian, Moralist, Lover," in *Gerald Griffin (1803-1840): A Critical Biography,* Cambridge University Press, 1978, pp. 70-109.

[*In the following excerpt, Cronin analyzes several of Gerald Griffin's novels, demonstrating Griffin's interest in and deep compassion for the Irish peasantry. Cronin argues that while Griffin's work is often flawed by melodrama, he nevertheless paints disturbing and realistic portraits of the wretched conditions endured by Irish peasants.*]

In 1829 Griffin published, in addition to *The Collegians,* another three-volume work containing two stories of about equal length, *The Rivals* and *Tracy's Ambition.* Both make clear his growing interest in and profound compassion for the wretched state of the Irish peasantry. In spite of the intrusive melodrama of *The Rivals,* both that story and its companion piece give a memorably realistic picture of the grim world inhabited by the Irish peasant of the first quarter of the nineteenth century.

The Rivals *(1829)*

The melodramatic story concerns a Methodist beauty named Esther Wilderming, loved by two suitors, Francis

Riordan and Richard Lacy. The former is a romantic young rebel who gets into trouble when he interferes with the police work of the more conservative and calculating Lacy. Riordan has to flee the country and take refuge in South America but, before he goes, he binds Esther to be true to him forever. When his death is reported, she yields to family pressure and becomes engaged to Lacy. She dies of grief and Riordan returns from abroad to find that she has just been laid to rest in the family vault. He removes her from the tomb, she miraculously revives and they are married. Lacy does his fiendish worst but fails to prevail against his rival or his love for Esther. He dies repentant. Told like that it sounds the most arrant melodramatic rubbish. This absurd plot, however, is merely the necessary, novelistic façade for a really effective piece of rustic realism which is sometimes very funny and often disturbing. Griffin sets his story in County Wicklow, around the beautiful vale of Glendalough, and seizes the opportunity to describe the small and lively rustic world of the place. In the depiction of Mr Lenigan's hedge school he achieves some of his most celebrated comic effects.[1] So vividly is the schoolhouse brought to life that we find ourselves bitterly regretting that Griffin did not pursue this vein of his abilities and eschew the melodramatic effects in which he so often indulges. The lesson in 'consthering' Virgil's *Aeneid,* conducted by Mr Lenigan's Classical assistant, is both hilariously comic in itself and richly relevant to the entire history of verbal acrobatics in the Anglo-Irish novel. The teacher leads his rustic scholars vigorously through a passage from the *Aeneid,* contriving on the way a marvellous, forced marriage between the sonorous splendours of the Latin and the hilarious vividness of the Anglo-Irish idiom of the south of Ireland. Here, clearly, is beginning one notable strand of Anglo-Irish literature, the flamboyant, thrasonical, vigorous line which is to include Carleton, Lever, Boucicault, Joyce, Flann O'Brien and Brendan Behan. Griffin's polymaths are the harbingers of such complex achievements as the 'Oxen of the Sun' episode in *Ulysses.*

The world of *The Rivals,* however, though productive of such hilarities as these, is essentially a grim place. The author's tone is a combination of the sombre and the sardonic:

> About this time one of those provincial insurrections broke out, which were usual during the last few centuries, amongst the discontented peasantry. Arms were taken, contributions levied for ammunition, floggings and cardings inflicted on the part of the insurgents; while the usual preventives were adopted by the local government. The district was proclaimed, and some hundreds of people were transported, but, strange to say, they still continued discontented.[2]

The precise nature of the cause espoused by Riordan is never very clearly indicated. He is said to be the author of a clever escape plan which rescues some prisoners from Lacy's police custodians when they are on their way to deportation but, in the court-room scene at the climax of the novel, he denies that he has been a rebel against the crown: 'You have laid treason at my door, and I will point it out lurking behind your own. You have called me rebel, falsely called me so, but I will make the same charge good against yourself, by evidence as palpable as matter.'[3] Thomas Flanagan equates Riordan with Robert Emmet but, in fact, he hardly emerges in so clear a light.[4] His rebellious doings are on a local rather than a national level and he experiences no difficulty in taking his place in society at the novel's end. As often with Griffin, however, the highly-flavoured histrionics of the principal actors are based on a clearly observed foundation of reality. The miseries of the Irish poor are made constantly clear. In an early scene we are introduced to the home of Mr Kirwan Damer, Esther's uncle and guardian, a strict Methodist with a tendency to proselytise his Catholic dependants. His brother-in-law, Tom Leonard, instructs him in the facts of Irish life and the paradoxes which he has ignored:

> 'Ah, now, come, Damer, keep your cant for the preachers, and talk like a man. It is very easy for you and me to sit down by our coal fires, and groan over the sins and ignorance of the poor, starving, shivering cottagers, while we drink our champaign and hermitage; but, heaven forgive us, I'm afraid that we'll fare otherwise in the other world, for all our hypocrisy, while these poor devils will be reading the Bible in paradise.'

> 'Fie, fie, Leonard, you grow more profane.'

> 'Do you know what John Wesley said?'

> 'Any thing that escaped the lips of that saint must be comfortable.'

> 'Very well. He said it was impossible for a Christian to expect to ride in a coach on earth, and go to heaven afterwards. Pick comfort out of that if you can.'[5]

The turbulence of Irish life is reflected in lively discussions in shebeens and at death-beds. Mr Lenigan's brother, Davy, is made the spokesman of the sort of liberal conservatism which was probably Griffin's own political faith. In the scene at the inn, in the village of Roundwood, he delivers a lengthy harangue on the subject of the Vestry Bill Act and the Sub-letting Act which have been the company's principal topics of conversation and, in the course of his speech, manages to glance at Catholic disabilities generally:

> We surmounted the times, gentlemen, when the priest was hunted with more diligence than the

ravenous wolf, an' as for the schoolmasther—(there was some tittering amongst the girls)—an' as for the schoolmasther, he was searched for as a vigorous sportsman, on the banks of the Nore, would search for his game . . . The time is now past when the poor bewildered Catholic, in his state of starvation, would not be allowed to keep a horse worth more than five pounds, and when he would not be allowed to keep one foot of the land of his forefathers under a lase, an' even spakin' the language of his country was a crime.[6]

He concludes his harangue by warning his listeners that violence will only play into the hands of their enemies:

the surest and most expeditious way to break all those chains, is to live paceable with those savages that daily want to raise us to rebellion, to observe the laws in the sthrictest manner, to avoid nightwalkin' as the root of all our misfortunes, and, of all the world, to beware of any secret societies, for I can assure you, with truth, that all who belong to any such community are of little consequence in any concerns, inless in violating the laws, an' going headlong to the gallows.[7]

In a sense, therefore, Griffin manages to have his 'rebelly' cake and eat it. He effectively brings home to his readers the genuineness of the peasants' grievances while constantly managing to suggest that all would be well if the laws were decently administered. Corrupt local politicians are the villains of the piece and are, essentially, as much the enemies of all loyal, middle-class citizens as of the peasants whom they more obviously oppress. The novel constantly affords us revealing glimpses of the troubled tangle of the life of the Irish poor, living close to the breadline and subject to savage penalties for transgressions which their appalling conditions render inevitable.

Tracy's Ambition *(1829)*

This second story is in every way more successful than *The Rivals,* more powerfully imagined, more forcefully and succinctly realised. It is the first-person narration of one Abel Tracy who is ruined by falling into the grip of obsessive ambition. The work has an almost Jonsonian force, with Abel possessing the comprehensive significance of a 'humour'. In his rendering of the main character Griffin displays considerable sardonic insight into Abel's psychology and employs it to involve us both with Abel himself and the turbulent times in which he lives. Abel is in every way an in-between character. He is, first of all, neither gentleman nor peasant but uneasily placed between two social levels and at the mercy of both:

I was one of a race who may be considered the only tenants of land in my native Island. Our castle

owners, above us, and our cabin holders, below, are both men of estate; while we occupy the generous position of honorary agents to the former, serving to collect their rents in a troublesome country; and of scapegoats on whom the latter are enabled to repose the burthen of rent, tythes, and county charges.[8]

The admirable brevity of this compares favourably with the much more leisurely and flaccid style of the corresponding description of that other 'middleman', Mr Daly, in Chapter 4 of *The Collegians.* Abel, himself a Protestant, compounds his median status by marrying a well-to-do Catholic, Mary Regan, whom he rescues romantically when her horse bolts. Griffin drives through these necessary preliminaries with unaccustomed speed and skill and in his short opening chapter manages to introduce Abel, marry him to Mary Regan and sketch effectively the well-bred scorn with which her brother, Ulick Regan, greets the match. Abel is to continue to smart at his elegant brother-in-law's contempt throughout the story. Ulick chides his sister for marrying secretly without his consent and promptly departs from Ireland, while Abel and his bride settle down at Cushlanebeg in reasonable comfort and set about rearing a family. Mary plays the part of intermediary for the local peasantry in any suit they make to her husband and for a long time he heeds her advice and, as a consequence, is highly regarded by the people.

His difficulties begin with the arrival in the area of a magistrate named Dalton whose express business it is to sniff out disaffection and generally play the part of government spy. He holds out to Tracy the promise of preferment, playing on Tracy's desire to climb the shaky ladder of a turbulent and disordered society:

A magistrate himself, and toiling hard for preferment, he had expressed a wish for my co-operation, and opened to my view prospects of personal advantage which I found it difficult to regard with that indifference of which I boasted. The influence which a little exertion, such as he recommended, would procure me among the people of the neighbourhood; the emoluments, trifling indeed in appearance, but yet capable of being improved into a return worthy of consideration; the rank to which it would lift me among the gentry of the country; the post which perhaps it would become my right to occupy among the representatives of ancient families, at sessions and assizes; no insolent bailiff nor Peeler to slap the court-house doors in my face; no impertinent crier to pick me out of a crowd with his long white wand, and bid me 'Lave that, an' make room for the gentlemen o' the Bar—' I figured to myself all these flattering circumstances, while I passed up and down our flagged hall, under such an agitation of spirits as I had seldom before experienced.[9]

Dalton's adored son, Henry, falls into debt and the besotted father calls on Abel Tracy for help. To retain

Dalton's favour Tracy hands over his daughter's dowry of six hundred pounds and from then on is at Dalton's mercy since the money is not repaid at the time agreed and Tracy's domestic affairs begin to disintegrate. Dalton continues to dangle before him the promise of preferment, and Tracy, conscious of his folly but driven on by his fatal flaw, soon passes from comfort and happiness to wretchedness and destitution. Dalton is engaged in persecuting the local people in the name of law and order and is prepared to go to any lengths to obtain convictions, planting evidence, suborning informers, bribing and threatening. Once he allows himself to be identified with Dalton, Tracy earns the hatred of the local people who had previously trusted and depended upon him. He falls victim to the terrorism which is inevitably bred of the vile social conditions and the cynicism of Dalton's administration. His wife, Mary, is killed by a band of masked attackers and he himself gravely wounded. He loses everything he has treasured until he is left with no object in life except the unmasking of Dalton. The hero's emotional turbulence is well charted by Griffin. At various points in the narrative Tracy perceives and even analyses accurately his own decline but always makes the necessary compromise with evil which forces him yet another step along the road to moral disintegration:

> Yes, I thought, I will first withdraw myself from his power, and secure a compensation for my losses, and then I will denounce and cast him off. Until then, until I am secure from the effects of his resentment, beware, my temper, how you suffer your vulgar prejudices to appear!

> I listened, meanwhile to a long dissertation of Dalton's, on the state of the Island, on the weakness of my nature, on the gain to be acquired by activity and *firmness,* and other stimulating subjects. But his pains were superfluous, for I had already determined to sacrifice my consciousness of right, and enter into a compromise with treachery.[10]

An effective part of the novel's moral structure is that Tracy's machinations are made finally to founder in total absurdity. Ulick Regan returns from exile to take a hand in his niece's fortunes. Tracy fails to recognise him, changed as he is by long residence in a tropical climate, and in any case fails utterly to comprehend Ulick's plans for his niece, Tracy's daughter, Eileen. Tracy absurdly jumps to the conclusion that Ulick wishes Eileen to marry a ridiculous drunken bachelor named Purtill and, labouring under this complete misapprehension, Tracy introduces this gaby into his house as Eileen's accepted suitor. He persuades his daughter to dismiss her fiancé, Rowan Clancy, who is, unknown to Tracy, the suitor favoured by Ulick. Tracy needlessly distresses his daughter, throws his house into an uproar with the silly doings of the egregious Purtill and is made to look wonderfully foolish when his

mistaken assumptions are exposed. Ulick's long-standing contempt for his brother-in-law seems justified by this climax and indeed by Tracy's weakness of character throughout the novel but, in spite of this, Griffin succeeds in retaining our regard for his all too vulnerable narrator. He is always more victim than villain and it is impossible to dislike altogether a character who is so often depicted at a disadvantage in his own account of his adventures. His enemy, Dalton, is brought low by the same forces which murdered Tracy's wife. Young Henry Dalton is brutally murdered by a peasant whom Dalton has repeatedly wronged and the broken-hearted father never recovers from his terrible loss. Tracy's ambition and the net of intrigue and calculation in which it involves him are ultimately exposed as the trivial irrelevancies they really are, and Abel Tracy himself complacently reveals at the very end how little he has learnt after all:

> For myself, I now lead a peaceful life among a circle of merry friends. My ambition is entirely set at rest, and I think if I could only succeed in obtaining the commission of the peace, which I am at present using every exertion to procure. I should be a contented man for the remainder of my days.[11]

It is appropriate that Griffin should have woven one of his most successful stories around the idea of an obsessive ambition. Intensely ambitious himself at the outset of his career, he gradually lost his taste for worldly success and found his work as a writer becoming increasingly distasteful to him. More and more he came to feel that his pursuits as an author were somehow irrelevant to the real concerns of a busy world in which he found himself sharing a house with two hard-working doctors, his brothers William and Daniel. For the depiction of Abel Tracy he reached within himself and applied profound convictions and insights concerning excessive human aspirations to his keen perception of the social ills of his day. In his effectiveness as a narrator, Abel Tracy recalls Maria Edgeworth's Thady Quirke in *Castle Rackrent*. Dangerously balanced between two classes, two religions, he inhabits a moral no-man's-land which Griffin charts with instinctive skill. This short and powerful work is altogether lacking in the longueurs which affect the much better-known novel, *The Collegians. Tracy's Ambition* possesses an impressive moral coherence and offers convincing glimpses of small-town life and the day-to-day existence of the country people. Griffin's Ireland often appears as a pullulating pit of restless helots but the depiction of their miseries is made all the more convincing by the fact that the novel is far from unrelievedly sombre. Indeed, there is a generous measure of the sort of comedy which would be at home in the 'R.M.' stories of Somerville and Ross when Griffin recounts the hilarious doings of the corps of yeomanry of which Abel Tracy is a member. His eye for comic detail is nicely evidenced in the second lieutenant who brushes his eyebrows against the grain to give himself an appearance of military ferocity. At the same time, the comedy is effectively used to suggest the chaotic state of the forces of law and order.

The malign attitude of authority to the Irish poor is voiced with memorable viciousness by Dalton:

> I think them a base, fawning, servile, treacherous, smooth-tongued and black-hearted race of men; bloody in their inclinations, debauched and sensual in their pleasures, beasts in their cunning, and beasts in their appetite. They are a disgusting horde, from first to last. I enquire not into causes and effects; I weigh not the common cant of misrule and ignorance; I look not into historical influences; I speak of the men as I find them, and act by them as such . . . I hate the people.[12]

The savage bitterness of the oppressed is voiced by the old hag, Mrs Shanahan, whose son has been shot dead by Tracy during a midnight attack by insurgents:

> You did this for me, Abel Tracy, an' the prayer I was goin' to offer, 'till you hindred me, was that the Almighty might do as much for you. If I had the arms or the sthrength of a man, I would'nt be talkin' to you this way. But though I'm weak, I have strong friends, an' they have you marked. You can't sthrike a bush in the country from this day, but a friend of Shanahan will start from it against you. Ah, Abel Tracy, there is no law for the poor in Ireland, but what they make themselves, and by that law my child will have blood for blood before the year is out.[13]

Maria Edgeworth had seen the peasantry through the eyes of Thady Quirke as that dangerous serf had gazed out through the cracked panes of Castle Rackrent. Griffin, through his narrator Abel Tracy, brings the people Thady saw to vivid life for us, and in this short but powerful novel we stumble with them along the muddy roads of a barbarous and bitter land, we feel them huddling their wretched rags about them, we inhabit with them their miserable cabins and feel their winter cold. Many of Griffin's personal tensions must have been generated by the clash between his powerfully realistic vision of the Irish world about him and the demands of his comfortable, middle-class background. A different sort of man would have either joined in the exploitation or perhaps undertaken an active campaign against it. Griffin, intelligent, sensitive, peace-loving, separated by birth and fortune from the mass of his countrymen but utterly unable to identify with their oppressors, worked out the logic of the situation and came to his own conclusion, that the only hope for his country and its people lay in improving their lot by educating them. He would have agreed with Davis's cry, 'Educate that you may be free', and we can see in the tragic vision he displays in *Tracy's Ambition* the reason for his eventual decision to join a teaching Order dedicated to the educational betterment of the Irish poor.

His lenghty concluding note to the work makes clear his attitudes and his didactic purpose. He first distinguishes between his own work in fiction and that of the Banim brothers, John and Michael, in their well-known *Tales by the O'Hara Family:*

> They were the first who painted the Irish peasant sternly from the life; they placed him before the world in all his ragged energy and cloudy loftiness of spirit, they painted him as he is, goaded by the sense of national and personal wrong, and venting his long pent up agony in the savage cruelty of his actions, in the powerful idiomatic eloquence of his language, in the wild truth and unregulated generosity of his sentiments, in the scalding vehemence of his reproaches, and the shrewd and biting satire of his jests.[14]

His own intention, he says, has been to depict a gentler Ireland:

> We have endeavoured in most instances, where pictures of Irish cottage life have been introduced, to furnish a softening corollary to the more exciting moral chronicles of our predecessors, to bring forward the sorrows and the affections more frequently than the violent and fearful passions of the people.[15]

He then goes on to convey his views on the course of Irish history and on the character of the Irish people as it has revealed itself through the ages. The Irish character, he states, has been astonishingly consistent in its fidelity to its native leaders, its devotion to the Church, its hatred of the conqueror. The credulity of the Irish has been matched only by the fury of their resentment when that credulity has been betrayed:

> It might be an interesting investigation to examine into the origin of those varieties in character which appear to be so hereditary, and which can only be broken up by a difference of political situation, and by a more extended system of education. But at present we only wish to speak of the character and condition of the Irish peasant as he is.[16]

When he goes on to consider what steps should be taken to improve the lot of the Irish peasant, Griffin is in no doubt as to what needs to be done:

> Poverty in nations, as in individuals, is the parent of licentiousness, and man must cease to feel the pangs of hunger before he can find leisure to embrace goodness. Will England, then, remain insensible to the personal afflictions, to the continued agonies of this long-suffering and long-neglected class of men? Will she permit their natural protectors, untaxed, to squander their resources abroad, and to return at long intervals only to increase the oppressions of the people?[17]

The immediate need, clearly, is for an improvement in the political position of the Irish peasant and for a radical revision of attitude by the holders of the land. Only then will Ireland cease to be a drain on the British Treasury and a source of English ignominy before the nations of the world.

In both *The Rivals* and *Tracy's Ambition,* Griffin writes with a powerful realism which is undimmed by the occasional melodrama of the plots. Both stories provide the reader with an unusual insight into the daily harshness of the lives of the Irish poor. Country roads with their travelling people, small towns with their poor markets and their beggars and prostitutes, paupers' cabins and paupers' graves, informers, 'nightwalkers', all pass before us in a sombre panorama of national desperation. Griffin has come a long way from the youthful detachment of his London days.

The Christian Physiologist *(1830)*

In Chapter 12 of the *Life,* Daniel describes the growth of Gerald's religious scruples in regard to his work. More and more, he became convinced that he was wasting his time and that it was impossible for the writer of fiction to control the creative passion and direct its power to proper, moral ends. Daniel reports him as saying: 'I see you, and William, and every one around me constantly engaged in some useful occupation, and here am I spending my whole life in the composition of these trashy tales and novels, that do no good either to myself or anybody else.'[18] It is clear from the account in the *Life* that Daniel struggled hard to combat his brother's moral and aesthetic scruples but it is equally clear that his arguments fell on deaf ears. As the situation worsened, Gerald began to impose upon himself a Dedalus-like regimen of regularity, the very strictness of which is symptomatic of his increasing distaste for the literary vocation:

> He became more systematic than ever in the disposal of his time; punctual as the striking of the clock in his hours of rising and retiring to rest; and, singular to say, though his interest in his literary labours had nearly lost all its freshness and force, he went through them each day with a most exact and scrupulous industry, looking on them as his only occupation, and therefore feeling that, as a matter of duty, they ought to be done well.[19]

It was at this time that he began work on *The Christian Physiologist,* an overtly didactic work with a specific moral aim which is clearly programmed in the Preface to the book: 'We have sought, by adding to that knowledge of his moral nature which his religious education supplies to the young Christian, such a knowledge of his physiological existence, of the wonders of his own frame, as might assist him in the observance of his heavenly duties.'[20] That Griffin himself was far from

confident that the public would take kindly to his fictional moralisings is indicated by his account of the curtailment of the original project for a much more elaborate work:

> It was intended at first to arrange in a popular form, and illustrate by amusing fables, the whole science of physiology; but it soon appeared that such a design must necessarily extend to a greater length, and demand a greater sacrifice of time, than would be warranted by the uncertainty of its reception with the public. We have therefore confined the undertaking at present, to the five external senses; which, if the public approbation should not warrant the completion of our design, will form a little work, complete in itself.[21]

In a lengthy footnote to the Preface, Griffin adverts to the erroneous views he had held at an earlier stage of his life and expresses profound regret for the mistaken opinions of his youth and for the bad example he may have set some of his young friends.

The Christian Physiologist contains, in addition to the five tales 'illustrative of the five senses', a long chapter entitled *Of the Intellect* and a concluding tale, *A Story of Psyche,* which is 'intended to represent the human Soul, or Will'. The second story in the book, *The Day of Trial,* illustrative of the sense of Hearing, had earlier appeared, under the title *The Deaf Filea,* in *The Juvenile Keepsake* in 1829. The first two stories in the volume are prefaced by an account of the functioning of the organs in question (the eye and the ear) and Griffin seems to have drawn freely on his brother's medical text-books in this connection, as Daniel indicates in his biography:

> The portions of this work which related to the structure and functions of the organs of sense, showed such an intimate knowledge of anatomy and physiology, that many persons imagined they could not have been written without the assistance of some medical man, and therefore that Dr Griffin or I must have had some hand in them; but this was so far from being the case, that though we could not help wondering what it was that made him every day pull down our medical books, and give himself so deeply to the study of anatomy, neither of us had the slightest conception what he was at until the work was completed.[22]

Each of the five tales is also prefaced by a chapter on the use and government of the sense under review.

The stories themselves are generally unimpressive. *The Kelp Gatherer* is a moral tale about a patient widow who endures blindness until, as a reward for her submission to God's will, she is cured of a cataract by a surgeon and is thus enabled to see her son, his wife and children for the first time since their return from America. It is noticeable that, although the story is set in Ireland, Griffin does not here equip his characters with a regional idiom. They are made to speak a correct, indeed formal English. *The Day of Trial,* the only story not specifically prepared for this volume, is rather more elaborately constructed and more effective. Madaghan, chief poet to the arch-king of Erin, has one son who is both deaf and dumb. Unknown to the despairing father, the son's disabilities are miraculously cured and he sets about training as a minstrel in secret. He enters for the contest which is to decide his father's successor as chief poet and, having won, reveals his secret to his delighted parent. Some of the ornate detail of this story resembles that of the long historical novel, *The Invasion,* which was soon to follow and for which Griffin had been collecting material for some time.

The Voluptuary Cured is, as its title suggests, an account of the reform of a nobleman bored by worldly pleasures. On the advice of his physician, he abandons the frivolous gaieties of the London season and sets out for his estates in Ireland. He puts up at a dreadful hotel in Waterford where his pocket-book is stolen and from which he eventually sets out, penniless, to travel to his agent's residence. He arrives in time to save a peasant from eviction and then discovers that his physician and the inn-keeper have been benevolently in league against him for his own good. The 'theft' of his money has been a hoax and Lord Ulla, in returning to his responsibilities as landlord, discovers the pleasures of a simple life and the satisfaction of doing one's duty. Mild fun is poked throughout at the Englishman's notion of Ireland as a wild country full of brigands and thieves. Lord Ulla, like Maria Edgeworth's Lord Glenthorne, has his eyes opened to his duties and to his own best interests. Despite its heavily moralistic tone, this is one of the more effective stories in the book and, in Lord Ulla's distaste for London and in the mild satire at the expense of English ignorance of Irish life, one occasionally catches a glimpse of Griffin's own sensations and attitudes. *The Self-Consumed* is a short and improbable tale illustrative of the evils of self-indulgence and luxury. Its detail is, once again, similar to that of *The Invasion,* with considerable emphasis on items of antique ornament, weapons and dress. This type of description is even more lavishly employed in *The Selfish Crotaire,* the story illustrative of the sense of Taste. This is set in the same era as *The Invasion,* the period of the Viking invasions of Ireland, and is clearly indebted to the lengthy researches Griffin was making in preparation for his historical novel, details of which were included in his *Common-Place Book A,* which is described and discussed at a later stage of this chapter.

The Christian Physiologist concludes with a chapter on the Intellect and the long, fanciful allegory of the progress of the Soul, *A Story of Psyche.* The account of the intellect is interestingly premonitory of Griffin's eventual flight from the world, and *A Story of Psyche*

is really an extension into the theological and moral fields of the old argument carried on between Hardress Cregan and Kyrle Daly about the conflicting claims of 'elegance and simplicity'. Psyche, or the Soul, thrust out of Paradise, is torn between the conflicting claims of Imagination (Hardress Cregan) and Judgement (Kyrle Daly). Imagination bedazzles Psyche into ignoring the sober warnings of Judgement, and, when Psyche has sickened of the delights of the senses and begun to fear the consequences of the evil she has perpetrated in the world through surrender to sensual delights, Imagination proves her greatest foe, filling her mind with horrid images of punishment and terror. Psyche is beset by images of the torments of Hell and, in desperation, turns to Philosophy for help but Philosophy is lost in the mists of scientific enquiry and can offer no true help to the questing spirit. Finally, the Almighty takes pity on Psyche and guides the searching Soul to the path of righteousness. Judgement is discovered at the foot of the Cross, and Psyche takes up the Cross and lives a life of self-denial and patient virtue. This, Griffin's brief version of a pilgrim's progress, is in no way theologically startling but the whole piece is interestingly analogous to Griffin's own life and very revealing of the type of thinking which lay behind some of his major decisions. At times the language employed anticipates passages from his later correspondence. Psyche, at the end, is thus depicted: 'Psyche has often been heard to say, that her life is happier than when abandoned to the dominion of her own servants, she trod the fertile valleys of the world, inhaling its sweetest perfumes, and banquetting upon its richest fruits.'[23] Years later, Griffin was to write to a friend in very similar vein, after he had himself retired from the world and was working as a teacher in the Christian Brothers' house at Cork: 'it seems curious even to myself, that I feel a great deal happier in the practice of this daily routine than I did while I was roving about your great city, absorbed in the modest project of rivalling Shakespeare, and throwing Scott into the shade'.[24]

Thus, *The Christian Physiologist,* even if of no great literary merit in itself, suggests something of the flavour of his next novel, throws considerable light on the kind of thinking which had shaped Griffin's past development and, further, forecasts his eventual retirement from the world.

Common-Place Book A: The Invasion *(1832)*

At the Christian Brothers' house at North Richmond Street, Dublin, where Griffin was received as a novice in 1838, there is preserved a most interesting common-place book of the author. Since Griffin attempted to destroy the bulk of his papers before retiring from the world, anything which survived the holocaust acquires thereby a kind of Sibylline interest merely by virtue of its survival. *Common-Place Book A,* however, is of absorbing interest in itself and in relation to the novel of which it is the basis, as it will be the purpose of the rest of this section to demonstrate. It is written in a copy of Taylor's printed form of common-place book, rebound in black half-leather with black grained paper boards, and has a printed paper label on the front board inscribed *Common-Place Book A.* It measures nine inches by seven and contains 330 pages, with a two-leaf insertion and coloured map at the beginning and a single-leaf insertion between pp. 292 and 293. The entries are written in dark ink and remain clear and easy to read. One short pencilled entry on p. 3 has faded somewhat. There are remarkably few corrections or erasures. The volume is equipped with an alphabetical Index of two letters on a leaf and had a set of eight labels, A to H. The labels B to D are missing which suggests, tantalisingly, that there may have been three other such books which are now lost. On the *verso* of the marbled end-paper there are the following inscriptions:

> Common-Place Book of Gerald Griffin presented to St Mary's Library by the Very Revd B. T. Russell, Prov. O.S.D. Presented by the Prior and Community of St Mary's to the Christian Brothers, North Monastery, Easter, 1921.

Enquiries to the Prior of St Mary's, Cork and the Rev. Br. Superior of the North Monastery, Cork have failed to uncover any other such volumes.

In *Common-Place Book A* the novelist recorded the mass of material which he collected for his historical novel, *The Invasion,* published in 1832. Daniel relates how Gerald embarked on preparations for this historical novel soon after the publication of *The Collegians* in 1829:

> Gerald had no sooner completed *The Collegians* than he began to turn his attention to the study of ancient Irish history, believing that there were many peculiarities in the usages of early times which would admit of being blended with a story, and would keep up that interest in the public mind, about the decline of which he was always apprehensive. He was deeply taken with this study, and says, in a letter to his brother, 'I am full of my next tale— quite enthusiastic—in love with my subject, and up to my ears in antiquities at the London Institution.'[25]

In March 1829 his researches took him to Dublin. He wrote to his brother William:

> I have done a great deal here at the Dublin Library, which is a tolerable collection, and I am promised an introduction to the Dublin Institution—also rather extensive. I do not wish to leave Dublin until I have smelted all the antiquarian lore in those two mines, which, by the way, is much more abundant than I expected. I have already learned to think enough for my first purpose, but as in architecture 'a little stronger than strong enough'

is the great maxim, so a little more learned than learned enough is a grand requisite for a historical work.[26]

So determined was he to prepare himself properly for his historical novel that he deferred publication of it until 1832. With characteristic integrity he was determined that his novel should be based on genuine and painstaking research. It is interesting to speculate why Griffin, at the moment of his greatest success with the publication of his best-known novel, *The Collegians,* should have turned aside to such antiquarian pursuits as absorbed him from 1829 until the publication of *The Invasion* in 1832. There is a clue, perhaps, in a letter which he wrote from Pallaskenry to a friend in London in February 1828 in the course of which he has the following to say about Irish history:

> There is a history which the world wants—a history which would do service to a people, and confer immortality on a historian (if properly executed). If I had even a moderate degree of talent—and with this talent the opportunity, the industry, (*that* I should command, however, I think,) the wisdom requisite for a good historian, I would undertake it in preference to any work whatsoever—I mean, as you may conjecture, a history of Ireland . . . Are there not men who would feel a *pleasure* in painting the convulsions of a powerful people, labouring under a nightmare for ten centuries?[27]

It should be remembered that, when he wrote this letter, a year after his return to his own country, Griffin was still painfully close to the experiences of his London period, those three fateful years of struggle and bitter disappointment during which he lost for ever the first, fine, careless rapture of his early ambition and began to win for himself what he was to describe as the 'half of a name'. He had struggled in the alien capital to have his plays accepted and in this he had failed utterly. He had finally succeeded in making a living by working for the literary journals of the day, by parliamentary reporting, by all sorts of hack-work. His literary dreams had faded very fast and he had felt himself an outsider in a city he hated. It is possible to see his antiquarian studies and his determination to write an historical novel as a logical and integral part of his development. His deep consciousness (expressed in the letter of February 1828 quoted above) of the gloomy, disastrous nature of Ireland's history for the ten centuries preceding his own gives us our point of departure. *The Invasion,* set in the halcyon days *before* the invader ravaged Ireland is, in a sense, a grandiose piece of patriotic nostalgia on the part of this talented and rootless man in desperate search for an identity, personal, national and artistic. Thomas Flanagan has noted how, during his time in London, Griffin made friends principally with foreigners, other expatriates.[28] He never put down roots in England and his early difficulties and disappointments obviously gave him a particular horror of London.

Yet, as a writer, he knew that London was the place where he must make his mark. He is sometimes, in certain moods, strongly attracted to the society of his literary peers. An excited letter from Dublin to his brother William on April 11, 1829 says that he 'will take the world as it comes from henceforth, and crush ceremony to pieces. I long to meet Lady Morgan and to know Miss Edgeworth.'[29] His considerable success with *The Collegians* gave him the entrée to literary society. Scott praised him.[30] Maria Edgeworth wrote in a letter to a friend about '*The Collegians,* in which there is much genius and strong drawing of human nature'.[31] Griffin clearly felt the attraction of the cultivated literary world of his day. His own letter of April 11, 1829 contains this revealing passage:

> It would, after all, be a great advantage that people of rank and influence should know and be interested about one, and it is worth something to know what fashionable society is. They are the people whom one writes to please, and it is well to know what pleases amongst them.

> This is my sober, business-like reason for wishing to know them; but take the honest truth—the pleasure is more than half the motive. This, after all, is really the only rank in which I could ever feel *at home*— in which I could fling off the *mauvaise honte*—talk—laugh—and be happy. But once again—that pang! I must work hard and get the antidote.

> Why was I not born to a fortune?[32]

That is one of Griffin's voices, the voice with which he speaks when, for a brief space, success, professional and social, raises him to a pitch of delight and social confidence which he seldom attains. The other voice follows immediately, in the same letter:

> If you were, says a little voice, you would never have known the Irish peasantry—you would never have written *The Collegians*—nobody would know, nobody would care a fig for you.

> Thank heaven that I was born poor—but, oh! heaven, do not keep me so![33]

That last jocose prayer holds the secret of his restlessness. It is that which sends him back to the early history of his country to depict a period when Ireland was not a drab, misgoverned, English colony but a centre of learning and culture to which the people of the larger island sent their children to be schooled. Griffin had, after all, proved with *The Collegians* that he could cut a figure in the larger literary world of his time. He had had a great success but he was finding it increasingly difficult to treat his peasant countrymen merely as fodder for the regional novel. His drift is increasingly towards a genuine sympathy for his fellow-countrymen's

miseries. *The Invasion* is a search for his origins and a search for solace. He had written, in a Joycean phrase, of 'a powerful people, labouring under a nightmare for ten centuries'. For Griffin as for his more celebrated successor in the Irish novel history was a nightmare from which he was trying, in his own way, to awake.

Common-Place Book A and the novel based upon it form a remarkable record of his flight from an intolerable present into a richly romanticised past. It provides references to over sixty works on history and mythology, ranging from *The Book of Lecan* to Bede's *Martyrology,* from Alfred's *Translation of Orosius* to Holinshed's *Chronicles.* The book records detailed information on a wide range of topics connected with the ancient Irish and the Danes. The novel was to be set in the eighth century and the writer records masses of detail about the dress, weapons, architecture, fighting habits and character of the Danes and the Irish of that period. An old map of Ireland showing the country divided into Leath Mogha (in the south) and Leath Cuin (in the north) is inserted at the beginning and occasional reference is made to this map throughout. Interspersed here and there are brief suggestions about the plot of the novel, for example on p. 30:

> Chap. 1: The Vikingirs described. State of Northern Europe. Character of the Sea Kings. Descent of Thorgils and their subjugation of Ireland. Devastation of Armagh. Thorgils and Malachy become kings, under what circumstances. View of state of country etc.

This entry was clearly made at an early stage of his planning of the novel because, in the finished work, this sketch of the opening chapter is not adhered to and the novel, instead, opens quietly in Ireland, with the actual invasion and the account of the Vikings held over until considerably later in the book.

Although later editions of *The Invasion* (published by Duffy of Dublin) were to carry an apologetic note about Griffin's amateur status as an antiquarian, and Professor Eugene O'Curry was to be called in to contribute explanatory notes of a more academically respectable kind, nevertheless Griffin's preparatory reading was of an impressive nature and its range and extent explained the huge quantity of detailed information contained in *Common-Place Book A* and eventually fed into the novel itself. The origins and history of the Vikings are sketched, with an account of their character, their battle practices, their religion, their funeral customs. There is a great deal of information on the history of ancient Ireland and the development of Irish Christianity, with accounts of the dress, living conditions and practices of the early Irish, their schools and bardic courts. Considerable attention is paid to the Druids whom St Patrick displaced and much of this detail finds its way into the novel eventually (for example, the story of

Patrick's shocking the Druids by lighting his huge fire before theirs on the eve of Samhain). The notes lay considerable emphasis on the splendour of ancient Ireland and on the advanced state of its learning. Frequent reference is made to gold and gold ornaments being in common use among the rulers, and their patronage of poets and historians is stressed. The Irish contribution to learning and Christianity is frequently mentioned, a typical entry being as follows:

> When Charlemagne founded the universities of Pavia and Paris, in the eighth century, Claude Clement and John Scot, both Irishmen, were appointed directors and first introduced the Birede, Biretrum, or doctor's cap, and the gold ring or the insignia by which they preceded all ranks but the nobility. (p. 228)

The notes soon become a roughly chronological survey of early Irish history, from pre-Christian times to the period after the Danish invasions and the record seems to conclude on the book's final page (p. 300) as the last entries, which record the survival of the Danes in the trading towns, have a note of finality about them. There follow twenty-one pages of a carefully kept Index (two letters on a leaf) with entries from A to W.

The most obvious interest which attaches to *Common-Place Book A* is that it is the evident source-book for one of Griffin's later novels and the great mass of detailed information which the writer compiled was to give *The Invasion* and authenticity which is, in places, a great advantage to it but which is often a dead weight, particularly at the beginning of the novel where the writer grossly overindulges himself in antiquarian description at every possible opportunity. This aspect of the novel was glanced at tartly by a contemporary reviewer in the *Literary Gazette* for Saturday, January 7, 1832 who commented: 'An epic, a novel, a treatise on political economy, and an antiquarian essay, are materials that do not assimilate. We will first allow our author to speak for himself, and then say why we think his efforts will not be rewarded with popularity.'[34] The novel itself is rather better than the reviewer suggests. Admittedly it begins very tediously and one soon wearies of the writer's determination to load every rift with the results of his antiquarian researches. Once the story gets under way, however, there is a certain interest in the confident depiction of a remote period and Griffin's reading would seem to have had this beneficial result, that it enabled him to move naturally enough through the remote times he is describing. It is, of course, a sentimentalised Ireland, full of richly apparelled chieftains and exotic Druids. There is little mention of the common people who, if they appear at all, do so merely as extras in the crowd scenes of a very glamorous production. The novel is leisurely in the extreme and perhaps the most curious aspect of it is that the invasion from which it derives its title barely

happens. In this connection the entry on p. 30 of *Common-Place Book A* about the burning of Armagh (quoted earlier) is most revealing. In the book itself this incident never takes place. It was evidently abandoned by the novelist but would seem to indicate that he had, at one time, intended to write about the Vikings' devastation of the main centres of Irish Christian civilisation. In the novel as he eventually wrote it the Vikings make a landing (in Munster), but this action is subsidiary to the quarrel between the hero, Elim, and his uncle, Baseg, and the invaders are repulsed pretty rapidly in the closing chapters.

What seems to have happened is that the focus of Griffin's interest changed as he wrote the book and turned from antiquarianism into channels already familiar to us from his previous novels. The book's strongest focus is on the character of Elim's Saxon friend, Kenric, who is yet another in the gallery of proud, discontented solitaries already so familiar to us in the work of this novelist. Kenric is a Saxon who is sent by his parents to be schooled in the sister island and he meets Elim at school and forms the friendship which is at the centre of the book. In terms of *The Collegians,* Elim is the Kyrle Daly, Kenric the Hardress Cregan of this novel. Kenric is always proud, solitary, inflexible in his opinions. He travels in Europe and achieves a superficial scholarly fame with a slight treatise on astronomy. The turning-point of his career occurs when he enrages the local Saxon ruler, Duke Elfwin, by contradicting him stubbornly in a trivial debate about the dating of Easter, thus losing the duke's favour and having to set out on his travels which eventually lead him into a guilty involvement with the Norsemen, the enemies of his Irish friends. He melodramatically saves Eithne, Elim's betrothed whom Kenric also loves, from death at the hands of the Vikings and dies at his home after a melodramatic illness bordering on madness. Pride is his besetting sin and the passages in which he deplores this failing have a familiar ring for the reader of Griffin's novels. He is from the beginning an outsider. At school, only Elim's kindness saves him from himself and, once their ways divide, Kenric is doomed by his own proud, inflexible nature to live and die unhappily. Griffin's preoccupation with this sort of character is, perhaps, nowhere more startlingly displayed than in this book where the treatment of Kenric's character is allowed to take precedence even over the carefully amassed historical detail. In the last analysis this is, in spite of all early appearances, a novel about Kenric rather than an historical novel.

Judging from *Common-Place Book A,* it would seem to have been the novelist's intention to write a vigorous account of battles long ago. In the event, though the Vikings, their beliefs and practices are elaborately described, they barely touch the shores of Ireland and we get instead a novel about a tormented Saxon solitary. This change of direction on the writer's part also renders irrelevant his early insistence on the dangers of faction among the Irish chieftains (a theme which Griffin probably wished to relate to the factious politics of the Ireland of his own day). If the book had shown an Ireland ravaged by the Vikings from without and torn by dissensions from within, the point about the dangers of faction would have been forcefully demonstrated. Since, however, Elim successfully repels the brief Viking attack at the end, much of the earlier detail about differences among the Irish chieftains seems ultimately irrelevant and the novelist seems to be aware of this when he closes his story by glancing briefly into the future and refers to the larger and more successful Viking invasions which lie ahead. In the light of the revealing entry on p. 30 of *Common-Place Book A,* it would seem reasonable to suggest that Griffin set out to write an historical novel about an Ireland already occupied by Viking invaders but that he finally wrote instead yet another elaborate exploration of the proud solitary who is always, in the region of character, his most obsessive interest.

There is one section of *Common-Place Book A* which has no connection with *The Invasion* but is of peculiar interest to the biographer as it sheds much light on the way Griffin's ideas were developing at this time (about 1830). Between pp. 113 and 143 he breaks off his exploration of ancient times to note his views on two important works which he was then reading. These are Locke's *On Human Understanding* and Rousseau's *Emile.* On pp. 118 and 119 there is also a short section headed 'Edgeworth on Education'. It is fortunate that, on p. 118, Griffin inserted a note to indicate that he finished reading Locke's work on May 1, 1830. This is the only date in the book and helps to place it for us. Pages 113 to 118 are occupied with a discussion of Locke's views on religious differences as expressed in his treatise on *The Conduct of the Understanding.* This involves Griffin in a careful discrimination between 'faith' and 'belief'. He distinguishes between them by contending that, while belief can be erroneous, faith cannot, a point which evidently matters to him as he returns to it briefly much later on in a note on p. 287 where he states that belief 'implied trust, and there can be no trust where is a mathematical certainty . . . Certainty is not belief, it is knowledge.' Locke distinguishes between the religious zealot and the person who is prepared to survey all religions with 'an equitable and fair indifference', and Griffin rejects the notion of 'an equitable and fair indifference' as sophistical. If you have the true faith, he says, why play meaningless games by pretending that you haven't? Without enquiring too nicely into the theological intricacies, what importantly emerges for the student of Griffin, at this point, is the inflexible certitude of his views.

For all the sweetness and gentleness of his nature, this is a mind like a rat-trap. Once the spring has snapped

on a truth it will not again release it for further examination. He expresses himself in mathematical images of certainty:

> A faithful Catholic for instance is bound to believe as firmly in the truth of his creed as that *four* is the double of *two,* although the grounds of his conviction are different, the former belief being dependent on the will, the latter not. Now the less time a man expends in listening to the opinions of those who assert that two and two make five, the more time he will save for better purposes. (p. 114)

and again:

> if I hear a man gravely contending against the self-evident fact that the three sides of a rectangular triangle are equal and if I, for impatience, will not hear him this does not mean that I have a bias the other way, but merely that I have a bad temper. (p. 118)

The gulf between Griffin's purposeful certainty and Locke's equally purposeful uncertainty is profound. We begin to understand Griffin's often puzzling critical intolerance as displayed in such unfortunate jingles as the one about the Romantic poets:

> Wordsworth, and Coleridge, and Landor, and Southey,
> Are stupid, and prosy, and frothy, and mouthy.[35]

In fact, in the course of his discussion of Locke, he employs the adjective 'romantic' in a clearly pejorative sense:

> The idea that mankind could be taught to judge aright, when passion urges them to judge wrong, in cases where the matter is left to their own understanding appears to me no less romantic than Lord Shaftesbury's fancy of practising virtue for its own sake and not for the love of its Author or the influence of hope and fear. (pp. 116-17)

These are, once again, the arrogantly convinced tones of Hardress Cregan arguing for 'simplicity' as against 'elegance' and they show how close artistic disaster looms. Empathy of an authorial kind is going to be more and more difficult for this writer. Fresh light is thrown on the important passages in Chapter 12 of the *Life* in which Daniel describes Gerald's decline into an aesthetic paralysis and his own efforts to argue his brother into a more reasonable frame of mind with common-sense arguments which stood no chance against the novelist's compulsive idealism:

> I mentioned to him also what I was informed a certain clergyman, a man of genius and information,

and highly esteemed in his diocese, had said on the subject: 'That he conceived it one of the greatest misfortunes to society, that, by a sort of general consent, an engine like the drama, capable of influencing so many millions to good or evil, should be left in the hands of the vicious and corrupt. That, as it has existed, and will exist to the end of time in all civilised countries, the common sense and benevolence of the thing was to make it as available to the purposes of virtue as it is now to vice. As to its being at best imperfect, and not without danger to some, that was the fate of all human exertions at good. Our instruments are always imperfect, let our aims or objects be what they may . . . One can effect no good without the possibility of some evil, for which, when one does his utmost to avoid it, he cannot be responsible.' Gerald, though he would not admit the applicability of such reasoning, replied to it so slightly as showed what little interest he took in the subject, often dismissing the argument with some little pleasantry and a smile, which made it clear that the time when it could have affected him was gone by.[36]

It is clear that Griffin was no longer susceptible to suggestions that the writer is a necessarily imperfect instrument in an imperfect universe. His intellect also rejected Locke's idea of 'an equitable and fair indifference' on matters of belief and, more and more, Griffin was to find it impossible to assume the attitude of artistic 'indifference' to the behaviour of his fictional creatures. The human sympathy and devouring curiosity about man and the universe which are life to the novelist were going down before a clutch of intransigent religious and moral convictions. Immediately after the section of Locke comes a brief passage in which Griffin takes the Edgeworth system of education to task for proposing 'a too great worldliness' as its object. The following extract, recalling Griffin's youthful ambitions and their rapid decline, has a strongly personal tinge:

> This love of worldly distinction, of exaltation, so contrary to the Christian precept, is the cause of the ruin of many promising characters. I grant that it is a passion hard to be subdued in youth, particularly when it comes under the veil of a love of independence, but if we cannot subdue it, for heaven's sake let it not be fostered. (pp. 118-19)

Between pp. 120 and 143 Griffin discusses Rousseau's *Emile*. He professes not to share Rousseau's horror of boarding-schools, claiming that families must eventually be broken up and that 'it is good that the nestling should be accustomed to short flights at first since it is doomed eventually to be banished from the home of its infancy'. There are some overtones here, surely, of Griffin's response to his own youthful separation from his parents and the bulk of his family at the time of their emigration to America. He evidently finds Rousseau, at least in some ways, a more congenial

philosopher than Locke, as he writes about him in a more relaxed and friendly fashion:

> Where Rousseau is in the right no man is more delightful. He is easy—elegant—witty—profound— But where he merely speculates—merely theorizes— where in fact he is in the wrong it is easy to see it for he at once gets angry and scolds people. Compare for instance his irresistible denunciation of swaddling clothes and hired nurses with his phillipic against public schools. (p. 121)

There follows immediately after this a passage which is so revealing of Griffin's peculiar, solitary nature that it deserves to be quoted in full:

> Rousseau's notion of a perfect confidence between master and pupil is I fear chimerical. This perfect confidence could not be accomplished even if they were as he wishes they should be of the same age. There is only one state of perfect confidence on earth—it is that which exists between a Catholic penitent and his confessor. Here alone there is no reserve—here alone the heart is truly laid bare—and the soul exposed in its true colours. The confidence of the most intimate friendship must still have some reserve and it is right and necessary that it should. Even if a man were guiltless of any crime, they very suggestions of nature herself, and the temptations to which the purest minds are liable render it necessary there should be a degree of secrecy. (p. 121)

Here speaks the touchy, sensitive, lonely man who suffered so wretchedly in London and, towards the end of his life, sent so coldly dismissive a message to his beloved Lydia Fisher in the waiting room at North Richmond Street.[37]

There follow some twenty or more pages in which Griffin considers various parts of the *Emile* and faults many of the great Romantic's theories. There are sizeable quotations in the original French, which would seem to indicate that Griffin had acquired at least a competent reading knowledge of that language. He is sometimes quite penetrating in his comments. On facile philanthropy he writes:

> I cannot but think that there is more of self-love than of philanthropy in the mere spinning of theories. It is easier and more pleasing to indulge the imagination than to serve the public. It is one thing to do good and another to dream of it—one thing to be useful and another to be eloquent. (p. 122)

And, on the natural treatment of disease:

> It is lost time to talk of applying natural remedies in an unnatural state of society. To say 'let nature be the physician' is in a word to say 'let all the world be reformed' a very easy thing to say and

delightful to contemplate, but saying it and thinking it will cure nobody. (p. 122)

His strong dislike of many of Rousseau's notions about children lends unusual force to his comments:

> Vicious human nature—depraved nature—he knew well—but he has not even a conception of the good and healthy human heart, such as it is when filled with the love of God and regulated by principles of virtue. He is to the human mind what Dr Baillie was to the human body—its morbid anatomist. Of the sound subject he knows nothing. (p. 124)

Throughout, his remarks are based on a rejection of Rousseau's concept of the State of Nature and on his own belief in the doctrine of Original Sin. Sometimes an unexpected but very Irish gaiety breaks through:

> 'Ayez donc soins de le promener souvent, de le transporter d'une place à l'autre, de lui faire sentir le changement de lieu, à fin de l'apprendre à juger des distances.' Imagine a nurse hawking a child to and fro and telling you when you ask her what she is about, that she is *taichin' him distance, the crathur!* (p. 129)

His own formidable standards of rectitude are frequently revealed, as on p. 132: 'The agony which the remembrance of crime occasions is not always penitence. Remorse may sin on, repentance never will. The vengeance of God and of nature is not the merit of the criminal, it is his punishment.' There is a curious passage on p. 134 in which he traces the growth of piety, unexpectedly maintaining that manhood is less inimical to piety than childhood. Often his comments on both Locke and Rousseau reveal a keen intelligence which revels in argument and which can express itself with considerable force and some wit. Here and there, though, can also be seen glimpses of those aspects of his character which were to prove so stultifying to the artist in him: his absolute conviction of the essentially solitary nature of the human condition; his formidable, almost impossibly demanding standards of personal rectitude which sadly, as he more and more oversimplified them, prevented him from developing a constructive aesthetic and produced in him a disastrous attitude to his fictional creations.

Common-Place Book A is, clearly, a document of the most absorbing interest and value for the student of Griffin and it is indeed fortunate that it has survived when so much else has perished. As evidence of his careful preparation for the writing of *The Invasion* it is a monument to his impressive professional conscientiousness and is of evident importance in relation to the novel for which it is the source-book. It also makes clear a revealing historical nostalgia on Griffin's part. It is evidence of a certain kind of patriotic escapism, a flight from the harsh realities of an intolerable Irish present to the halcyon days of a glorious past. Finally,

the thirty pages of comment on Locke and Rousseau between pp. 113 and 143 bring us close to the writer's mind and thought in a most revealing manner. It is, perhaps, too much to hope that *Common-Place Books B, C and D* will now be found but it is fortunate that this one at least survives, to bring us into contact with a considerable talent whose early decline is one of the great tragedies of early nineteenth-century Irish fiction. This phase of Griffin's career, from the publication of *The Collegians* to 1832, shows evidence of a changing attitude to his native country and a deepening sympathy for the terrible plight of the Irish poor. It also reveals in him an increasingly moralistic bent, allied with a growing tendency to indulge in a revealing kind of escapist historical nostalgia. . . .

Notes

[1] *The Rivals and Tracy's Ambition,* I, 146-53.

[2] Ibid. I, 36-7.

[3] Ibid. I, 81-2.

[4] Flanagan, *Irish Novelists,* 242.

[5] *The Rivals and Tracy's Ambition,* I, 59-60.

[6] Ibid. II, 37.

[7] Ibid. II, 40-1.

[8] Ibid. II, 111-12.

[9] Ibid. II, 131-2.

[10] Ibid. II, 276.

[11] Ibid. III, 292.

[12] Ibid. II, 188-9.

[13] Ibid. II, 206-7.

[14] Ibid. III, 296.

[15] Ibid. III, 297-8.

[16] Ibid. III, 299.

[17] Ibid. III, 300-1.

[18] *Life,* 271-2.

[19] Ibid. 276-7.

[20] *The Christian Physiologist* (London, 1830), x.

[21] Ibid. xi-xii.

22 *Life,* 277.

23 *The Christian Physiologist,* 375.

24 *Life,* 381.

25 Ibid. 231.

26 Ibid. 235.

27 Ibid. 286.

28 Flanagan, *Irish Novelists,* 235.

29 *Life,* 239.

30 *Journal of Sir Walter Scott,* ed. Anderson, 444.

31 *Life and Letters of Maria Edgeworth,* ed. A. J. C. Hare (2 vols., London, 1894), II, 167.

32 *Life,* 238.

33 Ibid. 238-9.

34 *Lit. Gaz.* 781 (Jan. 7, 1832), 4-5.

35 *Life,* 216.

36 Ibid. 272-3.

37 Ibid. 383. . . .

Barton R. Friedman (essay date 1982)

SOURCE: "Fabricating History, or John Banim Refights the Boyne," *Eire-Ireland,* Vol. XVII, No. 1, Spring, 1982, pp. 39-56.

[*In the following essay, Friedman contends that John Banim's* The Boyne Water *(1826) represents Banim's effort to correct the English and Protestant historical view of a particular period in Irish history.*]

In *The Politics of Irish Literature,* Malcom Brown observes that, during the 19th century, literary pleaders of Ireland's case against England devised a special mode of indirect discourse, pretending to engage in a dialogue on Ireland between Irishmen while intending to "be overheard by hesitant English well-wishers."[1] Though Brown devotes scarcely a word of his book to the Banims, the delightfully disingenuous letter from "Abel O'Hara" (Michael) to "Barnes O'Hara" (John) introducing *The Boyne Water* (1826) nicely exemplifies this indirect discourse at work. One eye fixed on their eavesdropping English well-wishers, Michael Banim records his brother's part in the dialogue as well as his own:

You inform us, yourself, "that Englishmen of almost every party, who may honor our book with a perusal, are now prepared to recognize the truth of the historical portraits and events we venture to sketch and allude to: that, since some late publications, and particularly, since that of 'the life of James II., king of England, collected out of memoirs, writ of his own hand,' . . . Englishmen have ceased to attribute to the deposed monarch such civil tyranny, and such plotting against their religion, as his hostile contemporaries found it politic to lay at his door; that, necessarily, if . . . James did not deserve all the hatred lavished on him by their forefathers, neither should living Englishmen continue to hate [his] sect for a spirit thus wrongfully charged against it; and lastly, that, inasmuch as the least perfect parts of the British constitution were not only allowed to remain by James's successor, but other parts, perhaps more objectionable, added to them, Englishmen at present see, in the zeal of the adherents of that successor, as much selfishness as patriotism; as much thirst of monopoly as thirst of righteousness; as much hunger for the loaves and fishes, as for the bread of life; as much indifference to freedom, when freedom could have been secured, as emptiness in the clamour they raised in her name; in a word, as much cant as truth; as much real jesuitism as the jesuitism they professed to oppose.

(I, ix-x)[2]

The kind of Englishman who may honor *The Boyne Water* with a perusal materializes in the book's chief protagonist, Robert Evelyn—the more because Evelyn is not an Englishman but an Irish Protestant, his mind formed by an English education. Evelyn's letter to his exiled Roman Catholic friend and brother-in-law, Edmund M'Donnell, lamenting Parliament's disregard of the Treaty of Limerick, closes the novel as "Abel O'Hara's" letter to "Barnes O'Hara" opens it. And Evelyn repeats the optimism about English justice professed by the Banims: "Englishmen will yet pay their fathers' debt to Ireland. The treaty of Limerick will yet be kept" (III, 436).

For John Banim in 1826, keeping the Treaty of Limerick meant legislating Catholic Emanicipation. As his few critics have pointed out, he wrote *The Boyne Water* to add his voice to those in England and Ireland supporting Emancipation, which Parliament in fact passed three years later.[3] Catholic Emancipation Banim views as an essential step toward healing the breach dividing Irishmen, the achievement of which Evelyn urges on M'Donnell as part of the program for fulfilling Ireland's aspirations to nationhood: "From the present hour, Ireland must become an united country, fairly and nobly rivalling England in all that makes England truly great, or remain, for ages, a province of England, poor, shattered, narrow-minded, contemptible, and, party with party as she stands, contemned by the world, and by England, too" (III, 435).

The division threatening to lock Ireland into a provinciality—poor, shattered, narrow-minded, and contemptible—is symbolized as Evelyn writes by the sea separating him from M'Donnell; its consequences symbolized not only by Edmond's banishment—with that of Sarsfield and the defenders of Limerick—to service in foreign armies, but also by the collapse of his hopes for domestic happiness through the death of his fiancée, and Evelyn's sister, Esther, in the siege of Londonderry. Banim uses the courtship of Edmund and Esther and of Evelyn and Edmund's sister Eva to dramatize the tension between public affairs and private feelings. The reconciliation of Evelyn and Eva, as Limerick is about to fall, suggests the potential of love to overcome the most deeply rooted of historical hatreds and show the way to making Ireland a united country.

Marriage between Roman Catholic and Protestant seems, indeed, the conventional resolution to dramatic conflicts with political implications for Irish novelists throughout the first half of the 19th century. This resolution forms, allowing for differences in the political and religious rivalries he addressed, part of the legacy conferred on them by Scott. Banim himself is accused by Robert Lee Wolff—implausibly, in my view—of patterning *The Boyne Water* with a fidelity "almost comic at times" on *Redgauntlet* (1824). Thomas Flanagan more reasonably proposes *Waverley* (1814) as Banim's model.[4]

But neither recognizes that, however much Banim has borrowed from Scott, he has reversed Scott's emphasis. In *Waverley,* the history of the Forty-Five is subordinate to the *bildungsroman* tracing Edward's growth from youthful dreamer to responsible adult, and Culloden enters the narrative only by inference. Scott even apologizes, if with a somewhat satirical edge, "for plaguing [his readers] so long with old-fashioned politics, and Whig and Tory, and Hanoverians and Jacobites," explaining that he cannot render his story "intelligible, not to say probable, without it" (I, 37).[5] In *The Boyne Water,* Evelyn is the same mature, moderate, tolerant citizen entering Carrickfergus after the accession of James II in 1685 as he is when writing to Edmund years after William's triumph is complete. Beyond his role as one of the principals in Banim's double love plot, he functions chiefly as witness to most of the major events in James's campaign to hold Ireland—from Londonderry to the Boyne to Limerick—thereby enabling his author to narrate each battle in detail. His capture at the Boyne reduces him to an all but passive observer; and in the last stages of the narrative much of its focus shifts to a real historical figure, Patrick Sarsfield.

That *The Boyne Water* is more concerned with history than fiction is implied by "Abel O'Hara's" letter to "Barnes," which could readily serve as the introduction to a scholarly treatise: while historians have traditionally accepted the Whig reading of the Glorious Revolution—the letter in effect runs—new perspectives like those opened by James's memoirs require that the case for the Stuarts, at least in Ireland, be reassessed. And "Abel" goes to great lengths, by way of repeated assertions to his brother, to assure their "hesitant English well-wishers" that the crucial episodes of the narrative, from the tornado bringing the Evelyns and the M'Donnels together to the circumstances determining the outcome of the struggle, are reliably documented: "Every statement of facts, or allusion to them, which we are compelled incidentally to put forward, is authorized by historians, whom both sides are bound to admit; and . . . nothing can be objected to us which must not also be objected to Dalrymple, or Harris, or Burnet, or Hume, or Smollett, or James's memoirs, or Walker's diary of the siege of Derry . . ." (I, xxv).

"Abel O'hara's" historians comprise, for the most part, a roll-call of the chief Protestant commentators on the Glorious Revolution available to a student in 1826. In their authority lies the Banims' claim to a fairness and balance they find lacking in English versions of James's Irish debacle. For they are acutely aware that—as Brown, following Cecil Woodham-Smith, remarks in *The Politics of Irish Literature*—viewing history through Irish eyes entails turning some of the greatest English heroes, among them William III, into villains.[6] If they are to hold the sympathy of that English reader whose well-wishes, however hesitant, "Abel O'Hara's" letter solicits, they must refrain from awakening his prejudices by firmly repressing their own. The magnitude of their problem is illustrated by a modern historian trained in scholarly objectivity: David Ogg, in *England in the Reigns of James II and William III.* Ogg attacks James's Declarations of Indulgence, arguing that, had he achieved his aim of placing as many Roman Catholics as possible in public office, he would have reconstituted England as a country in which, though Protestants might still practice their religion, they lived as "helots," kept from participating in their own government.[7] What Ogg describes—though without acknowledging or perhaps even realizing it—is precisely the state to which long-standing English policy had relegated Catholics in Ireland.

Bitterness at this policy manifestly underlies *The Boyne Water,* despite John Banim's efforts to mute it in his characterization of another English hero Brown lists as an anathema to the Irish, Oliver Cromwell, who makes his one appearance in the narrative as "ruthless Cromwell" (I, 19). In Banim's polemical design this epithet becomes a virtual, if nonetheless Freudian, slip of the pen. He pitches his narrative voice not as a rallying cry to the survivors of Ninety-Eight or, somewhat before its time, to the bold Fenian men, but as a call for moderation. Again, "Abel O'Hara's" letter alerts the reader to the *via media* he and his brother stake out for the novel:

> One side regards William as a persecutor, which he was not; as a Church-of-England champion, which

he was not; and as a religious bigot, which he was not: the other, as an amiable and chivalrous hero of romance, appointed, first to England, and next to Ireland, especially for the purpose of rooting out popery. . . . James, too—both agree in one point concerning him; namely, that he was a coward, or something very like it; and then, his hereditary haters call him tyrant, butcher, fanatic; or if that is not enough, his most vivid identity, in their comprehensive minds, changes into a brass sixpence, or a pair of wooden shoes; while the descendants of those who fought by his side, scarcely take the trouble of denying one of the leading charges; either because, in as much "contented ignorance" as those that talk more, (on this one subject, at least) they have listened until repetition worries them into assent, or because one of the leading charges, if allowed to be true, seems to afford, by throwing upon James's shoulders the blame of occasional defeat, some unction for their wounded vanity.

(I, xiii-xiv)

Proposing *The Boyne Water* as a corrective to history's portraits of William and James sums up one of the novel's main strategies. In his treatment of what J. G. Simms calls "The War of the Two Kings," John Banim anticipates the method of a historian for whom he and his brother would have little use, Lord Macaulay, who, as George Levine observes, narrates the Glorious Revolution in his *History of England* (1849-61) from the perspectives of the two men embodying its conflict: one the last of the feudal, the other the first of the modern, monarchs.[8]

Projecting history as an almost allegorically balanced construct leads Banim to build a symmetry into events which, Flanagan argues, reflects the influence of *Waverley*.[9] But Macaulay stresses this symmetry too, finding it in history itself:

The history of the first siege of Limerick bears, in some respects, a remarkable analogy to the history of the siege of Londonderry. The southern city was, like the northern city, the last asylum of a Church and of a nation. Both places were crowded with fugitives from all parts of Ireland. Both places appeared to men who made a regular study of the art of war incapable of resisting an enemy. Both were, in the moment of extreme danger, abandoned by those commanders who should have defended them. Lauzun and Tyrconnel deserted Limerick as Cunningham and Lundy had deserted Londonderry. In both cases, religious and patriotic enthusiasm struggled unassisted against great odds; and in both cases, religious and patriotic enthusiasm did what veteran warriors had pronounced it absurd to attempt.

(III, 1920)[10]

Paralleling the stand of Limerick against William to the stand of Londonderry against James expresses the admiration Macaulay shares with Banim for "the brave Sarsfield . . . [whose] exhortations diffused through all ranks a spirit resembling his own" (IV, 1913). Despite strident attacks on his *History* by Jacobite apologists like Demetrius Charles Boulger, who adjudges Macaulay's indictment of James's Irish infantry at the Boyne "as near historical truth as a fairy tale is to the hard realities of life," Macaulay shows some of the imaginative capacity R. G. Collingwood attributes to the ideal historian: participating in the consciousness of a native Irish witness to the Glorious Revolution; establishing that, in 1688, the orange riband was already "the emblem to the Protestant Englishman of civil and religious freedom, to the Roman Catholic Celt of subjugation and persecution"; urging, in a sentiment worthy of the Banims themselves, that "History must do to both parties the justice which neither has ever done to the other, and must admit that both had fair pleas and cruel provocations" (III, 1180, 1431).[11]

The Banims would surely deny that Macaulay does justice to the Irish party. He interprets William's seizure of the crown as a triumph of order over anarchy; and in extolling that triumph he turns history's cast of heroes and villains once more English-side-up: "England was again the England of Elizabeth and Cromwell; and all the relations of all the states in Christendom were completely changed by the sudden introduction of this new power into the system" (II, 1248).

Macaulay's William is precisely the amiable and chivalrous hero of romance the Banims had sought to exorcise from history, portrayed not only as the brave commander, ignoring a shoulder wound to ford the Boyne with his left wing, his arrival deciding the day, but also as a political genius:

It was no easy thing to subvert the English government by means of a foreign army without galling the national pride of Englishmen. It was no easy thing to obtain from the Batavian faction which regarded France with partiality, and the House of Orange with aversion, a decision in favour of an expedition which would confound all the schemes of France, and raise the House of Orange to the height of greatness. It was no easy thing to lead enthusiastic Protestants on a crusade against Popery with the good wishes of almost all Popish governments and of the Pope himself. Yet all these things William effected. All his objects, even those which appeared most incompatible with each other, he attained completely and at once. The whole history of ancient and of modern times records no other such triumph of statesmanship.

(III, 1060)

This William little resembles Banim's sullen, near reclusive monarch, shielded from his subjects by Bentinck and his Meerschaum-smoking Dutch officers, granting Evelyn a reluctant audience at Kensington Palace. Nor does James skilfully managing his prancing horse—encountered by Evelyn when he accompanies the delegation from Londonderry to the Jacobite camp at Johnstown—resemble Macaulay's frightened truant, throwing the Royal Seal in the Thames, abandoning his kingdom to its own devices:

> As he sat erect in his saddle, he seemed a man about fifty years of age, above the middle size, well, and rather squarely made; his features large and rigid; but wearing, instead of the mild and melancholy his father's wore, or the grave voluptuousness of his brother's, a somewhat bolder and haughtier expression; with perhaps more enterprize [*sic*] than was at once apparent in the countenance of either. His flowing periwig descended over his shoulders and back; his round grey hat, looped up at front, displayed a red and white plume, that was secured by a brilliant cross; many orders, foreign and national, surrounded the royal star that blazed on his breast; the holsters at his saddle-bow were richly embroidered; his horse nobly caparisoned; his boots furnished with golden spurs; and it was altogether evident that Louis's attention to the outfit of his king-brother, left naked but for him, had been worthy of the respect he always professed for the exiled monarch.

> (II, 268)

Instead of exorcising the amiable and chivalrous hero of romance from history, *The Boyne Water* recreates him in its portrait of James presenting a royal face to the world while his throne crumbles beneath him; or, rather, the novel extends him to apprehend both kings. William inspecting his troops before the Boyne assumes similarly heroic stature:

> He sat erect and motionless in the saddle, as if he were a compound identity with the foaming and noble animal he bestrode; his usually languid eyes glared and flashed; excitement sent a high colour to his wasted cheeks, and every limb of his body expressed energy, as, with a drawn sword occasionally moved around his head, he addressed, in his rapid transit along the line, brief but spirit-stirring words of approbation and encouragement, to the officers and soldiers that waved their hats and plumes, and shouted as he past.

> (III, 197-98)

Levine argues that Macaulay's narrative blends ingredients of the novel of manners with at least one essential ingredient, "old fashioned heroism," of chivalric romance.[12] Banim attempts a comparable blending. But he never quite bridges the gap between the novel of manners inherent in the courtships of Evelyn and Eva, Edmund and Esther, and the romance he fashions from history. Though he might have succeeded had he been able to build his plot around Edmund who, stripped of land and father by the brutal Kirke, abjures his name

and turns Rapparee, his polemical design required him to find his central intelligence in the moderate Protestant, Evelyn; and Evelyn is descended in a direct literary line from Waverley, of whom Flora MacIvor justly concludes: "high and perilous enterprise is not [his] forte. He would never have been his celebrated ancestor Sir Nigel, but only Sir Nigel's eulogist and poet" (II, 108).

Because high and perilous enterprise is not Evelyn's forte either, Banim renders the last part of his narrative a eulogy for another Sir Nigel, Sarsfield. Its major action, besides the Siege of Limerick itself, consists of the famous raid by the Lucan Horse on William's artillery train, during which Evelyn, as Sarsfield's prisoner, is carried along like an appendage to his saddle. Banim needs Evelyn's presence as a device not only for controlling point of view but also for expressing the political moderation he urges on Englishmen vintage 1826 in a voice, he assumes, more convincing than his own native Irish Catholic voice. Evelyn serves, that is, to question those simplistic moral labels ingrained in Englishmen by their historical traditions. In one of his several ideological debates with George Walker he thus accuses Bishop Burnet—praised by Macaulay as "a man of such generosity and good nature, that his heart always warmed towards the unhappy" (III, 1247)—of playing "your own jesuit . . . at the Hague . . . by his and your admission, instigating the daughter to dethrone—it may be—murder her father" (I, 318).

Before his transformation into the Rapparee leader Yemen-acknuck, Edmund, moreover, bespeaks a tolerance toward the grievances of Protestants comparable to Evelyn's toward those of Catholics, arguing with the Dominican extremist, O'Haggerty, at the pub in Carrickfergus that James is "infatuated—mad—in his measures on our behalf" (I, 285). O'Haggerty persuades Edmund, despite his reservations, to accept a commission in Antrim's regiment, as Walker persuades Evelyn to sign his assent, also despite reservations, to membership in the "counter association" organizing to guard Protestants against "popish massacre" (I, 313). The two clergymen seduce their young coreligionists with appeals to faith and friendship, as the radical Covenanter, Burley, in *Old Mortality* (1816)—in some respects more a model for *The Boyne Water* than *Waverley*—seduces Henry Morton.

Banim has split Scott's characters, importing them into *The Boyne Water* in binary form to accommodate his historical allegory. Burley becomes O'Haggerty and Walker, as Henry Morton becomes Edmund and Evelyn. Though Lord Evandale in the end pursues a career similar to Edmund's, joining Claverhouse in rebellion, just as Edmund joins the Rapparees, the wilds of Ireland are for Edmund only a way-station along his route into banishment. Whereas the vagaries of

British politics leading to 1688 make Morton—like Edmund but on the opposite side—first an exile serving in the wars between William of Orange and Louis XIV, and then, like Evelyn settling down to domestic tranquility with his Catholic bride, Eva M'Donnell, the accepted suitor of Edith Bellenden, daughter of a Tory family.

Banim's reincarnation of characters in *Old Mortality* into doubles mirroring each other extends to Claverhouse, who, as "bloody Claverhouse," ruthless scourage of Scots Covenanters, survives in Kirke, and as benefactor of Morton, wishing no better death them a soldier's in victorious battle, survives in Sarsfield. Claverhouse, Scott well knew, had his wish granted at Killiekrankie; Sarsfield, Banim well knew also, and has Edmund inform Evelyn, had already died Claverhouse's death at Neerwinden. Like Scott, Banim does not so much falsify history as shape it to his own ends. He found no need to invent a tyrant to justify Edmund's embrace of outlawry because he had Kirke, whom even David Hume, strong Williamite partisan as he was, labels a "wanton savage," ready to hand.[13] He found no need to invent a tempter to explain Evelyn's embrace of revolution or a leader to account for Londonderry's embrace of resistance because he had the Reverend George Walker ready to hand.

The conflict between Walker and Father O'Haggerty, which begins with their meeting at the pub in Carrickfergus and ends when they kill each other at the Boyne, sums up Banim's historical theme and exemplifies his method of representing history. If Walker, whom Macaulay describes as assisting by his eloquence to rally the people of Londonderry (III, 1483), figured prominently in real events, O'Haggerty seems a fiction nonetheless true to life. The admonitory sermon Edmund and Evelyn hear him delivering as they enter Carrickfergus—that "as God abandoned Saul, in his lukewarmness, and for his treatment of the Amalekites took his kingdom from him, and ruined his family . . . [so] would He punish all . . . guilty of a similar disobedience" (I, 245)—is attributed generally by Macaulay (III, 1442) to priests in the neighborhood of Londonderry and specifically by Cecil Davis Milligan to an unnamed friar addressing Catholic members of Mountjoy's regiment in Derry's marketplace.[14] No historian, to my knowledge, identifies Walker's killer as a militant priest in arms for James. Macaulay simply observes (IV, 1881-82) that Walker was shot urging his fellow Ulstermen on during their crossing of the Boyne at almost the same moment as Marshall Schomberg died performing the same service for the Huguenots; and Robert H. Murray agrees.[15]

Murray also records William's unsympathetic response—"What took him there?"—to the news of Walker's death, a response which had earlier found its way, the harshness of its rhetoric amplified, into *The Boyne Water*. "The fool!" says Banim's William, "what did he there?" (III, 248). Banim carefully footnotes William's remark, specifying its source as Dalrymple, for Banim's strategy requires that he induce the reader, presumably conditioned by Protestant historians of the Glorious Revolution, to adjudge Walker as much a villain as Scott's Burley. In this Banim set himself a formidable task. Even Hilaire Belloc, among the few English apologists for James, concedes Walker's achievement in imposing on the citizens of Londonderry an order and discipline that made their resistance possible.[16]

About the nature and importance of Walker's role in the defense of Derry, however, influential treatments of the siege differ. While Macaulay describes William conferring a reward of £5,000 on Walker and assuring him "that I consider your claims on me as not at all diminished" (IV, 1766), he also characterizes him as "an aged clergyman . . . who had taken refuge in Londonderry" (III, 1483), and suggests that his contribution amounted largely to providing moral support for the garrison. Murray, who repeatedly seems to follow Macaulay's version of events, again agrees.[17] Milligan's Walker comes closer to the energetic figure who dominates Protestant councils in *The Boyne Water*: raising a regiment to hold Dungannon for William, riding to Londonderry to warn Governor Lundy of the approach of James's troops.[18] But Milligan's Walker, too, occupies a position both more modest and more moderate than the unyielding hater of Catholics, who recruits Evelyn, rallies Derry's apprentices to shut the gates against Antrim's Redshanks, and hardens the wills of the citizenry to keep their vow of "No Surrender." In Milligan's account of the siege, while both Walker and Baker receive the title of governor after Lundy's flight, Walker remains subordinate to his fellow officer, exercising authority only over supplies; and when James, advancing under a flag of truce, is fired on from the walls, Walker joins Baker in apologizing for the city's transgression.[19]

In *The Boyne Water*, Walker engineers the attempt on James:

> "Yonder," resumed Mr. Walker, still in a low voice, and addressing himself to one of the enterprizing [*sic*] apprentices who had before done him a service—"yonder is the cruel tyrant, in person."
>
> "Where?" asked James Spike, standing to the side of his saker, a ready match in his hand.
>
> "See you not the crowd of gay officers who push on before the army?—See you not two of them that ride alone, surrounded by the others? The man on the grey horse, to the right, is the tyrant."
>
> James Spike rested his match across the saker, and he and Walker looked earnestly at each other.

"Touch her," at last whispered the clergyman—"but no—not yet; bear her muzzle down, a little; softly; none need note you—there, that allows for your elevation; touch her now."

(II, 285-86)

Once more like Burley, Walker vacillates between zealot and Machiavel. Faced with the confusion of his irregulars after their triumph over Claverhouse's Life Guards at Loudon-hill, Burley calls on Gabriel Kettledrummle to preach, "as a means of engaging the attention of the bulk of the insurgents, while he himself, and two or three of their leaders, held a private council of war, undisbturbed by the discordant opinions, or senseless clamour, of the general body" (II, 17-18). Seeing James, who had received Derry's assent to terms of surrender, appear before the walls with his escort, Walker exclaims, "throwing into his manner more vivacity than was natural to him, 'we are betrayed. . . . it was promised not to march a papist army within four miles of our town—but the false papists come!' " (II, 279-80).

Scott blurs the line between Burley's zeal for the cause of the Covenant and his use of revolt as a tactic to evade reprisal for the murder of Archbishop Sharpe. Burley shoots Cornet Grahame, cutting off the attempt at parley preceding Loudon-hill, because he knows he cannot share in the amnesty Claverhouse offers the rebels. Similarly, Walker inflates Kirke's pledge of aid to Derry, insuring the violation of yet another treaty between the garrison and its besiegers, in part because he would not be left "to the mercy of the merciless' (II, 373).

Walker's contempt for treaties negotiated with papists, and especially for the treaty concluded on the eve of Kirke's relief of the city, parallels Sarsfield's scrupulous adherence to the Treaty of Limerick, concluded under like circumstances, and anticipates his emergence as the real amiable and chivalrous hero of *The Boyne Water*. Exploiting the license allowed the historical novelist, as distinct from the historian, Banim on no authority places Sarsfield among the officers escorting King James within range of James Spike's cannon; and when Spike's shot forces their retreat, Sarsfield remains behind "as if astonishment and indignation kept him motionless; or as if to dare another shot in his own person" (II, 287).

Alerted in Ginkle's tent, the completed Treaty of Limerick before him on the table, to the approach of Chateau Renault's fleet; provoked by Colonel Loyd's assumption, seconded by the bishop of Meath, that, "perfidious papist" as he is, he will break the treaty even in the hour of signing it, Sarsfield recalls Derry's breach of military promise: "Nay, gentlemen, be not so quick, nor so hard with us; you, Colonel Lloyd, be merciful, in particular; for though your city of Derry

sent a shot in King James's face, when it was expected to keep a treaty with him—yet shall this treaty stand" (III, 424). His assurance grows into what amounts to a rhetorical set piece, by which Banim established him as spokesman for the integrity of Catholic Ireland:

"Though an ally's fleet, bearing us help enough to hold all Ireland in our hands, be now entering the mouth of the Shannon, yet shall it stand. Though our country be lost to us—though we bid farewell to her forever—though she exist for us, but in our recollections and our sorrows;" a manly tear glazed his eye—"yet shall it stand. And so, fare you well, gentlemen. We cannot save even our country at the price of our honor—of that honor, which, along with our love and efforts for her, alone makes us worthy of our being called her children. . . . " (III, 424-25)

Despite the Banims' claim to balance in their handling of the Glorious Revolution, Sarsfield's concern with honor shows *The Boyne Water* to be no less biased than Macaulay's *History*. His admonishment to his Protestant compeers—"Keep ye your part of this covenant as well as we keep ours, and there needs no ill-blood between us" (III, 425)—ominously foreshadows not only the implied indictment of English policy in Evelyn's letter to Edmund, but the whole course of events, especially within John Banim's lifetime, from the Rising that took place the year he was born, 1798, to the struggle for Catholic Emancipation that he entered by writing the novel.

The consequences of ill-blood manifest themselves dramatically in the estrangement of both pairs of lovers and the death by starvation of the innocent Esther; the potential of good will appears in the efforts of Sarsfield, exerted on behalf of an enemy, to abet the reconciliation of Evelyn and Eva. While Banim, like Scott, if less successfully, shapes his plot to explore the relationship between public and private worlds and, in periods of crisis, the often conflicting demands they make on the individual, Banim's didactic intent requires that, beyond crystallizing these stresses in fiction, he demonstrate their existence in history itself.[20] To this end, the unfortunate James II serves him perfectly. Wrenched from Eva at the very altar, as Esther is from Edmund, by the news of William's landing at Torbay and the disclosure of the commitments the young men have made to their misguiding spiritual lights, Evelyn retires to his house at Glenarm, where Walker regales him with an account—listing defections by friends and family—of James's setbacks at court; the severest of which he represents as the Churchills' subornation of Princess Anne. Embittered by the collapse of his own domestic hopes, but also outraged by the disloyalty of those closest to James, Evelyn pronounces their conduct "monstrous . . . unparalleled in the history of human nature, or of the human heart" (II, 24). In this conviction Evelyn is joined, through a narrative parenthesis, by Banim himself:

"succeeding generations will acknowledge" (they *have* on all sides acknowledged it)—"that this prince, whose chief errors were those of temper, judgment, and fanaticism, has met, from his most obliged friends, and the nearest members of his family, worse treatment than even Nero, Domitian, or the blackest tyrants of the world ever experienced."

(II, 24, italics Banim's)

The parenthesis, which no modern critic would consider other than a scandalous breach of novelistic decorum, reflects Banim's concern to break down the Williamite, Protestant prejudices of his contemporary English readers, while reinforcing the sympathies of those hesitant well-wishers toward Ireland lurking among them. In fact, the degree to which William had relied on betrayers of the royal trust has often provided a rhetorical club to his detractors and proved an embarrassment to his apologists. Belloc flatly asserts that perhaps no conspirators in history were so steeped in falsehood as those who dethroned James.[21] And Macaulay, contemplating Clarendon's turnabout, feels compelled to rationalize not only his behavior but the behavior of numerous compatriots among England's powerful and well-born who followed his example:

In revolutions men live fast: the experience of years is crowded into hours: old habits of thought and action are violently broken; and novelties, which at first sight inspire dread and disgust, become in a few days familiar, endurable, attractive. Many men of far purer virtue and higher spirit than Clarendon were prepared, before that memorable year [1688] ended, to do what they would have pronounced wicked and infamous when it began.

(III, 1150)

But Macaulay refuses the same indulgence to Richard Hamilton, who, assigned to present William's terms to Tyrconnell, presents his sword instead: "This man had violated all the obligations which are held most sacred by gentlemen and soldiers, had broken faith with his most intimate friends, had forfeited his military parole, and was now not ashamed to take the field as a general against the government to which he was bound to render himself up as a prisoner" (III, 1457).

Banim is equally, if less harshly, critical of Evelyn, who, by Jacobite standards, has taken the field against the government to which he is bound as a subject. Both Banim and Macaulay use betrayal as a device for stressing the magnanimity of their rightful kings: William, in an incident evoked by both, forgoes vengeance against Hamilton after his capture at the Boyne, instead sending for a physician to dress his wounds; James courteously welcomes Evelyn to his evening at Dublin Castle, demanding of him only the reasons for his disloyalty. When Evelyn can manage no better than the weak response that "his majesty's abdication had . . . seemed to release him from allegiance" (III, 173), James attacks him energetically and persuasively: declaring that abdication entails an act of free will, whereas he was driven from the throne over his own vigorous protests; that, "deserted by all upon whom [he] could have placed reliance," he had no power to resist William; that cognizant of the lesson taught him by his royal father—*"there is little distance between the prisons and the graves of princes"*—he chose flight as the one course left him (III, 173-77, italics Banim's).

Banim has put the whole Jacobite case against the legitimacy of William and his successors into James's reply to Evelyn. His speech constitutes another set piece, comparable in polemical import to Sarsfields's speech on honor, and it reduces Evelyn to silence, whereupon James dismisses him, again courteously but also patronizingly:

" . . . now, stripling, if you have truly stated your only or chief cause for rebellion, to arise from the abdicating, by us the throne of our ancestors, return to those who helped you to such a reason, and tell them, that from the sovereign prince they have caused you to wrong, and disposed you to destroy, you have heard his own apology. Tell them that to yourself, an undistinguished subject, he has—in all the humility that becomes his humbled situation, and in all the earnestness that becomes an injured man and a christian king, vouchsafed to vindicate himself, and the infant son who suffers with him, from their cruel slander. . . . "

(III, 173)

That the argument for rebellion is carried by a youth, who, whatever his virtues, is definable as a stripling, an undistinguished subject, appears to the critical eye a painfully unsubtle device for weighting history in James's favor. His confrontation with Evelyn is hardly a war between two kings. It is consistent, however, with Banim's treatment of the Derry apprentices denying entrance to Antrim's troops, which he trivializes as largely an adolescent prank: "In another moment the young crowd scampered by, to shut the other gates, some serious, some frightened at their own daring, but the greater number chuckling and laughing in such a way as told that there was as much fun as patriotism, as much whim as bigotry, in their important frolic" (II, 53). Banim characteristically claims truth for his rendering of the event by marshalling as much fact, including the identities of the apprentices, as the narrative will bear, and then calling the reader's attention to his practice: craving him "to observe, that all the names we have mentioned here, are, together with Mr. Walker's, historical names; and 'immortal' ones, too—in Derry" (II, 49). He employs the same stratagem in depicting the Protestant fear of massacre, incorporating the actual letter by which an anonymous peasant informer supposedly warned Lord Mount Alexander of a Roman Catholic plot "to fall on and murder man, woman, and child," then announcing: "Here is quoted, word for word, the document that, such as it is, produced the real or feigned shew of terror which, beginning in professions of loyalty to King James, ended in openly resisting his dominion in Ireland" (II, 27).

Banim tries in effect to have it both ways. While he accurately renders the causes of James's downfall in Ireland, he develops those causes within a rhetorical frame calculated to discredit their perpetrators: the Derry apprentices have earned immortal names, but only in Derry; the letter to Lord Mount Alexander provokes a show of terror, real or feigned. And he underscores the ambivalence with which he would have even his English reader view these details through the skepticism of Evelyn. Shown the letter by Walker—whom no historical account, to my knowledge, lists as receiving a copy—Evelyn observes that, though "It purports to be written by a vulgar Irishman . . . it rather seems to me like the diction of a vulgar Englishman; or, perhaps, an affectation of the latter by an educated person" (II, 28).

Evelyn's capacity for moral judgment derives partly, that is, from his sensitivity to language. Though himself victimized by language, as Walker deploys it, he grasps its potential to distort and corrupt. The subversive power of language comprises, indeed, one of Banim's pervasive themes. *The Boyne Water,* thus, opens with a confrontation between Evelyn's acerbic aunt and a peasant of Carrickfergus, incorrigible bigots both:

> "There," remarked Mrs. Evelyn, using gross language, no doubt, yet the common language of her day, even in parliament; "there goes a murdering and damnable papist."

> "An' there hur sits, a heretic jade, wid the fire ready kindled an' roarin' fur hur," retorted the man, also using the charitable expressions in vogue amongst the vulgar and bigotted of his persuasion. . . .

(I, 9)

Their exchange foreshadows Banim's recurrently allegorical use of characters, whereby even his major adversaries—Walker and O'Haggerty, William and James—become voices bespeaking rival ideologies. Mrs. Evelyn's hatred of papists is echoed by her attendant, an old Roundhead trooper, significantly named Oliver, who fondly recalls Cromwell's slaughter of Irish Catholics in 1641, and who is rebuked for his bloodthirstiness by Evelyn: "the times are altered; and altered, I hope, for the better, since they afford opportunities to men of all parties to hold out to each other the hand of brotherhood" (I, 11).

Banim essentially adumbrates his whole novel in this brief episode: the potential of good will to promote brotherhood is realized, literally, in the bond between Evelyn and Edmund; the potential of ill will to provoke conflict is realized in history itself. As an instrument of prophecy, history outweighs fiction. The reconciliation of Edmund and Eva with Evelyn affects no one but Edmund, Eva, and Evelyn. Though Edmund survives, he survives only as an exile—Esther and Ireland lost to him forever. Though Walker dies, his spirit persists in Parliament's refusal to honor the Treaty of Limerick. Though "Abel O'Hara" confidently predicts to "Barnes O'Hara" that "Facts will rout out delusions; and, with them, all disposition to consider as friends those who have endeavoured, and who still endeavour to perpetuate them, or to regard as enemies those who, in the spirit and love of truth, would humbly but zealously put them to flight for ever" (I, xviii), a reading of Macaulay or the Whig historians following him suggests that John Banim's revision of the facts changed little. Though Catholic Emancipation became law three years after *The Boyne Water* appeared, Ulster, where most of the novel is set, remains a sectarian battleground.

Notes

[1] Malcom Brown, *The Politics of Irish Literature* (Seattle: University of Washington Press, 1972), p. 36.

[2] The text of *The Boyne Water* cited in this essay is that of the edition published as part of the series, "Ireland From the Act of Union, 1800 to the Death of Parnell, 1891," under the general editorship of Robert Lee Wolff (New York: Garland Publishing, 1978).

[3] See Wolff's Introduction to *The Boyne Water,* "The Fiction of 'the O'Hara Family'," I, xiv; and Thomas Flanagan, *The Irish Novelists, 1800-1850* (New York: Columbia University Press, 1959), p. 191.

[4] "The Fiction of 'the O'Hara Family'," p. xiii; *The Irish Novelists,* p. 194.

[5] Citations of the Waverley Novels are to the edition published by Porter and Coates (Philadelphia, n.d.).

[6] *The Politics of Irish Literature,* p. 4.

[7] David Ogg, *England in the Reigns of James II and William III* (London: Oxford University Press, 1955), pp. 181-82.

[8] George Levine, *The Boundaries of Fiction* (Princeton: Princeton University Press, 1968), p. 140. Simms's phrase forms the title of his essay on the Glorious

Revolution in *A New History of Ireland,* II, ed. T. W. Moody, F. X. Martin, and F. J. Byrne (London: Oxford University Press, 1976).

⁹ *The Irish Novelists,* p. 194.

¹⁰ Citations of Macaulay's *The History of England from the Accession of James II* are to the Macmillan edition, ed. Charles Harding Firth (London, 1914).

¹¹ For Boulger's attack on Macaulay, see his *The Battle of the Boyne* (London: Martin Secker, 1911), p. 155.

¹² *The Boundaries of Fiction,* p. 127.

¹³ David Hume, *The History of England. From the Invasion of Julius Caesar to the Revolution of 1688,* VI (New York: Merril and Baker, n.d. [originally published between 1754 and 1762]), p. 245.

¹⁴ Cecil Davis Milligan, *History of the Siege of Londonderry. 1689* (Belfast: H. R. Carter, 1951), p. 19.

¹⁵ Robert H. Murray, *Revolutionary Ireland and Its Settlement* (London: Macmillan, 1911), p. 158.

¹⁶ Hilaire Belloc, *James the Second* (Freeport, N.Y.: Books for Libraries Press, 1928), p. 239.

¹⁷ *Revolutionary Ireland and Its Settlement,* p. 98.

¹⁸ *History of the Siege of Londonderry,* pp. 58, 77-78.

¹⁹ *Ibid.,* pp. 158-59, 134.

²⁰ For observations on this element in Scott, see Frances R. Hart, *Scott's Novels: The Plotting of Historical Survival* (Charlottesville: University Press of Virginia, 1966), p. 11.

²¹ *James the Second,* p. 212.

John Kelly (essay date 1996)

SOURCE: Introduction to *The Black Prophet* by William Carleton, Woodstock Books, 1996

[*In the following essay, Kelly investigates how the socio-political and religious atmosphere in which William Carleton was raised affected his writing.*]

'There never was', claims William Carleton in his uncompleted *Autobiography,* 'any man of letters who had an opportunity of knowing and describing the manners of the Irish people so thoroughly as I had.' This is a boast that critics have been happy to accept, with two qualifications: for 'Irish people' he should have written 'Irish peasantry', and the manners he described were those that flourished before the Great Famine of 1845-48. That famine, which was to alter forever Irish social, cultural and, eventually, political life, was already beginning when Carleton took up his pen in the spring of 1846 to write the first instalment of *The Black Prophet* for the *Dublin University Magazine,* a fact that accounts for the anguished engagement of its theme and descriptions, and, incidentally, for the strains in its form and execution. The famine described in the book is not the Great Famine; rather, Carleton draws on two earlier famines of 1817 and 1822, which he had witnessed at first hand, but which, if more local than that of the 1840s, exhibited and anticipated all the horrific scenes that were beginning to unfold even as he wrote. The novel is in this aspect not merely a witness to earlier suffering, but (as the dedicatory letter to Lord John Russell suggests) a message to present legislators, as Carleton vividly depicts the personal, social and national horror of endemic starvation and the deadly fevers and diseases that flourished in its wake.

Carleton understood the manners of the Irish peasantry so throughly because he was the first Irish novelist to be drawn from their ranks. Born in 1794 near Clogher, in the northern county of Tyrone, he was the youngest of fourteen children (six of whom died in infancy) of a poor but respectable Catholic tenant farmer. Educated at unofficial 'hedge-schools', and at a rather better organized 'classical school', he seemed destined for the priesthood, and actually set out for the Catholic seminary at Maynooth but turned back. He spent his later youth in a happy period of *dolce far niente,* living off his relatives until they threw him out, when, inspired by La Sage's picaresque hero, Gil Blas, he set out to make a name for himself in the world. Steadfastly refusing to contemplate any kind of manual work, he lived on his wits, and took a number of temporary teaching jobs, before finally arriving in Dublin. Here he converted to Protestantism, and began to create a network of contacts, through which he got a steady job in the Sunday School Society. This enabled him to marry, but he soon lost his job, and spent time running schools in Mullingar (where he was imprisoned for debt), and in Carlow, before returning to Dublin. Back in the capital, he was taken up by the evangelical proselytizer, the Rev. Caesar Otway, who encouraged him to submit stories and pen sketches to his anti-Catholic paper *The Christian Examiner.* These quickly gained Carleton a literary reputation, especially when some of them were collected as *Traits and Stories of the Irish Peasantry.* In 1839 he published his first full-length novel, *Fardorougha the Miser,* and shortly afterwards became acquainted with Thomas Davis and other Young Irelanders. Although he never subscribed to their nationalist policies, these contacts caused him to reflect more carefully on his position as an Irish novelist. He made a public apology for the sectarian bias of some of his earlier work and in the late 1840s produced a burst of novels which dealt with specific Irish ills: the curse of drink in *Art Maguire* (1845), Orange bigotry in *Valentine M'Clutchy* (1845), the danger of violent Catholic societies in *Rody the Rover* (1845), Irish laziness and complacent incompetence in *Parra Sastha* (1845), famine and the abuses of land tenure in *The Black Prophet* (1847), emigration in *The Emigrants of Ahadarra* (1848), and agrarian violence in *The Tithe Proctor* (1849). In 1848 he obtained the government pension which he had long sought, and his subsequent novels turned from the peasantry to the middle and upper classes, a milieu in which he was less at home. Despite his pension, Carleton never escaped debt and his later work, written to boil the family pot and pay for his whiskey, is too often slip-shod and conventional. He died, disgruntled and still in debt, in Dublin in 1869.

To understand more fully the nature of Carleton's achievement, and the reasons why his fiction took the direction it did, it is worth examining three aspects of his career—his cultural inheritance, the political atmosphere in which he grew up, and his attitude to religion—in more detail. His family, although poor in the possessions of the world, was unusually rich in its cultural inheritance. Both of Carleton's parents were bilingual in Gaelic and English, his mother was famous throughout the locality for her singing voice, while his father was no less celebrated for his unrivalled fund of songs and stories. Carleton inherited his father's story-telling gifts and his retentive memory, a memory he stocked with the songs, tales, and characters he met with in his daily life and at the frequent rural festivities: fairs, 'patterns', wakes, and dances of various kinds. 'My native place was a spot rife with old legends, tales, traditions, customs and superstitions', he wrote, and also recalled that his father told him so many folk-stories that he never in the rest of his life heard an Irish story that was new to him. By the age of twenty Carleton's mind was furnished with enough knowledge and experience to give him material for his fiction for the rest of his life, to the extent that one of his biographers claims that his memory rather than his imagination was his greatest resource as a writer. Certainly, many of the characters and incidents in his stories are taken from life, and in this novel Carleton in presenting Dick o' the Grange and Jemmy Branigan is 'certain that many of our readers will, at first sight, recognize these two remarkable originals'.

The way in which his parents could switch from Irish to English and back again for particular effects also alerted him to the force and influence of idiom and language. These resources of language and lore were augmented by his education at 'hedge-schools', curious Irish institutions which he describes in several of his stories. These schools were set up literally in a hedgerow, often by roofing over the top of a ditch, and they were presided over by men who compensated for their lack of formal education with wild claims for their scholarly prowess expressed in extravagant rhetoric, based on classical tropes and allusions. Thus Carleton grew up in a linguistically diverse culture: although English-speaking, he had access to Irish expressions and idioms where no English equivalents would do. Moreover, even his English had a distinctive tang, a Hiberno-English into which numerous racy Irish idioms and expressions had been directly translated as it supplanted the old tongue. To these linguistic advantages, he added the self-conscious and high-flown rhetoric of the hedge-schools, and a thorough knowledge of Latin and Greek gained through attendance at a small classical school in Monaghan, where, he claimed, the daily language was Latin. This diversity gives vividness to the language and style of his *Traits and Stories* and remains, if not so vibrantly, in the idiom of *The Black Prophet,* as, for instance, in the exchanges between Jemmy Branigan and the pedlar, and in the use of Gaelic expressions to give nuance to a situation or character. The comic potentialities of the hedge-schoolmaster mixture of pedantry and magniloquence are exploited to effect in the petition that Hanlon and the pedlar present to Travers, while the grounding in the classics they provided encouraged Carleton to reach for an epic dimension in his characters, with Sarah standing 'like the Pythoness, in a kind of savage beauty', while Mave's 'unparalleled heroism' in subduing her fear of fever would 'have won her a statue in the times of old Greece, when self-sacrifice for human good was appreciated and rewarded'.

Secondly, it should be remembered that Carleton grew up in the divided and violent province of Ulster. He was born just four years before the great uprising of 1798, in which nationalist forces with some limited French support threatened British rule in Ireland, and with it the Protestant hegemony. In that terrible year of blood-letting savage sectarian pogroms were carried out by both sides, and the brutality with which the Rising was finally crushed left an abiding legacy of bitterness and violence. Nowhere did feelings run higher than in Ulster, of all the four Irish provinces the one most extensively colonized by Protestant settlers. Carleton grew up in an atmosphere of sectarian violence and as a Catholic he and his family were at the mercy of Orange militias and paramilitary gangs. One of his most traumatic memories was of the night Protestant yeomen (all close neighbours) used the pretext of a toy cannon to raid his house, threaten his father with their muskets, and wound his sister with a bayonet. Orange power was ascendant: all the Justices of the Peace were Orangemen and so were the members of the Grand Juries, which were responsible for all aspects of local government. 'There was then', he complained, 'no law *against* an Orangeman, and no law *for* a Papist'. Inevitably, the Catholics tried to respond in kind. Carleton recalled the great sectarian pitched battle at Clogher Lammas fair, which left several dead and many severely wounded, and which he used as the basis of his story, 'The Party Fight'. He himself was initiated, reluctantly he says, into the secret Ribbon society, the Catholic organization which mirrored the Orange Order, and on a trip to Louth as a young man he found the country studded with gibbets and festooned with the tarred bodies of executed Ribbonmen, oozing obscenely in the unusually hot autumn sun. This background of casual but lethal communal and political violence informs his fiction and makes it more stark not only than contemporary French or English novels, but also than the fiction of his Irish contemporaries from more southerly counties. A double murder is the mainspring of the plot of *The Black Prophet,* but violence is endemic throughout the novel. Charlie Hanlon is in the vicinity of his murdered father because he is fleeing the consequences of his part in a sectarian Party Fight. It is clear that Red Roddy Duncan is the leader of a gang of Ribbonmen, and he, one of the 'vagabonds' and 'politicians' Carleton both despised and feared, orchestrates and inflames the outbreaks of famine violence, most notably against Skinadre's house. The violent ambience of the novel is set immediately both in imagery and action: the first chapter graphically describes a murderous assault on a mother by her step-daughter, a 'young tigress' who lunges 'with a growl like that of a savage beast', and blood also flows freely in the second chapter when young Dalton knocks the Black Prophet down. That Carleton flirts dangerously with melodrama in his descriptions is undeniable, but the world he was describing, stripped of any civilized veneer by the imperatives of starvation, 'the tyrannical instinct of self preservation', confounds the facile meliorist philosophies of the Victorians: 'There is no beast, however, in the deepest jungle of Africa itself, so wildly savage, and ferocious, as a human mob, when left to its own blind and headlong impulses.'

Much of the violence that Carleton encountered as a young man derived from the sharp religious divide which was (and is) particularly acute in the North of Ireland. But Carleton, who had once set out for Maynooth with the intention of becoming a priest, crossed that divide when he alone of his family converted to Protestantism. His apostasy, and the subsequent anti-Catholic propaganda in some of his stories, seriously damaged his reputation and popularity, not only with his contemporary Irish readers but also with future generations of Irish critics. Such critics have tended to explain it as a piece of self-interested materialism, whereby an intelligent, ambitious, struggling and unemancipated young Catholic sought to throw in his lot with the ruling establishment so as to gain a network of influential connections. No doubt such considerations did weigh, and perhaps weighed heavily, with the young Carleton, but we mistake him if we see this as his only motive for his change of religion. And this is the third element to be considered when assessing his writings, and perhaps particularly when considering *The Black Prophet.*

He tells us that he had begun to entertain doubts about Catholic dogma long before he was 'out on the world' in Dublin, as far back in fact as his youthful pilgrimage to the holy island in Lough Derg. And even as a child he had shown a precocious scepticism: told how a devout priest had escaped drowning with a boatload of pilgrims by walking over the surface of a storm-tossed lake, he coolly enquired why, possessing such powers, the priest had not also saved his fellow-travellers. His father, he recalls dryly, 'paused and looked at me, but said nothing'. As he grew older a sense of religious melancholy was added to this apparently innate scepticism. He increasingly felt that he had been singled out by Providence for particular punishment. At its most superficial this may be thought no more than the indulgent self-pity of a young man who had been spoilt (as the youngest child he was his father's favourite), and who felt frustrated because the greatness that should have been guaranteed to him as a seventh son seemed curiously elusive. But his gloom went deeper than this. 'I have often thought that man's life is divided or separated into a series of small epics; not epics that are closed by happiness, however, but by pain', he wrote in his *Autobiography,* and recalled that his unfair dismissal from a job made him 'reconsider my relation to Providence', and question why 'ill-fortune and human enmity' dogged his heels. This close scrutiny of Providence, and the need for Atonement, was not confined to Carleton: it was a characteristic of the contemporary evangelical movement in both Britain and Ireland, and it was by the evangelical wing of the Church of Ireland that Carleton was taken up when he converted and when he began to write. Evangelicalism was a reaction to the political upheavals and secularization that followed the French Revolution, and for which the optimistic natural theology of the eighteenth century seemed to offer no explanation. The evangelicals believed that the sinfulness of mankind had perverted God's design for the world with horrendous consequences: economic slumps, social and political unrest, Catholic emancipation, cholera outbreaks, and famines. Only through the atonement of sins could salvation be won, only through the example of Christ's Atonement on the cross for man's Original Sin could salvation come.

Of all Carleton's novels, *The Black Prophet* is the one most saturated in this essentially Protestant theology. It informs and shapes the theme and style of the novel in ways, as we shall see, that pull against the ostensible Realist agenda that Carleton has set himself. There is hardly a page in which Providence is not invoked or questioned. The pious characters trust (although sometimes more in hope than expectation) that 'the hand of God' is directing the tortuous train of events that constitutes the plot, but, if so, God evidently moves in mysterious ways, and in this book of famine, murder and suffering He appears as a vengeful rather than merciful Deity. The brooding presence of supernatural causes and occult forces working out mysterious and perplexing purposes challenge, complicate, and even subvert the Realist aspects of the book, not least because they seem to engage Carleton's imagination at a deeper level.

The very function of the Black Prophet's prophecies is, of course, to interpret and anticipate the actions of Providence through his mysterious power, and although his predictions are dismissed as bogus by the Realist narrator, they (like the dreams in the book) all turn out to be true. It is significant that his prophetic powers derive from, among others, Nebuchadnezzar, whom Jewish prophets thought the agent of God's wrath on a sinful Israel when he sacked the Temple and led them into Babylonian captivity. Two of Nebuchadnezzar's three 'Books' cited by the Prophet relate to Death and Judgement. The notion, central to evangelicalism at this time, that national suffering is a consequence of human sin, appears as early as chapter II when the Prophet, in predicting (correctly) that the famine will grow worse, ascribes this to 'the Almighty, in his wrath', a proposition to which Jerry Sullivan readily assents: 'Everything we can look upon appears to have the mark of God's displeasure on it'.

Nor are these predominantly Protestant and evangelical sentiments confronted by any Catholic alternative. Indeed, although nearly all the characters are Catholic, the Catholic presence in the book is curiously muted. We see the Sullivans saying their rosary, and there is a litany to the Blessed Virgin to intercede for Peggy Murtagh, but no one attends Mass. No Catholic priest appears until very late in the narrative, and then more in the guise of a glorified social worker than a spiritual comforter. Dalton as a Catholic could have shriven the sin of his supposed crime—if not its memory—in Confession, but he remains haunted by it, and is convinced that his deteriorating material circumstances are directly due to it. This belief is shared by both the narrator and the 'public mind', which, 'extremely acute' in some matters, 'began to perceive the just judgments of God as manifested in the disasters which befell' the Dalton family.

The theme of Providence impacts most obviously and least happily on the novel through its influence on the plot. The Judge comments directly on this: the sequence of events that finally bring the Prophet to justice 'is another proof of the certainty with which Providence never . . . loses sight of the man who deliberately sheds his fellow-creature's blood'. But to bring this about, Carleton has to devise an extraordinarily cumbersome story. That the plot is so labyrinthine and unsatisfactory is, of course, due to a number of factors, besides the theme. Carleton made his reputation as a

writer of novellas and short-stories. He found it more difficult to manipulate the various strands of a longer narrative. What remains in the memory at the end of this novel are the sketches, for instance the first description of Skinadre as a hypocritical country miser, and the set-piece descriptions of want and destitution. At other times the narrative becomes laborious, as when Carleton insists on explaining exactly how Sarah passed herself off as Mave during the abduction, and on those occasions when he pauses to sum up the story so far, one feels it is more to remind himself than the reader of where he has got to.

This problem was aggravated by serial publication. Carleton tells us in the Introduction that he did not revise the text which had appeared in the *Dublin University Magazine* when he republished it in book form, and internal evidence suggests that when he published the first instalment in May 1846 he still had no very clear idea of how his plot would unfold. Important characters such as Red Roddy Duncan and the pedlar do not appear until late in the story, while the motivation and even characterization of Sarah (called Sally for a few chapters) and Hanlon undergo such extreme swings that the narrator feels obliged to comment on it. The plan to rob the Grange seems a late invention, and other possible subplots (such as Skinadre's son and his desire for Mave) are introduced only to be left hanging. Some inconsistencies occur when theme comes into conflict with realism. Thus the beautiful heroine Mave retains her 'extraordinary symmetry', natural grace, abundant hair and—even more remarkably—her 'rounded figure', while starvation has reduced the rest of her family to lassitude and emaciation. Here verisimilitude surrenders to mild eroticism; elsewhere it gives way to the gothic elements of mystery, guilt and retribution. The Prophet's reaction at seeing the coat of the murdered Bartle Sullivan (extreme agitation, followed by a nightmare) seems out of proportion, seeing that he had nothing to do with that supposed crime. But the most grievous complications in the plot arise from Carleton's thematic need to show 'the wisdom manifested by an over-ruling Providence . . . the wondrous manner in which the influence of slight incidents is made to frustrate the subtlest designs of human ingenuity, and vindicate the justice of the Almighty in the eyes of His creatures'. This involves, among other improbabilities, prophetic dreams, extraordinary coincidences, unlikely behaviour, obscure motivation, and contrived incidents. An account of the adventures of the tobacco-box alone would sufficiently illustrate Carleton's limitations as a manipulator of plot.

We do not then read *The Black Prophet* for its formal qualities, but there is more to narrative than plot. Yeats said that in reading *The Black Prophet* he seemed 'to be looking out at the wild, torn storm-clouds that lie in heaps at sundown along the western seas of Ireland; all nature, and not merely man's nature, seems to pour out for me its inbred fatalism'. This rendering of an elemental and primitive world is one of the powerful achievements of the novel. The effects are bold, sometimes crude, but even in their theatricality they retain their effectiveness, because they enforce a central and controlling theme. Yeats speaks of clouds at sundown, and the central and recurrent metaphor in the book is of light and dark. This is not merely an exercise in the effects of chiaroscuro, but echoes and intensifies the opposition of good and evil, sin and redemption, guilt and atonement that lie at the heart of the book's concerns. This atmosphere is established from the outset: as the Prophet and Jerry Sullivan journey home in the second chapter a lurid and angry sunset gives the clouds the appearance of coffins and hearses, while the sun itself resembles an Old Testament prophet 'clothed with the majesty and terror of an angry God . . . commissioned to launch his denunciations against the iniquity of nations'. Such imagery and associations are repeated throughout the book, and if Carleton cannot resist exploiting their melodramatic potential (on one occasion Sarah's eyes glow like the 'coruscations of the Aurora Borealis', and no significant incident or discovery can occur without a bolt of lightning and a prolonged roll of thunder to emphasize its importance), the cumulative effect is powerful and elemental: even the thunder and lightning seem to be 'uttering the indignation of heaven against our devoted people'.

This last quotation opens up what is perhaps the fundamental question posed by the book, the relationship between the 'local' story of murder and retribution and the national catastrophe of the famine, and how far that catastrophe had been deserved. In introducing the large theme of Providence and Atonement in a book about a famine, and within the confines of a supposedly realist novel, Carleton found himself confronted by a number of theological and aesthetic problems. Speculation as to how far famine was a mark of God's wrath on a sinful people much exercised evangelical thought at the time he was writing. While there was that in Carleton's cosmic imagination prepared to entertain such a proposition, he also knew as a realist that the situation in Ireland, although it might derive ultimately from God's anger, owed a great deal to governmental neglect and to the mortal greed of landlords and middlemen. Thus his novel is not merely a representation of Irish life and character, it is also a tract, a desperate appeal to indifferent legislators, absentee landlords and uninformed English opinion to correct the terrible things that are happening in Ireland. Carleton saw it as his imperative to alert his readers to the situation, to alter opinion, and so save his country from the social, economic and possibly political catastrophe that was already in process. This is the message of his dedication to Lord John Russell, this is the theme of the Introduction, this is the reason

for the authorial interventions on the iniquities of middlemen and absentee landlords, on rabble-rousing men of no property, on the overdependence on one fragile vegetable. It is essential for moral and political purposes that he show famine *as it is* to waken the sympathy and action of rulers: 'The sufferings of that year of famine we have endeavoured to bring before those who may have the power in their hands of assuaging the similar horrors which have revisited our country in this. The pictures we have given are not exaggerated, but drawn from memory and the terrible realities of 1817.'

Carleton's analysis of the causes of famine, although incomplete, does not lack perspicacity. As well as his animadversions on the folly of over-dependence on one crop, he also points to the extraordinary anomaly whereby Ireland continued to export food while her people were starving to death in their thousands. He also apprizes us of the fact that while the poor are being reduced to unimaginable destitution and misery, other classes of Irishmen — strong farmers with bursting granaries, mealmongers and misers like Skinadre who have hoarded against times of want—are doing very well out of the famine. Such exploiters may be reprehensible, but they are not responsible. They take advantage of a bad situation, but the situation is so bad because the 'system' is rotten, 'the long course of illiberal legislation and unjustifiable neglect' by the British government. For Carleton this is exemplified by 'one of the worst and most cruel systems that ever cursed either the country or the people', whereby irresponsible and greedy head-landlords sublet their estates to middlemen, who, without lasting attachment to, or tenure of, the land take as much as they can as quickly as they can, and in the process destroy the social and economic fabric of Irish rural life. This system, if allowed to continue with its inevitable consequences, will be exploited by parish-pump rabble-rousers, 'unprincipled knaves, known as "politicians" — idle vagabonds, who hate all honest employment themselves, and ask no better than to mislead and fleece the ignorant and unreflecting people, however or whenever they can. These fellows read and expound the papers on Sundays and holidays; rail not only against every government; no matter what its principles are, but, in general, attack all constituted authority, without feeling one single spark of true national principle, or independent love of liberty.'

The novels of the 1840s in both Britain and Ireland are haunted by fear of the mob, and especially the mob roused and organized by unscrupulous agitators, who exist either on the margins of their societies or who come in from outside. In English novels they tend to be trade unionists, but for Carleton they are Ribbonmen, who, given the parlous state of Ireland and the dangerous neglect of the ruling classes, have the potential to wreak far more disruption and damage than their English counterparts.

But, just as Providence resolves the murder case and confounds the machinations of evil, so an unlikely instrument of providence, 'Robert James Travers, Esq', an unbribable agent, sorts out the agrarian injustices, and restores the Daltons to their rightful farm. In terms of Irish agrarian life in the early nineteenth century, Travers is perhaps hardly less miraculous and unbelievable than the prophetic dreams and amazing coincidences that settle the murder-plot, but he nevertheless inhabits the Realist part of the novel, that part which insists upon the authenticity of its descriptions and the rationality of its arguments to further its reforming and didactic purpose. There is inevitably a mismatch between this aspect of the novel and the elemental vision of Carleton's folk imagination, a mismatch which might be exemplified in Charlie Hanlon's dream: it was a mysterious but true dream, and his acting upon it set in motion that train of events that led to the Prophet's sentence for a murder 'discovered under circumstances little short of providential'. Yet the dream is not admissible as evidence in the Realist world, and cannot be put before the jury.

That Carleton was unable to reconcile these two aspects of the novel, nor to resolve the question of whether the famine was inflicted by mortal misgovernment or divine displeasure, is hardly surprising. There was a wide division between Carleton the primitive, the peasant, awed at the unfathomable mystery of the world, at the awesome indifference of famine, fate, and suffering to human endeavour, who understood how flimsy the veils of civilization are against the dictates of appetite and want, and Carleton the would-be Dublin gentleman, the soon-to-be government pensioner, with his trimming rationalization of famine riots, his careful footnotes, and rational analysis of agrarian ills. In this latter mode Carleton could be fickle in allegiance and petulant in attitudes. He is not so in this book: on the eve of one of the greatest human tragedies, not merely in Irish history but in the history of civilization, he launches an impassioned and courageous plea to an uncomprehending world to save the Irish people before it is too late. But it is not in that plea or in the social and economic arguments he advances in its support that the value of this book lies; rather it is in the scenes where he makes us see and feel the consequences of famine: the Murtaghs driven to the edge of insanity, desperately grubbing for food as their daughter lies dead; the dying mother amid her starving children, sunk to the mere condition of animal life; the brooding sense of hopeless suffering in which the elements act as a correlative for what cannot be otherwise expressed, the rain 'pouring down in that close, dark, and incessant fall which gives scarcely any hope of its ending, and consequently throws the heart into

that anxious and gloomy state which everyone can feel, and perhaps no one describe.'

ARISTOCRATIC IRISH AND ANGLO-IRISH NOVELISTS

Lewis Melville (essay date 1906)

SOURCE: "Charles Lever," *The Fortnighty Review,* Vol. CCCCLXXV, July 2, 1906, pp. 235-46.

[*In the following essay, Melville asserts that while Charles Lever has been charged with sacrificing his characters in his attempts to amuse his readers, and while many Irish critics in particular fault Charles Lever for perpetuating cultural stereotypes in his novels, Lever's writing is characterized by his "easy humour and natural tenderness." Melville concludes that Lever's "rollicking, madcap stories" have earned "an honoured place in English literature."*]

With just so much right as Scotsmen claim Sir Walter Scott as their national novelist, many admirers of Charles James Lever demand that the latter be regarded as the national Irish romancer. But while the works of Scott are beloved by his compatriots, those of Lever are by no means popular with his countrymen. The reasons are not far to seek: Scott glorified his characters, making his heroes and heroines the noblest of their race; Lever, the possessor of a sense of humour far keener than that of the greater writer, sacrificed everything in the endeavour to amuse. Those of Lever's detractors who hail from the Emerald Isle complain bitterly that he has done much "to perpetuate the current errors as to Irish character," yet it cannot truthfully be asserted that he has on the whole been guilty of gross misrepresentation; and the various accusations, carefully examined, amount to little more than a charge of having depicted only certain classes of society. It is true that except *en passant,* as in the opening chapters of *Tom Burke of "Ours,"* Lever did not treat of the political aspect of the Irish question; but that was not because he was unpatriotic, but because he had little interest in the problem; and it must be admitted that he did not portray the hard-working clerk or the honest business man of everyday life. He was at his best when describing the men who drank deep, rode hard, gamed heavily, fought bravely, and led a devil-may-care life; but also he depicted with graphic pen the wretched state of the peasantry, and drew with no unskilful hand the pitiful lot of the decayed Irish gentleman.

The humorist cannot but poke kindly fun at the weaknesses of his fellows, and Lever could not refrain from good-humoured laughter at his countrymen's foibles.

In his earlier books he made fun of most things, but he never wrote irreverently of sacred subjects, and always showed himself keenly alive to the holiness of the affection between parents and children, and to the beauty of love between man and woman. He wrote of youth and its joys: of the days *qu'on est bien à vingt ans,* when ambition is much but love is more, when frankness has not given place to diplomacy, when rash bravery rather than discretion is the rule. He wrote not of philosophy, nor of morality, but of the joyous times before high-spirited men come to forty year, and abandon "wine, woman, and song" for the serious business of life. He wrote, it must be remembered, of an era when existence was not so strenuous as it is now, when less was expected from a man and less consequently was forthcoming, when the duel was of frequent occurrence, drunkenness regarded only as a venial fault, and practical joking an everyday occurrence.

It has been well said that Lever rollicked through life rather than lived, and when writing his books there is no doubt he drew largely on his experiences. One hears of his establishing in Dublin a *Burschenschaft,* the members of which wore scarlet vests with gilt buttons and a red skull-cap adorned with white tassels when they assembled for the suppers, songs, and conversational jousts that formed the staple of the night's entertainment. One hears how he took a party of friends to a ball at a house some miles distant in a furniture van, a hearse, and a mourning carriage; and of how, when practising as a doctor at Coleraine, and riding to visit a patient, he leaped his horse over a turf-cart that blocked the way. This latter exploit is introduced into many of the stories, and was cleverly parodied by Thackeray and Bret Harte. "Knowing my horse, I put him at the Emperor's head, and Bugaboo went at it like a shot. He was riding his famous white Arab, and turned quite pale as I came up and went over the horse and the Emperor, scarcely brushing the cockade which he wore." And, lest you should doubt the likelihood of such a jump, Thackeray has given you a picture showing Phil Fogarty clearing, not only Napoleon, but Murat and Sieyès as well! " 'Cut him down!' said Sieyès, once an *abbé* but now a gigantic cuirassier; and he made a pass at me with his sword. But he little knew an Irishman on an Irish horse. Bugaboo cleared Sieyès, and fetched the monster a slap with his near hind hoof which sent him reeling from his saddle—and away I went, with an army of a hundred and seventy-three thousand eight hundred men at my heels." It is splendid fooling and not unjustifiable caricature.

It was in those early days, when full of the *joie de vivre,* that Lever wrote the ballad which Thackeray declared he would rather have written than any one of his own composition.

> The Pope he leads a happy life,
> He fears not married care, nor strife,

> He drinks the best of Rhenish wine—
> I would the Pope's gay lot were mine.

> But then all happy's not his life,
> He has not maid, nor blooming wife,
> Nor child has he to raise his hope—
> I would not ask to be the Pope.

> The Sultan better pleases me,
> His is a life of jollity,
> His wives are many as he will—
> I would the Sultan's throne then fill.

> But even he's a wretched man,
> He must obey the Alcoran,
> And dares not drink one drop of wine—
> I would not change his lot for mine.

> So then I'll hold my lowly stand,
> And live in German *Vaterland;*
> I'll kiss my maiden fair and fine,
> And drink the best of Rhenish wine.

> Whene'er my maiden kisses me,
> I'll think that I the Sultan be;
> And when my cheery glass I fill,
> I'll fancy then I am the Pope.

Lever studied medicine at Göttingen and Dublin, took his degree at the university in the latter city in 1831, and afterwards practised for some years in various parts of Ireland. It does not appear that he served any apprenticeship to letters, and, so far as it is known, he began his artistic career by the contribution to the *Dublin University Magazine* in 1837 of some sketches, afterwards issued in monthly parts with numerous additions as well as with illustrations by "Phiz," and in 1839 published in book form. This was, of course, *The Confessions of Harry Lorrequer,* which almost at once secured a favourable review in *Fraser's Magazine.* But what must have pleased Lever much more was a fierce fight in the Rugby school-close between two boys for a number of the *Dublin University Magazine* containing an instalment of the story. Sweet incense indeed to burn before an author! "That success was very intoxicating to me; and I set to work on my second book with a thrill of hope as regards the world's favour which—and it is no small thing to say it—I can yet recall," Lever wrote so late as the year of his death. "I felt, or thought I felt, an inexhaustible store of fun and buoyancy within me, and I began to have a misty, half-confused impression that Englishmen generally laboured under a sad-coloured temperament, took depressing views of life, and were proportionately grateful to any one who would rally them, even passingly, out of their despondency, and give them a laugh without much trouble for going in search of it."

Lever was not yet prepared to abandon his original profession, and an opening being found for him to practise in Brussels, he repaired thither. He had thought he would be appointed physician to the English Embassy, but in this he was disappointed, although he secured a fair number of patients; and being discontented, was easily seduced by the offer of the shrewd manager of the *Dublin University Magazine* to return to the Irish metropolis to edit that periodical at the handsome salary of twelve hundred a year. The manager was moved to this proposal by the success of the story Lever wrote for him while in Brussels, *Charles O'Malley, the Irish Dragoon* (1840), and the desire to retain for the magazine the services of the popular writer. He never had cause to regret the step, while the success of *Jack Hinton, the Guardsman* (1842) must have removed any lingering doubt he may have had as to the wisdom of the course he had taken.

Thackeray, however, thought Lever could do better for himself than remain in Dublin, where he was surrounded by third-rate writers, and tried to persuade him to come to London, where, in addition to other advantages, he would be able to improve his pecuniary position. Indeed, Thackeray thought his brother novelist would derive so much benefit from this change of residence that he backed his advice with offers of monetary and other assistance, if such were needed. Lever for various reasons declined this proposal, and afterwards told Major Dwyer that Thackeray was the most good-natured man in the world, "but that help from him would be worse than no help at all . . . He was like a man struggling to keep his head above water, and who offers to teach his friend to swim," adding that "Thackeray would write for anything and about anything, and had so lost himself that his status in London was not good." Looking back, it is amusing to recall the fact that this conversation took place in 1842, when Thackeray was in Ireland fulfilling a commission of Messrs. Chapman and Hall to write an "Irish Sketch-Book," and before the man who had lost his status in London had begun to write any of his great novels!

Thackeray was disappointed by Lever's decision, but their friendship remained unimpaired, and *The Irish Sketch-Book* was dedicated to "My dear Lever," who was much blamed by his countrymen for allowing his name to be associated with a work which they declared to be full of blunders and exaggerations. A more important result of the intercourse between the great men was that Lever, warned by Thackeray, infused a more cosmopolitan spirit into his work, which hitherto had been essentially Irish. But Thackeray was to influence Lever even more powerfully, for, when five years later he wrote *Phil Fogarty, a Tale of the Onety-Oneth,* Lever, appalled by the truth of the parody, declared he might as well shut up shop, and actually altered the character of his novels.

Following *Jack Hinton* came in quick succession *Tom Burke of "Ours," The Adventures of Arthur O'Leary,*

and *The O'Donoghue,* with the publication of which terminated the author's connection with the *Dublin University Magazine.* It may be said at once that all these books lack plot. "Story! God bless you, I have none to tell, Sir," is the quotation prefixed to *Harry Lorrequer,* and this might as well have been taken for the motto of the rest, which are absolutely formless, and consist merely of a great number of stories hung together upon the slightest connecting thread possible.

Charles O'Malley is, perhaps, the most popular of the early books. The characters are unusually bright, even for Lever, and each has an amazing superabundance of animal spirits, while the verses interspersed through the volumes are fresh and merry, and the anecdotes are related with peculiar gusto. Nowhere are there better stories than that which tells how Lady Boyle won the election for Tom Butler, and than that of "the man in the sewer," while the episode of the undergraduate has been thought worthy of repetition, with slight variations, by almost every novelist who has since portrayed life at a university. The gem of the book is the account of the pretended death and mock funeral of Godfrey O'Malley, a device adopted to enable that worthy man to escape his creditors and seek re-election for his constituency; and most amusing is the letter in which the news is conveyed to his nephew. "Your uncle Godfrey, whose debts (God pardon him!) are more numerous than the hairs of his wig, was obliged to die here last night. We did the thing for him completely; and all doubts as to the reality of the event are silenced by the circumstantial detail of the newspaper 'that he was confined six weeks to his bed, from a cold he caught ten days ago while on guard, repeat this, for it's better we had all the same story, till he comes to life again, which maybe will not take place before Tuesday or Wednesday. At the same time, canvass the country for him, and say he'll be with his friends next week, and up in Woodford and the Scariff barony: say he died a true Catholic; it will serve him on the hustings. Meet us in Athlone on Saturday, and bring your uncle's mare with you—he says he'd rather ride home; and tell Father MacShane to have a bit of dinner ready about four o'clock, for the corpse can get nothing after he leaves Mountmellick."

Lever most nearly approached failure with *Arthur O'Leary,* a sort of Baedeker's guide to the Continent, hopelessly overweighted with very long and rather tiresome interpolated narratives. On the other hand, the best of the books already mentioned—the best, perhaps, of all the books Lever ever wrote—is *Tom Burke of "Ours."* In that story there is a great variety of scenes and graphic descriptions, especially of Paris in 1806 and the Court at the Tuileries; while the whole is more than usually dramatic in treatment. Tom, when little more than a child, gets mixed up in an Irish plot against the Government, is arrested, contrives to escape, and flees to France, where he enters the *école militaire* and is given a commission by Napoleon himself. Subsequently he is unjustly suspected of complicity in the Chouan conspiracy in which Georges Cadoual loses his life, takes his trial with the leaders, and is saved only by the intercession of personages in high places. This is an historical novel of the old school, in which an obscure Irishman mixes in the best society, is always on the spot at the right moment, and is invariably in the confidence of his generals. Napoleon—the Napoleon of fiction, tender at one moment, cruel at the next—figures largely in the tale, and Tom is frequently in his presence, on one occasion actually saves his life, and at the end meets him by accident at Fontainebleau on the eve of his abdication. On the following day Tom witnesses the fallen monarch bidding farewell to the Old Guard prior to his departure for St. Helena; and there is nothing in any of Lever's books so touchingly described as this episode, and nothing so well written.

> Wearied with a wakeful night, I fell into a slumber towards morning, when I started suddenly at the roll of drums in the court beneath. In an instant I was at the window. What was my astonishment to perceive that the courtyard was filled with troops. The grenadiers of the guard were ranged in order of battle, with several squadrons of the *chasseurs* and the horse artillery, while a staff of general officers stood in the midst, among whom I recognised Belliard, Montesquieu, and Turenne—great names, and worthy to be recorded for an act of faithful devotion. The Duc de Bassano was there, too, in deep mourning, his pale and careworn face attesting the grief within his heart. The roll of the drums continued—the deep, unbroken murmur of the salute went on from one end of the line to the other. It ceased, and ere I could question the reason, the various staff-officers became uncovered, and stood in attitudes of respectful attention; and the Emperor himself slowly, step by step, descended the wide stair of the "Cheval Blanc," as the grand terrace was styled, and advanced towards the troops. At the same instant the whole line presented arms, and the drums beat the salute. They ceased, and Napoleon raised his hand to command silence, and throughout that crowded mass not a whisper was heard.
>
> I could perceive that he was speaking, but the words did not reach me. Eloquent and burning words they were, and to be recorded in history to the remotest ages. I now saw that he had finished, as General Petit sprang forward with the eagle of the first regiment of the guards, and presented it to him. The Emperor pressed it fervently to his lips, and then threw his arms around Petit's neck, while, suddenly disengaging himself, he took the tattered flag that waved above him and kissed it twice. Unable to bear up any longer, the worn, hard-featured veterans sobbed aloud like children, and turned away their faces to conceal their emotion. No cry of *"Vive l'Empereur!"* resounded now through those ranks where each had willingly shed his heart's blood for

him. Sorrow had usurped the place of enthusiasm, and they stood overwhelmed by grief.

> A tall and soldier-like figure, with head uncovered, approached and said a few words. Napoleon waved his hand towards the troops, and from the ranks rushed many towards him and fell on their kness before him. He passed his hand across his face and turned away. My eyes grew dim, a misty vapour shut out every object, and I felt as though the very lids were bursting. The great stamp of horses startled me, and then came the roll of wheels. I looked up; an equipage was passing from the gate; a *peloton* of dragoons escorted it; a second followed at full speed; the colonels formed their men, the word to march was given, the drums beat out, the grenadiers moved on, the *chasseurs* succeeded, and last the artillery rolled heavily up: the court was deserted, not a man remained—all, all were gone. The Empire was ended, and the Emperor, the mighty genius who created it, on his way to exile.

In each of these books is a dashing hero, in spite of the author's intention not always a gentleman, and often not far removed from a scamp, doing things that are unpardonable, and behaving in a way that no other novelist's hero ever does. The fact of the matter is, as has already been said, Lever subordinated everything to humour, and without a twinge of compunction would make a "bounder" of his best-beloved character for the sake of a good story. There is, too, a strong family likeness about the heroes. Each gets into trouble, usually when he is in no way to blame; each falls invariably on his feet; each fights duels with the most famous swordsman or the most renowned shot, and at worst escapes with a more or less severe wound; and each seems to be unsuccessful in love, but never fails—in the last chapter—to win for his wife the woman he desires. In each book there is also one villain—for choice, a scoundrelly attorney; and numberless officers, army doctors, priests, briefless barristers, horsedealers, and smugglers, all of whom have "yarns" to relate, practical jokes to engineer, and a marvellous, never-flagging flow of high spirits. The female characters rarely emerge from shadow, and, though but barely outlined, are usually of one of two types: the rather worldly-minded woman, and the well brought up, pure, honest, and, it must be confessed, generally uninteresting young girl; though occasionally he extended his limits, as when he drew the *vivandiére* Minette, the laughable Madame Lefevbre, and the inimitable Mrs. O'Reilly. When dealing with men, however, his characterisation, though never subtle, was frequently vigorous; and he has given us the delightful Bubbleton, who could never open his mouth but to utter some absurdity; the humorous Major Monsoon; the Knight of Gwynne, one of the most lovable and pathetic figures ever depicted; and the wily, cunning, humorous Mickey Free—by which last portrait Lever may be content to stand or fall as a creator.

. . . . . . My companion was my own servant, Michael, or, as he was better known, "Mickey" Free. Now, had Mickey been left to his own free and unrestricted devices, the time would not have hung so heavily, for, among Mike's manifold gifts, he was possessed of a very great flow of gossiping conversation. He knew all that was doing in the country, and never was barren in his information wherever his imagination came into play. Mickey was the best hurler in the barony, no mean performer on the violin, could dance the national bolero of "Father Jack Walsh" in a way that charmed more than one soft heart beneath a red wolsey bodice, and had, withal, the peculiar free-and-easy, devil-may-care kind of off-hand Irish way that never deserted him in the midst of his wiliest and most subtle moments, giving to a very deep and cunning fellow all the apparent frankness and openness of a country lad. He had attached himself to me as a kind of sporting companion, and, growing daily more and more useful, had been gradually admitted to the honours of the kitchen and the prerogative of cast clothes without ever having been actually engaged as a servant, and, while thus no warrant officer, as, in fact, he discharged all his duties well and punctually, was rated among the ship's company, though no one could say at what precise period he changed his caterpillar existence and became a gay butterfly, with cords and tops, a striped vest, and a most knowing prig hat, who stalked about the stableyard and bullied the helpers. Such was Mike. He had made his fortune, such as it was, and had a most becoming pride in the fact that he had made himself indispensable to an establishment which, before he entered it, never knew the want of him. As for me, he was everything to me. Mike informed me what horse was wrong, why the chestnut mare couldn't go out, and why the black horse could. He knew the arrival of a new covey of partridges quicker than the *Morning Post* does of a noble family from the Continent, and could tell their whereabouts twice as accurately, but his talents took a wider range than field sports afford, and he was the faithful chronicler of every wake, station, wedding, or christening for miles round, and, as I took no small pleasure in those very national pastimes, the information was of great value to me. To conclude this brief sketch, Mike was a devout Catholic, in the same sense that he was enthusiastic about everything—that is, he believed and obeyed exactly as far as suited his own peculiar notions of comfort and happiness; beyond *that* his scepticism stepped in and saved him from inconvenience, and though he might have been somewhat puzzled to reduce his faith to a rubric, still it answered his purpose, and that was all he wanted. Such, in short, was my valet, Mickey Free.

Shortly after severing his connection with the *Dublin University Magazine*, Lever went to live in Florence, where he wrote several books, among which may be mentioned *The Martins of Cro' Martin* (1847), a picture of life in the West of Ireland, *The Diary and Notes of Horace Templeton* (1849), and *Roland Cashel*

(1850). There appeared also, as a serial in *Household Words, A Day's Ride,* which was so unpopular with the readers of that periodical that Dickens adopted the unusual course of announcing beforehand the date of its conclusion. A careful perusal of the novel, which was brought out in book form in 1863, does not suggest any reason for its signal failure, and, though it is by no means a masterpiece, the author wrote worse books that achieved a certain amount of success. Lever made the daring experiment of publishing *Con Cregan* anonymously, and was much amused by the fact that, while favourably criticised, it was spoken of as the work of "a new author dangerous to Mr. Lever's supremacy." In 1857 Lever was appointed British Consul at Spezzia, a post which in those days was practically a sinecure, and in that city wrote nearly a dozen novels, including *Davenport Dunn* (1859) and *Sir Brooke Fosbrooke* (1866)—which latter was the author's favourite, although it has never taken any particular hold of the public. After ten years at Spezzia, he was promoted to Trieste. "Here is six hundred a year for doing nothing," Lord Derby said to him, "and you are just the man to do it." Though he still continued to write, his heart was not in his work, although his books do not show any marked signs of feebleness. His dearly-beloved wife had died, his health was bad, he disliked Trieste and its inhabitants, and his financial affairs were a source of worry. He paid a farewell visit to Ireland in 1781, and he died on June 1st in the following year.

The books of Lever's second period differ considerably from those written in earlier years. The style is less rugged, the construction better, the characters more carefully drawn, and the author's greater experience of life is evident throughout. But the anecdotes are fewer, there are none of the delightful songs; the martial scenes, dashing heroes, rollicking officers, and jolly priests have disappeared; and to most readers without these Lever is not Lever. The high spirits have gone, too, and the amusing practical joke and the merry quip and crank are things of the past; but the old humour is there, not so gay, indeed, and more reflective, but not a whit less agreeable, though appealing perhaps to a more delicate taste in letters.

Roland Cashel shows Lever in a state of transition, between his two manners, and with *The Fortunes of Glencore,* which followed it, he reached for the first time the later style. Then came *Davenport Dunn,* the story of a clever commercial swindler of that name and of Grog Davis, a "lag" who is almost redeemed by the great love he bore his daughter. *Davenport Dunn* is good, but best of all is *The Dodd Family Abroad,* a series of letters written by members of an average middle-class Irish family, with no unusual gifts and few special opportunities for observation, who have gone on the continent with crude and ridiculous notions of what awaited them there.

They dreamed of economy, refinement, universal politeness, and a profound esteem for England from all foreigners. They fancied that the advantages of foreign travel were to be obtained without cost or labour; that locomotion could educate, sight-seeing cultivate them; that in the capacity of British subjects every society should be open to them, and that, in fact, it was enough to emerge from home obscurity to become at once recognised in the fashionable circles of every Continental city. They affected to despise the foreigner while shunning their own countrymen; they assumed to be votaries of art when merely running over galleries; and, lastly, while laying claim for their own country to the highest moral standard of Europe, they not unfrequently outraged all the proprieties of foreign life by an open and shameless profligacy.

So Lever describes the Dodds in an admirably written preface, and he knew so well what he was writing about that the truth of it makes one almost forget that the correspondence is imaginary. At Brussels, at Florence, and elsewhere abroad he had seen many self-satisfied, half-educated, underbred visitors from Great Britain and Ireland, and had seen how it had come to pass that the middle-class Englishman *en voyage* had earned the hatred and contempt of the foreigner; but while his sympathies were in such cases obviously with the latter, he did not resist the opportunity to laugh at the social conditions of more than one European country.

The Dodd family consists of a husband and wife, a son, James, and two daughters, Mary Anne and Catherine. The husband is a fairly sensible man, brought away rather against his will, level-headed enough as a rule, but somewhat thrown off his balance by the complete change of surroundings; the wife is a silly woman who dearly loves a lord, in which particular she is resembled by James, a weak young man, inclining to dandyism, extravagant, and entirely inexperienced. Mary Anne is a splendid example of the *genus* snob, who cuts an old friend because he looks dowdy, and is for every complaining that Dublin is "terribly behind the world in all that regards civilisation and *ton*"; delighting to flirt with all and sundry—but there fate gets even with her by letting her "carry on" with a *table d'hôte* acquaintance who turns out to be not the nobleman whose title he assumes, but a common thief. It is a relief to turn to Catherine, agreeable, sensible, refined, tender—Lever's favourite female character, said to have been drawn from his wife. The great merit of *The Dodd Family Abroad* is the way in which each person, while chronicling the doings of the party, is made to expose his or her character. Lever believed he never wrote anything to equal this book, and certainly without fear of contradiction it may be said he never wrote anything better. Indeed, for sustained interest, quiet satire, reflective humour, and brilliant analysis of character, it stands among his works unrivalled.

Humour rather than pathos was Lever's *forte*. He admitted that his stories were wanting in scenes of touching and pathetic interest, but he consoled himself, as he characteristically told his readers, remembering to have heard of an author whose paraphrase of the Book of Job was refused by a publisher if he could not throw into it a little more humour. "If I have not been more miserable and unhappy, I am sorry for it on *your* account, but you must excuse my regretting it on my own," Harry Lorrequer said in the preface to his *Confessions,* and to that was added a humorous "publisher's note": "We have the author's permission to state that all the pathetic and moving incidents of his career he has reserved for a second series of *Confessions,* to be entitled *Lorrequer Married.*" But Lever could write well enough of tender incidents, and with a delicacy not equalled by many authors whose fame rests upon novels of misery or sad sentiments. Take, for example, the description of Tom Burke's thoughts as his father lay dying.

> I am writing now of the far-off past—of the long years ago, of my youth—since which my seared heart has had many a sore and scalding lesson; yet I cannot think of that night, fixed and graven as it lies in my memory, without a touch of boyish softness. I remember every waking thought that crossed my mind—my very dream is still before me. It was of my mother. I thought of her, as she lay on a sofa in the old drawing-room, the window open, and the blind drawn—the gentle breeze of a June morning flapping them lazily to and fro, as I knelt beside her to repeat my little hymn, the first I ever learned; and how at each moment my eyes would turn and my thoughts stray to that open casement, through which the odour of flowers and the sweet song of birds were pouring; and my little heart was panting for liberty, while her gentle smile and faint words bade me remember where I was. And now I was straying away through the old garden, where the very sunlight fell scantily through the thick-woven branches loaded with perfumed blossoms; the blackbirds hopped fearlessly from twig to twig, mingling their clear notes with the breezy murmur of the summer bees. How happy was I then! and why cannot such happiness be lasting? Why cannot we shelter ourselves from the base contamination of worldly cares, and live on amid pleasures pure as these, with hearts as holy and desires as simple as in childhood?

Lever was well aware of his faults. "I wrote as I felt—sometimes in good spirits—sometimes in bad—always carelessly—for, God help me! I can do no better," he said at the beginning of his career in *Harry Lorrequer;* and nearly a score of years later he remarked sadly: "I have only to look back upon great opportunities neglected and fair abilities thrown away, capacity wasted and a whole life squandered. Yet if it were not for the necessity that has kept me before the world, perhaps I should have sunk down wearied and exhausted long ago: but as the old clown in the circus goes on grinning and grimacing even when the chalk won't hide his wrinkles, so do I make a show of lightheartedness I have long ceased to feel, or, what is more, to wish for." The necessity was, it must be admitted, owing to a fondness for cards, in his case fatal because of his singularly bad luck, and the resultant urgent need of money. This explains why he wrote so much and so quickly, but, though it has more than once been pleaded in extenuation, it was not haste that gave him a loose style, although Lever himself wondered if he had written less he would have written better. This was, in great part, due to lack of revision, and he would not revise his manuscript because, knowing himself not to be a capable artist, he dreaded lest possibly he might at first, by happy chance, make the right impression, and then carefully improve it away. On the other hand, Lever possessed imagination of no mean order, rising at times to outbursts of real poetry; he had considerable descriptive power, and drew splendid pen-pictures of landscape and seascape, besides depicting vividly scenes in Irish and French life; and he was *facile princeps* in his particular field—the narration of humorous incident. There can be no doubt—although at present a spirit of reaction is evident in critical circles—that, in spite of all their faults of omission and commission, by virtue of the genuine raciness that inspired them, the easy humour, the natural tenderness, the best of Lever's rollicking, madcap stories will for all time have an honoured place in English literature.

O. Elizabeth McWhorter Harden (essay date 1971)

SOURCE: *"Castle Rackrent,"* in *Maria Edgeworth's Art of Prose Fiction,* Mouton, 1971, pp. 43-71.

[*In the following essay, Harden focuses on Maria Edgeworth's* Castle Rackrent *(1800), extolling the novel as the first in which Irish provincial life and character are carefully observed and depicted. Harden examines the biographical and political events which shaped Edgeworth's views and writings and argues that of Edgeworth's novels,* Castle Rackrent *best demonstrates her literary talent.*]

The year 1800 was a history-making year for Maria Edgeworth and for Ireland which she now claimed as her own, for it was in this year that the "minnicin lion" produced the work which critics of the novel consider as the most influential narrative prose between the death of Smollett (1771) and the publication of *Waverly* (1814). It presented the first careful study of provincial life and manners; pointed the way to a more penetrating and respectful treatment of peasant life; introduced the first "saga" novel into prose fiction, tracing the history of a family through several generations; and virtually established the detached narrative point of view of a minor character, viewing the material consistently from this angle. This work was to influence writers much greater than Miss Edgeworth—Scott in Scotland, Turgenev in Russia, and Cooper in America.[1] While Richard Lovell Edgeworth was away, fulfilling his duties in Parliament, his daughter remained at home and wrote the work which began the course of Irish fiction, and which has assured her of a secure place in the history of prose fiction.

Miss Edgeworth proved to be a capable representative for her country, for she had reached the mature age of thirty-three when *Castle Rackrent* was published; she had now lived in Ireland for eighteen years. During this time she had become vitally interested in all the striking peculiarities of Irish life and manners and had broadened her range of experiences by serving as her father's trusted accountant and agent. She thus obtained an insight into the lives and characters of the humble peasants on her father's estate, which she transcribed vividly into the pages of her Irish novels. She could not ignore the sordid conditions of her country—a striferidden country, which had long suffered from economic, religious, and political turmoil. She was among the hopefuls who had faith that the union of Ireland with Great Britain would result in a renewed prosperity for Ireland and a freedom from the burdens which had harassed the country since the reign of William III. Since in *Castle Rackrent* Miss Edgeworth portays Irish society largely as it was in the latter half of the eighteenth century, a brief review of the historical events and political conditions of Ireland seems essential to the understanding of the distinctive social types and curious manners found in the novel.

The basic reason for most of Ireland's disturbances was a problem both religious and political in nature—the conflict between Catholicism and Protestantism and the struggle of each for supremacy. While James II was still King of England, he had encouraged the Irish cause by making the Irish Catholic gentry sovereign in civil and military affairs; he hoped by this act to force the Protestant English settlers to accept Catholicism and the policies of his government. In 1689, he returned from exile in France, bringing with him military resources which Louis had supplied. Aside from his ambition to regain his throne, James hoped to restore Catholicism and recover Irish lands for Irishmen. But he and his followers achieved only nominal success, and with William's victory there began a long and continuous period of Catholic suppression.

The misery of Ireland increased rapidly during the eighteenth century because of its political, economic, and religious burdens. The Irish parliament had little power since it retained a position subordinate to the British parliament, a position which was reaffirmed by the Declaratory Act of 1719. The economic burdens were similar. Since Ireland was not recognized as a part of the empire, she was treated as an alien state in regard to British and imperial trade. She was impeded by numerous trade restrictions imposed by the British legislature. Her agricultural exports were forbidden entrance into Great Britain, and in 1699 her woolen industry (which promised to be a serious rival to the English) had been destroyed. Thus, the Irish market was the only outlet for Irish agriculture and industry.[2]

The question of land ownership posed a hardship of colossal severity,[3] for the greater part of Irish land was owned by absentee English landlords who carelessly and harshly administered their affairs through local agents and whose only interest in Ireland was to make money. Further hardships found expression in a code of Penal Laws which were designed to disinherit the Catholics and, as far as possible, to stamp out the Roman Catholic religion altogether. Under these laws Catholics were prevented from sitting in parliament and deprived of elective suffrage. They were excluded from any of the liberal professions. They could not own arms without a license, and they could not possess a horse of the value of more than £5. They were forbidden to have schools of their own or to educate their children abroad. They could not buy lands or hold leases for more than thirty-one years. A member of a Catholic family, by simply turning Protestant, could dispossess the rest of that family of the majority of the estate to his own advantage. In essence, the Catholic was deprived of almost every political and social right, almost every duty and privilege of a citizen.[4] The code left little hope for men of promise in Ireland. The most promising Catholic gentlemen withdrew to the mainland of Europe; two courses were open to those who remained: they could turn Protestant and become members of the privileged class, or they could hold fast to the old faith and suffer from intolerable conditions which reduced them to a status not far above peasantry.

The American War of Independence brought Great Britain to the necessity of bargaining with Ireland, and in 1780 Ireland was recognized as a state within the British Empire and given the protection and benefits of the Navigation Act policy. The Irish parliament gained nominal independence from British control with the repeal of the Declaratory Act of 1782. Although these measures were significant advances, Ireland was still plagued with economic difficulties, and Catholics were still excluded from Parliament. It was not until the Napoleonic war that the Irish took advantage of Great Britain's difficulties to seek rights hitherto denied them. The fear that Ireland might become a base for operations against Great Britain persuaded the British to come to terms. In 1800, the union of Great Britain and Ireland was accomplished. Although the Act of Union removed the most oppressive restrictions upon Ireland's trade, it did nothing to satisfy the wish of Irish Catholics to sit in Parliament.

The code of Penal Laws was the great factor in shaping the wealthy, extravagant gentry and the rebellious, lawless peasantry which Miss Edgworth describes memorably in her Irish novels. The Protestant nobility and the Catholic peasantry were the opposing extremes in the structure of Irish society, separated by a small and relatively unimportant middle class. The imprudence and apathy of the Protestant rulers were a natural outgrowth of the power, privilege and wealth thrust into their possession and made possible by the Penal Code:

> These gentry, as was natural to men in whose favor the laws were made and against whom they were scarcely operative, were a lawless class, overbearing, unused to contradiction in their domains at home and impatient of it abroad. Many of them, new to the duties and responsibilities of land proprietors, which were most trying in Ireland even to the patient and experienced, came by royal grant suddenly to great estates. Sudden accession to great possessions could not fail to stimulate and give play to all the tendencies of recklessness and extravagance so marked in the Irish upper classes. As masters, though often indulgent, they were autocratic, irresponsible, reckless, and violent, ruling their estate literally as despots, binding and loosing as they chose.[5]

The life of fashion centered in Dublin where rabble rousings, street brawls, violence, hard drinking, debt, and duelling were common occurrences in the lives of the ruling class. Hardly less striking than these incidents was the insatiable love of elegance and luxury which foreshadowed the crash that came with the Union:

> The leaders of fashion in the days of 1782 kept up princely establishments and gave entertainments on the grand scale. The court of the viceroy set the pace, and the rest were not slow to follow. The seeds of extravagance had been sown in the past by the social conditions under which many of the nobility and gentry grew up, and they flowered at this time. All seemed running a wild race to ruin, the effects of which were felt far into the following century. Coaches-and-six and coaches-and-four were plenty. These, with long rows of carriages and horsemen, made gay the fashionable drives of Dublin. But the pace was too rapid to be sustained. The Rebellion and the Union brought the revel abruptly to an end.[6]

The life of the distressed peasantry was a thing apart from this life of gay profusion and extravagance:

> The eighteenth century was for the peasant, crushed into quiescent misery by the code, a time of wretched discontent. The legal tyranny under which the peasants groaned left them, as Swift bitterly said, "hewers of wood and drawers of water to their conquerors." They were mainly cotters, sunk into extreme poverty. Cold and famine killed them by the thousands.[7]

Castle Rackrent is thus a telling introduction to the Irish squirearchy of the last half of the eighteenth century and displays with humor and pathos, mingled with wit and perception, the vices and follies that long afflicted the Irish nation. The novel is a revealing understatement of one of the great national grievances—a gentry made irresponsible by the same social conditions which reduced the peasantry to pariahs and outcasts. Indeed, Sir Patrick, Sir Murtagh, Sir Kit, and Sir Condy Rackrent take on a twofold significance: they function as characters in the action of the novel, considered as a work of art, and they are accurate historical transcriptions of a variety of distinctive social types among a gentry which flourished during the latter half of the eighteenth century.[8]

Sir Patrick represents the jovial, festive, hard-drinking country gentleman whose greatest feats were giving "the finest entertainment ever was heard of in the country" and consuming more Irish whiskey than any of his guests—"Not a man could stand after supper but Sir Patrick himself, who could sit out the best man in Ireland, let alone the three kingdoms itself."[9] His house was filled throughout each year with landed gentlemen from nearby estates who guzzled his whiskey, broke his punchbowls, consumed enormous quantities of food—who came early and stayed late, and Sir Patrick was so honored by their presence and merrymaking that he fitted out the chicken house for the overflow of unexpected guests! Finally, Sir Patrick's birthday arrived, and raspberry whiskey was an essential part of the birthday celebration—especially since Sir Patrick was the undisputed inventor of it. With a great shake in his hand, he lifted the bumper to his lips, and "died that night". It is ironic that Sir Patrick could not be present at his own funeral, an occasion more extravagant than any of those which had formed the picturesque kaleidoscope of his life:

> His funeral was such a one as was never known before or since in the county! All the gentlemen in the three counties were at it; far and near, how they flocked: my great grandfather said, that to see all the women even in their red cloaks, you would have taken them for the army drawn out. Then such a fine whillaluh! you might have heard it to the farthest end of the county, and happy the man who could get but a sight of the hearse! (pp. 5-6)

And while Sir Patrick's funeral offered an occasion for rejoicing, his body was seized for debt, with a murmur of curses from the mob as the last pathetic tribute to his memory.

Sir Murtagh, the new heir, represents a reaction to this thriftlessness among the gentry, for he is hot-tempered, selfish, and given to avarice. Hoping to gain an easy fortune by marrying into the Skinflint family, he succeeds only in becoming a frustrated skinflint himself; he inconveniently dies young in a fit of temper to leave a complacent wife, secure in her jointure. While Sir

Murtagh has his personal misfortunes, the tenants feel that his being their landlord is their greatest disaster: "The cellars were never filled after his [Patrick's] death, and no open house, or any thing as it used to be; the tenants even were sent away without their whiskey." (p. 6)

Sir Murtagh's treatment of the tenants is one of Miss Edgeworth's many examples of the evils of the Irish economic system. His merciless demands in "making English tenants of them", his "driving and driving, and pounding and pounding, and canting and canting and replevying and replevying", his seizure of the tenants' cattle which trespassed his land, his insistence on strict clauses in the tenants' leases, his enforcement of penalties, his demand for duty work—all culminate in the height of absurd injustice. The compulsive requirement of duty work must have appeared among the greatest oppressions to a peasantry, squalid and ignorant, yet capable of kindliness and great loyalty. Miss Edgeworth has explained this tyrannical custom of duty work for her readers:

> It was formerly common in Ireland to insert clauses in leases, binding tenants to furnish their landlords with labourers and horses for several days in the year . . . Whenever a poor man disobliged his landlord, the agent sent to him for his duty work, and Thady does not exaggerate when he says, that the tenants were often called from their own work to do that of their landlord. Thus the very means of earning their rent were taken from them: whilst they were getting home their landlord's harvest, their own was often ruined, and yet their rents were expected to be paid as punctually as if their time had been at their own disposal. (p. 103)

The one aspect of Sir Murtagh's character that might have saved him from total damnation is his brilliant knowledge of the law. But his attitude toward it finds expression in a daemonic love of knowledge as an instrument of power, as a means of wielding influence over his fellow beings. The simple conjecture of Thady, the old family steward, reveals a profound insight into Sir Murtagh's nature, a nature governed by misplaced ambition, while at the same time it juxtaposes a confirmed epicurean and a discerning, faithful old steward: "I made bold to shrug my shoulders once in his presence, and thanked my stars I was not born a gentleman to so much toil and trouble." (p. 10) Sir Murtagh dies just as he has lived, a symbol of corruption, and Thady's evaluation is an apt summingup of a misspent life: "Sir Murtagh in his passion broke a bloodvessel, and all the law in the land could do nothing in that case." (p. 12)

Sir Kit represents the irresponsible, gay, impecunious swashbuckler and is reminiscent of Miss Austen's villains; for Miss Edgeworth's Sir Kit and Miss Austen's John Willoughby and George Wickham all find pleasure in life by discarding scruples and candor.[10] However, while Willoughby and Wickham exist solely for their roles as villains, Sir Kit becomes the symbol of a deeply-ingrained evil in Irish society — the evil of absentee landlordism and of the serious consequences which the problem entails. With the eye of the artist, the accuracy of the historian, the experience of the observer, Miss Edgeworth sketches in the sordid details. Although old Thady is always loyal to the family, he cannot distort the truth:

> Sir Kit Rackrent, my young master, left all to the agent; and though he had the spirit of a prince, and lived away to the honour of his country abroad, which I was proud to hear of, what were we the better for that at home? The agent was one of your middle men, who grind the face of the poor, and can never bear a man with a hat upon his head: he ferreted the tenants out of their lives, not a week without a call for money, drafts upon drafts from sir Kit; but I laid it all to the fault of the agent; for, says I, what can sir Kit do with so much cash, and he a single man? but still it went. Rents must be all paid up to the day, and afore; no allowance for improving tenants, no consideration for those who had built upon their farms: no sooner was a lease out, but the land was advertised to the highest bidder, all the old tenants turned out, when they spent their substance in the hope and trust of a renewal from the landlord. All was now set at the highest penny to a parcel of poor wretches, who meant to run away, and did so, after taking two crops out of the ground. Then fining down the year's rent came into fashion; any thing for the ready penny; and with all this, and presents to the agent and the driver, there was no such thing as standing it. (pp. 14-16)

Thady relates the facts just as he remembers them.

Thus life continues at home while Sir Kit is abroad, appeasing his fondness for young ladies, watering places, and the gambling table. When payments to satisfy his indulgent appetites can no longer be extracted from the poor tenants, Sir Kit, like Sir Murtagh before him, seeks a solution to his financial embarrassment in a marriage with a rich heiress. Sir Kit's marriage is only a repetition of Sir Murtagh's failure, for his rich Jewess will not part with her diamond cross, and Sir Kit finds compatibility with his "stiffnecked Israelite" only by locking her in her room for seven years. Sir Kit resumes his old habits of sportive play while the "pretty Jessica" enjoys her diamond cross in isolation. Her illness during her confinement and a false report of her death increase Sir Kit's attractiveness as a possibility for marriage—at least, in the minds of three hopeful aspirants. Like his ancestors before him, Sir Kit lacks self-discipline and self-control, and proving a boast is as important in his topsy-turvy scale of values as any other feat. But luck plays him false, and he loses his life in a duel with the brother of one of his prospective lady-loves. Jessica, Sir Kit's rich prize,

"returned thanks for this unexpected interposition in her favour when she had least reason to expect it".

Sir Condy, described by Thady as "the most universally beloved man I had ever seen or heard of", confirms the truth that the wrong-doing of one generation lives into the successive ones. In repeating the pattern of thriftlessness and endless prodigality established by his ancestors, Sir Condy becomes the type of irresponsible Irish gentleman whose "settle it any how" and "bid 'em call again tomorrow" attitude reduces the Rackrent estate to total ruin. The fate of Sir Condy, like the fate of the Rackrent estate itself, is governed by a game of chance; a tossed-up coin determines Condy's choice of a wife, but the incident is symbolic of a series of reckless moves which bring to a climax the tragedy of four pleasure-seeking knaves and the decline and fall of an estate which had flowered with early hopes of prosperity.

Since Sir Condy is Thady's favorite among the four landlords of the Rackrent estate, over half of the narrative is concerned with the unfolding of his character and with the details of his proprietorship. Thady lingers nostalgically over his recollections of Sir Condy's childhood, and it is this love of an old man for a child, this allegiance and affection of an aging steward for a landlord, long since grown corrupt, that mark the expression of greatest tenderness in the novel:

> I remember him bare footed and headed, running through the street of O'Shaughlin's town, and playing at pitch and toss, ball, marbles, and what not, with the boys of the town, amongst whom my son Jason was a great favourite with him. As for me, he was ever my white-headed boy: often's the time when I would call in at his father's, where I was always made welcome; he would slip down to me in the kitchen, and love to sit on my knee, whilst I told him stories of the family, and the blood from which he was sprung, and how he might look forward, if the *then* present man should die without childer, to being at the head of the Castle Rackrent estate. (pp. 33-34)

Sir Condy's life is one long series of squandered opportunities. Not born to an estate, he is given "the best education which could be had for love or money"; yet he has very little knowledge of practical affairs and defiantly protests assuming even minimum responsibility for business matters. When his accession to the Rackrent estate is assured, since Sir Kit has no heirs, he foolishly accumulates debts against the estate before he ever comes into his inheritance. His failure to learn the intricacies of law and his lack of concern for economy and management make him easy prey for Jason—that shrewd, discerning, learned vulture who gloats over the carrion of Sir Condy's remains at the end of the novel. Sir Condy's marriage is more than a repetition of the marital failures of his ancestors; for whereas Sir Patrick, Sir Murtagh, and Sir Kit all married with the deliberate purpose of supplementing their fortunes and alleviating their financial embarrassments, they were at least not worsened by their choices. Sir Condy who lacks even their strength of purpose, however misguided that purpose may have been, is directed by his "devil-may-care" attitude into making a wrong choice. Isabella's family is wealthy, but because she marries Condy, her family withholds her dowry; accustomed to wealth, she is as extravagant as Condy and contributes greatly to his rapid financial decline and eventual degradation. Sir Condy's single personal triumph is the winning of a post in a general election, but it is a sad triumph for the candidate who is made a "laughingstock and a butt for the whole company". This incident is only another milestone toward the defeat of a landlord and his estate:

> My master did not relish the thoughts of a troublesome canvass, and all the ill-will he might bring upon himself by disturbing the peace of the county, besides the expense, which was no trifle; but all his friends called upon one another to subscribe, and they formed themselves into a committee, and wrote all his circular letters for him, and engaged all his agents, and did all the business unknown to him; and he was well pleased that it should be so at last, and my lady herself was very sanguine about the election; and there was open house kept night and day at Castle Rackrent, and I thought I never saw my lady look so well in her life as she did at that time; there were grand dinners, and all the gentlemen drinking success to sir Condy till they were carried off; and then dances and balls, and the ladies all finishing with a raking pot of tea in the morning. Indeed it was well the company made it their choice to sit up all nights, for there were not half beds enough for the sights of people that were in it, though there were shakedowns in the drawing-room always made up before sunrise for those that liked it. For my part, when I saw the doings that were going on, and the loads of claret that went down the throats of them that had no right to be asking for it, and the sights of meat that went up to table and never came down, besides what was carried off to one or t'other below stairs, I could'nt but pity my poor master, who was to pay for all; but I said nothing, for fear of gaining myself ill-will. (pp. 50-51)

While the creditors continue to clamor for their past-due accounts and the estate's needed repairs go unheeded, while Isabella chooses the wealth of her family rather than her marriage to Sir Condy, while Jason plans and plots and calculates the exact moment when the Rackrent estate will be his, Sir Condy increases his consumption of whiskey punch and postpones his day of reckoning. But the inevitable day of reckoning must come, and Miss Edgeworth, through the sheer accumulation of details, reveals the seriousness of Sir Condy's disaster:

> To cash lent, and to ditto, and to ditto, and to ditto, and oats, and bills paid at the milliner's and linen draper's, and many dresses for the fancy balls in Dublin for my lady, and all the bills to the workmen and tradesmen for the scenery of the theatre, and the chandler's and grocer's bills, and tailor's, besides butcher's and baker's, and worse than all, the old one of that base wine merchant's, that wanted to arrest my poor master for the amount on the election day, for which amount sir Condy afterwards passed his note of hand, bearing lawful interest from the date thereof; and the interest and compound interest was now mounted to a terrible deal on many other notes and bonds for money borrowed, and there was besides hush money to the sub-sheriffs, and sheets upon sheets of old and new attorneys' bills, with heavy balances, *as per former account furnished,* brought forward with interest thereon; then there was a powerful deal due to the crown for sixteen years' arrear of quit-rent of the town-lands of Carrickshaughlin, with driver's fees, and a compliment to the receiver every year for letting the quit-rent run on, to oblige sir Condy, and sir Kit afore him. Then there was bills for spirits and ribands at the election time, and the gentlemen of the committee's accounts unsettled, and their subscription never gathered; and there were cows to be paid for, with the smith and farrier's bills to be set against the rent of the demesne, with calf and hay-money; then there was all the servants' wages, since I don't know when, coming due to them, and sums advanced for them by my son Jason for clothes, and boots, and whips, and odd moneys for sundries expended by them in journeys to town and elsewhere, and pocket-money for the master continually, and messengers and postage before his being a parliament man; I can't myself tell you what besides . . . (pp. 68-69)

Sir Condy's death, like his marriage, is the result of a wager staked and lost. For three hundred golden guineas, he gladly signs away to Jason his last claim to the Rackrent estate. And the last of the Rackrents wagers his last guinea on the same type of feat which had caused the death of Sir Patrick, the first of his ancestors: he consumes the contents of Sir Patrick's great horn and "drops like one shot". The realization that his death is approaching arouses in Sir Condy the first flicker of self-realization during his entire lifetime: "Brought to this by drink," says he; "where are all the friends?—where's Judy?—Gone, hey? Ay, sir Condy has been a fool all his days," says he. (p. 93) Old Thady, burdened by the weighty cares of all that he has seen in the world, tired of wishing for its improvement, and almost glad that it is all over with his beloved master, utters that strange, sad, melancholic pronouncement, the grand finale to Sir Condy's life and the annals of the Rackrent history: "He had but a poor funeral, after all." (p. 93)

Thady Quirk is the most alive and complete of all Miss Edgeworth's character creations, and one critic has considered him "the most subtly drawn and skillfully presented character in the whole course of the Irish novel."[11] In his efforts to please his masters, his willingness to serve, and his obedience to duty, Thady affirms his unyielding allegiance to the lords of the Rackrent estate and to all that the estate represents.[12] His general attitude toward the family—however great their faults have been—is one of wholesome acceptance; he takes pride in recognizing the Rackrent family as "one of the most ancient in the kingdom". He is honored to have shared the family heritage, and he feels confident that the world will be as interested in each intimate detail of his narrative as he is.[13] Thady has learned early in life the wisdom of reticence, and because of his discretion he becomes the peacemaker, the friend, and the confidant to the members of the discordant households. "I said nothing, for I had a regard for the family", Thady remarks, or "I put my pipe in my mouth and kept my mind to myself; for I had a great regard for the family." The "family" has become the symbol of a way of life for Thady, and even of the iniquitous Sir Kit, Thady remarks, "I loved him from that day to this, his voice was so like the family." (p. 14)

Thady is poignantly real because Miss Edgeworth understands him completely and exposes both his inner and outer life—his inner life through the transparency of his nature, his outer life through his assertions and external manner. The author is able to identify herself with him completely, to capture the fleeting subtleties of his mind and the psychological motives of his behavior with remarkable precision. In her last novel, *Helen,* Miss Edgeworth, the teacher, converts the subject of truth into a thesis and urges the explication of the thesis as the primary goal in the novel. In her first novel, *Castle Rackrent,* Miss Edgeworth, the artist, concentrates first on creating a character, and because that character is Thady Quirk—distinct, individual, unlike any other creation—the qualities of truth, sincerity, and sobriety become indispensable requisites to his nature and are all the more appealing because they emanate from the depths of his character. "There's nothing but truth in it from beginning to end", Thady says at the close of his narrative, and his strikingly simple introduction of himself is the first of the many proofs of his assertion:

> My real name is Thady Quirk, though in the family I have always been known by no other than *"honest Thady"*—afterwards, in the time of sir Murtagh, deceased, I remember to hear them calling me *"old Thady,"* and now I'm come to *"poor Thady;"* for I wear a long great coat winter and summer, which is very handy, as I never put my arms into the sleeves; they are as good as new, though come Holantide next I've had it these seven years; it holds on by a single button round my neck, cloak fashion. To look at me, you would hardly think "poor Thady" was the father of attorney Quirk; he is a high gentleman, and never minds what poor Thady says, and having better than fifteen hundred a year, landed estate, looks down upon honest Thady; but I wash

my hands of his doings, and as I have lived so will I die, true and loyal to the family. (pp. 1-3)

Thady unhesitatingly confesses his personal prejudices; he cannot forgive Sir Murtagh's wife because he suspects that she "had Scotch blood in her veins"; yet he compliments his lady on her charity. He is proud that Sir Kit "lived away to the honour of his country abroad", but he candidly admits that business matters at home fared badly, because his master "was a little too fond of play". He dislikes his new lady, Sir Kit's wife, because she is Jewish: "Mercy upon his honour's poor soul, thought I, what will become of him and his, and all of us, with this heretic blackamoor at the head of the Castle Rackrent estate!" But he eases the tension between her and his master by explaining to her the nature and purpose of the trees, planted near the bog of Allyballycarricko' shaughlin. Thady perceives Sir Condy's folly in accepting Isabella Moneygawl rather than Judy M'Quirk as a wife; for the affected, presumptuous Isabella appears to Thady as a "mad woman for certain, which is . . . bad". But he accepts her unquestionably as his master's choice and is thankful that she is not a skinflint like Sir Murtagh's wife.

Thady's "mellow goodness", his freshness, his innocence spring from the uniformity of his temperament and an incomparable disposition to be happy with his lot in life. He would not exchange the contentment of his commonplace existence for the prestige of having been born a gentleman. Yet in his sympathy with human beings more unfortunate than he and in his capacity for pity, in his ability to negate or lose his identity in something larger than himself, he becomes heroic in stature. His sympathetic openness is most apparent in his feelings toward Sir Condy. He reprimands the creditor's agent who would interrupt the rejoicing over Sir Condy's victory in the election: "Put it [a written order for Sir Condy's arrest] in your pocket again, and think no more of it any ways for seven years to come, my honest friend . . . he's a member of Parliament now, praised be God, and such as you can't touch him: and if you'll take a fool's advice, I'd have you keep out of the way this day, or you'll run a good chance of getting your deserts amongst my master's friends, unless you choose to drink his health like every body else." (p. 53) Thady's reverence and admiration for Sir Condy and his duty toward his son create within him an acute psychological conflict when Jason is ready to force Sir Condy off of the estate: "Oh, Jason! Jason! how will you stand to this in the face of the county and all who know you?" says I; "and what will people think and say, when they see you living here in Castle Rackrent, and the lawful owner turned out of the seat of his ancestors, without a cabin to put his head into, or so much as a potatoe to eat?" (p. 73) Sir Condy must at last pay for the accumulated doom of the Rackrent generations and sign away the deed of the estate to Jason; Thady, realizing that his son takes possession of the estate because of his guile rather than because of his ability, describes the transaction with suppressed emotion:

> So he signed; and the man who brought in the punch witnessed it, for I was not able, but crying like a child; and besides, Jason said, which I was glad of, that I was no fit witness, being so old and doting. It was so bad with me, I could not taste a drop of the punch itself, though my master himself, God bless him! in the midst of his trouble, poured out a glass for me, and brought it up to my lips. "Not a drop, I thank your honour's honour as much as if I took it though," and I just set down the glass as it was, and went out; and when I got to the street-door, the neighbours' childer, who were playing at marbles there, seeing me in great trouble, left their play, and gathered about me to know what ailed me; and I told them all, for it was a great relief to me to speak to these poor childer, that seemed to have some natural feeling left in them . . . (pp. 74-75)

Thady has the incalculability of life about him, and he is never more real, never more human than in his moments of loneliness: "I had nobody to talk to, and if it had not been for my pipe and tobacco, should, I verily believe, have broken my heart for poor Sir Murtagh", a bewildered Thady remarks when the household is topsy-turvy and all is mass confusion with the accession of sir Kit. During the winter when Sir Condy is away in Dublin, attending his duties in Parliament, Thady is left alone at the estate with boards that creak, hangings that flap, winds that meet little resistance. His loneliness, which never descends into self-pity, assumes a universal quality:

> I was very lonely when the whole family was gone, and all the things they had ordered to go, and forgot, sent after them by the car. There was then a great silence in Castle Rackrent, and I went moping from room to room, hearing the doors clap for want of right locks, and the wind through the broken windows, that the glazier never would come to mend, and the rain coming through the roof and best ceilings all over the house for want of the slater, whose bill was not paid, besides our having no slates or shingles for that part of the old building which was shingled and burnt when the chimney took fire, and had been open to the weather ever since. I took myself to the servants' hall in the evening to smoke my pipe as usual, but missed the bit of talk we used to have there sadly, and ever after was content to stay in the kitchen and boil my little potatoes, and put up my bed there; and every post-day I looked in the newspaper, but no news of my master in the house; he never spoke good or bad . . . (pp. 56-57)

Thady is the one flawless product of Miss Edgeworth's creative imagination, for she was conscious of a method that directed her in his creation—a method which she adapted so skillfully to her medium that Thady's naive utterances frequently attain an eloquence that is all the more convincing because it is entirely consistent with his character. Miss Edgeworth's lengthiest comment on the composition of *Castle Rackrent* is found in a letter to Mrs. Stark, who had sent to Maria Colonel Stewart's long criticism of *Helen*. While the comment is not indicative of any clear-cut literary theory, it does intimate that Miss Edgeworth's effort was highly conscious, but not self-conscious, and it reveals an approach based on the freedom to feel and say—a liberty which Miss Edgeworth never again presumed completely in her writings:

> The only character drawn from the life in *Castle Rackrent* is Thady himself, the teller of the story. He was an old steward (not very old, though, at that time; I added to his age, to allow him time for the generations of the family). I heard him when I first came to Ireland, and his dialect struck me, and his character; and I became so acquainted with it, that I could think and speak in it without effort: so that when, for mere amusement, without any idea of publishing, I began to write a family history as Thady would tell it, he seemed to stand beside me and dictate; and I wrote as fast as my pen would go, the characters all imaginary. Of course they must have been compounded of persons I had seen or incidents I had heard; but how compounded I do not know: not by "long forethought," for I had never thought of them till I began to write, and had made no sort of plan, sketch, or framework. There is a fact mentioned in a note, of Lady Cathcart having been shut up by her husband, Mr. McGuire, in a house in this neighborhood. So much I knew, but the characters are totally different from what I had heard. Indeed, the real people had been so long dead, that little was known of them. Mr. McGuire had no resemblance, at all events, to my Sir Kit; and I knew nothing of Lady Cathcart but that she was fond of money, and would not give up her diamonds. Sir Condy's history was added two years afterwards: it was not drawn from life, but the good-natured and indolent extravagance were suggested by a relation of mine long since dead. All the incidents pure invention: the duty work and duty fowls, facts . . . [14]

The critical reader of *Castle Rackrent* wishes that Miss Edgeworth had said more. For Thady's great appeal lies in his simple charm and unconscious naivete, made possible by the artistic device of "transparency"—the ironic presentation of external fact in such a manner that the reader may see the truth underneath the external statement and draw his own conclusions.[15] Essentially, the events of Thady's narrative may be viewed from a three-dimensional level: the factual level in which the author has selected and arranged the events, typical of the world from which they are taken; the interpretative level of Thady, in which the events are filtered through his understanding; the interpretative level of the reader, who is able to see through and beyond Thady. For example, while the false report of Jessica's death is being circulated and the county speculates on three different ladies for Sir Kit's second wife, Thady remarks:

> I could not but think them bewitched; but they all reasoned with themselves, that sir Kit would make a good husband to any Christian but a Jewish, I suppose, and especially as he was now a reformed rake; and it was not known how my lady's fortune was settled in her will, nor how the Castle Rackrent estate was all mortgaged, and bonds out against him, for he was never cured of his gaming tricks; but that was the only fault he had, God bless him. (p. 27)

On the factual level, Sir Kit's being a reformed rake, his insecure financial status, and his weakness for gambling render him a complete rogue and an unfortunate marital prospect for any lady of consequence. As the statement filters through Thady's understanding, it becomes ironic understatement because of his complete failure to understand its serious implications. The reader, while he recognizes the impact of the statement, can at the same time appreciate Thady's simplicity; the plus or minus x, the unknown quality of the reader's imagination, makes up the totality of his conclusion.

Again, in denouncing Jessica for bringing only confusion to the Rackrent household, Thady proclaims: "Her diamond cross was, they say, at the bottom of it all; and it was a shame for her, being his wife, not to show more duty, and to have given it up when he condescended to ask so often for such a bit of trifle in his distresses, especially when he all along made it no secret he married for money." (p. 31) The assertion obviously un-masks the deceptive nature of Sir Kit who unsuccessfully used marriage as an instrument toward his financial salvation, while at the same time it justifies Jessica in her obstinate refusal to become such an instrument. But Thady shows no surprise at what would otherwise seem incredible, and the reader finds pleasure in the recognition of incongruities while he forms his own opinion.

In *Castle Rackrent,* Thady serves as the novel's center of vision. The point of view, then, is that of a minor character who tells the main characters' story; but Thady also functions as a character within the narrative and becomes the focal point of the interest and inspiration of the novel. Since the annals of the Rackrents are cast in the form of memoirs, with Thady acting as the author and Miss Edgeworth posing as the editor, the point of view is highly suitable for the kind of effect which Miss Edgeworth seeks to establish within this particular framework. The work is designed with no greater purpose in view than to serve "as a specimen of Irish manners and characters, which are, perhaps, unknown in England". But a faithful, realistic portrayal of such manners and characters could not present an appealing picture—a gentry, grown apathetic, irresponsible, and degenerate; a peasantry, poor squalid, and illiterate; an economic and political system grown hopelessly corrupt.

Chekov has said, "When you depict sad or unlucky people, and you want to touch your readers' hearts, try to be cold—it gives their grief a background against which it stands out in greater relief."[16] By delineating the events in the mirror of Thady's reflective consciousness, Miss Edgeworth is able to give them the appearance of bold relief and to sustain the illusion of seriousness, of heightened objectivity, which the story requires. Presenting the picture through the mellow mind of Thady also gives it a warm, glowing appeal. The expanse of life in the novel—the history of a family through four generations—is too extensive to be shown in a series of dramatic scenes. The events, then, are Thady's impressions, pictured and summarized by him for the reader.

Generally, the use of a first-person narrator imposes restrictions, both on the writer, who must reflect the world beyond and outside of his narrator, and on the reader, who is limited to the narrator's thoughts, observations, and feelings. But in *Castle Rackrent,* Thady's unique character and the very limitation of his opportunity for observation and interpretation gives unity to the story, since he provides a frame of reference for all of the events. He has had the opportunity of observing or experiencing all that is finally relevant to the story and is the one most capable of reporting the Rackrent history. Since his views are colored by his own emotional bias, and especially by his misconception of "family honor", the reader may question his ability as the chief interpreter of the events. We have seen, however, that Miss Edgeworth provides a "threefold vision" through Thady's transparency, and he thus becomes a very capable spokesman who powerfully suggests the outlying associations of events and who provides the sufficient balance of comedy and seriousness in the plot. As Sir Walter Scott has observed, "And what would be the most interesting, and affecting, as well as the most comic passages of *Castle Rackrent,* if narrated by one who had a less regard for the family than the immortal Thady, who, while he sees that none of the dynasty which he celebrates were perfectly right, has never been able to puzzle out wherein they were certainly wrong."[17]

The consistency with which Miss Edgeworth sustains the comic effect in an otherwise serious tale is one of her finest achievements. Since she chose to treat the Irish peasant seriously, and since, furthermore, she made an old peasant—crude, alien, superstitious, naive—the hero of her work, she was able to capture the distinct provincial peculiarities which puzzle, attract, and entertain the reader of *Castle Rackrent.* The comedy, then, arises from the nature of Thady's character, from the quaintness of his Irish idiom, from the strange varieties of Irish character in general, whether serious or gay, and from the tone of ironic detachment, which never changes throughout the narrative. Thady frequently prepares the reader for a scene of great sadness or hopelessness, only to neutralize the effect with a change to comedy or even farce. Instead of lingering over the pathos of Sir Patrick's death, Thady hurries on to describe the lavish funeral. Instead of paying his respects to the deceased Sir Murtagh, Thady emphasizes his eagerness to see his mistress depart from the Rackrent household. When Thady has remarked at length on the hopelessness and desolation of Sir Condy's state of affairs, he changes abruptly to Sir Condy's ambition to see his own funeral before he dies. The grimmest scene in the novel is thus followed by the scene of greatest farce:

> "Thady," says he, "all you've been telling me brings a strange thought into my head; I've a notion I shall not be long for this world any how, and I've a great fancy to see my own funeral afore I die." I was greatly shocked, at the first speaking, to hear him speak so light about his funeral, and he, to all appearance, in good health, but recollecting myself, answered, "To be sure it would be as fine sight as one could see, I dared to say, and one I should be proud to witness, and I did not doubt his honour's would be as great a funeral as ever Sir Patrick O'Shaughlin's was, and such a one as that had never been known in the county afore or since." But I never thought he was in earnest about seeing his own funeral himself, till the next day he returns to it again. "Thady," says he, "as far as the wake goes, sure I might without any great trouble have the satisfaction of seeing a bit of my own funeral." "Well, since your honour's honour's so bent upon it," says I, not willing to cross him, and he in trouble, "we must see what we can do." So he fell into a sort of a sham disorder, which was easy done, as he kept his bed and no one to see him; and I got my shister, who was an old woman very handy about the sick, and very skilful, to come up to the Lodge, to nurse him; and we gave out, she knowing no better, that he was just at his latter end, and it answered beyond any thing; and there was a great throng of people, men, women, and childer, and there being only two rooms at the Lodge, except what was locked up full of Jason's furniture and things, the house was soon as full and fuller than it could hold, and the heat, and smoke, and noise wonderful great; and standing amongst them that were near the bed, but not thinking at all of the dead, I was started by the sound of my master's voice from under the great coats that had been thrown all at top, and I went close up, no one noticing. "Thady," says he, "I've had enough of this; I'm smothering, and can't hear a word of all they're saying of the deceased." "God bless you, and lie still and quiet," says I, "a bit longer, for my shister's afraid of ghosts, and would die on the spot with fright, was she to see you come to life all on a sudden this way without the least preparation." So he lays him still, though well high stifled, and I

made all haste to tell the secret of the joke, whispering to one and t'other, and there was a great surprise, but not so great as we had laid out it would. "And aren't we to have the pipes and tobacco, after coming so far tonight?" said some; but they were all well enough pleased when his honour got up to drink with them, and sent for more spirits from a shebeanhouse, where they very civilly let him have it upon credit. So the night passed off very merrily, but, to my mind, sir Condy was rather upon the sad order in the midst of it all, not finding there had been such a great talk about himself after his death as he had always expected to hear. (pp. 77-79)

The characters all become alive and sufficiently individualized because Thady's accounts of them are unfolded through concrete, descriptive details which are supplemented by direct, vivid transcriptions of dialogue. Thady is never better than in his descriptions of the mistresses of the Rackrent estate. When Sir Condy brings his new wife Isabella to the Rackrent estate, Thady—who is already prejudiced against her—gives a sprightly, humorous review of his first impression:

> My new lady was young, as might be supposed of a lady that had been carried off, by her own consent, to Scotland; but I could only see her at first through her veil, which, from bashfulness or fashion, she kept over her face. "And am I to walk through all this crowd of people, my dearest love?" said she to sir Condy, meaning us servants and tenants, who had gathered at the back gate. "My dear," said sir Condy, "there's nothing for it but to walk, or to let me carry you as far as the house, for you see the back road is too narrow for a carriage, and the great piers have tumbled down across the front approach; so there's no driving the right way by reason of the ruins." "Plato, thou reasonest well!" said she, or words to that effect, which I could no ways understand; and again, when her foot stumbled against a broken bit of a car-wheel, she cried out, "Angels and ministers of grace defend us!" Well, thought I, to be sure if she's no Jewish like the last, she is a mad woman for certain, which is as bad: it would have been as well for my poor master to have taken up with poor Judy, who is in her right mind any how.

> She was dressed like a mad woman, moreover, more than like any one I ever saw afore or since, and I could not take my eyes off her, but still followed behind her, and her feathers on the top of her hat were broke going in at the low back door, and she pulled out her little bottle out of her pocket to smell to when she found herself in the kitchen, and said, "I shall faint with the heat of this odious, odious place." "My dear, it's only three steps across the kitchen, and there's a fine air if your veil was up," said sir Condy, and with that threw back her veil, so that I had then a full sight of her face; she had not at all the colour of one going to faint, but a fine complexion of her

own, as I then took it to be, though her maid told me after it was all put on . . . (pp. 41-42)

The skillful use of dialogue helps to reveal the characters of Thady's landlords in their roles as husbands, while it is also a telling exposure of their marital failures. The following dialogue between Sir Kit and his wife discloses the forced politeness, the incompatibility of temperaments in a union which began as a business venture for Sir Kit:

> "And what is a barrack-room, pray, my dear?" were the first words I ever heard out of my lady's lips. "No matter, my dear!" said he, and went on talking to me, ashamed like I should witness her ignorance. To be sure, to hear her talk, one might have taken her for an innocent, for it was, "what's this, sir Kit? and what's that, sir Kit?" all the way we went. To be sure, sir Kit had enough to do to answer her. "And what do you call that, sir Kit?" said she, "that, that looks like a pile of black bricks, pray, sir Kit?" "My turf stack, my dear," said my master, and bit his lip. Where have you lived my lady, all your life, not to know a turf stack when you see it, thought I, but I said nothing. Then, by-and-bye, she takes out her glass, and begins spying over the country. "And what's all that black swamp out yonder, sir Kit?" says she. "My bog, my dear," says he, and went on whistling. "It's a very ugly prospect, my dear," says she. "You don't see it, my dear," says he, "for we've planted it out, when the trees grow up in summer time," says he. "Where are the trees," said she, "my dear?" still looking through her glass. "You are blind," my dear, says he; "what are these under your eyes?" "These shrubs," said she. "Trees," said he. "May be they are what you call trees in Ireland, my dear," says she; "but they are not a yard high, are they?" (pp. 21-22)

Jason, the villain of the story, is one of the most powerfully visualized of the characters, for the reader is constantly made to feel his presence or his influence. It is fitting that he is the son of Thady, for since Thady recognizes his son's cunning and deceit, he naturally exercises great restraint in disclosing the real truth about his son. This restraint provides just the right shading necessary for the gradual unveiling of Jason's roguish nature. The last trap which Jason sets for Sir Condy is indicative of his consistent behavior pattern. Jason realizes that Sir Condy has left to Isabella a sizable jointure; when he hears that she has been involved in a serious accident, he hastily settles the jointure with Sir Condy, since he fears that Isabella may recover before this transaction is concluded. Thady describes the transaction:

> I soon found what had put Jason in such a hurry to conclude this business. The little gossoon we had sent off the day before with my master's compliments to Mount Juliet's town, and to know how my lady did after her accident, was stopped early this morning, coming back with his answer through O'Shaughlin's town, at Castle Rackrent, by my son Jason, and questioned of all he knew of my lady from the servant at Mount Juliet's town; and the gossoon told him my lady Rackrent was not expected to live over night; so Jason thought it high time to be moving to the Lodge, to make his bargain with my master about the jointure afore it should be too late, and afore the little gossoon should reach us with the news. My master was greatly vexed, that is, I may say, as much as ever I *seen* him, when he found how he had been taken in; but it was some comfort to have the ready cash for immediate consumption in the house, anyway. (p. 87)

Judy M'Quirk adds a masterly touch of irony to the story; once young and pretty and Sir Condy's favorite, she has become coarse and hardened in spirit, and her youth and beauty have fled with the passage of time. No longer interested in her former admirer once he is dying, she centers her marital aspirations on Jason, the next man in power, and thus, like Jason, is guilty of moral bankruptcy:

> "Hold up your head," says my shister to Judy, as sir Condy was busy filling out a glass of punch for her eldest boy—"Hold up your head, Judy; for who knows but we may live to see you yet at the head of the Castle Rackrent estate?" "May be so," says she, "but not the way you are thinking of." I did not rightly understand which way Judy was looking when she makes this speech, till a-while after. "Why, Thady, you were telling me yesterday, that sir Condy had sold all entirely to Jason, and where then does all them guineas in the handkerchief come from?" "They are the purchase-money of my lady's jointure," says I. Judy looks a little bit puzzled at this. "A penny for your thoughts, Judy," says my shister; "hark, sure sir Condy is drinking her health." He was at the table in *the room,* drinking with the exciseman and the gauger, who came up to see his honour, and we were standing over the fire in the kitchen. "I don't much care is he drinking my health or not," says Judy; "and it is not sir Condy I'm thinking of, with all your jokes, whatever he is of me." "Sure you wouldn't refuse to be my lady Rackrent, Judy, if you had the offer?" says I. "But if I could do better!" says she; "How better?" says I and my shister both at once. "How better?" says she; "why, what signifies it to be my lady Rackrent, and no castle? sure what good is the car and no horse to draw it?" "And where will ye get the horse, Judy?" says I. "Never mind that," says she, "may be it is your own son Jason might find that." (pp. 88-89)

Since the plan of *Castle Rackrent* called for a first-person narrator, the selection and arrangement of the details must depend upon Thady. On one hand, the method is advantageous, for it gives free sway to Thady's surmises, doubts, musings, and rambling digressions. At the same time, the method imposes few restrictions on the structure of the plot, which is loose and episodic.

The four generations of the Rackrents comprise the major episodes of the novel and are connected by the character of the narrator. The plot is more closely unified than the method would seem to permit, however, since Thady's tale is concerned with a single family estate and with four generations of *one* family. The Rackrent estate is the fixed, recurring symbol which helps to impose order, for it is indispensable in revealing character, in expediting the passage of time, and in delineating the remnants of a dying era. Its gradual downfall and deterioration over the years are a result of its mismanagement by the four generations. Consequently, in each instance, the estate is juxtaposed with its owner, whose character is unfolded in his handling of it. Over a period of years, the estate comes to symbolize a specific way of life of a family who have left their marks upon it. It also suggests a movement in time from apparent integration at the beginning to total disintegration at the end—a disintegration which is marked by the dissolution of a family unit and by the collapse of the estate itself. The death of Sir Condy, then, brings to a close the history of a family, of an estate, and of a way of life. The estate constitutes an important thematic element in the novel, for it illuminates the problems of inheritance by tying together the action of the past and present and by pointing always to the future.

The family lineage also provides unity in the plot, since the repetition of similar character traits establishes a continuous pattern; each generation recalls the reader directly to the central interest of the plot—the decay, disintegration, and final extinction of a family over several generations.[18] The similarities of Sir Patrick and Sir Condy, the first and last of the representatives, are especially significant, for they solidify into one mysterious image the "monument of old Irish hospitality".[19]

Castle Rackrent is undeniably the best evidence of Miss Edgeworth's literary merits. It is all of one texture; brisk in movement, lively in interest, filled with humor and pathos, it arouses our compassion and deepens our tolerance and understanding of a bygone age. It seizes a crucial era in the history of a nation and illuminates a world of forgotten customs and beliefs; it presents a direct impression of a people "fighting like devils for conciliation, and hating one another for the love of God".[20]

Castle Rackrent is noticeably free from all the faults which were to mar Miss Edgeworth's later works— heavy didacticism, wearisome repetitions, improbable exaggerations, elementary discussions, forced catastrophes. The most substantial and remarkable thing about the novel is the richness—the depth, complexity, and subtlety of its implications. It is therefore especially significant that Miss Edgeworth succeeded in giving the most accurate delineation of character and the most convincing expression of her country's problems in a novel which sought only the presentation of a "specimen of manners and characters". And the measure of her success is the difference between two methods— the method of statement and the method of representation. The major argument which runs throughout Henry James' prefaces to his novels is that in art "what is merely stated is not presented, what is not presented is not vivid, what is not vivid is not represented, and what is not represented is not art".[21] Instead of letting her story suggest the moral, Miss Edgeworth too often lets her moral suggest the story. But in *Castle Rackrent* she took a holiday from her duties as moral teacher, and instead of concentrating on teaching a safe and practical moral lesson, she allowed her characters to fulfill their own destinies and relinquished the duty of pointing a moral to the story itself. She made no attempt to explain human nature, but only to illuminate it. Consequently, what gives the work its ever-present air of reality is that rewards and punishments are the logical outcome of the characters' actions. Nothing is forced, nothing is wearisomely contrived, nothing is bound by the restrictions of theory or conscious moral purpose.

It is apparent, then, why Miss Edgeworth's readers from her own generation to the present day have always felt greatest affection for *Castle Rackrent*. On September 27, 1802, Miss Edgeworth wrote to Mrs. Mary Sneyd, "My father asked for *Belinda, Bulls,* etc., found they were in good repute—*Castle Rackrent* in better— the others often borrowed, but *Castle Rackrent* often bought."[22] Sir Walter Scott's warm praises of the work are well known. On one occasion he remarked, "If I could but hit Miss Edgeworth's wonderful power of vivifying all her persons and making them live as *beings* in mind, I should not be afraid."[23] In his "Preface" to *Waverly,* he generously expressed his indebtedness to Miss Edgeworth: "It has been my object to describe these persons, not by a caricatured and exaggerated use of the national dialect, but by their habits, manners, and feelings; so as in some distant degree to emulate the admirable Irish portraits drawn by Miss Edgeworth, so different from the "Teagues" and "dear joys," who so long, with the most perfect family resemblance to each other, occupied the drama and the novel."[24] And Anne Thackeray Ritchie praised Miss Edgeworth for a quality which Sir Walter Scott also possessed: "Her own gift, I think, must have been one of perceiving through the minds of others, for realising the value of what they in turn reflected; one is struck again and again by the odd mixture of intuition, and of absolute matter of fact which one finds in her writings."[25]

In *Castle Rackrent,* Miss Edgeworth drew directly from nature; only in *Castle Rackrent* was she a poet, at least in the sense in which Rupert Brooke used the term: "It consists in just looking at people and things in themselves—neither as useful nor moral nor ugly nor anything else; but just as being."

Notes

[1] Sir Walter Raleigh, *The English Novel* (New York, 1901), p. 267; Grant C. Knight, *The Novel in English* (New York, 1931), pp. 149-150; Ernest A. Baker, "Maria Edgeworth", *The History of the English Novel,* VI (London, 1935), 32; Percy Howard Newby, *Maria Edgeworth* (Denver, 1950), p. 39; Edward Wagenknecht, *Cavalcade of the English Novel* (New York, 1954), p. 138; Walter Allen, *The English Novel* (New York, 1958), p. 108.

[2] Sir James O'Connor, *History of Ireland, 1798-1924,* 2 vols. (New York, 1926), I, 40-41.

[3] O'Connor points out that three-fourths of the population at this time were Catholic; nine-tenths of the population were engaged in agriculture. Consequently, "it is to the condition of the workers on the land [that] we must look if we are to form a just conclusion as to the social and economic state of the country". See *History of Ireland, 1798-1924,* I, 8, 18.

[4] *ibid.,* pp. 48-49.

[5] Horatio Sheafe Krans, *Irish Life in Irish Fiction* (New York, 1903), pp. 2-3.

[6] *Ibid.,* p. 20.

[7] *Ibid.,* p. 21.

[8] In her "Preface" to *Castle Rackrent,* Miss Edgeworth says that "the race of the Rackrents has long been extinct in Ireland" and that her Rackrent squires "could no more be met with at present in Ireland, than squire Western or parson Trulliber in England". The statement is more accurate as an expression of the author's faith in the future of Ireland than as a comment on contemporary Irish society. She hopes that with the union of Great Britain and Ireland, her countrymen can "look back with a smile of good-humoured complacency" at the Rackrent squires of Ireland's former existence. For the relationship between Irish life and Irish fiction, see Krans, pp. 1-24; and Thomas Flanagan, *The Irish Novelists, 1800-1850* (New York, 1958), pp. 1-50.

[9] *Castle Rackrent, Tales and Novels by Maria Edgeworth,* 2nd ed., 18 vols. (London, 1832), I, 3. All citations from the works—excluding the earliest writings (considered in Ch. I), *Helen,* and "Orlandino"—are taken from this edition. Each work is initially identified in a footnote by title and volume number in the edition. Page references are subsequently given in parentheses following the quoted material. References to other sources are given in footnotes.

[10] See *Sense and Sensibility,* Chs. 29, 44; *Pride and Prejudice,* Chs. 35, 41, 46, 51, 52. Miss Edgeworth is more skillful at creating a "thoroughly bad" character than Miss Austen. Since Miss Austen's novels deal predominantly with fashionable life, the foibles of her villains are primarily departures from the accepted etiquette of the society which she creates. She obviously did not understand villains, and they rarely come alive in her hands. Miss Edgeworth's scoundrels are nearly always convincing, for the evil stems naturally from the characters themselves. Her inconsistencies in character development appear in the works after *Castle Rackrent* and arise significantly from a warping of the fable itself in order to point a moral.

[11] Krans, p. 276.

[12] In his recent study, *Maria Edgeworth the Novelist* (Fort Worth, 1967), James Newcomer attempts to refute two centuries of criticism by offering a new interpretation of the character of Thady Quirk. According to Newcomer, Thady is not the uncomplicated, sincere, and loyal retainer but rather a dissembling, crafty, and calculating villain who, in assisting his son Jason, expedites the ruin of the Rackrents. That Newcomer's judgments are false and misleading can be readily seen by placing them within the context of *Castle Rackrent.* In attempting to disprove Thady's simplicity, Newcomer states: "What are the loyalties of the man who tells us that when Sir Kit came home with his bride 'I held the flame full in her face to light her, at which she shut her eyes, but I had a full view of the rest of her, and greatly shocked I was'?" (p. 146) Newcomer does not indicate that his excerpt is incomplete. The original text continues: " . . . for by that light she was little better than a blackamoor, and seemed crippled, but that was only sitting so long in the chariot". (*CR,* p. 19) Thady is reflecting a commonly-held prejudice against Jews, a prejudice further substantiated by Miss Edgeworth's frequent preference for the Jew as villain. Newcomer insists that the "calculating mind of Thady" can be seen in his urging Sir Condy to marry Judy M'Quirk, Thady's great niece ("advancing a Quirk to the position of mistress of the estate") and that Condy, *at Thady's suggestion;* decides to flip a coin which will decide Condy's choice between Judy and Isabella Moneygawl. (p. 147) Yet Miss Edgeworth says earlier that Condy "had no liking . . . to miss Isabella" and that Thady "could not but pity [his] poor master, who was so bothered between them . . . ". (*CR,* p. 38) Condy, not Thady, decides to flip the coin, and Condy is as disappointed as Thady when the choice is Isabella. (*CR,* p. 41) Newcomer argues that the father-son relationship between Thady and Jason is conclusive evidence of Thady's guile; (pp. 147-151) but the open verbal conflicts between the two and Thady's increasing dislike for his son—near the end he says that they "have scarce been upon speaking terms" for some fifteen weeks (*CR,* p. 71)—these facts Newcomer ignores. Valid judgments cannot be derived from a reduction and a distortion of the text.

[13] Cf. John Galt's *Annals of the Parish* (1821). Galt employs the point of view of a single character much in the manner of Miss Edgeworth. An aging minister, Rev. Micah Balwhidder, is the narrator who chronicles the events of his parish from the time of his appointment until his retirement. Like Thady, he looms large in his own narrative because of his whimsicality and his humorous simplicity, which are augmented by his mellow view of life. Galt's *The Entail* (1823) is similar to *Castle Rackrent* in that it covers the fortunes of a family through several generations.

[14] *Chosen Letters,* ed. F. V. Barry (New York, 1931), pp. 243-244.

[15] The term "transparency" is used by Brander Matthews to describe Miss Edgeworth's method. See Matthews' "Introduction", *Castle Rackrent* and *The Absentee* (New York, 1952), p. xv.

[16] Cited by Newby, p. 44.

[17] *The Lives of the Novelists,* Everyman ed. (New York, 1910), p. 376.

[18] See the discussion of the four Rackrent squires, pp. 48-55.

[19] For a comparison of Sir Patrick and Sir Condy, see p. 55.

[20] The phrase is Helen Zimmern's. See *Maria Edgeworth,* pp. 74-75.

[21] Richard P. Blackmur, "Introduction", *The Art of the Novel* by Henry James (New York, 1962), p. xi.

[22] *Life and Letters,* p. 83.

[23] Samuel Austin Allibone, *A Critical Dictionary of English Literature and British and American Authors* (Philadelphia, 1886), p. 542. In a letter from James Ballantyne to Maria Edgeworth, respecting her commendation of *Waverly,* 11th November, 1814.

[24] "A Postscript Which Should Have Been a Preface", *Waverly* (Boston, 1857), pp. 367-368.

[25] "Miss Edgeworth, 1767-1849", *A Book of Sibyls* (London, 1883), p. 121.

William Howard (essay date 1979)

SOURCE: "Regional Perspective in Early Nineteenth-Century Fiction: The Case of *Ormond,*" *The Wordsworth Circle,* Vol. X, No. 4, Autumn, 1979, pp. 331-38.

[*In the following essay, Howard analyzes Maria Edgeworth's treatment of Irish issues in her 1814 Ormond. Howard demonstrates how in this novel, an increasingly larger gap between Edgeworth's own views and those of the native Irish is revealed.*]

The Romantic belief that human nature could best be observed in the life of the lower classes presented a fundamental problem to writers like Sir Walter Scott and Maria Edgeworth: as members of a higher order of society they were barred by birth and education from speaking with what the age considered the genuine voice of their region. As an Irish landowner in contact with the native peasantry Miss Edgeworth could describe their customs, dialect, and living conditions, but born and educated in England and a member of the Ascendancy she could not speak from the peasants' social vantage point or with the limited perspective which their stationary life dictated. Her early familiarity with at least two cultures and the extensive travel which broadened her experience prevented her from identifying with the peasants for whom she tried to speak. Nor could an Edinburgh Clerk of Session, in spite of his childhood familiarity with the border country, speak with much conviction for the smugglers of the Solway or the Highland drovers.

This predicament is reflected in the central characters of their fiction. Often these characters are also narrators, but they are either English, like Waverley and Mannering, and therefore only mediators between the regional characters and the reader, or such a mixture of birth and upbringing as to preclude their adopting a purely regional viewpoint (e.g., Glenthorn or Colambre). They express an attitude invariably sympathetic with, but never identical to that of the region. As long as fiction took the form of a traveller's comments on a region the narrator's point of view was transparent enough for the reader to accept its limitations, without demanding an intimate view of the common people. The value of regional fiction over geographical or anthropological documentation, on the other hand, has always been its ability to convey the human spirit of the region, the native's way of thinking, sources of pleasure, and opinion of himself in relation to the world outside. Since no peasant writer emerged—at least before Carleton began writing in 1829—to give an inside view, Scott, Miss Edgeworth, and John Galt were forced to devise a variety of strategies to overcome their inherent deficiency.

Scott takes the direct approach of identifying himself as much as possible with the peasants' attitudes and projecting the regional voice through the dialogue of peasant characters. But his elaborate attempt to establish a local point of view in the prefaces to *Tales of My Landlord* (1816) and *Chronicles of the Canongate* (1827) is never carried over consistently into the narrative technique of the two books, and neither narrator is a peasant. Occasionally, though, a character such as Chrystal Croftangry, out of touch with the region by virtue of his profligate life in cosmopolitan society, reveals a conscience which speaks obliquely for the region. Exulting in the downfall of the purchaser of his family's estate, an industrialist who had brought commerce to the area and rejected the old family house to build a modern one, Croftangry's better self reminds him "how this poor man's vanity gave at least bread to the labourer, peasant and citizen; and his profuse expenditure, like water spilt on the ground, refreshed the lowly herbs and plants where it fell. But thou! whom hast thou enriched, during thy career of extravagance, save those brokers of the devil, vintners, panders, gamblers, and horse-jockeys?"[1] More often a person like Meg Dodds in *St. Ronan's Well* (1824), a character whose sentiments are obviously those of the natives, embodies the voice of the region. Her description of the intrusion of "foreigners" which has transformed their town is typical of Scott's technique:

> My Leddy Penelope Penfeather had fa'an ill, it's like, as nae other body ever fell ill, and sae she was to be cured some gate naebody was ever cured, which was naething mair than was reasonable—and my leddy, ye ken, has wit at wull, and has a' the wise folk out from Edinburgh at her house at Windywa's yonder.... So, after her leddyship's happy recovery, as they ca'd it, down came the hail tribe of wild geese, and settled by the Well, to dine thereout on the bare grund, like a wheen tinkers; and they had sangs, and tunes, and healths, nae doubt, in praise of the fountain, as they ca'd the Well.... And so up got the bonnie new Well, and down fell the honest auld town of St. Ronan's, where blithe decent folk had been heartsome eneugh for mony a day before ony o' them were born, or ony sic vapouring fancies kittled in their cracked brains. (*Waverly Novels,* XXXVIII, 40-41)

The rest of the novel presents a regional view of fashionable life by juxtaposing the two communities in a single location. Scott reveals a significant innovation in his attempt to convey regional attitudes, here, because much of his message is contained in the simple structural device of juxtaposition rather than outright statements by regional characters. Unfortunately this innovation came at the end of his career.

In most of his work, Scott attempted to convey what I have called the "voice" of the region, a more or less direct statement of the attitudes and opinions of the region as a distinct entity. A study of *St. Ronan's Well* or many of John Galt's novels, however, reveals that this term is not adequate to describe such complex techniques as juxtaposition, irony, and context which were also used to communicate native attitudes. It is even less useful for describing Maria Edgeworth's work. Her attempt to convey a relatively consistent regional outlook, which would supersede not only the level of individual characters but also her own cosmopolitan bias, leads her to adopt techniques which can best be collected under the term "regional perspective." By this concept I mean the perception, through the prism of a set of values which the author identifies with a particular region, of modes of life and ideas current outside its boundaries. Whereas "voice" indicates direct statements by a character, "perspective" implies a bias contained in the organization and texture of the novel which, through contact of various kinds with other views of life, makes an indirect comment either on itself or, more often, on that which it is observing. As such it can be conveyed through a multiplicity of individual points of view, but is distinct from narrative point of view in that it exists independently of the predominant position of either the author or his narrator. To a certain extent it is governed by reality outside the fictional world, since it must relate to the actual values prevalent in a real geographical area; therefore it need not always be approved by the author or by all the regional characters in the book, although it reflects attitudes which the author has not been able to ignore. It may not even add up to a logical conclusion by the end of the novel, but it is an element of the work to which the reader will often be called upon to respond. In short it is a spatial corollary to the "time" perspective in historical novels where life in a particular era is examined through eyes conditioned by life in another age.

Maria Edgeworth employs a number of techniques which enable her to present more realistically the opinions and attitudes of the native Irish without either approving of them or trying to pass them off as her own. They do not enable her to speak for the peasantry, any more than Scott's sympathy with his peasants enables his characters to speak precisely with the approval of contemporary peasants, but they do liberate her from the necessity of imposing overmuch the Ascendancy view of Ireland. She tackled the problem of point of view as early as her first novel, *Castle Rackrent* (1800), by creating a peasant narrator to relate the Rackrents' story in the first person. Thady's success as a character, however, was not matched by his ability to assert the multifarious attitudes of that part of Ireland. He was too strikingly individual; his extreme loyalty to the family and his personal eccentricities impaired his value as a regional spokesman. Although the obvious discrepancy between his view and the author's did allow Miss Edgeworth to convey something of the ambivalence which resulted from her position in Ireland, her life was too far removed from his to assimilate fully the social and racial biases which a story direct from John Langan himself would have instinctively expressed. Consequently, she turned to an aristocratic narrator in *Ennui* (1809) and an omniscient one in her remaining Irish novels. But her abandoned experimentation with a limited point of view did not rule out a quest for more subtle methods of transmitting regional attitudes. *Ormond* proves that.

The regional perspective in *Ormond* (1814) is revealed initially through the carefully wrought intrigue of the opening chapters. The scene is a party at the country home of Sir Ulick O'Shane, a local gentleman of never quite specified position in Irish national affairs, who now finds himself out of work "by the change of ministry" ([1972], p. 5; all references are to this edition). Emanating from the conversation of the party is a sense of impending danger which gradually emerges to dominate the evening's activities. Sir Ulick's third wife, chosen by her husband "from necessity, for money, at five-and-forty" (p. 4), sets the tone of the chapter with her English prejudices: "She dreaded Irish disturbances much, and Irish dirt more; she was persuaded that nothing could be right, good, or genteel, that was not English. . . . Her experience had been confined to London life, and in proportion as her sphere of observation had been contracted, her disposition was intolerant" (p. 5). As the evening progresses the gaiety of the party is threatened by repeated tremors of anxiety, especially Lady O'Shane's fear that the gates "ought to be locked! There were disturbances in the country" (p. 15). The eventual arrival of Sir Ulick's son, Marcus, and ward, Harry Ormond, both covered in blood from a violent encounter with a local peasant, finally exposes the undercurrent of hostility and paranoia that has existed in the scene to this point. Lady O'Shane's attitude to life outside Castle Hermitage is shared by Marcus—"insolent to his inferiors, especially to his Irish inferiors" (p. 265)—and is emphasized by the cause of the recent fight. Begun as a simple dispute over the right of way on a country lane, the argument soon escalated to vague charges from Marcus that "all the Carrolls were bad people—rebels" (p. 20), and to some reciprocal "expressions about tyranny" (p. 20) from Moriarty Carroll, the local peasant alluded to by Marcus. Ormond's consequent, though accidental, shooting of Moriarty launches the plot of the novel, just as the verbal sparring that preceded it offers the most concrete indication of the state of the neighborhood.

The establishment point of view in this scene is that of the world Maria Edgeworth knew intimately, Ascendancy life on a rural Irish estate, but by her construction of the scene she draws our attention to the perspective of the surrounding natives. The undertone of anxiety is not only a reflection of Lady O'Shane's paranoia, but an acknowledgment of the true regional perspective on her husband's style of life. And it forces the reader to contemplate that outside view without, save for the brief reference to tyranny, direct verbal statement from any of the regional characters. The tension is conveyed by the situation, the locked gates at the big house and the volatility of a chance nocturnal encounter on the road, rather than by any direct statement about the feelings of the native people. Moreover, Lady O'Shane's English-based prejudice is not the issue; nothing more is made of English-Irish

prejudice in the novel and the lady herself soon vanishes. It serves the more immediate function of illustrating the lower class's propensity to judge those above them. Their opinion is important not because it accords with the author's beliefs—it often does not—but because the activities of people like the O'Shanes are only understandable when viewed in relation to those of others who inhabit the same environment. This reference to the collective expression of a geographically defined group of people is one ingredient which distinguished the early regional novel from its predecessors.

The remainder of the first half of *Ormond* is dominated by the contrasting characters of Sir Ulick and his cousin Cornelius O'Shane. The difference is of personality—the urbanity and ambition of Sir Ulick distinguished from the eccentricity and self-sufficiency of Corny—and of conflicting relationships to the people in their region. Sir Ulick considers "the necessity of keeping up a neighbourhood, and maintaining his interest in the county, as the first duties of man" (p. 6). He needs local support to maintain his position in Dublin, and he subordinates both his regional and natural responsibilities to "the improvement of his fortune and the advancement of his family" (p. 6). His character embodies traits which Richard Lovell Edgeworth viewed with contempt in his remarks on the role Edgeworth played in the debate surrounding the Irish Act of Union:

> I might have obtained a seat in the imperial parliament, and might have dedicated the remainder of my life to what is fondly called the good of my country; or which, under this name, is often meanly pursued, *the advancement of my family and fortune.*

> I now feel most sincerely grateful to Providence, for having given me sufficient prudence and resolution, to resist these temptations, to follow a different course, to cultivate my estate, to improve my tenantry, and to educate my children.[2]

This statement, dictated to his daughter at the time she was submitting sections of *Ormond* to him as she wrote them, reflects the major character division contained in the novel. It also explains Miss Edgeworth's gradual desertion of the initially affable Sir Ulick as he manifests more of the exploitation her father scorns.

On the other hand, King Corny of the Black Islands remains a regionally oriented character. Much has been written in praise of his superbly drawn eccentricity, but Maria Edgeworth herself considered him more than just a carbon copy of an "oddity" she knew: "Not one word I ever heard said by the living man, or had ever heard repeated of his saying, except 'Drop what you have,' etc., went into my King Corny's mouth—would not have suited him. I was obliged to make him according to the general standard of wit and acuteness, shrewd humour and sarcasm, of that class of *unread* natural geniuses, an overmatch for Sir Ulick, who is of a more cultivated class of acute and roguish Irish gentlemen."[3] He is also an extreme example of what Mr. Edgeworth's document was, in a milder form, advocating. Living in isolation from the national scene, Corny concentrates on the cultivation of his estate, the "improvement" of his tenantry, and the education of his child. But even his conviviality and popularity with the natives, not to mention his casual adherence to Catholicism, cannot mask the fact that his methods of cultivation rely on "a mule, a bull, and two lean horses" (p. 67); that the improvement of his tenantry is restricted to handouts of food and a surfeit of drinking, riding and shooting; or that the education of his daughter consists of reluctantly sending her to a dancing master on the mainland.

In another and more essential way the two men are different—Sir Ulick, a political animal, possesses the "capability of adapting his conversation to his company and his views" (p. 3); Corny is a man of almost absurd adherence to his own word. Considerable emphasis is laid on oaths and resolutions in the Black Islands section of the novel, especially on Ormond's rather fragile vows of personal improvement and Corny's promise to give his daughter in marriage to the son of an old drinking companion. The emphasis is not accidental; it is the major attribute of the primitive life in this area which is not shared either by Sir Ulick and the national set, or later by the fashionables of Paris. We laugh with the author at Corny's persistence—"No; my word is passed—when half drunk maybe, but no matter; it must be kept sober. Drunk or sober, a gentleman must keep his word" (p. 56)—but we recognize it as the expression of a rural faith in a man's word which accompanies his suspicion of legal documents, banks, and politicians. Here as elsewhere Corny speaks for the region while Ulick is busy trading off its interests as his own.

These contrasting characters are brought together in a verbal sparring match which is unsurpassed in Maria Edgeworth's writing and would do credit to many a greater writer. "A sort of single combat," she calls it, "without any object but to try each other's powers and temper, . . . in which the one on the offensive came on with a tomahawk, and the other stood on the defensive parrying with a polished blade of Damascus" (p. 64). The argument takes place while Corny is mending the toy whistle of one of his dependents, a fact which is lost on neither of the combatants. The country cousin is trying to force the other to "woodcock," to inadvertently disclose his real reason for expelling Ormond from Castle Hermitage, but he takes the opportunity to inflict as much pain as possible in the process. As they argue Corny continues to work on the whistle, reducing all the while the importance of prize cattle, jobbery, and sundry other topics to the level of that

ignominious toy. He speaks for the regional values in this scene, though not always for Miss Edgeworth's, and his personal limitations in such comments as "my jobs, good or bad, have cost my poor country nothing" (p. 69), are also the limitations of the region: isolated, feudal, and noncontributory to the national good. But the whole scene has been utilized to point out from a regional perspective the short-sightedness of Sir Ulick's unbridled desire for national recognition. Quite apart from Corny's direct statements in the dialogue, this perspective is supported by the context in which the dialogue takes place. In Corny's domain, which is also an integral part of Ulick's native region and heritage, the Dublin oriented political hack resembles a fish out of water. His weaknesses are cruelly exposed. In the end not only of this scene but of the novel itself, he "woodcocks," exposing the sordid reality of his principles to his astounded erstwhile admirers.

The antithesis revealed through character is also embodied in the geography of the region. Because the region, an area of the central plateau surrounding Lough Ree and including the islands in the lough, is the first of Maria Edgeworth's Irish settings to be specifically named, we can assume that its location is crucial to her purpose. Situated in the geographical centre of Ireland, it is where we would expect to find the heart of its traditional and national life as well as the communications hub of its commerce. Instead we find a region which is neither Gaeltacht, nor Pale, neither industrial nor commercial; an area combining the primitive life of the Black Islands with the somewhat urbane but inconsequential life of Castle Hermitage. In short, it is an area waiting for a future. And Ormond's auspicious entry at the end of the whistle scene reminds us not only that he is the current toy of the two cousins, but that he represents the chance of reconciling the extreme inclinations they embody. If, as Ian Watt says of eighteenth-century fiction in *The Rise of the Novel* (1972), "triumph in the big city has become the Holy Grail in the individual's secular pilgrimage" (p. 204), Ormond and others like him reverse the trend in the nineteenth century by combining experience gained in their metropolitan visits with preference for regional life.

Meanwhile Sir Ulick's visit to the Black Islands is followed by that of Black Connal, one of a large number of characters in the novel who have rejected the regional way of life, either for national politics like Sir Ulick, English life like Marcus, or French society like Miss O'Faley, Corny's sister-in-law, "that thing, half Irish, half French, half mud, half tinsel" (p. 310). By inserting this representative of Parisian society into the context of regional life Miss Edgeworth extends the examination of civilized values through a regional perspective which Corny had initiated in the previous scenes.

The regional voice is apparent in Sheelah's comment on Connal's birth—"French! Sure Black Connal's Irish born, . . . that much I know anyway"; the regional perspective is continually suggested by different views we are given of the pseudo-Frenchman in a variety of situations. Briefly we see him through the eyes of a servant boy, as M. Connal talks on at the table, "sure of the applause of mademoiselle, and as he thought, secure of the admiration of the whole company of natives, from *le beau pere,* at the foot of the table, to the boy who waited, or who did not wait, opposite to him, but who stood entranced with wonder at all that M. de Connal said, and all that he did; even to the fashion in which he stowed trusses of salad into his mouth with his fork, and talked through it all" (p. 157). We are later informed of *le beau pere*'s opinion of his future son-in-law—"all he says that way is in the air, no substance . . . too full of himself, that youngster, to be a friend to another" (p. 177)—and we can imagine the waiting-boy's view from the deftness of the painting in the above scene. The final brush stroke, that last phrase, deflates what Connal interprets as respect for the content of his thought into a small boy's fascination with the stranger's ability to talk with his mouth full.

The technique throughout this section is especially interesting because it seems to separate the perspective of the region itself from that of its principal character, Ormond. While Ormond and Corny, as well as Sheelah and Moriarty, often speak with the voice of the region, several of the scenes are constructed to show the fallibility of their personal view and the independence of the regional outlook from both their personal, and the author's omniscient, view. A good example is Ormond's lengthy and highly entertaining metaphysical *tête a tête* with Connal:

> "Each nation has its taste. Everything is for the best in this world for people who know how to make the best of it. You would not think, to look at me, I was so philosophic; but even in the midst of my military career I have thought—thought profoundly. Everybody in France thinks now," said M. de Connal, taking a pinch of snuff with a very pensive air. . . .
>
> "That is to say, of your rank?" said Ormond.
>
> "Nay, I don't give myself as an example; but you may judge. I own I am surprised to find myself philosophising here in the Black Islands; but one philosophises everywhere."
>
> "And you would have more time for it here, I should suppose, than at Paris."
>
> "Time, my dear sir? No such thing! Time is merely an idea . . ." (pp. 168-9).

Ormond's naivete in this scene is partially regional innocence of cosmopolitan affairs but it is primarily personal, since it does not correspond to the no-nonsense attitude of other regionals like Corny or Sheelah. On the other hand, the fact that Connal misses Ormond's one comment on the virtues of a regional life as he launches into another philosophical monologue does not remove the validity of its presence. The artificial "thinking" of fashionable French society is belied by the simple reminder of the natural pace of life in a rural setting and by the refreshing simplicity of Ormond's approach to things.

That Miss Edgeworth's view also diverges from the regional perspective is evident in more than one instance in this scene. Although she disapproves of characters such as Connal, for example, she uses him to express those of her own thoughts which are based on experiences which regional characters generally lack. In opposition to Corny's satisfaction with isolation in the region, and in spite of her distaste for Connal's egocentric personality, she agrees with his criticism of the circumscribed perspective often advanced by regional characters: "You will lose this little *brusquerie* of manner, . . . when you have mixed more with mankind. We are all providentially dependent on one another's good opinion. Even I, you see, cannot live without yours" (p. 175). As subsequent events show, an enlarged view of life is her prerequisite for an enlightened life in the region. Eventually even Corny is converted to the idea of travel as a means of educating Ormond; though before his scheme can be activated, he is killed in a hunting accident.

With Corny's death the first movement of the novel ends. The regional perspective has been conveyed through the contrast of the two major characters as well as through the incongruity of the fashionable Connal in the context of Black Island society. The regional voice has been expressed by King Corny at times, by Ormond, Sheelah, or Moriarty at others. In addition, though, we have been given other indications of the way in which the region perceives events and characters. We are told directly by the author, for example, what the region would have thought about Ormond's riding and hunting exploits which are "to this hour recorded in the tradition of the inhabitants of the Black Islands" (p. 106), but we are not allowed to confuse this admiring view with the author's: "to be popular among the unknown, unheard of inhabitants of the Black Island: could this be an object to any man of common sense?" (p. 79). We can detect in these details a desire to convey the regional view of life as an independent entity, a collective attitude which more often than not corresponds with that of the author, but which at increasingly important junctures is left to stand on its own.

After Corny's death Sheelah speaks for the region when she justifies the mode of mourning and burial for their departed monarch: " 'Tis the custom of the country, and what else can we do but what the forefathers did?

How else for us to show respect, only as it would be expected, and has always been? And great comfort to think we done our best for him that is gone; and comfort to know his wake will be talked of long hereafter, over the fires at night, of all the people that is there without; and that's all we have for it now; so bear with it, dear" (p. 196). Funerals play an important part in Maria Edgeworth's fiction because they are a dramatic way of indicating the judgment of characters from a collective point of view. They act as a final demonstrable ballot in which the creatures that share a person's life are called upon to give their judgment. Corny is buried in the tradition of his ancestors and, as Sheelah notes, in the hearts of those who knew him. Popularity among the peasants of the Black Islands is not one of Maria Edgeworth's criteria of greatness, but it is a fact of her regional perspective, which she presents as an independent assessment of her characters.

With Corny's burial we move into the second half of the novel, dominated not by a great character contrast as the first was, but by the personal development of Ormond and the simultaneous decline of Sir Ulick. Critical attention to this novel has underlined the influence of *Tom Jones* and *Sir Charles Grandison* on the formation of Ormond's character and stressed the relationship between the Edgeworths' educational theories and the delineation of his character; the regional content of the novel substantiates these findings by demonstrating the role of personal experience on his maturing mind. When the author acknowledges her dual purpose near the end of the novel by implying "that the mind is a kingdom of yet more consequence than even that of the Black Islands" (p. 400), she is also admitting the role of geographically orientated experience in his development. His eventually admirable qualities of mind are the product of his contact with several different cultures and they reach their culmination when he returns to the Black Islands. But for all the theory in the first part of the book, the isolation of regional life has left Ormond very little improved at the death of his mentor. His experience with the resolution-prone Corny has "practised and strengthened" his resolution, but resolution is a "quality or power of mind totally independent of knowledge of the world" (p. 231). What is added in the second half of the novel is a determination to improve himself not so much by the making and keeping of vows, but by widening his horizons through travel, not "merely to see the world, but to distinguish himself in it" (p. 232).

He now exchanges his inside view of the region for an outside one, gaining a new insight into the public character of Sir Ulick and the achievements of King Corny. Thus, "after a day or two's journey from Castle Hermitage, when he had got beyond his own and the adjoining counties" (p. 245), he hears of Sir Ulick's reputation in the country at large. He fights a duel in Ulick's defense only to be rebuked by Sir Ulick for his

naivete. Thus apprised of the narrowness of his regional view of life, his veneration of Ulick as the most important man in the region and the area's major link with national affairs is shaken; from the national perspective the finest man in the region is nothing more than a petty jobber—"pay by the job, you have his vote" (p. 248). The emphasis of the novel is beginning to turn away from the virtues of regional life to an appraisal of its weaknesses, such as the parochialism that enables Sir Ulick to maintain his position, and the narrow perspective that stationary life in the region fosters.

As the emphasis shifts, Ormond becomes less reliable as the voice of regional values. Each addition to his experience points out the need for an even wider perspective, and the destruction of many of his naive attitudes only proves the limitations of his early education. This process is accentuated by his acquisition of a private fortune which strengthens his ambition and elevates him socially above the bulk of regional characters. Conversely it offers him the opportunity to see more of the world and to observe regional life in an enlarged context. As his connections with the region wane, therefore, the role of perspective replaces that of the direct regional voice. A series of literary devices ensures that the reader sees events and manners from a regional vantage point even when the wayward hero fails to.

The major device, a pattern of imagery, is established just before Ormond's visit to Paris and provides a frame of reference to which his activities there are to be related. The central image arises out of Ormond's observations on the west coast estate of Sir Herbert Annaly. Here he finds a profligate tenantry whose chief activity is the deliberate destruction of passing ships and the theft of their cargo: "The best of the set were merely idle fishermen, whose habits of trusting to their luck incapacitated them from industry; the others were illicit distillers, smugglers, and miscreants who lived by waifs and strays—in short, by the pillage of vessels on the coast. The coast was dangerous; there happened frequent shipwrecks, owing partly, as was supposed, to the false lights hung out by these people, whose interest it was that vessels should be wrecked" (p. 273). Sir Herbert has employed a group of his tenants to construct a permanent lighthouse in the area to eliminate the practicability of these artificial lights. The scene would merely illustrate the capacity for an understanding landlord to improve his peasantry if it were not for the complex of ideas which Miss Edgeworth creates around the lighthouse image. Sir Herbert's words to Ormond in this scene, for example, have implications beyond their immediate meaning. When he tells Ormond not to "trust to outward appearances too much" (p. 300), he is referring to the misleading evidence of his physical appearance in relation to his decaying health, but it is a theme that persists throughout the scene.

Ormond's ensuing gullibility when trying to search out the contraband from a shipwreck which occurs shortly thereafter, merely reinforces its larger application.

This motif recurs in a similar, though subtler, test of Ormond's powers of discrimination. In the shipwreck scene Miss Edgeworth had introduced another aspect of Sir Ulick which was related to the "false lights" image. Unlike Sir Herbert, Ulick "was the man to live under; he was the man that knew when to wink and when to blink; if he shut his eyes properly, sure his tenants filled his fist" (p. 274). As a party to their plunder his offer to handle Ormond's affairs on his departure for Paris is ominous for Ormond's financial security. An echo of the peasantry, "whose interest it was that vessels should be wrecked," can be heard in the description of Sir Ulick, "seizing precisely the moment when Ormond's mind was at the right heat, aiming with dexterity, and striking with force, [he] bent and moulded him to his purpose" (p. 317). Accordingly Ulick makes a great show of "proving that all was exact" in their accounts and of placing Ormond under his gratitude before assuming control of "a large sum which Ormond had in the English funds" (p. 318). Direct judgment is suspended here, but more will be heard of Sir Ulick's false lights later.

Ormond proceeds to Paris where the full impact of the shipwreck image is exploited. Initially the reader is reminded of it in the figurative language used to describe Ormond's first impressions of the French scene, impressions which are carefully manipulated by M. de Connal. Connal's purpose is "only to win all the young man's fortune at play" (p. 328), and his method is to incite Ormond to remain long enough in Paris to squander his money at a faro bank in which Connal has a substantial stake. In order to win Ormond's fortune at the gaming table, Connal lures the young Irishman with the magnificence of Parisian life. He shows him the Hotel de Connal, the salon of which is "blazing with lights, reflected on all sides in mirrors, that reached from the painted ceiling to the inlaid floor" (p. 328). He allows Ormond to "take a fancy to madame" (p. 328), by encouraging a revival of Ormond's childhood affection for her. Finding her "shining in the salon" (p. 331), and "blazing with crosses and stars" (p. 330), Ormond is "dazzled by the brilliancy of Dora's beauty" (p. 328). This emphasis on light extends to Connal's introduction of Ormond to Versailles, also: "well might the brilliancy dazzle the eyes of a youth fresh from Ireland, when it amazed even old ambassadors, accustomed to the ordinary grandeur of courts" (p. 341). But in all this Connal "did not seem to have any design upon Ormond" (p. 331). Like Sir Ulick, he is skilled at wrecking ships.

Eventually the image begins to emerge from the almost casual language of physical description into distinct metaphors. Faced with the danger of succumbing to Dora's charms, for example, Ormond "sought for safety in a course of dissipation" by vowing to meet her only in crowded assemblies (p. 343). In a similar image, Connal describes Ormond's social success: "I give you joy, . . . you are fairly launched! You are no distressed vessel to be taken in tow, nor a petty bark to sail in any man's wake. You have a gale, and are likely to have a triumph of your own" (p. 343). Likewise he concludes that Ormond "seemed to be quite in his natural element in this sea of pleasure" (p. 344). Little does he realize the accuracy of his appraisal. Not a "petty bark to sail in any man's wake," Ormond demonstrates—in a society where vows of any kind have been shown in incident after incident to be mere formalities—that the principles gained from contact with the firm resolution of King Corny are capable of protecting him from unsuspectedly false lights wherever he goes. He sticks to an oath never to gamble beyond his pre-established limit as firmly as ever Corny stood by one of his arbitrary resolutions. The result of Ormond's action in the Parisian context reinforces the reader's confidence in the regional values of the early part of the book. His strength of mind—the phrase is a favourite with the Edgeworths—indicates more than simply personal maturity; it implies, since it is particularly associated in this novel with Ormond's native region, a Black Island commentary on the society which attempts to subvert personal integrity.

And the imagery provides a non-rational, non-argumentative, but omnipresent, touchstone of regional values in a society far removed geographically from the Black Islands. It enables the author to sustain her intended contrast in the reader's mind even at times when her only regional character is temporarily distracted. The lighthouse image, applied equally to what we often consider the savage and uncivilized and to what represents the epitome of sophistication, reveals a message which the hero often fails to recognize himself. We see that deception in a wealthier, more genteel, society is only another manifestation of the same human frailty usually condemned only in more primitive living conditions. Because Ormond never fully appreciates his danger in Paris, he never applies his same condemnation of the west coast Irish pirates to that society. The reader, with the aid of explicit imagery, is left to do that for himself.

On Ormond's arrival in Ireland, "the first news he heard . . . was that Sir Ulick O'Shane was bankrupt" (p. 382). Even here the shipwreck image continues to embody Sir Ulick's treatment of Ormond, his neighbours, and the country at large. It surfaces in the language of a rumour that "an estate had been made over to Marcus, who would live in affluence on the ruin of the creditors" (p. 383). In effect Sir Ulick has been a national false light, luring creditors onto the rocks of his own bankruptcy. "It was a public calamity, a private source of distress, that reached lower and farther than any bankruptcy had ever done in Ireland" (p. 382). As Ormond walks the streets of Dublin, then travels the road to Castle Hermitage, he is confronted with the public view of Sir Ulick's deception: "His house in Dublin, fit for a duke! Castle Hermitage full of company to the last week; balls, dinners, champagne, burgundy! Scandalous!" (p. 383)—and not a penny for those who trusted him with their investments. In contrast to the national outcry, however, the attitude of those in his own region who had also lost money in the crash, is a more forgiving one. A cottager living on the hill overlooking Castle Hermitage, for example, inquires of Ormond, "did you hear it?" cried she, "and the great change it caused him—poor Sir Ulick O'Shane" (p. 385). This sympathy with one of their own is a regional trait which supersedes the misdemeanors of people like Sir Ulick, though it is not sufficient to blind their final judgment.

The voice of the region speaks on two important occasions at the end of the novel. Perhaps their vioce does correspond with the author's when they pass judgment on Sir Ulick by avoiding his funeral—"this was considered by the country people as the greatest of all the misfortunes that had befallen him; the lowest degradation to which an O'Shane could be reduced" (p. 389). She almost certainly approves of their assessment of the relative merits of the two O'Shane cousins: " 'See the difference,' said they, 'the one was the true thing, and never changed; and after all where is the great friends now? . . . See, with all his wit, and the schemes upon schemes, broke and gone, and forsook and forgot, and buried without a funeral, or a tear, but from Master Harry' " (pp. 389-90). But it is doubtful that she fully endorses the region's view in this case. The reclusive policy of King Corny is as detrimental to the region as the constant yearning for power outside the region that motivated his cousin. The people have always admired Corny, but Maria's approval of Sir Herbert Annaly could not accommodate all of Corny's practises.

On the second occasion, we can be certain that the neighborhood speaks independently of the author. Ormond's decision to settle in the Black Islands is greeted by the people and by Miss Edgeworth from antithetical motives: "For the Black Islands he had a fondness; they were associated with all the tender recollections of his generous benefactor. He should hurt no one's feelings by this purchase; and he might do a great deal of good, by carrying on his old friend's improvements, and by further civilizing the people of the islands, all of whom were warmly attached to him. They considered Prince Harry as the lawful representative of their King Corny, and actually offered up prayers for his coming again to reign over them" (p. 399). Maria Edgeworth's admiration for the Annalys, combined with her disapproval of mere popularity with the lower classes, places her in agreement with Ormond's reforming tendencies. On the other hand she

recognizes in the attitude of the people themselves a desire for a return to the days of King Corny. By the end of the novel they speak an independent mind, not one that is admired by the author, but one that she recognizes as a fact of life nevertheless. The frequent divergence of perspective in the novel acknowledges the difference between the cosmopolitan and Ascendancy view of regional life and the view which people isolated and stationary in their own habitat express.

Ormond is Maria Edgeworth's best novel. It transcends her society novels because it places the equivalents of Lady Delacour, the brilliantly conceived character in *Belinda* (1801), into a multi-level social structure in which their foibles are demonstrated to have repercussions beyond their own insulated sphere. Miss Edgeworth was never at her strongest when depicting love plots, and society novels without love intrigue have little to offer. On the other hand her painting of the milieu in which these actions take place was her forté. In the last of her Irish novels she portrayed it with a greater complexity of vision and a deeper understanding of regional issues. Such is her honesty that she depicts the gap between her own perspective of regional life and that which is firmly entrenched in the regional mentality. Thus the novel ends not with the sentimental ambivalence of *Castle Rackrent* or the facile optimism of *Ennui* or *The Absentee,* but with the hint of a finely tuned conflict awaiting the reforming hero as he returns to the region where his own dissipation is recorded in local tradition. Unlike Glenthorn and Colambre, Ormond has been presented as a human hero, capable of weak-minded fascination with what the author considers trivial, and capable of total immersion in the hedonistic revelry of King Corny's court. But he is also capable of maturing in the course of the novel beyond the one-dimensional conversion of Glenthorn and the consistent virtue of Colambre.

Perhaps it is no accident that Maria Edgeworth wrote no other regional fiction after *Ormond*. Her father, a moving force behind most of her fiction, died a few days before its publication and she found it difficult to write fiction of any kind after his death. But when she did return to writing it was to non-regional work. No doubt her comment that *Helen*'s (1835) lack of Irish character was due to the harshness of realities was part of the explanation, as we can see from the differing conclusions to *The Absentee* and *Ormond*. Larry's letter at the end of the earlier work expresses the confidence of the peasantry that Colambre's return will benefit them, but it also implies that they welcome the opportunity of an "improved" life. By the end of *Ormond,* however, the peasants are welcoming a continuation of the primitive existence they had experienced under King Corny. Maria Edgeworth was realizing more and more the gap between her own views and those of the native Irish. She saw little evidence in real life of the reforming landlord she advocated in her fiction.

Notes

[1] Sir Walter Scott, *The Waverley Novels,* 48 vols. (1848), XLI, 47.

[2] *Memoirs of Richard Lovell Edgeworth,* 2 vols. (1969), II, 444. (R. L. E.'s italics).

[3] Augustus J. C. Hare, *The Life and Letters of Maria Edgeworth,* 2 vols. (1894), II, 252.

Colin B. Atkinson and Jo Atkinson (essay date 1980)

SOURCE: "Sydney Owenson, Lady Morgan: Irish Patriot and First Professional Woman Writer," *Eire-Ireland,* Vol.XV, No. 2, Summer 1980, pp. 60-90.

[*In the following essay, Colin B. Atkinson and Jo Atkinson review the Irish novels written by Sydney Owenson, Lady Morgan, and demonstrate how Morgan's work was typical of that of the new and growing body of professional women writers. At the same time, the critics point out that Morgan, unlike her contemporaries, combined in her novels feminist and Irish patriotic themes, while establishing both personal and social success.*]

A Biographer wrote of Julia Kavanagh (1824-1877), an Anglo-Irish author, that "in her twentieth year she returned to London, and adopted literature as a profession."[1] A great distance separates Julia Kavanagh from Aphra Behn (1640?-1689), the first Englishwoman to wrest a living from writing. How much society and women and literature had to change before a woman could simply choose to be a professional writer, and before a biographer could mention that decision so casually! In the 18th century, it was only extraordinary women who, as Eliza Haywood (1693?-1756) put it, would "exchange the needle for the quill." Some were in desperate need of money; others had had a superior education and encouragement.[2] But it was not until the beginning of the 19th century that one may properly speak of professional women writers, and even then they were far different from their male contemporaries. Nor were they a homogeneous group: there were those who did not need to earn money, such as Fanny Burney; there were the "journeywomen," who wrote what would sell; there were the teachers, the propagandists, and the early professional women writers. Few made large amounts of money, but many did well enough: Charlotte Smith (1749-1806) supported ten children by her novels and Felicia Hemans (1793-1835) educated five sons with her poetry.[3]

One of the most fascinating was Sydney Owenson, later Lady Morgan (1776-1859). While not completely forgotten like most of her contemporaries, largely because of her influence on both Irish politics and the Irish novel, she is the epitome of the woman writer of this period. Lionel Stevenson called her "the first successful professional woman author—the first to ride to social, intellectual and financial prestige entirely through her business-like exploitation of her literary talent."[4] During the most active part of her writing career, from 1800 to 1840, she published some 70 volumes, including verse, nine novels, a comic opera, two travel books, one biography, several collections, a history of women in the ancient world, part of an autobiography, and numerous articles, pamphlets, and feuilletons.

The emergence of these early 19th-century professional women writers was the result of a number of social forces in the 18th century which overcame, or helped women to overcome, the hostility or the patronizing of the literary establishment. The significance of Lady Morgan's achievement can only be seen in the context of the rise of women writers and their increasing awareness that they could and should write not merely "women's books" but books on any topic that a man might choose. In the development from the "exceptional," like Aphra Behn, to the "ordinary" professional writer, like Julia Kavanagh, Lady Morgan and her sisters of the early 19th century are pivotal figures.

Women were never welcomed into the writing profession. As the popular but rakish novelist Eliza Haywood wrote in 1725:

It would be impossible to recount the numerous difficulties a Woman has to struggle through in her Approach to Fame: If her Writings are considerable enough to make any Figure in the world Envy pursues her with unweary'd Diligence; and if, on the contrary, she only writes what is forgot, as soon as read, Contempt is all the Reward her Wish to please excites; and the cold breath of Scorn chills the little Genius she has, and which, perhaps cherished by encouragement, might, in Time, grow to a Praise-worthy Height.[5]

One hundred years later, Charles Lamb called "clever" women "impudent, forward, unfeminine, and unhealthy in their minds," and said of the writer Letitia Landon that,

if she belonged to me I would lock her up and feed her on bread and water till she left off writing poetry. A female poet, or female author of any kind, ranks below an actress, I think.[6]

Yet, in spite of constant disapprobation, throughout the 18th century women continued to enter the writing profession. They would not have done so had not certain changes come about during this century. There was a great expansion in the number of readers of both sexes, especially those who did not have a classical education and whose reading needs therefore differed from those of the upper-class men whose requirements had largely dominated literature.[7] Literature had been written by men from their own experiences and education, from both of which women were largely excluded.[8] The education of girls of all classes, both in theory and in practice, had always lagged far behind that of boys. It was not till the Restoration that it can be said with certainty that all girls of the middle and upper classes could read and write, and Dr. Johnson remarked at the "amazing progress made in literature by women" because in his youth "a woman who could spell a common letter was regarded as all accomplished."[9]

The birth in 1740 of the circulating library, its rapid growth, the increase in the number of women writers and readers, and the better repute of the novel all coincided:

> In general the low repute of fiction and of women who wrote it reinforced each other. Not until, in 1740, the novel had been raised to respectability by Richardson, and not until respectable women novelists achieved fame—Sarah Fielding, Charlotte Lennox, and Fanny Burney—were the two respectabilities joined.[10]

Under the impetus of this changing audience, the novel developed, a form which did not require a classical education or wide experience either to read or to write. Women seized upon it and had a large share in its growth and direction. Thus, they scrambled to a toehold in the masculine world of letters, for "Though history itself has only grudgingly accommodated the aspirations of women, literary history has moved through a series of emancipations and expanding fields of conquest."[11] As the number of women writers increased, the proportion of the desperate, the rakish, and the educated "lady" among them decreased. The male criticism, both literary and personal, altered as well: from a mixture of condemnation of her audacity and wonder at her capacity, gentlemen critics grudgingly began to make room for the woman writer, though it would be decades before the writer who happened to be a woman found reasonable acceptance.

At first the room made for her was a special province, a ghetto of sensibility, in which she was thought to excel. Critics would comment on her excellencies, or shortcomings, in these limited areas, those of domesticity, love, religion, and morality.[12] As a gentleman admirer said to Anna Maria Porter (1780-1832), a successful author of novels which taught "universal purity,"

> So dedicating female talents . . . is fulfilling the end for which they were bestowed; a peculiar Christian duty, lady, in your sex, when so endowed; a grateful debt to that religion, which alone has elevated woman again to that station which she had lost by the fall.[13]

Women, it was acknowledged, were especially fitted to handle these themes:

> Women in general have a quicker [social] perception [which] . . . partly arise[s] from the restraints on their own behavior, which turn their attention constantly on the subject, and partly from other causes. The surface of their minds, like that of their bodies, seems of a finer texture than ours; more soft, and susceptible of immediate impression. They have less muscular power—less power of continued voluntary attention,—of reason—passion and imagination. . . . They learn the idiom of character and manner, as they acquire that of language, by rote merely, without troubling themselves about its principles.[14]

Some women, of course, tried to stay within their allotted areas; for many, their narrow experiences and education made impossible any attempt to go beyond. A few, while remaining within, made everything outside seem almost coarse, but there were not many Jane Austens. Women had many different reasons for writing, but few wrote without diffidence, without some qualms; all were well aware of the disapproval that surrounded them. Their writings were most acceptable when they wrote to instruct the young, or from poverty, preferably to support families. What Sarah Fielding (1710-1768) wrote in the preface to *David Simple* (1744) was equally true 75 years later: "Perhaps the best Excuse that can be made for a Woman's venturing to write at all, is that which really produced this Book: Distress in her circumstances: which she could not so well remove by any other Means in her Power."[15] And it should be noted that Sarah Fielding wrote for children.

So long as women remained within their sphere, reviewers treated them as "ladies," and a certain language of gallantry was often affected. If, however, they ventured beyond into, say, the political realm, they were attacked, often viciously, especially if the critic were on the other side. Political discussions were considered "subjects too grave for a female pen . . . ,"[16] because "We cannot allow them strength of mind, deep reasoning powers, nor, in every instance, that firm solid judgement found in the other sex."[17] Most men felt it would be better if women did not write at all: their true sphere was the home. As late as 1850, an article in *The Leader* expressed the opinion of many:

> It is a melancholy fact, and against all political economy, that the group of female authors is becoming every year more multitudinous and more successful. . . . Wherever we carry our successful pens we find the place preoccupied by a woman. How many of us can write novels like Currer Bell, Mrs. Gaskell, and fifty others, with their shrewd and delicate observations of life? What chance have we against Miss Martineau, so potent in many directions? Women have made an invasion of our legitimate domain; they write dramas, they write treatises; . . . . This is the march of mind, but

where, oh, where are the dumplings? Does it never strike these delightful creatures that their little fingers were meant to be kissed, not to be inked? Women's proper sphere of activity is elsewhere. Are there not husbands, brothers, friends, lovers to coddle and console? Are there no stockings to darn, no purses to make, no braces to embroider? *My idea of a perfect woman is one who can write, but won't.*[18]

However, women writers would not stay in their special province. They could not be prevented from intruding into male dominions. For example, Jane Marcet (1769-1858) published her first book, *Conversations on Chemistry . . . Especially for the Female Sex* in 1806 and continued the *Conversation* series for forty years. Her most popular was *Conversations on Political Economy* (1816), which gave Harriet Martineau (1802-1876) the idea of writing her *Illustrations of Political Economy* (1832-1834), a series which made her one of the most influential people of her time.[19] Such women could not accept the limited subjects assigned to them, the very subjects which men often considered demeaning.

Aiding these "uppity women" was the feminist consciousness that had been growing throughout the 18th century, particularly during the last three decades. The American and French Revolutions; the theoretical and actual breakdown of hierarchies; the questioning of religion, which held women responsible for the fall of humanity; the numerous books on the rights of man; and Mary Wollstonecraft's *Vindication of the Rights of Women* (1792) all served to broaden the interests and understanding of many women, and men. Increasingly, women and their place in the world became an important topic of discussion:

> Wollstonecraft's radicalism, however, makes only one end of the spectrum of opinion that colors the writings of the self-conscious women of her day. In the 1780's, 1790's, and 1800's, feminism touched them all, from those who supported to those who opposed its doctrines, with all the range of possible attitudes (including apparent indifference to controversy) that is between: the elitism of Mme de Staël, the Evangelicalism of Hannah More, the conservatism of Maria Edgeworth, the cautious prudery of Fanny Burney, the pedagogical hauteur of Mme de Genlis, the Americanism of Susanna Rowson, the escapism of Mrs. Radcliffe, the irony of Jane Austen.[20]

George Lillie Craik wrote in 1847 that "everybody is aware of the racket that has been kept up on this subject in our own day and every since the breaking out of the French Revolution,"[21] but the "racket" had only increased—it had not begun then. For several centuries the *querelle des femmes* had amused or angered French and English writers, both hack and serious, with women only rarely entering the battle. But from the time of Mary Astell's *A Serious Proposal to the Ladies, for the Advancement of Their True and Greatest Interest* (1697), women became less defensive about championing their own sex and increasingly addressed themselves to other women. The consciousness of women that they were unfairly subordinated was old; what was new was a vague but growing idea—on the part of some members of both sexes—that something could and even ought to be done to change the situation. This can particularly be seen in the novel:

> Upon every aspect of the question of the relations of the sexes there is a significant difference in the attitudes of the men and women novelists. The men (except for Richardson . . .) incline to take male opportunism and irresponsibility as normal manifestations of male character. But from Mrs. Haywood down to Mrs. Inchbald, Mary Wollstonecraft and Amelia Opie . . . women's subservient and often humiliating role is presented by women writers with increasing resentment. At the end of the century even the serious men novelists—Bage and Godwin, for example—contend not only for political and legal equality for women, but for everyday decency in the treatment of wives and daughters. . . . [22]

Attitudes toward women were changing in the early 19th century; the place of women in the social world was being discussed with seriousness. There was no "women's movement" in our sense, in any sense, except perhaps during the French Revolution.[23] But there was "widespread dissatisfaction with the condition of women that found various expression in satire and in sober counsel, in theoretical arguments, practical proposals, and practical action."[24] Patricia Meyer Spacks finds a "'special female self-awareness' that makes of every woman writer in every age a member of an unconscious sisterhood."[25] While the statement may be exaggerated, it is born out by such critics as Ellen Moers.[26]

It was not only writers who were affected. The end of the 18th and the beginning of the 19th centuries was a period when women were greatly influential in many areas of English life; they affected the aristocracy in their salons and the middle classes through their writings on education, religion, economics, and politics, as well as their fiction. Working-class women were also changing: industrialization and the egalitarian ideas of the time were irrevocably altering their lives, and many became involved in the radical political movements.[27] Women of all classes became increasingly aware of their subordination: "Before men could be expected to recognise that women had a point of view of their own, it was necessary for that fact to be brought home to women themselves."[28] And it was the women writers who brought the fact home to women, and to many men as well. Women wrote most of the light literature, the novels, the verse, the children's stories, that other women read. Literature was the only field for a woman of talent and ambition, even if her talent was not for writing. As Harriet Martineau wrote, "I want to be doing something with the pen, since no other means of action in politics are in a woman's power."[29] Many others acted on this concept, as well, and bookshops were full of women's efforts to instruct in all sorts of fields. Henry Crabb Robinson, however, was puzzled by this:

> How strange it is, that while we men are modestly content to amuse by our writings, women must be didactic! Miss Baillie writes plays to illustrate the passions, Miss Martineau teaches political economy by tales . . . and Miss Edgeworth is a schoolmistress in her tales.[30]

Crabb Robinson was not alone; few people understood the changes that women were going through. We now know that the Women's Rights Movement did not begin in the latter 19th century with the agitation for the vote. No such movement could have taken place without the changes of the earlier decades, especially without the professional women writers, whose contributions to the emancipation of their sex fill the first four decades of the 19th century.

In these decades the professional woman writer came into her own—her opportunities increasing, her fields expanding, all by her own efforts. The first decade began splendidly with the publication of *Delphine* (1803) and *Corinne* (1807), both of which influenced women writers for the rest of the century.[31] Madame de Staël (1766-1817) was concerned above all with political, moral, and social ideas. She believed that literature had "ceased to be a mere art; it had become a means to an end, a weapon in the service of the spirit of man."[32] Like Harriet Martineau, she used her books as political weapons; like Hannah More (1745-1833), the "bishop in petticoats," she was a propagandist. And she was, all through her turbulent career, well aware of the difficulties of being a woman writer. In 1800, in *Literature Considered in Its Relationship to Social Institutions*, she wrote that "the entire social order . . . is arrayed against a woman who wants to rise to a man's reputation,"[33] and in *Delphine* and *Corinne* she showed the tragic lives of women who possessed superior abilities in a society which punished them. No woman writer was quite the same after reading Mme de Staël, and her influence was as great in England as on the Continent. Lady Morgan, who was delighted to be occasionally referred to as "the Irish Corinne," and who loved to meet great women, just missed knowing her, and wrote, "I thus was prevented from seeing one of the most distinguished women of the age; from whose works I had received infinite pleasure, and (as a woman, I may add), infinite pride."[34]

The second decade saw the beginning of the remarkable prison ministry of Elizabeth Fry (1780-1845), whose book *Observations on . . . Female Prisoners* was published in 1827. The decade ended with the sensational trial for adultery of Queen Caroline (1820). Few women were unmoved by the queen's position; it caused the daughter of Mary Wollstonecraft to change her name from Mary Shelley to Mary Wollstonecraft Shelley, the form she retained for the rest of her life. James Mill's article on government in the *Encyclopedia Britannica* (1820)—in which he dismissed the need of women's direct representation in a democratic government, since they were represented by husbands or fathers—was a further stimulant, along with the agitation, at the end of the decade, about the Reform Bill.

The 1830s were a decade of great importance to women. On the extreme left, radicals in France and England challenged their subjection.[35] Journals began to publish large numbers of articles on various aspects of the Woman Question, and they took a share in the work for the Reform Bill:

> We may say that the general public first began to think seriously on the matter [women's rights] after the epochmaking Reform Act of 1832. This celebrated measure admitted £ 10/- householders to the right to vote and carefully excluded females; yet it marked a new era in the awakening of civic consciousness: women had taken active part in the attendant campaigns; and the very fact that 'male persons' needed now to be so specifically designated in the bill, whereas hitherto 'persons' and 'freeholders' had been deemed sufficient, attests to the recognition of a new factor in political life.[36]

In the working classes, women were active among the Chartists, and the first Charter of Rights and Liberties (1838), included female suffrage as one of the demands. And, in 1837, a woman ascended the throne which "provided feminism with exactly the sort of glaring anomaly that Englishmen so often need before an argument is felt to have any practical force."[37]

The unfortunate life of Caroline Norton (1808-1877) summed up much of woman's wrongs. The beautiful granddaughter of Richard Brindsley Sheridan, she had made an unfortunate marriage with a younger son in 1827. Though she had been writing since childhood, it was "her husband's ungracious reminders that she had brought him no fortune"[38] and a lack of money for her first confinement that began her long, successful career as an author. From 1829 onwards she poured out verses and novels, but it was her pamphlets which changed English law and English women. Her husband sued her for adultery with Lord Melbourne in 1836 and lost, but he first claimed her earnings and then removed her three sons, both of which were his legal rights. She began a campaign for the rights of a mother, beginning in 1837, and in spite of the usual outcries from Parliament and the conservative journals that the family and England would be destroyed, her agitation led to the passage of the Infants' Custody Act (1839), which permitted, but did not require, a judge to assign children under seven to the mother, when she was innocent.[39] The discussions of this question, and other pamphlet agitations of hers, extended and reinforced those on the Reform Bill.

Mrs. Norton's custody fight was greatly helped by her fame as a writer. Indeed, it was Harriet Martineau's belief that the ablest advocates of women's rights would be the successful professional women writers. And, if few of these women are known or read today, if some even border on the unreadable, yet they had much influence in their own time both on literature and on history. They broke through more barriers than they even knew existed. One such woman, Anna Jameson (1794-1860), a prolific writer on many subjects, published her *Characteristics of Women, or Shakespeare's Heroines* in 1832:

> To women readers . . . it had more than a literary appeal; till then most critics had taken it for granted that Shakespeare, like themselves, thought women's characters less important than those of men. Anna Jameson put forward a different opinion.[40]

An important circle grew up around Mrs. Jameson; it included Lady Byron and Julia Smith—the latter aunt to both Florence Nightingale and Barbara Leigh Smith (later Barbara Bodichon), both leaders in the next generation of feminists.

The professional woman writer of the early 19th century often had a greater impact on her contemporaries than those who preceded and followed her. She enjoyed an audience which was larger and more receptive to new ideas about women than her predecessors, and she had the advantage of some novelty, without all the difficulties of being a pioneer. Yet, she also had freedom to experiment that later generations did not have. The new genre of annuals and most of the verse were largely hers; the journals' anonymous articles were open to women; and the novel was one field in which the woman writer could and did exist equally with men. Modern readers have seen far better works, and the novels of this period, with a few exceptions, will strike them as "too long, too didactic, a little too stiff in style, a little too puritanical, a little too commonplace, or in a word, a little too uninteresting." Yet, with these long-forgotten creations that many women earned a decent living, and changed history in a small way.[41]

The professional woman writer of the early 19th century neither belonged to a bluestocking circle nor lingered in a garret. She was more visible, not only socially, but in her dealings with the new publishing houses, which had replaced subscription publishers.[42] For an enterprising woman, with even slight talent but much perseverance, for one who could learn to bargain with publishers, to "hustle" and to "puff," it was perhaps an ideal time. Sydney Owenson, Lady Morgan, was just this sort of woman. She is both typical of these new professional women writers and unique in her successful fusion of feminism, Irish patriotism, and personal and social success.

Sydney Owenson was never the lady dilettante. She wanted financial success and prestige, and was proud when she had achieved them. Her childhood experiences with poverty made her determined to be financially independent and, after a short period as a governess, she became a writer. Several years and novels later, she wrote a best seller, and from then on "the indomitable energy and indefatigable industry which characterized her"[43] kept her successful. She wrote:

> I am sick of the jargon about the idleness of genius. All the greatest geniuses have worked hard at everything—energetic, persevering, and laborious. . . . Nothing but mediocrity is slothful and idle.[44]

A woman who felt strongly about everything, and who threw herself into whatever she did, she wove the two guiding passions of her life: the wrongs of Ireland and the importance of women in the history of the world, into virtually everything she wrote. Proud of her efforts, she said in old age to a younger writer:

> I know I am vain, but I have a right to be so. . . . I wrote books when your mothers worked samplers, and demanded freedom for Ireland when Daniel O'Connell scrambled for gulls' eggs among the wild crags of Derrynane.[45]

The forms and settings of her novels often anticipated later literary fashion, as did many of her political beliefs. Long before Harriet Martineau, Sydney Owenson recognized the power inherent in the pen of a politically minded woman, and was attacked viciously for her championing of Ireland and her outspoken liberal opinions. She never regretted her adherence to what were often considered radical ideas. In 1836, after recovering from delirium, she wrote in her diary:

> How my head worked! what books I wrote! what plans I laid. . . . But did I recant one opinion? Not one! I thought I should have died, and yet repeatedly said to myself, had I the sorry battle of life to fight over again, I should just take my old ground![46]

Her last major work was *Woman and Her Master* (1840), though several volumes of memoirs, some pamphlets, and a revised novel were later published. There would have been far more, but serious eye problems prevented her from the hard work she had always done. But she did not just fade away: a great lover of and giver of parties, she entertained friends on her eighty-second birthday, in 1858, with the rendition of a ribald song in Dublin slang, "The Night before Larry Was Stretched." A few months later she died, after whispering to her devoted maid, "Put just a touch of rouge on my cheeks; one might as well look one's best at the last."[47] Her memoirs came out shortly before she died, and the *Atheneum* wrote of her:

> Praised by Byron, traduced by Croker, petted by . . . La Fayette, and spoiled by the whole Whig aristocracy, Sydney, Lady Morgan has lived through the love, admiration and malignity of three generations of men. A literary Ninon, she seems as brisk and captivating now as when George was Prince . . . , and the author of 'Kate Kearney' divided the laureateship of society and song with Tom Moore. As she then sang she still sings. Some harps seem never worn and never out of tune. . . . This faculty of liveliness and good humour is as strange as it is admirable in one whose long life has been a succession of siege and storm. In her youthful time Lady Morgan was less a woman of the pen than a patriot and partizan. Her books were battles. . . . Through more years than we care to say, her name was a sign among the combatants, her voice sounded a trumpet through Whig and Tory camps, and a new book from her hand drummed a host of friends and enemies to arms. She wrote, too, in an age when to be a woman was to be a[n Irish] patriot was to be a criminal.[48]

Her early life prepared her for independence. She was born in Dublin on Christmas, 1776, to an improvident Irish actor and a devoutly Protestant English mother who had never reconciled herself either to Ireland or the stage, and who died when her daughter was twelve. The unsentimental Sydney later wrote: "My Mother! there is something infinitely dear and tender in that name, and though all mothers may not be equally dear and tender, still it is the declared intention of Nature that they should be so."[49] None of her heroines have mothers; all the early ones have close, even protective relationships to their fathers, and the later ones have no parents at all. Her heroines become increasingly independent with each novel. Some years later, Florence Nightingale observed that the "secret charm" of novels was that "the heroine has *generally* no family ties (almost *invariably* no mother), or, if she has, these do not interfere with her entire independence."[50] The combination of the exigencies of the stage and her father's cheerful fecklessness brought the family to poverty and debtors' prison. Sydney Owenson grew up desiring to "be *somebody* and to place herself *somewhere*. . . ," as the *Atheneum* later put it.[51]

Until she was twelve, her education was haphazard. Her father brought home various instructors who never lasted long, until he finally literally picked up Thomas Dermody, a ragged street beggar of about fourteen, who later became a poet. He taught Sydney and her younger sister to read and write. After their mother's death, the girls were sent to a strict Huguenot boarding school, where they studied foreign languages, geography, arithmetic, drawing, and music. A short period and another boarding school completed the girls' slight formal education, but Sydney never ceased to study on her own.

Her name was often linked, and not only by the *Atheneum,* to that of Tom Moore. They were both physically very small, about the same age, and both were adopted by a Whig aristocracy which found them entertaining. Moore played the piano and sang his songs; Sydney Owenson played the Irish harp, sang old Irish airs, and danced Irish jigs. Both made a good living as professional writers, and it is instructive to compare their educations. Although Moore's father, a grocer, was far more financially secure than was Sydney's, that is not the major reason for the differences in their education. Tom Moore was educated to fit him for the world of politics, literature—the world of men. Sydney Owenson was, in effect, excluded from the learning and the intellectual discipline that would have aided her career immeasurably.

Tom Moore went early to a good elementary school until he was six, and then to an excellent grammar school, whose headmaster loved poetry, music, and the stage. There Moore had a through grounding in Latin and Greek as well as French and Italian. He entered Trinity College, Dublin, where he was a member of the Historical Society, founded by Edmund Burke, which had at various times virtually every brilliant student as a member. He was surrounded by fellows and tutors who appreciated and wrote contemporary literature. From there he went to the Middle Temple, and at every step he made friendships which helped him greatly in his later professional life.

Tom Moore had an excellent education, especially when it is considered as a preparation for a writing career. Sydney Owenson would have profited by the same, for though a classical education was no longer a necessity for readers or writers, yet the overall training, the discipline, the opportunities for friendships, the broader scope, would have enabled her to have made greater use of her talents. Though her writing style improved over the years, it was seldom felicitous and occasionally turgid. "An early nineteenth century reviewer once remarked that women writers must possess more than ordinary talent, since they could produce such excellent work without having benefited from a classical education."[52] And Sydney Owenson wrote, without comment, of a dinner party which Moore attended, where he

> declaimed against the spread of knowledge and the diffusion of cheap literature, as destructive to wit and talent . . . ; above all, he said, the unclassical and uneducated people meddling with literature

(Gad-a-mercy, fellow!), and the dilettanteisms of the age were destroying genius. . . . He exclaimed bitterly against writing-women, even against the beautiful Mrs. Norton. 'In short,' said he, 'a writing-woman is one unsexed;' but suddenly recollecting himself, and pointing at me, said to my sister, 'except her,' (me), ... [53]

Financial independence was a major concern and a major theme in Sydney Owenson's work. It was against her father's wishes that she decided to earn her living as a governess. He tried, without her knowledge, to get a patron to take care of her. She was angry and humiliated: "She told him plainly she would rather support herself honestly by teaching than be the dependent of a patron."[54] From that time on she took over the direction of her family, which included her sister and their old nurse as well as her father. Though the two or so years she spent as a governess were good ones—she was treated as a member of the family and remained friends with her employers—the difficulties and uncertainties of a woman earning a living occur in nearly all her novels. In *Woman, or, Ida of Athens* (1809), a young Greek girl finds herself penniless in England, responsible for the support of two young brothers and an aged father, but "she was so totally a stranger to the manners of the country . . . that she knew not in what way the talents of women could contribute to her subsistence, and support."[55] Ida can, of course, embroider, and she spends her last money on fancy materials only to find her handiwork of no use in earning a living. Though Sydney Owenson made her own clothes and had contempt for women who could not sew, she detested the "busywork" taught to girls, and in one novel she described it contemptuously: "Cloth fruit and filagree baskets, daubed velvet and paper card-racks, French mottoes and English devices, with all the industrious arts which bad taste supplies to unoccupied mediocrity. . . ."[56] Though Ida was saved by an unbelievable manipulation of plot, her later heroines work as governesses, artists, and writers, and almost all have difficulties at some point. In her last novel, *The Princess, or, the Beguine* (1834), the heroine tries to find work as a governess:

Helpless, hopeless, with none to vouch for or to recommend her, her talent and acquirements availed her nothing. Still she strove to work her way to an honest subsistence. But in that most humiliating, that only line open to female industry, which unites all that is confidential in trust with all that is servile in position,—her very appearance was against her. . . .[57]

Years later, having achieved success in several ways, but particularly as an artist, Sydney Owenson rejects the "tardy liberality" from the family which had wronged her, and writes the most satisfying answer:

You will offer me (as to a poor relation) some certain means of existence for the future. The past renders it impossible that I should accept of such tardy liberality; the present leaves it unnecessary for me to do so. I am as wealthy as yourself; for my means are equal to, and even beyond, my wishes. They are within myself, a faculty which the world can neither give nor take away.[58]

Sydney Owenson firmly believed what she wrote in her best-selling *The Wild Irish Girl* (1806), that "happiness is to be purchased, and labour is the price; fame and independence are the natural result of talent united to diligence. . . ."[59] But there were those who felt that such independence was unbecoming to a woman. William Hepworth Dixon, her friend and literary executor, wrote:

She was a courageous, indomitable spirit; but the constant dependence on herself, the steady concentration of purpose with which she followed out her own career, without letting herself be turned aside, gave a hardness to her nature, which, though it did not destroy her kindness and honesty of heart, petrified the tender grace which makes the charm of goodness. No one can judge Sydney Owenson, because no one can know all the struggles, difficulties, temptations, flatteries, and defamation which she had to encounter, without the shelter or support of a home, or the circle of home relatives. She remained an indestructably honest woman; but every faculty she possessed had undergone a change, which seemed to make her of a different species to other women.[60]

In later years she would insist that every girl should be trained to do something well, something which could serve to earn her a living.

Her early writing career is shaped by her independent spirit. After a conventional start, she soon began embodying her Irish patriotism in her novels. She had begun by publishing a volume of verse by subscription, the usual method of young women:

Given . . . the smallest modicum of the 'gift of song,' as it was the fashion then to call it, you could safely decide to be a poet. And if you happened to catch the public ear, you could make quite a decent living. You wrote poetry to order, you supplied it by the yard. You engaged, as "L.E.L." and Mrs. Norton did, to furnish a dozen or more poems to accompany the drawings. You edited Annuals, and you could reckon quite safely upon a substantial yearly sum.[61]

But Sydney Owenson ventured into other territory; the only poetry she published after the first were two volumes of Irish melodies and translations in 1805 and 1807.

Inspired, she later said, by reading of the financial successes of Fanny Burney, she used her free time while a governess to write two novels. The first, *St. Clair; or, First Love,* appeared in Dublin in 1803 and in London the following year. It had a lively heroine, different from the current fashion of languishing ladies, and showed her enthusiasm for Ireland's scenery, legends and history. *The Monthly Mirror* pronounced it "the production of a man of distinguished abilities. . . ."[62] Like many women writers, she concealed her authorship at the beginning. Some continued to do so, like Jane Austen; Sydney Owenson, however, soon signed her own name to her work. Her first novel was sufficiently successful to encourage her to continue, and she published *The Novice of Saint Dominick* in 1805. Set in 16th-century France with a resourceful heroine who has heroic adventures disguised as a troubador, the novel is really about Ireland:

> The praises of Provençal minstrelsy, and the elaborate account of how the language and culture of Provence survived in definance of oppression, could be transferred to Ireland by any alert reader. The sufferings of the poor, under a system of absentee landlordism, were shown with similar insinuation. Even more prominent was the insistence on the evils of a religious antagonism which filled otherwise admirable people, Catholics and Protestants alike, with prejudice, hatred, and vengeance, leading to the horrors of civil war. The eloquent pleading for tolerance and cancellation of ancient feuds had as much relevance to contemporary Ireland as to France of two centuries before.[63]

In 1806 she published *The Wild Irish Girl,* a best seller and the most famous of her books. With it Sydney Owenson achieved her desired fame, fortune, and social acceptance, which remained hers for the rest of her long and active life. *The Wild Irish Girl* was two different novels, depending on the audience. To the English reader, it was a romantic tale, the story of a young Englishman sent over to his father's Irish estate to study. There he gradually falls in love with a mysterious, brilliant, beautiful Irish girl, the daughter of a proud and eccentric old aristocrat now virtually a pauper. To the Irish reader, the romance was between the young Protestant, the son of an absentee landlord, who gradually falls in love not simply with the heroine but with Ireland, in the person of Glorvina, an Irish princess, daughter of an ancient house which lacks material goods but is wealthy in tradition, learning, music—all that Ireland once had and lost, but faintly remembers. In this, as always, the author was thoroughly professional: she did her research. She studied everything she could find on Irish music, history, archaeology, costume, ornament, legend. All of these she introduces to the reader, in the footnotes if not in the text, so that the English may learn that Ireland is not merely a land of illiterate and brutish peasants and pigs, and that the Irish may recall their ancient heritage. At the end, the romance satisfactorily dealt with, the author pleads for a union of sympathy and understanding between the two countries, the two religions, and asks that all landlords live on their estates to improve them.

The Irish reader accepted the book "as a political document," while "Dublin Castle marked her down as an enemy and the enemies of Dublin Castle acclaimed her as a valuable ally."[64] Both the novel and the author became immensely popular; *The Wild Irish Girl* went through seven editions in two years in England and several in the United States. Sydney Owenson, with her newly purchased harp and black cloak, which became her trademarks, was called Glorvina and accepted as a species of Wild Irish Girl in the salons of the Whig aristocracy. Thus, the romance achieved all of her aims, giving her money and fame, giving the English reader "a sympathetic interest in Ireland's plight," and giving . . . "first form to the rhetoric of Irish nationalists."[65]

A book of essays on Ireland appeared next, followed by two poorly received novels in 1809 and 1811, one set in Greece and the other in India. She returned to Ireland for *O'Donnell, A National Tale* (1814). It was another best seller, not as romantic as *The Wild Irish Girl,* with considerable humor and satire. The heroine is a governess who later reappears as a duchess, and the hero a poor Irishman whose rightful estates belong to another. The plot is involved but meagre, and the best character is Patrick MacRory, the "ancestor of all the talkative, witty, resourceful man-servants in the works of Lever and others."[66] What made the book important was that the hero was an Irish *gentleman,* and a Roman Catholic. The public was used to Irish peasants being Catholics, and the better sort being Protestants, but to treat of a gentleman Catholic was unheard of. In all her Irish novels she unites a Protestant to a Catholic. And not only did she show Catholics who were gentlemen and ladies, she portrayed priests who were educated and nuns who had happily chosen the convent. Of religion she said, "for myself, though one among the many in my own country who have been educated in the most rigid adherence to the tenets of the Church of England, I should . . . think myself endowed with very few 'sketches and shadows of Christianity' were I to confine virtue to sect; or make the speculative theory of opinion the test of moral excellence; or proof of human perfection."[67] It is perhaps difficult for some today to realize how extravagant and extreme was the hatred and distrust of Roman Catholicism in England during this period, and how much venom was directed at Sydney Owenson for her toleration. She felt the Church of Ireland was grasping and greedy, riddled with nepotism and criminally avid for the tithes the Irish were forced to pay. Indeed, she was the first to point out this "greatest of all Irish grievances." Unaffected by the evangelicalism, which steadily increased in the Church of England throughout her life, she remained an 18th-century skeptic who tried to counter the bitter antagonisms in Ireland in her writings.

In 1812 she married Sir Charles Morgan, M.D. (1783-1843), an Englishman. Eton and Cambridge educated, a widower with one daughter, he held liberal, even radical views, and taught her a great deal. Shortly after her marriage, which proved to be an extraordinarily happy one, she wrote a friend that her days of authorship were over—she had to spend time setting up a house. In fact, she was hard at work on the research for a new book. She kept up the same pace of work after her marriage as before, simply adding more active politicking and entertaining to her well organized and industrious life.

The Morgans' marriage settlement gave each full control over all money acquired before and after marriage: she kept all earnings from her writing; his private fortune reverted to his daughter on his death. Although he was English, they chose to live in Dublin and work for Catholic Emancipation, and "their house on Kildare Street gradually became Dublin's most powerful literary salon, and a center of political activity."[68] She adored him, but since he did not have her boundless energy, she believed him to be lazy, and under her urging he wrote two books, over a hundred articles, numerous book reviews, and added sober chapters to her books on Italy and France. He gave her support when she was attacked by the Tory reviewers, even writing a satirical poem against the "hireling hacks" at one point. Their enemies considered them a team: "In fact, the match between Sydney Owenson and Sir C. Morgan was an active literary speculation—no sleeping partnership, but a brisk business, in which the medical man concocted doses of democratic doctrines, and made up bitter pills for royalists; while his helpmate wrote pretty labels for the one, and silvered the other."[69] Even in her marriage, an egalitarian partnership, she was the independent professional writer, something still considered a radical feminist goal today.

The Irish problem was not the only controversial political subject Lady Morgan tackled: in 1817 she published *France,* and the wrath of the Tories fell upon her. The English had spent more than twenty years hating and fearing the French, and had not forgotten the Irish revolt of 1798 to whose hopes the revolutionary French had contributed. She and her husband were among the first to visit France after it was open again to British travelers, and they were not only pro-French, virtually without reservations—not only in favor of the French Revolution and all it had done including the overthrow of the monarchy, the aristocracy, and the Church—but she stated clearly in her book that the English had been treacherous to Napoleon after his surrender. *France* was a lively book, full of interviews which showed plainly that the author respected the opinions of a laundress as much as that of a duchess.

John Wilson Croker attacked Lady Morgan in a "twenty-five page review that exceeded even its own

usual level of ferocity."[70] She was ridiculed because she had to earn a living; she was accused of "licentiousness, profligacy, irreverence, blasphemy, libertinism, disloyalty, and atheism. . . ."[71] But worst of all her faults: she was a woman. She had first been attacked in 1809 for her novel *Ida*—a poor book and her own least favorite. She had been instructed, among other things, to get married. She continued to be the target of vicious and *ad feminam* vituperation for many years, even after her death. She was castigated for writing of Roman Catholic priests as "gentlemen of refined manners, and most Anglified conversation," when the renewer stated.

> . . . the reverse would be the truth. A nobler race than the Anglo-Norman, or Cromwellian, or Williamite conquerors of Ireland . . . does not exist. A baser, meaner, more creeping and crawling banditti of conquered slaves than the Celtic population of that island, never disgraced the face of the earth.[72]

Croker got up a mock Royal Commission to inquire into her age and tried to have the knighthoods of her husband and brother-in-law overturned. In Croker's journal for 1821 and 1822, her biographer counted 27 different "animadversions on her. . . . , ranging from full page diatribes down to passing references to her squint or her childlessness."[73] The vehemence, the exaggeration of the criticism of that period is almost beyond comprehension today. Though legitimate criticism could certainly have found fault with Lady Morgan for occasional factual sloppiness, an inability to get foreign languages quite right, her often obtuse style, and improbabilities of plot, the true principle of Tory criticism was "to denounce as evil and mischievous the work (and the character as well) of any writers whose doctrines were set against the 'ancient order of things.' "[74]

While others were cowed by such attacks, Lady Morgan was not.[75] She knew that it was better to be attacked than to be ignored, she felt she was right in her opinions, and she loved a good fight. Letting it be known that she was "pickling a rod for her critics," she caricatured John Wilson Croker in her next novel, *Florence MacCarthy* (1818). To make satire more pointed, the Irish heroine is a writer. Though Benjamin Disraeli pilloried him in *Coningsby* as Mr. Rigby, "one of whose talents was for 'massacring a she liberal (it was thought that no one could lash a woman like Rigby)'," and Macaulay also retaliated in a review of Croker's edition of Boswell, Tom Moore said that "Croker winced more under the caricature [in *Florence Macarthy*] than any of the many direct attacks which were made upon him."[76] Lady Morgan outlived most of her attackers and, in an assessment in 1868, the judgment was pronounced that "on most of the great political questions touched upon in her writings, she was as clearly in the right, as time has proved the *Quarterly* and her other antagonists wrong."[77]

France was very successful, going into four English editions, two French, and four American. It had created a great deal of talk, and the Morgans decided to write a similar book on Italy—Lady Morgan writing background, interviews, and social history, while her husband investigated other matters. Further, under his tuition she had matured politically, and was tackling some of the major issues of the day. Fully aware of the powers of her pen, especially after *France,* she set out to aid "the great cause, the regeneration of Italy."[78] The Italians had been abysmally governed by their non-Italian masters, and Napoleon had thrown them out. His appointees had in turn been ousted and, as Lady Morgan put it, the previous incompetents had been "restored, grim, suspicious, determined to maintain their ancient rights by censorship and repression."[79] The Morgans' reputation preceded them, and the Italian police kept them under constant surveillance, noting that they "both show themselves to be the most determined constitutionalists and reformers."[80] In *Italy* (1821) Lady Morgan defended the acts of Napoleon, criticized the Austrians for their oppressive rule, attacked hereditary monarchy and the obscurantism of the Catholic Church, and again attacked the English government's treachery, this time for their having broken the agreement to help Italy attain independence.

The *Edinburgh Review* was beside itself with rage:

> When a woman of violent and irrepressible passions, and inordinate conceit and vanity, has the mortification to receive a severe but just castigation for her broadly-blazoned offences against good taste, correct feeling, and sound morals, it is no more than natural that she should rave and vociferate a little, and that, in the orgasm of her rabid but impotent fury, she should even rake into the stercoraceous and putrescent puddles of Billingsgate for filthy missiles to hurl at the head of her antagonist.[81]

The French government had passed a decree against her because of *France,* but it was *pro forma;* the Italian reaction was much harsher. The Papal and Austrian governments banned *Italy* in all countries of the Empire, and Lady Morgan was prohibited from traveling there. Sadly, several of the liberal Italians to whom she had spoken were sent to prison. *Italy* did not sell well. There was little interest in England in the struggle of the Italian people for independence. After the abortive revolt of 1821, many Italian exiles came to the Morgans for help, and the couple worked tirelessly to provide assistance.

Lady Morgan's next book, a biography of the Italian painter Salvator Rosa, was not successful, and she returned to writing about Ireland in her next novel, *The O'Briens and the O'Flahertys: A National Tale* (1827). It is by far her best and might even be considered an unjustly forgotten book. It has charm, humor, and believable, even lovable, characters. To be sure, she does not forget Ireland's wrongs, but she gives the reader a "moving and perceptive representation of Irish life."[82] The background is 1798, the action is involved, but it is the picture of an Ireland painted almost without regard to its propaganda purposes or to influencing the English to understand Ireland, which makes the book her most memorable.

All in all, her Irish novels were the best books she wrote. No doubt she needed the stimulation of a good fight and the knowledge that she was contributing to the cause of her beloved country. But there is another theme which never failed to spark her imagination: women. Had she lived a decade later, her cause might have been feminism. As we have seen, Lady Morgan had all the instincts of the professional writer and all the courage and determination necessary for a woman to attempt to go beyond merely ekeing out a living or dabbling in *belles lettres* or editing annuals. She was, in fact, the first Irish professional woman writer. It now remains to examine her claim to a significant position in the tradition of "feminist" writers.

Certainly Lady Morgan's mind and her work had always been concerned with women. Her heroines dominate the action and become increasingly independent. Romance was never their aim; patriotism informed their hearts more than love, and independence more than marriage. Her interest in women culminated in *Woman and Her Master* (1840), a history of women in the ancient world. She hoped to bring it up to the 19th century, but failing eyesight prevented her from publishing more than the first volume.

She always observed what women did: "I am always studying eminent persons, women above all—eminent no matter for what, de Staël, or Taglioni, *c'est égal.*"[83] She was always inspired to read women's work. While still a governess, she read of the poet Helen Maria Williams (1762-1827), and immediately wrote her an ode. She decided to write a book about Belgium after visiting the atelier of a young Belgian artist, who became the heroine. She read women's work consciously, with "sincerest gratitude for the amusement and instruction they afforded me."[84] In her turn, she would work to instruct and amuse. Not only are her heroines strong women, but she also mentions women writers, painters, patriots, and artists whenever possible. The young Greek heroine of the deliberately titled *Woman, or, Ida of Athens* (1809) tells her young compatriots of their glorious history, and "of those eminent persons, *of either sex,* who had distinguished themselves by their wisdom, their virtues, their talents, their patriotism."[85] When women writers are named, it is not only Sappho and Aspasia, but lesser known poets such as Praxyla and Erinne. In her most obviously feminist novel, *The Princess, or, the Beguine* (1835), the heroine is working on a book "with a view to the illustration of the lives of the able stateswomen to whom Belgium is so deeply indebted."[86] Even a double entendre is twisted into a lesson: the artist heroine speaks of the Flemish masters to the Englishman who would like to seduce her:

> 'And where are we to find . . . the Flemish mistresses?'
>
> 'Which of our female artists?' she asked with naivete. 'We have produced many eminent women in the arts. To begin with Marguerite Van Eyck, the sister of Hubert and John. She cultivated her art with such devotion, that she made a vow to St. Beghe, the patroness of the Beguines, never to marry. And she stuck to it, though she had many offers.[87]

Surely no woman writer, before or since, has labored so hard to introduce her readers to the history of women.

The wrongs of women are also made clear in her books, though Lady Morgan is more determined to illustrate the good than the evils. But in *Woman and Her Master* she wrote a work which should be placed in the feminist tradition which includes Mary Astell's *A Serious Proposal,* Mary Wollstonecraft's *Vindication,* and John Stuart Mill's and Harriet Taylor's *Subjection of Women.* As with her novels and her nonfiction, however, the book is marred by her weaknesses: her rather turgid style, her lack of a systematic education, but most of all her fierce combativeness in the service of a cause. Nonetheless, *Woman and Her Master* was a pioneering attempt to trace women's agency in history, to demonstrate their power for civilizing that, despite all handicaps, always emerged.

Her analysis begins with the means by which men have subjugated women. In the past and among "savages" it is by greater physical strength, but now other means are used to keep her down, what "*he* calls philosophy and science. . . . "[88] Women are given an education in "the arts which merely please, and which frequently corrupt," and if she tries to do more than she is permitted by social customs, "she is denounced as a thing unsexed. . . . "[89] She cannot make the laws which govern her, has no rights to her own property unless she "is protected by the solitary blessedness of a derided but innocent celibacy, or by an infamous frailty."[90] Matters have not changed over the centuries: "Society, then as now, excluded women from all legitimate sources by which they might provide for their subsistence; and opened its portals only to reward the exercise of their frailties."[91] What was expected of women was the impossible:

> Educating her for the Harem, but calling on her for the practices of the Portico, man expects from his odalesque the firmness of the stoic, and demands from his servant the exercise of those virtues which, placing the elite of his own sex at the head of its

muster-roll, give immortality to the master. He tells her, 'that obscurity is *her* true glory, insignificance her distinction, ignorance her lot, and passive obedience the perfection of her nature.' yet he expects from her, . . . that conquest over the passions by the strength of reason, that triumph of moral energy over the senses and appetites, and that endurance of personal privations and self-denials, which with him . . . are qualities of rare exception, and practices of most painful acquirements.[92]

Despite this "corrupting influence of oppression," woman's true nature has always manifested itself. She has, even in the most primitive society, been the civilizing and humanizing force, and Lady Morgan called on men to allow "the just development and mutual influence of the two sexes . . ." which alone can effect the further civilizing of humanity.[93]

The knowledge of woman's true nature, her very identity, had almost been lost, Lady Morgan insisted, by the way men wrote history. The wickedness of queens was relished. Women's good qualities were overlooked, if indeed they were mentioned at all by male historians except in "rare instances, and through the eminence of the men with whom they were associated."[94] Those who shone through no reflected male glory left only traces, if that, and the author saw the task of what we could now call a feminist revision to recover the lost history of women. Nor was Lady Morgan the first to call for this attempt at rewriting women's history: in 1705 Mary Astell complained of the male historians' distorted picture:

> Some good Examples [of women] are to be found in History, though generally the bad are ten for one; but how will this help our Conduct, or excite in us a generous Emulation? Since the Men being the Historians, they seldom condescend to record the great and good Actions of Women; and when they take notice of them, 'tis with this wise Remark, That such Women *acted above their Sex.* By which one must suppose they wou'd have their readers understand, that they were not Women who did those Great Actions, but that they were Men in Petticoats![95]

As might be expected, Lady Morgan's history lacks scholarly objectivity. She had done her research, but her temperament was combative, and she had much to say in what she thought would be her last book. She gave no quarter: where a woman was heroic, it was the result of her own doing; where she was evil, she could not be blamed: "Her faults belonged to the bad men and bad age in which she lived—the worst on record; her virtues and her genius were her own."[96] Men, when cornered, revert to brute force, to tyranny, to the exercise of power. Women, being the embodiment of intelligence and progress, cannot commit the range or magnitude of crime which men can. Woman's position is always insecure for she is always at the mercy of the ruling males. Lady Morgan shocked reviewers by singling out for praise not only the Sarahs and the Deborahs, but also Eve and Jezebel and some of the more blood-thirsty Roman empresses. Where she could not defend, she stated that some women had a more evil effect on history than was allowed by male historians. Though some of her defenses are highly polemical, at best, one at least deserves closer attention. In 1840, one of the main reasons given for women's subordinate position in society, and morally, was Eve's responsibility for the Fall. Lady Morgan defended Eve on the grounds that she was tempted by the promise of knowledge, of God-like intelligence, unlike her lump of a spouse, and to the readers of her time this bordered on blasphemy.

The critical reception of *Woman and Her Master* resembled that given her other books, ranging from a vicious review through judicious criticism to high praise. The attack, as usual, was *ad feminam,* one reviewer castigating her for her great age—she was then in her sixties—and her looks, likening her to an ugly and venomous toad. Her scholarship was slighted, and it was said she praised Jezebel because they resembled each other. The critical reception of *Woman and Her Master* is worthy of closer study for its revelation not only of contemporary attitudes to the "woman question," but also of the hostile atmosphere of literary journalism generally. An aggressive and radical woman was fair game not only as any partisan writer would be to those in other camps, but also doubly vulnerable as an "unsexed creature" and someone outside the "old boys' network."

From the time she began to write until 1840, Lady Morgan had published a book every two or three years, plus articles, verse, stories, and countless book reviews. She was constantly studying and researching for future books. She had worked continually for more than forty years, and if failing eyesight slowed her literary industry, it did not end it completely. Writing was her life, and she continued, with the aid of a secretary, until she died. She was a solid professional; what she promised, she delivered. Her research was as extensive as she could make it in the days before public libraries, and she was shrewd and practical with her publishers, to their distraction. In fact, her relations with her publishers were a model of careful professionalism and a sound business mind. In 1837 she was granted the first pension given to a woman writer, £ 300 a year. As she wrote in a new preface when *The Wild Irish Girl* was reissued in 1846:

> The pension granted by Sir Robert Peel to the illustrious Mrs. Somerville (the expounder of La Place to the English scientific reader, as Madame du Chatelet was of Newton to the French, . . .) and that allowed to the author of the following pages, being I believe the first assigned to female writers, so far, make an epoch in the history of letters. . . . [97]

She was proud of what she had accomplished, and she had a right to be. She wrote once, after a long illness, that one of her greatest blessings was that she was aware "that I never lost an occasion of working or rendering a service during my long life, to the best of my ability. . . . "[98]

Sydney Owenson, Lady Morgan, has been called the first professional woman writer, and perhaps she was. As more feminist literary histories are written, the concept of "first" becomes less useful. There is a tradition of literary women stretching back long before Lady Morgan. However, coming when she did, she is an important figure. She maintained her economic independence and expressed her unique self through the profession of letters. She worked at it, researched and planned her works, shrewdly marketed her writing, helped aspiring young writers whenever she could, and was innocently proud of her achievements. But more than that, she was a woman with causes, most notably the celebration of the greatness of Ireland's history and culture, and the greatness of women's. No historian concerned with the history of Ireland in the early 19th century, the feminist literary tradition, or the development of the professional writer can afford to overlook her. Her novels may not be great literature, but they are significant period pieces. Though she is not a Jane Austen or a Charlotte Brontë, Lady Morgan has her honorable place in literary history.

Notes

[1] Catherine J. Hamilton, *Notable Irishwomen* (Dublin: Sealy, Bryers and Walker, [1904]), p. 191.

[2] Miriam Leranbaum, "Mistresses of Orthodoxy: Education in the Lives and Writings of Late Eighteenth Century Women Writers," *Proceedings of the American Philosphical Society,* 121 (1977), 281-301, *passim.*

[3] Other women who earned a sufficiency or more during this period were Mrs. Barbault (1743-1825); Mrs. Inchbald (1753-1821), who supported several members of her family; Susan Ferrier (1782-1854); Mary Wollstonecraft (1759-1797); Mary Mitford (1787-1855), who supported a n'er-do-well father; and Susan Ferrier (1782-1854). Hannah More said she had made over £30,000 from her books.

[4] Lionel Stevenson, *The Wild Irish Girl, The Life of Sydney Owenson, Lady Morgan* (London: Chapman & Hall, 1936), Preface, n.p.

[5] From the Preface to *The Memoirs of the Baron de Brosse* (1725), quoted in George F. Whicher, *The Life and Romances of Mrs. Haywood* (New York: Columbia University Press, 1915), p. 20.

[6] First quotation from E. V. Lucas, *The Life of Charles Lamb* (London: Methuen, 1905), II, 32-33; second from

P. G. Patmore, no source given; both from H. E. Haworth, "Romantic Female Writers and the Critics," *Texas Studies in Literature and Language* (Winter, 1976), 724.

[7] In H. S. Bennett, *English Books and Readers 1603-1640* (Cambridge: Cambridge University Press, 1970), one may find the following catagories of books published during the 16th and 17th centuries, few of which women had either the experience, the education, or the temerity to write: sermons, law, medicine, religious controversy, translations from the classics, education, astronomy, popular science, geography, travel, adventure, history, news, and literature.

[8] See Walter J. Ong for his discussions of the exclusively male world of classical education in "Latin Language Study as a Renaissance Puberty Rite," *Rhetoric, Romance and Technology* (Ithaca: Cornell University Press, 1971), pp. 113-141; and "Agonistic Structures in Academia: Past to Present," *Daedalus,* 103 (Fall, 1974), 119-238.

[9] Robert Halsband, " 'The Female Pen,' Women and Literature in Eighteenth-Century England," *History Today,* 24 (October, 1974), 703. Thomas Macaulay summed up Fanny Burney's writing life in 1843, when he wrote, "She vindicated the right of her sex to an equal share in a fair and noble province of letters," in "Madame D'Arblay," *Critical and Historical Essays* (London: J. M. Dent, 1909), II, 612.

[10] Halsband, " 'The Female Pen,' " 706.

[11] Nina Auerbach, *Communities of Women: An Idea in Fiction* (Cambridge, Mass.: Harvard University Press, 1978), p. 6.

[12] Haworth, p. 729.

[13] Anne Katherine Elwood, *Memoirs of the Literary Ladies of England* (New York: Ams Press, 1973 [London 1843]), II, 303.

[14] From *The Edinburgh Review* (February 24, 1815), 336-337, quoted in Haworth, pp. 729-730.

[15] Robert Halsband, *Ladies of Letters in the Eighteenth Century,* papers read at a Clark Library Seminar, January 8, 1969 (Los Angeles: William Andrews Clark Memorial Library, University of California, 1969), p. 34.

[16] *Monthly Review* (October, 1817), 121.

[17] From *The Critical Review,* 3s, 2 [July, 1804], 458, quoted in Haworth, p. 734.

[18] Janet Dunbar, *The Early Victorian Woman: Some Aspects of Her Life 1837-1857* (London: Harrap, 1953), p. 132.

[19] Dorothy Thomson, "Jane Haldimand Marcet," *Adam Smith's Daughters* (New York: Exposition Press, 1973), pp. 9-28.

[20] Ellen Moers, *Literary Women* (Garden City, New York: Doubleday & Company, 1976), p. 125.

[21] *The Pursuit of Knowledge under Difficulties, Illustrated by Female Examples* . . . (London, 1847), p. 23.

[22] Harrison R. Steeves, *Before Jane Austen, The English Novel in the Eighteenth Century* (New York: Holt, Rinehart and Winston, 1965), p. 100.

[23] Scott H. Lytle, "The Second Sex (September, 1793)," *Journal of Modern History,* 27, 1 (1955), 14-26; and Margaret George, "The 'World Historical Defeat' of the *Republicaines-Revolutionnaires,*" *Science and Society,* XL, 4 (Winter, 1976-77), 410-437.

[24] Regina Janes, "Mary, Mary, Quite Contrary, Or, Mary Astell and Mary Wollstonecraft Compared," *Studies in Eighteenth Century Culture,* Vol. 5, ed. Ronald C. Rosbottom (Madison: University of Wisconsin Press, 1976), pp. 121-139.

[25] Auerbach, p. 13.

[26] Moers, see especially her discussion of Ann Radcliffe, pp. 190-213.

[27] E. P. Thompson, *The Making of the English Working Class* (New York: Random House, 1964), pp. 162-3, 415-17, 730-31.

[28] W. Lyon Blease, *The Emancipation of English Women* (New York: Benjamin Blom, 1971 [London, 1910]), P. xi.

[29] From R. K. Webb, *Harriet Martineau, Radical Victorian* (1960), p. 114; from Moers, p. 20.

[30] Inga-Stina Ewbank, *Their Proper Sphere: A Study of the Bronte Sisters as Early Victorian Female Novelists* (Cambridge, Mass.: Harvard University Press, 1966), p. 23, from *Diary, Reminiscences and Correspondence of Henry Crabb Robinson,* ed. Thomas Sadler (1872), II, 144.

[31] See Moers, pp. 264-319 and *passim;* and J. Christopher Herold, *Mistress to an Age: A Life of Madame de Staël* (New York: The Bobbs-Merrill Company, 1962 [1958]), *passim.*

[32] Herold, p. 193.

[33] Herold, p. 233.

[34] William John Fitzpatrick, *The Friends, Foes, and Adventures of Lady Morgan* (Dublin: W. B. Kelly, 1959), p. 96.

[35] Richard Pankhurst, *The Saint Simonians, Mill and Carlyle: A Preface to Modern Thought* (London: Sidgwick & Jackson, [1956]), *passim.*

[36] Eugene Hecker, *A Short History of Women's Rights* (Westport, Conn.: Greenwood Press, 1971 [1914]), p. 145.

[37] John Kilham, *Tennyson and "The Princess," Reflections of an Age* (London: The Athlone Press, 1958), p. 104.

[38] Janet Courtney, *The Adventurous Thirties: A Chapter in the Women's Movement* (Freeport, N.Y.: Books for Libraries Press, 1967 [1933]), p. 75.

[39] In 1925 custody was given to the mother by law.

[40] Beatrice O'Malley, *Women in Subjection: A Study of the Lives of Englishwomen before 1832* (London: Duckworth, 1932), p. 350.

[41] Steeves, p. 1.

[42] Lady Morgan's relations with her various publishers deserves fuller treatement than is possible here. She was always in control and by charm and tough mindedness was able to master an aspect of publication difficult for most authors, especially at that time.

[43] Lady Morgan, *Passages from My Autobiography* (New York: D. Appleton and Company, 1859), I, 212.

[44] *Passages,* II, 255.

[45] Stevenson, p. 313.

[46] *Lady Morgan's Memoirs: Autobiography, Diaries and Correspondence,* ed. W. Hepworth (London: William H. Allen, 1863), II, 410.

[47] Stevenson, p. 316.

[48] "Passages from My Autobiography" review, *Atheneum* (January 25, 1859), 73.

[49] *Memoirs,* I, 69.

[50] From *Cassandra,* p. 397, in Ray Strachey, *The Cause: A Short History of the Women's Movement in Great Britain* (Port Washington, N. Y.: Kennikat Press, 1969 [1928]).

[51] "Sydney, Lady Morgan," obituary, *Atheneum* (April 16, 1859), 516.

[52] Dunbar, p. 132.

[53] *Memoirs,* II, 403-404.

[54] Stevenson, p. 43.

[55] *Woman, or, Ida of Athens* (London, 1809), IV, 89.

[56] *Florence MacCarthy: An Irish Tale* (New York: P. J. Kenedy, 1895 [1818], p. 206.

[57] *The Princess, or, The Beguine* (Paris: Baudry's European Library, 1835), p. 351.

[58] *Ibid.,* p. 355.

[59] *The Wild Irish Girl* (London: Henry Colburn, 1846 [1806]), p. 7.

[60] Owens Blackburne [Elizabeth Casey], *Illustrious Irishwomen,* (London: Tinsley Brothers, 1877), II, 180-181.

[61] Courtney, p. 4.

[62] Stevenson, p. 57.

[63] Stevenson, p. 65.

[64] Thomas Flanagan, *The Irish Novelists 1800—1850* (New York: Columbia University Press, 1958), p. 125.

[65] *Ibid.,* p. 119.

[66] Stevenson, p. 164.

[67] *Irish Quarterly Review,* 9 (July, 1859), 406.

[68] Flanagan, p. 130.

[69] "Sir Charles and Lady Morgan," *Dublin University Magazine* (September, 1860), 277.

[70] Stevenson, p. 189.

[71] *France,* 2nd ed. (London: Henry Colburn, 1817), Preface, p. ix.

[72] "Lady Morgan's *Dramatic Scenes from Real Life,*" *Fraser's Magazine,* 8 (November, 1833), 617.

[73] Stevenson, p. 240.

[74] Walter Graham, *Tory Criticism in the Quarterly Review* (New York: Columbia University Press, 1921), p. 39.

[75] Among the many other writers attacked for their politics was Mrs. Barbauld, whose poem "Eighteen Hundred and Eleven," on the destruction of England, was also attacked by the *Quarterly.* She published nothing further for the rest of her life, some thirteen years. Mona Wilson, *Jane Austen and Some Contemporaries* (London: Cresset Press, 1938), p. 75.

[76] Stevenson, p. 191.

[77] Stevenson, p. 101.

[78] Letter to her sister, *Autobiography,* I, 382.

[79] Beatrice Corrigan, Three Englishwomen in Italy," *Queen's Quarterly,* 79 (1972), 155.

[80] Stevenson, p. 213.

[81] Quoted in Stevenson, p. 228. She wrote a pamphlet in reply, saying that the campaign against her was inspired and organised by hired agents of the reactionary party in power in the hope of preventing her books from being read," (Stevenson, p. 226), and the *Edinburgh Magazine* devoted twelve pages of vituperation to her.

[82] Flanagan, p. 151.

[83] *Autobiography,* II, 367.

[84] Lady Morgan, *The Book of the Boudoir* (New York, 1829), pp. 126-127.

[85] *Ida,* II, 43, italics author's.

[86] *The Princess,* p. 305.

[87] *The Princess,* p. 187.

[88] Lady Morgan, *Woman and Her Master* (Westport, Conn.: Hyperion Press, 1976 [1840]), I, 19.

[89] *Ibid.*

[90] *Ibid.,* I, 18.

[91] *Ibid.,* I, 170.

[92] *Ibid.,* I, 19, italics author's.

[93] *Ibid.,* I, 216.

[94] *Ibid.,* II, 95.

[95] From *The Christian Religion, As Profess'd by a Daughter of the Church of England* (London: R. Wilkin, 1705), pp. 292-293. Quoted in Janes, p. 129.

[96] *Woman and Her Master,* II, 50.

[97] *The Wild Irish Girl,* p. xxxvii.

[98] *Autobiography,* II, 473.

Tom Dunne (essay date 1987)

SOURCE: "Fiction as 'the Best History of Nations': Lady Morgan's Irish Novels," in *The Writer as Witness: Literature as Historical Evidence,* edited by Tom Dunne, Cork University Press, 1987, pp. 133-59.

[*In the following essay, Dunne defends Lady Morgan's work against charges that it is "wildly imaginative and essentially frivolous," arguing that her Irish novels combine realism with Morgan's understanding of the forces which created distinct and contrasting perceptions of Irish history.*]

In so far as there is a modern image of Lady Morgan, it tends to reflect that common among her contemporaries, of a rather bizarre society hostess, who wrote romantic and eccentric historical novels, all of whose heroines resembled herself, while she in turn imitated the best known of them, Glorvina of *The Wild Irish Girl* (1806), in terms of dress and ornamentation, and a proclivity for bringing her harp to parties. Her Irish novels, four in all, published between 1806 and 1827,[1] are precisely the kind of literature from which most historians tend to recoil, as wildly imaginative and essentially frivolous, while literary critics have ignored them as badly written popular romances. This paper hopes to show that Morgan was less a romantic than a realist writer, one whose flamboyance masked a serious intent, and whose novels should be seen by historians as valuable documents for understanding important elements of Irish political culture and intellectual life between the Union and the Famine. It may also be of interest to those who work in the highly specialised and exciting area of historical inquiry, which literary criticism is, at least in part, because these novels offer a particularly interesting case study of a novelist who employed historical perspectives to explain, and even to influence, contemporary reality. Her argument that fiction constituted 'the best history of nations', made in the preface to her second Irish novel, *O'Donnel* (1814), referred less to its ability to recreate the past, than to the fact that it 'exhibited a mirror of the times in which it is composed: reflecting morals, customs, manners, peculiarities of character and prevalence of opinion'.[2] This view that the imaginative writer is, of necessity, a historian of his or her own time, however much this may be disguised by the nature of the literary genre involved, must form the basis of any belief in the value of literature as historical evidence. It is also basic to some modern hermeneutic approaches to literary theory and criticism. Paul Ricoeur has tried to provide a common theoretical framework for both disciplines, arguing that history writing and fiction are related and comparable forms of discourse, in terms of narrative structure, as well as the location of each in historical time.[3] Marxist literary critics, like Frederic Jameson, make the connection in a different way, in arguing for a historically informed criticism, and especially for 'the priority of the political interpretation of literary texts'.[4]

Concern about the relationship between writings which were subjectively imaginative and those which claimed to be objectively historical, had a particular importance in the evolution of the novel in the eighteenth century. Awareness of a resistance on the part of readers to the very idea of invented or imagined worlds led novelists like Defoe, Richardson and Fielding to disguise their works as autobiographies, memoirs, real-life adventures or eyewitness accounts. The new popular historical works they counterfeited, on the other hand, were regarded as a branch of literature and only slowly developed critical approaches to evidence and documentation.[5] While very influenced by the eighteenth-century tradition, Morgan did not go so far as to claim that her novels were 'true' histories, but she constantly interwove her fiction with historical 'facts', and appealed to the authority of historians and historical documents. She described her novels as 'my Irish histories', and herself as a 'collator of Irish chronicles', an 'Irish antiquarian', and was mocked by Hazlitt for 'strutting the little Gibbon of her age'.[6] Her failure to make any absolute distinctions between fiction and history can also be seen in the ease and pragmatism with which she moved from one genre to the other. She began what became her biography of the Italian painter-patriot Salvator Rosa as a novel, while what was begun as a history of the Belgian revolution was turned instead into a novel, called *The Princess*.[7] Her Irish novels, in particular, combine three distinct but interdependent texts. As well as the fictional text, and the inevitable authoritative authorial voice commenting on it, there is a large and often obtrusive historical subtext, made up of references to and quotations from both historians and historical sources, and in the form of footnotes or end of volume notes. This subtext, acting in support of the authorial commentary, directs the reading of the fictional text, and has a wide and interesting range of reference, reflecting the intense and, as Donal McCartney has shown, increasingly partisan contemporary debate among historians.[8] This paper is concerned mainly with the nature of Morgan's historical understanding, and its relationship to her political attitudes and intent, but it will also discuss an important shift in her later novels, from an appeal to the eighteenth-century Catholic antiquarians, the so-called 'native historians' like O'Halloran and O'Connor, to an ever-greater reliance on the work of more modern historians, mainly Irish Protestant and English. This was, doubtless, influenced by the new critical approach to sources begun by Ledwich, though Morgan's liberal Protestantism disdained the sectarian obsession with the 1641 rising, to which this was mainly applied. Nevertheless, her novels, like the histories to which they appealed, can properly be regarded, in Oliver MacDonagh's phrase, as 'politics by other means'.[9]

While she wrote only one Irish historical novel, in the conventional sense—*The O'Briens and the O'Flahertys* (1827), set in the 1770s and 1790s—the rest, although they had contemporary settings, were dominated by historical perspectives and obsessed with historical explanations. The first of them, *The Wild Irish Girl*, while romantic in tone, was heavily didactic in intent, and this tendency was intensified when in the next Irish novel, *O'Donnel: a national tale,* she moved away, as the preface put it, from 'pure abstraction', to concentrate on 'the flat realities of life'.[10] In fact, all her novels, including the first, belong properly to the realist tradition and their concern with history owed less to romanticism than to a recognition that clashing perceptions of Irish history formed a central element of the reality she wished to confront and to influence. In this, as in other respects, her fiction reflected the profoundly colonial nature of Irish society, and her primary concern was to encourage a reappraisal of the colonial past, as an essential means of dealing with its contemporary legacy of conflict and division. Her perspective was a liberal colonist or ascendancy one, akin to Maria Edgeworth's in important respects, but in a distinctively different tradition,[11] closer to Thomas Davis whose proposal of a dialogue between past and present as the key to reconciliation, she anticipated. Terry Eagleton has argued recently, that modern hermeneutic theory, which proposes a similar type of dialogue, has the problem that it cannot 'tolerate the idea of a failure of communications . . . It cannot, in other words, come to terms with the problem of ideology'.[12] Such a failure, charged with ideological difference, led, as we will see, to Lady Morgan's ultimate disillusionment with the healing potential of history within Ireland. At the same time, the achievement of Catholic Emancipation robbed her of the cause that she had long urged on English liberal opinion. This English audience was, for her, the primary one, and thus the one which most shaped her fiction. Following in the long tradition of Irish colonial writing, her main concern was to explain the Irish historical experience, and through it, contemporary violence and poverty, to English readers, who would thus be persuaded to support the demand for Irish reforms, particularly Catholic Emancipation. This tradition was reinforced by the Act of Union which made Irish affairs the direct responsibility of the Westminster Parliament. It involved, among other things, a sensitivity to English historical perspectives, in this case the English Whig tradition, with which Morgan, in any case, identified and appealed to as an Irish Whig. The nature and purpose of her appeal to this English opinion changed from a favourable presentation of the Gaelic past to combat traditional anti-Irish prejudice, in her first novel, to a harsh but limited indictment of 'six centuries of oppression' in the remaining three, 'a series of national tales', as she described them, 'undertaken with a humble but zealous view to the promotion of a great national cause, the emancipation of the Catholics of Ireland'. She defended this overt political ambition for fiction, on the basis that, 'Novels, like more solid compositions are not exempted from the obligation to inculcate truth. They are expected, in their idlest trifling to possess a moral scope, and politics is but morals on a grander scale'.[13]

Morgan used history in three principal ways. Most simply, and often most memorably, it provided colour or atmosphere—history as entertainment. In all of her novels this was associated particularly with her passion for ruined castles, abbeys and churches, 'at once so melancholy and so interesting'.[14] While *The Wild Irish Girl* was the most colourful of her novels in this respect, even here, history had a second and more serious purpose, that of explanation and authority; the key to understanding the present. 'The causes of Ireland's misfortunes are so deep-rooted', declared her hero in *Florence Macarthy* (1818) 'that every page in her history is a palliation of her faults'.[15] Morgan's marshalling of evidence and authority for her historical account recognised the persistence of the tendency in the reading public to distrust fiction on important matters, while deferring to historians—a tendency long since reversed! It also underlined the political as well as the literary purpose of her novels. The third, and perhaps most interesting use of history by Lady Morgan was as a dynamic element in the story—historical understanding forwarded the action, and transformed situations and lives. When the Anglo-Irish hero, Mortimer, in *The Wild Irish Girl* arrived on the estate of his absentee father in the west of Ireland, he discovered a locked study, full of books on Irish history, and in liberating them, so to speak, he began the process of freeing himself from his prejudiced views of Gaelic Ireland. He was soon 'deep in the study of the language, history and antiquities of this ancient nation', helped by a series of lectures from the Prince of Inismore, the descendant of the 'Milesian' lord, dispossessed and indeed killed by Mortimer's ancestor. This novel largely comprises a series of such lectures, and whatever their effect on the modern reader might be, they galvanised the hero into a determination to reconcile his father and the Prince.[16] In a key scene of her second Irish novel, *O'Donnel,* the hero of that name used the 'few shrivelled parchments and mouldering papers' that remained from his ancestors, the Gaelic lords of Tír Conaill, to prove the legal rights of an English heiress to lands alienated from his father by the penal code.[17] In *Florence Macarthy,* ancient documents are also important in a court case, when an attempt to frame the local Whiteboy leader for an entirely fictitious 'rebellion', was foiled by one of the judges demonstrating that the key prosecution document was from the sixteenth century.[18] Finally, in *The O'Briens and the O'Flahertys,* the hero's father, Terence O'Brien became a wealthy lawyer due mainly to his antiquarian lore, and resurrected his family title 'on the evidence of an old tombstone'.[19] In his case, the fruits of historical research were to be megolomania and ruin, though even in this last and most pessimistic of her Irish novels Morgan preserved the primary dynamic function of her characters' confrontations with the past and its legacy—that it should be a healing process, and lead to reconciliation. This found its ultimate symbol in all the novels in the marriages of hereditary enemies—that of the Gaelic Glorvina and 'Cromwellian' Mortimer in *The Wild Irish Girl,* of the Gaelic heroine, Florence Macarthy, to the Norman Fitzadelm, of O'Donnel and his English Duchess, and of Murrough O'Brien to Beavoin O'Flaherty. In her account of why she had abandoned her original project of a historical novel based on the life of Red Hugh O'Donnel, she explained that history *had* to have a healing effect, or it had no place in her fiction. Once convinced that the story of Red Hugh instead of promoting 'conciliation' would let loose 'discord', she abandoned it in favour of a story of 'more modern and more liberal times'.[20]

This emphasis on Morgan's *uses* of history helps to point up the contrast between her fiction and that of her great contemporary, Sir Walter Scott. Both were preoccupied with historical explanation, and Scott too provided an authoritative, if less pedantic, subtext of historical references and footnotes. The central historical event for both was the destruction of traditional Gaelic societies over the previous three centuries, and the complex social and political revolution which accomplished and accompanied this. The explanation provided by both aimed at a reconciliation of past and present, in part to aid a national consensus, in part to explain the author's country to an English audience. Both were essentially conservative and supporters of the status quo. The differences between them, however, are more revealing, and go much further than Victor Hugo's acid judgment that Morgan had 'much more love of celebrity than love of her country', and that, 'beside Scott's pictures, full of life and warmth, Lady Morgan's studies were only pale and chilly sketches'.[12] They had fundamentally different approaches to, and understandings of, historical process, reflecting in part, perhaps, their different political allegiances. While Scott's Toryism encouraged an emphasis on organic growth and continuity, Morgan's Whiggism saw history more as a series of revolutions leading to the achievement of 'liberty'. Scott's theme was no less than the nature of historical change itself, as Lukacs has argued so brilliantly.[22] His characters represented major historical forces and social trends, and his emphasis was on the transformation of social life at all levels, and the interaction of class interests with political events. Morgan lacked Scott's depth of historical understanding, as well as his sophistication in handling historical themes. Scott, as recent research has emphasised, was aided by a remarkable school of eighteenth-century Scottish 'philosophical' historians, like Stewart, Hume, Fergusson and Smith.[23] The contrast with the traditionalism and limited concerns of the historians on which Morgan had to rely can be seen at a glance in that between titles, such as Adam Ferguson's *An essay on the history of civil society* (1767) or John Miller's *Origins of ranks* (1771) compared with John Curry's *A historical and critical review of the civil wars in Ireland* (1775) or

Ierne defended (1774) by Sylvester O'Halloran. The revolution in Irish historiography from the 1790s, despite its more critical approach to sources, continued with the narrowly political and partisan concerns of the antiquarians. For Morgan, as for most Irish historians, history was a storehouse of argument to be used, rather than a process to be understood. Her main concern, as she put it, was to explain 'national grievances' as 'borne out by historic fact'. Thus, even though she also tried to portray characters, 'such as identify a class or represent a genus',[24] she could not, as Scott did, root her characters in a sustained way, in the historical process. This failure, common to most contemporary Irish novelists, to transcend the particularism of the Irish experience and produce fiction of universal appeal, can also be explained in tems of the nature of Irish society. While Scott was the product of a society which was relatively prosperous, self-confident and socially cohesive. Morgan's more fractured historical sense reflected a divided and impoverished country, traumatised as well as mesmerised, by a revolution few felt to be complete or secure. The Irish Whig interpretation of history could not have the self-confidence long developed by the English. Ireland's abrasive and continuing colonial experience, in marked contrast to the experience of Scotland, ensured that historical conflicts persisted into current politics. Thus, Morgan could accept the historical necessity and ultimate benefit of the Irish 'revolution', but could not shut it up in a 'completed' past, as Scott did that of Scotland. This may be why Scott could write historical novels, while Morgan, for the most part, could only write contemporary novels suffused with history—though she could write historical novels on non-Irish themes.[25] The Irish experience, and the Irish Whig tradition also meant that Morgan's heroes, rather than coming from the common people, as so many of Scott's do, were all aristocratic, and indeed she saw historical change largely in terms of a conflict between aristocracies, and its ultimate resolution in the substitution of an enlightened for a corrupt ruling class.

There were other and perhaps more prosaic influences, which helped to shape Lady Morgan's historical perspectives; notably her family background, her Whig politics, her adoption by Dublin's Viceregal society, and her involvement with the Catholic emancipation campaign. Daiches has explained Scott's psychology and outlook in terms of the tensions between his mixed aristocratic and bourgeois ancestry.[26] Those inherent in Morgan's origins were far more complex, and extreme, and yet, as we will see, there is little enough evidence for tensions flowing from her mixed Gaelic, Anglo-Irish and English background, in her novels. The tradition that she was born on the Irish Sea, as her bourgeois English methodist mother travelled to Dublin to join her flamboyant Connaught father, an actor-singer who specialised in stage-Irish parts, has at least a symbolic validity. In her *Memoirs,* she gave this mixed

parentage a characteristically romantic gloss, 'My father was a Celtic Irishman, my mother was a Saxon',[27] but the rality was more confused. She obviously disliked her mother, though she was glad ultimately to have inherited her practical common sense. Her mother's early death was a decisive event, bringing her even more strongly under her father's influence, and accelerating the collapse of the family's fortune, which in the end drove the young Sydney Owenson to become a writer. Her engaging, impractical and ultimately pathetic father was the centre of her life, 'my child as well as my father, the object for which I laboured and wrote and lived', as she wrote after his death.[28] The comparison in this, as in so many other respects, with Maria Edgeworth, is interesting, and in her strong distaste at being mentioned in the same breath as Lady Morgan, Edgeworth pitied her for having a father so different from her own and saw this influence as the basis of the contrast in their literary styles.[29] Morgan, however, seemed proud of him and was certainly protective. Her account of his history seems a romanticised version of his own and centred on the transformation of Robert MacOwen, Irish-speaking son of a Catholic tenant farmer and a harp playing mother from the Protestant gentry family, the Croftons, into Robert Owenson, a moderately successful actor on the English stage, with the help of his distant cousin, Oliver Goldsmith. Her pride in her ancestry came to be focused almost entirely on her paternal grandmothers' Protestant connections, and the influence on her of the Anglicised Gaelic background of her father, while clearly great, was also complex.[30] He had a fund of folklore and legend, as well as a notable repertoire of Gaelic songs, which formed the basis of his daughter's important collection of Irish airs, with English words, published the year before *The Wild Irish Girl,* and an influence on Moore. It was clear, however, from her introduction, and other comments,[31] that despite being so close to this authentic Gaelic source, her attitude was that of the sympathetic outsider, as distanced in its own way as that of Charlotte Brooke from the Bardic poetry she published. Even though she mimicked her father's Irish in her singing, she clearly had no understanding of the Irish language, beyond a few phrases used to charm servants.[32] Similarly, while her father's background gave her a romantic interest in the west of Ireland, her perspective on it was more that of Longford House, the residence of her Crofton relations, where she stayed while gathering materials for *The Wild Irish Girl.*[33] This ambivalent attitude to her Gaelic background only reflected that of her father, who was a fascinating combination of the authentic and theatrical—even to the extent of singing traditional songs in Irish while playing stage-Irish parts.[34] His major dramatic roles, like Sir Lucius O'Trigger or Major O'Flaherty, clearly influenced his daughter's writing and characterisation, and in a more general sense, both her fiction and her view of history retained a theatrical quality. Her father also introduced her to

Whig politics. His reconstruction of the Fishamble Street theatre, renamed The National Theatre Music Hall, was inspired, his daughter believed, by the 'Irish nationality' of the Volunteers and the corps to which he belonged filled the pit in full uniform on the opening night in 1784. Later that year, a benefit performance, organised by Napper Tandy for an imprisoned patriotic printer led to the theatre losing its licence.[35]

This political connection was strengthened by the support given to her by the Irish Whig establishment after *The Wild Irish Girl* became the object of Tory attacks. Looking back to that time in 1846, in the preface to the new popular edition of the novel, she proudly listed those of 'her gallant and liberal countrymen' together with 'the English members of the Irish government', who had come to her aid, and in a remarkable footnote, she added,

> Last and least of the "mere Irishry" drawn within the English pale of this truly delightful society, was an obscure girl, whose sole passport into circles so brilliant was that she had written an Irish tale, in the Irish interest, sung Irish songs, translated by herself from Irish poems and played the Irish harp.[36]

Her adaptation of her father's 'Irish' performances, both genuine and theatrical, from the stage to the pages of the novel, and to Dublin drawingrooms, was certainly a major factor in her social success in Whig and Viceregal circles. However, though she may have been at first simply another focus for the current aristocratic fashion for the Gaelic past, she eventually became an insider and a major political hostess. Her description of herself as one of the 'mere Irishry' was more colourful than accurate, and the rapidity of her absorption into Dublin society can be seen in another opening night audience, this time for her 'impromptu little play', written as a vehicle for her father, and produced three years later, in 1809. Her description of that scene can be read as a paradigm of her vision of Irish society as a whole.

> The Viceregal box and dress circle were exclusively occupied by the court and officers of the garrison, who were headed by the commander-in-chief. The whole of the liberal part of the Irish bar, and their friends, filled the upper circle, and the pit and galleries were filled by a popular Catholic Irish audience, whose fun and humorous sallies filled up the intervals of the acts, while their frequent cheers for the Lord Lieutenant, and frequent calls for "Patrick's Day" and "Kate Kearney" . . . produced a sort of national drama.[37]

At the end of the same year, her social metamorphosis was completed when she accepted the invitation to live in the household of the great Tory magnate, Lord Abercorn, putting up with the irritations of being patronised as an exotic family retainer for the entrée it

gave her into the highest social circles in England, and which she later extended to those of the Continent. The Abercorns also rather bullied her into marriage with their family doctor, Charles Morgan, and by procuring him a knighthood gave her the necessary independent social standing of a title. However, even before Sydney Owenson became Lady Morgan, her politics, like her views of history were markedly aristocratic.

The extension of her promotion of Catholic emancipation from writing novels to some involvement with O'Connell's campaign underlined her Whiggism. In 1826, together with her English and 'ultra liberal husband', she became part of the liberal Protestant support group, 'the friends of civil and religious liberty', as she described them. Deeply distrustful of O'Connell, and 'that nest of hornets', the Catholic Association', her role, even by her own exaggerated account[38] was confined mainly to providing part of the social milieu in which some of the Catholic leadership met their Protestant supporters, and sympathetic members of the Irish government. Her only attendance at a Catholic Association meeting was at the final one which, to her relief, decided on 'the prompt extinction of this great engine of popular opinion'. She hoped that the granting of emancipation would end popular agitation and her chagrin when this proved not to be the case, and her alarmism during the years following about 'revolution . . . from below', showed the extent to which she regarded emancipation as a boon to be conferred by the English government, at the instigation of liberal Protestant opinion in both countries.[39] This was not only in the Irish Whig tradition of her beloved Grattan, but also in a particular colonial tradition going back to the early sixteenth century and beyond. If, as I have argued elsewhere, Maria Edgeworth belonged to the Spencer tradition of colonial writing about Ireland, Morgan belonged to that of Anglo-Irish reformers and historians of the Pale.[40] Thus, her portrayal of Irish history featured the Anglo-Irish of Norman origin as both heroes and victims, a corrupt and essentially 'New English' aristocratic clique as villains, while the passive Gaelic Irish were patronised as well as sympathised with, and the English both castigated and appealed to. Lady Morgan may have belonged to this Anglo-Irish tradition less simply than Edgeworth belonged to hers, but it nonetheless offers an indispensable key to her writings.

The influence of Morgan's aristocratic and Whig ambiance on her fiction and politics was evident in her second Irish novel, *O'Donnel,* dedicated to the Duke of Devonshire who was described as the foremost among Ireland's

> great English landholders . . . whose conduct towards a grateful and prosperous tenantry best evinces in its effects how much the happiness and improvement of the lower classes of the

nation depend upon the enlightened liberality and benevolent attentions of the highest.[41]

The preface revealed her decision to change to a more overtly political and realist fiction, and explained why she had abandoned her initial plan to base the novel on 'the romantic adventures and unsubdued valour of O'Donnel the Red, Chief of Tir Conaill in the reign of Elizabeth', in favour of one which featured his latterday descendant.[42] She had, in fact, done a lot of research on Red Hugh, and had written one volume of the projected historical novel, before she abandoned it, partly under the influence of her newly acquired and fastidiously rationalist husband. 'As for me, I am every inch a wife', she wrote to a friend, 'and so ends the brilliant thing that was Glorvina'.[43] The death of her father, the original of 'the Prince of Innismore', in the same few months, may also have been a factor. Most important, however, was her changing historical perspective, which reflected the Anglo-Irish tradition of deep hostility to as well as fascination with the Gaelic world. In her own explanation, as well as the fear of encouraging 'discord' rather than 'conciliation', she instanced the disappointment of her hope 'to extenuate the errors attributed to Ireland, by an exposition of their causes, drawn from historic facts'. Instead, she found that she would be holding up 'a glass to my countrymen, reflecting but too many fearful images . . . for I discovered, far beyond my expectations, that I had fallen upon "evil men and evil days" '.[44] It is clear from the synopsis of her original plot, which she preserved in the text of the rewritten novel as the O'Donnel family history, that she had recoiled from the ultimate response of Red Hugh to the appalling injustices he had suffered, his joining with O'Neill in a major rebellion against the Crown, a response that 'the interests of humanity require to be buried in oblivion'.[45] O'Flanagan has argued that *O'Donnel* broke new ground in having a Gaelic Catholic aristocrat as hero,[46] but it is even more significant that, unlike his famous ancestor, the modern O'Donnel not only accepted the colonial settlement, but also helped to preserve it.

Morgan's retreat from the largely favourable view of the Gaelic world and the Gaelic past in *The Wild Irish Girl* was also influenced by the new critical approach to the Gaelic sources, evident in contemporary historians, and which was reflected in the increasingly hostile portrayal of antiquarians in her novels. Even in *The Wild Irish Girl*, the Prince's romantic antiquarianism, with its constant references to Keating and O'Halloran, is balanced somewhat by his daughter Glorvina's defence of McPherson's translations of Ossian. While her 'fancy is sometimes dazzled' by reading them in the original, she also thinks them spoiled by 'wildly improbable' and 'ridiculously grotesque details' and often prefers 'the refined medium of McPherson's genius.[47] The heroine of *Florence Macarthy,* a writer of Irish novels like her creator, has

an antiquarian library and lives in the half-ruined castle of her MacCarthy More ancestors. Yet she declares that, 'the present state of this poor country interests me more than its ancient, real or fabled, greatness'. In this novel Morgan's attack on Irish antiquarians commenced in earnest in her portrayal of Terence Oge O'Leary, pedantic schoolmaster and author of the 'Genealogical history of MacCarthy More, written in the Phoenician tongue, vulgo-vocato Irish, it being more precise and copious than the English and other barbarous dialects', as he described it. He is an archaic figure, though having some influence on the peasant mind, and is portrayed as in turn ludicrous, fanatical, pathetic, and sinister. Lest the reader miss the point, the author explains that O'Leary is 'an ancient Seanachy' of Ireland, 'credulous of her fables and jealous of her ancient glory; ardent in his feelings and fixed in his prejudices . . . living only in the past, contemptuous of the present and hopeless of the future'.[48] The father of Murrough O'Brien, the hero of *The O'Briens and the O'Flahertys* is 'a profound Seanachy, antiquarian and an Irish Philologist'. Despite his learned contribution to the recently established Royal Irish Academy, he too lived in the past, 'knowing nothing of modern Ireland but her sufferings and her wrongs', knowing little of ancient Ireland but her fables and her dreams'.[49] The reader is hardly too surprised to learn that he was also a secret Jesuit, dedicated to restoring the ancient high-kingship in the Catholic cause! Even after Lady Morgan, like Maria Edgeworth ten years earlier, had found both the Irish present and the Irish past too disturbing as subjects for fiction, she continued her attack on Ireland's 'learned and patriotic antiquarians', most notably in an interesting essay on 'Irish historians' published in 1841. This made the perceptive point that 'the native antiquarians stop short where fable ends and history begins, at the English invasion', and that most of the history of the later period and up to the present was written by Englishmen whose work gave them access to official records. She was also at pains to defend her own use of 'such images from the vasty deep of doubtful story' as she described material taken from Keating, O'Halloran and others, arguing that it was 'not only patriotism but sound policy' to use 'rhyme and reason, fact and fable, poetry and prose alike', to achieve the indispensable reform, Catholic Emancipation. This done, however, Ireland should look to the future, and not to the past,[50]—a naive if understandable hope, and a nice example of the fallacy that there can be a clear dividing line between 'history' and 'the present'.

Having, thus far, looked at the relationship of history to fiction in Lady Morgan's writings, and having discussed the main factors which influenced her historical understanding, it remains to examine her version of the Irish past, and the consequences for her of the ultimate failure of Catholic Ireland to share it. Her novels have contemporary settings, except for *The O'Briens and the O'Flahertys,* and even that is set within the timespan of her own lifetime. Instead, each reflects on the Irish historical experience over centuries, as a commentary on contemporary problems. Nonetheless, it is possible to construct from them her cumulative portrayal of that experience, which for the purposes of this paper, can be divided into three distinct phases:

(a) Her account of the conquest from the twelfth century to the seventeenth, and in particular, its impact on the old Gaelic elite.

(b) Her depiction of the more recent past, especially of 1782-1800, as the golden age of Irish Whiggism, its frustration and betrayal.

(c) The history of the Catholic cause and its championship by Irish Whigs, the final phase, as she believed, or rather hoped, of Ireland's revolution.

The regret of the hero Mortimer, in *The Wild Irish Girl* that his Cromwellian ancestors had taken possession of the land of the Prince of Innismore by force, was not to be repeated in Lady Morgan's fiction.[51] Instead there was an insistence that the colonial past, despite the acts of injustice associated with it, should be accepted as an accomplished fact and a commonplace of history. This sentiment was, appropriately, most clearly expressed by the sophisticated Europeanised descendant of the O'Donnel, who argued with a tired fatalism 'that in Ireland, as in all nations, what is won by the sword becomes legitimate property; that time sanctions usurpations, and that possessions long maintained, however gotten, are consecrated by the lapse of ages, and held by the best of all tenures, prescriptive right'. He went even further, stating 'the O'Donnels were not, *even anciently,* the original possessors of the land over which they reigned for centuries, which they won by the sword and which the sword partly won in turn from them'[52]—a sentiment in line indeed with the Gaelic tradition of pragmatic fatalism, articulated, for example, in similar language by Tadhg Dall Ó hUiginn in the late sixteenth century poem written in defence of the claims of the Anglo-Norman Mac Uilliam Burc.[53] It adds to the sense of piquancy, perhaps, that among Ó hUiginn's Gaelic patrons were the O'Donnells! While the results of conquest should be accepted, however, Morgan voiced criticism of its various stages. The main attack on the Normans came, again appropriately, from the 'true Geraldine' hero of *Florence Macarthy,* Fitzadelm, who described them as adventurers who 'took the sanction of heaven for their deeds of violence'. This was essentially a literary device, part of the process of reconciliation between the descendants of Norman and Gaelic Irish nobility, which was the main concern of the novel. Her belief that the quarrels of the thirteenth and fourteenth centuries were an enduring source of friction was articulated mainly

by the seanachy O'Leary, who regularly confused events from that period with those of his own day.[54] This recognition of the importance of what Oliver MacDonagh has called 'the elision of time' in 'the Irish habit of historical thought' formed in this period,[55] persisted in all Morgan's novels. One of its main functions was to explain the sense of grievance felt by the victims of the different stages by which Ireland became, in the words of the learned chaplain to the Prince of Innismore, 'a colonised or a conquered country'.[56] Naturally, this sense of historical wrong was expressed in a manner which aided the argument in favour of Catholic emancipation as reparatory justice. Thus the Ulster O'Donnells, although 'a people unsophisticated and unrefined', had a 'hereditary fealty and attachment' to the English crown, and were driven to rebellion by the unjust persecution inflicted by new English officials like Perrott, Bagnal and Bingham, who acted against the express wishes of the Queen. Red Hugh's response therefore, was understandable, although it went too far.[57] Morgan's particular heroes, 'the descendants of the princely Geraldines'[58] were also the victims of the Tudor reconquest. In *Florence Macarthy,* for example, Walter Raleigh is attacked as a 'freebooter', and 'little better than the captain of licensed banditti' for his attacks on the Roches and the Barrys, and others

> of English origin, men who still inherited from their ancestors some recollection of Magna Carta. They therefore . . . either protected or burnt their castles and were consequently 'rebels'. The persecution of the illustrious family of the Fitzgeralds, in the persons of the celebrated Earl of Kildare and the great Earl of Desmond, whose crime was being the richest subject in the empire, are too well known to need comment.[59]

In the same vein, the wars of the 1640s were described in *The O'Briens and the O'Flahertys* as being between the 'loyal Irish and English rebels', and the Cromwellian period as an unlawful tyranny. William of Orange had 'wise and benevolent intentions' towards the Irish, and was distanced carefully from the persecution of Irish Catholics under the Penal Code as he was in John Banim's major historical novel, *The Boyne Water* (1826). In a well-pitched appeal to English Whig prejudice as well as the Whig sense of justice, the worldly Gaelic Irish exile, Count O'Flaherty, reflected on the events of the seventeenth century.

> I shall never dispute that the English might not have acted wisely in exterminating the Irish at the time of the revolution, and thus getting rid of a race which they looked upon as armed in the cause of despotism and bigotry . . . Having, however, permitted the Irish to live, they should not have deprived them of all the rights which give life its moral dignity.[60]

This emphasis on 'the demoralisation of the people it persecuted and brutified'[61] was central to Morgan's interpretation of the colonial process.

Her reiterated categorisation of Irish history as one of 'misrule and oppression', indeed of 'six hundred years of oppression'[62] also had a traditional Anglo-Irish focus. The villains of the piece are English governments (though not English monarchs) and even more, the corrupt, *arriviste* 'new English' adventurers who dominated Irish government from the mid-seventeenth century. She quoted as Grattan's description of them, that they were 'one of the worst of oligarchies . . . a plebeian oligarchy'[63] and also portrayed them in party terms as Irish Tories, 'advocates of their own arbitrary power', who corrupted the 'Whiggish toast' to William of Orange to mean, 'the subjection of the Catholic population, an unequal distribution of rights and the supremacy of a narrow, bigotted and impolitic intolerance'.[64] To a poor Dubliner in *Florence Macarthy* they are 'the Ascendancy, sir; only for it . . . wouldn't we be this day hand in glove, orange and green; sorrow one colour you'd know from the other, Och! but that would not do—where would the Ascendancy be? only all Irish men then'.[65] This 'banditti of dictators' came under heaviest fire in *The O'Briens and the O'Flahertys,* as 'an oligarchy, in whose members the sense of irresponsible power engendered a contempt for private morals, as fatal as their political corruption'. They are represented especially by the Knockloftys, 'dull as the Dutchmen from whom they were descended, tasteless as they were talentless', and the amoral leaders of a corrupt viceregal court, which is compared to that of Versailles, in being 'at once puerile and licentious'. These 'political vampires', were thus part of the 'proconsular despotism' against which the Anglo-Irish Whigs had to contend.[66]

The manner in which Morgan portrayed the impact of colonialism on the native Irish was also charged with moral judgment. Unlike Scott, her interest in the social dimension of the Gaelic collapse was minimal, and confined largely to answering Protestant fears about the stability of the land settlement. She concentrated instead on the psychological response, and in a way which conveyed a distinct impatience, even contempt. The hero in *Florence Macarthy* encompassed the theme in general terms when he spoke of 'that demoralisation which the misrule of centuries has impressed upon all branches of its [i.e. Ireland's] population'.[67] This was discussed in greatest detail in *The O'Briens and the O'Flahertys,* in which the hero's father, the apostate Baron Terence O'Brien, was described as a typical figure,

> with thoughts ever retrospective to the glories of "ancient old Ireland", and with that religious tendency to passive obedience with which . . . Catholics are accursed, he is a rebel and a royalist

on the same principles. These conflicting opinions he veils under an exterior of the most unlimited submission of the powers that be . . . In a word, he is only a "brief abstract" of a large class of his countrymen, such as six centuries of degradation had made them.[68]

Later in the novel, his idealistic son, Murrough, was urged by the heroine to leave the country, as it offered no hope for patriots. 'Here the fortitude of long endurance corrupts into obsequiousness; and the spirit of the gallant maddens into lawless intemperance'. Frustrated in his attempt to establish United Irish activity in Connaught, he was forced to agree, and he echoed the view that native demoralisation was largely self-induced, and due to the combined effects of Catholicism and a warped view of history. Thus, the Catholic gentry

> slept over the degradation of their caste . . . Six hundred years of oppression were producing their moral effects. The conscientious notions of passive obedience of the Catholic were then fortified by the seared and calloused feelings of the man; while . . . pride and ambition . . . were exchanged for a silly, but too national vanity, which centred itself on the oft cited past.

Among such people he concluded, 'no political impression was feasible'.[69]

This perspective dominated the native Irish stereotype that emerges from these novels. *The Wild Irish Girl* in setting out to dispel the initial 'decided prejudice' of the hero against the 'semi-barbarous, semi-civilised Irish' developed one typical form of colonial stereotype, that of the reverse image. Thus the Irish were portrayed in this novel as heirs to a great, if destroyed civilisation, and despite their poverty were hospitable, enlightened and good-humoured. This stereotype also had its negative side; for example the explanaton as to why there were so few architectural remains of the pre-Christian era was double-edged

> The ancient Irish, like the modern, had more soul, more genius, than worldly prudence, or cautious, calculating forethought . . . works of imagination seduced them from pursuing works of utility[70]

—including one can infer, uniting to resist outside aggression. In the later novels the stereotype was designed to reflect the colonial experience rather than to deny it. When the Anglo-Irish hero of *Florence Macarthy* arrived at the Dublin quays, he employed a native porter. He was 'miserably clad, disgustingly filthy, squalid, meagre and famished'. He was at the same time both 'debasingly acquiescent' and 'yet preserved the vindictiveness of conscious degradation'. Such dangerous duality was stressed several times in the novel, and was particularly threatening in the figure of Owney Rabragh, the peasant leader, who displayed 'qualities inherent in the lower Irish. Warm friends and revengeful enemies, inviolable in their secrecy, devoted in their attachments, inexorable in their resentments'. It was also emphasised, however, that the less savoury aspects of the Irish stereotype were the products of injustice, as in the explanation of Glentworth, the liberal Protestant landlord in *O'Donnel,* of the linguistic cunning of the poor as, 'the natural qualities of a people who long had nothing but address to oppose to force or to disarm oppression'—an interesting echo of Edgeworth's analysis of peasant speech.[71] A more flamboyant embodiment of the stereotype, and also an amalgam of the traditional 'wild Irish' figure with that of the fashionable 'noble savage', was Shane na Brien, the hero's foster-brother in *The O'Briens and the O'Flahertys.* He was 'a fine specimen of the mere Irish animal in its highest spiritual perfection', and an example of the degeneracy of the old native aristocracy 'to desperate outlaws'. Combining fanatical loyalty to his friends, with murderous revenge against his and their enemies, 'this last specimen of the Raparees of the earlier part of the last century, had the true Irish spirits, formed for every excitement, to madden into riotous gaiety, to sink into gloomy despondency'.[72] There were some positive elements in her portrayal of aspects of the threatening Gaelic subculture in the later novels, particularly of fosterage. There are also some surprising insights, like that into the dual loyalty of Terence Oge O'Leary, being, in his own words, 'tributory and seanachy . . . to the McCarthys' while 'servitor in the great Norman family of the Fitzadelms'—an almost uncanny echo of the position of Aogán Ó Rathaille, the great Gaelic poet of a century before, who also venerated the broken McCarthys as his hereditary lords, while depending on Anglo-Irish patronage.[73]

Lady Morgan had been fascinated by the tragedy of the dispossessed Gaelic nobility ever since meeting some real-life examples as a child. She based the Prince of Innismore partly on the McDermott of Coolavin, O'Donnel on 'the celebrated Charles O'Connor of Ballinagar', and Murrough O'Brien partly on Lord Cloncurry. Yet despite the fact that she liked to talk, even late in life, of 'my friend the O'Connor Don of Ballynagar, as legitimate a representative of the true kings of Ireland as any sovereign on or off his throne, at this moment in Europe',[74] her fictional presentation of the older generation of such people was as archaic, pathetic and obsessive figures—their ruined castles and museums full of symbols of long vanished greatness, their quarrels and ambitions rooted in an irrecoverable past.[75] The younger generation, however, were more enlightened and forward looking; made so by the tragedy of exile, the men having 'to fight on foreign grounds for foreign interests', while all her heroines after 'the purely national and natural' Glorvina[76] had

been educated in Europe. Rory O'Donnell and Murrough O'Brien represented a different romantic tradition than did the Prince of Innismore, not of the broken Gaelic past, but of the adventurous European present—the former a supporter of the ancient regime in France, just as he is an apologist for the colonial system in Ireland; the latter a modern liberal and a veteran of the French revolution, who became a United Irishman. While both suffer from 'mortified pride' at their present poverty and their family's historic wrongs, they turn their backs resolutely on the past. O'Brien does so as a result of reading the 'Annals' of his family history, compiled by his antiquarian father, and rejecting them as the 'fables' of 'a barbarous people . . . their boasted learning a tissue of monkish legends; their government, the rudest form of the worst of human institutions, feudality'.[77] While O'Brien finally despaired of changing Ireland and returned to France, Morgan's earlier young Gaelic heroes and heroines had stayed on. Their role was to be that of enlightened landlords, who had particular advantages, as will become clear, when we examine her odd treatment of one of the main worries that opponents of Catholic emancipation claimed to have, that is, the attitude of Catholics to the colonial land settlement.

In *The Wild Irish Girl,* the chaplain to the Prince dismissed 'the erroneous claim' made by the peasantry that they were 'the hereditary proprietors of the soil they cultivate', and the author in a footnote stated that the Irish of superior rank, whose ancestors had indeed been dispossessed, accepted the status quo.[78] The conformist hero of the next Irish novel, *O'Donnel,* demonstrated her contention admirably, defending the prescriptive rights of conquest, and even substantiating the claims of an English heiress to what had remained of his family's property, in court. He also repudiated the popular belief that he was, 'by the law of nature, the true heir'. And yet, at the end of the novel, by his marriage to the heiress, he *did* become, in the author's words, 'reinstated in some part of the vast possessions of his ancestors, forfeited at various periods, by the vicissitudes of property, incidental to the former unhappy state of Ireland'. In the same way, the heiress to the Macarthys repossessed their 'ancient castle and vast possessions' by her marriage to the Marquis of Dunore, while Glorvina had similarly restored to her family the land taken from them by the Cromwellian Mortimers.[79] This apparent contradiction is interesting, and reflected, in part at least, a tension between the separate aims of answering Protestant fears and of exploiting the classic symbol of reconciliation. It is also, perhaps, less of a contradiction than it seems. The alliance of the young, liberal Anglo-Irish and Gaelic nobility was an unequal one, the Gaelic partner being in a clearly subordinate position in terms of property and inheritance but still fulfilling an important role in acting as a link between the now loyal tenantry and the Anglo-Irish enlightened landlord, and thus achieving social cohesion as well as 'national unity'. Thus, for example, Florence McCarthy, after her marriage was, doubtless, able to exploit what she had earlier described as 'the prejudice which runs so strongly in favour of the representatives of [the tenants'] ancient chiefs, on my side, born and reared among them, speaking their language and assimilated to them in a thousand ways'. A similar exploitation of traditional loyalties is suggested by Maria Edgeworth at the end of *Ormond* (1817).[80]

The theme of Catholic repossession was dealt with differently in Morgan's darkest, and on the Catholic question, most confused novel, *The O'Briens and the O'Flahertys*. In this, the Catholic exile, Count O'Flaherty, recovered land at the beginning rather than at the end of the book, and he did so in accordance with stereotyped Protestant fears, by a court case over title, adding insult to injury by establishing a convent on the land! The portrayal of Catholicism throughout the novel as a sinister, Jesuit-run conspiracy also sits oddly with the declared intention of promoting the Emancipation cause, and serves as a reminder that Morgan, in the Irish Whig tradition, viewed Catholicism in itself with intense dislike, and the removal of the Penal Code as a great libertarian cause, to be achieved under the auspices of an enlightened Anglo-Irish leadership. The celebration of their time of greatest achievement and saddest defeat, the story of Ireland's lost revolution, was her real objective in what was to be, not inappropriately, her final Irish novel.

It was also appropriate that Henry Grattan should make a brief appearance, as he played a major role in the creation of the myth of the revolution achieved in 1782 and betrayed in 1800. His rhetoric echoes in her survey of the period between the 1770s, where the novel begins, and the 1790s, where much the greater part of it is set. 'America had revolted, and England, in her hour of peril, fearing Ireland as the aggressor in times of danger always fears the oppressed, reluctantly abandoned a part of that all-pervading and comprehensive system of tyranny'. The Volunteers were described in similarly extravagant and misleading rhetoric. 'Permitted to arm in their own defence, the Irish stood forth with all their ancient valour and with more than their ancient unity, to protect their native land from foreign aggression, and to realise that splendid dream of political philosophy, a national army'. Her heroes, having won 'Free Trade' and 'legislative independence', continued to fight against the corrupt Ascendancy clique, who are determined to destroy them, especially after, 'The French revolution, at its dawn so splendid and so temperate, produced in Ireland an effect the most powerful and electric'. Even thus embattled, the Irish revolution had an instantaneous and even physical impact, as 'from the year 1782 . . . the city [Dublin] rose from its rubbish and the hovel of mud became a palace of marble'. On a different level, 'never did any country give to the world a more splendid or more intellectual generation as that which now burst forth to illustrate the benefits of political independence'.[81] The Volunteer Review in the Phoenix park, which began the second part of *The O'Briens and the O'Flahertys,* was graphically and affectionately portrayed as a great popular demonstration, led by Lord Charlemont, 'one of those men who hallow a whole people', and who had helped to establish this 'revolution without blood'. The portrayal of real historical characters in this book was simply as great public figures, looked at from a distance, very different from the brilliant psychological portraits of such people in Scott. Thus Grattan, as he marched past, was only described as 'one of the greatest men that Ireland ever produced . . . the Irish Cicero'.[82]

The most interesting aspect of Morgan's version of the 'Golden Age' of Anglo-Ireland was the inclusion of the United Irishmen, or rather the moderate aristocratic elements in that movement, firmly within the tradition. This, again, followed trends in history writing, a number of apologias by United Irish leaders having already appeared, while Moore was contemplating a life of his friend Lord Edward Fitzgerald and Madden was working on his monumental account. Her view of the early United Irish leadership as a frustrated younger generation of Irish Whigs had much validity, in terms both of their own self-perception and their ideology.[83] Its claimed aristocratic character was certainly decisive for her hero, Murrough O'Brien, proud of his descent from Brian Boru, and expelled from Trinity as 'the Irish Mirabeau', on the evidence of letters which discussed 'the separation of Ireland from England', and were believed to be his, though belonging in fact to Lord Walter Fitzwalter—clearly modelled on Lord Edward Fitzgerald. Fitzwalter, in fact, rejected separatism, which was 'as physically impossible at the moment as it would always be politically unwise', but he enthused about 'a national union, the brotherhood of affection, that community of interest, which . . . effect a regeneration by means as constitutional as they are effectual', and urged O'Brien to join the United Irishmen whose members, he assured him, came from 'the most illustrious families'. Despite some reservations, O'Brien agreed, mainly because Fitzwalter was a member, 'the descendant of the princely Geraldines, the brother of a peer of the realm'.[84]

The theme of aristocratic Anglo-Irish leadership of the movement was continued in the description of the Tailors Hall meeting that evening, presided over by Simon Butler, a descendant of 'the great Anglo-Norman Lords of the Pale'. Tone, Tandy, Drennan, Emmet and Rowan, were all described—as seen from the gallery— and their Protestantism stressed. The details and the rhetoric were based on contemporary sources, most remarkable being her echoing of an image from Tone, in her description of the rank and file at this meeting, 'the stern brow of uncompromising Presbyterianism, contrasting to the mobile, varying muscle of downtrodden Catholicism; the latter drawling forth its plaintive discontents, the former announcing its immovable resolutions'. When she described O'Brien and Fitzwalter as 'two representatives of the Norman and Milesian races of Ireland', united at 'the shrine of national independence', Morgan clearly saw such a 'national union' in terms of aristocratic leadership, just as Tone saw it in terms of the middle classes. Given her romantic view of the United Irishmen, it is not surprising that Morgan avoided the traumatic class and sectarian violence of 1798 in this novel, beyond a brief reference to 'the reign of terror which preceded the horrible epoch of the rebellion'.[85] Earlier, in *Florence Macarthy* she had given the Grattanite version of it being a reaction against ascendancy tyranny, and 'excited for the purpose of effecting a ruinous Union'. The first volume of that book gave an exaggerated account of the effect of the Union (always described as a 'betrayal') on Dublin, its trade ruined, its suburbs a sea of poverty, its magnificent centre 'still, silent and void'. It was, in the words of the Grattan-type character, Hyacinth Daly, a 'fallen capital'; its tragedy being best summed up by 'the many hotels which now succeed in the patrician streets of Dublin to the mansions of the banished nobility'. The contrast with the bustling, if vulgarised Dublin of Maria Edgeworth's, *The Absentee,* underlines their differences in political perspective as well as in literary purpose.[86]

The Union also meant an end to the Irish Whigs' shadowy dream of 'national independence' and their cause reverted to the more prosaic matter of completing the Irish revolution by emancipating the Catholics. The author herself became part of this historical phase through her roles as Whig hostess, qualified supporter of the Catholic Association, and above all, as political novelist, whose 'national tales' were intended as vivid arguments for this 'great national cause'.[87] She saw Catholic emancipation in a dual historical perspective, as both the culmination of the seventeenth-century 'revolution' in favour of civil and religious liberty, and as a necessary guarantee for the permanence of the colonial settlement, with which that revolution had a close and tension-filled relationship in Ireland. Some elements of her novels were more simply, even crudely propagandistic in the Catholic cause, like the wildly exaggerated catalogue of horrors she portrayed as the operation of the Penal Code in the 1770s, in the first part of *The O'Briens and the O'Flahertys.*[88] This was balanced, however, by the anti-Catholic tone of the novel as a whole, and its emphasis on the Anglo-Irish leadership of a passive Catholicism. The very different reality of the O'Connellite campaign, with its dynamic bourgeois Catholic leadership, its liberal Protestant auxiliaries, and its terrifyingly disciplined mass politics, had already begun to distress her, as she wrote what was to be her last Irish novel. In the aftermath of

Emancipation, her diary and correspondence became strident with warnings about 'revolution' and 'terrorism', and when these subsided, querulous with disenchantment at a country she described as being 'between bedlam and a jail'. In the end, she quit 'wretched Dublin, the capital of wretched Ireland' altogether in 1837, and went to live in London, helped by a pension from the Melbourne government.[89] Her dilemma was, of course, the classic Whig one. What she believed and wanted to be the end of a revolution turned out to be the start of an entirely different one, under new auspices. The initiative having clearly passed to others within Ireland, she concentrated in her later years on urging support for the English Whigs, 'Ireland's longtime friends', and above all, for an end to agitation.[90]

While she wrote no more Irish novels after 1827, Lady Morgan did write a fictional representation of post-emancipation Irish society and politics in a play, *Manor Sackville,* published in an odd collection entitled *Dramatic Scenes of real life,* in 1833. This dark and pessimistic work featured a liberal and enlightened Englishman who, inheriting an Irish estate, tried to run it on just and humanitarian principles, only to be attacked and driven out by Orange bigots, Catholic politicians and the very peasants he had tried to help and who repaid him by an attempt on his life. Of particular significance was the connection clearly made between the activities of the agrarian secret society and the inflated rhetoric of the preposterous lower middle class catholic 'pathriots'—who disliked the hero because 'he took part with the base Whigs and talked of conciliaytion'. Safely back in London Sackville rejected the 'pathriot' argument that Ireland suffered under despotic government. 'Emancipated Ireland . . . is free . . . repose is now her most urgent necessity'. Earlier, in a key scene in the play, he had argued with the young Maynooth-trained curate for a particular form of 'repose'—that Ireland should 'forget the past'. The priest not only argued for 'the importance of keeping up the national spirit by preserving the glorious remembrance of past times', he stressed particularly that the Irish people should remember their saints and martyrs, 'who were deprived of their liberty and their ancient, national and venerated Church'. Sackville abandoned the argument, making little impression with the assertion that Ireland needed 'not saints, but citizens; not heroes, but peacable, industrious and calculating utilitarians'.[91] Not only had the political revolution failed to stop at Catholic emancipation, but Irish history, Morgan's own favoured political weapon, had been hijacked by a new Catholic nationalism. She even worried that she might have been responsible for releasing a genie, which had now run amok, and in many of her later writings was at pains to defend the use she had made of Irish history and legend in the interest of achieving Catholic Emancipation, while insisting that the success of that reform meant that 'such signs and images of the worst times in the history of humanity', which had been 'new burnished', should 'now be returned to the old property room of Irish vanity, as no longer applicable to the wants of the times'.

The implication that history could be so easily manipulated, and that her version of it should prevail, tells us much about Lady Morgan's fiction as well as her politics. She was not, of course, altogether mistaken on either count, and we can see what she could not, that her political and her historical perspectives were to continue as important elements in Irish constitutional and cultural nationalism. Like Liberalism in Britain a century later, Anglo-Irish Whiggism was to become a dominant ideology even while it declined as a political force. Lady Morgan's novels may have had no discernible political impact, but they reflected and contributed to an increasingly popular political culture. Through such writings, at least in part, the work of antiquarians and historians entered the arena of political discourse, and the rhetoric of O'Connell, as well as of Young Ireland bristled with the symbolism and the shorthand that recur in all her novels—harps and wolfhounds, 'six hundred years of oppression', the dark despairing eighteenth century relieved by the Golden Age of Grattan's Parliament and ending in the catastrophe of the Union. Her advocacy of a confrontation with Ireland's colonial history as a basis for reconciliation anticipated Davis; but her version of that history, like his, itself became a weapon in the process of polarisation which she had aimed to reverse. In literary terms she deserves more attention than she has received, and may benefit from the current interest in feminist literature, as one of the first truly professional women novelists and one whose heroines were dominant and intellectual. She is also an important, and sometimes very good novelist of her native Dublin, despite her normal association with the romantic west. Her main importance as a writer, however, may lie precisely in the area on which this paper has focused—the manner in which she made historical sources and historical themes the raw material and the subject matter of a political fiction. While Scott's inferior in terms of both historical understanding and literary skill, she too developed a distinctive form of historical fiction, which exploited and reflected the shadowy boundary that then existed between these two related forms of literary discourse. The contrast between Morgan and Scott reflected even more the extent to which the nature of a society's historical experience shapes its literature. The Irish novel, then and since, has been haunted by history, and, with the possible exception of Joyce, has been unable to put it into the kind of perspective achieved by Scott. 'A nightmare from which I am trying to awake', as Dedalus called Irish history,[92] produced a less coherent, and in many ways more interesting fiction.

Notes and References

[1] Lady Morgan, *The Wild Irish Girl*, 3 vols (London, 1806); *O'Donnel. A national tale*, 3 vols (London, 1814); *Florence Macarthy. An Irish tale*, 4 vols (London, 1818); *The O'Briens and the O'Flahertys. A national tale*, 4 vols (London, 1827).

[2] *O'Donnel*, i, p. vii.

[3] P. Ricoeur, *Hermeneutics and the human sciences. Essays on language, action and interpretation* (Cambridge, 1981), pp. 274-96.

[4] F. Jameson, *The political unconscious. Narrative as a socially symbolic act* (London, 1981), p. 17.

[5] cf. Leo Braudy, *Narrative form in history and fiction: Hume, Fielding and Gibbon* (Princeton, 1970), esp. Ch. 1.

[6] H. Hepworth Dixon (ed.), *Lady Morgan's memoirs: autobiography, diary and correspondence*, 2 vols (London, 1863), ii, p. 324; L. Stevenson, *The Wild Irish Girl. The Life of Sydney Owenson, Lady Morgan* (London, 1936), pp 242-3; W. J. Fitzpatrick, *Lady Morgan, her career, literary and personal, with a glimpse of her friends and a word to her calumniators* (London, 1860), pp. 285-6; Stevenson, *Life*, p. 237.

[7] Stevenson, *Life*, pp. 234, 287; *Morgan's Memoirs*, ii, pp 381-3.

[8] D. McCartney, 'The writing of history in Ireland, 1800-1830', *Irish Historical Studies*, x, 1957, pp. 347-62.

[9] O. MacDonagh, *States of Mind. A Study of Anglo-Irish conflict 1780-1980* (London, 1983), p. 6.

[10] *O'Donnel*, i, pp. vii-xii.

[11] cf. T. Dunne, *Maria Edgeworth and the colonial mind* (O'Donnell Lecture, National University of Ireland, 1984).

[12] T. Eagleton, *Literary Theory. An introduction* (Oxford, 1983), p. 73.

[13] *O'Donnel* (1846 ed.), Preface.

[14] *O'Donnel*, iii, p. 259.

[15] *Florence Macarthy*, i, pp. 133-4.

[16] *Wild Irish Girl*, ii, p. 117.

[17] *O'Donnel*, iii, pp. 192-3, 267-8.

[18] *Florence Macarthy*, iii, p. 39.

[19] *The O'Briens and the O'Flahertys*, i, p. 85.

[20] *O'Donnel*, i, pp. vii-xii.

[21] Stevenson, *Life,* p. 202.

[22] G. Lukacs, *The historical novel* (English ed., 1962), pp. 30-63.

[23] D. Brown, *Walter Scott and the historical imagination* (London, 1979), esp. Ch. 3.

[24] *Wild Irish Girl* (1846 ed.), p. xxv; *The O'Briens and the O'Flahertys,* i, p. ix.

[25] *The novice of St Dominic* (1806); *The missionary, an Indian tale* (1811).

[26] Brown, *op. cit.,* p. 184.

[27] Stevenson, *Life,* p. 3; *Morgan's Memoirs,* i, p. 40.

[28] Stevenson, *Life,* p. 159.

[29] M. Butler, *Maria Edgeworth, a literary biography* (Oxford, 1972), p. 448.

[30] *Morgan's Memoirs,* i, Ch. VII; ii, p. 529.

[31] Miss Owenson, *The lay of the Irish harp* (London, 1807), esp. the preface; *Morgan's Memoirs,* i, pp. 258-67; Stevenson, *Life,* p. 67.

[32] *Morgan's Memoirs,* i, p. 164. For her misuse of Irish words, cf. ibid., pp. 14, 165; *The O'Briens and the O'Flahertys,* ii, p. 293.

[33] *Morgan's Memoirs,* i, pp. 258-60.

[34] Stevenson, *Life,* p. 1.

[35] *Morgan's Memoirs,* i, Ch. 4; Stevenson, *Life,* pp. 11-24.

[36] *Wild Irish Girl* (1846 ed.), pp. xxxiii-iv.

[37] Ibid., p. xxxv, footnote.

[38] *Wild Irish Girl,* ii, pp. 224 ff.

[39] Ibid., pp. 274-319.

[40] Dunne, *Edgeworth and the colonial mind;* B. Bradshaw, *The Irish constitutional revolution in the sixteenth century* (Cambridge, 1979); C. Lennon, *Richard Stanihurst, the Dubliner 1547-1618* (Dublin, 1981).

[41] *O'Donnel,* i, dedication page.

[42] Ibid., pp vii-xii.

[43] *Morgan's Memoirs,* i, p. 519; ii, p. 5.

[44] *O'Donnel,* i, pp. x-xi.

[45] Ibid., ii, pp 7-36; i, p. xi.

[46] T. Flanagan, *The Irish novelists 1800-1850* (Connecticut, 1958), p. 133.

[47] *Wild Irish Girl,* ii, pp. 92-5.

[48] *Florence Macarthy,* ii, p. 247; i, pp. 265, 284-5.

[49] *The O'Briens and the O'Flahertys,* i, pp 30, 55-6; ii, pp. 211-12.

[50] Sir T. C. and Lady Morgan, *The book without a name,* 2 vols (London, 1841), ii, pp. 163-5, 171-2.

[51] *Wild Irish Girl,* i, p. 129.

[52] *O'Donnel,* iii, pp. 274-5, 271-2.

[53] E. Knott, *A bhfuil againn dar chum Tadhg Dall Ó h Uiginn,* 2 vols (Dublin, 1921, 1926), i, No. 17.

[54] *Florence Macarthy,* i, pp. 312-3; iii, p. 119, 198.

[55] MacDonagh, *States of Mind,* Ch. 1.

[56] *Wild Irish Girl,* iii, pp. 15-16.

[57] *O'Donnel,* iii, pp. 7-36, 333-9.

[58] *The O'Briens and the O'Flahertys,* iii, p. 77.

[59] *Florence Macarthy,* i, pp. 321-7, 14-16.

[60] *The O'Briens and the O'Flahertys,* ii, pp. 273-85.

[61] *Florence Macarthy,* i, pp 326-7. Cf. also ibid., iii, pp 119, 271; iv, p. 268; *The O'Briens and the O'Flahertys,* i, pp 26, 68-9; iv, pp. 283-4.

[62] e.g. *Florence Macarthy,* i, p. 95; ii, pp. 231-2. *The O'Briens and the O'Flahertys,* i, pp. 68-9; iv, pp. 283-4.

[63] *Wild Irish Girl* (1846 ed.), p. xxxix, footnote. The phrase was originally Edmund Burke's, in *Letter to a peer of Ireland on the Penal Laws against Irish Catholics* (1782). For a recent discussion of Burke's argument see S. Deane, *Celtic Revivals. Essays in modern Irish literature* (1985), pp. 23-31.

[64] *Florence Macarthy,* ii, pp. 109-10.

[65] Ibid., i, p. 53.

[66] *The O'Briens and the O'Flahertys,* i, pp. 142-5, and p. vii of preface; ii, pp. 149, 154, 5.

[67] *Florence Macarthy,* ii, p. 119. Also, ibid., p. 271; iv, p. 268; *O'Donnel,* i, p. 203.

[68] *The O'Briens and the O'Flahertys,* i, pp 68-71.

[69] Ibid., iv, pp. 244-6, 283-4.

[70] *Wild Irish Girl,* i, p. xxix; ii, p. 72.

[71] *Florence Macarthy,* i, pp. 21, 92; iii, p. 136; iv, p. 8; *O'Donnel,* i, p. 204; Dunne, *Edgeworth and the colonial mind,* pp. 17-21.

[72] *The O'Briens and the O'Flahertys,* i, pp. 30-32; ii, pp. 286 ff.

[73] *Florence Macarthy,* iii, p. 62. S. Ó Tuama, *Fili faoi sceimhle* (Dublin, 1978), pp. 83-184; T. Dunne, 'The Gaelic response to conquest and colonisation: the evidence of the poetry', *Studia Hibernica,* No. 20, 1980.

[74] Stevenson, *Life,* p. 73; *O'Donnel,* ii, pp. 317-19 (footnote); *Morgan's Memoirs,* ii, p. 195; i, p. 65.

[75] e.g. *Wild Irish Girl,* i, pp. 138 ff., 194-8; ii, pp. 50 ff.; iii, p. 229. *The O'Briens and the O'Flahertys,* i, pp. 253 ff.; ii, pp. 191 ff.; 329 ff.

[76] *The O'Briens and the O'Flahertys,* i, pp. 71-2; Florence Macarthy, iii, p. 149; *Wild Irish Girl,* ii, p. 109.

[77] *O'Donnel,* ii, p. 39; *The O'Briens and the O'Flahertys,* ii, pp. 256-7.

[78] *Wild Irish Girl,* iii, p. 65.

[79] *O'Donnel,* iii, pp 150-61, 267-8, 304-5; *Florence Macarthy,* iv, p. 282; *Wild Irish Girl,* iii, pp. 258-9.

[80] *Florence Macarthy,* iii, p. 276. Cf. also *O'Donnel,* iii, pp. 304-5; *Wild Irish Girl,* iii, p. 259. Cf. Dunne, *Edgeworth and the colonial mind,* pp. 13-14.

[81] *The O'Briens and the O'Flahertys,* i, pp. 138, 140-46, 253; iii, pp. 6-7.

[82] Ibid., i, pp. 146-7, 163.

[83] e.g. T. A. Emmet et al., *Memoire, a detailed statement of the origin and progress of the Irish union . . .* (1802). T. Moore, *The life and death of Lord Edward Fitzgerald* appeared in 1831, while R. R. Madden's multi-volume series on *The United Irishmen, their lives and times* appeared between 1842 and 1846.

[84] *The O'Briens and the O'Flahertys,* i, pp. 161-4; iii, Ch. 2.

[85] Ibid., iii, pp. 112-14; iv, p. 324. Theobald Wolfe Tone, *An argument on behalf of the Catholics of Ireland* (Dublin, 1791), p. 10. T. Dunne, *Theobald Wolfe Tone: Colonial Outsider. An analysis of his political philosophy* (Cork, 1982), Ch. iv.

[86] *Florence Macarthy,* i, pp. 21 ff. Maria Edgeworth, *The Absentee,* 2 vols (1812), ii, Ch. 1. Cf. W. J. McCormack, *Ascendancy and Tradition in Anglo-Irish Literary History from 1789 to 1939* (Oxford, 1985), Ch. 4.

[87] *O'Donnel* (1846 ed.), preface.

[88] *The O'Briens and the O'Flahertys,* i, pp. 22-6, 54-73, 98-102.

[89] *Morgan's Memoirs,* ii, pp. 313-19, 379-81. Stevenson, *Life,* p. 299.

[90] *Morgan's Memoirs,* ii, pp. 313-14; *Wild Irish Girl* (1846 ed.), preface; Lady Morgan, *Dramatic scenes from real life,* 2 vols (London, 1833), i, pp. 244-6.

[91] *Manor Sackville,* comprising Vol. i, and pp. 1-30 of Vol. ii of *Dramatic scenes of real life.* Cf. especially i, pp. 233-49; ii, pp. 27-8; i, pp. 154-63.

[92] James Joyce, *Ulysses* (1922), p. 40 (Penguin ed.).

FURTHER READING

Anonymous. *"The Complete Works of Gerald Griffin."* Brownson's *Quarterly Review* IV, No. XV (July 1859): 342-72.

Offers a largely favorable appraisal of Griffin's writing.

Cahalan, James M. *Great Hatred, Little Room: The Irish Historical Novel.* Syracuse: Syracuse University Press, 1983, 240 p.

Traces the origins and development of the Irish historical novel as a specific genre of modern Irish fiction. The book follows this development through the 1970s; the chapters focusing on the nineteenth-century novel feature John and Michael Banim, Sheridan Le Fanu, and William Carleton.

——. "Discovering Voices: The Irish Novel before 1830," and "Variations on Irish Themes, 1830-90." In *The Irish Novel: A Critical History,* pp. 1-45 and 46-84. Boston: Twayne Publishers, 1988, 364 p.

The two chapters survey the history of criticism of the nineteenth-century Irish novel beginning with the publication of Maria Edgeworth's *Castle Rackrent* in 1800.

Cronin, John. *The Anglo-Irish Novel, Volume One: The Nineteenth Century.* Totowa, N. J.: Barnes and Noble Books, 1980, 157 p.

Offers brief biographical comments on several authors and provides a critical introduction to one of each of their works. The nineteenth-century novelists surveyed include: Maria Edgeworth, John Banim, Gerald Griffin, and William Carleton.

Davis, Robert. *Gerald Griffin.* Boston: Twayne Publishers, 1980, 150 p.

Examines Griffin's life and works, exploring the social and political forces which shaped Griffin's writing. Davis focuses on Griffin as a novelist, rather than as a poet or journalist. Two of Griffin's major works, *Tales of the Munster Festivals* and *The Collegians* each have a chapter devoted to them.

Flanagan, Thomas. *Irish Novelists: 1800-1850.* New York: Columbia University Press, 1959, 362 p.

Reviews the major works of the most notable Irish novelists of this period, including Maria Edgeworth, Lady Morgan, John Banim, Gerald Griffin, and William Carleton.

Harmon, Maurice. "Cobwebs before the Wind: Aspects of the Peasantry in Irish Literature from 1800 to 1916." In *Views of the Irish Peasantry, 1800-1916,* edited by Daniel J. Casey and Robert E. Rhodes, pp. 129-59. Hamden, Conn.: Archon Books, 1977.

Examines the way the Irish peasantry was portrayed in fiction by both upper class and peasant Irish writers.

MacDonagh, Thomas. "Anglo-Irish Literature," and "Anglo-Irish Authors." In *Literature in Ireland: Studies Irish and Anglo-Irish,* pp. 21-29 and 57-63. New York: Frederick A. Stokes Company, 1916.

Analyzes the influences on and development of Anglo-Irish literature, focusing in particular on the tension felt by Irish authors writing for English audiences.

McCormack, W. J. *Sheridan Le Fanu and Victorian Ireland.* Oxford: Clarendon Press, 1980, 310 p.

Studies the life and a selection of the works of Sheridan Le Fanu, a Protestant middle class Irish author. McCormack notes in the introduction to this book that due to the repetitive nature of some of Le Fanu's fiction, "a full study of all his novels and stories cannot be justified."

Newcomer, James. "*Castle Rackrent:* Its Structure and Its Irony." *Criticism* VIII, No. 2 (Spring 1966): 170-79.

Argues that *Castle Rackrent* has been praised for the wrong reasons, maintaining that the novel's "subtle" construction and its irony are often overlooked and that instead the novel is lauded as being "a work of spontaneous ebullience" and for "an ingenuousness that is noteworthy for its total absence."

Sloan, Barry. *The Pioneers of Anglo-Irish Fiction 1800-1850.* Totowa, N.J.: Barnes and Noble Books, 1986, 277 p.

Studies the major works by prominent nineteenth-century Irish authors, including Maria Edgeworth, the Banim brothers, Gerald Griffin, Lady Morgan, and William Carleton. Concludes with a summary of the merits and deficiencies of the Irish novel from 1800 to 1850.

Sullivan, Eileen A. *William Carleton.* Boston: Twayne Publishers, 1983, 146 p.

Analyzes Carleton's literary career, beginning with a "sketchy biography, describing the chaotic conditions of Carleton's life as they related to his art." The study focuses on Carleton's short stories and novels.

Nineteenth-Century Captivity Narratives

INTRODUCTION

A genre specific to North America during the seventeenth, eighteenth, and nineteenth centuries, the captivity narrative reflects the diversity and complexity of American self-images during the period when the newly-evolving nation began to take shape. In contrast to the commonly held belief that white Americans and Native Americans interacted primarily through major military conflicts, the captivity narratives reveal a greater frequency and more fluid series of encounters—encounters that began with the violent kidnapping of white families but ended in a variety of ways: from the "Indianization" of whites, to arranged exchanges of captives, to successful escapes from imprisonment. The political and cultural views guiding these narratives vary considerably as well: while many stories describe the brutality and cruelty of captivity, others insistently portray their captors as gentle and benevolent.

The body of extant captivity narratives provides access into tensions within early American identity, which was, as many scholars have claimed, dominated by the problem of "the frontier," or the confrontation with an "uncivilized" people who resisted the physical and cultural migration of European Americans. June Namias has observed that Native Americans commonly employed captivity as a strategy, but whites did not. For them, capture "employed elements not found in European warfare in the early modern or modern periods—a forced, prolonged imprisonment with the enemy, a fearful contamination, a separation from one's community, a loss of spouse and children, and a communion with or at least relentless exposure to representatives of the devil." Central themes of these narratives include the dichotomy between civilization and wilderness and the decision between heroic resistance and redemptive suffering.

The earliest narratives were generally autobiographical accounts (sometimes related to a more literate editor) by captives returned to their communities by exchange or through rescue. In the nineteenth century, although factual or semi-factual accounts continued to be published, fictional narratives—primarily sensationalistic, popular "dime novels"— became common. However, despite the association of the captivity narrative with popular fiction, works such as James Fenimore Cooper's *The Last of the Mohicans* (1826)

also exhibit the influence of major elements of the captivity narrative. In addition, as Richard Slotkin and John Saillant have noted, during this period the structure and sentiment of captivity narratives were also employed in a modified form by abolitionist authors, who emphasized the parallels between white captives and black slaves.

Due to the differential treatment of captives—men were much more likely to be killed than women— many of the first-person accounts were authored by women. As a result, captivity narratives have informed historical analyses of images of femininity: women and young girls, considered by European culture to be the most innocent and vulnerable of captives, are portrayed alternatively as stoically and passively awaiting rescue; as heroically staging their own escapes and those of their children; or as adapting to native life without attempting—and sometimes even actively resisting—a return to Anglo-American life. Captivity for many women, as these narratives suggest, offered a kind of freedom unavailable in "civilized" society; whereas in white society women were economically dependent and confined to the home, as captives they often displayed strength, endurance, and fortitude and performed feats of which they were not previously believed capable. The threat of sexual assault on white women by Native American men, often euphemized as forced marriage, pervades many of the most popular captivity narratives. This threat, as Christopher Castiglia has contended, is linked in the popular imagination to the corruption of civilized sensibilities through integration into a native lifestyle: this possibility, to the minds of early settlers, emphasized the malleability of European American identity, existing as it did on the frontier of a vast wilderness. A standard element of these narratives is the establishment of either the most extreme difference between white and Native cultures, or the subtle similarity between the two.

In opposition to the straightforward accounts of earlier periods, nineteenth-century narratives more deliberately expressed political and cultural views, whether violently anti-Indian or more conciliatory. Richard VanDerBeets has argued that the captivity narrative may be read as propaganda that became increasingly vehement and incendiary in order to justify westward expansion. In the popular "dime novels," both Native and white characters were highly stylized, and the plots melodramatically followed the same general pattern of suffering and redemption established by the first American captivity narrative, *A True History of the Captivity and Restoration of Mrs. Mary Rowlandson,* published in 1682. The captivity narrative also became a significant genre in children's literature, in which form it self-consciously offered moral and religious lessons. Thus the captivity narrative reflected and contributed significantly to the self-conception of the nation, and became a major genre in early American literature. Although the popularity of the captivity narrative waned with the stabilization and effective erasure of the frontier toward the end of the nineteenth century, the genre continues to influence literary constructions of American identity.

REPRESENTATIVE WORKS

Harriet V. Cheney
    A Peep at the Pilgrims in Sixteen Hundred Thirty-Six. A Tale of Olden Times (novel) 1824

Lydia Maria Child
    Hobomok. A Tale of Early Times (novel) 1824

James Fenimore Cooper
    The Last of the Mohicans (novel) 1826

Fanny Kelly
    Narrative of My Captivity among the Sioux Indians (non-fiction) 1871

Susanna Rowson
    Reuben and Rachel (novel) 1798

James Everett Seaver
    A Narrative of the Life of Mrs. Mary Jemison (non-fiction) 1824

Catharine Maria Sedgwick
    Hope Leslie; Or, Early Times in the Massachusetts (novel) 1827

Sarah Wakefield
    Six Weeks in the Sioux Tepees: A Narrative of Indian Captivity (non-fiction) 1863

OVERVIEW

Richard VanDerBeets (essay date 1973)

SOURCE: Introduction to *Held Captive by Indians: Selected Narratives, 1642-1836,* edited by Richard VanDerBeets, University of Tennessee Press, 1973, pp. xi-xxxi.

[*In the excerpt that follows, VanDerBeets provides a general introduction to the American literary tradition of the captivity narrative, which in the nineteenth century became increasingly sensationalistic and fictionalized.*]

Civilized peoples have long recognized the value of tempering their joys with a play or story chronicling the misfortunes and tragedies of others. Because the earliest Americans countenanced neither playacting nor the unhealthy influences of the novel, they wrote and read true tales of tragedy and horror in the form of disasters, plagues, and shipwrecks—and of Indian massacres and captivities. As the frontier pushed westward under continuing conflict the tales of Indian captivity accompanied it, gradually becoming our first literature of catharsis in an era when native American fiction scarcely existed. The immense popularity of the Indian captivity narrative in its own time is unquestionable; first editions are rare today because they were quite literally read to pieces, and most narratives went through a remarkable number of editions. There are some thirty known editions of the Mary Rowlandson narrative; Jonathan Dickenson's account went to twenty-one, including translations into Dutch and German; there are over thirty editions of the Mary Jemison captivity; and the popularity of Peter Williamson's narrative carried it through forty-one editions.

American Indians took white or non-Indian captives for four principal reasons: to use as slaves; to ransom (to the English and, later, Americans); to sell (to the French or to other tribes); and to replace, by adoption, those members of the tribe lost or slain in battle. Except for the fur trader, who did not as a rule publish his observations, the captive shared Indian life more intimately and for a longer time than all other colonials or settlers. In addition to providing fascinating popular reading in America for over two centuries, the narratives of Indian captivity have from the beginning proved valuable documents for the ethnologist, historian, and cultural historian. The four surviving sixteenth-century captivity accounts—*Relation of Alvar Nunez Cabeza de Vaca* (1542), *The Captivity of Juan Ortiz* (1557), Hans Staden's *Warhaftige Historia* (1557), and Job Hortop's *The Travailes of an Englishman* (1591)—are not only remarkable firsthand tales of ordeal and adventure but also provide the earliest descriptions of the Indians of Texas, Florida, and Brazil. Captain John Smith's account of his three-week captivity (1607-1608) in Virginia contains excellent detail on Pamunkey Indian manners and customs, although this is never so well remembered as the description of his famous encounter with Powhatan and Pocahontas, first fully reported in his *General History of Virginia* (1624). While Smith's account is not technically a separately published captivity narrative, it does stand as the generic precursor of the later and discrete narratives of Indian captivity in America. A succession of later narratives such as Jonathan Dickenson's (1699) and those of John Gyles (1736), Robert Eastburn (1758), Marie LeRoy and Barbara Leininger (1759), Thomas Morris (1791), James Smith (1799), Mary Jemison (1824), Charles Johnston (1827), Rachel Plummer (1839), and Nelson Lee (1859) all contain, in addition to their personal adventures, significant and detailed observations of aboriginal life and customs—Seminole, Maliseet, Mohawk, Ottawa, Miami, Seneca, Shawnee, Comanche, and Apache, among others. Many captive-narrators were excellent observers, and their accounts of Indian warfare, hunting, customs and manners, religion, and council procedures are in some cases our only glimpses of these past realities. In this way their narratives constitute valuable specimens of ethnological reportage. For the historian, many of the narratives of Indian captivity are repositories of eyewitness information relating to the major Indian-white conflicts throughout the course of American history. The narrative of Mary Rowlandson (1682) provides additional insight into King Philip's War and even Philip himself, whom Mrs. Rowlandson met and spoke with during her captivity. Such eighteenth-century narratives as John Williams (1707), John Gyles (1736), Peter Williamson (1757), and Robert Eastburn (1758) give added dimension to the French and Indian War generally and to many campaigns and battles specifically. Also, such nineteenth-century accounts as those of Rachel Plummer (1839), Nelson Lee (1859), and Fanny Kelly (1871) underscore the conflicts arising from the later westward movement.

In the context of American cultural history, however, the significances of the narratives of Indian captivity are shaped and differentiated largely by the society for which the narratives were intended. These cultural significances are in many ways discrete impulses and range from expressions of religious sentiment, to vehicles for anti-Indian propaganda, to blatantly visceral penny dreadfuls or pulp thrillers. The earliest Indian captivity narratives published in America, those of the seventeenth and early eighteenth centuries, are straightforward and generally unadorned religious documents, for the most part Puritan; a number of surviving Jesuit relations illustrate the Catholic experience. The captivity here takes on a typically symbolic and even typological value, reinforced by frequent scriptural citations. There are over fifty-five such references in the narrative of Father Isaac Jogues. The religious and largely didactic function is generally made explicit either in a prefatory note or very early in the narrative proper, though title pages more often than not provide succinct indicators: Mrs. Rowlandson's *The Soveraignty and Goodness of God, Together With the Faithfulness of His Promises Displayed* (1682); Jonathan Dickenson's *God's Protecting Providence Man's Surest Help in the Times of the Greatest Difficulty and Most Imminent Danger* (1699); John Williams' *The Redeemed Captive Returning to Zion* (1707). Interestingly, the first American Negro "slave narratives" are in fact Indian captivities of distinctly religious orientation: *A Narrative of the Uncommon Sufferings and Surprising Deliverance of Briton Hammon, A Negro Man* (1760), and *A Narrative of the Lord's Wonderful Dealings with John Marrant, a Black, Taken Down from His Own Relation* (1785). The religious expressions deriving from the captivity experience treat the salutary effects of the captivity, especially in the context of redemptive suffering; the captivity as test, trial, or punishment by God; and, finally and most demonstrably, the captivity as evidence of Divine Providence and of God's inscrutable wisdom.

Calvinists believing themselves to be God's chosen people newly arrived in the Promised Land to establish a New Zion, the Puritan settlers extended their typology to encompass a view of the Indian inhabitants of the continent as Canaanites who the Lord had promised Moses would be driven from the land to make way for the Neo-Israelites. "Thus the Lord was pleased to smite our Enemies in the hinder Parts," concluded the 1638 report of the extermination of the Pequots at Fort Mystic wherein six hundred Indians were killed at the cost of two English lives, "and to give us their Land for an Inheritance." Believing also that the last great struggle between good and evil was to take place in their wilderness, a struggle between God's chosen and the agents of the Devil, they considered the natives of the wilderness to be under the direction of Satan and consequently enemies of God and His instruments in that struggle. Seventeenth-century records clearly reveal the extent to which the Puritans held the conception of Indian as Devil. Cotton Mather firmly believed in the magical powers of the Indian Powaw (powwow), an example to him of heathen black arts. The common view was that through the Devil's help, the Indians' charms were of force to produce effects of wonderment, and it was a widespread belief that the Devil held the Indians in thrall and even appeared in bodily shape to them. In *God's Controversy with New England* (1662), Michael Wigglesworth described the Indian forest, the scene of the prophesied last struggle between good and evil, as a "Devil's den" wherein "none inhabited / But hellish fiends, and brutish men / That devils worshipped."

If the savages were directly the instruments of Satan and indirectly so of God, then the torments of Indian captivity could be, and were, viewed as one of God's ways of testing, punishing, or instructing His creatures. "God strengthened them [Indians] to be a scourge to his People," writes Mary Rowlandson; "the Lord feeds and nourishes them up to be a scourge to the whole Land." The scriptural citation she uses for support is Hebrews 12:6: "For whom the Lord loveth he chasteneth, and scourgeth every Son whom he receiveth." In the course of her narrative, Mrs. Rowlandson turns to the Scriptures for comfort over sixty-five times, occasioned by reflections on a variety of incidents ranging from the death of her child (Genesis 42:36: "Me have ye bereaved of my Children . . .") to her staying dry while fording a river (Isaiah 43:2: "When thou passeth through the waters I will be with thee . . ."). Most of her citations are strikingly appropriate to her captivity experience: Jeremiah 31:16: "Refrain thy voice from weeping, and thine eyes from tears, for thy work shall be rewarded, and they shall come again from the land of the Enemy"; or Psalms 106:46: "He made them also to be pittied, of all those that carried them Captives." Father Isaac Jogues sees punishment for weakness even in the small details of his captivity. When his bonds give him pain and he asks to have them loosened, "God justly ordained that the more I pleaded, the more tightly they drew my chains." For the Jesuits, particularly, physical suffering was a redemptive and intensely religious aspect of captivity, an experience to delight in: "How long they spent their fury on me," relates Jogues, "he knows for whose love and sake I suffered all, and for whom it is delightful and glorious to suffer." When the Mohawks force a Christian Huron prisoner to cut off Jogues's left thumb, the priest observes that "surely it is pleasing to suffer at the hands of those for whom you would die, and for whom you chose to suffer. . . . " He then takes the severed thumb in his other hand and offers it to God.

For Protestant captives, however, the salutary effects of captivity generally lay in areas other than suffering, principally the morally instructive nature of the experience. There were spiritual lessons to be drawn. "How evident is it that the Lord hath made this Gentlewoman a gainer by all this affliction," runs the preface to the second edition of the Rowlandson narrative, "that she can say 'tis good for her yea better that she hath been, then that she should not have been thus afflicted . . . the worst of evils working together for the best good." Mrs. Rowlandson validates this theme in matters both large and small. On the first Sabbath of her captivity she recalls "how careless I had been of God's holy time, how many Sabbaths I had lost and misspent. . . . Yet the Lord still shewed mercy, and upheld me; and as he wounded me with one hand, so he healed me with the other." When, after her release, she is troubled with small matters ("a shadow, a blast, a bubble, and things of no continuance . . ."), she thinks upon her recent captivity: "It was but the other day that if I had had the world, I would have given it for my freedom. . . . I have learned to look beyond present and smaller troubles."

Perhaps the chief spiritual significance for both the captive-narrator and his reader lay in interpreting the captivity as an illustration of God's providence. "God was with me, in a wonderfull manner, carrying me along and bearing up my spirit . . . that I might see more of his Power," writes Mrs. Rowlandson. "Thus God wonderfully favored me," John Gyles reflects, "and carried me through the first year of my captivity. . . . Though

I underwent extreme difficulties, yet I saw much of God's goodness." Father Jogues views his captivity as an opportunity, willed by God, to baptize and instruct the heathen in their very camp. Robert Eastburn blesses God for the "gracious interposure of Providence, in preserving me both from sin and danger" during his captivity. At one point, being interrogated about the strength of Fort Williams, Eastburn gives false information in the hope that the Indians will not attack the fort; when they do not, he sees the workings of a divine plan in his capture: "Hereby it evidently appeared that I was suffered to fall into the hands of the enemy to promote the good of my countrymen."

If the captive drew such lessons from his experience, he also felt obliged to pass them on to others who might profit from the morally instructive nature of Indian captivity. "One principall ground of my setting forth these lines," writes Mrs. Rowlandson, is "to declare the Works of the Lord, and his wonderfull power in carrying us along, preserving us in the Wilderness, while under the Enemies hand, and returning us to safety again. . . . " In the introduction to his narrative, John Gyles states that one reason for compiling his "private memoirs" is "that we might have a memento ever ready at hand, to excite in ourselves gratitude and thankfulness to God." More importantly, he continues, "may the most powerful and benificent Being accept of this public testimony . . . and bless my experience to excite others to confide in his allsufficiency." Elizabeth Hanson suggests the instructive, edifying design of her narrative by asserting that she related her "remarkable trials and wonderful deliverances" for one reason only: the hope that "thereby the merciful kindness and goodness of God may be magnified, and the reader hereof provoked with more care and fear to serve him in righteousness and humility." As test or punishment by God, as opportunity for redemptive suffering, and as evidence of divine providence, the Indian captivity experience was viewed by Puritan and Catholic captives as salutary and morally instructive. Late Protestant captives of firm religious convictions made comparable apprehensions, though principally that of the captivity as illustration of God's providence. Explicit or implicit in their narratives are the spiritual lessons they drew from captivity, lessons intended as well for the moral edification of the reader. In this mode and by these apprehensions, the Indian captivity narrative served as an intense and satisfying expression of profoundly felt religious experience.

From animosities dating back to Indian encounters during the Forest Wars of the later seventeenth century and aggravated by the initial conflicts of what was to become the French and Indian War, the captivity narratives of the early and middle eighteenth century became vehicles less for religious expression than for hatred of the Indian and, later, his French master in the struggle with England for control of the continent.

Again, title pages are more than suggestive: *French and Indian Cruelty Exemplified in the Life and Various Vicissitudes of Fortune of Peter Williamson* (1757); *A Narrative of the Sufferings and Surprizing Deliverances of William and Elizabeth Fleming . . . Wherein it Fully Appears, That the Barbarities of the Indians is Owing to the French, and Chiefly their Priests* (1756). The propaganda value of the captivity narrative became more and more evident and was increasingly a factor in narratives treating experiences during the eighteenth century. The French and Indian War produced narratives markedly anti-Indian, anti-French, and anti-Catholic. The Revolution (often called "The British and Indian War"), during which many tribes shifted allegiance to the English against the settlers, called forth equally inflammatory accounts of Indian outrages, depredations, and captivities.

When John Gyles is offered a biscuit by a Jesuit, he is afraid to eat it and buries it, believing that the priest "had put something into it to make me love him. Being very young, and having heard much of the Papists torturing the Protestants," he relates, "I hated the sight of a Jesuit." Gyles's mother, also a captive, thinking that her son would be sold to the Jesuit, cries out: "I had rather follow you to your grave or never see you more in this world, than you should be sold to a Jesuit; for a Jesuit will ruin you, body and soul!" Gyles is instead sold to a French merchant and laments later that he has been turned over to "a people of that persuasion which my mother so much detested." Differences between the 1754 and 1760 editions of the narrative of Elizabeth Hanson illustrate the intrusion of specific anti-French sentiment into updated accounts of Indian captivity. In the 1754 version, Mrs. Hanson describes the scalping of her children, adding only the fact that the Indians were accustomed to "receiving sometimes a reward for every scalp." In the 1760 edition the phrase is replaced by propaganda: "And it has been currently reported, that the French, in their wars with the English, have given the Indians a pecuniary reward for every scalp they brought to them." Robert Eastburn's narrative, one of the most overtly anti-French and anti-Catholic, reports that "the pains the papists take to propagate such a bloody religion is truly surprising. . . . The zeal they employ to propagate superstition and idolatry should make Protestants ashamed of their lukewarmness." Eastburn tells of young boys taken at Oswego who were "delivered up a sacrifice to the Indian enemy, to be instructed in popish principles, and be employed in murdering their countrymen, yea, perhaps their own fathers, mothers, and bretheren! O horrible! O lamentable!" He suggests that the "insatiable thirst of the French for empire" is aided by the pardons they receive from the Pope and their priests for whatever crimes committed in the course of conquest. Eastburn especially damns the conduct of the French governor of Quebec, who even in time of peace had given the Indians encouragement to murder and capture the inhabitants of the frontiers: "a scandal

to any civilized nation, and what many pagans would abhor." Observing that "our enemies seem to make a better use of a bad religion than we do of a good one" because they are united as one man while America is divided against itself, Eastburn warns that the French "leave no stone unturned to compass our ruin. They pray, work, and travel to bring it about, and are unwearied in the pursuit, while many among us sleep in a storm which . . . has laid a good part of our country desolate and threatens the whole with destruction."

Peter Williamson is equally assertive but more graphic. During his captivity he encountered other captives who gave him "some shocking accounts of the murders and devastations committed in their parts; a few instances of which will enable the reader to guess at the treatment the provincials have suffered in years past." There follows a catalog of horrors to demonstrate French-inspired Indian cruelties: entire families slaughtered and scalped; victims cut in pieces and given to the swine; a trader scalped, roasted while still alive, and his whole body eaten (including his head, of which is made an "Indian pudding"). These "instances of savage cruelty" lead Williamson to his main polemic: such horrors must "cause in every breast the utmost detestation," not only against the Indians but against those who, through "inattention, or pusillanimous or erroneous principles, suffered these savages at first, unrepelled, or even unmolested, to commit such outrages and incredible depradations and murders."

One of the "repeated injuries" cited in the Declaration of Independence is the British endeavor "to bring on the inhabitants of our frontiers the merciless Indian Savages, whose known rule of warfare is an undistinguished destruction of all ages, sexes, and conditions." It is not surprising, then, that Revolutionary War narratives of Indian captivity during the late eighteenth century serve in many ways as vehicles for anti-British propaganda of the kind directed against the French in the earlier French and Indian captivities. The "Account of the Destruction of the Settlements at Wyoming," one of the tidbits in the Manheim anthology of captivities, is largely designed as an attack on the British and Tories for their employment of Indian allies in the Revolution. "The following are a few of the more singular circumstances of the barbarity practiced in the attack upon Wyoming [the Wyoming Valley in western Pennsylvania]," the account begins, and then develops a tale of treachery, cruelty, and horror calculated to elicit the reader's wrath against the British and Royalists. The Reverend William Rogers, in his preface to John Corbly's narrative, also in the Manheim collection, refers to Great Britain during the Revolution as "a power, at that time, so lost to every human affection, that, rather than not subdue and make us slaves, they basely chose to encourage, patronize and reward, as their most faithful and beloved allies, the savages of the wilderness." The military, religious, and nationalistic considerations of both the French and Indian and the Revolutionary wars, then, find forceful expression in propagandistic narratives of Indian captivity and as such constitute another of their significant cultural impulses.

The infusion of melodrama and sensibility into the narratives, appropriately ornamented and stylistically embellished, capitalized on what became an increasingly profitable commercial market for properly "literary" narratives of Indian captivity in the later eighteenth and early nineteenth centuries. To be sure, the earlier propagandistic impulse deliberately played up Indian horrors and outrages, but more to solicit strong anti-Indian sentiments than to evoke pity and terror for the captive himself. It was but a short and almost inevitable step from narrative excesses for the purpose of propaganda to excesses in the interest of sensation and titillation, from promoting hatred to eliciting horror, from inspiring patriotism to encouraging sales, from chauvinism to commercialism. The chief concern was not for accuracy or fidelity to the hard facts of frontier life but rather for the salability of pulp thrillers, such penny dreadfuls as *Affecting History of the Dreadful Distresses of Frederic Manheim's Family* (1793), *An Affective Narrative of the Captivity and Sufferings of Mrs. Mary Smith* (1818), or *An Affecting Account of the Tragical Death of Major Swan, and the Captivity of Mrs. Swan and Infant Child* (1815). This particular application of the captivity narrative can be seen in three overlapping developments: accounts became more stylized, with every effort toward literary correctness; they became sensationalized, with an emphasis upon "effect" and the sensibility of horror; and, finally, they became so factually exaggerated and ultimately fictionalized that in some cases they were outright novels of sensibility based only slightly and speciously on actual captivities.

An illustration of the subtle shift toward more literary effect in the narratives is found in the versions of the captivity of Elizabeth Hanson. The 1754 edition, less simple and direct than the first (1728) edition but still a relatively straightforward account, was altered through "improved" diction and other rhetorical embellishments for the 1760 edition, the account of Mrs. Hanson's experience that was "Taken in Substance from her own Mouth" by one Samuel Bownas:

> [1754] In a few days after this, they got near their journey's end, where they had more plenty of corn, and other food. But flesh often fell very short, having no other way to depend on it but hunting; and when that failed, they had very short commons. It was not long ere my daughter and servant were likewise parted, and my daughter's master being sick, was not able to hunt for flesh; neither had they any corn in that place, but were forced to eat bark of trees for a whole week.

> [1760] Accordingly, in a few days after this, they drew near their journey's end, where they found greater plenty of corn and other food; but flesh often fell very short, as they had no other way of procuring it but hunting.

> It was not long before my daughter and servant were parted also; and my daughter's master falling sick, he was thereon disabled from hunting. All their corn was likewise spent; and so great were their distresses, that they were compelled to feed on the bark of trees for a whole week, being almost famished to death.

The worst offenders at this kind of stylistic embellishment were journalists or opportunists who "edited" for publication the accounts of captives. The development of sensationalism in the narratives can be discerned in two separate appeals: one to the reader's sensibilities through stylistic excesses and melodrama, the other to his capacity for horror through excesses of descriptive detail. Many narratives contain passages well within the tradition of the sentimental novel: in the Manheim anthology, Jackson Johonnot begins the narrative of his captivity as if it were indeed an affecting fiction, expressing his confident expectation that "the tender hearted will drop the tear of sympathy, when they realize the idea of the sufferings of such of our unfortunate country folks as fall into the hands of the western Indians, whose tender mercies are cruelties." Johonnot's attempt to confirm this expectation is in part stylistic: "Alas! how fluctuating are the scenes of life! how singularly precarious the fortunes of a soldier!" And, "Good God! what were my feelings when, starting from my slumbers, I heard the most tremendous firing all around, with yellings, horrid whoopings and expiring groans in dreadful discord. . . . "

Given the circumstances and conditions of Indian captivity, it was an easy matter to elicit horror from the reader by playing up "barbarities terrible and shocking to human nature" as Peter Williamson did. This narrative, like others of its kind, displays many elements of the Gothic novel—depicting the reactions of a character to trying or appalling situations, holding the reader in suspense with the character, and the heaping of a succession of horrors upon the reader in order to shock and alarm him. The Williamson narrative very quickly plunges into a veritable orgy of horrors, excessively and even lovingly described. Two prisoners with Williamson have their bellies ripped open, entrails removed and burnt before their eyes; a third captive is buried upright to his neck, scalped, and a fire laid along-side his head until his brains boil and "till his eyes gushed out of their sockets." Jackson Johonnot describes the scalping of a companion, who is then stripped naked and stabbed with knives "in every sensitive part of the body" and left "weltering in blood, though not quite dead, a wretched victim to Indian rage and hellish barbarity." Such incidents had, for the most part, a basis in actual occurrence; it is the excessive and sensational treatment of them that affronts the modern reader. There are numerous examples, on the other hand, of incidents in many narratives that are either so greatly exaggerated as to strain credibility, such as Isaac Stewart's encounter with Welsh-speaking Indians or the circumstances surrounding Rachel Plummer's cave visitation, or are, in some cases, outright fictions lacking the all-important sense of authentically human experience that characterizes the earlier, genuine captivities. Because of these known fraudulent and fictionalized accounts, many writers of authentic narratives felt obliged to attest the veracity of their own accounts. As early as 1758, the Reverend Gilbert Tennent's preface to Robert Eastburn's narrative points out that Eastburn is a deacon of the church and that his testimony "may with safety be depended upon." The 1792 version of Jemima Howe's captivity ("A Genuine and Correct Account . . .") given to the Reverend Bunker Gay was issued to remedy the excesses of a previously published version thought by Mrs. Howe to be "romantic and extravagant," containing errors of fact as well as excesses of style. By the early decades of the nineteenth century the credibility of captivity narratives was definitely in question, so much so in fact that one narrative was actually accompanied by an affidavit. Published in the 1820's, the later editions of the captivity of Matthew Bunn contained this testimony: "I, Matthew Bunn, the author of the above Narrative am duly sworn, and testify that the above Narrative is a true statement of the Life and Adventures of the above named Matthew Bunn. . . . " Many nineteenth-century captives were reluctant to publish their stories at all. The most recently published original narrative of Indian captivity, the account of Frank Buckelew—who was taken in 1866 at the age of thirteen by Lipan Indians in Texas—was not related until 1932. The preface states that he "long hesitated to present his story as an Indian captive lest it be condemned as fiction, like so many Indian stories, and cast aside as worthless."

An egregious example of the entirely fictionalized captivity narrative is *An Account of a Beautiful Young Lady, Who Was Taken by the Indians and Lived in the Woods Nine Years* (1787), by Abraham Panther [pseud.]. Pure fiction in a pamphlet of less than a dozen pages, it was a best seller of sorts, running through twenty-five editions printed by small village presses and hawked by Yankee peddlers. Its popularity is not surprising in a time when reading fiction was improper but reading "true" stories was legitimate. The *Narrative of the Singular Adventures and Captivity of Mrs. Thomas Berry* (1800) is also regarded as another piece of "Indian fiction." Very likely the first novelist to work an Indian captivity into his narrative and pass it off to the public as a true adventure was W. R. Chetwood, whose *The Voyages, Dangerous Adventures and Imminent Escapes of Captain Richard Falconer* (1720) went through nine editions. The most elaborate

eighteenth-century captivity in novelized form is Ann Eliza Bleecker's *The History of Maria Kittle. In a Letter to Miss Ten Eyck* (1797). This novel, a fictionalized story of the captivity of Maria Kittlehuyne and the massacre of her family during King George's War, is an outright novel of sensibility. Mrs. Bleecker's unabashed goal is to "open the sluice gate" of the reader's eyes by achieving "the luxury of sorrow" in her story. "O hell! are not thy flames impatient to cleave the center and engulph these wretches in thy ever burning waves?" soliloquizes her heroine at the high point in this tale of Indian devastations and cruelties; "Are there no thunders in Heaven—no avenging Angels—no God to take notice of such Heaven-defying cruelties?" The captivity narrative has here become whole-cloth sentimental fiction, a forerunner of many of the tales in Erastus Beadle's celebrated series of formularized dime novels, the first of which using the captivity experience appeared in 1860: Edward S. Ellis' *Seth Jones; or, The Captives of the Frontier,* followed by such others as Joseph E. Badger's *The Forest Princess; or, The Kickapoo Captives,* and *Nathan Todd; or, The Fate of the Sioux' Captive.* It is at this point and with this mode that, for all practical purposes and with few exceptions, the development of the narratives of Indian captivity culminates—in the travesty of the penny dreadful. . . .

THE POLITICAL SIGNIFICANCE OF CAPTIVITY NARRATIVES

Richard VanDerBeets (essay date 1972)

SOURCE: "'A Thirst for Empire': The Indian Captivity Narrative as Propaganda," in *Research Studies,* Vol. 40, No. 3, September, 1972, pp. 207-15.

[*In the following essay, VanDerBeets discusses captivity narratives as vehicles for propaganda, employed to incite anti-Indian sentiment during the period dominated by the idea of Manifest Destiny.*]

> These few instances of savage cruelty . . . must strike the utmost horror, and cause in every breast the utmost detestation, not only against the authors, but against those who, through inattention, or pusillanimous or erroneous principles, suffered these savages at first unrepelled, or even unmolested, to commit such outrages, depradations, and murders.
>
> *French and Indian Cruelty; Exemplified in the Life and Various Vicissitudes of Fortune of Peter Williamson* (1757)

While American anti-French and anti-British propaganda during both the French and Indian and Revolutionary Wars exploited the conventional and better-known modes of promulgation in tracts, military "histories," broadsides, and sermons, another and little-examined vehicle for such sentiment may be discerned in the narratives of Indian captivity published throughout these periods of conflict. Further, the use of the captivity narrative as propaganda continued well into the nineteenth century, largely in the context of Manifest Destiny.

Although the officially declared phase of the French and Indian War spanned only the period from 1755 to 1762, there had been continual warfare between the colonies of New England and France long before European armies actually set foot on the North American continent. As early as 1689 the French governor of Canada sent a force from Montreal to attack the English in Albany, and a Massachusetts "Act of Reward" in 1696 suggests the degree of feeling against the French foe and his allies by announcing that "To prosecute the French and Indian enemy, the General Court offers fifty pounds p. head for every Indian man and 25 pounds p. head for any Indian woman or Child, male or Female, under the age of fourteen years taken or brought in Prisoner, the Scalps of all Indians to be produced." The Indian allies of the French were chiefly Huron, Shawnee, Ottawa, and some Iroquois from the western end of the Confederacy. Because the Indians were never wholly loyal to the French, their ultimate influence in the outcome of the war proved negligible. With the official declaration of war in 1756 and the appearance of European armies on the scene, the importance of the Indian as ally quickly diminished. If the Indian role in a conflict so inaccurately named for him was of little military consequence, it nonetheless provided a focal point for English sentiment against the French enemy in the struggle for control of the continent. Such sentiment, directed against the Indians, their French masters, and, with equal vehemence, the Jesuits, found an especially suitable and powerful vehicle in the narratives of Indian captivity during the period.

The Redeemed Captive Returning to Zion; or, A Faithful History of Remarkable Occurrences in the Captivity and Deliverance of Mr. John Williams (1707)[1] provides details of the Indian attack and massacre at Deerfield in 1703, but then becomes largely a recitation of Jesuit abuses and guile during Reverend Williams' stay at Montreal, Quebec, and Chateauviche. He describes the Jesuits as "cunning, crafty enemies, using all their subtilty to insinuate into young ones, such principles as would be pernicious." Williams laments that "the consideration of such crafty designs to ensnare young ones, and to turn them from the simplicity of the gospel to Romanish superstition, was very exercising." With grim irony, he reports the speech of a Jesuit in command of an Indian war party who told him: "When the savages went against you, I charged them to baptize all children before they killed them; such was my desire of your eternal salvation, though you were our enemies." When an Indian "proselyted to the Romish faith" tries to force him to make the sign of the cross and kiss a crucifix, Williams refuses even

when threatened with having his brains dashed out with a hatchet. "I told him I should sooner choose death than to sin against God." Although admittedly "unused to, and unskilful in poetry," Williams composed a short poem for inclusion in his narrative on the circumstances of his experience and the situation of his scattered flock. Entitled "Some Contemplations of the poor and desolate state of the church at Deerfield," it bears quoting in part, outlining as it does the attack, forced march to Canada, and trials of his congregation:

> Many, both old & young, were slain out-right;
> Some, in a bitter season, took their flight.
> Some burnt to death, and others stifled were;
> The enemy no sex or age would spare.
> The tender children, with their parents sad,
> Are carried forth as captives, some unclad.
> Some murdered on the way, unburied left,
> And some, through famine, were of life bereft.
> After a tedious journey, some are sold,
> Some kept in heathen hands, all from Christ's
>   fold:
> By popish rage, and heath'nish cruelty,
> Are banished. Yea some compell'd to be
> Present at mass. Young children parted are
> From parents, and such as instructors were.
> Crafty designs are us'd by papists all,
> In ignorance of truth, them to inthrall.
> Some threat'ned are, unless they will comply,
> In heathen's hands again be made to lie.
> To some, large promises are made, if they
> Will truths renounce, & choose their popish
>   way.
>   Oh Lord! mine eyes on thee shall waiting
> be,
> Till thou again turn our captivity.

In *Memoirs of Odd Adventures, Strange Deliverances, Etc., In the Captivity of John Gyles, Esq.* (1736)[2] John Gyles reports being offered a biscuit by a Jesuit and burying it in the belief that the priest "had put something into it to make me love him. Being very young, and having heard much of the Papists torturing the Protestants," he relates, "I hated the sight of a Jesuit." Gyles' mother, also a captive and thinking that her son would be sold to the Jesuit, cries out: "I had rather follow you to your grave or never see you more in this world, than you should be sold to a Jesuit; for a Jesuit will ruin you, body and soul!" Gyles is instead sold to a French merchant, turned over to "a people of that persuasion which my mother so much detested."

Nehemiah How, in the French prison at Quebec with several hundred other captives, reports on the poor treatment afforded them by their French captors. His journal, *A Narrative of the Captivity of Nehemiah How* (1748),[3] is a stark record of the deaths from illness of his fellow captives during the winter 1746-47. On November 24, 1746, he reports thirty sick and dying.

How's narrative ends on May 19, 1747, and he himself died in captivity at Quebec from "the prison fever" on May 25 of that year. *A Genuine and Correct Account of the Captivity, Sufferings, and Deliverance of Mrs. Jemima Howe*[4] relates the experience of Jemima Howe, captured in 1755 and taken with her infant to be sold to the French. In the home of a prospective French buyer, the lady of the house exclaims: "Damn it, I will not buy a woman that has a child to look after." Nor will the couple feed her while at the house, and she is able to have food only by skimming bread crusts from a greasy swill-pail in the room. When finally bought by a French family, she reports that both the father of the household and his son lusted after her, a greatly embarrassing and perplexing situation in which she was hard put to secure her own virtue. Mrs. Howe is even more exercised when her two daughters are ransomed from the Indians by the French and put in a Canadian nunnery: "In this school of superstition and bigotry they continued" until the war ended, she writes. To her great chagrin, Mrs. Howe found that one of these daughters refused to leave the nunnery and return home, doing so finally only under the threat of force: "So extremely bigoted was she to the customs and religion of the place, that, after all, she left it with the greatest reluctance."

Anti-French sentiment in captivity narratives was, of course, strongest during the actual period of the French and Indian conflict. The title page of the 1756 Fleming narrative, *A Narrative of the Sufferings and Surprising Deliverances of William and Elizabeth Fleming,*[5] carries the following notice: "Wherein it fully appears, that the barbarities of the Indians is owing to the French, and chiefly their priests." Differences between the 1754 and 1760 editions of the narrative of Elizabeth Hanson illustrate the intrusion of specific anti-French sentiment into "updated" accounts of Indian captivity. In the 1754 version, *God's Mercy Surmounting Man's Cruelty, Exemplified in the Captivity and Surprising Deliverance of Elizabeth Hanson,* Mrs. Hanson describes the scalping of her children, adding only the fact that the Indians were accustomed to "receiving sometimes a reward for every scalp." In the 1760 edition, *An Account of the Captivity of Elizabeth Hanson,* the phrase is replaced by "And it has been currently reported, that the French, in their wars with the English, have given the Indians a pecuniary reward for every scalp brought to them."[6]

"The pains the papists take to propagate such a bloody religion is truly surprising," writes Robert Eastburn in *A Faithful Narrative of the Many Dangers and Sufferings, as well as Wonderful and Surprising Deliverances of Robert Eastburn,*[7] one of the most overtly and violently anti-French and anti-Catholic narratives of Indian captivity. "The zeal they employ to propagate superstition and idolatry should make Protestants ashamed of their lukewarmness." Eastburn tells of young boys taken at Oswego, "delivered up a sacrifice to the Indian enemy, to be instructed in popish principles, and be employed in murdering their countrymen, yea, perhaps their own fathers, mothers, and bretheren! O horrible! O lamentable!" He suggests that the "insatiable thirst of the French for empire" is aided by the pardons they receive from the Pope and their priests for whatever crimes committed in the course of conquest.

Eastburn details the callous treatment he received at the hands of the French as well as Indians. Forced to travel through New England winter naked except for a vest, he is refused relief by the French general leading the invading army, who tells him that he will have clothes when he reaches Canada. "Cold comfort to one almost frozen," Eastburn recalls bitterly. He also relates that when news came of the fall of the fort at Oswego in 1756, his French captors rejoiced and took to "mocking us, poor prisoners, in our exile and extremity, which was no great argument either of humanity or true greatness of mind." He especially damns the conduct of the French governor of Quebec, who even in times of peace had given the Indians great encouragement to murder and capture the inhabitants of the frontiers ("a scandal to any civilized nation, and what many pagans would abhor"), and tells of an incident when Indians brought a lame captive before the governor and were reproved by that worthy for not having killed him for his scalp instead.

Observing that "our enemies seem to make a better use of a bad religion than we do of a good one," because the French are united while America is divided against itself, Eastburn momentarily despairs. "Our case appears to me indeed gloomy," he warns, but expresses the hope that God will graciously incline his countrymen to unite in "the rigorous and manly use of all proper means" to defeat the French. The task will not be an easy one in the face of the French threat, he counsels. "I may with justice and truth observe, that our enemies leave no stone unturned to compass our ruin. They pray, work, and travel to bring it about, and are unwearied in the pursuit, while many among us sleep in a storm which . . . has laid a good part of our country desolate and threatens the whole with destruction."

Thomas Brown, a member of Rogers' Rangers captured on patrol from Fort William Henry in 1757, recounts in *A Plain Narrative of the Uncommon Sufferings and Remarkable Deliverance of Thomas Brown* (1760)[8] the attempts of the French to enlist his aid against his own people. The French commander is portrayed as a man ruthless and without principle who tells Brown that he wants him to serve as guide to the Fort and show where the walls can be scaled. When young Brown answers that he will not be a traitor to his country and help in destroying his friends, the commander replies with a smile that "in war you must not even show consideration for your father or mother." Further, when he is sold to a French merchant in Montreal, Brown reports being subjected to constant attempts to convert him to Catholicism. Jonathan Carver, a volunteer in General Webb's expedition to strengthen the garrison at Fort William Henry, was present when the Fort fell to Montcalm in 1757 and recorded the details of the infamous massacre that followed during his brief captivity *(Travels Through the Interior Parts of North America)*.[9] The survivors of the garrison, permitted to leave with guns but no ammunition, are promised a guard to protect them from the Indian allies of the conquering French. Instead they are left unprotected and surrounded by savages. The sick and wounded are slaughtered without mercy, and Carver himself reports running up to a French sentinel and asking for help only to be cursed as "an English dog" and given back to the Indians. Reflecting on the massacre, Carver wishes that this "flagrant breech of every sacred law" was the result of the French commanders simply being unable to control the savages, rather than premeditated design. But he suggests that "an unprejudiced observer would, however, be apt to conclude, that a body of ten thousand Christian troops had it in their power to prevent the massacre from becoming so general."

Peter Williamson *(French and Indian Cruelty; Exemplified in the Life and Various Vicissitudes of Fortune, of Peter Williamson, a Disbanded Soldier)*[10] is more direct. During his captivity he encountered other prisoners who gave him "some shocking accounts of the murders and devastations committed in their parts; a few instances of which will enable the reader to guess at the treatment the provincials have suffered in years past." There follows a catalog of horrors to demonstrate French-inspired Indian cruelties: entire families slaughtered and scalped; victims cut in pieces and given to the swine; a trader scalped, roasted while still alive, and his whole body eaten (including his head, of which is made an "Indian pudding"). These "instances of savage cruelty" lead Williamson to his main polemic: such horrors must "cause in every breast the utmost detestation," not only against the Indians but against those who, through "inattention, or pusillanimous or erroneous principles, suffered these savages at first, unrepelled, or unmolested, to commit such outrages and incredible depradations and murders." The title page of the third edition (1758) of the Williamson narrative adds this: "Together with a description of the most convenient roads for the British forces to invade Canada in three divisions, and make themselves masters of it the next campaign, 1759."

Enmity toward the French lasted after the surrender of New France. Alexander Henry, an English fur trader and hunter captured by Chippewas in 1763 during attacks occasioned by the Conspiracy of Pontiac, was present at the massacre at Fort Michilimackinac. Henry places the blame for the outrage on the passivity of the French Canadians who, smouldering with hatred for their former enemies, disregarded rumors of the Indian

uprisings and then stood idly by when violence flared. "Amid the slaughter which was raging, I observed many of the Canadian inhabitants of the fort calmly looking on," he relates in his *Travels and Adventures in Canada and the Indian Territories Between the Years 1760 and 1776*,[11] "neither opposing the Indians nor suffering injury."

If the American phase of the Seven Years War is to be known as the French and Indian War, then the War of the Revolution might just as accurately be called the British and Indian War. Because the effect on the Indians of the treaty concluding the French and Indian War was to replace the French king with a British king as authority, because the rising revolt in the colonies constituted a threat to the only authority they acknowledged, and because they were dependent on that authority for trade and help, it was only natural that the Indians would side with the British in the War of the Revolution. As in the previous conflict, Indian allies proved more a hindrance than a help, but as before they also became the focus for sentiment against their military masters—in this instance the British. One of the "repeated injuries" cited in the Declaration of Independence, for example, is the British endeavor "to bring on the inhabitants of our frontiers the merciless Indian Savages, whose known rule of warfare is an undistinguished destruction of all ages, sexes, and conditions."

Revolutionary War narratives of Indian captivity during the late 1770s and 1780s serve in many ways as vehicles for propaganda and anti-British sentiment of the kind directed against the French in the earlier French and Indian captivities. The "Account of the Destruction of the Settlements at Wyoming," one of the tidbits in the Manheim anthology *(Affecting History of the Dreadful Distresses of Frederic Manheim's Family)*,[12] is largely designed as an attack on the British and Tories for their employment of Indian allies in the War of the Revolution. "The following are a few of the more singular circumstances of the barbarity practiced in the attack upon Wyoming," the account begins, and then develops a tale of treachery, cruelty, and horror calculated to elicit the reader's wrath against the British and Royalists. Reverend William Rogers, in his preface to John Corbly's narrative in the same collection, refers to Great Britain during the Revolution as "a power, at that time, so lost to every human affection, that, rather than not subdue and make us slaves, they basely chose to encourage, patronize, and reward, as their most faithful and beloved allies, the savages of the wilderness." Other captivity accounts during and immediately after the revolutionary period deploring the Indian as British ally include those of Moses Van Campen, Daniel Boone, Dr. Knight and John Slover, and Mary Jemison. An indicative and especially overblown example is to be found in the narrative of the captivity of Mary Kinnan *(A True Narrative of the Sufferings of Mary Kinnan)*:[13]

"O Britain! how heavy will be the weight of thy crimes at the last great day! Instigated by thee, the Indian murderer plunges his knife into the busom of innocence, piety, and of virtue; and drags thousands into a captivity, worse than death."

By the turn of the century, however, Indian captivity narratives, devoid of either anti-French or anti-British sentiments, take on a tone of general Indian hatred that foreshadows the full blooming of nineteenth-century Manifest Destiny and the irresistible force of American nationalism. The first significant collection of captivity narratives, Archibald Loudon's *A Selection of Some of the Most Interesting Narratives of Outrages, Committed by the Indians, in Their Wars, with the White People* (1808-11),[14] betrays a markedly anti-Indian bias. In his preface to the collection, Loudon remarks: "The philosopher who speaks with delight of the original simplicity, and primitive innocence of mankind, may here learn, that man, uncivilized and barbarous, is even worse than the most ferocious wolf or panther in the forest." Loudon also quotes Indian-hater Hugh Henry Brackenridge to the effect that "all that is good and great in man, results from education; an uncivilized Indian is but a little way removed from a beast who, when incensed, can only tear and devour, but the savage applies the ingenuity of man to torture and inflict anguish." In this collection, interspersed between actual captivities, editor Loudon provides his own accounts of Indian barbarity (*e.g.,* "Some of the Modes of Torture Practised by the Indians"), always inflammatory but often undocumented in specifics and sources.

While it had been a three-hundred-year task to break completely the resistance of the Indians of eastern America, it was but a thirty-year enterprise to "clean up" the prairies and Western tribes to make way for the westering Spirit of Progress in the nineteenth century. Ante-bellum emigration inspired both punitive expeditions against the Indians and, ultimately, near wars of extermination. The postwar campaigns against the tribes of the Plains focused on the Sioux, from 1866 to 1875, and against the Apaches in the final phase, from 1882 to 1887. Not surprisingly, narratives of Indian captivity throughout this period of expansion and nationalism in the nineteenth century reflect attitudes consistent with this spirit. Nelson Lee (*Three Years among the Comanches, the Narrative of Nelson Lee the Texas Ranger; Containing a Detailed Account of His Captivity among the Indians*),[15] for example, a captive of the Comanches in 1856, complains of the then-current Indian policy of the United States because it does not take into account the Indians' "unwavering faith in the future ascendancy of the red man" that prompts them to perpetual resistance. Lee's solution is a simple one: instead of maintaining a line of military posts on the frontier, the government should send out a punitive expedition through Indian territories, demonstrate its military

might, arrest "turbulent" chiefs, and, in general, "teach them a lesson too impressive to be forgotten."

The most blatantly chauvinist and racist of all nineteenth-century accounts is R. B. Stratton's narrative of the captivity of the Oatman Girls, *Life among the Indians, or: The Captivity of the Oatman Girls among the Apache and Mohave Indians.*[16] While Stratton registers the typical disgust at the Indian life style (the Apaches live in "all the extremes of filth and degradation"; their mode of dress is "needlessly and shockingly indecent"), a more telling indictment is his implication that their nomadic existence is downright unAmerican: "These Apaches were without any settled habits of industry. They tilled not. . . . They had soil that might have produced, but most of them had an abhorrence of all that might be said of the superior blessings of industry and the American civilization." Stratton brings the narrative to a close by contrasting the "blessings of civilization, and a superior social life" of the whites with "those whose ignorance will not suffer them to let go their filth and superstition," observing with fervor that the frontier "is already begirt with the light of a higher life; and now the foot-fall of the pioneering, brave Anglo-Saxon is heard upon the heel of the savage," and suggesting in the obvious spirit of Manifest Destiny that "the march of American civilization . . . will yet, and soon, break upon the barbarity of these numerous tribes, and either elevate them to the unappreciated blessings of a superior state, or wipe them into oblivion, and give their long undeveloped territory to another."

It seems but a short step, then, and a step that, in fact, closes a full circle, from the seventeenth-century Calvinist, typology-inspired conception of Indian land as a prophesied and deserved "inheritance" to the nineteenth-century Progress-inspired conception of Indian territory as a rightful "possession." These apprehensions and the attitudes they fostered, as well as the military and nationalistic considerations of the French and Indian and Revolutionary Wars, find forceful expression in the accounts of Indian captivity to an extent that renders this impulse one of the most significant applications of the narratives collectively.

Notes

[1] All quotations are from the Sixth Edition (Boston, 1795). Williams, pastor of the church at Deerfield, saw his two youngest children killed and his wife tomahawked on the march to Canada. His daughter Eunice remained in Canada, became a Catholic, and married an Indian.

[2] Boston, 1736. Reprinted in S. G. Drake, *Indian Captivities* (Auburn, 1850). Gyles was captured at the attack on Pemaquid on August 2, 1689, held by the Indians for six years, then sold to a Frenchman with whom he lived for three more years.

[3] Boston, 1748. How was taken on October 11, 1745, at Great Meadow Fort (now Putney, Vermont).

[4] Boston, 1792. Mrs. Howe was captured in an attack on Bridgman's Fort, New Hampshire, on July 27, 1755.

[5] Boston, 1756.

[6] London, 1760. This "improved" version bears the notice: "Taken in Substance from her own Mouth, by Samuel Bownas."

[7] Boston, 1758. Eastburn was captured at Fort Williams, New York, on March 27, 1756.

[8] Boston, 1760.

[9] London, 1778. This volume contains one of the most spirited accounts of the Fort William Henry massacre.

[10] London, 1759. Williamson was captured by Shawnee Indians on October 2, 1754, on his farm in Berks County near the forks of the Delaware.

[11] The New York, 1809 edition.

[12] The Manheim anthology (Philadelphia, 1794) is a collection of assorted earlier Indian captivities and massacres. The Wyoming Settlements were located in the Wyoming Valley of Pennsylvania.

[13] Elizabethtown, 1795. Mary Kinnan was taken by Shawnees in 1791 and sold into several other tribes.

[14] 2 vols. Carlisle, Pa., 1808-11.

[15] Reprinted, Norman: University of Oklahoma Press, 1957.

[16] Second edition, San Francisco, 1857.

Wilcomb E. Washburn (essay date 1983)

SOURCE: Introduction to *Narratives of North American Indian Captivity: A Selective Bibliography,* by Alden T. Vaughan, Garland Publishing, 1983, pp. xi-lviii.

[*In the excerpt that follows, Washburn traces the development of the captivity narrative from the seventeenth to the nineteenth century, and links this development to the shifting national identity.*]

The most prominent aspect of Indian-white relations as expressed in American literature of the seventeenth, eighteenth, and nineteenth centuries was the captivity experience. Yet the occupation of Indian land by whites with its by-product of conflict is surely the most *important* aspect of Indian-white interaction. Louise K.

Barnett attributes the disproportionate attention given to the captivity experience to the need to rationalize and justify the English presence in the New World.[1] It was easier to express outrage at the cruelty of the Indian in capturing white women and children than to defend the policy of separating the Indian from his land. However, the attraction of the captivity narrative surely derives from the fact that it combined dramatic form, thrilling adventure, exotic context, and personal relevance. Three of the four "best-selling" narratives published between 1680 and 1720 were captivities; the fourth was *Pilgrim's Progress.*[2] Four captivity narratives—Rowlandson, John Williams, Jonathan Dickinson, and Mary Jemison—are listed by Frank Luther Mott, *Golden Multitudes: The Story of Best Sellers in the United States* (New York, 1947), pp. 20-22, 303-305, as among the great best-sellers of American publishing. It was easy to imagine oneself swept away from one's loved ones and captured by strange Indians whether or not that event was likely to occur. Surely it was this ability to touch every individual imagination that made the captivity narrative such a persistently popular literary form. . . .

Scholars of the captivity experience have tended to overemphasize the degree to which white captives became Indianized as a result of the captivity experience. According to the most thorough and scholarly analysis of the subject, that by Alden Vaughan and Daniel Richter in "Crossing the Cultural Divide: Indians and New Englanders, 1605-1763," "There is conclusive evidence of only 24 prisoners who became 'white Indians'—just 1.5 percent of the total number of cases. . . . " Allowing for other possible examples of prisoners remaining with their Indian captors, Vaughan and Richter conclude that no more than 52 of the 1,641 New Englanders captured between 1675 and 1763, or 3.2 percent "underwent completely the cultural transition from British American to American Indian."[6] Vaughan and Richter's study, which utilized a computer and sophisticated categories of age, sex, duration, identity of captor, etc., corrects the most sophisticated previous study, that of James Axtell in his "The Scholastic Philosophy of the Wilderness," which estimated that 15 percent of captured New Englanders may have become "full-fledged Indians."[7] Vaughan and Richter's analysis indicates that those most likely to remain with either the French or the Indians were captives between the ages of 7 and 15; 40 percent were assimilated into their captor's society. Girls aged 7 through 15 were the most likely of all groups to be "transculturated": almost 54 percent of this group refused to return to New England compared with less than 30 percent of the boys in the same age group. Vaughan and Richter's work provides a sobering corrective to the belief, expressed so eloquently by Hector St. John de Crevecoeur, in his *Letters from an American Farmer* (London, 1782), p. 295, that "thousands of Europeans are Indians, and we have no examples of even one of these

Aborigines having from choice become European!" This belief, echoed by Cadwallader Colden and Benjamin Franklin among others, also had historical and literary support both in the nineteenth and twentieth centuries, but Vaughan and Richter's computerized analysis has forced a revision of the unqualified assertions of the numbers, at least in New England, who can be considered "white Indians."[8]

No similar sophisticated studies of captives taken in other places and other times have been made. The trend toward a decline in the number of whites who refused to be repatriated—documented by Vaughan and Richter for the latter part of the period they studied—probably continued in the period of the American Revolution and beyond, as attitudes toward Indians changed from what Vaughan and others have characterized as "cultural bias" into "racial prejudice," and as Indian power withered before white military supremacy.[9] Nevertheless, the captivity experience continued to be important, whether or not the captive sought or was offered an accommodation with his captors. Captain John Rogers, writing from the Mero District of Kentucky, on August 5, 1792 (repr. Garland, vol, 21a; item 228), for example, lists an extraordinarily high number of individuals killed, wounded, or taken prisoner in the preceding seven months.

Nineteenth-century captivity estimates also indicate the continued high incidence of captivities. The Southern Plains tribes—Comanches, Kiowas, and until driven further west by the Comanches in the eighteenth century, the Apaches—held the greatest number of captives in the nineteenth century. An estimated 900 to 1,000 Mexican captives, and a much smaller though not insignificant number of Anglo captives, were among the Comanches in 1850. Organized in loose autonomous bands, early masters of the horse culture introduced by the Spaniards, led by leaders chosen for demonstrated military prowess, the Plains tribes utilized captives as they did horses: to possess or to sell. A flourishing trade in slaves of any race (equaled only by that which took place in the seventeenth-century Southeast) made captives useful and valuable. They might be held within the tribe, either as adopted members or as slaves, sold to other Indian tribes, or used—by sale or donation—as negotiating counters in Indian dealings with the white man. Ransoms as high as $2,000 were sometimes paid for captives who thus served as the economic equivalent of a large amount of guns, liquor, or other durable goods.[10]

The evolution of the captivity narrative between 1750 and 1800 expressed the changing attitudes of the white inhabitants of the American land. The figure of the captive came to blend imperceptibly with that of the hunter, the trader, and the Indian himself. The captive became part of the wilderness landscape and the wilderness landscape became part of the psyche of the white American. As Slotkin puts it, "just as the idea of seeking greater intimacy with the natural landscape emerged in the exploration narratives, the idea of accepting greater intimacy with the Indians gained ground in the captivity narratives written between 1750 and 1800."[11] The shift was also from a God-centered narrative in which the victim escapes to return to the ordered society from which he or she had been abducted to a more man-centered narrative in which the captive uses his knowledge of the wilderness to facilitate the destruction of his captors. Slotkin finds the model of this new humanistically oriented narrative in Daniel Boone's *Adventures* (1784, 1786, 1824; repr. Garland, vol. 14a, b, and c; item 105). The hero of the eighteenth-century narrative may have thanked the Lord for his salvation, protection, or escape, but his principal reliance (and pride) was upon himself and the skills he had acquired to pit himself against his wilderness foe. The role of the protagonist of the late eighteenth- and early nineteenth-century captivity narrative was normally played by the hunter, a solitary figure locked in an intimate embrace with the natural wilderness and its denizens.

Slotkin has pointed out how closely the American myth of the hunter resembles the creation myths of the Indians. In both, the hunter is not an object of reproach (as in Christian thought) for his "insatiable incontinence." Rather, he is more nearly the culture hero who lifts his people to a higher state of being. The acceptance of the myth by later writers, and particularly by the great figures of the American literary Renaissance, distinguishes the Boone and post-Boone accounts from the earlier Puritan views of the wilderness. In Rowlandson and other New England captivities, deliverance consists not in grappling with and overcoming the satanic forces of the wilderness, but in providential escape from those forces and a return to the order of transplanted European communities on the edge of the American forest. Both the early Puritans and the first trans-Appalachian frontiersmen feared the wilderness, but later frontiersmen, building on the experiences of their ancestors in the New World, saw salvation in their power to control and shape the wilderness environment themselves. "The growth of this confidence," Slotkin notes, "is the central theme of the evolution of the literature of human frontier heroes out of the Puritan literature of human subjection to God and natural forces."[12]

Boone's life as a captive and/or adopted son of the Shawnees was both an evocation of the perils faced by the American pioneer and a demonstration of his ability to educate himself in the life of the forest. What gave Boone's narrative its mythic quality was the utilization of his "Indianness" to bring civilization to the wilderness. Although a hunter and warrior, he was the willing vanguard of the agriculturalist and judge. More importantly he represented the new man—half Indian, half European—who emerged on the international stage as "the American."

Slotkin relates the evolution of the Boone narratives between 1793 and 1824 to the varying cultural presuppositions of the Eastern seaboard and the Western interior, as well as to the emerging character of the new American "type" represented by Boone. The initial myth of Boone as recorded in Filson's narrative was gradually purged of its literary and romantic qualities and suffused with realism and strength (1784, 1786, 1824; repr. Garland, vol. 14a, b, and c; item 105). A Western audience demanded a literature more reflective of the reality of the frontier than of the literary conventions of Europe. Yet Samuel Metcalf's use of the Boone narrative in his 1821 *Collection of Some of the Most Interestting Narratives of Indian Warfare in the West* (repr. Garland, vol. 38; item 199) continued to reflect the earlier Eastern emphasis upon the "civilized" rather than the "hunter" hero. It was not until John A. McClung's *Sketches of Western Adventure* (Maysville, Kentucky, 1832; repr. Garland, vol. 50; item 191) that Boone (and the Western hero generally) emerged as a man of action rather than a man of thought. The "wild West" was finally welcomed as a positive alternative to the ordered East.[13]

Horatio Greenough's sculpture, "Rescue Group," commissioned in 1838 and finished in 1851, graced the East Front of the Capitol in Washington until that facade was extended in 1962 and the statue put in storage. The statuary graphically portrays the image that nineteenth-century literary versions of the captivity experience established in the American mind. In the composition, the arms of an Indian about to attack a white woman and her baby are pinioned by the gigantic figure of a frontiersman. The size of the figures represents the significance of each. The woman is tiny and frail, the Indian powerful in comparison with her, but diminutive in comparison with the Bunyanesque rescuer. Called informally "Daniel Boone Protects His Family," as Slotkin as noted, the statue portrays Boone in his social role protecting the values of civilization and progress rather than in his solitary, violent, pathfinder role.[14]

The growing physical and cultural closeness of the Indian and the new "American" at the end of the eighteenth century was illustrated not only in Boone but in the person of James Adair, author of *The History of the Indians of America* (London, 1776). Risking frequent capture while living with the Chickasaw Indians, Adair experienced both the dangers and pleasures of life in the forest. Like Boone, Adair is representative of the American type that emerged in the eighteenth century, half Indian, half transplanted European, a harbinger of the new man who would soon throw off the shackles of a European past.[15]

As Americans became less bound to the dogmas of a European religious and political past and more familiar with the dark interior of the American forest, the captivity theme emerged in increasing numbers of *fictional* captivity narratives. How can one explain the transition from the realistic captivity narrative to its imaginative use in the literature of the eighteenth and nineteenth centuries? In effect, Americans discovered that the captivity theme provided an instant tradition for a society that, in a European sense, lacked a past. Though America could boast of no ancient buildings and no classical heritage, it was not bereft of the traditions upon which literature is based. Its colonial past, short as it was, included more than humdrum daily rounds of toil and activity. Its wars, while not as dramatic as Europe's in terms of numbers involved and stakes at issue, did pit a European people against a strange and unorthodox foe. The captivity experience contained the most dramatic aspect of that conflict, when the European was taken to the bosom of his Indian enemy. It was just a short step from the historical impact of the captivity to its imaginative use in literature. Dorothy Forbis Behen found fifteen American novels with captivity episodes published before 1823. Eight were published in 1823, 1824, or 1825. Their influence on James Fenimore Cooper's *The Last of the Mohicans,* she observes, has been too little noticed.[16]

The formal literary landmark concerning the use of the Indian captivity theme in American fiction is Charles Brockden Brown's *Edgar Huntley: or, Memoirs of a Sleep Walker.* Not included in the Garland collection because of its easy availability elsewhere, *Edgar Huntley* is a complex and difficult romance for today's reader but significant because of its conscious use of the Indian captivity theme. As Brown put it in his celebrated introduction:

> America has opened new views to the naturalist and politician, but has seldom furnished themes to the moral painter. That new springs of action, and new motives to curiosity should operate; that the field of investigation, opened to us by our own country, should differ essentially from those which exist in Europe, may be readily conceived. The sources of amusement to the fancy and instruction to the heart, that are peculiar to ourselves, are equally numerous and inexhaustible. It is the purpose of this work to profit by some of these sources; to exhibit a series of adventures, growing out of the condition of our country, and connected with one of the most common and most wonderful diseases or affections of the human frame.

> One merit the writer may at least claim; that of calling forth the passions and engaging the sympathy of the reader, by means hitherto unemployed by preceding authors. Puerile superstition and exploded manners; Gothic castles and chimeras, are the materials usually employed for this end. The incidents of Indian hostility, and the perils of the western wilderness, are far more suitable; and, for a native of America to overlook these, would admit of no apology. These, therefore, are, in part, the ingredients of this tale,

and these he has been ambitious of depicting in vivid and faithful colours. The success of his effort must be estimated by the liberal and candid reader.[17]

The development of American literature as an art form and as a commercial venture inevitably had a distorting effect upon the captivity narrative. As Richard VanDerBeets has put it, captivity narratives in the early nineteenth century became "more stylized . . . sensationalized . . . and ultimately fictionalized."[18] Behen, without specifically commenting on the trend to sensationalism, has documented the increasing literary use of the captivity tale in the late eighteenth and early nineteenth centuries, not only in fictitious accounts but in the revision and expansion of earlier, more straightforward accounts.[19] The scholar most skeptical about the realism of the later captivities has been Roy Harvey Pearce. Pearce deplores the increasingly "journalistic" character of the narratives as they descend toward the "penny dreadfuls" and "pulp thrillers" of the later nineteenth century.[20] However, James G. Meade has insisted that the captivity narratives of the period demonstrate a higher level of authenticity and realism than Pearce and VanDerBeets allow. Meade finds the conventions of the genre more often imposed by the Indians than by literary tradition and insists that the narratives long remain a vital form and natural outgrowth of their writers' experiences. It is unjust, Meade asserts, to dismiss the later captivity narratives because of the growing "literary" qualities they reveal, but there is no doubt that both the burgeoning market for fiction and the public thirst for tales of Indian captivity spurred the captivity genre in the directions indicated by VanDerBeets and Pearce.[21] A recent student of captivity narratives—James Arthur Levernier, author of "Indian Captivity Narratives, Their Functions and Forms," University of Pennsylvania Ph.D. dissertation (item 326)—attributes the changed form of the captivity narrative in this period to changing American cultural needs, specifically (p. 38) the need to support "the theory of Manifest Destiny then emerging in the popular American imagination." Levernier's theory lacks substantial support in the documentary record.

One of the most popular captivity narratives and one representing the transition to the more self-confident and imaginative form of narrative emerging in the early national period appeared under the pseudonym of Abraham Panther (1787, 1794; repr. Garland, vol. 17g and h; item 210). What gives the Panther narrative its special interest is its blending of the traditional captivity theme of return to the bosom of one's original culture with the fertility theme in which the captive girl slays her captor—who represents a sort of earth god—to restore fertility to the soil. Slotkin interprets the Panther narrative as expressing the choice open to Americans at the close of the colonial period of (1) seeking union with and absorbing the virtues of the native kings of the soil or (2) continuing to cling to inherited values

(as the early Puritans did). The Panther narrative concerns a young lady whose lover is killed by the Indians; she is captured by them, only to escape and become lost in the wilderness. She finally wanders into the cave of a gigantic Indian and is forced to choose between love and death. Like Hannah Dustin in colonial times, she leaps over the horns of the dilemma by killing the giant with his own sword and hatchet. She does not immediately return to civilization, however, but finding a kind of Indian corn she plants it in the wilderness and continues to live in the cave until discovered by the authors of the narrative. The lady then returns with them to her father's house and, after being reconciled with him, inherits his lands.

It is doubtful that most of the readers of the Panther captivity understood, even subconsciously, the implications seen by Slotkin. Moreover, as Behen has pointed out, readers of this narrative may have been bewildered by the joining of the tradition of female hardihood exemplified in Hannah Dustin's earlier scalping of her Indian captors and the traditions of the sentimental novel of the late eighteenth and early nineteenth centuries. As Behen notes, the heroine of the Panther narrative killed her captor with a hatchet, cut off his head, and quartered his body. "But for the man who found her in the wilderness she gave a performance of sensibility complete with a fainting fit and a 'plentiful shower of tears.'" Whether one reads the Panther narrative realistically, symbolically, or sentimentally, it seems appropriate to the confident American mood of the period. It is hard to imagine the Panther narrative appearing either in the seventeenth or in the late nineteenth century.[22]

An increased sympathy for Indian life was incorporated in some Indian captivity narratives in the early nineteenth century. Alexander Henry's *Travels and Adventures in Canada and the Indian Territories Between the Years 1760 and 1776* (1809; repr. Garland, vol. 31; item 127) illustrates the point. Captured during Pontiac's Rebellion, Henry was adopted by a member of the Chippewa tribe. Henry became a close and affectionate brother and son to his captor, and his tearful farewell expressed the bonds of love that grew between them.[23] Even those who saw the Indians primarily as a hated foe frequently expressed admiration for their fighting abilities. Colonel James Smith, who was captured at Fort Duquesne in 1755 and held captive for six years, in his *Account of the Remarkable Occurences* in his life (1799; repr. Garland, vol. 24e; item 223) urged Americans to emulate the Indians if they wished to conquer them.

The captivity experience in the nineteenth century became the theme of both hack writers and literary geniuses. Run-of-the-mill writers sought to present the experience as their audience expected to see it; the formula was stock. Creative writers, like Cooper, used the captivity narratives in a different way, giving their readers insights into the meaning of the experience that they would not otherwise have received. Such writers communicated the mythical significance of the white captive's immersion in a savage culture and environment. The experience might be attractive or repulsive. Hawthorne saw the wilderness in Puritan terms as the dark force that lured civilized men away from their religion and reason. Western writers like Timothy Flint, on the other hand, celebrated the immersion of the white hunter/captive into the wilderness as a way of imbibing and absorbing the spirit of the place, of displacing the Indian occupant rather than escaping from him.[24]

The great literary figures of the time were familiar with the captivity literature of the colonial and early national periods. James Fenimore Cooper, in particular, made extensive use of this literature. As Slotkin has pointed out, in Cooper's Leatherstocking tales, "The capture of white women by Indians and associated villains and their rescue by Leatherstocking and his associates is the recurrent theme of the action in all the novels save *The Pioneers*." Yet Cooper, as a true literary artist, rose above the simple events of captivity with which popular writers satisfied their readers' expectations. Cooper, rather, pulled his readers to a perception of the mythic significance of the hunter/captivity experience for the American people. The character of Leatherstocking, in effect, incorporated the virtues of both civilized and uncivilized ways of life.[25]

What were the motives that led captives to publish or to allow their accounts to be published? The reasons are extraordinarily varied.

The reasons for publication of the early Puritan narratives reflected the religious life of the community. As incorporated in the works of such theologians as Cotton Mather, they were used as illustrations of the dangers of the corrupt natural man and the untamed natural environment. Indeed, Mather told one returned captive sitting in his audience that if he could not throw off the bonds of the Devil and be born again in Christ it would be better that he should have remained among the Indians. It was the "improvement upon" the captivity narrative—the religious message to the community—that was the important motive for publication of the early narratives.

Increasingly, publication of captivity narratives was directed against an external enemy: sometimes the French, sometimes the Indians, sometimes both. The intention was to stir up patriotism at home and direct hatred against the enemy responsible for the captivities. Thus John Williams' *Redeemed Captive, Returning to Zion* (1707, 1758, 1853; repr. Garland, vol. 5a, b, and c; item 275), first printed shortly after the actual captivity in 1704, was reprinted in 1758 partly for patriotic purposes. In the last paragraph of the 1758 edition, Thomas Prince of Boston, the distinguished New England historian, supplied this bristling justification for the elimination of the French presence in Canada:

> And by the Accounts above, we may learn, from the Instance of *This one town only* in *our Western Frontiers* of the *Province* of the *Massachusetts-Bay* in *New-England*—what horrible Murthers and Desolations *This Province* has suffered from the *French* and *Indians* in all our Wars with them ever since the year 1675, when the *Indians* first broke out upon us—and *what Numbers* of the *present People* in *Canada* are the *Children* of This province, or *Descendents* from them—Which, in case the sovereign *GOD* should ever lead a victorious Army of ours into *Canada,* will clearly justify us to all the World, if we should bring every child & descendent of *New-England,* yea of *all* the *British Colonies,* away.—Especially considering we should bring them into a much pleasanter and more plenteous Land and agreable Climate; out of a wretched land of Darkness & Slavery, both Religious and Civil, into a Land of glorious Light and Liberty. And may the ALMIGHTY hasten it in his Time!

The justification for publishing Robert Eastburn's *Faithful Narrative* (1758; repr. Garland, vol. 8c; item 99) bridges the pious motives of the seventeenth century and the anti-French concerns of the early eighteenth century. Introduced with a reference to the revivalist Presbyterian clergyman Gilbert Tennent, who pronounced the narrative to be pious in design and in its execution "entertaining and improving," Eastburn's narrative of his capture in 1756 by the French and Indians was, as he noted in his introduction, never intended to be published. "But a number of my friends were pressing in their persuasions, that I should do it; with whose motion I complied, from a sincere regard to God my king and country, so far as I know my own heart." Eastburn, a deacon of his church, was shocked by the dedication of his Catholic French and Indian captors who, he observed, "seem to make a better use of a bad religion than we of a good one." While "our enemies are inconsiderable in number, compared with us," he noted, "yet they are united as one man, while we may be justly compared to a house divided against itself, and therefore cannot stand long, in our present situation."

The "chief aim" in publishing the narrative of the Flemings, husband and wife (1756; repr. Garland, vol. 8a; item 106), was "to give an idea of the distresses of such as are so unfortunate as to fall into the hands of our savage enemies, to those who may seem disinterested in these matters, who make light of them." The introduction contrasts the comfort of Pennsylvania's secure city dwellers with the sufferings of "some hundreds of our poor back settlers," and the narrative is designed to evoke sympathy for the latter while it generates patriotism in the former.

How significant was the group alluded to in the Fleming introduction who "made light of" the tales of captivities in the mid-eighteenth century? At first glance it would seem unlikely that any significant number of colonists would make fun of the real sufferings of those who experienced the torments of Indian captivity. But with the increasing appearance of fictional as well as factual accounts of captivity in the eighteenth century, skepticism and cynicism about such adventures mounted. One of the most valuable narratives—James Smith's 1799 account (item 223) of his captivity among the Indians after his capture at Fort Duquesne in 1755—was not published immediately after Smith's return from captivity because, as Smith put it, "at that time the Americans were so little acquainted with Indian affairs, I apprehended a great part of it would be viewed as fable or romance."

Revenge was a continuing motive for publishing captivity narratives. When Hugh Henry Brackenridge published the narrative of Colonel Crawford's expedition against the Ohio Indians in 1782 (1783, 1843; repr. Garland, vol. 12c and d; item 57), his motive was clearly stated in the appended "Observations with regard to the animals vulgarly called Indians." Brackenridge's bitter diatribe concluded: "the tortures which they [the Indians] exercise on the bodies of their prisoners, justify extermination."

The war between the United States and the Sac and Fox tribe in 1832, in which Abraham Lincoln participated, was also the occasion for utilizing a captivity narrative—that of the two Hall sisters—to justify a harsh response against the Indians. As John A. Wakefield, in the conclusion to his *History of the War between the United States and the Sac and Fox Nations of Indians* (1834; repr. Garland, vol. 49b; item 263), observed:

> The author has been led to the foregoing reflections, from seeing in many of the eastern prints, that many erroneous statements have gone abroad, respecting the origin and management of this war; and some of them casting reflections on the Governor of our State, and crying out, "poor Indians." But as I have before observed, none but the reckless and abandoned hearted man, would have the hardihood to cast imputations upon our Executive, and cry out, "poor Indians," after a thorough perusal of the many outrages these hell-hounds committed on our frontier settlements.

The captivity theme seems to have been adopted by religious writers in the early nineteenth century as a dramatic and effective way of presenting an otherwise dull and conventional message. The narrative of Thomas Baldwin is an example (repr. Garland, vol. 52c; item 44). Baldwin is pictured on the cover of the account in his old age as "the Christian Philosopher," hand on head, who has drunk deep of the cup of sorrow because his wife and children were massacred while he escaped the dreaded captivity. Linked to Colonel Daniel Boone in the narrative (which describes events in Kentucky in the 1780s), Baldwin's adventures are narrated by the editor who records the old man's final exhortation "to you, Sir, and to all, I would then say, whatever may be your or their rank in life, if you wish to be happy in this world, and to secure certainty of being infinitely more so in the world to come, I pray thee cherish Religion." In an afterword the editor links Baldwin's willingness to record his captivity with his belief that permanent happiness can be found only in "the religion of a crucified redeemer."

Other captivity narratives were put to a similar religious purpose. Deerfield minister John Williams' *Redeemed Captive, Returning to Zion* (item 275) narrative appeared in numerous Sunday School versions in the nineteenth century, such as that prepared by Titus Strong, *The Deerfield Captive: an Indian Story, being a Narrative of Facts for the Instruction of the Young* (item 249),[26] which went through several editions in the 1830s and 1840s.

Profit to the publisher was a significant motive for the publication of captivity narratives. This fact is illustrated by the publishing history of Mrs. Susannah Johnson's account of her four years of suffering following her capture by the French and Indians at Charlestown, New Hampshire, in 1754 (1796, 1797, 1814; repr. Garland, vol. 23a, b, and c; item 124). The first edition of her account was published in Walpole, New Hampshire, in 1796, and was quickly reprinted in Glasgow, Scotland, in 1797, with the note that "The Publishers of this Narrative bought it of an American Gentleman who arrived at Greenock in the Bark Hope, a few weeks ago; and as he assured them that there was not a copy of it to be procured in Europe, and that it sold in America for four shillings and sixpence, they deemed it worthy of re-printing." Other editions followed before and after Mrs. Johnson's death in 1810. The editor of the Windsor, Vermont, edition of 1814, Abner Kneeland, a minister, noted that Mrs. Johnson "was very anxious to have this work revised and republished before her death." Kneeland reported that she wished him to "get the copy right secured to her daughter Captive (Mrs. Kimball); which I told her I would do if time and opportunity would permit." Kneeland preached a sermon at Mrs. Johnson's funeral and incorporated that and other material into the edition that followed. The new enlarged edition was the basis for still another edition of the work published in Lowell, Massachusetts, in 1834.

The author of *A Journal of the Adventures of Matthew Bunn* (1796, 1827; repr. Garland, vol. 21f and g; item 66) attributed the reprinting of his journal of St. Clair's defeat by the Indians of the old Northwest Territory, and his subsequent capture, to the desire to inform the public "of the barbarity and inhumanity of the red and white savages" as well as to amuse and make some money. That such narratives served at least the latter purpose is indicated by the fact that after publishing the 1827 edition, the Batavia, New York, publisher got out another edition ("7th Edition, Revised—4000 Copies") in the following year.

The publishing history of the story of the Oatman girls, captured by Yavapais in 1851 near Fort Yuma while they with their parents were endeavoring to reach California, illustrates the continuing popularity and profitability of captivity narratives in the second half of the nineteenth century. Two editions (item 248) of the narrative, written by Royal B. Stratton at the request of the afflicted brother and son, were published in California in 1857. The first edition was quickly exhausted and the second, in a printing of 6,000 copies, was also devoured by the California and Oregon trade within a few months of publication. To satisfy the continuing demand, a third edition was published in New York in 1858. In the preface to the second edition (San Francisco, 1857), Stratton noted that "It was with borrowed means that Mr. Oatman published the first edition, and it is to secure means to furnish himself and his sister with the advantages of that education which has been as yet denied, that the narrative of their five years' privations is offered to the reading public."

The justification for publishing Nelson Lee's account of his capture by the Comanches in 1858 was to recoup the finances of Lee, who had returned in poverty, and to lead to the ransom of others still held by the Comanches (1859; repr. Garland, vol. 75; item 173). Lee, who was illiterate, relied on an editor to take down the story of his three years' captivity. The preface to his account was dated January 1, 1859, sixty days after his return. He was originally spared because his alarm watch fascinated his captors, but he also amused them by his "what the hell" attitude. When released from the bonds with which he was confined, he hurled objects at his tormentors. Instead of killing him for his presumption, they laughed.

Captivity accounts were also written to educate the ignorant and unwary. Mary Barber, who had wanted to be an Indian missionary and who had ultimately married Squatting Bear, a Sioux chief, in 1867, gave the following reason for writing the *True Narrative* of her five years among the Indians (1872; repr. Garland, vol. 86b; item 47):

> If my narrative has proved interesting I am well satisfied, but if in its perusal some silly girl may change her mind regarding the noble red men and relinquish all thoughts of going among them, for any purpose whatever, then I am fully satisfied.

The publishers of Joseph Barker's *Interesting Narrative* of the sufferings of Barker and his wife among the Comanches (1848; repr. Garland, vol. 63a; item 48) provided a multipurpose justification for their publication:

> In the first place, it will operate as a salutary warning to those who are prone to listen to the syren voice of the deceitful land speculator, and wander away in search of happiness, taking their sorrowing families with them, far into the pathless wilderness; secondly, it presents a true picture of Indian life, showing that the savage of the forest is not that harmless, dignified character we sometimes see drawn by the hand of benevolent philanthropy, but a cruel and barbarous being who may not be trusted till his temper has been broken and his nature changed by the hand of civilization.

The publishers of Clara Blynn's account of her captivity among the Plains Indians (1869; repr. Garland, vol. 81; item 13) attempted to justify one of the less savory American attacks on the Indians by the dramatic device of having Mrs. Blynn and a number of other females captured and violated by Cheyennes under a chief named Santana near Sand Creek, site of the infamous massacre of unoffending Cheyennes in November 1864 by Colonel Chivington and the Colorado volunteers. In Mrs. Blynn's narrative two girls, aged 12 and 14, were stripped and violated by a dozen Indians. "And more horrible yet to relate, as each brute sated his passions, he would draw his knife and cut a deep score on the quivering body of the victim." Mrs. Blynn herself was saved from such treatment because Santana fancied her for himself. Generals Sheridan and Custer eventually came to the rescue, defeating Santana and freeing Mrs. Blynn. In a final comment, the editors noted:

> So, in his short but determined winter campaign, General Sheridan actually saved a vast effusion of bloodshed, outlay of public money, and did more than all the Peace Commissions that were ever held—to ensure at least the safety of thousands of helpless women and children on the frontiers. And we firmly believe that if the whole Indian business were placed in the hands of Lieutenant General Sherman and Major General Sheridan, we should have no more trouble with the savages.

An unusual justification for publishing a captivity narrative was that of Mrs. Sarah Wakefield, taken prisoner during the Sioux uprising of 1863 (1863; repr. Garland, vol. 79a; item 264). While the first of her stated reasons for publishing what she claimed was not originally written for the public eye was to benefit her young children in case of her death, the third and last reason seems to be the most significant. "I do not publish a little work like this in the expectation of making money by it," she wrote, "but to vindicate myself, I have been grievously abused by many, who are ignorant of the particulars of my captivity and release by the Indians." Mrs. Wakefield's favorable comments concerning her treatment by the Indians displeased many of the white citizens of Minnesota and it does not take a great stretch of the imagination to think how her "six weeks in the Sioux tepees" became the butt of sly and lascivious comments by those whose racial antagonism to the Sioux was intense. Mrs. Wakefield wrote under particularly poignant circumstances. The Indian who had spared her from suffering was later hung "by mistake" though Mrs. Wakefield implied that it might have been by design. Even the innuendos about her sexual "fall" among the Indians—a common assumption directed against female captives by an unforgiving male-dominated white world—could not be dispelled even by her insistence that "The Indians were as respectful towards me as any white man would be towards a lady: and now, when I hear all the Indians abused, it aggravates me, for I know some are as manly, honest, and noble, as our own race."

An even more unusual motive for publishing a captivity narrative was that of Edwin Eastman, author of *Seven and Nine Years among the Camanches and Apaches: An Autobiography* (1873), Jersey City, 1873 and 1874, and London, 1878; repr. Garland, vol. 88; item 100) whose book served primarily as a vehicle to sell the patent medicine called Eastman Indian Blood Syrup, which was described in notices appended to the book as "the most remarkable purifier of the blood that I have ever known; it is a tonic, diuretic, a nervine, and a gentle laxative. It is alterative, sudorific, soporific, and deobstruent." The syrup, conveniently, was advertised as available throughout England and the United States. . . .

Ethnological data was an incidental product of seventeenth- and eighteenth-century captivity narratives, usually expressed in the captive's account of exactly what happened to him or her. Nineteenth-century captivity narratives, on the other hand, occasionally included separate sections on the culture of the Indians among whom the captive lived. The nineteenth-century narratives were influenced by, and competed for the reader's attention with, the emerging literature of travel novels (for example Melville's *Typee* and *Omoo*), of scientific literature (such as the account of the Wilkes expedition), and of "dime novels." Ethnological sections helped the captivity narratives compete with this literature.[27] Nevertheless, the bulk of the narratives, whether of the seventeenth, eighteenth, or nineteenth centuries, consisted primarily of the exciting incidents of capture, escape, and return, not the details of everyday life among the Indians or observations of great ethnological significance.

Aside from the descriptions of techniques of torture at the stake, perhaps no ethnological detail is more frequently described than running the gauntlet, a practice characteristic of the Eastern Algonquian tribes. One of the most detailed descriptions of the process is contained in Freegift Patchin's 1833 account of his captivity and

sufferings during the American Revolution (1833; repr. Garland, vol. 52a; item 221). As the captives were brought to each Indian village or encampment they were forced to run between two rows of irate villagers who beat them as they attempted to reach the safety of a fixed refuge at the end of the line. Once, passing between the two lines of women, Patchin reported that one saluted him with the comment "poor *shild*, poor *shild*" and thereupon gave him a blow that "nearly split my head in two." At another camp, Patchin noted that a whole regiment of British troops lined up in two parallel rows to protect the American captives "as here were many young lads of the natives, quite able, if an opportunity was given them, to hack and club us to death, before we reached the fort."

The use of the gauntlet as a form of retaliatory response by those aggrieved by the previous actions of the captives and as a test of the prisoners' fortitude is a subject explored by only a few historians. In James Axtell's interpretation, the gauntlet is seen primarily as an initiation rite into Indian society. Axtell emphasizes the educational effect of the gauntlet on the captive rather than its purgative effect (through vengeance) on his captors. The evidence supporting either interpretation of the practice is ambiguous. Certainly many whites perceived murderous intent when in fact cultural transformation was intended. The evidence shows protective behavior and soft or symbolic blows on the part of some Indians forming the gauntlet. Possibly the testing process that the gauntlet represented is amenable to interpretation from both points of view simultaneously. The Indians did tend to eliminate those who could not adapt to the harsh existence of a warrior society, as sufficient examples of their cruelty to children who could not keep up with retiring war parties attest. Possibly their cruelty to some of those captured sated their thirst for vengeance. At the same time the gauntlet tested and revealed the qualities that they expected to find in those whites they would adopt into their society. A gauntlet ceremony was, until the late 1930s, a feature of the initiation rites of freshmen at Dartmouth College, originally founded as an Indian school. Its use in this college context can perhaps be equated to its historical use as an initiation and testing rite by a potentially accommodating society rather than as a venting of hostility and rage upon helpless victims by a hostile and vindictive society.[28] The captivity narratives supply data essential to proper interpretations of the subject.

The narrative of Mary Jemison, the "White Woman of the Genessee," is one of the captivity narratives most significant ethnologically, yet it sold as well as the novels of Scott and Cooper during the 1820s and in the year of its appearance sold better than the works of either novelist. Of the many editions published, the one edited by the pioneer ethnologist Lewis Henry Morgan in 1856 has been chosen for reproduction along with the original 1824 edition (repr. Garland, vol. 41a and b; item 237). While full of specific ethnographic details about the Iroquois, Mary Jemison's account also incorporates the "marriage metaphor" that, Slotkin asserts, lies at the bottom of the captivity genre. Jemison, captured while a young girl, was married to an Indian warrior (and subsequently married to another Indian after his death). Her love and admiration for her Indian spouses, her acquisition of Indian traits, her suspicion of white settlers, are all brought out effectively in James Seaver's account of her captivity. Slotkin points out that her description of her second Indian husband is "strikingly like current descriptions of Boone" and Cooper's Natty Bumppo. Both as an ethnological account and as a piece of literature, Seaver's account of Mary Jemison's captivity is important in marking the growing acceptance of the native American as a legitimate American character rather than as a hostile force from which Western man must escape.[29]

A consistent theme throughout the Indian captivity narrative (both actual and fictional) is that of revenge for injuries sustained. In white eyes revenge was seen as vindictiveness, unwarranted in terms of Christian values even if directed against the very parties guilty of injustices against the natives. In Indian terms, revenge was seen as justice, warranted in terms of Indian values, which required that such obligations to one's fellow men as well as to the Great Spirit not be forgotten or excused. The torture of prisoners at the stake, so often rehearsed in the captivities, was carried on deliberately and formally, however much white narratives perceived only "frenzy" and casual cruelty in the event. It was little comfort to the unfortunate victim to know that he or she was serving as an offering to the imperatives of Indian culture, but it is important to recognize the ritualized context within which such acts of apparently gratuitous cruelty took place.

The case of Colonel William Crawford in the 1780s provides perhaps the best example of this cultural imperative. On March 8, 1782, Pennsylvania militia murdered 90 Christian Indians at Gnadenhütten. On June 4, 1782, Colonel Crawford, commanding about 250 men of the Pennsylvania militia, fought a battle with an equal number of Indians. The next day Crawford was surrounded by 140 newly arrived Shawnees and some of Butler's Rangers. All of Crawford's men were killed or captured. Crawford was roasted slowly at the stake in retaliation for the massacre of Gnadenhütten.[30]

Most difficult for English readers to understand was the extreme cruelty visited upon the hapless captive by the women and children of the village to which he was taken. The thrusting of burning splinters into the victim's body was frequently cited by horrified editors as an expression of the Indians' innate and diabolical cruelty. Few perceived the action as a form of catharsis for the non-combatants whose loved ones had been destroyed on the battlefield. At times the catharsis might be provided by the venting of fury against a captive, but at other times it might be satisfied by his adoption into the bosom of the Indian family that had lost a member. Catharsis by fury rather than love was evident among whites as well as Indians placed in similar situation. The classic example may be the action of the women of Marblehead who seized two bound Indian captives from the hands of their English escorts during King Philip's War and beat them so savagely with stones and "billets of wood" that they were found after the attack "with their heads off and gone, and their flesh in a manner pulled from their bones."[31]

The opposite side of the coin of Indian revenge for ill treatment was Indian remembrance of good treatment. The captivities are replete with examples of Indian gestures of friendship and good will toward white captives. The motives for good treatment ranged from pure sympathy to calculated gain, but centered primarily on recognition of earlier good will and generous conduct displayed by the captive and/or his or her associates. At work was the converse of the philosophy of retaliating for injustices received: it was to reward good actions. In both cases, Indian value systems demanded that justice be done. There could be no vicarious atonement or escape from the consequences of one's actions, as in Christian philosophy. The person who acted badly must be punished; he who acted justly was to be rewarded.

The fear and loathing with which Europeans viewed the tortures incident to captivity were not entirely owing to their novelty. Cruel torture was a part of the European heritage of the earliest settlers. Such ecclesiastical or judicial punishments as burning of heretics and criminals, breaking on the rack, etc., did not begin to recede into memory until the eighteenth century. The agent of cruelty in the New World, however, was more often the native American than European institutions of government or the church. Even writers who praised the natives as kind and hospitable also noted their cruelty to their enemies.[32] That the Indians could be both cruel and kind, however, was not always recognized by the captives, who were unlikely to appreciate the ritualistic—even religious—significance of the cruel fate meted out to them. Since the treatment of captives was an expression of retribution for grievances suffered—a value supreme in most Indian religious systems—both the apparently "gratuitous" cruelty and the occasional "ceremonial" cannibalism were logical elements in Indian eyes, however revolting and horrifying to whites. While comprehended in a partial fashion by perceptive observers like Montaigne, the religious significance of the process of revenge on captives was never fully understood by most white observers. While an understanding would not have diminished the fear of those subject to such a capture, it might have given that fear a more rational and philosophic character.

The potency of revenge in Indian life was often seen in the Indian response to false commercial dealings by whites, a frequent cause of Indian wars. Thus in Charles Saunders' narrative of the eighteenth century (1763; repr. Garland, vol. 10a; item 233), the author notes the Indians' lack of avariciousness in trade, "they being usually complacent and abundantly reasonable, excepting when they imagine themselves imposed upon or affronted, and in this case a ten-fold restitution would make no atonement, they being implacable in their resentment, and entire strangers to the dictates of humanity."

The popular white view of the experience of a woman captive among the Indians included the assumption of brutal and mass rape. While more a projection of white fears than a common experience, rape of female captives was not unknown among nineteenth-century Plains Indian captors. Plains practice thus contrasted sharply with tribal practices in the Eastern Woodlands, particularly in colonial times, when rape of captives was virtually unknown. Captured females rarely acknowledged the experience of rape, perhaps to avoid the stigma attached to a female captive, thus used, upon being restored to polite society.[33] The repugnance directed at white women "spoiled" by sexual intercourse with their Indian captors has been documented by Rayna Green in her study of Indian-white interaction in the American vernacular tradition. In the folktales upon which she draws, Green finds frequent expression of the theme of white women made unfit for white men after sexual contact with Indian men.[34]

James Axtell suggests two explanations for the absence of any rape reports in the early colonial period: (1) the Indians (of New England at least) esteemed black rather than white the color of beauty, and (2) the incest taboo forbade a warrior from attempting to violate his potential (by adoption) future sister or cousin.[35] Both of these assertions seem to me only partially plausible. I suggest that the warrior ethic which enforced continence, even with their wives, upon members embarking on an expedition, and the rejection of European cultural patterns that stimulated an aggressive sexual attitude even while attempting to repress such an attitude, are more explanatory of Indian behavior. However, the subject needs further study, and other scholars may mine the narratives for additional hypotheses.

More often than not, the role played by the captive white woman among the Plains Indians was that of wife or slave of her captor or buyer. Cynthia Ann Parker, the wife of Quannah Parker, a Comanche chief, is the best-known example of a captured white woman integrated into one of the Plains tribes. . . . In considering the important roles played by whites in Indian society (as opposed to Indians in white society) it is important to remember that the integration of the white into Indian society, however traumatic for the white, was genuine and binding upon the Indian. By contrast, the integration of the Indian into white society was often more formal than real.

The experiences of Anglo or Mexican boys captured by Plains Indians were little different from the experiences of girl captives. J. Norman Heard has concluded that captives became more or less integrated into the capturing tribe depending upon the age at which they were taken. The younger and more impressionable captives were more likely to remain with their adopted families rather than return to the white world, even if given the opportunity. As in the case of colonial New England . . . , young boys more often resisted return to a white society than females, but often both men and women were sufficiently conditioned by Indian upbringing to remain strongly attached to their adopted culture.[36]

The process by which Indians successfully converted English captives to the Indian way of life has been well described by James Axtell. While this phenomenon has long been recognized by students of this subject, Axtell has brought together the evidence from the captivity narratives *and* the public records and woven this material into an analysis that establishes the highly sophisticated character of the process. Beginning with a physical substitution of Indian moccasins for European shoes, the captive who was adopted progressed through the ceremony of running the gauntlet or equivalent trials to a ceremony in which his "white blood" was symbolically washed and scrubbed away by his new Indian brothers and sisters. He was thereupon received into the wigwam of the family adopting him and was thereafter treated with perfect equality by his fellow tribesmen.

Though challenged by critics who question the use of data drawn from those who returned to white society from Indian society to explain what happened to those who remained captives, Axtell's arguments have established a new level of interpretation of the events of captivity.[37] In a genre that has tended to be dominated by literary scholars, Axtell, a historian, has shown how ethnographic and historical detail from the captivity narratives, combined with related documentary material, can provide an interpretation of Indian and white behavior that cannot otherwise be recovered from the record of the past.

A more modest effort to test the ethnographic content of the captivity narrative against modern anthropological knowledge was made jointly by A.L. Kroeber (1876-1960), the distinguished anthropologist from the University of California, Berkeley, and Clifton B. Kroeber, associate professor of history at Occidental College. The Kroebers examined the nineteenth-century account of the Oatman sisters, Olive and Mary, who were carried away by the Yavapai Indians after their family was attacked while traveling alone on the Gila

Trail about eighty miles east of Yuma, on March 18, 1851. Father, mother, and five other Oatman children were killed; a brother was left for dead but saved by friendly Indians. The two sisters were sold to the Mohave Indians after a year's time; one died of starvation during a famine in the Mohave Valley; the survivor, Olive, was sold to the whites in 1856 and her story published by the Reverend Royal B. Stratton of Yreka, California. The Kroebers compared the sensational narrative with the evidence of Olive's life among the Indians collected by Army authorities at Fort Yuma immediately after her release. That evidence consists primarily of a careful interrogation (debriefing in today's terminology) of Olive one day after her arrival in 1856. The Kroebers concluded that it is necessary to apply a corrective to the Stratton account. Stratton embroidered Olive's story with assumptions of Indian treachery and inhumanity not borne out by the evidence. He also projected on his readers the assumption that the girls were adolescents rather than children although in fact Olive was only eleven when captured.[38]

After her recovery Olive Oatman occasionally lectured about her experience. Her lecture notes concerning her experience followed the traditional captivity format from the time of Mrs. Rowlandson, complete with reference to the providential nature of her delivery from her cruel fate. She described her captors, for the most part, as cruel and treacherous, though she gave instances of their genuine sympathy and concern for her fate. In keeping with the delicacy of the day, she made no reference to her sexual life, if any, but only to the drudgery of her work. In her lecture, Indian customs were passed over quickly: "They have a few superstitions, but of these & their traits I have spoken in my book."[39]

An effective attempt to measure the ethnographic veracity of a literary treatment of the captivity experience is Maurice Schmaier's "Conrad Richter's *The Light in the Forest:* An Ethnohistorical Approach to Fiction."[40]

The rescue of Captain John Smith by Pocahontas, daughter of the Indian chief Powhatan, has proved a durable "type" for many captivity narratives. Just as the accuracy of Smith's account has been questioned, so have many subsequent accounts of a captive's rescue by an Indian maiden been subject to historical doubt or literary embellishment. Among the narratives in which the male captive is spared by the intervention of an Indian girl was Jonas Groves' account of his capture during the later stages of the French and Indian wars (1820; repr. Garland, vol. 37c; item 34).

By the end of the nineteenth century, use of the Pocahontas rescue theme could be treated humorously, even by the captive himself. Thus Josiah Mooso, in describing his rescue by a sixteen-year-old Indian girl who took him to her lodge, could write in his later reminiscences (1888; repr. Garland, vol. 97; item 202):

My conscience, even now, smites me to think of the deception I practiced upon the woman, to whom I owe my life, but as an excuse I will plead that being a white man and she an Indian was sufficient grounds for not wishing to take her as my wife, and the only way that seemed to suggest to me a path out of the difficulty was to take my flight, and the way of liberty must be through her agency.

A companion theme to that of the white male being saved by the Indian female was that of the white female being spared by the Indian male. The extent to which this theme could be romanticized in late nineteenth-century narratives was expressed in Mrs. L. G. Benton's account of her grandfather Daniel Howe's captivity and escape during the French and Indian wars (18—; repr. Garland, vol. 103b; item 52). As Mrs. Benton put it:

Poor little Rachel soon grew faint and began to cry. One of the savages raised his tomahawk and was about to strike her. As her sunbonnet hung back and her long golden curls shone in the sun, Daniel thought her the most beautiful creature he had ever seen; but he could do nothing for her. However, when the chief saw the uplifted tomahawk he gave the fierce savage a blow which nearly felled him, then he patted the little weeping girl on her shoulder and taking her up in his strong arms, he carried her many a mile as he went in his own wild way. After a time Rachel dropped her head on the Indian's shoulder and went to sleep.

The evolution of the texts of the various editions of the captivity narratives is a fit subject for more detailed analysis by literary scholars. An amusing example of a revision in the interest of greater "veracity" is the modification of the passage in the 1786 edition of Philip M'Donald and Alexander M'Leod's *Surprising Account* (1787, 1794; repr. Garland, vol. 17e and f; item 193) describing their captivity. In the 1786 edition the travelers come across "a monstrous creature in human shape, but nearly twelve feet in height [who] jumped from a rock in the road and taking us both up, almost dead with fear, into his hand, exclaimed in the Hebrew language, 'What creatures can these be.'" The 1794 edition noted that

we were suddenly surprised by a human figure, who with amazing agility jumped from a rock into the road, and walked towards us in seeming astonishment. His stature and bulk appeared to be equal to that of the Patagonians, as related by modern voyagers; his aspect open, and free from that savage fierceness so conspicuous in the American Indians in general.

The figure went on to exclaim in Hebrew, "'What creatures can these be,'" though he spoke the language "imperfectly."

These giants among whom M'Donald and M'Leod had fallen were presented as amiable descendants of the migrants who came from Asia soon after the flood. They were shocked to hear of the quarrels of European Christians. The editor of the later edition must have doubted that many readers would accept the reality, let alone the good nature, of these people in the monstrous form in which they were originally presented.

The pious pen of the editor also moved when a narrative failed to make conventional obeisance to the workings of Divine Providence. Thus the editor of the 1811 edition of Frances Scott's narrative of her capture in 1785 (1786, 1799, 1800, 1811; repr. Garland, vol. 16b, c, d, and e; item 22) added the note that "She expresses her thankfulness to Divine Providence, for its kind interpositions in her favour in aiding and effecting her escape from the Indians, in supporting her, when she descended the precipice, and preserving her from the poison of the venemous snake, and sending the birds to direct her course." This sentence was added to the earlier editions that merely reported Mrs. Scott in a low state of health after her ordeal and "inconsolable for the loss of her family, particularly bewailing the cruel death of her little daughter."

Captivity narratives, while a single genre, show an almost kaleidoscopic complexity. They span the gap between the simple, pious, reportorial, admonitory accounts of the seventeenth century to the breezy, sentimental, cliché-ridden fictitious "dime novels" of the late nineteenth century. Perhaps the importance of the genre derives from the fact that captivities were always *popular*. Whether factual or fictitious, religious or secular, propagandistic or naive, they gripped the imagination of their contemporary audiences. They were bought by the thousands and often read to pieces.

Are captivity narratives merely an interesting chapter in the literary history of the United States or do they provide a key to the understanding of American character and history? Interpretations of the narratives by leading scholars leave no doubt that the captivities throw a profound light on American life. What that light illuminates is subject to widely varying interpretations. . . . While the captivity experience is now remote from the contemporary American public, it remains a body of information that unlocks some of the mysteries of the American past.

Notes

[1] Louise K. Barnett, *The Ignoble Savage: American Literary Racism, 1790-1890* (Westport, Conn., 1975), p. 4.

[2] Richard Slotkin, *Regeneration through Violence: The Mythology of the American Frontier, 1600-1860* (Middletown, Conn., 1973), pp. 144-145. . . .

[6] Alden T. Vaughan and Daniel K. Richter, "Crossing the Cultural Divide: Indians and New Englanders, 1605-1763," American Antiquarian Society, *Proceedings* 90, pt. 1

(April 1980): 23-99, especially pp. 23, 60-62, 64, 97. This article takes issue with the findings of James Axtell, *The School upon a Hill: Education and Society in Colonial New England* (New Haven, Conn., 1974), pp. 276-277.

[7] James Axtell, "The Scholastic Philosophy of the Wilderness," *William and Mary Quarterly,* 3rd ser. 29 (1972): 361-362, 361n.

[8] Vaughan and Richter, *op. cit.,* pp. 23-99.

[9] On the shift in attitudes toward Indians between the seventeenth and nineteenth centuries, see Alden T. Vaughan, "From White Man to Redskin: Changing Anglo-American Perceptions of the American Indian," *American Historical Review* 87 (1982): 917-953.

[10] Georgia David Xydes, "The Noble Ravage: Captivity Narratives of the Southern Plains," report presented to the faculty of the Graduate School of the University of Texas at Austin in partial fulfillment of the requirements for the degree of Master of Arts, December, 1975, pp. 5-6.

[11] Slotkin, *op. cit.,* p. 247.

[12] *Ibid.,* pp. 412, 475-478, 488-490.

[13] *Ibid.,* pp. 398-412.

[14] *Ibid.,* pp. 441-442.

[15] Wilcomb E. Washburn, "James Adair's 'Noble Savages,'" in *The Colonial Legacy,* edited by Lawrence H. Leder, vol. 3 and 4 (New York, 1973), pp. 91-120.

[16] Dorothy Forbis Behen, "The Captivity Story in American Literature, 1577-1826: An Examination of Written Reports in English, Authentic and Fictitious, of the Experiences of White Men Captured by the Indians North of Mexico," Ph.D. dissertation, University of Chicago, 1952, pp. 388-389. See also David T. Haberly, "Women and Indians: *The Last of the Mohicans* and Captivity Tradition," *American Quarterly* 28, no. 4 (Fall 1976): 431-443.

[17] Charles Brockden Brown, *Edgar Huntley: or, Memoirs of a Sleep Walker,* Philadelphia, 1799, 1:3-4.

[18] Richard VanDerBeets, ed., *Held Captive by Indians: Selected Narratives, 1642-1836* (Knoxville, Tenn., 1973), Intro., p. xx.

[19] Behen, *op. cit.,* especially chap. 3.

[20] Pearce, *op. cit.,* pp. 3, 6, 11, 20.

[21] James G. Meade, "The Indian Captivity Narrative in Colonial America," unpublished term paper for

Lawrence W. Towner, Director, The Newberry Library, Chicago, June 1, 1968, in the possession of Mr. Towner, pp. 2, 8-9, 14; see also Meade's "The 'Westerns' of the East: Narratives of Indian Captivity from Jeremiad to Gothic Novel," Ph.D. dissertation, Northwestern University, 1971.

[22] Slotkin, *op. cit.,* pp. 257-259; Behen, *op cit.,* p. 143.

[23] Slotkin, *op. cit.,* pp. 328-329.

[24] *Ibid.,* pp. 470, 475-478.

[25] *Ibid.,* pp. 470, 485, 502. See also Vaughan and Richter, *op. cit.,* pp. 86-87.

[26] (Greenfield, Mass., 1832), 68 pp.

[27] Xydes, *op. cit.,* p. 25.

[28] James Axtell, "The White Indians of Colonial America," *William and Mary Quarterly,* 3rd ser. 32 (1975): 55-88, reprinted in Axtell, *The European and the Indian: Essays in the Ethnohistory of Colonical North America* (New York, 1981), pp. 168-206, especially pp. 185-188. See also Vaughan and Richter, *op. cit.,* pp. 80-81.

[29] Slotkin, *op. cit.,* pp. 446, 449.

[30] John K. Mahon, article in forthcoming volume on the history of Indian-white relations in the *Handbook of North American Indians,* revised edition, to be published by the Smithsonian Institution, Washington, D.C.

[31] James Axtell, "The Vengeful Women of Marblehead: Robert Roules's Deposition of 1677," *William and Mary Quarterly,* 3rd ser. 31 (1974): 647-652.

[32] Cornelius J. Jaenen, *Friend and Foe: Aspects of French-Amerindian Cultural Contact in the Sixteenth and Seventeenth Centuries* (Ottawa, Canada, 1976), p. 137.

[33] Xydes, *op. cit.,* pp. 37-38,

[34] Rayna D. Green, "Traits of Indian Character: The 'Indian' Anecdote in American Vernacular Tradition," *Southern Folklore Quarterly* 39, no. 3 (September 1975): 233-262, at 238,

[35] James Axtell, "White Indians of Colonial America," p. 67. See also other essays in Axtell's collection.

[36] J. Norman Heard, *White into Red: A Study of the Assimilation of White Persons Captured by Indians* (Metuchen, N.J., 1973).

[37] Paula A. Treckel, letter to the editor, and response of Axtell, *William and Mary Quarterly,* 3rd ser. 33 (1976): 143-153.

[38] A.L. Kroeber and Clifton B. Kroeber, "Olive Oatman's First Account of Her Captivity among the Mohave," *California Historical Society Quarterly* 41 (1962): 309-317. An expended consideration is contained in the forthcoming University of Nebraska Press edition of the Oatman captivity narrative, edited by Wilcomb E. Washburn.

[39] Edward J. Pettid, S.J., ed., "Olive Ann Oatman's Lecture Notes and Oatman Bibliography," *San Bernardino County Museum Association Quarterly* 16 (1968): 1-39 (at 15).

[40] *Ethnohistory* 7 (1960): 327-398.

Michelle Burnham (essay date 1997)

SOURCE: "The Imperialist Audience: Nationalism and Sympathy in the Frontier Romance," in *Captivity and Sentiment: Cultural Exchange in American Literature, 1682-1861,* University Press of New England, 1997, pp. 92-117.

[*In the following excerpt, Burnham interprets captivity narratives as "national" narratives, which attempt either to challenge or to solidify the unity and identity of the newly independent and newly imperialist nation.*]

Near the end of Ann Eliza Bleecker's 1793 *History of Maria Kittle,* three Englishwomen, all rendered homeless and husbandless after hostile encounters with the Indians, share their sentimental stories with a group of Frenchwomen in Montreal. The three women tell stories that would have been familiar ones to captivity narrative readers, and their stories produce the profusion of tears that increasingly characterized such narratives. Bleecker's text takes the form of a letter written by one of Kittle's female relations, which recounts the heroine's blissful domestic life, her husband's reluctant departure from their home just before it is subjected to an Indian raid, the conflagration of her home, the death of her children and relatives in the attack, and her subsequent grueling journey through the wilderness with her captors. After her redemption, Kittle repeats this tale to her companions in Montreal, who respond by indulging "some time spent in tears, and pleasing melancholy" (52). A Mrs. Bratt follows with a mournful account of her own captivity and the death of her beloved son at the hands of the Indians, an event that causes her violently to "execrate their whole race, and call for eternal vengeance to crush them to atoms" (55). Moved by Bratt's story, the Frenchwoman Madame de R——requests yet another narrative from Mrs. Willis since, as one Frenchwoman claims, "my heart is now sweetly turned to melancholy. I love to indulge these divine sensibilities, which your affecting histories are so capable of inspiring" (73). Mrs. Willis relates to her now captive audience her escape from captivity by concealing herself and her children inside a hollow tree and her subsequent pilgrimage across Canada to locate her husband, only to find that he died in a Montreal jail before her arrival.

Stories such as Mrs. Willis's observe a sentimental temporality that resembles what Franco Moretti has labeled a "rhetoric of the too late," in which the continual deferral of reunion, confession, or agnition produces a "moving" effect (160). Moretti offers as an example of this narrative strategy a scene in which a young son and his father realize at last their mutual affection but only at the father's deathbed. What provokes tears at a scene such as this is not just the moment of agnition but the fact that such agnition arrives too late, in the same way that Mrs. Willis arrives too late to be reunited with her spouse. Maria Kittle's narrative, however, eventually recuperates what is lost from the "too late" by finding resolution in what might be called the more optimistic but equally moving rhetoric of "just in time." For after the conclusion of these three "affecting histories," the narrative advances to the sudden arrival of Kittle's husband, who only moments before had been informed that the wife he believed dead was in fact residing in a nearby home, to be reunited with his wife. During this melodramatic moment "the spectators found themselves wonderfully affected—the tender contagion ran from bosom to bosom—they wept aloud" (65).

This unexpected reunion, in which feeling circulates between French and English subjects alike, recalls the passionate expression of political and national sympathies encouraged by the women's accounts. Each of these three narratives maligns the Indians in direct proportion to its praise of the French for their recognizably European hospitality and benevolence. As grief for the captive Englishwomen converts into anti-Indian rage, the weeping audience becomes an incensed one. Madame de R——marks this transition and defines these national bonds when she fervently wishes "that the brutal nations were extinct, for never—never can the united humanity of *France* and *Britain* compensate for the horrid cruelties of their savage allies" (63). The military alliance of the French and Indians against the British is redefined here as an opposition between European "humanity" and Indian "brutality." It is the impossibility of balancing this new national equation that leads the audience to fantasize Indian extinction. But the passive construction and subjunctive tense of her (death) sentence—"that the brutal nations were extinct"—grammatically refuse to attribute any agency to that accomplishment.

Bleecker's *History,* written in 1779 and published posthumously in 1793, is one of many late-eighteenth-century captivity narratives that emphasize less the detailed experience of captivity among the Indians than the dramatic sensations that the telling of that experience produces. The multiplication of feeling within these successive final scenes suggests what attracted readers to Bleecker's text and other like it: as Madame de R——insists, spectatorial melancholy is an indulgence, a form of pleasure. Julie Ellison suggests in her analysis of Bleecker's poetry that these "affecting histories" are doubled histories, histories at once of the family and of the French and Indian wars. Ellison argues further that because the discourse of sensibility forges associations between emotion and historical events, eighteenth-century women writers turned to that discourse as a way of moving between the realm of feeling and that of history.[1] I would add that such writers turned more specifically to sentimental narratives of Indian captivity, which offered an ideal entry point into the discourse of history and into the project of nation-building.

The melancholy pleasure that Kittle's Montreal audience and, by the same token, Bleecker's American readers experience from these captivity histories serves as an affective model of what I shall call the imperialist audience, a model that takes on new proportions in the early nineteenth century, when attitudes toward the Indians emerged that would eventually find voice in Andrew Jackson's later rhetoric of Manifest Destiny and his policy of Indian removal. The Jeffersonian project of assimilation that had dominated national Indian policy began to falter in the early 1820s, when southern calls for active removal reached Congress (Horsman 194-95) and the hopeful tone of philanthropists began to shift toward doubt (Sheehan 145). Central to this Jacksonian-era model of the imperialist audience is the subtraction of agency from the historical stage, so that causal aggression looks like inevitability. In his analysis of imperialist fiction, Abdul R. JanMohamed points toward such a formulation when he suggests that "those who have fashioned the colonial world are themselves reduced to the role of passive spectators in a mystery not of their own making" (87). In other words, the imperialist nation imagines itself as an unaccountable audience, affected by a tragic disappearing act that no perceptible agent has effected. The convenient elision of agency allows mourning to be free of responsibility. But it is the accompanying sensation of pleasure that points toward the violence otherwise obscured by tears. Thus, Bleecker's sentimental prose and her narrative's tearful closure in marital reunion are strategies crucially intertwined with her text's imperialist and nationalist politics. In sentimental frontier romances of the later Jacksonian era, the narrative of Amerindian nations always observes the melancholic rhetoric of "too late," while the narrative of the American nation always claims the pleasurable rhetoric of "just in time."

The Frontier Romance and the Captivation of History

More than a century before the publication of Bleecker's *History of Maria Kittle,* captivity narratives maintained and relied on the interpenetration of family history and national history. Mary Rowlandson, for example, inscribes an often detailed record of the battles, conditions, and progress of King Philip's War as she records her personal history of maternal loss, spiritual trial, and domestic return. Furthermore, Rowlandson simultaneously tells these twinned histories and foretells, through the predictive logic of Puritan typology, a redemptive history of the Anglo-American project in New England. Likewise, many colonial American histories, including such massive tomes as Cotton Mather's *Magnalia Christi Americana* and pamphlet-size accounts of the Indian wars, integrate events of Indian captivity into their narratives. Repeatedly, the scene or event of Indian captivity metonymically links, with chains of feeling, the micropolitical realm of the family to the macropolitical representation of America's current state and future condition. From their outset, captivity narratives were intimately involved in the construction as well as the prediction of a "moving" history whose typical narrative logic of inevitability positioned their readers as an imperialist audience.

By the later eighteenth century and the publication of texts like Bleecker's *History,* when captivity narratives and sentimental novels were increasingly indistinguishable from one another, the historical and nationalist components of these texts remain central to their narrative design as well as to their continuingly popular cultural appeal. If the remarkable elasticity of the sentimental trope of captivity operated so effectively—and affectively—during the revolutionary era, it continued strategically to serve the construction of a deliberately national history in early-nineteenth-century novels. Louise Barnett significantly situates Bleecker's *History,* along with Susanna Rowson's 1798 *Reuben and Rachel,* at the beginning of the frontier romance genre so often identified with the later James Fenimore Cooper, his southern counterparts Robert Montgomery Bird and William Gilmore Simms, and their reputed European forebear, Sir Walter Scott. Although Barnett finally echoes a host of critics by dismissing these early women's texts, her chronology nonetheless suggests the possibility of an alternative—and surprisingly matriarchal—genealogy for the American frontier romance, which the effacement of such texts suppresses.[2] While Bleecker's and Rowson's texts owe their own significant debts to the captivity narrative tradition, they also crucially transform the captivity narrative, as Carroll Smith-Rosenberg argues, into a love story ("Subject Female" 500). That love story, however, is as much a national romance as it is a family one.

Two events of Indian captivity are contained in the elaborate family and national history that unfolds in Rowson's novel. Her central characters are the descendants of Columbia, the great-granddaughter of Christopher Columbus and the granddaughter of Orrabella, a Peruvian princess.[3] Four generations later in this genealogy, William Dudley marries Oberea, the daughter of

Susanna Rowson

a Narragansett Indian chief who captured him from his childhood home. Dudley, who counts among his paternal ancestors Lady Jane Grey, becomes the chief sachem of the tribe upon the death of his captor-turned-father-in-law. Not until Dudley's son marries into the Quaker Penn family and produces twin children do the Reuben and Rachel of Rowson's title appear. This complex and fantastic genealogy, which begins with the matriarchs Columbia and Orabella, takes up the entirety of the novel's first volume and weaves together into a single heritage European conquerors, Algonquin Indians, British royalty, Peruvian royalty, Protestants, and Quakers. It furthermore weds family history to American history through a series of romantic marriages.

Rowson's second volume traces the attempts of Reuben and Rachel on the one hand to reclaim their rightful inheritance of land on the Pennsylvania frontier and on the other each to marry and settle into domestic respectability. While Reuben's romance is deferred by his captivity among Amerindians, Rachel's is nearly destroyed by her captivity within European perceptions of proper womanhood. Separated by the Atlantic, the twins attempt parallel escapes: the pregnant Rachel circulates around the English countryside in an effort to escape social censure and poverty, while her disinherited brother awaits an opportunity to escape from his Indian captors. Like earlier captivity narratives and novels such as Richardson's *Pamela, Reuben and Rachel* positions the unity and reproduction of both family and nation after the escape from captivity.

Published four years after the American printing of *Charlotte Temple, Reuben and Rachel; or Tales of Old Times* marks Rowson's self-conscious adoption of a specifically American audience, as well as an explicit focus on the discipline of American history. In her preface, Rowson claims that she wrote this novel to interest and to educate young women not only in "history in general; but more especially the history of their native country" (iii). It may have been this early textbook-novel as much as Cooper's 1823 *Pioneers* that inspired a next generation of women novelists to write frontier romances, which combine a romantic marriage plot with events in the nation's historical past.[4] The majority of such novels, which flourished in America between the War of 1812 and the Civil War (Barnett 42), typically begin with familial disruption by historical events of conflict with native Amerindians and end with familial reunion. Two frontier romances of the 1820s, Harriet V. Cheney's *A Peep at the Pilgrims in Sixteen Hundred Thirty-Six. A Tale of Olden Times* (1824) and Catharine Maria Sedgwick's *Hope Leslie; Or, Early Times in the Massachusetts* (1827), echo not only the subtitle of Rowson's earlier work but also its complex dynamics of romance and history, of the family and the nation. In both novels, a romance narrative of deferred marital union coincides with an imperialist narrative of Amerindian dispossession. The narrative movement of erotic deferral seduces the reader into a sympathy that obscures the violence of racial displacement.[5] The attendant sensations of pleasure and melancholy are repeatedly organized and resolved around the scene of Indian captivity.

Surprisingly little attention has been paid to Cheney's book, despite the fact that Sedgwick's novel, which has received a great deal of critical attention in the past decade, depends, to some extent, on Cheney's earlier novel.[6] In fact, *Hope Leslie* offers a critical response to and revision of the historical constructions and evasions of *A Peep at the Pilgrims,* whose author Sedgwick obliquely acknowledges in her book. The sentimental event of captivity is, in both texts, the site of historical construction and revision, as well as the scene that produces an imperialist audience who watch, with pleasurable melancholy, a violent spectacle that both is and is not of their own making.

The Historical Gaze in A Peep at the Pilgrims

Harriet Cheney's *A Peep at the Pilgrims* begins in 1636 with the arrival in Plymouth of the Englishman Edward Atherton, an Anglican who has left a distinguished military career behind after the death of his Anglican father and his Puritan mother. If his parents did not share the same religious identity, however, we learn

that they did share similar histories of family disinheritance as well as a sense of "forbearance and liberality" that their only son inherits. In fact, it is the "unprejudiced" (1: 20) Atherton's refusal to meet Puritans on the battlefield that leads him to resign his military commission. He subsequently departs on a ship for the New World, watching "with his eyes fixed" (1: 26) the receding shores of the Old World. As soon as he lands on the shores of Plymouth, he hears and is immediately captivated by the disembodied voice of Miriam Grey, emerging from the open window of her home. Atherton attempts to get a look at the source of this voice, but because the inhabitants of the home are "screened from observation by a curtain" (1: 11), he fails. However, Atherton easily locates her at church service the next day, where—although her face is then hidden beneath a scarf and hood—he "scanned" with "diligence every article of her dress and every motion of her person" (1: 33). The intensity and fixity of Atherton's vision is matched only by its persistent failure to catch direct sight of its object, and this inaccessibility generates a longing that fuels the novel's romance plot.

But this initial romance is quickly thwarted by Miriam's orthodox Puritan father, who, quite in contrast to Atherton's own parental examples, will not tolerate his daughter's union with a non-Puritan. In an effort to dispel his romantic disappointment and recover from his thwarted hopes, Atherton leaves Plymouth for Boston. On his approach to the city, in a scene that echoes his departure from England, he gazes from a hilltop on the receding "seat of Indian empire" from which, he notes, the Indians "were still retreating before the advance of civilization, and resigning their territories to the white people" (2: 9). Atherton embarks on a new path of American empire when he joins John Underhill's Boston army in its excursion to defend the Connecticut settlements from attacks by the Pequot Indians. But what might seem at Atherton's departure from Plymouth the novel's abandonment of the romance plot for a historical one becomes instead a collision between them. Located at the site of that collision is the scene of captivity, a scene that, like Miriam's obscured face or the receding terrain of empire, seductively attracts as it retreats from the spectatorial gaze.

When Atherton departs and while her father is absent on a journey to England, the lovelorn but duty-bound Miriam decides to accompany her newly married cousin to her home on an outlying Connecticut farm. There, along with a young girl, Miriam is taken captive by the Pequots.[7] The collision of history with romance at the moment of captivity in Cheney's novel immediately becomes a collusion of interests as well, for the English military desire to defeat the Pequots becomes inseparable from Atherton's desire to protect Miriam and to rescue her from captivity in the wigwam of the Pequot chief Mononotto. Thus, Atherton ostensibly joins the Boston militia less to further unseat Indian empire than to gain empire over Miriam Grey. The romance narrative, here as elsewhere in the novel, displaces history precisely at the moment of agency, of political accountability. On the one hand, the romance narrative and its movement toward domestic union depends on the unfolding of historical events, for it is only by virtue of the Pequot War and Miriam's captivity that the distance between the separated lovers begins to close. At the same time, however, the romance plot is forever eclipsing the historical narrative, distracting the imperialist audience away from the scene of violence. Romance alternately depends on and obscures history as both narratives move toward a teleological end of marital/national union. Captivity serves here not only as the structural and affective link between these two narratives but as the visual and narrative aperture for Cheney's descent into national history.

The captive Miriam, confined in the wigwam of the Pequot sachem Mononotto, is supervised by the sachem's wife Mioma and their daughter, who remains unnamed in the novel. Cheney characterizes the relationship between captive and captor in affectionate, almost maternal terms, for we learn that it was only Mioma's wild grief and pleading to her husband for the lives of the two girls that has kept them alive thus far. Though it is not typical, such affection between Anglo captives and their Indian mistresses is not uncommon in many captivity narratives.[8] In nearly every other respect, however, the portrayal of this captivity departs significantly from the experience documented in earlier narratives. In comparison to long, arduous journeys through the wilderness, Miriam's captivity is a stationary, domestic one. Her greatest trial is not the destruction of her home and family, not the violent deaths of family and friends, not even the rigorous test of physical endurance in a trek through the forest. Rather, Miriam's greatest trial is one of boredom, a boredom generated by her immobile confinement within the wigwam among the Indian women.

Significantly, she does not escape from captivity but is rescued from it. Such rescue is typically legitimated in revolutionary-era narratives by the Indian and British threat of rape, but that threat is often subsumed in the frontier romance by the desire for marital, and American, union. If earlier captivity narratives like Rowlandson's or Bleecker's generally end with the promise of a reunited family, frontier romances end with the prospect of a future family. This shift coincides with a historical shift in national sensibility. What once were seen as external threats to the colonies, such as the Indians, are now seen as internal threats to the unity of the American republic. National stability in the 1820s appeared to depend on eliminating domestic regional, class, and racial factions.[9] This shift must also be seen, however, in the context of the nineteenth-century cult of domesticity, that "empire of the mother," for Miriam's captivity is virtually an Indian version of frontier domesticity. Cheney's strategy of immobilizing the experience of captivity effectively holds Miriam captive in a home not her own and at the site of racial and historical conflict. Although her fondness for her captors would seem to suggest the possibility of transcultural sympathy, her captivity and rescue in fact work to displace sympathy away from the Pequot Indians and the violent scene of their massacre.

Atherton's rescue of Miriam and her young co-captive is thwarted at the last minute, when his ship—captained by a "cowardly Dutchman" (2: 192)—pulls away from the shore and the Indians recapture the group on the shoreline. Mononotto later returns Miriam to the ship, to be exchanged for several Pequots held captive there; but when Miriam reaches the site where Atherton was captured and separated from her, she "covered her face to exclude every object from her view—for every object was associated with the most painful recollections" (2: 222). Miriam averts her gaze here in an attempt to repress memory, a gesture in contrast to earlier descriptions of Atherton's aggressive gaze. Together, however, these scenes point toward a tropology of the gaze that operates throughout the novel. One of the characteristics of Miriam's behavior—and much of her appeal to her several suitors—is her refusal either to bestow or receive gazes. After first hearing her voice through the window in Plymouth, Atherton spends much of the first part of the novel attempting to get a "peep" at Miriam. When he later rescues her from a boating accident, she thanks him full-faced only briefly, until she realizes her error and looks away. When she is brought onto the ship by Mononotto, she and the other redeemed female captive are sent below deck to a cabin, for "they were embarrassed by the gaze of curiosity" (2: 221). Even when Miriam is restored to the house of John Winthrop's son, she does not appear at dinner "from a natural aversion to encounter the gaze of strangers" (2: 234).

By contrast, one sign of Atherton's masculine bravery is his ability to withstand any gaze. While the two females are returned and exchanged, Atherton is retained as a captive by the Pequots, filling the space left void by Miriam's rescue. The violence of the captivity experience as it was represented in captivity narratives emerges only when Atherton takes Miriam's place. It is Atherton, not Miriam, who is bound to a stake, circled by a "horrid war-dance" (2: 224), subjected to torture, and "condemned to pass the night surrounded by his vindictive enemies, whose disfigured countenances glared upon him like demons" (2: 222). Yet unlike Miriam, Atherton is fully able to withstand and return these glares, just as he "sustained the haughty gaze of Mononotto with dignified composure" (2: 223).

This succession of gazes might be taken as instances that exemplify the novel's project as a whole. Cheney's title presents the text as a "peep" at Pilgrim life, suggesting a secretive and forbidden gaze into America's past, backward to an event that retroactively becomes an early monument to national history. Indeed, the audience's peep back nearly a century to "olden times" is, no less than the lovers' romantic gazes, characterized by the dynamics of captivation and foreclosure. If the audience's historical peep is the text's most overarching gaze, however, that gaze is conspicuously and deliberately averted from the novel's central historical event, the Pequot massacre. Cheney describes the English army's preparation for battle and their trying journey through the wilderness to the Pequot fortresses in careful detail, almost as though the physical mobility and suffering absent from Miriam's captivity are sympathetically transferred to the army. All the stereotypical trials of a captive's trek—physical weariness, hunger or an utter distaste for Indian food, passage over difficult terrain and through a hostile climate, laden with infants or provisions—are experienced by the troops: "The English endured excessive fatigue and suffering throughout the day; the weather was oppressively warm; they were almost destitute of suitable provisions, and obliged to travel through a pathless wilderness, encumbered with heavy arms and ammunition" (2: 246). The infant has been replaced by artillery, but this moving story of resistant mobility works as effectively for the English army as it did for English captives.

By the time the narrative reaches the battle itself, the romantic and historical narratives move inseparably toward their progressive ends. The event of captivity has made the reunion of Miriam and Atherton contingent on the English defeat of the Pequots; historical events have been seductively co-opted and justified by romantic desire. And yet when the narrative does reach the battle, it abruptly draws back, refusing to represent the scene by pleading—quite suddenly and rather illogically, given the novel's otherwise unhesitant depiction of historical events and figures—a refusal to tread into the discourse of history: "it is not our intention to invade the province of the historian, by entering into the details of this sanguinary conflict, from which the feelings of humanity recoil with horror. Suffice it to say, a complete victory was achieved by the conduct and intrepidity of the English" (2: 250). The horror that leads Cheney herself to shield her eyes here is reminiscent of Miriam's "covered . . . face" at the site of "the most painful recollections." This novel's effort to construct retroactively a historical memory for the American nation relies on an act of deliberate forgetting that is inscribed in its very center.[10] The imperialist audience is both attracted to and repelled by this unsightly yet significant symptom on the body of national history.

Despite Cheney's horrified refusal to gaze on what we might identify as the face of this historical scene of genocidal violence, she does go on to explain, in an agentless past tense, that

the laurels of the conqueror were unhappily stained with the blood of the innocent and defenceless. In little more than an hour, a flourishing village of seventy wigwams was reduced to ashes, and upwards of six hundred Indians,—the aged, and the feeble infant, the warrior in his strength, and the mother with her helpless children, were destroyed by the sword, or perished in flames.

The English had only two killed. . . .   (2: 250-51)

The only grammatical agents of anti-Indian violence here are swords and flames, not English subjects, and even then such agency is further displaced into the passive voice. This unwatchable event is ambivalently presented as both a horror and as cause for national celebration. Cheney notes that "considering the weakness of the colonies . . . their success appears almost miraculous; and under the smiles of Heaven can only be attributed to the prompt and cheerful exercise of th[eir] intrepid valour" (2: 256). The tentative return to a providential Puritan mode of historiography here strategically invokes the agentless grammar of divine intervention. Mention of the subsequent swamp battle, in which most of the Pequots who survived the fire were either killed or taken captive, is concluded with the satisfied claim that "[t]his second victory was complete, and the brave and powerful tribe of Pequods was totally exterminated" (2: 256). This sentence literally pauses midway between "victory" and "extermination," not to link the two events but to shift from the register of pleasure to that of melancholy. The sentence, like Cheney's narrative, would seem to pose a contradiction between "the theoretical justification of exploitation and the barbarity of its actual practice" (JanMohamed 103). JanMohamed argues that imperialist fiction relies on a manichean opposition that subordinates before it disposes of the colonized other. Cheney's novel, however, relies equally on a sentimental discourse that does not justify barbarity by subordinating the other so much as it screens the very problems of justification and barbarity beneath the irresistible forces of passive inevitability. If Cheney and her audience can indulge in pleasurable melancholy, it is because the grammar as well as the gaze of her narrative effaces agents.

The contradictions and evasions that mark the representation of Anglo-Indian contact and conflict persist to the end of the novel, when Atherton exhibits a sudden and surprising sympathy toward the captured Indians—now described as "children of the forest"—who "are to be sent to Bermuda as slaves" (2: 267). Given his vehement role in their genocidal defeat only pages earlier, Atherton's response is unexpected even if it is supported by the sympathetic logic of his own captivity. Such contradictions call to mind narratives like Rowlandson's, but the tension between her typological representation of the Indians as agents of Satan and her "realistic" representation of humane Indians remains unresolved in a way that Cheney's contradictions do not. Cheney's text, which indulges both in racial stereotype and transracial sympathy, relies on the sentimental affect of imperialist spectatorship, which not only accommodates but in fact requires both Atherton's violence and his pity. His passive response of "being moved" by Indian removal effaces active aggression, just as romantic desire effaces historical violence. It is this structure of imperialist affect that allows Cheney to appropriate the historical event of the Pequot massacre for nationalist purposes while remaining critical of its excesses; her novel struggles to build a national memory on an event whose details she would rather forget. Just as it had during the postrevolutionary era, the distracting mechanism of captivity launches a progressive and sentimental narrative of the American nation precisely by obscuring its violent and colonialist origins.

Pequots, Seminoles, and National Unity

To the 1824 readers of Cheney's novel, the fate of the Pequot Indians may well have resonated as a potential future for the American nation itself. An example of a failed and fragmented nation, the Pequots and their vanished empire function as a kind of negative model and critical warning to the troubled American union. The Pequot War, in fact, would no doubt have recalled Andrew Jackson's Seminole War, resolved just years before amid much dispute over the legislative as well as the moral legitimacy of his actions. And Jackson's political discourse, no less than frontier romance novels, linked nation and family through affective rhetoric. If Atherton's role in the Pequot massacre is emotionally justified by his desire to protect Miriam, Jackson's rationale for the Seminole War was likewise a defense of American women and children from Indian violence, a logic that, according to Michael Paul Rogin, "freed Jackson to urge American attacks on Indian women and children" (196) and to burn Seminole villages. Only once the war ended, Rogin notes, did Jackson begin to refer to the Indians as his children, a discursive and sentimental shift reminiscent of the victorious Atherton's sudden reference to the Pequots as "children of the forest." Jackson's Indian Removal Act of 1830 simply brought together into policy proremoval attitudes that had been circulating for decades in the South and West and conceptions of Indian extinction and European expansion that were gaining ground with proponents of scientific racialism.[11] When agents of Indian removal used Atherton's phrase "children of the forest," they were repeating the sentimental strategies as well as the language of frontier romances. . . .

Historical Revisionism in Hope Leslie

By complicating Cheney's representation of the Pequot War and of Anglo-Indian race relations, Catharine Maria Sedgwick's *Hope Leslie* problematizes the founding of Jacksonian national romance on events of anti-Indian

violence. *Hope Leslie* was published three years after *A Peep at the Pilgrims,* and Sedgwick acknowledges the earlier novel when she marks the absence of particular historical events in her own text with a reference to Cheney's. In the chapter that offers a recollection of the 1636 Pequot massacre, Sedgwick notes that "the anecdote of the two English girls, who were captured at Wethersfield, and protected and restored to their friends by the wife of Mononotto, has already been illustrated by a sister labourer" (56).[12] The "sister labourer" is, of course, Cheney, the center of whose novel is the unseen scene of that massacre. The narrative of *Hope Leslie* begins after the Pequot War has ended, and Sedgwick's acknowledgment of Cheney's novel suggests that she deliberately begins where Cheney leaves off in an effort to add to, rather than repeat, the historical narrative begun by her "sister labourer." But the project of *Hope Leslie* is historical restitution as much as it is historical continuation, for Sedgwick repeatedly turns her narrative gaze toward those scenes from which Cheney's gaze was averted. Whenever Sedgwick's novel works to restore agents to the stage of empire, it places her audience in an affective quandary.

Hope Leslie begins not with the sole arrival of an English son to the colonial settlements but with several arrival narratives. Years earlier, we learn, the orphaned Puritan William Fletcher left England, where he was forbidden to marry his Anglican cousin and true love, Alice Fletcher. When the narrative begins, Alice's two daughters, Hope and Faith Leslie, arrive from England after the death of their parents to become the wards of Fletcher's New World family. This transatlantic arrival is paired, however, with the arrival of Mononotto's daughter, who was captured during the Pequot War, at the Fletchers' frontier home. If orphaned English subjects repeatedly arrive in the colonies to found family and national histories, the Indian subject arrives at this site severed from her family and her now fragmented tribe in order to work as a servant for the Fletchers. At the end of *A Peep at the Pilgrims,* when the captured Indians are exiled into slavery, John Winthrop assures Atherton that Mononotto's daughter, who assisted in the attempt to rescue Miriam, would remain in safety. Sedgwick not only adopts Cheney's character at this moment of narrative abandonment, but she furthermore names the daughter of Mononotto and Mioma (or Monoca, as Sedgwick calls her) Magawisca. This initial substitution signals Sedgwick's recognition of the successive acts of oblivion that make Cheney's construction of a national memory possible, even if it is only to replace oblivion with another fiction. By giving Magawisca a central and heroic role as well as a historical memory and voice, *Hope Leslie* counters even as it repeats the romantic history constructed in *A Peep at the Pilgrims.*

Sedgwick, like Cheney, employs events of captivity as a point of entry into the realm of history, and it is through the affective manipulation of such events that she embarks on the task of historical revision. There are a multitude of successive captivities in *Hope Leslie,* beginning with the captivity of Alice Fletcher by her Anglican and royalist father in order to prevent her from marrying her Puritan cousin and emigrating with him to the colonies. This early error and failed romance will ultimately be remedied by the prospective marriage of Fletcher's son Everell and his adopted daughter Hope Leslie. As Alice's early captivity suggests, this novel does not always situate the scene of captivity at the site of racial conflict and cross-cultural contact.[13] My focus here, however, is on those specifically transcultural captivities through which Sedgwick constructs a counter-memory to Cheney's national narrative, captivities that work to reopen the text of history in order to expose the details from which Cheney's peep is averted.

Magawisca's arrival as a servant in a Puritan home is an example of the kind of English philanthropy and protection promised by Winthrop at the end of *A Peep at the Pilgrims.* But Sedgwick's portrayal of Magawisca's condition reverses the operation of sympathy by insisting that her audience watch not their own benevolent reflection on the historical stage but Indian actors. When Magawisca is invited into the Fletcher cabin, she appears as an alien cultural curiosity, bare-armed, with feathers and "rings of polished bone" in her hair, dressed in garments painted "with rude hieroglyphics" and wearing beaded moccasins (23). Mrs. Fletcher responds with domestic displeasure at receiving an "Indian girl for household labor," and the hostile maid Jennet refers to her as "Tawney" and "savage." These subordinating gestures are undercut, however, by the displeasure and hostility of Magawisca, whose "eyes had turned on Jennet, flashing like a sun-bean through an opening cloud," and by Everell's sympathy toward the Indian's "natural feeling," which "touched the heart like a strain of sad music" (24-25). This first scene of contact moves toward a reversal of the positions of cultural dominance and subordinance that it initially seems to reproduce.

When Magawisca finally speaks in her own language, to an Indian messenger who arrives with the scalp of the Pequot chief Sassacus, she overturns her employers' benevolent claim that she has been fortunately rescued from "the midst of a savage people" to be "set in a christian family" (24). Far from being rescued, Magawisca asserts that she has been taken captive. This exchange is conducted in her own language, thereby alienating her captors, who "could not understand" and who look on "with some anxiety and displeasure" (26). Magawisca gives the Indian messenger her bracelet with instructions to take it to her father, Mononotto, and to "[t]ell him his children are servants in the house of his enemies" (26). In a racial reversal of the captivity narrative scenario, the Indian Magawisca is the figure

enslaved by her military antagonists, the English. In fact, Magawisca's message and token is much like the one sent by Miriam and delivered by Mioma's daughter in *A Peep at the Pilgrims.* Atherton learns that Miriam is held captive only after Mononotto's daughter offers him a note scratched into bark. Just as this handwriting sample, a token of Miriam's identity, encourages Atherton to rescue her, so does Magawisca's bracelet result in Mononotto's attack on the Fletcher home to rescue his captive children and to avenge the family and tribal deaths suffered in the Pequot War. But here the Indian is a direct agent of her own escape rather than an indirect agent for the rescue of an English captive. Just as Miriam wants both to escape and to ensure that her former captors be treated kindly, Magawisca is torn between loyalty to her father and tribe and a desire to protect her Puritan captors from harm.

The chapter in which Sedgwick expressly refers to Cheney contains two accounts of the Pequot War that figures so centrally, if only by its descriptive absence, in *A Peep at the Pilgrims.* The first is given to Everell Fletcher by the servant Digby, whose participation in that war authorizes his claim that "these Pequods were famed above all the Indian tribes for their cunning" (43). Though Digby's narrative is reputedly engrossing as well as authentic, Sedgwick does not directly represent it in her text. She notes only that

> [t]he subject of the Pequod war once started, Digby and Everell were in no danger of sleeping at their post. Digby loved, as well as another man, and particularly those who have had brief military experience, to fight his battles over again; and Everell was at an age to listen with delight to tales of adventure and danger. They thus wore away the time. (43)

What might seem simply a vague repetition of Cheney's averted gaze, however, becomes supplanted by a second narrative of that same event, offered to Everell this time by Magawisca.

While secretly awaiting the appearance of Mononotto outside the Fletcher home, Magawisca informs Everell that "[i]t was such a night as this—so bright and still, when your English came upon our quiet homes" (46). Her subsequent narrative of the English attack on the Pequot village, presented in a direct discourse and detail lacking in Digby's account, forces a crisis in the political and national sympathies generated by texts like Cheney's or Ann Eliza Bleecker's. In Magawisca's account the beleaguered army is an Indian one, and the helpless captives are a family of Indians. Sedgwick argues in her preface for a revision in the representation of "[t]he Indians of North America," whose "own historians and poets, if they had such, would as naturally, and with more justice, have extolled their high-souled courage and patriotism" (6). Magawisca serves as Sedgwick's imagined Indian historian, who exposes what is obscured in Cheney's representation of the Pequot War. Her Indian history employs the affective logic of Cheney's text to reassess Cheney's historical narrative. In Magawisca's version emotion links not family to the American nation but Indian family to American family. This alternative history, furthermore, turns Jacksonian rhetoric against Jacksonian policies by paralyzing nationalist sympathies at a crucial moment, just before the expected arrival of Mononotto "determined on the rescue of his children" (57). Magawisca's vivid memory reconstructs the violent destruction "in our own homes, [of] hundreds of our tribe" and her vision of "[t]he bodies of our people . . . strewn about the smouldering ruin" (49). Because this image precedes the subsequent Indian attack on the Fletcher homestead, the reader's response of sentiment is prevented from converting into anti-Indian rage. Such rage instead belongs to the defeated Pequots.

The friendship that Cheney proclaims was bred between the English and the Indians following the Pequot War is contested by Sedgwick's portrayal of the shamed and enraged Mononotto, intent on "the infliction of some signal deed of vengeance, by which he hoped to revive the spirit of the natives, and reinstate himself as head of his broken and dispersed people" (57). The outcome of this violent attack poses the problem of emotional undecidability: Mrs. Fletcher and her infant son are killed, and the child Faith Leslie and Everell are taken captive, while Magawisca and her brother Oneco escape from captivity to be reunited with their father. Mononotto announces his victory when, disposing of his son's English dress, he claims that "[t]hus perish every mark of the captivity of my children" (65). Affect extends here in two irreconcilable directions; the sensations of pleasure and melancholy are not wedded but divorced, not reconciled but disturbingly at odds. This conflict of feeling remains unresolved because it is unaccompanied by the imperialist temporality of the inevitable; here Indian disappearance is replaced by Indian resistance. The Amerindian narrative briefly adopts the rhetoric of "just in time," while the Anglo-American one succumbs, momentarily, to the grief of the "too late." Only at the end of her novel—when, in the wake of Magawisca's departure, Everell and Hope plan their wedding—will Sedgwick reverse these rhetorics.

Despite her ultimate escape from physical captivity, however, Magawisca remains in another sense captive within the discursive constraints of Sedgwick's Anglo-American textuality. Indeed, despite "her Indian garb" (22), Magawisca appears in many ways as a Europeanized and thus familiarized Indian woman. Like Mary Jemison, held captive in her own enormously popular captivity narrative (published, significantly, the same year as Cheney's novel), Magawisca is a sentimental heroine who speaks English

and feels sympathy for her white captors. But for its racial reversal, her narrative of Indian "courage and patriotism" otherwise resembles Cheney's account of English "intrepidity." Magawisca's history, too, is a seductive romance that disrupts the discourse that contains her only by employing that discourse against itself. In other words, Magawisca's sentimental history of the Pequot War repeats Cheney's but with a critical difference. This strategic repetition resembles the mimicry that Homi Bhabha associates with the colonized and that articulates cultural difference from a site located "between the lines and as such both against the rules and within them" (*Location* 89). When these scenes from *Hope Leslie* are read against Harriet Cheney's earlier novel, the particular effects of such mimicry on historical representation become evident. Sedgwick's text does not replace American with Pequot history so much as it radically questions the construction of authoritative history altogether.

Everell responds to Magawisca's counter-memory of the Pequot War by realizing that he had previously only heard its details "in the language of the enemies and conquerors of the Pequods; and from Magawisca's lips they took a new form and hue" (53). "This new version of an old story" seems to Everell not simply a different version but the right one, for it "remind[s] him of the man and the lion in the fable. But here it was not merely changing sculptors to give the advantage to one or the other of the artist's subjects; but it was putting the chisel into the hands of truth, and giving it to whom it belonged" (53). When sculptor and sculpture, author and text, exchange roles, historical representation is exposed as a fiction, as an undecidable romance. This undecidability mirrors the affective conflict inspired in Sedgwick's audience. Sympathy can no longer translate into justifiable rage, and the temporality of history abruptly stalls. Everell's national sympathies—formed by official accounts of Indian wars by William Bradford and William Hubbard—suddenly shift their identification, for his "imagination, touched by the wand of feeling, presented a very different picture of these defenceless families, pent in the recesses of their native forests, and there exterminated, not by superior natural forces, but by the adventitious circumstances of arms, skill, and knowledge" (54). Everell restores causality to the agentless grammar of Jacksonian manifest destiny. When, on the following page, Sedgwick quotes descriptions of the Pequots and of their massacre from Bradford's *Of Plymouth Plantation* and Hubbard's *A Narrative of the Indian Wars in New England,* she invites a critical rereading of these texts by exposing the textuality and thus the undecidability of any narrative of American history.[14]

The discursive constraints on Sedgwick's project of historical restoration are perhaps most evident in her portrayal of the novel's central captivity episode. Like the unseen Pequot battle at the center of *A Peep at the*

Pilgrims, Faith Leslie's captivity remains unwitnessed. This aperture into Amerindian history and culture simply will not open, much like the historical captivity on which it is based—the 1704 capture of Eunice Williams, daughter of the Puritan minister John Williams and a distant relation to Sedgwick herself.[15] Hope Leslie's desperate and continuing attempt to meet with her sister—who, seven years after her capture, has abandoned any English identity, married Magawisca's brother Oneco, converted to Catholicism, and speaks only in tribal dialect—recalls the attempts of Eunice Williams's family to encourage her to leave the Indians and return to her biological family and culture. On first sight of her "lost sister," at a meeting reluctantly arranged by Magawisca,

> Hope uttered a scream of joy; but when, at a second glance, she saw her in her savage attire, fondly leaning on Oneco's shoulder, her heart died within her . . . and instead of obeying the first impulse, and springing forward to clasp her in her arms, she retreated . . . , averted her eyes, and pressed her hands on her heart, as if she would have bound down her rebel feelings. (227)

Hope's averted eyes here mirror Sedgwick's narrative gaze and recall Cheney's repetition in *A Peep at the Pilgrims* of Miriam's refusal to look. Sedgwick attempts to represent neither Faith's "captivity" nor her life among the Indians. But whereas Cheney and Miriam refuse to look, Sedgwick and Hope finally look, only to see nothing.

After refusing to discard her Indian clothes for English ones, Faith speaks to her sister through Magawisca, who translates her responses into English. When Hope asks, in the language of captivity narratives, whether her sister "remembers the day when the wild Indians sprung upon the family at Bethel, like wolves upon a fold of lambs? . . . when Mrs. Fletcher and her innocent little ones were murdered, and she stolen away?" Magawisca translates Faith's reply that "she remembers it well, for then it was Oneco saved her life" (229). Repeatedly, Hope's sentimental appeals to family history fail to reach her sister; although they translate linguistically, they fail to translate affectively. What to Hope seems Faith's inability to remember is for her Indianized sister simply the memory of a different family history, like Magawisca's alternative memory of national history. Faith Leslie remains unrepresented because unrepresentable, her history a silent void that escapes both her sister's pleas and Sedgwick's Anglo-American discourse.

Debt, Loss, and Magawisca's Missing Limb

Faith Leslie, as a subject and a body reinscribed by cultural exchange, is rendered unreadable. Her captivity is a border crossing without return, and this transgression inverts the cultural logic of escape and revenge. When the national enemy appears as a family, in Magawisca's moving Pequot War narrative as in Faith's refusal to leave home, imperialist affect stumbles over its own contradiction. Pleasure and melancholy will not be reconciled. Everell's captivity, unlike Faith's, ends with his return. But he returns to family and nation with a surplus, a cross-cultural debt that crucially alters the affective economy of captivity. In her earlier narrative to Everell, Magawisca recounts her eldest brother Samoset's heroic defense of the Pequot fort before being taken prisoner by the English. When Samoset refused to exchange military information for his life, his captors "with one sabre-stroke . . . severed his head from his body" (51). This familial and national loss through death operates emotionally, as it does in Bleecker's *History of Maria Kittle,* to justify revenge. Thus, Mononotto, obeying the "natural justice" (92) of the Indians, determines to sacrifice Everell Fletcher in exchange for the death of his son Samoset.

Magawisca's appeals to her father and her attempts to facilitate Everell's escape all fail to alter the course of this justice. In a final attempt to save the life of her friend, who was taken captive in the effort to allow her own escape from captivity, Magawisca actively intervenes to repay her debt. When Mononotto raises his hatchet over Everell's head in the act of retributive violence, "Magawisca, springing from the precipitous side of the rock, screamed—'Forbear!' and interposed her arm. It was too late. The blow was levelled—force and direction given—the stroke aimed at Everell's neck, severed his defender's arm, and left him unharmed. The lopped quivering member dropped over the precipice" (93). Magawisca's action settles her account, but the weight of her severed arm falling over the cliff measures the debt incurred by the escaped Everell. Loss can only be mourned or revenged, possibilities combined in the response of melancholy pleasure. Debt, on the other hand, can only be repaid or forgiven and inspires the responses of anxiety and accountability. When the white captive's escape is accomplished by the sacrificial agency of an Indian woman rather than the agency of a male Anglo-American patriot, the Jacksonian imperialist equation between Anglo-Americans and Amerindians is radically reconfigured.

The image of Magawisca's severed body, quite literally "rent by a divided duty" (80), recalls popular revolutionary-era iconography representing Britain and America. The colonies were frequently portrayed as an Indian woman, and one 1782 print represents her with a knife thrust into her bloody and "mangled breast," prevented by British imperial violence from feeding her children The colonies also frequently appeared as a snake hewn into pieces, and this image's imperative caption, "Join or Die," called for the national healing of this amputated body Another revolutionary image of imperial Britain, circulated in prints by Benjamin Franklin and others, is that of a woman whose colonial limbs have been severed from her body [16] The image of Magawisca's amputated arm fuses and revises these earlier images to suggest the threat of Anglo-American imperialism to the coherence of the Amerindian body.

But this iconography of divided bodies also illustrates the effect of imperial violence on the fluid movement of commerce. This corporeal imagery of national or communal integrity appears as early as 1630, in John Winthrop's corporate metaphor of the body. In "A Model of Christian Charity," Winthrop portrays the successful Company of Massachusetts Bay in New England as a body whose various parts are in a relation characterized by "the sweete Sympathie of affeccions" (290) and are held together by "the sinewes and other ligaments" (292) of Christian love. This sympathetic relation, however, is also an economic one, for this body is further kept intact by the divinely sanctioned (im)balance between rich and poor. Debt, Winthrop insists, must be repaid according to the laws of commerce and can be forgiven only when the debtor has "noething to pay thee"; "[e]very seaventh yeare," he suggests, "the Creditor was to quitt that which hee lent to his brother *if* hee were poore" (286; emphasis added). Debt becomes loss by the rule of mercy but only after the rules of commerce and repayment fail. By insisting that both affection and wealth circulate together to keep the communal corpus whole, Winthrop's metaphor underwrites the colony's stability with an economic sentimentalism that precludes the possibility of perpetual debt.

The narrative of *Hope Leslie* resumes precisely seven years after Magawisca sacrifices her arm to save Everell's head. Everell returns from an education in England with a sensibility of this debt, for when Digby suggests that he once believed Everell "as good as mated with Magawisca," the youth replies that "you do me honour, by implying that I rightly estimated that noble creature; and before she had done the heroic deed, to which I *owe* my life" (214; emphasis added). When, during Hope Leslie's later meeting with her sister Faith, Magawisca is unexpectedly taken captive and—suspected of mobilizing Indian retaliation against the English—imprisoned in the Boston jail, the opportunity for repayment is staged. Magawisca pleads at her trial for release from an indefinite imprisonment by arguing, through the use of the rhetoric of the captivity narrative, that such a fate is a "death more slow and terrible than your most suffering captive ever endured from Indian fires and knives." In a final appeal, Magawisca discards her mantle to expose "[h]er mutilated person" before recalling Governor Winthrop's own debt to her family: "to my dying mother, thou didst promise, kindness to her children" (293).

Torn between the anti-Indian sentiments of national defense on the one hand and transnational sympathy on the other, Magawisca's audience encounters an emotional undecidability similar to the one generated by Mononotto's attack/rescue at the Fletcher home. By unveiling what cannot be seen, the unrestorable missing limb, Magawisca produces "in the breasts of a great majority of the audience, a strange contrariety of opinion and feelings" (294). Once again, this conflicted response will not resolve into the imperialist sensation of a pleasurable melancholy. The audience does not gaze passively on an obscured scene of cultural loss, on the inevitability of Indian disappearance; instead, they are paralyzed by their unobscured vision of cultural debt, of an unrepayable Indian dispossession.

Andrew Jackson built his early legal career on a complete dismissal of John Winthrop's rule of mercy, on the refusal to convert debt to loss regardless of the debtor's poverty or the duration of the debt. As a lawyer, Jackson represented creditors in suits against those refusing to pay their debts. He spent years repaying debts of his own, an experience that, according to Rogin, fostered Jackson's lifelong hostility to debt evaders. Rogin suggests that only Jackson's obsession with debt equaled his obsession with Indian removal. The two were, of course, inseparable, since Indian lands were repeatedly possessed in exchange for unrepaid tribal debts. The laws of the market, which were characterized by that same passive inevitability ascribed to Indian "extinction," both justified Indian dispossession and, by eliminating agency, erased the guilt of accountability. By so displacing aggression by inevitability, Rogin notes, Jackson became a "passive spectator of a policy he had actively advocated" (213).[17] If Indian monetary debts to the whites were paid by land, forcing Indian removal, the white moral debt for the Indian deaths caused by removal was sometimes repaid with money. But more often, Indian deaths were represented not as a debt but as a spectacle of loss, which the imperial nation could only watch and mourn. The discourse of manifest destiny allowed the imperialist audience to paradoxically forgive their own debt.

Hope Leslie reflects the anxiety of debt current in Jacksonian America but radically counters Jacksonian absolution by refusing to balance and therefore to close this cultural account. Before Magawisca's trial, Hope Leslie reminds Governor Winthrop of "the many obligations of the English to the family of Mononotto—a debt, that has been but ill paid." When Winthrop replies, "That debt, I think was cancelled by the dreadful massacre at Bethel," Hope invokes Magawisca's absent arm when she recalls "another debt that never has been—that scarce can be cancelled" (274). Everell's attempts at both "open intercession" and "clandestine effort" on his creditor's behalf fail miserably. When he attempts to remove the bars to Magawisca's cell, early detection causes him to flee. When he tries to persuade Esther Downing, to whom he is engaged, to assist him, her "religious duty" prevents her from interfering without "scripture warrant" (278). It is finally through the agency of Hope Leslie that Magawisca is rescued and Everell redeemed from his own botched rescue attempts. In fact, as Carol J. Singley notes, it is always "through the wits and magnanimity of the female characters" that the errors of patriarchal leaders are corrected in this novel (116). It is as though Sedgwick takes advantage of Jackson's own imperialist refusal of historical agency to deed agency to Anglo-American and Amerindian women.

Hope Leslie ends with Magawisca's departure in a canoe to the uncertain future of her family and tribe. After she "disappeared for ever from their sight" (334), Hope and Everell finally confess their love and move toward the union that corrects the intolerance of their parents' generation. In the end, this novel repeats the national romance that it elsewhere complicates and resists. But *Hope Leslie* finally closes not with the promise of this future marriage but with Esther Downing's spirited defense of her refusal to marry. Her example, writes Sedgwick, "illustrated a truth, which, if more generally received by her sex, might save a vast deal of misery: that marriage is not *essential* to the contentment, the dignity, or the happiness of woman" (349-50). This ending refuses the romance of marital union and, by implication, national union. In the frontier romance tradition these paired resolutions enable a national narrative to progress by suturing events of imperialist violence. Esther's resistance therefore upsets the affective logic on which the historical romance relies, and by doing so it recalls the empty scene of Faith Leslie's refusal to return and the void of Magawisca's unrepayable debt. Sedgwick ultimately leaves her audience captive in the affective predicament on whose resolution imperialist and nationalist sentiment relies.

Notes

[1] Ebersole's claim that Bleecker's "is a history of the heart, not a political history" (135) separates the interdependence of the emotional and the political to which Ellison points.

[2] In addition to Barnett, see Dekker and Bell. Including writers like Bleecker and Rowson might position Sir Walter Scott and his 1814 *Waverly* as a later descendant of a transatlantic tradition of historical captivity fiction.

[3] It is as though Rowson literalizes Herman Mann's symbolic 1797 claim that Deborah Sampson is the daughter of Columbia, who was figured in contemporary iconography as both the American nation and an Amerindian woman.

[4] See also Castiglia on the role of women writers in this genre (112). The term *frontier romance* simply denotes a more specific type of historical romance, and

since the texts on which I focus belong to both categories, I use the two terms more or less interchangeably in this chapter. Historians and anthropologists have critiqued the term *frontier* for its imperialist and ethnocentric assumptions, assumptions reproduced in most frontier romances. I follow June Namias in retaining a redefined notion of the frontier as a transcultural and transracial site of contact (12).

[5] Doris Sommer outlines a model of the Latin American historical romance that similarly stresses the narrative interdependence of eroticism and nationalism, in which there is "a metonymic association between romantic love that needs the state's blessing and political legitimacy that needs to be founded on love" (41). Like the Latin American novels Sommer reads, nineteenth-century North American romances emphasize national and familial reproduction, but that narrative also depends on an Amerindian narrative of failed reproduction.

[6] Castiglia's brief analysis of *A Peep at the Pilgrims* is the only critical work done on the book, to my knowledge, though he does not note its relation to *Hope Leslie*. *A Peep at the Pilgrims* was popular enough to be reprinted the year after its 1824 publication and to appear in a second edition in 1826. Its next American printing, in 1850, was also its last, although one London edition appeared in 1841. Cheney was the daughter of the early American novelist Hannah Webster Foster and sister of Eliza Lanesford Cushing, another writer of historical romances. Later Cheney and Cushing were co-editors of the *The Literary Garland,* a magazine published in Canada, where both women lived after marrying merchants who settled in Montreal. See Story (254) and MacDonald for biographical information on Cheney.

[7] This captivity, which is briefly recounted in Underhill's 1638 narrative of the war, *Newes from America,* is the first documented captivity in North American literature in English. Underhill's mention of it, however, is brief and utterly without details, so Cheney's reconstruction of it is conjectural, though no doubt based on other captivity experiences documented in narratives.

[8] See, for example, Elizabeth Hanson's and Mary Jemison's narratives (Seaver).

[9] For a concise account of the developing divisions that threatened social coherence in the Jacksonian era, see Smith-Rosenberg (*Disorderly Conduct* 79-89). Like Smith-Rosenberg, I take "the age of Jackson" to encompass a period extending from at least the early 1820s to the 1840s and beyond.

[10] See Renan and Anderson for discussions of the crucial role of forgetting in the construction of a national memory.

[11] See Horsman on the development of scientific racialism and removal attitudes.

[12] Kelley first identified Cheney as this "sister labourer" (Sedgwick n. 358).

[13] Alice Fletcher's kidnapping, for example, like the peculiar captivity of Sir Philip Gardiner's cross-dressed page, Rosa, suggests rather the confinement of women within a system of patriarchal authority, whereas Thomas Morton's imprisonment in the Boston jail suggests authority of a different kind.

[14] See Dana Nelson on Sedgwick's revision of Puritan histories through the strategies of sympathy ("Sympathy").

[15] Mary Kelley considers the similarity between Faith Leslie and Eunice Williams, who was captured by Indians as a child, remained among them, married a Caughnawaga Indian, converted to Catholicism, and resisted her family's effort to return to New England ("Introduction" xxxviii, n. 4). For an account of Eunice Williams's story, see John Demos, *The Unredeemed Captive.*

[16] See Olson for discussions of these images in their revolutionary context.

[17] I have relied on Rogin's study in my discussion of Jackson and debt.

Works Cited

Anderson, Benedict. *Imagined Communities: Reflections on the Origin and Spread of Nationalism.* Rev. ed. London: Verso, 1991.

Barnett, Louise. *The Ignoble Savage: American Literary Racism, 1790-1890.* Westport: Greenwood Press, 1975.

Bell, Michael Davitt. *Hawthorne and the Historical Romance of New England.* Princeton: Princeton UP, 1971.

Bhabha, Homi K., ed. *Nation and Narration.* London: Routledge, 1990.

Bleecker, Ann Eliza. *The History of Maria Kittle.* Hartford, 1797.

Castiglia, Christopher. *Bound and Determined: Captivity, Culture-Crossing, and White Womanhood from Mary Rowlandson to Patty Hearst.* Chicago: U of Chicago P, 1996.

Cheney, Harriet V. *A Peep at the Pilgrims in Sixteen Hundred Thirty Six: A Tale of Olden Times.* Boston, 1824. 2 vols.

Dekker, George. *The American Historical Romance.* Cambridge: Cambridge UP, 1987.

Demos, John. *The Unredeemed Captive: A Family Story from Early America.* New York: Knopf, 1994.

Ebersole, Gary L. *Captured by Texts: Puritan to Postmodern Images of Indian Captivity.* Charlottesville: UP of Virginia, 1995.

Horsman, Reginald. *Race and Manifest Destiny: The Origins of American Racial Anglo-Saxonism.* Cambridge: Harvard UP, 1981.

JanMohamed, Abdul R. "The Economy of Manichean Allegory: The Function of Racial Difference in Colonialist Literature." *"Race," Writing, and Difference.* Ed. Henry Louis Gates, Jr. Chicago: U of Chicago P, 1985. 78-106.

Kelley, Mary. Introduction. *Hope Leslie.* By Catharine Maria Sedgwick. New Brunswick: Rutgers UP, 1987. ix-xxxix.

MacDonald, Mary Lu. "Harriet Vaughan Cheney." *Canadian Writers before 1890.* Ed. W. H. New. Vol. 99 of *Dictionary of Literary Biography.* Detroit: Gale Research, 1990.

Mann, Herman. *The Female Review; or, Life of Deborah Sampson.* New York: Arno P, 1972.

Mather, Cotton. *Magnalia Christi Americana.* New York: Russell and Russell, 1967. 2 vols.

Nelson, Dana. "Sympathy as Strategy in Sedgwick's *Hope Leslie.*" Samuels 191-202.

Olson, Lester C. *Emblems of American Community in the Revolutionary Era: A Study in Rhetorical Iconology.* Washington: Smithsonian Institution P, 1991.

Renan, Ernest. "What Is a Nation?" Trans. Martin Thom. Bhabha, ed. *Nation* 8-22.

Rogin, Michael Paul. *Fathers and Children: Andrew Jackson and the Subjugation of the American Indian.* New Brunswick: Transaction, 1991.

Rowlandson, Mary. *Narrative of the Captivity of Mary Rowlandson.* 1682. Lincoln 107-67.

———. *A Narrative of the Captivity, Sufferings and Removes of Mrs. Mary Rowlandson.* Boston, 1771.

Rowson, Susanna. *Charlotte Temple.* Ed. Cathy N. Davidson. New York: Oxford UP, 1986.

———. *Reuben and Rachel; or, Tales of Old Times: A Novel.* Boston, 1798.

Samuels, Shirley, ed. *The Culture of Sentiment: Race, Gender, and Sentimentality in 19th Century America.* New York: Oxford UP, 1992.

Scott, Sir Walter. *Waverley; or, 'Tis Sixty Years Since.* Ed. Claire Lamont. New York: Oxford UP, 1986.

Sedgwick, Catharine Maria. *Hope Leslie; or, Early Times in the Massachusetts.* 1824. Ed. Mary Kelley. New Brunswick: Rutgers UP, 1987.

Seaver, James E., ed. *The Narrative of the Life of Mrs. Mary Jemison.* Syracuse: Syracuse UP, 1990.

Sheehan, Bernard W. *Seeds of Extinction: Jeffersonian Philanthropy and the American Indian.* Chapel Hill: U of North Carolina P, 1973.

Smith-Rosenberg, Carroll. *Disorderly Conduct: Visions of Gender in Victorian America.* New York: Knopf, 1985.

————."Subject Female: Authorizing American Identity." *American Literary History* 5 (1993): 481-511.

Sommer, Doris. *Foundational Fictions: The National Romances of Latin America.* Berkeley: U of California P, 1991.

Story, Norah. *The Oxford Companion to Canadian History and Literature.* Toronto: Oxford UP, 1967.

Underhill, John. *Newes from America.* London, 1638.

IMAGES OF GENDER

David T. Haberly (essay date 1976)

SOURCE: "Women and Indians: *The Last of the Mohicans* and the Captivity Tradition," in *American Quarterly,* Vol. XXXVIII, No. 4, Fall, 1976, pp. 431-43.

[*In the following essay, Haberly considers the influence of the captivity genre on James Fenimore Cooper's portrayal of femininity in* The Last of the Mohicans.]

Despite considerable new interest in narratives of Indian captivity, this large genre remains somewhat isolated within American literary history—more interesting to bibliographers and ethnohistorians than to critics.[1] Some recent studies of captivity narratives have ably elaborated basic ideas first presented by Roy Harvey Pearce a generation ago; new and highly imaginative approaches to the captivities have also been attempted, but the critics' eagerness to fit one or more narratives into universal mythic structures or into psychosexual theories of American culture has often distracted them from the fundamental question about the captivities—the specific influence of this vast and enormously popular genre upon the development of literature in the United States.[2]

Yet it is only logical that such influence must have existed. Bibliographers have catalogued more than a thousand separate captivity titles, published fairly steadily from the sixteenth century to the first decades of the twentieth; many of the best-known narratives were reprinted in dozens of editions.[3] For roughly a hundred years, from 1750 to 1850, the Indian captivity was one of the chief staples of popular literary culture; as Phillips D. Carleton noted, such narratives "took the place of fiction, of what might be called escape literature now."[4]

The frontier between fact and fiction, moreover, was often very vague indeed, and it is sometimes difficult today to separate the authentic accounts of redeemed captives from the works of writers eager to make a quick buck by milking a well-established market—Ann Eliza Bleecker's *History of Maria Kittle* is a notable example—or dimly conscious of the fictional possibilities inherent in the totally violent and alien reality of Indian captivity—as in the cryptic narrative of "Abraham Panther"[5] or Charles Brockden Brown's *Edgar Huntly.*

These fictional captivities, however, are at best of marginal interest. I would suggest, rather, that an important and neglected aspect of the captivity tradition is its influence upon major works of nineteenth-century American fiction.[6] And my purpose here is to define and analyze the impact of that tradition upon James Fenimore Cooper's *The Last of the Mohicans*—for several generations one of the most popular of all American novels and a work which created an idea of America which put down deep and permanent roots in Europe, in Latin America, and in the recesses of our own minds.

I believe, further, that a number of the most controversial aspects of the structure and the thematics of Cooper's novel are only tangentially related, at best, to such generalities as the theory and practice of myth-making or the suggested homoeroticism of American literature. These aspects, rather, flow directly from the very concrete difficulties Cooper faced in adapting the traditional and clearly-defined captivity narrative to his new and very different purposes.

By 1825, Cooper had tried his hand at a range of novelistic genres, seeking to identify his own strengths and weaknesses and to find a way to use fiction to foster America's "mental independence," a goal he was to describe—in a letter of 1831—as his chief object.[7]

He had written a novel of manners (*Persuasion.* 1820); two patriotic historical novels (*The Spy,* 1821, and *Lionel Lincoln,* 1825); a sea story (*The Pilot,* 1824); and a semicomic, semi-autobiographical novel of the local gentry (*The Pioneers,* 1823). It was natural that, in shuffling through the available genres, he should attempt a fictionalized captivity. A concrete link between parallel incidents in Cooper's fiction and in one authentic captivity has only recently been established,[8] but his passionate interest in the American past and the ready availability of such narratives—some dealing specifically with his own area of upstate New York—would inevitably have led him to the captivities.

And *The Last of the Mohicans,* despite the shift in narration away from the traditional first person, is above all a captivity narrative—more exactly, as we shall see, it is two separate captivity narratives. First, however, it is important to look back at the tradition those narratives had created, the tradition Cooper necessarily inherited when he sought to use the genre.

The purpose of many captivities, by 1825, was often frankly commercial. Rescued captives not infrequently found themselves without family or funds, and their accounts of life in Indian hands served both to bring in a little cash and to advise their neighbors—as well as generous readers throughout America—of their heroism, their suffering, and their present need. There must also have been, for many returned captives, a kind of therapy in the recounting of their adventures, a way to exorcise their darkest memories—particularly by Cooper's time, when the changing stylistic conventions of the narrative had placed a barrier of verbal commonplaces between experience survived and experience described.[9]

In the early narratives of Puritans like Mary Rowlandson, captivity, suffering, and final redemption were all part of God's plan, and the publication of these events was a Christian duty.[10] By the nineteenth century, that sort of easy metaphoric structure had disappeared; what remained, in its essence, was violence—the total and almost incomprehensible violence of captives scalped and beaten, women starved or tortured to death, babies drowned or bashed against blood-spattered rocks, children with faces burned into unrecognizable scars.

The physical environment of the captivity narratives linked all of this violence and suffering to the frontier; one wonders anew that Americans moved westward in the face of these tracts, the most readily obtainable and believable accounts of the fate that might await them there. And the captivity narratives were filled with raw and burning hatred of the Indian—a hatred so intense that the motives and even the reciprocal violence of the Indian-hater seem understandable and even, for a moment, wholly justified.

Cooper's own ideas, as he sat down to write his fictionalized captivity, were very different indeed. He was conditioned by his background and by his nationalism to idealize the frontier—the endless forests that appear in *The Last of the Mohicans* as the image of all of the American West. As George Dekker has noted, " . . . in Cooper's mind American nationhood and the Westward Movement . . . were intimately connected; each new clearing furnished a sign of the increasing temporal greatness of the nation. . . . "[11] Further, Cooper's ethnological readings and a patriotic fervor that transcends chronology and even race both determined him to idealize the American Indian.

Cooper's problem, then, was to reconcile his own ideals—the beauty of the American wilderness, the glory of the Westward Movement, and the native heroism and goodness of at least a part of Indian America—with the powerful captivity tradition of horrendous barbarities committed on the western frontier by Indians unspeakably vile. The key to the fictional resolution of these antitheses, I believe, lay for Cooper in a basic feature of the captivity narratives—the role of women.

A large proportion of the authentic narratives of captivity were written by women; deprived by Indian violence of the protection of husbands or family, female captives were often more pressingly in need of the financial support a successful narrative might provide. But women captives were also central figures in many of the captivities produced by males, and by Cooper's time had become preeminent in the increasingly popular anthologies of captivities and in the fictional offspring of the tradition.

In these works, women suffered the cruelest torments, and it was those torments which most sorrowed and enraged readers. Beyond this, however, female-centered captivity narratives had a special interest for readers—and for potential romancers—because they were inherently more suspenseful than the stories of males taken by Indians. For quite apart from the common perils of torture and death, three important additional dangers might await female captives.

There was, first, the possibility that a white woman captured by Indians might be defeminized; that is, that her suffering and her separation from civilization might lead her into patterns of behavior suitable only for males. This danger had not greatly preoccupied the Puritans, who applauded Hannah Dustin's massacre of her captors, but it did worry nineteenth-century readers. Bravery, quickness of action, mental and physical independence—and even the shedding of blood—were totally at odds with the ideal of the sentimental heroine. Leslie Fiedler has documented the hostile reactions of Hawthorne and Thoreau to Hannah Dustin's heroics; Hawthorne's attitude was the more important and more typical. While Thoreau was concerned that Hannah had axed Indian children,

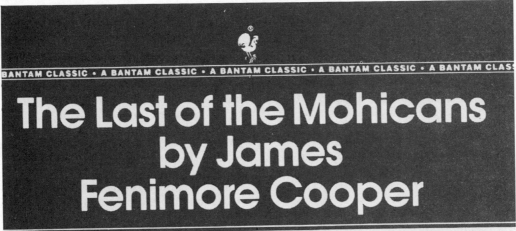

Title Page from The Last of the Mohicans *by James Fenimore Cooper*

Hawthorne was merely distressed that she had acted as a man, shoving her husband into the background.[12]

Similar reservations about unfeminine reactions to even the most horrifying situations were expressed by the editors of nineteenth-century captivity anthologies. John Frost, for example, in his *Thrilling Adventures among the Indians,* criticized and even ridiculed some acts of heroism by white women, since he found such tales "little pleasing or amiable. Woman, as an Amazon, does not appear to advantage. Something seems to be wanting in such a character; or, perhaps, it has something too much."[13]

Considerably more frightening for the readers of captivity narratives was the possibility that a white woman might be raped—or, more genteelly, forced into marriage with an Indian. The factual evidence on Indian sexual abuse of captive women in the East is contradictory. Mary Rowlandson declared that during her captivity, " . . . by night and by day, alone and in company: sleeping all sorts together, and yet not one of them [the Indians] ever offered me the least abuse of unchastity to me, in word or action."[14] Elizabeth Hanson hedged a little, writing that " . . . the Indians are seldom guilty of any indecent carriage towards their captive women, unless much overtaken in liquor."[15]

Cooper clearly did not believe that Indians were as chaste as was claimed,[16] and it is likely that his readers had serious doubts as well. It was hardly to be expected, after all, that redeemed female captives would openly confess the loss of their virtue. And the genteel disclaimers of seventeenth- and eighteenth-century captives are repeated, during a later western expansion, in the accounts of women captured by tribes for whom rape appears to have been an established practice.[17] One Mrs. Horn, for example, wrote, "In conclusion, perhaps I ought to say, that with reference to a point, of all others of the most sacred importance to a captive female, (with gratitude to my Maker I record it.) my fears were in no part realized."[18] But, as a modern scholar notes, " . . . most white women redeemed from captivity in the West charged that sexual abuse of their fellow captives was common but claimed that because of some unusual circumstance they, themselves, had been spared the ordeal."[19]

Female captives might not only lose their femininity and their virtue; they might also lose their very whiteness. The Indianization process has been of great interest to twentieth-century anthropologists and psychologists,[20] but it also troubled thoughtful students of America, like Franklin, who feared that the rapid Indianization of large numbers of white captives—in sharp contrast to the pitifully few recorded cases of Indians civilized by white society—bore some worrisome lesson about the comparative value and permanence of two very different cultural systems.[21]

The Indianization of white females, however, posed a particular problem, since it suggested willing acceptance of Indian sexual mores and of an Indian spouse. The chief characters in many of the most popular captivity narratives—Eunice Williams, Mary Jemison, Frances Slocum, and Cynthia Ann Parker, for example—were Indianized white women who declined to be redeemed and who established enduring relationships with Indian males;[22] other captive white females struggled desperately to flee their rescuers and return to their Indian husbands and children.[23] The existence of such Indianized female captives did not merely raise doubts about the values of white civilization; it could also imply the far more disturbing possibility that white women might find Indian men sexually superior.

When Cooper began his fictional captivity, therefore, he quite naturally chose to focus the book on the perilous adventures of white women in the wilderness. In order to describe and discuss a full range of possible reactions to captivity, Cooper used the fictional technique that Henry Nash Smith—in his study of the Leatherstocking character—called "doubling."[24] The two sisters, Alice and Cora Munro, represent two very different types of captivity heroine, and two divergent reactions to captivity.

The doubling process, however, is not confined to the Munro sisters; it also defines the structure of the novel, for *The Last of the Mohicans* is composed of two separate captivity narratives. The first captivity—the happy captivity, to borrow the title of a seventeenth-century Chilean example of the genre[25]—ends with the safe arrival of Alice and Cora at Fort William Henry, at the close of Chapter XIV; it derives from the simplest and most pleasant of the captivity narratives, those in which the captive or captives return safely to the bosom of family and friends. After two intercalary chapters, the second narrative begins with the Fort Henry Massacre in Chapter XVII; this captivity—the tragic captivity—represents another, grimmer tradition.

The first, happy captivity, as Donald Darnell has pointed out, takes place between forts, within the outer limits of the white world.[26] The violence it contains is almost always potential rather than actual—shouted threats, a drop of blood on a leaf, the loss of a few of Alice's tresses. The purpose of this narrative is not to describe blood-baths—those follow later on in the novel; through this recreation of one type of captivity, Cooper sets out to define and differentiate the characters of Cora and Alice, before they enter the second captivity and the dark, alien world that belongs to the Indian alone.

Cooper begins this process when fair Alice and dark Cora first appear, using the established equation of complexion and character as a kind of novelistic shorthand, suggesting to his readers exactly where their fullest sympathies should lie.[27] This cosmetic characterization is immediately reinforced as Cooper gets down to the business of defining the disparate "gifts" the sisters possess—"gifts" as different as those of Natty Bumppo and David Gamut. Alice is lighthearted, weak, and innocent; she is the ideal sentimental heroine of a captivity narrative, weeping and fainting as she confronts a series of purely physical dangers. Cora, however, is prey to the three important moral perils—defeminization, rape, and Indianization—and the "gifts" that expose her to these dangers are made clear in her first reactions to Magua. The sudden appearance of the Indian startles Alice, but she quickly recovers to banter coyly with Duncan. Cora, on the other hand, gazes at Magua with "an indescribable look of pity, admiration, and horror, as her dark eye followed the easy motions of the savage." (21) In Cora's pity lies her "gift" for unwomanly seriousness and strength of character; her horror foreshadows the rape motif; and her admiration for "the easy motions of the savage" reveals a sensuous miscibility that will lead to her relationship with Uncas and the gradual Indianization that relationship implies.

Cora's unfeminine "gifts" of courage, logic, and self-reliance are more fully developed as the first captivity progresses; even Duncan comes, rather grudgingly, to admire these traits: " . . . your own fortitude and undisturbed reason," he tells her, "will teach you all that may become your sex." (104) By the time the captives reach the security of the fort, Cora actually longs for adventure—like a seasoned trooper. "I sicken at the sight of danger that I cannot share," she proclaims; Natty welcomes her as an equal, "with a smile of honest and cordial approbation," and wishes for "a thousand men, of brawny limbs and quick eyes, that feared death as little as you!" (179)

Cora is also far more sensual than Alice, as her "rather fuller and more mature" figure suggests (21); Magua's threats to her virtue are the direct result of this "gift." She is threatened by rape—in Cooper's terms, forced marriage and sexual submission to Magua—in large part because she is conscious of its possibility. Thus, in the cave scene in the first captivity, the two sisters react in very different ways when suddenly awakened by Duncan. Alice murmurs in her sleep: "No, no, dear father, we were not deserted; Duncan was with us!" Cora's dreams, however, are not those of innocence: " . . . the motion caused Cora to raise her hand as if to repulse him, . . ." (81-82)

When the captivity begins, Alice and Cora appear "to share equally in the attentions of the young officer" (21), but it gradually becomes clear that Duncan belongs to Alice alone. While some critics have seen Cora as a case of unrequited love, pining after Heyward, this seems a misreading of the novel. Cora is disappointed that she is not Duncan's choice, but she is also increasingly attracted to Indian men, as her thoughtful contemplation of Magua first suggests. In the cave,

when the captives first see Uncas in all his glory, Alice's reaction is that of an art student gazing upon a Greek statue; Duncan considers the young brave a remarkable anthropological specimen; but Cora sees Uncas as a man, without consideration for race and color—and that perception embarrasses her white companions (65-66).

And Cora must have a potential mate, as Alice has Duncan. Natty might seem a reasonable candidate, but Cooper clearly felt that the scout—while suited to Cora by character and by color—was too much her social inferior. Natty's dialect would have made this class distinction obvious to contemporary readers, and Cooper drives the point home, towards the end of the book, when he describes the scout's "deference to the superior rank of his companions, that no similarity in the state of their present fortune could induce him to forget." (373)

Social class, then, is more important than race, and Cooper provides Cora with two suitors of equal rank—a chief of the Mingoes, Magua; and the last prince of the Mohicans. If we ignore, for a moment, the fact that both Uncas and Magua are Indians, a perfectly commonplace sentimental triangle emerges. Cora is sought after by two suitors of her class—one a handsome and good nobleman of long and illustrious ancestry; one a violent and lecherous type, born a chief but more recently a drunken servant. In these terms, it is only natural that Cora should prefer Uncas.

Because Uncas is an Indian, however, the progress of the Cora-Uncas romance necessarily implies her Indianization. It is Cora who adopts the Indian techniques of leaving a trail, and the full development of the relationship with Uncas is symbolized in a passage at the very end of the first captivity; as the party approaches the fort, "Duncan willingly relinquished the support of Cora to the arm of Uncas, and Cora as readily accepted the welcome assistance." (183)

During the Fort William Henry interlude, Cooper takes pains to reassure readers worried and perplexed by Cora's "gifts." "Gifts," in Cooper, are not the result of conscious choices, but are preordained by genetics or by environment; even the satanic Magua's character is the result of his tribal ancestry and his sufferings among the whites. Cora, as we discover in Chapter XVI, is of African descent, the daughter of a West Indian mulattress with whom Colonel Munro formed a connection and whom he later married; the future mother of pure Alice, of course, was still in Scotland, "a suffering angel [who] had remained in the heartless state of celibacy twenty long years, . . ." (201-02) This background immediately explains Cora's "gifts," assures us that she is not really a bad person after all, and makes her relationship with Uncas seem both natural and permissible.

The established characters of Cora and Alice are not altered in any important way during the second captivity, deep in the Indian world. Alice is ever more dependent, a tear-stained and insensible bundle dragged from place to place by her male protectors. Cora is still self-reliant, fatally attractive, and increasingly Indianized—as her adoption of Indian oratory shows. In her plea to Tamenund, in fact, Cora strongly identifies the curse of her ancestors—African slavery—with the sufferings of the Indians, like her the victims of white racism (386).

Cooper finally gives Uncas a forced and tightly-structured opportunity to choose between two worlds—between his love for Cora and his respect for Indian traditions. Uncas cannot overcome the force of tradition and environment; he allows Magua to take Cora away once again, and by that choice all hope for a conventional happy ending is destroyed. Cora's Indianization is complete with her death; she receives an Indian burial, beside Uncas, while the native maidens sing prophecies of a marriage consummated in heaven—a standard resolution of the miscegenation issue in novels from other New World cultures.[28]

Through this juxtaposition of two kinds of captivity narrative and through the development of the different "gifts" of his two captivity heroines, Cooper explores the multiple fictional possibilities of the genre. The deaths of Uncas and Cora, moreover, allow the novelist to make several self-righteous but highly comforting statements about race. First, he can claim to be free from the racial prejudice he describes as a Southern trait, since he admits the possibility of interracial love. Miscegenation, however, is still an impossibility, precluded by unalterable barriers of culture and tradition. This reassured white Americans worried about the development of mixed races and cultures, like those found in other parts of the Americas, and about the possible miscibility of the two victimized races—the Indians and those of African descent.

Cooper's exposition of the disparate "gifts" of his characters explains *what* happens in the novel; but it does not explain *why* such things occur. And his fundamental problem remains: how to reconcile his idealized vision of the frontier with the violence implicit in the captivity tradition and explicit in this, the most violent of the Leatherstocking tales.

The gap between idealism and the reality of violence could be bridged only by an explanation based upon immutable "nature," not upon the deterministic "gifts" of individuals. And Cooper therefore took the central role of white females in the captivity tradition and in his own novel, and subtly changed the focus in order to provide such an explanation. It is not mere chance and coincidence that women appear as the chief objects of captivity violence; that violence does not flow from the realities of frontier life or from the evil lusts of Indian males. White women, rather, are the direct cause of all the violence that surrounds

their passage through a world in which they do not belong; it is their "nature."

Cooper and his contemporaries believed that the power of white women was the result of their powerlessness; as he wrote in *The Sea Lions,* most of their " . . . real power and influence . . . arises from their seeming dependence. . . . "[29] And *The Last of the Mohicans* is above all a study of the enormous, ironic power of those consistently described as "tender blossoms" and "harmless things."

This power, while interesting and perhaps amusing in the drawing rooms of civilization, becomes immensely destructive when transferred to the frontier wilderness. White men and red, Cooper believed, could sublimate their different genetic and environmental "gifts" and exist in something approaching harmony in the haven of the American wilderness; the very presence of white women makes such harmony impossible. As Natty says, in one of the novel's most significant speeches, " . . . it would not be the act of men to leave such harmless things to their fate, even though it breaks up the harboring place for ever." (55)

White women have this effect because it is their "nature" to excite passion among men—all sorts and kinds of men. No matter how superficially civilized in dress and speech, no matter how sharply their different "gifts" are defined, Cora and Alice are both inherently and potentially sexual, designed above all else for procreation—a point Cooper makes obliquely through his description, in the lines just before our introduction to the sisters in all their finery, of the "low, gaunt, switch-tailed mare," whose foal is "quietly making its morning repast, . . ." (20) As soon as Cora and Alice appear, they artlessly exhibit their charms; such is their "nature," as it is the "nature" of males to react. And such brief moments of exhibitionism in fact become a kind of predictable motif in the novel, inevitably introducing violence.[30]

This inherent power of attraction upsets the balance between man and nature, between white and Indian. To preserve and to please white females, the harboring places are broken up; horses are trained to ungainly and unnatural paces (154–55); and the decorative creatures of the wilds are slaughtered (378). And men of both races willingly take enormous and totally irrational risks in order to possess or to defend the virtue of white women.

Thus, merely because these "flowers, which, though so sweet, were never made for the wilderness" (55) have presumed against all advice to travel where they do not belong, violence will replace harmony and death will come to Cora, to Magua, and to Uncas—the last of the Mohicans, the last hope in Tamenund's vision for a rebirth of Indian America. No less is the natural culpability of Alice and Cora.

In the first captivity, Alice and Cora are only intuitively conscious of their power. Of the male characters, only Magua fully understands the potential of white women—the power, as he expresses it, to make white men their dogs. He seeks to possess Cora because he is attracted to her, but he also comprehends her importance as a symbol and as a means to control the actions and reactions of other men.

Magua's expectations are realized. Duncan becomes so distraught at the thought of "evils worse than death" (100), of a fate "worse than a thousand deaths" (138), that he is almost incapable of rational thought and action. Uncas too becomes, in Magua's terms, a dog to the women, providing menial services for the two sisters and amazing and amusing the others (69). By the mere presence of white women, Uncas is led to deny "his habits, we had almost said his nature, . . ." (145); his contact with Cora and Alice has "elevated him far above the intelligence, and advanced him probably centuries before the practices of his nation." (146) In fact, Natty complains that Uncas' behavior, in his eagerness to rescue the girls, has been "more like that of a curious woman than of a warrior on his scent." (152)

Once the women are safe within Fort William Henry, Cooper suggests the deep cultural roots of their power. Alice coyly calls Duncan to task—in terms of the chivalric tradition: " . . . thou truant! thou recreant knight! he who abandons his damsels in the very lists!" (189) She is surprised when Heyward is deeply wounded by the accusation. References to chivalry continue to crop up in these intercalary chapters—and it is this tradition which forms the powerless power of Cora and Alice and all other white women.

Just as the first captivity began with the mare-foal image and with the sisters' artless display of their charms, the tragic captivity begins with women and children—the latter serving as symbols of the sexual nature and purpose of women. An Indian is attracted by a shawl one of the women wears and tries to grab it. "The woman, more in terror than through love of the ornament, wrapped her child in the coveted article, and folded both more closely to her bosom." The Huron then grabs the child, teases the woman with it, and dashes the head of the infant against a rock; he then kills the mother. At that point the massacre of the innocents and the second captivity commence; once again women appear as the cause of violence as well as its object (221-23).

Magua seizes Alice—"he knew his power, and was determined to maintain it" (225)—and the two girls disappear with him into the forest. Their power remains, however, affecting their rescuers. Uncas is uncharacteristically excited by the discovery of Cora's veil, and begins to act "as impatient as a man in the settlements; . . ." (235) Duncan embarks on the insane and dangerous adventure as a sham witch doctor: "I

too can play the madman, the fool, the hero; in short, any or everything to rescue her that I love," he declares (288). Natty is amazed by Heyward's irrational daring, but such is the power of the women that the young officer for the first time takes command: "But Duncan, who, in deference to the other's skill and services, had hitherto submitted somewhat implicitly to his dictation, now assumed the superior, with a manner that was not easily resisted." (288)

Natty continues to ponder this power, and tries to define it. "I have heard," he muses, "that there is a feeling in youth which binds man to woman closer than the father is tied to the son. It may be so. I have seldom been where women of my color dwell; but such may be the gifts of nature in the settlements. You have risked life, and all that is dear to you, to bring off this gentle one, and I suppose that some such disposition is at the bottom of it all." (336)

The power of Cora and Alice increases in its scope as the second captivity progresses. Magua loses his cool, cunning appreciation of the symbolic and strategic value of his captives, and begins himself to be controlled. Natty too falls under the influence of the power he cannot explain, and offers Magua an increasingly illogical set of bargains in exchange for Cora. While the scout knows that " . . . it would be an unequal exchange, to give a warrior, in the prime of his age and usefulness, for the best woman on the frontier," he is nonetheless prepared to sacrifice himself when all else fails. Magua, with equal irrationality, refuses the trade (397-98). Even David Gamut, the pacifist hymnmaster, is overpowered, and prepares to go to war for Cora, reminded "of the children of Jacob going out to battle against the Shechemites, for wickedly aspiring to wedlock with a woman of a race that was favored of the Lord." (413)

When the last battle begins, Cora challenges Magua—confident that he too is now her "dog." He tries to kill her, but cannot: "The form of the Huron trembled in every fibre, and he raised his arm on high, but dropped it again with a bewildered air, like one who doubted. Once more he struggled with himself and lifted the keen weapon again. . . . " (426) As he hesitates, another Huron kills Cora—and Magua delays his escape and slays one of his own men to avenge her death. Magua and Uncas then struggle; Uncas allows himself to be killed—since Cora is dead. Magua makes a mad, suicidal attempt to escape, and Natty kills him.

The final victory of the Delawares over the Hurons is itself yet another example of Cooper's doubling. Magua consistently refers to the Delaware-Mohican tribes as "women"—a pejorative epithet that Cooper took from Heckewelder's writings, but which fully conforms to his own cultural prejudices. As Paul Wallace has demonstrated, Cooper's use of this epithet was conditioned by a misunderstanding of the complex intertribal relationships of Indian America. The Delawares were defined as "women" in their agreements with the Five Nations; that role, however, was one of honor and of power.[31] For Cooper, however, women were necessarily dependent and inferior. But the concept of the natural powerless power of white women is transferred, in the novel, to the Delawares and Mohicans. Like Cora and Alice, they cannot escape violence, and cannot control their own destinies; but they do retain the power to destroy.

The ending Cooper chose for the novel is a direct result of his transmutation of the captivity tradition. White women and their intrusive, destructive power must be removed before the ideal harmony of the frontier can exist once again; Cora is buried, and Alice departs for civilization, sobbing in the seclusion of her litter. With her go her white "dogs," like her the creatures of the civilized world. Natty and Chingachgook must stay behind, since the harmony of their grief for Uncas represents all that is possible in the absence of white women. The crude woodsman and the drunken Indian of *The Pioneers* are no longer merely local color, quaintly useful in forcing philosophical discussions about the nature of government; they are the final proof of Cooper's reconciliation of his idealized frontier with the tradition of the captivity narratives. And from this artificial, novelistic pairing—from these "two childless womanless men of opposite races," in Lawrence's phrase[32]—issue Huck and Jim, the Lone Ranger and Tonto, and all the other offspring, cultured or popular, of *The Last of the Mohicans.*

Notes

[1] Major bibliographical sources for the captivities include: the Newberry Library's list of books in the Edward E. Ayer Collection (Chicago: Newberry Library, 1912) and Clara A. Smith's supplement to that list, *Narratives of Captivity among the Indians of North America* (Chicago: Newberry Library, 1928); R. W. G. Vail, *The Voice of the Old Frontier* (Philadelphia: Univ. of Pennsylvania Press, 1949); and C. Marius Barbeau, "Indian Captivities," *Proceedings of the American Philosophical Society,* 94 (1950), 522-48. Also see Dwight L. Smith, "Shawnee Captivity Ethnography," *Ethnohistory,* 2, No. 1 (Winter 1955), 29-41.

[2] To date, by far the most interesting response to this question is Richard Slotkin's massive and always stimulating study of the captivities, *Regeneration Through Violence* (Middletown, Conn.: Wesleyan Univ. Press, 1973).

[3] Four captivity narratives—those of Mary Rowlandson, John Williams, Jonathan Dickinson, and Mary Jemison—are listed among the great best-sellers of American publishing by Frank Luther Mott, *Golden Multitudes* (New York: Macmillan, 1947), pp. 20-22 and 303-05.

[4] Phillips D. Carleton, "The Indian Captivity," *American Literature,* 15 (1943 44), 170.

[5] R. W. G. Vail, "The Abraham Panther Indian Captivity," *The American Book Collector,* 2 (1932), 165-72.

[6] The importance of the captivity tradition in the formation and popularization of the figure of the Indian-hater—in Bird's *Nick of the Woods,* Melville's *Confidence Man,* and elsewhere—has not yet been fully studied. The captivity theme also crops up elsewhere within Cooper's Leatherstocking novels, notably in *The Deerslayer,* and is central to his *Wept of Wish-ton-Wish.* However, its first and most forceful appearance, in Cooper's works, is in *The Last of the Mohicans.*

[7] Cited by Robert E. Spiller, *James Fenimore Cooper* (Minneapolis: Univ. of Minnesota Press, 1965), p. 8.

[8] Richard VanDerBeets, "Cooper and the 'Semblance of Reality': A Source for *The Deerslayer,"* *American Literature.* 40 (1971), 544-46.

[9] See Roy Harvey Pearce, "The Significances of the Captivity Narrative," *American Literature,* 19 (1947-48), 4-5; and Richard VanDerBeets, "A Surfeit of Style: The Indian Captivity Narrative as Penny Dreadful," *Research Studies,* 39 (1971), 297-306.

[10] Pearce, "The Significances," pp. 2-3; and David L. Minter, "By Dens of Lions: Notes on Stylization in Early Puritan Captivity Narratives," *American Literature,* 45 (1973), 335-47.

[11] George Dekker, *James Fenimore Cooper* (New York: Barnes and Noble, 1967), p. 65.

[12] Leslie A. Fiedler, *The Return of the Vanishing American* (New York: Stein and Day, 1968), pp. 95-108.

[13] John Frost, *Thrilling Adventures among the Indians* (Philadelphia: J. W. Bradley, 1851), p. 84.

[14] Mary Rowlandson, from *The Sovereignty and Goodness of God,* in *Held Captive by Indians,* ed. Richard VanDerBeets (Knoxville: Univ. of Tennessee Press, 1973), p. 84.

[15] Samuel Bownas, ed., *An Account of the Captivity of Elizabeth Hanson,* from the English edition of 1760, in *Held Captive by Indians,* p. 147.

[16] Natty claims, at one point, that not "even a Mingo would ill-treat a woman, unless it be to tomahawk her," but this statement is contradicted by Magua's insistence that Cora become his squaw and by the reactions of Heyward and of Natty himself. J. F. Cooper, *The Last of the Mohicans* (New York: W. A. Townsend,

1859), p. 273. All page references in the text are to this, the Darley edition.

[17] See Dee Alexander Brown, *The Gentle Tamers* (New York: Putnam, 1958); Carl Coke Rister, *Border Captives* (Norman, Okla.: Univ of Oklahoma Press, 1940); and J. Norman Heard, *White into Red* (Metuchen, N.J.: Scarecrow Press, 1973).

[18] From Mrs. Horn's narrative, in Carl Coke Rister, *Comanche Bondage* (Glendale, Calif.: A. H. Clark, 1955), p. 197. The punctuation is Mrs. Horn's.

[19] J. Norman Heard, *White into Red,* p. 101.

[20] A. Irving Hallowell, "American Indians, White and Black: The Phenomenon of Transculturalization," *Current Anthropology,* 4 (1963), 519-31.

[21] See Franklin's famous letter of May 9, 1753, to Peter Collinson, in Alfred Owen Aldridge, "Franklin's Letter on Indians and Germans," *Proceedings of the American Philosophical Society,* 94 (1950), 392-93; and J. Hector St. John Crèvecoeur, *Letters from an American Farmer* (New York: Fox, Duffield, 1904), Letter XII, pp. 304-08.

[22] John Williams, *The Redeemed Captive* (Boston: Printed by B. Green for S. Phillips, 1707); *A Narrative of the Life of Mrs. Mary Jemison* (Canandaigua, N.Y.: J. D. Bemis, 1824); John Todd, *The Lost Sister of the Wyoming* (Northampton, Mass.: J. H. Butler, 1842)—the first account of the Frances Slocum captivity, subsequently retold by a number of other authors; *Narrative of the Perilous Adventures, Miraculous Escapes and Sufferings of Rev. James W. Parker* (Louisville: Morning Courier, 1844), which includes Cynthia Ann Parker's story.

[23] Heard, *White into Red,* pp. 2-4.

[24] Henry Nash Smith, *Virgin Land* (Cambridge, Mass.: Harvard Univ. Press, 1950), p. 69.

[25] Francisco Nuñez de Pineda y Bascuñán, *Cautiverio feliz* (Santiago, Chile: Imp. de El Ferrocarril, 1863).

[26] Donald Darnell, "Uncas as Hero: The *Ubi Sunt* Formula in *The Last of the Mohicans.*" *American Literature,* 37 (1965), 261-62.

[27] The best general discussion of Cooper's female characters and his use of cosmetic symbolism is Nina Baym's "The Women of Cooper's Leatherstocking Tales," *American Quarterly,* 23, No. 5 (Dec. 1971), 696-709.

[28] For a very similar example from Brazil, see José de Alencar's *O Guarani* (Rio de Janeiro: Tip. do Diário do Rio de Janeiro, 1857).

[29] Cited by Kay Seymour House, *Cooper's Americans* (Columbus, Ohio: Ohio State Univ. Press, 1966), p. 27.

[30] See, for example, p. 110.

[31] Paul A. W. Wallace, "Cooper's Indians," in *James Fenimore Cooper: A Re-Appraisal* (Cooperstown, N. Y.: New York State Historical Association, 1954), pp. 63-77.

[32] D. H. Lawrence, *Studies in Classic American Literature* (New York: T. Seltzer, 1923), p. 86.

Annette Kolodny (essay date 1984)

SOURCE: "Mary Jenison and Rebecca Bryan Boone: At Home in the Woods," in *The Land Before Her: Fantasy and Experience of the American Frontiers, 1630-1860,* University of North Carolina Press, 1984, pp. 68-89.

[*In the essay that follows, Kolodny examines the conflict between the nineteenth-century ideal of white womanhood and the captivity narratives authored by "Indianized" women.*]

Always disturbing to a white society determined to replace the forests and their native inhabitants with "a civilized Manner of Living" was the specter of white children, once having experienced Indian ways, forever attached to them. At a prisoner exchange between the Iroquois and the French in upper New York in 1699, Cadwallader Colden observed that "notwithstanding the French Commissioners took all Pains possible to carry Home the French, . . . few of them could be persuaded to return." "The English had as much Difficulty. No Arguments, no Intreaties, nor Tears of their Friends and Relations, could persuade many of them to leave their new Indian Friends and Acquaintance." Even among those who were so persuaded, Colden continued, "several . . . in a little Time grew tired of our Manner of living, and run away again to the Indians, and ended their Days with them."[1] In the next century, Benjamin Franklin echoed Colden's observations, noting that

> when white persons of either sex have been taken prisoners young by the Indians, and have lived a while among them, tho' ransomed by their Friends, and treated with all imaginable tenderness to prevail with them to stay among the English, yet in a Short time they become disgusted with our manner of life, and the care and pains that are necessary to support it, and take the first good Opportunity of escaping again into the Woods, from whence there is no reclaiming them.[2]

It was a situation that called into deepest question the Europeans' claim to a superior cultural organization, especially because, as Colden also noted (with no little chagrin), the reverse was never the case. "Indian Children have been carefully educated among the English, cloathed and taught, yet," he conceded, "I think, there is not one Instance, that any of these, after they had Liberty to go among their own People, and were come to Age, would remain with the English, but returned to their own Nations, and became as fond of the Indian Manner of Life as those that knew nothing of a civilized Manner of Living."[3]

As I have suggested earlier, the eagerness with which Americans purchased books like John Filson's *Adventures of Col. Daniel Boon* (along with its many reprintings), Alexander Henry's *Travels and Adventures in Canada and the Indian Territories, Between the Years 1760 and 1776* (first published in 1809), and, beginning in 1823 with *The Pioneers,* James Fenimore Cooper's Leatherstocking novels, was no doubt due—at least in part—to these texts' reassuring response to the gnawing Euro-American fear of Indianization and the accompanying distrust of "escaping . . . into the Woods." For all their temporary adoption into Indian families, and their knowledge of Indian woodcraft, both the real-life Boone and Henry clearly retained their white manners and their allegiance to the settlements; and Cooper's Natty Bumppo always insisted on his "white gifts."[4] All three, moreover, refrained from sexual contact with the Indian. Boone asserted an adoptive family of parents and siblings; Henry lived and hunted with several tribes, but accepted only the brotherhood (and surrogate fatherhood) of Wawatam; and, in *The Last of the Mohicans* (1826), the single novel in which he approached the notion of miscegenation, Cooper had Natty repeatedly insist on his identity as "a man without a cross."[5]

If such were the heroes that white society would publicly take to its bosom, in private that same society wondered and gossiped about the others, those who had escaped "into the Woods" and embraced Indian life to its fullest. For over half a century, for example, Eunice Williams inspired both rumor and curiosity in her native New England. The daughter of the Reverend John Williams, Eunice was taken captive as a small child in the winter of 1704, during the famous French and Indian raid on the town of Deerfield, Massachusetts.[6] She was then adopted by her Indian captors, and, despite many entreaties from various family members, it was more than thirty years before she returned to New England. When she did, first in the autumn of 1740 and then again the next summer, she came accompanied by her Indian husband and their two daughters. She would not, however, make any other concessions to the world of her birth. In consequence, for over fifty years following her visits, local legend attested that she had preferred the Indian blanket to the white woman's dress and had insisted on a tepee pitched on her brother's lawn rather than sleep within his house.[7]

But if stories like these—and there were many others—caught local fancies, they were never the stuff of legend or myth. There were no doubt several reasons for this. In the case of Eunice Williams, the story of her life with the Indians would have been difficult (albeit not impossible) to record since she no longer spoke English and had to communicate with her white family through an interpreter. More important, perhaps, though her marriage to an Indian may have fascinated the residents of Deerfield, few English colonials were as yet prepared to accept the fact of apparently willing miscegenation, especially where the white partner was a woman. (That male hunters and traders often took Indian "squaw wives," as they were scornfully termed, was common knowledge; but most whites preferred to see these as temporary unions of convenience, or else wrote off the white hunter as hopelessly "Indianized.") At the heart of such denials, however, may have been something more than the habitual white terror of interracial mixings. For, to accept a white woman's intimacy with the Indian was, as well, to accept her intimacy with the forest spaces he inhabited. And from the eighteenth century through the first quarter of the nineteenth, as we have seen, those spaces were imaginatively being wrested from the Indian in order to be given over exclusively to the white male hunter. In 1823, exploiting precisely this aspect of the burgeoning Boone mythology, Cooper's Natty Bumppo declared himself "form'd for the wilderness."[8]

Into Americans' studied literary silence on the subject of white-red intermarriage, and into the wilderness preserve of the white male hunter, there intruded in 1824 two landmark texts: Lydia Maria Child's historical romance, *Hobomok: A Tale of Early Times,* and James Everett Seaver's *Narrative of the Life of Mrs. Mary Jemison.* Completed in six weeks and signed only "by an American," *Hobomok* enjoyed immediate success and quickly established its nineteen-year-old author as the toast of the Cambridge and Boston literati.[9] Daring as was its assertion of a white woman's willing marriage to an Indian, the novel nonetheless escaped censure by portraying its heroine as lonely and despondent— ill-treated by a narrowly Puritanical father, grieving over the recent death of her mother, and convinced that her true love (an Englishman) has been lost at sea. Her marriage to the Indian, whose name served as the novel's title, is thus an act of desperation rather than an assertion of love or desire. At the same time, since Hobomok leaves his native village in order to marry Mary Conant, now pitching his wigwam on the shore outside of Plymouth plantation, he and his bride inhabit neither the Indian wilderness nor the European settlement. Thus, Child was not called upon to imagine a white woman's accommodation to life in the forest.

In the end—despite the fact that the union results in a son, called "little Hobomok" (but named "'according to the Indian custom, . . . Charles Hobomok Conant'")—

the heroine's white lover returns. Aware of his wife's unshakable attachment to her former fiancé, the noble Indian divorces her (Indian-style, by burning "'the witche hazel sticks, which were givene to the witnesses of my marriage'"), and disappears into the forest, never to be seen again. Mary Conant then returns to the Plymouth settlement, reconciles with her father, marries her white suitor and, at the last, sees her mixed-blood son "a distinguished graduate" from Harvard. Her marriage to the Indian is, in a sense, obliterated. The son's real father, we read, "was seldom spoken of; and by degrees his Indian appellation was silently omitted."[10]

Much though he might have preferred it, James Everett Seaver could succeed in no analogous obliteration because, as his subject insisted of her first husband, "strange as it may seem, I loved him!"[11] Indeed, at the heart of *The Narrative of the Life of Mrs. Mary Jemison [MJ]* was the experiential texture of the world that Child, for all her daring, simply could not imagine— the world of a white woman contentedly adopted into Indian society and happily adapted to life in the wilderness.

In 1823, a small printer and bookseller in upstate New York arranged a meeting between a schoolteacher named James Everett Seaver and an Indianized white woman known locally as "the White Woman of the Genesee." Her name was Mary Jemison. On the Pennsylvania frontier in 1758, at the age of thirteen or fourteen, she had been captured by a raiding party of French and Indians and thereafter adopted into the tribal life of the Seneca. At the time of the interview, Jemison had been residing for over forty years on what had once been tribal land, near modern Geneseo, New York, attracting to herself, among her white neighbors, a reputation for being "the protectoress of the homeless fugitive" and locally "celebrated as the friend of the distressed" (*MJ,* p. viii). Since Jemison was believed to have "arrived at least to the advanced age of eighty years," the purpose of the interview was to elicit from her an accurate account of her life "while she was [still] capable of recollecting and reciting the scenes through which she had passed" (*MJ,* pp. v, ix). In this, Seaver served as amanuensis, for three days diligently recording "her narrative as she recited it" (*MJ,* p. x). For, though she spoke "English plainly and distinctly," Jemison could neither read nor write (*MJ,* p. xi).

In his preface to the narrative that appeared the next year, Seaver claimed a "strict fidelity," assuring readers that "no circumstance has been intentionally exaggerated by the paintings of fancy, nor by fine flashes of rhetoric; neither has the picture been rendered more dull than the original" (*MJ,* p. v). But, in fact, the very circumstances of its composition militated against the narrative's fidelity. The "many gentlemen of respectability" responsible for initiating the project, Seaver revealed in his introduction, did so, among other reasons, "with a view . . . to perpetuat[ing] the remembrance of the atrocities of the savages in former times" (*MJ,* p. ix). A glance at the title page suggests that the printer, J. D. Bemis, thought he had arranged for a conventional captivity narrative. "An Account of the Murder of her Father and his Family; her sufferings; her marriage to two Indians," it promises, and then— with a sensational flourish—the title page added, the "barbarities of the Indians in the French and Revolutionary Wars."

In agreeing to the interview, Jemison may have had her own, quite different purposes, to which Seaver only dimly alludes. "The vices of the Indians, she appeared disposed not to aggravate," he noted in his introduction, while she "seemed to take pride in extoling their virtues" (*MJ,* p. xiii).

Seaver, clearly, had his own agenda. Defining "biographical writings" as "a telescope of life, through which we can see the extremes and excesses of the varied properties of the human heart" (*MJ,* p. iii), Seaver claimed both a didactic and a moral import for the work. Jemison's story, he asserted, "shows what changes may be affected in the animal and mental constitution of man; what trials may be surmounted; what cruelties perpetrated, and what pain endured, when stern necessity holds the reins, and drives the car of fate" (*MJ,* pp. iv-v). "The lessons of distress" to be derived from Jemison's biography, he hoped, would have "a direct tendency to increase our love of liberty; to enlarge our views of the blessings that are derived from our liberal institutions; and to excite in our breasts sentiments of devotion and gratitude to the great Author and finisher of our happiness" (*MJ,* p. vi). That such lessons might not be lost on the children whom he counted in his audience, Seaver "render[ed] the style easy" and gave "due attention" to the "chastity of expression and sentiment." Above all, he promised, "the line of distinction between virtue and vice has been rendered distinctly visible" (*MJ,* p. v).

To insure these *improving* effects, Seaver exploited all the racial assumptions of his era, thus making certain that the subject from whose life the lessons were to be drawn would be clearly identifiable as white. Only then, he seems to have felt, could she attract a sympathetic reading, the image of the "squaw" or the Indianized white woman having as yet gained neither currency nor approbation. If he could not wholly camouflage the fact that both her dress and "her habits are those of the Indians"—since this was well known to the many whites living in the area—he could, even so, clothe her in sturdy virtue and a "naturally pleasant contenance, enlivened with a smile." He repeated the testimony of white neighbors who "give her the name of never having done a censurable act," and, for his own part, he called her demeanor during the three-day interview "very sociable" (*MJ,* p. xiv). He even attributed to her the stock responses of the sentimental heroine—as opposed to the stereotypic notion of the impassive Indian—by noting that "her passions" were "easily excited. At a number of periods in her narration," Seaver wrote, "tears trickled down her grief worn cheek, and at the same time a rising sigh would stop her utterance" (*MJ*, p. xi).

That Seaver resorted to such devices suggests that he was trying to prepare his audience for what he knew to be a most unusual text; but it suggests also that he himself may not have been fully prepared for the narrative he received. Certainly, nothing in his previous reading experience could have so prepared him. And the fact is, for all its wealth of detail derived from Jemison's experiences among the Seneca and for all its fascinating store of historical information, *The Life of Mrs. Mary Jemison* is an inconsistent, often perplexing document. At times, it simply echoes the conventions of the earlier female captivity narratives or introduces moralizing elements from the sentimental romances with which Seaver was obviously familiar. At other times, it seems almost gratuitously to focus on "the barbarities which were perpetrated upon" white prisoners by their Indian captors (*MJ*, p. 149), as though it were a standard Indian War narrative. But every now and then what seems authentically to have been Jemison's story breaks out of the molds to which Seaver and his backers would consign it, evading the narrative conventions of captivity and sentimental romance alike and becoming, instead, the story of a woman who, in the forested wilderness of upstate New York, knew how to "take my children and look out for myself" (*MJ*, p. 74).

Unusual in a captivity narrative, the opening chapter offers information about Jemison's parents and their immigration from Ireland to a prosperous farm amid "the then frontier settlements of Pennsylvania" (*MJ*, p. 19). In the second chapter, this "little paradise" (*MJ*, p. 20), is rudely disrupted by a "party . . . of six Indians and four Frenchmen" (*MJ*, p. 25), at which point the conventional captivity design takes over. The Jemison family (with the exception of two older brothers) and some neighbors are taken prisoner and, with their Indian captors, "soon entered the woods" (*MJ*, p. 25). The cruelty of their captors and the hardships of their journey are carefully detailed, the language of these passages echoing, like a refrain, features that could be traced back to the earliest Puritan captivities. As they advance deeper into the forest and away from English settlements, for example, the landscape becomes increasingly threatening; on the second night, reminiscent of Rowlandson, they camp "at the border of a dark and dismal swamp" (*MJ*, p. 26).

At this second encampment, the Indians offer the first clue to their intentions. Mary's shoes and stockings are removed and, in their place, she is given "a pair of mocassins." The only other member of the party accorded this treatment is a young boy, son of a neighbor woman who has also been taken. Jemison's mother apparently correctly interpreted these gestures to mean that the Indians intended to "spare" the lives of the two children, "even if they should destroy the other captives." Accordingly, she took the first opportunity to bid her daughter a kind of admonitory farewell. Among other things, she adjured the girl "not [to] forget your English tongue" and to remember "your own name, and the name of your father and mother" (*MJ*, p. 27). The mother's premonitions proved correct. In short order the two children were separated from the rest of the captives, and within two days Mary's fears for the fate of her family are corroborated: the Indians clean and dry her parents' scalps ("yet wet and bloody") in her view (*MJ*, p. 30).

Fearful though she is, escape seems impossible. To leave the Indians would place her "alone and defenceless in the forest, surrounded by wild beasts that were ready to devour us" (*MJ*, p. 34). It was a situation that called forth all the pathos of the sentimental heroines into which the Puritan *Judea capta* had finally degenerated. However Jemison may have actually phrased her dilemma, Seaver had done his homework in other texts. In answer to her question, "But what could I do?," he put into his subject's mouth an assemblage of phrasings repeated from Hannah Swarton through Francis Scott: "A poor little defenceless girl; without the power or means of escaping; without a home to go to, even if I could be liberated; without a knowledge of the direction or distance to my former place of residence; and without a living friend to whom to fly for protection, I felt a kind of horror, anxiety, and dread" (*MJ*, p. 29). Like Rowlandson, Swarton, and the fictional Maria Kittle who followed them, Jemison tells us, "I durst not cry—I durst not complain. . . . My only relief was in silent stifled sobs" (*MJ*, p. 29).

Possibly because there were no available literary models for what followed, beginning with the third chapter Jemison's *Life* swerved radically from conventional formulae and freed itself from most of the rhetorical flourishes that had dominated the second chapter. For in Chapter 3, Mary Jemison is given new clothes, a new name, and is ritually adopted by two sisters of the Seneca tribe, by whom "I was ever considered and treated . . . as a real sister, the same as though I had been born of their mother" (*MJ*, p. 39). Slowly and patiently, her adoptive sisters teach her the Seneca language and train her to the tasks appropriate to Indian women. The Indians' earlier cruelties are now set aside, even effaced, as Jemison describes her new life with these "kind good natured women; peaceable and mild in their disposition; temperate and decent in their habits, and very tender and gentle towards me" (*MJ*, p. 40).

Although her adoptive "sisters would not allow me to speak English in their hearing," Jemison remained faithful to her mother's entreaties, taking the opportunity, "whenever I chanced to be alone . . . of repeating my prayer, catechism, or something I had learned in order that I might not forget my own language." This, along with opportunities to talk with whites who came among the Indians either as prisoners or as traders, permitted her to retain her spoken English. At the same time, with her "sisters . . . diligent in teaching me their language," Jemison soon found that she "could understand it readily, and speak it fluently" (*MJ*, p. 40). In short, despite efforts to hold onto the English tongue, she was fast becoming acculturated to her new life. Having been "with the Indians something over a year," she recalled, she became "considerably habituated to their mode of living, and attached to my sisters" (*MJ*, p. 43).

Only once during her first year among the Seneca does she seem to have regretted that habituation. When the tribe paid its annual trading visit to Fort Pitt, Jemison confided, "the sight of white people who could speak English inspired me with an unspeakable anxiety to go home with them, and share in the blessings of civilization." But when her adoptive family begins to suspect that the whites may have designs on the girl, they spirit her away and hide her. It "seemed like a second captivity," Jemison told Seaver, but, with "time, the destroyer of every affection," her "unpleasant feelings" faded, "and I became as contented as before" (*MJ*, p. 43). The contentment seems to have been genuine. For, contradicting then current notions of the arduousness of the Indian woman's life, Jemison described a world that—at least until the horrific disruptions of the Revolutionary War—appeared almost idyllic in its repeated seasonal routines.

Her new home, she says, was "pleasantly situated on the Ohio. . . . The land produced good corn; the woods furnished a plenty of game, and the waters abounded with fish." On the upper banks of the Ohio, "we spent the summer . . . where we planted, hoed, and harvested a large crop of corn, of excellent quality" (*MJ*, p. 40). In the autumn, the Seneca moved "down the Ohio . . . till we arrived at the mouth of the Sciota river; where they established their winter quarters" (thus making Jemison the first white woman known to have traveled the Ohio). Hunting—both for food and for "peltry" for trade—sustained the tribe through the winter. "The forests on the Sciota were well stocked with elk, deer, and other large animals; and the marshes contained large numbers of beaver, musk-rat, &c. which made excellent hunting for the Indians." When the hunting season was over, the Seneca "returned in the spring . . . to the houses and fields we had left in the fall before. There we again planted our corn, squashes, and beans, on the fields that we occupied the preceding summer" (*MJ*, p. 41). To these cyclical repetitions, in which "one year was exactly similar, in almost every respect, to that of the others," Jemison seems easily to have

adapted, commenting approvingly that they were "without the endless variety that is to be observed in the common labor of the white people" (*MJ*, pp. 46-47).

During her first two years with the Seneca, Jemison was regarded as still a child, and so the only work she records is joining "with the other children to assist the hunters to bring in their game" during the winter months (*MJ*, p. 41). When she achieved the status of an adult, in her view, again her labor "was not severe." "Notwithstanding the Indian women have all the fuel and bread to procure, and the cooking to perform, their task is probably not harder than that of white women, who have those articles provided for them," she told Seaver, "and their cares certainly are not half as numerous, nor as great. In the summer season, we planted, tended and harvested our corn, and generally had all our children with us; but had no master to oversee or drive us, so that we could work as leisurely as we pleased" (*MJ*, pp. 46, 47). The same theme is repeated in a later chapter. While males of the tribe attended to ritual functions and hunting, "their women," she noted, "attended to agriculture, their families, and a few domestic concerns of small consequence, and attended with but little labour." As far as Jemison was concerned, then, "no people can live more happy than the Indians did in times of peace" (*MJ*, p. 64).

What irretrievably tied her to life among the Indians was her marriage, after two years with the Seneca, to a Delaware named Sheninjee: "a noble man; large in stature; elegant in his appearance; generous in his conduct; courageous in war; a friend to peace, and a great lover of justice." Whether what follows indicates the interpolations of her uneasy scribe, or whether Jemison herself inserted the qualifications as a way of softening the implications of her subsequent declaration, we shall never know. "Yet," she hesitates in the narrative we now have, for all these fine traits, "Sheninjee was an Indian. The idea of spending my days with him, at first seemed perfectly irreconcilable to my feelings." Nonetheless, marry him she does, "according to Indian custom," and soon enough she finds herself won over by "his good nature, generosity, tenderness, and friendship towards me," so much so that he "soon gained my affection." "Strange as it may seem," she concludes, "I loved him!—To me he was ever kind in sickness, and always treated me with gentleness; in fact, he was an agreeable husband, and a comfortable companion" (*MJ*, p. 44).

Though the union with Sheninjee was happy, it was not long-lived. After three years of marriage (and the birth of a son), Jemison was persuaded by her Seneca brothers to join them on a trek from the Ohio to the tribal homeland on the Genesee, to winter there with her two sisters (who "had been gone almost two years"). To this, Sheninjee consented, determining in the meanwhile "to go down the river [and] . . . spend the winter in hunting with his friends, and come to me in the spring following" (*MJ*, p. 51). For Jemison, the trip to western New York proved long and difficult. Her clothing was inadequate to the rain and cold weather she encountered and, as a result, she recalled being "daily completely wet, and at night with nothing but my wet blanket to cover me, I had to sleep on the naked ground, and generally without a shelter, save such as nature had provided." "In addition to all that," she emphasized, "I had to carry my child, then about nine months old, every step of the journey on my back, or in my arms." "Those only who have travelled on foot the distance of five or six hundred miles, through an almost pathless wilderness," she concluded, "can form an idea of the fatigue and sufferings that I endured on that journey" (*MJ*, p. 53). Happily, her "brothers were attentive," helping her where they could, and, in due course, the little party "reached our place of destination, in good health, and without having experienced a day's sickness" (*MJ*, p. 54).

Having spent the winter "as agreeably as I could have expected to, in the absence of my kind husband," Jemison then suffered "a heavy and unexpected blow." "In the course of the summer" she received "intelligence that soon after he left me . . . [Sheninjee] was taken sick and died." The "consolation" of her Seneca family helps her through this period so that "in a few months my grief wore off and I became contented" (*MJ*, p. 58). Sufficiently contented that, when a year or two later, the king's bounty offered her the opportunity to be returned to the whites, she remained "fully determined not to be redeemed at that time" (*MJ*, p. 58). Sticking to her resolution, she successfully eludes both the white man and the Indian chief who have decided to return her. Chapter 5 then ends with the information that when her son "was three or four years old, I was married to an Indian, whose name was Hiokatoo, . . . by whom I had four daughters and two sons" (*MJ*, p. 62).

With Chapter 6, the cyclical idyll of Indian life is forever disrupted by warfare between the would-be independent colonies and the English, a contest in which the Seneca sided with the crown. And, at the same time, this chapter reveals that Jemison's second marriage enjoyed little of the mutuality of affection that had marked the first. "During the term of nearly fifty years that I lived with [Hiokatoo]," Jemison insisted, "I received, according to Indian customs, all the kindness and attention that was due me as his wife." But this hardly bespeaks the quality of attentiveness she had received from Sheninjee. Even so, Jemison was apparently reluctant to speak negatively of her second husband (certain, perhaps, that her biographer, on his own, intended to cast the man in no favorable light), and so she simply insisted that Hiokatoo "uniformly treated me with tenderness and never offered an insult" (*MJ*, p. 104). Intent, however, on exploiting the Revolution as the basis for a traditional Indian War

narrative, Seaver sought other sources of information about Hiokatoo and, from neighbors and former military men, pieced together the portrait of a formidable "warrior, [whose] cruelties to his enemies perhaps were unparalleled" (*MJ*, p. 104). Large sections of Chapters 7 and 11, in fact, are given over to sometimes lurid details of Hiokatoo's exploits against the Americans.

The same Revolutionary War that gave ample scope to Hiokatoo's prowess as a warrior also forced Mary Jemison to make good use of every survival skill she had learned among the Indians. For her, the test came during General Sullivan's campaign against the tribes of western New York State in 1779. "A part of our corn they burnt, and threw the remainder into the river. They burnt our houses, killed what few cattle and horses they could find, destroyed our fruit trees, and left nothing but the bare soil and timber" (*MJ*, pp. 73-74). The Indians themselves, however, had earlier escaped across the river. After ascertaining that Sullivan's troops were gone from the area, the Seneca returned, only to discover "not a mouthful of any kind of sustenance left, not even enough to keep a child one day from perishing with hunger" (*MJ*, p. 74).

From the war narrative that Seaver now seems eager to pursue, Jemison's own story insistently emerges. With the weather "cold and stormy" and the remnant of her tribe "destitute of houses and food too," Jemison resolves "to take my children and look out for myself, without delay. With this intention," she continues, "I took two of my little ones on my back, bade the other three follow, and the same night arrived on the Gardow [or Gardau] flats, where I have ever since resided" (*MJ*, p. 74). Her independent removal from the rest of the tribe advances the narrative to yet another recounting of adaptive survival—only this time, it is not a white woman's adaptation to life among the Indians but, in its place, an Indianized white woman's successful adaptation to fending for herself on the cleared and open "flats" along the banks of the Genesee River. (Hiokatoo, for most of the war, was away, leading raiding parties against the American frontier settlements.)

Upon her arrival at the Gardau flats, Jemison encounters "two negroes, who had run away from their masters. . . . They lived in a small cabin and had planted and raised a large field of corn, which they had not yet harvested." In exchange for food and shelter for herself and her children, Jemison husks their corn "till the whole was harvested." Residing with the blacks through the "succeeding winter, which was the most severe that I have witnessed since my remembrance," Jemison and her family survive, while other Indians, for want of food, do not. "The snow fell about five feet deep, and remained so for a long time, and the weather was extremely cold; so much so indeed, that almost all the game upon which the Indians depended for subsistence, perished, and reduced them almost to a state of starvation. . . . Many of our people barely escaped with their lives, and some actually died of hunger and freezing" (*MJ,* p. 75).

The following spring she builds her own dwelling on the flats and here, on "extremely fertile" land (*MJ,* p. 96), she has continued to reside until the time of the interview with Seaver. The blacks had remained only two more years and then taken off (probably for Canada). (Hiokatoo had died in 1811.) Though relatively few whites had even seen the area when Jemison first removed there, by the time of the narrative it is well populated, and Jemison now leases part of her considerable holdings (deeded to her by the Indians) "to white people to till on shares" (*MJ,* p. 96).

What is striking about her description of the intervening years—aside, of course, from the drama of their warfare—is the relative absence of Hiokatoo as a presence in the household and the sense that, with Jemison's arrival, the Gardau flats ceased to be part of the wilderness. "My flats were cleared before I saw them," Jemison explains, proffering the Indian legend that they had once been inhabited by "a race of men who a great many moons before [the Indian], cleared that land and lived on the flats" (*MJ,* p. 76). Whether or not a reader accepts such speculation, the impact is immediate and undeniable: the uninhabited flats become a part of the human world, and the reader thereafter ceases to think of Jemison as living in an unremitting wilderness.

No less striking is her emphasis upon her ability to manage for herself. "For provisions I have never suffered since I came upon the flats; nor have I ever been in debt to any other hands than my own for the plenty that I have shared," she boasts (*MJ,* p. 143). With the aid of her children only, she insists, she carried the boards that were to become her permanent home; with her children, she built that home; and even into the present year, she continues the yearly planting of corn:

> I learned to carry loads on my back, in a strap placed across my forehead, soon after my captivity; and continue to carry in the same way. Upwards of thirty years ago, with the help of my young children, I backed all the boards that were used about my house from Allen's mill at the outlet of Silver Lake, a distance of five miles. I have planted, hoed, and harvested corn every season but one since I was taken prisoner. Even this present fall (1823) I have husked my corn and backed it into the house. (*MJ,* p. 142)

Of the eight children to whom she has given birth, three now survive—all daughters. The youngest, with her husband and their three children, also live on the Gardau Tract, while the rest of her family, including "thirty-nine grand children, and fourteen great-grand children," live nearby, "in the neighborhood of Genesee River, and at Buffalo" (*MJ,* p. 143). "Thus situated in the midst of my children," Mary Jemison concluded the narrative of her uncommon life (*MJ,* p. 144).

Richard Slotkin has observed that, "wittingly or unwittingly," Seaver designed this closing to imitate contemporary popular images of a patriarchal Daniel Boone, "seated," at the end of his life, "in the midst of his happy brood of unspoiled 'children of the woods,'"[12] It is an astute observation—except that, once again, Slotkin ignores the crucial fact of gender. A comfortable and secure life "in my own house, and on my own land" (*MJ,* p. 143) bespoke the reward for surmounting wilderness hardships that had previously been accorded to men—but never to a woman—in American literary history. As such, Jemison's *Life* was "revolutionary" not for the generic alterations Slotkin cites,[13] but because it represented the first text in American literature to move a real-world white woman beyond the traditional captivity pattern to something approaching the *willing* wilderness accommodations of a Daniel Boone.[14]

With that switch in gender, moreover, the nature of the accommodation also changed. For, with Jemison, the baggage of familial and communal domesticity began to enter the wilderness preserve of the male hunter-adventurers. To be sure, following the Boone original, many narratives of western exploration had expressed their protagonist's eagerness to locate sites for future settlement, and, in this sense, they too made claims to familial and communal interests. But in point of fact, most of these narratives concentrated on the private pleasures of and solitary intimacy between the white male protagonist and his wilderness surroundings, thus emphasizing the romance of high adventure rather than the prosaic realities of cabin-building and hoeing corn.[15] In sharp contrast to the Adamic paradisal longings of the men, and unlike her fictional prototype in the Panther Captivity, Mary Jemison brought home and family into the cleared spaces of the wild—an act of survival, if not of romance.

It was a transformation for which the American public was ready and eager. Originally conceived of by its first printer, James D. Bemis of Canandaigua, New York, as a volume that would attract readers in the northern and western sections of his home state, *A Narrative of the Life of Mrs. Mary Jemison* did not for long remain "distinctively a New York state book." Publishers across the country recognized its wider appeal, and pirated editions by English printers were soon being sold on both sides of the Atlantic. According to Frank Luther Mott, Seaver had succeeded in producing the unrivaled best-seller of 1824, and throughout the rest of the decade his rendering of Jemison's life continued to sell as well as the novels of Scott and Cooper.[16] In 1842 a revised and extended version was published, which also enjoyed several subsequent reprintings. And in 1856 there appeared yet another enlarged edition, also with supplementary and corroboratory materials, called forth, as its publishers noted, by "frequent inquiries . . . for the work."[17]

The public acceptance—indeed, acclaim—with which Child's *Hobomok* and Seaver's *A Narrative of the Life of Mrs. Mary Jemison* had been received in 1824 may well have prompted James Fenimore Cooper's willingness to approach similar themes in *The Last of the Mohicans,* which appeared in 1826. But Cooper's was, at best, only a hesitant approach. Following Child rather than Jemison, he permitted his white heroine no taint of Indianization, let alone any real accommodation to the wild. And, drawing back from the consummation of Indian-white sexuality that had marked both Child and Jemison, Cooper preferred to have his protagonists die and reunite, if at all, in the "'blessed hunting-grounds of the Lenape'"—rather than grapple with the worldly implications of the suggested attraction between Uncas and Cora. So reticent was he on the subject, in fact, that even the unconsummated attraction had to be justified by the hint that the dark-eyed Cora herself carried the blood of darker races (her West Indian mother having been "descended, remotely," from slaves).[18]

Women writers did not share these reticences. Taking full advantage of what Child and Jemison had made imaginatively possible, Catherine Maria Sedgwick offered a white heroine whose romantic attachment to an Indian included a happy accommodation to life in the woods. To be sure, Sedgwick's *Hope Leslie: Or, Early Times in the Massachusetts* depicts almost nothing of the details of Faith Leslie's life among the Indians and thereby, as Dawn Lander Gherman has pointed out, it emphasizes little of "her attachment to the Indian culture in general."[19] But it does at least assert, even if only sentimentally, the appeal of her woodland transformation. As the Indian maiden Magawisca explains to Faith's sister, "When she flies from you, as she will, mourn not over her . . . ; the wild flower would perish in your gardens; the forest is like a native home to her, and she will sing as gayly again as the bird that hath found its mate."[20] Sedgwick had apparently judged popular reading tastes correctly: upon its first appearance in 1827, *Hope Leslie* rivaled the sales of Cooper and Scott. Such was the legacy of Child and Jemison.

Because of its unique emphasis on a white woman's domestic accommodation to the wilderness, the Jemison narrative, by itself, may have also pointed the way to a renewed interest in the history of Rebecca Bryan Boone. For where Rebecca Boone shared with Jemison the stature of a white woman successfully adapted to life in the wilderness, as the wife of America's mythic frontiersman, she attained that stature without assuming any of Jemison's Indian associations. In preparing his *Biographical Memoir of Daniel Boone* [*DB*], then, Timothy Flint—a man whose eye was always on the main chance—undoubtedly took his cue from the continuing

popularity of the Jemison narrative and attributed to his hero's wife "the same heroic and generous nature" he gave her husband.[21] That he did not thereby succeed in delineating a radically new heroine for the frontier west, nor even achieve a portrait with the strengths of Seaver's Jemison, should not surprise. Flint's subject, after all, was Daniel, not Rebecca Boone; and Flint's purpose was to promote settlement of the agricultural frontier. As a result, Rebecca inevitably shrank to a symbolic appurtenance in the face of her husband's overpowering mythic resonances, just as she also shrank to an exemplary elder in the face of Flint's primary concern to attract readers westward. That said, Flint must nonetheless be credited with resurrecting Rebecca Bryan Boone in 1833 from what had then been a half century of almost nameless obscurity.

Although John Filson's 1784 narrative had recognized Boone's "wife and daughter [as] being the first white women that ever stood on the banks of the Kentucke river,"[22] it never named either woman or otherwise gave them prominence. Throughout that spurious first-person narrative, in fact, Rebecca Bryan Boone is denominated simply as "my wife," and her participation in the initial difficulties and dangers of first settlement is nowhere detailed. Only once is she credited with independent action. "During my captivity with the Indians," Boone reports, "my wife, who despaired of ever seeing me again, expecting the Indians had put a period to my life, oppressed with the distress of the country, and bereaved of me, her only happiness, had, before I returned, transported my family and goods, on horses, through the wilderness, amidst a multitude of dangers, to her father's house, in North Carolina."[23] Boone then returns to his recounting of the Indian Wars along the Kentucky frontier and makes no further mention of the wife and family he had brought back from North Carolina and resettled again in Boonsborough in 1780. Filson's *The Adventures of Col. Daniel Boon,* of course, set precedents that subsequent Boone accounts would follow. Printer John Trumbull's shortened version of Filson, which appeared two years later, even further reduced Rebecca Bryan Boone's (still nameless) role in her husband's story. And in 1813, the year of her death, one Daniel Bryan, claiming kinship, published a verse epic celebrating Daniel's adventures, but Rebecca hardly figures in *The Mountain Muse: Comprising the Adventures of Daniel Boone; and the Power of Virtuous and Refined Beauty.*[24]

Thus, until Daniel Boone's death in 1821, the only published information regarding his wife had to be gleaned from the various reprintings of the Filson or Trumbull narratives and the occasional newspaper interview granted by Boone or by one of his sons. Following Boone's death, the Providence, Rhode Island, printer, Henry Trumbull, brought out yet another version of the Filson text to which he added "a continuation of the life of Col. Boon, from the conclusion of the American and Indian Wars" to the time of his death, attributed "to a near relation of the Colonel . . . who received it from his own mouth." This 1825 expanded version of Boone's life and adventures underscored anew the image of Boone as a gifted hunter and "a great friend to the Indians," but it offered barely a word about Rebecca—beyond, that is, noting her acquiescence to her husband's preference for the "perfect Wilderness." Seeking the society of "the wild animals of the forest . . . in preference to that of his fellow countrymen," this "continuation" narrative explained, Boone removed "with his family," at age 65, "to the Tennessee Country, then almost a perfect Wilderness." Of the family's reaction to the move we learn only that "it is a remarkable fact that the family of Colonel Boon, which was comprised of his wife, two sons and a daughter, were not less pleased with a secluded life than himself."[25] Following Boone to the year of his death in 1821, the Henry Trumbull text did not even mention Rebecca's passing in 1813.

Despite these printed omissions, as a rich fund of oral lore grew up around the great hunter, so too—if to a lesser degree—Rebecca Bryan Boone attracted popular interest. It was said by some that she was a fair shot, by others that she rivaled her husband in marksmanship; and the rumor persisted that she, not her husband (who was often away from home), had taught their sons the use of the gun. As Boone grew older and increasingly enfeebled by rheumatism, moreover, it became common knowledge that Rebecca accompanied him into the woods, helping her husband to bring down the game, aiming and firing when his knotted fingers could not, and generally proving as valuable a companion as any son or Indian might be.[26] But, beyond the occasional newspaper article, little of this made its way into print. Nor did Timothy Flint, when he essayed a comprehensive *Biographical Memoir of Daniel Boone,* make much use of this material—with one prominent exception: out of the oral tradition he plucked the fire-hunt story and thereby forever assured Rebecca a place in the mythic matrix surrounding her husband.

In addition to his literary pretensions, Timothy Flint saw himself as a beneficent promoter of western settlement. In this sense, the 1833 *Biographical Memoir of Daniel Boone* was simply a more dramatic continuation of his earlier, two-volume *Condensed History and Geography of the Western States, or the Mississippi Valley* (1828).[27] Both works, after all, celebrated the struggling early history of a frontier area and then made clear its current appeal to prospective settlers. Where Flint differed from other promotional writers of his day was in his understanding of the need to address women as well as men on the subject of emigration. He did not address them in the same way, however, since, in his view, "men change their place of abode from ambition or interest; women from affection" (*DB,*

p. 30). For male readers, therefore, he elaborated the economic gains of emigration and played to their fantasies through the figure of Daniel Boone. For women, he offered Rebecca Bryan Boone, the exemplary model of a woman who, from affection, willingly "follow[ed] her husband to a region where she was an entire stranger" (*DB,* p. 30). Indeed, wherever Flint introduced women in the *Biographical Memoir* he introduced, as well, an embedded exemplum.

His account of the attack on Bryant's Station is a case in point. One of several fortifications along the Kentucky border (near present-day Lexington), Bryant's Station was attacked by Indians in August of 1782. Unable to penetrate the outer fencing, the Indians settled in for a prolonged siege, surrounding the little fort and cutting off its inhabitants from their single source of water, a spring located just outside the perimeter. When the station ran low on water, as Flint tells it, the women, "these noble mothers, wives, and daughters, assuring the men that there was no probability that the Indians would fire upon them, offered to go out and draw water for the supply of the garrison; and that even if they did shoot down a few of them, it would not reduce the resources of the garrison as would the killing of the men" (*DB,* p. 115). Following the historical facts, Flint then pictured the women marching "out to the spring, espying here and there a painted face, or an Indian body crouched under the covert of the weeds. Whether their courage or their beauty fascinated the Indians to suspend their fire," he does not pretend to guess (thus feigning ignorance of Indian fighting habits that—as the Kentuckians had rightly guessed—insured the women's safety). If, historically, the women probably made only a single trip to the spring, each filling her bucket once, Flint would have it "that these generous women came and went until the reservoir was amply supplied with water" (*DB,* p. 115). He was, of course, trying to heighten the drama of the scene.

But he was also, if illogically, designing his exaggeration so as to draw a moral for those "modern wives, who refuse to follow their husbands abroad." If the women of early Kentucky were willing to risk the dangers of Indian attack, he challenges, then how dare "modern wives" object to western migration only on the grounds "of the danger of the voyage or journey, or the unhealthiness of the proposed residence, or because the removal will separate them from the pleasures of fashion and society." These are but selfish and self-indulgent objections, he suggests, and, in their place, he admonishes his female readers, "contemplate the example of the wives of the defenders of this station" (*DB,* p. 115). Or, throughout the *Memoir,* he implies, contemplate the model of Rebecca Bryan Boone: "she" who "followed [her husband] from North Carolina into the far wilderness, without a road or even a trace to guide their way—surrounded at every step by wild beasts and savages" (*DB,* p. 247).

Flint's stories of the "noble" women of Bryant's Station, the women "running balls" in defense of McAfee's Station the following year (*DB*, p. 196), and his assertion that Rebecca Bryan Boone shared with her husband "the same heroic and generous nature" (*DB*, p. 247) should have generated images of strong, independent womanhood on the frontier. But such was not the case. Like his contemporaries, wary of what might be seen as the hardening, or masculinizing, effect of the frontier on women, Flint backed away from these implications of the historical record. And again, Rebecca Bryan Boone proved the vehicle for his intentions. Acknowledging that she had shared with her husband "in all his hardships, perils, and trials," Flint suppressed what might otherwise be concluded from that remark and asked readers to see Rebecca first as "a meek" and then, only secondarily, as a "yet courageous and affectionate friend" to her mate (*DB*, pp. 247-48).

He even discounted what was supposedly Boone's first-person testimony and denied Rebecca her role as the adult responsible for safely returning her little family to North Carolina after her husband's captivity (and presumed death) among the Shawnee. Flint wrote:

> At the close of the summer of 1778, the settlement on the Yadkin [River in North Carolina] saw a company on pack horses approaching in the direction from the western wilderness. . . . At the head of that company was a blooming youth, scarcely yet arrived at the age of manhood. It was the eldest surviving son of Daniel Boone. Next behind him was a matronly woman, in weeds, and with a countenance of deep dejection. It was Mrs. Boone. (*DB*, p. 165)

Contradicting all the earlier Boone narratives derived from Filson, in which Boone clearly credited "my wife" with "transport[ing] my family and goods on horses through the wilderness, amidst many dangers,"[28] Flint here attributes leadership to a "youth" whom he must concede had "scarcely yet arrived at the age of manhood." The resourceful Rebecca, meanwhile, who in 1778 would have been forty-one, is reduced to "a matronly woman" in widow's weeds, passively following her son as she had once meekly followed his father. But so important was it for Flint to project an acceptable femininity, especially in the wilderness, that he thus rewrote what was already familiar and ignored any oral lore that might challenge his (he supposed) comforting stereotype.

Finally, however, it was the myth of Daniel Boone that, in Flint's pages, overwhelmed and buried the reality of Rebecca Bryan. For Timothy Flint, a New Englander lately transplanted to the Ohio, as for others before him, the figure of Daniel Boone took shape around the image of a loner from his earliest days "formed to be a woodsman" (*DB*, p. vi). In the "solitary and trackless wilderness" of Kentucky, according to Flint, Boone experienced "a kind of wild pleasure" (*DB*, p. 44) that is nothing short of erotic. In the woods, "the paradise of hunters" (*DB*, p. 227), Boone grasps at a "fresh and luxuriant beauty" (*DB*, p. 36), enjoying there a solitary winter later recalled as "the happiest in his life" (*DB*, p. 64). Little wonder, then, that the legend that Flint preserved from the oral tradition, concerning Boone's courtship of Rebecca Bryan, projected yet another instance of the hero's "darling pursuit of hunting, . . . which in him amounted almost to a passion" (*DB*, p. 227).

Purporting to record Rebecca's and Daniel's first meeting, the "fire hunt" legend hints at much older literary sources even as it describes a method of stalking deer adopted by the whites from Indian practice. As it begins, a youthful Daniel Boone is engaged "in a fire hunt" one night with a young friend, and Flint carefully explains what this entails:

> The horseman that precedes, bears on his shoulder what is called a *fire pan*, full of blazing pine knots, which casts a bright and flickering glare far through the forest. The second follows at some distance, with his rifle prepared for action. . . . The deer, reposing quietly in his thicket, is awakened by the approaching cavalcade, and instead of flying from the portentous brilliance, remains stupidly gazing upon it, as if charmed to the spot. The animal is betrayed to its doom by the gleaming of its fixed and innocent eyes. This cruel mode of securing a fatal shot, is called in hunter's phrase, *shining the eyes.* (*DB*, p. 26)

When two eyes had thus been shined, Boone—who was the second horseman, with his rifle at the ready—dismounted and approached his quarry. "Whether warned by a presentiment, or arrested by a palpitation, and strange feelings within, at noting a new expression in the blue and dewy light that gleamed to his heart," Flint declines to guess. "But," he continues, whatever the reason, "the unerring rifle fell," its bullet still in the chamber, "and a rustling told [Boone] that the game had fled. Something whispered him it was not a *deer;* and yet the fleet step, as the game bounded away, might easily be mistaken for that of the light-footed animal" (*DB*, p. 27).

Presuming "that he had mistaken the species of the game," the resolute hunter doggedly pursues his quarry—all the way to the house of his neighbor, "a thriving farmer, by the name of Bryan" (*DB*, pp. 27, 25). Here he discovers Bryan's daughter, "a girl of sixteen, . . . panting for breath and seeming in affright," because she believes she has just been chased out of the woods by a panther. The two are introduced and, as Flint describes it, "the ruddy, flaxen-haired girl stood full in view of her terrible pursuer, leaning upon his rifle, and surveying her with the most eager admiration." The moment takes on the colors of a Scott romance: "Both were young, beautiful, and at the period when the affections exercise their most energetic influence" (*DB*, p. 28). With the close of the chapter, the romantic expectations are fulfilled and the informing metaphor completed. As Boone "was remarkable for the backwoods attribute of *never being beaten out of his track,* he ceased not to woo, until he gained the heart of Rebecca Bryan. In a word," Flint concludes, "he courted her successfully, and they were married" (*DB*, p. 29).

If the fire-hunt legend calls to mind medieval allegories in which the hunting of the hart plays out a lover's pursuit of his *dear,* it does so with a difference. In medieval allegories, the hunt begins with the wounding of the hart and terminates with its capture, the symbolic uniting of the lovers thus displacing the prior pursuit. In Flint's *Biographical Memoir of Daniel Boone,* however, the hunting never ceases. The imputed consummation that closes the story does not, in fact, bind Daniel to Rebecca's side. For Boone's "darling pursuit of hunting" is not metaphorical: it *is* his controlling "passion" (*DB*, p. 227). The "unexplored paradise of the hunter's imagination" (*DB*, p. 48) is the forest here, not the marriage bed. As a result, the Rebecca Bryan of the fire-hunt legend emerges not as a person beloved in her own right but, instead, as a human cipher who has managed, if only briefly, to take on the erotic appeal of the wilderness that defined her husband's meaning.

Although family members have insisted that the Boones themselves often repeated the story, it is also said that their children refused to believe it. The Boone children were no doubt aware that their father had first seen his future bride when his older sister, Mary Boone, married into the neighboring Bryan family. Fifteen-year-old Rebecca Bryan, of course, had attended that wedding.[29] The modern reader must discount the story on other grounds. For its mythic and medieval sources notwithstanding, the "fire hunt" finally represents not a symbolic courtship but a travesty of courtship, reducing Rebecca to a fleeing incarnation of Daniel Boone's true and overriding love: the hunt.

But Timothy Flint seems to have been both unaware of the story's darker implications and unmindful of the Boone children's well-known skepticism. Therefore, when he included the fire hunt in what was to become what Henry Nash Smith has termed "perhaps the most widely read book about a Western character published during the first half of the nineteenth century,"[30] Flint forever attached the legend's symbolic significations to the woman, thus stylizing what others, after him, would make of her. To be fair to Flint, even if the modern reader cannot rest satisfied with the portrait, it must be said that he did, after all, grant Rebecca Bryan Boone her name and an attentiveness accorded in no previous text. In so doing, he at least made her available to history (even if not to literature).

In *The Pioneer Women of the West* (1852), for example, Elizabeth Fries Ellet repeatedly acknowledged Flint as the source for her chapter on Rebecca Boone.[31] But even without that acknowledgment, Flint's influence would be obvious. Several passages from the *Biographical Memoir* are quoted whole in Ellet (including the fire-hunt legend), while elsewhere Ellet expands on hints taken directly from Flint. Where Flint had maintained the imaginative codes that defined the forests as "the paradise of hunters" (*DB*, p. 85) and relegated to women "a garden spot" (*DB*, p. 85), Ellet personalized Flint's generalization, assigning the "garden spot" specifically to the charge of "Mrs. Boone and her daughters": "They had brought out a stock of seeds from the old settlements and went out every bright day to plant them."[32]

Where Flint and Ellet differed was where the feminine models of their respective decades differed. If, in 1833, Flint had harked back to the passively "meek" sentimental heroines of earlier decades, in 1852 Elizabeth Fries Ellet dropped the word from her description and, instead, cut Rebecca's figure to match the fashion of her own decade's reigning cult of domesticity: "A most faithful and efficient helpmeet had she proved to the pioneer, possessing the same energy, heroism, and firmness which he had shown in all the vicissitudes of his eventful career, with the gentler qualities by which woman, as the centre of the domestic system, diffuses happiness and trains her children to become useful and honored in after life."[33]

The publication of Flint's *Biographical Memoir of Daniel Boone* meant that, as of 1833, Americans enjoyed—for the first time—published access to two real-life white women who had learned to survive in the wilderness and convert it into a home for themselves and their families. It did not mean that Rebecca Boone would henceforth inspire the kind of mythologizing that her husband had, or that either she or Mary Jemison would independently become figures of legend in the nation's shared cultural imagination. All her wilderness survival skills notwithstanding, Jemison had willingly married—indeed, *loved!*—where white society would see only savagery and brutality. Enormously and continuously popular though it was, therefore, Seaver's portrait of Mary Jemison fell short of myth, its white heroine forever tainted by her Indianization. In Flint's pages, an exemplary Rebecca Boone appeared all too infrequently and all too indistinctly to stand proof against the many and changing stereotypes in which others, in the future, would cast her. And by portraying her first and most dramatically as reflected in the flickering and distorting torchlight of her husband's predominating myth, Flint effectively annihilated any possibility that she might achieve mythic status on her own.

Notes

1 Colonial observations on the successful adoption of whites by Indians are quoted and discussed in Frederick Turner, *Beyond Geography: The Western Spirit Against the Wilderness* (New York: Viking Press, 1980), p. 244.

2 Ibid.

3 Ibid. For an excellent discussion of the successful adoption of whites by Indians, see also James Axtell's "The White Indians of Colonial America," *William and Mary Quarterly,* 3d ser. 32 (January 1975): 55-88.

4 See James Fenimore Cooper's "Preface to the Leather-Stocking Tales, New York, 1850," in *The Last of the Mohicans* (1826), ed. William Charvat (Cambridge, Mass.: Houghton Mifflin, 1958), p. 12.

5 See John Filson, *The Discovery, Settlement And present State of Kentucke . . . To which is added, An Appendix, Containing, The Adventures of Col. Daniel Boon, one of the first Settlers . . .* (Wilmington, Del.: James Adams, 1784), p. 65; Alexander Henry, *Travels And Adventures in Canada and The Indian Territories, Between The Years 1760 and 1776* (New York: I. Riley, 1809), p. 161; Cooper, *The Last of the Mohicans,* p. 284.

6 The details of the 1704 raid on Deerfield were preserved by John Williams, Eunice's father, who, upon being ransomed in 1706, composed a narrative of his captivity experience, *The Redeemed Captive Returning to Zion: Or, A Faithful History of Remarkable Occurrences in the Captivity and Deliverance of Mr. John Williams, Minister of the Gospel in Deerfield,* first published in Boston in 1707 and many times reprinted thereafter.

7 For a full discussion of the Eunice Williams captivity and the gossip aroused by her subsequent visits to Massachusetts, see Dawn Lander Gherman, "From Parlour to Tepee: The White Squaw on the American Frontier," Ph.D. dissertation, University of Massachusetts, 1975, pp. 70-91.

8 James Fenimore Cooper, *The Pioneers; or, The Sources of the Susquehanna: A Descriptive Tale* (1823; reprint, New York: G. P. Putnam's Sons, 1893), p. 475.

9 See Susan Phinney Conrad, *Perish the Thought: Intellectual Women in Romantic America, 1830-1860* (New York: Oxford University Press, 1976), p. 105.

10 Lydia Maria Child, *Hobomok. A Tale of Early Times* (Boston: Cummings, Hilliard and Co., 1824; facsimile reprint, New York: Garrett Press, 1970), pp. 186, 182, 187, 187-88.

11 James Everett Seaver, *A Narrative of the Life of Mrs. Mary Jemison, Who was taken by the Indians, in the year 1755, when only about twelve years of age, and has continued to reside amongst them to the present time* (Canandaigua, N.Y.: J. D. Bemis and Co., 1824), p. 44 (hereafter cited in the text as *MJ*).

12 Richard Slotkin, *Regeneration through Violence: The Mythology of the American Frontier, 1600-1860* (Middletown, Conn.: Wesleyan University Press, 1973), p. 450.

13 Slotkin finds the Jemison narrative "revolutionary" because its unconventional ending radically diverged from the "restoration scene that concluded the captivity tales of the Puritans" (p. 450). That the Jemison narrative did not offer the conventional restoration scene is true, but it was hardly the first captivity narrative to abandon the convention.

14 At the close of the Revolution, Jemison turned down yet another opportunity to be repatriated to the white community, preferring to remain near her Indian relations and on the Gardau flats. The reason she gives in Seaver, *Narrative,* is "that I had got a large family of Indian children, that I must take with me; and that if I should be so fortunate as to find my relatives, they would despise them, if not myself; and treat us as enemies; or, at least with a degree of cold indifference, which I thought I could not endure" (p. 93).

15 See Filson; also "A true and faithful Narrative of the surprizing Captivity and remarkable Deliverance of Captain Isaac Stewart," in E. Russell, comp., *Narative of Mrs. Scott and Capt. Stewart's Captivity* (Boston: E. Russell, 1786), pp. 19-24.

16 See Frank Luther Mott, *Golden Multitudes: The Story of Best Sellers in the United States* (New York: Macmillan Co., 1947), pp. 97, 96-97, 305.

17 James Everett Seaver, *Life of Mary Jemison: Deh-He-Wä-Mis* (New York and Auburn: Miller, Orton and Mulligan; Rochester, N.Y.: D. M. Dewey, 1856), p. 9.

18 Cooper, *The Last of the Mohicans,* pp. 364, 172.

19 Gherman, p. 193.

20 Catharine Maria Sedgwick, *Hope Leslie: Or, Early Times in the Massachusetts,* 2 vols. (New York: White, Gallaher, and White, 1827), 2:262.

21 Timothy Flint, *Biographical Memoir of Daniel Boone, The First Settler of Kentucky: Interspersed with Incidents in the Early Annals of the Country* (Cincinnati: N. and G. Guilford and Co., 1833), p. 247 (hereafter cited in the text as *DB*).

22 Filson, p. 60.

[23] Ibid., p. 72.

[24] See *The Adventures of Colonel Daniel Boon, One of the first Settlers at Kentucke . . . Written by the Colonel himself* (Norwich, Conn.: John Trumbull, 1786). In Daniel Bryan, *The Mountain Muse: Comprising the Adventures of Daniel Boone; and the Power of Virtuous and Refined Beauty* (Harrisonburg, Va.: Davidson and Bourne, 1813), Rebecca Bryan Boone makes her most dramatic appearance when she attempts to dissuade her husband from first going off to explore Kentucky, crying "My Boone! / How can you leave your Home, your Wife and Babes" (p. 56).

[25] *Life and Adventures of Colonel Daniel Boon, The First White Settler of the State of Kentucky* (Providence, R.I.: H. Trumbull, 1824), pp. 19, 27, 22.

[26] I am indebted in this discussion to materials in John Bakeless, *Daniel Boone: Master of the Wilderness* (New York: William Morrow, 1939), esp. pp. 26-30, 38, 347.

[27] Timothy Flint, *A Condensed History and Geography of the Western States, Or the Mississippi Valley,* 2 vols. (1828; reprint, Gainesville, Fla.: Scholars' Facsimiles and Reprints, 1970).

[28] *Life and Adventures of Colonel Daniel Boon* (H. Trumbull, 1824), p. 15.

[29] See Slotkin, p. 300; and Bakeless, pp. 26-27.

[30] Henry Nash Smith, *Virgin Land: The American West as Symbol and Myth* (1950; New York: Random House, Vintage Books, 1961), p. 59; also see Mott, p. 318.

[31] See Elizabeth Fries Ellet, *The Pioneer Women of the West* (1852); facsimile reprint, Freeport, N.Y.: Books for Libraries Press, 1973), pp. vii, 43. Although John Frost did not acknowledge Flint as his source, his debt to both Filson and Flint is clear enough in his remarks on Rebecca Boone in *Heroic Women of the West: Comprising Thrilling Examples of Courage, Fortitude, Devotedness, and Self-Sacrifice, Among the Pioneer Mothers of the Western Country* (Philadelphia: A. Hart, 1854), pp. 26-31.

[32] Ellet, p. 49.

[33] Ibid., p. 56.

Christopher Castiglia (essay date 1996)

SOURCE: "The Wilderness of Fiction: From Captivity Narrative to Captivity Romance," in *Bound and Determined: Captivity, Culture-Crossing, and White Womanhood from Mary Rowlandson to Patty Hearst,* University of Chicago Press, 1996, pp. 106-36.

[*In the excerpt that follows, Castiglia studies female-authored captivity narratives in terms of gender relations and identity, finding that the works, which combine elements of both sentimental fiction and the wilderness tale, question culturally accepted notions of home and domesticity.*]

Captivity Narratives . . . have repeatedly transgressed boundaries between cultures and identities. As these historical narratives became fictionalized, they allowed white women authors to cross literary boundaries as well, combining conventional genres and challenging distinctions between fact and fiction. As Carter's "Our Lady of the Massacre" and editorial rewritings of the captives' accounts show, captivity narratives from their inception have complicated the apparently transparent overlap of experience and representation. Editorial tampering as well as more subtle restrictions in the available language result in the filtering of captives' experiences through cultural stories circulated in myth, folklore, expansion pamphlets, abolition tracts, and legal, scientific, and liturgical discourse, among other sources. Resisting an easy equation of autobiography and experientially supported "fact," captivity narratives have reproduced dominant constructions of the social world, but they have also imagined new stories—and hence new "realities"—for white women's lives in America.[1] . . .

. . . . .

The privileging of female community in white women's fiction occasioned a strikingly different textual closure than that imagined in most autobiographical accounts. In the captivity narratives, the greatest threat to the captive's extra-vagant imagination typically came neither at the moment of capture nor during her trek through a new physical and cultural terrain but on her return. ["Extra-vagant" comes from what Thoreau in *Walden* calls *extra-vagance,* a desire "to wander far beyond the narrow limits of my daily experience" so as "to speak somewhere *without* bounds" (1854, 240).] No matter how far a captive went toward joining the lives of her captors or challenging the assumptions of her home culture, such revision usually ceased once return appeared inevitable. Extraordinary exceptions notwithstanding, for captive white women going home meant acquiescing, if only partially and in the eleventh hour, to models of representation that supported the colonialist and patriarchal desires their texts previously resisted.

Typically, the captive's return—both physical and textual—is ensured and enforced by a human agent, a "rescuer," whose duty is not only to convey home the white captive but to supervise the reinscription of conventional narratives of identity on her body. Narratives such as K. White's, in which captives are either self-protected or returned home by other women, are rare; while captives frequently survived captivity with the help of other women, they were ultimately "rescued" only by a white man or a group of white men. Since, as the narratives of captives such as Patty Hearst demonstrate, the captive's body and her text become interchangeable through captivity, her reliance on men for rescue *in* the text determines her anticipation of a masculine readership *of* the text. Male rescuers thus become privileged readers, with equal access to the captive's body and to her text. Forced by historical necessity to anticipate and appeal to a masculine audience, white women frequently conclude their captivity by depicting themselves as passive, vulnerable, and xenophobic—in short, as "rescuable"—in marked contrast to their earlier self-representations.

A brief return to Fanny Kelly's *Narrative of My Captivity among the Sioux Indians* reveals both the historic necessity of anticipating a masculine audience and the disastrous consequences of "rescuability" for white women and their Indian captors. Kelly describes the surprise attack by a war party of Indians on an American wagon train escorted by Captain Fisk, who keeps the braves at bay for three days. The Sioux, waiting for the train to recommence its journey in order to ambush it from behind, urge Kelly to write a letter assuring Fisk of the Indians' friendly intentions. Recognizing that her only chance of rescue lies in keeping Fisk alive, Kelly forms a plan of her own.

> Knowing their malicious design, I set myself to work to circumvent them; and although the wily chief counted every word dictated, and as they were marked on paper, I contrived, by joining them together and condensing the information I gave, to warn the officer of the perfidious intentions of the savages, and tell him briefly of my helpless and unhappy captivity. (1871, 149)

Fisk answers that he has no intention of trusting the Indians, and the Sioux force Kelly to write a more convincing assurance.

> Again I managed to communicate with them, and this time begged them to use their field-glasses, and that I would find an excuse for standing on the hills in the afternoon, that they might see for themselves that I was what I represented myself to be—a white woman held in bondage. (150)

Kelly's strategy proves immediately gratifying both to herself and to the soldiers.

> The opportunity I desired was gained, and to my great delight, I had a chance of standing so as to be seen by the men of the soldier's [*sic*] camp. I had given my own name in every communication. As soon as the soldiers saw that it truly was a woman of their own race, and that I was in the power of their enemies, the excitement of their feeling became so great that they desired immediately to rush to my rescue. (150)

As Kelly's narrative makes clear, to be rescued women must first arouse desire—the desire to rescue—in men, which they accomplish by shaping themselves and their texts so as to be acceptable to the masculine audience on which rescue depends. Desire is awakened in Kelly's audience through the suggestion of a traditional rescue plot, the key elements of which are contained in her phrase, "in the power of their enemies." Manipulating both the Indians and the United States military by presenting herself as helpless, Kelly's self-representation is obviously paradoxical. Yet having survived life in captivity through a combination of fortitude and understanding, Kelly can return to her home culture only by asserting her vulnerability, her powerlessness, and her disdain for her culture's "enemies."

In presenting herself to male spectators, Kelly also becomes what female captives historically have been: an object of exchange in a power struggle between two groups of men. Kelly's objectification and its relation to the desire of the male soldiers become clear when she writes, "As soon as the soldiers saw that it truly was a woman of their own race . . . the excitement of their feeling became so great that they desired immediately to rush to my rescue." The same sentence that relates the arousal of the soldiers' desire witnesses the captive's transformation from an "I" to an "it," her prose registering her change from a subject to an object of both physical and textual exchange.[16] Having stripped herself of agency by representing herself as "helpless and unhappy," Kelly tries to maintain her independence by asserting her signature, noting, "I had given my own name in every communication." Yet Kelly is no longer in control of her text; her "name" is not hers to own. Like other captive white women, Kelly had little choice in anticipating a masculine audience, since the power of physical rescue lies with the strongholds of patriarchal authority: the government and the military. Yet in presenting her text to a masculine audience, Kelly perpetuates a narrative of female dependency and racial depravity, thereby transcribing the social and economic agenda of white men.

The dangerous irony of Kelly's transformed self-representation is that, in seeking "rescue" from Fisk's soldiers, she is threatened by further appropriation and powerlessness: her apparent passivity in relation to her rescuers places Kelly, as it would later place Patty Hearst, in a narrative of sexual objectification and control as well. The soldiers' "desire" to rescue Kelly on viewing her through their binoculars arises from the scopophilic dynamic of masculine/active/gaze and feminine/passive/spectacle that Laura Mulvey describes as characteristic of the fetishistic masculine gaze.[17] Kelly's letter fails to receive the "proper" response until her vulnerability is "embodied." Desire awakened by her letter therefore becomes connected to desire awakened by her body, while both are effective only insofar as they represent female powerlessness in the face of masculine vision and agency.

Kelly's transformation into a powerless object of sexualizing surveillance undertaken in the guise of rescue epitomizes the representational crisis encountered by numerous captive white women, who repeatedly resist the objectifying prurience not of their captors but of their countrymen. Mary Rowlandson refused the sexualization of vulnerability in the minds of her readers, asserting

> I have been in the midst of those roaring lions and savage bears that feared neither God nor man nor the devil, by night and day, alone and in company, sleeping all sorts together, and yet not one of them ever offered me the least abuse or unchastity to me in word or action. Though some are ready to say I speak it to my own credit, I speak it in the presence of God and to His glory. (1682, 70)

Two hundred years later Kelly made a similar assertion: "I had never suffered from any of [the Indians] the slightest personal or unchaste insult. Let me bear testimony to this redeeming feature in their treatment of me" (1871, 178). Following her arrest, Patty Hearst complains that the prison psychiatrists are interested in hearing only the sexual details of her kidnapping, despite her insistence that the SLA spent more time planning revolution than fornicating (1982, 376). That Rowlandson, Kelly, and Hearst all needed to refute the suggestion of rape, despite the fact that the Indians reportedly did not rape captives, points to an identification in the minds of their white audiences between captivity, race, and sexual vulnerability.[18] That connection, which perhaps lay behind what Rowlandson's ministerial editor refers to as the "coy phantasies" (Lincoln 1913, 115) of her readers, is articulated in the 1962 introduction to the reprint of in theirnarrative, where the editor reports, "The female captive, because of her greater potential for pathetic effects and because of the excitement she created as an object of sexual interest, all but crowded the male captive off the scene" (Zanger 1962, vi). The captive's efforts notwithstanding, something about "rescuability" suggests to white, male readers—both then and now—sexual availability, powerlessness, and hence "interest."

White male (super)vision has destructive consequences not only for the captive but for her captors as well. Dominant narratives of manifest destiny, from the colonial era through the present day, have relied for dramatic tension on the threatened sexualization of white women by men of color who possess uncontrollable, violent, and animalistic lusts. The persistent belief in the sexual "tainting" of white women through captivity, which exposes the captive to men of color, is revealed in the etymology of "rape," the root of which is the Latin verb, *rapere,* to seize, to capture, or to carry away. Yet captivity narratives repeatedly show that the depiction of captors as lurid threats to white innocence serves both to disguise white, male control of women's bodies and to justify the extermination of the Indians and the appropriation of their lands. Sarah Wakefield describes the pressure white soldiers put on redeemed captives to produce rape narratives that activated retaliatory "rescue" campaigns, bringing large profits to white men. White women who believe that "rescue" is undertaken on their behalf, and not in the service of imperialism, pay a heavy price for their naïveté. Kelly relates the story of Mrs. Blynn, a captive who sends a letter to her father urging him to have the governor of Kansas sign a peace treaty with the Sioux so she may return home. Instead, Custer's men "came charging with loud huzzahs upon the village" (1871, 248), resulting not only in the murder of Mrs. Blynn by her captors but in the slaughter of the entire Sioux tribe.

Kelly's narrative ends by dramatizing these losses suffered by women and Indians due to "rescuability." After her redemption, Kelly finds herself alone and destitute; her husband has died of cholera, and her narrative appears in a pirated edition before Kelly can enjoy any profits from its publication. Her only means of support is government compensation, promised to her by one of her most avid readers, President Ulysses S. Grant. But Kelly encounters "difficulties" in receiving her money, and while Congress eventually passes a bill granting Kelly five thousand dollars, no one tells her of the proposed bill until after it is passed. Ironically, in Kelly's financial support comes not from the United States government or her white countrymen but from her former captors. Kelly one day encounters on the streets of Washington a group of familiar Sioux who have come to collect money for lands appropriated by the government. Appalled by her financial distress, the Sioux ask Kelly to draw up a bill of losses suffered at their hands, which they immediately present to the Secretary of Indian Affairs, demanding that she be paid from monies owed to the tribe. The final depiction of shared litigation challenges the faith Kelly has placed in a white, male audience and in the rescue it provides. Far from having gained "insider" status by anticipating that audience, Kelly finds herself like her captors relying for definition and sustenance on a government she could not elect and which is interested in her only as a symbol of powerlessness and suffering.

The authors of the captivity romances were as aware of the dangers posed to their heroines by masculine rescue as they were of the adventures offered by captivity in the wilderness. In *A Peep at the Pilgrims,* for example, Edward Atherton launches a campaign to rescue Miriam Grey that results in a bloody war between the Pequods and the Plymouth colony. When Atherton later boasts of rescuing Miriam, Miles Standish responds, "'I cannot learn that she was in any danger, till you provoked the Indians to vengeance'" (1824, 454). Cheney contrasts Atherton's "private and romantic enterprise" (386) with a more peaceful and effective plan: Miriam's Indian "mother," Mioma, works diligently to ensure the captive's release and is near success when Atherton's actions force the chief back into an adversarial role.

Never having been captured themselves, the authors of captivity romances were at greater liberty to reimagine rescue and the modes of self-representation it offers the captive heroine. As Cheney's alternative to masculine rescue suggests, in the wilderness of fiction women rescue other women, bringing the heroine not from Indian captivity to the "freedom" of white society but from isolation in households dominated by fathers to communities imagined through the enabling fiction of shared gender identity.[19] Like their narrative sources, furthermore, captivity romances equate rescue with reading, although again they differ in inscribing a readership of women. In the captivity romances, rescue does not come through the solitary heroics of men like Atherton, leading to alienation or to the loss of agency, as in Kelly's. Rather, rescue arises from a community composed of "sisters" who are in turn invited to share a literary meeting place and a coded indictment of the constraint and coercion in women's daily experiences.

America's first captivity fiction, Ann Eliza Bleecker's *The History of Maria Kittle* (1793), presents an instructive contrast to the rescue depicted in Fanny Kelly's narrative. Bleecker begins her tale by critiquing the masculine agency at the center of conventional rescue plots. Bleecker depicts men as stubborn and rash, motivated by a self-destructive fatality that renders "protection" and desertion at their hands equally calamitous to women. Despite his distrust of the Indians, Mr. Kittle (he never receives a first name) leaves his wife alone with the Indians when they come to warn the Kittles of an imminent raid, and then, believing their warning, again deserts Maria while he travels to Albany to seek a safer house for his family. When Mr. Kittle plans to leave his family alone a third time, Maria expresses her frustration with male adventure, "'Is it not enough . . . that you have escaped one danger, but must you be so very eager to encounter others?'" (31). Other husbands who, like Mr. Kittle, abandon their wives to captivity have received justification from male authors. When Mr. Duston left his wife Hannah to battle the Indians alone, Hawthorne rose to his defense. In "The Duston Family," Hawthorne writes that Hannah, who rescued herself when she murdered and scalped her Indian captors, will be "remembered as long as the deeds of old times are told" as "the bloody old hag" who should have "drowned in crossing Contocook River," while her husband will be recalled as a "tender-hearted yet valiant man" (1900, 238). Bleecker offers no such defense. When Mr. Kittle cries, "Burst—burst my shrinking heart, and punish a wretch for not having died in the defense of such lovely and innocent beings! Oh! why was I absent in this fatal hour?" (1793, 46), Bleecker meets his question with pointed silence.

The same self-destructive rashness characterizes Mr. Kittle's life after Maria's capture. Rather than attempting to find his wife, Mr. Kittle throws himself into a suicidal stint in the army; "in hopes of ending a being that grew insupportable under the reflection of past happiness, he tempted death in every action wherein he was engaged, and being disappointed, gave himself up to the blackest melancholy" (85). Other men prove more dramatically destructive in their fatality. When the Indians come to the Kittle home, Maria is in the company of her sister-in-law, Comelia, and Comelia's husband. As the Indians attempt to break down the door, Comelia's "'rash, rash, unfortunate husband'" opens the door to the attackers, urging his distraught wife to "'be resigned to the will of God'" (35). The tempering of "rash" with "unfortunate" does not disguise the blame Comelia (or Bleecker) puts on her husband for their imminent deaths. Most disturbing is Comelia's final plea—"'Have mercy on yourself, on me, on my child'" (35)—made not of the Indians, but of her nominal "protector."

Rather than relying on masculine agency for their rescue, Bleecker's women—represented, in contrast to the men, as rational and courageous—are either aided by other women or are self-delivered. Mrs. Willis makes the difficult journey to Montreal to redeem her husband, "flushed with hope, and with indefatigable industry and painful solitude" (80) (after his friends point out the dangers, Mr. Kittle abandons the very same plan for redeeming Maria). During her captivity Maria never loses her "stoical composure" (52). When the Indians surrender Maria and her brother to the governor of Montreal, he begins questioning them harshly. From the crowd curiously observing the interview emerges Mrs. D——, an Englishwoman "whom humanity more than curiosity had drawn to the place" (63). Mrs. D——, moved by "the soft impulses of nature" (63), intercedes with the governor and is granted permission to take Maria to her home, where she shows her new "sister" so much tenderness that Maria "again melted into tears; but it was a gush of grateful acknowledgment" (66-67). Rescue comes to Maria, finally, not through masculine heroics, but through female sympathy and "sisterly" affection. Even Maria's role as narrator is created through her bond with Mrs. D——. During the governor's questioning, Maria remains petrified and mute. Under the Englishwoman's care, however, the "tempest of [Maria's] soul subsided in a solemn calm; and though she did not regain her vivacity, she became agreeably conversable" (66). Moved not by "curiosity" but "humanity," not prurience but empathy, Mrs. D——rescues Maria not only from her period of captivity but from a debilitating silence as well.

Just as Maria's story is "redeemed" by a sympathetic female auditor, so Bleecker's new rescue plot is enabled by an equally new, specifically female audience capable of recognizing and drawing strength from the codes of the captivity story. Bleecker inscribes a female readership first through the epistolary form of her text, composed as a letter from the narrator to her sister. Bleecker constructs an even wider female audience within the events of the narrative. When Mrs. D——arranges a tea in Maria's honor, the women who attend—French and English gentlewomen as well as other American captives—call upon each other to tell their stories, which are heard amid "tears, and pleasing melancholy" (68). Although not all the women assembled at Mrs. D——'s have been abducted, the degree to which *all* female auditors appear to identify with the captives highlights the captivity narrative's particular significance for audiences of women. Sharing their feelings of isolation and powerlessness, the women of Bleecker's text have their less tangible constraints embodied and validated. Women reading Bleecker's text are encouraged to witness the powerful benefits of female community, to sympathize with female suffering, and to admire female strength, endurance, and resolution. They are also offered, through the representation of a female audience, membership in that community. In the end the women declare sisterhood that crosses class and national (although not racial) barriers:[20] ' "I now reject (interrupted MRS. BRATT) all prejudices of education. From my infancy have I been taught that the French were a cruel perfidious enemy, but I have found them quite the reverse" ' (73). Where Kelly's relationship to her spectators hinges on gender difference, Bleecker's is predicated on an empathy—a faith in shared experience—between speaker and audience.

The women of Bleecker's text arguably form America's first literary consciousness-raising group. Teresa de Lauretis describes consciousness raising as "the process of self-representation which defines 'I' as a woman, or, in other words, en-genders the subject as female" (1984, 159). The political potential of this en-gendering, according to de Lauretis, lies in the critical revision of social reality, undertaken in two stages. In the first, a woman "places [herself] or is placed in social reality, and so perceives and comprehends as subjective (referring to, even originating in, oneself) those relations—material, economic, and interpersonal—which are in fact social and, in a larger perspective, historical" (159). Having found her subjectivity in the "social world," a woman may then share her narrative with others who have had similar experiences, collectively constructing a discourse that at once validates female subjectivity (showing that her interactions with society are not aberrant or neurotic) and enacts "a continual modification of consciousness; that consciousness in turn being the condition of social change" (184). The change brought about by consciousness raising need not be "in 'concrete action,'" de Lauretis notes, "but in a disposition, a readiness (for action), a set of expectations" (178).

The narrators of autobiographical accounts undertake the first stage of consciousness raising, understanding the experience of captivity, enacted on their bodies, to represent social and historical relations. At the point of return, however, they surrender their participation in the second stage, in which female subjectivity is validated and changed. The female community inscribed in Bleecker's text returns the captive to the second stage of consciousness building, thereby transforming both the captivity narrative and its heroine. If her newfound community does not "change" patriarchal discourses of gender, it does enable the heroine to articulate her social experience of constraint in ways that transform her from an object to a subject of interpretation. Put another way, if Kelly's interaction with a masculine audience marks the end of her self-inscriptions, Maria Kittle, in finding a female audience, has just begun to speak. For Maria's audience, her powers of narration are her primary attraction, rendering the captive heroine visible as the subject of discourse and desire, not solely as their object.

Of course, the very community that rescues both captive and author from masculine appropriation simultaneously binds them to dominant representations of "true womanhood" as well. To appeal to an emerging female readership, both the captive and her creator must conform to certain conventions: the former must be emotional and nurturing, temperamentally attached to all other women, while the latter must communicate in the language of sentiment and triumphant sisterhood. The very concept of "female community," as Nancy Cott and others have argued, emerges from a discursive "separation of spheres" that, while it gave women a common identity that allowed them to come together in imagined commonality, also represented them as unsuited for the "public sphere" of men and masculinity. Rendering rescue as restrictive as well as liberating, even when it comes at the hands of other women, the captivity romances demonstrate the impossibility of any ultimate "freedom" for women characters. The inescapability of representational overdetermination in the romances thus echoes the continual "captivity" of the autobiographical narrators who, held hostage in their own society by tyrannical fathers and lovers, again become captives in the "wilderness," often in the same way as at home—as surrogate mothers, daughters, and housekeepers.

At the same time, however, the heroine's captivity ends in a cultural liminality from which she criticizes the conventions of her own society and explores alternative narratives for women. For example, the captivity romances show the gender conventions apparently policed through "female community" to be contradictory constructions, capable of leading women into the very discursive "spheres" they were designed to foreclose. Women's domestic and nurturing nature suits them for lives outside the home, free of their families, while the communities borne of "sameness" increasingly permit the heroine to articulate her salutory knowledge of transcultural "difference." In the captivity romance, then, one can never return to the community one has left behind, nor can one enter one's newfound community, without exceeding the representational—and hence the ideological—borders of both. From that excess, however, arises the possibility for what Leigh Gilmore, in reference to women's autobiographies, calls "unruly subjects who are unevenly objectified and who represent identity in relation to other values and subjectivities" (1994, 12). Unlike the masculine romantic dream of life "without bounds," female extra-vagance, gained through the captivity story, thus resists the utopian impression of "freedom" that, as D. H. Lawrence notes, is the surest sign of one's imprisonment.[21] Rescue leaves women not in a state of antesocial liberty but in the moment of articulation arising between two forms of confinement.

At least one community, however, must grant the female subject permission to experiment, to exceed her objectification and speak. As long as autobiographical narrators could imagine a return only to the patriarchal community they had left behind, no such experimentation was possible. Fanny Kelly at one point in her narrative attempts, like Maria Kittle, an epistolary escape. As she is carried into captivity, Kelly leaves a trail of letters so her rescuers can find her. When after some time she realizes that no rescuer is following her paper trail, Kelly, who dedicates her *Narrative* to Fisk's soldiers, admits, "my great fear was that my letter had not fallen into the right hands" (1871, 205). To ensure that her text fell into the "right" hands, Bleecker advertised for her desired readership, one that could imagine more complex social arrangements and subjective identifications, for whom "rescue" would not mean "return." Within the circle of her captive audience, Maria Kittle is returned neither to a false promise of liberty nor to absolute overdetermination. Rather, she tells a tale that resists the naturalized binaries of white, middle-class America and concludes, if not with freedom, then with a more authorizing mode of rescue.

The critique enabled through liminality in the plot is echoed in the captivity romance's liminality of genre. The captivity romance was never entirely distinct from the more "acceptable" female genres of each period. Susanna Rowson, author of America's most renowned sentimental novel, *Charlotte Temple,* cast *Reuben and Rachel* within the Richardsonian tradition. Two authors of captivity romances, Eliza Cushing and Harriet Cheney, were daughters of another well-known sentimental novelist, Hannah Foster, author of *The Coquette,* and drew on their mother's literary style in their novels. Catharine Sedgwick was one of the most successful domestic novelists of the early nineteenth century and used many conventions of that genre in *Hope Leslie.* These authors introduced the captivity narrative into already existing narrative structures, modifying both. Just as the heroine exists in a liminality between

cultures that allows us to "read" both of her captivities, so the text exists in a liminality that reveals how certain genres reflect and perpetuate the cultural attitudes the heroine encounters in a more immediate and threatening manner within the events of the narrative.

From its inception, the captivity romance has crossed traditional generic boundaries particularly in order to contrast, and hence denaturalize, depictions of "womanhood." On one level, Ann Eliza Bleecker's *The History of Maria Kittle* is a novel of sensibility.[22] Describing Mr. Kittle's actions on finding his home destroyed and his family either murdered or captured, Bleecker interrupts her narrative to address her female reader: "But doubtless, my dear, your generous sensibility is alarmed by my silence about Mrs. Kittle" (1793, 48). Within the narrative, one of Maria's auditors cries, "'my heart is now sweetly tuned to melancholy. I love to indulge these divine sensibilities, which your affecting histories are so capable of inspiring'" (73), while Maria, even in the midst of her captivity, indulges in "the luxury of sorrow" (56). By introducing "sensibility" as a privileged concern of her captivity story, Bleecker places the wilderness tale within the realm of women's authority—emotion—and puts the suffering heroine in a central and sympathetic position.

Yet Bleecker also contradicts and modifies the expectations produced by the appearance of "sensibility" in *The History of Maria Kittle,* thereby avoiding a seeming endorsement of female suffering.[23] As Mary Poovey argues, the novel of sensibility with its "emotional indulgence served not only to sublimate frustrated sexual desire but also to inflame emotion and thus keep [the heroine] hostage to passion" (1984, 54). Carroll Smith-Rosenberg argues that women writers of the 1790s frequently warned female readers of the dangers of sentimental romances, not only "because they taught women sex and passion for men but because they taught women to renounce their own reason and independence" (1988, 177). Bleecker resists these dangerous renunciations by consistently contradicting the signifiers of suffering: "the *eloquence* of sorrow," "the *luxury* of sorrow," "*sweetly* tuned to melancholy." Suffering is no longer imposed from without on an unwilling female subject who lacks all agency in the drama of seduction and/or abandonment; rather, it becomes a relished and cultivated form of expression. Exaggerating their emotional suffering, furthermore, the women of Bleecker's text make their role as victims apparent *as* role, thereby denaturalizing their position in oppressive social dramas.

Beyond her play with the content of sensibility, Bleecker complicates the sentimental depiction of women as domestic, emotional, and spiritual, juxtaposing the world of feeling and its genre—the novel of sensibility—with the world of action and its genre—the wilderness tale. By contrasting genres, Bleecker foregrounds the ideological contradiction between cultural prescription and resistance experienced within the narrative by Maria herself. The moment of greatest generic conflict in *The History of Maria Kittle* occurs precisely when Maria is faced with the difficult choice between a return to her previous domestic life or a commitment to the adventure and community she has found in the wilderness. During the course of Maria's captivity, from the time of Comelia's death to the entrance of Mrs. D——, Bleecker's language remains measured, the prose mirroring Maria's "stoic" composure. Even in the company of Mrs. D——and her friends, Maria and her prose remain relatively controlled. Maria becomes a heroine of (overwrought) sensibility only when reunited with her husband. Seeing Mr. Kittle, "The tide of joy and surprise was too strong for the delicacy of her frame; she gave a final exclamation, and stretching out her arms to receive him, dropped senseless at his feet" (1793, 82). The Kittles' reunion effects a representational transformation, as a woman who has survived captivity in the wilderness suddenly becomes delicate of frame. While Maria must be strong to survive captivity and tell her tale, she must be inscribed within the role of a delicate, fainting wife if she is to fit culturally acceptable models of womanhood. In short, Maria is caught in the crossover from the wilderness to the parlor, from her existence as a strong survivor to her reemergence into her "proper sphere." The tension between the two worlds—one of action and the other of feeling—is represented in *The History of Maria Kittle* by a conflict of genres.

Later captivity romances, following Bleecker in her use of the captivity narrative to modify existing literary genres and the cultural ideologies they inscribe, provide one of the most striking enactments in American literature of what M. M. Bakhtin has called "heteroglossia." When a text usually considered "nonliterary" yet also essential to the novel's development (Bakhtin here includes the confession, the diary, the conversion narrative—all forms the captivity narrative has taken at one time or another) enters a more traditionally "literary" genre, the author deploys two languages "to avoid giving himself up wholly to either of them; he makes use of this verbal give-and-take, this dialogue of languages at every point in his work, in order that he himself might remain as it were neutral with regard to language, a third party in a quarrel between two people (although he might be a *biased* third party)" (1981, 314). Bakhtin's description of the conflict between languages and of the author's position as a fought-over subject attempting to free himself (Bakhtin assumes the author is male) from the confines of either, accurately describes the situation of the heroine *within* the captivity romance. Fought over by white and Indian men, in whose economy she serves as metonym for the land and capital at stake, the captive attempts to remain neutral—or to carve out a third subjectivity, identified with neither of the masculine parties—in order to escape domination by either. The social restrictions imposed by either of her captivities (within a domestic or sentimental ideology on one hand, or as a passive item of exchange on the other) battle each other through their respective, representative genres, the result being that both sides begin to lose their definitive claim on "truth," giving rise instead to a cultural relativism in which the heroine can reimagine her status in both worlds.

This is the process Bakhtin, moving beyond the plane of the strictly literary, calls "social heteroglossia": a "dialogue of two voices, two world views, two languages" (325). Through the creation of social heteroglossia, the novel deconstructs the illusion of "a sacrosanct, unconditional language" (324)—thereby also questioning the cultural hegemony represented by that language—by "making available points of view that . . . exist outside literary conventionality" (323). Heteroglossia serves in the captivity romances not to replace one view of/from womanhood with another, substituting and universalizing the frontier novel's representation of women in place of that contained in domestic or sentimental literature; rather, it seeks, by putting two often conflicting depictions of women side by side, to question whether "womanhood" can ever be definitively fixed in literature. Through the layering of genre, the authors of the captivity romance therefore introduce difference into the construction of white womanhood as well.

With its combination of the emotion and the female community so central to domestic or sentimental fiction and the extra-vagance that lies at the heart of the wilderness tale, the captivity romance occupies a final liminal space: the uncharted territory between the terrains mapped out by critics of American literature. This final liminality has proven less beneficial, however, for the genre's refusal to follow either a "masculine" or a "feminine" plot has ensured its invisibility in both traditional and revisionist considerations of American literary history. The captivity narratives unfortunately prove Nancy K. Miller's insight that to "depart from the limits of common sense (tautologically, to be extravagant) is to risk exclusion from the canon" (1988, 25).

Traditionally, the wilderness has been the domain of the American Adam. Literary criticism has neglected women writers in general but has been particularly reluctant to consider women in the wilderness. In her groundbreaking "Melodramas of Beset Manhood, or How Theories of American Fiction Exclude Women Authors," Nina Baym exposes the sexism of critics who have made stories of the frontier the central myth of America. Baym's quarrel with traditional literary history is not, however, that it excludes women writers who wrote wilderness tales. Rather, Baym accepts the traditional critical premise that the mobility required for wilderness adventure is "a male prerogative" (1985,

72), placing the entire genre of wilderness fiction beyond the reach of women. Baym's assessment is understandable if one considers only the wilderness tales accounted for in traditional literary history—the novels of Cooper and the tales of Daniel Boone—in which women are indeed rendered as essentially immobile, unfit for life outside "civilization." When one considers the captivity romances, however, a different "wilderness' emerges, and consequently a different configuration of gender outside the home.

The women-authored captivity romances have been overlooked because the central binary of traditional literary history—in which men thrive in the wilderness while women rule at home—has been circulated even in feminist revisions of the American canon.[24] Many recent discussions of women and American literature present domesticity as empowering rather than—or at least at the same time as—confining, but do not challenge the inherited equation of women and the home. Claiming that the "ethic of sentimental fiction, unlike that of writers like Melville, Emerson, and Thoreau, was an ethic of submission," Jane Tompkins, for example, contends that American women "lacked the material means of escape or opposition. They had to stay put and submit" (1985, 161). In response to this "lack," Tompkins concludes, "the domestic novelists made that necessity the basis on which to build a power structure of their own" (161).

Tompkins' analysis, like the novels she discusses, seems to make a virtue of a perceived necessity, rather than challenging the association of women with the home or questioning the "fact" of women's powerlessness in the face of social prescription. Tompkins ignores that several of the novelists whom she claims "had to stay put and submit" also wrote wilderness novels that express both a dissatisfaction with domesticity and an ability to partake in a supposedly "masculine" resistance. Reclaiming domesticity as a site of women's culture and a source of strength has led to valuable reassessments of nineteenth-century women's literature, but it has simultaneously diminished the work of authors who expressed in their wilderness novels a strong dissatisfaction with domesticity, no matter how enobling that realm might be.[25]

A response from within feminist literary criticism has argued the dangers of assuming that women moved without resistance into their domestication, or that domesticity itself was a singular and uncomplicated phenomenon.[26] Karen Sanchez-Eppler, for instance, has noted that a model of literary history that "accepts the notion of domesticity as a separate, enclosed sphere" (1992, 348) perpetuates "the two basic presumptions of the cult of domesticity . . . : not only does the home remain essentially separate from the public realm, but in its adherence to a moral, nurturant, and noncompetitive ethos the domestic sphere is itself construed as

inherently undivided" (348). Literary histories that assume generic "purity" based on conceptions of a self-contained, undivided sphere thereby perpetuate gender essentialism, argues Sanchez-Eppler, who favors instead the model of domesticity marked by division or contradiction, the "self-divided and therefore anti-essentialist domestic scene" (353).

A consideration of the captivity romances, which depict a highly complicated "domesticity" and jarringly combine supposedly "separate" spheres, provides an ideal opportunity to reconsider not only cultural constructions of gender but the ways in which literary histories inscribe those constructions through their framings of "appropriate" mythologies. In their combination of domestic or sentimental fiction and the wilderness tale, the captivity romances question essentialist constructions of "identity" in terms of both individual characters and cultural mythologies, and thereby open the way for new revisions and reinscriptions of gender and of literary history. Until we recognize women's place in creating the wilderness of fiction, a realm that complicates the very binarisms criticism has unwittingly perpetuated, we have refused women writers their most important form of extra-vagance: "the extravagant wish," as Nancy K. Miller writes, "for a *story* that would turn out differently" (1988, 40).

Notes

[1] For a fuller discussion of how women's autobiographies, particularly those employing cultural "crossing," blur distinctions between fact and fiction in order to achieve agency for women, see Leigh Gilmore (1994). . . .

[16] Kelly again refers to herself in the third person throughout the concluding chapter of her narrative, in which she recounts General Sully's campaign against the Indians. Whenever she enters the discourse of struggle "between men," as Eve Kosofsky Sedgwick notes, a woman can be no more than an object of exchange; Kelly's choice of pronouns registers that objectification in her text.

[17] "In a world ordered by sexual inbalance," Laura Mulvey writes, "pleasure in looking has been split between active/male and passive/female. The determining male gaze projects its fantasy onto the female figure, which is styled accordingly. In their traditional exhibitionist role women are simultaneously looked at and displayed, with their appearance coded for strong visual and erotic impact so that they can be said to connote to-be-looked-at-ness" (1989, 19).

[18] The claim that Indians did not rape white women captives is made by Ulrich (1980) and by Vaughan and Clark (1981). James Axtell attributes the Indians' lack of sexual interest in white female captives to a differ-

ent aesthetic standard ("the New England Indians, at least, esteemed black the color of beauty"), a strong incest taboo (most captives were adopted into families as female relatives), and to "a religious ethic of strict warrior continence" (1985, 310). Susan Brownmiller argues that materials published subsequent to the Kelly narrative suggest that she and other captives *were* raped (1975, 140-53). Among the narratives I have read, one captive—Ann Coleson—reports being raped by her Sioux captors, while several claim they never experienced or heard reports of Indian rape. Gertrude Morgan writes that "the crime of ravishing captive women, so common and hellish a vice among civilized nations, *is entirely unknown.* That statement may dissipate the romance many writers have imparted to their stories of the Indians and beautiful white captive maidens, but it is nevertheless a fact" (1866, 29).

As Morgan indicates, at work in reports of Indians raping white women is less a concern for white women's safety than a prurient white fantasy. The sexualization of the captive's vulnerability can be analyzed through Catharine MacKinnon's connection of stereotypical female gender roles and the subordinated position women occupy in heterosexuality. As MacKinnon writes, "Vulnerability means the appearance/reality of easy sexual access; passivity means receptivity and disabled resistance, enforced by trained physical weakness; softness means pregnability by something hard. Incompetence seeks help as vulnerability seeks shelter, inviting the embrace that becomes the invasion, trading exclusive access for protection . . . from the same access" (1982, 530). That the terms MacKinnon chooses to describe women's sexual position—"seeks help," "invasion," "trading exclusive access for protection"—so closely parallel the language of "rescue" is itself telling. The narratives of Rowlandson, Kelly, and Hearst bear out MacKinnon's thesis, as each shows the narrative of masculine rescue leading to the discourse of sexual desire and ultimately of rape.

[19] I borrow the concept of the "imagined community" from Benedict Anderson's 1983 study of the rise of nationalism. For a fuller discussion of Anderson's argument and its relationship to the imagined gender communities inscribed in the captivity romances, see chapter 5.

[20] Subsequent captivity romances explore the bonds between white women and Indians left unexamined in Bleecker's text. See chapters 5 and 6.

[21] In "The Spirit of Place," D. H. Lawrence writes, "Men are free when they belong to a living, organic, *believing* community, active in fulfilling some unfulfilled, perhaps unrealized purpose. Not when they are escaping to some wild west. The most unfree souls go west, and shout of freedom. The shout is a rattling of chains, always was" (1923, 6).

[22] Pearce first made the case for Bleecker's text as "simply a captivity narrative turned novel of sensibility" (1947, 13).

[23] While some critics, most notably Jane Tompkins and Nancy Armstrong, have persuasively argued that sentimentalism potentially empowers women, Bleecker, working within a wider repertoire of genres, appears to have associated the language of sentimentalism with female frailty and domestic confinement.

[24] Annette Kolodny is one of the few critics to consider carefully women's writings on the American frontier; yet even Kolodny argues that frontier women never left their homes behind, striving to create domesticated gardens in the wilderness.

[25] For a fuller critique of Tompkins' argument, see Myers (1988).

[26] Gillian Brown's *Domestic Individualism* (1990) argues that nineteenth-century gender ideologies were far more complex than "separate sphere" history would lead contemporary readers to believe.

Works Cited

Anderson, Benedict. 1983. *Imagined Communities: Reflections on the Origin and Spread of Nationalism.* London: Verso.

Armstrong, Nancy. 1987. *Desire and Domestic Fiction: A Political History of the Novel.* New York: Oxford University Press.

Axtell, James. 1985. *The Invasion Within: The Contest of Cultures in Colonial North America.* New York: Oxford University Press.

Bakhtin, M. M. 1981. *The Dialogic Imagination: Four Essays.* Ed. Michael Holquist. Trans. Caryl Emerson and Michael Holquist. Austin: University of Texas Press.

Baym, Nina. 1985. "Melodramas of Beset Manhood: How Theories of American Fiction Exclude Women Authors." Pp. 63-80 in *The New Feminist Criticism: Essays on Women, Literature and Theory,* ed. Elaine Showalter. New York: Pantheon.

Bleecker, Ann Eliza. 1793. *The Posthumous Works of Ann Eliza Bleecker, in Prose and Verse.* Ed. Margaretta V. Fangeres. New York: T. and J. Swords.

Brown, Gillian. 1990. *Domestic Individualism: Imagining Self in Nineteenth-Century America.* Berkeley and Los Angeles: University of California Press.

Brownmiller, Susan. 1975. *Against Our Wills: Men, Women and Rape.* New York: Simon and Schuster.

Cheney, Harriet. 1824. *A Peep at the Pilgrims.* Boston: Phillips, Samson.

Coleson, Ann. 1864. *Miss Coleson's Narrative of Her Captivity among the Sioux Indians.* Philadelphia: Barclay.

de Lauretis, Teresa. 1984. *Alice Doesn't: Feminism, Semiotics, Cinema.* Bloomington: Indiana University Press.

Drake, Samuel Gardiner. 1851. *Indian Captivities; or, Life in the Wigwam.* Auburn: Derby and Miller.

Drimmer, Frederick. 1961. *Scalps and Tomahawks: Narratives of Indian Captivity.* New York: Coward-McCann.

Gilmore, Leigh. 1994. *Autobiographics: A Feminist Theory of Women's Self-Representation.* Ithaca, N.Y.: Cornell University Press.

Hawthorne, Nathaniel. 1900. "The Duston Family." *The Complete Writings of Nathaniel Hawthorne.* Vol. 17, pp. 229-38. New York: Houghton, Mifflin.

Hearst, Patricia Campbell. 1988. *Patty Hearst.* With Alvin Moscow. New York: Avon.

————. 1982. *Every Secret Thing.* With Alvin Moscow. Garden City, N.Y.: Doubleday.

Kelly, Fanny. 1871. *Narrative of My Captivity among the Sioux Indians.* Hartford: Mutual Publishing. Also reprinted in Drimmer (1961) and Peckham (1954).

Kolodny, Annette. 1984. *The Land before Her: Fantasy and Experience of the American Frontiers, 1630-1860.* Chapel Hill: University of North Carolina Press.

Lawrence, D. H. [1923] 1969. *Studies in Classic American Literature.* New York: Viking.

Lincoln, Charles. 1913. *Narratives of the Indian Wars, 1675-1699.* New York: Charles Scribner's Sons.

MacKinnon, Catharine A. 1982. "Feminism, Marxism, Methodology, and the State: An Agenda For Theory." *Signs* 7 (spring): 515-44.

Miller, Nancy K. 1988. *Subject to Change: Reading Feminist Writing.* New York: Columbia University Press.

Morgan, Gertrude. 1866. *Gertrude Morgan; or, Life and Adventures among the Indians of the Far West.* Philadelphia: Barclay.

Mulvey, Laura. 1989. *Visual and Other Pleasures.* Bloomington: Indiana University Press.

Myers, D. G. 1988. "The Canonization of Susan Warner." *The New Criterion* (December): 73-78.

Pearce, Roy Harvey. 1947. "The Significances of the Captivity Narrative." *American Literature* 19:1-20.

Peckham, Howard H. 1954. *Captured by Indians: True Tales of Pioneer Survivors.* New Brunswick, N.J.: Rutgers University Press.

Poovey, Mary. 1984. *The Proper Lady and the Woman Writer: Ideology as Style in the Works of Mary Wollstonecraft, Mary Shelley, and Jane Austen.* Chicago: University of Chicago Press.

Rowlandson, Mary. 1682. "The Sovereignty and Goodness of God." Pp. 31-75 in Vaughan and Clark (1981); also reprinted in Drake (1851); Peckham (1954), and VanDerBeets (1973).

Sanchez-Eppler, Karen. 1992. "American Houses: Constructions of History and Domesticity." *American Literary History* 4 (Summer): 345-53.

Sedgwick, Eve Kosofsky. 1985. *Between Men: English Literature and Male Homosocial Desire.* New York: Columbia University Press.

Smith-Rosenberg, Carroll. 1988. "Domesticating Virtue: Coquettes and Revolutionaries in Young America." Pp. 160-84 in *Literature and the Body: Essays on Populations and Persons. Selected Papers from the English Institute, 1986,* ed. Elaine Scarry. Baltimore: The Johns Hopkins University Press.

Thoreau, Henry David. [1854] 1958. *Walden; or, Life in the Woods.* New York: Harper and Row.

Tompkins, Jane. 1985. *Sensational Designs: The Cultural Work of American Fiction, 1790-1860.* New York: Oxford University Press.

Ulrich, Laurel Thatcher. 1980. *Good Wives: Image and Reality in the Lives of Women in Northern New England, 1650-1750.* New York: Oxford University Press.

VanDerBeets, Richard. 1973. *Held Captive by Indians: Selected Narratives, 1642-1836.* Knoxville: University of Tennessee Press.

Vaughan, Alden T. and Edward W. Clark. 1981. *Puritans among the Indians: Accounts of Captivity and Redemption, 1676-1724.* Cambridge, Mass.: Harvard University Press.

Zanger, Jules, ed. [1873] 1962. *Narrative of My Captivity among the Sioux Indians.* By Fanny Kelly. New York: Corinth.

MORAL INSTRUCTION

James A. Levernier (essay date 1978)

SOURCE: "The Captivity Narrative as Children's Literature," in *The Markham Review*, Vol. 8, Fall, 1978, pp. 54-59.

[*In the following essay, Levernier maintains that nineteenth-century captivity narratives written specifically for children and young adults were intended to convey moral, religious, and political lessons.*]

Between 1820 and 1860 the wave of cultural nationalism that profoundly affected the writings of Washington Irving, James Fenimore Cooper, and Nathaniel Hawthorne also influenced literature written primarily for America's rising generation of young people. Prior to the 1820s, American children's literature had been, as R. Gordon Kelly notes, "simply a variant of English taste" but the spirit of achievement, pride, and cultural satisfaction that spread throughout America during the decades preceding the Civil War gave shape to a type of children's literature that, according to John C. Crandall, reflected "the nationalistic spirit which nurtured it."[1] Affirmations of the American Dream—stories of frontier life and adventure, biographies of American heroes, and tales of the rise from rags to riches—replaced Old World sagas about the exploits of kings, princesses, knights, and aristocrats as the literature that mid-nineteenth-century Americans, anxious to preserve and to foster their country's democratic ideals, encouraged their youth to read.[2] Even religious institutions, whose primary goal was to teach the Bible, not nationalism, insisted that Sunday School tracts be "thoroughly American in their coloring and environment."[3]

It should come as little surprise, then, that a significant number of children's stories written in America during the decades between 1820 and 1860 are about the true and fictitious experiences of Indian captives. Narratives of Indian captivity were a uniquely New World tradition which, by the 1820s, was thoroughly a part of American lore and popular culture. During the sixteenth and seventeenth centuries, narratives about the captivities of explorers like Captain John Smith provided Europeans with their first glimpse of the lifestyle and character of the American natives. Seventeenth-century Puritans, Catholics, and Quakers used captivity narratives to illustrate the mysterious workings of divine providence. With the onset of the French and Indian Wars, the Revolutionary War, and the later Indian wars, captivity narratives were converted into propaganda for the expulsion, assimilation, or destruction of the Indian and his French and British allies. They also stimulated the imaginations of literary artists like James Fenimore Cooper, whose Leatherstocking Tales, with their series of Indian wars, pursuits, and captures, participate in a tradition which could be easily and, as was thought, profitably adapted to the needs and forms of children's literature.[4] Written or rewritten for children, narratives of Indian captivity afforded a decidedly American medium for the entertainment and instruction of the young in such subjects as reading, writing, history and moral behavior—though not necessarily in that order—as well as for the perpetuation of conventional attitudes, among them the conviction of white, Protestant, Anglo-Saxon superiority.

Because nineteenth-century educators considered fact more edifying than fiction,[5] captivity stories written for children were usually about the experiences of an actual Indian captive, and, since these experiences usually occurred on the frontier during times of border warfare, such stories provided an excellent opportunity to teach children about their American heritage. *The Deerfield Captive* (1831), for example, is "a narrative of facts for the instruction of the young" that recounts the captivity of John Williams, a Puritan minister taken captive by a band of French and Indian warriors who plundered the Massachusetts outpost of Deerfield during the winter of 1704 and who forced the survivors, among them Williams and his family, to march through the snow to Canada. Based on *The Redeemed Captive Returning to Zion* (1707), Williams's classic account of the incident, the children's version clarifies obscure points of colonial history that serve as background to the narrative. Among the historical material it contains are discussions of the French and Indian Wars, the settlement of Plymouth by the Pilgrims, and the early histories of several towns in western Massachusetts, including those of Springfield, Northampton, and Deerfield.

Children's stories about Indian captivity also contain lessons in geography and folklore. In *The Lost Sister of Wyoming* (1842), an "authentic narrative" about the experiences of Frances Slocum, a famous Indian captive who so appreciated the lifestyle of her captors that she chose to spend her life among them,[6] the Reverend John Todd, author of the book, describes at length the location and topography of the valley in northeastern Pennsylvania where Frances was taken captive. Interspersed throughout the narrative are folktales about the area, among them the story, common on the frontier, about the exploits of a local who escapes captivity by submerging himself under a log-jam, which his Indian pursuers pass without noticing him.[7]

Reprinted from *The New Mirror for Travellers* (1828), James Kirke Paulding's satire on fashionable summer resorts in the Hudson River region, "Murderer's Creek," a selection in both *The Child's Picture Book of Indians* (1833) and McGuffey's *Newly Revised Eclectic Third Reader* (1846), uses folklore to explain how the Otterkill, a stream which flows into the Hudson River at a juncture a few miles northwest of West Point, received its more romantic cognomen of "Murderer's Creek." According to local legend, a pioneer family by the name of Stacey was living near the banks of the Otterkill when the Indians of the area, long enraged by incessant white encroachments on their lands, planned a surprise attack upon all white inhabitants of the region. No one, not even women and children, was to be spared. In order for the attack to succeed, secrecy was an absolute necessity, for if the settlers learned beforehand of the uprising, they would have time to warn their neighbors, and not only might the rebellion end in failure, but it also might very well result in the needless slaughter of many Indians. Fearful for the safety of the Staceys, whose friendship and hospitality he had long enjoyed, Naoman, an elderly Indian chieftain, warned the family of the uprising and urged them to leave the area at once. While fleeing down the Otterkill, the Staceys were captured by the hostile Indians and threatened with torture and death if they refused to tell who had warned them of the impending disaster. Faithful to the Indian who had been faithful to them, the Staceys remained silent even when the Indians prepared to execute their children. Moved by this gesture of fidelity, Naoman confessed his complicity in the incident, and the Indians, by this time in a frenzy of uncontrollable rage, massacred both Naoman and the Staceys. Thus, the legend informs us, in memory of the place where the Stacey family lived and died, the Otterkill "is called 'Murderer's Creek.'"[8]

Because Indian captivity could easily be seen as an act of God, who, for some reason known only to Him, might elect to test the religious fortitude of His servants by subjecting them to the trial of Indian captivity, captivity narratives provided a convenient means for dramatizing the works of providence in a manner which children could understand.[9] Explicit about what he wished to achieve, the Congregationalist missionary, Elias Cornelius, wrote *The Little Osage Captive* (1821) in the hopes that it might persuade children and youth "to embrace the gospel themselves, and do what they can to send it to others." About the experiences of Lydia Carter, a child ransomed from captivity by a group of "Christian missionaries," who, before her tragic and untimely death from tuberculosis, converted her from the "deep darkness of heathenism" to the "blessings" of Christianity, *The Little Osage Captive* discourses on the value of missionary efforts to convert the world's pagan population, particularly those "heathen" who were fortunate or unfortunate enough to live in North America, within easy reach of zealots like Cornelius. "Had there been no missionaries to instruct her," states Cornelius about Lydia, "she would have died without a knowledge of the Savior, who we may hope cheered and supported her in the departing hour."

By emphasizing the fact that American pioneers willingly faced and in some instances endured ordeals like Indian captivity so that their country might eventually become a place where democracy and the values that it symbolized might prosper, captivity narratives could also be used to foster patriotism among the young, an important dimension of the majority of children's literature written in America during the decades immediately preceding the Civil War.[10] *The Deerfield Captive,* for example, "shows, in a striking manner, what trials our ancestors were compelled to endure in laying out these fair settlements which it is our lot to inherit." Its anonymous author hopes that "the sufferings of the first civilized inhabitants of New England" will fill "the tender minds" of his readers with "gratitude for the privileges and the blessings" which the "labors and privations" of their forefathers have secured for them. "In order to possess the liberty of worshipping God, according to the dictates of their own consciences," explains the author of *The Deerfield Captive,* the Pilgrims and Puritans who first colonized America "sailed across the Atlantic ocean, a distance of three thousand miles, to a new and uncivilized country," forsaking a "land of comfort and plenty for an unknown wilderness" where, "surrounded by beasts of prey and savage barbarians," they "would have to encounter all manner of hardships"—captivities, of course, included.

Indian captivity could also teach that the cardinal virtues were intrinsically worth cultivating. John Williams "was a good man" because "he was patient and submissive." Rather than "murmur or complain" about his fate, he "put his trust and confidence in God" and "was supported by his faith and his piety." According to Elias Cornelius, Lydia Carter "was an excellent example to children who have had, from their infancy, a thousand comforts and privileges which she had not enjoyed." Unlike "many children who do not remember the kindnesses which they receive, nor feel thankful for them," Lydia "was a *very grateful little girl.*" Among the questions appended to McGuffey's "Murderer's Creek" is one which asks, "Which is better, to do harm, or to suffer harm?" The story teaches that friendship and trust are qualities worth dying for and that bravery and self-sacrifice transcend the boundaries of sex and age.

Indian captivity could also function to perpetuate racial and religious prejudices, which, though gratuitously noticeable to the modern reader, apparently did not disturb the moral certitude of nineteenth-century pedagogues whose function it was to indoctrinate young Americans with a lifelong respect for the values, admirable or otherwise, of their elders.[11] Because they threatened the spread of American culture westward, southward, and northward, the Spanish, the French, and especially the Indian were depicted as retrogressive, anarchic, and, at least in the case of the Indian, degenerate and possibly subhuman. In *The Stolen Boy* (1830), a story about the adventures of a Spanish youth captured by "Cumanche" Indians, Barbara Hofland takes every possible opportunity to expound on the degenerate nature of the Indian. While she begrudgingly admits that Indians can sometimes be "punctual" and occasionally even "hospitable" Mrs. Hofland states that their vices "more than counter-balance their virtues." These vices, which Mrs. Hofland is quick to enumerate, include larceny, murder, revenge, bigotry, superstition, laziness, cruelty, cannibalism, and, of course, drunkenness, which, states Mrs. Hofland, is the favorite pastime of even the "wisest and gravest chiefs" and which is the most nearly universal "trait" which Indians can be said to possess.

In her haste to condemn them, Mrs. Hofland even goes so far as to accuse the Indians of being in league with Satan. This opinion was first articulated by the Puritans,[12] and became, when translated into secular terms, the basis for the image of the Indian as "savage beast" or "brute barbarian"; the stereotype flourished in hundreds of nineteenth-century captivity narratives written by hack writers in a predictable alliance with land speculators who, in the interest of real estate development, wanted to rid the West of Indians.[13] When the Indians who capture Manuel (*The Stolen Boy*) use their knowledge of woodcraft to escape a detachment of soldiers that is hot on their trail, Mrs. Hofland credits their success to supernatural powers obtained from the devil. Nevertheless, when Manuel escapes from captivity by means of wilderness skills that he acquired from the Indians, Mrs. Hofland appreciatively comments that he exhibited a "firmness of endurance" which was "worthy of the highest praise" and "admiration." Not only is the Indian incapable of doing good, but Indian vices become virtues, according to Mrs. Hofland, when practiced by whites.

Mrs. Hofland is also critical of the Spanish. Like the Indians, the Spanish are "destined to be vanquished" because, as she informs us, they are "much too indolent." Without industry, she explains, it is possible to "starve in the midst of plenty" and to "want" while "in possession of an immense expanse of fruitful country." No doubt Mrs. Hofland, like many of her contemporaries, wished to secure that land for Anglo-, not Spanish-, American culture. As *The Stolen Boy* reveals, as early as 1830, Americans had pointed the flag of Manifest Destiny toward Mexico, and many of the soldiers who later died while defending American claims to lands north of the Rio Grande may very well have been inspired to do so, at least in part, from youthful memories of tales like that by Mrs. Hofland.[14]

The Casco Captive (1837) casts an equally covetous glance toward Canadian lands. Based on an episode in Cotton Mather's *Magnalia* (1702), *The Casco Captive* recounts the experiences of Hannah Swarton, a Puritan woman taken captive during King William's War (1689-96) and forced to march to Canada, where she lived for five years among her French and Indian captors. Like the Spanish who control Mexico, the French

who inhabit Canada are depicted as "intolerant, cruel, and vicious." Because they are under the influence of the "Church of Rome"—whose "artful priests" encourage "fraud, violence, and blood-shed"—the French, like the Spanish, have failed to prosper, at least in contrast to their American neighbors. "While the Roman Catholic religion keeps the French of Canada from improvement and growth," states the anonymous author of *The Casco Captive,* "we, with the Bible, the preacher, and the schoolmaster, shall spread and spread over the wilderness, till, with a peaceful population, we crowd to the St. Lawrence, and scatter over the hills and valleys the cheerful school-house and the sacred place of public worship." Within this context, Catholic Indians were, of course, the ultimate affront to Anglo-American social decorum. They combined, as the author of *The Casco Captive* tells us, the "innate depravity" of their race with the "bigotry" and "superstition" of their French proselytizers and were, therefore, "immoral and wretched, as the heathen generally are."[15]

The Civil War saw a decline in the cultural nationalism that had previously encouraged the writing and publication of children's stories about Indian captivity, and the captivity narrative was no longer considered appropriate reading for impressionable young minds. Among the factors which contributed to this shift in sensibilities were the gradual assimilation of the Indian into a consciously cultivated historical heritage,[16] and, as R. Gordon Kelly has pointed out, a growing post-war spirit of sectionalism, industrialism, and urbanism which challenged the New England values that had dominated children's literature prior to the 1860s.[17] So profound was this change in attitudes that by the early decades of the twentieth century Congress had established the Boy Scouts of America, whose goal was to encourage American youth in the practice of crafts and values which had been learned from the Indian.[18]

Notes

[1] R. Gordon Kelly, "American Children's Literature: An Historiographical Review," *American Literary Realism,* 6 (1973), 95; John C. Crandall, "Patriotism and Humanitarian Reform in Children's Literature, 1825-1860." *American Quarterly,* 21 (1969), 3-4.

[2] For discussions of the differences between American children's literature and its British counterpart, see Rosalie V. Halsey, *Forgotten Books of the American Nursery* (Boston: Goodspeed, 1911) and Cornelia Meigs et al., *A Critical History of Children's Literature* (New York: Macmillan, 1953; rev. ed., 1969).

[3] Quoted from Edwin W. Rice, *The Sunday School Movement and the American Sunday School Union* (Philadelphia, 1917), pp. 143-44, by Crandall, 4.

[4] For a general overview of the various cultural and literary phases of the captivity narratives, see Phillips D.

Carleton, "The Indian Captivity," *American Literature,* 15 (1943), 169-80; Roy Harvey Pearce, "The Significances of the Captivity Narrative," *American Literature,* 19 (1947), 1-20; and Richard VanDerBeets's introduction to his collection of captivity narratives, *Held Captive by Indians!* (Knoxville, Tennessee: University of Tennessee Press, 1973). Studies which concentrate on individual aspects of the captivity tradition include David Minter, "By Dens of Lions: Notes on Stylization in Early Puritan Captivity Narratives," *American Literature,* 45 (1973), and Richard VanDerBeets's sensitive and thorough articles, "A Surfeit of Style: The Indian Captivity Narrative as Penny Dreadful," *Research Studies* 39 (1971), 297-306, and "'A Thirst for Empire': The Indian Captivity Narrative as Propaganda," *Research Studies,* 40 (1972), 207-15. For an analysis of the impact of the captivity tradition on the development of American literature, particularly the novels of Cooper, Simms, and Brown, see Leslie Fiedler, *The Return of the Vanishing American* (New York: Stein and Day, 1968); Richard Slotkin, *Regeneration Through Violence* (Middletown, Connecticut: Wesleyan University Press, 1973); VanDerBeets, "Cooper and the 'Semblance of Reality': A Source for *The Deerslayer,*" *American Literature,* 40 (1971), 544-46; and, more recently, David T. Haberly, "Women and Indians: *The Last of the Mohicans* and the Captivity Tradition," *American Quarterly,* 28 (1976), 431-43.

[5] It is a well documented fact (see, for example, Alexander Cowie, *The Rise of the American Novel* [New York: American Book Company, 1948] and Henri Petter, *The Early American Novel* [Columbus, Ohio: Ohio State University Press, 1971]) that not until late in the nineteenth century did Americans overcome a distrust for fiction which had been ingrained into their sensibilities by the Puritans who had considered fiction to be frivolous if not immoral. Sharing the suspicions of their culture for works which relied on artifice for a structure, authors of early American children's literature naturally felt more comfortable when writing biography or history than they did when writing fiction, and stories about Indian captivity which are written for children proudly display in their titles that they are "authentic narratives" which are "based on fact." See, for example, *The Deerfield Captive* (Greenfield, Massachusetts, 1831) and Barbara Hofland, *The Stolen Boy* (New York, 1830).

[6] Born in Warwick, Rhode Island, in 1773, Frances Slocum, daughter of Henry Warner and Margaret Olivia Slocum, was captured in November of 1778 by Delaware Indians who attacked the Wyoming Valley in northeastern Pennsylvania where her family had settled the previous year. Adopted into the tribe and given the name "Maconaquah" or, in English, "Little Bear," Frances accepted the lifestyle of her captors, grew up and married in the tribe, and eventually had several children by an Indian husband. In 1835 a visitor to the Miami Indians living on the Wabash River near what is now Peru, Indiana, heard about Frances and wrote to the postmaster at Lancaster, Pennsylvania, in the hopes of locating her white family. When they learned of her existence, they set out to persuade her to come and live with them. Accustomed to the ways of the Indians and fearful of the brothers and sisters she had almost forgotten, Frances Slocum, by then affectionately nicknamed "The Lost Sister of the Wyoming," chose to remain with her Indian children and grandchildren. She died in 1847 at age seventy-four. For other accounts of her life and captivity, see John F. Meginnes, *Biography of Frances Slocum* (Williamsport, Pennsylvania: Heller Brothers, 1891) and Charles E. Slocum, *History of Frances Slocum* (Defiance, Ohio, 1908).

Like Frances Slocum, many Indian captives preferred life among the Indians to that of so-called white civilization. Benjamin Franklin, Cadwallader Colden, and J. Hector St. John de Crevecoeur were among the many colonial Americans who expressed concern about the alarming number of captives who refused to return to white society when offered the opportunity to do so. Tribalized, these "hybrid offspring of civilization and barbarism," as Francis Parkman termed them in an essay on James Fenimore Cooper, discarded their white identity and took up Indian ways and culture to the point of sometimes participating in wars against the race of their birth. For discussions of the phenomenon of Indianized whites, see Irving Hallowell, "American Indians, White and Black: The Phenomenon of Transculturation," *Current Anthropology* 4 (1963), 519-31; J. Norman Heard, *White into Red: A Study of the Assimilation of White Persons Captured by Indians* (Metuchen, New Jersey: Scarecrow Press, 1973); and James Axtell, "The White Indians of Colonial America," *The William and Mary Quarterly,* 32 (1975), 55-88.

[7] Among the many frontier heroes to whom this motif has been attributed is John Colter, a member of the Lewis and Clark expedition who had been captured by Blackfeet Indians at the headwaters of the Missouri in 1808. Like the hero in the Slocum narrative, Colter escaped his captors by hiding in a river under a raft of logs. Memorialized by Washington Irving in *Astoria* (1836), Colter's dramatic escape from the Blackfeet helped elevate him to the status of a giant of western legend.

[8] The story of the Stacey family is a curious example of the complex relationship between folk and literary cultures in America. While the people of Orange County, New York, insist that the legend is based on fact, there is no mention of the Staceys or the legend prior to Paulding. The earliest reference to the Otterkill as "Murderer's Creek" is recorded on a map dated 1656 (see E.M. Ruttenber, *History of the Indian Tribes of Hudson's River* [Albany, New York: J. Munsell, 1872]), before which the stream was called "Martelaer's

Rack Creek," in reference to a treacherous stretch of water near a large rock on which travelers might easily have been "martyred" or "murdered" (see E.M. Ruttenber and L.H. Clark, *History of Orange County, New York* [Philadelphia: Everts and Peck, 1881], p. 41). In researching *Koningsmarke, the Long Finne* (1823), a novel about Scandinavian pioneers which contains a truncated version of the Stacey saga, Paulding might easily have come across a similar legend about a tributary of the Delaware, also called "Murderer's Creek," which he afterwards, perhaps inadvertently, associated with the New York stream of the same name. In this legend, a text of which can be found in *Documents Relative to the Colonial History of the State of New York* (Albany, New York: Weed, Pearsons, and Co., 1853-87; V. 3, p. 342; V 5, p. 283), white settlers are waylaid and murdered by Indians near a stream thereafter known as "Murderer's Creek." The people who lived near Murderer's Creek accepted Paulding's story as fact, for they were enchanted by his narrative and anxious to preserve local lore, especially stories praising the heroism and fortitude of their pioneer forefathers. Like Washington Irving's account of Rip Van Winkle's ill-fated encounter with Henry Hudson and the crew of the *Half Moon*, Paulding's tale of Murderer's Creek began as literature and later became the substance of folk tradition.

[9] From the onset, religious concerns form a major motivation for the writing and publication of captivity narratives. For a discussion of this aspect of the captivity tradition, see Pearce, "The Significance of the Captivity Narrative;" Minter, "By Dens of Lions: Notes on Stylization in Early Puritan Captivity Narratives"; and the introduction to VanDerBeets, *Held Capture by Indians!*

[10] See, for example, Crandall, "Patriotism and Humanitarian Reform in Children's Literature, 1825-1860."

[11] For informative discussions of how children's literature can be used, inadvertently or otherwise, to foster and perpetuate racial stereotypes and prejudices, see John P. Shepard, "Treatment of Characters in Popular Children's Fiction," *Elementary English,* 39 (1962), 672-76; and David K. Gast, "Minority Americans in Children's Literature," *Elementary English,* 44 (1967), 12-23. Using twentieth-century materials as the basis for their studies, Shepard and Gast conclude that while the heroes and heroines of children's stories "strongly tend to be clean, white, healthy, handsome, Protestant Christian, middle-class people," villains are generally "persons of non-Caucasian races," particularly blacks, Indians, Japanese, Chinese, and Spanish-Americans.

[12] Many Puritans, Increase and Cotton Mather among them, considered Indians to be instruments of Satan, if not devils themselves. For a discussion of Puritan attitudes toward Indians, see Roy Harvey Pearce, *The Savages of America* (Baltimore: The Johns Hopkins Press, 1953; rev. ed., 1965); Slotkin, *Regeneration Through Violence;* and G.E. Thomas, "Puritans, Indians, and the Concept of Race," *New England Quarterly,* 40 (1957), 3-27.

[13] For a discussion of the use of the captivity narrative as anti-Indian propaganda, see VanDerBeets, "'A Thirst for Empire': The Indian Captivity Narrative as Propaganda."

[14] Since the time of John Quincy Adams's presidency, the United States had tried to gain territorial rights to the land which now constitutes the state of Texas. American colonization of Texas began in 1821 under a grant issued to Moses Austin by the Spanish government. As more and more Americans moved into Texas, it became apparent that if they were to retain their rights as citizens of the United States, the territory must declare its independence from Mexico. An armed confrontation (now known as the Texas Revolution) began in 1835, and within a year, Texas had won its independence—at the cost, however, of many lives. In 1846 the Republic of Texas was annexed into the United States.

[15] It is curious to note that these same racial prejudices appear in nineteenth-century literature intended for adult audiences. The patrician writers, James Fenimore Cooper and Francis Parkman, for example, disapproved of any culture—French, Spanish, or Indian—which was not Anglo-Saxon in origin. Inter-racial marriages were especially frowned upon because they corrupted the purity of traditional bloodlines. In *The Prairie* (1827), Cooper groups French *coureurs de bots,* whom he calls "semibarbarous hunters from the Canadas," along with Spanish-Indian "half-breeds, who claimed"—wrongly of course—"to be ranked in the class of white men." According to Parkman, whose monumental study of the final years of the French and Indian Wars—*The Conspiracy of Pontiac* (1851)—contains an extended analysis of the plight of white captives who refuse to return to civilization, the offspring of Indians and whites are doomed by virtue of their mixed ancestry to be like the biblical Ishmael, "outcasts" and "wanderers" from both "civilization" and "the savage state."

[16] The decision of President Ulysses S. Grant to give control of the Bureau of Indian Affairs to the Quakers, a sect that had been known for its benevolent treatment of Indians since colonial times and the popularity of novels like Helen Hunt Jackson's *Ramona* (1884), a sentimentalized depiction of the plight of Western Indians, both indicate that by the latter part of the nineteenth century public attitudes toward the Indian had greatly softened, especially in the East, where he no longer posed a military threat. Instead of a ruthless opponent of civilization, the Indian was imaged as a pathetic anachronism, cast aside as civilization marched forward.

[17] Kelly, "American Children's Literature: An Historiographical Review," 101.

[18] Originally called "the Woodcraft Indians," the Boy Scouts of America, under the supervision of Daniel Carter Beard and Ernest Thompson Seton, encouraged American youth to emulate Indian ways: hunting, camping, fishing, hiking, and other outdoor activities. Organized according to the principles of tribal government, the Boy Scouts are divided into local and regional groups which regularly convene to form a "pow-wow." The original scout handbook, as formulated by Seton, was called *Two Little Savages* (1902), and even today in order for a scout to advance in standing among his peers he must master a series of activities, roughly equivalent to Indian initiation rites, which, in the terminology of scouting, are respectively labeled: 1) "wolf," 2) "bear," and 3) "lion."

June Namias (essay date 1993)

SOURCE: "Sarah Wakefield and the Dakota War," in *White Captives: Gender and Ethnicity on the American Frontier*, University of North Carolina Press, 1993, pp. 204-61.

[*In the excerpt below, Namias claims that Sarah Wakefield, who was captured during the Dakota War of 1862, wrote a narrativized "act of conscience" in attempting to portray her captors realistically and sympathetically, in conflict with prevailing popular opinion.*]

Sarah Wakefield's career as author and reporter of her own experience as a captive began shortly after the hangings [of her captors] at Mankato. Why did she write her book? What is its history and what does it tell us about this woman, the historical event in which she participated, and the role of conscience? Wakefield's decision to write her narrative was infused with her sense of guilt and her inability to overlook what appeared to her as a deliberate attempt to get rid of Chaska [the Indian who protected Wakefield and her children while they were held captive]. In it she wrote, "Now I will never believe that all in authority at Mankato had forgotten what Chaska was condemned for, and I am sure, in my own mind, it was done intentionally." Which others in authority Wakefield held responsible, she only vaguely implied. As to her own role, her own conscience, she first wrote, "Now I will always feel that I am responsible for that man's murder, and will never know quietness again." She later changed the end of the sentence to read, "and will reproach myself for urging him to remain."[92]

Six Weeks in the Sioux Tepees: A Narrative of Indian Captivity first appeared in print within months after the release of Wakefield and her children. The printing history of this book was short; to date only two imprints are known, one in 1863, published in Minneapolis by the Atlas Printing Company, and the second, issued in Shakopee by Argus Book and Job Printing in 1864. Even in the print shop, Sarah Wakefield was "subjected to many embarrassments," including the "malice and gross carelessness of the printer," who produced a first edition with many "omissions and misprintings" and any number of misspelled Indian names.[93]

From the few extant copies of both editions, we can tell that Wakefield's was one of those captivities which, in the grand tradition, was read to pieces. The small pamphlets came with colored paper covers, printed on rough, inexpensive paper. They were made to sell fast, not to endure as classic literature. The second edition added a frontispiece with a picture of Little Crow. Its back cover announced:

AGENTS WANTED

Local Traveling Agents wanted in every section of this and adjoining States, to whom a liberal discount will be made.

Address

MRS. SARAH F. WAKEFIELD,
Shakopee, Minnesota[94]

Besides the desire to sell the work, an examination of these editions uncovers their author's intent and her crisis of conscience. Those first printing errors were corrected, but other changes took place between the 1863 and 1864 editions, in both length and content. The 1863 edition had fifty-four pages, the 1864 edition, sixty-three. This nine-page addition might appear insignificant; quite the opposite is the case. Nine pages of tiny print in the 1860s would be closer to eighteen pages in today's more readable typefaces. The expansion of the booklet, even in its own day, adds nearly 18 percent new material to the original.

In the new, enlarged edition, with 50 lines to a page, a total of 653 lines were added. The new material falls into four categories, each adding greater detail and depth to the original story; they are the mother/survivor role, Chaska and Dakota life, the threatening nature of Indian life in captivity, and issues of conscience.

The sequences dealing with her as mother-survivor and with Chaska as protector of mother and children constitute a central plot and an expanded defense of Chaska. But the intervention of a heroic Indian figure in the position of rescuer of white womanhood and savior of helpless white children did not fit the mythic archetype for rescue of the maiden in distress from the dragon or animal-like man-beast. Her appeal here and elsewhere seems especially aimed at the female reader. She describes her actions as those of a virtuous mother defending her young with Chaska's help. The soldiers and others hold her virtue suspect. Along with themes of protection and virtue, Wakefield included threatening aspects of Indian life which mirrored the sentiment more typical of other Minnesota captives, earlier captivity stories, and the popular press. Such anti-Indian statements probably functioned to buy credibility with the Minnesota public, allowing Wakefield to attack the government and agency whites for bringing on the conflagration.

But despite traditional captivity elements, Wakefield's argument amounts to three indictments of the government: she assigns it responsibility first for the Dakotas' state of starvation and misery; second, for the hanging of an innocent man; and finally, for dispossessing the Dakotas and leaving them to die on the prairie. The combined impact of these charges elevates the original narrative from a white woman's defense of her own actions to a moral critique of the Minnesota and federal authorities. Their sins of commission, all deliberate, all avoidable, are delineated by her as an act of Christian conscience, a plea by a Christian mother for mercy in support of Minnesota's Indian community.

In the preface to both editions Sarah Wakefield tells the reader that the work was not intended for public consumption, but rather for the eyes of her children, and she continues: "I do not pretend to be a book-writer," warning the reader not to expect "much to please the mind's fancy." Apologies and disclaimers aside, in the second edition she persuasively sets up her story, tracing in the setting, the backdrop of the first night of fright, the first July 4 incident, the habits of the traders. This takes up six pages in the later edition, amplifying the plea for sympathy into the fuller context of a dramatic story. Rather than an anti-Indian tract we have a pro-Indian story, constructed with the realization that compassion can more easily flow from understanding and empathy.[95] In a metaphorical sense it is the story of a mother to her children but also of a mother in the wider community.

From the first page of the first edition, Wakefield is clear as to how she sees the Indian people with whom she found herself. After a single sentence about her husband's appointment to Yellow Medicine, she says of her relationship with the Dakotas: "I found them very kind, good people. The women sewed for me, and I have employed them in various ways around my house, and began to love them and respect them as if they were whites. I became so much accustomed to them and their ways that when I was thrown into their hands as a prisoner, I felt more easy and contented than any other white person among them, for I knew that not one of the Yellow Medicine Indians would see me and my children suffer as long as they could protect me."[96]

By August 1862, there had been "murders committed among them by the Chippewas," and the Dakotas came in for their annuities and "camped out" a mile from the agency buildings. "Here they remained many weeks, suffering hunger: every day expecting their pay so as to return to their homes."[97] Her sympathy for them in a time of starvation dominates her opening words. This is different from the second edition in which she writes a more romantic lead-in to the Wakefield family arrival. But even here, one expects that the scenes coming into the pristine Dakota prairie prepare the reader for the violent events that ensue.

Through its discussion of the murder of George Gleason and her children's escape from death, Wakefield's narrative sets up the dichotomy of the good and the bad Indian, with Chaska taking the role of the good Indian and Hapa [Hapan] appearing as the "horrid, blood-thirsty wretch." Although she was arguing with a "dual vision" that dates back to early seventeenth-century America, she couched it in the language of the debate informing nineteenth-century white-Indian discourse. In this environmentalist view, Indians were inferior because of their lack of Christian religion and membership in an "inferior" racial group. But the missionaries and "liberal" whites of Wakefield's day thought that Christianization and civilization could change people. Chaska represented the potentially "civilized" Indian, as opposed to Hapa, who stood for the worst of the old Indian ways. In her text Wakefield sees the two as foils and says, "Here can be seen the good work of the Missionaries. The two men were vastly different, although they both belonged to one band and one family; but the difference was this: the teaching that Chaska had received; although he was not a Christian, he knew there was a God, and he had learned right from wrong."[98]

From the moment Wakefield and her children arrived in the Dakotas' camp she was treated with great respect. They recognized her as the woman they knew from their winter camp in Shakopee when they had come to her house and she had given them food. During fighting between the Dakotas and the Ojibwas in 1858, her husband had treated Dakota wounded, "and they often said he saved many of their lives."[99] Now they greeted each other as "old friends." She describes how, in exchange for these good works, "they would protect me and mine." The old women helped her down from the wagon, crying when they saw her and spreading carpets for her, giving her a pillow and asking her to rest herself. They made supper for her and her children and assured her she was safe. She was then told to go with Chaska and to trust him as a "good man."[100] She followed him and explains how she could survive by following along and not complaining. She laughed and joked with the Dakotas, helped prepare meat for the warriors by pounding it into leatherlike strips they could wear around their waists into battle, painted blankets, and braided ribbons to ornament the horses. She explains how her behavior would "conciliate them, and a different course would have caused different treatment."[101]

Sarah Wakefield tells us that her main motive was to protect herself and her children. On Thursday, August 21, the Indians got up early to attack Fort Ridgely. Chaska explained that for her protection she and the children should go with him to his grandfather's, "who lived in a brick house about a mile away." His sister Winona "painted my cheeks and a part of my hair. She tied my hair (which was braided like a squaw's down my back) with several colored ribbons and ornamented me with fancy colored leggins, moccasins, etc. My children were painted in like manner. . . . Who would have known me to be a white woman?"[102] She disguised her boy James by rubbing dirt on him so that those Indians who she had heard would kill them would not know he was white. She tore the dress from baby Lucy to show her dark skin. When a Dakota woman warned her they would kill her and hold the children for ransom, she said she would rather see them dead and begged for a knife to kill her daughter. "What I suffered, let every mother imagine, when you think of my trying to cut my child's throat myself." In describing many of these trials of motherhood, she plays on the reader's sentiment to highlight her will to survive and protect her children.[103]

But some of the white captive women around her judged Wakefield's behavior to be too cooperative. Mary Schwandt remembered that "Mrs. Dr. Wakefield and Mrs. Adams were painted and decorated and dressed in full Indian costume, and seemed proud of it. They were usually in good spirits, laughing and joking, and appeared to enjoy their new life. The rest of us disliked their conduct, and would have but little to do with them."[104] In the second edition Wakefield adds piece after piece about her protective role as a mother and her willingness to sacrifice everything for her life and her children's: she worked, gave away, and changed clothing. "They asked me to take off my hoops, which I did. I think I should have cut off my right hand if I could have saved my life."[105]

After emphasizing motherhood, Wakefield turns pleas for sympathy into forums for describing how Chaska and his family saved her and the children. When she was about to kill her child, Chaska's mother came and took the baby on her back, gave her crackers and a cup, and urged Sarah and the boy to hurry to the woods. There the Indian mother told her they should hide themselves in the high grasses until morning. When danger threatened, Chaska carried her son James to his aunt's home.[106]

As a result of these experiences, Wakefield tries to convey the necessity and rightness of helping Indians in return: "I was anxious to do all I possibly could for them when they needed assistance." While others attribute her behavior to love and misdirected passion for Chaska, Wakefield places her actions on the field of conscience: "I could never love a savage, although I could respect any or all that might befriend me, and I would willingly do everything in my power to benefit those that were so kind to me in my great hour of need."[107] Her sense of duty to others is based on a Christian dictum: "Do unto others as you would have them do unto you." The civilization of a Christian woman could be no less generous than that of a newly Christianized Indian.

Along with its Christian impetus, perhaps her way of dealing with her grief and guilt was to transpose the personal story into a political one. Unlike the usual captivity narrative, Indian action and damage done have *causes* other than God's or the Devil's work or savagery or malevolence. As the Dakotas' forces and their captives moved miles up the river valley past the Upper Agency at Yellow Medicine and on past Lac qui Parle, Wakefield saw the destruction wreaked on Dr. T. S. Williamson's mission—an effort of over twenty years which Wakefield admired and respected. She ponders the rubble and Williamson's life work thus repaid after years among the Indians. Why had this happened?[108] "I could not think of any other cause than this—it may be right, it may be wrong; but such is my belief—: That our own people, not the Indians, were to blame. Had they not, for years, been cheated unmercifully, and now their money had been delayed; no troops were left to protect the frontier and their Agent, their 'father,' had left them without money, food or clothing, and gone off to the war."[109]

At the end of her narrative, in the second longest addition to the second edition, Wakefield expands the scope of her story.[110] She says that when H. H. Sibley arrived at Camp Release with the Minnesota military forces, many women changed their stories. One woman who used to complain that she was overfed by the Indian women told the soldiers how she was nearly starved, going for days without food. Wakefield claimed such lies were made up to "excite the sympathy of the soldiers."[111] "My object was to excite sympathy for the Indians and in so doing, the soldiers lost all respect for me, and abused me shamefully; but I had rather have my own conscience than that of those persons who turned against their protectors, those that were so kind to them in that time of great peril."[112] Her narrative closes with an attack on the contemporary state of affairs in Minnesota. She refers to the members of the expeditions mounted in 1863 to capture those Dakotas who escaped onto the plains as profit mongers, not heroes. Describing the situation of the Dakotas in their new reservation on the South Dakota plains, she points out that thirty-six hundred Dakotas lived on poor land with alkali water, waiting for government food supplies and dying in great numbers. She is also concerned about the Winnebagos, former enemies of the Dakotas, who lived in the southern part of Minnesota and northern Iowa. Although they did not fight in the war, they were leaving Minnesota under threats of extermination and, according to Wakefield, risked death on the high plains at the hands of their enemies the Tetons and Brules.[113]

Sarah Wakefield felt guilt for Chaska's death but also sorrow for "my neighbors," who "lived like the white man; now they are wanderers, without home, or even a resting place." "Their reservation in this State was a portion of the most beautiful country that was ever known, and they had everything they wished to make them comfortable if they could have only stayed there; but a few evil men commenced their murderous work, and all has gone to ruin."[114]

Though more than two centuries away from Mary Rowlandson's narrative, like her predecessor, Sarah Wakefield closed her book by calling upon her maker to set things straight. She tells of an Indian family recently passing through Shakopee. Recognizing them, she ran down to talk and bring them food. "For this," she laments, "I have been blamed; but I could not help it. They were kind to me, and I will try and repay them, trusting that in God's own time I will be righted and my conduct understood, for with Him all things are plain." [115]

. . . . .

"My object was to excite sympathy for the Indians and in so doing, the soldiers lost all respect for me, and abused me shamefully; but I had rather have my own conscience than that of those persons who turned against their protectors, those that were so kind to them in that time of great peril."[147] Perhaps there is much in Wakefield's story to excite sympathy for her own fate, to justify herself, and to have readers overlook her own moral shortcomings. Her anguish at Chaska's arrest at Fort Release, her own leaving, and then his subsequent death had a profound enough effect on her to galvanize her to write her story. She says that the night before she left, Captain Grant "gave me his word as a gentleman" that Chaska "would not be executed, but would be imprisoned for five years." At the time she says she "was very well contented, and troubled myself no further."[148] But why was she "contented" if he was to be imprisoned and she and her children went free? Why did she not stay longer, get assurances from others and in writing? Or is this expecting too much? Apparently, her own conscience, her own guilt that she was ineffective in saving a man who saved her came upon her after Chaska's death, and her own narrative, as much as it tries to clear her name, is a plea for conscience and an attempt to clear her conscience as well.

In the past, the genre of the captivity narrative has been examined as an original, perhaps quintessential American form often interpreted as functioning from the first as a mythic justification for Protestant Anglo-America's violent defeat of the infidel

and "savage."[149] But a careful examination of Sarah Wakefield's narrative indicates that if it was used to help her own credibility, it was not written or used primarily as anti-Indian propaganda, a white-supremacist polemic, or an ethnographic work. On the contrary, it was the statement of one white woman's conscience and sympathy, and it tells us something of the complex nature of such conscience in the world of Indian-white relations.[150]

The narrative is important because it is one of the few to be written and published by a female captive almost immediately after the Dakota War of 1862. At least eight other narratives exist of or by white women, a few others by white men. Only one other was published by its author as a separate piece in the first years following the event.[151] Most were published as part of nineteenth-century white settler histories, some twenty, forty, or sixty years later in varying editions in Minnesota newspapers and local histories.[152] Wakefield's narrative, like Mary Jemison's, offers an alternative vision of Indian-white relations on the frontier.

The Dakota War was something of a civil war, in this case, an Indian-white communal war. Christian conversions, Indian acculturation, years of intermarriage, and the taking of part-Indian hostages had simultaneously blurred and sharpened cultural divisions along communal lines.[153] Along with land hunger and race hatred, a subtext of the war became sexual and racial fear, a fear of relations between white women and Indian men. Sarah Wakefield's story is remarkable for the unusual nature of the narrative itself, its author, and her relationship to the Dakotas who protected her and her family through the six weeks of the uprising and the man who likely died because of this relationship.

In an essay on Harriet Beecher Stowe's *Uncle Tom's Cabin,* Jane P. Tompkins urges us to look again at popular literature by women. She sees Stowe's work as a critique of American society, representing "a monumental effort to reorganize culture from the woman's point of view." The popularity of sentimental novels is a good reason "for paying close attention to them."[154] Like Stowe's, Wakefield's work appealed to women's sense of justice. Both appeared in a world in which it was presumed that women had greater moral and spiritual power than men. Like Stowe, Wakefield was a New England woman who saw the lie behind white dealings with a people of color. She too wrote of duplicity, and her work called out for fairness. And she wrote in a popular genre, read by both men and women and, in the nineteenth century, often written by women. Unlike Stowe, the world she described came from her own experience and observation. And unlike Stowe, Wakefield's work did not ride a crest of feeling open to changing oppression, rather it appeared in a place and time that favored Indian extermination. Yet hers was not a work of Indian hatred but an act of conscience, posed in the wider framework of a woman who, in defense of her own self-interest, also recognized a set of wrongs against the other. Wakefield's life and work blended the genre of captivity with a Christian message of compassion. Hers was a woman's story, which included an attack on political and economic domination and an attempt to understand one who was like a brother. Like Stowe, she believed it to be her Christian duty to speak out against these evils. "They were kind to me, and I will try and repay them, trusting that in God's own time I will be righted and my conduct understood, for with Him all things are plain."[155] In the world in which she lived, her action and her writing were dangerous but, she felt, necessary.

The social relations between people of different races, classes, nations, sexes, and ethnic groups define us profoundly. Individuals can and do work for change, but the forces that maintain these systems of dominance are strong. Most of us think that if our country or community acted unjustly toward others we could stand up, protect those falsely accused, do the right thing. We hope we are not irrevocably bound to the social categories in which we were born and raised. Sarah Wakefield was put to such a test. Under the intense pressure of war, racism, and hysteria, under the immediate pressures of other captives and the commanding officers and soldiers at Camp Release, she was expected to keep to the party line, to say that Indians were fiends, worse than beasts—rapists and murderers. She was expected to consent to the nearly unanimous view of Minnesota whites that they should be exterminated, one and all, or at least banished from the state onto the prairie—the farther away the better. We can only guess that she may have been under unexpected pressure as well from her husband, who aside from having lost his books, his instruments, and his job and fearing the death of his wife and two children in the melee that was Minnesota, wanted to take his family by the hand and lead them away. Instead he found a wife whose life had taken an additional turn. She not only had rejected the story of savage Indians, she had become close to one of "them," in fact a whole family of "them." Who knew how close? She had responsibilities to her husband. She had not seen him. Given the rumors about her life, they needed a lot of time to clarify what had happened. And there were likely his expectations that as a mother with two children, who had undergone the traumas of war, she would want to protect them, be the "good mother," take them away to a safe place where they could put these weeks of murder, disruption, and parental separation behind them.

Part of her must have wanted to move away from the recriminations of other women prisoners and the men of the military as fast as possible. But this was not what the doctor's wife did. It was her clear intent to defy the common view of wife, mother, and Indian, not just privately but publicly. She would not just resume the protection of her husband's custody, take her children and go home. No, she would stay and publicly take the stand in Chaska's defense in a set of trials that saw next to no defense for nearly four hundred Dakotas.

Sarah Wakefield, woman of privilege, did not walk away from a man, a family, and a people who had saved her life and had made it as comfortable as possible under the circumstances. She was the recipient of a respect and appreciation she was seen as deserving based on the years of care she and her husband had dispensed to the Dakota community. Now she was intent upon showing reciprocity and a Christian woman's sense of compassion. First at the military commission trials, later with the publication of her narrative, the costs for this public stance were great. It is true, however, that she did not stay long enough. Why did she not stay longer? Could she have done more? She had no effect in reversing the verdict against the life of one Dakota man and against the ultimate fate of his family and his people. Chaska died; his family was part of the Dakota community that was banished onto the prairie and died in droves on reservations in South Dakota and Nebraska. The "Indian problem" was moved on to a further frontier, the Indian people soon to experience another wave of decimation.

In the closing words of her narrative, Sarah Wakefield said she would "bid this subject farewell." It was not so easy then, nor is it easy now.

Notes

. . . . .[92] Wakefield, *Six Weeks* [*in the Sioux Tepees: A Narrative of Indian Captivity*] (1864) [*Garland Publishing,* vol. 79 (New York: Garland, 1977)], 59, 42, 48.

[93] Wakefield, *Six Weeks* (1863), Preface. The Dakota War produced other instant publications besides histories and captivities. There were instant dime novels of the most lurid type such as Ann Coleson, *Miss Coleson's Narrative of Her Captivity among the Sioux Indians!* (Philadelphia: Barclay, 1864); Edward S. Ellis, *Indian Jim: A Tale of the Minnesota Massacre* (London: Beadle, [1864]); and Ellis, *Nathan Todd; or The Fate of the Sioux Captive,* vol. 4 (London: George Routledge and Sons, 1861).

[94] Wakefield, *Six Weeks* (1863), and Wakefield, *Six Weeks* (1864).

[95] Wakefield, *Six Weeks* (1864), 3-8, and Preface to this and the 1863 edition.

[96] Wakefield, *Six Weeks* (1863), 3.

[97] Ibid., 3.

[98] Wakefield, *Six Weeks* (1864), 14.

[99] "The wounded are under the care of Drs. WAKEFIELD and WIESER of Shakopee." In the one-hour battle with 176 Ojibwa, 3 Dakota were killed and 14 wounded. It was reported that 4 of these might survive ("The Battle between the Sioux and Chippewas at Shakopee," *Shakopee Pioneer Democrat,* June 3, 1858, Shakopee, Scott County, Writers' Project Annals files, [Minnesota Historical Society, Division of Manuscripts]).

[100] Wakefield, *Six Weeks* (1864), 14.

[101] Wakefield, *Six Weeks* (1863), 14-15.

[102] Wakefield, *Six Weeks* (1864), 22, and in the first edition as well.

[103] Ibid., 18.

[104] There is the possibility that it is Mrs. Adams to whom Sibley refers in letters to his wife. Schwandt continued, "Mrs. Adams was a handsome young woman, talented and educated, but she told me she saw her husband murdered, and that the Indian she was then living with had dashed out her baby's brains before her eyes. And yet she seemed perfectly happy and contented with him!" ("The Story of Mary Schwandt. Her Captivity during the Sioux 'Outbreak,'—1862," July 26, 1894, *Minnesota Historical Society Collections* 6 [1896]: 461-74, esp. 472-73; "Narrative of Mary Schwandt" in Charles S. Bryant and Able B. Murch, *A History of the Great Massacre by the Sioux Indians, in Minnesota* [Cincinnati: Rickey & Carroll, 1864], 335-42). On multiple editions see Namias, "White Captives," 548, n. 125, for listings in the Brown County Historical Society.

[105] Wakefield, *Six Weeks* (1864), 11, 16. Wakefield never talks about the trunk full of clothes, which were probably distributed around the camp. But Mary Butler Renville does in *A Thrilling Narrative of Indian Captivity.* Mrs. J. E. De Camp Sweet describes warriors decked out in "ladies bonnets," "furs," "brooches and chains," "silks . . . made into skirts," "shawls . . . used for saddle cloths" on the march from Little Crow's camp near the Lower Agency to the Upper Agency ("Mrs. J. E. De Camp Sweet's Narrative of Her Captivity in the Sioux Outbreak of 1862," *Minnesota Historical Society Collections* 6 [1899]: 368). Also see White, "Captivity among the Sioux," 405.

[106] Wakefield, *Six Weeks* (1864), 18, 29.

[107] Ibid., 19, 55.

[108] Williamson was a Carolina missionary who was part of the American Board of Commissioners for Foreign Missions' effort to convert the Dakotas. He set up his first mission in Lac qui Parle and later near the Upper Agency. Williamson learned Dakota and began to translate the Bible into Dakota between 1837 and 1842 (Riggs, *Memorial Discourse,* 4-16).

[109] Wakefield, *Six Weeks* (1864), 40-41.

[110] Ibid., 3-7, 61-63.

[111] Ibid., 60. Wakefield may mean Minnie Buce Carrigan, who shared a tent with her at Camp Release. Carrigan wrote of sharing a tent with other captives: "We were nearly starved, as we had eaten almost nothing all that day" (*Captured by the Indians* [1907 and 1912], *Garland Library,* vol. 106 [New York: Garland, 1977]). But Benedict Juni of New Ulm (aged ten, almost eleven at the time) said that meat, cattle, sheep, and hogs were in "abundance" as Dakotas took them "and held them in common" (*Held in Captivity,* 11, 19).

[112] Wakefield, *Six Weeks* (1864), 60.

[113] Ibid., 62. The Riggs and Williamson papers discuss these issues. Also see William E. Lass, "The Removal from Minnesota of the Sioux and Winnebago Indians," *Minnesota History* 38, no. 8 (1963): 353-64.

[114] Wakefield, *Six Weeks* (1864), 62-63.

[115] Ibid., 63.

. . . . .

[147] Wakefield, *Six Weeks* (1864), 60.

[148] Ibid., 56.

[149] Richard Slotkin, *Regeneration through Violence: The Mythology of the American Frontier, 1600-1860* (Middletown, Conn.: Wesleyan University Press, 1973). Harry J. Ross traces captivity themes in history and literature, indicating a dual paradigm of freedom and escape within the genre ("Trapped by Society, Imprisoned in the Wilderness: Captivity in American Literature, 1680-1860" [Ph.D. dissertation, Northwestern University, 1989]).

[150] Wakefield, *Six Weeks* (1863).

[151] The other contemporary captive narrative written by a woman is Renville, *Thrilling Narrative.* References to the many versions of Minnesota women's narratives: Mrs. Helen Carrothers [Helen Mar Paddock Carrothers, later Tarbel], Mattie Williams, Mary Schwandt, Minnie Buce Carrigan, Mrs. N. D. [Urania S. Frazer] White; "Mrs. J. E. De Camp Sweet's Narrative" [Janette E. Sykes also Mrs. J. E. De Camp]; Nancy McClure [Mrs. Nancy McClure Faribault Huggan] (Namias, "White Captives," 555-57, n. 169). There are also heroic stories of

women such as Mrs. Alomina Hurd, Justina Kreiger, and Mrs. Eastlick (somewhat in the Amazonian tradition) who got away, and George C. Allanson's account, which focuses on his mother, Suzanne Frenier Brown. For George Spencer's manuscript and other male accounts of those who had been children or adolescents at the time of their capture see Juni, *Held in Captivity,* Samuel J. Brown, "In Captivity," and Parker I. Peirce, *Antelope Bill.* Alan Woolworth and Darla Schnurrer helped me find these accounts.

[152] The most popular of these histories are Bryant and Murch, *History of the Great Massacre;* Connolly, *Thrilling Narrative of the Minnesota Massacre;* McConkey, *Dakota War Whoop;* Fred M. Hans, *The Great Sioux Nation: A Complete History of Indian Life and Warfare in America* (n.d.; rpt. Minneapolis: Ross and Haines, 1964); Heard, *History of the Sioux War.*

[153] Anderson, *Kinsmen.*

[154] Jane P. Tompkins, *Sensational Designs: The Cultural Work of American Fiction, 1790-1860* (New York: Oxford University Press, 1985), 122-46.

[155] Wakefield, *Six Weeks* (1864), closing paragraph, 63.

Gary L. Ebersole (essay date 1995)

SOURCE: "Rebinding the Bonds: Mixed Motives and Bodies in Captivity Narratives, 1750-1900," in *Captured by Texts: Puritan to Postmodern Images of Indian Captivity,* University Press of Virginia, 1995, pp. 144-89.

[*In the following excerpt, Ebersole discusses the role of gender and religion in the captivity narratives of the nineteenth century, with particular emphasis on the peculiar combination of entertainment and moral instruction that characterizes these works.*]

The Gendered Bodies of American Heroes and Female Captives

In the wake of the American War of Independence, and again after the French and Indian War and the War of 1812, captivity narratives were used to feed a growing desire among American readers for homegrown heroes and heroines. In these narratives, the hero's body is not a site of divine affliction but is selflessly offered up for the greater good of the nation's citizenry. At the same time, scenes of suffering are narrated not only to move the readers to tears of sympathy but often to develop a profound respect for these heroic men and women, models of patriotic self-sacrifice.

One example of this trend is the short captivity *The Remarkable Adventures of Jackson Johonnot, of*

Massachusetts (1791). A former footsoldier in the Continental army, Johonnot maintains that a traditional religious motive lay behind his decision to bring his story to the public's attention, but this is mixed with the expectation that sentimental reading practices would be brought to bear on his tale. Addressing his reader directly, he writes, "As the dispensations of providence towards me have been too striking not to make a deep and grateful impression, and as the principal part of them can be attested to by living evidences, I shall proceed, being confident that the candid reader will pardon the inaccuracies of an illiterate soldier, and that the tender hearted will drop the tear of sympathy, when they realize the idea of the sufferings of such of our unfortunate country folks as fall into the hands of the western Indians, whose tender mercies are cruelties" (*The Garland Library of Narratives of North American Indian Captivities* 18:3).

While the title page notes that the text had been "written by [Johonnot] himself, and published at the earnest request and importunity of his friends, for the benefit of American youth," the narrative does not provide moral guidance for this readership. Instead, it warns young men against foolishly enlisting in the military with dreams of glory and false hopes of realizing easy fame and fortune, as he had done. Johonnot does not represent himself as a model of Christian piety or resignation but as a loyal and patriotic citizen willing to risk his life in order to protect the residents on the frontier. He harnesses the traditional religious motives for recording and publishing a captivity tale to a new cult of nationalism and patriotism (*Garland* 18:5, 17).

Similarly, other captivity narratives were published as part of an effort to memorialize American heroes. Moses Van Campen's *A Narrative of the Capture of Certain Americans, at Westmoreland* (1780?) was composed, according to the author, because "my Mind was so struck with the rare specimens of Enterprize, Bravery, and Conduct which were exhibited in these little Adventures" (*Garland* 13:2).[10] This attitude is characteristic of a broader cultural movement away from seeking paradigmatic figures exclusively in the Bible or in antiquity and toward lifting up native heroes. Historical societies grew rapidly in number in the United States after the Revolutionary War. The Massachusetts Historical Society, founded in 1793, was the first such state society; by 1860 there were 111 historical societies in the United States, almost all publishing their proceedings.

After it was first submitted to the Society of the Cincinnati in Connecticut, David Humphreys's *Essay on the Life of the Honorable Major-General Israel Putnam* was presented to the general reading public in 1788. "An essay on the life of a person so elevated in military rank, and so conversant in extraordinary scenes," he asserted, "could not be destitute of amusement and instruction, and would possess the advantage of presenting for imitation a respectable model of public and private virtues" (*Garland* 19:iii-iv). This text illustrates the emergence in the late eighteenth century of a new literary type—the self-contained male hero—which served as a counter to the representations of the sentimental male.

Humphreys voices concern over what he feels to be the deleterious consequences of the explosion in the number of sentimental historical romances and purported histories of scenes from the Revolutionary War written by persons far removed from the actual scene of battle. He sees his own historiographic activity as a necessary corrective to this deplorable situation and promises to provide the reader with the real meaning of recent American history by presenting an objective account. Significantly, in this history the true source of General Putnam's courage and heroism is found in his natural constitution.

Humphreys rails against the danger that romantic historical fictions pose to the social order. They threaten to undermine the moral foundations of the nation by finally leading the good but easily duped citizens of the republic to lose their faith in historical writing and, consequently, in the truth. The "mischief" caused by fictional works of history was such that "the easy-believer of fine fables and marvellous stories will find, at last, his historical faith change to scepticism and end in infidelity" (*Garland* 19:8-10).

Humphreys holds the inculcation and maintenance of public morality to be the responsibility of the historian. The cultural work of historical biographies is to promote the reader's "historical faith." Significantly, this moral crusade for truth is linked with a strident opposition to the core assumptions held by many persons in the culture of sensibility, most especially the belief that one's moral sense is activated and then cultivated only by responding to external sensory stimuli. Humphreys's male hero, General Putnam, needs no such external goad; he is constitutionally virtuous:

> Courage, enterprize, activity and perseverence were the first characteristics of his mind. There is a kind of mechanical courage, the offspring of pride, habit or discipline, that may push a coward not only to perform his duty, but even to venture on acts of heroism. Putnam's courage was of a different species. His undaunted feelings depended, less than the feelings of most others, on external objects, adventitious aids, or the influence of example. He stood alone, and collected within himself, always possessed intrepidity equal to the occasion. His bravery, that appears to have been constitutional, never for a moment deserted him in the trying situations. (*Garland* 19:17-18)

Putnam is cast as an ideal hero, a man of refined sensibility but one who is cool rather than emotionally heated and who acts out of his innate character. The moral nature of this hero is hermetically sealed, as it were, within the hero's body, a body quite distinct from the tremulous sentimental body.

This depiction of the heroic male was in part a reaction against certain sentimental representations of the moral role women play in culture. Most especially, it denies that men need to be reformed by women, who smooth the rough edges of their harsh or brutal nature. The male hero Humphreys presents as a model for emulation is not subject to swooning, groaning, or any involuntary affective responses to the scenes of life and death, pleasure and pain, or unwarranted suffering which he encounters. Rather, Putnam's character was

> a species of cool, deliberate fortitude, not affected by the paroxism of enthusiasm, or the phrenzy of desperation. It was ever attended with a serenity of soul, a clearness of conception, a degree of self-possession and a superiority to all the vicissitudes of fortune, entirely distinct from any thing that can be produced by the ferment of blood, and flutter of spirits. . . . The heroic character, thus founded on constitution and animal spirits, cherished by education and ideas of personal freedom, confirmed by temperance and habits of exercise, was completed by the dictate of reason, the love of his country and an invincible sense of duty. (*Garland* 19:18)

Humphreys argues that it was this innate character that had allowed Putnam "to pass in triumph through the furnace of affliction." He makes no appeal to any external agency, including divine providence, in this regard. Here, the providential interpretive frame has completely vanished, and in its place one finds a controlling set of gender constructions. The male hero is self-contained and in control of his reason and his libido, while the female is emotional and weak, with her only defense against violence being her ability to appeal to the sympathy of others precisely by displaying her feminine virtues and her pitiful vulnerability. The myriad representations, in nineteenth-century works of literature, in prints and paintings, in sculpture, and on the stage, of women on their knees, with eyes lifted up and hands clasped in prayer in a gesture appealling for mercy before a raised tomahawk, participated in this process of constructing new gendered bodies.

These distinctive gender traits inform the descriptions of General Putnam and Mrs. Howe. Putnam is represented as having been fearless and ever in control of his senses, even when faced with overwhelming odds on the battlefield or the immediate prospect of being burned at the stake by his Indian captors. His calm demeanor and silent courage then were such that the Indians soon came to believe him to be a god, or at least to be under the direct protection of the Great Spirit. With the flames licking around Putnam, as he was bound to the stake, he was stoic and resigned to his death, regretting only that he would be separated from his wife and children. Physical pain held no power over him. Finally, when Putnam was miraculously saved at the last moment, it was not by the agency of divine providence but through the "interposition" of a French officer, who had earlier been the recipient of the kind solicitude of the general (who always recognized individuals of like class). Thus, Putnam's character is represented as having ultimately been the source of his own salvation (*Garland* 19:62, 69-70).

Humphreys introduces a second captivity tale into his narrative as well, that of a Mrs. Jemima Howe. As a counterpoint to the male hero, he sketches her in the complementary terms of a sentimental heroine in distress. Unlike General Putnam, she does not so much act as react to events and the actions of others around her. Her face and body are a text to be read by sensitive observers, for a record of her suffering has been inscribed in her features. One of the dictums of sentimental moral anthropology was that the innate virtue of a person of sensibility would not be adversely affected by the vicissitudes of life, rather, a person's character would be strengthened by such testing. Yet if the inner person could not be changed by adversity, it was widely believed that the effects of having experienced scenes of horror and suffering were registered externally in one's carriage and on one's body—in scars, in a furrowed brow, in the look of one's eyes. All of these were assumed to be clear markers of a person's moral character and personal history. Thus, when Mrs. Howe is introduced for the first time, a discerning eye could read her sad history in her facial features. She is not hysterical (a popular image of the female) but someone who has composed herself and thus who is prepared to narrate an engaging story, even as her body has been textualized:

> Distress, which had taken somewhat from the original redundancy of her bloom and added a softening paleness to her cheeks, rendered her appearance the more engaging. Her face, that seemed to have been formed for the assemblage of dimples and smiles, was clouded with care. The natural sweetness was not, however, soured by despondency and petulance; but chastened by humility and resignation. This mild daughter of sorrow looked as if she had known the day of prosperity, when serenity and gladness of soul were the inmates of her bosom. That day was past, and the once lively features now assumed a tender melancholy, which witnessed her irreparable loss. She needed not the customary weeds of mourning or the fallacious pageantry of woe to prove her widowed state. She was in that stage of affliction, when the excess is so far abated as to permit the subject to be drawn into conversation without opening the wound afresh. It is then rather a source of pleasure than pain to dwell upon the circumstances in narration. Everything conspired to make her story interesting. (*Garland* 19:74-75)[11]

The sentimental female body is morally instructive precisely insofar as it is "interesting" to others. In the late eighteenth century, this term meant that the scene of the former captive narrating her tale had the power to attract the attention of others and to evoke a sympathetic response from them. Insofar as Howe's body-in-pain and her mind have been composed (and thus her person and history transformed into a stable body-as-text), her narrative has the power to interest other persons and to evoke their moral sensibilities. Howe is described as having come to terms with her past suffering and loss so that her affliction is no longer painful to recall, especially when she has a congenial audience of persons of like sensibility. The pleasure to be found in narrating one's past pain and suffering here is not understood as a stage in the grieving process; rather, it comes from the knowledge that the moral sensibilities of the audience can be sharpened and instructed through the affective transaction involved in the act of narration. By sharing her sad story of suffering and woe, the former captive contributes to the softening of the audience's hearts and minds and to the further cultivation of their tenderhearted humanity. In giving expression to her pain and suffering, she provides the opportunity for her listeners' sympathy to find expression as well. Innumerable examples from history demonstrate that intense pain can be borne and can even be a source of ecstatic pleasure for the sufferer when it is located within a meaningful structure. The paradox represented by the composed body-in-pain has fascinated people over the ages.

Overdetermined gendered bodies are found in other captivity narratives from the late eighteenth and early nineteenth centuries. *French and Indian Cruelty* (1757), the story of Peter Williamson's captivity, was one of the most popular captivities in this period and was regularly reissued down through the nineteenth century. Initially, Williamson published his tale in order to move his readers to sympathize with his plight as a wounded veteran and former captive and thus to open their purse strings. By telling and selling his story, he hoped to earn enough money to set himself up in some kind of gainful employment. He seems to have been much more successful in this endeavor than most former captives because he managed to earn a living from sales of his narrative and other writings while exhibiting himself in Indian costume at his coffeeshop in Edinburgh for many years until his death in 1799 (*Garland* 9).

Williamson's tale is representative of works that offered various sorts of captivity to readers. Mrs. Howe, for instance, was represented not only as an Indian captive but also, à la Pamela, as a helpless and vulnerable female captive in Montreal, where she had to ward off unwanted sexual advances from two Frenchmen. Other tales tell of individuals who had been kidnapped and sold into virtual slavery, or of persons who had fallen into poverty through circumstances outside their control and been forced to become indentured servants or otherwise lost their freedom, autonomy, and social position. Whatever the case, such tales sought to evoke the sympathy of readers for the plight of the protagonists and the sufferings they experienced. In doing so, they sought to exercise and cultivate the reader's moral imagination.

The remarkable popularity of Williamson's captivity narrative over the years was due in no small part to his skillful appeal to multiple audiences and their reading practices. He appealed at once to religious sensibilities, sentimental ideals, and the anti-French and anti-Indian feelings that had been stirred up in the Anglo-American world by the French and Indian War. He claims to have been kidnapped as a child of eight in Aberdeen, imprisoned onboard a ship, and sold as an indentured servant in Pennsylvania. In his twenties he had managed to gain his freedom, married, and was living on a three-hundred-acre farm on the Delaware River. In his own words, he was at this time "blessed with an affectionate and tender Wife, who was possessed of all amiable Qualities to enable me to go thro' this World with that Peace and Serenity of Mind, which every Christian wishes to possess." Predictably, his idyllic domestic life was soon destroyed by an Indian attack (*Garland* 9:10).

Williamson describes various sorts of torture he was subjected to in captivity and claims to have borne these in silence by putting his faith in God. Like many other writers before and after him, he narrates scenes of the infliction of pain and suffering, including Indians dashing the brains of infants on rocks and butchering pregnant women, as a means of demonstrating the inhumanity of the Indians and the French, who were hardhearted and unmoved by "the Tears, the Shrieks, or Cries of these unhappy [and innocent] Victims."

The ubiquitous scenes in Indian captivities of infants, children, and women being "knocked on the head" with a tomahawk when they cried or moaned frequently do not reflect actual occurrences. These scenes are too common and too stereotyped to inspire any confidence in their actuality. Such scenes were composed of two elements designed precisely to evoke sympathy for the victims and hatred for the Indians: the victims are inevitably depicted as innocent and helpless, and the savages are unmoved by their tears or cries, as any person of feeling and moral sensibility would be. Such scenes, then, were constructed with an understanding of the moral significance of the circulation of feeling in sentimental reading practices; they were part of the currency in the economy of feeling and sympathy in the eighteenth- and nineteenth-century culture of sentiment.

Time and again Williamson describes the suffering of a poor captive alone among the Indians only to conclude with such an observation as "to all which, the poor Creature could only vent his Sighs, his Tears, his Moans, and Intreaties, that to my affrighted Immagination, were enough to penetrate a Heart of Adamant, and soften the most obdurate Savage. In vain, alas! were all his Tears." While the savages were portrayed as unfeeling brutes, Williamson represented himself and other white males as persons of sensibility. In the culture of sentiment, heightened sensitivity could itself be a source of intense, albeit "exquisite," pain, as in the following passage, describing a party of soldiers as they discovered the female captive, beloved of the captain, naked, bloody, and bound to a tree:

> No Heart among us but was ready to burst at the Sight of the unhappy young Lady. What must the Thoughts, Torments, and Sensations, of our brave Captain then be, if even we, who knew her not, were so sensibly affected! For, oh! what Breast, tho' of the brutal savage Race we had just destroy'd, could, without feeling the most exquisite Grief and Pain, behold in such infernal Power, a Lady in the Bloom of Youth, bless'd with every Female Acomplishment which render'd her the Envy of her own Sex, and the Delight of ours, enduring the Severity of a windy, rainy Night! (*Garland* 9:19, 45)

Here Williamson recreates a typical sentimental scene of female virtue-in-distress, a scene guaranteed to evoke "the most exquisite Grief and Pain" in the spectators and readers. He continues, addressing the reader directly, a device that evolved from oral forms such as the jeremiad and other kinds of preaching. Like Cotton Mather before them, preachers in the Great Awakening and the Second Awakening in America directly challenged their audiences to contemplate scenes of death or the suffering of souls in hell. Williamson asks his audience to gaze on this scene of an innocent female body-in-pain and to respond appropriately, which now means in gendered terms:

> Behold one nurtur'd in the most tender Manner, and by the most indulgent Parents, quite naked, and in the open Woods, encircling with her Alabaster Arms and Hands a cold rough Tree, whereto she was bound with Cords so straitly pull'd, that the Blood trickled from her Finger Ends! Her lovely tender Body, and delicate Limbs, cut, bruis'd, and torn with Stones and Boughs of Trees as she had been dragg'd along and all besmear'd with Blood! What Heart can even now, unmoved, think of her Distress, in such a deplorable Condition? having no Creature with the least Sensations of Humanity near to succour or relieve her, or even pity or regard her flowing Tears and lamentable Wailings!

As the woman's lifeless form is restored to consciousness, "eagerly fixing her Eyes on her dear Deliverer, and smiling with the most complacent Joy, [she] blessed the Almighty and him for her miraculous Deliverance." The pitiful tale she proceeds to tell of her captivity proves to be a "pleasing, painful Interview" (*Garland* 9:45, 46).

It is, perhaps, hard for us today to appreciate how and why such pain and grief could be considered pleasing, interesting, or beautiful. But throughout the eighteenth and nineteenth centuries, the readers of works of sentimental literature undoubtedly found such scenes to be so. The "pleasure" spoken of here was usually not located in immediate sensory perceptions but was the result of reflective activity. Philosophical and epistemological support for such a position was found, among other places, in *A Treatise of Human Nature,* where Hume held that "no passion of another discovers itself immediately to the mind. We are only sensible of its causes or effects. From *these* we infer the passion: And consequently *these* give rise to our sympathy."[12] Whatever the precise source of support for the widespread understanding of the moral efficacy of sentimental reading practices, however, it is important to recognize that Williamson's captivity narrative found a ready audience not only because it was linked to "the metaphysics of Indian-hating and empire-building" but because it was linked to sentimental reading practice. The scenes of death and suffering were effective because of the widely shared understanding of how reading such works could be a form of rational entertainment and a means of moral improvement.[13]

Readers of such captivity tales seem to have come from all socioeconomic levels of society, including the lowest. A few captivities sold cheaply on the streets have survived and may be taken to be representative of a much larger number of similar works. *The Travels and Surprising Adventures of John Thompson, who was taken and carried to America, and sold for a Slave there:—How he was taken Captive by the Savages.— With an Account of his happy delivery, after Four Months slavery, and his return to Scotland* (1761) is typical. This work was pilfered almost directly from the Williamson narrative, with only the name of the author and a few other details altered. It was no doubt the product of a modest scheme to make some quick money on the street.

At times the purchasers of such street literature could have an oral account of the author's captivity along with the printed pamphlet. *A full and particular Account of the Sufferings of William Gatenby,* a short pamphlet of only eight pages from 1784, for instance, announces that "if any person has a desire to have any further particulars, by applying to the said Hawker of this paper, they may have their curiosity satisfied with the greatest pleasure." The author authorized the street hawker to sell his narrative, "hoping all well-disposed christians will contribute a trifle to my relief, by purchasing this small book." The hawker apparently took a share of the sales receipts (*Garland* 9:24).[14]

While Humphreys held the moral edification of the people to be the sacred duty of the historian, other authors offered captivity narratives to the public as suitable material for the poet, the novelist, the playwright, and the moral philosopher. *A Brief Narrative of the Captivity and Sufferings of Lt. Nathan'l Segar* (1825) is an example of a work which had these multiple audiences in mind. This edition is a reissue of a work originally penned by Segar (1755-1847) in an effort to gain full compensation for his military service in the Revolutionary War and his captivity in Maine. The editor argues in the introduction that the work is of both local and national historical interest. Moreover, because it accurately represents the respective characters of the Indian and the frontiersman, it is an important chapter in the history of the moral development of man. "The character of the aboriginal inhabitants of this country is a curiosity in the history of human nature," he writes, "and is falling among the antiquities of moral remains and monuments. The station of the settler, the pioneer of the forest, is also singular and interesting." Figures such as Segar "are men, the incidents of whose lives are frequently of the most romantic cast, and whose habits are, from necessity, often so peculiar as to furnish a fine theme for contemplation and description of the novelist, the poet, the historian, and the observer of human nature" (*Garland* 37:5, 3).

It was believed that the tales of captives, who had been deprived of the company of civilized persons and the amenities of civilization and forced to live in virtual isolation, were both "amusing and instructive" when they were compared with "the condition of him who hears around him the din or the arts and mingles in the bustle of the busy and social scene." Captivity tales, especially those based (however loosely) on fact, were offered as an invitation to readers to engage in an inquiry into the human condition and, with the comparative knowledge gained, to meditate on the blessings and the costs of civilization. Still other tales were presented as affording the reader "an opportunity of observing the mind of man in its progress from the original savage to civilized life; as well as in its retrograde movements from civilization to the savage state" (*Garland* 37:4; 26:25).

The presence of large numbers of white Indians in these centuries could not be ignored and led to a wide variety of responses, including some efforts to explain the phenomenon scientifically and others to explain it away. Some persons maintained that the divide between the "primitive" and "civilized" man was the result of an evolutionary process; others claimed that there was an ontological distinction between the savage and the civilized peoples. The possibility that the distinction between these states had not yet been finally won was both fascinating and frightening and has stimulated fictional explorations of "going native," ranging from Cooper's Leatherstocking Tales and Conrad's *Heart of Darkness* to Burroughs's Tarzan.

Some fictional captivities attempted to mediate between hard history and fiction as narrative vehicles of moral improvement. James Russell's pocket-sized novel *Mathilda; or, The Indian's Captive* (1833) was offered to the public as a means of chasing away the reader's despondency and "unmerited grief," of furnishing amusement and moral instruction, and of demonstrating the workings of divine providence in history. The form and style of the work were crafted with the female reader's delicate sensibilities and susceptibility to seduction in mind. Russell claims to have obtained the outline of his tale firsthand from a former female captive who became the model for his heroine. In apologizing for his limited literary skills, he also claims (unconvincingly, it must be said) that he himself had been abducted and made an Indian captive "at an age when the human mind is most susceptible of improvement" (*Garland* 51:iii).

If Russell claims that his work is not deserving of the designation "novel" because it is based on fact, the editor of *Sketches of Aboriginal Life* (1846), the inaugural volume of a series of historical romances called "American Tableaux," defends the moral efficacy of fiction. He boldly claims that while not "authentic history," works of historical fiction alone could bring the past to life and speak to readers (*Garland* 62:iii).

History and fiction were blurred genres in the first half of the nineteenth century. While many persons were deeply concerned over the negative social consequences of works of fiction and historical romances, others considered these forms to be more truthful and better vehicles of moral instruction than factual historical accounts, insofar as well-written works of fiction were more apt to evoke sympathetic responses from readers. Our present generation was clearly not the first to recognize the literary nature of history.[15]

Female Heroines, Maternal Instinct, and Redemptive Suffering

A large number of nineteenth-century captivity narratives illustrated ideal gender roles and virtues. We have seen how female captives served as historical instances of feminine virtue-in-distress. Such figures were usually passive, waiting to be rescued by male heroes, while the narrative scenes of these suffering innocents were designed to evoke sympathy in the reader or, at other times, a ferocious anger and thirst for revenge against the cruel and inhuman savages who had inflicted such suffering on the women.

We will now turn to a representative selection of captivities from the second half of the nineteenth century in which the central themes are a specifically female heroism, associated with maternal instinct, and redemptive suffering by women and children. Such texts are generally a mix of religious sentiments, a historiographical impetus to record examples of female heroism, and the prevailing gender constructions. *Miss Coleson's*

Narrative of Her Captivity Among the Sioux Indians! (1864), an anonymous work of fiction, is representative of the inexpensive novels then widely available. While not a pure work of sentimental literature, it shares many of the same informing values, as selected structural elements of the sentimental genre are incorporated in a tale otherwise reminiscent of earlier religious narratives of suffering, providential escape, and heroism. The author relies upon the reader's familiarity with and affirmation of the values of sentimental literature in crafting his characters and his depiction of the Indians.

This novel employs negative stereotypes of the Indians throughout, most importantly in descriptive scenes and "factual accounts" of savage Indian customs and brutal atrocities—innocent women tomahawked, "mutilated in a shocking manner," and scalped; infants' brains dashed out against trees or rocks; cannibalism; captives forced to run the gauntlet; and sadistic acts of cruelty and torture. The prevailing white cultural constructions of gender and gender roles are also invoked to further damn the Indians as uncivilized. Indian women, for instance, are represented as possessing some of the attributes of female feeling and sympathy, although in insufficient measure. If Pocohantas had once been able to intercede successfully on behalf of Capt. John Smith, the Indian women here have largely lost their powers of moral suasion. The wife of the Indian chief protests without success against her husband's forcing Miss Coleson to watch the torture of a white male prisoner.

The characterization of all Indians, regardless of age or sex, is uniformly negative. Indian children lack the charm, intellect, and moral aptitude of their white counterparts; moreover, their education and even their forms of play are declared to be such that the limited potential the Indian children begin with is never developed. In sum, Indians are found to be closer in nature to animals than to civilized human beings, since "their sense of hearing, sight and smell, are much more acute than those of white people, and enables them to distinguish objects at an incredible distance" (*Garland* 79:36-38).

In a descriptive passage dictated by the joint values of refined femininity and sentimental mores, the author introduces another incidental character—a young woman, born of a Canadian mother and an Indian father—who helps Miss Coleson escape. This woman's inherited nature as a "mixed Blood" is used to explain both her good looks and her kind civility. Yet while the immediate mutual sympathy this young Indian maiden and Miss Coleman feel for each other signals the recognition of a certain shared nature, the young woman's share of Indian blood finally keeps her from spurning Indian society for civilization.

A mysterious male figure, who suddenly appears as Miss Coleson is attempting to escape, kills her pursuer, and assists her to return to the white world, is introduced in the conventional terms of a sentimental romantic hero—polite, solicitous of female needs, desires, and delicate nature. Physically, he is dark and ruggedly handsome, with a "roman nose and fine intelligent countenance." With this physiognomic validation of the man's good character and trustworthiness, Coleson is certain that she is in good hands (*Garland* 79:38, 45).

Although Coleson undergoes "unbearable suffering and fatigue" in captivity, she is never too tired to respond to the beautiful and the sublime in nature in a manner appropriate to a woman of her sensibilities. The body of the sentimental heroine is not only a site of suffering, it is also always atingle, sensitive to the scenery and persons around her:

> Notwithstanding the pain in my limbs, and the fatigue of drawing my sledge, I could not help remarking on the loveliness of nature peculiar to these northern latitudes, and which seemed sufficient to dissipate every sensation of pain and weariness; such a rare combination of frost and sunshine, without being seen and felt, could hardly be imagined. The wind, which had blown fiercely all the morning, came to a perfect lull in the afternoon; even the deep roar of the pine woods hushed to a gentle murmur—and as we walked along, our hair, our faces, our eyebrows, and even our eyelashes, were as white as a powdering of snow could make them— while the warmth of the sun gave a sensation of peculiar purity to the air. (*Garland* 79:34)

Even under the extreme duress of captivity, this sentimental and romantic heroine's refined sensibilities are both irrepressible and indestructible. If this portrait seems artificial, unnatural, and unrealistic to modern readers, this was not the case for nineteenth-century readers. In the face of many counterexamples of captives, both male and female, having gone native, the author of this work seeks to deny the very possibility of this happening to anyone who was truly civilized. Coleson had little thought of escaping, not because she could ever be reconciled to a savage life, but because she was so moved and taken by the remarkable sights and extraordinary experiences of captivity that she forgot all else temporarily (*Garland* 79:33).

In both works of fiction and nonfiction the sentimental heroine is frequently paired with the complementary male hero. This is the case even in male adventure stories, which became very popular in the second half of the nineteenth century. Cheap novels, such as Sylvester Crakes's *Five Years a Captive Among the Blackfeet Indians* (1858), mix tales of western adventure with racial stereotypes, information on Indian life and customs, sentimental scenes, and occasionally even religious sentiments. The figures of the heroic rugged frontiersman and the lone cowboy owe much to Filson's Daniel Boone and Cooper's Leatherstocking Tales, as

they find life in nature to be spiritually rewarding and invigorating. The following passage illustrates the mix of romanticism and male freedom in the wilderness:

> In the wild roaming of the hunter, amid the freedom of the forest, mountains, hills, and valleys, there is a species of ennobling adventure and enlarged liberty that is calculated to fill the soul with admiration for the vast and grand in nature—where the looming of the hoary mountain, the roaring of the river, the whispering of the forest, and the murmuring of the gentle rivulet, speak, in accents bold and grand, the praises of that God who commanded, and they stood fast. Cut off from of the conventionalities of civilized life, the trapper feels somewhat like Robinson Crusoe, on the island of Juan Fernandes. (*Garland* 74:19)

Like Daniel Boone before him, John Dixon, the hero-narrator, found his life as a hunter and trapper to be "actually captivating." His own condition as a captive mirrored the human condition in important ways, while his response to captivity was a model of and for living with life's vicissitudes. In this way, the author manages to combine a standard Christian moralism, a sentimental male-female relationship, and an action-packed male adventure story (*Garland* 74:19, 36). Although he makes no appeal to divine providence, he presents a familiar rationale for telling a captivity tale—by presenting the utter degradation of the heathen Indian, he will rekindle the reader's gratitude for having enjoyed the civilizing influence of Christianity.

The introduction of the character of Roxana, a female captive, permits the author to portray ideal male-female relationships, as well as her eventual "beautiful death." Dixon acts as the noble civilized male, ever attentive in the midst of savagery and unfeeling cruelty to the needs and the nature of the suffering incarnation of female virtue-in-distress. Selflessly, he vows to stay among the Indians in order to nurse Roxana back to health until such time as he can lead her back to civilization. Theirs is not a sexual relationship, however; the hero's reward is in serving this paradigm of female purity and humility (*Garland* 74:157, 170).

Roxana, who is dying of consumption, is presented as a model of perfect Christian resignation in the face of her illness, pain, and suffering in captivity. The beautiful death of a pale, innocent woman (or, alternatively, a child) was a popular theme throughout the nineteenth century, guaranteed to evoke tears in the readers' eyes and to turn their thoughts to the power of purity in the world. Because the Bible had promised the meek would inherit the earth, nineteenth-century authors frequently used pale, sickly, pious women to illustrate this truth for millions of readers. The figure of the innocent woman suffering in captivity immediately suggested itself as an ideal model of perfect resignation to the will of God.

In *Two Months in the Camp of Big Bear* (1885), a first-person narrative, Theresa Gowanlock and Theresa Delaney seek to correct incomplete and inaccurate accounts of their captivity that had appeared in the press, including the suggestion that they had been sexually violated. These Canadian women style themselves as being content with Victorian ideals of womanhood; Gowanlock even suggests that only the memories of her domestic life "within the sacred precincts of the paternal hearth" had kept her from sinking into despair during her captivity. This phrase captures the extent to which the patriarchal ideal of domestic life had taken on religious overtones in the nineteenth century. For her part, Delaney invokes divine providence to explain what had befallen her, while justifying the publication of her tale for reasons found earlier in Adam Smith's *The Theory of Moral Sentiments:* "I look upon the writing of these pages as a duty imposed upon me by gratitude. When memory recalls the sad scenes through which I have passed, the feeling may be painful, but there is a pleasure in knowing that sympathy has poured a balm upon the deep wounds, and that kindness and friendship have sweetened many a bitter drop in the cup of my sorrow and trouble" (*Garland* 95:6, 5).

When Delaney recalls how she had become an object of the male gaze, she invites the female reader to imagine herself into her situation. She assumes that the leering gaze of the male voyeur is universally known by women, as the female body is exposed to the male "naked eye." Interestingly enough, this lurid feeling of being exposed and watched is then compared to the knowledge that one's actions are being watched by God:

> Imagine yourself seated in a quiet room at night, and every time you look at the door, which is slightly ajar, you catch the eye of a man fixed upon you, and try then to form an idea of my feelings. . . . I know of no object so awe-inspiring to look upon, as the naked eye concentrated upon your features. Had we but the same conception of that "all seeing eye," which we are told, continually watches us, we would doubtlessly be wise and good; for if it inspired us with a proportionate fear, we would possess what Solomon tells us i[s] the first step to wisdom— "The fear of the Lord is the beginning of wisdom." (*Garland* 95:117-18)

In an 1854 anthology of captivity narratives, *Heroic Women of the West,* the editor, John Frost, claims that the blessings then enjoyed by the American people were a direct result of the toil, suffering, and heroism of the first settlers, including pioneer women. The stories of the latter provided, he maintained, "the most splendid examples of that [female] spirit of self-sacrifice and devotion which can only be prompted by disinterested affection" (*Garland* 66:8). The symbolic complex of female self-sacrifice, "disinterested affection" or selfless action, and redemptive suffering took on a religious

aura in the nineteenth century. Whereas men might at times be motivated by visions of glory to perform acts of courage, women's heroism was understood to be of a purer nature, precisely because female acts of courage and self-sacrifice were assumed to be selfless. Female maternal instinct and love led to egoless actions in which all thought of oneself was overridden by concern for the welfare of others.

The representation of female virtue expressed spontaneously in a time of need was found in innumerable works of literature. In many captivity narratives women often willingly risk their own lives and suffer physical pain in order to protect their children and husbands. In Margaret Hosmer's *The Child Captives,* issued in 1870 by the Presbyterian Publication Board, one finds the following example: "Beyond her power of suppression, [Mrs. Bright] uttered a shriek of horror, which redoubled its agony when she saw [the Indians] approach the bed of her husband. Instinctively she sprang before it to save him, and received in her own breast the ball of a pistol lowered and pointed at him by the leading savage. She fell, and covered his face with her own lifeblood" (*Garland* 83:45).

In *The Capture and Escape* (1870), Sarah Larimer presents herself as always having been motivated by maternal love. In describing how she had successfully escaped from the Indians, carrying her small son, Larimer says that only a mother's love could have driven her to act as she had. Her text, like so many others, is heterogeneous, drawing at points on structuring devices found in earlier captivity narratives, including sentimental and religious ones. The following passage, lifted directly from the manuscript of Fanny Kelly, a fellow captive, deals with the death of Kelly's young daughter, Mary.[16] While it goes on at undue length for modern sensibilities, nineteenth-century readers apparently enjoyed the "luxury of pain and grief" such as this scene produced:

> The body of little Mary had been found pierced by three arrows, and she had been scalped by the ruthless knife. . . . When discovered by a traveller, her body lay with its little hands stretched out, as if she had received, while running, the piercing, deadly arrow. None but God knew the agony of that young heart in its terrible extremity, and surely He, who numbers the sparrows and feeds the ravens, was not unmindful of her in that awful hour, but allowed the heavenly kingdom, to which her trembling soul was about to take flight, to sweeten, with a glimpse of its beatific glory, the bitterness of death—even as the martyr Stephen, seeing the bliss above, could not be conscious of the torture below. (*Garland* 84:113-14)

The understanding informing the composition and reception of scenes such as this was that the pain and suffering visited upon innocent children won them immediate entry into heaven, without their having to wait for the Second Coming. Moreover, the children's memory of their pain was graciously erased by God, who, at the moment of death, granted them a foretaste of the blissful eternal life in heaven that awaited them. Like Harriet Beecher Stowe's depiction of Little Eva's death, the death of little Mary also participated in what Jane Tompkins has called "a pervasive [nineteenth-century] cultural myth which invests the suffering and death of an innocent victim with . . . the power to work in, and change, the world."[17] The significance of Mary's death is presented to the reader as follows:

> Of all strange and terrible fates, no one, who had seen her gentle little face in its loving sweetness, the joy and comfort of her adopted parents' hearts, would ever have predicted such a barbarous one for her. But it was only the passage from death into life, from darkness into daylight, from doubt and fear into love and endless joy. Those little ones, whose spirits float upward from their downy pillows, amid the tears and prayers of broken-hearted friends, are blest to enter into at heaven's shining gate, which lies as near little Mary's rocky, blood-stained pillow in the desolate waste as the palace of a king; and when she had once gained the great and unspeakable bliss of heaven, it must have blotted out the remembrance of the pain that won it, and made no price too great for such delight. (*Garland* 84:115)

Kelly structured her own account of her captivity in large part by drawing a sharp contrast between her expectations of what the family's migration westward would be like and the reality they subsequently encountered. She writes of having set out on the journey "with high-wrought hopes and pleasant anticipations of a romantic and delightful journey across the plains, and a confident expectation of future prosperity among the golden hills of Idaho." Even life in a tent was experienced as an enjoyable extension of homelife before the Indian attack destroyed her family (*Garland* 85:12-14).

Chapter 16, "Scenes on Cannon Ball Prairie—Reflections," is a sustained meditation on the landscape of captivity, blending memories of her childhood and mother, her present state of captivity, and the uncertainty of the future into a general religious statement about human life. Because it encapsulates so many of the cultural values of the time, it bears our careful attention. Kelly narratively sketches the contours of her emotional responses to the landscape, noting each change and shifting shadow. "Well do I remember my thoughts and feelings when first I beheld the mighty and beautiful prairie of Cannon Ball River," she writes. "With what singular emotions I beheld it for the first time! I could compare it to nothing but a vast sea, changed suddenly to earth, with all its heaving, rolling billows; thousands of acres lay spead before me

like a mighty ocean, bounded by nothing but the deep blue sky. What a magnificent sight—a sight that made my soul expand with a lofty thought and its frail tenement sink into utter nothingness before it!" (*Garland* 85:154).

As memories of the past roll over Kelly, the landscape before her—"heaving, rolling"—comes to resemble her own body through an affective affinity. Nature and its scenes could move persons of sensibility in the same way that witnessing the suffering of other persons did. As a result, it was believed that one's affective responses to changes in the scenery and landscape, if carefully noted, could provide moral instruction. Kelly participated fully in the culture of sentiment and invited her reader to share her vision and experience of the landscape and the human condition. Most importantly, she invokes the cult of motherhood, with its emotional complex of selfless love and pain in her didactic reverie:

> I stood and marked every change with that poetical feeling of pleasant sadness which a beautiful sunset rarely fails to awaken in the breast of the lover of nature. I noted every change that was going on, and yet my thoughts were far, far away. I thought of the hundreds of miles that separated me from the friends that I loved. I was recalling the delight with which I had, when a little girl, viewed the farewell scenes of day from so many romantic hills, and lakes, and rivers, rich meadows, mountain gorge and precipice, and the quiet hamlets of my dear native land so far away. I fancied I could see my mother move to the door, with a slow step and heavy heart, and gaze, with yearning affection, toward the broad, the mighty West, and sigh, wondering what had become of her lost child. (*Garland* 85:155)

The vision of her mother, conjured up by the landscape, overwhelms Kelly. In a similar situation in captivity almost two centuries earlier, Mary Rowlandson and Hannah Swarton had been moved to lament the fact that they had failed to keep the sabbath, had been less than ardent in their prayers, or had forsaken a churched community to pursue a desire for more farmland. Kelly, though, is moved to lament her failure to appreciate the sacrifices her mother had willingly made for her. We are in the realm of the cult of motherhood:

> Mother! what a world of affection is comprised in that single word; how little do we in the giddy round of youthful pleasure and folly heed her wise counsels, how lightly do we look upon that zealous care with which she guides our otherwise erring feet, and watches with feelings which none but a mother can know the gradual expansion of our youth to the riper years of discretion. . . . How deeply then we regret a thousand deeds that we have done contrary to her gentle admonitions! How we sigh for those days once more, that we may retrieve what

we have done amiss and and make her kind heart glad with happiness! (*Garland* 85:156)[18]

Kelly's thoughts, memories, and regrets lead her to burst into tears, while, her body trembling, she cries out to her mother. She then reflects on her husband's probable captivity, the murder of her daughter, and the utter destruction of their "short, happy spring-time of life, so full of noble aspirations." She moves quickly to generalize from her immediate situation, suggesting that all life was full of such vicissitudes. Like so many authors before her, she finds all that has befallen her to be part of a divine plan. If her "cup of calamity," as Increase Mather called it, has been full, she claims that nevertheless she has found peace in a state of perfect resignation before life (and death) as these are known in the world (*Garland* 85:158). . . .

Notes

. . . . .[10] Van Campen himself became the subject of a lengthy heroic biography, written by a grandson, who sought to preserve the family's oral history of the Revolutionary War. See John Niles Hubbards, *Sketches of the Life and Adventures of Moses Van Campen* (1841), in [*The Garland Library of Narratives of North American Indian Captivity*. (311 titles in III volumes. Selected and arranged by Wilcomb E. Washburn. New York & London: Garland, 1976-77)] 13.

[11] Apparently, the real Mrs. Howe was not among those readers who found Humphreys's version of her life "interesting." In *A Genuine and Correct Account of the Captivity, Sufferings & Deliverance of Mrs. Jemima Howe* (1792), Humphreys was himself charged with having misrepresented some of the facts of the case and, more seriously, of having besmirched Mrs. Howe's reputation (*Garland* 19:19).

[12] Hume, [David,] *A Treatise of Human Nature,* [ed. Ernest C. Mossner (London: Penguin Books, 1969)] p. 627.

[13] Not everyone seems to have been taken with Williamson's tale of woe, afflications, and the vicissitudes of life. In June 1758 Williamson was imprisoned briefly in Aberdeen at the instigation of some local merchants, who charged him with having libeled them by implying that they were behind the kidnapping of children in the city. More than 350 copies of his narrative were seized by the authorities, threatening the author's livelihood. In prison he was forced to sign a retraction and, as a condition of his release, made to promise to insert this retraction in every copy of his work. After his release, however, the scrappy Williamson went on the offensive again, charging in an expanded edition of his captivity that he had signed the retraction under duress. He also collected and reprinted a number of depositions, sworn before magistrates, to the effect that he had, indeed, been kidnapped as a child and, thus, had not misrepresented the facts. Thus, retelling his tale was a means of attempting to restore his good name. Later, his text was also used in an effort to affect British foreign policy toward the colonies (1758 ed., *Gerland 9*).

[14] See Shepard [Leslie], *History of Street Literature* [(Detroit: Singing Tree Press, 1973).].

[15] James Fenimore Cooper spoke for many members of his generation when, in a laudatory review of Royall Tyler, he quoted the novelist Fielding to the effect that political historians wrote fiction, while novelists, like himself, captured the *real* world in their writing (Davidson) [Cathy N.,], *Revolution and the Word: The Rise of the Novel in America* (New York: Oxford University Press, 1986)], p. 220.

[16] Larimer had announced that because of considerations of length she had been unable to include the full story of her friend Mrs. Kelly, but she promised to do so in a forthcoming work entitled "Mrs. Kelley's Experience among the Indians." Apparently Fanny Kelly did not appreciate her "friend's" effort to tell her story in print, for in her own account, *Narrative of My Captivity,* she writes: "Some explanation is due the public for the delay in publishing this my narrative. From memoranda, kept during the period of my captivity, I had completed the work for publication, when the manuscript was purloined and published" (*Garland* 85:vi).

In October 1870, Kelly filed suit against the Larimers in court. The case was contested in various venues until the summer of 1876, when the parties finally settled out of court, with the Larimers paying approximately $2,000 to Kelly. Details of the legal battle between Kelly and Larimer may be found in Farley, "An Indian Captivity" and in the "Epilogue" (pp. 323-32) to the 1990 reprint of Kelly, *Narrative of My Captivity Among the Sioux Indians.*

[17] Tompkins [Jane,], *Sensational Designs: The Cultural Work of American Fiction, 1790-1860* (New York: Oxford University Press, 1985)], p. 130.

[18] The literature on the cult of motherhood in the eighteenth and nineteenth centuries is extensive. See, for example, Cott [Nancy,], *Bonds of Womanhood: "Woman's Sphere in New England, 1780-1835* (New Haven: Yale University Press, 1977)]; Ryan, [Mary P.,] *Empire of the Mother: American Writing about Domesticity, 1830-1860* (New York: Haworth Press, 1982)] Epstein [Barbora,], *Politics of Domesticity: Women, Evangelism, and Temperance in Nineteenth-Century America* (Middletown, Conn.: Wesleyan University Press, 1981)] and Douglas [Ann.], *Feminization of American Culture* [(New York: Knopf, 1977)]. . . .

FURTHER READING

Carleton, Phillips D. "The Indian Captivity." *American Literature* 15 (April 1943): 169-80.

> Traces the general form, in terms of plot and style, of captivity narratives of the nineteenth century.

Derounian-Stodola, Kathryn Zabelle, and James Arthur Levernier. *The Indian Captivity Narrative, 1550-1900.* New York: Twayne Publishers, 1993, 236 p.

> Analyzes the historical context and popular success of captivity narratives, paying particular attention to gender constructions, the myths and popular images commonly associated with the Indian captors, and the application of the narratives in folklore and children's literature.

Fitzpatrick, Tara. "The Figure of Captivity: The Cultural Work of the Puritan Captivity Narrative." *American Literary History* 3, No. 1 (Spring 1991): 1-26.

> Examines the conflict between "the promise of the wilderness," and the religious and cultural xenophobia that characterizes the earliest American captivity narratives, and continued to inform the genre in its later manifestations.

Griffin, Edward M. "Patricia Hearst and Her Foremothers: The Captivity Fable in America." *The Centennial Review* 36, No. 2 (Spring 1992): 311-26.

> Links the structure and tone of Mary Rowlandson's seventeenth-century account of captivity to Patricia Hearst's 1982 *Every Secret Thing.*

Kestler, Frances Roe, ed. *The Indian Captivity Narrative: A Woman's View.* New York: Garland Publishing, 1990, 588 p.

> Collects the major captivity narratives of the eighteenth and nineteenth centuries.

Levernier, James, and Hennig Cohen, eds. *The Indians and Their Captives.* Westport, Conn.: Greenwood Press, 1977, 291 p.

> Compiles both popular accounts and more literary narratives of captivity from 1557 to 1846.

Pearce, Roy Harvey. "The Significances of the Captivity Narrative." *American Literature* 19, No. 1 (March 1947): 1-20.

> A seminal essay that revived critical interest in the captivity narrative; considers these narratives as literary history.

Saillant, John. "'Remarkably Emancipated from Bondage, Slavery, and Death': An African American Retelling of the Puritan Captivity Narrative, 1820." *Early American Literature* 29, No. 2 (1994): 122-40.

> Discusses the appropriation of the language and tropes of the captivity genre by Lemuel Haynes, a black Calvinist minister, in his *Mystery Developed* (1820).

Thorne, Melvin J. "Fainters and Fighters: Images of Women in the Indian Captivity Narratives." *Midwest Quarterly* 23, No. 4 (Summer 1982): 426-36.

> Studies two contradictory portrayals of women in captivity narratives.

VanDerBeets, Richard. "Captivity Narratives and the Westward Movement." In *The Matter of the Red Man in American Literature,* edited by John J. McAleer, pp. 5-7. Hartford: Transcendental Books, 1984.

> Contends that the captivity narrative served the political aim of inciting nationalistic anti-Indian feeling during the westward expansion of the nineteenth century.

Zanger, Jules. "Living on the Edge: Indian Captivity Narrative and Fairy Tale." *Clio: A Journal of Literature, History and the Philosophy of History* 13, No. 2 (Winter 1984): 123-31.

> Argues that the issue of the frontier or borderland informs the two seemingly disparate genres of fairy tales and captivity narratives.

The Sensation Novel

INTRODUCTION

Corpses, secrets, adultery, insanity, prostitution—all are key elements of the sensation novels of the 1800s. Called sensation novels because they are designed to make the reader feel basic sensations—shock, disbelief, horror, suspense, sexual excitement, and fear—these novels offer unexpected twists and turns within a framework of predictable conventions. These recurring conventions include deathbed confessions, family secrets, mistaken identity, inheritance, bigamy, and female villains. This combination of the predictable and the chaotic is representative of the clash between rigid Victorian society and the changing societal and gender roles that accompanied the emergence of industry and capitalism in England and America. With their exciting plot lines and easily readable format, sensation novels explored unspoken fears and anxieties in a rapidly changing world.

In the mid-1800s, women had few rights and were expected to be subservient to men. Not only were women denied the vote, they were denied the right to own property. Cultural expectations required that women refrain from expressing themselves openly in the presence of men. Rather they were expected to be pure, pleasant, and supportive of men at all times. But, as reflected by the controversial sensation novels, these rigid roles were changing. Feminist critics of the 1980s and 1990s are quick to point out the unusual prevalence of strong female characters in sensation novels, and the way their independent and often sexual behavior was harshly criticized by contemporaries of the novels. Modern critics also point out the way in which female sexuality was often used to denote strength, rebelliousness, and evil. Appearing as nefarious seductresses, female characters were often villains who were punished or made to see the error of their ways at the story's end. Feminist critics also claim that while women in earlier novels had been portrayed as victims waiting to be rescued, in sensation novels the roles were often reversed and the male characters were victimized. Other scholars see the validation of marriage as a common theme of sensation novels and still others argue that the genre allowed women readers of the mid-1800s to enjoy independence vicariously through the actions of the female characters.

With the urbanization that accompanied the industrial boom of the mid-1800s, the big city also played a central role in many sensation novels. Some critics assert that the city provides the setting where men were tempted by villains and seduced by fallen women. These critics also argue that the urban sensation novel celebrated domesticity and the home as sources of renewal, faith, and morality. Female characters were, more often than not, encouraged to remain at the center of home life while men ventured out into the dangerous city with all of its temptations. The city was also the setting wherein shocking secrets about one or more of the characters were revealed. These secrets commonly .involved murder, bigamy, or adultery and often came to light in a deathbed confession scene. This motif arose directly out of the breakdown of rigid Victorian social mores and attitudes toward social class—a breakdown caused in part by the growth of capitalism and urbanization, which offered a variety of new attitudes and opportunities for class mobility.

Major authors of the genre include Mary Elizabeth Braddon, Wilkie Collins, Charles Dickens, Charles Reade, George Meredith, Mrs. Henry Wood, Susan Warner and Caroline Norton. There seem to be differences not only between the styles of male and female writers of the genre, but also in how the work of each was received. For example, Dickens and Reade wrote novels in which elements of detective and crime fiction predominate, while Braddon and the other female novelists most often wrote about strong independent heroines. Some modern critics argue that women novelists were central to the genre while male writers like Dickens merely anticipated it, employing elements that would eventually become associated with sensation fiction. Others argue that Wilkie Collins's *The Woman in White* (1860) was the first genuine sensation novel although that distinction has also been claimed for Mary Elizabeth Braddon's *Lady Audley's Secret* (1862). In addition, critics contemporary to the sensation genre held male novelists in higher esteem than their female counterparts, possibly because women novelists often wrote unconventional plots that featured women as main characters and were more likely to be socially unsettling while male novelists wrote more conventional mysteries. Another reason for this difference may be that in general women in the mid-1800s were not expected to succeed at serious literary endeavors. In any case, male and female novelists were generally categorized into two distinctly separate groups. Wilkie Collins, who was often associated with the female novelists, is the exception. This association was probably due to the strong presence of female heroines in Collins's work. Collins's reaction to being grouped with female novelists and associated with the "feminine" category of sensationalism is explored in Tamar Heller's essay, "Writing After Dark: Collins and Victorian Literary Culture."

Sensation novels were closely tied to the melodramatic theater of the same period. In fact, such writers as Charles Reade and Wilkie Collins wrote drama as well as novels and many of the most well-known sensation novels were written for or adapted to the stage. While conventional dramas were often set in distant castles or far-away lands, sensation theater was set in the present day and location, giving it a proximity and reality that was new to theater-goers.

This sense of reality and proximity was also heightened in the sensation novel by its origins in journalism. Many scholars claim that sensation novels grew out of newspaper stories involving murder, assault, and other crimes that people found especially shocking in Victorian times. Often, these stories revealed the involvement of upstanding, even well-known, citizens in dangerous or immoral behavior. In a culture that valued appearances, revelations of crime among the upper class disrupted idyllic Victorian ideas about society. Failure to be shocked by these events was considered in bad taste—and to write about them was even worse. But the relationship between the new style of fiction writing and the new style of journalism went both ways. Because many of the sensation novelists claimed to get their material straight from the newspaper, they felt justified in writing about it. Meanwhile, newspaper stories suggested that, like the characters in sensation novels, anyone's nextdoor neighbor could turn out to be a murderer or an adulterer, or to have some other scandalous secret. Reading about crimes in the newspaper brought fictional crimes closer to home, made the improbable events of sensation novels seem more real, and made everyday life a little more exciting—all of which helped to make sensation novels immensely popular. Marketed cheaply, sensation novels sold very well at train stations, small stores, kiosks, and newspaper stands and were widely discussed in magazines and newspapers and among ordinary citizens.

Although sensation novels were widely read, they were often criticized by literary critics of the day on the grounds that they were conducive to immorality and vice. Often, the same critics claimed that sensation novels were poorly written. Many believe this reaction was due to the novels' indirect challenge of rigid Victorian social roles and modes of thinking which were well established in the 1860s. In the oncoming industrial age, this play on the undercurring fear of the unknown in the face of change made the sensation novel popular among the masses and unacceptable to high-minded critics. While nineteenth-century critics attacked the genre on moral grounds, later critics found it too common to warrant scholarly attention. In fact, with the exception of T. S. Eliot's well known essay, "Wilkie Collins and Dickens" written in the 1930s, sensation novels were largely ignored by the critics until the 1970s. Although many scholars agree this lack of criticism results from the genre's close relationship with popular culture, critics today are interested for the same reason that critics in the 1960s were indifferent. Focusing on how these novels reflect Victorian thought and social change, modern critics have resurrected the sensation novel and reinstated it as a valuable part of literary history.

REPRESENTATIVE NOVELS

Mary Elizabeth Braddon

Lady Audley's Secret 1862
Aurora Floyd 1863
John Marchmont's Legacy 1863
The Doctor's Wife 1864
Only a Clod 1865

Wilkie Collins
The Dead Secret 1857
The Woman in White 1860
No Name 1862
Armadale 1866
The Moonstone 1868
Man and Wife 1870
Poor Miss Finch 1871-2

Charles Dickens
Nicholas Nickleby 1838-9
The Old Curiosity Shop 1840-1
Barnaby Rudge 1841
Bleak House 1852-3
Great Expectations 1860-1

George Eliot
The Mill on the Floss 1860
Daniel Deronda 1876

Mrs. S. C. Hall
Can Wrong be Right? 1862

Thomas Hardy
Desperate Remedies 1871

Elizabeth Lynn Linton
Grasp Your Nettle 1865

George Meredith
Evan Harrington 1860
Rhoda Fleming 1865

Caroline Norton
Lost and Saved 1863

Ouida
  Held in Bondage 1863

Charles Reade
  It is Never too Late to Mend 1856
  White Lies 1857
  Love me little, Love me long 1859
  Foul Play 1868-9
  A Terrible Temptation 1871
  A Perilous Secret 1883

Susan Warner
  The Wide, Wide World 1850
  Queechy 1852

Mrs. Henry Wood
  East Lynne 1861

OVERVIEWS

Temple Bar (essay date 1870)

SOURCE: "Our Novels," in *Temple Bar*, Vol. XXIX, No. CXV, April, 1870, pp. 410-24.

[In the following essay, the author discusses conventions and themes of the sensation novel from a nineteenth-century perspective.]

The Sensational School.

In attempting to treat the second branch of our subject—the School of Sensational Novels—we are confronted on the very threshold with a challenge, if not, indeed, with a difficulty. What is a sensational novel? And by what principle of discrimination do we affix to any existing class of romance this special and scarcely complimentary title? (There is yet another difficulty; but it is one which must accompany our inquiry into each school of novels, and which indeed attends nearly all attempts at classification. Is So-and-so a sensational novel? And, if it is, is Such-and-such, which differs from So-and-so in a conspicuous manner, also a sensational novel? In roughly settling this difficulty, injustice, we are aware, may very possibly be done; but no critic professes to have perfectly faultless balances. For instance, while the exceedingly clever authoress of 'Cometh up as a Flower' may seem to share some of the peculiarities of this school, it would be the height of blindness not to recognise the fact, that in many respects she is brilliantly distinguished from those writers.) Our answer to this very proper question—which has been put over and over again by extremely reasonable objectors, and to which, as far as we know, there has never yet been given an adequate and satisfactory reply—shall be forthcoming in due time. But

we must first address ourselves to a brief literary retrospect, in the course of which we make no doubt some of our readers will conceive that we are providing evidence of the antiquity of the sensational novel amply sufficient to cut the ground completely from under our feet. We must, however, ask them to be good enough to suspend their judgment until they have heard us out.

It stands to reason, as much as it accords with tradition, that the very earliest storytellers must have appealed to the particular human emotions on whose still sensitive chords our sensational novelists delight to play. In this sense, but (as we shall see later) only in this sense, the sensational novel may claim the honour of a very remote ancestry. We possess no learning on the subject which is not open almost to everyone; and if we seem to dip into deep wells for our illustrations, it is, in reality, that others have brought their water for us to the surface; and we offer our readers a taste of it, only in order that they may, a little later, be able to compare it with the flavour of those modern productions which, we maintain, alone deserve the epithet popularly given to them. At first sight, the old 'Erotikoi' (as they are called), or writers of erotic adventures, would seem to have as much in common with the authors of one kind of romance as with those of another, since love is the indispensable hinge on which the tales of all novelists alike turn; but it is on account of this very community of interest as far as love is concerned, that we must seek for differences of character in some other department of the emotions. Now, if we may be allowed to speak of the 'Erotikoi' as a whole, and to take no note of the exceptions which could no doubt be adduced against our rule, we may say that they have certain broad features in common which will be recognised as having considerable affinity with the modern school called sensational. Unkind fates sever heroes and heroines devotedly attached. If domestic fortune forbears to frown, fierce bandits swoop down upon them at the moment of their union, and bear them away into bitter captivity. If separated by evil chance, their days are spent in adventurous wanderings. They travel in unknown climes; they pass through perils by land and perils by sea; they are a thousand times within a second of eternity, when the *deus ex machinâ,* so warmly deprecated by Horace, invariably intervenes to snatch them from destruction. Their final reunion is brought about by agency thoroughly miraculous, though not more so than that with which many recent examples have made the public familiar; and though the stories of the 'Erotikoi' resemble nearly all works of fiction by their happy termination, their special affinity to the school of which we are treating is seen afresh in their hero or heroine constantly turning out to be a person of much greater importance and much higher rank than had been supposed. Poison plays a considerable part in their pages, as it has done in those of writers with whom we are more closely acquainted; magic takes the place of that somnambulism and of those spiritualistic phenomena which nowadays come so copiously to the rescue of the involved sensationalist. Nor in the romances of chivalry shall we seek in vain for some similarity to certain stories of our own time, which assuredly cannot be called chivalrous, though the similarity is much slighter than in the case we have just been considering. As has been well observed, the 'Erotikoi' employed Fate and its ministers to drive their personages into the domain of excitement and adventure; whereas in the romances of chivalry, the heroes are their own fate, and spontaneously wander in search of peril and bloodshed. Their exploits are extraordinary—magical—incredible; but their tone is healthy, and it is evident that the writer has exerted his imagination to exalt a brave and sanguine audience, and not, as in the case of the 'Erotikoi,' to stimulate a worn-out and depressed people. In the middle of the sixteenth century we seem to come upon fresh representatives of the Sensational School, in such writers as Giovanni Giraldi Cinthio, to whom, probably, Shakespeare was indebted for the story of Othello. We have to traverse two centuries before we again meet with any body of romances which can even be said to be ancestors in a direct line of our Sensational School. Horace Walpole's 'Castle of Otranto,' Clara Reeve's 'Old English Baron,' and the wonderful works of Mrs. Radcliffe, to which may be added those of Lewis and Maturin, revived the love of romantic horrors; and the readers of fiction were once more led through secret and gloomy passages, made familiar with haunted sleeping-chambers, carried into the recesses of dismal forests in order to preside over the execution of fiendish murders, initiated into the mysteries of frowning castles, and freely admitted into the company of tremendous bandits. A quarter of a century later, thieves, highwaymen, and desperadoes were introduced to public notice through the medium of the novel; and Dick Turpin, Claude Duval, and Jack Sheppard engaged the sympathies of a crowd of readers.

With these few but salient facts in our mind—which we have purposely set in a light most favourable to the theory that the Sensational School of to-day (of which so much has been said) is no novel phenomenon, but only the continuation of a school which has existed from time immemorial—let us turn to the works which form our immediate subject, and see, by an analysis of them, how far that theory is from the real truth. We can pass but a very few of them in review; but we shall select the best known, the most read, and the most warmly applauded. We shall, however, be able to see, from the community of the features of those we do analyse, how applicable the judgment passed upon them probably is to those we leave untouched.

The first noticeable peculiarity in the novels of the time which are called sensational, is that their story is always laid in the present day. They are invariably supposed to depict contemporary incidents and contemporary manners. We shall have something to say on this point later; but we will not interrupt our account of their characters, plot, situations, and *mises en scène,* by any desultory criticisms. Suffice it to say, that proximity of time is deemed indispensable to the effect they are intended to create. If the novel is printed about 1860, care is taken to inform us, early in its pages, that "three days after this, the 14th of June, 1856," such an event occurred to the heroine; and then, to bring us still nearer, we are informed, a little further on, that it is late in the August of 1857. The reader may thus well hope to reach 1860 before the end of the third volume, by which means the mysterious occurrences detailed in all three will be brought almost to his own door; and that is a great advantage. Similarly, the scene is invariably laid in our own country. Every publisher affirms, that for a novelist to take his personages abroad, is to damn his book irretrievably; yet one would have thought that when something exceptionally terrible and mysterious had to be made credible, the more distant and unknown the locality, the more easily would the wonder-telling author be believed. That is a stage we have long since passed. The *omne ignotum pro mirifico* maxim is no longer needed. We are prepared to believe in wonders only if they happen hard-by. Our sensational novelists, accordingly, stick to their native land; and as a very large proportion of subscribers to the circulating libraries live in London or its vicinity, they usually restrict themselves to the metropolis for their town-life, and to the home-counties for their rural life. In London itself, they find it difficult to make the *mise en scène* of rich and fashionable existence gloomy and suggestive of horrors; so there they devote themselves to contrast, and place a female murderess or a man haunted with the memory of crime amid light and joyous surroundings. But when they get into the country, they can more easily prepare the reader for shocking disclosures. Fish-ponds, dry moats, and ruinous walls covered with dark moss, surround a house surmounted by chimneys broken down by age and long service, and which would topple down but for the ivy which supports them. They have doors studded with great iron nails, and so thick that the sharp iron knocker strikes upon it with a muffled sound; and the visitor, fearing that the noise of his knocking will even penetrate these strongholds, rings a clanging bell nestled in the gloomy ivy aforesaid. So deathlike is the tranquillity of all around, that he feels a corpse must be lying somewhere in that grey pile of building. When a servant makes her appearance, she speaks of it as "a mortal dull place," adding, "I've heard tell of a murder that was done here in old times." It has rustic beauty, we are told, and its owner has done all he can to make it a fit habitation for his bright young wife; but nothing can save it from being hopelessly dreary. In one of its chambers there is a secret passage, with, which everybody save the person who sleeps in it is acquainted. To judge our climate from the description of our sensational novelists, a foreigner would suppose that the wind howled six days out of every seven. Boreas is made to do considerable duty by writers of the Sensational School. It has its own way, we are told, and makes cruel use of its power. It batters and beats the low thatched roofs of outhouses and stables, till they lean over and lurch forward. It shakes and rattles the wooden shutters before the narrow casements, till they hang broken and dilapidated on their hinges. And having done all these things, it flies away, shrieking, to riot and glory in its destroying strength. If, after all this, the reader is not prepared to be poisoned, stabbed, blown into the air; to find a skeleton in every cupboard, and a lost will in every drawer; to meet with an inconvenient number of husbands, and a most perplexing superfluity of wives; and to get rid of them by arson, strangulation, or a deep well, he must be very insensible to the influence and charm of situation.

Having prepared us by these well-known arts not to be surprised at anything, our sensational novelists then introduce us to domestic relations of an exceedingly peculiar character. The means are various, though only slightly various, but the end invariably one—to make the reader very tolerant of whatever strange thing may happen beneath the roof of the home to whose secrets he is introduced. On one occasion he will find that its master, a man of title and of conspicuous position in his county, has married a young woman without a single relation, and of whose antecedents he knows absolutely nothing, and never, makes any inquiry. The circumstance might, we should imagine, excite some surprise, but it is casually mentioned as the most natural thing in the world. She comes as governess to a neighbouring family, in answer to an advertisement, and no one—it is said with exquisite *naïveté,* or the imitation of it—knew anything more about her. Her lord is quite happy in his mind in the matter, though he knows as little as anybody else, and his silence stops the mouths of all others. Yet this 'waif-and-stray,' who comes from nowhere, is a perfect phœnix. Her accomplishments, we are told, are strangely numerous and brilliant: she is the chief attraction of every gathering in the neighbourhood, and she returns home from local races wearied out with the exertion of fascinating half the county; she does water-colour drawings with exquisite taste, and she plays and sings divinely. Such a personage is well calculated to secure the interest of minds more excitable than critical; but the attraction of mystery is heightened by her wearing a narrow black ribbon round her neck, with something or other attached to it—but what nobody knows, for she always keeps it hidden under her dress. She plays with the ribbon when she is meditating; she clutches at it, as though it is strangling her, when she is the victim of a great temptation to which she ultimately yields. In a word, she already has a husband living when the man with the title, ignorant of the fact, proposes to and is accepted by her. The whole interest of the story depends upon the situations which can be made to follow from this entanglement. Sometimes the case is modified by a bigamist heroine being the victim of an error. She marries, believing her first husband to be dead—but she is mistaken; and as he is one of the lowest of his species, whilst her second lord is a gentleman of rank and fortune, here again there is ample room for the exciting and the improbable. The contempt of the probable has, as a matter of course, to be carried to a high pitch, and is one of the most striking features of these novels. Men passionately in love with their wives, and whom wind, tide, or steam cannot carry fast enough to them, let months on months pass by without writing to them, simply because a single letter would have rendered the plot of the story impossible. A country bumpkin, improperly admitted into the bigamist wife's boudoir, accidentally opens a secret drawer, finds a baby's shoe and a lock of child's hair, which places the secret of the life of the mistress in the keeping of the maid. The former pretends to be dead and buried so successfully, that even her first husband erects a tombstone over her. He finds that she is alive only by accidentally visiting the house in which she now lives—by casually, and without any special object, crawling into her apartment through a low narrow passage—and by finding himself in front of a portrait which he recognises as hers. As he then seeks an interview with her, and refuses to leave her to her agreeable life of luxury, she manages to drop him into a deep well, from which, however, he escapes even more wonderfully than he got into her boudoir. He then abandons her and everybody, leaving the whole world to suppose that he is dead. A careful scrutiny would probably show that nearly all the novels of the Sensational School are built, so to speak, on the same lines. Open which of them we will, we are infallibly reminded of the one we have just closed. This time the father of the heroine, again a person of considerable social position, has married an actress, and the mother's bohemian blood filters through into the veins of her daughter. You are already quite sure that she is about to turn out a bigamist; and the only surprise left you is the discovery that she is an amiable one. But how can an amiable young lady marry a second husband, her first one being still alive? Nothing more easy to the sensational novelist. Dead, yet not dead, is one of their favourite resources—which, it may be observed, is only another use of the double-edged device displayed in the situation produced by a bigamous marriage. The amiable young lady reads in a newspaper that the low wretch whom she ran away from school to marry, and who, although he married her for her money, has allowed her to leave him and return to her father, has broken his neck over a stiff hurdle, and been taken up stone-dead. Forthwith she accepts a lover who has long been urging his suit, and who, like the rest of the world, with the exception of her father, herself, and a confidant of her husband, knows nothing of her history. Very shortly after the engagement, her ponies are violently stopped in her father's park by a dog-fancier—her husband's confidant, to wit; and though her *fiancé* is by her side, she descends, and enters into a long private conversation under the trees with her assailant. She refuses to give her lover any explanation of the extraordinary incident; and though he is a very mettlesome person, he tolerates her silence, and the horrible suspicions to which the circumstance has given rise. Very shortly, however, the situation becomes so mysterious, that he does break off the engagement; and the amiable young lady consoles herself by marrying another rich flame of the good simpleton sort, who is perfectly aware that there is a mystery connected with her, and that her former lover discarded her for it—but who takes her to his heart and home, notwithstanding. Almost immediately after the marriage, the amiable young lady discovers that the report of her first husband's death was a mistake. Amiability—to say nothing of common honesty and common sense—would have dictated an avowal of the unhappy but innocent situation. That, however, would have brought the sensational story to a premature close; so the amiable young lady enters upon a couple of volumes of courageous subterfuge and deception. The most admirable coincidences occur to aggravate her case—the most notable one being that the second husband engages the first one as his stud-groom. Still the amiable young lady holds her peace and braves it out. Here another stock-device is employed in order to pile up the agony and superadd to the sensation. We have said that in the stories we are discussing there is always a wonderful detective; a superhumanly shrewd barrister, who has nothing else to do but to go about and unravel the mysterious threads that envelope the lives of his friends; or some seeming fool, who is in reality devoting himself to the solution of personal problems apparently insoluble. In the case of the amiable young lady, there is an anything-but-amiable lady-companion and housekeeper of middle-life, who constitutes herself a spy upon the movements and conduct of the wife, and who, thoug both the wife and the husband (who is devotedly attached to her) are perfectly well aware what she is doing, is permitted by them to remain in the establishment. A single word from either would have been sufficient for her dismissal; but then, what would have become of the situation? With the same contempt of the probable—nay, of the possible—the stud-groom is allowed to retain his situation, even though the wife manifests great emotion on his arrival, and though she tells her husband, *tout bonnement,* that the groom is acquainted with the secret which from him she keeps jealously concealed. But why should we pursue this particular specimen of the Sensational School? We have been travelling over well-known ground—only bringing, during the journey, its most monstrous features into more salient relief. That such a situation should culminate in a murder is, we own, natural enough, and equally so is it that the amiable young lady should be suspected as the perpetrator of it. The wonderful detective is once more introduced, to trace the crime to its real source; and the heroine is, in the end, amply rewarded for all this remarkable amiability.

We have said that the 'time' of these sensational dramas is to-day; and on this point we shall yet have a good deal to observe. For the present, however, we desire to note only the plausible uses made in them of certain convenient resources essentially modern. The old romancer could, it is true, send his personages into distant climes, when it was necessary for a short time to get rid of them; but, in that case, he was obliged to send them nobody knew where—to the Hesperides, to the inhospitable Caucasus, to Ultima Thule, to the back of the North Wind. The modern reader would not stand that. Not that such a mode of treatment would be too improbable an improbability for his stomach, but for quite another reason. He knows nothing of the Hesperides, the inhospitable Caucasus, Ultima Thule, or the back of the North Wind; and he does not suppose that he knows anything about them. Moreover, he does not want to know anything about them. But he does know something about Australia, or he fancies he does; and he wants to know something more—or, at least, to hear it talked about—because he has a brother, son, cousin, or former servant there, and he is aware that hundreds of people have there made large fortunes. Accordingly, Australia is the very thing for the sensational novelist to conjure with. If such a distance does not quite lend enchantment to the view, it makes bigamy, missing letters, the rapid accumulation of money, and misreported deaths amazingly feasible. Australia has been a true goldfield to the Sensational School of novelists, and many a good 'find' has it provided for them. The daily newspaper is another invaluable modern ally. In it may be inserted false announcements of births, false announcements of deaths, and false announcements of marriages; and the well-known 'agony column' is the sensational novel in embryo. Nor any less invaluable are the penny post and the telegraphic wires. Assisted by such agents, the trusted wife "can smile and smile and be a villain" without the smallest chance of detection before the end of the third volume. A lady wishes to leave her home for the day on some plausible excuse. What more easy? At breakfast the servant brings her a telegraphic message. She is much surprised, and wonders what it can be. It is from an old governess, who is dangerously ill, and who begs the favour of her presence before dying. Of course she must comply with the request, and her husband accompanies her. The telegram bears no address, but they very naturally go to the house where the governess was living when the wife last saw her. She is not there, and nobody in the neighbourhood can give any information on the subject. In other words, the telegram was a deception from beginning to end, devised by the wife to hoodwink her husband and baffle an amateur detective.

The part played by this last species of person is an almost undeviating feature of the novel sensational. He is made to act the part of an analytical chorus, the writer not trusting the unaided faculties of his readers to find out where, at any particular stage of the artificial perplexity and convolutions, they precisely are. He periodically sums up the situation—an operation which, speaking for ourselves, we confess to have found very convenient, since in reading sensational novels our memory has a trick of deserting us, and our attention of playing truant. It is therefore highly consoling and commodious to find, when you are about a third through the story, and it has made so little, or so confused, an impression on you, that you fear you must either read it all over again or give it up as a bad job—that the amateur detective has drawn up a schedule of facts, enumerated under some fifteen or twenty headings, just as in a barrister's brief, or a case for opinion. We may add that his good-luck is even more remarkable than his ability for what is popularly called "putting two and two together." He will stumble, for instance, on an annual which seems to be the most innocent of its kind, and which he is just about to lay down, when he casually discovers that two blank leaves in it are stuck together. He separates them with his paper-knife, and what he discovers between them for ever places the villain of the story in his power. Of course he does not avail himself of his knowledge as yet. We are only in the middle of the second volume, and the interest must be sustained by his gratuitous longsuffering. Should he be in want of a bit of handwriting with which to compare a letter in his possession, he has but to go and lodge at the seaside, and, lo! it is forthcoming. If he should happen to need a chronological record of a lady's travels, he has the good fortune, far away from her present abode, to stumble on an old trunk of hers, to which still adhere legible railway labels. None of them give any clue to the facts he is striving to verify. However, he gets a sponge and a little water, removes one of the labels, and underneath it is another which lets the required cat out of the bag. The clever person—and she is very clever—who does everything she can conceive to do away with the traces of her identity, and indeed of her entire past, leaves these convenient threads, by which the history of her previous obscure career is successfully tracked. But every fresh discovery only starts a fresh mystery. When you have every reason to suppose that you have reached the heart of the secret, you are then allowed to see that within that secret is yet another secret, without which the explanation of the first is not an explanation. In many cases there is no real secret, no real mystery at all; and the confiding temper of the reader has, in vulgar parlance, been made a fool of by the—let it be acknowledged—very remarkable ingenuity of the writer. If a jewel—on the possession of which the whole story turns—is missing, and the cardinal question is, who has got it? surely the reader may justifiably consider himself 'sold' when he is at length allowed to know that one of the characters of the story has, in a somnambulistic state, removed it from the ordinary place of deposit, and unconsciously hidden it. In the instance to which we are referring, the consummate craft with which the interest is sustained, and the excellence of the language in which the story is told, should be frankly acknowledged; but, for all that, the reader has been sucking in the east-wind, and we may infer, with the Scotchman, that he will not get fat on it.

The lurid light which we have spoken of as being purposely thrown over the inanimate scenes amid which the action of the sensational novel usually takes place, is in them often made to surround the leading characters. The study of imagination and character is one of the favourite pursuits of our time, and it can boast of novelists who have done some striking work for it in that direction. But it is not in the novels of the Sensational School that we must look for true instances, though a hasty shallow criticism has over and over again ascribed to them a quality they do not possess. There is a vast distinction between character and characteristics; and the 'lurid' people in sensational novels are only people with characteristics. We yield to no one in admiration for the genius of Charles Dickens; but as he never, by any chance, encounters genuine criticism, and as, if he were to write the most arrant nonsense in the world (which we fear he now not unoften does), nobody would have the candour to say so in print, we may, perhaps, venture to observe, that this trick of substituting characteristics for character, and palming off the one for the other, is borrowed from a man whose exquisite sense of the ludicrous, mastery over pathos, and discriminating judgment in the employment of terror, these writers have, unfortunately, not imitated. A squint, a limp, a hump, a peculiarity of speech, an eccentricity of hair—any obvious and salient external idiosyncracy—does duty nowadays, both in novels and on the stage, to make a man or woman a character. All exaggeration, it has been said, is weakness, and grotesqueness is the resource of feeble artists. Few people can pretend to know any single one of their most intimate acquaintances as thoroughly as George Eliot has made them know Tito in 'Romola.' Yet Tito—base bad Tito!—has the exterior of an angel, and is as free from personal peculiarities and distinctive tricks as is a statue. Tito is a magnificent specimen of character-portraiture; none better exists in this world. All George Eliot's novels—'Felix Holt,' perhaps, excepted—are filled with kindred examples; but in no one single instance is there the faintest attempt to bring the character more home to us, by attaching to the person some conspicuous and externally-protruded and reiterated peculiarity. George Eliot is too strong for that. Turn to our sensational novels, and they swarm with these feeble and, as it seems, often befooling devices. We have singular old men, first exhibited to us in the vastness of a room, with wainscoting behind them, and with the light so falling on them that their faces and figures come out into forcible relief. They have vivid strange eyes, silver hair that hangs down to their shoulders, but withal black eyebrows. They wear peculiar garments, and either stoop noticeably, or stand supernaturally upright. Their children are as peculiar, externally, as themselves. They are gentlemen and ladies of birth; but they will be made to talk the broadest provincial English, so that they may be accepted as characters at once. If a governess has to play a leading part in a domestic tragedy, she is the oddest figure in the world—has large and hollow features, wears the most extraordinary clothes conceivable, has bleached and sallow skin, and is a foreigner who talks English peculiarly. She pronounces child *'cheaile,'* and on the strength of it is a character for the rest of the book. If the writer wants to make her a very characteristic personage, he adds blindness and the smallpox, and the reader must be dull indeed who does not then accept her as a very remarkable character indeed. In fact, these sensational characters are nothing but puppets, which, as in a Punch-and-Judy show, we know by their dress or distinguish by their speech.

Puppets, however, hung with characteristics have this advantage over genuine characters, that the wire-man below—that is to say, the writer—can make them do anything he likes, without disturbing the credulity of the average reader, or transmuting his gape into a stare. Sensational novelists avail themselves of this advantage with striking prodigality. "As accessories to this story," we read the other day in a review of a book proceeding from the Sensational School, "there are three midnight murders, a ruined girl trapped in a lunatic asylum" [lunatic asylums are a mine of wealth to these authors and authoresses], "some wholesale knocking-down in a gaming-house, the elopement of a married woman disguised as a boy; and in the course of the narrative we are treated to no less than eleven deaths." We have not read the novel in question, for this species of literature is inexhaustible; but we have come across very well-known samples of sensational art where the agony is piled up equally high. In one of these, which has had hundreds of thousands of fashionable readers, the first hundred pages favour us with a murder, a seduction, a suicide, and the transformation into a drawing-room maiden of a low street-singer. One of the characters commits a murder in each volume. We do not know that we could put its remaining contents into language more succinct than that in which they were described in a weekly review at the time the book appeared. Testimony other than our own on the subject will, perhaps, not be amiss: "We have a sailor accusing his honest father-in-law of murder, a husband accusing his wife of adultery; the disappearance of a baby heiress, who lives in a castle, and is protected by a great iron door; the achievements of a London detective"—*ecce iterum Crispinus!*—"and the ignominious failures of a husband-hunter. Marvellous, too, are the adventures of the heroine, who sings in low publichouses at Wapping, is said to be the child of a wretch whom she knows to be a murderer, is picked out of a gutter by a baronet worth £40,000 a year, is transferred to a thoroughly aristocratic seminary presided over by two maiden sisters, marries the baronet, is made a widow in a few weeks through the devices of one of the personages of the story, devotes herself to purposes of revenge, and discovers at last that she is the stolen child of a lady of title and distantly connected with her husband's family." The description is enough to take away one's breath. But (as many of our readers will know) we have not been speaking of a serial story of 'Reynolds's Miscellany' or the 'London Journal,' but of a novel, "large numbers" of which, it was advertised on its appearance, would be "taken" by the circulating libraries, where well-appointed carriages most do congregate.

Now, are such novels, plentiful too as blackberries, a satisfactory feature of the time? And if we answer in the negative, in what respect does their unsatisfactory character differ from that of all the novels, romances, and stories ever written to excite interest, appeal to sustained curiosity, gratify the appetite for the marvellous, and answer the human demand for imaginary horror? We take it that the broad line of distinction between the writers of the Sensational School of to-day, and the writers in various past ages whose works would, on a hasty classification, be by many catalogued with those of the former, is that they despise that distance which not only lends enchantment to the view, but which justifies both writer and reader for accepting as likely the grossly improbable. Suppose an Athenian had laid the horrors of tragedy on the shoulders, not of imaginary or of semimythical ancestors, but on those of people to be seen every day in the temple or the marketplace—would he have impressed his contemporaries with a high sense of his dramatic powers, or would they have accepted his parricides, matricides, fratricides, and incests as the result of a judicious use of imaginative ingenuity? There is a very considerable difference, no doubt, between tragedies and novels; but the difference, as far as the right of violating probability is concerned, is all on the side of the former. The mask, the buskin, and all the other accessories of stage art, reconcile one to the improbable far more easily and successfully than does paper covered with mere print. But to compare novels with novels, and not with a higher and more advantageous mode of exciting emotion, when before did it ever enter the head of the writer of romance to find a field for the exercise of his more awful powers just at his own door or round the corner? With a due sense of the fitness of things, rather did he travel far afield, and seek, in remote and somewhat obscure regions, for a reasonable arena wherein to make men and women act outrageously. Outrageous their actions did not seem, happening in places where personal experience had not gone before, and set the boundaries of the probable and the improbable. In the domain of romance, as in that of theology, there is a particular sphere, where the doctrine *Credo quia impossibile*—"I believe the thing because it is impossible"—solves every difficulty. But it is not a sphere within one's own cognisance. When we know nothing, we are ready to believe anything—and very properly so. The most extravagant of fairy-tales offends no one, but delights all. When we are told that—

"The air hath bubbles as the water hath,
And these are of them,"

we experience no difficulty in conceding the assumption. We cannot know that it is not so; and we are pleased, instead of shocked, at a bold surmise that is more than equivalent to the discovery of another land.

In these days of fiction, however, a change has really come over the spirit of our dreams. It is on our domestic hearths that we are taught to look for the incredible. A mystery sleeps in our cradles; fearful errors lurk in our nuptial couches; fiends sit down with us at table; our innocent-looking garden-walks hold the secret of treacherous murders; and our servants take £20 a year from us for the sake of having us at their mercy. Describe these things as happening last century, or even thirty years ago, or as taking place in Asia Minor or Calabria, and no one will pay you the slightest heed. Publishers will probably decline to entertain it. You have misapprehended the taste of the time. Turn Calabria into St. John's Wood, and for Asia Minor substitute Mayfair—then double the improbable incidents, and be a popular sensational novelist.

What is the cause of this very pronounced taste on the part of the novel-readers of England? No one cause will account for it; the causes are many. The first that occurs to us is that we are becoming more insular than ever we were, narrowing the sphere of our interests, and carrying into literature the practice of non-intervention first started in connection with politics. It would be but a shallow answer to remark, that for one Englishman who went abroad thirty years ago, ten, or perhaps twenty, do so now. Granted; but what Goldsmith said last century is more than ever true in this—that most people travel to confirm their prejudices. They explore a continent, and return more insular in sentiment than before they had passed the rolling limits of their native island. It is not from the number of people who make passing excursions into foreign parts that we must gather the amount of general interest taken in the phenomena of foreign life. Novels are a much surer test; and let one or two good instances stand for many. It is not merely our own opinion (though we hold it strongly), but that of several competent judges, that there are few novels in the English language so charming as the Italian stories of Mr. Thomas Adolphus Trollope. No novelist writes with a more intimate acquaintance with the scenes in which the action of his books is laid, and

none with a more shrewd familiarity with peculiarities of national character. Moreover, the emotional interest in such books as 'La Beata' is of the highest prose order, and of the most intense kind. Yet, though warmly appreciated by a select circle, Mr. T. A. Trollope's Italian novels have certainly not had the success they deserve. An English novel by that writer, 'Lindisfarne Chase,' has, we believe, been far more largely read; but it is markedly inferior to his Italian stories. It is the choice of locality that has settled their respective popularity. Thousands of people who devour the English novels of Mr. Trollope's brother, Mr. Anthony Trollope, are not aware that he too has written stories of foreign lands. His name is not on the titlepage; but, even if it were, the fact that Bohemia, not England, is the home of the characters would amply suffice to give him but one reader where he usually has a hundred. Again, what has been the least successful of George Eliot's novels?—Romola? Why? because it was the least meritorious?—Not at all; but because its interest was centred in past times and in foreign lands. Of 'Esmond,' immeasurably the best of Thackeray's novels, the same tale might almost be told; though, in its case, England was still its theme, though not the England of to-day.

To put the thing compactly, the interests of the public are narrow interests—narrow in point of place, narrow in point of time. But, in proportion as they have grown narrowed, they have become intensified. There are very few things about which the novel-reading public wants to know anything at all; but when it wants to know at all, it wants to know everything, and, if possible, more than everything. Deeply curious as to the affairs of its immediate neighbours, whilst profoundly indifferent to those of people who stand to it in a more remote relationship, the public will, in the case of the former, invent mystery, strangeness, and interest, where in reality there is none of the three, and insist upon investing the honest British householder, his passionless materfamilias, and simpering girls, with volcanic feelings, dark designs, and a tragic fate. Certain social distinctions somewhat assist the process. We have such hard-and-fast lines in this country, that to people who live in Bloomsbury, people who live in Belgravia may easily be made a mystery, and *vice versâ*. Quite ignoring the fact that there is a great deal of human nature in men and women—indeed, more of that than of anything else, no matter what their sphere—the sensational novelist invites his bourgeois readers to believe that people of title are an exception to all human rules; young ladies of fashionable life, that poor governesses are far more fearfully and wonderfully made than themselves; and the respectable classes of society, that they are surrounded by creatures who are ever ready for treason, treacheries, and toils. Nor need it be denied, that there is just enough foundation in actual experience to give these fantastic pictures a colourable excuse. Every now an then some strange domestic incident of modern life is revealed to the universal gaze in our courts of law, and in the communicative columns of the daily papers. On that small substratum of the strange, horrible and revolting, the Sensational School build their tremendous castles in the air. Furnished with the Ten Commandments, and the occasionally startling breaches of them disclosed by the police, they picture to us an entire society swarming with thieves, murderers, adulterers and bigamists. It has been said, that there is always something agreeable to us in the misfortunes of our neighbours. It would certainly seem as though a record of their vices is eminently pleasing. But if people will persist in prying overmuch into the affairs of their immediate acquaintance, they are sure to end by imputing to them a host of faults and vices, perhaps of crimes; and the modern sensational novel gratifies the same petty taste that hungers for depreciatory tittle-tattle and scandalous gossip. We remember to have once seen a sensational novel described as 'kitchen literature.' We thought the epithet appropriate. Unhappily, the sensational novel is that one touch of anything but nature that makes the kitchen and the drawing-room kin.

As in the case of the Fast School, let the ability displayed by many writers of the Sensational School be frankly acknowledged; and when we come to consider the ethical drift of their work, we must absolve them from the charge of immorality that has been brought against them by some critics—unless, indeed, we take the word "immoral" in an unusually wide signification. No doubt the reading of sensational novels must have a deteriorating effect on the mind, and we doubt if a single human being has ever reaped one iota of benefit from them. They stimulate only to depress. They are the worst form of mental food, if we except that which is absolutely poisonous. As we have already said, they represent life neither as it is nor as it ought to be; and, therefore, while they fail to instruct, they do not even attempt to elevate. In a word, they are neither exact nor exalting; and the world may congratulate itself when the last sensational novel has been written and forgotten.

Patrick Brantlinger (essay date 1982)

SOURCE: "What is 'Sensational' about the 'Sensation Novel'?" In *Nineteenth-Century Fiction,* Vol. 37, No. 1, June, 1982, pp. 1-28.

[*In the following essay, Brantlinger offers an in-depth overview of the sensation novel.*]

Even though "sensation novels" were a minor subgenre of British fiction that flourished in the 1860s only to die out a decade or two later, they live on in several forms of popular culture, obviously so in their most direct offspring—modern mystery, detective, and sus-

pense fiction and films. The sensation novel was and is sensational partly because of content: it deals with crime, often murder as an outcome of adultery and sometimes of bigamy, in apparently proper, bourgeois, domestic settings. But the fictions of Wilkie Collins, Sheridan Le Fanu, Mary Elizabeth Braddon, Charles Reade, Mrs. Henry Wood, and some other popular authors of the 1860s have special structural qualities as well, which can perhaps be summed up historically as their unique mixture of contemporary domestic realism with elements of the Gothic romance, the Newgate novel of criminal "low life," and the "silver fork" novel of scandalous and sometimes criminal "high life."

The best sensation novels are also, as Kathleen Tillotson points out, "novels with a secret," or sometimes several secrets, in which new narrative strategies were developed to tantalize the reader by withholding information rather than divulging it.[1] The forthright declarative statements of realistic fiction are, in a sense, now punctuated by question marks. This structural feature is crucial for the later development of the mystery novel, though it also points backward to both Gothic and Newgate fictions. Crimes do not always involve mysteries in earlier fictions, but sometimes they do, as in *Oliver Twist* and *The Mysteries of Udolpho.* The emergence of the protagonist as detective or of the detective as an aid to the protagonist—most obviously in the case of Sergeant Cuff in *The Moonstone*—marks the evolution of a genre of popular fiction which refuses to follow the path of direct revelation prescribed by realism but instead hides as much as it reveals. Jacques Derrida argues that it may be "impossible not to mix genres" because "lodged within the heart of the law [of genre] itself [is] a law of impurity or a principle of contamination."[2] Derrida suggests that the peculiar mark or structural feature that defines any genre can never belong exclusively to that genre but always falls partly outside it. The element of mystery in a sensation novel I take to be such a distinguishing feature, one that both sets sensation novels apart from more realistic fictions and points to their relatedness to some other romantic and popular forms.

Without drawing hard-and-fast lines between it and earlier Gothic romances or later detective fictions, the sensation novel can be defined from at least three different but complementary perspectives. The most familiar is historical, involving the situating of certain novels and novelists in their 1860s context of Gothic and domestic realism in fiction, the powerful influence of Dickens, stage melodrama, "sensational" journalism, and bigamy trials and divorce law reform. A second perspective involves isolating those structural features of the sensation novel genre that, in Derrida's terms, represent its peculiar mark or marks, even while recognizing that such features may partially characterize some other genres as well—or in other words, that it may be "impossible not to mix genres." In the second section, I argue that an apparent disintegration of narrative authority, caused by the introduction of secular mystery as a main ingredient of plots, is an especially significant trait of the sensation novel. The third perspective is psychological. Perhaps no genre of high or popular culture has so often been subjected to psychoanalytic scrutiny as the mystery novel. I shall suggest in the final section that, as a forebear of modern detective fiction, the sensation novel shares several of its psychological properties. Taken together, these perspectives should provide a fairly comprehensive definition of a genre of fiction that stands midway between romanticism and realism, Gothic "mysteries" and modern mysteries, and popular and high culture forms—a genre, in other words, that like all genres is itself a mixture of sometimes contradictory forms, styles, and conventions.

I

In a review entitled "The Enigma Novel," a writer in *The Spectator* for 28 December 1861 declared: "We are threatened with a new variety of the sensation novel, a host of cleverly complicated stories, the whole interest of which consists in the gradual unravelling of some carefully prepared enigma."[3] Although not every tale that has come to be labeled a sensation novel involves a mystery—Charles Reade, for example, rarely withholds the sources of villainy from his readers, qualifying as a sensationalist chiefly on the grounds of content—many imply by their very structures that domestic tranquility conceals heinous desires and deeds. And although its subject is no more sensational than those of *The Woman in White* (1860), *No Name* (1862), and *Armadale* (1866), Collins's *The Moonstone* (1868) is often called the first mystery-cum-detective novel which, according to Dorothy Sayers, set a standard of perfection that later mystery writers have failed to meet.[4]

Just as much as the introduction of sex and violence, about which the first reviewers of sensation novels raised a great hue and cry, the introduction of mystery into a novel form that seems otherwise to follow the conventions of domestic realism posed disturbing questions. These questions arise on both the thematic and structural levels. On the former level, there is the problem of the relation of mysteries of crime, adultery, skeletons in family closets to religious mystery. By a kind of metaphoric sleight of hand, the Gothic romance had managed to make secular mystery seem like a version of religious mystery. *The Monk*, for example, straddles the fence between a gruesome, sadomasochistic thriller and a religious fantasy with horrific but just religious penalties visited upon Ambrosio at the end. The mysteries in *Uncle Silas* (1864), *Lady Audley's Secret* (1862), *East Lynne* (1861), and *The Moonstone*,

however, have not even a quasi-religious content. Le Fanu perpetuates the supernatural elements of Gothic as metaphors (Silas Ruthvyn as werewolf or vampire), and Collins links speculations about fate to the accidental turnings of his multiple plots. Everything that happens in *The Moonstone,* for example, can be interpreted as the fulfillment of the curse that follows the diamond, while everything that happens in *Armadale* seems predestined either because it is wildly coincidental or because it has been predicted by Allan Armadale's dream. But the sensation novel involves both the secularization and the domestication of the apparently higher (or at any rate, more romantic) mysteries of the Gothic romance. Ironically, just as novel-writing seems to be growing more "sensational" in the 1860s, it is also growing tamer. From one perspective, the sensation novel represents an infusion of romantic elements into realism. From another, it represents the reduction of romance to fit Biedermeier frames.

During the 1860s "sensation" and "sensational" were attached—usually with more than a dash of sarcasm—to artifacts other than novels. There were "sensation dramas" at least as early as Dion Boucicault's melodramatic hit of 1861, *The Colleen Bawn,* and also "sensational" advertisements, products, journals, crimes, and scandals. Theatrical "sensations" like Boucicault's or like Tom Taylor's *The Ticket-of-Leave Man* (1863), which features the professional detective and master disguise artist Hawkshaw, suggest the connection between stage melodrama and the sensation novel that foreshadows the relationship between best sellers and the cinema today.[5] Most of the writers of sensation novels also wrote melodramas, and best sellers like *East Lynne* and *Lady Audley's Secret* were quickly dramatized. With his enthusiasm for all things theatrical, Dickens set the pattern. "Every writer of fiction," he declared, " . . . writes, in effect, for the stage."[6] In the preface to his early novel, *Basil* (1852), Collins asserted that "the Novel and the Play are twin-sisters in the family of Fiction" and invoked the poetic license for "extraordinary accidents and events" that he associated with the theater.[7] And Charles Reade thought of himself as a "philosophical melodramatist" first, a novelist second. Any piece of fiction—his own, Smollett's *Peregrine Pickle*, Trollope's *Ralph the Heir*, Zola's *L'Assommoir*—was grist for Reade's melodramatic mill. In more than one instance he even converted a play into a novel, rewriting *Masks and Faces* (1852) as *Peg Woffington* (1853) and extracting *White Lies* (1857) from an earlier script.[8] In his analysis of sensation fiction for the *Spectator*, Richard Holt Hutton states what was often literally the case: "The melodrama of the cheap theatres is an acted sensational novel."[9]

As with melodrama, so with the sensation novel: violent and thrilling action, astonishing coincidences, stereotypic heroes, heroines, and villains, much sentimentality, and virtue rewarded and vice apparently punished at the end. As Winifred Hughes argues, however, "With the rise of the sensation novel, melodrama . . . lost its innocence." Partly because of its moral ambiguity, the sensation novel was felt to be dangerous by many of its first critics, while stage melodrama seemed less threatening. Traditional melodrama celebrated virtue and domesticity, but the sensation novel questions them, at least by implication. Of course the subversive qualities of novels like *Lady Audley's Secret* are not overt. As Hughes points out, bigamy—that favorite "sensation" crime (next to murder)—"has the advantage of making sexual offense" or "vice" punishable. And it also validates the institution of marriage in a backhanded way.[10]

Bigamy, adultery, and the problem of divorce law were much on the minds of Victorians in the 1860s. Jeanne Fahnestock has shown the influence of—among other "sensational" events—the 1861 Yelverton bigamy-divorce trial on the fiction of Braddon, Reade, and others. "After the Yelverton revelations, the public was painfully aware of the disgraceful accumulation of laws governing marriage . . . which made bigamy legally possible" (Captain Yelverton himself escaped without serious legal penalty).[11] Even in those sensation novels whose plots do not hinge upon bigamy, there is a strong interest in sexual irregularities, adultery, forced marriages, and marriages formed under false pretenses. But rather than striking forthright blows in favor of divorce law reform and greater sexual freedom, sensation novels usually tend merely to exploit public interest in these issues. Wilkie Collins's concern with marriage and divorce law in *No Name* and *Man and Wife* (1870) is exceptional, as are Charles Reade's themes of social reform and sexual conflict in stories like *Hard Cash* (1863) and *Griffith Gaunt* (1866).

Partly because of its generally exploitative approach to controversial issues like bigamy and adultery, the sensation novel was felt to be disreputable by most contemporary reviewers. Henry James, for example, writes about *Aurora Floyd* and *Lady Audley's Secret* with half-contemptuous admiration, as "clever" and "audacious" literary tricks that their author has managed to bring off by applying a "thoroughgoing-realism" to the "romance" of "vice."[12] Especially when they dealt with bigamy, sensation novels seemed to be a British equivalent of the suspect "French novels" that Robert Audley carries about with him and sometimes reads in *Lady Audley's Secret* (or, as *Punch* called it, *Lady Disorderly's Secret*). One reviewer of Collins's *No Name* mistakenly declared the sensation novel to be "a plant of foreign growth":

It comes to us from France, and it can only be imported in a mutilated condition. Without entering on the relative morality or immorality of French and

English novelists, one may say generally that, with us, novels turn upon the vicissitudes of legitimate love and decorous affection; while in France they are based upon the working of those loves and passions which are not in accordance with our rules of respectability.[13]

This hardly gives British fiction prior to the 1860s its due with regard to the illegitimate and indecorous. But subjects were broached in sensation novels that many good Victorians thought inappropriate, and the fact that these subjects seemed not to be addressed seriously but merely "sensationally" made them all the more disreputable. No doubt the greatest sensation of all was the discovery by many respectable readers in the 1860s (though hardly unknown in prior decades) that crime paid in fiction, as Count Fosco in *The Woman in White* says it pays in life. James understands this; as he says in his review of *Aurora Floyd,* "The novelist who interprets the illegitimate world to the legitimate world, commands from the nature of his position a certain popularity."[14]

James is content to analyze the clever though shallow artistry by which Braddon produces best sellers, but other reviewers saw in the sensation novel something much more disturbing. The Archbishop of York preached a sermon against sensation novels in the Huddersfield Church Institute in 1864, in which he declared that "sensational stories were tales which aimed at this effect simply—of exciting in the mind some deep feeling of overwrought interest by the means of some terrible passion or crime. They want to persuade people that in almost every one of the well-ordered houses of their neighbours there [is] a skeleton shut up in some cupboard." W. Fraser Rae, who quotes the Archbishop in the *North British Review* (September 1865), describes sensation novels as "one of the abominations of the age."[15]

Negative responses to the sensation novel often echo negative responses to Dickens. What Thackeray said in *Catherine*—that Dickens romanticizes crime and dwells upon the most sordid and "extravagant" aspects of life—was repeated many times over in the reviews of Collins, Braddon, Wood, and Ouida. And just as the sensation novel was felt to exercise a corrupting influence on higher culture, Dickens's novels were often similarly viewed, as when Dr. Thomas Arnold told Wordsworth that "his lads seemed to care for nothing but Bozzy's next No., and the Classics suffered accordingly."[16] All of Dickens's major novels involve crime and detection at least tangentially, and many of the other ingredients of sensation fiction are present in his work at least as early as *Oliver Twist* and *Barnaby Rudge.* Thus, the former comes close to being both a Newgate and a mystery novel: in unraveling the secret of Oliver's parentage and thwarting Monks, Mr. Brownlow plays the role of the full-fledged detectives in later novels. *Oliver Twist* also contains foreshadowings of professional detectives in the Bow Street runners, Blathers and Duff. Moreover, at least the metaphors in *Oliver Twist* give it a magical, quasi-Gothic coloring, albeit more probably derived from such sources as *Grimm's Fairy Tales* than from *The Mysteries of Udolpho* or *Melmoth the Wanderer*. Oliver's entrapment in the underworld slums of the thieves is in one way not so different from the entrapment of Mrs. Radcliffe's heroines in their picturesque alpine castles and abbeys, for despite the changes of location, sex, and social message, they share the archetypal pattern of youthful innocence threatened by deviltry. In any case, next to Dickens's fiction, the Gothic tales of mystery, suspense, erotic awakening, and quasi-supernatural terror of Mrs. Radcliffe and her successors were the most important antecedents of the sensation novel of the 1860s.

Some sensation novels are indistinguishable from Gothic romances. Many of Le Fanu's stories of terror and the occult should perhaps be categorized as Gothic rather than sensation fictions, if only because of the dominance of supernatural over realistic elements. In the preface to *Uncle Silas,* Le Fanu rejects the new label and invokes an older tradition:

> May [the author] be permitted a few words . . . of remonstrance against the promiscuous application of the term "sensation" to that large school of fiction which transgresses no one of those canons of construction and morality which, in producing the unapproachable "Waverley Novels," their great author imposed upon himself? No one, it is assumed, would describe Sir Walter Scott's romances as "sensation novels"; yet in that marvellous series there is not a single tale in which death, crime, and, in some form, mystery, have not a place.[17]

Scott may be the ancestor whom Le Fanu would most like to claim, but his thinly veiled sadomasochistic tale of the captivity, deception, near-seduction, and near-murder of an adolescent heroine points more directly to Mrs. Radcliffe. Maud Ruthvyn suggests as much when, about to explore the decaying mansion of her Uncle Silas, she tells her maid: "I feel so like Adelaide, in the 'Romance of the Forest,' the book I was reading to you last night, when she commenced her delightful rambles through the interminable ruined abbey in the forest" (ch. 54, p. 358).

In the sensation novel, the Gothic is brought up to date and so mixed with the conventions of realism as to make its events seem possible if not exactly probable. In "sensationalizing" modern life, however, the novelists paradoxically discovered that they were making fictions out of the stuff that filled the newspapers every day. Indeed, on one level they could even claim that to sensationalize was to be realistic. In *Victorian Studies in Scarlet,* Richard D. Altick points out that "every good new Victorian murder helped legitimize,

and prolong the fashion of sensational plots."[18] Historically there is a direct relationship between the sensation novel and sensational journalism, from the extensive crime reporting in the *Times* and the *Daily Telegraph* to such early crime tabloids as the *Illustrated Police News.* Collins based some of the details of *The Moonstone* on the sensational news stories of the Constance Kent murder in 1860 and the Northumberland Street murder in 1861. As Dickens modeled Bucket on Inspector Field, so Collins modeled Sergeant Cuff on Inspector Whicher, the chief detective in the Kent affair. And Henry James writes of *Lady Audley's Secret:*

> The novelty lay in the heroine being, not a picturesque Italian of the fourteenth century, but an English gentlewoman of the current year, familiar with the use of the railway and the telegraph. The intense probability of the story is constantly reiterated. Modern England—the England of to-day's newspaper—crops up at every step.[19]

Much more disparagingly, Henry Mansel complained about the emergence of "the criminal variety of the Newspaper Novel, a class of fiction having about the same relation to the genuine historical novel that the police reports of the 'Times' have to the pages of Thucydides or Clarendon." All a writer of a sensation novel needed to do, said Mansel, was to "keep an eye on the criminal reports of the daily newspapers," which would virtually write his fiction for him.[20]

Mansel's outcry against "the Newspaper Novel" comes especially close to Charles Reade. Of all the sensation novelists, Reade was most dependent on the newspapers, just as he was also the most involved in stage melodrama. When the *Times* criticized his *A Terrible Temptation* (1871), partly for its portrayal of the "scarlet woman" Rhoda Somerset, Reade wrote two letters to the editor protesting that he had merely "dramatized" facts reported by the *Times.* Indeed, all of his best novels, he said, were inspired by the *Times:* "For 18 years, at least, the journal you conduct so ably has been my preceptor, and the main source of my works— at all events of the most approved." Reade proceeds to list several of his works inspired by the *Times.* Of *It Is Never Too Late to Mend,* he says, "a noble passage in the *Times* of September 7 or 8, 1853, touched my heart [and] inflamed my imagination." Of *Hard Cash,* he says that "an able and eloquent leader on private asylums" gave him the main theme for his exposé novel. And *Put Yourself in His Place* grew out of Reade's perusal of *Times* articles "upon trades unions and trade outrages."[21] Reade is incensed that his favorite paper should complain about the subjects of his novels when he takes those subjects straight from that paper. He could argue that his novels were based upon the "great facts" of the age and were therefore thoroughly realistic. As he frequently declared, he was a writer of "romances founded on facts." Those who wanted to dismiss his novels as melodramatic, crude, or worse, had first to show that the facts were not melodramatic or crude.

II

Winifred Hughes points out that Reade's obsessive insistence on the factual basis of his stories implies a lack of faith in the authority of fictive imagination.[22] A similar difficulty in claiming authority marks the narrative structures of many sensation novels. Because they blended romance with realism, the sensational with the domestic and contemporary, improbable or at least infrequent events with probable settings and characters, sensation novels posed difficulties for their writers as well as their first readers. Murders and conspiracies do not lurk down every dark street, in the shadows of every dark house. Or do they? Newspapers suggested otherwise, and how could a sensation novelist who imitated the newspapers fail to be realistic? Here is one way in which the conventions of fictional realism come to be punctuated with question marks. Mary Elizabeth Braddon states part of the creed of the sensation novelist when she makes her amateur detective-hero, Robert Audley, tell his villainous aunt:

"What do we know of the mysteries that may hang about the houses we enter? If I were to go to-morrow into that commonplace, plebeian, eight-roomed house in which Maria Manning and her husband murdered their guest, I should have no awful prescience of that bygone horror. Foul deeds have been done under the most hospitable roofs; terrible crimes have been committed amid the fairest scenes, and have left no trace upon the spot where they were done. . . . I believe that we may look into the smiling face of a murderer, and admire its tranquil beauty."[23]

The reference to Maria Manning emphasizes the credibility of such a character as Lady Audley, who is herself an incarnation of this creed: her outward beauty—the blonde, blue-eyed, childlike but also coquettish stereotype of female loveliness and innocence—masks insanity, bigamy, homicide.

The plots of sensation novels lead to the unmasking of extreme evil behind fair appearances. In doing so, they threatened their first readers' cherished assumptions about women, marriage, and the fair appearances of the Victorian scene. "Bigamy novels" clearly played upon their readers' own marital frustrations and disillusionments. As James explains, an author like Braddon—aggressive, clever, familiar with the ways of the world—herself represents an antithesis to the Victorian ideal of innocent and unchallenging womanhood: "Miss Braddon deals familiarly with gamblers, and betting-men, and flashy reprobates of every description. She knows much that ladies are not accustomed to know, but that they are apparently very glad

to learn."[24] Braddon could be taken as going beyond the genteel realism of a Trollope or a Thackeray to unlock the true mysteries of life—those that more proper Victorians thought should be walled off from the reader. Perhaps the overriding feature of both melodrama and the sensation novel is the subordination of character to plot; in the novel, not just plot but also descriptive detail and setting can deduct from character. Collins seems to belie this when, in the preface to the first edition of *The Moonstone,* he says:

> In some of my former novels, the object proposed has been to trace the influence of circumstances upon character. In the present story I have reversed the process. The attempt made, here, is to trace the influence of character on circumstances. The conduct pursued, under a sudden emergency, by a young girl, supplies the foundation on which I have built this book.[25]

The "young girl" is undoubtedly Rachel Verinder, though Collins might also mean Rosanna Spearman, who hides the chief clue—Franklin Blake's paint-smeared nightgown—in the quicksand. But Collins's point is hardly persuasive. Rachel's failure to confront Franklin with what she has seen prolongs the mystery, but the mystery itself is largely independent of character. If character were really central, her rejection of Franklin should serve as a tip-off to a clever detective like Cuff, who instead suspects Rachel. The initial "circumstance" is the bequest of the diamond to Rachel by her uncle, from which everything else follows. The lives of all the characters are dramatically—indeed, melodramatically—altered by this circumstance; the accursed diamond casts a spell on everyone, only broken by the unraveling of the mystery and the sensational events at the end.

In fiction as in melodrama, the sensational derives much more from plot than from character. Boucicault's plays were famous for their "sensation scenes," like the rescue from drowning in *The Colleen Bawn* and the explosion on the steamboat in *The Octoroon,* and sensation novels contain equivalent episodes, like the arson scenes in *The Woman in White* and *Lady Audley's Secret.* Only a well-conceived villain or villainess—Collins's Count Fosco, Braddon's Lady Audley, Le Fanu's Uncle Silas—seems strong enough both to shape circumstances and to rival sensational events in interest. But even they are doomed to fall prey to circumstances: an inadvertent clue, a startling coincidence is all that melodramatic justice seems to need to unravel their secrets. The world of melodrama and of the sensation novel is very much one in which circumstances rule characters, propelling them through the intricate machinations of plots that act like fate. "A hand that is stronger than my own is beckoning me onward upon the dark road," says Robert Audley, several times over, in Braddon's tale (ch. 23, p. 131). He is the amateur detective of the story, but he performs that role reluctantly, contradicting both his placid character and some of his better inclinations.

Early in her story, Braddon intrudes as narrator to make the same point that her hero makes about crime and mystery "amid the fairest scenes." What is remarkable about this narrative interpolation is that it seems itself out of context, coming long before the reader is certain that any crime has occurred, and even well before the disappearance of Lady Audley's first husband, George Talboys. On one side of the intrusion, Talboys and Robert Audley are peacefully fishing. On the other side, they return peacefully to their rustic inn. The narrative interruption seems therefore abrupt, gratuitous, shocking, like its subject matter:

> We hear every day of murders committed in the country. Brutal and treacherous murders; slow, protracted agonies from poisons administered by some kindred hand; sudden and violent deaths by cruel blows, inflicted with a stake cut from some spreading oak, whose every shadow promised— peace. In the county of which I write, I have been shown a meadow in which, on a quiet summer Sunday evening, a young farmer murdered the girl who had loved and trusted him; and yet, even now, with the stain of that foul deed upon it, the aspect of the spot is—peace. No species of crime has ever been committed in the worst rookeries about Seven Dials that has not been also done in the face of that rustic calm which still, in spite of all, we look on with a tender, half-mournful yearning, and associate with—peace. (ch. 7, p. 36)

This passage is a microcosm of the sensation novel— indeed, of all mystery novels—not just in its content, but in its structure of abrupt revelation. And not merely fiction but life is like this, Braddon says: peace masks violence; innocent appearances cloak evil intentions; reality itself functions as a mystery until the sudden revelation of guilt, which is always lurking in the shadows. The passage also serves as a foreshadowing; even before we are aware of specific crimes, Braddon makes us listen to the jingling of the keys to the mystery, all of which are in the narrator's possession. We learn at the outset how ignorant we are about the story to come—and consequently about life and the nature of evil—and how much knowledge and power the narrator has.

Sensation novels involve not radically new techniques but manneristic extensions of features from earlier novels. Braddon's key jingling is a case in point. Without any consciously experimental intention, she pushes third-person omniscient narration to its logical limits. The narrator, even while foreshadowing with fatalistic implications, ceases to convey all information and begins to disguise much of it as hints, clues, hiatuses, as when Lady Audley orders her maid to send what would be, if revealed, an incriminating telegram: "'And now listen, Phoebe. What I want you to do is very simple.' It was so simple that it was told in five minutes, and then Lady Audley retired into her bed-room" (ch. 7, p. 39). The central mystery, the disappearance of George Talboys, involves the same pattern. We sense that the narrator is being willful and even capricious when George and Robert view Lady Audley's portrait, but George—and the narrator—give no sign of recognition. And when George wanders away from Robert and from us, not to reappear until the end of the novel, the same feeling of narrative willfulness arises.

In *The Woman in White* and *The Moonstone,* Collins escapes from the logical awkwardness of Braddon's narrative hide-and-seek by a pattern of multiple first-person narrations roughly similar, as Kathleen Tillotson suggests, to the overlapping and conflicting voices of *The Ring and the Book* (itself almost a versified sensation novel, though set in the past). But it would be a mistake to overemphasize the uniqueness of this pattern or to fail to recognize the many aspects of Collins's novels that are quite familiar within the general context of Victorian fiction. T. S. Eliot suggests as much when he says that the distinction of genre between *East Lynne* and *The Mill on the Floss* is much less than the modern distinction between "highbrow" and detective fiction.[26] Nevertheless, to some extent sensation novels represent extreme elaborations and almost parodic inversions of works like *Middlemarch* and *Barchester Towers*. The distinction is not a sharp one, but it approximates Trollope's description in his *Autobiography:*

> Among English novels of the present day, and among English novelists, a great division is made. There are sensational novels and anti-sensational, sensational novelists and anti-sensational. . . . The novelists who are considered to be anti-sensational are generally called realistic. I am realistic. My friend Wilkie Collins is generally supposed to be sensational.[27]

Trollope goes on to say that he thinks this division a mistake on the part of the critics; "a good novel should be both" realistic and sensational, "and both in the highest degree." But realism and sensationalism are still antithetical in his usage, and he clearly prefers the probable and commonplace to their opposites. *The Eustace Diamonds* (1873), for example, may itself parody *The Moonstone,* partly by removing the mystery and keeping no secrets from the reader.[28]

At the same time that the narrator of a sensation novel seems to acquire authority by withholding the solution to a mystery, he or she also loses authority or at least innocence, becoming a figure no longer to be trusted. Just as character is subordinated to plot in the sensation novel, so the narrator is diminished by no longer communicating with the reliability of the tellers of more forthright tales. From a presiding mentor, sage, or worldly wise ironist guiding us through the story as in *Middlemarch* or *Barchester Towers,* the narrative persona must now become either secretive or something less than omniscient, perhaps slipping back into the interstices of the story as unobtrusively as possible. If the content of the sensation novel represented a challenge to bourgeois morality, one way that challenge shows up structurally is in the undermining of the narrator's credibility. When the story is still told through third-person omniscient narration, as in *Lady Audley's Secret* and *Armadale,* the problem is most acute: the narrative persona shares the knowledge of the crime with the criminal characters but does not share it directly with the reader. The narrator therefore takes on a shady, perhaps even criminal look reminiscent of the old idea that a detective must be in secret sympathy with criminals in order to catch them (and metaphorically, at least, detectives are often portrayed as being in league with the devil).[29] This moral ambiguity is a bit like the relationship between Vautrin and the narrator of *Père Goriot:* both are men of the world, both have penetrated the "mysteries" of Paris in ways undreamt of by Eugène Rastignac, and both are interested in Eugène's journey from innocence to experience. Vautrin, of course, is a diabolical tempter, but it is also clear that the narrator's variety of experience is not exactly angelic.

Structurally the detective emerges in the sensation novel as a substitute for the forthright narrative personae of more realistic novels, or as a personification of the morally ambivalent role of the narrator. Like their prototypes, Inspector Bucket and Sergeant Cuff, most fictional detectives have at the outset a kind of reduced omniscience, similar to Vautrin's worldly knowledge: they are familiar with society, crime, and criminals, but about the causes of the particular crime in a story they are at first as much in doubt as the reader. They do not have a solution but they know how to arrive at one. They can follow the clues that the no longer trustworthy narrator-author places in their path, leading towards a restoration both of social order and of some semblance of narrative omniscience, often through a recapitulation of the hidden events by the detective, at the end of the story.

Of course the emergence of the detective in fiction can be explained historically as well as structurally. Walter Benjamin has analyzed the evolution of detective fiction as a corollary of the growth of urban anonymity and alienation.[30] To such a general analysis must be added the more specific details of the creation of the police and detective forces in nineteenth-century cities and of the fascination of Dickens, Collins, and other writers with them. Bucket and Cuff represent a penetration of criminal low life and of "the mysteries of

London" that their creators both envied and identified as part of their own novelistic equipment. Mystery and detection in nineteenth-century fiction also appear to be correlatives of the growth of professional and technical specialization. As the specialist—like the detective—acquires knowledge in one area, other areas become opaque, mysterious. The detective as a specialist who unravels criminal mysteries expresses a wish fulfillment shared by all of us, to be able to know or to read just a few things very well, like clues, but through reading them very well to penetrate the deepest mysteries of life.

The early, naïve development of omniscient narration in fiction breaks down partly from the intrusion of mystery into it, but partly also from the recognition of the conventional—and logically preposterous—nature of omniscience. Within Jane Austen's compass of "two or three families in a country village," omniscient narration proceeds without apparent difficulty. Within Dickens's London it begins to seem more artificial, both because the idea of a narrative persona knowing everything about such a vast place implies something close to supernatural authority (clearly an uneasy fit in fiction purporting to be realistic) and because from the outset Dickens wants to show us the "mysteries" of the city while still rendering them mysterious. Dickens's occasional experiments with narrative structure—the double narration of *Bleak House,* for example—can be seen as attempts to deal with these contradictions. So, too, can the even more radical experiments in Wilkie Collins's novels: the multiple narrations of *The Woman in White* and *The Moonstone,* the odd mixture of narrative patterns and effects in *No Name* and *Armadale.* In the latter, Collins achieves something close to multiple narration by interjecting correspondence without authorial comment (the letters between Lydia Gwilt and Maria Oldershaw), long passages of dialogue in which characters recount their life stories (the opening confession of Allan Armadale), condensations of long periods of time as viewed through the memories of a single character (the Rev. Mr. Brock's recollections in the first chapter of the second book), and Lydia's diary at the end of the tale. At the same time, the supposedly omniscient narrator of *Armadale* does not often intrude into the story either to moralize or to speculate about events.

The strange world of the Armadale "doubles" and of the dream which comes true seems thus to exist in a kind of vacuum. Because of the dream and the heavy doses of coincidence, everything in *Armadale* seems to be laden with a preternatural—if not quite supernatural—significance. Because of the unobtrusiveness of the narrator, however, this potential significance is never explained, even while the reader—in common with the characters—witnesses the unraveling of the secular mysteries that constitute the plot. The story's emphasis on "fate" or "destiny" does not finally point beyond the labyrinthine windings of its plot to something more than accident or chance. When Collins does at last intrude as narrator, presumably to explain the higher mysteries to which the secular mysteries seem to point, it is only in an appendix in which he gives no answers: "My readers will perceive that I have purposely left them, with reference to the Dream in this story, in the position which they would occupy in the case of a dream in real life—they are free to interpret it by the natural or the supernatural theory, as the bent of their own minds may incline them."[31] Of course Collins is only dodging the questions about dreams and predestination that his novel has so elaborately raised. The passage thus represents an abdication of omniscience and a backhanded acknowledgment of the diminished stature of the narrative persona in contrast to, say, those in George Eliot's novels.

As in *Armadale,* the introduction of mystery—the self-conscious withholding of any important information from the reader—necessarily both diminishes and complicates the role of narrator. The narrator must seem either to connive with criminals, thereby sacrificing moral legitimacy, or to suffer a kind of structural amnesia, only recovering something close to omniscience as a version of memory or recapitulation at the end of the story. The detective—in the sensation novel, often the protagonist like Walter Hartright of *The Woman in White* rather than a professional—appears to fill the vacuum created by the at least partial abdication of authority by the narrator. Even when the conventions of third-person omniscient narration are maintained, as in *Armadale* and *Lady Audley's Secret,* once detection begins the information supplied to the reader tends to be reduced to the information possessed or discovered by the detective. The mystery acts like a story which the narrator refuses or has forgotten how to tell; the detective must now "put the pieces together." The plot unwinds through the gradual discovery—or, better, recovery—of knowledge, until at the end what detective and reader know coincides with what the secretive or somehow remiss narrator-author has presumably known all along. But this coincidence of knowledge is no longer "omniscience" of the kind present, say, in *Middlemarch.* The diminution—indeed, perhaps even criminalization—of the narrator is also linked to a diminution of the kind of knowledge hidden and recovered: he or she can now hold the keys only to a secular mystery, ordinarily of the criminal, most sordid kind, and can no longer make any very credible or consistent claim to be able to unlock the higher mysteries of life, nature, society, God. The equivocations and silences of Collins's narrative personae suggest these transformations of metaphysical-religious knowledge into the solution of a crime puzzle and of the omniscient narrator into a collaborator with his disreputable character doubles, the criminal and the detective.

The detective, moreover, is not so much the antithesis of the narrator, trying to recover what the narrator

secretes, as one of his personifications in the text, presiding over the plot and leading the reader down several false paths before discovering—or recovering—the true one. That is, just as the narrator in the sensation novel must simultaneously reveal and withhold information, so the detective: his knowledge is usually greater than the reader's, but it is incomplete; he may finally know even less than the reader. Sergeant Cuff, for example, solves only parts of the mystery in *The Moonstone,* sets up some false leads, and then leaves the scene until near the end; he is not exactly more successful at providing information than the missing third-person narrator. In W. S. Gilbert's comic opera spoof, *A Sensation Novel in Three Volumes,* the Scotland Yard investigator, Gripper, seems mainly bent on delaying the solution of mysteries and allowing criminals to escape. Disguised as a North American Indian, Gripper says:

> When information I receive that Jones has been a-forging,
> And on the proceeds of his crime is prodigally gorging,
> Do you suppose I collar my friend and take him to the beak, m'm?
> Why, bless your heart, they wouldn't retain me in the force a week, m'm.
>
> In curious wig and quaint disguise, and strangely altered face, m'm,
> Unrecognised I follow my prey about from place to place, m'm;
> I note his hair, his eyes, his nose, his clothing and complexion,
> And when I have got 'em all into my head, I set about detection.[32]

And thus Jones slips through Gripper's fingers. Gilbert is right: fictional detectives seem often to be in collusion with both criminals and narrators, functioning as much to blow smoke in the reader's eyes as to provide solutions. They mimic the ambivalence of their at least partially abdicated narrators. Their roles are largely dictated by the central structural ambiguity upon which all mystery and detective fiction is based, an ambiguity suggested by the idea of "telling a secret"—you must first be a party to holding the secret in order to tell it.

III

Despite the air of preternatural significance in a novel like *Armadale,* mysteries in most sensation novels do not clearly connect with anything higher than a particular case of arson or bigamy or murder. The mysteries in *Bleak House* point to the larger mysteries of community and isolation, love and selfishness in the society that Dickens anatomizes. But the mystery of *The Moonstone,* even though serious attitudes about crime and poverty, religious hypocrisy, the law, and the empire can be inferred from it, does not explicitly point beyond itself to larger issues.[33] And unlike the Dedlocks and their followers in *Bleak House,* who represent everything that Dickens thinks is wrong with the decaying aristocracy of the 1850s, Sir Percival Glyde and Count Fosco in *The Woman in White* are not bearers of social or even very weighty moral messages. Sir Percival is a stereotypic melodrama villain from whose career of deceit and crime Collins asks us to draw only the most obvious of morals. Count Fosco is much more interesting as a character, but the shadowy Italian politics that destroy him at the end of the novel are only a deus ex machina to bring on his just deserts. Collins is not interested in saying anything about secret societies, or Mazzini, or the Orsini affair. He does not even take the occasion to deplore the terrible conditions in private insane asylums, as Charles Reade does in *Hard Cash.* Several of Collins's other novels—*No Name* and *Man and Wife* with their treatment of the injustice of the marriage laws, for example—take up social reform themes in the Dickens manner. And no matter how melodramatic, Charles Reade's novels put social reform in the forefront.

The mysteries in *Lady Audley's Secret, Uncle Silas, The Woman in White,* and *The Moonstone,* however, function like those in later mystery novels and do not connect with anything outside themselves. In each case, though much that is violent and terrifying happens along the way, the mystery turns out to be soluble, unlike the larger mysteries raised by *Bleak House* and *Our Mutual Friend.* The worst evils that can be perpetrated by individuals are unmasked, but the instant of their revelation is usually also the instant of their exorcism. The paradox is that sensation novels—and mystery novels after them—conclude in ways that liquidate mystery: they are not finally mysterious at all. The insoluble is reduced to the soluble, just as the social evils that most concern Dickens are reduced to the level of personal villainy. Guilt is displaced onto others, which is to say onto scapegoat characters whom we are quite glad to see punished, and the good characters with whom we most strongly identify "come out clean" and are rewarded with happy endings. W. H. Auden describes the process in his essay on mysteries, "The Guilty Vicarage":

> The magic formula is an innocence which is discovered to contain guilt; then a suspicion of being the guilty one; and finally a real innocence from which the guilty other has been expelled, a cure effected, not by me or my neighbors, but by the miraculous intervention of a genius from outside who removes guilt by giving knowledge of guilt. (The detective story subscribes, in fact, to the Socratic daydream: "Sin is ignorance.")[34]

Auden suggests the ritual nature of detective fiction, with the detective as the priest who performs the exorcism. But the pattern is not fully developed in sensation novels, which are more flexible and various than modern detective novels and, as T. S. Eliot points out, closer to serious fiction.[35] Their structures are consequently less reassuring; the detectives in them, for example, are usually not Auden's "genius from outside" but a character or characters directly involved in the story. Indeed, Sergeant Cuff, the prototype of later professional sleuths, is not the chief detective in *The Moonstone.* That role belongs to Franklin Blake, the protagonist, who turns out also to have stolen the diamond. And the piecemeal process of detection depends heavily on luck and coincidence, as in *Oliver Twist* (the most striking coincidence in *The Moonstone,* of course, is also the most baffling: that Franklin Blake himself is the thief).

The paradox of Franklin Blake, or of the detective in pursuit of himself, points to the essence of later mystery novels. Most serious novels—manifestly in a *Bildungsroman,* for example—involve a search for the self, the attempt of at least one character to stake out a career or an identity in the social wilderness. In sensation and mystery novels, however, just as the intractable problem of evil is reduced to a neatly soluble puzzle on a personal level, so the search for self is short-circuited. The unraveling of the mystery, as in *The Moonstone* where Franklin Blake works his way through the labyrinth of clues and false leads only to discover that he himself has stolen the diamond, mimics self-revelation but points the other way. The mystery revealed exonerates both the protagonist and the reader from guilt: Franklin's act was unconscious; the real villain is his rival, Godfrey Ablewhite, whom we are only too glad to have murdered by the convenient Indians, the rightful owners of the gem.

Few works of fiction have been more psychoanalyzed—as opposed to criticized and admired for their serious qualities—than *The Moonstone.* This is due partly to its approximation to fullness and seriousness. It is a big novel, with many characters, with an unusual narrative structure, and with an intricate plot—nearly as full and complicated, say, as *Bleak House.* But it is a big novel with a hole in the middle, tunnel vision, represented symbolically by the obsessive object named in its title: only find the Moonstone and all questions are answered. *Bleak House* is among other things a murder mystery, but the noose of guilt is ultimately drawn around everyone, around society at large, as symbolized by the upward spreading smallpox and by the all-engulfing Chancery suit. For its victims, there is usually no way out of Chancery, just as there is no escape from guilt and the law in *The Trial.* But in *The Moonstone,* the short circuit from Franklin Blake the detective to Franklin Blake the unconscious thief (albeit after many pages of twists and implications) and thence to Franklin Blake the rewarded and happy protagonist is eminently satisfying and finally too neat.

Collins makes brilliant use of the conventions of the best Victorian novels while undercutting their most serious implications. In much the same way, other sensation novels and mysteries mimic serious fiction.

In the best of the psychoanalytic essays on *The Moonstone,* Albert D. Hutter grants too much to detective fiction when he likens it to the process of psychoanalysis itself:

> Detective fiction involves the transformation of a fragmented and incomplete set of events into a more ordered and complete understanding. As such it seems to bridge a private psychological experience, like dreaming, and literary experience in general. And like a psychoanalysis, the detective story reorders our perception of the past through language.[36]

The idea that detective fiction acts as a bridge between dreams "and literary experience in general" may be correct, but Hutter's next sentence seems to contradict what I have just said about the reduction of mystery to a soluble level and the short-circuiting of the search for the self. Leo Löwenthal's dictum that "mass culture is psychoanalysis in reverse" is closer to the mark than the idea that detective fiction acts like a psychoanalysis.[37] Detective fiction only mimics the processes that are like psychoanalysis in serious fiction; it is both diverting and diversionary, and inevitably reductive. Hutter appears to recognize this when he says that Collins "adopts . . . the device so common to the Victorian novel of splitting hero and villain and giving one the crime and punishment so that the other may be free to enjoy his rewards without guilt."[38] While this may call into question the analytic power of all fiction where such character splitting occurs, it also suggests why it means very little to say that detective fiction follows the pattern of a psychoanalysis. It only mimics that pattern, just as it mimics aspects of serious fiction.

A distinction must be made between trait or character splitting in sensation novelists like Collins and in more realistic novelists like George Eliot. In the former, character splitting is more pronounced, again partly reflecting the influence of the Gothic romance. The two Allan Armadales, Anne Catherick as ghostly double-goer in *The Woman in White,* and the two lives, two husbands, and two personalities of Lady Audley hark back to the patterns of doubling in a Gothic tale like James Hogg's *Confessions of a Justified Sinner.* These patterns can be partly explained psychoanalytically as expressive of narcissistic regression. Such tendencies exist mainly on a metaphoric level in most realistic novels, whereas they are given much more literal expression in romantic fiction, including the sensation novel. As Winifred Hughes says, sensation novels "reveal a recurrent preoccupation with the loss or duplication of identity. . . . Everywhere in the lesser sensation novels

the unwitting protagonists experience their strange encounters with the empty form of the *doppelgänger.*"[39]

Hughes goes on to point out that "incident as well as character is subject to the principle of duality." The plots of sensation novels "are typically structured around a recurrence of similar or identical situations, not infrequently in the shape of dreams or omens and their ultimate fulfillment."[40] A structural explanation for this doubling of incidents emerges from the realization that mystery stories are necessarily two-fold. Hutter points to Tzvetan Todorov's essay on detective novels in *The Poetics of Prose,* in which Todorov shows that they are always double narratives. The first narrative concerns the past and the crime that has been committed; it is wound up and unraveled in the second narrative, which concerns the present and recounts the detection of the cause of the crime. Todorov relates this pattern of double narration to the Formalist distinction between "fable," which corresponds to "what happened in life," and "subject" or plot, which corresponds to "the way the author presents it to us."[41] But in the detective novel "what happens in life" is virtually reduced to a variant of "the way the author presents it to us." Whereas serious literature imitates life partly by reducing and simplifying its scale and complexity, the mystery novel imitates serious literature by carrying its reductive and simplifying tendencies to extremes. Like the sensation novel from which it evolved, the mystery novel shrinks "fable" to a single event or a few related ones (a crime or crimes, murder or theft often combined in sensation novels with bigamy and the assumption of false identities), just as it also shrinks mystery to a soluble level and diverts the problem of self-identity into a pattern of exorcism or of the projection of guilt onto another. "Plot" then follows the path of detection through conveniently placed clues to the final explanation of this simplified version of "fable," correctly identifying the culprit—the personified cause of the "fable"—and dishing out punishment and rewards. Like the fatal "hand" that keeps pointing Robert Audley down the path of detection, or like the pattern of improbable coincidences in most melodramas and sensation novels, the unraveling of the plot seems dimly to represent the working out of destiny: everything is put back in order at the end, all questions have been answered.

Hutter proceeds to analyze the unconscious sexual symbolism in *The Moonstone* and to consider both the oedipal theory of mystery stories and the more interesting—because less obvious and perhaps less reductive—theory that mysteries are symbolic re-creations of the primal scene. No doubt both theories can help to explain all fictions, but the primal scene idea seems especially relevant to mysteries, and perhaps even more to sensation novels, in which the mysteries occur within families, than to many later detective novels. The theory, as Hutter explains it, "reads detective fiction as an expression of primal scene fears and wishes, that is, as an expression of the conflicts of the child who witnesses parental intercourse." Hutter's application of this theory to *The Moonstone* is especially insightful, partly because it is a novel "built around a visual tension . . . the characters watching a crime committed in a bedroom at night, not understanding it, and suffering because they are forced into a new view of a loved object."[42] Obsessive curiosity and voyeurism characterize all mystery stories, but the theory fits best where the mystery is confined to a family and the voyeurism is a matter of life and death to the voyeur, as in both *Lady Audley's Secret* and *Uncle Silas,* for example, and also in much Gothic fiction. Such a thesis involves interpreting both the victims or corpses and the villains as surrogate parent figures, seen dimly through the childhood memory of the fearful vision (whether real or imagined) which both misconstrues the parental intercourse as an act of violence and secretly wishes it to be such an act. In *Uncle Silas,* which has, if anything, even more "visual tension" and horror related to that tension than *The Moonstone,* the Bluebeard and vampire-werewolf metaphors attached to Maud Ruthvyn's terrifying uncle point towards the regressive pattern suggested by the primal scene theory, although it is Silas's son, Dudley, who aims at marrying Maud, seducing her, or having her any way he can. The terrific finale points even more clearly in the same direction: Maud watches from the shadows as Dudley drives home the strange pick axe, with its "longish tapering spike," meant for Maud herself, time after time into the breast of the apparently sleeping Mme. de la Rougierre, whose body heaves with "a horrible tremor" and "convulsions," "the arms drumming on the bed," until "the diabolical surgery was ended" (ch. 64, pp. 426-27). It is a "sensation scene" to match anything in Boucicault's plays—anything in the entire literature of sensation, in fact—for its combination of grisly terror with erotic suggestion. The regressive quality of *Uncle Silas* and Le Fanu's other fiction is unmistakable, whether it is better explained by the primal scene idea or some other psychological theory; that quality is the chief source of its very considerable power.

Most sensation novels confine their voyeuristic, primal scene revelations to family circles, but the family itself was the mainstay of Victorian bourgeois values. Sensation novels were therefore subversive without ordinarily addressing political issues. They stripped the veils from Victorian respectability and prudery, exposing bigamists and adulterers, vampires and murderesses. They did so not by pushing the conventions of realistic fiction to the limits, as Zola was soon to do in France, but by subverting those conventions themselves, importing romantic elements back into contemporary settings, reinvesting the ordinary with mystery (albeit only of the secular, criminal variety), and undoing narrative omniscience to let in kinds of knowledge that realistic fiction had often excluded. In place of the empiricist

realism that strives for objective, direct mimesis, the sensation novel seems to substitute a different measure of reality, based on primal scene psychology, that now reads objective appearances as question marks or clues to mysteries and insists that the truth has been hidden, buried, smuggled away behind the appearances. But this subversive attitude is also felt to be regressive, inferior to traditional realism: the sensation novel never directly challenged the dominance of more serious, more realistic fiction, and sensational authors and narrators seem forever to be backing away from the deepest truths in their stories, abdicating or undermining their own authority. Precisely because of their reductive and regressive properties, however, sensation novels often approach the quality and complexity of more serious Victorian fiction. Perhaps it would be best to say that sensation novels seize upon and exaggerate the reductive properties that are already present in serious fiction. In terms like Derrida's on the impurity of genres, T. S. Eliot writes:

> You cannot define Drama and Melodrama so that they shall be reciprocally exclusive; great drama has something melodramatic in it, and the best melodrama partakes of the greatness of drama. *The Moonstone* is very near to *Bleak House.* The theft of a diamond has some of the same blighting effect on the lives about it as the suit in Chancery.[43]

The development of the sensation novel marks a crisis in the history of literary realism. At the same time that George Eliot was investing the novel with a new philosophical gravity, the sensationalists were breaking down the conventions of realistic fiction and pointing the way to the emergence of later popular forms and perhaps also to later, more conscious assertions of the need to go beyond realism into all those mysterious areas of life and art that supposedly omniscient narrators often seem not to know. Although anything "sensational" is by definition not to be taken too seriously, the word itself points to a source of immediate excitement or surprise, the realm of the unexpected. As T. S. Eliot remarks, "we cannot afford to forget that the first—and not one of the least difficult—requirements of either prose or verse is that it should be interesting."[44] Whatever else they are, sensation novels are certainly that. In his defense of literary sensationalism in *Belgravia* (a journal edited by none other than Mary Elizabeth Braddon) George Augustus Sala launched an assault on "the dolts and dullards and envious backbiters" for whom "everything is 'sensational' that is vivid, and nervous, and forcible, and graphic, and true." If these "anti-sensationalists" had their way, Sala declared in his final terrific sentence, then life itself would be a sorry affair, for they would establish a new reign of dullness: "Don't let us move, don't let us travel, don't let us hear or see anything; but let us write sonnets to Chloe, and play madrigals on the spinet, and dance minuets, and pray to Heaven against Sensationalism, the Pope, the Devil, and the Pretender; and then let Dullness reign triumphant, and Universal Darkness cover all."[45] Sala's sensational protest points forward to the fuller, more profound rebellions of the decadent and modernist writers who wrote the final epitaphs for the safer kinds of realism and for the Victorian pieties of hearth and home.

Notes

[1] "The Lighter Reading of the Eighteen-Sixties," Introduction to Wilkie Collins, *The Woman in White*, Riverside ed. (Boston: Houghton, 1969), p. xv.

[2] "The Law of Genre," trans. Avital Ronell, *Critical Inquiry*, 7 (1980), 57.

[3] "The Enigma Novel," rpt. in *Wilkie Collins: The Critical Heritage*, ed. Norman Page (London and Boston: Routledge, 1974), p. 109.

[4] Introd., *The Omnibus of Crime*, ed. Dorothy L. Sayers (New York: Harcourt, Brace, 1929), p. 25.

[5] There is a brilliant exposition of this idea in T. S. Eliot, "Wilkie Collins and Dickens," *Selected Essays*, new ed. (New York: Harcourt, Brace, 1960), pp. 409-18; originally published in *TLS*, 4 Aug. 1927, pp. 525-26.

[6] Dickens, quoted by J.W.T. Ley, *The Dickens Circle* (New York: Dutton, 1919), p. 87.

[7] "Letter of Dedication," *Basil*, 3 vols. (London: R. Bentley, 1852), I, xiii. Also see *Basil* (1862 rev. ed.; rpt. New York: Dover, 1980), p. v.

[8] According to Wayne Burns, Reade thought of fiction "as a lesser form of the drama" (*Charles Reade: A Study in Victorian Authorship* [New York: Bookman, 1961], p. 113; see esp. ch. 4).

[9] [Richard Holt Hutton], "Sensational Novels," *Spectator*, 8 Aug. 1868, p. 932.

[10] *The Maniac in the Cellar: Sensation Novels of the 1860s* (Princeton: Princeton Univ. Press, 1980), pp. 71, 31.

[11] "Bigamy: The Rise and Fall of a Convention," *NCF*, 36 (1981), 58. See also Arvel B. Erickson and Fr. John R. McCarthy, "The Yelverton Case: Civil Legislation and Marriage," *Victorian Studies*, 14 (1971), 275-91; and Mary Lyndon Shanley, "'One Must Ride Behind': Married Women's Rights and the Divorce Act of 1857," *Victorian Studies*, 25 (1982), 355-76.

[12] "Miss Braddon," rev. of *Aurora Floyd*, in *Notes and Reviews* (Cambridge, Mass.: Dunster House,

1921), pp. 108-16; originally published in the *Nation*, 9 Nov. 1865, pp. 593-94.

[13] Unsigned review, rpt. in *Wilkie Collins: The Critical Heritage*, pp. 134-35; originally published in the opening number of the *Reader*, 3 Jan. 1863, pp. 14-15.

[14] James, "Miss Braddon," p. 115.

[15] The archbishop of York's sermon is quoted by W. Fraser Rae in "Sensation Novelists: Miss Braddon," *North British Review*, 43, NS 4 (1865), 203 (British ed.).

[16] Wordsworth to Edward Moxon, April 1842, excerpted in *Charles Dickens: A Critical Anthology*, ed. Stephen Wall (Harmondsworth: Penguin Books, 1970), p. 61. See also George Ford, *Dickens and His Readers: Aspects of Novel-Criticism since 1836* (New York: Norton, 1965), pp. 39-43 and 177-79.

[17] Joseph Sheridan Le Fanu, "A Preliminary Word," *Uncle Silas: A Tale of Bartram-Haugh*, introd. Frederick Shroyer (New York: Dover, 1966), p. xvii; further citations in my text are to this edition.

[18] *Victorian Studies in Scarlet* (New York: Norton, 1970), p. 79.

[19] James, "Miss Braddon," pp. 112-13.

[20] [Henry Mansel], "Sensation Novels," *Quarterly Review*, 113 (1863), 501.

[21] *Readana* in *The Works of Charles Reade*, 9 vols. (New York: Peter Fenelon Collier, n.d.), IX, 377-78.

[22] Hughes, *The Maniac in the Cellar*, p. 75

[23] *Lady Audley's Secret*, introd. Norman Donaldson (New York: Dover, 1974), ch. 18, p. 94; subsequent references in my text are to this edition. An excellent study of Braddon is Robert Lee Wolff, *Sensational Victorian: The Life and Fiction of Mary Elizabeth Braddon* (New York and London: Garland, 1979).

[24] James, "Miss Braddon," pp. 115-16.

[25] Preface to the First Edition, rpt in *The Moonstone*, ed. J. I. M. Stewart (Harmondsworth: Penguin, 1966), p. 27.

[26] Eliot, *Selected Essays*, pp. 409-10.

[27] Anthony Trollope, *An Autobiography*, introd. Bradford Allen Booth (Berkeley and Los Angeles: Univ. of California Press, 1947), p. 189.

[28] H. J. W. Milley, *"The Eustace Diamonds* and *The Moonstone,"* Studies in Philology, 36 (1939), 651-63.

[29] Ian Ousby, *Bloodhounds of Heaven: The Detective in English Fiction from Godwin to Doyle* (Cambridge, Mass.: Harvard Univ. Press, 1976), pp. 3-18.

[30] *Charles Baudelaire: A Lyric Poet in the Era of High Capitalism,* trans. Harry Zohn (London: New Left Books, 1973), pp. 40-48.

[31] Appendix, *Armadale* (New York: Dover, 1977), p. 597.

[32] *A Sensation Novel in Three Volumes* (London: Joseph Williams, 1912), pp. 22-23.

[33] For a contrasting argument see John R. Reed, "English Imperialism and the Unacknowledged Crime of *The Moonstone,"* Clio, 2 (1973), 281-90.

[34] *The Dyer's Hand and Other Essays* (New York: Vintage Books, 1968), p. 158.

[35] Eliot, *Selected Essays,* pp. 417-18.

[36] "Dreams, Transformations, and Literature: The Implications of Detective Fiction," *Victorian Studies,* 19 (1975), 191.

[37] Löwenthal, quoted by Martin Jay, *The Dialectical Imagination* (Boston: Little, Brown, 1973), p. 173.

[38] Hutter, "Dreams, Transformations, and Literature," pp. 202-3.

[39] Hughes, *The Maniac in the Cellar,* p. 21.

[40] Ibid.

[41] *The Poetics of Prose,* trans. Richard Howard (Ithaca: Cornell Univ. Press, 1977), p. 45.

[42] Hutter, "Dreams, Transformations, and Literature," pp. 203-4. The first crude version of this theory is Geraldine Pederson-Krag, "Detective Stories and the Primal Scene," *Psychoanalytic Quarterly,* 18 (1949), 207-14. See also Charles Rycroft, "The Analysis of a Detective Story," *Imagination and Reality,* introd. M. Masud R. Khan and John D. Sutherland (New York: International Universities Press, 1968), pp. 114-28.

[43] Eliot, *Selected Essays,* pp. 417-18.

[44] Ibid., p. 418.

[45] "On the 'Sensational' in Literature and Art," *Belgravia,* 4 (1868), 457, 458.

Richard D. Altick (essay date 1986)

SOURCE: "The Novel Experience," in *Deadly Encounters: Two Victorian Sensations,* University of Pennsylvania Press, 1986, pp. 145-58.

[*In the following essay, Altick provides a general overview of the sensation novel and its components and origins.*]

The "sensation" in the melodrama of the 1860s involved not only the addition of athletic and mechanical devices as sources of excitement but the historical context in which these were presented. In deference to a shift in the audience's tastes, playwrights had been gradually turning away from stories laid in the past and making a point and virtue of locating their actions in the present time. This intensified interest in using the stage as a mirror of contemporary life affected the melodrama as much as it did other theatrical genres. Now that realistic sets were available to reproduce the visual aspects of modern everyday life, sensation dramatists were able to present melodramatic events, new or from stock, in plausible settings, the novelty of which was itself a sensation. In enlisting what might be called "the shock of actuality"—of recognizable present-day scenes and characters in contemporary dress—as opposed to "romance," which implied another time, another locale, the sensation drama sought to authenticate the unlikely plot and the extraordinary incidents of which it was composed. And this is what sensation fiction also sought to accomplish, on the printed page.

Again, it was the label that was new, not, for the most part, the product itself. The sensation novel was a not too precisely differentiated subgenre of fiction distinguished by a high content of melodramatic narrative. Readers in quest of agreeable shocks had been well served, in their respective times, by the Gothic tale of terror, Sir Walter Scott's romances with their copious perils, accidents, and confrontations, and popular fiction, mostly historical romances, by such of Scott's successors as William Harrison Ainsworth. Whatever other powerful appeals they had, Dickens's novels were devoured for their frequent use of melodramatic situations and events—the "circle of fire," as Ruskin called it—which brought the thrills of the theater to the fireside. In 1868, George Augustus Sala, writing in the *Belgravia* magazine (edited, incidentally, by the reigning monarch of sensation fiction, Miss Braddon), pointed out what should have been obvious seven years earlier, when the term was first applied to fiction:

> The only wonder is that the charitable souls [some of Dickens's critics] have failed to discover that among modern "sensational writers" Mr. Charles Dickens is perhaps the most thoroughly, and has been from the very outset of his career the most

persistently, "sensational" writer of the age. There is sensation even in *Pickwick:* the "Madman" and the "Stroller's" story, the death of the "Chancery Prisoner," and the episode of the "Queer Client," for example. *The Old Curiosity Shop* is replete with sensation, from the extravagant pilgrimage of Nell and the old man to the death of Quilp. *Barnaby Rudge* begins with the sensation of an undiscovered murder, and ends with the sensation of a triple hanging and a duel *à mort.* In *Nicholas Nickleby* the end of Mr. Ralph Nickleby and the shooting of Lord Frederick Verisopht by Sir Mulberry Hawk are sensational enough to suit the strongest appetite. And the murder of Tigg Montague by Jonas Chuzzlewit; and the mysterious husband of Miss Betsy Trotwood in *David Copperfield;* and the convict millionaire in *Great Expectations;* and the grinding of the "National Razor" in the *Tale of Two Cities;* and Monks's confession, and the murder of Nancy, and the death of Sykes; in *Oliver Twist;* and finally, the spontaneous combustion in *Bleak House;* (Dickens considered several titles for the novel before he decided on *Bleak House.* Among them was not *Lady Dedlock's Secret,* which would have contributed to the strong case that could be made for *Bleak House* as a proto-sensation novel.) and the tumbling down of the house in *Little Dorrit;* and Mr. Carker's death in *Dombey and Son.* Are not all these pure "sensation"?

Sala's catalog illustrates how broadly the term had come to be applied by that time. But most of its examples fall into two categories, secrets on which the plots hinge and violent deaths, especially murders. These had been familiar components not only of some fiction read by the middle classes, including the "Newgate novels" (narratives of criminal careers) by Bulwer-Lytton and Ainsworth, but the flood of cheap pot-boiled fiction for the lower-middle and working classes, the crude pabulum that scandalized many concerned observers of the cultural scene.

Although many novels published before 1860 qualified as examples of sensation fiction, the first new one to be so called was Wilkie Collins's *The Woman in White,* which was serialized in Dickens's weekly paper, *All the Year Round,* between 26 November 1859 and 25 August 1860, published in book form in the latter month, and reissued in one volume in 1861, just months before the Murray and Vidil affairs (the preface was dated February). It is not certain as yet just when the adjective was first extended from the drama to fiction, but an allusion to the genre in the *Morning Herald*'s valedictory to the Vidil case on 25 August shows that it was current by that time: "the moral disorganisation of which all classes in society are now complaining, and which forms the staple of most of our sensation novels."

Less than a year later, in *Blackwood's Magazine* for May 1862, the term was so well established as to serve

as the title of a double-columned twenty-page review, by the well-known novelist Margaret Oliphant, of *The Woman in White* and Dickens's *Great Expectations,* which latter book she explicitly called a "sensation novel" because of its "incidents all but impossible, and in themselves strange, dangerous, and exciting." Buyers of *All the Year Round* had been reading the last weekly installments of the novel the preceding summer. Magwitch, the returned convict, had revealed his secret to an appalled Pip in the issue for 25 May. On 22 June, just a week before Baron de Vidil attacked his son, Miss Havisham, still dressed in her decayed bridal gown, suffered fatal burns in a fire at Satis House. On 6 July there was an account of Pip's perilous confrontation with the murderous Orlick; and on 13 July—the very day that the newspapers carried the first reports of the two sensations—the issue of *All the Year Round* that was being snatched up at the newsagents' and bookstalls contained the climactic event of *Great Expectations,* Pip's and Herbert Pocket's attempt to smuggle Magwitch out of the country, which ended in the melodramatic night scene of the rich old convict being fatally injured during a death struggle with the evil Compeyson under the keel of a speeding Thames steamer. Even before the novel's serial run was concluded on 3 August, the finished book had been published and was reviewed on the weekend of 20 July in the *Examiner* and the *Saturday Review,* side by side with their editorials on the two great crimes of the moment.

Dickens's latest novel, therefore, the work of the era's most popular writer of fiction, provided an immediate literary background to the developing sensation craze. (It is possible that the writer of the *Standard*'s editorial on the Vidil case on 22 July, referring to the public's reluctance to undergo "the ordeal of wasting whole days in the company of policemen and about the purlieus of the police courts, attended by the knowing clerk of a gentleman most improperly designated the 'thieves' attorney,'" had Wemmick and Jaggers in mind.) *Great Expectations,* like *Bleak House* (1852-53), had been intended, as Dickens said in the preface to the latter, to dwell "upon the romantic side of familiar things," a phrase that might well stand as a definition of what the ensuing school of sensation novelists was about.

And school it was—an informal collection of novelists, men and women, mostly second-rate or worse, unified in their sense of what the reading public most wanted at the moment and their readiness to oblige. In April 1863, a long review-essay in the *Quarterly Review* by the philosopher and historian Henry Mansel, dealt with no fewer than twenty-four examples of sensation novels, including two or three, published in 1859-60, to which the name was applied retroactively. Although sensation fiction, so called, continued to be ground out as late as the 1880s, the vogue reached its peak in the mid-1860s. An unidentified writer in the

Westminster Review (October 1866) described its hectic intensity and scope as well as anyone:

> There is no accounting for tastes, blubber for the Esquimaux, half-hatched eggs for the Chinese, and Sensational novels for the English. Everything must now be sensational. Professor Kingsley sensationalizes History [in *Hereward the Wake*], and Mr. Wilkie Collins daily life. One set of writers wear the sensational buskin, another the sensational sock. Just as in the Middle Ages people were afflicted with the Dancing Mania and Lycanthropy, sometimes barking like dogs, and sometimes mewing like cats, so now we have a Sensational Mania. Just, too, as those diseases always occurred in seasons of dearth and poverty, and attacked only the poor, so does the Sensational Mania burst out only in times of mental poverty, and afflict only the most poverty-stricken minds. From an epidemic, however, it has lately changed into an endemic. Its virus is spreading in all directions, from the penny journal to the shilling magazine, and from the shilling magazine to the thirty shillings volume.

Preeminent in the shoal of lesser writers who swam in the wake of Collins and Dickens in those first years of the sensation craze was Mary Elizabeth Braddon, whose *Lady Audley's Secret,* serialized in the monthly *Sixpenny Magazine* from January to December 1862 and published in three volumes in October of the same year, was regarded by contemporary critics as the prototype of the new genre. Henry James, indeed, credited Miss Braddon rather than Collins with having "created the sensation novel." It was a huge success at the circulating libraries, eight editions being called for during the first three months after publication in book form. The novel was full of appropriately thrilling accessories, such as a secret passage in a country house (a holdover from innumerable Gothic romances) and a thunderstorm in which lightning plays around the razors of a gentleman's dressing case, "a phenomenon," said a reviewer, "of which we never heard before, and shall never read of again except in a 'sensation' novel."

But these were trivial matters. The two daring features that set *Lady Audley's Secret* apart from preceding melodramatic fiction and, through it, determined the nature of the sensation novel to come were the figure of the beautiful Lady Audley, a female Mephistopheles as one critic called her, and the crimes she either committed or contemplated. At a time when, in crime-ridden fiction, women were almost always cast in victimized roles—Marian Halcombe and Laura Fairlie in *The Woman in White,* for instance—she was depicted as an out-and-out villain. By that single stroke, Miss Braddon defied convention, challenging the prevailing estimate of women as angels in the house, almost by definition incapable of crime, and of murder least of all. Lady Audley was the prey of murderous instincts, and if she failed to achieve her goal of killing her first husband,

it was not for want of trying: she threw him down a well, and it was not her fault that, unknown to her, he managed to climb out and escape to America. She did succeed in being an arsonist on one occasion. Both murder and arson, however, were commonplace crimes, even if not ordinarily associated with women. Lady Audley's third crime, by contrast, was bigamy, a violation of law one party to which was of necessity a woman. Two distinguished novels had set a precedent for the use of this comparatively rare crime as plot material. In *Jane Eyre* (1847) Mr. Rochester, his insane wife still living, made an abortive attempt to marry Jane. And in *Pendennis* (1848-49) Lady Clavering was married to her second husband in the erroneous belief that her first, a convict named Amory, was dead. Thackeray got her out of her difficulty by revealing that her first marriage was no marriage at all, Amory having already become a multiple bigamist with wives scattered from Newcastle to New Zealand. Moreover, in the past three years the murder trial of the bigamous Dr. Smethurst and the Yelverton case had sharpened public enthusiasm for stories whose complications mirrored the real-life ones that had been exposed at the Old Bailey and in the Dublin courtroom, and while *Lady Audley's Secret* was running in the *Six-penny Magazine, All the Year Round* was serializing Collins's *No Name,* which also hinged on the issue of whether a marriage had legal force.

Bigamy quickly became a spécialité de la maison in sensation fiction; of the twenty-four novels Mansel listed in his *Quarterly Review* article, no fewer than eight had plots hinging on that titillating crime.

> No novel [said the *Westminster* reviewer, 1866] can now possibly succeed without it. In real life money is sometimes obtained by marriage, but in literature only by bigamy. When Richardson, the showman, went about with his menagerie he had a big black baboon, whose habits were so filthy, and whose behaviour was so disgusting, that respectable people constantly remonstrated with him for exhibiting such an animal. Richardson's answer invariably was, "Bless you, if it wasn't for that big black baboon I should be ruined; it attracts all the young girls in the country." Now bigamy has been Miss Braddon's big black baboon, with which she has attracted all the young girls in the country. And now Mr. Wilkie Collins has set up [in *Armadale*] a big black baboon on his own account.

Beyond bigamy lay a tract of liberal conduct that novelists and their reviewers could only hint at, in novels, said Mansel, "which, instead of multiplying the holy ceremony, betray an inclination to dispense with it altogether. . . . The chief interest centres on a heroine whose ideas on this subject are rather on the side of defect than of excess." Although the novelists who introduced such spicy hints of sexual irregularity doubtless valued them for their scandalous potential, they also discovered that they supplied useful plot material. As a reviewer in *The Reader* (3 January 1863) observed, "Unlawful passions are inevitably replete with a variety of sensational situations, of which authorized love, however fervent, is devoid, and the consequence is that a sensation novel which cannot dwell upon seductions, intrigues, infidelities, and illegitimate connections, is like Hamlet, not only without the Prince, but without the Ghost and without Ophelia."

The final ingredient in the sensation brew was relatively conventional. The sensation drama might have an element of mystery and detection—the legendary Hawkshaw appeared in Tom Taylor's *The Ticket of Leave Man* in 1863—but it could do well enough without it so long as suspense was supported by other means. In sensation fiction the element of secrecy, to be followed in due course by revelation, was considerably more important, often taking the form of guilty knowledge or missing documents. But the mysteries that engaged the patrons of the circulating libraries were mysteries of event, not of motive. Here the imaginative reach of journalism far exceeded that of popular fiction. We have seen the newspaper commentators playing amateur psychologist as they speculated on the motives behind the baron's and Roberts's murderous conduct, especially on the possibility of madness. In the Vidil trial, Serjeant Ballantine pursued as far as he could a line of inquiry tending to suggest that the son suffered from an unbalanced mind. But although the sensation novelists made madness a frequent visitant in their pages (Lady Audley attributed her criminal impulses to paroxysms of insanity, and she ended her days in a Belgian madhouse), they used it merely as a convenient plot device, not as a mysterious abnormality to be described and examined. In the sensation novel formula, suspenseful plot and exciting incident were all, character nothing. The men and women, usually titled, endowed with the social graces and adequate money, and dressed in the latest fashion, served only as puppets to advance the story and as models for the book's engraved illustrations. Few of them, Wilkie Collins's sometimes excepted, had the three-dimensional authenticity of the dauntless major, his devoted mistress, the fixated Roberts, the adventurous baron, or his neurotic son, or, for that matter, the reality of the miscellaneous witnesses who were tangled by accident in a pair of sensational proceedings in law. The depth and variety of psychological interest that lend so much permanent vitality to the fiction of Dickens, Thackeray, the Brontës, Trollope, and George Eliot were alien territory to the sensation novelists of the 1860s and after.

Nor were they concerned with probability; the strange but (as it proved) true story of Major Murray dispensed them from the obligation that normally binds the writer of realistic fiction. Thackeray was right: "After this, what is not possible?" The plain evidence of the newspapers was infinitely more impressive than Dickens's specious effort to justify the wild coincidences he so freely employed when they were needed. In Northumberland Street crumbled into dust the limits placed on the degree to which novelists—not romancers, but writers purporting to mirror contemporary life—were entitled to strain their readers' credulity. In sensation fiction the timely distribution of accidents, barring the supernatural, knew no bounds. If Dickens could invoke "scientific" authority for the spontaneous combustion that incinerated the junk dealer Krook in a shop not far from Fleet Street, or if Wilkie Collins and Trollope could avail themselves of obscure legal quirks for plotting purposes, sensation novelists had behind them the undeniable precedent of Northumberland Street.

What lent the final piquancy to all these bold deviations from the prevailing line of morality and the ordinary odds of likelihood was the implication, deliciously terrifying to every reader of sensation fiction, that they could happen to you and me, if not as actual participants then as vitally interested witnesses. Henry Mansel, writing ironically at the moment, made the same observation that had flowed from the pens of newspaper writers in the summer of 1861, dwelling on the peculiarly modern flavor of the Murray and Vidil cases: "The man who shook our hand with a hearty English grasp half an hour ago—the woman whose beauty and grace were the charm of last night, and whose gentle words sent us home better pleased with the world and with ourselves—how exciting to think that under these pleasing outsides may be concealed some demon in human shape, a Count Fosco [in *The Woman in White*] or a Lady Audley!"

Henry James put it more picturesquely two years later, when, in the pages of the American *Nation* (9 November 1865), he credited Wilkie Collins with "having introduced into fiction those most mysterious of mysteries, the mysteries which are at our own doors. This innovation gave a new impetus to the literature of horrors. It was fatal to the authority of Mrs. Radcliffe and her everlasting castle in the Apennines. What are the Apennines to us, or we to the Apennines? Instead of the terrors of *Udolpho,* we were treated to the terrors of the cheerful country-house and the busy London lodgings. And there is no doubt that these were infinitely the most terrible. Mrs. Radcliffe's mysteries were romances pure and simple; while those of Mr. Wilkie Collins were stern reality. . . . Of course, the nearer the criminal and the detective are brought home to the reader, the more lively his 'sensation.'"

James's jaunty tone was at odds with the deeper concerns expressed, or implicit, in what his English contemporaries wrote on the same subject. It was no light matter to see fell purposes and deeds attributed to the social class that by the mid-Victorian era had become the prime wielder of political, social, and economic power and the center of attention in imaginative literature, above all fiction: the self-consciously and proudly moral middle class. Its primary interest in literary matters was to read about itself, to find its comfortable world mirrored in fiction. To the distress of most arbiters of taste and morality in such matters, it did not resent the action of sensation novelists in revealing its world to be not so comfortable and safe after all. In fact, the welcome it gave to sensation fiction was striking evidence that it actually relished so drastic a shattering of its illusions. Ironically, in an era when most novelists worshiped, in behalf of their readers, at the altar of domesticity, sensation novelists turned the reverential ideal of home and family inside out, purporting to discover lurking behind the innocent façade of decorous life a prodigious quantity of illicit behavior.

During its feverish run in the 1860s, sensation fiction did not enjoy a very good press, though occasional critics minimized its defects even if they did not linger to praise it. Moral objections aside, the main charge against the genre was that it was written for, and devoured by, a middle-class clientele whose literary taste should be the exemplar of wholesomeness, proof against the seductions of romancers. In sensation fiction, the principal ingredients of the despised street literature, stories that sold in penny and halfpenny slices, moved up-market, so to speak, finding their way into staid households and corrupting the imaginations of susceptible readers. "These tales," said Mansel, "are to the full-grown sensation novel what the bud is to the flower, what the fountain is to the river, what the typical form is to the organised body. They are the original germ, the primitive monad, to which all the varieties of sensational literature may be referred." The customary reading fare of the workingman did have its counterpart in sensation fiction, but Mansel was indulging in a grossly oversimplified form of literary genetics: the sensation novel also had a far more reputable ancestry. But by the 1860s, cheap working-class fiction, which had previously depicted crime for its shock value alone, ironically was hedged with a certain morality, its authors purporting to depict it only to warn against its dangerous allure. In the sensation novel, by contrast, it went unreproved. Whatever purposes the authors had in mind did not include any ambition to strengthen their readers' moral principles.

It was this spectacle of the solid, educated middle class accepting and indeed reveling in the sensation novelists' picture of its own corruption that the archbishop of York deplored when he spoke before the Huddersfield Church Institute in the autumn of 1864. In an address widely reported in the newspapers (the *Times* for 2 November, for example, devoted a whole long column to it), he denounced the genre for the immoral influence it supposedly exerted on its readers. By implicitly glorifying crime as a frequent occurrence in the everyday life of the class to which they belonged, it tempted them to commit crimes themselves, or, if they were less suggestible, at least induced them to look upon other people's crimes with callous indifference rather than suitable revulsion. Sensation novels, the archbishop continued, "want to persuade people that in almost every one of the well-ordered houses of their neighbours there was a skeleton shut up in some cupboard; that their comfortable and easy-looking neighbour had in his breast a secret story which he was always going about trying to conceal; that there was something about a real will registered in Doctors' Commons and a false will that at some proper moment should tumble out of some broken bureau."

The *Times* reported that the audience responded to this observation with laughter, an indication of the spirit in which it was both offered and received. The archbishop, allowing himself to descend to drollery for a moment, was simply restating in an up-to-date context the ancient charge, heard in every Puritan campaign against a literary target since Tudor times, that fiction was to be eschewed because it provided a gravely false picture of actuality. There was no truth, he maintained—and by their laughter his auditors seemed to subscribe to its absurdity—in the impression that sensation novelists conveyed, of a respectable, mentally healthy middle class rife with melodramatic secrets, demonic creatures garbed in frock coats or crinolines, and criminal impulses.

But, as we have seen, the Murray and Vidil cases had induced newspaper commentators to adopt a quite different view: the everyday presence of dark mysteries and of social corruption was not a figment of sensation novelists' diseased imaginations but a hard fact to be faced. The newspaper coverage of the cases dramatically substantiated the premise that crime, including murderous assaults on the person, could very well occur in settled, highly respectable social circumstances. Like their colleagues in the somewhat more raffish profession of the theater, where sensation dramas were likewise sometimes set in fashionable society, the novelists found in the daily press constant warranty for the implied message, "it can happen to you," which added immeasurably to their stories' appeal.

Like the journalists who sought to read larger significance in particular criminal events, the people who commented at length on the popularity of sensational fiction freely generalized about what it seemed to imply about the national character at the moment, whether or not its picture was true to the facts. Both parties shared a common anxiety: what would the French, Britain's severest critics, think of that character as revealed, on the one hand, by the prevalence of crime and the workings of the English system of justice, and on the other, by sensation novels? Margaret Oliphant's voice (in *Blackwood's Magazine* for August 1863) was typical:

> Supposing our French neighbours were likely to judge us, as we are greatly apt to judge them, by the

state of national affairs disclosed in our works of fiction, these lively observers must inevitably come to the conclusion that murder is a frequent occurrence in English society, and that the boasted regard for human life, which is one of the especial marks of high civilisation, exists only in theory among us. The charm of killing somebody, of bringing an innocent person under suspicion of the deed, and gradually, by elaborate processes of detectivism, hunting out the real criminal, seems to possess an attraction which scarcely any English novelist can resist.

"For the service of the modern novelist," Mrs. Oliphant said, "every species of moral obliquity has been called in to complicate the neverending plot."

What is piquant on the other side of the Channel is out of the question within "the four seas." We turn with a national instinct rather to the brutalities than to the subtleties of crime. Murder is our *cheval de bataille;* and when we have done with the Sixth Commandment, it is not the next in succession which specially attracts us. The horrors of our novels are crimes against life and property. The policeman is the Fate who stalks relentless, or flies with lightning steps after our favourite villain. The villain himself is a banker, and defrauds his customers; he is a lawyer, and cheats his clients—if he is not a ruffian who kills his man. Or even, when a bolder hand than usual essays to lift the veil from the dark world of female crime we give the sin itself a certain haze of decorum, and make that only bigamy which might bear a plainer title. . . . Murder, conspiracy, robbery, fraud, are the strong colours upon the national palette. . . . Law predominates over even romance and imagination. If we cannot frame a state of affairs unexceptionably right, which is impossible to humanity, we can at least take refuge in the construction of circumstances which are legally and punishably wrong; and this expedient seems satisfactory to the national conscience.

Was this truly, then, to borrow the phrase Trollope would later use as the title for a novel, the way we live now? On the whole, the observers analyzing the Murray and Vidil cases had more to say on the topic of the national malaise of which they were taken to be symptoms than did the critics of sensational fiction. The latter were concerned instead with the morality of the genre and its presumed effects on that of its readers. The sternest view was Mansel's, who called it one of the "morbid" phenomena of contemporary literature, "indications of a widespread corruption, of which they are in part both the effect and the cause; called into existence to supply the cravings of a diseased appetite, and contributing themselves to foster the disease, and to stimulate the want which they supply."

Of the several major authors who wrote fiction with a sensational cast, Collins was the only one to whom the term "sensation novelist" was customarily applied during his lifetime. He went on to exploit the fashion he had helped stir in *No Name* (1862), *The Moonstone* (1868), and several later, less successful novels. In *The Moonstone* occurs one of the few recognizable fictional uses of the Northumberland Street episode, a half-and-half mixture of fact and invention. (There had already been a faint echo of Northumberland Street in Trollope's *Can You Forgive Her?* (1864-65). The rivals for Alice Vavasor's hand, her villainous cousin George and the loyal, steady John Grey, fight in the latter's rooms over a tailor shop in Suffolk Street, Pall Mall. In a return engagement, George actually tries to shoot Grey with a pistol.) One Friday, Geoffrey Ablewhite meets a perfect stranger in a bank in Lombard Street; he is lured to an apartment at the back of the first floor of a house in (yes) Northumberland Street; while he has his back turned to the closed folding doors communicating with the front room he is assaulted. So far, except for shifting the scene of the initial encounter, Collins was faithful to the Murray story. But in other respects he freely adapted it. The room that in real life was cluttered with Louis Philippe furnishings became almost empty, apart from "a faint odour of musk and camphor" and "an ancient Oriental manuscript, richly illuminated with Indian figures and devices, that lay open to inspection on the table"; instead of being shot, Ablewhite is blindfolded, gagged, and searched, but not otherwise harmed by his attacker, one of three mysterious Orientals who had rented the apartment a short time earlier; and he is summoned to Northumberland Street by letter, not to receive an offer of a large loan to the Grosvenor Hotel Company but with the prospect of a large donation to the Mothers'-Small-Clothes-Conversion Society, a charity devoted to redeeming fathers' trousers from the pawnbroker and preventing their further use as collateral by altering them to fit a child. It is Ablewhite, not his assailant, who is found when "two respectable strangers" break into the room where he is bound to a chair. But the authentic flavor of the first phase of the Murray case comes through when he asks them, "What does it mean?" and they reply, "Exactly the question we were going to ask you." For good measure, Collins has the polite stranger whom Ablewhite met in the bank, Septimus Luker, fall into the hands of the three Orientals on the same day and under identical circumstances, this time in a byway off the Tottenham Court Road. Like Charles Reade, another sensation novelist who has some place in the history of Victorian fiction but not on the same level as Collins and (above him) Dickens, Collins heeded the sardonic advice critics repeatedly offered to the aspiring sensation novelist: "Let him only keep an eye on the criminal reports of the daily newspapers, marking the cases which are honoured with the special notice of a leading article, and become a nine-days' wonder in the mouths of quidnuncs and gossips; and he has the outline of his story not only ready-made, but approved beforehand as of the true sensation cast."

In *Our Mutual Friend* (1864-65), the novel that followed *Great Expectations,* Dickens used a variety of sensational material, and in fact may have drawn the outlines of the plot involving Bradley Headstone, the "respectable" schoolmaster whose mind has "gloomy and dark recesses" and outside his hours of work "broke loose . . . like an ill tamed animal," from the story of William Roberts. The parallels are striking. Headstone is as obsessed with young Lizzie Hexam as Roberts was with Mrs. Murray, and in trying to locate her he shadows her lover and protector, Eugene Wrayburn, as relentlessly as Roberts shadowed Mrs. Murray. At the climax of the action, at the Plashwater Weir Mill lock on the Thames, Headstone waylays Wrayburn and attacks him with a murderous ferocity reminiscent of the Northumberland Street confrontation, but his badly injured victim, like the major, manages to survive.

Dickens was well into writing what might have been the most sensational of all his novels, appropriately titled *The Mystery of Edwin Drood,* when he died in 1870. Meanwhile, Trollope had fallen into the mode, though in his autobiography he would be at pains to distinguish his "realistic" fiction from the "sensation fiction" of writers whom he regarded as his antagonists. The plot of *Orley Farm,* published in monthly numbers in 1861-62, hinged on a disputed will, and many of Trollope's succeeding novels would contain incidents, if not actual story lines, that were obviously crafted in deference to the public demand. Thomas Hardy was affected by the sensation vogue at the outset of his career, and echoes of it are found in isolated episodes in most of his novels, half a dozen of which, for example, use murder as a plot device. Even the fastidious George Eliot was not exempt from the fever; there are elements of sensationalism in both *Felix Holt* (1866) and *Daniel Deronda* (1876-77). The most enduring heritage of the sensation fiction of the 1860s is found in these scattered aspects of Trollope's, Hardy's, and Eliot's novels. Recent critics have discovered there significant indications of the way the realistic impulse developed in English fiction and affected its form from 1860 onward.

The sensation vogue constituted a colorful and curious chapter in the history of English popular literary culture. Perhaps it would not have had the same impetus, or taken the shape it did, had its earliest pages not been in process of composition at that moment in July 1861 when the newspapers blazoned the occurrence of two real-life sensations in a single day's editions. In unconscious collaboration, Roberts, the driven loan shark, and Baron de Vidil, the somewhat dubious intimate of French royalty and English peers, set the tone, if not the stage, for the Victorian Age of Sensation.

PRINCIPAL FIGURES

T. S. Eliot (essay date 1932)

SOURCE: "Wilkie Collins and Dickens," in *Selected Essays,* Harcourt, Brace and Company, 1932, pp. 409-18.

[*In the essay that follows, Eliot discusses melodramatic elements in the novels of Dickens and Collins.*]

It is to be hoped that some scholarly and philosophic critic of the present generation may be inspired to write a book on the history and aesthetic of melodrama. The golden age of melodrama passed, it is true, before any person living was aware of its existence: in the very middle of the last century. But there are many living who are not too young to remember the melodramatic stage before the cinema replaced it; who have sat entranced, in the front stalls of local or provincial theatres, before some representation of *East Lynne,* or *The White Slave,* or *No Mother to Guide Her;* and who are not too old to have observed with curious interest the replacement of dramatic melodrama by cinematographic melodrama, and the dissociation of the elements of the old three-volume melodramatic novel into the various types of the modern 300-page novel. Those who have lived before such terms as "highbrow fiction," "thrillers" and "detective fiction" were invented realize that melodrama is perennial and that the craving for it is perennial and must be satisfied. If we cannot get this satisfaction out of what the publishers present as "literature," then we will read—with less and less pretence of concealment—what we call "thrillers." But in the golden age of melodramatic fiction there was no such distinction. The best novels *were* thrilling; the distinction of *genre* between such-and-such a profound "psychological" novel of today and such-and-such a masterly "detective" novel of today is greater than the distinction of *genre* between *Wuthering Heights,* or even *The Mill on the Floss,* and *East Lynne,* the last of which "achieved an enormous and instantaneous success, and was translated into every known language, including Parsee and Hindustani." We believe that several contemporary novels have been "translated into every known language"; but we are sure that they have less in common with *The Golden Bowl,* or *Ulysses,* or even *Beauchamp's Career,* than *East Lynne* has in common with *Bleak House.*

In order to enjoy and to appreciate the work of Wilkie Collins, we ought to be able to reassemble the elements which have been dissociated in the modern novel. Collins is the contemporary of Dickens, Thackeray, George Eliot; of Charles Reade and almost of Captain Marryat. He has something in common with all of these novelists; but particularly and significantly with Dickens. Collins was the friend and sometimes the collaborator of Dickens; and the work of the two men ought to be studied side by side. There is, unhappily for the literary critic, no full biography of Wilkie Collins; and Forster's *Life of Dickens* is, from this point of view, most unsatisfactory. Forster was a notable biographer; but as a critic of the work of Dickens his view was a very narrow view. To any one who knows the bare facts of Dickens's acquaintance with Collins, and who has studied the work of the two men, their relationship and their influence upon one another is an important subject of study. And a comparative study of their novels can do much to illuminate the question of the difference between the dramatic and the melodramatic in fiction.

Dickens's "best novel" is probably *Bleak House;* that is Mr. Chesterton's opinion, and there is no better critic of Dickens living than Mr. Chesterton. Collins's best novel—or, at any rate, the only one of Collins's novels which every one knows—is *The Woman in White*. Now *Bleak House* is the novel in which Dickens most closely approaches Collins (and after *Bleak House, Little Dorrit* and parts of *Martin Chuzzlewit*); and *The Woman in White* is the novel in which Collins most closely approaches Dickens. Dickens excelled in character; in the creation of characters of greater intensity than human beings. Collins was not usually strong in the creation of character; but he was a master of plot and situation, of those elements of drama which are most essential to melodrama. *Bleak House* is Dickens's finest piece of construction; and *The Woman in White* contains Collins's most real characterization. Every one knows Count Fosco and Marion Halcombe intimately; only the most perfect Collins reader can remember even half a dozen of his other characters by name.

Count Fosco and Marion are indeed real personages to us; as "real" as much greater characters are, as real as Becky Sharp or Emma Bovary. In comparison with the characters of Dickens they lack only that kind of reality which is almost supernatural, which hardly seems to belong to the character by natural right, but seems rather to descend upon him by a kind of inspiration or grace. Collins's best characters are fabricated, with consummate skill, before our eyes; in Dickens's greatest figures we see no process or calculation. Dickens's figures belong to poetry, like figures of Dante or Shakespeare, in that a single phrase, either by them or about them, may be enough to set them wholly before us. Collins has no phrases. Dickens can with a phrase make a character as real as flesh and blood—*"What a Life Young Bailey's Was!"*—like Farinata

    Chi fur gli maggior tui?

or like Cleopatra,

      I saw her once
Hop forty paces through the public street.

Dickens's characters are real because there is no one like them; Collins's because they are so painstakingly coherent and lifelike. Whereas Dickens often introduces a great character carelessly, so that we do not realize, until the story is far advanced, with what a powerful personage we have to do, Collins, at least in these two figures in *The Woman in White,* employs every advantage of dramatic effect. Much of our impression of Marion is due to the words in which she is first presented:

> "The instant my eyes rested on her I was struck by the rare beauty of her form, and by the unaffected grace of her attitude. Her figure was tall, yet not too tall; comely and well developed, yet not fat; her head set on her shoulders with an easy, pliant firmness; her waist, perfection in the eyes of a man, for it occupied its natural place, it filled out its natural circle, it was visibly and delightfully undeformed by stays. She had not heard my entrance into the room, and I allowed myself the luxury of admiring her for a few moments before I moved one of the chairs near me as the least embarrassing means of attracting her attention. She turned towards me immediately. The easy elegance of every movement of her limbs and body, as soon as she began to advance from the far end of the room, set me in a flutter of expectation to see her face clearly. She left the window—and I said to myself, 'The lady is dark.' She moved forward a few steps—and I said to myself, 'The lady is young.' She approached nearer, and I said to myself (with a sense of surprise which words fail me to express), 'The lady is ugly!'"

The introduction of Count Fosco—too long to quote in full—requires many more small strokes; but we should observe, Marion Halcombe being already given, that our impression of the Count is made very much stronger by being given to us as Marion's impression of him:

> "There are peculiarities in his personal appearance, his habits, and his amusements, which I should blame in the boldest terms, or ridicule in the most merciless manner, if I had seen them in another man. What is it that makes me unable to blame them, or to ridicule them in *him?*"

After this who can forget the white mice or the canaries, or the way in which Count Fosco treated Sir Percival's sulky blood-hound? If *The Woman in White* is the greatest of Collins's novels, it is so because of these two characters. If we examine the book apart from Marion and Fosco, we must admit that it is not Collins's finest work of construction, and that certain of his peculiar melodramatic gifts are better displayed in other books. The book is dramatic because of two characters; it is dramatic in the way in which the dramatic differs from the melodramatic. Sir Percival Glyde is a figure of pasteboard, and the mystery and the plot of which he is the centre are almost grotesque. The one of Collins's books which is the most perfect piece of construction, and the best balanced between plot and character, is *The Moonstone;* the one which reaches the greatest melodramatic intensity is *Armadale.*

The Moonstone is the first and greatest of English detective novels. We say *English* detective novels, because there is also the work of Poe, which has a *pure* detective interest. The detective story, as created by Poe, is something as specialized and as intellectual as a chess problem; whereas the best English detective fiction has relied less on the beauty of the mathematical problem and much more on the intangible human element. In detective fiction England probably excels other countries; but in a *genre* invented by Collins and not by Poe. In *The Moonstone* the mystery is finally solved, not altogether by human ingenuity, but largely by accident. Since Collins, the best heroes of English detective fiction have been, like Sergeant Cuff, fallible; they play their part, but never the sole part, in the unravelling. Sherlock Holmes, not altogether a typical English sleuth, is a partial exception; but even Holmes exists, not solely because of his prowess, but largely because he is, in the Jonsonian sense, a humorous character, with his needle, his boxing, and his violin. But Sergeant Cuff, far more than Holmes, is the ancestor of the healthy generation of amiable, efficient, professional but fallible inspectors of fiction among whom we live today. And *The Moonstone,* a book twice the length of the "thrillers" that our contemporary masters write, maintains its interest and suspense at every moment. It does this by devices of a Dickensian type; for Collins, in addition to his particular merits, was a Dickens without genius. The book is a comedy of humours. The eccentricities of Mr. Franklin Blake, the satire on false philanthropy in the character of Mr. Godfrey Ablewhite (to say nothing of the Life, Letters and Labours of Miss Jane Ann Stamper), Betteridge with his "Robinson Crusoe," and his daughter Penelope, support the narrative. In other of Collins's novels, the trick of passing the narration from one hand to another, and employing every device of letters and diaries, becomes tedious and even unplausible (for instance, in *Armadale,* the terrific villain, Miss Gwilt, commits herself to paper far too often and far too frankly); but in *The Moonstone* these devices succeed, every time, in stimulating our interest afresh just at the moment when it was about to flag.

And in *The Moonstone* Collins succeeds in bringing into play those aids of "atmosphere" in which Dickens (and the Brontës) exhibited such genius, and in which Collins has everything except their genius. For his purpose, he does not come off badly. Compare the description of the discovery of Rosanna's death in the Shivering Sands—and notice how carefully, beforehand, the *mise-en-scène* of the Shivering Sands is prepared for us—with the shipwreck of Steerforth in *David Copperfield.* We may say, "There is no comparison!"

but there *is* a comparison; and however unfavourable to Collins, it must increase our estimation of his skill.

There is another characteristic of Wilkie Collins which also brings him closer to Dickens, and it is a characteristic which has very great melodramatic value: compare the work of Collins with the work of Mrs. Henry Wood, already mentioned, and one sees how important for melodrama is the presence or absence of this. Forster, in his *Life of Dickens,* observes:

> "On the coincidences, resemblances and surprises of life Dickens liked especially to dwell, and few things moved his fancy so pleasantly. The world, he would say, was so much smaller than we thought it; we were all so connected by fate without knowing it; people supposed to be far apart were so constantly elbowing each other; and tomorrow bore so close a resemblance to nothing half so much as to yesterday."

Forster mentions this peculiarity early in the life of Dickens, long before Dickens became acquainted with Collins. We may take it that this feeling was common to Dickens and Collins, and that it may have been one of the causes of their being drawn so sympathetically together, once they had become acquainted. The two men had obviously in common a passionate feeling for the drama. Each had qualities which the other lacked, and they had certain qualities in common. It is perfectly reasonable to believe that the relations of the two men—of which Forster gives us only the barest and most unsatisfactory hints—affected profoundly the later work of each. We seem to find traces of it in *Little Dorrit* and *The Tale of Two Cities.* Collins could never have invented Durdles and Deputy; but Durdles and Deputy were obviously to play their part in a whole, *bien charpenté* as Collins's work is, and as the work of Dickens prior to *Bleak House* is not.

One of the minor works of Collins which illustrates especially this insistence upon the "coincidences, resemblances and surprises of life" is *The Frozen Deep.* The story, as we read it, was patched up from the melodrama which Collins wrote first; which was privately performed with great success on several occasions, and in which Dickens took the leading part. Collins was the cleverer at writing stage pieces; but we may imagine that Dickens was the cleverer at acting them; and Dickens may have given to the *rôle* of Richard Wardour, in acting it, an individuality which it certainly lacks in the story. This story, we may add for the benefit of those who have not read it, depends upon coincidence with a remarkably long arm; for the two men who ought not to meet—the accepted and the rejected lover—do meet, and under the most unlikely conditions they join, without knowing each other's identity, the same Polar Expedition.

In *The Frozen Deep* Collins wrote a piece of pure melodrama. That is to say, it is nothing but melodrama.

We are asked to accept an improbability, simply for the sake of seeing the thrilling situation which arises in consequence. But the frontier of drama and melodrama is vague; the difference is largely a matter of emphasis; perhaps no drama has ever been greatly and permanently successful without a large melodramatic element. What is the difference between *The Frozen Deep* and *Oedipus the King?* It is the difference between coincidence, set without shame or pretence, and fate—which merges into character. It is not necessary, for high drama, that accident should be eliminated; you cannot formulate the proportion of accident that is permissible. But in great drama character is always felt to be—not more important than plot—but somehow integral with plot. At least, one is left with the conviction that if circumstances had not arranged the events to fall out in such and such a way, the personages were, after all, such that they would have ended just as badly, or just as well, and more or less similarly. And sometimes the melodramatic—the accidental—becomes for Collins the dramatic—the fatal. There is one short tale, not one of his best known, and far from being his best—a tale with an extremely improbable ghost— which nevertheless is almost dramatic. It is called *The Haunted Hotel;* what makes it better than a mere readable second-rate ghost story is the fact that fatality in this story is no longer merely a wire jerking the figures. The principal character, the fatal woman, is herself obsessed by the idea of fatality; her motives are melodramatic; she therefore compels the coincidences to occur, feeling that she is compelled to compel them. In this story, as the chief character is internally melodramatic, the story itself ceases to be merely melodramatic, and partakes of true drama.

There is another characteristic of certain tales of Collins's, which may be said to belong to melodrama, or to the melodramatic part of drama. It consists in delaying, longer than one would conceive it possible to delay, a conclusion which is inevitable and wholly foreseen. A story like *The New Magdalen* is from a certain moment merely a study in stage suspense; the *dénouement* is postponed, again and again, by every possible ingenuity; the situations are in the most effective sense theatrical, without being in the profounder sense dramatic. They are seldom, as in *The Woman in White,* situations of conflict between significant personalities; they are more often conflicts between chessmen which merely occupy hostile positions on the board. Such, for instance, is the prolonged battle between Captain Wragge and Mrs. Lecomte at Aldburgh, in *No Name.*

The one of Collins's novels which we should choose as the most typical, or as the best of the more typical, and which we should recommend as a specimen of the melodramatic fiction of the epoch, is *Armadale.* It has no merit beyond melodrama, and it has every merit that melodrama can have. If Miss Gwilt did not have

to bear such a large part of the burden of revealing her own villainy, the construction would be almost perfect. Like most of Collins's novels, it has the immense— and nowadays more and more rare—merit of being never dull. It has, to a very high degree, the peculiar Collins merit above mentioned, which we might call the air of spurious fatality. The machinery of the book is operated by the Dream. The mind of the reader is very carefully prepared for acceptance of the Dream; first by the elaborately staged coincidence of the two cousins getting marooned on the wreck of the ship on which the father of the one had long before entrapped the father of the other; secondly by the way in which the Dream is explained away by the doctor. The doctor's explanation is so reasonable that the reader immediately reacts in favour of the Dream. Then, the character of the dreamer himself is made plausibly intuitive; and the stages by which the various parts of the Dream are realized are perfectly managed. Particularly is this true of the scene in which, after some excellent comedy of humours on the boating party, Miss Gwilt arrives at sunset on the desolate shore of the Norfolk Broads. By means of the Dream, we are kept in a state of tension which makes it possible to believe in characters which otherwise we should find preposterous.

The greatest novels have something in them which will ensure their being read, at least by a small number of people, even if the novel, as a literary form, ceases to be written. It is not pretended that the novels of Wilkie Collins have this permanence. They are interesting only if we enjoy "reading novels." But novels are still being written; and there is no contemporary novelist who could not learn something from Collins in the art of interesting and exciting the reader. So long as novels are written, the possibilities of melodrama must from time to time be re-explored. The contemporary "thriller" is in danger of becoming stereotyped; the conventional murder is discovered in the first chapter by the conventional butler, and the murderer is discovered in the last chapter by the conventional inspector—after having been already discovered by the reader. The resources of Wilkie Collins are, in comparison, inexhaustible.

And even if we refused to take Collins very seriously by himself, we can hardly fail to treat him with seriousness if we recognize that the art of which he was a master was an art which neither Charles Reade nor Dickens despised. You cannot define Drama and Melodrama so that they shall be reciprocally exclusive; great drama has something melodramatic in it, and the best melodrama partakes of the greatness of drama. *The Moonstone* is very near to *Bleak House.* The theft of a diamond has some of the same blighting effect on the lives about it as the suit in Chancery; Rosanna Spearman is destroyed by the diamond as Miss Flite is destroyed by Chancery. Collins's novels suggest questions which no student of "the art of fiction" can afford to neglect. It is possible that the artist can be too conscious of his "art." Perhaps Henry James—who in his own practice could be not only "interesting," but had a very cunning mastery of the finer melodrama—may have had as a critic a bad influence. We cannot afford to forget that the first—and not one of the least difficult—requirements of either prose or verse is that it should be interesting.

Lyn Pykett (essay date 1992)

SOURCE: "Mary Elizabeth Braddon: The Secret Histories of Women," in *The 'Improper' Feminine,* Routledge, 1992, pp. 83-113.

[*In the following essay, Pykett examines the novels of Mary Elizabeth Braddon to discuss the relationship between Victorian gender roles and the convention of the family secret in sensation novels.*]

> [Sensation novelists] wanted to persuade people that in almost every one of the well-ordered houses of their neighbours there was a skeleton shut up in some cupboard; that their comfortable and easy-looking neighbour had in his breast a secret story which he was always going about trying to conceal.
>
> (Ray 1865:203)

> Had every creature a secret, part of themselves, hidden deep in their breasts, like that dark purpose which had grown out of the misery of her father's untimely death—some buried memory, whose influence was to overshadow all their lives?
>
> (EV I:3)

This fearful question, asked by Eleanor Vane, heroine of *Eleanor's Victory,* lies at the heart of the sensation novel. It both exposes and plays on the fear of respectable Victorian society that social and familial normality had some dark secret at its core. The secrets of the family and the secret histories of families are the source of the typical sensation plot, which, as Henry James noted, is concerned with 'those most mysterious of mysteries, the mysteries that are at our own doors' (1865:594). Indeed, the power of sensationalism, as Elaine Showalter has pointed out, derives 'from its exposure of secrecy as the fundamental enabling condition of middle-class life' (1978b:104). As both Showalter and Anthea Trodd (1989) have demonstrated, the sensation novel's characteristic preoccupation with domestic crimes is the focus of a range of anxieties about the nature and structure of the family, and the problematic relationship of this private (feminine) sphere with the public (masculine) domain.

In particular, the sensation novel habitually focuses on the secrets and secret histories of women. All of Mary Elizabeth Braddon's early novels are structured around women with a concealed past: women who, for a variety of reasons, conceal their present motivations and

desires, and who have a hidden mission which drives their lives. In most cases these feminine concealments both result from, and foreground, a tension between the proper and the improper feminine. The secret at the heart of Braddon's novels usually involves a former transgression of the bounds of the proper feminine, or it involves a guilt by association, which taints or threatens the heroine's respectability. The concealment most often results from a conflict between a particular woman's self-appointed mission and the accepted codes of the proper feminine, or from the necessity for women to act by stealth, and often through male agents, in a society which casts them in a passive, dependent role. Except in the case of Braddon's two best-known novels, the secret involves a conflict between the heroine's mission to avenge a wronged father (or father-substitute) and that code of the proper feminine which defines woman as self-sacrificing, loving and forgiving. Revenge thus serves as a generalised metaphor for a commanding secret passion, a hidden desire which motivates a woman's actions.

Often, several forms of secrecy converge to generate a particular narrative. In *Eleanor's Victory,* for example, Eleanor Vane conceals and bears the guilty burden of her impoverished past with a dissolute father who is addicted to gambling. Although this 'guilty' past (and its convergence with the family secrets of others) is the origin of the story, it is Eleanor's own deliberate concealments which sustain—and provide the necessary complications for—the narrative trajectory. In the earlier part of this novel Braddon rewrites *The Old Curiosity Shop,* tempering Little Nell's preternatural goodness, which is all suffering and endurance, with a more realistic sense of the moral and psychological consequences of the experience of observing and being involved in the downward spiral of the obsessive gambler. The secret of Dickens's heroine is an ultra-'feminine', passive goodness which passes all understanding, and which cannot survive in this fallen world. Eleanor's secret, on the other hand, is her 'unwomanly' desire for revenge and her active pursuit of the man who has driven her father to suicide.

A similar set of secrets lies at the centre of the particularly complex (even cumbersome) plot and sub-plots of *Run To Earth,* whose heroine, Jenny Milsom, is literally rescued from the gutter (where she has been earning a precarious living as a street-singer) by Sir Oswald Eversleigh, who renames her and remakes her as a genteel woman. Jenny/Honoria's secret history is her ignoble birth (she is the daughter of a desperado called Black Milsom), her association with low-life criminals, and her dark knowledge of hideous crimes. However, an even darker secret sustains the second half of the novel; Honoria compromises her 'womanly' nature by apparently forsaking her infant daughter in order to unravel the secret of (and avenge) her husband's death.

The sins of the father also lie at the root of the concealments of Margaret Wilmot/Wentworth in *Henry Dunbar*. Margaret not only bears the taint of her father's criminality and poverty, but is also implicated in his guilt through her dutifully filial concealment of his murder and impersonation of his former employer. The plot of *Henry Dunbar,* like those of several of Braddon's novels, turns on women's position as 'relative creatures' (Basch 1974) and on the complexities and contradictions resulting from their conflicting loyalties as daughters, wives and mothers. This conflict is repeatedly foregrounded in direct comments by the narrator. In *Eleanor's Victory,* for example, we are told that Eleanor's life 'had fashioned itself to fit that unwomanly purpose [of avenging her father]. She abnegated the privileges, and left unperformed the duties of a wife' (EV II:152); or again, 'She had neglected her duty as a wife, absorbed in her affection as a daughter; she had sacrificed the living to the dead' (EV III:173). Unsurprisingly, the narrative trajectory of this novel, as of most of Braddon's fictions, is directed towards the proper feminisation of the heroine. The 'victory' of the title turns out 'after all' to be 'a proper womanly conquest, and not a stern, classical vengeance. The tender woman's heart triumphed over the girl's rash vow' (EV III:321). Ultimately Eleanor declines to exact her long-desired retribution from her father's destroyer, and wholeheartedly embraces her wifely and womanly role. However, as in other women's sensation novels, without the heroine's 'unwomanly purpose' there would have been no story.

Family secrets and the secret histories of women are most spectacularly present in *Lady Audley's Secret* and *Aurora Floyd*. It is significant that Braddon's most successful novels should each involve the secrets of a woman's own transgressive past, rather than her concealments of the guilty secrets of others. In fact, Braddon's most famous heroines are actually criminals; both are bigamists, and one attempts, and the other is suspected of, murder. Like a number of sensation heroines, Lady Audley and Aurora Floyd are used both to exploit and explore the fear expressed by another bestselling woman novelist, that all women 'possess a sleeping potentiality for crime, a curious possibility of fiendish evil' (Ouida 1895:324).

Aurora Floyd, Braddon's second bestseller, is built around the simplest and most commonplace of secrets: that of an impetuous and misspent youth. According to the double standard of sexual morality such a secret in a man's life may be of little interest; there is no story, unless it be in the return of the repressed feminine, as in Bertha's embodiment of Rochester's past in *Jane Eyre*. In the case of a woman, however, the secret of youthful transgression is the origin of a proliferation of narratives. Aurora, the motherless and hence improperly socialised and improperly feminised heroine

of the novel, has extended her masculinised interest in horses and racing to her father's groom, Conyers, with whom she elopes. Rumours of her youthful misdemeanours subsequently prevent her marriage to Talbot Bulstrode, a scion of the Cornish aristocracy. The need to conceal this early misjudgment is compounded (and plot complications proliferate) when, erroneously believing Conyers to be dead, Aurora subsequently marries John Mellish, only to discover that her first husband is still alive, and indeed has come to work on her second husband's estate.

It is worth noting, incidentally, that all of Braddon's heroines (indeed the heroines of most sensation novels) share Aurora's lack of a mother. As the speaker of Florence Nightingale's fragment 'Cassandra' observes: 'the secret of the charm of every romance that ever was written . . . is that the heroine has *generally* no family ties (almost *invariably* no mother), or, if she has, these do not interfere with her entire independence' (quoted in Strachey 1978:397). It is certainly a defining characteristic of the sensation heroine that she has not been 'educated to that end [of the good wife] by a careful mother' (AF:41). As in so many nineteenth-century novels by women, the motherless heroine is both more vulnerable and more assertive than was the norm for the properly socialised woman. Socially sanctioned mothering, as an extended horticultural metaphor in *Aurora Floyd* has it, is required to 'train and prune' the 'exuberant branches' sometimes found in women in their natural state, so that they may be 'trimmed and clipped and fastened primly to the stone wall of society with cruel nails' (AF:42).

Aurora Floyd moves from hidden transgression to concealed criminality more by accident than by design, as a result of her inadvertent bigamy. Lady Audley's secret criminality is, apparently, a matter of cold calculation. Helen Talboys, disguised as Lucy Graham, marries Sir Michael Audley knowing that she is still legally married to George Talboys. When she learns of Talboys's imminent return from Australia she carefully stage-manages the death by consumption of 'Helen Talboys', and places an obituary announcement in *The Times*. Accidentally discovered by her first husband, she pushes him down a well—she assumes to his death—and subsequently attempts to dispose of her second husband's nephew, Robert Audley, whom she fears will reveal her guilt.

These two women, each possessed of a secret past which compromises the marriage on which they embark in the narrative present, become the focus of a range of questions and tensions about the nature of femininity, the domestic ideal, women's role in marriage, and the state of modern marriage, which were central preoccupations in sensation fiction in general. I want to look first at some of the ways in which Braddon's two bestselling novels represent femininity.

Staging The Feminine: Braddon's Melodramatic Style

Most critics were and are agreed that the power of *Aurora Floyd* and *Lady Audley's Secret* lies in their transgressive heroines. Indeed, both contemporary reviewers and later readers have focused on the transgressive nature of these heroines rather than on their criminality. This tends to reinforce the view that the bigamy novel was used either to develop the adultery plot in a displaced form, or as a way of representing a sexually active female character whilst keeping within that framework of law and custom which was designed to regulate female sexuality. In what ways are Braddon's best-known heroines transgressive? What does their transgressiveness signify? How does it function within the narrative economy of the text?

The characterisations of Aurora Floyd and Lady Audley both involve an elaborate play with fictional female stereotypes. Both characters, in different ways, embody the contradictory discourse on woman (discussed in I, 2 above) in which woman is figured as either a demon or an angel. The two heroines embody and exploit the fear (which pervaded middle-class culture) that women are 'wild beasts' whose lusts and licentiousness run riot if unconstrained by the patriarchal family.[8]

Aurora Floyd is represented from the outset as very obviously transgressing the boundaries of the proper feminine. Her physical appearance is itself a sign that she belongs to the category of the dangerous, improper feminine. Moreover, like her creator, Aurora (in James's memorable phrase) 'knows much that ladies are not accustomed to know' (1865:593). She is represented as a prototypical 'Girl of the Period': her behaviour is generally fast, she uses coarse language, and has a passion for (and unwomanly knowledge of) horseracing. The verve with which this stereotype is represented in Braddon's novel has the paradoxical effect of portraying the culture's demon, the masculinised 'unwomanly' woman, as the desirable and desired feminine. However, Aurora's secret (as revealed in the rapidly unfolding narrative) is that beneath this racy and, apparently, criminal exterior beats the eternal heart of domestic, maternal woman. Aurora's story is the story of the gradual taming of the wild beast of the improper feminine.

On the other hand (an irony not lost on her contemporary readers), Braddon's first *femme fatale,* the bigamous, murderous and possibly insane Lady Audley, seems, at least on the surface, to be contained within the boundaries of the proper and respectable feminine. This feminine ideal is elaborated and, it appears, celebrated in an early descriptive passage:

> Wherever she went she seemed to take joy and brightness with her. In the cottages of the poor her fair face shone like a sunbeam. She would sit for a quarter of an hour talking to some old woman, and apparently as pleased with the admiration of a toothless crone as if she had been listening to the compliments of a marquis; and when she tripped away, leaving nothing behind her (for her poor salary gave no scope to her benevolence), the old woman would burst out into senile raptures with her grace . . . For you see Miss Lucy Graham was blessed with that magic power of fascination by which a woman can charm with a word or intoxicate with a smile.
>
> (LAS:5-6)

The direct narratorial address of this extract, with its familiar, even banal, formulae for feminine charms, involves the reader in shared assumptions about the nature of feminine fascination. A typical example of Braddon's descriptive technique, this passage (which continues in the same vein for some length) engages in an excess of description and an overemphasis on Lucy's embodiment of the feminine ideal, with the effect of making her the object of the reader's gaze. Thus, at the level of textual or narrative representation, Lucy Graham is staged as spectacle, just as within the narrative the character is staging herself. This latter kind of performance is central to Braddon's novels, since, like Lucy Graham, virtually all of her heroines have something to hide, and are to that extent actresses.

Lady Audley shares with a number of Braddon heroines the 'shame' of an ignoble father and humble and impoverished family circumstances. To this is added a more fundamental fear about her parentage: the fear that she may have inherited her mother's madness. This taint, passed on from mother to daughter like a mark of Eve, represents an association between madness and the feminine which was pervasive in nineteenth-century culture.[9] In fact the question of Lady Audley's madness (is she mad, or is she simply clever and/or wicked?) becomes one of the key secrets of the narrative. The repeatedly postponed uncovering of the mystery of Lady Audley is one of the major sources of narrative pleasure, as the main plot of this novel persistently promises to get at the hidden truth of its heroine/villain, and of woman.

As far as the character of Lady Audley herself is concerned, her fear of her secret destiny adds another dimension to the determining conditions of a woman's life. The habits of self-surveillance developed by Helen Maldon/Lady Audley in response to her fears of inheriting her mother's madness are an exaggerated form of that self-scrutiny enjoined upon every woman by prevailing ideas of the proper feminine. Braddon's emphasis on her heroines' concern to protect their secrets, like her habitual minute focus on their sensations and feelings, is in part a foregrounding of the process of self-surveillance endemic in a culture in which the 'supremacy of the woman's moral nature and her potential degeneracy were the twin poles of a representation which had already transposed a panic about the social body—its ordered regulation and reproduction—into moral terms' (Rose 1986:111).

In fact 'Lucy Graham' and 'Lady Audley' are both roles played by Helen Maldon, who has repeatedly remade her identity with each rise in the social scale from the impoverished daughter of a disreputable half-pay naval officer; to the wife of George Talboys, heir to a considerable fortune (from which he is disinherited as a result of his father's displeasure at his imprudent marriage); to Lucy Graham, the quiet, respectable governess. In her final incarnation as Lady Audley, 'every trace of the old life [is] melted away—every clue to identity melted and forgotten', as marriage to Sir Michael promises to put an end to 'dependence . . . drudgery . . . [and] humiliations' (LAS:12).

Braddon not only shows Lady Audley adopting a series of different roles, but also focuses on the way her heroine plays a number of different parts within one apparently stable role. That of 'Lady Audley', the respectable gentlewoman, child-bride of a wealthy baronet, is itself fraught with contradictions; it is a kind of masquerade. By foregrounding Lady Audley's impersonation of proper femininity, the novel does more than simply focus attention on the feminine duplicity in which the entire narrative originates. It also explores and exploits fears that the respectable ideal, or proper feminine, may simply be a form of acting, just one role among other possible roles. Even more seriously, the representation of Lady Audley, like that of some of Braddon's other heroines, raises the spectre that femininity is itself duplicitous, and that it involves deception and dissembling.

Such fears are exploited in one of Braddon's favourite narrative procedures—the construction of a narrative of unmasking. This strategy is most frequently used in a process of progressive revelation of the 'real' nature of a particular female character. In *Lady Audley's Secret* the unmasking narrative is found in its most extreme form in Robert Audley's attempt to expose his uncle's wife. One of the key points in this narrative of the contest between Lady Audley and her husband's nephew—the viewing of Lady Audley's portrait in Chapter 8—is worth looking at in some detail, since it is a very good example of the way in which Braddon's narratives habitually stage the feminine as spectacle. The strategy is one in which the excess of the melodramatic style is extremely important (I shall return to both of these points shortly).

In his eagerness to improve upon his 'imperfect notion of her face' Robert Audley, accompanied by his friend George Talboys, gains entry to Lady Audley's private rooms, which contain her unfinished portrait. The men's method of entry (by a secret passage) has clear sexual overtones, and the scene is presented as a stealthy, illicit, masculine invasion of a feminine domain. The reader is invited to share in the voyeuristic male gaze upon the exotic and intimate feminine space of Lady Audley's dressing room. The *mise-en-scène* is extremely elaborate and detailed, and emphasises sexual difference. On glimpsing his bearded face in the mirror, Talboys 'wondered to see how out of place he seemed among all these womanly luxuries' (LAS:69). The room, 'almost oppressive from odours', is full of flowers, exquisite china, jewels and gorgeous dresses carelessly abandoned (and suggesting a feminine abandon); all are traces of the feminine presence of the absent Lady Audley.

The scene builds to its climax as the male invaders proceed from the boudoir, through the dressing room, to the antechamber and approach Lady Audley's portrait. Unlike the other objects in her apartments the portrait is not just a sign or trace of Lady Audley, it is representation as revelation. The objects in the room are signs of the absent female body, but signs too of the social masquerade which that body adopts. The discarded clothes function both as erotic traces of femininity and as the abandoned costumes of the actress. The portrait, on the other hand, represents the body itself as sign. In viewing the portrait the characters in the narrative acquaint themselves with Lady Audley's face, while the readers are granted access to the secrets of her being. In this scene readers are positioned as spectators of the portrait which is both displayed to their gaze and 'read' for them. Our gaze is fixed firmly on the Pre-Raphaelite detail, while the narrator both satirises Pre-Raphaelitism and appropriates its sensuous and sensual gaze.

The elaborate description and reading of the painting suggest that, just as Audley and Talboys (and hence the reader) have glimpsed something of Lady Audley's inner, private self through their penetration of the recesses of her private rooms, so too the painter has penetrated the inner recesses of her identity and revealed its awful truth (and, perhaps, a feared truth about the nature of femininity): the inner reality that lies behind the mask of respectable femininity.

> It was so like and yet so unlike; it was as if you had burned strange-coloured fires before my lady's face, and by their influence brought out new lines and new expressions never seen before in it . . . [It] had something of the aspect of a beautiful fiend.
>
> (LAS:71)

The portrait scene prefigures the progressive narrative exposure of Lady Audley's secrets. In the narrative, as in the portrait, the angel in the house is revealed as the demon in the house. Long before the end of the novel the domestic idyll of Audley Court is unmasked as a hollow sham, and through this unmasking the economic and power relations of an aristocratic marriage (and the passions it represses) are also exposed. Ultimately the transgressive Lady Audley, too, is unmasked and 'Buried Alive' (to quote the title of the chapter which narrates this event) in a *maison de santé* (a madhouse) in the appositely named Belgian town of Villebrumeuse. Her incarceration and her subsequent death after a prolonged *maladie de langeur* (which is reported in a chapter ironically entitled 'At Peace') are the means by which the trangressive heroine (and the improper feminine) is expelled from the narrative.

However, the improper feminine remains as a repressed trace in the text's narration, in the linguistic excess of the melodramatic style. The physical manifestation of the improper feminine—Lady Audley's body—which has persistently been represented and read as spectacle, is finally represented simply by means of the Pre-Raphaelite painting that had promised to yield up her secrets. In the final paragraphs of the novel the reader's attention is directed once more to this portrait, now hidden behind a curtain from the prurient gaze of 'the inquisitive visitors . . . [who] admire my lady's rooms, and ask many questions about the pretty fairhaired woman, who died abroad' (LAS:446). The curtain which hangs before the portrait is at once a shroud which hides the improper feminine from the society whose equilibrium it has threatened, and also a veil which tantalisingly conceals and maintains the improper feminine's alluring mystery. Thus, even after her death, Lady Audley remains as a disturbing presence.

Lady Audley's Secret deliberately blurs the issue of whether its heroine's acting—her process of self-construction—is the product of her madness, or the result of cool calculation. In either case it is explicitly associated with the process of self-fashioning required by any respectable Victorian girl seeking to make her way in the world. (This is equally true of the way in which Aurora's dissembling is represented in *Aurora Floyd*.) Lady Audley's self-proclaimedly heartless attitude to her situation is, from one point of view, simply a more than usually honest assessment of the nature of the choices open to the would-be genteel woman:

> I had learnt that which in some indefinite manner or other *every schoolgirl learns sooner or later*—I learned that my ultimate fate in life depended upon my marriage, and I concluded that if I was indeed prettier than my schoolfellows, I ought to marry better than any of them.

> (LAS:350, my italics)

The reader is also implicated in this common-sense view of Lucy's situation (and thus aligned with the views of a criminal and/or madwoman) through those representative characters 'the simple Dawsons' (Lucy's employers), who encourage her marriage to Sir Michael and who 'would have thought it more than madness in a penniless girl to reject such an offer' (LAS:9). The notion that normal, sane femininity is built upon

prudential calculations of this kind is endorsed by Dr Alwyn Mosgrave, the medical expert called in by Robert Audley in his attempts to deal with the problem of Lady Audley. When in possession of only part of Lady Audley's story—the part relating to her bigamous deception of Sir Michael—Mosgrave delivers a medical verdict that is unequivocal:

> She ran away from her home, because her home was not a pleasant one, and she left it in the hope of finding a better. There is no madness in that. She committed the crime of bigamy, because by that crime she obtained fortune and position. There is no madness there. When she found herself in a desperate position, she did not grow desperate. She employed intelligent means, and she carried out a conspiracy which required coolness and deliberation in its execution. There is no madness in that.

> (LAS:377)

Robert Audley's definitions of the feminine are more conventional and less capacious than Mosgrave's. Audley seeks to prove Lady Audley's madness partly to save his friend and his uncle's family from scandal, but largely because his notions of the feminine cannot reconcile *sane* femininity with the criminally duplicitous behaviour of which he intuitively knows Lady Audley to be guilty. The readers' definitions of sane femininity are destablished by the way in which they are invited, by turns, to share Mosgrave's and Robert Audley's view of the heroine. The readers' view of normal, sane femininity is similarly challenged by their changing emotional investments in the character, which are engineered by the narrator's constantly shifting point of view.

When acquainted with the full extent of Lady Audley's crimes, the expert on insanity agrees to incarcerate her, not because she is mad, but because she is 'dangerous'.

> There is latent insanity! Insanity which might never appear; or which might appear only once or twice in a life-time . . . The lady is not mad; but she has the hereditary taint in her blood. She has the cunning of madness, with the prudence of intelligence. I will tell you what she is, Mr. Audley. She is dangerous!

> (LAS:379)

Lady Audley is dangerous because she is not what she appears to be, because she cannot be contained within the bounds of the proper feminine. Mosgrave's diagnosis seems to hold the key to an understanding of the way in which Braddon uses madness in her novels.

Braddon structures several novels (most notably *Lady Audley's Secret* and *John Marchmont's Legacy*) around characters who are, appear to be, or become mad or deranged. In each of these novels madness is used as a way of figuring the dangerous, improper feminine, which is both formed by and resists the management and control of the middle-class family and the self-regulation which is the internalisation of those broader social forms of control. *Lady Audley's Secret* and *John Marchmont's Legacy* both raise the question of whether female insanity may simply be 'the label society attaches to female assertion, ambition, self-interest, and outrage' (Showalter 1987:72). In addition *John Marchmont's Legacy* asks whether madness is, in fact, a *symptom* of bourgeois femininity.

Lady Audley is represented in terms of a contemporary medical discourse in which women's behaviour is related to the vagaries of the female body: her strange career dates from the birth of her son, and the onset of puerperal fever.[10] The figure of Lady Audley—the angel in the house turned domestic fiend—is also produced within and by a socio-medical discourse in which the image of female purity always contains within itself the antithetical image of female vice. Such a figure represents and explores fears that (actual, historical) women cannot be contained within dominant definitions of 'woman', or of normal femininity.

Olivia Arundel, the female villain in *John Marchmont's Legacy,* is in some ways an even more interesting representation of the feminine and of madness, or indeed of the feminine as madness, since her insanity seems to be actively produced by the norms of respectable femininity. Like Lady Audley, Olivia is used to raise the question of whether the proper feminine is a cover for, or the cause of, madness (the improper feminine). Lady Audley's story ends with her incarceration in an asylum modelled on the bourgeois household in order that the domestic ideology and its definitions of femininity may be defended. Olivia's story, on the other hand, is the story of a woman's incarceration within and by that ideology and those definitions. On a number of occasions the narrator focuses directly on this aspect of Olivia's predicament.

> Olivia Arundel had lived from infancy to womanhood . . . performing and repeating the same duties from day to day, with no other progress to mark the lapse of her existence than the slow alternation of the seasons, and the dark hollow circles which had lately deepened beneath her grey eyes . . .

> These outward tokens, beyond her own control, alone betrayed the secret of this woman's life. She sickened under the dull burden which she had borne so long, and carried out so patiently. The slow round of dull duty was loathsome to her. The horrible, narrow, unchanging existence, shut in by cruel walls, which bounded her on every side, and kept her prisoner to herself was odious to her. The powerful intellect revolted against the fetters that bound and galled it. The proud heart beat with murderous violence against the bonds that kept it captive.
>
> (JML I:135-6)

I have quoted this passage at such length because it is outwardly a direct and open analysis of 'the problem' of the frustrations and constraints of the domestic woman's lot. However, closer scrutiny (and the narratorial perspective is all about *close scrutiny*) reveals Olivia's situation not as a generalised female predicament but as one which is peculiar to the woman of 'powerful intellect'. This aspect of the representation of Olivia reveals, once again, the sensation novel's preoccupation with the blurring and instability of gender categories. The combination of passively endured suffering and the latent aggression of the murderous violence of her captive heart is precisely not what any *normally gendered* woman was supposed to feel about the frustrations of a dull life. The secret of Olivia's predicament seems to be that she is like a man. She is a 'mistake of nature', who has 'the brow of an intellectual and determined man' (JML I:125); she lacks the 'tenderness which is the common attribute of a woman's nature. She ought to have been a great man' (JML III:54).[11]

The above passage also provides another interesting example of the functions and effects of the melodramatic style. The omniscient narrator appears to be in complete control of the character, whose inner secrets are fathomed and anatomised with forensic care and detail. However, Olivia is also constituted as a disturbance, and thus beyond anatomisation and control. As the agent of disruption and confusion she is a disturbance in the narrative, but she is also a disturbance at the level of narration. The stance of narratorial control is disrupted by the melodramatic excess, not only of Olivia's actions, but also of the way in which she is represented in and as language. The narrator's forensic representation is overwhelmed by the melodramatic style, and the anatomising stance is abandoned at the end of the long passage quoted earlier.

> *How shall I anatomise* this woman, who, gifted with no womanly tenderness of nature, unendowed with that pitiful and unreasoning affection which makes womanhood beautiful, yet tried, and tried unceasingly, to do her duty, and to be good . . . ?
>
> (JML I:136, my italics)

Anatomising is replaced by display. As is so often the case in Braddon's fiction, the narrator announces the difficulty or impossibility of articulating a particular example of the feminine, only to embark on a surplus of articulation.

The Melodramatic Style and the Spectacle of Woman

This melodramatic excess is one of the hallmarks of Braddon's style, as it is of the sensation novel in general. It is an irruption into narration of that feeling (particularly the erotic feeling) which is repressed in the narrative. This excess—as Jane Feuer (1984) argues of television melodrama—opens up a 'textual space, which may be read against the seemingly hegemonic surface' (8). It appears in its most highly wrought form in setpiece scenes and dramatic tableaux which stage the heroine/villainess as a spectacle; she may be presented as the object of a public gaze within the text, or the scene may be staged directly for the reader. In such scenes the female body becomes a sign (or system of signs) which is imperfectly read, or misread, by the characters within the text, but which is legible to the narrator, and hence to the reader—even if what is legible is finally the sign's elusiveness.

Again and again in Braddon's novels female characters are represented by means of an intense focus on their physical appearance. For example, the mystery of Olivia's failure to conform to the feminine ideal is both 'explained' and inscribed in this description of her hair (a passage which, incidentally, typifies Braddon's habitual fetishisation of women's hair):

> Those masses of hair had not that purple lustre, nor yet that wandering glimmer of red gold, which gives peculiar beauty to some raven tresses. Olivia's hair was long and luxuriant; but it was of that dead, inky blackness, which is all shadow. It was dark, fathomless, inscrutable, like herself.
>
> (JML I:141)

Braddon's women rise up from the page like the heavily sensualised female subjects of Pre-Raphaelite paintings, and are offered as the object of the reader's rapt gaze. This staging of a particular version of the feminine for the gaze of the reader is also prominent in *Aurora Floyd*. Aurora's mother, who plays no part in the narrative present of the novel (she died at Aurora's birth), is, nevertheless, a powerful narrative presence, and provides a way of representing and viewing the feminine which anticipates the presence of the heroine herself.

> The banker's wife was a tall young woman, of about thirty, with a dark complexion, and *great flashing black eyes* that lit up a face, which might otherwise have been *unnoticeable,* into the splendour of absolute beauty.
>
> (AF:7, my italics)

Noticing this flashing incandescence is precisely what the text requires readers to do, as the narrator invites them to gaze admiringly at Eliza. As in the description of Olivia's hair, the passage works by addressing and invoking a particular cultural awareness of the female body. The reader is co-opted into the role of co-creator of the spectacle.

> *Let the reader recall* one of those faces, whose chief loveliness lies in the glorious light of a pair of magnificent eyes, and *remember* how far they

surpassed all others in their power of fascination. The same amount of beauty frittered away upon a well-shaped nose, rosy pouting lips, symmetrical forehead, and delicate complexion, would make an ordinarily lovely woman; but concentrated in one nucleus, in the wondrous lustre of the eyes, it makes a divinity, a Circe.
>
> (AF:7, my italics)

The speaking presence of the body in the text was a much-discussed aspect of sensation fiction. Their tendency to dwell on the (female) body was generally regarded as one of the improprieties of sensation novels; the intense physicality of their representation of the heroine was the source of their perceived transgression. Braddon's deployment of a familiar repertoire of physical traits and ways of describing the seductive feminine was one of the formulaic aspects of her novels which were much criticised by reviewers. Since these formulae are such a prominent feature of her work, one can only assume that such writing was also an important source of pleasure to readers, and hence that it is worth examining more closely.

As I have suggested, the reader is repeatedly required to *notice* Braddon's central female characters. Aurora, for example, is first brought to notice (although it is not the first time she appears in the text) when she is the object of the fascinated gaze of Talbot Bulstrode, to whom she appears as, 'A divinity! imperiously beautiful in white and scarlet, painfully dazzling to look upon, intoxicatingly brilliant to behold' (AF:29). The rest of this passage simultaneously indulges in and satirises the practice of spectating femininity, by representing Bulstrode's fluctuating and contradictory reponses to (and revisions of) his vision, before it is punctured by the bathetic 'reality' of Aurora's enquiry about the result of a horse race.

Aurora is sometimes presented as the direct object of the reader's gaze, and sometimes mediated through a male gaze, while at other times the reader spectates a more or less public spectating of the character. Several of these perspectives are present in the following scene, which stages Aurora's arrival at Mellish Park upon her marriage to its owner:

> They [the Yorkshire servants] could not choose but admire Aurora's eyes, which they unanimously declared to be 'regular shiners;' and the flash of her white teeth, glancing between the full crimson lips; and the bright flush which lighted up her pale white skin; and the purple lustre of her massive coronal of plaited hair. Her beauty was of that luxuriant and splendid order which has almost always most effect upon the masses, and the fascination of her manner was almost akin to sorcery in its power over simple people.
>
> (AF:110)

This passage moves from physically displaying Aurora to the reader through the eyes of the Yorkshire servants, to implicating the reader directly in the process of spectatorship. The feminine power of the character not only bewitches simple people (like the servants) but also (by the end of the passage) intoxicates the discriminating narrator: 'I lose myself when I try to describe the feminine intoxications, the wonderful fascination exercised by this dark-eyed siren' (AF:111). Aurora Floyd possesses the text. The effect is one of simultaneously exploiting and satirising those mid-Victorian 'regimes of representation' which 'signify in the historical process of redefinition of woman as *image, as visibly different*' (Pollock 1988:120).

Like Lady Audley, Aurora Floyd is continually presented as spectacle, as a speaking picture of power, pride and beauty. The reader is repeatedly invited to join a character (usually a male character) in a voyeuristic spectating of the unwitting heroine—as when John Mellish discovers his wife asleep in her dressing room:

> Aurora was lying on the sofa, wrapped in a loose white dressing-gown, her masses of ebon hair uncoiled and falling about her shoulders in serpentine tresses that looked like shining blue-black snakes released from poor Medusa's head to make their escape amid the folds of her garment.

(AF:227)

Here, the heroine is 'pictured' in the 'sleeping-woman' pose much favoured by male artists of the later nineteenth century. She is represented by a heavily sexualised word-painting which is typical of Braddon's sixties novels. This aspect of Braddon's melodramatic style, like the paintings it replicates, offers a representation of woman as simultaneously 'an object of erotic desire and a creature of self-containment, not really interested in, and hence not making any demands upon, the viewer's participation in her personal erotic gratification' (Djikstra 1986:69).[12]

The effect is a representation of female sexuality as voyeuristic spectacle, which offered both male and female readers pleasurable images of female erotic power. The potential danger of this power is defused through the fetishisation of the text's gaze, and through the melodramatic style. As in the portrait scene from *Lady Audley's Secret* (see pp. 91-2) and in numerous other passages in Braddon's novels which represent female figures in private female spaces (especially boudoirs and dressing rooms),[13] such writing (like the painting styles it both replicates and satirises) combines sexual frisson with the promise of a privileged access to feminine interiority.

Braddon's writing both panders to a contemporary taste created by Rossetti and his followers and, at the same time, foregrounds in its satiric excess the way in which the Pre-Raphaelites figured woman as fantasy, the 'sign of masculine desire' (Pollock 1988:21). As Griselda Pollock has suggested, the Pre-Raphaelite representation of woman as difference was a direct intervention in the complex process of renegotiation of gender roles which was taking place throughout the latter half of the nineteenth century.

> In the visual sign, woman, [which was] manufactured in a variety of guises in mid-nineteenth-century British culture, this absolute difference is secured by the erasure of indices of real time and actual space, by an abstracted . . . representation of faces as dislocated uninhabited spaces which function as a screen across which masculine fantasies of knowledge, power, and possession can be enjoyed in a ceaseless play on the visible obviousness of woman and the puzzling enigmas, reassuringly disguised behind the mask of beauty. At the same time, the face and sometimes part of a body are severed from the whole. Fetish-like they signify an underlying degree of anxiety generated by looking at this sign of difference, woman.

(Pollock 1988:123)

The cumulative effect of those scenes in which Braddon writes the body is complex. Ultimately, however, they work to destabilise the category of the feminine by simultaneously reinscribing and satirically undercutting conventional codes for describing and representing the female body.

The staging of the heroine as spectacle is also the site of another important destabilising factor in Braddon's novels, and a source of their subversive potential. Within the narrative economy of a particular text, the heroine usually has a functionally transgressive role as subject or agent. However, this active transgression is undercut or negated at the level of narration, where the heroine is the passive object of the text's gaze, placed in a specular relationship to the reader, who, in turn, occupies a position of mastery *vis à vis* the heroine. On the other hand, the frequent changes in point of view involve the reader in constantly shifting power relations with the heroine. The reader moves from spectating her as the object of the text's or narrator's gaze, to seeing her through the eyes of one or more of the other characters, to sharing her own perspective, or being co-opted by the narrator to a moral judgement or sympathetic understanding of her heroine. These constant shifts tend to keep the heroine's meaning and significance in a state of flux. As in the contradictory or double discourse on woman, Braddon's heroines constantly shift from being active agents to passive sufferers, from transgressors to victims.

Masculinity, The Feminine Ideal, and Modern Marriage

Although most of Braddon's sixties novels, especially *Lady Audley's Secret* and *Aurora Floyd*, focus on different kinds and differing degrees of feminine transgression, they are not simply stories of the thrills and spills of errant femininity (or, as it would sometimes seem, stories about reforming or expelling it). Rather they use the transgressive woman as both a trigger and a focus for a range of narratives of uncertainty about gender, class, marriage and the family.

Uncertainties about gender are not confined to the definitions of femininity, but are also demonstrated in the representation of masculinity. Braddon's novels habitually reproduce and satirise contemporary anxieties about the blurring of gender boundaries and gender functions. Robert Audley in *Lady Audley's Secret* is used to focus attention on the social construction of gender as he progresses from a period of 'feminised' indolence to a fully 'masculinised' role as head of the bourgeois family. Audley plays a crucial role in *Lady Audley's Secret:* the unmasking of a duplicitous female by a feminised male. This unmasking provides the novel's central narrative dynamic—the cat-and-mouse game in which Robert tries to penetrate and unmask the secrets of his aunt, and she tries first to ensnare him sexually and then to kill him. Both ploys are equally threatening to Robert's masculine identity.

The parrying relationship between nephew and aunt both focuses on gender instabilities, and ultimately stabilises them. Robert's suspicions of his aunt are represented as a privileged insight into her nature, which derives, in part, from his quasi-incestuous attraction to her. His insight into Lady Audley's secrets is also associated with his own feminised identity. The Robert Audley of the early stages of the narrative is a version of the improper masculine, that is to say, he has not been properly socialised into an acceptable masculine role. Audley is an example of that recurring spectre of Victorian fiction, the young man whose active energies and purpose are sapped by 'expectations' and by the lack of a necessity to earn his own living. His brooding, sensitive nature is formed by his 'feminine' habit of reading decadent French novels; his lack of vocation or employment supplies him with extensive leisure in which to brood on the situation at Audley Court with the heightened sensitivity and imagination produced by this reading.

In his pursuit of the secret of Lady Audley, Robert discovers manhood and his vocation. He embarks on a chivalric quest, to solve the mystery of George Talboys's disappearance and Lady Audley's role in it. This chivalric quest is transformed into bourgeois epic as, in his detective role, Robert increasingly develops the legal skills which had merely bored him when he was ostensibly practising at the Bar. Robert's obsessive knightly detective quest, a central strand of the narrative, derives, in part, from a masculine camaraderie and loyalty to George Talboys. However, more importantly for the narrative and sexual economy of the novel, Robert's

quest is also (and increasingly) motivated by his love for George's sister Clara. This relationship functions to some extent as a displacement of the homoerotic bonding of Robert and George. (There is a great deal of narratorial insistence on Robert's attraction to Clara's close physical resemblance to her brother.) However, its main function is its role in the novel's investigation and satirisation, as well as reproduction and naturalisation, of a particular social construction of masculinity. The movement from male bonding to male-female bonding is presented as part of a process of maturation and socialisation. As both motivator and reward of the novel's bourgeois epic, the transparent Clara becomes the foundation of Robert's emergence into a properly socialised masculinity; his quest to unmask and expel Lady Audley becomes the route to that destiny.

Clara is the true embodiment of the domestic ideal which Lady Audley merely impersonates. She also embodies many of its contradictions. Robert's discovery of Clara comes at a crucial stage in the repression and expulsion of his attraction to the dangerous, duplicitous femininity of the *femme fatale* in Lady Audley. It also plays a vital part in his conversion to the roles of defender of the proper feminine, and of the patriarchal, aristocratic family from the threat of dissolution.[14] In this last respect Robert acts as his uncle's proxy as well as Clara's. In fact Robert's quest ends in a subtle displacement and merging of aristocratic and bourgeois values, which is complex in its effects. Robert does indeed expel the disrupter of his uncle's household but, significantly, his actions do not result in the restoration of equilibrium, or the reinstatement of the aristocratic family. The patriarch Sir Michael retires from the scene, a broken man, and Audley Court remains empty.

The aristocratic family is not so much restored as remade, in the genial companionate union of Alicia Audley (Sir Michael's daughter) and Sir Harry Towers. The main focus of the novel's closure, however, is the bourgeois, suburban idyll 'in a fairy cottage . . . between Teddington Lock and Hampton Bridge' (LAS:445), where Robert becomes the head of an idealised affective family and a rising man of the legal profession. The idealised family of Robert, Clara, George and their respective offspring not only replaces the aristocratic one of Sir Michael Audley, but is also a renewal of the bourgeois family, in which warmth and affection replace the cold formality of the motherless family of Harcourt Talboys.

The concluding idyll of *Lady Audley's Secret* is partly a fantasy resolution of the contradictions of the Victorian bourgeois family: a patriarchal institution which is, nevertheless, persistently represented as a private feminised space. The Thamesside cottage is a feminised domestic world in which, paradoxically, men can be men. It is a world purged of the improper feminine of illegitimate desire, passion and French novels. However, Braddon's use of the conventional closure of a marriage which reinstates the order of the bourgeois family and the domestic ideal, also foregrounds the contradictions of that institution and that ideal, and destabilises them through satire. The beginning of the novel's concluding chapter has an element of self-conscious excess, of over-perfection, as the redeemed and redeeming younger generation eat strawberries and cream in 'pretty rustic harmony', and everything is 'pretty', 'merry' or 'generous-hearted'.

The proper feminine of the domestic ideal is further undercut, in both *Aurora Floyd* and *Lady Audley's Secret,* through the juxtapositioning of problematic representatives of the improper feminine with equally problematic representatives of the proper or respectable feminine. In *Lady Audley's Secret,* Clara's capacity to motivate the lethargic Robert Audley is a testimony to the power of the proper feminine, but her dull, enduring passivity and her subjugation to her father's will clearly demonstrate the negative aspects of this version of femininity. The norms of respectable femininity are similarly questioned in the counterpointing of Aurora Floyd's story with that of her virtuous cousin Lucy. Like Braddon's transgressive women, the angelic Lucy is also subjected to the specularity of the narrator's gaze, for example in the treatment of the agonies of her initially unrequited love for Talbot Bulstrode. Bulstrode's dilemma over the competing charms of Lucy and Aurora serves as a focus for a review of the limitations as well as the strengths of the respectable feminine and the domestic ideal. His 'ideal woman' is a powerful cultural stereotype:

> . . . some gentle and feminine creature crowned with an aureole of pale auburn hair; some timid soul with downcast eyes . . . some shrinking being, as pale and prim as the mediaeval saints in his pre-Raphaelite engravings, spotless as her own white robes, excelling in all womanly graces . . . but only exhibiting them in the narrow circle of a home.
>
> (AF:34)

Lucy is, in fact, the very pattern of the domestic ideal, 'exactly the sort of woman to make a good wife'.

> Purity and goodness had looked over her and hemmed her in from her cradle. She had never seen unseemly sights, or heard unseemly sounds. She was as ignorant as a baby of all the vices and horrors of this big world . . . and if there were a great many others of precisely the same type of graceful womanhood, it was certainly the highest type, and the holiest, and the best.
>
> (AF:41)

Aurora Floyd contrives simultaneously to endorse this ideal and satirise it, but above all to make it seem much duller than its alternative, Aurora.

Lucy and Clara are, of course, common fictional stereotypes, of the kind one expects to find in formulaic fiction such as Braddon's. Perhaps more unusual is the self-consciousness of Braddon's use of stereotypes, and the way in which this self-consciousness foregrounds the ideological power of generic conventions. Braddon's novels also explore, from a variety of perspectives, the hypocrisies, self-deceptions and repressions of the aristocratic, or would-be aristocratic, male, and the social codes over which he presides. These male stereotypes are often used for satirical purposes, but here, as in other matters, the effects of Braddon's satire are complex. Masculine stereotypes or values which are satirically undercut are, in several cases, finally endorsed. Such complexity (even contradiction) is evident in the treatment of Talbot Bulstrode and John Mellish in *Aurora Floyd:* the former, rigidly proud, jealous of his social position and fiercely moralistic; the latter, a more open, frank and generous version of masculinity, a 'big, hearty, broadchested Englishman' in whom 'the Rev. Charles Kingsley would have delighted' (AF:48). The self-satisfied conservatism of the social code of each of these men is satirised, but both are ultimately vindicated. Partly this is an endorsement of a specifically contemporary masculinity.

> Surely there is some hope that we have changed for the better within the last thirty years, inasmuch as we attach a new meaning to this simple title of 'gentleman'. I take some pride, therefore, in the two young men of whom I write, for the simple reason that I have no dark patches to gloss over in the history of either of them.
>
> (AF:51)

Like that of Robert Audley, the fully-formed masculinity of each of these characters is constructed, finally, through complex engagements with various versions of the feminine. Robert Audley, as I have noted, is made as a man by detecting the improper feminine in Lady Audley, by hunting down and containing her secret, and expelling the improper feminine from both himself and the family. In *Aurora Floyd,* where the improper feminine is less alien and masculinity rarely as compromised or threatened as in the earlier novel, Mellish negotiates (rather than confronts) Aurora's secret and domesticates rather than expels the improper feminine. Bulstrode's cold, aristocratic masculinity is challenged and destabilised by his encounter with the dangerous feminine of Aurora, and humanised by learning to accept and forgive feminine transgression (the ministrations of his wife, Aurora's cousin Lucy, are crucial here).

Gender and class are always complexly intertwined categories in Braddon's novels. The focus on specific versions of the masculine and feminine is also a scrutiny of specific versions of class. Ambivalences and anxieties about gender categories and boundaries are, similarly, related to anxieties about class. Braddon's feminised males and transgressive or masculinised women often have ambivalent class positions: they are socially ambitious, their class origins are more lowly than their current or desired social position, or they have not been properly socialised to the class to which they belong. As I noted earlier, Braddon's sensation plots are driven by family secrets, especially women's secrets, which are often connected with lowly social origins and/or social ambition. The typical Braddon novel of the 1860s involves a threat to the family (usually the aristocratic family) from destabilising forces such as a lower-class woman or a socially ambitious male. Such plots serve as a focus for numerous anxieties about the mores of mid-nineteenth-century marriage.

On marriage, as on gender, Braddon's novels offer a range of voices and perspectives. The narrator repeatedly addresses the understanding reader on the way things generally are in marriage in the modern world. This is usually articulated in the woman-to-woman address, which both Braddon and Wood use to position the reader as a feminine subject and as a member of a community which shares common feelings and values. This strategy is used in the address to careless wives, which provides a context for Aurora's predicament.

> Ah, careless wives! who think it a small thing, perhaps, that your husbands are honest and generous, constant and true, and who are apt to grumble because your next-door neighbours have started a carriage . . . stop and think of this wretched girl, who in this hour of desolation recalled a thousand little wrongs she had done to her husband, and would have laid herself under his feet to be walked over by him could she have thus atoned for her petty tyrannies . . . Think of her in her loneliness, with her heart yearning to go back to the man she loved.
>
> (AF:290)

Such writing works to reinforce normative womanly virtues by positioning the reader in a socially or sexually trangressive role, and making her experience vicariously the frisson of having lost the benefits (taken for granted by the ordinary bourgeois wife) of the love of a good man. Although it has the effect of 'talking up' the value of ordinary marriage, this confident pontification is, to some extent, destabilised by the particularities of the situations which the novels dramatise, and by the use of a number of different points of view.

The predicament of the woman who has married into a superior social class is one important focus for Braddon's critique of modern marriage. It is treated satirically in the depiction in *Aurora Floyd* of Eliza

Prodder's self-confident negotiations of the snobbery of the County families when she marries the banker Archibald Floyd. Her years as an actress have accustomed her to playing a part and to mixing with stage duchesses, and her fears that 'I shall die of my grandeur, as the poor girl did at Burleigh House' (AF:13) are unfounded. Elsewhere Braddon focuses minutely on the rigours of the role of wife to the upper-middle-class or aristocratic male, and particularly on the wife's learning to play the part expected of her by her husband and the society in which she finds herself. The novels repeatedly focus on a wife's anxieties about being on public view—displayed by her husband to his family and neighbours, or observed or spied on by servants or other members of the household.[15]

Male fears and anxieties about marriage are also explored. They are staged structurally through plots which focus on threats to the patriarchal family by transgressive women. In addition the reader is, from time to time, positioned within a male perspective from which she views male expectations of women and of marriage, and male fears about the social realities of the marriage market. I have already noted Braddon's focusing on the fears and feelings of Mellish and Bulstrode in *Aurora Floyd;* the bathetic scrutiny of Sir Michael Audley's disappointments following his proposal to Lucy is another interesting example:

> He walked straight out of the house, this foolish old man, because there was some strong emotion at work in his heart . . . something almost akin to disappointment; some stifled and unsatisfied longing which lay heavy and dull at his heart, as if he had carried a corpse from his bosom . . . He must be contented, like other men of his age, to be married for his fortune and his position.
>
> (LAS:111-12)

The contradictions inherent in Victorian views of marriage, notably the attempt to hold together a belief in the nobility and sanctity of marital love with a belief in economically prudential alliances, are the source of the narratives of marriage at the centre of most of Braddon's novels. They are seen at their most extreme in the scrutiny of Gilbert Monckton's almost masochistic fantasies about wifely betrayal in *Eleanor's Victory.*

> Yes, Gilbert Monckton had [apparently] discovered the fatal truth that marriage is not always union and that the holiest words that were ever spoken cannot weave the mystic web which makes two souls indissolubly one . . . Did not girls . . . marry for money, again and again, in these mercenary days?
>
> (EV II:140)

In Braddon's fiction marriage is not merely a device of closure but, as in the New Woman fiction of the nineties, a source of story. One of her dominant plots (with the notable exception of *Lady Audley's Secret*) is that in which a wife who has married for prudential reasons (whether these be financial or as a means to some other desired end) learns to love her husband within marriage. Marriage is thus not the goal of romantic love, but the site upon which it is constructed.

Braddon's narratives of marriage are usually structured around a series of scenes from a marriage which is threatened by secrecy and lack of understanding between the partners. The most common narrative situation involves the suspicions of one of the partners about the past or present secrets of the other. Although these difficulties are causally linked to specific plot situations, they are also seen as being inherent in the way women and men are socially constructed along rigid lines of difference. Men and women are shown as being foreign countries to each other, largely as a consequence of the fact that they view each other through stereotypes and ideals. In such narratives marriage, the presumed site of union and mutual understanding, is revealed as, in fact, a state of mutual isolation, secrecy and misunderstanding.

Viewing the consequences of such secrecy is a major source of narrative pleasure in Braddon's fiction. Readers are invited to observe and/or participate in the sufferings of characters who have to endure the 'tortures known only to the husband whose wife is parted from him by that which has more power to sever than any . . . wide extent of ocean—a secret'. (AF:145). The preoccupation with secrecy in marriage adds another layer of spectating to Braddon's plots. The novels make frequent use of scenes in which a fearful and suspecting spouse watches his or her partner in a scene with another, or others, from which the spectating spouse feels excluded. Such scenes almost always involve the spectating character in misreading what is being seen.

Such misreading is particularly prominent in *Eleanor's Victory,* in which husband and wife are separated by the secrets of their past and by their different social experience. Both habitually misread the signs of each other's behaviour. Gilbert, in particular, misreads a number of scenes in which he is the jealous and masochistic spectator, such as this scene between Eleanor, her friend Richard Thornton, and Launcelot Darrell, the man she suspects of being responsible for her father's death:

> Following every varying expression of her face, Gilbert Monckton saw that she looked at [Thornton] with an earnest questioning appealing glance, that seemed to demand something of him . . . Looking from his wife to Richard, the lawyer saw that Launcelot Darrell was still watched . . . Mr Monckton felt very much like a spectator who looks on at a drama which is being acted in a language that is unknown to him.
>
> (EV II:209)

Such scenes of spectating are even more important in Ellen Wood's novels, and I shall return to the function of this spectatorship in the next section.

Another aspect of secrecy that is foregrounded in Braddon's novels, and in sensation fiction generally, is its ability to transform the home, in Victorian middle-class ideology a domestic shrine, into a prisonhouse of suspicion. Indeed, as in some popular women's genres of the twentieth century, such as the woman's film and the family melodrama of the 1940s and 1950s (and possibly for similar reasons), the domestic setting of the sensation novel is an extremely important part of its message and its pleasures. One of these pleasures is the opportunity afforded by the *mise-en-scène* for a sort of fictional equivalent of a visit to a stately home. Many of Braddon's novels are set in, or involve visits to, rather grand houses, which are described in lavish detail. The use of such settings offers two important sources of narrative pleasure. First it is a kind of voyeurism, allowing the reader to spy on the lives of those in a superior social class. Secondly, and more importantly for the ideological work of sensation fiction, it reconciles the reader to the limitations of her own marriage, home and social circle by means of what one might call the 'Dallas' effect. Like melodramatic television soap opera and cinematic family melodrama, sensation fiction displays to its readers people with money, status and power who, despite their possession of these desired attributes, do not possess happiness. Moreover, since the admired wealth and position are often built on guilty secrets they are insecure and are easily lost. This both articulates social insecurity in a time of rapid change, and also opens a space for the reader to believe that, like femininity, class and social status are a form of masquerade.

Braddon's sensation novels thus play upon their readers' social and material ambitions only to turn them back on themselves and reconcile readers to the mundane securities (however limited) of their own lot. Each portrait of the beautiful, beloved and/or powerful woman is matched by a scene focusing on her misery and powerlessness. Every elaborate description of a lavish interior is matched by a scene of disenchantment in which an aspiring character is pictured in the setting which had previously been the goal of his or her ambitions. Thus Honoria, the child of the gutter (and worse), is pictured surveying the lands and woods she has inherited from her husband only to discover that 'the possession of them means nothing to me' (RE II:32). Similarly, although 'there was a time' when the Bovaryiste Isobel Gilbert in *The Doctor's Wife* 'would have thought it a grand thing to be rich' (347), it has passed when she inherits the house and lands she had once dreamed of.

By juxtaposing the glamorous domestic setting with the scene of disenchantment, Braddon's novels articulate the contradictions of the Victorian view of the home. On the one hand the bourgeois home exists in the public sphere as a sign of social status and site of conspicuous consumption. On the other hand, it belongs to the private sphere of the moral and emotional life. Braddon's sensation novels variously negotiate, resolve, or merely display those contradictions, but in certain cases they work to reposition the woman as a domestic creature. Thus at a key moment in her transformation from racy Girl of the Period to reconstructed domestic woman, Aurora re-views the grand rooms of Mellish Park, not as the potential theatre for her public display but as the setting of a domestic life endangered by revelations about her secret past: 'How pretty the rooms look! . . . how simple and countrified! It was for *me* that the new furniture was chosen . . . Good-bye, dear home, in which I was an impostor and a cheat' (AF:278-9). When she has repented, and paid for, her transgressive past, Aurora can reoccupy her 'dear home' as a doting wife and mother. However, she does so on new terms. The narrative constructed around Aurora works to translate her marriage and her possession of her home from (to adapt Cixous's terms) the economy of property to the realm of the gift. Anxieties about marriage being a form of prostitution are thus foregrounded by aspects of the sensation plot, but those anxieties are ultimately dispelled as the novel's central marriage is transformed from an economic transaction to a freely given exchange of love. The effect of this process in *Aurora Floyd* (and perhaps in the sensation novel in general) is, in part, simply to mask the real economic relations of marriage, but it also involves an attempt to reassure (male and female) readers that these relations are capable of transformation.

Notes

. . . [8] See Kemble 1838.

[9] Showalter (1987) suggests that this association of madness and the feminine is endemic 'within our dualistic systems of language and representation', and that 'madness, even when experienced by men, is metaphorically and symbolically represented as feminine: a female malady' (3-4).

[10] The resemblance between Braddon's plot and a contemporary case study of this condition has been much commented upon. Showalter quotes from John Connolly's *Physiognomy of Insanity* the case of a 'sensitive woman whose mother had been insane . . . [and who] became deranged and melancholic almost as soon as her poor little child came into this world of want' (Showalter 1987:71-2).

[11] The terms of this description closely resemble those in which M. Héger recalled Emily Brontë: 'She should have been a man—a great navigator . . . ' (quoted in Gérin 1972:127).

[12] The Medusan snakes are losing themselves in Aurora's clothing rather than turning outwards towards the spectator.

[13] See, for example, *Lady Audley's Secret,* pp. 294-5: 'If Mr. Holman Hunt could have peeped into the pretty boudoir I think the picture [of Lady Audley in thoughtful pose before the fire] would have been photographed upon his brain to be reproduced by-and-by upon a bishop's half-length. My lady in that half-recumbent attitude, with her elbow resting on one knee, and her perfect chin supported by her hand, the rich folds of drapery falling away in long undulating lines from the exquisite outline of her figure . . . Beautiful in herself, but made bewilderingly beautiful by the gorgeous surroundings which surround the shrine of her loveliness.' The passage continues with an elaborate inventory of the gorgeous objects.

[14] This is a recurring situation in Braddon's novels. Both Paul Marchmont (JML) and Victor Carrington (RE) are feminised men who seek to defend a version of the family which they identify closely with their mother. While Robert Audley polices the (improperly) 'feminished' family to protect it from the criminality of Lucy, Paul Marchmont and Victor Carrington turn to crime to wrest the family from (what they perceive to be) usurping females.

[15] The role and significance of the 'household spies we call servants' (AF:19) are discussed in Trodd 1989. . . .

NINETEENTH-CENTURY REACTION

Christian Remembrancer (essay date 1863)

SOURCE: "Our Female Sensation Novelists," in *Christian Remembrancer,* Vol. CXXI, July, 1863, pp. 209-36.

[In the following essay, the anonymous author presents an overview of the sensation novel and evaluates the works of Wood, Norton, and Braddon—in the negative manner characteristic of critics of the period.]

We have been counselled not to ask why the former times were better than these, and are thus instructed to beware of enhancing the past in peevish depreciation of the present, the scene of our labours and trials. The check is constantly needed by those whose past is long enough ago to melt into harmonious, golden, defect-concealing distance; but we are disposed to think that such check is never more required than when a comparison is forced upon us of the popular ideal of charming womanhood in the times we remember, and what seems to constitute the modern ideal of the same thing. This ideal may be gathered from the poetry, the romance, and the satire of both periods, as well as from closer experience. There was a time when the charge against young ladies was a morbid love of sermons and a too exclusive devotion to the persons that preached them; then they were the subjects of tender ridicule for a fantastic refinement; then they doted upon Fouqué and his Sintram, and were prone to sacrifice solid advantages and worldly good things to a dream of romance; then it was interesting and an attraction, at least to seem to live in ignorance of evil; then they felt it good taste to shrink from publicity, and submitted to the rules of punctilio and decorum as if they liked them. Those were the days when the red coat was not unreasonably jealous of the academic gown, when dash was not the fashion, when the ordinary gaieties of life were entered into not without a disclaimer, and an anxiety to assert an inner preference for something higher and better, fuller of heart and sentiment, satisfying deeper instincts. Those were the days before *Punch's* generation of 'fast young ladies' were born; while it would still have been a wild impossibility for the *Times* to announce beforehand that an Earl's daughter would, on such an occasion and in such a theatre, dance an Irish jig, and a still wilder impossibility for the lady to keep her engagement, and for the illustrated papers afterwards to represent the feat in the moment of execution.

We are not saying that the generation of which this is a feature is really a falling off from that other generation which furnishes us with such pleasant memories. Each has its developments for good or evil, sense or nonsense. The one is composed of the daughters of the other. The history of society is a series of reactions from faults it has become alive to. We know all this; but the popular literature of the day, which undertakes to represent the thought and impulses of its own time, almost forces us into a frame of disparaging comparison. The novels of twenty and thirty years ago, which told us a good deal we did not like of the society of the period, have passed into oblivion; the notions and tendencies of to-day find their exponents in novels in everybody's hands. They are peopled with characters which, if they go beyond our observation, and exceed anything we have seen, yet indicate plainly enough the direction manners have taken, and are accepted as a portrait of life by the general reader, through his very act of taking them into favour.

The 'sensation novel' of our time, however extravagant and unnatural, yet is a sign of the times—the evidence of a certain turn of thought and action, of an impatience of old restraints, and a craving for some fundamental change in the working of society. We use the popular and very expressive term, and yet one much more easy to adopt than to define. Sensation writing is an appeal to the nerves rather than to the heart; but all exciting fiction works upon the nerves, and Shakspeare can make 'every particular hair to stand on end' with anybody. We suppose that the true sensation novel feels the popular pulse with this view alone—considers any close fidelity to nature a slavish subservience injurious to effect, and willingly and designedly draws a picture of life which shall make reality insipid and the routine of ordinary existence intolerable to the imagination. To use *Punch's* definition in the prospectus of the *Sensation Times,* 'It devotes itself to harrowing the mind, making the flesh creep, causing the hair to stand on end, giving shocks to the nervous system, destroying conventional moralities, and generally unfitting the public for the prosaic avocations of life.' And sensationalism does this by drugging thought and reason, and stimulating the attention through the lower and more animal instincts, rather than by a lively and quickened imagination; and especially by tampering with things evil, and infringing more or less on the confines of wrong. Crime is inseparable from the sensation novel, and so is sympathy with crime, however carefully the author professes, and may even suppose himself, to guard against this danger by periodical disclaimers and protests.

The one indispensable point in the sensation novel is, that it should contain something abnormal and unnatural; something that induces, in the simple idea, a sort of thrill. Thus, 'Transformation,' where a race of human beings inherit the peculiarities of the Faun, and in whom a certain conformation of ear characteristic of the Greek myth crops out at intervals, is sensational. The very clever story 'Elsie Venner' is sensational in the same way, where the heroine is part rattlesnake, and makes us shudder by her occasional affinities in look and nature with the serpent race. All ghost-stories, of course, have the same feature. In one and all there is appeal to the imagination, through the active agency of the nerves, excited by the unnatural or supernatural. But the abnormal quality need not outrage physical laws; exceptional outrages of morality and custom may startle much in the same way. Bigamy, or the suspicion of bigamy, is sensational as fully, though in a lower field, as are ghosts and portents; it disturbs in the same way the reader's sense of the stability of things, and opens a new, untried vista of what may be. All crime that seems especially incongruous with the perpetrator's state and circumstances is of this nature, and offers a very ready and easy mode of exciting that surprise and sense of novelty which is the one indispensable necessity. Of course no fiction can be absolutely commonplace and natural in all its scenes and incidents; some extraordinary conditions seem unavoidable in its machinery. Thus, story-writers of every age and style seem, by one consent, to ignore for their heroines the most universal and inevitable of all relationships. The heroines of fiction have no mothers. Every rule has its exception, of course; but the exception in this case proves the rule. Thus, the only mother we can think of in Sir Walter Scott's series of novels is Lady Ashton, a monstrous and unnatural mother, performing the very opposite of the maternal part. In the same way, Richardson's Clarissa Harlowe has as good as none. Harriet Byron and her friends are motherless. Dickens has very few. None of Miss Bronte's or George Eliot's heroines have mothers, nor have Miss Ferrier's. Miss Edgworth has one or two model mothers, but most of her heroines are without. Miss Yonge, it must be granted, has one charming mother, who performs a mother's work, in the 'Heir of Redclyffe;' but the majority of her young people make all their mistakes for the want of one, and show their goodness by overcoming the evil consequences of that supreme deprivation. Those who write for children find it easier to devise probable and excusable scrapes without the maternal guardian of discipline and order. The moral story-teller can somehow inclucate principles, and supply examples more to his mind without. The mere novelist finds the mother a dull and unmanageable feature, except, indeed, where the scheming or tyrannical mother of the fashionable novel brings about the necessary tragic element, drives her daughter to despair by enforcing good matches, or oppresses her for mere envy of her youth and virgin graces. Miss Austin, who looked on life as it *is,* and shut her eyes to none of its ordinary conditions, *has* some mothers—Mrs. Bennet, the silly mother, who would drive any sensitive child wild with shame, and Mrs. Dashwood, who encouraged her daughter in sentimentalism—but her essential heroines are without. Mr. Thackeray's mothers merge into mothers-in-law. It is quite a feature of Mr. Trollope's course of fiction that he now and then gives us a real mother and does not feel embarrassed by the relation. However, we need not further pursue the inquiry.

This exceptional condition of early life—freedom from restraint, and untimely liberty of choice and action—then, belongs to the youth of all fiction. Of course, in sensational novels, this liberty is exaggerated indefinitely. There is nothing more violently opposed to our moral sense, in all the contradictions to custom which they present to us, than the utter unrestraint in which the heroines of this order are allowed to expatiate and develop their impulsive, stormy, passionate characters. We believe, it is one chief among their many dangers to youthful readers that they open out a picture of life free from all the perhaps irksome checks that confine their own existence, and treat all such checks as real hindrances, solid impediments, to the development of power, feeling, and the whole array of fascinating and attractive qualities. The heroine of this class of novel is charming because she is undisciplined, and the victim of impulse; because she has never known restraint or has cast it aside, because in all these respects she is below the thoroughly trained and tried woman. This lower level, this drop from the empire of reason and self-control, is to be traced throughout this class of

literature, which is a consistent appeal to the animal part of our nature, and avows a preference for its manifestation, as though power and intensity came through it. The very language of the school shows this. A whole set of new words has come into use, and they are caught up and slipped into, as a matter of course, to express a certain degradation of the human into the animal or brutal, on the call of strong emotion. 'One touch of nature makes the whole world kin,' says the poet; the whole world of this school includes things that Shakspeare never dreamed of. Thus the victim of feeling or passion sinks at once into the inspired or possessed animal, and is always supposed to be past articulate speech; and we have the *cry,* the *smothered cry of rage,* the *wail,* the *low wailing cry,* the *wail of despair,* with which, if our readers are not familiar, *ad nauseam,* we can only say we *are.* The curious thing is, that probably no writer ever heard a woman utter this accepted token of extreme emotion, which would indeed be a very intolerable habit in domestic life; but it is evidently accepted by a very large circle as *the* exponent of true, thorough-going passion. It is the same with motion. It is man's privilege to walk; in novels men, or at any rate the women, *creep.* In love, in helplessness, in pity, in tenderness, this abject, fawning, cat-like movement is found the most expressive sign of a mental posture. Again, these people *writhe* and twist and coil themselves. 'This self-sustained and resolute woman writhed in anguish.' They have 'serpentine arms,' and 'snake-like, Medusa locks.' On occasion they will stand rampant, erect, with glittering serpent eyes. They are prone to blows. It is one of the privileges of reason and cultivation that men can be angry through their minds and tongues alone, but the people in all sensation writing rush to blows at once. Whatever training they may have had, it all drops from them on provocation, and the wild animal proclaims itself. Most readers are familiar with Aurora Floyd's castigation of her stable-boy; indeed, this fascinating lady is so ready with her natural weapons, that we find her on one occasion in the presence of two men, on whom she has inflicted stripes and scratches, the scars of which they will carry to their graves. And the writer of 'East Lynne' is not behind her more impetuous sister authoress in her belief in the possibility of blows in civilized circles, for she makes a countess strike her heroine furiously on each cheek, while that interesting young lady was her guest, stimulated solely by the jealousy of one pretty woman for another. But what will not Mrs. Wood's countesses do?—though, indeed, Mrs. Norton, who should know what grand ladies are made of, brings her marchioness to very much the same pass of animal *abandon.* Blows imply passion, so perhaps it is needless to speak of the previous uncontrolled passion, which is another characteristic of the sensational heroine in common with brute nature; but Miss Braddon enlarges on it, as a feature of the temper that most interests her, in terms which we prefer to our own:—

'Have you ever seen this kind of woman in a passion?—impulsive, nervous, sensitive, sanguine. With such a one passion is a madness—brief, thank Heaven!—and expending itself in sharp, cruel words, and convulsive rendings of lace and ribbon, or coroner's juries might have to sit even oftener than they do.'—*Aurora Floyd,* vol. ii. p. 264.

And the scene in 'East Lynne,' where Barbara, with vehement hysterical passion, upbraids the innocent and unconscious Carlyle for having married somebody else, is another example of the disgraceful unrestraint which some writers think a feature of the ideal woman. Another characteristic is the possession by one idea—an idea so fixed and dominant that the mind impregnated by it has no choice but to obey. The faithful or the vicious animal is so influenced, but a man thus out of his own control is on the high road to madness. However, it is thought sublime, and the reader is expected to be awed by the strength of a character led by some immoveable and absorbing notion, amenable neither to time nor place nor manners, nor to any of the influences that turn our thoughts from one thing to another, and multiply and divide our interests. And it is certain that a good many people think this a very grand form of nature; and an index of power in a writer even to conceive such a thing, whether natural or not, as something colossal, overshadowing their imagination. It is a refreshing change, for instance, from the monotony of easy reasonable social life to follow the moods, or rather the mood—for she has but one—of a woman of this type, who is for ever apostrophising herself 'with a smothered cry of rage,' 'Is there no cure for this disease? is there no relief except madness or death?' In a current story by the same hand ('Eleanor's Victory'), we have a girl of sixteen devoting her life to vengeance in the following strain; and we know Miss Braddon's style too well to doubt she will keep her word:—

' "I don't know this man's name (with whom her father had played his last game at ecarté); I never even saw his face; I don't know who he is, or where he comes from; but sooner or later I swear to be revenged upon him for my father's cruel death."

' "Eleanor, Eleanor!" cried the Signora, "is this womanly? is this Christian-like?"

' "I don't know whether it is womanly or Christian-like," she said, "but I know that it is henceforth the purpose of my life, and that it is stronger than myself." '
                                        —*Once a Week,* April, p. 415.

In like manner, instinct is a favourite attribute: reason may be mistaken, but instinct never. In one story we have two girls, within a page or two of one another, who read characters like a book, and see villany at a glance in persons who have passed for respectable all their lives. 'When I look at people,' says one, 'I

always seem to know what they are;' while the other, with inane simplicity, apologises for her insight, 'I cannot help seeing things.' Another characteristic closely allied to all these is fatality. It is no use trying to be good; they do try; but Elsie Venner can no more eradicate the rattlesnake-malice out of her nature than can these less avowedly fated women their evil propensities. Thus, in 'East Lynne,' Lady Isabel is impelled to the worst wrong against her will:—

'She (the wife of Carlyle) was aware that a sensation all too warm, a feeling of attraction towards Francis Levison, was waking within her; not a voluntary one. She could no more repress it than she could her own sense of being; and mixed with it was the stern voice of conscience, overwhelming her with the most lively terror. She would have given all she possessed to be able to overcome it, &c. &c.'

                                        —*East Lynne,* vol. ii. p. 2.

And again, we are bid not to doubt the principles of a lady whose practice was undoubtedly open to question:—

'Oh! reader, never doubt the principles of poor Lady Isabel; her rectitude of mind, her wish and endeavour to do right, her abhorrence of wrong; and her spirit was earnest and true, her intentions were pure.'

She did not, in fact, encourage the temptation which overcame her:—

'She did not encourage these reflections—from what you know of her you may be sure of that—but they thrust themselves continually forward.'

'On what a slight thread do the events of life turn,' is the favourite language of this school, which, as they interpret it, means, or seems to mean, that there are temptations that are irresistible. Thus, 'Olivia Marchmont' might have made a saint but for unluckily falling in love with a good-natured cousin, provokingly unconscious of his conquest. As it was she was a fiend; but she had not succumbed without many struggles to her sin and despair. 'Again and again she had abandoned herself to the devils at watch to destroy her, and again and again she had tried to extricate her soul from their dreadful power; but her most passionate endeavours were· in vain. Perhaps it was that she did not strive aright; it was for this reason, surely, that she failed so utterly to arise superior to her despair; for otherwise that terrible belief attributed to the Calvinists, that some souls are foredoomed to damnation, would be exemplified by this woman's experience. She could not forget. She could not put away the vengeful hatred that raged like an all-devouring fire in her breast, and she cried in her agony, "There is no cure for this disease!" '

We have placed 'East Lynne' at the head of our series not as the most marked example of the school, but as first in time. This story was brought into notice—and, indeed, extensive notoriety, by a puff in the *Times,* which represented it as a work of extraordinary power, dealing with the depths of our nature in a master's spirit. This imprimatur might not have told as it did, but for the authoress's real power of telling a story; but it unquestionably invested it with a credit and reputation which must have cost the docile reader some trouble to reconcile with his own impressions, and which strike us as grossly beyond the actual merits of the work. When we say that a writer's style is vulgar, there may, unquestionably, be the excuse of a pardonable and inevitable ignorance. A person may have many of the qualities of a novelist, and yet neither have the *habits* of the circle it pleases him to describe, nor be familiar with pure English as it is spoken and written. Still, genius is a keen, quick-witted power; it possesses the principle of selection, and instinctively perceives and holds by the best. Mrs. Wood's persistent use of certain vulgarisms, such as the uniform substitution of *like* for *as*—'Like I did;' 'He was deep in the business of packing, *like* his unfortunate brother had been;' and, above all, her unconscious use of the word 'party' for a single person, are telling facts; as where the stately hero, in some crisis of fate, alludes to the *'party'* who is working mischief and ruin; or where a ghost alarms a neighbourhood, and the clergyman has to mention with reluctance a family name: 'the—the *party* that appears to be personating Frederick Massingberd;' and again another, in great perplexity, 'I cannot say if it be the *party* I suspect;' and so on. We maintain that observation, that first requirement in those who are to picture human nature, as well as ear, must be wanting where such habits as these can be persisted in. It is of a piece with those descriptions of spring which bring the fragrant violet, and the fresh green of the oak together, and with those pictures of manners which represent the town clerk as asking the bench of magistrates to pipes and ale, announcing his attention in these dignified terms, 'I entertain the bench of justices to-night, Barbara, to pipes and ale;' and carrying it out to the fortunate recipients of these favours with ' "I have been considering that you had better all five come and smoke your pipes at my house this evening, when we shall have time to discuss what must be done. Come at seven, not later, and you will find my father's old jar replenished with the best broad-cut, and half a dozen churchwarden pipes. Shall it be so?" The whole five accepted the invitation eagerly.'—(*East Lynne,* vol. i. p. 68). With manners which make it natural in a courtly earl to ask as his first question, after introducing his daughter to this same young attorney, 'Is she not handsome?'

We do not know what to say of the courage which shall plunge boldly into the manners of a society of which the writer has not the remotest experience. Success must be the only test of the right to do so. Shakspeare made kings talk, and kings are willing to

be so drawn by him; they know, at any rate, that they are not more kingly than he represents them. Whether earls and earls' daughters will be content with the figure they make in Mrs. Wood's pages is another question. At any rate, Mrs. Wood is very much at her ease when she sets fine ladies and gentlemen talking, and thinks nothing of making a Lady Mary not only accept a lout of an apothecary, who is for ever pounding drugs on a counter, but eagerly jump at him, and express a wish he had asked her years before. There are no misgivings, no timidity in her portraiture; the fashionable flirt breaks into vituperation as fluently as Lady Carolina Wilhelmina might have done, and is jealous in five minutes' time of the looks of admiration cast at the younger beauty. The fatally fascinating Captain, a scion of the aristocracy, makes quick work of it, and before the end of the first evening, by dint of profuse compliments, pointed by glances from 'eyes of the deepest tenderness,' 'draws vivid blushes' from the delicate, sensitive heroine, not of offended maiden pride, but from a heart touched by an indelible impression. This is the sort of writing we might very well expect from the preliminary training of a temperance novel ('Danesbury House'), in which, by unflinching, conscientious adherence through every page to the subject of strong drinks and different forms and degrees of drunkenness, Mrs. Wood won the hundred pound prize, but it materially detracts from her right to any high stand in our literature. It is perhaps inevitable that the self-taught and guess-work novelist should jumble ranks and utterly confuse our notion of the social standing of the *dramatis personœ;* and this is especially the case in all Mrs. Wood's writings. Barbara, the second wife, who succeeds Lady Isabel, with her flippancy, her vulgar finery, her outspoken declaration of love, might be supposed to be some milliner's apprentice, but we believe is really intended to be an English lady. We observe an appreciation of out-of-door successes, an expectation from chance and irregular introductions, which marks a certain class. If the hero gets into a train in an anxious preoccupied state of mind, it is supposed that his silence, indifference, and failure in *petits soins,* will be felt an injury by any young and handsome woman in the same carriage, who, it is taken for granted, regards every public place a scene of conquest.

When this lady gives herself up to the odd and eccentric, we still less know where we are. Each of her novels has a humorist. In 'East Lynne' it is a Miss Corny, a sister of the heroic attorney, a violent woman, who assaults her suitors, shakes the breath out of her brother's clerk on the slightest provocation, and dresses like a madwoman, but who is still treated with marked respect as well as awe by her neighbours, and allowed by the attorney to force herself upon his wife and be virtual mistress of his household. This low and wild virago is the companion to the Lady Isabel, and it strikes the refined and devoted husband as a good arrangement on the whole. Humour is not a common feminine gift, so that we ought to be indulgent of mere failure; but, unfortunately, this lady fails not only in execution, but in the first idea of a fit subject for jest. The ordinary routine of the toilet, for instance, seems to be regarded as an inexhaustible field for mirth. We might say, she is most particularly amiss when she dwells on the details of masculine attire; except that the betrayal of her own sex, and all the little expedients by which the inroads of age may be warded off, is, perhaps, still more unpleasing, and is especially unfair upon the single ladies she holds up to ridicule—first, for being single; next, for being no longer young; next, for losing with youth itself some of the charms of youth; and last, for having recourse to any means of arresting Time's ravages. These are all such common characteristics of third-class novels, sensational or otherwise, that we should not notice them but that more than one leader of opinion has committed itself to a wholesale approval of 'East Lynne,' and one has gratuitously pronounced it *not* vulgar.

The acknowledged new element of this order of fiction is the insecurity given to the marriage relation. Unless we go with the bride and bridegroom to church, and know every antecedent on each side, we cannot be at all sure that there is not some husband or wife lurking in the distance ready to burst upon us. When once the idea enters the novel-writer's mind, it is embraced as a ready source of excitement, and capable of a hundred developments. Except that the circumstances are actually impossible, and would, we think, be very revolting if they were possible, the predicament is invested with real interest in 'East Lynne.' The moral fault of the book is, that the heroine has imputed to her a delicacy and purity of mind in utter variance with her whole course. None but a thoroughly bad woman could have done what Lady Isabel did. She had not the ordinary temptation to wrong; and as for those fine distinctions between affection and love which some ladies are prone to refine upon, we count them among the most mischievous of sentimental speculations. Lady Isabel, for example, marries the attorney, has a great *affection* for him, is exacting of his attention and devotion to herself, is capable of passionate jealousy, and all the while, we are ashamed to say, *loves* somebody else. At last she runs off with the Captain—then behold! instantly, in five minutes, she finds out her mistake, and begins to *love* the attorney and hate the other; and finally, on this connexion breaking in the usual way, she disguises herself, being supposed by the outraged and re-married husband to be dead, engages herself as governess to her own children, and dies, we may almost say, of jealousy of the new wife who succeeds to her old privileges; for the first time being thoroughly in love with him who had been her husband. Her first conception of this scheme is thought an occasion for some religious sentiment, and so we read—

'She had a battle to do with herself that day—now resolving to go, and risk it; now shrinking from the attempt. At one moment it seemed to her that Providence must have placed this in her way, that she might see her children in her desperate longing; at another, a voice appeared to whisper that it was a wily, dangerous temptation flung across her path—one which it was her duty to resist and flee from. Then came another phase of the picture—How should she bear to see Mr. Carlyle the husband of another?—to live in the same house with them, and witness his attentions, possibly his caresses? It might be difficult; but she could force and school her heart to endurance. Had she not resolved in her first bitter repentance to *take up her cross daily,* and bear it? No; her own feelings, let them be wrung as they would, should act as the obstacle.'

She had not been long in her new post when we read—

'When Lady Isabel was Mr. Carlyle's wife, she had never wholly loved him. The very utmost homage that esteem, admiration, affection, could give was his; but that mysterious passion called by the name of love (and which, as I truly and heartily believe, cannot in its refined etherialism be known to many of us) had not been given to him. It was now, I told you some chapters back, that the world goes round by the rule of contrary—conter-rary, mind you, the children have it in their game—and we go round with it. We despise what we have, and covet that which we cannot get. From the very night she had come back to East Lynne, her love for Mr. Carlyle had burst forth with an intensity never before felt. It had been smouldering almost ever since she quitted him. "Reprehensible!" groans a moralist. Very. Everybody knows that, as Aby would say. But her heart, you see, had *not* done with human passions, and they work ill and contrariness (let the word stand, critic, if you please), and precisely everything they should not.'

—*East Lynne,* vol. iii. 252.

The predicament is undoubtedly one fruitful of singular situations. Mr. Carlyle, to do him justice, is faithful to each obligation as it arises, and the same scenes that interested the reader when Lady Isabel was his wife are repeated to the letter when Barbara succeeds to that place which had been the object of such outspoken solicitude. In old times Barbara had peeped and listened in torture to Lady Isabel's singing of Mr. Carlyle's favourite songs, he standing by her chair and turning her leaves, with many tender interruptions. Now the process is reversed. It is Lady Isabel who peeps and listens, and Barbara sings the very same song, which must, we should say, be of very commanding merit to continue a favourite under such an awkward weight of unpleasant association. The thing is degrading to all parties, more so than the writer has any thought of; and her heroine is sunk still lower by the contempt that is thrown on her betrayer, to whom we are first introduced as a fascinating lady-killer, but who develops into a pitiful, abject, blundering wretch, talking the lowest slang, and finally dragged through a horse-pond, in the very sight of Lady Isabel, who, we are so often told, had been endowed with a sensitively refined delicacy. This, no doubt, is all done for the moral; but what must the woman have been to sacrifice heart and soul to so poor a creature?

Some scenes there are of interest and of such power as belongs to thoroughly realizing a conception. The authoress is best in tragedy. She has a vivid picture before her, though of the sentimental sort. There are indeed no close touches as far as we see; nor anything of which we can say, 'This is true to nature,' but the situation is well sustained. At the close of the story the erring wife watches the deathbed of her boy, whom she dare not claim as her own child:—

'William (her dying child) slept on silently. *She* thought of the past. The dreadful reflection, "If I had not—done—as I did, how different would it have been now!" had been sounding its knell in her heart so often, that she had almost ceased to shudder at it. The very nails of her hands had, before now, entered the palms with the sharp pain it brought. Stealing over her more especially this night as she knelt there, her head lying on the counterpane, came the recollection of that first illness of hers. How she had lain, and, in her unfounded jealousy, imagined Barbara the house's mistress. She dead— Barbara exalted to her place—Mr. Carlyle's wife— her child's step-mother! She recalled the day when her mind, excited by certain gossip of Wilson's—it was previously in a state of fever bordering on delirium—she had prayed her husband, in terror and anguish, not to marry Barbara! "How could he marry her," he had replied in soothing pity. "She!—Isabel was his wife; who was Barbara? Nothing to them." But it had all come to pass. *She* had brought it forth; not Mr. Carlyle—not Barbara; she alone. Oh! the dreadful memory of the retrospect. Lost in thought, in anguish past and present, in self- condemning repentance, the time passed on. Nearly an hour must have elapsed since Mr. Carlyle's departure, and William had not disturbed her. But— who is this coming into the room? Joyce.

'She hastily rose up, and, as Joyce advanced with a quiet step, drew aside the clothes to look at William. "Master says he has been wanting me," she observed. "Why—oh!"

'It was a sharp, momentary cry, subdued as soon as uttered. Madame Vine sprang forward to Joyce's side looking also. The pale, young face lay calm in its utter stillness; the busy little heart had ceased to beat. Jesus Christ had come, indeed, and taken the fleeting spirit.

'Then she lost all self-control. She believed that she had reconciled herself to the child's death;

that she could part with him without too much emotion. But she had not anticipated it would be quite so soon. She had deemed that some hours more would at least be given him; and now the storm overwhelmed her. Crying, sobbing, calling, she flung herself upon him; she clasped him to her; she dashed off her disguising glasses; she laid her face upon his, beseeching him to come back to her, that she might say farewell—to her, his mother—her darling child—her lost William.

'Joyce was terrified, terrified for consequences. With her full strength she pulled her from the boy, praying her to consider, to be still. "Do not, do not, for the love of Heaven! *My lady! my lady!*"

'It was the old familiar title that struck upon her fears, and induced calmness. She stared at Joyce, and retreated backwards, after the manner of one retreating from a hideous vision.

' "My lady, let me take you into your room. Mr. Carlyle is coming; he is but bringing up his wife. Only think if you should give way before him! Pray come away!"

' "How did you know me?" she asked in a hollow voice.

' "My lady, it was that night when there was an alarm of fire. I went close up to you to take Master Archibald from your arms; and as sure as I am now standing here, I believe that for the moment my senses left me. I thought I saw a spectre, the spectre of my dead lady. I forgot the present, I forgot that all were standing round me; that you, Madame Vine, were alive before me. Your face was not disguised then; the moonlight shone full upon it, and I knew it, after the first few moments of terror, to be, in dreadful truth, the *living one* of Lady Isabel. My lady, come away; we shall have Mr. Carlyle here."

'Poor thing, she sank upon her knees in her humility, her dread. "Oh! Joyce, have pity upon me! don't betray me. I will leave the house, indeed I will. Don't betray me while I am in it."

' "My lady, you have nothing to fear from me. I have kept the secret buried within my heart since then—last April! It has nearly been too much for me. By night and by day I have had no peace, dreading what might come out. Think of the awful confusion, the consequences, should it come to the knowledge of Mrs. Carlyle. Indeed, my lady, you ought never to have come."

' "Joyce," she said, hollowly, lifting her haggard face, "I could not keep away from my unhappy children. Is it no punishment to *me*, think you, the being here?"

she added vehemently. "To see him—my husband—the husband of another! It is killing me."

' "Oh, my lady, come away! I hear him! I hear him!"'

'Partly coaxing, partly dragging, Joyce took her into her own room, and left her there. Mr. Carlyle was at that moment at the door of the sick one. Joyce sprang forward. Her face, in emotion and fear, was one of livid whiteness, and she shook, as William had shaken, poor child, in the afternoon. It was only too apparent in the well-lighted corridor.

' "Joyce," he exclaimed in amazement, "what ails you?"'

' "Sir! master!" she panted, "be prepared; Master William—Master William—"'

' "Joyce; not *dead?*"'

' "Alas! yes, sir." '

—East Lynne, vol. iii. p. 250.

When Lady Isabel is about to die, and it becomes necessary to inform Carlyle who has been his inmate all this while, the effect the news takes upon him shows a realization of the usual position: 'The first clear thought that came thumping through his brain was, that he must be a man of two wives.' Happily, the embarrassment does not last long, and the lady dies after an interview of penitence and explanation.

The same perplexity forms one main point in the hero's trials in the authoress's next work, 'Verner's Pride.' In this there is an estate of which we never know who is the master, and a lady of whom we cannot tell who is the husband, and, indeed, Lionel is put in about as delicate a dilemma, and his conscience as oddly tried, as we remember to have known it. He is represented as a person of peculiarly scrupulous honour, yet we find him making two offers in one day—the one to the woman he likes, the other to an old love who had jilted him for some one else, for no reason at all that we can see, except that it occurred to him as the most convenient thing to do at the moment. Of course it is a fatal mistake, and he gets punished for his temporary hallucination. The lady is by no means ill drawn, only she is not worth drawing with the elaboration bestowed upon her. Sibylla is silly and vain, a vulgar flirt, and ruinously extravagant, and a woman thus endowed, we all know, can say and do things called incredible. She tests her husband's heroic virtue and forbearance to the uttermost, and the moment comes when there seems a road of escape for him. A ghost appears on the scene who drives the rustics out of their wits, and presently convinces wiser observers that the lady's first husband (for Sibylla was a widow) was in life. The news reaches

Lionel, and also the lady, who manifests very little concern at the reappearance, when she ascertains that whoever is her husband, she still remains mistress of Verner's Pride. Some persons of scrupulous mind recommend the withdrawal of the lady into retirement until the mystery is solved; but it seems considered a noble generosity in the hero that he stands by his wife, who, whenever she is in a pet, declares her preference for her first choice; though the whole point of the merit lies in the fact that he really likes the ill-used Lucy best, and, in fact, tells her so whenever they are together.

We have innumerable passages like the following:—

'He crossed over to her and laid his hand fondly and gently on her head as he moved to the door. "May God forgive me, Lucy," broke from his white trembling lips. "My own punishment is heavier than yours." '

—Verner's Pride, vol. ii. p. 127.

After such scenes we find him indeed making the amende to his wife, 'My little wife, if you cared for me as I care for you, &c. &c.,' with the explanation—'And there was no sophistry in this speech. He had come to the conviction that Lucy ought to have been his wife; but he did care for Sibylla very much.' The above fatherly and benedictory caress we observe to be coming very much into fashion upon paper, as a sort of disinfectant of questionable scenes, rendering harmless a good deal of flirtation which might otherwise be deemed of very doubtful propriety. In the matter of the ghost Lionel proved to be right, as the apparition turned out not to be the first husband, but his elder brother, also supposed to be dead, assuming his likeness. So Sibylla loses Verner's Pride after all, and tries her husband's indomitable patience, till she conveniently kills herself by going to a ball in a critical state of health. The story of course ends in the union of Lucy and Lionel, who agree that they have had long to *wait* for their present happiness, an ill-chosen word surely where a living wife has been a hindrance.

There is much in Verner's Pride entirely beneath criticism—irrelevant matter, awkwardly brought in and awkwardly expressed. Indeed, both in grace of style and aptitude to embrace the variety and poetry of any scene she describes, this writer in her best efforts falls greatly short of the two ladies we have classed with her, as illustrating a certain literary phase of our day—the Hon. Mrs. Norton and Miss Braddon—though the moral tone, in profession, and as entertaining the idea of duty when opposed to feeling, is superior to either.

Mrs. Norton's best friends are obliged to admit that her story, 'Lost and Saved,' is unfit for the drawing-room table, and ought to be kept out of the way of young ladies. In fact, in urging a great wrong upon the world, she is supposed to be compelled to disregard minor proprieties. The alleged purpose of the book is to show, that while the faults of women are visited as sins, the sins of men are not even visited as faults. She fights the battle of her sex by showing the injustice of the world, in its severity towards a certain class of errors, if committed by the helpless and the weak, and the tolerance of the same and much worse when perpetrated by the powerful and strong. Its highest morality as we see it is, that to sin with feeling is better than to sin without. There is the artifice of making a certain class of errors look light, by contrasting them with extremes of egotism, malignity, and positive crime; and the exigencies of the argument require society to be painted in the strongest and harshest colours. We observe that her admirers assume the leading characters to be, if not actual portraits, at least very intimate studies; and it is certainly more charitable to suppose that certain individuals are indicated by these 'studies' than that they represent to the writer's mind the prevailing characteristics of noble and fashionable society in our own day. Mrs. H. Wood writes about great people in artless and transparent ignorance of the gay world she describes. Mrs. Norton cannot be ignorant, but something else may make her pictures as little trustworthy. When a writer has opportunities of knowing that he is writing about superiors, perhaps, to his reader, that reader is apt to put on a deferential state of mind; but the deference may be wholly misplaced. If Sir Bulwer Lytton, though familiar with statesmen, may present to us the expansive exuberant prime minister we meet with in his novels, and nowhere else; if a college fellow draw a picture of university life absolutely at variance with his experience; and if a schoolmaster delineate impossible boys, then may a fine lady paint society such as she has never seen it, knowing better all the while, but doing it simply for amusement, or because there is wanting the power to see things as they are, or because a theory demands it, or the plot of a story must have it, or because it would be pleasant if it were so, or from disappointment, or temper, or malice. Any of these causes are, we see, sufficient to make an author reverse, and utterly defy his knowledge. In Mrs. Norton's case, it need only be that some bitter and angry soreness has tempted her to extreme limits of exaggeration and caricature. Her peeresses have certainly a body and a tone about them very different from the dressed-up milliners of courageous inexperience; but she shows them through distorted glass, and in blue and lurid lights. Hence a veritable glimpse of Pandemonium. While page after page denounces the ill nature, scandal, and harsh judgment of the world, what is technically called society is shown us in an aspect which might lead us to suppose we had opened a cynical French novel in mistake. There are the same horrors of profligacy attributed to a class, and the same shameless intrigue as the habitual practice of persons receiving the respect and homage of the world.

All vice seems to culminate in a certain Milly Nesdale. Milly is the wife of Lord Nesdale, and the mother of lovely children, whom she professes to foster and care for. She maintains the faint externals of duty and respectability and religion, but is in fact more of an atheist than M. About's hero who believed in *Fridays,* and has no more faith in Christianity than in Vishnu. Under a thin cloak of propriety she is a serpent, a witch, a fiend, betraying her trusting husband with malignant triumph, and doing and saying things which it is better to glance at than repeat. This lady is a universal favourite, courted by the hero's friends, as keeping him out of what their worldliness fears more, and sustaining her credit and fascinations undisturbed to the end.

'And how the world loved Milly.'

. . . . .

'For there is a little society in a corner called "The Society for the Suppression of Vice," but there is a much larger society for its protection; and in that larger society Right and Wrong do not signify, but Success and Non-Success.'—*Lost and Saved,* vol. ii. 86.

And Milly is loved by the world in no ignorance of her real qualities. All her friends would have recognised her in the description—

> 'Her body was lithe as the liana, and her soul was the soul of the snake—rampant, watchful, cautious— till a safe noiseless spring and a sudden coil gave her her prey.'—P. 88.

While to her lover, who listens to her treacherous and base words, lightened by

> 'The wily Hindoo smile which still lingered in Milly's features; it seemed that he had sold his soul to a species of charming water-witch rather than given his heart to a woman.'

The heroine, in contrast to this complicated wickedness, is a sweet, impulsive, highly-gifted, unsophisticated girl, who is the victim of a mock marriage, which the world will not believe her to have been the dupe of. There is an air of this mock marriage being in deference to English prejudice. We cannot help thinking, had the story been written for French readers, it would have been dispensed with, for the whole tone of the book points to another state of things, and certainly pleads for those, unhappy and betrayed, who can pretend to no such extenuation. Otherwise, why hits, in the tone of the author of 'No Name,' at our 'cruel laws,' involving illegitimate children in 'intolerable misfortune,' for the ordinary victims of these laws have nothing to do with even the pretence of marriage. Moreover, when Beatrice learns that the so-called marriage was not legal, it makes no difference in her course of action; she waits where she is till the real marriage shall be performed. Mrs. Norton can draw a graceful picture of innocent, happy simplicity. Her heroine, though conventional, as are her father, her saintly sister, her midshipman brother, is often interesting. But she identifies her too closely with *some one else* for the simplicity to be genuine; her language, when moved and excited, is that of a passionate woman of the world. There are curious experiences given to her, true we dare say, but which really come at a much later date than the heroine stage. We must own to some surprise, how any cultivated mind, refined by poetry, and even genius, can possibly reduce a heroine to such extremities of degradation as are brought about in Beatrice's search for a living, after she is abandoned by Treherne. The belief in intrinsic purity ought to preserve any favourite conception of the imagination from such contacts, such base suspicions; but, we believe, wherever there is unrestraint, whether the undisciplined element is found in a writer who talks of earls and marchionesses in blindest ignorance, or absolute knowledge, there is vulgarity: the vulgarity of recklessness as to exact truth, or its consequences; a resolution to say your say, to produce its effect, to prove your point, and to secure readers at all hazards. In this unrestrained spirit is executed the portrait of the Marchioness of Updown, with all the details of her 'corpulence,' her 'snorting,' and coarsely-selfish *abandon*. It has the air of a caricature of some person unfortunate enough to have incurred a lively authoress's ill will, and, as it stands, seems as little likely to be a correct likeness of an individual as it is of a class. However, the Marchioness forms the life of some spirited scenes; and though she is one of the respectable people who sanction the disreputable Nelly, her own errors are so far in a presentable form, that we need not scruple to lay them before our readers. This great lady is aunt of the wicked hero, Montague Treherne, and had known Beatrice in her happier days. Now, through a humble companion and amiable dependant, who had helped Beatrice in her sorest need, she comes again, though unknowingly, in contact with her as the purchaser of some valuable lace. Some slight error of the much-bullied companion had flurried the great lady's temper. Beatrice, who is now a lace-cleaner, had not returned the precious fabric as soon as expected. The Marchioness of Updown, flustered and furbelowed, and accompanied by the policeman she had summoned, makes her way to the heroine's poor lodgings.

'The Marchioness breasted the narrow staircase as though she were about to scale the battlements of a surrendering fortress. "Go before me into this den," she said to Parkes, "and show me where my lace is! I'm not going to be put off with false excuses any longer, I can tell you. Get me my lace. Mr. Sergeant, you are to follow me; you, John, stand at the door. We'll soon see if people are to be kept out of their property this way." She pushed the door wide open

as Parkes crept in before her; and Parkes had only time to murmur that she hoped Beatrice would not feel frightened; and to hear the word "frightened" in proudest contempt, before the bulky and bulkily-dressed Marchioness stood in the small room.'

Beatrice refuses to give back the lace, and returns the money which had been sent for it.

"Ho!" almost screamed the Marchioness; "you dare, you bad, bad girl. Policeman, this is a bad girl who knew my nephew abroad, and tried to give me the plague. Take the lace from her. It's my lace; I bought it; I gave a hundred and seventy guineas for it. Take it from her: take her into custody. Take Parkes into custody; they are both accomplices."

Beatrice struck her open palm on the packet of bank-notes that lay on the table. "Here," she said, "is the money you paid for that lace. I refuse to sell it to you. It is mine. This room is mine. Leave it."

"You wicked girl; you bold bad hussy! I insist on my lace. You want to sell it to somebody else, because you're found out now. It was worth a great deal more than I gave for it! Oh! you cheat, you; but it won't do. I'll have my rights. Policeman, I bought the lace; get me the lace. Search the place; take this young woman into custody. Why don't you take her when I order you?"

The sergeant of police half smiled. He said in a deprecatory sort of manner: "You see, my lady, if the young woman declines to receive the money, and won't part with the lace, I really don't know how I can act."

"She *did* receive the money; and the lace was mine, and I *will* have it! She's a cheat; her father was a cheat before her, and her brother fired at the Queen; and I will have my lace!"

Beatrice looked scornfully up at her: "You selfish, prosperous, cruel woman," she said. "Tyrannize over your own household! this room is mine, humble as it is; it is no place for you. Go away and leave me in peace. The lace will never be yours. I sent it away this morning, and I will never let you have it again."

"Where? where? Policeman, make her say *where* she has sent it! You wicked toad, I don't believe you! I don't believe it's sent away. You want to wear it, I suppose. You want to dress yourself up in frippery and finery to seduce more young men of good family, and try to get them to admire you, as you did my fool of a nephew. You seem to have had a pretty come down since then! Give me my lace," shouted she, her rage apparently increasing in the dead silence, with which she was permitted to rise; and she made a sort of angry movement in advance, pushing the table at which Beatrice was seated.

"Come, come, my lady, there really must be none of this! Now do pray compose yourself. Your ladyship had better come away;"—and the sergeant of police actually laid his hand on the august and obese arm, whose bracelets quivered with the wearer's passion.

"How *dare* you touch me, MAN!" gasped the Marchioness. "If you can't do your duty, and take people into custody when you're told to take them, at least don't dare meddle with ME, you impudent stupid."

"Policeman," said Beatrice, "I take you and the lady who is here present to witness, that I return to the Marchioness of Updown the money she sent for the lace she desires to buy, and which I refuse to sell. I can bear no more of this: I have been ill for some time." And so saying, Beatrice vanished into a little bed-closet, from which a tiny staircase led to M. Dumont's workroom below.

The Marchioness positively shook with rage at her disappearance. She stood for a moment her eyes glaring with amazement and anger. Then seizing the bank-notes in the envelope, and turning suddenly on little Miss Parkes, she said, "I discharge you, you vile, you wicked minx! I discharge you. You are discharged! I hope you will starve. *I* shan't recommend you, I promise you. It's a pity you can't do like your beauty there, and wear lace and coral to make gentlemen fall in love with you. I discharge you, mind! I forbid you to come back. I'll have the doors shut upon you. Any rags you may have left in my house can be packed up and sent to you by Benson; and you don't deserve even that much kindness; nor—only your salary was paid yesterday—you would not get that, you cunning thief, you!"

"Come, come, milady," remonstrated the sergeant. "Really such words are actionable. I'm here to keep the peace, you know. Your ladyship musn't forget yourself this way."

' "You go away, man! I ordered you here—now I order you to go away. I order you away. You've done no good: you haven't got my lace; you let all these low people have the best of it; you won't take people into custody, though you're told ever so; and I don't want you any more. Go away. John! call the carriage. John, do you hear me, or not?" '

The Marchioness returns to her splendid carriage, which had attracted a London mob.

'Into that carriage the baffled tyrant got, and was driven rapidly away, the sergeant of police saying quietly to a brother-constable—after giving vent to his feelings in a low whistle of contempt—"Curious now, ain't it, Brown, how like females are one to t'other? This one's a real marchioness, with a real sort of a marquis, dining with the Queen, and all that, and here she's been a behaving for all the world like Betsy Blane, the fishwoman, as I had in the lock-up last night. She's as like her—as like as one oyster-shell is to another!" and the brother-constable gave a smiling grunt of assent.'

—*Lost and Saved,* vol iii. p. 20.

Nor does Mrs. Norton fail to make good her place in the modern sensational school, by conceiving scenes in its extremest development. Not only does she give us one peeress, a fish-wife, and another carrying on correspondences which would sink her into lowest infamy, through the medium of advertisements in the *Times'* second column; but what has been called our Arsenical Literature has been enriched by a very thorough-going scene from her pen. The wicked peeress has, if possible, a more wicked aunt who has mated herself, not without a sense of degradation, to an honest attorney, supercifiously indicated by his titled employers as 'that fellow Grey.' Mrs. Myra Grey shares some of that Hindoo blood, fruitful of intrigue, which gives a wild charm to her niece, and possesses an ivory jewel-hafted dagger with which she opens her husband's letters, and becomes possessed of his client's secrets. On one occasion she betrays knowledge thus surreptitiously obtained, and the consequences threatening to be disagreeable to herself, she proceeds, as though the means were at hand any moment, to poison an inconvenient witness. This is Maurice Lewellyn, the good genius of the story: he sits at her luncheon-table previous to an interview with her husband, but refuses to eat.

"Take at least a glass of wine—let me mix you some sherry and seltzer-water."

He bowed and stretched out his hand for the tumbler, struggling for at least some outward courtesy to this cunning and corrupt woman. She filled it and moved slowly away.

Mr. Grey's youngest boy burst merrily into the room—"I say, papa—where's papa? ain't he coming out this fine Sunday?"

Then seeing the guest, he came up smilingly, and said, "Give me some of your wine for a treat."

"May you?" said Maurice.

"Oh! yes, papa gave me some last Sunday for a treat."

Maurice held the glass to the child's lips. Mrs. Myra Grey was settling some flowers on the mantel-piece: she heard the boy's last words.

"Gave you what?" she said, turning towards them. Then she darted forward, and exclaiming, "Oh my God!" she vehemently seized the child by both arms and drew him back from Lewellyn.

"I beg your pardon," she said, with a strange smile, "but my children never taste wine."

"Oh mamma—last Sunday."

"Come away, you are a naughty riotous boy, and must go upstairs." She led the child away. As she opened the door, Lewellyn heard her say, "Did you swallow any of it? Spit! spit out upon the door-rug;" and the child said, "La! mamma, I had not even got my lips to the glass when you pulled me away."

Lewellyn, who is an acute lawyer, has his suspicions, and in her absence takes out of his pocket an empty flask, and pours into it half the contents of the tumbler. When he gets home he administers the mixture to a dog, which after some hours, dies of convulsions. In the meanwhile, a second guest, Montague Treherne, the betrayer of Beatrice, arrives at the same luncheon-table, and, after angry words with Mrs. Myra, drinks off the remaining contents of the tumbler—a curious thing, by the way, for a very fastidious fine gentleman to do. The lady witnesses the act.

> Her eyes were riveted upon the glass in his hand. Her countenance assumed a strange expression of mingled defiance and terror. As he turned angrily from her, and ran down the stairs with the light quick step that was habitual to him, she passed her handkerchief, dipped in water, over her own forehead with a slight shudder.

"BOTH!" she said, in a sort of frightened whisper. "Both! what shall I do?"

> 'Then rising once more, with a ghastly face, she proceeded carefully to rince the goblet out of which he had drunk, the glass Maurice had used, and the small decanter that stood by them.'

—*Lost and Saved*, vol. iii. p. 249.

Montague Treherne sails next day in his yacht, is seized with spasms, procures the assistance of a doctor who pronounces it poison, not cholera as the sailors had supposed, and dies. The doctor brings the body to England, and informs Lewellyn of his opinion. Lewellyn has his strong suspicions, which might in fact be certainties, but—

> 'What end, indeed, could it have served to bring to doubtful trial, and probable acquittal, the wife of the family solicitor? . . . to disturb with an immense scandal the society in which Montague and his relatives moved; and to receive no guerdon, when all was done, but resentment and reproach from his family?'

—Vol. iii. p. 296.

The murderess, therefore, is let alone, learns caution, and along with all the other bad people of the book, is taken leave of by the reader in unabated prosperity and confirmed social credit and standing. 'The Marchioness is still the person who 'occupies most attention (and most space) at all the balls given 'by royalty and by the subjects of royalty.' And Nelly, in spite of a letter to her angry and malignant aunt, which sounds like an imprudence, is in greater favour with her husband and the world than ever. Beatrice is taken up and restored to society by kind friends, marries an Italian count, not handsome, but with a voice, 'unutterably sad, unutterably sweet,' who has been forsaken by his wife, and the curtain closes on the young mother hanging over the cradle of her baby. For calm, serene, domestic felicity, the very last thing these heroines of many stormy adventures are fit for, is always the haven assigned to them. It is easier, in fact, to turn nun, hospital nurse, or sister of mercy, to take up and carry through the professed vocation of a saint, than to work out the English ideal of wife, mother, and presiding spirit of the house, after any wide departure from custom and decorum; and it is one of the most mischievous points of a bad moral that leads the young and inexperienced reader to suppose otherwise.

If Mrs. Norton attacks apparent and recognised respectability, professes to unmask false pretences, and shows that the worst people are those most in the world's good graces, Miss Braddon, the first and, at present, pre-eminent sensation writer, sets herself to defy and expose the real thing. Her bad people don't pretend only to be good: they *are* respectable; they really work, nay slave, in the performance of domestic duties and the most accredited of all good works. The moral proper of her stories may be good or bad; as thus,—Lady Audley is wicked, and comes to a bad end; Aurora Floyd does a hundred bad things and prospers in spite of them, both in her own fate and in the reader's favour; but the real influence of everything this lady writes is to depreciate custom, and steady work of any kind whatever; every action, however creditable, that is not the immediate result of generous impulse. She disbelieves in systematic formal habitual goodness. She owns to a hatred of monotonous habit even in doing right. She declares for what she calls a Bohemian existence. She likes people to be influenced by anything rather than principle and cold duty; in fact, nerves, feeling, excitement, will, and inclination are the sole motive powers of every character she cares for. The person who goes on day after day doing stated duty-work because it is duty, not because she likes it, is a monster to her, a something hardly human. She regards such an one (that is in her books) as a painful, oppressive phenomenon. Not believing in the pleasures of habit of any sort, she can no more understand that there may be alleviations, hopes, nay positive joys, in a life of conscientious observances than could Timothy's Bess, in 'Adam Bede,' conceive it possible for life to have a single satisfaction to a person who wore such a cap as Dinah's. The recoil from dulness is evidently too strong, and all regularity, all day by day uniform occupation is dull to her; and she has such a way of putting it that we confess there is danger of its seeming dull to the reader also.

In a story now coming out, this feeling is shown in the portrait of a clergyman's daughter working her father's parish. Olivia is a model visitor of the poor—a sort of typical and transcendent district-visitor—who never lets a day pass unimproved, who allows no impediments, still less her own ease, to interfere with the work and duty before her. Most people learn to like such occupations even if not congenial; habit and the sense of usefulness make them more than tolerable. Olivia hates them with an ever-growing hatred, and they turn her into a fiend. Of course there is a good deal about the work not being done in a right spirit, being done as duty, not in love; but this is a conspicuous salve, a necessary reservation, which does not seem to us to mean much. Any woman plodding in good works as Olivia does, would produce a shudder and revulsion in such a mind, be she ever so earnest and sincere in her task. And to those outside we grant this sort of life does seem a dull one. Miss Braddon, no doubt, finds abundance of young readers to echo her sentiment, though habit coming upon a sense of usefulness makes such lives more than tolerable, the happiest of all lives to those that live them. In fact, Olivia represents the 'moral man' as familiar to us under the handling of a certain class of preachers, saying prayers, reading the Bible, going three times a day to church:—

> 'Mrs. Marchmont made an effort to take up her old life, with its dull round of ceaseless duty, its perpetual self-denial. If she had been a Roman Catholic she would have gone to the nearest convent, and prayed to be permitted to take such vows as might soonest set a barrier between herself and the world; she would have spent the long weary days in perpetual ceaseless prayer; she would have worn deeper indentatious upon the stones already hollowed by faithful knees. As it was she made a routine of penance for herself, after her fashion; going long distances on foot to visit her poor when she ought to have ridden in her carriage; courting exposure to rain and foul weather; wearing herself out with unnecessary fatigue, and returning footsore to her desolate home, to fall fainting in the strong arms of her grim attendant Barbara. But this self-appointed penance could not shut Edward Arundel and Mary Marchmont from the widow's mind. Walking through a fiery furnace, their images would have haunted her still, vivid and palpable, even in the agony of death. . . . . No good whatever seemed to come of her endeavours, and the devils, who rejoiced at her weakness and her failure, claimed her as their own. They claimed her as their own.'—*Temple Bar,* February, 1863, p. 157.

Olivia Marchmont to be sure was impeded not only by a wild indomitable passion, but by a fund of unused energy and genius. She is one of Miss Braddon's favourites, possessing—

> 'The ambition of a Semiramis, the courage of a Boadicea, the resolution of a Lady Macbeth.'

She was—

> 'Devoured by a slow-consuming and perpetual fire. Her mind was like one vast roll of parchment whereon half the wisdom of the world might have been inscribed, but on which was only written, over and over again, to maddening iteration, the name of Edward Arundel. . . .

'Olivia Marchmont might have been a good and great woman. She had all the elements of greatness. She had genius, resolution, an indomitable courage, an iron will, perseverance, self-denial, temperance, chastity. But against all these qualities was set a fatal and foolish love for a boy's handsome face and frank, genial manner. If she could have gone to America, and entered herself amongst the feminine professors of law and medicine—if she could have set up a printing-press in Bloomsbury, or even written a novel—I think she might have been saved.'—P. 477, April, 1863.

But even where there is not this disproportionate greatness of soul, where the task is in exact measure with the worker, Miss Braddon shows an equal repugnance to the humdrum and to the ordinary feminine ideal. Her odious females are all remarkable for conformity to the respectable type, whether as 'religious women doing their duty in a hard uncompromising way,' or writing a 'neat' letter, or cutting their husband's bread and butter, or 'excelling in that elaborate and terrible science which woman paradoxically calls plain needlework.'

Three things seem to have aided in this war against steady unexcited well-doing, a familiarity at some time or the other with the drudgery of learning, and an equal familiarity with horses and with theatricals, not simply play-going, but life behind the scenes. Her heroines have all been disgusted by a routine education, some in their own person, some inflicting it on others. It is an excuse for Aurora's flight from school with her father's groom, that she was kept strictly to her lessons. Lady Audley was teacher in a school; Olivia Marchmont imposes an intolerable amount of dates, Roman history, and all the rest, on her hapless charge; and Eleanor, in 'Eleanor's Victory,' on one happy holiday—

> 'Looked back wonderingly at the dull routine of her boarding-school existence. Could it be possible that it was only a day or two since she was in the Brixton schoolroom hearing the little ones, the obstinate incorrigible little ones, their hateful lessons—their odious, monotonous repetitions of dry facts about William the Conqueror and Buenos Ayres, the manufacture of tallow candles, and the nine parts of speech.'—*Once a Week,* p. 335, March 1863.

The ordinary well-educated young lady, the flower and triumph of civilization, who has mastered her lessons, the languages, the history, the difficult passages in the sonata in C flat, and liked them all, is alternately an object of amusement and contempt. In contrast with the glowing Aurora, we have a good-natured portrait of the model heroine of another school, learned in geography and astronomy and botany and chronology, and reading one of the novels that *may* lie on a drawing-room table. 'How tame, how cold, how weak, beside that Egyptian goddess, that Assyrian queen, with her flashing eyes and the serpentine coils of purple-black hair.'

> 'The long arcades of beech and elm had reminded him, from the first, of the solemn aisles of a cathedral; and coming suddenly to a spot where a new arcade branches off abruptly on his right hand, he saw, in one of the sylvan niches, as fair a saint as had ever been modelled by the hand of artist and believer—the same golden-haired angel he had seen in the long drawing-room at Feldon Woods—Lucy Floyd, with the pale aureola about her head, her large straw-hat in her lap, filled with anemones and violets, and the third volume of a novel in her hand. A High Church novel, "it is explained," in which the heroine rejected the clerical hero because he did not perform the service according to the Rubric.'—*Aurora Floyd,* vol. ii. p. 16.

How different from this serene inanity the unrestrained 'expansive natures,' unchecked by system of any sort, whose youth has been suffered to run wild, do what they like, form their own opinions, get into scrapes, and compromise themselves while still in their teens, which charm this writer's fancy! Nothing is so purely conventional an idea as that young girls untaught or ill-taught can be graceful or attractive, however favourite a notion it is with writers of fiction. But this clever, bright writer can describe an unattached, vagrant, slipshod existence with touches of truth, with admissions of the necessary condition of such an existence, which give a greater air of reality to her pictures than we often see. Thus, her Eleanor, whose childhood has been passed with a disreputable, self-indulgent spendthrift of a father, with whom she had lived in occasional luxury and habitual destitution, whose companion

has been a good-natured, slovenly scene-painter and theatrical supernumerary, who is now, at fifteen, a teacher in a third-rate boarding-school, shows in the following pretty picture nothing at variance with her bringing up. The health and spirits of the solitary girl are exciting the spleen of the sea-sick passengers of the Dieppe steamer:—

> 'Eyes dim in the paroxysms of sea-sickness had looked almost spitefully towards this happy radiant creature, as she flitted hither and thither about the deck, courting the balmy ocean-breezes that made themselves merry with her rippling hair. Lips blue with suffering had writhed as their owners beheld the sandwiches which this young school-girl devoured, the stale buns, the flat raspberry tarts, the hideous, bilious, revolting three-cornered puffs, which she produced at different stages of the voyage from her shabby carpet-bag. She had an odd volume of a novel, and a long dreary desert of crochet-work whose white cotton monotony was only broken by occasional dingy oases, bearing witness of the worker's dirty hands; and they were such pretty hands, too, that it was a shame they should ever be dirty; and she had a bunch of flabby faded flowers, sheltered by a great fan-like shield of newspaper; and she had a smelling bottle which she sniffed at perpetually, though she had no need of any such restorative, being as fresh and bright from first to last as the sea-breezes themselves.'

It is in the existence of the real with the impossible that this writer's power lies. This tart-loving child of fifteen is the girl who, three days later, devotes herself to vengeance, and lives for years in the unchanging hope of seeing the sharper who got her father's money hanged through her instrumentality. People are apt to think, though it is no such thing, that the knowledge of ordinary custom-loving human nature is a much easier thing than knowledge of the waifs and strays of humanity, and this lady's experiences are ostentatiously of this exceptional kind. She would have us think that she views human nature generally in a scrape. Thus, she will ask, as if familiar with detectives and their mode of noting down their pencil memoranda, When they begin their pencils? and 'how it is that they always seem to have arrived at the stump?' Again, one of her characters is intoxicated: 'his head is laid upon the pillow, in one of those wretched positions which intoxication *always* chooses for its repose,' as though she had seen so much of it. And it is with people in a scrape, or ready at any moment to fall into one, that she sympathises. Blind passion gets them into difficulties, blind trust carries others along with them; and *trust* is a quality in wonderful favour with some people, as it indeed ought to be with all the heroines of the Aurora type—a trust which leads the big Yorkshireman thus to declare himself, in answer to the insinuations of the envious and respectable Mrs. Powell:—

> ' "You are a good husband, Mr. Mellish," she said, with a gentle melancholy. "Your wife *ought* to be

happy," she added, with a sigh, which plainly hinted that Mrs. Mellish was miserable.

' "A good husband!" cried John; "not half good enough for her. What can I do to prove that I love her?—what can I do? Nothing—except to let her have her own way. And what a little that seems! Why, if she wanted to set that house on fire, for the pleasure of making a bonfire," he added, pointing to the rambling mansion in which his blue eyes had first seen the light, "I'd let her do it, and look on with her at the blaze." '—*Aurora Floyd,* vol. ii. p. 237.

The whole idea of life and love in writers of this class is necessarily mischievous and, we will say, immoral. Independent of the fact that 'John' was duped by his wife all this time, that she knew her first husband was living, and that therefore she was not his wife, the picture of the relation between these two is one really incompatible with the weight and seriousness of matrimonial obligations. There is a praise and sympathy for unreasoning blind idolatry very likely to find a response in young readers, whether of the vain or romantic type; and the better it is done—the more sweetness and feeling is thrown into it—the more dangerous if it gets a hold, and keeps its ground. Husbands and fathers at any rate may begin to look about them and scrutinize the parcel that arrives from Mudie's, when young ladies are led to contrast the actual with the ideal we see worked out in popular romance; the mutual duties, the reciprocal forbearance, the inevitable trials of every relation in real life, with the triumph of mere feminine fascination, before which man falls prostrate and helpless. Take the following scene.

Aurora has to go up to London to buy off the interference of her real husband the groom, whom her father supposes to be dead, and of whom her husband knows nothing. The idolizing father welcomes her to the disturbed and interrupted dinner:—

'Aurora sat in her old place at her father's right hand. In the old girlish days Miss Floyd had never occupied the bottom of the table, but had loved best to sit by that foolishly doting parent, pouring out his wine for him, in defiance of the servants, and doing other loving offices which were deliciously inconvenient to the old man.

'To-day Aurora seemed especially affectionate. That fondly-clinging manner had all its ancient charm to the banker. He put down his glass with a tremulous hand to gaze at his darling child, and was dazzled with her beauty and drunken with the happiness of having her near him.

' "But, my darling," he said by-and-by, "what do you mean by talking about going back to Yorkshire to-morrow?"

' "Nothing, papa, except that I *must* go," answered Mrs. Mellish, determinedly.

' "But why come, dear, if you could only stop one night?"

' "Because I wanted to see you, dearest father, and talk to you about—about money matters."

' "That's it!" exclaimed John Mellish, with his mouth half full of salmon and lobster sauce, "that's it!—money matters! That's all I can get out of her. She goes out late last night and roams about the garden, and comes in wet through and through, and says she must come to London about money matters. What should she want with money matters? If she wants money, she can have as much as she wants. She shall write the figures and I'll sign the cheque; or she shall have a dozen blank cheques to fill in just as she pleases. What is there upon this earth that I'd refuse her? If she dipped a little too deep and put more money than she could afford upon the bay filly, why doesn't she come to me, instead of bothering you about money matters? You know I said so in the train, Aurora, ever so many times. Why bother your poor papa about it?" '—*Aurora Floyd,* vol. ii. p. 139.

So far as real life sees, or ever has seen anything like this, it is among the Cleopatras and other witch-like charmers who have misled mankind; not among wives and daughters of repute in Christian or even in heathen times. No doubt discipline, self-restraint, and moral training, stand in the way of this fascination: in every conspicuous example these have all been wanting; still there are people, no doubt, to agree with the sporting community of Doncaster, who, we are told, one and all liked Aurora all the better for breaking her whip over a stable-boy's shoulder, and who are led willing captives by the varied and opposite manifestations of unchecked feeling, passion, and impulse, when there is beauty and grace enough to smooth over and conceal their real repulsiveness.

The series of books before us happen to be from female pens, and sensation writing in their hands takes a peculiar hue. Thus with them, love is more exclusively the instrument for producing excitement, and they have the art of infusing greater extravagance of sentiment in its expression. A certain Mr. Fullom has complained bitterly that Miss Braddon has stolen the outline of one of his novels, and has reproduced incident after incident in 'Lady Audley's Secret' with scarcely the affectation of disguise; the real bitterness of the transaction lying no doubt in the fact that his precursory tale had been too little read for the plagiarism to be known to any but the two authors. The successful appropriation of another's plot no doubt shows that quality of prompt assimilation attributed to Aurora, 'who was such a brilliant creature, that every little smattering of knowledge she possessed appeared to such good account, as to make her seem an adept in any subject of which she spoke.' This is no doubt a power of the feminine nature, to take in at a glance, and to make apparently her own, what has cost hard labour to slower, though original, thinkers. Probably nobody could read Mr. Fullom's book; we do not pretend to have heard of it, but he makes out an excellent case, which just proves Miss Braddon's dramatic power. Play wrights take anybody's story—it belongs to them to make it fit for the stage; and the world is essentially a *stage* to Miss Braddon, and all the men and women, the wives, the lovers, the villains, the sea-captains, the victims, the tragically jealous, the haters, the avengers, merely players. We could extract pages, fit, as they stand, for the different actors in a melodrama, vehemently and outrageously unnatural, but with a certain harmony which prevents one part exposing the other.

We ought possibly to apologize to the readers of a theological review for intruding on their notice scenes with certainly no direct bearing on the subjects to which its columns are as a rule devoted. But we have thought it well to enter our protest against the form of fiction most popular in the present day, because we conceive it to fail both positively and negatively in the legitimate uses of fiction. Negatively, because it asks least from the sense, feeling, and thought of the reader; and positively, because instead of quickening the imagination it stimulates a vulgar curiosity, weakens the established rules of right and wrong, touches, to say the least, upon things illicit, raises false and vain expectations, and draws a wholly false picture of life. Every true and honest observer of human nature adds something to the common experience, but if anything new is to be learnt from the sensational novel, as far as our observation goes, it is in that field of knowledge which emphatically is not wisdom.

Tamar Heller (essay date 1992)

SOURCE: "Writing After Dark: Collins and Victorian Literary Culture," in *Dead Secrets: Wilkie Collins and the Female Gothic,* Yale University Press, 1992, pp. 82-185.

[*In the following essay, Heller examines the nineteenth-century division of sensation novels into "serious" or "popular" and "male" or "female." Heller focuses on Wilkie Collins's collection of short stories published in 1856,* After Dark, *to explore the way in which the presence of these divisions affected Collins's work.*]

Although Collins' novels after *Basil* continued to engage "modern life," he still wrote historical fiction, returning in the mid-1850s to the subject of revolution that had been thematically important in his earliest works. Recalling the setting of his ghost story about the French Revolution, "Nine O'Clock!" he serialized

a lengthy tale about the Reign of Terror, "Sister Rose," in Dickens' journal *Household Words* in 1855, including it the next year in his collection of short stories *After Dark.* In *After Dark,* he embeds this historical fiction within the collection's frame narrative, in which a male artist and his female scribe become both collaborators and rivals in the literary marketplace. This juxtaposition of a tale about revolution with an allegory of the marketplace foregrounds the Victorian writer's relation to history, even as it continues to figure Collins' ambivalent relation to the Gothic genre. Within the frame narrative, the wife, who is an amanuensis, suggests that her husband write for money and then transforms his stories into Gothic narratives, a plot that encodes Collins' anxiety about the female voice and the status of Gothic fiction in the Victorian literary establishment.

Although this narrative about the literary marketplace and the rivalry between male and female artists sounds familiar after *Basil,* both the frame narrative of *After Dark* and the story "Sister Rose" represent a significant development in this plot rather than simply another look backward. Even as the history that the endings of both *Antonina* and *Basil* had tried to repress returns in "Sister Rose"—itself a tale about a kind of resurrection—the subtle shifts between masculine and feminine perspectives in the frame narrative complicate Collins' revision of the female Gothic. Whereas the first-person narrative of *Basil* privileges the male viewpoint (and a misogynist one at that), the frame narrative of *After Dark* is written instead by a figure for the woman writer. Although this narrative strategy does not simply substitute a female for a male perspective, it does render Collins' allegory of the writer in the marketplace more complex, since in his own preface to the work he adopts some of the metaphors for storytelling used by his female narrator. In order to explore why Collins could identify with a female narrator as well as be anxious about that identification, the first part of this chapter will place the relation between writing and gender so often figured in his fiction in the context of Victorian literary culture. In particular, this reading will examine how the development of Collins' career in the 1850s and 1860s intersected with the rise both of the literary marketplace and of a growing gap between "popular" and "serious" fiction. In debates over the status of Victorian fiction, the difference between popular and serious is defined most obviously in class terms—"high" and "low"—but also in gendered terms, contrasting a masculine professional ethos with sensation fiction identified as feminine. Thus before turning to the figuration of Collins' own literary situation in *After Dark,* I will examine the tensions inherent in his desire to identify with masculine professionalism while being identified by his critics with feminine sensationalism.

"No Character at All": The Sensation Novel and Literary Professionalism

At the beginning of the 1860s, the decade that witnessed the craze for and critical debate over the sensation novel, a reviewer wrote about *The Woman in White* that "Like the women in Pope, most of Mr. Wilkie Collins's characters have no character at all."[1] On the surface, this statement endorses an opinion about Collins' fiction that was to become a critical commonplace: his works, like other examples of Victorian sensation or melodramatic fiction, are concerned with plot rather than with character. As this reviewer claims, the readers are "much less interested in the people than in what happens to the people."[2] Yet the argument that Collins "does not attempt to paint character or passion,"[3] although it expels him from the canon of the realist novel, is as much an ideological as an aesthetic judgment. Surely many readers of Collins' fiction would disagree that his characters are any less memorable than those of other Victorian novelists (and if, as the reviewer claims, the figures in Collins' novels have "characteristics, but not character,"[4] those in the works of more securely canonical authors like Dickens and Thackeray are often types rather than psychological portraits).[5] Yet "to have a character" in the Victorian period also meant to have a reputation; when Ezra Jennings says in *The Moonstone*, "I am a man whose life is a wreck, and whose character is gone," he means that he is an outcast because scandalous rumors about his past prevent him from obtaining the written recommendations of character that were a prerequisite for a job.[6] The degraded class status of not having a character may be compared with definitions of femininity as lack or absence. The verse from Pope's "Epistle to a Lady" to which the reviewer of *The Woman in White* refers proclaims that "Nothing so true as what you once let fall / 'Most Women have no Characters at all.'"[7]

Collins' reviewer thus puns on the social, as well as the literary, definition of character, since in *The Woman in White* (as in such later novels as *No Name* and *The Moonstone*) Collins often portrays women and other outcasts who have no "character," because of either their gender or their ambiguous class status (or both, as with the illegitimate daughter who is the central figure in *No Name*). This characterlessness is troped not just through femininity but through a sexually fallen femininity; in Pope's verse, the important word is "fall." Just as the reviewer of *Basil* condemned the novel by exclaiming in horror over its plot of the "adultery of a wife," critics like the reviewer of *The Woman in White* imply that the lack of securely defined social and gender identity among Collins' characters reflects on the aesthetic value of the novels in which they appear. Not only are Collins' characters compared with women without reputation, but he himself is likened to a member of the working class rather than to one of a literary elite, the reviewer from the *Saturday Review*, after claiming that Collins is a "story-teller" rather than a "great novelist," says that "he is, as we have said, a very ingenious constructor; but ingenious construction is not high art, just as cabinet-making and joining are not high art."[8]

To claim that Collins' novels embody the "lowness" of his characters obviously is ironic, since in *Basil* the figure for the male writer tries to escape the contamination of female influence and of Mannion's demonic ressentiment. That Collins returned to *Basil* in 1862 to revise it is appropriate, since the narrative would have been popular in the heyday of the sensation novel, and its story about trying to escape from literary and social "lowness" would have been a compelling one for him amid critical disagreement concerning the value of his fiction.

That fiction deemed sensational should be considered marginal or subliterary attests to a debate about the changing status and definition of Victorian fiction. As Walter Phillips argues in his pioneering study of Dickens, Collins, and Reade as sensation novelists, the Victorian literary marketplace changed drastically during the period in which these writers established their careers. With fiction no longer available only to an elite, the writer became more dependent on appealing to an audience than in the past, a dependency which the demands of serial publication only exacerbated.[9] The previous chapter traced *Basil*'s association of writing for the marketplace with wage slavery and the degradation of aesthetic value. Yet the discourse about the devaluation of fiction in the marketplace that *Basil* reflects appears simultaneously with a new emphasis within the Victorian literary establishment, by writers and critics alike, on the moral and aesthetic value of writing and on the professionalism (not the wage slavery) of the novelist.

The claim that, in the words of a reviewer of *Basil,* the writer has a "high and holy mission"[10] mystifies the economic reality in which that writer creates. This mystification serves to protect and even to enhance the status of the intellectual and, in so doing, to preserve other hierarchies that social and economic changes might threaten. The association of Victorian fiction with democratization, with being available even to the working and lower classes, is countered by a critical discourse that uses aesthetic terms to condemn the content of fiction, particularly if that content is read as subversive of gender and class roles.

Discussing the growing separation between "popular" and "great" literature during the Victorian period, Winifred Hughes notes that "Curiously, some thought ominously, the rise of the sensation genre coincided with the height of the novelist's newly-won prestige, his new presence as a social and ethical force."[11] Yet the timing of the rise of sensation fiction is not curious at all when the genre is viewed as a construction by the literary establishment (reviewers were the first to coin the phrase) of a fiction that contrasts with prestigious, or "great" art. Certainly, the very term *sensation fiction* implies a dichotomy between fiction that, as this label suggests, appeals to the bodily senses—"excitement, and excitement alone, seems to be the great end at which they aim," claimed H. D. Mansel[12]—and that which appeals to the mind. (Would the opposite of sensation fiction be cerebral fiction?) Yet the boundary between high and low reproduces other social dichotomies: male and female, upper class and lower class, even white and nonwhite. A critic for the *Westminster Review* likened the sensation novelist, including Mary Elizabeth Braddon and Collins, to a showman exhibiting a "big black baboon, whose habits were so filthy, and whose behavior was so disgusting, that respectable people constantly remonstrated with him for exhibiting such an animal." According to the critic, the showman's answer was, "If it wasn't for that big black baboon I should be ruined; it attracts all the young girls in the country."[13]

This anecdote conflates all those who are "low" in the body politic: the black baboon, who embodies the racial Other, the showman, an image for the working class, and the young girls whose sexuality is stimulated. In this allegory of the literary marketplace, the writers of sensation fiction (the showman selling a look at his baboon) purvey works that dangerously arouse the sexuality of women—particularly, it is implied, middle-class women, who are supposed to be sexually repressed—the same charge that used to be leveled at writers of earlier Gothic literature. That women were associated with writing and reading such sexually charged fiction (sensation novels, indeed) is evinced by such reviews as the one entitled "Our Female Sensation Novelists." This review, which focuses on women writers like Mrs. Henry Wood, author of *East Lynne,* and Braddon, author of *Lady Audley's Secret,* complains that "the sensation novel . . . is a sign of the times—the evidence of a certain train of thought and action, of an impatience of old restraints, and a craving for some fundamental change in the working of society."[14] This association of women's Gothic writing with revolution is also made by Margaret Oliphant in a lengthy review of sensation novels in *Blackwood's Magazine,* which compares the "hectic rebellion against nature" in the sensation novel with Hester Prynne's adultery in *The Scarlet Letter* and claims that such novels represent "frantic attempts by any kind of black art or mad psychology to get some grandeur and sacredness restored to life—or if not sacredness and grandeur, at least horror and mystery, there being nothing better in earth or heaven; Mesmerism possibly for a make-shift, or Socialism, if perhaps it might be more worthwhile to turn ploughmen and milkmaids than ladies and gentlemen."[15]

Oliphant's link between sensation fiction and frustrated revolutionary aspirations—aspirations that are even

Wilkie Collins

millenarian ("nothing better in earth or heaven")—undermines the distinction made between sensation and cerebration by critics of the sensation novel. That sensation novelists crave some "fundamental change in the working of society" implies that they think too much rather than (as their lust for "excitement" presumably suggests) that they do not think at all.[16] Whereas those who believed that fiction should be serious were influenced by Carlyle's vision of the writer as prophet and social critic, popular fiction like the sensation novel was associated with having the wrong type of social vision, or one that blurred social hierarchies. Jonathan Loesberg argues that the debate over the literary status of sensation fiction, by reflecting concerns about the stability of class definition, has many parallels to debates over the parliamentary reforms in the 1850s and 1860s that attempted to expand suffrage.[17] He locates this mid-Victorian "class fear" in such important and highly popular sensation novels as *The Woman in White, Lady Audley's Secret,* and *East Lynne,* which all contain socially displaced characters; Collins' Laura Fairlie descends to the level of a working-class woman, Wood's Isabel Vane becomes a governess, and Braddon's central figure rises above her station.[18] Because all these characters are women, however, this anxiety about the miscegenation of classes is also linked to anxieties about gender definition. In this sense, these novels reproduce ideological tensions inherent in the period—"class fear," a fear that women will become insubordinate or lose their "place"—without necessarily being as subversive as they have been called both by their contemporaries and by some recent critics.[19] Still, less important than the radical content of the sensation novel is the perception that it was revolutionary because it depicted types of ambiguity (moral, social, gender) rather than stable and unambiguous ideological definitions.[20] And, equally important, the low status assigned sensation fiction within generic hierarchies reproduces the increasing stratification of literature during the second half of the nineteenth century.

Joining the Gentleman's Club: Collins' Career in the 1850s

Collins' prefaces to his works indicate his desire to be classified as a serious, rather than simply as a popular, novelist. The vehemence of this desire has led critics to describe his prefaces to *Basil* in particular—he revised the original preface for the second edition—as "belligerent," "polemical," and "truculent."[21] Yet if Collins' prefaces in general are, as Sue Lonoff claims, "exercises in self-defense,"[22] they are most importantly a defense against the often dismissive reviews which, like that of *The Woman in White*, impugned his ability to craft "high art." In the 1862 preface to *Basil,* Collins responds to criticism of the novel as both "revolting" and subliterary by repeating a passage from the 1852 edition in which, echoing his father's Romanticism, he depicts himself as a writer who not only exposes social ills but also transforms them into art: "Is not the noblest poetry of prose fiction the poetry of every-day truth?" (xxxvi).

In an admiring review written in the late 1850s, the French critic Emile Forgues, who also translated several of Collins' novels into French, forecast for Collins a career as an author of note and, most significant, as the author who would tell the story of Victorian authors in his fiction: "Who is better qualified than he . . . to depict for us the life of the artist in England and in our period?"[23] Yet it is telling that Forgues compares *Basil,* the novel that concerns the male artist's attempts to differentiate himself from women writers, with the work of Charlotte Brontë and Elizabeth Gaskell. Even though they predate the coining of the term, the novels with which Forgues compares *Basil—Jane Eyre* and *Mary Barton*—share many of the attributes of sensation fiction: Brontë's novel was condemned for its immorality and, like *Lady Audley's Secret* and *East Lynne,* contains a heroine who rises in class position, whereas *Mary Barton* was criticized for its portrayal of working-class unrest. The comparison between *Basil* and these novels demonstrates a tendency, which was to be emphasized in the debate over sensation fiction, to class Collins' works with those of women writers, and specifically to compare supposedly subversive tendencies

in his novels with those in the works of women. Nuel Pharr Davis points out that the comparison of *Basil* with *Jane Eyre* and *Mary Barton,* even in the context of an admiring review, may have galled Collins: "To Wilkie, sensitive about women authors, it must have been irksome to think that the kindest appraisals of *Basil* would call it, as the French critic, Forgues, did, 'quelque chose d'approchant *Jane Eyre.*'"[24]

Davis refers to comments Collins made that resemble Hawthorne's famous line about "scribbling women"; for example, a character in a Collins sketch written for Dickens' periodical *Household Words* in 1858 claims he has been told by "persons of experience in the world of letters" that "Ladies of the present century have burst into every department of literature, have carried off the accumulated raw material under men's noses, and have manufactured it to an enormous and unheard of extent for the public benefit. I am told that out of every twelve novels or poems that are written, nine at least are by ladies."[25] The comparison between writing and manufacturing here, as well as the raw note of rivalry with women, recalls the link in *Basil* between women writers and the degradation of the marketplace in which male writers must now compete. As in *Basil,* too, what is significant about this hostility to women writers is how it expresses in a displaced form anxieties about writing in the marketplace, anxieties that, as Collins' career was being established during the 1850s and 1860s, could only have been exacerbated by the classification of his works with the sensation novel.

In her study of the growth of Victorian literary professionalism, Julia Swindells describes the ways in which the literary establishment was male dominated and male defined; those women who succeeded in obtaining recognition, like George Eliot and the Brontës, did so only after struggles to ingratiate themselves with male patrons or by assuming a masculine professional identity.[26] Swindells refers to literature in the Victorian period as a "gentleman's club,"[27] and Walter Phillips describes the "literary fraternalism" of Dickens, Collins, and Reade.[28] Certainly, this fraternalism may be seen as an attempt to distinguish the gender roles that the rise in the number of women novelists may have threatened. Since professionalism was male defined (as most Victorian women were barred from a career), it was easier to associate "serious" art with male novelists, or with a woman novelist like Eliot who took a male name and conformed to aesthetic standards favored by the male literary establishment. In this context, Collins' relationship with Dickens, who was a formidable embodiment of literary professionalism, may be read as symptomatic of Collins' need to be taken seriously as a professional writer.[29]

Since his career represented many of the same difficulties in professional definition, Dickens was a particularly appropriate model for Collins. As the title of

Phillips' study makes clear, Dickens, an enormously popular writer, was classified by some as a sensation novelist. (*Great Expectations,* for instance, was considered an example of sensation fiction.)[30] Yet, more successfully than Collins, he was able to transcend the category of the popular to be recognized as a great novelist and social prophet. In the letter he wrote to Collins about *Basil,* Dickens claimed that it was the seriousness of the younger writer's efforts that pleased him:

> It is delightful to find throughout that you have taken great pains with it [the novel] besides, and have "gone at it" with a perfect knowledge of the jolter-headedness of the conceited idiots who suppose that volumes are to be tossed off like pancakes, and that any writing can be done without the utmost application, the greatest patience, and the steadiest energy of which the writer is capable.[31]

The language of this letter combines elitism with what may be a covert sexism: although the idiots Dickens refers to presumably do not know the difference between a literary work and a product of trade—they are bakers, not writers—to call badly written volumes pancakes implies that such volumes are the product of domestic labor and that the jolter-headed idiots may be women writers. In any event, with the words "utmost application," "greatest patience," "steadiest energy," Dickens demonstrates how, as James Brown has argued, he associates the labors of the professional writer with the apotheosis of industry, thrift, and perseverance that Lukács identifies as characteristic of the "heroic epoch of bourgeois development."[32]

Dickens' praise of Collins' labor and his denigration of those who do not take time to write well echoes the language of the 1852 preface to *Basil,* where Collins claims he is not one of the "mob of ladies and gentlemen who play at writing" (i, xv [1852]). This reference to a "mob of ladies and gentlemen," although it recalls the moment in the text where Basil's voice is literally overpowered by a lower-class mob and symbolically overwhelmed by feminine influence, associates bad writing with a kind of aristocratic decadence. The association of this mob with an aristocratic indolence that the bourgeois writer must overcome is underscored by Collins' objection to these lady and gentleman authors as essentially "holiday authors, who sit down to write a book as they would sit down to a game at cards—leisurely-living people who coolly select as an amusement 'to kill time,' an occupation which can only be pursued, even creditably, by the patient, uncompromising, reverent devotion of every moral and intellectual faculty, more or less, which a human being has to give" (I, xvi [1852]). That Collins identifies writers in the marketplace with effete aristocrats rather than with people struggling for a living is part of a discourse of empowerment for the bourgeois writer, whose hard work does not make him a wage slave but rather

guarantees him a professional identity. The casual attitude toward authorship displayed by "leisurely-living people" contrasts with the "humble, work-a-day merit" that Collins claims for his own writing, since he argues that his "painstaking" care (I, xv [1852]) ranks him among those authors who share "the homely but honourable distinction of being workers and not players at their task" (I, xvii [1852]).

The language of a shared literary mission in Dickens' letter and Collins' preface suggests how empowering the relationship between the two writers was to the younger one. Collins' intellectual friendship, and even at times partnership, with Dickens gave him access to the world of literary professionalism in which the elder author had so brilliantly succeeded; during the 1850s Collins first joined Dickens' journal *Household Words* and later (after skillful negotiations on his part) became a staff member. This close bonding between two male artists was reminiscent of that between Collins' father and the Scots painter Sir David Wilkie. Yet the friendship was (at least at first) not so much egalitarian as paternal. Eliza Linton characterized Dickens' relationship to Collins as that of "a literary Mentor to a younger Telemachus,"[33] and in many ways Dickens filled for Collins the place that had been vacated by his father. Although, as a liberal reformer who supported the revolutions of 1848, he was more ideologically congenial to Collins than his father had been, Dickens' career emblematized the rigorous professionalism and bourgeois industry that Collins ascribes to William in the *Memoirs.*

Significantly, however, Dickens' advice to Collins underscored a conflict between politics and professionalism. In *Basil,* the writer in the marketplace is associated both with wage slavery and with the veiling of subversive writing to appeal to an audience. The ideal of professionalism that Dickens and Collins shared may have seemed to elevate the male writer from the position of wage slave, but it did not liberate him from dependency on his readers. In the *Memoirs* Collins describes how his father had claimed that "a painter should choose those subjects with which most people associate pleasant circumstances. It is not sufficient that a scene pleases *him*" (I, 59). In his own role as mentor, Dickens was to advise Collins how to please his audience, even if it meant diluting elements in his fiction that a predominantly middle-class readership would find subversive. As Collins' employer at *Household Words* and *All the Year Round,* Dickens even played the part of censor himself, directing his editor W. H. Wills to delete anything from Collins' articles that might, as he said in one letter, "be sweeping and unnecessarily offensive to the middle class. He has always a tendency to overdo that."[34]

Sue Lonoff suggests that, even given what was positive in his influence, Dickens may have "stunted"

Collins' potential by urging him to curb his frank portrayal of sexuality and his critique of the Victorian middle class.[35] Certainly, the very act of writing for Dickens on the staff of *Household Words* may have represented a political choice on Collins' part. Before Collins switched over completely to writing for Dickens' journal, he had been writing for the *Leader,* a socialist journal founded by Thornton Hunt and George Henry Lewes in 1850. Collins contributed to the *Leader* between 1851 and 1856, during the period in which he wrote *Basil* and first began to work for Dickens.[36] Kirk Beetz claims that Collins was a "warm supporter of *The Leader*'s 'Red Republicanism,'"[37] but a sympathy with socialism would not have been unusual among intellectual circles; Dickens called himself a radical during the 1848 revolutions, and even Carlyle, in most ways a political conservative, supported them. Still, the transition during the latter part of the 1850s from writing for a radical journal to writing for middle-class publications like *Household Words,* which spoke to and for bourgeois domesticity, is significant in Collins' career. This choice mirrors the allegories in many of his novels of the male writer's choice between allying himself with radical causes and affirming his identity as part of the bourgeoisie.[38]

Gothic and the Marketplace: The Frame Narrative of After Dark

These tensions in Collins' artistic self-definition are particularly marked in his work of the 1850s and 1860s, the period in which his reputation and his career became firmly established. Even as his revision of Gothic was increasingly associated with "feminine" sensationalism and subversiveness, he was paradoxically placed in a position, like that of Mannion in *Basil,* of having to veil subversive elements in his writing so as not to tell "bitter truths" too bitterly. Yet, if Collins found himself in a position like that of marginalized groups (women and the working classes), who if they were not silent, were criticized for speaking too loudly, he also strove to achieve a voice through a literary professionalism that bespoke masculine and middle-class identity.

Whereas later chapters will discuss this kind of complexity in Collins' most famous works of the 1860s, *The Woman in White* and *The Moonstone,* the short-story collection *After Dark,* published in 1856, is an important early example of a split between a masculine and a feminine perspective. Different works of Collins' enact this tension between strands of masculine and feminine, of being politically engaged or of censoring politics, by embodying different viewpoints: a work with misogynist overtones like *Basil* is followed in 1857 by *The Dead Secret,* which takes as its central, and sympathetically rendered, character a working-class woman with an illegitimate child. Although Collins' novels are famous for their critiques of Victorian

women's lack of legal and economic rights, even the most daring have misogynist elements, such as *Armadale* (1866), in which the remarkable and thoroughly Gothic Miss Gwilt attempts to murder her writer husband.

As if to emblematize this multivocal art, the frame narrative of *After Dark,* the collection compiled during the period when he left the *Leader* to write for Dickens, confuses the different voices that define it. In his preface Collins claims that he wishes to provide in the frame narrative "one more glimpse of the artist-life which circumstances have afforded me peculiar opportunities of studying":

> This time I wish to ask some sympathy for the joys and sorrows of a poor traveling portrait painter— presented from his wife's point of view in "Leah's Diary," and supposed to be briefly and simply narrated by himself in the Prologues to the stories. I have purposely kept these two portions of the book within certain limits; only giving, in the one case, as much as the wife might naturally write in her diary at intervals of household leisure; and, in the other, as much as a modest and sensible man would be likely to say about himself and the characters he met with in his wanderings.[39]

Collins asks for sympathy for the "poor traveling portrait-painter" who is the figure for the male artist in the frame narrative. Yet the joys and sorrows of the artist are only "supposed" to be narrated by himself in the prologues to the stories, an uncertainty about the male voice that draws attention to the strength of the female one: it is the wife of the artist whose point of view predominates within the frame narrative itself.

As Collins says, the frame narrative of *After Dark* tells the story of the male artist through excerpts from his wife's journal entitled "Leaves from Leah's Diary." In this diary Leah Kerby describes her husband William's unemployment: an itinerant portrait painter, he is temporarily blinded by an inflammation of the eyes that prevents him from pursuing his trade until he is cured and that threatens to reduce his family to destitution. A benevolent doctor helps the Kerbys find cheap lodging with a farmer's family, but Leah is the one who devises a scheme to make money: she will copy by dictation the amusing stories her husband has gathered from sitters while he paints their portraits, and the resulting book, if popular, will alleviate their financial crisis. Although William Kerby initially resists this plan, he eventually succumbs to his wife's overwhelming enthusiasm, and only the title of the collection remains in doubt. Leah acknowledges that she will not be able to write down the stories until "after dark" (30) because of her daytime chores in the house and the nursery, and the doctor triumphantly seizes on this phrase as the perfect title. When the frame narrative resumes briefly at the end of the stories, the husband has been cured and the book is about to be published.

Since the stories in the collection are tales of mystery and the Gothic, Collins' fictive description of how he came to write them compares his own endeavors with a feminine experience: the interstices of domestic labor are a suitably eerie time in which to create Gothic. Leah's transcribing Gothic stories after dark recalls Basil's reference to how he has "contracted the bad habit of writing at night." The sex of the Gothic writer has been changed, however, for even if Leah only tells her husband's stories, her idea for the title of the narrative she must write at night suggests that she, rather than he, is the originator of the Gothic. Yet Collins' own preface implies that the female perspective becomes central only when male vision fails: William can neither see nor write because he is blinded, so Leah must take his place.

Even as this partnership dilutes female linguistic authority by making Leah an amanuensis, like Clara in *Basil,* it also reduces male power. William Kerby is a diminished version of William Collins: both are painters, yet the homely surname Kerby testifies to the drop in social status between the William of the *Memoirs* and this destitute artist, referred to by his wife pityingly (and with an unintentional pun) as "poor William" on the first page of her narrative (9). This "poorness" is underscored in comically hyperbolic terms during his wife's narrative: "poor William . . . looking so sickly and sad, with his miserable green shade" (17). At another point the husband and children are implicitly lumped together: "the children difficult to manage; William miserably despondent" (21). Yet, despite this pathos, William Kerby does share William Collins' artistic vision. Just as Collins portrayed his father in the *Memoirs* as studying the minutest details to record Nature's truth, so William Kerby claims that portrait painting is "nothing but a right reading of the externals of character recognizably presented to the view of others" (36). In fact, Kerby asks his sitters to tell stories so that he can read their characters correctly, a sequence which implies that fiction making is a form of the father's art.

In the frame narrative's chronology, however, the precondition for fiction making is the male artist's weakness. Kerby's artistic vision is obscured by a blinding that, as a symbolic castration, repeats the imagery of sight and blindness in *Basil.* This image of the blinded male artist, however, recalls a scene within the *Memoirs* themselves, where Collins remembers that William was afflicted near the end of his life by a similar "inflammation of the eyes," which also had a temporarily blinding effect and had to be treated in the same way as William Kerby's malady (II, 165-67).

Whereas William Kerby's situation echoes William Collins', Leah's diary is apparently inspired by one written by Harriet Collins. According to William Clarke, Harriet had shared with her son a diary based on her experiences as an artist's wife, and Collins discussed the possibility of its publication with Dickens, concluding that it would be necessary to "make a story to hang your characters and incidents on."[40] The extent to which Harriet's diary reemerges as Leah's, however, is ambiguous, since Leah's story seems vastly different (William Collins' eye problems came later in life and never reduced the family to the dire straits of the Kerbys). What is significant about Harriet Collins' contribution to the idea of the frame narrative, however, is how it causes Collins to take a role similar to Kerby's. In the frame narrative, Leah is originator of a literary idea for which (since her husband writes the stories) she gets only secondary credit as scribe, a position similar to that of Harriet Collins, who evidently inspired the plot of her son's frame narrative. The status of the mother's writing here recalls the descriptions of Collins' father's paintings in the *Memoirs,* which Collins heard from her though he does not acknowledge this fact, any more than he admits any debt to his mother in his preface to *After Dark* (where he claims that the stories are "entirely of my own imagining" [6]). Whatever the extent of Harriet's contribution to Collins' plot, then, his relation to his mother's writing embodies the anxiety about the male artist's feminine rivals that shapes the frame narrative.

Yet at the same time, the presence of a maternal voice—Leah's if not Harriet's—in the frame narrative enhances the artistic innovation of *After Dark* by replacing Kerby's incapacitated masculine art with an image for feminine art. A narrative strand in the leaves of Leah's diary—which are necessarily fragments broken off by her domestic duties and not completed pieces of writing—records the story of a bead purse that her daughter is sewing, under her supervision, as a present for the daughter of the benevolent doctor-patron who has helped them. The story of the bead purse becomes such a refrain in the entries of Leah's diary—first it is "getting on fast" (15), and then there is a momentary crisis about the steel rings and tassels needed to complete it—that Leah comments when it is done, "So much for the highly interesting history of the bead purse" (17). Leah intends the phrase "highly interesting history" to resound ironically, since she assumes this domestic history would bore anyone not involved in it. Yet this type of history, even if private and domesticated, has a literary significance. The history of the bead purse becomes, like Leah's journal itself, the story of a type of feminine narrative; a craft taught by a mother to a daughter and given to another young girl would seem to symbolize the transmission of creativity between women writers in such feminine genres as the female Gothic, with which Leah, who writes after dark, has already been associated.

Leah's image of netting the bead purse is repeated by Collins in his preface to the collection, where he claims, "I have taken some pains to string together the various stories contained in this Volume on a single thread of interest" (5). This parallel between his own creativity and feminine domestic art—a parallel already suggested by the title *After Dark*—echoes in his own narrative method in the book, since the structure of the collection, with story after story and stories within stories, weaves a multiplicity of voices in place of a strictly linear literary unity. This type of multivoice narrative, a more positive version of the fragmentation of narrative voice in *Basil* because it stresses coherence amid diversity rather than simply a failure of aesthetic unity, anticipates the series of narrators in such later Collins works as *The Woman in White* and *The Moonstone;* in these narratives women and working-class characters often have as significant a voice as do middle-class men.

Yet although it is tempting to read the feminization of the writer in *After Dark* as empowering both for Collins and for the female voices within his works, this feminization, as in *Basil,* still expresses an ambivalence about being an artist in the marketplace. That Leah helps her daughter net a purse for the daughter of a male patron emphasizes the distance in economic status between the two families, since the doctor's daughter would have more to put in the purse than would her own child. That a purse is an image for the woman's text, which we know to be a Gothic one, implies that the genre is itself a commodity: like a woman writer of sensation fiction, Leah hopes that the book bought by her other patrons, the reading audience, will be a popular one so as to garner the most money.

Moreover, read as a symbol for the female genitals, the purse conflates sexual and economic meanings to suggest that selling writing in the marketplace is a form of prostitution. The doctor, who abets the book project, hints at such a reading when he claims that Leah is worth her weight in gold and that she is "all ready to get into the bookseller's scales and prove it" (29). This image of his wife selling herself as well as her book reinforces the emasculation of William Kerby that is suggested not only by his blindness, but also by his wife's ingenuity at making the money he can no longer earn. Although Leah's scheme is formed in response to the doctor's worry that William will fret at "the prospect of sitting idle and being kept by his wife" (15), it strengthens her power within the household, although at the price of her symbolic prostitution in a system of exchange outside the home. Through this image of prostitution, Leah becomes a figure not only for the working woman but also for Victorian anxiety about that figure; as Leonore Davidoff and Catherine Hall have argued in *Family Fortunes,* by laboring outside the home the working woman threatened both domesticity and the class identity of bourgeois men, defined by their ability to provide for women and children.[41]

Although this image of Leah's selling herself for money reveals an anxiety about female economic autonomy, it more specifically targets the autonomy of the woman writer who usurps her husband's role as provider with her "ready pen" (33). The figure of the writer as prostitute, however, represents the degradation of male, as well as female, writing, as Catherine Gallagher argues when she identifies the image of "the author as whore" as one that is "disabling, empowering and central to nineteenth-century consciousness."[42] Although Gallagher, reading *Daniel Deronda,* focuses on attitudes about professional women writers in Victorian England, she claims that the image of prostitute, like that of the Jewish usurer, can also be applied to men: "the activities of authoring, of procuring illegitimate income, and of alienating oneself through prostitution seem particularly closely associated with one another in the Victorian period."[43] Especially since we can read Leah as a figure who is more closely aligned than her husband is with what Collins himself does—she writes for money and she embodies a new type of female Gothic—the prostitution image describes the position of the male writer in the marketplace: if a man is like a woman, it is because what Gayle Rubin calls "the traffic in women," or their sexual barter, becomes an apt metaphor for the Victorian male writer's economic vulnerability.[44]

At the same time that it echoes the image of the mother as harlot in *Antonina,* prostitution in *After Dark* is linked to the theme of declining paternal authority, and the waning power of male literary authority, that Collins had explored in earlier works. Gallagher claims that the figure of literary paternity is associated with the idea of the "procreative Word," unlike prostitution, which becomes an image for "the written word as an arbitrary and conventional sign multiplying unnaturally in the mere process of exchange."[45] Yet just as she also argues that the prostitution image could be "empowering" for the women writers who transform it into a figure for their newfound linguistic creativity, Collins' metaphors for writing in the marketplace are not sheerly negative. For one thing, Leah is associated with a new type of literary generativity. Although she begins her journal by asserting that she is happy she has no more children to feed (9), the book becomes her baby in that its conception, as she says, "originated with *me*" (22). In a domesticated version of Mary Shelley's command in the 1831 preface to *Frankenstein* to her "hideous progeny" to "go forth and prosper," Leah calls the book her "third child," which has "gone out from us on this summer's day, to seek its fortune in the world" (540).

Still, it is uncertain whether Leah's book-baby—which after all is Collins'—is a monster offspring or not. In his preface to *After Dark,* Collins uses the metaphor of procreation to describe his work:

> Let me, once for all, assure any readers who may honor me with their attention, that in this, and in all other cases, they may depend on the genuineness of my literary offspring. The little children of my brain

may be weakly enough, and may be sadly in want of a helping hand to aid them in their first attempts at walking on the stage of this great world; but, at any rate, they are not borrowed children. The members of my own literary family are indeed increasing so fast as to render the very idea of borrowing quite out of the question, and to suggest serious apprehension that I may not have done adding to the large book-population, on my own sole responsibility, even yet. (7)

For Collins to call his books "the little children of my brain" does not necessarily feminize him, since the metaphor attests to his masculine potency. (By stressing his originality, it certainly excludes his own mother as coauthor.) Yet Collins' paternal authority may, like William Kerby's, become diluted if he is unable to provide for his "weakly" children who are part of a vast array of books in the marketplace ("the large book-population") that multiply like a Malthusian vision of the lower classes.

In spite of Collins' protests to the contrary, this ceaseless multiplication of books suggests a kind of unoriginality, or repetition of meaning, caused by the need of the writer in the marketplace to produce a "numerous" family. Yet Collins' use at the beginning of the preface of Leah's image of stringing together threads implies a more positive and innovative version of literary creativity than does his image of literary paternity. Similarly, when the act of generating books within the narrative is associated with Leah's motherhood rather than with William's fatherhood, it signifies a revolutionary originality. Developing the image implicit in her description of how the idea for the book "flashed" upon her, Leah asks: "Did Friar Bacon long to dance when he lit the match and heard the first charge of gunpowder in the world go off with a bang" (25). The violence of this image underscores the inversion of gender roles that Leah's idea has brought about—she is the head of the household now—even as it likens the figure for the woman writer in the marketplace to the "great men" of which Friar Bacon is one (Leah also compares herself to Isaac Newton). Elsewhere, William admits that his wife's idea is "an ingenious idea, and a bold idea" (28). Rather than merely initiating a system of exchange in which signs are arbitrary, Leah's entry into the marketplace thus signifies the advent of radical new ideas.

"Sister Rose": Revolution and the Female Voice

Leah implies that her writing is a revolutionary innovation, and the longest story that her husband tells is a tale about the French Revolution entitled "Sister Rose." Although this story was originally published in *Household Words* in 1855, as the central tale in *After Dark* it reflects the gender and class anxieties expressed in the frame narrative and represents, through the displaced form of the historical narrative, the tensions in Collins' professional self-definition during the 1850s and 1860s.

In particular the tension between masculine professionalism and feminine writing is figured by the confusion between male and female voices in the telling of the story. Within the frame narrative Collins suggests that Leah's voice may overwhelm her husband's, an anxiety about women's writing that resurfaces later. Although William's voice succeeds Leah's as he introduces each story, the tale of Sister Rose is related to him by a woman, a sitter whom he calls the French Governess. In the introduction to "Sister Rose," William explains how he came to tell this feminine narrative after meeting the governess, an employee of an English family who had become a substitute mother to its motherless daughters. As he paints a picture of Mademoiselle as a gift for one of the daughters, who is moving to India, his sitter tells him the story of a woman she calls Sister Rose, whose likeness she wears in a miniature that she insists William reproduce in her own portrait. Although the story of Rose, who is now dead, takes place during the French Revolution, the governess herself is a living embodiment of revolutionary history, quoting *Candide* and mixing her narrative with "outbursts of passionate political declamation, on the extreme liberal side" (117).

That these political outbursts are not repeated within William's version of the governess' tale testifies to his attempt to modulate her voice by imposing his own on it. As he explains, he must modify Mademoiselle's words both because of her political remarks and because of her general manner of telling the tale in "the most fragmentary and discursive manner" (117). Whereas this fragmentary female speech recalls the fragmenting of conventional narrative coherence in the leaves of Leah's diary, William's attempt to retell the governess' tale by "rigidly adhering to the events of it exactly as they were related" (117) substitutes a masculine form of narrative for a feminine one. Yet since we know that Leah rewrites the words her husband repeats, the voice of the male artist is actually sandwiched between those of two women.

These complex concentric circles of narrative add several layers of irony to the tale of Sister Rose. The hidden voice of the female amanuensis undermines the male narrator's attempts to reassert the primacy of his voice over a woman's. Having been pushed to the periphery of the narrative, however, Leah's voice wields its power only from a distance, as does the voice of the governess herself.[46] This marginalization of the female voice is represented through the relation of the miniature of Sister Rose, the female subject of the tale, to the story she inspires. This miniature, bequeathed to the governess who was her "dearest friend" (113), recalls the picture of Caroline Beaufort in *Frankenstein* willed to Elizabeth Lavenza. As in Shelley's novel, a legacy transmitted from one woman to another is intercepted by a male figure who here repaints the miniature in his own portrait of the governess. This symbolic appropriation of the female voice by the male artist anticipates the struggle for primacy between male and female voices within the story itself.

The story that the French governess tells is not, as its title might imply, about a nun, but about a woman named Rose Danville, who is the sister of the major male character, Louis Trudaine, who promises to look after her at their dying mother's request. Trudaine, a scientist, even rejects an offer from the French Academy for an important position because he is concerned about Rose's mistreatment by her haughty aristocratic husband, Charles Danville. The story begins in 1789, on the verge of the outbreak of the revolution, and continues during the period just before the end of the Reign of Terror in 1794, when Danville, who resents Trudaine's influence over his sister, denounces him to the revolutionary tribunal. Unbeknown to Danville, however, the suspicious behavior of Trudaine and Rose that he has observed and intends to use as a way of revenging himself on his wife's brother represents their joint efforts to help Danville's mother, an unabashed royalist, escape to safety outside France. Although Trudaine and Rose are arrested and condemned, they are saved from the guillotine by a former servant of the Danvilles named Lomaque, who has become a major official in the secret police but retains a loyalty to Trudaine, whose father helped his own, and to Rose, who was once kind to him. In a final confrontation after the Terror, Trudaine denounces Danville, who is unwittingly about to commit bigamy because he assumes that his wife and brother-in-law perished during the revolution. When the full extent of Danville's treachery is revealed (he helped to convict Rose and Trudaine by pretending that he knew of the plot to save his mother and acted as a fervent patriot by informing on her rescuers), his mother rejects him and the father of the woman he was about to marry kills him in a duel. The story ends with Rose, Trudaine, and Lomaque—adopted by the grateful pair he has saved—living together as one family.

In its focus on an incestuously close relationship between a brother and a sister, this narrative is indebted most obviously to *Basil,* but also through that novel to *Frankenstein,* with its plot concerning the bond between Frankenstein and his sisterlike spouse, Elizabeth Lavenza. The figure of Lomaque also recalls both Frankenstein's monster and Mannion; his "wrinkled, haggard face" (142) is reminiscent of the seamed face of Shelley's monster, but Lomaque's ressentiment of his servile status determines his later allegiance to the revolution. Yet Lomaque is a revision of the kind of monstrous outcast embodied both by the monster and by Mannion because he domesticates

revolution, betraying the revolutionary government he serves to save a family. His situation reverses Mannion's because he saves the son of a man who had been kind to his father (rather than, like the earlier character, revenging himself on the son of a man who hadn't). Moreover, Lomaque is touched by the kindness Shelley's monster never receives: he helps Rose for no other reason than because she once kept a cup of coffee hot for him.

Lomaque, however, is not the only male character whose rebellion against the family is tamed, since Trudaine himself is a domesticated Frankenstein figure. Although he is an "amateur professor of the occult arts of chemistry" (127), whose research Danville sneeringly characterizes as a search for the "Elixir of Life," Trudaine is not, like Frankenstein, so much a figure for the revolutionary metaphysician as he is for an emergent bourgeois professionalism. His devotion to chemistry, which causes him to be courted by the French Academy, recalls Collins' description in the original preface to *Basil* of professional writers as those who "follow Literature as a study and respect it as a science" (I, xvii [1852]). Yet Trudaine, who claims that the best elixir of life is the "quiet heart" and "contented mind" he has found in his sister's company (127), abandons professional ambitions to live, like Basil, in the private world of women.

This decision, although it indicates the extent of Trudaine's allegiance to domesticity, is implicitly emasculating. Although Trudaine claims that he has learned to feel toward his orphan sister "more as a father than as a brother" (134), fulfilling his mother's deathbed promise—"Be all to her, Louis, that I have been" (145)—has placed him in a feminine role. His assumption of his mother's position, in fact, makes him like the French governess, who tells his sister's story and who is a "second mother" to the motherless daughters in her charge (108). The most dramatic way that Trudaine's association with the feminine effaces his career, however, is through his rescue from the guillotine. Lomaque borrows a chemical formula from Trudaine to erase the names of both brother and sister from the death list, an erasure that symbolizes how Trudaine's profession and his masculinity have been made into a blank. This blankness in turn links him with the femininity associated with absence and blankness through Rose, whose gentle self-effacement embodies an idealized femininity.

Yet, as in the female Gothic, the power of women is as terrifying to men as their powerlessness. Although Rose is terrorized by her marriage to a brutal aristocrat, the revolution that triumphs over the aristocracy liberates her from that marriage to transform her, albeit temporarily, into a symbol for the Terror itself. Her nervousness, a signifier for the female Gothic plot of imprisonment and claustrophobia that engulfs her, blossoms into a shrill and hysterical voice during her imprisonment and trial. Trudaine's arrest in her husband's presence causes Rose to resist her cruel husband openly for the first time, as she seizes his arm in the "recklessness of terror . . . with both hands— frail, trembling hands—that seemed suddenly nerved with all the strength of a man's. 'Come here—come here! I must and will speak to you!'" (174). The outbreak of both Rose's violence and her voice coincides with the eruption of a revolution associated with women as well as with figures for class ressentiment like Lomaque. At Rose's trial the major part of the audience are women: "all sitting together on forms, knitting, shirt-mending, and baby-linen-making, as coolly as if they were at home" (183).

While she is defending herself, Rose's voice resembles that of this female audience, which often shrilly interrupts the proceedings. Although her brother does not want her to talk and further incriminate herself (even claiming that her efforts to speak reflect a temporary madness), Rose becomes an image for the revolutionary virago as she speaks over his voice, which had momentarily "overpowered" her own (190): "Her hair lay tangled on her shoulders; her face had assumed a strange fixedness; her gentle blue eyes, so soft and tender at all other times, were lit up wildly. A low hum of murmured curiosity and admiration broke from the women of the audience" (190). This female audience even clears the way for Rose's voice: "'Let her speak! let her speak!' exclaimed the women" (191). Earlier the "winning gentleness of her voice" (166-67) had been described as Rose's most remarkable feature, but that voice now is conflated with that of the Terror.

After the trial, however, Rose is silenced, "her head sunk on her bosom, her hands crossed listlessly on her lap" (206). Collins ascribes this silence to "that spirit of resignation, which is the courage of women in all great emergencies" and which now seems like "the one animating spirit that fed the flame of life within her" (213-14). This transformation of Rose's feminine flaming eloquence into feminine silent resignation prepares for her brother's assuming the role of her savior: she does not even know of Lomaque's plan to save their lives until some time afterward. This attempt to contain the female power associated with the revolution is mirrored by the way the revolutionary women themselves are relegated to signifiers of domesticity. Although the female audience seem to be monstrous mothers as they sew baby linen at the revolutionary tribunal, they are horrified by Danville's boast that he would inform on his own mother: "the fiercest woman-republican on the benches joined cause at last with the haughtiest woman-aristocrat on the platform. Even in that sphere of direst discords . . . the one touch of Nature preserved its old eternal virtue, and roused the mother-instinct which makes the whole world kin" (201).

This invocation of a universal feminine nature dovetails with the mission of the journal that first serialized the story, *Household Words,* which similarly valorized domesticity as the ideology that, although bourgeois in origin, nonetheless spoke to and united all classes. Still, in "Sister Rose," even the "mother-instinct" that allies "the fiercest woman-republican" with the "haughtiest woman-aristocrat" escapes from the boundaries of a conventional domesticity to threaten men. Besides the unnervingly dangerous makers of baby linen at the trial (predecessors of Dickens' *tricoteuses*),[47] the story's figure for a disruptive rather than an angelic mother is Madame Danville, Rose's mother-in-law, disapprovingly called "that passionate woman" by Trudaine (145). Madame Danville's voice, however, is silenced by terror: paralyzed with fear at the end of the story when she spots Rose, whom she thought dead, "She neither spoke nor moved" (255). She is stricken by the evidence of her son's perfidy with an illness that "affects her mind more than her body" (260), a mental imbalance that recalls the hysterical near-madness that Trudaine ascribes to Rose when she wants to speak at the trial.

This diagnosis of femininity as disease associates masculinity with the diagnostic power of reason. Unlike Basil, who could not see, discriminate, or know, Trudaine, for all his association with feminine blankness, is nonetheless possessed of a knowledge that saves both himself and his sister from the guillotine. Similarly, the crabbed police agent Lomaque, despite the belatedness for which he castigates himself—"too late to speak—too late to act—too late to do anything!" (136)—becomes the tale's figure for detection and plotting, uncovering the "impenetrable mystery" of Madame Danville's escape and planning Trudaine and Rose's. The rise of this figure for male detection, Collins' most important narrative innovation and one he would develop in such later novels as *The Woman in White* and *The Moonstone,* represents an attempt to reassert male authority by emphasizing men's analytical power and their ability not only to be differentiated from, but also to read and control the feminine. In "Sister Rose," however, this strategy is only partially successful, for though it silences Rose, both Trudaine and Lomaque (whose "weakness of the eyes" suggests the tenuous nature of his reading skill and recalls the weakened figure of William Kerby) end their days with Rose in a domestic obscurity that banishes history.

By effecting what by now seems to be Collins' trademark ending—a containment both of female power and of history—"Sister Rose" apparently invokes revolution in order to extinguish it. This pattern is emphasized by two of the tales that surround "Sister Rose" in *After Dark,* which are even more conservative parables about the French Revolution. In "A Terribly Strange Bed," the first story of the collection and one of Collins' most extraordinary mystery tales, an Englishman is almost robbed and murdered by a group of charlatans who arrange for the canopy of a bed to descend upon him in his sleep—an image that suggests sexual suffocation. It is telling that one of the architects of the murderous plan is a veteran of Napoleon's army, and hence a relic of the threat the French Revolution posed to the English. (Not surprisingly, it is the English narrator's skill at detecting the danger of his situation that saves him.) Although "Gabriel's Marriage," the second story after "Sister Rose," is told by a female narrator, it similarly celebrates the Catholic reaction against the French Revolution in a plot about the reconciliation of fathers and sons. The mingling of different types of discourse about revolution in these tales mirrors the mixture of male and female voices in the frame narrative and tales like "Sister Rose."

In spite of her silencing, however, the figure of Sister Rose in some sense bridges the ideological gaps within *After Dark* and, particularly, within the story that bears her name. The pun implicit in Rose's name—she rises from the dead to confront her oppressive husband—suggests that the ghostly presence of revolution in *After Dark* persists despite its attempted erasure. William Marshall sees Rose's apparent resurrection as an example of the theme of "the return to life of those presumed by someone to be dead," which repeats itself continually in Collins' fiction, most famously in *The Woman in White*, where Laura Fairlie must reestablish her legal identity after her double is buried in her place.[48] In "Sister Rose," this resurrection of the dead is a return of the repressed, since Rose's story, told by the French governess, provokes a resurrection both of feminine power and of revolutionary history.

As if haunted by these ghosts, William Kerby ends his retelling of Rose's story by confessing that he finds it difficult to end:

> I linger over these final particulars with a strange unwillingness to separate myself from them, and give my mind to other thoughts. Perhaps the persons and events that have occupied my attention for so many nights past have some peculiar interest for me that I cannot analyze. Perhaps the labor and time which this story has cost me have especially endeared it to my sympathies, now that I have succeeded in completing it. However that may be, I have need of some resolution to part at last with Sister Rose, and return, in the interests of my next and Fourth Story, to English ground. (263-64)

As if he finds the spell of Rose's femininity particularly compelling, William admits to needing masculine "resolution" in order to leave her story. The trancelike hold of the story, however, paralyzes even his ability to choose another to tell, precipitating his wife to make that decision "on her own responsibility" (264). Since we know that his wife is writing down the story of Sister Rose and that the "labor" in crafting the story is partly hers, this resurrection of a female voice renders

ironic both Kerby's relief at returning from the foreign ground of the story to comfortable English safeness, and the attempt within the story to contain female power.

Yet William Kerby's lingering over the story of Sister Rose is important not just for the resurrection of female power that this moment implies. That William claims he cannot analyze the attraction the story has for him suggests that he refuses to do so, possibly because the narrative is compelling for him as an artist who has (albeit unwillingly) entered the marketplace. As a story that, through Lomaque, contains a narrative about class ressentiment, "Sister Rose" might be a compelling tale for a male artist who is economically marginalized. The juxtaposition of a historical fiction about revolution with the frame narrative, which so obsessively figures the blurring of gender and class boundaries in the marketplace, underscores how "Sister Rose" figures the ambiguous status of the Victorian male writer. The Gothic governs this symbolic narrative: William ponders on the story that he, like his wife, has told after dark—"for so many nights past." The writing of Gothic again represents the ideological choices available to the male writer. Within the story Rose's voice, like Leah's, figures kinds of subversive feminine narratives, yet if the figure for the male artist (Trudaine or William) does not identify himself with this revolutionary voice, he nonetheless resembles women in their economic and social vulnerability. When Leah's voice resumes the frame narrative at the end of *After Dark,* she does not describe the restoration of her husband's power with the cure of his blindness. Instead she reveals a dependency on the marketplace that causes the narrative to end in a limbo only emphasized by the final reference to Gothic obscurity: "Oh, Public! Public! it all depends now upon you . . . our future way in this hard world is to be smoothed for us at the outset, if you will only accept a poor painter's stories which his wife has written down for him After Dark!" (543-44).[49]

Notes

[1] Review of *The Woman in White,* by Wilkie Collins, *Saturday Review,* 25 August 1860, in *Wilkie Collins: The Critical Heritage,* ed. Norman Page (1974; reprint, London: Routledge, 1985), 84-85.

[2] Ibid., 84.

[3] Ibid., 83.

[4] Ibid., 85.

[5] As realism became more firmly established as a critical standard in the second half of the nineteenth century, Dickens, like Collins, was criticized for the implausibility of his characters. See, e.g., George H. Ford,

Dickens and His Readers: Aspects of Novel-Criticism since 1836 (Princeton: Princeton University Press, 1955), 129-55.

[6] Wilkie Collins, *The Moonstone,* ed. Anthea Trodd (Oxford: Oxford University Press, 1982), 420.

[7] Alexander Pope, "Epistle to a Lady," in *The Poems of Alexander Pope: A One-Volume Edition of the Twickenham Text with Selected Annotations,* ed. John Butt (New Haven: Yale University Press, 1963), 560, ll. 1-2. Referring to this poem to condemn Collins' supposed inability to create character seems to have been standard procedure for his critics. An article in the *Westminster Review* claimed ("to slightly alter Pope's words") that: "Nothing so true, as what you once let fall, / His novels have no character at all; / Matter too soft a lasting mark to bear, / And best distinguished by black, brown, or fair." "Belles Lettres," *Westminster Review* (American ed.), n.s., 86 (July 1866): 127.

[8] Review of *The Woman in White,* in *Critical Heritage,* ed. Page, 84.

[9] See Walter Phillips, *Dickens, Reade, and Collins: Sensation Novelists* (1919; reprint, New York: Russell and Russell, 1962), particularly chap. 2, "The Background of Sensationalism," 37-108.

[10] Review of *Basil,* in *Critical Heritage,* ed. Page, 53.

[11] Winifred Hughes, *The Maniac in the Cellar: Sensation Novels of the 1860s* (Princeton: Princeton University Press, 1980), 39.

[12] H. D. Mansel, "Sensation Novels," *Quarterly Review* (American ed.), n.s., 113, no. 226 (1863): 252.

[13] "Belles Lettres," *Westminster Review* (American ed.), n.s., 86 (July 1866): 126.

[14] "Our Female Sensation Novelists," *Living Age* 78 (1863): 352. This essay originally appeared in the *Christian Remembrancer* in 1863.

[15] [Margaret Oliphant], "Sensation Novels," *Blackwood's Edinburgh Magazine* 91 (May 1862): 565.

[16] The writer of the essay "Our Female Sensation Novelists" divides the reader's body into two oppositional and implicitly feminized sites: "Sensation writing is an appeal to the nerves rather than to the heart" (p. 352). This symbolic map pits the heart, a synecdoche for domesticated sentiment, against the nerves, the neurasthenic impulses that similarly define femininity in the language of Victorian biological determinism, but which are associated with the disruptive side of women's nature—hysteria, madness, and sexuality—rather than with the domestic.

[17] Jonathan Loesberg, "The Ideology of Narrative Form in Sensation Fiction," *Representations* 13 (Winter 1986): 115-38.

[18] Ibid., 118-19.

[19] Critical attention has recently been directed at the subversive nature of sensation fiction; see, e.g., Thomas F. Boyle, *Black Swine in the Sewers of Hampstead: Beneath the Surface of Victorian Sensationalism* (New York: Viking, 1989). For the gender ideology of sensation narratives, see Elaine Showalter, *A Literature of Their Own* (Princeton: Princeton University Press, 1977), 153-81; Hughes, *Maniac in the Cellar,* 106-36; and Elizabeth Helsinger, Robin Lauterbach Sheets, and William Veeder, *Literary Issues,* vol. 3. of *The Woman Question: Society and Literature in Britain and America, 1837-1883* (Chicago: University of Chicago Press, 1983), 122-45.

[20] See Hughes, *Maniac in the Cellar,* 55-72, for how the sensation novel replaces the dialectics of melodrama with moral ambiguity. Keith Brown Reierstad examines this kind of ambiguity in Collins' heroines in "Innocent Indecency: The Questionable Heroines of Wilkie Collins' Sensation Novels," *Victorian Institute Journal* 9 (1980-81): 57-69.

[21] Respectively, by Phillips, *Dickens, Reade, and Collins,* 129; Sue Lonoff, *Wilkie Collins and His Victorian Readers: A Study in the Rhetoric of Authorship* (New York: AMS Press, 1982), 18; and Keith Reierstad, "The Demon in the House: or, The Domestication of Gothic in the Novels of Wilkie Collins" (Ph.D. diss., University of Pennsylvania, 1976), 131.

[22] Lonoff, *Wilkie Collins and His Victorian Readers,* 18.

[23] Emile Forgues, "William Wilkie Collins," *Revue des deux mondes,* 15 November 1855, in *Critical Heritage,* ed. Page, 66.

[24] Nuel Pharr Davis, *The Life of Wilkie Collins* (Urbana: University of Illinois Press, 1956), 120; for Forgues' comparison, see *Critical Heritage,* ed. Page, 63.

[25] Wilkie Collins, "A Shy Scheme," *Household Words* 17 (March 1858): 315; quoted in Davis, *Life of Wilkie Collins,* 70.

[26] Julia Swindells, *Victorian Writing and Working Women: The Other Side of Silence* (Minneapolis: University of Minnesota Press, 1985), particularly 45-113. N. N. Feltes locates the publication of *Middlemarch* as a case study of the difficulty with which a woman writer defined herself as a professional in "One Round of a Long Ladder: Gender, Profession, and the Production of *Middlemarch,*" chap. 3 in his *Modes of Production of Victorian Novels* (Chicago: University of Chicago Press, 1986), 36-56.

[27] See Swindell's discussion, "The Gentleman's Club, Literature," in *Victorian Writing and Working Women,* 91-113.

[28] Philips, *Dickens, Reade, and Collins,* 109.

[29] For an illuminating survey of the working friendship between Dickens and Collins, see Sue Lonoff, "Charles Dickens and Wilkie Collins," *Nineteenth-Century Fiction* 35 (September 1980): 150-70, and her *Wilkie Collins and His Victorian Readers,* 42-55.

[30] See Margaret Oliphant's discussion of *Great Expectations* as a sensation novel in "Sensation Novels," 574-80.

[31] Charles Dickens to Wilkie Collins in *Critical Heritage,* ed. Page, 49.

[32] James M. Brown, *Dickens: Novelist in the Marketplace* (London: Macmillan, 1982), 41.

[33] Eliza Lynn Linton, quoted in Lonoff, *Wilkie Collins and His Victorian Readers,* 42.

[34] Charles Dickens to W. H. Wills, 24 September 1858, *Charles Dickens as Editor: Being Letters Written by Him to William Henry Wills, His Sub-editor,* ed. R. C. Lehmann (London: Smith, Elder, 1912), 247.

[35] Lonoff, *Wilkie Collins and His Victorian Readers,* 50-51.

[36] See Kirk H. Beetz, "Wilkie Collins and *The Leader,*" *Victorian Periodicals Review* 15 (1982): 20-29, for Collins' association with the journal, and also Anne Lohrli, "Wilkie Collins and *Household Words,*" *Victorian Periodicals Review* 15 (1982): 118-19. Both articles are useful for discussing Collins' early journalistic experience, and Beetz in particular provides valuable evidence about Collins' politics.

[37] Beetz, "Wilkie Collins and *The Leader,*" 25.

[38] One of the reasons that Collins left the *Leader* illustrates this point. As Beetz describes it, Collins quarreled with Edward Pigott over a satire on religion that the journal had published. In a letter to Pigott, Collins proclaimed, "You have made your confession of political faith (and I agree in it, as you know)—but you have made no confession of religious faith" (quoted in Beetz, ibid., 24). Beetz reads this letter as proof of Collins' Christianity that refutes the common view that he was an atheist, or at least an agnostic. Yet the letter sheds light not only on Collins' religious beliefs but also (more significantly in my view) on his ambivalence about being associated with radical politics. Although he parenthetically declares his sympathy with Pigott's socialist

views, Collins balks at the journal's identification with the religious skepticism attributed to radicals.

[39] Wilkie Collins, preface to *After Dark,* vol. 19 of *The Works of Wilkie Collins* (New York: Peter Fenelon Collier, [1900]), 5-6. All references will be to this edition and are cited by page in the text.

[40] William M. Clarke, *The Secret Life of Wilkie Collins* (London: Allison and Busby, 1988), 78.

[41] Leonore Davidoff and Catherine Hall, *Family Fortunes: Men and Women of the English Middle Class, 1780-1850* (Chicago: University of Chicago Press, 1987), especially pt. 2, "Economic Structure and Opportunity," 193-315.

[42] Catherine Gallagher, "George Eliot and *Daniel Deronda:* The Prostitute and the Jewish Question," in *Sex, Politics, and Science in the Nineteenth-Century Novel,* ed. Ruth Yeazell, Selected Papers from the English Institute, 1983-84, n.s., no. 10 (Baltimore: Johns Hopkins University Press, 1986), 40.

[43] Gallagher, "George Eliot and *Daniel Deronda,*" 43. As she says: "The author . . . does not go to market as a respectable producer with an alienable commodity, but with *himself* or *herself* as commodity. The last half of the eighteenth century is the period both when the identity of text and self begins to be strongly asserted and when the legal basis for commodifying texts (as distinct from books) comes into being in copyright law. This combination puts writers in the marketplace in the position of selling themselves, like whores" (43).

[44] Gayle Rubin, "The Traffic in Women: Notes on the 'Political Economy' of Sex," in *Toward an Anthropology of Women,* ed. Rayna R. Reiter (New York: Monthly Review Press, 1975), 157-210.

[45] Gallagher, "George Eliot and *Daniel Deronda,*" 40.

[46] The one moment where Leah draws attention to her own voice in the stories simultaneously undercuts its authority. At the end of "A Terribly Strange Bed," there appears a "note by Mrs. Kerby" in which she claims that she cannot resist mentioning the incident that caused her husband to remember the tale. After supplying this information, she says that William thought it "scarcely worth while to mention such a trifle in anything so important as a book": "I cannot venture, after this, to do more than slip these lines in modestly at the end of the story. If the printer should notice my few last words, perhaps he may not mind the trouble of putting them into some out-of-the-way corner" (72).

[47] Henry J. W. Milley examines "Sister Rose" as an influence on *A Tale of Two Cities* in "Wilkie Collins and 'A Tale of Two Cities,'" *Modern Language Review* 34, no. 4 (1939): 525-34.

[48] William Marshall, *Wilkie Collins* (New York: Twayne, 1970), 42.

[49] The frame narrative of Collins' short-story collection *The Queen of Hearts* (1859) emphasizes the writer's dependency on the audience. Three elderly brothers, each a retired professional (clergyman, doctor, lawyer), have no idea how to entertain their young and fashionable niece, who is foisted on them for some time as an odd condition of her father's will. Their Scheherazade-like plan to tell her stories culled from their past figures the audience of the professional writer (the brothers are very proud of their seriousness) as a kind of demanding female despot, a Queen of Hearts.

FEMINIST CRITICISM

Jeanne B. Elliott (essay date 1976)

SOURCE: "A Lady to the End: The Case of Isabel Vane," in *Victorian Studies,* Vol. XIX, No. 3, March, 1976, pp. 329-44.

[In the essay that follows, Elliott evaluates the ways in which the attitudes and influences of a period are revealed through its popular literature. Focusing particularly on East Lynne *by Mrs. Henry Wood, Elliott discusses the presence of a desire for change in women's roles in the domestic novels of the 1800s.]*

Many of the best-known novels of the Victorian period are distinguished by a concern for the problems of women's duties and spheres of action. Perhaps the most brilliant exposition of the conflict between the established patterns of domestic life and an intense if formless yearning for wider horizons can be found in the struggles of George Eliot's ardent heroines, Dorothea Brooke, Romola, and Maggie Tulliver. Also memorable, though depicted on a less elevated scale, are the young women of Anthony Trollope's Parliamentary series, such as Alice Vavasour and Glencora Palliser, who find themselves in a state of decorous rebellion against convention because of their desire to participate in the world beyond the confines of the home. Meredith and Hardy, too, involved themselves with the debate, though their interests turned to special problems of the relationship between the sexes. Clearly one of the significant topics of the day concerned the role of women in contemporary life, and the nineteenth-century novel, with its strong ethical and social emphasis, responded in depth to a controversy that was agitating the world of the intellectuals as well as the middle-class reading public.

Although the richest insights into woman's nature and destiny naturally occur in the major novels, it is to the lesser fiction of the period that the modern reader turns for a direct knowledge of the underlying moral assumptions that determined the philosophical climate in which the debate on "the woman question" flourished. The popular novel is an excellent source for ascertaining contemporary value systems. A book which sells in quantity almost invariably displays a structure of belief congenial to a majority of its readers; it speaks directly of ideas so fundamental that they are seldom discussed openly even in serious fiction. Thus almost any Victorian best-seller provides for later generations an almost inexhaustible storehouse of information about the beliefs and attitudes which were widely accepted at the time it was written. In no area of investigation is the Victorian popular novel richer in allusive materials than in its presentation of the conflict between the burgeoning aspirations of women and the demands of the domestic ideal.

Among nineteenth-century best-sellers, none surpassed in popularity *East Lynne* by Mrs. Henry Wood. Published in 1861, it became the literary success of the decade, selling over a million copies by the end of the century.[1] The reasons for *East Lynne*'s success are clear; the author offers her readers a reliable combination of humor, mystery, mother love, sin, repentance, and death. But the blend of sensationalism and sermonizing which is Mrs. Wood's trademark should not obscure the extent to which her novel provides, on a different level, an insight into the same problem of "woman's sphere" which occupied George Eliot and Anthony Trollope. Mrs. Wood presents the conventional response to questions which her great contemporaries considered in a far more profound and searching manner. Herself the daughter of a successful Shropshire manufacturer, Mrs. Wood wrote for the wives and daughters of the newly prosperous and upwardly mobile mercantile classes. In every way she shared the ethical assumptions and moral convictions of her readers, and she always directed her sensational plots to the ends of traditional morality. In *East Lynne* the present-day reader may see in pure form many of the existing stereotypes of Victorian femininity, and understand more fully the nature of the society which created them.

East Lynne is one of the few popular novels of the nineteenth century still remembered today, at least by title. At first glance, it appears to demonstrate little concern with the deeper social issues of the day; the aristocratic heroine, Isabel Vane, and her middle-class husband, Archibald Carlyle, are involved in a situation as improbable as it is harrowing. But upon closer consideration, the difficulties which beset the heroine show a very real connection with the problems facing any woman of the educated and leisured classes. Lady Isabel Vane confronts a not uncommon Victorian dilemma: she is caught between the demands of her own nature and the rigid standards imposed upon her sex and class. In brief, her tragic fate (and it would have appeared tragic to almost all of the contemporary readers of the book) arises from her inability to live up to the ideal of the Lady. *East Lynne,* in fact, may stand as a kind of overstated summary of the immense Victorian problem of Woman versus Lady.

In *East Lynne* the lesson to be learned from the downfall of the unfortunate Isabel is emphasized for the modern reader—probably without the author's conscious intent—by the fact that the heroine is a Lady in both senses of the word. Isabel Vane begins her life as the adored daughter of the Earl of Mount Severn, and although she closes her unhappy existence as the disguised and disfigured governess, Madame Vine, to Mrs. Wood (and no doubt to her reading public) she is Lady Isabel to the end.

Much of the power of *East Lynne* as a novel lies in its dramatization of the whole ideal of the Lady, in its general application to any woman of gentle birth who embodied the desired attributes of Maiden, Wife and Mother, of course in the proper order. The theory of the Lady exerted a profound influence in creating the self-image of the typical Victorian woman, even though she might not belong to the "gentle classes."[2] The notion of "ladylike behavior" was central in determining the social and emotional climate in which the Victorian daughter, wife, or mother worked out her destiny and chose her social role—at least insofar as a choice was available to her.

Thus *East Lynne* presents in dramatic and highly-colored form an extended parable of the problems of the gentlewoman in Victorian England. In Lady Isabel every Victorian female reader could encounter an idealized version of herself and a dramatic view of her own conflicts. In the role of Archibald Carlyle, every middle-class person, male or female, could read a justification and an idealization of the husband's role as protector, arbiter, guide, and judge. And of course many Victorian wives found in the extravagant drama of Lady Isabel's ill-omened choices a clear-cut moral lesson and a personal warning. Mrs. Wood makes clear her intent to produce a cautionary tale with an aside to the reader on the occasion of Lady Isabel's first attack of remorse after her flight with her seducer:

> Lady—wife—mother! should you ever be tempted to abandon your home so will you awaken! Whatever trials may be the lot of your married life, though they may magnify themselves to your crushed spirit as beyond the endurance of woman to bear, *resolve* to bear them; fall down upon your knees and pray to be enabled to bear them; . . . bear unto death rather than forfeit your fair name and your good conscience! for be assured that the alternative, if you rush on to it, will be found far worse than death![3]

For any thoughtful reader of Victorian fiction, it is perhaps unnecessary to repeat at length the immense importance of social class in the novel. Hero and heroine were typically of gentle birth; subordinate roles might be assigned to the working class, to servants, or to other representatives of the "respectable poor."[4] A few specimens of the aristocracy could be added to give a becoming gloss to the narrative, with a certain number of them designed as cautionary types, representative of the bad old Regency days, and others among the group amiable and high-principled, as a tribute to the present Queen. Nevertheless, the personages of the central plot were almost always middle class, in ideals if not in origin. And it was among the middle classes of Victorian England that the ideal of the Lady was taken most seriously.[5]

The ideal of the Lady, like most powerful and influential stereotypes, is easier to discuss than to define. In the 1860s particularly, the term seems to have been accepted unself-consciously, and much of the analysis of its meaning belongs to later dates. Most writers agree, however, in a cluster of indispensable traits, without which no woman could approach the ideal.[6] By definition, of course, the Lady was of gentle birth, and as a direct consequence of her membership in the leisure classes, she had a role, but not an occupation. In an age which exalted work as an anodyne for most evils, personal and social, the Lady was permitted no work outside the home, and in the more extreme versions of the ideal, was barred from any fatiguing or demeaning activity within it. She was nearly always required to be self-disciplined and self-contained to an extent which the modern woman would regard as repressed. In dress and demeanour she was modest; she was restrained from any ostentatious or flamboyant behavior, even in the society of her equals. Inevitably she was patient and long-suffering, passive under injustice and unfair treatment.

The mind of the Lady was supposed to be as underdeveloped as her emotions. Although a bit of polite learning was permitted some of the more fortunate daughters of the upper middle classes (languages, music, art, and literature seem to have been acceptable), any young woman who aspired to lady-like status was well advised to remain ignorant of Latin and Greek, science, business, and finance. Above all, the Lady was supposed to be sexually neuter: not only ignorant of physiology (at least before marriage) but also largely devoid of sexual drives. She was expected to love her chosen husband, but it must be assumed that it was a selfless and disinterested love capable of persuading her to overlook, for his sake, the distasteful nature of the act of procreation.[7] Frequently, though not inevitably, the ideal of the Lady included a degree of physical frailty. Some of Trollope's heroines enjoy radiant health without forfeiting their status as Ladies, and none of them is given to undue languishing. In general, however, it is clear that a degree of physical weakness was never unbecoming in a Lady, and in certain circles might be regarded as highly desirable.

Against the background of this widely accepted ideal, Isabel Vane, in the opening chapters of *East Lynne,* appears to be the embodiment of the perfect Lady as well as the perfect heroine. She comes from an aristocratic background, and is the only daughter of a titled family. She has been educated in a manner befitting her station, with the full range of elegant accomplishments demanded by the standards of the day. She plays the piano with considerable skill, sings beautifully, and speaks excellent French. The sweetness and charm of her manner impress all observers. She is devoted to her father, charitable and benevolent to those in need, and displays a sincere and commendable piety. Her beauty is described in the quasi-religious terms frequently used by Victorian writers who supported the sentimentalized ideal of domestic virtue that received its apotheosis in Coventry Patmore's *The Angel in the House* (1862). Isabel is full of generous impulses (though she has no money of her own) and demonstrates a proper awareness of her obligations to her social inferiors. Even her rival, Barbara Hare, finds no fault with Isabel's behavior and admits that she has the dress and demeanour of a Lady (part I, chap. 7). Any nineteenth-century reader would immediately recognize her as the Innocent Maiden, the first phase of the Lady. If it were not for Mrs. Wood's rather heavy-handed hints, (part I, chap. 1 and 2) it would be logical to assume that anyone fortunate enough to begin in life with such a range of advantages would certainly undergo a natural transformation into the two subsequent phases of the Lady, namely, the Devoted Wife and the Dedicated Mother.

With Isabel Vane's marriage to Archibald Carlyle, she moves from her relatively simple role as Maiden to grapple (unsuccessfully, as it turns out) with the problems inherent in fulfilling as a mature woman the duties of the Lady. As a modern observer notes, "Marriage could often prove a sexual and emotional disaster for those trained to be affectionate, yet asexual and mentally blank."[8] What is there in Isabel's situation that leads to the failure of her marriage and brings Isabel herself to a fate that most Victorian women would have regarded, in the much-battered phrase, as worse than death? Since Isabel has begun her marriage as the perfect Maiden, what goes wrong?

The answer appears in *East Lynne* on two distinct levels, one stated directly by the author and the other apparent only to the reader who analyzes the implications of the narrative. The overt reason is Isabel's jealousy of her husband's frequent meetings with Barbara Hare, who was in love with Archibald before his marriage. In fact, Mrs. Wood creates a typical nineteenth-century subplot to account for the extended conferences between the blameless Archibald and the virtuous Miss Hare: her brother, Richard, has been falsely accused of a murder, and only Barbara believes in his innocence enough to seek legal counsel. However, a more significant answer appears below the surface of the novel as Mrs. Wood creates a detailed picture of the married life of the Carlyles. We discover that poor Isabel is beginning to suffer for the elegant education that has made her in every sense of the word a real Lady. Unlike some contemporary heroines of middle-class origin, she finds herself in difficulty not from aspiring above her station, but by acting out the role to which she was born. She strives in a literal fashion to live up to the demands of the Victorian ideal of the Lady as Wife and Mother, and the emotional strain becomes too great for her.[9] Isabel's frustration with her social environment and the demands of her domestic situation create the central conflict in *East Lynne,* and her injudicious solution to her problem generates the pathetic ending so much admired by nineteenth-century critics. For the modern reader the improbable and lugubrious ending may be less rewarding than Mrs. Wood's analysis of a mid-Victorian marriage.

Mrs. Wood, in her scenes of domestic life at East Lynne, presents a revealing picture of the circumscribed existence of a woman who takes the ideal of the Lady with complete seriousness. First of all, Isabel Carlyle has no occupation. Her situation is more encompassed by ennui than that of most women of her station. She does not direct her own servants, order the family dinner, or even choose her personal clothing. Not for her is the command of an extensive staff of domestics, which Mrs. Isabella Beeton in her *Book of Household Management* likens to the generalship of an army. East Lynne is run by Archibald Carlyle's overbearing half-sister, Cornelia, who firmly pushes Isabel out of the control of her own establishment. On the morning after she and Archibald return from their wedding journey, Isabel confesses, "I don't think I know anything about housekeeping" (part I, chap. 15). From that moment onward all important decisions are made by Miss Carlyle. In the next few months, Isabel earns Miss Corny's enmity and contempt because of her ineptness in simple household tasks, such as the "plain sewing" which the latter's idea of domestic economy makes mandatory (part I, chap. 17). Contemporary readers might have remembered the warning of Mrs. Ellis, writing in 1839, to "avoid, as far as you can do so with prudence . . . any very close contact with your husband's nearest relatives" (Ellis, *Women,* p. 23). But no doubt the Earl of Mount Severn had not considered Mrs. Ellis required reading for his aristocratic daughter.

In addition to her lack of occupation, Lady Isabel finds herself severely limited in her opportunities for social life within the restricted circle of the village of West Lynne. As the wife of a country lawyer, lacking any fortune of her own, Lady Isabel is cut off from the fashionable upper-class world into which she was born. She has no near relatives and did not attend a girls' school, at which she might have initiated friendships which would continue after her marriage. According to the custom of the time, the Lady could not mingle socially with her inferiors, except by way of opening a bazaar or ornamenting a church festival in a spirit of graceful condescension. Her visiting circle must be restricted to family, old friends, and the wives of her husband's associates. Archibald Carlyle, though educated at Rugby and Oxford, dislikes fashionable society and most of his business involves the farmers and tradesmen of the immediate area. Thus Isabel is thrown more and more into the company of her unsympathetic sister-in-law, and cut off from any opportunity for friendship with other women of her own age and class.

The only adults whom Isabel sees on a regular basis are the servants. Joyce, who functions as a kind of superior nursemaid, becomes devoted to Isabel, but because of the restrictions imposed upon the conduct of a Lady, Isabel cannot confide in her. This situation is particularly unfortunate, because Joyce is one of the few persons who recognizes the difficulties of Lady Isabel's existence. Furthermore, in the class structure of the day, a servant cannot go directly to her master and call his attention to his wife's unhappiness. It is only after Isabel has finally fled from her home, that Joyce, believing her mistress is dead, pours out her feelings to the shocked husband.

> "I say she has been driven to it. She has not been allowed to indulge a will of her own, poor thing, since she came to East Lynne; in her own house she has been less free than any one of her servants. . . . All these years she has been crossed and put upon; everything, in short, but beaten . . . and she has borne it all in silence, like a patient angel. . . . "
>
> (part II, chap. 9).

And of course as the Perfect Lady, Isabel has not dared to complain of her sister-in-law's tyranny.

In viewing the domestic difficulties of Lady Isabel, it is interesting to speculate whether her problems were created by particular circumstances, or whether they might be typical of Victorian wives who aspired to be Ladies. Considerable contemporary evidence suggests that the problems of boredom and limited social horizons must have been widespread. Mrs. Ellis found discontent more prevalent than it had been a decade earlier. "By far the greater portion of the young ladies (for they are no longer *women*) of the present day, are distinguished by a morbid listlessness of mind and body" (Ellis, *Women,* p. 15). As an antidote she prescribes a vigorous course of domestic duties, but then Mrs. Ellis opposed the growing cult of the Lady in all of her books of advice. The fact that she felt obliged to denounce it with such incessant energy suggests the extent to which it had permeated all ranks of society.

In another way, Lady Isabel faces a problem common to her middle-class contemporaries. She lacked money,

and so did the majority of Victorian wives, even those from relatively affluent families. Not until 1870 with the Married Woman's Property Act did the law guarantee a wife's right to her own earnings, and secure to her use any inheritance she might receive, as well as money gifts of more than two hundred pounds. Up to that date nearly all women of the middle class were dependent upon fathers or husbands for a household allowance and sufficient money to meet personal needs. However, it should be noted that most women of Lady Isabel's background and station would have possessed money in their own right, and in all probability their control of it would have been protected by a marriage settlement. This important preliminary to upper-class marriages was a contract between the future husband and the bride's family, reserving certain property for the exclusive use of the wife, frequently with the stipulation that it should pass, in event of her death, directly to her children and not to her husband. Needless to say, Isabel has no such safeguard. Her father died penniless, having dissipated an ample fortune; he also failed to make any provision for his daughter, assuming that Isabel, gifted with unusual beauty, would marry young (part I, chap. 1). With her complete ignorance of financial matters, Isabel does not understand the problems she faces, but she does know that she brought her husband no money. When she is continually reminded of this fact by the constitutionally stingy Miss Corny, she retreats into timidity and self-reproach.

Although the problems of boredom, social isolation, and lack of money are accentuated for Isabel Carlyle because she has married out of her own social class, many of her other difficulties must have been shared by nearly all of her real-life contemporaries who aspired to the status of Lady. The intense self-discipline and forebearance required of the Lady probably ranks as the most frustrating problem faced by Isabel and the numerous Victorian readers who suffered vicariously with her through the pages of *East Lynne*. The ideal prescribed rigorous suppression of all impulses of self-assertion or anger. In theory, at least, the Lady should demonstrate flawless manners and constant self-control in the presence of those of lower social rank. Among her equals, the Lady must always show deference to all masculine opinions, and especially to those of her husband. As a gently-born Maiden, she was expected to obey her parents, and with marriage she changed only her allegiance, not her habits. Many women in nineteenth-century fiction suggest that this ideal remained largely (and fortunately) unachieved; Lady Isabel seems extraordinarily passive and lacking in ego strength in comparison with the heroine of almost any novel by George Eliot, Anthony Trollope, or the Brontë sisters.

Most middle-class women educated for Ladyhood remained completely ignorant of the practical realities of life, and Isabel is no exception. To an almost absurd degree she is unaware of the value of money, the way it is earned, and the requirements of domestic economy. She has no idea of her husband's income. When Miss Carlyle tells her she is ruining Archibald by her extravagance, she accepts the accusation, and suffers prolonged feelings of guilt. Mrs. Wood sets the reader straight with frequent mention of Carlyle's "comfortable fortune" and his sister's lifelong stinginess (part 1, chap. 17). Isabel has no conception of the work of a country lawyer or the demands which his profession may make upon him. As bride, she often asks why Archibald cannot remain at home with her all day; she finds it suspicious that Barbara Hare comes to see him on business. Admittedly, the secrecy which surrounds Carlyle's attempts to aid Barbara seems excessive by present-day standards, but it is clear that Barbara also has her struggles with the code of the Lady and worries about appearances every time she visits the law offices of Archibald Carlyle. Unlike Lady Isabel, though, she has sufficient spirit to defy the rules when it is necessary for her brother's welfare.

Another attribute of the ideal Lady appears to be strongly marked in Isabel Carlyle. She is repeatedly described as physically frail. Though it is always difficult to ascertain how far the contemporary novel reflects an existing situation and how far it merely represents an ideal, any reader of Victorian fiction will recall the frequent and elaborate descriptions of illness, as well as the protracted deathbed scenes which occur in novels representing every level of society. It seems clear that recurrent illness and lack of physical vitality must have been common among nineteenth-century women, regardless of social level. Undoubtedly nineteenth-century fashions and domestic habits did little to promote good health, even in the affluent classes. Lack of sunshine, inadequate exercise, ill-ventilated and drafty houses, overfeeding and lack of fresh foods, heavy clothing and tight corsets— all must have contributed to the incidence of illness among women. Public health measures and modern medical techniques were largely undeveloped. Childbearing still constituted a very real hazard. Even so, the ideal of the Lady seems to have included delicate health as a desirable, if not an inevitable concomitant of superior social status and moral sensitivity. Mrs. Ellis, in one of her many strictures upon the cult of the Lady refers to " . . . the sickly sensibilities, the feeble frames, and the useless habits of the rising generation" (Ellis, *Women,* p. 15). It is interesting to notice how often, in Victorian literature, the terms "vulgar" or "rude" are used in conjunction with the word "health," and the implications of the term "delicacy" are open to further speculation. The correlation of high social status and physical weakness was well established prior to Victorian times, but in the nineteenth century women seem to have assumed the symbolic function of indicating family gentility, both in personal dress and in bodily weakness.

Of all the women depicted in *East Lynne,* Lady Isabel is clearly the weakest in physical constitution and general good health. She is also, perhaps not coincidentally, the highest in rank. It might, of course, be argued that the author has prudently created a character who can gracefully expire in order to solve one of the major plot complications, but the emphasis upon Isabel's delicacy seems fundamental to the development of her nature as essentially finer, if more frail, than the ordinary personalities who surround her. She is gravely ill at the birth of her first child. Several times her concerned husband sends her to the seaside to recover her health, and it is at one of these visits that she renews her fatal friendship with Captain Levison (part II, chap. 2). After her return to East Lynne in the disguise of Madame Vine, she is frequently too ill to assume her duties. Gradually she grows weaker, but Mrs. Wood emphasizes that her decline is caused by the anguish of observing her former husband in scenes of domestic felicity with her one-time rival, Barbara, and by the maternal anguish created as she nurses her eldest son through the final stages of consumption, unable to reveal herself to him, even when he is dying (part III, chap. 21). At the novel's climax she expires from the traditional broken heart, comforted by Archibald's forgiveness and one final chaste kiss; Barbara is fortunately away at the seaside.

Finally, one difficulty which the Lady shared with almost all Victorian women was the necessity for appearing completely asexual. In the plot structure of *East Lynne,* Mrs. Wood is careful to demonstrate that Lady Isabel's motives for leaving her husband have nothing whatsoever to do with erotic frustration or illicit sexual desire. In fact, one of the chief contemporary criticisms of *East Lynne* centers around the fact that Isabel's motives for elopement seem terribly inadequate.[10] But Mrs. Wood's need to create a sympathetic heroine leads her to emphasize that Isabel, as an embodiment of the ideal Lady, has no interest in sex, even when it is comprehended within the acceptable framework of love and marriage. After accepting Archibald Carlyle's proposal, she tells him, "I like you very much; I esteem and respect you; but I do not yet love you" (part I, chap. 12). A year of domestic bliss with the exemplary Archibald produces the desired result. Although Isabel never manages real romantic love for her husband, she develops a reasonable wifely affection:

> When she compared him with other men, and saw how far he surpassed them, how noble and how good he was, how little the rest looked beside him, her heart rose up with pride at the consciousness of being his wife; a princess might have deemed it an honour to be the chosen of such a man as Archibald Carlyle.

> (part II, chap. 1).

At this point the modern reader might logically assume that Isabel's long-suppressed sexual instincts erupt when she meets again the fascinating Captain Levison, for whom she had once entertained a girlhood fancy. However, Mrs. Wood is eager to spare her heroine this calumny. In several passages she makes it quite clear that Isabel is not moved by the virile charm of her seducer:

> Instead of the garden of roses it had been her persuader's pleasure to promise her (but which, in truth, she had barely glanced at, for that had not been her moving motive) she had found herself plunged into an abyss of horror. . . .
>
> (part II, chap. 10).

At the time when Captain Levison finally persuades Isabel to elope with him, he appeals primarily to her jealousy, which has long been smouldering because of her husband's secret meetings with Barbara Hare: "'Be avenged on that false hound, Isabel. He was never worthy of you. Leave your life of misery and come to happiness'" (part II, chap. 8). The motive for the elopement is repeatedly shown as Isabel's overwhelming jealousy of her husband's secret interview with Barbara, which Captain Levison exploits for his own purposes. It is clearly unthinkable that a real Lady could leave her husband because of sexual preference for another man; all women, and especially Ladies, were not supposed to have "animal instincts." Mrs. Wood is completely in accord with the beliefs of her own day in her attitude toward Isabel's transgression. Ladies feel no sexual impulse, and Isabel is a real Lady—so runs the syllogism which underlies the action of *East Lynne*. Therefore, Isabel could not have been motivated by physical desire for her seducer. In spite of its melodramatic excesses, the novel accurately reflects a prevailing view of women, and Mrs. Wood creates her heroine in the image of the Lady, with all of her essential attributes.

A few nineteenth-century critics apparently noticed the relationship of Isabel Carlyle to the Ideal Lady. Some of them expressed a generalized approval of the portrait, finding Mrs. Wood's heroine particularly appealing and true to life. Samuel Lucas's influential review in *The Times* for 25 January 1862, which probably insured the popular success of *East Lynne,* praises the construction of the book, and pays particular tribute to Mrs. Wood's "skill in characterization" (Lucas, p. 6). A reviewer for the *Athenaeum,* writing shortly after the book's publication, discusses the personal fascination which Lady Isabel exerts upon other characters of the novel, and dwells at length upon a charm of manner which is sufficient to affect even Barbara Hare: " . . . she [Barbara] looks upon Isabel only with envy and the most unfeigned admiration."[11] On the other hand, a few of the more intransigent critics of what was popularly called "sensation fiction" found the entire novel distasteful precisely because the heroine was presented as an embodiment of the Victorian Lady. "The moral fault of the book is, that the heroine has imputed to her a delicacy and purity of mind in utter variance with her whole course."[12] Mrs. Margaret Oliphant writing in the pages of *Blackwood's* also voices doubt about the book, arising principally from the sympathy given to the heroine, which she found an example of dubious morality.[13]

Finally, an interesting nineteenth-century estimate comes from the journalist Adeline Sergeant, writing from the vantage point of the 1890s. Her article on Mrs. Wood in *Women Novelists of Queen Victoria's Reign,* takes a different view:

> *East Lynne* owes half its popularity, however, to that reaction against inane and impossible goodness which has taken place since the middle of the century. Just as Rochester and Paul Ferrol are protests against the conventional hero, so Lady Isabel is a protest against the conventional heroine— and a portent of her time. We were all familiar with beauty and virtue in distress, from Clarissa Harlowe downwards. It is during later years that we have become conversant with beauty and guilt as objects of our sympathy and commiseration.
>
> (Sergeant, p. 181).

She remarks further:

> Now that the mists of prejudice have cleared away, we can see very well that no more praise of wrong doing was implied by Mrs. Wood's portrait of Lady Isabel than by Thackeray's keen-edged delineation of Becky Sharp or George Eliot's sorrowful sympathy with Maggie Tulliver. . . .
>
> (Sergeant, p. 182).

In her final estimate, she sees in *East Lynne* the working of the modern spirit "which leads to the comprehension of the sufferings of others, to a new pity for their faults and weaknesses . . ." (Sergeant, p. 182). Lady Isabel, she suggests, fascinated contemporary readers because they saw reflected in her character an indistinct but unmistakable image of themselves as they might have been in other circumstances.

However, the strongest evidence that *East Lynne* presents the tragedy of a widely recognized type, rather than an individual, occurs within the novel itself, in the treatment which Mrs. Wood accords another female character who strays from the path of virtue. Afy Hallijohn (christened Aphrodite) is a young person of ambiguous social status; she is the daughter of a law clerk and a woman described as a "lady," despite her somewhat eccentric taste in given names (part I, chap. 16). Richard Hare, Barbara's brother, becomes enamoured of her over the violent objections of his family and seeks her hand in marriage. At the same time Afy is pursued with less honorable intentions by a mysterious personage named Captain Thorn, temporarily residing in a nearby town. Afy, who has a clear eye to the main chance, prefers her elusive suitor, who is handsome and aristocratic, to the plodding if well-meaning Richard, whom she describes as "half-baked" (part II, chap. 15).

During the unravelling of the subplot concerning the murder of Afy's father (the crime of which Barbara's brother is accused), the solicitors acting for Richard Hare unearth the information that Afy has resided in London for over two years with Captain Francis Levison, the villainous seducer of Lady Isabel. Although the information is presented in an indirect way, and the court accepts Afy's fiction that she "happened" to reside in London, and that Levison "happened" to pay a "morning call" now and then, there can be no doubt that Afy is, in the classic Victorian phrase, no better than she should be (part III, chap. 16). Of course Afy's guilt is less than Isabel's, in that she is involved in fornication rather than adultery. Of greater significance to the Victorian audience, she has no children to consider, and her affair with Levison does not injure a family structure nor damage any reputation except her own. Lady Isabel, on the other hand, has failed in her deepest obligations. She has violated her marriage vows, deserted her young children, and inflicted injury on that most sacred of Victorian ideals, the family.

Even though Lady Isabel has been the greater sinner, the punishment meted out to her seems totally out of proportion. As it turns out, Afy is not punished at all. She undergoes a temporary loss of status in West Lynne, but by maintaining a pose of stiff-necked innocence, she suffers no permanent damage in social position. Of course she is deprived of Richard Hare's attentions; he bluntly rejects her, saying, "You must pardon me for intimating that from henceforth we are strangers" (part III, chap. 22). However, she is sought as a wife by the prosperous tradesman Joe Jiffin, and at the end of the novel, vanishes into triumphant matrimony. Her yielding to the sins of the flesh only causes her a few months of embarrassment and the loss of her gentlemanly suitor.

For Lady Isabel the punishment is social ostracism, the loss of her children, forfeiture of her good name, misery, humiliation, and death. After her elopement with Levison, she undergoes a kind of ostracism which is difficult for the modern reader to comprehend. She cannot visit England except in disguise. Her nearest relative, the Earl of Mount Severn, affords her a measure of sympathy and a small allowance, but he assents in the general belief that providence has been merciful when he hears of her supposed death in a railway accident (part II, chap. 14). From the moment she leaves her home, her name can no longer be mentioned by any of the inhabitants of East Lynne. Her six-year-old daughter is from that time onward called Lucy, not

Isabel. Her children are told that she is dead. She lives in fear that her daughter will be prevented from marrying well because of the obloquy associated with her name. When at last the unfortunate Lady Isabel expires under the roof of her old home, she is conveniently buried in a corner of the churchyard, her grave marked only by the initials IMV. Meanwhile, we assume, Afy lives happily as Mrs. Joe Jiffin. But she is not a Lady.

The wages of sin, Mrs. Wood suggests, are not always death. As far as sexual transgressions are concerned, the grim warning applies only to the Lady. She bears the burden of her class, very much as her male counterparts took up the White Man's Burden later in the century. The Lady's conduct is ever in the public eye. She functions as an example to the "lower orders." On her rests the responsibility for preserving two great Victorian ideals, the Family and Private Property, for she represents both. Most of the archetypal power of *East Lynne* is invested in its heroine, the erring Lady Isabel. She appears first as the symbolic figure of the Maiden, and later as Wife and Mother. In both roles she reflects the ideal of the period, and even more significantly, the overwhelming problems inherent in the maintenance of that ideal. In her movement from innocence to worldly knowledge, she serves as an example and a warning to the mid-Victorian reader.

From the vantage point of a later century, it is clear that Mrs. Wood does not possess the insight of a major novelist. She never sees the implications of her heroine's failure to conform to the prevailing ideal. For her, Lady Isabel is an unfortunate victim of a single ill-considered decision, rather than the scapegoat of a repressive code of behavior. Nowhere in *East Lynne* does she recognize the significance of the long sequence of emotional distortion which leads Isabel to break with society, though she accurately depicts many elements in that sequence. In her personal philosophy she supported prevailing morality, and in her numerous asides to the reader she took every opportunity to point out the terrible results of rebellion against the established pattern. For the modern reader, however, the moral of the story is totally different but equally clear. In the overstated drama of *East Lynne,* Mrs. Wood presents us with an insight into the power of a social ideal and the potential for personal disaster which it encompassed. If the demands of gentility are still strong upon the present-day woman, it may be that the ideal of the Lady has not wholly vanished from the modern world.

Notes

[1] The figure of one million copies sold is probably a conservative one. See Frank Luther Mott, *Golden Multitudes* (New York: R. R. Bowker Company, 1947), p. 144; and Adeline Sergeant, "Mrs. Henry Wood," *Women Novelists of Queen Victoria's Reign,* edited by Margaret Oliphant (London: Hurst & Blackett, Ltd., 1897), p. 183.

[2] Mrs. Sarah Stickney Ellis, *The Women of England* (New York: D. Appleton & Co., 1839), p. 87.

[3] Mrs. Henry Wood, *East Lynne* (London: Cassell and Company, Ltd., 1909), part II, chap. 10. (Future references to the novel, identified by part and chapter, will be indicated in the text.)

[4] Margaret Dalziel, *Popular Fiction 100 Years Ago* (London: Cohen & West, 1957), p. 86. Dalziel gives an interesting comment on this tendency, which appeared in the penny press as well as in standard novels.

[5] Ellis, *The Wives of England* (London: Fisher, [1843]), p. 208.

[6] See C. Willet Cunnington, *Feminine Attitudes in the Nineteenth Century* (New York: Haskell House, 1973), pp. 135-136; and J. A. and Olive Banks, *Feminism and Family Planning in Victorian England* (New York: Schocken Books, 1964), pp. 62-76.

[7] Françoise Basch, *Relative Creatures,* translated by Anthony Rudolf (New York: Schocken Books, 1974), pp. 8-9.

[8] Martha Vicinus, "The Perfect Victorian Lady," Introduction, *Suffer and Be Still: Women in the Victorian Age* (Bloomington: Indiana University Press, 1972), p. x.

[9] For a slightly different view of the emotional pressures upon Victorian women, see Mary S. Hartman, "Murder for Respectability: The Case of Madeleine Smith," *Victorian Studies,* XVI (1973), 381-400.

[10] [Samuel Lucas], *"East Lynne,"* The Times (25 January 1862), p. 6.

[11] "New Novels," *Athenaeum,* no. 1772 (12 October 1861), 474.

[12] "Our Female Sensation Novelists," *Living Age,* LXXVIII (1863), 357.

[13] [Mrs. Margaret Oliphant], "Novels," *Blackwood's,* XCIV (1863), 170.

Sally Mitchell (essay date 1981)

SOURCE: "Sensation, Sex, and the 1860's," in *The Fallen Angel: Chastity, Class and Women's Reading, 1835-1880,* Bowling Green University Popular Press, 1981, pp. 73-99.

[In the essay that follows, Mitchell explores the ways in which sensation novels—particularly George Meredith's Rhoda Fleming *and Thomas Hardy's* Desperate Remedies—*reflect and react to changing roles for women in the Victorian period.]*

The literary phenomenon of the 1860s was the sensation novel.[1] Sensationalism meant excitement, secrets, surprises, suspense; it meant strong emotion aroused by strong scenes, violent death by murder, train, fire, and poisons ranging from chloroform to nightshade; and it meant continual shocks provided by violating decorum. One critic in 1863 complained that eight of the twenty-four recent novels he was reviewing were about bigamy,[2] and his selection did not include some entries by leading novelists, such as Charles Reade's *Griffith Gaunt (Argosy,* 1865-66; 3 vols. 1866) or William Makepeace Thackeray's *Phillip (Cornhill,* 1861-62; 3 vols. 1862). One can hardly open a novel written at the height of the vogue without discovering a woman unchaste in fact, in reputation, or by desire, whether with intent, by accident, or through a technicality.

Of course the decade had no monopoly on the sort of light literature that depends on exciting incident, strong emotion, and characters who vary from the stereotype only in the particular perversion that expresses their villainy. The Gothic, the Newgate, and the penny dreadful had preceded the sensation; the detectives, the spies, the cinema, and television were to follow. The difference in the sixties was the serious critical attention paid to the kind of novel which we have for the past hundred years considered a sub-species: fiction, not literature. Sensation novels were reviewed in respectable quarterlies and denounced from the pulpit. The second generation of Victorian writers began under their influence; George Meredith's *Rhoda Fleming* and Thomas Hardy's *Desperate Remedies* are both treatments of the unchaste woman written in the shadow of sensationalism.

With so many portraits of the unchaste placed before the public eye, and with such a supply of causes, motives and consequences for her actions there is—even in the restoration of justice at the end—a remaining substratum of ambiguity. That, in itself, is significant. Writers who saw enlarged possibilities for a woman of less than immaculate purity were both reflecting and reacting to changes in the role of women in society.

One striking feature of the sensation novels of the 1860s, as a group, is the centrality of female characters. The form requires a villain to move the plot, and an astonishing number of the villains are, in the words of an 1866 review, "beautiful women of elegant figure and golden locks, whose fascinating exterior only hides a subtle brain and a pitiless heart."[3] Justice punishes the villainess; her strength is demonstrated, feared, and crushed. Often her sexual misbehavior provides the clinching proof of her viciousness.

Other centrally placed female characters, however, are neither chaste, victimized, nor anathematized. Adeline Sergeant explained that *East Lynne* was popular because people were tired of "inane and impossible goodness" in heroines.[4] Really interesting women—women worth writing a whole book about—had sexual experience. The subterfuges that novelists had to invent so heroines could have freedom of action and still be pure enough to marry the hero reveal the strain that social limitations imposed on the feminine role.

The typical novel of the 1860s was about contemporary life. "Proximity," as one reviewer said, is "one great element of sensation. It is necessary to be near a mine to be blown up by its explosion."[5] Writers are very specific about street names and railway timetables and the nearest town with a telegraph office (and they probably expected their readers to check up on them); they often drop in references to scandals or murders that have recently been in the news. This intense awareness of contemporary detail also encouraged sensation novelists to reflect immediately on the changes they perceived in social standards and modes of behavior.

A good deal of the sexual frankness is conservative—or even reactionary—in effect. Divorce, for example, was legally possible for the middle class after 1857, but sensation novelists seldom use it to solve their characters' problems; instead they protest that the law can not possibly divide two people who have literally been merged into one. Even a woman victimized by a fake wedding is not usually allowed to marry while the man who took her virginity remains alive.

Middle-class virgins are unchaste in sensation novels, as they had not been in earlier popular fiction. Changing social patterns provided new opportunities. Girls attend Eights Week at Oxford and the system of chaperonage breaks down; they walk across the fields unaccompanied to pay a call and find only the young man of the house at home. Most significantly, they ride—an occupation which makes the company of a suitably mature chaperone particularly difficult to obtain. The woman riding with only a groom to protect her provides new plots: she can, like Bella in Annie Thomas' *On Guard* (3 vols. 1865), get lost and have to spend the night at an inn twenty-seven miles from home, or she may, even more scandalously, elope with the groom himself, like Mary Elizabeth Braddon's *Aurora Floyd*.

Aside from the new plots she creates, the figure of a woman riding gives clear evidence of conservative reaction to a new social phenomenon. When a woman is introduced in a riding habit—or even more dangerously, on the hunting field—we can be virtually certain that trouble and impropriety will follow. Bella (in *On Guard*) and Kate Gaunt (of Reade's *Griffith Gaunt*) manage to avoid unchastity but not dishonor; Adelaide in Henry Kingsley's *Ravenshoe* (*Macmillan's*, 1861-62) and Caroline Eversfield in Elizabeth Grey's *Passages in the Life of a Fast Young Lady* (3 vols. 1862) both

marry, but not soon enough after they have eloped for the county ladies to visit them. One cause of the reaction can be seen in the first description of Aurora Floyd: "At six years of age she rejected a doll and asked for a rocking-horse."[6] Women who ride horses are also apt to use slang—that is, to talk men's language. Before a riding heroine can reach a happy ending, she must suffer enough weakness, illness and humiliation to melt her down into chastened femininity. (In *On Guard*, we know that Bella will be saved when she compassionately lets the fox live.)[7]

Besides the general reaction against women who assume masculine traits, there is also a specific contemporary phenomenon that gave an aura of impropriety to the horsewoman: the "pretty horsebreakers" of Rotten Row. At the beginning of the 60s the English demimonde appeared publicly in the Park, in letters to the *Times,* in alluring portraits in newsagents' shops and, indeed, in Sir Edwin Landseer's Royal Academy picture for 1861, of which Skittles was the subject. Towards the middle of the decade a series of two-shilling yellowbacks purported to tell the life stories of the most notorious women about the town. Though they imitated the format of the railway novel they were not carried by Smith's bookstalls or, of course, by Mudie's, but they were available elsewhere—curiously, more easily in the provinces.[8] The books pretend half-heartedly to be journalistic exposes. The parties in St. John's Wood which break up suddenly when a division is called in the House are described in pornographically opulent terms but there are no scenes of actual sexual encounter, and even these books usually come down on the side of conventional roles, sometimes with amusing suddenness. *The Soiled Dove* ends with a melodramatic tableau of Laura frozen to death in the snow after the sound of hymns sung in the street has kept her from murdering the "Honorable" who ruined her. *Anonyma* finally marries the man who rouses her respect so much that she will not even kiss him until she has proved that she can reform.[9]

The most common type of sinful, sexual, evil woman in sensation novels is the adventuress. The whole race are Becky Sharp's children: women who pursue money, position, power and security by the socially acceptable route of marriage. The adventuress marries without love and therefore submits to sex without love. Even though the submission takes place within marriage, the adventuress is often shown to be evil because of her sexual willingness; she later commits adultery or reveals that she was not a virgin when she married.

Bracebridge Hemyng's *Held in Thrall* (yellowback, [1869]) is typical of the cheap railway books that reduce the story to its essentials by leaving out such subtleties as psychology. By the second page we have learned that Mona Seafield is a governess who would willingly sell her soul to the devil in order "to raise herself above the necessity of working . . . and to compel others to render her the homage due to rank and wealth." She fails to attract the heir to a neighboring estate, persuades an old poacher to force his submissive wife to "remember" switching the babies she had nursed, blackmails the newly-elevated pseudo-heir into marrying her, makes sure of her settlement, and elopes with a captain who deserts her to sink "from one depth of degradation to another" (p. 149).

In thoughtful hands the figure is more complex and reveals how difficult it was to reconcile the work-ethic with the genteel distrust of pushiness and ambition. The adventuress admits her goal, which, in these novels, heroes generally do not. It is admirable for a man to work hard, but he does not deliberately seek riches and power—the money is an accidental by-product and the seat in Parliament a gracious recognition of an effort which was virtuous for its own sake. The conflict is further complicated by the realization that woman's state is anomalous: she can "work" her way to the top only by putting her person (as opposed to her hands and brain) in trade. Significantly, the character named Magdalen in Wilkie Collins' *No Name (All the Year Round,* 1862-63; 3 vols. 1862) is not the unmarried mother of Vanstone's children but the daughter who cold-bloodedly contrives to recapture the inheritance lost through her illegitimacy by committing matrimony with the heir-at-law.

The treatment of the adventuress also reveals an underlying fear of woman's sexual attractiveness once she decides to use her body for what it is worth and adopts the aggressive role. She can succeed because she violates the understood conventions. Men are not used to supplying restraint; they can therefore be ruined by seductive females. William Winwood Reade's *Liberty Hall, Oxon.* (3 vols. 1860) has a whole phalanx of man-trapping women, from the three shopgirl sisters in Woodstock whose father earns a living by threatening undergraduates with breach-of-promise suits to the ladies at a county ball who make bets with each other about which men they will be able to capture by the end of the evening. Lucy (another woman who rides to the hounds) loses her virginity without any sense of shame. She does, however, make a clear calculation of its value:

> "I have lost a woman's chief treasure, and I have lost it like a fool, I have lost it for nothing, I have lost it for itself. *Itself,* ha! ha! what a prize, for so great a stake—Ah, if we young girls knew. . . .but when we know, it is too late . . . all is lost, lost, lost!"

> She drooped her head, and she thought. Then her eyes flashed: a proud smile curled upon her lips.

> "Lost for others, not for me! I have still a stern will, a strong brain: I have still resolution to conquer,

and cunning to hide. I have been a child, I have fallen; I will be a woman, and I will rise. But I must forget that I have a heart, that heart which has so nearly lost me all." (II, 283)[10]

Men were threatened by riding women, by ambitious women, by women who used sexuality for their own ends. The most reactionary novelists sensationally exaggerated the masculine-serving qualities of the old ideal. James McGrigor Allan objects, in *Nobly False* (2 vols. 1863), that

> the woman who can unite in herself, the graces and charms peculiar to her sex, with sufficient intellectual power to comprehend and sympathise with a superior man, and with sufficient moral worth to sacrifice self, and make her life subservient to that of the man she adores—is extremely rare, and can hardly ever be met with in *Society!*

> The tone of society and modern female education are fatal to the gentleness, yielding disposition, and disregard of self, which are absolutely essential to a woman who wishes to be the companion of a man of thought. The women to be met with in ball-rooms, are all educated to *Queen* it through life . . . (II, 76-77)

Fortunately, the novel's hero finds Miriam, a self-taught ferryman's daughter, who not only is willing to live with him without marriage so that he can keep a promise made to his dying mother, but also drinks lye in compromising circumstances so that he will hate her and marry a social equal for his own good. In the book's introduction, Allan says that Miriam embodies the ideal of womanhood which had obsessed him for years: unchaste not through weakness but because of "the unfathomed depths of woman's capacity of suffering and self-negation for a man she loves" (I, v-vi). We are not surprised to discover that Allan later wrote *Woman Suffrage Wrong in Principle and Practice* (1890).

The plot that introduces the widest variety of sexual scandal is also, though more ambiguously, conservative. This plot is one of the stand-bys of English fiction: the discovery of rightful inheritance. The sexual incident usually takes place offstage. Illegitimate children—often in the best of families—have been concealed under polite fictions or farmed out to foster parents. Babies have been switched for motives pure or impure. The sexual adventure in the past generation was evil because it confused the social fabric and introduced the uncertainty consequent to not knowing who people really are. The outcome is conservative; the rightful heir is at last recognized.

This conservatism is ambiguous because it tends to confirm middle-class values by giving them the sanction of aristocratic "legitimacy." The plot frequently provides moral elevation for a socially inferior girl at the expense of her betters. The legitimate child who ultimately inherits is the offspring of an early mesalliance. When the social climber or younger son comes into the property, he convinces the milliner or farmer's daughter or nurserymaid who had valiantly held out for the church and the ring that their marriage was invalid because he signed the register with a false name, or the license was not in order, or the clergyman not in orders. Then he bigamously marries a woman who brings him an aristocratic connection to go with his money or money to go with his encumbered estate. (A girl could be fooled even if she were not particularly naive. One section of the 1867 Consecration of Churchyards Act had the purpose of "affirming the validity of certain marriages supposed to have been doubtful on account of the position of the communion table being changed.")

Thackeray's *Henry Esmond* (3 vols. 1852) is a good example of the pattern, though the plot is so ubiquitous in the sixties it can hardly be said to have a source. It is, of course, the male version of the Cinderella story. The hero, usually thought to be illegitimate, has been raised in obscurity and earned his own way in the world. The delayed inheritance rewards the hardworking heir and provides a magic symbol of gentility to confirm his virtue—and his mother's.

The wicked seducers who deliberately ruin girls to gratify their own sensuality are almost invariably aristocrats who also display the other vices of idleness—gaming, racing, ruinous debt. Sensation novelists do not just silently disapprove of the villainy by showing the ironic contrast between the victim's suffering and the man's prosperity; they are more apt to punish the man overtly. Thus they demonstrate a sense of justice more rigorous than novels of previous decades. We are meant to infer that society approves of the moral rigor. The gamekeeper in A. J. Barrowcliffe's *Normanton* (1862) murders his daughter's seducer and is sentenced to only one year's imprisonment. The aristocratic despoiler in *The Soiled Dove* commits suicide. The girls in novels of this sort are young, poor, uneducated, innocent and pitiable and sometimes, therefore, survive. In *Jessie's Expiation* (3 vols. 1867), by Oswald Boyle, the poor victimized girl is forced by her titled seducer to marry a lunatic; she (being a true woman) grows to love him "because he is miserable" (III, 246) and they are treated kindly by the novel's admirable people, a young middle-class couple who made a love-match on slender means and have to work hard. But wicked Lord Rendover poetically drowns at the very spot where he had kidnapped Jessie.

Mrs. Henry Wood's *East Lynne (Colburn's New Monthly Magazine*, 1859-61; 3 vols. 1861) is the most famous of the sensational bourgeois moralities about sex and unearned money. The curse of both looms over the opening words: "In an easy-chair of

the spacious and handsome library of his town house sat William, Earl of Mount Severn. His hair was grey, the smoothness of his expansive brow was defaced by premature wrinkles, and his once attractive face bore the pale, unmistakable look of dissipation" (Ch. 1). William Vane had been an industrious, steady, legal student until three unexpected deaths gave him a title and sixty thousand a year on which to ruin himself. Meantime he went to Gretna Green with the woman he loved. Because of the elopement there was no settlement; because of the title there was waste and indolence. When the earl dies his daughter Isabel is penniless and homeless. She marries Mr. Carlyle, who buys Mount Severn's home (East Lynne) with the money he earns as a country lawyer, who continues to work even after he becomes a man of property, and whose neighbors recognize his worth by electing him to Parliament. Isabel falls prey to idleness (Carlyle's sister lives with them and manages the household), jealousy (because her husband keeps necessary business secrets from her), and physical proximity to a man who stirs her blood. Her punishment is instantaneous:

> Never had she experienced a moment's calm or peace, or happiness, since the fatal night of quitting her home. She had taken a blind leap in a moment of wild passion; when, instead of the garden of roses it had been her persuader's pleasure to promise her, (but which, in truth, she had barely glanced at, for that had not been her moving motive), she had found herself plunged into an abyss of horror from which there was never more any escape . . . a lively remorse, a never-dying anguish, took possession of her soul for ever. O reader, believe me! Lady—wife—mother! should you ever be tempted to abandon your home, so will you awake! Whatever trials may be the lot of your married life, though they may magnify themselves to your crushed spirit as beyond the endurance of woman to bear, *resolve* to bear them; fall down on your knees and pray to be enabled to bear them: pray for patience; pray for strength to resist the demon that would urge you so to escape; bear unto death, rather than forfeit your fair name and your good conscience; for be assured that the alternative, if you rush on to it, will be found far worse than death. (Ch.10)[11]

The novel's second half is effective because Mrs. Wood manages the emotional effects so that even the reader who agrees with every word of the moral homily remains sympathetic towards Isabel. Her flaws (the biggest was to marry a man she respected but did not love) are clearly shown in the first half of the book. In the second part, Mrs. Wood puts much more emphasis on Levinson's villainy—he refuses to marry Isabel and make their child legitimate; he is shown to be a practiced seducer and, ultimately, a murderer—so that Isabel comes to seem more of a victim. Her most noble quality—her love for her children—provides both the vehicle for her punishment and the opportunity for purification through suffering.

That punishment is most harrowing which involves the loss of that which is most valued. A generation earlier the heaviest burden on the unchaste woman had been the sense of sin (the fear that she would not go to heaven), the physical threats of poverty and further degradation into prostitution, and the loss of place in society. Isabel suffers from loss of place in the family. Disfigured in a railway accident which kills her bastard child and leads Carlyle to think that she is dead, she returns to East Lynne as governess. She sees her husband happy with his second wife. She must give her children the cool attention of a governess instead of a mother's passionate embraces. Daily and hourly she lives with the awareness of what she has lost.

The reader always knows a good deal more than Isabel about what is really going on, realizes that Levison is a villain, knows that her jealousy is unfounded, and thus never doubts that Isabel acts wrongly. But Mrs. Wood's portrait of her character and of the marital relationship leads to sympathy, not pity. Isabel is conscious of her utter dependence on Carlyle. She stands to him as child to parent; she is afraid to ask questions because he might laugh at her for not understanding the obvious; she is constantly on her good behavior. She is protected, cherished, and not allowed to grow up. She feels hurt when he pays less attention to her after the honeymoon year is over; he has a business to attend to but the business of a woman's life, so far as she can see, is to maintain a perfect relationship with her husband. She feels inferior: if she were a better woman, somehow, he would love her more.

The husband and marriage bond are the focus of her feelings of inferiority. Her elopement is, if only momentarily, an act of revenge; like Edith Dombey, she uses the weapon most effective in the battle between the sexes. Isabel's crime and punishment show how much social retrictions shape woman's nature. The role traps Isabel; she has no independent goal but can only leave vengefully in the company of another man. Furthermore, as Margaret Maison has pointed out, the divorce law is essential to the story. Carlyle is morally free to marry again because he thinks Isabel is dead, but if he had not divorced her first, his marriage to Barbara would be invalid.[12] Divorce set up a legal barrier against any hope that the adulteress might work out a reconciliation; it ensured that she would be permanently cut off from her family.

When *East Lynne* first went the rounds of publishers it was rejected by both Smith and Elder and Chapman and Hall. George Meredith, the reader for the latter, called it "foul."[13] By the end of the century it had sold almost half a million copies and had been translated, according to Mrs. Wood's son, "into every known tongue."[14] The review by Samuel Lucas in the *Times* for 25 January 1862 is a study in qualified enthusiasm by a man who—like many another reader with a sense of literary standards—loved the book and felt that he shouldn't: "It would, perhaps, be invidious to say that, in our opinion, *East Lynne* . . . is the best novel of the season," he begins, and goes on to point out Levinson's fortuitious and unexplained villainy and the large role played by coincidence in keeping the plot afloat. And yet, he admits, "as regards its satisfaction of the indispensible requirement which is the rude test of the merits of any work of fiction . . . *East Lynne* is found by all its readers to be highly *entertaining.*"

One reason characters like Isabel engage the reader's attention is that we sense they are right in objecting to their role. Elfrida in Florence Marryat's *Love's Conflict* (3 vols. 1865) is shy and timid and afraid that her husband will stop loving her unless she makes a doormat of herself. When she admits that she was attracted to a man who treated her decently, her husband demands a separation; emotional faithlessness is enough for him.

Thus even while moralists are horrified by unchaste behavior and use its consequences to punish aggressive women, they realize uncomfortably that continued oppression will lead to acts of rebellion. Lucy of *Liberty Hall, Oxon.* marries the man she had her eye on, despite her lost virginity, and then reaps misery because he brings up her past every time they quarrel. The narrator's tone is ambiguous: "When a girl, she was bound by those chains to which women submit, because they are slaves. This girl attempted to break her bonds, and she has suffered" (III, 362). A slender thread of sympathy glints momentarily even in the portrait of the most devious adventuress, the slight, childish, golden-haired Lady Audley who, in the interval between being terrified by a thunderstorm and coming home with a skirt full of wildflowers, has shoved her lawful husband down a well in order to preserve her bigamous marriage.[15] The reader had earlier seen her in her bare governess's room after Sir Michael Audley proposed, saying to herself: "No more dependence, no more drudgery, no more humiliations . . ." (Ch. 1). Elaine Showalter suggests that Lady Audley is allowed to end her life in a madhouse instead of on the gallows because both Braddon and the reader have, in many ways, identified with her.[16]

Marriage was the only way that a woman could improve her social position. In William Starbuck's *A Woman against the World* (3 vols. 1864) "Pretty Sally" is a cheeky, vain, farm laborer's daughter who lives in a cottage with two rooms and eight people. Even though she has a baby, she sets her cap at the doting old squire: "she would live to triumph over her enemies; those who sneered should yet be made to curtsey in her presence. Not mere vulgar ambition animated her mind, but the wild feverish longing to obtain a woman's victory" (I, 274). She wins financial security and social place, but ultimately achieves a crucial realization:

To be lost in the light of a true man's love was once her dream. Hers had been a sad awakening. All other affections save that of and for her children had been in her experience a delusion, and she began to think that a woman's destiny is not necessarily dependent for its fulfilment on possessing a greater or less amount of marital . . . love. (III, 353)

Starbuck hedges Sally's sexual guilt by disclosing that there had been a secret and supposedly invalid wedding with the baby's father and, for the sake of his readers' romantic expectations, gives her a happy marriage after all (though only in a footnote to the end of the book), with the village schoolmaster who starts a communal farm where degraded farm laborers are transformed into clean, enlightened citizens. Starbuck's book is an attack on the persistence of "this ridiculous notion of caste . . . in spite of the evidence afforded by almost every town and village, that the secret of the change that transmutes the boor naturally into the gentleman accidentally, is education" (II, 256). The sensational story of Sally and her bigamous entanglements may simply be sauce to keep the reader interested, but it has the effect of adding sex to the other accidents of birth that unjustly limit human aspirations and achievements.

The novels we have been considering emphasize the social sources of woman's unchastity, but few are problem novels that show the woman as a victim of society. Rather, the problem is that women use their bodies for social ends; they try to dispose of their own persons in their own best interests. Physical passion is not often mentioned. Rhoda Broughton's *Not Wisely but Too Well (Dublin University Magazine,* 1865-66; 3 vols. 1867) was shocking not because the heroine fell but because she wanted to, continuously, in a series of climactic scenes of encounter and renunciation repeated for three volumes. The novel was first published as a serial in *Dublin University Magazine,* a relatively expensive and small-circulation periodical edited by Broughton's uncle, Sheridan LeFanu. No English publisher would accept it as a library novel until it had been extensively revised. The crucial revision is intriguing. In the three-volume edition the heroine's married lover is fatally injured on the way to a ball, and she sits solicitously by his deathbed trying to provide religious comfort. She then joins a charitable sisterhood. In the first version he gets to the ball, takes her out into the garden, and shoots her—dead. Why is that more shocking? Perhaps because violent martyrdom in defense of her virginity would make Kate a saint, and she had already been too passionate to go to heaven without spending some time repenting. But there is also a social consideration. In the previous confrontation, which is nearly the same in both versions, Kate refuses to yield for the good of his soul; she loves him too much to let him damn himself by ruining her. That is an acceptable heroic role for a woman. In the rejected version's garden scene, she will not yield because she does not want to lose her own chance of heaven. When the conflict between herself and a man comes to the last extremity, she puts herself first. For the publisher, heroic martyrdom was not permissible but compassionate sacrifice was.

The religious emphasis itself was probably also shocking. The book seems to imply that only fear of God keeps women chaste; that without religion Kate would listen to the animal promptings of her body. Most of the sensation novels have a worldly frame of reference. Women commit human errors and are punished by human consequences: loss of caste, inability to bear children, unhappy marriage. The death penalty is no longer inevitable. Nor did the earthly punishment have to be so severe that sexual error became the one central fact of woman's existence. The heroic scale is diminished; women remain women even with imperfections.

The most common punishment is loss of the opportunity to fill woman's natural role. Only rarely does an unchaste heroine have Ruth's motive to rise. It is almost as if the link between intercourse and pregnancy had been broken. Motherhood, like inheritance, is a magic reward reserved for the virtuous. Aurora Floyd has no children until her unintentional bigamy is relieved by the death of her first husband; the child that Griffith Gaunt got bigamously on Mercy Vint dies so that she can marry Sir George Neville and have nine that are healthy and sound. The Fast Young Lady's son is born dead. Elfrida Treherne's child is deformed because of the passion she felt for her husband's cousin while carrying it. Adelaide, in *Ravenshoe (Macmillan's* 1861-62; 3 vols. 1862), who had become Lord Welter's mistress in order to force him to marry her, breaks her back in a fall while hunting and grows softened, beloved and sterile. (We might also notice that Rosamond Lydgate's ill-fated horseback ride in *Middlemarch* [4 vols. 1871-72] is an act of defiance towards her husband and leads to miscarriage.)

Motherhood has a simple symbolic value instead of exerting a moral or psychological influence on woman's character. Good women have children and bad women reject them. Lady Audley leaves her legitimate child with her drunken father; Lucy of *Liberty Hall, Oxon.* gives her illegitimate one to its father because she has "had enough" of "the brat" (III, 202). The hero of *Land at Last (Temple Bar,* 1865-66; 3 vols. 1866)[17] makes a daringly unconventional marriage to a woman rescued from the streets, and the reader knows for certain that the marriage was a mistake when she refuses to nurse their child.

The good mother was still a standard image for the good woman. But the sentimental novel's innocent heroine virtually disappeared. The lengthy pursuit of a helpless girl by a vicious man is one sensational plot conspicuous by its absence. The fair fragile virtuous innocent, when she remains, is reduced to the role of ingenue, waiting quietly in the drawing room to marry the hero when he gets free of all those interesting entanglements. The sensation novel depended on action, and an admirable, matrimonially negotiable middle-class virgin could not do much; the code of chaperonage required that even in her own house a single woman under thirty could not talk to an unrelated man unless a married gentlewoman or mature servant was in the room. But a married woman had freedom of movement, affairs to direct, and servants to order around. She might have a settled income at her disposal. And she also had, like lower-class girls, an aura of sexual knowledge. George Treherne (in Marryat's *Love's Conflict)* has an image of the girl he wants to marry, "a pure, half-celestial being, refined and delicate in the extreme, with a mind cultivated and attuned to be the companion of his own. He had not thought of her as very beautiful so much as very pure in mind and body . . ." (I. 78). The woman he falls in love with is his cousin William's pregnant wife, Elfrida.

Marriage gave women freedom of action; motherhood, as in novels of previous decades, allowed them to exhibit acceptable strength. The husband, however, had to be removed from the scene so that the woman could demonstrate her self-sufficiency—and so that she could play a romantic role. Even the ingenue was sometimes married; in Ouida's *Under Two Flags* (3 vols. 1867) the woman who eventually marries the hero is introduced first as a child and reappears later as a rich virgin widow—her husband died before the wedding night, leaving her plenty of money, a changed name, and the status to roam around North Africa. Both Wilkie Collins and Charles Reade (as well as many lesser novelists) used the complications of Scots, Irish, medieval, civil, and foreign marriage ceremonies to provide heroines with sexual experience. A husband's bigamy was often simply a device for supplying a woman who was "neither maid, wife, nor widow."[18] These legal technicalities show a certain slippage in moral absolutes; the moralist uses crime in order to show that it does not pay, but the sensationalist has a tendency to reveal that it was not actually crime.

Some sensation novelists must have resorted to intentional and cold-blooded pervarication to make their own conceptions about women acceptable to the mid-Victorian audience and publishers. The leading female authors could hardly sympathize with retiring helpless women even if society said they ought. Most of them wrote for a living because they had incompetent or incapable men (either husbands or fathers) dangling somewhere in the background. Some, in addition, had their own secrets to conceal. Florence Marryat was separated from her husband. The five children of Mary Braddon and John Maxwell were born before

1874, when the death of Maxwell's first wife (who was in a mental asylum) allowed them to marry.[19] Both of the leading male sensationalists had semi-public unorthodox private lives; Reade kept house for twenty-five years with an actress, Mrs. Seymour,[20] and Wilkie Collins lived for the latter half of his life with Caroline Graves, the original Woman in White, though in the meantime Martha Rudd bore him three children.[21]

The fascination with women's strength touches on the scene that dominates the pornography of the period. Most of the riding women carry a whip; Anonyma brings it down across the face of a gentleman who looks rudely at her in the park; Lucy of *Liberty Hall, Oxon.* is said to have horsewhipped a man; Aurora Floyd beats a stableboy for kicking her dog. Charles Reade was so obsessed by strong-armed women that one recent biographer explains nearly the whole canon as a sadomasochistic fantasy resulting from the suppression of Oedipal love. The pattern was noticed by contemporaries.

> Mr. Reade's *repertoire* is limited. He has one brilliant, splendid woman, full of noble instincts, of passion and generosity . . . and he has another simple, tender, wise feminine creature who is the rival, the conqueror, the defender . . . and between these two he has a fancy for placing a very weak, sometimes contemptible, man.[22]

Reade subsumes sexuality in the maternal function. In *The Cloister and the Hearth* (4 vols. 1861) Margaret is pregnant and socially compromised after a medievally binding betrothal of which she has no proof. She practices medicine to support her child and her senile father until the law catches up and stops her. When her betrothed reappears—he had become a priest because he thought Margaret was dead—she stage-manages a "miracle" to scare him out of his hermit's cell and convince him that his duty is to relieve misery in the parish. She becomes his housekeeper and district visitor and promises that she will make sure he keeps his vow of celibacy even if he should be tempted by living in the same house with her.

The woman in a conventional social role—who was totally dependent on a man—was little use to the sensation novelist. The striking thing about Reade's Margaret is the complete reversal: she takes care of her child and her husband and even her father. Her practical abilities are held up for us to admire. The unchaste girl who was forgiven in novels of the thirties and forties was always in some measure a victim; those qualities that the male novelist (like Bulwer-Lytton or Froude) adored derived from her submissiveness, her naturalness, her innocence, her quality of being presocial—uncorrupted by society. She was an ideal child. Collins and Reade, on the other hand, portrayed

Charles Reade

the ideal mother, who chose not to be a victim, and whose strength lay in her social skills. The men are unworldly; the women can cope. They manipulate society instead of abjuring it.

Collins' *No Name (All the Year Round,* 1862-63; 3 vols. 1862) hurries through the illegal connection of the elder Vanstones retrospectively in the opening chapters. "Mrs. Vanstone," even at forty-four, is more interesting and more refined than either of her daughters. A generation earlier, she had chosen to save Vanstone from ruin; he was drifting into hopelessness and dissipation after he had pensioned off the adventuress who "led him on, with merciless cunning" (Ch. 13) into matrimony. The second Mrs. Vanstone uses woman's superior capacity for social maneuvering towards a good end:

> she set herself from the first, to accomplish the one foremost purpose of so living with him, in the world's eye, as never to raise the suspicion that she was not his lawful wife. The women are few indeed, who cannot resolve firmly, scheme patiently, and act promptly, where the dearest interests of their lives are concerned. . . . she took all the needful precautions, in those early days, which her husband's less ready capacity had not the art to devise— precautions to which they were largely indebted for the preservation of their secret in later times. (Ch. 13)

One other feature of the sensation novel also tended to weaken the ethereal image of womanhood. In their search for ever greater and greater emotional effects, novelists touched on taboos for the sake of the response that they generated. There was a run on scenes of women nursing their infants. Birth became a physical process and not merely a spiritual one; morning sickness and postpartum weakness were used as plot devices; new fathers emerged shaken and restored to moral rectitude by realizing what their wives had gone through in the birth chamber. Things that could not be talked about were approached by innuendo; the abortion den in *Armadale (Cornhill,* 1844-66; 2 vols. 1866) might have been shielded from all but the very knowing by Collins' description of it as "a house rightly described as filled with wicked secrets, and people rightly represented as in danger of feeling the grasp of the law" because they are "skilled in criminal concealment" (Bk. 4, Ch. 4) but many novelists counted on readers' ability to gauge the suitable date of a marriage by counting off nine months backwards. W. W. Reade described Lucy, who had made a sudden trip to France and was gone for over a year, on her wedding day: "Her face was pale but beautiful; her arms were white, and finely molded; her bosom displayed more embonpoint than is usually found in young unmarried women."[23] Novelists used blood as well as sex; accidents are gory; heroines (even virtuous ones) die laboring for breath and coughing up blood; poison-takers have their stomachs pumped; and the final reconciliation in *Griffith Gaunt* is underlined when Griffith supplies a transfusion for Kate after a difficult childbirth.

Novelists had evidence of public interest in these topics. One secondary effect of the 1857 Divorce Act was that divorce court proceedings—which tended to be messy, since adultery had to be proven—were reported in the press. Though careful families probably did not let unmarried girls read the newspaper, women did buy Cecil Beeton's *The Queen,* a sixpenny weekly journal first issued in September 1861. It offered fashions and needlework, reports from Buckingham and Balmoral and, almost every week, a long illustrated account of a railway or steamship disaster and a column of criminal news headed "The Black Book":

> A Mr. John Grayson Farquhar, of Grange-road, Smallheath, shot, on the evening of Thursday week, a girl of 20, named Elizabeth Brooks, who had been living under his roof as housekeeper, and had borne him a child, which is dead . . .

> A respectable young woman, at Littleborough, near Rochdale, having incurred public disgrace by concealing the birth of a child (which was found dead), the brother went out and hanged himself, and the reputed father of the child has done the same.[24]

Novelists could be witty in pointing out the distance between people's taste in excitements and the brittle surface of prudery, as when Henry Kingsley carefully referred to "Br—ch-s" in a novel about bastardy, seduction and the death-throes of a whore.[25] Editors constantly imposed standards of taste. Florence Marryat removed a good deal the caressing from *Love's Conflict* at Geraldine Jewsbury's insistence.[26] Charles Dickens' eye was apparently caught by a questionable phrase in *No Name.* Chapter 13 of the three-volume edition says that "The accident of their father having been married, when he first met with their mother, has made them the outcasts of the whole social community." A reviewer protested that "we have often heard an illegal connexion and its result euphemistically designated as a 'misfortune;' but this is the first time, as far as we are aware, in which a lawful marriage has been denominated an 'accident.'"[27] The objectionable phrase had not appeared in the serial chapter that Dickens printed in *All the Year Round* on 10 May 1862.

The revisions made for the London publication of *Not Wisely but Too Well* reveal some details about the standard of propriety in the sixties. Many of the corrections come under the heading of good taste. In the earlier version Dare describes his last meeting with his legal wife thus:

> "I could have split laughing if I had not felt so inclined to be sick. I thought she'd never have done slobbering over me; and I can tell you, Kate, it is a serious thing to have a great female six feet six hanging all her weight round your neck. Such a strapper she is, Kitty!"[28]

For book publication the passage was altered to:

> "I should have died laughing if I had been spectator instead of sufferer. I thought she would never have ended the enacting of the Prodigal Son over me. Six fatted calves would not have been too many to slay in honour of my return. Such a giantess as she is, too, Kitty!" (II, 16-17)

The heroine is made more refined—she says "O nonsense" instead of "Oh bother"—and the niceties of physical propriety are observed: at one point in the original Dare catches Kate by the arm, while in the novel it is by the hand. In the revision, Broughton added paragraphs of commentary to assure the reader that she is not "defending the girl" or trying to make Dare attractive (I, 273).

In doing so she violates her original conception. Removing the physiological detail forces Broughton to deny her heroine's sensual experience and keeps the reader from realizing that Kate was physically attracted to Dare. In this passage, for example, the italicized phrases appear only in the first published version:

> . . . and he wrapped his arms around her as she stood before him, tighter, tighter, *till they were like fetters of iron binding her; and the strain that fulfilled all the wild longing, the burning dreams of weeks, was quite painful;* and *he* bent down his head from his stately height to her small uplifted face, nearer, nearer, till their lips met . . . [29]

The words Broughton had to leave out—the italicized words—are for me a fairly accurate description of the sexual tension that precedes orgasm, even in a virgin: kissing, masturbating, fantasizing. Many similar emendations indicate that the description of a woman's feelings that came from the experience or imagination of a rural clergyman's twenty-two-year-old daughter was not, in the eyes of a London publisher, fit to be read. The *Times* found even the revised version "unreal and repulsive."[30] Yet the book was highly successful, which suggests that Broughton found a responsive chord among readers. *Not Wisely but Too Well* was published anonymously, and it was reported that the Reverend Broughton strictly forbade his daughter Rhoda to read it.[31] In point of fact, he had died in 1863, before the novel came out, which destroys the truth of the anecdote but makes its wide circulation perhaps even more significant, because it reveals the subversive glee with which some women looked at men's opinions about what they ought to know and feel.

Few of these sensation novels have any claim to literary survival except as a reflection of the decade's interests. Changes in the publishing business and the reading audience that were not wholly understood at the time explain why sensationalism received more serious critical attention than we now give to similar kinds of entertainment.

The important innovation in publishing, which took place almost exactly at the beginning of the decade, was the shilling monthly magazine. The older monthlies had been so expensive (two shillings and sixpence, or even three shillings and sixpence in the case of the *New Monthly Magazine*) that they were read primarily by the gentry and the upper reaches of the middle class. The old monthlies saw their public as the educated, the cultured, the influential; most supported an identifiable political philosophy through articles on economics and public policy. Even *Bentley's Miscellany,* which was founded in 1837 on the strength of its editor's *Oliver Twist* and later passed from Dickens' hands into Ainsworth's, printed only one serialized novel at a time. Throughout the fifties none of the monthly magazines had a circulation of more than six or eight thousand copies per issue.

Around 1860 paper prices dropped sharply and, as with the penny magazines two decades earlier, many publishers saw the potential profits to be made from larger sales of a cheaper article. *Cornhill* began in 1860 with an astonishing circulation of 120,000. That figure could not hold—it depended on novelty and lack of competition—but by late in the decade *Argosy, Belgravia, Cornhill, Macmillan's, St. James, St. Paul's* and *Temple Bar* were each selling around twenty thousand copies an issue.[32]

Financially, the readers must largely have overlapped with the library audience; people who could afford a shilling a month for a magazine could also spend a guinea a year to subscribe to Mudie's. The difference is that choosing which magazine to buy gave them a more direct influence over what was published. The two authors whose sensation novels were smash hits early in the decade soon had their own magazines: Braddon founded *Belgravia* in 1866 and Mrs. Wood took over *Argosy* in 1867. Magazine serials had a tremendous impact on book sales, because a three-volume edition was usually published just before the end of the periodical run. *No Name* concluded in *All the Year Round* on 17 January 1863. When the book was published complete in an edition of four thousand on 31 December 1862, all but four hundred copies were sold by the end of the day.[33]

The shilling monthly colored the style and content of sixties writing. The number of competing magazines created a great demand for novels. Serialization encouraged the accumulation of incident (as opposed to the leisurely development of character) and the construction of an exciting peak in each installment. (The pace, not the subject matter, of *Adam Bede* made Blackwood decide to publish it in volumes rather than, as he had first intended, in *Blackwood's Edinburgh Magazine*.) The dramatic withholding of secrets kept the reader buying until the last issue. And the audience that influenced style, topic and moral standards by choosing what to buy was no longer simply the educated reading class.

The greatly expanded magazine-buying audience was made up of people who had lacked either the half-crown or the serious interest to subscribe to the older periodicals. Both factors had an influence. The less weighty format ate into sales of the established monthlies; *Blackwood's* circulation declined steadily throughout the sixties, and *Bentley's* first tried running more fiction and then merged with the shilling *Temple Bar* in 1868. But there were also many, especially in the lower to middling ranks of the commercial and administrative middle class, who had been priced out of the market at half a crown.

We do not need to go so far as the *Quarterly Review* article which found the penny novel of the forties and fifties to be "the original germ . . . to which all varieties of sensational literature may be referred"[34] to realize that the new novel-buying public was partly composed of those who might have been reading penny weekly magazines twenty years earlier. The economy was expanding; one historian says that three-fifths of the people who could be described as middle class in 1880 entered the class since 1840.[35] The story of an apparently false marriage made valid by discovering the truth, the "have your cake and eat it too" morality that criticizes the aristocracy and yet gives the heroine a title at the end, and the paradoxical combination of frankness with family-centered morality are all features of the *Family Herald* or the *London Journal*. Indeed, even the dramatic method reminds us that puzzles were popular in the penny magazines; with any sensational author less skillful than Wilkie Collins the reader generally figures out the answers long before the characters do. In the sixties we can see some direct overlap in audiences. *Lady Audley's Secret* was "second serialized" in the *London Journal* in 1863[36] and was successful enough to be followed by another story of Braddon's.[37] A few years later a *Family Herald* reader wrote to ask who Ouida really was.[38] In 1868 Reade reissued in hard covers the novel he had written for the *London Journal* eleven years earlier; he retitled it *The Double Marriage* to emphasize the bigamy theme. Many sensation novels were translated immediately to the other mass form and were successful as melodramas.

Until the 1860s it had been possible to assume that literature very successful with the novel-reading audience was probably worth reading. If books of the sensational type ceased to attract critical notice by the end of the decade, it was not because they had disappeared but because "bestseller" was on its way to becoming a pejorative term. In another ten years the future poet laureate, Alfred Austin (who had himself tried his hand at a sensation novel) told the public that "High Art" could not be written in a democracy because commercial success was "in the hands of a clever, pushing, semi-educated middle-class."[39] George Eliot was the last English novelist to enjoy both immediate popularity and lasting acclaim. After the 1860s writers and critics alike began to assume that the majority were Philistines.

Moralizers throughout the sixties believed that sensation literature was a symptom of rot at the core of society. But others defended the vogue. "E. B." wrote in Mrs. Wood's *Argosy* that people sought fiction to relax with because of "the very thoughtfulness of the age."[40] Escape reading gives us a clue about what is being escaped from; it may reflect a reverse image of the tone of the times.

At the turn of the nineteenth century the sensational form of literature was the Gothic. The novel of the sixties, like the Gothic, had an aristocratic cast of characters, used suspense to elicit terror, introduced perversion and abnormality, and depended heavily on the inheritance theme. It differed, however, in two important ways: the much smaller role of the supernatural—which was central to most Gothic novels—and the disappearance of the vapid, vapoury, helpless heroine.

The Gothic novel's supernaturalism was a reaction to the age of reason; it suggested that there were forces abroad in the world which could not be comprehended. The domesticated or urbanized Gothic tale of the 1840s—often published in penny numbers for poorer readers—used the real terrors of city life as a substitute for the imagined terrors of haunted castle and ruined monastery. James Malcolm Rymer's *The White Slave* (penny numbers, 1844-45) has a poor girl pursued through number after number by a villainous colonel. Her additional hazards include the poor law, misguided charitable ladies, needlework contractors, pompously respectable employers whose sons take liberties on the back stairs, and wretched prison conditions. Here, as in much of Dickens, the very geography of the city is as frightening as the subterranean passages of a medieval castle.

W. H. Ainsworth's *Old Saint Paul's* (1841)—the first novel to be serialized in an English newspaper—is an interesting transition-piece. Ainsworth uses the standard Gothic plot of the chased chaste as a string to hold together scenes of urban horrors magnified by fire and plague. Amabel is an innocent victim, but the grocer's apprentice who had tried for month after month to save her wins a knighthood for his role in halting the fire and marries an heiress.

The Gothic novel gave readers helplessness as an escape from rationalism and responsibility. In Ainsworth, in 1841, the heroine is still helpless, but the hero is an incarnation of initiative and self-help. By the 1860s helplessness, even of women, had apparently lost its attraction. The sensation novel provided escape from an increasingly complex urban economic and social environment that limited the individual's freedom of action, and from a decade colored by lack of certainty: by scientific questions about the special creation of the human race, by religious doubt. The sensation novel exorcised helplessness by ascribing evil to the actions of a single villain and then defeating that villain. The events that characters can't control arise not from social or supernatural forces but from deliberate human actions: wills, deathbed promises, secrets, intrigues. Detective skill and rational process and playing by the rules restore order at the end. The Gothic novel put the irrational in escapism; the sensational took it out again. It was a heroic literature for an age that had secret doubts about the individual's controlling role in the scheme of things.

George Meredith has been called the first "highbrow novelist."[41] His "plain story" about an unchaste woman is anything but plain; his hero and villain are the same person; social conventions and rigid morality are to

blame but there is no alternative good to praise; and the interpretation of Dahlia's purification through suffering is open to doubt.

Rhoda Fleming (3 vols.) was published in 1865, five years after Meredith had become a reader for Chapman and Hall. In it he abandoned the highly individual style and restricted social milieu of his earlier books for what seems in part a deliberate attempt to use his new understanding of a publisher's business relationship with the customers and in part a serious reflection inspired by the manuscripts he had been reading by the gross. Virtually every element of character and situation might be duplicated in any number of novels from the early 1860s: the farmer's daughter drawn to the city by her search for excitement, the son of a baronet-banker who abandons her because of class and family, the widowed adventuress over whom two duels have been fought, the bigamist who ships his wife off to America so he can marry for money, the misappropriated funds and intercepted letters.

Meredith was not, however, a sensationalist in technique. Many of the most gripping scenes (Robert's beating, his attack on Algy, the climactic moments of Dahlia's wedding to Sedgett) take place offstage. Some questions are never answered. Incomplete narration and shifting viewpoints had been used, of course, by Wilkie Collins (or, for that matter, by Mrs. Crowe a generation earlier) but in Meredith's book no detective comes along to pick up the loose ends. J. C. Jeaffreson's review in the *Athenaeum* raised a common contemporary objection; the story, he says, goes "slipping through the reader's fingers."[42] Meredith says in chapter 12 that the British public "will bear anything, so long as villainy is punished." The mass public will not, however, bear figuring out for themselves who the villains are and whether they have been punished or not.

Most of the characters accept class-based sexual codes. Edward abandons Dahlia because a lower-class wife would damage him socially, though his friends forgive "the lesser sin of his deceiving and ruining the girl" (Ch. 8). Public appearance and social prejudice also bind Dahlia's family; her father puts his farm on the market because—since everyone assumes that a man is responsible for his daughter's behavior—he can no longer hold up his head in front of the neighbors. Rhoda's part in the crucifixion of her sister reveals an absolute confusion between purity and respectability. Rhoda refuses to believe that Dahlia has done anything wrong. If her sister will only get married, her faith will be vindicated; Rhoda sees marriage as a proof of chastity rather than as a substitute for it.

Each marriage in the book is a symbol of woman's surrender. In the final movement of the story, the strong woman is humbled. Rhoda is caught between the horns of duty and desire, the same dilemma which led her to impale her sister's heart in the name of duty. Rhoda once exulted that "she, alone of women, was free from that wretched mesh called love" (Ch. 42). But faced with the promise to marry Algy—which she made to mitigate the consequences of her own action—and the realization that she loves Robert, she grows "weary of thinking and acting on her own responsibility and would gladly have abandoned her will." She tells Robert "'I am not fit to be my own mistress'" (Ch. 43).

Dahlia herself is shown almost entirely by indirection, and it is hard to know what we should make of her. Meredith insists that she not be seen in light of the "foul sentimentalism" of "soiled purity . . . lost innocence, the brand of shame" (Ch. 30). She avoids the victim role by taking responsibility for herself: "she had voluntarily stripped her spirit bare of evasion, and seen herself for what she was; pleading no excuse" (Ch. 30). She refuses to consider social judgments; she does not mind what people will say about her; she drinks poison rather than go with the "husband" who has been arranged for her. The cliche rendering of Dahlia's sanctification—that her soul "shone in her eyes and in her work, a lamp to her little neighbourhood"— and the moral of her final words—"'Help poor girls'"— were added to the novel when Meredith revised it for the collected edition of 1886. The original version of 1865 closes with Edward's puzzled realization that the purified woman—the woman free of society and sensuality—has escaped Eve's curse and is independent of man. Does the perfectly pure woman indeed have no heart? Is Dahlia something more or something less than human once she is "purified" of desire and emotion?

Thomas Hardy's *Desperate Remedies* (3 vols. 1871) is often considered an embarrassing beginner's piece to be explained away as a use of sensational material in order to secure publication. Hardy began as a social critic; Macmillan wrote him in 1869, when rejecting *The Poor Man and the Lady,* that "your pictures of character among Londoners, and especially the upper classes, are sharp, clear, incisive, and in many respects true"—but, he feared, in many respects comparable to the sort of thing printed in *Reynolds's Miscellany.*[43] Chapman and Hall were willing to publish but recommended against it; their reader, George Meredith, advised the aspiring novelist to forget about social reform and "attempt a novel with a purely artistic purpose, giving it a more complicated 'plot.'"[44]

And so he did. At first reading, Hardy's use of the sensation materials appears simply bungled. The changes of identity and secrets of the past are obvious; any reader of sixties novels knows what it means when an unmarried girl suddenly makes a long trip to the Continent for her health and looks as suspiciously at death certificates as at marriage lines. In comparison to Collins, Hardy seems plodding and self-conscious in dropping the clues, as, for example, when the otherwise

characterless housekeeper just happens to fold a hair left on a pillow into a scrap of paper so that it will be available, ten chapters later, when it is needed. Yet the method itself—arriving at a rational explanation for every detail, and using every detail to build the final situation—comes, in Hardy's hands, to imply cosmic interdependence. The characters' fortunes do not depend on individual efforts, or virtue, or villainy, or even on some dark and malignant fate but on half-chance events that arise from the intersection with other lives. One story's hero, the author muses, is a walk-on in the story of another life. Trains are delayed not by spectacular accidents but because it is Christmas and everyone is travelling; concealments arise from motives no darker than self-consciousness. The ultimate effect expresses the very sense of helplessness that popular sensationalists exorcised. Hardy's late novels are hardly less sensational than *Desperate Remedies* but the complaint ceased to be made, not only because the vogue for the term had passed but because, as Darwin, Marx and Freud seeped into intellectual consciousness, the sense of helplessness took on a philosophical dimension.

Hardy elaborates stock sensational conventions. Miss Aldclyffe displaces her maternal emotion onto Cytheria, the daughter of the man she did not marry because she knew that he would hate her when he' found out she was not a virgin. The situation is conventional, but the scene in which Miss Aldclyffe comes to Cytheria's bed, tries to turn her against all men, and pleads for her love extends Charles Reade's blurring of the distinction between maternal and sexual love into uncharted territory.

Chastity is not terribly high on Hardy's list of virtues. Anne Seaway is perhaps a conventional whore with a heart of gold: "Many of these women who own to no moral code show considerable magnanimity when they see people in trouble. To act right simply because it is one's duty is proper; but a good action which is the result of no law of reflection shines more than any" (Ch. 19). But duty, indeed, is the problem, because duty implies some one or some thing more important than the individual. When Cytheria discovers immediately after her wedding to Manston that she loves Edward, her brother speaks for society:

> "Many a woman has gone to ruin herself . . . and brought those who love her into disgrace, by acting on such impulses as possess you now. I have a reputation to lose as well as you . . . Besides, your duty to society, and those about you, requires that you should live with (at any rate) all the appearance of a good wife, and try to love your husband."

> "Yes—my duty to society," she murmured. "But ah, Owen, it is difficult to adjust our outer and inner life with perfect honesty to all! Though it may be right to care more for the benefit of the many than

for the indulgence of your own single self, when you consider that the many, and duty to them, only exist to you through your own existence, what can be said? . . . perhaps, far in time to come, when I am dead . . . they will pause just for an instant, and give a sigh to me, and think 'Poor girl,' believing they do great justice to my memory by this. But they will never, never realize that it was my single opportunity of existence, as well as of doing my duty, which they are regarding . . ." (Ch. 13)

The whole basis of the thematic movement has changed. There can be no sin, suffering, purification and redemption for the unchaste woman because there is no final reward, no eternal scale. Miss Aldclyffe is neither a tragic victim nor a wicked adventuress nor a purified heroine. She made a mistake, was sorry, and tried to rectify it, but good motives are not enough; her maternal love leads to further sorrow. "'Pity me—O pity me'" she says to Cytheria towards the end. "'To die unloved is more than I can bear!'" (Ch. 21) In a universe stumbling towards darkness human love takes on new significance, not as a cement for the family-based social order but as a temporary shelter against loneliness and doubt.

Neither Hardy's novel nor Meredith's was widely enough read at the time of publication to enter into the mass consciousness in any direct fashion; *Desperate Remedies* was remaindered by Smith's library after three months on the shelves and *Rhoda Fleming* was the most sparsely and unfavorably reviewed of Meredith's novels.[45] Though they grew from the same time and class conditioned consciousness and made use of the same plot material as the more ephemeral sensation novels, *Rhoda Fleming* and *Desperate Remedies* offered problems instead of solutions.

In the sensation novels proper, a woman's unchastity is used, often, simply to violate decorum for the sake of an emotional effect. The interesting moral issues are seldom followed to their conclusion; often they seem no more than the accidental insertions of an intelligent author writing at speed. In very broad terms, however, popular sensation novels react conservatively to changing mores. The woman who is, like a man, sexual is apt to be bad because she is also financially ambitious or power-mad or in other ways masculinized. The attacks are mitigated, however, by a recognition that economic dependence and social subordination are imposed by woman's conventional role and by a realization that propriety is not necessarily the same thing as chastity. When—as in Collins and Reade—the strong women are admired, it is because they have the power, motherlike, to intervene between men and a sometimes undesirable world.

Notes

[1] The term "sensation novel" was first used in September 1861 in the *Sixpenny Magazine,* according to Kathleen Tillotson, "The Lighter Reading of the Eighteen Sixties," preface to *The Woman in White,* by Wilkie Collins (Boston: Houghton Mifflin, 1969), p. xxi.

[2] H. L. Mansel, "Sensation Novels," *Quarterly Review,* 113 (1863), 490.

[3] "Recent Novels: Their Moral and Religious Teaching," *London Quarterly,* 27 (1866), 104.

[4] Adeline Sergeant, "Mrs. Crowe, Mrs. Archer Clive, Mrs. Henry Wood," in *Women Novelists of Queen Victoria's Reign* (London: Hurst and Blackett, 1897), p. 181.

[5] Mansel, p. 488.

[6] Mary Elizabeth Braddon, *Aurora Floyd* (London: Tinsley, 1863), I, 33.

[7] The sporting novelist Robert Smith Surtees also disliked women on horseback, though on slightly different grounds; his targets were the feminine types who joined the fox-hunt for romantic reasons and thereby interfered with masculine pleasures. See Ch. 15, "The Hunting Woman," in Frederick Watson, *Robert Smith Surtees: A Critical Study* (London: Harrap, 1933).

[8] *Athenaeum,* 22 Oct. 1864, p. 523.

[9] *Anonyma or Fair but Frail* (1864); *The Soiled Dove: A Biography of a Fast Young Lady Familiarly Known as "The Kitten"* (1865). Other titles include *Skittles, Incognita, The Beautiful Demon, Love Frolics of a Young Scamp, "Left Her Home",* and *Fanny White.* The series was originally published by George Vickers and reissued about 1884 by C. H. Clark. All were anonymous; the authorship has been attributed to W. Stephens Hayward, E. L. Blanchard, Bracebridge Hemyng, and others. Sadleir feels that Hemyng, who wrote the section on prostitution in London for Mayhew and also produced a great number of cheap railway novels, was probably responsible for at least the earlier books of the series; see Michael Sadleir, *Nineteenth Century Fiction: A Bibliographical Record* (Cambridge: Cambridge Univ. Press, 1951), II, 8.

[10] Elipses in the original. The *Saturday Review* called *Liberty Hall, Oxon.* "the filthiest book that has been issued by a respectable English publisher during the lifetime of the present generation"; see 21 Jan. 1860, p. 84.

[11] Punctuation is taken from the first edition, II, 107-08. The cheap editions tend to be more liberal with exclamation points and italics.

[12] Margaret Maison, "Adulteresses in Agony," *The Listener,* 14 Jan. 1961, p. 134.

[13] Amy Cruse, *The Victorians and Their Books* (London: Allen and Unwin, 1935), p. 325.

[14] Charles W. Wood, *Memorials of Mrs. Henry Wood* (London: Bentley, 1894), p. 248.

[15] *Lady Audley's Secret,* by Mary Elizabeth Braddon; serialized in *Robin Goodfellow* (6 July—28 Sept. 1861, unfinished) and in *Sixpenny Magazine* from March, 1862; published in three volumes by Tinsley on 1 Oct. 1862 with eight further three-volume editions by early 1863. The profits enabled Tinsley to build a villa which he graciously named Audley Lodge.

[16] "Desperate Remedies: Sensation Novels of the 1860's," *Victorian Newsletter,* No. 49 (1976), p. 4.

[17] *Land at Last* was published in *Temple Bar* under the name of the magazine's editor, Edmund Yates. William Tinsley, in *Random Recollections of an Old Publisher* (London: Simkin, Marshall, 1900), I, 143, says that most or all of the book was written by Frances Sarah Hoey.

[18] Charles Reade, *Griffith Gaunt,* Ch. 43.

[19] Robert Lee Wolff, "Devoted Disciple," *Harvard Library Bulletin,* 22 (1974), 6.

[20] Judging from Reade's character as interpreted in Wayne Burns, *Charles Reade: A Study in Victorian Authorship* (New York: Bookman Associates, 1961), the relationship with Mrs. Seymour could have been physically innocent. Reade did, however, have an early alliance with a fisher girl, and his will acknowledged their child.

[21] Kenneth Robinson, *Wilkie Collins* (New York: Macmillan, 1952), p. 36.

[22] Margaret Oliphant, "Charles Reade's Novels," *Blackwood's Edinburgh Magazine,* 106 (1869), 490.

[23] *Liberty Hall, Oxon.,* III, 205.

[24] *The Queen,* 7 Sept. 1861, p. 11.

[25] *Ravenshoe,* Ch. 66.

[26] The text of the first edition shows that Marryat has carried out Jewsbury's suggestions quoted in Jeanne Rosenmayer Fahnestock, "Geraldine Jewsbury: The Power of the Publisher's Reader," *Nineteenth Century Fiction,* 28 (1973), 253-72.

[27] Mansel, p. 296.

[28] *Dublin University Magazine,* 66 (1865), 505.

[29] I, 247; *Dublin University Magazine,* 66 (1865), 15.

[30] *Times,* 25 Dec. 1867, p. 4.

[31] Cruse, p. 332.

[32] Alvar Ellegard, "The Readership of the Periodical Press in Mid-Victorian Britain," *Victorian Periodicals Newsletter,* No. 13 (1971), p. 18.

[33] Robinson, *Wilkie Collins,* pp. 168-69.

[34] Mansel, pp. 505-06.

[35] H. J. Hanham, *The Reformed Electoral System in Great Britain, 1832-1914* (London: Historical Association, 1968), p. 12.

[36] *LJ,* 37 (21 Mar. 1863) - 38 (15 Aug. 1863).

[37] "The Outcasts," expressly written for the *London Journal* and commencing on 12 Sept. 1863, p. 161. Braddon also wrote for *Reynolds's Miscellany* and for other cheap magazines.

[38] *FH,* 31 (6 Sept. 1873), 300.

[39] Alfred Austin, "Art and Democracy," *Cornhill,* 40 (1879), 231.

[40] "The Sensation Novel," *Argosy,* 18 (1874), 142.

[41] L. T. Hergenhan, "The Reception of George Meredith's Early Novels," *Nineteenth Century Fiction,* 19 (1964), 214.

[42] *Athenaeum,* 14 Oct. 1865, p. 495.

[43] William R. Rutland, *Thomas Hardy: A Study of His Writings and Their Background* (Oxford: Blackwell, 1938), 353-54.

[44] Florence E. Hardy, *The Early Life of Thomas Hardy, 1840-1891* (London: Macmillan, 1928), p. 82.

[45] L. T. Hergenhan, "Meredith's Attempts to Win Popularity: Contemporary Reaction," *Studies in English Literature,* 4 (1964), 638.

Jane Tompkins (essay date 1985)

SOURCE: "The Other American Renaissance" in *Sensational Designs: The Cultural Work of American Fiction 1790-1860,* Oxford University Press, 1985, pp. 147-85.

[*In the following essay, Tompkins assesses the way in which women's lives in the 1860s play into some recurring elements of sentimental fiction and the sensation novel. She focuses particularly on* The Wide, Wide World *by Susan Warner.*]

If the tradition of American criticism has not acknowledged the value of *Uncle Tom's Cabin,* it has paid even less attention to the work of Stowe's contemporaries among the sentimental writers. Although these women wrote from the same perspective that made *Uncle Tom's Cabin* so successful, and although in the nineteenth century their works were almost equally well-known, their names have been entirely forgotten. The writer I am concerned with in particular is Susan Warner, who was born in the same year as Herman Melville, and whose best-selling novel, *The Wide, Wide World,* was published in the same twelve-month period as *Moby Dick.* But I am not interested in Warner's novel for the light it can shed on Melville;[1] I am interested in it because it represents, in its purest form, an entire body of work that this century's critical tradition has ignored.

According to that tradition, the "great" figures of the 1850s, a period known to us now as the "American Renaissance," were a handful of men who refused to be taken in by the pieties of the age. Disgusted by the clichés that poured from the pens of the "scribbling women," these men bore witness to a darker reality, which the mass of readers could not face. While successful female authors told tearful stories about orphan girls whose Christian virtue triumphed against all odds, the truly great writers—Poe, Hawthorne, Melville, Emerson, Thoreau—dared, according to Henry Nash Smith, to "explore the dark underside of the psyche," and to tackle "ultimate social and intellectual issues." And because they repudiated the culture's dominant value system, they were, in Perry Miller's words, "crushed by the juggernaut" of the popular sentimental novel.[2] The sentimental writers, on the other hand, were sadly out of touch with reality. What they produced, says Smith, was a literature of "reassurance," calculated to soothe the anxieties of an economically troubled age. To the "Common Man and Common Woman," fearful of challenge or change, they preached a "cosmic success story," which promised that the practice of virtue would lead to material success. Their subject matter—the tribulations of orphan girls—was innately trivial; their religious ideas were "little more than a blur of good intentions"; they "feared the probing of the inner life"; and above all were committed to avoiding anything that might make the "undiscriminating mass" of their middlebrow readers "uncomfortable."[3]

Those judgments are, in fact, amplified versions of what Hawthorne and Melville said about their sentimental rivals, whom they hated for their popular and critical success. My purpose here is to challenge that description of sentimental novels and to argue that their exclusion from the canon of American literature has been a mistake. For its seems to me that, instead of accepting uncritically the picture Hawthorne and Melville painted—of themselves as victims, of the sentimental novelists as negligible, and of the general public as, in Hawthorne's words, "that great gull, whom we are endeavoring to circumvent"—modern scholars ought to pay attention to a body of work which was so enormously influential and which drew so vehement a response from those who—successfully as it turned out—strove to suppress it.

The publication of Susan Warner's *The Wide, Wide World* in December of 1850, caused an explosion in the literary marketplace that was absolutely unprecedented—nothing like it, in terms of sales, had ever been seen before. Fifteen months later, *Uncle Tom's Cabin,* whose fame is still legendary, broke the records Warner's novel had set. Two years later, Maria Cummins' *The Lamplighter*—the direct literary descendant of *The Wide, Wide World,* and the novel that earned Hawthorne's special contempt—made another tremendous hit.[4] Critics have been at a loss to explain the enormous and long-standing popularity of these books, and one critic, who has devoted an entire study to the influence of popular fiction on classical American writing, dismisses the phenomenon, saying "it is impossible now to determine just what did happen to the market in the early 1850's."[5]

But it is not impossible to determine. The impact of sentimental novels is directly related to the cultural context that produced them. And once one begins to explore this context in even a preliminary way, the critical practice that assigns Hawthorne and Melville the role of heroes, the sentimental novelists the role of villains, and the public the role of their willing dupes, loses its credibility. The one great fact of American life during the period under consideration was, in Perry Miller's words, the "terrific universality" of the revival.[6] Sentimental fiction was perhaps the most influential expression of the beliefs that animated the revival movement and had shaped the character of American life in the years before the Civil War. Antebellum critics and readers did not distinguish sharply between fiction and what we would now call religious propaganda. Warner, for instance, never referred to her books as "novels," but called them stories, because, in her eyes, they functioned in the same way as Biblical parables, or the pamphlets published by the American Tract Society; that is, they were written for edification's sake and not for the sake of art, as we understand it. The highest function of any art, for Warner as for most of her contemporaries, was the bringing of souls to Christ. Like their counterparts among the evangelical clergy, the sentimental novelists wrote to educate their readers in Christian perfection and to move the nation as a whole closer to the city of God. They saw their work as part of a world-historical mission; but in order to understand the nature of their project, one has to have some familiarity with the cultural discourse of the age for which they spoke.[7]

The best place to begin is with a set of documents that, as far as I know, have never made their way into criticism of American Renaissance literature: the publications of the American Tract Society, one of the five great religious organizations of the Evangelical United Front.[8] These organizations were a concrete mobilization of wealth, energy, and missionary fervor designed to convert the entire nation and eventually the entire world to the truths of Protestant Christianity. That monumental effort, though it failed in its original purpose, did provide the nation with that "sameness of views" that, as Lyman Beecher, one of the movement's chief initiators, observed, was essential to the welfare of a nation torn apart by sectional strife.[9] The literature of the American Tract Society, the first organization in America to publish and distribute the printed word on a mass scale, is a testament both to the faith of evangelical Christians—to the shape of their dreams—and to what they experienced as everyday reality. It is only by attempting to see reality as they did that one can arrive at a notion of what gave sentimental fiction its tremendous original force.

I. The Closet

The conception of reality on which the reform movement was based is nowhere more dramatically illustrated than in the activities of the New York City Tract Society which, in 1829, undertook a massive experiment in what we would now call social welfare. The Society divided the city's fourteen wards into districts of about sixty families each and appointed teams of its members to visit every family in each district once a month.[10] The Tract Visiters, as they were called, ministered to the poor in a material way, helping them to find jobs and better homes; but this was not their primary purpose. Their major business was distributing Bibles and religious tracts, organizing prayer meetings, urging church attendance, and talking to people about the state of their souls. The Tract Visiters believed that the only real help one could offer another person, rich or poor, was not material, but spiritual, and the directions that guided them in their work insisted on this: "Be much in prayer," the directions said. "Endeavor to feel habitually and deeply that all your efforts will be in vain unless accompanied by the Holy Ghost. And this blessing you can expect only in answer to prayer. Pray, therefore, without ceasing. Go from your closet to your work and from your work return again to the closet."[11]

If one can understand what made these directions meaningful and effective for the people who carried them out, one is in a position to understand the power of sentimental fiction. For all sentimental novels take place, metaphorically and literally, in the "closet." Sentimental heroines rarely get beyond the confines of a private space—the kitchen, the parlor, the upstairs chamber—but more important, most of what they do takes place inside the "closet" of the heart. For what the word *sentimental* really means in this context is that the arena of human action, as in the Tract Society directions, has been defined not as the world, but as the human soul. This fiction shares with the evangelical reform movement a theory of power that stipulates that all true action is not material, but spiritual; that one obtains spiritual power through prayer; and that those who know how, in the privacy of their closets, to struggle for possession of their souls will one day possess the world through the power given to them by God. This theory of power makes itself felt, in the mid-nineteenth century, not simply in the explicit assertions of religious propaganda, nor in personal declarations of faith, but as a principle of interpretation that gives form to experience itself, as the records the Tract Visiters left of their activities show.

The same beliefs that make the directions to Tract Visiters intelligible structured what the Visiters saw as they went about their work. In one Tract Society report the Visiter records that a young woman who was dying of pulmonary consumption became concerned at the eleventh hour about the condition of her soul and asked for spiritual help. The report reads:

> She was found by the Visiter supplied with a number of tracts, and kindly directed to the Saviour of sinners. Some of her relatives—they cannot be called friends—attempted to impede the visiter's way to her bedside, and would often present hinderances which she could not remove. God, however, showed himself strong in her behalf. . . . For some time clouds hung over her mind, but they were at length dispelled by the sun of righteousness. . . . As she approached the hour which tries men's souls, her strength failed fast; her friends gathered around her; . . . and while they were engaged in a hymn her soul seemed to impart unnatural energy to her emaciated and dying body. To the astonishment of all, she said to her widowed mother, who bent anxiously over her, "Don't weep for me, I shall soon be in the arms of my Saviour." She prayed fervently, and feel asleep in Jesus.[12]

Like all the fiction we label "sentimental," this narrative blots out the uglier details of life and cuts experience to fit a pattern of pious expectation. The anecdote tells nothing about the personality or background of the young woman, fails to represent even the barest facts of her disease or of her immediate surroundings. For these facts, the report substitutes the panaceas of Christian piety—God's mercy on a miserable sinner, the tears and prayers of a deathbed conversion, falling "asleep" in Jesus. Its plot follows a prescribed course from sin to salvation. But what is extraordinary about this anecdote is that it is not a work of fiction, but a factual report. Though its facts do not correspond to what a twentieth-century observer would have recorded, had he or she been at the scene, they faithfully represent what the Tract Society member saw. Whereas a modern social worker would have noticed the furniture of the sick room, the kind of house the woman lived in, her neighborhood, would have described her illness, its history and course of treatment, and sketched in her socio-economic background and that of her relatives and friends, the Tract Visiter sees only a spiritual predicament: the woman's initial "alarm," the "clouds [that] hung over her mind," God's action on her heart, the turn from sin to righteousness. Whereas the modern observed would have structured the events in a downward spiral, as the woman's condition deteriorated from serious to critical, and ended with her death, the report reverses that progression. Its movement is upward, from "thoughtlessness" to "conviction," to "great tranquality, joy, and triumph."[13]

The charge twentieth-century critics have always leveled against sentimental fiction is that it presents a picture of life so oversimplified and improbable, that only the most naive and self-deceiving reader could believe it. But the sense of the real that this criticism takes for granted is not the one that the readers of sentimental novels had. *Their* assumptions are the same as those that structured the events of the report I have just quoted. For what I've been speaking about involves three distinct levels of apprehension: "reality itself" as it appears to people at a given time; what people will accept as an "accurate description" of reality; and novels and stories that, because they seem faithful to such descriptions, therefore seem true. The audience for whom the thoughtless young lady's conversion was a moving factual report, found the tears and prayers of sentimental heroines equally compelling. This is not because they didn't know what good fiction was, nor because their notions about human life were naive and superficial, but because the "order of things" to which both readers and fictions belonged was itself structured by such narratives.

The story of the young woman's death from pulmonary consumption is exactly analogous to the kind of exemplary tale that had formed the consciousness of the nation in the early years of the nineteenth century. Such stories filled the religious publications distributed in unimaginably large quantities by organizations like those of the Evangelical United Front. The American Tract Society alone claims to have published thirty-seven million tracts at a time when the entire population of the country was only eleven million. And the same kind of exemplary narrative was the staple of the McGuffey's readers and primers of a similar type on which virtually the entire nation had been schooled. They appeared in manuals of social behavior, and in instructional literature of every variety, filled the pages of popular magazines, and appeared even in the daily newspapers. As David Reynolds has recently demonstrated, the entire practice of pulpit oratory in

this period shifted from an expository and abstract mode of explicating religious doctrine, to a mode in which sensational narratives carried the burden of theological precept.[14] These stories were always didactic in nature—illustrating the importance of a particular virtue such as obedience, faith, sobriety, or patience—and they were usually sensational in content—the boy who plays hooky from school falls into a pond and drowns, the starving widow is saved at the last moment by a handsome stranger who turns out to be her son. But their sensationalism ultimately lies not so much in the dramatic nature of the events they describe as in the assumptions they make about the relation of human events to the spiritual realities that make them meaningful. One of their lessons is that all experience is sensational, when seen in the light of its soteriological consequences: the saving or damning of the soul. In their assumptions about the nature and the purpose of human life, these stories provided a fundamental framework for the ordering of experience. The following typical account of a sick child's conversion provides some sense of how that interpretive system worked.

"Ann Eliza Williams, or the Child an Hundred Years Old, an Authentic Narrative" by the Reverend William S. Plumer, D.D. (New York: American Tract Society, n.d.) records that a young girl of "exquisite nervous sensibility" and "an irascible, obstinate, and ungovernable temper" had become concerned about her soul after two attacks of tuberculosis. During the second attack, she is converted, joins the church, and from that time on becomes a model of Christian deportment. On one particular occasion, the sick child is asked by her doctor and pastor how she feels. But instead of reporting her physical sensations, she "seems to forget all her bodily pain" and gives an answer that ignores the question: "O Jesus is precious, I am happy in him; his favor is life and his loving kindness is better than life."[15] Far from ignoring the question, however, Ann Eliza implicitly rebukes her questioners by putting their question into its proper perspective. Her words can be paraphrased as follows: "My physical condition is not important; what matters is my soul, for that alone is immortal. And since Jesus by his death has redeemed my soul, I am happy because of him." This theological answer seems to deny the practical realities of Ann Eliza's situation—her sickness, her pain, her possible death—but in fact it deals with those realities directly by pointing to the means of overcoming them. The thought of Jesus' love transforms her experience, makes her happy, drives away her pain. Her recognition that God's love is the final fact of existence transforms Ann Eliza's situation: what she experiences now is not pain, but the knowledge of her salvation. And therefore when someone asks her how she feels, "O Jesus is precious" is not a pious evasion, but a truthful reply.

It is extremely difficult for modern readers to hold on to the perspective that makes Ann Eliza's answer seem true, both because its theological assumptions are different from ours and because those assumptions carry with them a correspondingly alien rhetoric. In the twentieth century, materialist notions about the ultimate nature of reality and faith in the validity of scientific method have given rise to strategies of persuasion that require institutionally certified investigators to argue in a technical vocabulary for conclusions based on independently verifiable evidence, gathered according to professionally sanctioned methods of inquiry. (The metaphysical assumptions behind this mode of argumentation are no less powerful for being unstated.) In the same way, a belief that reality is ultimately spiritual, and a conception of Jesus as a personal savior with whom one has a loving and intimate relationship, gave rise in the early nineteenth century to a rhetoric in which an individual (such as the Reverend Plumer) testifies in impassioned language to miraculous or sensational events bearing witness to the truths of religious faith. In this rhetorical tradition, a single representative case, strikingly presented, constitutes the most effective form of evidence because that is the form which the audience *expects* such demonstrations to take. The force of the demonstration, moreover, depends upon the miraculousness of the events it describes, not on their probability—as the subtitle "or the Child an Hundred Years Old" suggests—since the point of the story is to affirm the existence of supernatural powers by pointing to God's intervention in human affairs, and not to chart the course of natural, unregenerate behavior. There is no need, either, for independent verification of the evidence, because supernatural events, by definition, cannot be repeated experimentally. Other "authentic" cases just like this one—of which the tract literature is full—would be the best kind of auxiliary verification. The Reverend Plumer's credentials, moreover, are superb. He is a Christian minister and a doctor of divinity, and therefore can be presumed to have special insight into phenomena of the kind he relates, and he is vouched for by the prestigious American Tract Society, a bastion of the country's religious (and socio-economic) establishment. Finally, the language of his narration gives palpable proof of the spiritual realities he bears witness to, not because it is neutral and detached, but because it is so obviously the product of intense feeling. When the presence of the Holy Ghost is what is in question, spontaneous eloquence, Biblical and oracular in style, is the most persuasive form of rhetoric.

In short, the conditions within which Ann Eliza's story is heard as convincing are just as culturally determined as those that shape its theology. The same network of assumptions that supported the religious beliefs of evangelical Christians shaped their rhetorical and stylistic conventions as well. For a text depends upon its audience's beliefs not just in a gross general way, but intricately and precisely. It depends, to borrow a term from ethnomethodology, upon "the fine power of a culture," which "does not, so to speak, merely fill brains in roughly the same way, but fills them so that they are alike in fine detail."[16] And this means that the cultural conventions that make a narrative convincing inform not only the perception of nonmaterial concerns such as the existence of God or the shape of an argument, they also inform perception of the ordinary facts of existence.

The records people left of their lives in antebellum America suggest that the modes of thought underlying the Tract Society directions and the story of Ann Eliza Williams pervaded people's perceptions of their everyday affairs. The letters they wrote to one another, the diaries they kept, the way they thought about their work, their homes, and their families, reflect the same sense of millenarian purpose that drove the reform movement and inspired writers like Warner and Stowe. The Protestant-Republican ideology, which identified the spreading of the Gospel with the building of a nation, did not distinguish clearly if at all between activities that had a practical aim—such as the straightening of a room, the building of a school, or the starting of a business—and activities that were specifically spiritual—like reading the Bible or attending prayer meetings. The welfare of the nation, conceived in millenarian terms as the bringing of God's kingdom to earth, depended upon the virtue of the individual citizen; any task, no matter how small, could be seen as either helping or hindering the establishment of Christ's kingdom. As John Thompson declared in addressing the American Home Missionary Society's twenty-second annual meeting:

> no nation can either prosper or last without popular virtue— . . . the virtue of the Bible, in all its purity and life, and generous conviction! Religion, Protestant religion, is our great national want, as it is our greatest national security. . . . Our power lies in no gleaming spear, or gloating admirals; . . . it dwells in the workshops, the manufactories, in the open fields, by the firesides, in the homes and haunts of our widespread population; and this virtue comes not of nature; it is a foreign element and must first be implanted.[17]

The implantation of virtue was the primary goal of nearly everything nineteenth-century Americans read: textbooks, novels, poems, magazine stories, or religious tracts. As David Tyack and Elisabeth Hansot have recently argued, the entire educational system in this country was founded on the premise that a democratic republic depended on the Christian character of its citizens; the men who built the nation's common schools saw themselves as doing the Lord's work.[18] When the coming of God's kingdom depended on the private virtue of every citizen, even deciding when to get up in the morning, or what time to eat dinner had consequences that no Christian could afford to overlook. For example, in this time schedule printed in a child-rearing manual entitled *Thoughts on Domestic Education, The Result of Experience* by a "Mother," the sense of an overriding purpose entwines itself with the minute-by-minute organization of a young lady's typical day.

SCHEME
for the distribution of time.

Hours		o'Clock
	To rise, all the year round	—7 A.M.
1	Dressing, washing, bathing	—8
1	Prayer and Study	—9
1	Breakfast and conversation	—10
4	Studious occupation	—2 P.M.
2	Walking, riding, or dancing	—4
1	Light reading or drawing	—5
1	Dinner	—6
2	Music, needlework, or reading	—8
1	Tea and conversation	—9
1	Dancing, music, needlework, or reading	—10
	To be in bed by	—11
8	Sleep	—7 A.M.

The last question before going to sleep: What good have I done today?[19]

The question that ends the day is the key to understanding what the time schedule is for. So that the young lady will never be at a loss as to how to answer it, the Mother appends a table of virtues to her volume, starting with "Obedience," and including others such as "Humility" and "Industry," which the young lady can check off according to whether or not she has performed them. The organization of time into regular blocks of activity, beginning with prayer and ending with a checklist of virtues, provides a miniature example of how people in the antebellum era thought about their daily lives, and indeed about the whole of life. The cultivation of social skills like conversation, and of artistic accomplishments like drawing and needlework, the pursuit of "studious occupation" and of physical fitness through "walking, riding, or dancing" were conceived not as ends in themselves, but as part of the practice of virtue which had to be learned through conscious self-discipline. One had a "scheme" for the distribution of time the better to serve God and one's fellow man. The time schedule and the checklist of virtues were ways of building Christian character, the foundation stone of a democratic republic.[20] And this sort of instructional material was not merely theoretical in its consequences; people did not simply *talk* about virtue, they lived it. Just as whole families in the slums of New York wept and asked to be instructed in the Scriptures when they heard Visiters read aloud the story of "Bob, the Cabin Boy," so young ladies really did organize their days according to the principles the Mother recommended.[21] The best example I have found of how totally the evangelical movement had saturated American culture is this time schedule found in the pocket

of a girl's dress. Mrs. Lydia Sigourney reprints it in her biography of Margaret Flower, who died in Hartford, Connecticut, in 1834, at the age of fourteen.

> Rise at half past five. Take care of the rooms. Sew until two hours from that time. Practice my piano one hour, then study one hour. Work till three in the afternoon, then practice an hour, and study an hour, reserving time for exercise.[22]

Margaret Flower's schedule (composed, as Sigourney notes, when she was *on vacation*) shows that directions such as those that the Mother offered her readers, and which the Tract Society distributed to its members, really worked. They had traction because the readers they addressed already understood life according to the principles that these directions are attempting to inculcate. Margaret Flower follows the instructions she finds in a manual because she already wishes to make herself into a more effective agent of God's will. The didactic literature of the antebellum era was not an abstract set of standards designed to *force* life into a predetermined shape; rather, it helped its original audience to put into practice the aims they already had at heart.[23] As Robert Wiebe observed, the leaders of the reform movement "believed that they spoke *for* the nation rather than to it"; assuming that their audience "shared the same ethical system, the same dedication to public service," they attempted "not to convince people but simply to rouse them."[24] For Margaret Flower, as for the author of *Thoughts on Domestic Education*, taking care of the rooms, practicing an hour, then studying an hour were activities that had to be regulated because they were understood in the light of a great purpose: the saving of one's soul and the bringing of all souls to Christ.

When you turn from the tract society reports, religious narratives, educational manuals, and autobiographical documents to the fiction of writers like Stowe and Warner, you find the same assumptions at work. Those novels are motivated by the same millennial commitment; they are hortatory and instructional in the same way; they tell the same kinds of stories; they depend upon the same rhetorical conventions; and they take for granted the same relationship between daily activities and the forging of a redeemer nation. When critics dismiss sentimental fiction because it is out of touch with reality, they do so because the reality *they* perceive is organized according to a different set of conventions for constituting experience. For while the attack on sentimental fiction claims for itself freedom from the distorting effects of a naive religious perspective, the real naiveté is to think that that attack is launched from no perspective whatsoever, or that its perspective is disinterested and not culture-bound in the way the sentimental novelists were. The popular fiction of the American Renaissance has been dismissed primarily because it follows from assumptions about the shape and meaning of existence that we no longer hold. But once one has a grasp of the problems these writers were trying to solve, their solutions do not seem hypocritical or shallow, unrealistic or naive; on the contrary, given the social circumstances within which they had to work, their prescriptions for living seem at least as heroic as those put forward by the writers who said, "No, in thunder."

II. Power

If the general charge against sentimental fiction has been that it is divorced from actual human experience, a more specific form of that charge is that these novels fail to deal with the brute facts of political and economic oppression, and therefore cut themselves off from the possibility of truly affecting the lives of their readers. Tremaine McDowell, writing in *The Literary History of the United States,* dismisses Mrs. Lydia Sigourney—who epitomizes the sentimental tradition for modern critics—by saying that while she "knew something of the humanitarian movements of the day, all . . . she did for Negroes, Indians, the poor, and the insane was to embalm them in her tears."[25] Such cutting remarks are never made about canonical authors of the period, though they, too, did nothing for "Negroes, Indians, the poor," and wrote about them considerably less than their female rivals. But what this sort of commentary reveals, beyond an automatic prejudice against sentimental writers, is its own failure to perceive that the great subject of sentimental fiction is preeminently a social issue. It is no exaggeration to say that domestic fiction is preoccupied, even obsessed, with the nature of power. Because they lived in a society that celebrated free enterprise and democratic government but were excluded from participating in either, the two questions these female novelists never fail to ask are: what is power, and where is it located? Since they could neither own property, nor vote, nor speak at a public meeting if both sexes were present, women had to have a way of defining themselves which gave them power and status nevertheless, in their own eyes and in the eyes of the world.[26] That is the problem sentimental fiction addresses.

In his characterization of American women, Tocqueville accurately described the solution to this problem as it appeared to an outsider. He noted that the interests of a "Puritanical" and "trading" nation lead Americans to require "much abnegation on the part of women, and a constant sacrifice of her pleasures to her duties." But, he continues, "I never observed that the women of America consider conjugal authority as a usurpation of their rights. . . . It appeared to me, on the contrary, that they attach a sort of pride to the voluntary surrender of their own will and make their boast to bend themselves to the yoke, not to shake it off."[27] The ethic of sentimental fiction, unlike that of writers like Melville, Emerson, and Thoreau, was an ethic of submission. But the relation of sentimental authors to their subservient condition and to the dominant beliefs about the nature and function of women was more complicated than Tocqueville supposed. The fact is that American women simply could not assume a stance of open rebellion against the conditions of their lives for they lacked the material means of escape or opposition. They had to stay put and submit. And so the domestic novelists made that necessity the basis on which to build a power structure of their own. Instead of rejecting the culture's value system outright, they appropriated it for their own use, subjecting the beliefs and customs that had molded them to a series of transformations that allowed them both to fulfill and transcend their appointed roles.

The process of transformation gets underway immediately in Warner's novel when the heroine, Ellen Montgomery, a child of ten, learns that her mother is about to leave on a long voyage for the sake of her health and that she will probably never see her mother again. The two have been weeping uncontrollably in one another's arms, when Mrs. Montgomery recollects herself and says: "Ellen! Ellen! Listen to me, . . . my child—This is not right. Remember, my darling, who it is that brings this sorrow upon us,—though we *must* sorrow, we must not rebel" (I, 12).[28] Ellen's mother, who has been ordered to go on this voyage by her husband and her physician, makes no attempt to change the situation. She accepts the features of her life as fixed and instructs her daughter to do the same. The message of this scene, and of most sentimental fiction, is that "though we *must* sorrow, we must not rebel." This message can be understood in one of two ways. The most obvious is to read it as an example of how this fiction worked to keep women down. This reading sees women as the dupes of a culture that taught them that disobedience to male authority was a "sin against heaven."[29] When mothers teach their daughters to interpret the commands of husbands and fathers as the will of God, they make rebellion impossible, and at the same time, hold out the false hope of a reward for suffering, since, as Mrs. Montgomery says, "God sends no trouble upon his children but in love" (I, 13). In this view, religion is nothing but an opiate for the oppressed and a myth which served the rulers of a "Puritanical" and "trading nation." In this view, the sentimental novelists, to use Ann Douglas' phrase, did "the dirty work" of their culture by teaching women how to become the agents of their own subjection.[30]

The problem with this reading is that it is too simplistic. The women in these novels make submission "their boast" not because they enjoyed it, but because it gave them another ground on which to stand, a position that, while it fulfilled the social demands placed upon them, gave them a place from which to launch a counter-strategy against their worldly masters that would finally give them the upper hand. Submission, as it is presented throughout *The Wide, Wide World,* is never submission to the will of a husband or father, though that is what it appears to be on the surface; submission is first of all a self-willed act of conquest of one's own passions. Mrs. Montgomery tells Ellen that her tears of anger are "not right," that she must "command" and "compose" herself, because, she says, "you will hurt both yourself and me, my daughter, if you cannot" (I, 12). Ellen will hurt herself by failing to submit because her submission is not capitulation to an external authority, but the mastery of herself, and therefore, paradoxically, an assertion of autonomy.[31] In its definition of power relations, the domestic novel operates here, and elsewhere, according to a principle of reversal whereby what is "least" in the world's eyes becomes "greatest" in its perspective. So "submission" becomes "self-conquest" and doing the will of one's husband or father brings an access of divine power. By conquering herself in the name of the highest possible authority, the dutiful woman merges her own authority with God's. When Mrs. Montgomery learns that her husband and doctor have ordered her to part from Ellen, she says to herself, "not my will, but thine be done" (I, 31). By making themselves into the vehicles of God's will, these female characters become nothing in themselves, but all-powerful in relation to the world. By ceding themselves to the source of all power, they bypass worldly (male) authority and, as it were, cancel it out. The ability to "submit" in this way is presented, moreover, as the special prerogative of women, transmitted from mother to daughter. As the women in these novels teach one another how to "command" themselves, they bind themselves to one another and to God in a holy alliance against the men who control their material destinies. Thus, when Mr. Montgomery refuses his wife the money to buy Ellen a parting gift, it is no accident that she uses her own mother's ring to make the purchase; the ring symbolizes the tacit system of solidarity that exists among women in these books. Nor is it an accident that the gift Mrs. Montgomery gives her daughter is a Bible. The mother's Bible-gift, in sentimental literature, is invested with supernatural power because it testifies to the reality of the spiritual order where women hold dominion over everything by virtue of their submission on earth.[32]

The bypassing of worldly authority ultimately produces a feminist theology in which the godhead is refashioned into an image of maternal authority. When Mrs. Montgomery teaches Ellen what it means to trust in God, she asks her to describe her feelings toward herself:

> "Why, mamma:—in the first place, I trust every word you say—entirely—I know nothing could be truer; if you were to tell me black is white, mamma, I should think my eyes had been mistaken. Then everything you tell or advise me to do, I know it is right, perfectly. And I always feel safe when you are near me, because I know you'll take care of me. And I am glad to think I belong to you, and you

have the management of me entirely, and I needn't manage myself, because I know I can't; and if I could, I'd rather you would, mamma." (I, 18)

Mrs. Montgomery replies:

> "My daughter, it is just so; it is *just* so: that I wish you to trust in God. He is truer, wiser, stronger, kinder, by far, than I am, . . . and what will you do when I am away from you:—and what would you do, my child, if I were to be parted from you forever?" (I, 18)

Mrs. Montgomery's words produce a flood of tears from Ellen, but nevertheless Ellen has learned that when her mother dies she will not really be bereft, for God, who is just like her mother, will take her mother's place in her life; and conversely, the novel seems to suggest, Mrs. Montgomery will take the place of God. When the moment of parting comes, she writes in the flyleaf of Ellen's Bible:

> "'I love them that love Me; and they that seek Me early shall find Me.'"
>
> This was for Ellen; but the next words were not for her; what made her write them?—
>
> "'I will be a God to thee, and to thy seed after thee.'"
>
> They were written almost unconsciously, and, as if bowed by an unseen force, Mrs. Montgomery's head sank upon the open page. . . . (I, 49)

There are two ways of understanding this passage which parallel the double meaning of "submission" in the politics of sentimental fiction. We can read Mrs. Montgomery's inscriptions so that the "I" in "I love them that love Me" and "I will be a God to thee" are spoken by God, whose words she is just repeating. Or, we can read the inscriptions so that the words are spoken by Mrs. Montgomery herself. Indeed, it is this interpretation that is borne out by subsequent events in which Ellen's goodness, her devotion to duty, her piety, and Christian deportment are all attributed to the influence of her mother. The definition of the mother as the channel of God's grace, the medium through which he becomes known to mankind, locates the effective force of divinity in this world in women. Doing the will of God finally becomes identical with doing what one's mother wants. And if one is a woman, doing the will of God means obeying a divinity that comes to look more and more like oneself. Scene after scene in *The Wide, Wide World* ends with Ellen weeping in the arms of a kind mother-figure—a representative of God in human form. As Ellen matures, and her spiritual counselors grow closer to her in age—she calls them "sister" and "brother"—she finally learns to control her passions on her own and becomes her own mother. Not coincidentally, the one completely happy, whole, and self-sufficient character in this novel is an elderly woman who lives alone on a mountaintop and is, so to speak, a God unto herself. This is the condition toward which the novel's ethic of submission strives. While outwardly conforming to the exigencies of her social role, inwardly the heroine becomes master of her fate and subject to no one outside herself.

Read within the context of nineteenth-century American culture, the scene between Ellen and her mother reconciles women's need for power and status with a condition of economic and political subservience. This fiction presents an image of people dominated by external authorities and forced to curb their own desires; but as they learn to transmute rebellious passion into humble conformity to others' wishes, their powerlessness becomes a source of strength. These novels teach the reader how to live without power while waging a protracted struggle in which the strategies of the weak will finally inherit the earth.

III. Trifles

But while women were attempting to outflank men in a struggle for power by declaring that it was not the world that was important to conquer but one's own soul, they did in fact possess a territory of their own that was not purely spiritual, and they made maximum use of the one material advantage they possessed. The territory I am referring to is, of course, the home, which operates in these novels as the basis of a religious faith that has unmistakably worldly dimensions. The religion of the home does not situate heaven in the afterlife, but locates it in the here and now, offering its disciples the experience of domestic bliss. Just as the practice of submission, which looks like slavery to us, became, in the context of evangelical Christianity, the basis for a claim to mastery, so confinement to the home, which looks to us like deprivation, became a means of personal fulfillment.

Social historians have tended to take a dim view of the domestic ideology, regarding its promises of happiness as illusory and the accompanying restrictions as impossible to bear.[33] In the course of illustrating how women had to abandon any ambitions of their own, accommodating themselves to their husband's position in society, Barbara Epstein quotes a tale from a textbook for young girls about a man who had lost his fortune and was forced to move to a humble cottage in the country. As he walks home one evening with a friend, he worries aloud about his wife's state of mind. He is afraid she may not be able to cope with poverty, the fatigue of housework, and the absence of elegant appointments. But when the men arrive at the cottage, the wife

came tripping forth . . . in a pretty rural dress of white; a few wild flowers were twisted in her fine hair; a fresh bloom was on her cheek; her whole countenance beamed with smiles . . ."My dear George," cried she, "I am so glad you are home! I've set out a table under a beautiful tree behind the cottage; and I've been gathering some of the most delicious strawberries, for I know you are fond of them and we have such excellent cream, and everything is so sweet and still here.—Oh!" said she, putting her arm within his, and looking up brightly into his face, "Oh! we shall be so happy."[34]

Epstein comments that although domesticity protected women from the harsh economic world, "in real life drudgery and isolation were more prominent than strawberries and cream."[35] Epstein's sarcasm here is understandable, but it misses something important. Of course homelife was mostly drudgery, but the women who wrote scenes like the one I have just quoted knew that. The religion of domesticity could never have taken hold if it had not had something real to offer. And what it had to offer was an extraordinary combination of sensual pleasures, emotional fulfillment, spiritual aspirations, and satisfaction in work accomplished.

Of all the characters in *The Wide, Wide World*, the one who has achieved the greatest spiritual victory is old Mrs. Vawse, who lives in a house built into a cleft of rock on a windswept mountaintop. Though she has no one to lean on—her husband, children, and former mistress are all dead—she says "I am never alone . . . I have nothing to fear" because "my home is in heaven, and my Savior is there preparing a place for me" (XVIII, 201, 197). Though Mrs. Vawse says her home is in heaven, everything that the novel says about her goes to show how well she lives in her earthly one. Though deprivation is ostensibly the defining feature of this woman's existence—she has no money, no property, no relatives—her house is warm and comfortable, her surroundings are pleasant, she works at odd jobs to earn money when she needs it, and she obviously enjoys the company of her friends. She is always, says Warner, "cheerful and happy, as a little girl" (XIX, 203). While Mrs. Vawse claims that the secret of her contentment is "letting go of earthly things . . . for they that seek the Lord shall not want any good thing," (XVIII, 197) she in fact has everything she wants. Mrs. Vawse is the most completely happy and fulfilled person in the novel because economically, socially, and emotionally she is the most independent. When Ellen asks her why she lives so far away from everyone, she answers, "I can breathe better here than on the plain. I feel more free" (XVIII, 201). Autonomy and freedom, exactly what the lives of antebellum American women lacked, are the defining features of Mrs. Vawse's existence. Heaven, as it is figured in Warner's novel, is a place of one's own where one can be "happy, as a little girl" but without the dependency of childhood, or of most Victorian women.

Despite the novel's emphasis on Mrs. Vawse's spirituality as the source of her contentment, it is the physical features of her one-room house that, rightly understood, provide a lesson to those who would emulate her success. Everything in Mrs. Vawse's house shines with the consequences of her labor. The floor is "beautifully clean and white," the windows are "clean and bright as panes of glass can be," "the hearth was clean swept up," "the cupboard doors . . . unstained and unspoiled, though fingers had worn the paint off" (XVIII, 198). The work of scrubbing and polishing—women's work—has produced a spiritual purity and a physical beauty in which holiness and pleasure are combined, a combination repeated in the juxtaposition of her "large Bible" and "cushioned armchair" (XVIII, 198). Ellen and her friend, Alice, have come to Mrs. Vawse to "get a lesson in quiet contentment" (XVIII, 196). The lesson that they get—in addition to the one that Mrs. Vawse explicitly gives them—is that piety and industry, both activities over which a woman has control, can set you free. Mrs. Vawse's home presents an ideal of fulfillment toward which the readers of sentimental fiction could strive. It is full of material pleasures—cleanliness, attractive surroundings, warmth and good food (Mrs. Vawse gives Ellen and Alice delicious cheese, bread, and "fine tea" [XVIII, 200])—and it offers spiritual and emotional nourishment as well—Mrs. Vawse gives religious counsel and affection to her friends, and sends them on their way fortified in every sense. While the ethic of submission required a stifling of aggression, a turning inward of one's energies to the task of subduing the passions, the home provided an outlet for constructive effort, for *doing* something that could bring tangible results.

At the same time that the domestic ideal gave women a concrete goal they could work toward and enjoy the possession of, it gave them a way of thinking about their work that redeemed the particularities of daily existence and conferred on them a larger meaning. The triviality of sentimental fiction has, along with its morality and its tears, traditionally been the object of critical derision. But this triviality is the effect of a critical perspective that regards household activity as unimportant. Women writers of the nineteenth century, having been allotted one small corner of the material universe as their own, could hardly allow that area to be defined as peripheral or insignificant. Besides making the home into an all-sufficient basis for satisfaction and fulfillment in the present, they wrote about domestic routines in such a way that everything else appeared peripheral. Just as "submission" is transformed into "self-command," and the extinction of self into the assumption of a god-like authority, so the routines of the fireside acquire sacramental power in the novels of this period; the faithful performance of household tasks becomes not merely a reflection or an expression of celestial love but, as in this scene from Warner's novel, its point of origin and consummation:

> To make her mother's tea was Ellen's regular business. She treated it as a very grave affair, and loved it as one of the pleasantest in the course of the day. She used in the first place to make sure that the kettle really boiled; then she carefully poured some water into the tea-pot and rinsed it, both to make it clean and to make it hot; then she knew exactly how much tea to put in the tiny little tea-pot, which was just big enough to hold two cups of tea, and having poured a very little boiling water to it, she used to set it by the side of the fire while she made half a slice of toast. How careful Ellen was about that toast! The bread must not be cut too thick, nor too thin; the fire must, if possible, burn clear and bright, and she herself held the bread on a fork, just at the right distance from the coals to get nicely browned without burning. When this was done to her satisfaction (and if the first piece failed she would take another), she filled up the little tea-pot from the boiling kettle, and proceeded to make a cup of tea. She knew, and was very careful to put in, just the quantity of milk and sugar that her mother liked; and then she used to carry the tea and toast on a little tray to her mother's side, and very often held it there for her while she ate. All this Ellen did with the zeal that love gives, and though the same thing was to be gone over every night of the year, she was never wearied. It was a real pleasure; she had the greatest satisfaction in seeing that the little her mother could eat was prepared for her in the nicest possible manner; she knew her hands made it taste better; her mother often said so. (I, 13-14)

The making of tea as it is described here is not a household task, but a religious ceremony. It is also a strategy for survival. The dignity and potency of Ellen's life depend upon the sacrality she confers on small duties, and that is why the passage I have quoted focuses so obsessively and so reverentially on minute details. Ellen's preparation of her mother's tea has all the characteristics of a religious ritual: it is an activity that must be repeated ("the same thing was to be gone over every night of the year"); it must be repeated correctly ("she knew exactly how much tea to put in the tiny little tea-pot," "the bread must not be cut too thick, nor too thin," "and if the first piece failed she would take another"); it must be repeated in the right spirit ("all this Ellen did with the zeal that love gives"); and it must be repeated by the right person (Ellen "knew her hands made it taste better; her mother often said so"). Ellen's hands make the tea and toast taste better because the ritual has worked, but it works not only because it has been performed correctly, but because Ellen and her mother believe in it. The creation of moments of intimacy like this through the making of a cup of tea is what their lives depend on. What the ritual effects is the opening of the heart in an atmosphere of closeness, security, and love. The mutual tenderness, affection, and solicitude made visible in the performance of these homely acts are the values sacred to sentimental fiction and the reward it offers its readers for that other activity which must also be performed within the "closet"—the control of rebellious passion. While Ellen and her mother must submit to the will of God, expressed through the commands of husbands and doctors, they compensate for their servitude by celebrating daily their exclusive, mutually supportive love for one another.

That is why this ritual, although it resembles the Christian sacrament of holy communion, does not merely *promise* fulfillment; it offers consummation in the present moment. The tea and toast are real food, and the feelings that accompany them, like those that characterize the soul's relation to Christ in evangelical hymns, are feelings living human beings share with one another.[36] The exigencies of a Puritanical and trading nation had put women in the home and barred the door; and so in order to survive, they had to imagine their prison as the site of bliss. In this respect, the taking of tea is no different from hoeing a bean patch on the shores of Walden Pond, or squeezing case aboard a whaling ship; they are parallel reactions against pain and bondage, and a means of salvation and grace. The spaces that American Renaissance writing marks out as the site of possible transcendence are not only the forest and the open sea. The hearth, in domestic fiction, is the site of a "movement inward," as far removed from the fetters of land-locked existence as the Pacific Ocean is from Coenties Slip.

The happiness that women engender in the home is their prerogative and their compensation. But this felicity is not limited in its effects to women, although they alone are responsible for it. Like prayer, which must be carried on in solitude and secrecy in order to change the world, the happiness that women create in their domestic isolation finally reaches to the ends of the earth. "Small acts, small kindnesses, small duties," writes the Reverend Peabody, "bring the happiness or misery . . . of a whole generation. Whatever of happiness is enjoyed . . . beyond the circle of domestic life, is little more than an offshoot from that central sun."[37] The domestic ideology operates in this, as in every other respect, according to a logic of inversion whereby the world becomes "little more than an offshoot" of the home. Not only happiness, but salvation itself is seen to depend upon the performance of homely tasks. "Common daily duties," says the Reverend Peabody, "become sacred and awful because of the momentous results that depend upon them. Performed or neglected, they are the witnesses that shall appear for or against us at the last day."[38] By investing the slightest acts with moral significance, the religion of domesticity makes the destinies of the human race hang upon domestic routines. Margaret Flower makes out a time schedule when she is on vacation, and Ellen Montgomery treats the making of her mother's tea as "a very grave affair" because they know that "momentous results" depend upon these trifles. The measuring out of life in coffee spoons, a modernist metaphor for insignificance and futility, is interpreted in sentimental discourse as a world-building activity. When it is done exactly right, and "with the zeal that love gives," it can save the world.

It is easy and may be inevitable at this point to object that such claims are pathetic and ridiculous—the fantasies of a disenfranchised group, the line that society feeds to members whom it wants to buy off with the illusion of strength while denying them any real power. But what is at stake in this discussion is precisely what constitutes "real" power. From a modern standpoint, the domestic ideal is self-defeating because it ignores the realities of political and economic life. But those were not the realities on which Americans in the nineteenth century founded their conceptions of the world. As Lewis Saum has written: "In popular thought of the pre-Civil War period, no theme was more pervasive or philosophically fundamental than the providential view. Simply put, that view held that, directly or indirectly, God controlled all things."[39] Given this context, the claims the domestic novel made for the power of Christian love and the sacred influence of women were not in the least exaggerated or illusory. The entire weight of Protestant Christianity and democratic nationalism stood behind them. The notion that women in the home exerted a moral force that shaped the destinies of the race had become central to this country's vision of itself as a redeemer nation. The ethic of submission and the celebration of domesticity were not losing strategies in an age dominated by the revival movement. They were a successful bid for status and sway. Even as thoroughgoingly cosmopolitan a man as Tocqueville became convinced of this as a result of his visit to the United States from 1830 to 1831. "As for myself," he said, concluding his observations on American women, "I do not hesitate to avow that, although the women of the United States are confined within a narrow circle of domestic life, and their situation is in some respects one of extreme dependence, I have nowhere seen woman occupying a loftier position; and if I were asked, now that I am drawing to the close of this work, in which I have spoken of so many important things done by the Americans, to what the singular prosperity and growing strength of that people ought mainly to be attributed, I should reply—to the superiority of their women."[40]

IV. Pain

The claims that sentimental fiction made for the importance of the spiritual life and for women's crucial role in the salvation of the race were not spurious or self-deceiving, because they were grounded in and appealed to beliefs that had already organized the experience of most Americans. But while the sense of power and feelings of satisfaction that the religion of domesticity afforded were real, not just imagined, they were bought and paid for at an almost incalculable price. The pain of learning to conquer her own passions is the central fact of the sentimental heroine's existence. For while a novel like *The Wide, Wide World* provides its readers with a design for living under drastically restricted conditions, at the same time it provides them with a catharsis of rage and grief that registers the cost of living according to that model. When Melville writes that Ahab "piled upon the white whale's hump the sum of all the general rage and hate felt by his whole race from Adam down, and then, as if his chest had been a mortar . . . burst his hot heart's shell upon it," he describes the venting of a rage that cannot be named as such in Warner's novel, but whose force is felt nevertheless in the deluge of the heroine's tears.[41] The force of those passions that must be curbed at all costs pushes to the surface again and again in her uncontrollable weeping. For although these novels are thought to have nothing to say about the human psyche, and to be unaware of "all the subtle demonisms of life and thought" which preoccupied greater minds, in fact they focus exclusively on the emotions, and specifically on the psychological dynamics of living in a condition of servitude. The appeal of Warner's novel lay in the fact that it grappled directly with the emotional experience of its readership; it deals with the problem of powerlessness by showing how one copes with it hour by hour and minute by minute. For contrary to the long-standing consensus that sentimental novelists "couldn't face" the grim facts of their lives, their strength lay precisely in their dramatization of the heroine's suffering as she struggles to control each new resurgence of passion and to abase herself before God. It is a suffering which, the novelists resolutely insist, their readers, too, must face or else remain unsaved. And they force their readers to face it by placing them inside the mind of someone whose life is a continual series of encounters with absolute authority.

Warner's novel pulls the reader immediately into such a situation. As the novel opens, Ellen Montgomery is sitting quietly at the window of her parents' New York townhouse, watching the evening close in on a partially deserted street. Her invalid mother is resting and has asked her to be still. (Characteristically, the heroine is trapped in an enclosed space, is under an injunction *not* to do anything, has no direct access to the world she can see from her limited vantage point, and must make the best of her situation.) Ellen studies the scene outside the window with great concentration. It is pouring rain. She watches the last foot passengers splashing through the water, horses and carriages making their way through the mud, until finally, at the far end of the street, one by one, lights begin to appear. "Presently," Warner writes, "Ellen could see the dim figure of the lamplighter crossing the street from side to side with his ladder;—then he drew near enough for her to watch him as he hooked his ladder on the lamp irons, ran up and lit the lamp, then shouldered the

ladder and marched off quick, the light glancing on his wet oil-skin hat, rough great-coat and lantern, and on the pavement and iron railings" (I, 10). When the lamplighter has finally disappeared, Ellen sets herself to straightening the room: she adjusts the curtains, stirs the fire, arranges the chairs, puts some books and her mother's sewing-box back in their places. Finally, having done everything she can think of, Ellen kneels down and lays her head next to her mother's on the pillow and after a moment gently strokes her cheek. "And this succeeded," says Warner, "for Mrs. Montgomery arrested the little hand as it passed her lips and kissed it fondly" (I, 10).

What makes this scene work is the way it draws the reader into its own circuit of attention. Forced into the dark parlor with Ellen, the reader has to pay attention to what Ellen pays attention to—the tiny details of the lamplighter's progress down the street, parlor furniture, books, sewing-boxes, the moment of suspense when she lays her hand on her mother's cheek. These things become the all-engrossing features of the reader's world. The circumscribed materials of Warner's novel do not seem at all lacking in importance when seen from the heroine's perspective; instead, the restricted focus, which one might have supposed to be a disastrous limitation, works to intensify the emotional force of what takes place. At times, the vulnerability of the child, forced to live within the boundaries authority prescribes and constantly under the pressure of a hostile supervision, becomes almost too painful to bear.

Warner's refusal to mitigate the narrow circumstances of her heroine's existence is particularly striking when one compares this novel to the opening of *Huckleberry Finn*. When Huck is trapped by his drunken father near the beginning of Twain's novel, he concocts an elaborate ruse that allows him to escape. He kills a hog, scatters its blood around the cabin, drags a sack of meal across the threshhold to imitate the imprint of a body, and disappears, hoping that his father and the townspeople will think he has been murdered—and of course they do. *The Adventures of Huckleberry Finn* has for a long time stood as a benchmark of American literary realism, praised for its brilliant use of local dialects and its faithfulness to the texture of ordinary life. Twain himself is famous for his scoffing attacks on the escapism of sentimental and romantic fiction. But if one compares his handling of a child's relation to authority with Warner's, the events of *Huckleberry Finn* enact a dream of freedom and autonomy that goes beyond the bounds of the wildest romance. The scenario whereby the clever and deserving Huck repeatedly outwits his powerful adversaries along the riverbank acts out a kind of adolescent wish fulfillment that Warner's novel never even glances at. When Ellen is sent by her father to live with a sadistic aunt in New England, when she is deeded by him a second time to an even more sinister set of relatives, there is absolutely nothing she can do. Ellen is never for a moment out of the power of her guardians and never will be, as long as she lives. While the premise of Twain's novel is that, when faced by tyranny of any sort, you can simply run away, the problem that Warner's novel sets itself to solve is how to survive, given that you can't.

In the light of this fact, it is particularly ironic that novels like Warner's should have come to be regarded as "escapist." Unlike their male counterparts, women writers of the nineteenth century could not walk out the door and become Mississippi riverboat captains, go off on whaling voyages, or build themselves cabins in the woods. Nevertheless, modern critics, as we have seen, persist in believing that what sentimental novelists offered was an easy way out: a few trite formulas for the masses who were too cowardly to face the "blackness of darkness," too lazy to wrestle with moral dilemmas, too stupid to understand epistemological problems, and too hidebound to undertake "quarrels with God." But "escape" is the one thing that sentimental novels never offer; on the contrary, they teach their readers that the only way to overcome tyranny is through the practice of a grueling and inexorable discipline. Ellen Montgomery says to her aunt early in the novel that if she were free to do what she wanted she would run away—and spends the rest of the novel learning to extirpate that impulse from her being. For not only can you not run away, in the world of sentimental fiction, you cannot protest the conditions under which you are forced to remain. Ahab's cosmic protest "I'd strike the sun if it insulted me" epitomizes the revolutionary stance of the heroes of classical American fiction; sentimental heroines practice a heroism of another sort.

Learning to renounce her own desire is the sentimental heroine's vocation, and it requires, above all else, a staggering amount of work. Since self-suppression does not come naturally, but is a skill that can only be acquired through practice, the taking apart and putting back together of the self must be enacted over and over again, as each new situation she meets becomes the occasion for the heroine's ceaseless labor of self-transformation. It is, as Ellen often says to her spiritual mentors, "hard." And since, in any individual instance, crushing the instinct for self-defense and humbling oneself before God can only be accomplished through protracted effort, the scenes that enact this process are long and tortuous. Over and over again the heroine must overcome the impulse to rebel and justify herself, must throw herself on the mercy of the Lord and ask his help in forgiving those who have wronged her.

In a sense, these novels resemble, more than anything else, training narratives: they are like documentaries and made-for-TV movies that tell how Joe X, who grew up on the streets of Chicago, became a great pitcher for the White Sox, or how Kathy Y overcame polio and skated her way to stardom. They involve arduous apprenticeships in which the protagonist undergoes repeated failures and humiliations in the course of mastering the principles of her vocation. They always involve, prominently, a mentor-figure who initiates the pupil into the mysteries of the art, and enunciates the values the narrative is attempting to enforce. The trainer, who is simultaneously stern and compassionate, loves the protagonist most when she is being hardest on her. In sentimental fiction, the vocation to be mastered is Christian salvation, which, translated into social terms, means learning to submit to the authorities society has placed over you. In Ellen's case, her Aunt Fortune (a literal representative of fate), and later her Scottish relatives, are the authorities whom Ellen must learn to obey without a murmur. And her mentors are first her mother, then Alice Humphries, a young woman who befriends Ellen in her first exile, and then Alice's brother John, who takes over when Alice dies.

The role Ellen's mentors play in administering the novel's disciplinary program is a complicated and crucial one. Though they are her refuge and her loving saviors, it is they who put the "rock" in Ellen's soul by refusing to let her give way to her rebellious feelings. Whereas her Aunt Fortune exerts control over Ellen's life externally, her mentors control her inmost being; they alter her behavior at its source by teaching her how to interpret her feelings. Anger and indignation— no matter what the cause—are a disease of which she must be cured, and in order to be cured she must not "shrink" from her "physician." "No hand but His," they tell her, "can touch that sickness you are complaining of (XV, 158). Relentless in their determination that Ellen shall learn to humble herself before God, her mentors make demands of her that are excruciatingly intimate and exacting.

It is hard for people who have not read Warner's novel to understand the nature of the heroine's relation to her mentors. The claustrophobic atmosphere of the novel, its concentration on the moral consequences of even the smallest pieces of behavior, and above all the sense it conveys of someone utterly at the mercy of implacable authorities, trap the reader into the heroine's cycle of frustration, humiliation, and striving. The immediacy and force of her emotions invest the tiniest incidents with an intensity that a simple account of their features cannot recapture. What most eludes the attempt to portray these scenes is the passion that fills them—a passion that erupts continually and inarticulately in the flood of her tears, as repeatedly she is made to bare her soul to the gaze of her superiors.

When Ellen runs to her friend Alice, after her Aunt Fortune has treated her cruelly, at first Alice is all sympathy and affection. But what Ellen learns from

Alice, comforting and solicitous as she is, is that her protests are all pride and selfishness, and that she must learn not to stand up to her aunt even to *herself.* "For," as Alice says, "the heart must be set right before the life can be" (XVI, 173). The only way to set the heart right is through total self-abnegation, and the only way to achieve that is by praying to the "dear Savior." When Ellen asks "what shall I do to set it right?" Alice's answer is "Pray," (XVI, 173) and this will always be her answer. When Ellen says "But, dear Miss Alice, I have been praying all morning that I might forgive Aunt Fortune and yet I cannot do it," Alice's answer is still the same, "Pray still, my dear, . . . pray still. If you are in earnest the answer will come" (XVI, 173). Alice never gives an inch in these exchanges because her job is to teach Ellen that the self must *never* have its way, for "God resisteth the proud, but giveth grace unto the humble" (XVI, 174). When Ellen bursts into tears at such sayings, and cries out "but it is so hard to forgive," Alice is unmoved. "Hard, yes, it is hard when our hearts are so, but there is little love to Christ and no just sense of his love to us in the heart that finds it hard. Pride and selfishness make it hard. The heart full of love to the dear Savior cannot lay up offenses against itself" (XVI, 174).

Tears and prayers are the heroine's only recourse against injustice; the thought of injustice itself is implicitly forbidden. The anger that such a thought would arouse is Ellen's worst enemy and her besetting sin; that anger must be transmuted into humility and love for "the hand that has done it" (XLII, 461). And so, Ellen's mentors are immitigable in their insistence that Ellen turn to Christ for help when she is in distress. If she wants to be happy, she must learn to seek him. "Remember Him, dear Ellen," they always say, "remember your best Friend. Learn more of Christ, our dear Savior, and you can't help but be happy" (XVII, 183). When Ellen thanks Miss Alice for befriending her, exclaiming, "Oh, Miss Alice, what would have become of me without you!" Alice gently rebuffs her: "Don't lean upon me, dear Ellen," says Alice, "remember you have a better Friend than I always near you. . . . Whenever you feel wearied and sorry, flee to the shadow of that great rock" (XVI, 174; XVII, 183). Through constant and repeated reminders, Ellen's mentors establish Christ in Ellen's mind as an all-powerful internal "Friend" who watches everything she does. Thanks to her mentors, when Ellen goes to her room in tears, she is not retreating to a safe place any longer because, once in the privacy of her room, she must abase herself before the authority she has internalized.

Ellen's self-command increases as she learns to turn more frequently to prayer, to her Bible, to hymns, and to religious books for strength and solace. And from time to time, Warner notes with satisfaction the "progress" of the "little pilgrim" (XXXV, 368);[42]

"solitude and darkness saw many a tear of hers," says Warner, as she "struggled . . . to get rid of sin and to be more like what would please God" (XXXI, 331). But despite her constant progress in the business of self-renunciation, Ellen always needs more inner strength than she can muster. She is constantly being caught in some attitude of incomplete surrender which earns her the devastatingly mild rebukes of Miss Alice or Mr. John. The faintest signs of irritation or self-concern tell them that her devotion to Christ is not yet absolute. "Is seeking His face your first concern?" they ask, "be humbled in the dust before Him" (XLV, 489; XXVIII, 309).

But the massive tests of Ellen's faith are still before her. Ellen learns that her mother has died, and is inconsolable. She goes into a decline from which she is rescued only by Mr. John's tutelage and affection. Then Alice dies, and Ellen is desolate. But this time "she knew the hand that gave the blow and did not raise her own against it. . . . Her broken heart crept to His feet and laid its burden there" (XLI, 446). The final blow is separation from Mr. John. Her father dies and deeds her to some rich relatives in Scotland; Ellen is cast upon the wide world a second time, and this time she will have no mentors to rely on. Like all true Christians, she must learn to live on faith alone.

The final chapters of *The Wide, Wide World* require of the heroine an extinction of her personality so complete that there is literally nothing of herself that she can call her own. Whereas Ellen's aunt had subjected her to constant household drudgery and frequently hurt her feelings, she made no attempt to possess her soul. But Ellen's Scottish relatives are spiritual tyrants; they look upon Ellen as a "dear plaything, to be taught, governed, disposed of." "They would do with her and make of her precisely what they pleased" (XLVII, 524). What they please is that she give up her identity. Under their rule, in which the "hand that pressed her cheek," though "exceeding fond," is also the "hand of power," (XLVII, 530) submission reaches its acutest manifestations. The store of loyalties and affections that Ellen has garnered during her first exile is stripped from her methodically and completely. The Lindsays' authority will brook no appeal. Her uncle makes Ellen call him "father," changes her name from Montgomery to Lindsay, orders her to forget her nationality, forces her to drink wine, forbids her to speak of her former friends, refuses to let her talk of religion, and insists that she give up her sober ways and act "cheerful." After prolonged internal struggles, many prayers and tears, and much consulting of her Bible, Ellen bends submissively to every one of these commands; her time, her energies, her name, her nationality, her conversation, her friends are not hers to dispose of. "God will take care of me if I follow Him," she says to herself, "it is none of my business." "God giveth grace to the humble, I will humble myself" (XLVIII, 546). Absolutely friendless, with no one to understand and comfort her, Ellen (who is about thirteen years old by now) has only God to turn to. When the Lindsays try to take God away from her, it marks the turning point in her Christian education. Up to now, Ellen's Christian duty has required her to submit silently to every assault on her personal desires; the final test of her obedience will require that she disobey, because it is an attack not on herself but on "Him."

Ellen has been in the habit of spending an hour every morning in Bible reading and prayer; it is this hour that enables her to maintain her humble bearing in the face of the Lindsays' demands. When her grandmother learns of it, she forbids Ellen to continue, but this time Ellen says to her grandmother, "there is One I must obey even before you" (L, 563). Although it looks as though, in disobeying, Ellen has gone against everything she has been taught, in fact, the novel's lesson here is the same as it has been throughout: obey the Lord and He will provide. In her distress, Ellen behaves exactly as her mentors had instructed her—she "flees to the shadow of that great rock." She goes to her room, and cries, and then begins to sing:

> *When I draw this fleeting breath,—*
> *When my eyelids close in death,—*
> *When I rise to worlds unknown,*
> *And behold Thee on Thy throne,—*
> *Rock of Ages, cleft for me,*
> *Let me hide myself in Thee.*
>
> (L, 566)

Because Ellen has not asked anything for herself, her will, which is one with the will of God, prevails. Ellen's uncle overhears her singing, and, won over by her meekness and humility, intercedes for her with her grandmother; he arranges for her to have her precious hour alone if she will promise to be more cheerful and keep her "brow clear." Ellen keeps the promise. "Her cheerfulness," says Warner, "was constant and unvarying." Her "unruffled brow," "clear voice," and "ready smile" are the product of a pure heart and a broken will, for though "tears might often fall that nobody knew of," Ellen had "grasped the promises 'He that cometh to Me shall never hunger,' and 'Seek and ye shall find'" (L, 569).

To Warner's audience, steeped in the Christian tradition of self-denial and submission to God's will, Ellen's suffering, as she gradually gives up the right to *be* herself, is necessary. It is not only necessary; it is desirable. Ellen's mentors express their love for her in their willingness to inflict pain as God, in the Protestant tradition, loves those whom he chastises. After her mother has died, John asks Ellen, "do you love Him less since He has brought you into this great sorrow?" "No," Ellen replies, sobbing, *"more"* (XXXIV, 363). But the embrace of pain and the striving for

self-abandonment that characterize the heroines of sentimental fiction have, for the modern reader, psycho-sexual overtones that are inescapable and should at least be mentioned here. When Mr. John says to Ellen, "be humbled in the dust before Him—the more the better," (XXVIII, 309) his words, harsh and titillating at the same time, suggest the relationship between punishment and sexual pleasure, humiliation and bliss. The intimate relation between love and pain that Warner's novel insists on calls to mind nothing so much as *The Story of O,* another education in submission in which the heroine undergoes ever more painful forms of sexual humiliation and self-effacement, until finally she asks "permission" to die. In each case, when the heroine has learned to submit totally to one authority, she is passed on to a more demanding master, or set of masters, who will exact submissions that are even more severe.

The end point of the disciplinary process is the loss of self: either through physical death, as in O's case or Uncle Tom's, or psychological death, as in Ellen's, a sloughing off of the unregenerate self. By the end of Warner's novel, Ellen does not exist for herself any more, but only for others. Sanctified by the sacrifice of her own will, she becomes a mentor by example, teaching lessons in submissiveness through her humble bearing, downcast eyes, unruffled brow, and "peculiar grave look" (XLV, 494). Even the joy that Ellen gives her elders is not her own doing, but God in her. She is a medium through which God's glory can show itself to men. Like Alice, Ellen becomes a person who "supplied what was wanting everywhere; like the transparent glazing which painters use to spread over the dead color of their pictures; unknown, it was she gave life and harmony to the whole" (XX, 213). The ideal of behavior to which the novel educates its readers is the opposite of self-realization; it is to become empty of self, an invisible transparency that nevertheless is miraculously responsible for the life in everything.

Given the amount of pain that sentimental heroines endure, it is almost inconceivable that their stories should have been read as myths of "reassurance." But perhaps this reading, insofar as it arises from anything that is really in these novels, is based on the way they end. At the end of *The Wide, Wide World,* Ellen is rewarded for her suffering, like Job—to whom she is twice compared. Having given up everything, she now has everything restored to her a hundredfold. That restoration takes the form of Mr. John, whom Ellen loves, to whom she has "given herself," and who, Warner intimates, will marry her when she comes of age. In Mr. John the various authorities in Ellen's life are finally merged. Whereas before, the authorities over her had been divided into three separate realms—the earthly authority of her father, Aunt Fortune, and the Lindsays; the transcendent authority of God; and the authority of her spiritual mentors who mediated between the two—now they are all contained in a single person. Since, as Warner observes, Mr. John's commands are always "on the side of right," there will never again for Ellen be a conflict between duty and obedience. The male figure, representing both divine and worldly authority, who marries the heroine in the end, is the alternative to physical death in sentimental fiction; he provides her with a way to live happily and obediently in this world while obeying the dictates of heaven. He is the principle that joins self-denial with self-fulfillment, extending and enforcing the disciplinary regimen of the heroine's life, giving her the love, affection, and companionship she had lost when she was first orphaned, providing her with material goods and social status through his position in the world.

The union with Mr. John looks at first exactly like the sort of fairy-tale ending that sentimental fiction is always accused of fobbing off on its readers: Cinderella rescued by Prince Charming. One can see Aunt Fortune as the wicked stepmother who makes Ellen sweep and churn butter when she would rather be studying French, and Alice as the fairy godmother who provides supernatural help and leads her to the prince. But the real analogues to Warner's novel are not fairy tales, though they do have happy endings. The narratives that lie behind *The Wide, Wide World* are trials of faith—the story of Job and *Pilgrim's Progress*—spiritual "training" narratives in which God is both savior and persecutor and the emphasis falls not on last-minute redemption, but on the toils and sorrows of the "way." These narratives, like Warner's novel, teach the reader, by example, how to live. And their lesson, like Warner's, is that the only thing that really matters in this world is faith in God and doing his will: nothing else counts. Although Ellen will be united eventually with Mr. John, her submissiveness has become so complete that it hardly matters who is her master now. Through prolonged struggle, she has taught herself to be the perfect extension of another's will; because her real self is inviolate, having become one with God, she can accept whatever fate deals out. And in fact, Warner gives her "three or four more years of Scottish discipline" before restoring her to the "friends and guardians she best loved" (LII, 592). The education of the sentimental heroine is no more a fairy story than the story of Job or *Pilgrim's Progress*. Rather, it is an American Protestant *bildungsroman,* in which the character of the heroine is shaped by obedience, self-sacrifice, and faith. Warner's language in summing up her heroine's career makes this plain:

> The seed so early sown in little Ellen's mind, and so carefully tended by sundry hands, grew in course of time to all the fair stature and comely perfection it had bid fair to reach—storms and winds that had visited it did but cause the root to take deeper hold;—and at the point of its young maturity it happily fell into those hands that had of all been most successful in its culture. (LII, 592)

In an unfriendly review of Warner's book, Charles Kingsley quipped that it should have been called "The Narrow, Narrow World" because its compass was so small.[43] And in a sense he was right. Although the frontispiece of the first illustrated edition shows a ship tossing on a stormy sea, with the sun breaking through clouds in the background, all of the heroine's adventures take place indoors, in small enclosed spaces that are metaphors for the heart. Warner tells the reader as much in the novel's epigraph:

> Here at the portal thou dost stand,
>   And with thy little hand
> Thou openest the mysterious gate
>   Into the future's undiscovered land.
>   I see its valves expand
> As at the touch of Fate
>   Into those realms of Love and Hate.

The realms of love and hate are no less turbulent and suspenseful than those Kingsley described in *Westward, Ho!,* and considerably less given to the playing out of adolescent fantasies. The storms and winds of Warner's novel are those that nineteenth-century readers actually encountered in their lives. The wideness of this world is to be measured not by geographical or sociological standards, but by the fullness with which the novel manages to account for the experience of its readers. That experience, as I have argued, was shaped conclusively by the revival movement and by the social and economic condition of American women in the antebellum years. That is the condition that Ellen Montgomery's story represents, and it is "narrow" only in the sense of being confined to a domestic space, like most of Henry James' fiction, or Jane Austen's. But unlike Austen or James, the sentimental writers had millennial aims in mind. For them the world could be contracted to the dimensions of a closet because it was in the closet that one received the power to save the world. As the Reverend Dr. Patton, addressing the fifteenth annual meeting of the American Home Missionary Society, said:

> The history of the world . . . is the history of prayer. For this is the power that moves heaven. Yet it is the power which may be wielded by the humblest and obscurest saint. It will doubtless be found in the great day, that many a popular and prominent man will be set aside; whilst the retired but pleading disciple, will be brought forth to great honor, as having alone in her closet, wrestled with the angel and prevailed.[44]

Notes

[1] That is how twentieth-century critics have usually treated this work. See, for example, Henry Nash Smith, "The Scribbling Women and the Cosmic Success Story," *Critical Inquiry,* 1 (September 1974), pp. 47-49; John T. Frederick, "Hawthorne's 'Scribbling Women,'"

New England Quarterly, 48 (1975), pp. 231-240; Ramona T. Hull, "Scribbling Females and Serious Males: Hawthorne's Comments from Abroad on Some American Authors," *Nathaniel Hawthorne Journal,* 5 (1975), pp. 35-38.

2 Smith, p. 58; Henry Nash Smith, *Democracy and the Novel* (New York: Oxford University Press, 1978), p. 12; Perry Miller, "The Romance and the Novel," in *Nature's Nation* (Cambridge, Mass.: Harvard University Press, 1967), pp. 255-256.

3 Smith, *Democracy and the Novel,* pp. 13-15.

4 James D. Hart, *The Popular Book: A History of America's Literary Taste* (Berkeley: University of California Press, 1950), pp. 93, 94, 111; Frank Luther Mott, *Golden Multitudes* (New York: Macmillan, 1947), pp. 122-125.

5 Smith, *Democracy and the Novel,* p. 8.

6 Perry Miller, *The Life of the Mind in America from the Revolution to the Civil War* (New York: Harcourt Brace and World, 1965), p. 7.

7 Kenelm Burridge, *New Heaven, New Earth: A Study of Millenarian Activities* (New York: Schocken Books, 1969), provides a valuable account of the social content of millenarianism which has been crucial to my own thinking concerning the assumptions about power implicit in all kinds of evangelical writing, including Warner's novel.

Burridge's definition of religion makes sense in the context of nineteenth-century social thought, which was so intimately bound up with religious beliefs.

"For not only are religions concerned with the truth about power, but the reverse also holds: a concern with the truth about power is a religious activity" (p. 7). "Religious activities will change when the assumptions about the nature of power, and hence the rules which govern its use and control, can no longer guarantee the truth of things" (p. 7).

"The rules which govern the use of power can be determined. Both emerge from the ways in which individuals discharge or evade their obligations, what they do to counter or meet the consequences of evasion, how they cope with a pledge redeemed, what they say the consequences will or might be." "Salvation equals redemption equals unobligedness" (p. 8).

"'Feeling themselves oppressed' by current assumptions about power, participants in millenarian activities set themselves the task of reformulating their assumptions so as to create, or account for and explain, a new or changing material and moral

environment within which a more satisfactory form of redemption will be obtained" (p. 10).

"An adequate or more satisfactory way of gaining prestige, of defining the criteria by which the content of manhood is to be measured, stands at the very heart of a millennarian or messianic movement. And these criteria relate on the one hand to gaining or retaining self-respect, status, and that integrity which is implied in the approved retention of a particular status; and on the other hand to an acknowledged process whereby redemption may be won" (p. 11). "The redemptive process, and so redemption, bears significantly on the politico-economic process, particularly the prestige system" (p. 13). "A prestige system is based upon particular measurements of manhood which relate to gaining or retaining self-respect and integrity, and which refer back to the politico-economic process, the redemptive process, and assumptions about power" (p. 13). "Indeed, all religions are basically concerned with power. They are concerned with the discovery, identification, moral relevance and ordering of different kinds of power, whether these manifest themselves as thunder, or lightning, atomic fission, untramelled desire, arrogance, impulse, apparitions, visions, or persuasive words. . . . And all that is meant by a belief in the supernatural is the belief that there do exist kinds of power whose manifestations and effects are observable, but whose natures are not yet fully comprehended" (p. 5).

"Religions, let us say, are concerned with the systematic ordering of different kinds of power, particularly those seen as significantly beneficial or dangerous" (p. 5).

8 This is the term given to the movement by Charles Foster in his excellent account, *An Errand of Mercy: The Evangelical United Front, 1790-1837* (Chapel Hill: University of North Carolina Press, 1960).

9 As quoted by Foster, p. 273.

10 In March of 1829, for example, a pamphlet entitled *Institution and Observance of the Sabbath* was distributed to 28,383 New York families. See Foster, p. 187.

11 New York City Tract Society, *Eleventh Annual Report* (New York: New York City Tract Society, 1837), back cover.

12 New York City Tract Society, pp. 51-52.

13 New York City Tract Society, pp. 51, 52.

14 David Reynolds, "From Doctrine to Narrative: The Rise of Pulpit Story-Telling in America," *American Quarterly,* 32 (Winter, 1980), pp. 479-498.

15 Reverend William S. Plumer, "Ann Eliza Williams, or the Child an Hundred Years Old, an Authentic

Narrative," in *Narratives of Little Henry and His Bearer; The Amiable Louisa; and Ann Eliza Williams* (New York: American Tract Society, n.d.), pp. 4, 11.

[16] Harvey Sacks, "On the Analysability of Stories by Children," in *Ethnomethodology,* ed. Roy Turner (Middlesex, England: Penguin, 1974), p. 218.

[17] American Home Missionary Society, *Twenty Second Report* (New York: William Osborn, 1848), p. 103.

[18] David Tyack and Elisabeth Hansot, *Managers of Virtue: Public School Leadership in America, 1820-1980* (New York: Basic Books, Inc., 1982), pp. 15-104.

[19] *Thoughts on Domestic Education, The Result of Experience,* by a Mother (Boston: Carter and Hendee, 1829), p. 106.

[20] For a comparable example, see Lydia Maria Child, *The Mother's Book* (Boston: Carter and Hendee, 1829), which devotes an entire chapter to the "Value of Time."

[21] New York City Tract Society, p. 158.

[22] Mrs. Lydia H. Sigourney, *Margaret and Henrietta* (New York: American Tract Society, 1852), pp. 12-13.

[23] The expectation that children should order their lives for the furthering of God's kingdom is commonplace. See, for instance, Lydia Maria Child's New Year's message to children, *The Juvenile Miscellany,* I, 3 (January 1827), pp. 103-105, which urges children to "make a regular arrangement of time" and to be "always employed."

[24] Robert Wiebe, "The Social Functions of Schooling," *American Quarterly,* 21 (1969), pp. 147-150.

[25] Tremaine McDowell, "Diversity and Innovation in New England," in *The Literary History of the United States,* ed. Robert E. Spiller et al., 3rd ed., rev. (London: Macmillan, 1963), p. 289.

[26] In the first half of the nineteenth century, single women could own real property but married women could not. "Essentially," writes Lawrence Friedman, *A History of American Law* (New York: Simon and Schuster, 1973), p. 184, "husband and wife were one flesh; but the man was the owner of that flesh." For a good discussion of the growing discrepancy, from the seventeenth century onward, between anti-patriarchal theories of government and the reinforcement of patriarchal family structure, see Susan Miller Okin, "The Making of the Sentimental Family," *Philosophy and Public Affairs,* 11 (Winter 1982), pp. 65-88.

[27] Alexis de Tocqueville, *Democracy in America,* trans. Henry Reive, rev., 2 vols. (New York: Vintage Books, 1957), II, p. 223.

[28] Chapter and page references to *The Wide, Wide World* are to the undated, one-volume "Home Library" edition of the novel (New York: A. L. Burt).

[29] Reverend Orville Dewey, *A Discourse Preached in the City of Washington, on Sunday, June 27th, 1852* (New York: Charles S. Francis and Company, 1852), p. 13. Dewey's sermon on obedience is characteristic of a general concern that a democratic government was breeding anarchy in the behavior of its citizens, and that obedience therefore must be the watchword of the day. In European society, Dewey argues, where the law of caste still reigns, there is a natural respect for order and authority. But "*here* and *now,*" he continues, pp. 4-5, "all this is changed. . . . With no *appointed* superiors above us, we are liable enough to go to the opposite extreme; we are liable to forget that any body is to be obeyed—to forget even, that God is to be obeyed. . . . Only let every man, every youth, every child, think that he has the right to speak, act, do any where and every where, whatever any body else has the right to do; that he has as much right to his will as any body; and there is an end of society. That is to say, let there be an end of obedience in the world, and there is an end of the world." Since, in Dewey's eyes, pp. 13-14, the home is the source of anarchy in the state, family discipline is the source of all good civil order, and therefore the goal of domestic education must be "a patient and perfect obedience." "If the child is *never* permitted to disobey, it will soon cease to think of it as possible. And it should *never* be permitted! . . . Only when living under law—only when walking in obedience, is child or man, family or State, happy and truly prosperous. Selfish passion every where is anarchy, begetting injustice, and bringing forth destruction." Sentimental novels, along with advice books for young women, child-rearing manuals, and religious literature of all sorts, helped to inculcate the notion that obedience was a domestic as well as a civic virtue, especially in the case of women. Beginning in the 1830s, as Nancy F. Cott has shown in *The Bonds of Womanhood: "Woman's Sphere" in New England, 1780-1835* (New Haven: Yale University Press, 1977), pp. 158-159, clergymen directed their sermons on the need for order in family and society especially at women, "vividly emphasizing the necessity for women to be subordinate to and dependent on their husbands."

[30] Ann Douglas, *The Feminization of American Culture* (New York: Alfred A. Knopf, 1977), p. 11.

[31] Tocqueville, II, pp. 210, 212, describes the process of moral education of American women in very much the same terms. "Americans," he says, "have found out that in a democracy the independence of individuals cannot fail to be very great, youth premature, tastes ill-restrained, customs fleeting, public opinion often unsettled and powerless, paternal authority weak, and marital authority contested. Under these circumstances,

believing that they had little chance of repressing in woman the most vehement passions of the human heart, they held that the surer way was to teach her the art of combating those passions for herself." Thus, Tocqueville continues, having cultivated an extraordinary "strength of character" and learned to "exercise a proper control over herself," the American woman "finds the energy necessary for . . . submission in the firmness of understanding and in the virile habits which her education has given her."

[32] Harvey C. Minnich, ed. *Old Favorites from the McGuffey Readers* (New York: American Book Co., 1936), pp. 178-179, prints a poem, from the *Fourth Reader,* entitled "A Mother's Gift—The Bible." The first stanza reads as follows:

> *Remember, love, who gave thee this,*
> *When older days shall come,*
> *When she who had thine earliest kiss,*
> *Sleeps in her narrow home.*
> *Remember! 'twas a mother gave*
> *The gift to one she'd die to save!*

The Bible is the symbol of the mother in sentimental literature, taking her place, after she is dead, serving as a reminder of her teachings, and as a token of her love. To forget what the Bible says is to forget one's mother:

> *A parent's blessing on her son*
> *Goes with this holy thing;*
> *The love that would retain the one,*
> *Must to the other cling.*

[33] For example, Douglas; Barbara Epstein, *The Politics of Domesticity* (Middletown, Conn.: Wesleyan University Press, 1981); Barbara Welter, *Dimity Convictions* (Athens, Ohio: Ohio University Press, 1976).

[34] Epstein, p. 75. The original source is Irving's *Sketch Book.*

[35] Epstein, p. 75.

[36] Sandra Sizer, *Gospel Hymns and Social Religion* (Philadelphia: Temple University Press, 1978), p. 33, describes that relation as follows: "The secret of his saving power lies in a movement inward, not only toward shelter and refuge with Jesus and/or in heaven, but to a realm of intimacy. It is a sphere not only of passivity but of passion—the passion, the emotions, in nineteenth-century language the 'affections.'" Sizer's book is the best discussion I know of the relationship between the domestic ideal and evangelical Christianity. In summing up the relationship between the gospel hymns and popular fiction, p. 110, she writes:

> In short, the hymns incorporate the ordering of the world provided by the ideology of evangelical domesticity in the novels; the two rhetorics are

parallel and very nearly identical. Jesus and heaven, so central in the hymns, are being understood in terms of domestic descriptions. The tender affections, the feminine virtues, the home-haven which gives protection and generates inward strength through intimacy—all become part of the hymns' picture of Jesus and his heavenly realm.

[37] Reverend E. Peabody, "Importance of Trifles," in *The Little Republic, Original Articles by Various Hands,* ed. Mrs. Eliza T. P. Smith (New York: Wiley and Putnam, 1848), p. 120. The "importance of trifles" theme is ubiquitous in nineteenth-century inspirational literature. It is directly related to the Christian rhetoric of inversion ("The last shall be first"), to the cultivation of the practical virtues of honesty, industry, frugality ("A stitch in time saves nine"; "A penny saved is a penny earned"), and to the glorification of the mother's influence. In another essay in the same volume, "A Word to Mothers," pp. 210, 211-212, Thomas P. Smith writes: "Let us not forget that the greatest results of the mind are produced by small, but continued, patient effort." "As surely as a continued digging will wear away the mountain, so surely shall the persevering efforts of a Christian mother be crowned with success. . . . She is, through her children, casting pebbles into the bosom of society; but she cannot as easily watch the ripples made: no, they reach beyond the shore of mortal vision, and shall ripple on, in that sea that has neither shore nor bound, for weal or for woe, to them, and to the whole universal brotherhood of man."

[38] Peabody, in *The Little Republic,* ed. Smith, pp. 124-125.

[39] Lewis O. Saum, *The Popular Mood of Pre-Civil War America* (Westport, Conn.: Greenwood Press, 1980), p. 3.

[40] Tocqueville, II, p. 225.

[41] Herman Melville, *Moby-Dick or, The Whale,* ed., introd. Charles Feidelson, Jr. (New York: The Bobbs-Merrill Company, 1964), p. 247.

[42] *Pilgrim's Progress* is Ellen's favorite book.

[43] Charles Kingsley, *The Water-Babies* (London, 1903), p. 174, as cited by Foster, *Susan and Anna Warner,* p. 48.

[44] American Home Missionary Society, *Fifteenth Report* (New York: William Osborn, 1842), p. 104.

FURTHER READING

Boyle, Thomas. *Black Swine in the Sewers of Hampstead: Beneath the Surface of Victorian Sensationalism.* New

York: Viking, 1989, 273 p.

Discusses the Sensation Novel and its relationship to the cultural, social and political life of Victorian times.

Cvetkovich, Ann. *Mixed Feelings: Feminism, Mass Culture, and Victorian Sensationalism.* New Brunswick, N. J.: Rutgers University Press, 1992, 227 p.

Examines female characters, their roles in regard to emotion and behavior, and the way these roles are woven into the Sensation Novel. Focuses on *Lady Audley's Secret, The Woman in White, East Lynne* and George Eliot's *Daniel Deronda.*

Edwards, P. D. *Some Mid-Victorian Thrillers: The Sensation Novel, Its Friends and Its Foes.* St. Lucia, Queensland: University of Queensland Press, 1971, 34p.

Offers an overview of the Sensation Novel, discussing particularly *The Woman in White, East Lynne* and *Lady Audley's Secret* each in its own right as well as in comparison to other novels often categorized as "Sensational."

Reed, John R. *Victorian Conventions.* Ohio University Press, 1975, 561 p.

Provides a chapter on each of several main conventions of the Sensation Novel.

Taylor, Jenny Bourne. *In the Secret Theatre of Home: Wilkie Collins, Sensation Narrative, and Nineteenth-Century Psychology.* London: Routledge, 1988, 306 p.

Examines Collins' work and its place in Victorian times and the sensation genre.

The Well-Made Play

INTRODUCTION

Originating in France as the *pièce bien faite,* the well-made play is a style of dramatic writing characterized by a meticulous, methodological purposiveness of plotting. The logically precise construction of the well-made play is typified by a number of conventions. The plot is most often based on a withheld secret—known to the audience but unknown to the characters—which, when revealed at the climax, reverses the fortunes of the play's hero. During the course of the play, the overall pattern of the drama is reflected in the movement of the individual acts, in which a steadily mounting suspense is achieved through the battle of wits between the hero and the villain. The hero's fortune fluctuates during his conflict with the adversary until finally, at the climax, the secret is revealed in an obligatory scene (*scène à faire*) and the hero is benefitted in the final *dénouement,* or resolution.

By all critical accounts, the well-made play was originated by Eugène Scribe, who, over the course of his prolific career, gradually perfected the genre. Like those of Jean Racine, Scribe's plays focus on a small cluster of characters involved in a single action that builds steadily to a climax. Unlike Racine, however, Scribe infused his plays with a technical specificity, by which each particular action of a character is explained and justified so that it is made to seem inevitable. Over the course of his literary career, during which he produced over 420 dramatic works, Scribe was one of the most popular playwrights in France. He wrote dramas for the four major Parisian theaters of the day, and in the period from 1815 to 1830, Scribe's plays accounted for more than one-tenth of the new comedies and *vaudevilles* in Paris.

The French dramatists who followed Scribe adapted his formula to two very different uses. Victorien Sardou, a disciple of Scribe, used the well-made form in the service of a more realistic drama. For example, his *Daniel Rochat* (1880) depicts the confrontation between an atheist hero who marries an Anglo-American woman who wants to follow their civil ceremony with a church wedding; the entire play chronicles the struggle between these two and ends in an unsatisfactory conclusion. By contrast, Eugène Labiche applied Scribe's formula mainly for the purpose of arousing laughter; his farces present a picture of contemporary Parisian life, but offer little social commentary.

Scribean drama was extended by Émile Augier and Alexandre Dumas *fils.* Augier infused the form of the well-made play with romanticism and melodrama, and founded popular realism in France. In plays such as *L'aventurière, Gabrielle,* and *La gendre de M. Poirier,* Augier addresses the moral culture of his time, commenting on contemporary Parisian life, its mores and social distinctions. Dumas similarly used Scribe's style to comment on modern life, but Dumas went further than Augier in his realism. His characters are battered by their circumstances; Dumas used the form to critique the social conventions and class stratifications of France, to study the problems of modern capitalism and religion, and to comment on the literary process itself.

Despite Scribe's overwhelming popularity during his lifetime and his profound influence on his contemporaries, evaluations of the well-made play since then have been primarily negative. Literary critics have largely dismissed the well-made plays of Scribe, which they claim combine theatrical ingenuity in an intricate plot with a bare minimum of thought, a lack of poetry, and weak characterization. George Bernard Shaw said of Scribe in a famous comment, "Why the devil should a man write like Scribe when he can write like Shakespeare or Molière, Aristophanes or Euripides?" While most of Scribe's plays have been relegated to virtual obscurity, however, the profound effect the well-made form had on the historical development of modern European drama is undeniable. The plays of Scribe and Sardou were translated and performed in England and America as early as 1819, influencing such playwrights as Edward Bulwer-Lytton, Tom Taylor, and T. W. Robertson, all of whom adapted the form to their own purposes. Most notably, Scribe's influence extends to Henrik Ibsen, who directed a number of Scribe's plays in Norway before producing his own dramatic works; his early works clearly reflect a Scribean influence, while his later works adapt the style of the well-made play, infusing it with symbolism. Other critics have detected Scribe's influence on Henry James and, ironically, Shaw as well. Despite Scribe's dramatic weaknesses, then, the well-made play exerted an immeasurable influence in the history of theater well into the twentieth century, shaping the nature of drama in a variety of movements, including realism, naturalism, and symbolism.

REPRESENTATIVE WORKS

Émile Augier
  L'aventurière [*The Adventuress*] (drama) 1848
  Gabrielle (drama) 1849

Le gendre de M. Poirier [*The Son-in-law of M. Poirier*] (drama) 1854
Le mariage d'Olympe [*Olympia's Marriage*] (drama) 1855

Edward Bulwer-Lytton
　Richelieu (drama) 1839
　Money (drama) 1840

Alexandre Dumas *fils*
　La dame aux camélias [*Camille*] (drama) 1852
　Diane de Lys (drama) 1853
　Le demi-monde (drama) 1855
　Francillon (drama) 1887

Eugène Labiche
　Le chapeau de paille d'Italie [*The Italian Straw Hat*] (drama) 1851

Victorien Sardou
　Les pattes de mouche [*A Scrap of Paper*] (drama) 1860
　La patrie [*The Fatherland*] (drama) 1869
　Daniel Rochat (drama) 1880

Eugène Scribe
　Bertrand et Raton (drama) 1833
　La Calomnie [*Slander*] (drama) 1840
　Le Verre d'Eau [*The Glass of Water*] (drama) 1840
　Bataille de Dames (drama) 1851

Tom Taylor
　Plot and Passion (drama) 1853

OVERVIEWS

C. E. Montague (essay date 1925)

SOURCE: "The Well-Made Play," in *Dramatic Values,* Doubleday, Page & Company, 1925, pp. 62-74.

[*In the essay that follows, Montague discusses the dramatic techniques of the well-made playwrights, focusing on Sandeau, Augier, and Dumas.*]

During the long reign of the French "well-made piece" the voice of its makers was seldom stilled on the darling theme of how they did it. They lectured on it, and wrote prefaces, and the interviewer went not empty away. Like simple, truthful conjurors—men who are always admitting that rabbits come out of their hats without Divine interposition—"Simply the perfection of my method, ladies and gentlemen, nothing more"—they disclaimed inspiration; they made out that they were only doing a kind of sums; only, like naturalists, inferring the whole of a good-sized unknown beast from the modest premise of one knucklebone.

Then would follow technical instructions. An unwritten play, said Sardou, always appeared to him as a kind of philosophic equation from which the unknown term had to be disengaged; he held that "once the formula for this was found, the piece followed of itself." At this point young France is apt in these later days to interject idiomatically, *"Chansons!"* and yet there is a sense in what Sardou says. Consider his own play, "La Sorcière," how it grows. Imagine its germ, the first thought, the very practical thought—"What will make a good harrowing climax for Sarah Bernhardt?" Well, he might start from a standard melodramatic horror—a condemnation of the innocent to death. How, then, to sharpen its poignancy? Make the death burning; that's something. What next? Make her convict herself to save her lover. Good!—what next? Make her feel that in killing herself to save her lover, she is merely leaving him in a rival's arms. Excellent!—anything more? Yes, deprive her of the consolation of knowing or hoping that the lover will ever understand her sacrifice or value her memory. That is the way the climax of a tragic "machine" may be devised, by a cumulative process of invention. The climax once there, the plot issues out of it, backward; each step "disengages" itself. Burning?—that means the time of the Inquisition. A lover who shall be set free at a word from a mistress on trial herself and about to be burnt? How shall you make her word so potent to save him, so powerless to save herself? Only by making the lady a Moor, a heathen, the man a Christian Spaniard so framed to please the Holy Office that they will fairly jump at a chance to let him off. But how shall she be made, while clearing him, to damn herself quite in his eyes and to root out all love of her from his heart? Nothing for it but to make her avow herself, in his hearing, a witch, and confess she has used hellish arts to make him in love with her. Yes, but she must not have verily used hellish art; she must not be really a witch; else, where will your audience's sympathies be? And so, of necessity, this Moorish lady of 1507 must practice therapeutic hypnotism in order to scandalize 16th-century Toledo, but must also talk 20th-century science about it, so that the audience may know she is only a female Charcot, born rather soon, and not a veritable Witch of Endor. Thus are the unknown terms of Sardou's equation disengaged; the whole of "La Sorcière" follows of its own accord.

Or take another case of machine-making, that of Jules Sandeau's "Mademoiselle de la Seiglière." Sandeau, one fancies, started with a bright notion for a third-act situation in a four-act play—the sudden discovery of mutual love by a man and a woman of different social rank and political feeling, the man bound by a filial sentiment of revenge not to fall in love with the woman, and the woman bound by a previous betrothal not to fall in love with the man. When Augier lit on an idea like this, for the end of a last act but one, he chuckled.

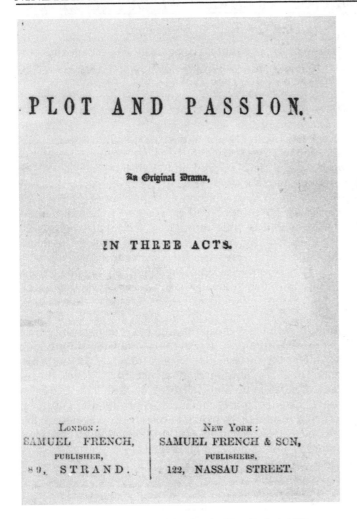

PLOT AND PASSION.

An Original Drama,

IN THREE ACTS.

LONDON:	NEW YORK:
SAMUEL FRENCH,	SAMUEL FRENCH & SON,
PUBLISHER,	PUBLISHERS,
89, STRAND.	122, NASSAU STREET.

Title page from Plot and Passion *by Tom Taylor, 1853*

"*L'affaire,*" he said, "*est dans le sac.*" Doubtless Sandeau did likewise. His fourth act needed small thought; it would come of itself, given the other three, it being the nature of last acts merely to sweep up the crockery smashed at the climax of last acts but one. The first act, of course, must be all explanations. But explanations of what? The answers disengage themselves from the very nature of the smash in Act III. Different social grades and political feelings? Clearly a case for the old clash of well-born Legitimist and plebeian Bonapartist. Filial vengeance to be wreaked by a son of one of these upon a daughter of the other? Plainly your chance is in the seismic dispossessions, redistributions and restitutions of French real estate between the outbreak of the Revolution and the final return of the Legitimist emigrants. When by this process, carried straight on, you have deduced a Royalist Marquis, with one fair daughter, in actual but not legal possession of an estate belonging, under the Code Napoléon, to the unexpectedly surviving son of an ill-used person of lowly origin, your first act begins to write itself, for it must unfold these circumstances. Characters, too, are disengaged from the "philosophic equation." Real property and the Code Napoléon imply a lawyer, to instruct the young claimant to the estates. But in a well-made cast a lawyer cannot be wasted on law alone. People in well-made casts have to work for their places. The obvious work for him to fill up his time with is that of the friend who, by old dramatic tradition, keeps up to the mark, the vindictive mark, the hero who wavers between love and vengeance. The child of the people having thus obtained a bottle-holder, balance necessitates one for the other combatant, the Marquis. Well, as his daughter was first to be betrothed to a man of her own rank, and as she and her father call out, in any case, to be balanced by this young man and his mother, why not make this dowager work double tides too, like the lawyer, and be the Marquis's second and adviser in the conflict. Then the lawyer and this lady, being thus set at one another, must be furnished with some vitriolic dispute of their own, to keep them hard at it; so the lawyer shall be her old, scornfully rejected suitor. And there, with just one footman to get people into rooms and say the things that have to be said but do not quite come rightly from any one else, is Sandeau's whole cast, and, in outline, his whole play; and the cohesion and compactness of plays thus evolved were, until the disturber Ibsen came, the modern European ideal of dramatic craftsmanship.

Of course you find considerable and often delightful differences between one well-made piece and another, as they unwind their orderly coils. Labiche is charmingly unlike Sandeau. "Le Voyage de M. Perrichon," a good Labiche, is very buxom, blithe, and debonair, and most alertly witty. It has, it is true, a rick in its back, caused by violent extension in infancy from three acts to four, but it has characterization and even a tincture of philosophy, and you enjoy the cunning of the good workman even in the act of spoiling his own work by lugging in the inorganic Zouave and the whole affair of the duel; it takes a master joiner to make such a mess of a play without making more. "Mademoiselle de la Seiglière," not so gay as Labiche, is a regular Kriegspiel of motives and counter-motives wilily set by the ears; the whole Landwehr and Landsturm of the armies of drawing-room intrigue march and countermarch, turn flanks and drive in fronts, like good ones; a silence sinks on the house as it bends up each intellectual agent to the feat of seeing why Destournelles first feared that Bernard would marry Hélène and then hoped it, and how the Baronne de Vaubert first brought Bernard into rivalry with her son, and then ceased to dread him, and then dreaded him again.

Again, in Pailleron's "L'Etincelle" lively comedy rests on quite sound psychology. Original and excellent comic use is made of the fact that speech and gesture are not merely symbols of feeling but modes of feeling, and that when you use them you do not merely interpret preexisting emotions, but also set emotional processes in operation, every emotion being modified by its own expression, while some emotions may be so rapidly developed by their expression, even their histrionic expression, that they seem almost to be born of it.

Bisson, without the sap and sunniness of the humane Labiche, or the pretty genial sparkle that Meilhac had "on his day," perfected a rather mechanical brilliancy and malice of comic invention. No one could imagine queerer fixes for his characters, or work them out with less waste of their comic possibilities. After his "Surprises du Divorce" the theatre ought to have relinquished, as a completed work, its immemorial preoccupation with the mother-in-law. All other dramatic handlings of that theme are leaflets to this treatise, mere tentative borings into that seam of comic effect, compared with this capacious and branching mine. With "Les Surprises du Divorce" a topic was played out, and though we may all be bored by later farcical hits at the mother-in-law, "Les Surprises" always seems piquant; it has the lasting freshness of the best thing of a kind.

And yet, granted the diverse animation of a score of 19th-century French dramatists, there does appear in that period a remarkable coexistence of elaborate and precise technical theory and of poorness or shallowness of spirit. Scribe's soul, where it ventures out at all, looks like that of some mean player for safety, a "sensible man of the world," a thinker of what may be thought with the least inconvenience, an exalter of the current, the accepted, the easy, as wisdom and virtue. The younger Dumas taught from half-knowledge and preached without elevation. Augier, a striking example, could not be content to purl and prattle like the agreeable minor brook that he was; he tried to play the Jordan, to be august, momentous, baptismal. The history of his play "L'Aventurière," which he wrote in his youth and re-wrote when past forty, is full of suggestion. There were those who thought, even in 1860, that second thoughts spoilt a quite good boyish play, a piece of the headlong felicity sometimes brought off by writers when young, just because they are young; their spirits are high; their delight in the way others write is so fresh that they copy with gusto, not tamely; they are not yet dulled by finding they scarcely know anything. The first draft of "L'Aventurière" was one of these April productions; it worked on the somewhat dust-strewn spirit of Sarcey, the critic, until he would babble of green fields, dew, the opening eyelids of the morn, auroral things of all sorts. Then a fatal wisdom entered into Augier. He had walked, more or less, in the ways of his heart and in the sight of his eyes; now he must needs bring himself into judgment, and half the world too; so he deepened, or thickened, the tone of his piece, turned comedy to *"drame"*—that thing so different from "drama"—made his old guy of a love-sick dotard a quite tragic person, and set up in form as a critic of life and a scourge of the wicked, or some of the wicked.

There may be a time to put away childish things; there is certainly one to refrain from so doing. Augier's was not the time to turn a light-hearted small play of intrigue into a mighty invocation of "vengeance on Jenny's case." Augier grew serious perversely, only to show what a foul wrong it was for "adventuresses" to derange the peace of substantial middle-class houses; the wretches, to Augier's gathering wrath, did not shrink from wishing that someone might marry them, rescue them out of the street; and how splendid it was when the son of the house used his air of the conquering *mâle,* and his wit, and his well-hung philandering tongue, and his own wide practice in streets (*"J'ai fatigué mon cœur,"* the noble fellow says, *"à tous les carrefours"*) to fool and abase and repel into outer darkness that troublesome asker for help to live well. So thought Augier, like the young Dumas; to them, adventuresses were so many Colorado beetles; art's duty was simply to keep them away from the crops, and the stronger the caustic treatment the better. Well, it still seems quite clever when Fabrice, the good son, the retired rake, dupes and confounds and finally lectures Clorinde. Yet something has gone wrong since 1860; one finds one is laughing upon the wrong side of one's mouth; whether it be Mr. Shaw, or the Zeitgeist, or mere continued incidence of evidence on reluctant ears, something tells people now that Clorindes are Clorindes partly because Fabrices are Fabrices. When a prodigal who "has had so many mistresses that one day he woke up to find he had nothing left but a sword," comes home and preaches on the text—

> On doit le même outrage
> Aux femmes sans pudeur qu'aux hommes sans courage,
> Car le droit au respect, la première grandeur,
> Pour nous c'est le courage et pour vous la pudeur,

one only feels now that the kicks already received by the preacher from fortune cry out to be supplemented by the human foot. Who is he, to wave a fellow sinner back to the husks that the swine do eat?

We have got so far past Jew-baiting in western Europe that Shakspere's intention in Shylock has to be turned inside out on the acting for people to stand it. When cleansing and virilizing work like "One of Our Conquerers" gets us past courtesan-baiting as well, we fear it will not be worth while to turn much of Augier inside out too, for he has an outside indeed, but no inside, or little. All that does not matter much he can do very well. How pat the rhymes are that the properly schooled French actors deliver so patly; how lucid the plot; how multitudinous the small sparkles of verbal vivacity; how droll, in an established way, the drinking-bout; how knowingly the touch of demi-semi-pathos is measured out to the adventures at last! Throw the first stone at her? Why, of course we must, and many more; only let us drop a magnanimous tear while we throw. Such was Augier, a soul like a bats-man who knows quite well how to walk to the wicket, buttoning a glove as he goes, and to pat the pitch flat with his bat, and to walk from the wicket again the right way, duly breaking into a run, and to raise his cap just at the right distance from the pavilion—who knows, in fact, everything but how to bat. Like his Fabrice he does *"un peu de tout, hors de ce qu'il faut faire."*

Let us not be unjust to these minor accomplishments. Still, they are minor. And that was the mark of the well-made piece as a whole—to be great in minor respects and minor in great ones. Not, of course, trivial in one way *because* it was fine in another. Always beware of the sentimental disdain of good craftsman-ship as something over against, and at war with, the soul's higher energies. But somehow the well-made pieces had brought technics and ideas—both of them things calling out to be perfected—into a wrong rela-tion. Was it that the trick of conceiving first of a play's emotional climax condemned that very climax to rela-tive poorness or middlingness, since the supreme things of this kind are conceived at a heat that only comes at the culmination of a sustained, ascending effort of imaginative architecture? Is it only when he is sweat-ing and glowing and breathing deeply with the fight against technical difficulties, against the half-thwarting, half-inspiring reluctancy of matter, as the artist knows matter, that visions like that of Desdemona's death scene will visit the dramatist's mind? Sardou and his kind thought to redeem dramatists from their share of Adam's curse—to convert into a smooth mathematical demonstration the obscure and desperate struggle of the craftsman with the obstacles to beauty in the thing that he dimly dreams he may fashion. Perhaps the curse is a condition of the glory; perhaps it is not a curse; we merely surmise, without any assurance.

Allardyce Nicoll (essay date 1949)

SOURCE: "The Coming of Realism," in *World Drama: From Aeschylus to Anouilh,* Harcourt, Brace and Com-pany, 1949, pp. 484-518.

[*In the following excerpt, Nicoll discusses the primary representatives of the well-made play.*]

. . . Scribe and the Well-Made Play

Meanwhile a significant development in dramatic tech-nique was being evolved in France. This came partly through the practice of the melodrama and of its asso-ciate, the *comédie-vaudeville,* partly through trends in the sphere of comedy.

From the time of the Revolution to the thirties of the nineteenth-century French comedy had been unsure of itself. The famous decree of 1791 established complete freedom for the theatres; decrees issued fifteen years later, in 1806 and 1807, not only limited the number of playhouses, but once more set up a censorship; still other decrees, continually changing the regula-tions, left those concerned with stage affairs never certain by what rules they would next be bound. Such were not conditions favourable for the flourishing of comedy, nor were the general moods of the age apt to encourage the thoughtful laughter of Molière. If, how-ever, little of intrinsic worth was produced, two move-ments deserve attention.

The first of these may be described as the mechani-zation of comic-character portrayal. This is marked particularly in the work of Charles Étienne and of Louis-Benoît Picard. As an example may be taken the latter's *Un jeu de la fortune, ou les marionettes (Play of Fortune; or, The Marionettes,* 1806), wherein men are depicted as creatures whose actions are deter-mined by the pulling of invisible strings. In a sense this trend may be regarded as the unconscious comic counterpart of the emphasis on fate in the poets' dismal tragedies.

The second movement is that towards realism. Such a play as *Un moment d'imprudence (An Imprudent Mo-ment,* 1819), by Alexis-Jacques-Marie Wafflard, shows a new realistic comedy in the making. Life is treated here with interesting vividity, and the adventures of Monsieur and Madame d'Harcourt are dealt with skil-fully. These adventures, ultimately determined by eco-nomic causes, are given theatrical complexity through the person of Madame de Montdésir, who lives a double life under her own name and under that of Madame d'Ange: to Madame d'Harcourt she is known in the latter guise, while her husband is acquainted with her in the former. Not without some true virtue, and informed with the same materialistically realis-tic spirit, is *Les comédiens (The Comedians,* 1820) of Casimir Delavigne, an author more famous for his rather melodramatic *Les vêpres Siciliennes (The Sicilian Vespers,* 1819).

Into this atmosphere stepped Eugène Scribe. A practi-cal man of the theatre, he realized that for the attain-ment of success a new, foolproof dramatic technique was required, a technique suited for a theatre so vastly different in potentiality and form from those that had housed the plays of Shakespeare or even the tragedies of Racine.

For Scribe that which matters in a play is the plot, and consequently he looks back, not towards Marivaux, whose stories were merely slim excuses for an op-portunity to probe the heart and reveal sentiments, but towards Beaumarchais, who, although he knew how to delineate character, was fundamentally inter-ested in intrigue and action. Being a practising writer for the theatre, Scribe realized that a popular audience wants, in the first instance, a vividly told dramatic tale; he realized, too, that many of the devices used in the telling of theatrical tales in the past no longer suited the changed stages of his time; and he set for himself the task of devising a formula by which narratives of all kinds—melodramatic, comic, and farcical—could, with a minimum of effort, be rendered appealing when presented on the boards. His success in this task may be gauged from the fact that he was able to set up what amounted to a play-factory, in which stories were found, invented, or paid for and turned, like sausages, into comestibles for which the public was eager to expend its money.

As Alexandre Dumas *fils* saw clearly, Scribe had no "inspiration of idea" and no sincerity save what he devoted to his commercial values. For Musset a play has an artistic being and, however fantastic, an inner reality: for Scribe a play is a play, to be prepared according to a mechanical plan, a thing without organic life. "No one," comments Dumas,

> knew better than M. Scribe—who was without conviction, without simplicity, without any philosophic end in view—how to set into action if not a character or an idea, at least a subject, and above all a situation, and to extract from that subject and that situation their logical theatric effect; none better than he understood how to assimilate the latest ideas and adapt them to the stage, sometimes on a scale and in a spirit absolutely opposed to the combinations of the one from whom he received the idea. . . . He was the most extraordinary improviser we have had in the history of our drama; he was the most expert at manipulating characters that had no life. He was the shadow-Shakespeare.

From this description of Scribe's ability Dumas proceeds to compare him with Musset:

> If, among the four hundred plays he wrote, either by himself or in collaboration, you place *Il ne faut jurer de rien,* or *Un caprice,* or *Il faut qu'une porte soit ouverte ou fermée*—that is to say, a tiny *proverbe* written by the most naïve and inexpert of dramatists—you will see all Scribe's plays dissolve and go up into thin air, like mercury when heated to three hundred and fifty degrees; because Scribe worked for his audience without putting into his labour anything of his soul or heart, while Musset wrote with heart and soul for the heart and soul of humanity. His sincerity gave him, though he was unaware of this, all the resources which were the sole merit of Scribe.

While this is true—that Scribe's many plays go up into thin air when compared with dramas written from the heart—Dumas was too wise to fail to see that the technical skill of the popular dramatist had its own value. The conclusion, he remarks, is that the playwright who knows

man as Balzac (or Musset) did, "and the *theatre* as Scribe did, will be the greatest of the world's dramatists."

Just as Musset perfected the work of his immediate predecessors, so Scribe, looking only at theatrical form, perfected the work of others. Fundamentally, his inspiration comes from the writers of melodramas—who, eschewing character studies, were forced to pay particular attention to action—and from those of the vaudeville-farce, a genre which became increasingly popular during the early decades of the nineteenth century. His earliest piece, *Une nuit de la Garde Nationale* (*A Night with the National Guard,* 1815), was called a *tableau-vaudeville,* and the vaudeville technique remained with him to the end of his career. This sketch already shows the main elements of his craft. The play begins with a clear presentation of the background, economically but firmly implants in the audience's mind knowledge of the facts on which the subsequent episodes are founded. These facts known by his public, all the author has to do is to start pulling the strings of his puppets: in and out they go, and the resultant intrigue holds the attention, almost makes us forget that they are puppets without life of their own. And the illusion is made the greater by the free use made by the playwright of material taken from the life of the day. Scribe, as Dumas noted, was nothing if not up-to-date.

This does not, of course, imply that Scribe always took his scenes from material familiar to, or closely associated with, the life of the time. Many of his pieces introduce historical matter—however unhistorically treated—and quite a number escape into the world of the fantastic. Towards the very beginning of his career he varied his pattern with a *folie-vaudeville* entitled *L'ours et le pacha* (*The Bear and the Pasha,* 1820), with exciting scenes in the seraglio, designed to titillate the public, and all the mechanism of Oriental wonder.

By this time the talented young author was the rage of Paris; by this time he had become sure of his art and was capable of applying it to subject-matter of any description. The formula of the well-made play—*la pièce bien faite*—was complete. Thenceforward for a period of thirty-odd years he kept the playhouses supplied with a constant series of dramas, nearly all accompanied by music, in which scenes serious, comic, and farcical were wrought into a skilful theatrical pattern. One after another his five hundred plays followed in a constant stream. Here were the sketches from life, such as *La petite sœur* (*The Little Sister,* 1821), *La seconde année* (*The Second Year,* 1830), and *Le chaperon* (*The Hood,* 1832); here were *drames,* such as *Rodolphe, ou frère et sœur* (*Rodolphe; or, Brother and Sister,* 1823) or (turn it about) *Camilla, ou la sœur et la frère* (*Camilla; or, The Sister and the Brother,* 1832); here were sentimental 'tragedies,' such as the once-famous *Adrienne Lecouvreur* (1849), penned in collaboration with Ernest Legouvé, and (with a happy ending) these two authors' *La bataille des dames, ou un duel en amour* (*The Ladies' Battle; or, A Duel of Love,* 1851); here were fantasies, such as *La chatte métamorphosée en femme* (*The Cat metamorphosed into a Woman,* 1827), *Le diable à l'école* (*The Devil at School,* 1842) or *La fée aux roses* (*The Rose Fairy,* 1849); here were Oriental spectacles, such as *Haÿdée, ou le secret* (*Haydee; or, The Secret,* 1847); here were pseudo-historical pieces, such as *La sirène* (*The Syren,* 1844) or *Marco Spada* (1852). With spirit, gaiety, and a sense of the sensational Scribe makes each one of these exciting and entertaining fare; there is hardly a real character in any, but, as many another author of the time discovered, there is a multiplicity of action and, above all, an almost infallible recipe for the production of similar works. As he showed so clearly in the extraordinarily popular *Une chaîne* (*A Chain,* 1841), Scribe was able to make people believe in his almost wholly synthetic situations, and naturally his companions eagerly examined the secrets of his art. The immediate imitators of Scribe are legion.

What is more important is that his formula for the construction of a *comédie-vaudeville* was found to be applicable also to the writing of more serious dramas. It is not too much to say that, mediocre though his own creations may be, he provided for others precisely what an age of romanticism most needed—a mould into which dramatic thought and passion might be poured. The romantic mind tends to be diffuse and sometimes vague, but diffuseness and vagueness are untheatrical qualities. Scribe accomplished an important task—albeit unwittingly—by emphasizing the importance of action and by showing how necessary for success is careful and deliberate planning of effect.

While the influence of Scribe's works was widespread, extending far beyond the boundaries of France, it is important to remember that even where the impress of his style is patent dramatists of many European lands preserved at least the main elements in their own native traditions and allowed the Scribe formula, when they employed it, merely to make more strongly theatrical qualities stemming from a different source.

Thus, for example, in Spain the Argentinian Ventura de la Vega, in introducing knowledge of the new style to Madrid, incorporated in it features of a purely Castilian sort: his *El hombre del mundo* (*The Man of the World,* 1845) owes its vigour to such a combination of forces. In these efforts he was companioned by Mariano José de Larra, whose *No más mostrador* (*Closing the Shop,* 1831) is confessedly an adaptation, with Spanish elements, of the French 'master.' In Italy, similarly, the spirit of Goldoni and of the *commedia dell' arte* prevented a merely slavish following of Paris models. There is a true breath of Venetian air in *La donna romantica e il medico omeopatico* (*The Romantic Lady and the Homeopathic Doctor,* 1858), by Riccardo Castelvecchio (Giulio Pullé), which deals, rather delightfully, with a young bride, Irene, who is wrapped in dismal sighs contracted from a reading of the best French love-romances.

Poland finds its characteristic spirit expressed in the various writings of Kazimierz Zalewski, with his *Bez posagu* (*Without a Dowry,* 1869), *Matżenstwo Apfel* (*The Apfel Marriage,* 1887), and other dramas of domestic interests. In Czechoslovakia the Scribe style is given an individual twist by Emanuel Bozděch, with his popular *Zkouška státníkova* (*The Politician's Trial,* 1874), and in Austria it is handled by Eduard von Bauernfeld in such plays as *Die Bekenntnisse* (*The Acknowledgments,* 1834) and *Bürgerlich und romantisch* (*Simple and Romantic,* 1835). Hungary too presents a peculiar comedy-drama variant of its own in such plays as the lively *A kérök* (*The Suitors,* 1819) and *Csalódások* (*Illusions,* 1828), by Károly Kisfaludy, and *Szökött katona* (*The Deserter,* 1845), by Ede Szigligeti, although the latter author is probably better known for his *A trónkeresö* (*The Pretender,* 1867), a tragic drama set in the thirteenth century. *Csalódások* is notable for its portrait of the blundering Mokány, *Szökött katona* for its effective pictures of peasant life. From Sweden comes *Ett resande teatersällskap* (*The Touring Company,* 1842), by August Blanche, a play confessedly built on a French foundation, yet made thoroughly Scandinavian in atmosphere and characters.

In looking at such plays it is evident that we must endeavour at once to estimate the force of that powerful French influence which made so many plays in so many lands merely pieces taken "from the French" and which is the expression of a mechanistic philosophy of the theatre, and to give full weight to the enduring national strains which even that influence could not completely banish from the stages of Europe.

Sardoodledum

Through a kind of amalgam of Scribe's technique, the suggestions given by the early experiments in mechanistic comedy and the resourcefulness of the melodrama—now directing its attention to materialistic themes—a new form of drama gradually came into being. From Lytton to Robertson in England, and from Augier to Sardou in France, diverse playwrights were engaged in preparing the theatres for what was to come—and, paradoxically, establishing a style against which later writers might react. Although the progress of realism is constant and uninterrupted during these years, yet the realism of one decade has ever seemed absurd to the realists of the next, and accordingly advance has taken the form continually of unacknowledged influence associated with public expressions of contempt. To Robertson Lytton appeared old-fashioned, and to Pinero Robertson was outmoded; nevertheless the line from the first author to the last is absolutely unbroken. Sardoodledum was both an inspiration and a menace for the dramatic authors at the end of the century.

It is, indeed, the prolific and successful Victorien Sardou who, although so much of his work belongs to the final years of the century, provides one of the chief links between the earlier styles and those that were to come. If we take a bird's-eye view of dramatic development in France and England within this period we can easily discern three main currents meandering downward and eventually forming one great stream. One is the melodramatic, represented by Sardou in France and by Boucicault in England. The second is the transformation of comedy-farce: here Eugène Labiche and H. J. Byron may be taken as representative. The third is the tentative introduction of contemporary themes—in particular those of marriage and money—not confined to one author or to one group of authors, but, as it were, welling up from the soil in diverse places almost imperceptibly until suddenly they take shape as a constantly flowing rivulet.

Victorien Sardou was a faithful disciple of Scribe, and his one endeavour was to produce plays likely to prove successful on the stage; he soared to success in 1860 with *Les pattes de mouche (A Scrap of Paper)*, which long held popular esteem. Accordingly he ranges over vast territory, embracing in his wanderings both the romantic-historical and the realistic. Plot is of more concern to him than either character or idea, and theatricality predominates in his writings. This very theatricality, however, has its values, since he succeeded in enlarging the Scribe formula so as to make it apply to a stage which was becoming increasingly rich in its resources. He knew well how to make use of new scenic effects, and he was even capable of making his own innovations—such as the dramatic use of crowds, the employment of groups of persons not as automaton-supers but as dynamic forces in the action. In this and other ways he prepared the path for his successors.

His historical pieces, such as *Théodora* (1884), *La Tosca* (1887), *Robespierre* (1899), *Madame Sans-Gêne* (written with Émile Moreau, 1893), and *La sorcière (The Witch,* 1903), need not detain us, although some of these are to be remembered because they were written for, and provided highly characteristic rôles for, Sarah Bernhardt. This sphere of playwriting, moreover, provided Sardou with what was one of the most successful and certainly one of the best among his plays, *La patrie (The Fatherland,* 1869), in which he piles melodramatic sensation upon realistic scenes and both of these upon the exhibition of tragic, tortured love. Typical is the scene in which Karloo discovers that his revolutionary friends have been betrayed through the ministry of Dolorès. Her husband is going to his death on the scaffold as Karloo and she plan to flee the country together, when suddenly the truth is revealed:

KARLOO: That woman—at the Duke's—this morning! That woman—at the Duke's—last night!

DOLORÈS: Last night?

KARLOO: It is she.

DOLORÈS: No!

KARLOO: It's you. It's you! You have betrayed us! You miserable——— Dare you deny that you are the one?

DOLORÈS: Ah, Karloo!

KARLOO: Leave me—don't touch me!

[*He disengages himself and darts towards the right, where he falls into a chair.*]

DOLORÈS: Pity me.

KARLOO: God's vengeance! And I have been looking for her! And here she is. Who else?

DOLORÈS [*who has fallen to the floor*]: Ah, Karloo! Don't curse me! Let the others do that—not you.

KARLOO: Fiend—traitress—coward—coward!

DOLORÈS [*on her knees, making her way towards him*]: You don't know all, my Karloo He wanted to kill you. When he left me he said: "I am going to kill him!" I was mad with terror—stark mad—Karloo! I swear I was raving mad! I only tried to save you—I loved you so much! It was for your sake, for you!

KARLOO [*taking her hands in his*]: Your love. Your love has made me a perjurer and a traitor! Your fatal love has brought these poor wretches to the scaffold, and a whole nation to its ruin! Your love is hellish, deadly! I *do* curse you! I execrate, I hate you!

[*He casts her to the floor.*]

DOLORÈS: Ah, Karloo, you are killing me!

KARLOO: No, not yet!

DOLORÈS: What are you going to do?

KARLOO [*dragging her to the window*]: Come here, Madam! First, look at your work.

DOLORÈS: Pity me!

[*The windows are red with the reflected light of the faggots. Screams and murmurs of horror are heard.*]

KARLOO: Look at it! Look at your faggot-heap—it's burning!

DOLORÈS: Pity me!

KARLOO: Look—count your victims!

DOLORÈS: Karloo—ungrateful———

KARLOO [*raising her and forcing her to look*]: You must accustom yourself to flames—you must have some notion of what hell is like—hell, where your love is dragging us!

DOLORÈS: Mercy!

KARLOO: Listen! They have caught sight of me! Listen now, listen!

THE PRISONERS: Karloo—traitor! Traitor!

KARLOO: Do you hear?

DOLORÈS: My God!

KARLOO: And do you not also hear the dead man crying out: "Remember your oath"?

DOLORÈS [*rising in terror*]: No. No.

KARLOO: "No matter who the guilty one may be, strike, have no mercy!"

DOLORÈS: Karloo, would you strike me?

KARLOO [*drawing his dagger*]: My oath!

DOLORÈS [*wild with terror, as she struggles to free herself*]: With your own hand—no! You wouldn't do that! Pity me—I'm afraid!

KARLOO [*losing his self-control*]: I have sworn!

DOLORÈS: No, no—don't—leave me!

KARLOO: I have sworn, I have sworn!

[*He plunges the dagger into her.*]

DOLORÈS [*falling to the floor*]: Now go—you have killed me. And I loved you so! I loved you so.

[KARLOO: *throws his dagger down.*]

KARLOO [*nearly out of his mind*]: I have killed you! I! I!

DOLORÈS: At least you can join me, now! Come.

KARLOO [*falling to his knees before her, an inanimate mass, and covering her with kisses, while he sobs*]: I will come with you—I am so miserable! Dolorès, my sweetest love! O God! O God!

DOLORÈS: Come, then.

KARLOO [*standing*]: Wait! I am coming! [*He runs to the window, stands in it, and cries out.*] Executioner [*excitement in the Square*]—you lack one man! Make way for me on your faggot-heap!

DOLORÈS [*rising in order to see him*]: Ah!

KARLOO [*to* DOLORÈS, *his voice full of loving tenderness*]: You see? I am coming, I am coming!

[*He goes swiftly from the room.* DOLORÈS *dies.*]

What popular audience would not be thrilled by such a scene? What lover of truth in the theatre can refrain from a smile or a sneer?

Play after play is cast in the same mould. *Spiritisme (Spiritualism,* 1897) exploits current interest in the occult by showing a young wife, Simone, angered at her husband's absorption in spiritualistic research, first taking a lover and later giving herself out as dead. Deserted by the lover, she finds a friend who so works on the husband's mind as to persuade him to summon her spirit back from the shades—whereupon, of course, the real Simone appears. This is the situation of *Much Ado about Nothing* without the poetry. Equally theatrical is *Marcelle* (1896), which, dealing with the story of a woman with a past, characteristically brings her safely out of her troubles to a conclusion vastly happier than any of the realists would have allowed her.

Yet this very theatricality was to be put to good use, both by Sardou himself and by his immediate followers, in the service of the realistic drama. Of such plays his *Daniel Rochat* (1880) may be regarded as typical. Here a free-thinking, 'atheist' hero marries, by a civil ceremony, an Anglo-American girl, Léa, but jibs at following this by a ceremony in church. The entire play is taken up with the struggle between these two, and in the end a somewhat unsatisfactory conclusion is reached. Although not by any means a masterpiece, and although now seen to be replete with many spurious sentiments, this drama illustrates well how the Scribe technique, applied in new ways, was being adapted to the requirements of contemporary themes. In himself Sardou is nothing but a later edition of Kotzebue or of Pixérécourt; as a 'barometer' of Parisian playhouse taste his works have prime historical value; for those who came after him he was a model to be imitated and an idol to be overthrown.

Closely associated with Sardou in his endeavour to feed the stage with successful entertainments is Eugène Labiche. Instead, however, of cultivating the melodramatic, he relies mainly upon comedy farce, applying the now familiar Scribe formula to plays designed mainly for the purpose of arousing laughter. Although he succeeded in presenting a delightful series of amusing pictures of contemporary life, most of his works have little intrinsic value. On the other hand, a few of them—notably *Le voyage de M. Perrichon* (*M. Perrichon's Journey,* 1860) and *La poudre aux yeux* (*Dust in the Eyes,* 1861)—betray qualities of a further kind. The former presents a definite thesis, suggesting that men are apt to detest those who do them a good turn, that their affection goes out rather to those whom they themselves have assisted. In *La poudre aux yeux* the plot is based on the idea of being and seeming—the complications arising from the social masks worn by the diverse characters. Perhaps Labiche does not contribute in these works much of great importance for the later development of the play of ideas, yet this incursion of a sense of purpose into the realm of farce is not unworthy of notice. Most of his work, however, is of the delightfully irresponsible kind represented by *Le chapeau de paille d'Italie* (*The Italian Straw Hat,* 1851), in which a worthy young hero is thrown into a maze of unexpected comic trials all because his horse happens to eat a straw hat that has been hung up on a tree.

Along with these two currents we must observe how topics based on contemporary conditions were beginning, even before 1829, to receive dramatic treatment. Two thoroughly minor playwrights, for example, Édouard-Joseph Mazères and Adolphe Empis, collaborated in this very year to produce *La mère et la fille* (*Mother and Daughter,* 1830), a play dealing with marriage in relation to money, while four years later they brought out *Une liaison* (1834), in which appeared a theme later to be more fully exploited—that of the prostitute in the family circle. Even before these dates another minor writer, Casimir Bonjour, wrote his *L'argent, ou les mœurs du siècle* (*Money; or, The Manners of the Age,* 1826), which by its very title indicates its interests.

These are early dramas: Sardou, starting his career in 1854, carries us on into the present century; the work of Labiche appears mainly in the sixties and seventies. Although diverse in date, the three streams may be viewed together if we regard Sardou not so much for himself as for what he symbolized, and if we see Labiche merely as the perfector of a line of comedy-farce the tradition of which he inherited. The realistic melodrama, the realistic farce, and the introduction of the 'thesis' in both laid the foundations of the typical drama of the latter half of the century.

Popular Realism in France

The fusion of these is well revealed in the work of Émile Augier. Starting in the mood of imaginative romanticism, tinged with melodramatic sentiment, pursuing technically the methods of Scribe, he became one of the principal founders of the new style. In 1844 he first came before the public with a verse drama, *La ciguë (Hemlock),* an unimportant piece, followed shortly afterwards by a couple of other works in the same medium, *L'aventurière* (*The Adventuress,* 1848) and *Gabrielle* (1849). The interest of these two dramas rests in their subject-matter. *L'aventurière* presents a picture (set in an historical past) of a prostitute, Clorinde, whose entire being is transformed because of her newly awakened love, and draws a sharp contrast between the good sense of the bourgeoisie and romantic follies: in it we are close to *La dame aux camélias.* In the second a definite thesis is introduced. The whole purpose of the play is to prove that it is better for a woman to extract joy and romantic pleasure from living respectably as a wife than to snatch at the illusory delights of being a mistress: here we have entered the sphere of the drama of ideas.

As yet, however, the form by no means harmonized with the content. The scenes, characters, and ideas belong to the social life of the mid-nineteenth century, but the thinkling verse carries us into the atmosphere of another age. Soon, however, Augier, no doubt inspired by Dumas *fils,* was prepared to find a truer harmony; and as a result of his determination came *Le gendre de M. Poirier (The Son-in-law of M. Poirier),* in 1854, written in collaboration with Jules Sandeau, from whose novel *Sacs et parchemins* its plot is derived. There can be no question but that this is a minor masterpiece. Its effervescent wit, allied to a serious purpose, gives it a distinction above most of its companions. Fundamentally, the story is based on the clash between two ideals. On the one hand stands the Marquis de Presles, representative of the ancient aristocracy; on the other is the wealthy, middle-class M. Poirier. The latter has caused his daughter, Antoinette, to marry Gaston, a scion of the noble house: Gaston is just on the point of coming to appreciate the virtues of his *parvenu* bride when Poirier starts to retrench, to speak vulgarly of money, to display all his lack of gentility. The conflict between the proud aristocrat, living in the past, idle, domineering, yet gifted with magnanimous qualities, and the hardworking, yet essentially vulgar, bourgeois is delineated with admirable balance and fine restraint. Perhaps the end may appear a trifle sentimental, when Antoinette's native dignity and nobleness of mind succeed in converting Gaston to look upon her with love, but until the very last scenes this play is innocent of the vices which so cluttered up and falsified the dramas of the eighteenth century. Here is a modern spirit: *Le gendre de M. Poirier* can still be read or seen with interest and profit.

Augier's stress on moral ideas is perhaps his greatest contribution to this mid-nineteenth-century realistic movement, and the moral idea becomes even more pronounced in *Le mariage d'Olympe* (*Olympia's Marriage,* 1855), which may be regarded as a kind of answer to *La dame aux camélias*. Augier had been prepared in *L'aventurière* to accept the concept of the reformed prostitute, but he was not prepared to allow her to stain family honour. His Olympe is a woman who, after a life of sin, allows her former life to vanish from memory by the device of taking another name. In her new rôle she marries Henri, nephew of the Marquis de Puygirou, by whom she is welcomed into the aristocratic circle. Her nature, however, is wholly evil: she yearns for the excitements of her early life, and through sheer boredom she starts a scandal concerning the innocent Geneviève. By her own actions she is revealed, and at the end the old Marquis, to protect the honour of his line, shoots her and is shown reloading his pistol, for the purpose of committing suicide, as the curtain falls.

Throughout the course of his later work Augier kept emphasizing his common-sense views on life. He was no revolutionary, and romantic excesses seemed to him a potent danger; his mission, as he regarded it, was to draw lifelike pictures of contemporary society and to plead for the basic virtues. The evils of city life are delineated both in *La jeunesse* (*Youth,* 1858), and *Les lionnes pauvres* (*Dissipation;* written in collaboration with Édouard Foussier, 1858); in *Les effrontés* (*The Impertinents,* 1861) he attacks the enormities of the modern newspaper and the power it puts into the hands of single men; discussion of politics and clericalism made *Le fils de Giboyer* (*Giboyer's Son,* 1862) a *succès de scandale* in its day; divorce is the theme of *Madame Caverlet* (1876). Finer than these is *Les Fourchambault* (1878), in which a study is made of an upper middle-class household, with a vulgar Mme Fourchambault, a libertine son, Léopold, who yet has some good in him, a poor relation, Marie, and a *deus ex machina* in the person of an illegitimate son, Bernard, who sentimentally saves the family from bankruptcy and wins the fair Marie's hand as the curtain falls. In all of these there is a skilful and interesting handling of character as well as a philosophy which, although maybe somewhat shallow, gives to the scenes an individual quality. The plays of Augier proved that the theatre could well serve as a platform for the enunciation of ideas, made interesting because of their incorporation in plots narrated with the technical brilliance which Scribe had taught his followers to cultivate.

Augier's chief companion in this sphere was Alexandre Dumas *fils,* whose career extends from the famous *La dame aux camélias* of 1852 to *Francillon* in 1887. Like Augier, he was serious in his intent; like him, he based his technique on that of Scribe, although to Scribe's influence in this way he added a strength based apparently on careful study of Corneille's style; like him, he set out to explore the reaches of contemporary life. In his writings, however, more clearly than in those of Augier, the characteristic trend of nineteenth-century realism becomes apparent. His persons are treated as creatures of their surroundings, puppets rudely battered as they are jerked to and fro by unseen strings in the blind power of circumstance, and there is a tendency in his writings to assume that the realistic resides only in the darker spheres of life. In their reaction against the prevailing themes of their romantic predecessors, the romantic realists of the age were impelled to abandon the colourful for the sordid.

His characteristic qualities are well revealed in that earliest of his plays, *La dame aux camélias* (played frequently as *Camille*), in which a prostitute, Marguerite Gautier, is made the heroine. Following the Scribe formula, the first act is devoted almost entirely to presenting the general *milieu* in which she moves. This set, the play is then made to march on towards its fatal conclusion. For the first time Marguerite's heart has been touched by love, and she arranges to go off with her Armand to spend the summer in the country. His father arrives, and by his skilful pleading persuades her that, if she truly loves him, it is her duty to give him up. Hereupon she makes the great sacrifice, writing to Armand that she has decided to leave him for another. In drunken anger he insults her publicly, and she, worn out from the passions of these events, falls into a decline. Just as the repentant Armand, having learned the truth, takes her to his arms she dies.

Like a thunderbolt this play descended upon Paris. The whole of the theatre public wept and sighed over the poor Marguerite, and when Augier tried to arouse consideration of other aspects of the problem his *Mariage d'Olympe* had short shrift. This particular kind of realistic drama was firmly established.

It was even more fully established in *Le demi-monde,* of 1855, a play that in its title introduced a new word into the French—indeed, into the international—vocabulary. The 'demi-monde' is the asylum of all those who have left their own social environment, welcoming alike men and women of rank whom fortune has cast down and other men and women who, usually for their own advancement, have climbed up the rungs of the social ladder, but have been unable to enter the closed windows of high life. In this world lives Suzanne, a self-seeking beauty whose one thought is of herself. She entangles in her snares the young hero, Raymond de Nanjac, who is, however, sternly warned of the menace by his gay and cynical friend, Olivier de Jalin, a former lover of Suzanne. A quarrel ensues between the two men, and a duel is fought; but in the end Suzanne's duplicity is revealed, and for the hero all is well.

What attracts our attention here is the manner in which Dumas has concentrated his attention almost entirely on environment. The stress of the play is not so much on the persons as on the social world in which they live: the demi-monde itself, rather than de Nanjac, may be regarded as the central character in the play.

La question d'argent (*A Question of Money,* 1857) followed a couple of years later. Here, instead of developing a *milieu,* Dumas turns to exploit a problem. Fundamentally, this problem is that of the rightness or wrongness of capitalistic finance. The story of the poor-born Giraud, who is prepared to marry Élisa de Roncourt simply for the purpose of obtaining a respectable position in life, does not matter in comparison with the basic question—whether a man has the right to employ duplicity (in this case a pretended absconsion designed to lower the value of company stocks) in order to make an enormous profit from his investments. The theme has been so frequently dealt with since Dumas' time—it has now even invaded the realm of the detective story—that it has ceased to make much impress on our minds, and maybe we must agree that in its structure *La question d'argent* does not exhibit such skill as was revealed in the earlier plays of this author; at the same time, we may readily imagine the impression made on contemporaries by this bold presentation of a problem, adumbrated before, but never so trenchantly expressed.

With *Le fils nature* (*The Illegitimate Son,* 1858) comes something new: it is now commonly recognized that in this work the modern 'thesis-play' was created. And it was created with conscious deliberation. "'Art for art's sake?'" cries Dumas. "Words devoid of meaning!" And he proceeds to enunciate his belief that it is the mission of the dramatist to preach. The sermon in *Le fils naturel* is illegitimacy, and one of the chief virtues of the drama is that the preacher, instead of merely giving his congregation what it expected to hear, dares to present an idea of his own. Through an exceedingly complex plot Dumas traces the fortunes of the base-born Jacques de Boisceny, who through his own fine qualities succeeds in becoming an outstanding political figure of his time. His father is Charles Sternay, a self-seeking individualist, who has deserted his mistress in order to marry into an aristocratic family. At first Sternay is merely annoyed when his paternity of Jacques is revealed, but as the young man becomes of greater and greater importance in the world of affairs he seeks, in vain, to recognize him as his son. Unquestionably the audience would have expected a sentimental reunion for the final curtain: Dumas, however, has caused his hero to adopt his mother's name and remain unreconciled.

After a number of largely insignificant plays Dumas proceeded to enlarge the scope of his new dramatic invention in *Les idées de Madame Aubray* (*Madame Aubray's Ideas,* 1867), in which appears a kind of study of true Christianity in modern social surroundings. The central character is Madame Aubray, a woman who believes in following the dictates of her own charitable soul rather than the codes of the world in which she lives. Her dearly beloved son, Camille, falls in love with a girl, Jeannine, a presumed 'widow' and in reality an unmarried mother. When Camille asks for his mother's approval Madame Aubray refuses, but after Jeannine, in a moment of noble renunciation, pretends to Camille that she has had many lovers she is so deeply touched that she gives the girl to her son. This is undoubtedly an interesting play, and Dumas has exhibited great skill, not only in revealing the mind of Madame Aubray herself, but, more importantly, in suggesting the influence of her character upon those with whom she comes into contact. Sentimentalism, no doubt, colours the general picture, and the situations are sometimes twisted to accord with the author's purpose, but among the plays of ideas written in the sixties and seventies this stands out for its directness of aim and its sincerity af purpose.

There follows a series of rather conflicting plays on the subject of illicit relations. In the ironical *Une visite de noces* (*A Honeymoon Call,* 1871) a husband is shown attracted towards a former mistress when he thinks she has had many lovers, but immediately repelled when he finds out that she is faithful to his memory: he prefers, rather than resume an illicit attachment to a woman of this kind, to remain with his wife. In *La Princesse Georges* (1871) the irony is of a different sort and bitter. Séverine's husband, a prince, has a liaison with Sylvanie, wife of the Count de Terremonde. Loving her husband, the injured woman informs the count, and then is dismayed to learn that he intends to kill his rival when he comes for his assignation. A shot is heard; Séverine is in despair; then suddenly it is revealed that the slain man is not her husband, but a wretched youth, de Foudette, to whom also Sylvanie had opened her arms and who had, all unwittingly, walked into the trap. The solution is clever—perhaps too clever; for, although in our minds we are prepared to recognize that the author has found an interesting twist for a hackneyed plot—even although we may admit that his purpose is being pursued by indication of the blind fate that operates in this world of the illicit in sex relations—the unexpectedness of the final scene undoubtedly invokes in us an impression of artificiality. Like so many plays of the same kind still to come, there is too much brain-work here.

It is of interest to note—especially when we compare Dumas' career with that of authors immediately following him—that from these purely realistic plays he now turned to a kind of drama which, although maintaining outward realism, became invested with a kind of mystical atmosphere. In his address to the public prefacing *La femme de Claude* (*Claude's Wife,* 1873) he speaks of his latest work as "purely symbolic." "Claude does not murder his wife," he declares; "the dramatist docs not murder a woman; together they destroy a Beast." Written after the outbreak of war with Prussia, *La femme de Claude* mingles a spy theme with that of adultery. Césarine is the thoroughly dissipated wife of a great inventor; she becomes involved in the toils of a German agent, Cartagnac, and turns the head of her husband's brilliant assistant, Antonin. In the end, just after she has been foiled in her attempt to steal some military plans, Claude shoots her dead—symbolically with the new rifle invented by Antonin—and the Beast is vanquished.

The symbolic style, no less than that of *La Princesse Georges,* shows at once Dumas' source of weakness and his source of strength. The strength lies in his mastery of what may be called theatrical logic. Although analysis may demonstrate the spurious sentiment apparent in many scenes of *La dame aux camélias,* that irresistible sweep accompanied by economy of means which the author learned from Scribe has made it a popular favourite. Above all other things, Dumas knew how to arrest and to hold the attention of his audiences. At the same time, in this strength lies potential weakness. So long as the dramatist keeps to the level of *La dame aux camélias* all is well; but when he tries to become profound the very artificiality inherent in the 'well-made-play' formula proves his undoing. The scaffolding and the machinery suddenly reveal themselves to us blatantly, and illusion is dispelled.

With Augier, Dumas may be accepted as one of the most influential members of that dramatic group which was intent on establishing the new realism, on introducing social problems into the playhouse, and on using the stage for the purpose of inculcating ideas; but neither was a genius.

Dozens of other writers applied themselves to the new style and wrote abundantly of the problems (mainly marriage and money) of the bourgeoisie. Among them are François Poinsard with his *L'honneur et l'argent* (*Honour and Money,* 1853), Paul Arène with his *Pierrot héritier* (*Pierrot the Heir,* 1865), Theodore Barrière with his *Malheur aux vaincus* (*Woe to the Vanquished,* 1870), Jacques Bornet with his *L'usurier* (*The Usurer,* 1870), Victor Séjour with his *L'argent du diable* (*The Devil's Coin,* 1854). Of such authors few deserve special note. Honoré de Balzac has quality, but even he warrants much more attention for his *Comédie humaine* than for his plays—*La marâtre* (*The Stepmother,* 1848) and *Mercadet* (1851)—although the latter is an incisively written study of financial chicanery, with some excellent scenes. So, too, individual mention may be made of the interesting *La révolte* (*The Revolt,* 1870) of Count Philippe de Villiers de l'Isle-Adam, a not ineffective anticipation of *A Doll's House.*

There are works of minor interest here, but the real triumphs of the realistic stage were still to come.

Realistic Gropings in England

While the English stage produced no Dumas or Augier, the same movements as dominated in Paris can be traced in London.

In the year 1840 appeared a play called *Money,* by Lord Lytton, and its very title tells its story. Here is the direct equivalent of those French plays which, then and later, explored the problems of wealth and sought to reveal some of the vices of bourgeois society. The scene in which the will of the rich Mr Mordaunt is read indicates its tone. The relatives are gathered, all eager and expectant, with, among them, the poor hero, Evelyn, and his love, Clara. One after another of the richer members of the company are woefully disappointed, and then comes the shock as the lawyer reads on:

> SHARP: "And, with the aforesaid legacies and exceptions, I do will and bequeath the whole of my fortune, in India Stock, Bonds, Exchequer bills, Three Per Cent. Consols, and in the Bank of India (constituting him hereby sole residuary legatee and joint executor with the aforesaid Henry Graves, Esq.) to Alfred Evelyn [*pause—a movement on the part of everybody but* SHARP], now or formerly of Trinity College, Cambridge [*universal excitement*], being, I am told, an oddity, like myself—the only one of my relations who never fawned on me; and who, having known privation, may the better employ wealth." And now, sir, I have only to wish you joy, and give you this letter from the deceased. I believe it is important.

[*All rise.*]

EVELYN [*looking over to* CLARA]: Ah, Clara, if you had but loved me!

CLARA [*turning away*]: And his wealth, even more than poverty, separates us for ever!

LADY FRANKLIN: I wish you joy.

OMNES [*crowding round to congratulate* EVELYN]: I wish you joy.

SIR JOHN [*to* GEORGINA]: Go, child—put a good face on it—he's an immense match! My dear fellow, I wish you joy; you are a great man now—a very great man! I wish you joy.

EVELYN [*aside*]: And *her* voice alone is silent!

GLOSSMORE: If I can be of any use to you———

STOUT: Or I, sir———

BLOUNT: Or I? Shall I put you up at the clubs?

SHARP: You will want a man of business. I transacted all Mr Mordaunt's affairs.

SIR JOHN [*rushing to centre of crowd, and pushing them aside*]: Tush, tush! Mr Evelyn is at home *here*—always looked on him as a son! Nothing in the world we would not do for him!

EVELYN: Lend me ten pounds for my old nurse!

OMNES: Certainly! Certainly!

[*Chorus put their hands into their pockets, producing purses, and offering them eagerly.*]

No more than this brief extract is required to indicate *Money*'s position in the history of the theatre. Without doubt it stems from the sentimental tradition: the situation in which Evelyn and Clara find themselves is similar to that of many an eighteenth-century hero and heroine. At the same time, its dialogue has not the strained artificiality associated with the names of Cumberland and Kelly, while its theme definitely aligns it with the work of the new realists.

In this way the play stands as an excellent example of transitional drama. Lytton was a writer who, like Scribe himself, was apt in sensing the trend of public taste. *Money* he wrote because he realized the craving for the realistic in measured doses: he was also the author of the immensely popular 'gentlemanly melodrama' *The Lady of Lyons* (1838) and the romantically historical *Richelieu; or, The Conspiracy* (1839), because he realized that the same public that craved for realism also craved for romance.

The contributions of Boucicault, Reade, and Taylor have been noted above, but something new enters into the theatre with the work of Tom Robertson (T. W. Robertson). It must be confessed that his plays have little intrinsic importance: he wrote no *Dame aux camélias* or *Gendre de M. Poirier*. On the other hand, the significance of his writings was, for the English stage, of very considerable extent, and accordingly their innovations must be surveyed, if not for their own worth, at least for what they meant to others.

Fundamentally Robertson, who started as a romantic melodramatist, was the first man in England to conceive of stage realism as a complete whole. Others before him had penned scenes taken (more or less) from ordinary life; others too had introduced real objects, or their theatrical semblances, to the boards. It remained for him to co-ordinate these efforts. He not only set forth to write plays in which he tried to reflect the ways of common life; he endeavoured to provide for those plays such settings and such interpretation as fitted their lines. He sought for actors prepared to abandon the old bold manner appropriate to melodrama

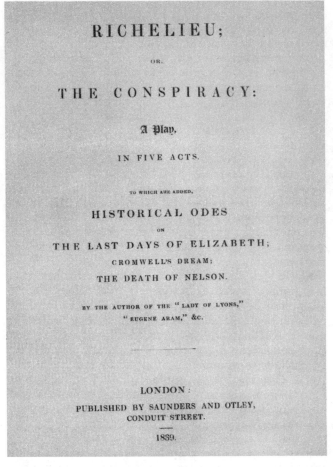

Title page from Richelieu: or, The Conspiracy *by Edward Bulwer-Lytton, 1939*

and the romantic play; he insisted that his doors should have real knobs on them and not simply painted forms.

An excellent, and an essentially truthful, picture of his struggles was presented by his successor, A. W. Pinero, in *Trelawny of the 'Wells'* (1899), and nowhere better could one find an indication both of what Robertson set out to accomplish and what he sought to banish from the playhouse. If this later comedy is read as a comment on his own works we shall have a clear mental image of his achievements. After a kind of transitional play, *David Garrick* (1864), he created in *Society* (1865) a drama that immediately fluttered Victorian audiences, and followed this with a series of similar pieces—*Ours* (1866), *Caste* (1867), and *School* (1869). Of these *Caste* shows his qualities at their best and most characteristic. Whiffs of sentimentalism and romance are to be breathed here certainly. The Honourable George D'Alroy is almost as pure as a hero of melodrama, and Esther Eccles is a true heroine. Beyond this, however, there is a flavour in this comedy-drama of which the melodrama remained innocent. Esther is in danger, but not from any dark-moustached villain: the menace to her life is the snobbery of D'Alroy's aristocratic family. Noting this, we realize that in *Caste* Robertson has moved into an entirely different mental and emotional world. Although he makes use of melodramatic devices, the service to which they are put is far other than that of a few decades before. The very title of his play shows his purpose: above and beyond the characters and the plot there exists a theme, and that theme is 'Caste.' In his own way Robertson was doing for London what Augier and Dumas *fils* were doing for Paris.

One further comment may be made on his significance for the modern stage. Not alone, certainly, yet nevertheless powerfully, he aided in the development of the present-day producer. As the drama increased its scope during the nineteenth century and as the theatres came to enjoy practical resources of which they had no knowledge in the past, the need arose for the appointment of officials responsible for co-ordination of effect. Such need came with the 'historical' productions of Shakespeare's plays by Charles Kean; it presented itself to Dion Boucicault with his new-style melodramas; Gilbert found it essential to exercise control of this kind in the production of his comic operas. Robertson was one of the first in England to demonstrate the need with respect to the realistic stage.

This, of course, is not to say that he achieved anything akin to what was accomplished by the German players who acted under the direction of the Duke of Saxe-Meiningen and whose methods so deeply impressed contemporary theatre workers, but his tentative efforts were in the same direction as theirs. In its tours during the seventies and eighties this company revealed in final form what the stage had been groping towards during the immediately preceding decades. The director became all-important, and every effort was made to secure unity of impression, where in the presentation of Shakespeare's plays in revival or in the production of the new realistic drama. . . .

SCRIBE'S STYLE

Patti P. Gillespie (essay date 1972)

SOURCE: "Plays, Well-Constructed and Well-Made," in *The Quarterly Journal of Speech,* Vol. 58, No. 3, October, 1972, pp. 313-21.

[*In this essay, Gillespie differentiates the well-made play from the well-constructed play, using the distinction to critically evaluate Scribe's dramatic style.*]

Critical allusions to the plays of Eugène Scribe (1791-1861) are confused, ambiguous, and often contradictory. The literature surrounding this playwright discloses several curious situations. The name of Scribe is well known to students of the drama; the plays of

Scribe are not. The success and esteem of Scribe in his own day were remarkable;[1] his subsequent reputation has been largely unfavorable.[2] Dramaturgical patterns which supposedly describe Scribe's practices are proposed;[3] a substantial number of Scribe's plays do not fit the patterns.[4] Eugène Scribe is the acknowledged "father" of something called the "well-made play"; the meaning of the phrase "well-made play" remains obscure, imprecisely defined, inadequately understood.

None of these problems is more vexing than the use which critics have made of the term "well-made play." Common usage for over a century has firmly linked the name of Scribe to the label "well-made play"; on the other hand, the phrase connotes a degree of excellence which makes its application to Scribean dramaturgy unacceptable to some critics. An anecdote related by John Russell Taylor illustrates the dilemma:

> Not long ago I was talking with a group of young British dramatists about the theatre and play-writing in general. The term 'well-made play' came up, as it will, in a derogatory sense, and suddenly one of them said 'Come to think of it, why shouldn't a play be well-made? What's wrong with that?' What indeed. And yet the phrase, which seems obviously designed as a compliment, is almost invariably used in modern criticism as an insult.[5]

The contradiction between intention and application, between the term and the thing, has given rise to many curious statements: "The well-made play is rather an ill-made play";[6] and, "the well-made play . . . [is] a product of artifice rather than art, dependent on incident and formulas rather than on character-study and truth to life."[7]

Some English writers, attempting no doubt to avoid the obvious contradiction, shun the term "well-made play" altogether when discussing the works of Scribe and his imitators. These critics reserve the term "well-made" for those plays of a superior construction; they use the French designation *"bien faite"* for plays constructed in the manner of Eugène Scribe. While often useful, this alternative is not wholly satisfactory, for it leaves French critics to wrestle alone with a problem not entirely of their making; moreover, the French have confronted the same problem with the term *"pièce bien faite"* that the English and Americans have faced with the phrase "well-made play."[8] Thus, in both languages the apparent disparity between the words used to describe and the object being described has resulted in ambivalence and confusion.

While critics have generally been aware of the seeming contradiction between the term and the thing *well-made play,* most have failed to recognize in what manner and to what degree this confusion has manifested itself within the critical literature. In criticism the single term "well-made play" (or *pièce bien faite*) is being used by different critics to designate different types of plays.

Although various subtleties of definitions appear, two major meanings can be isolated. For some critics the term denotes any skillfully constructed play whose action is formulated causally; the term is evaluative and is applicable to the works of many great dramatists. In this sense, the first known practitioner of the form was Sophocles, and the first critic to define the form was Aristotle. Donald Clive Stuart is a representative spokesman for this position:

> The expression [well-made play], when used approvingly, denotes a play in which the action develops through an inevitable sequence of cause and effect, in which every scene is so placed and so treated that to change it in the slightest degree would harm the total effect. Furthermore, the expression describes—and still with approval—a plot which unfolds with suspense and surprise and rises to several crises, as in *Oedipus Rex*.[9]

For other critics the term is not evaluative; it is descriptive. For these critics "well-made play" denotes more specific techniques and is applicable to the plays of relatively few dramatists, the first being Eugène Scribe. Many of these critics propose that, while Scribe really "invented" nothing, he did combine previously known elements in somewhat different ways; therefore, he may be considered as the creator of a new dramaturgy. Taylor summarizes this position:

> Nothing comes from nothing, and certainly all sorts of precursors can be found for Scribe and his form of play. But for our purposes it is sufficient to say that what had been done occasionally, patchily and empirically by others Scribe did regularly, consistently and in full consciousness of what he was doing.[10]

Clearly the phrase "well-made play" must be applied more exactly and with greater precision in the future. If ever the threads of confusion surrounding Scribe's dramaturgical contributions are to be untangled, an unequivocal distinction between the two meanings of the single term must be established and preserved.[11]

With that goal in view, I would propose a convenient, if somewhat arbitrary, differentiation. For a play whose action is formulated causally and skillfully, i.e., the position of the first critical group described above, the term *well-constructed* should be used. In this sense, *well-constructed* is to be understood as an evaluation of the results of a playwright's efforts; he has made a good play.[12] For a play written in and after the nineteenth century and written in the manner of Eugène Scribe, i.e., the position of the second critical group, the term *well-made* should be used. In this sense

well-made is to be understood as a description of the techniques used by the playwright; he has made a certain kind of play. Obviously using these guidelines, a play can be well-constructed without being well-made (*Oedipus Rex);* or a play can be well-made without being well-constructed (*A Scrap of Paper).*

A distinction between well-constructed and well-made having been proposed, the responsibility of delimiting these terms remains. Available critical writings are of little value in this regard. William Archer, for example, implies that the crucial distinction is inherent in the relationships between the play's complexity and its clarity.[13] For George Bernard Shaw the difference rests upon the inclusion of the unexpected.[14] For Francis Ferguson the definitions depend upon differentiating "the plot as the rationalized series of events, and the plot as 'the soul of the tragedy'."[15] Among the critics who have attempted to contradistinguish the well-constructed and the well-made play, Elder Olson is at once the most correct and the most precise:

> The whole probability of the . . . [well-made plot] depends upon the probability that one event as cause will produce another as effect. The probability of the . . . [well-constructed plot] includes not merely this, but the probability . . . that the agent, as a person of given character, will or will not do a given thing.[16]

These brief but perceptive remarks are tantalizingly close to the central issue, but still they fail to isolate the primary flaw in Scribe's plays, the flaw which would make critics unwilling to call them "well-made" when "well-made" is perceived as evaluative and complimentary. Equally significant is Olson's failure to enunciate clearly why that flaw is a flaw. Therefore, although agreeing with the direction of Olson's comments, I would insist upon the need for further elaboration.

If a play is well-constructed, its six parts as identified by Aristotle (plot, character, thought, diction, music, and spectacle) will exist in an intimate interrelationship based on both material and formal causation.[17] To illustrate: because incidents in plays are composed of actions performed and articulated by human-like agents, because human speech and action result necessarily from emotional or intellectual decisions, and because decisions are a necessary consequence of desires, it follows that character, thought, and diction are parts of the whole, the plot; they are also means to the end, the plot; that is to say, they are the materials out of which the plot is constructed. Since in a play, the diction is rendered orally (spoken dialogue) and the physical actions are represented visually (moving actors), then music and spectacle are also parts of and means to the plot. Plot, then, includes the other five parts of a play; it is the whole of which they are the parts, the end of which they are the means.

But conversely and simultaneously, plot determines the form which each of the parts will assume. The characters are teleologically determined by the kinds of actions in which they will participate; the thoughts of the characters are determined by the kinds of characters possessing, articulating, and acting upon them. Diction necessarily is determined by the situation in which it is being spoken, but further it is used to reinforce the thoughts being expressed and the character of the agents expressing them, and so on. Both the formal-material causation of the six parts and the complexity of the inter-connections among the six parts are evidently necessary if a good play is to result.

So long as the dramatist maintains this delicate balance among the six parts, he may construct a good play in a variety of ways. By choosing and arranging incidents and characters in one way, a playwright can construct a drama evocative of pity and fear; by formulating the six parts in other ways the dramatist can write plays productive of laughter-evoking emotions or of suspense, fear, hatred. Thus tragedies, comedies, melodramas are common forms of drama.

Different forms are not the only options open to the playwright. To effectuate any form, he can choose from among several possibilities the devices he desires for unifying his play. In some plays a mood may be a significant device of achieving unity; Maeterlinck's *Pelléas et Mélisande* has an aura of mistiness about it which contributes to the convincingness of the action. Or character may be a device of unity, as it is in *Faust, From Morn to Midnight,* and *Abe Lincoln in Illinois.* Aristophanes traditionally built his comedies around the element of thought; *The Frogs,* for example, explores the impending disintegration of Athenian society and poses suggestions for halting the decline. *Uncle Tom's Cabin,* a melodrama, and *Andromache,* Euripides' somewhat schematized tragedy, both gain unity by the device of thought. Perhaps the most common device of all for obtaining unity, however, is the construction of the probability that one event as an antecedent will lead to another event as its consequence. This is unity of action, the unity which Aristotle preferred for tragedy and so meticulously described in chapters seven through eleven of the *Poetics. Oedipus Rex* displays this type of unity.

Since most critics assert that well-made plays are unified by action, a brief review of the essential features of unity of action seems in order. Unity, in this kind of plot, is the result of the presentation of one complete and whole action with the constituent incidents connected in such a way that the removal or transposition of one incident would markedly change the whole play. The well-constructed plot which is unified by action must have a beginning, a middle, and an end. The proper magnitude of the plot, although limited externally by the memory span of the audience, is determined internally by two factors: the significance of the respective actions being represented, and the desirable realization of the affective powers of the play. Each incident in the play must have a magnitude commensurate with its peculiar function in the play as a whole.

In well-constructed plays which gain unity through action, then, there is an essential interconnection among the incidents represented within the plot; and there is the material-formal interdependency among the six constituent elements of the play. Theoretically, to disrupt or distort any of the consociations will result in a drama which is flawed, which is not well-constructed.

Nonetheless, depending upon the *form* (tragedy, comedy, melodrama) of the well-constructed play, certain subtle differences in the nature of these relationships can be seen. In tragedy, the seriousness of the action being imitated requires that the characters deliberate and decide upon issues of ethical importance. Early in a tragedy, an agent's character will make probable his actions; later in the tragedy his actions together with his character make probable his subsequent decisions and actions. An early decision of the protagonist, for example, may cause him to undergo certain experiences; these experiences, in turn, may produce subtle changes in his character which will affect all of his later decisions and actions. Character in tragedy, in this way, remains an integral part of the probability being constructed by the playwright and remains intimately connected both with what has happened previously and with what will happen presently. Indeed, the action of a well-constructed tragedy most often progresses by means of a series of fundamental and ethical decisions by the main characters.

In well-constructed comedies and melodramas, on the other hand, no such intimate and profound relationship exists between characters' thinking and acting. The kinds of actions being imitated in these forms preclude successive moral choices of a fundamental nature, that is, questions involving the nature of good and evil, right and wrong. Actions in comedy, being contrary to the serious, and those in melodrama, being either temporarily or even only seemingly serious do not require, indeed do not allow for, character change and development of the sort found in tragedy. Only at the end of a play is an agent in comedy or melodrama apt to show marked alterations in his character. For example, a villain who made successive moral choices during the action of a play would not long remain a villain; the melodrama would therefore most probably sacrifice its own unique powers, that is, the melodrama would cease to be a melodrama. Instead of undergoing basic changes of an ethical nature, the characters in melodramas and comedies usually select a purpose, or goal, early in the action; this goal remains largely unchanged during the course of the action and provides the motivation for a series of attempts to attain it. Unity of plot is achieved less by the interaction of character and situation than by the thought of a character expressed as intent. Since the evocative powers of both forms are related in an inverse proportion to the degree of understanding and pity for the participating agents, and since the action may be formulated as a series of attempts and defeats, characterization in comedy and melodrama may be rather superficial and the organization of the action may be episodic. The less exacting relationship between character and incident also allows chance to assume a greater role as a determinant of action in comedy and melodrama than in tragedy. Although inappropriate for tragedy, such conditions are quite acceptable in melodramas and comedies because the nature of the action and the desired evocative powers permit characters to be delineated sufficiently by relatively few indices, action to progress on the basis of the intent of a character, and the formulation of the whole to be episodic—all without damaging the unique powers of these forms.[18]

Summarizing, in a well-constructed play, the constituent parts of the whole exist in a definite and definable interrelationship regardless of the probability scheme which the poet chooses to construct in order to unify his work of art. Depending upon the form of the play, however, the dramatist may relax or tighten the connections among the parts; but he must not distort them.

Well-made plays, although bearing certain superficial resemblances, are not well-constructed and should not be confused with plays like *Oedipus Rex*. Scribe appropriated for his plays (most of which are comedies) part, but not all, of the methods of probability and unity which Aristotle recommended as the best possible constructions for tragedy.[19] Scribe constructed plays which seem to move from a beginning, through a middle, to an end, by means of an antecedent-consequence progression of incidents. He constructed plays which appear not to be episodic because his agents make decisions which on the surface seem to be the antecedents for further actions.[20] His characters, therefore, apparently are important participants in their situations. Thus, Scribe's comedies and melodramas display a superficial similarity to tragic formulations. The ramifications are immense.

First, because his action seems to progress in a cause-to-effect manner, the anticipations aroused by his plays differ markedly from the expectations established when a construction is frankly and unashamedly episodic. Indeed his plays arouse a set of expectations which are generally considered inappropriate, or at the very least inessential, for other comic and melodramatic constructions. For example, that special kind of interaction between the characters and their situation, normally reserved for the tragic form, is expected in plays by Scribe. As a consequence, his characterizations seemingly need to be subtle and multifaceted to allow the agents to participate meaningfully in their situations. The prospect of a close interaction between the characters and the actions also suggests that the play's content should be probed for a serious purpose or an ethical statement.

Reinforcing such assumptions is the comic tone of the plays. Scribe preferred a sophisticated, restrained comedy and seldom abandoned, even temporarily, his established schemes of probability in order to indulge in scenes of rollicking farce or broad humor. His audience is therefore constantly confronted with a sense of the inevitability of the action, action at once unrequired by any character's development and unrelieved by an exuberance of robust comedy. The implications are clear. By selecting techniques of probability and unity which superficially resemble those normally associated with tragedy, Scribe seems to imply that his comedies and melodramas may be something else, something more.

Scribe's arousal of the wrong set of anticipations led to yet another problem. When Scribe chose a method of formulation so closely associated with tragic constructions, he altered significantly the criteria against which his plays would be measured. No reputable critic seriously suggests that Aristophanes should motivate the appearance of the dung beetle or the adoption of the sex strike. Critics seldom find objectionable the train of fools to Volpone's bed and are generally unconcerned that more or fewer could as easily have been depicted, or that the number and placement of the episodes is quite arbitrary. Few scholars interrupt the hilarious comic scenes between Titania and the ass-headed Bottom to complain that Chance caused Titania to fall in love with the weaver. How absurd, too, would appear a critic who railed against Molière for providing insufficient preparation for Acaste and Clitandre's acquisition of Célimène's letters in *The Misanthrope*. In each of these plays, the action as it unfolds is quite acceptable in terms of its own scheme of probability and its own method of plot unification. But Scribe by his unfortunate choices of method seems to invite comparisons with tragic constructions; such comparisons have not been to Scribe's advantage.

Critics past and present have applied evaluative standards to Scribe's plays which differ from those applied to other comic and melodramatic formulations. For example, Olson, in his discussion of the well-made play writes:

> You have met the well-made plot before, in the *Poetics* of Aristotle; it is simply a form of the characterless play, the kind, as Aristotle puts it, that may exist without character. The personages in a well-made play are puppets because they have no chance to choose, because the logic of events rules

all, because their characters have been reduced to mere circumstances of the incidents; human agency has been reduced to natural force, and action has been reduced to event.[21]

Olson seems unaware that he is applying criteria which are generally considered inapplicable or non-essential for good comedies. Thus while it is true, as Olson observes, that Aristotle spoke of a characterless play, it is equally true that Aristotle had confined himself very rigorously to a discussion of tragedy. Critical comments on Scribe's plays very often seem to lose sight of the fact that almost all of the plays are comic or melodramatic, not tragic constructions. When critics condemn Scribe for using stock characters,[22] are they suggesting that Plautus, Beaumarchais, Molière, and Shakespeare did not? When complaining that Scribe's stories are farfetched and fantastic, exceedingly dependent on chance and coincidence,[23] do the critics wish to imply that those of Aristophanes, Terence, and Shaw are not? When denying that Scribe wrote his plays for a serious moral or ethical purpose,[24] do they claim to see such goals paramount in the constructions of Congreve? The point here is certainly not that Scribe was a comedist of the stature of Aristophanes, Molière, or Shakespeare; he was of course no such thing. The point is that *the flaws which most critics cite* as the reasons for Scribe's poor constructions are not perceived as flaws when they occur in the formulations of master comedists. One must conclude, I think, that the present critical explanations are both inadequate and misleading.

But Scribe's dramatic agents are not well-characterized; the exigences of incident do determine overmuch the qualities ascribed to the agents. What is the true nature of the quite palpable flaws in technique?

It has been demonstrated above that the kind and depth of characterization required by comedies and melodramas differ from those needed in tragedy. Regardless of form, however, the agents in any well-constructed play will embody traits which are suitable to and material for the actions in which they participate. In a well-made play, by contrast, the agent's traits do not contribute substantially to that agent's actions. A few examples will clarify.

In *Oedipus Rex,* the inquiring mind of the king is established as a major character trait. This trait translates directly into the action of the tragedy: it is the quality which leads Oedipus to question the source of the plague, to seek the killer of Laius, and to unearth the secret of his own birth. In *Adrienne Lecouvreur,* Scribe's only tragedy,[25] the prince is characterized in Act I as an amateur chemist only because Adrienne must be poisoned in Act V by the princess. The problem was: the princess must plausibly have access to a deadly poison; Scribe's solution was: the prince might

be a chemist with his analytical laboratory in his home. Thus, the prince is a chemist not because he needs an inquisitive mind to justify a discovery which he will make, nor because he needs a certain scientific objectivity to allow him particular insight into a problem confronting him, but rather because his wife must have access to poison with which she can murder an actress. In Molière's *Tartuffe,* the gluttony of the hypocrite is a sign of and a reinforcement for his sexuality; the trait is central to the meaning of the play. In Scribe's *Bertrand et Raton,* on the other hand, Raton's taste for excellent wines is introduced merely to provide a convenient cellar in which he can be locked out of the action for a bit; this quality has not relationship to the play's central concern or to the remaining traits of Raton. Jonson in *Volpone* uses Corbaccio's deafness for its farcical potentialities; in *Feu Lionel,* Scribe renders Brémontier myopic so that Alice can be required, plausibly, to read aloud two letters which contain expository and preparatory information necessary if the audience is to grasp the intrigues which follow.

To compound examples is unnecessary. The point is that in Scribe's plays, whether comedy or tragedy, the exigences of incident dictate (formally determine) the agents—their traits, their speeches, their emotions; and agent (his traits, speeches, and emotions) do not, however, contribute substantially to that character's decisions or actions. Moreover, the qualities and traits are not often included for their own sake, either for what they might contribute to the central issue of the play or for their worth in terms of sheer comic potentiality; they are assigned instead to accord with the rigorous demands of the many and complicated lines of action. Character in Scribe's plays, then, is only minimally material to plot, while plot (in the sense of the sequence of incidents) is rigorously determinative of character. Thus, it is not low levels of characterization in Scribe's plays which are undesirable. The real problem in dramatic technique is the failure of an individual agent's several traits to relate to one another mutually and integrally, and the tendency of traits to contribute more significantly to incident than to agent. That he *distorts rather than loosens* the relationship among the actions, characters, and emotions is the source of Scribe's errors.

These errors, once recognized, are the differentia between well-made and well-constructed plays (see footnote 12). If these distinctions are then reflected in the vocabulary of critics in the future, many of the confusions surrounding the phrase "well-made play" will be eliminated.

Notes

[1] A few facts will illustrate. Between 1815 and 1830, Scribe's plays accounted for more than one-tenth of the new comedies and *vaudevilles* played in the Parisian

theatre. In 1834, works by Scribe were performed one hundred thirty-five times, a record not equalled for more than fifteen years. In 1836, Scribe was invited to join the French Academy. See Maurice Albert, *Les Théâtres des boulevards: 1789-1848* (Paris: Société française d'imprimerie et de librairie, 1902), p. 285; and, Neil C. Arvin, *Eugene Scribe and the French Theatre, 1815-1860* (Cambridge, Mass.: Harvard Univ. Press, 1924), p. 220.

[2] See for example Oscar G. Brockett, *The Theatre: An Introduction* (New York: Holt, Rinehart, and Winston, 1964), p. 263; John Russell Taylor, *The Rise and Fall of the Well-Made Play* (London: Methuen and Co., Ltd., 1967), p. 9; William A. Nitze and E. Preston Dargan, *A History of the French Literature: from the Earliest Times to the Present,* 3rd ed. (New York: Holt, 1938), p. 680.

[3] The most influential of those recently proposed is by Stephen S. Stanton, "Introduction," *Camille and Other Plays* (New York: Hill and Wang, 1957), pp. xii-xiii.

[4] Stanton's "seven structural features," for example, when literally and strictly applied *exclude over two-thirds* of the thirty-five plays which Scribe wrote for the non-musical stage. In this regard also it is well to remark that these thirty-five plays are not all "full length" as asserted by Dr. Stanton in his encyclopedia article. Stephen S. Stanton, "Eugène Scribe," in *The Reader's Encyclopedia of World Drama,* ed. John Gassner and Edward Quinn (New York: Thomas Y. Crowell Co., 1969), p. 752.

[5] *The Rise and Fall of the Well-Made Play,* p. 9.

[6] Elder Olson, *Tragedy and the Theory of Drama* (Detroit: Wayne State Univ. Press, 1961), p. 79.

[7] Nitze and Dargan, p. 680.

[8] The observations of Henri Ghéon are pertinent here: "There still was the dogma of 'the well-made play.' 'The well-made play' of Racine, had become little by little, 'the well-made play' of Scribe, then of Victorien Sardou." Henri Ghéon, *L'Art du théâtre* (Montreal: Éditions Serge, 1944), p. 132. Translation my own.

[9] *The Development of Dramatic Art* (New York: Dover Publications, 1960), p. 552. For other examples of this position see Oscar G. Brockett, *History of the Theatre* (Boston: Allyn and Bacon, 1968), p. 371; Maurice Valency, *The Flower and the Castle* (New York: Macmillan, 1963), p. 40.

[10] *The Rise and Fall of the Well-Made Play,* p. 11. For other examples of this position see Winton Tolles, *Tom Taylor and the Victorian Drama* (New York: Columbia Univ. Press, 1940), p. 114; Thomas H. Dickinson,

The Contemporary Drama of England (Boston: Little, Brown, and Co., 1931), p. 34; Geoffrey Brereton, *A Short History of French Literature* (London: Cassell, 1954), p. 325.

[11] Stuart seems aware of the problem inherent in the term: he speaks of its use either "approvingly" or "disapprovingly." Curiously he does not explore the confusions resulting from the dual use of the term nor does he pursue the ramifications of this confusion in the critical literature. Most importantly, he proposes no escape from the existing dilemma, if in fact he recognized it as such.

[12] To prevent a possible misunderstanding: any number of good (well-constructed) plays are not causally organized. But of all the well-constructed plays, only the causally organized are typically confused with well-made plays. This fact accounts for the focus of the following discussion.

[13] *Playmaking: A Manual of Craftsmanship* (Boston: Small, 1912), p. 213.

[14] "The Author's Apology to *Mrs. Warren's Profession,*" in *Plays by George Bernard Shaw,* ed. Eric Bentley (New York: New American Library, 1960), p. 44.

[15] "*Ghosts* and *The Cherry Orchard:* The Theatre of Modern Realism," in *Essays in the Modern Drama,* ed. Morris Freedman (Boston: Heath and Co., 1966), p. 22.

[16] *The Theory of Comedy* (Bloomington, Indiana: Indiana Univ. Press, 1968), p. 117.

[17] *On the Art of Poetry,* chs. 3-4.

[18] Professor Hubert Heffner, Indiana University, has provided invaluable assistance in the formulation of these ideas.

[19] The evidence for this study was the thirty-five non-musical plays of Scribe. From Scribe's complete dramatic output (something around four-hundred works), the non-musical plays were selected as the sample because (1) critics do not customarily cite Scribe's opera libertti, comic operas, or *vaudevilles* as examples of well-made plays, and (2) music introduces a unique constraint upon the dramatist's construction and determines in large measure the structures open to him. The non-musical plays are available in Eugène Scribe, *Les Oeuvres complètes de Eugène Scribe* (Paris: Dentu, 1874), I-IX.

[20] Closer examination reveals that Scribe's plays are not so unified and are in fact episodic.

[21] Olson, *Comedy,* p. 117.

[22] See, for example, Tolles, p. 23.

[23] See, for example, Brander Matthews, *Principles of Playmaking* . . . (New York: Scribner, 1919), pp. 143ff., who summarizes such positions.

[24] See, for example, Hugh Allison Smith, *Main Currents of Modern French Drama* (New York: Holt, 1925), pp. 112-117.

[25] It could be forcefully argued that this play is melodrama rather than tragedy and I would not quarrel with this assessment. I chose to consider it a tragedy because critics contemporary with Scribe so designated it.

Douglas Cardwell (essay date 1983)

SOURCE: "The Well-Made Play of Eugène Scribe," in *The French Review,* Vol. LVI, No. 6, May 1983, pp. 876-84.

[*In this essay, Cardwell argues that, contrary to general critical opinion, Scribe's dramas include an imaginative use of "the elemental aspects of drama" rather than a mere "mechanical application of a formula."*]

Eugène Scribe has long been acknowledged as the developer, or inventor, of what is commonly called the well-made play, and there is an abundance of literature on translations, adaptations, and imitations of his works as well as general agreement on the importance of his influence on both French and foreign playwrights well into this century. The reaction against his plays—which began during his lifetime and continues today in the revolt against the "bourgeois" theater that he typifies for many, and of which he is indeed a primary source—serves as additional proof of his importance in the history of theater and of the power of the forces he organized and directed, as does also the viewing of many current films and television programs, which bear his stamp as clearly as do the plays of Augier, Feydeau, Ibsen, or Shaw.

The essence of that power, the nature of that stamp, however, have generally defied definition; his admirers have had as little success as his detractors. Both groups have tended to emphasize his technical skill, usually without explaining it and without considering other factors that might have contributed to his success. Alexandre Dumas *fils* dismissed him as a "prestidigitateur de première force,"[1] while others commented on the absence of style and character development, but these typical generalities fail to answer satisfactorily the question raised so often and so despairingly by Théophile Gautier:

> Comment se fait-il qu'un auteur dénué de poésie, de lyrisme, de style, de philosophie, de vérité, de naturel, puisse être devenu l'écrivain dramatique le plus en vogue d'une époque, en dépit de l'opposition des lettrés et des critiques?[2]

Gautier correctly perceives that Scribe's undeniable technical skills do not adequately explain his success but cannot do better than to blame the philistine audiences of the time who made Scribe the first Frenchman to get rich by writing plays while neglecting the playwrights favored by the crimson-vested defender of *Hernani*. Most critics have been kinder to the audiences, but not to Scribe, and they have continued to refer to technical skill, theatrical tricks, a basic structure, a formula, which would define the well-made play and explain its success.

The most recent and most elaborate attempt to reduce the well-made play to a formula comes from Stephen S. Stanton, who claims that "True examples of such drama display seven structural features," which he lists.[3] The list is apparently based on a small number of Scribe's plays, especially *Le Verre d'eau,* which is included in his anthology. While one might use the phrase "true examples" to imply that any Scribe play that fails to exhibit the listed features is not "well-made," it is not logical to suppose that, having found a formula for success, Scribe used it only a few times and ignored or abandoned it in the remainder of his plays. Surely any attempt to define the well-made play as exemplified by Scribe must take into account the thirty-five plays included in the series *Comédies-Drames* by the editors of the only complete edition of this works.[4] Stanton's list is at the same time too specific and too general: too specific, because it excludes many of those plays; too general, because one could follow it to the letter and still not produce a well-made play. A few adjustments will not solve the problem, for the difficulty lies not simply in finding a more accurate formula, but in the fact that accuracy is incompatible with the brevity of a formula. The most remarkable feature of these plays, when viewed collectively, is their variety. The lowest common denominator is just not low enough to be of much use. Thus the search for a formula that will explain the structure of the well-made play is doomed to failure. There is no general structure that is common to all such plays. One can, however, describe common practices and tendencies in order to understand better the meaning of that term as it applies to Scribe. The emphasis will be on the typical rather than on the exceptional, but the fundamental fact remains that the range of possibilities is too broad for the description to serve as a prescription. It takes more than the application of rules to construct a well-made play.

Scribe's works include several types of play. Not only are there the expected comedies with various themes and settings—social, historical, political—but also a play that anticipates the *pièce à thèse (La Calomnie)* and a serious drama (*Adrienne Lecouvreur*). *Dix ans de la vie d'une femme* is a pre-naturalist play that traces in dismal detail the decline and death of a woman who falls under the influence of the wrong friends, and there is even a melodrama *(Les Frères invisibles)*. It is certainly not possible to deny the flexibility and variety of the well-made play.

For the exposition there are some clearly defined principles. It must be complete, not in the sense that every detail about previous events that is to be included in the play must be in the exposition, but rather that there must be at least an allusion to every event, though the details may be filled in later if it suits the purposes of the playwright. The exposition must not precede all the action, but be mixed in with the first part of it. The play begins with an event that precipitates a crisis in an already unstable situation, which arouses the interest and curiosity of the audience and gives more life and energy to the exposition. Often an action illustrates the exposition: when an unexpected visitor shows up for breakfast in the first act of *Les Trois Maupin,* the tip he gives the "servant" is used to buy the groceries needed to feed him, thus graphically demonstrating the previously-mentioned poverty of the family. Scribe avoided monologues and dialogues in which the characters exchange information already known to both of them in favor of scenes that seem more natural and that often help to advance the action. The "dilution" of the exposition with action obviously prolongs it, and in the longer plays, which require a great deal of exposition, it is not unusual for it to extend into the beginning of the second act. Generally it is spread over the first quarter of the play.

The action of the well-made play is made up of attempts to overcome a series of obstacles, culminating in the major obstacle that will hold up until the dénouement. Obstacles can be of any type, though they very often have to do with communication-either achieving it or preventing it. There must be several obstacles in each play, and they must be arranged in ascending order of difficulty, except that a major obstacle may have satellite lesser obstacles that serve to make it more imposing, in which case it is the total weight of the problems a protagonist faces that increases as the play progresses as much as the weight of the individual problems. The reversals associated with each obstacle usually come in pairs, the first favorable and the second unfavorable, so that the hero's difficulties afford only brief respites before the final victory. Often the action includes a near-solution (in some cases one that would result in an unsatisfactory dénouement) to add excitement and suspense as well as to prepare the real solution. The action also includes situations, known as *scènes à faire,* that the audience longs for but regards as uncertain, or dreads but believes to be unavoidable. They usually involve a direct confrontation between protagonist and antagonist, or their representatives, from which one will emerge the victor (at least provisionally). The *scène à faire* generally comes fairly late in the action and points the way to the dénouement. There are usually secondary *scènes à faire*

as well; sometimes one becomes part of the dénouement, as does the threatened *scène à faire* that is avoided at the last minute to save the happy ending. Though the antagonist may get his just desserts in some other fashion, the scene usually depends upon the decisive communication of a key piece of information, or upon its prevention. The scene is carefully prepared, highly dramatic, and, despite its structural importance, designed primarily for the emotional satisfaction of the audience.

In its broadest formulation, the structure of a Scribe play usually centers around a single character whose decisions and actions vitally affect the fates of the other characters. In many of the plays a decision is made and then changed several times, with appropriate reactions by the other characters, before the final curtain. The action swings back and forth without making any real progress until the end. In another group of plays, the action is linear, with steady progression from beginning to end. In *Rêves d'amour,* for example, Jeanne flees from Henri throughout the play, while Henri overcomes obstacle after obstacle before finally catching her in the last scene. And in *Dix ans de la vie d'une femme,* the morals and situation of the title character go down steadily from beginning to end, with only the most illusory upswings.

Scribe's basic dramatic device is the *quiproquo.* There are usually several in one play; one may be the basis for the main action, but this is not always the case (in *Les Contes de la reine de Navarre,* for example, there is a succession of *quiproquos,* as Marguerite tries one scheme after another to try to free her brother). Usually the misunderstanding is an accident, often without the knowledge of any of the parties to it, but sometimes it is induced with intent to deceive, and often exploited. The use of the *quiproquo* is part of a broader pattern in which the revelation or continued concealment of a secret, the receipt of certain information by the correct person, or the prevention of its discovery by the wrong person is essential to the proper outcome of the action. Various bits of information may, in the course of the play, be communicated, withheld, distorted, falsified, or invented, causing the many ups and downs in the action. One visible indication of the importance of communication in Scribe's plays is the constant use of letters and various documents and papers. (Over one-fourth of all scenes involve some form of paper stage property, and only eleven of the one hundred thirty-three acts have no such scene.) The secret or *quiproquo* is usually made obvious to the spectator from the beginning, or at least early, but not always (in *Oscar* the audience must wait until the end of the play to learn the true identity of the woman with whom Oscar had a rendezvous, after two other candidates are implicated, then cleared). In this Scribe follows the policy that he reportedly claimed to be the secret of his art. Octave

Feuillet, in the speech he gave when taking Scribe's seat at the Académie Française, quotes him as saying:

> Le publique m'aime parce que j'ai soin de le mettre toujours dans ma confiance; il est dans le secret de la comédie; il a dans les mains les fils qui font jouer mes personnages; il connaît les surprises que je leur ménage, et il croit les leur ménager lui-même; bref, je le prends pour collaborateur; il s'imagine qu'il a fait la pièce avec moi, et naturellement il l'applaudit.[5]

He may indeed have done this for the reason he states, but there is also more potential for drama and suspense when the audience knows the secret than when it does not, for then it is constantly aware of what is at stake. Nevertheless, this does not prevent Scribe from springing a few surprises on the audience.

Each scene must make a definite contribution to the development of the action. As could be expected in plays where communication is so important, the combination of characters to be found onstage at a given moment is determined mainly by the potential for the transfer of information. Some bit of information received or imparted, some act or failure to act, some decision or indecision marks every scene. A very important part of the structure of the well-made play is thus determined by the arrangement of the entrances and exits of the characters and the onstage combinations that result. The scenes are usually tightly linked together, as each prepares the next; the author must thus ensure that each succeeding scene has a combination of characters that will permit the action to move forward according to plan. He avoids, however, certain necessary combinations as long as possible or, even more tantalizingly, permits and then interrupts them, before finally satisfying the carefully cultivated desire of the audience to witness the expected outcome. He must also avoid excessive and increasingly hard-to-justify entrances and exits by any of the characters. In Scribe's plays, major characters average at least three scenes per appearance, sometimes more than four—scarcely a frenzied pace. Though there should be two or three characters onstage most of the time in order to control the spread of information properly, more are needed here and there for the sake of variety. Often most or all of the main characters are on stage for the last scene, for the long-awaited revelation of the facts that will make possible the happy ending, or that will give certain characters (and the audience) some anxious moments before the danger of a fatal revelation is dissipated, often by means of the artful lie. At the end of *Le Verre d'eau,* for example, disastrous scandal is averted when Bolingbroke asserts that he has sent Masham to see his wife Abigail in the queen's apartments. In fact Masham is not married and has come to see the queen.

Typically, one character will dominate each act, but the same person does not dominate all the acts in a play. In *Adrienne Lecouvreur,* the dominant characters are, in turn, the princess, Michonnet, Adrienne, the princess, and Adrienne. This domination is indicated by the fact that the character is onstage through most or even all of the scenes of the act, but it is not usually limited to that constant presence. The character may be actively seeking to affect the outcome of the action, or undergoing successive shocks as others act for or against him, or merely looking on as others struggle (as a prelude, of course, to more direct action later on). The act usually ends on a definite shift in the fortunes of a main character and often has as its purpose the preparation of that shift.

One of the most obvious areas of structural variation is in the number, length, importance, and relationship to the main plot of the sub-plots. Most plays have at least one sub-plot, and there may be as many as seven, usually quite solidly linked to the main plot. In *Le Verre d'eau,* for example, the love-plot of Masham and Abigail and the plot of Bolingbroke to return to power become interdependent as the three characters work together to obtain their several ends. In other plays, the sub-plot is more parallel than dependent (in *Les Trois Maupin* the rise of Henri in society and in the military, due to the protection of amorous ladies at court, is independent of his sister's rise to fortune while masquerading as a famous singer, also at Versailles, though their contemporaneous presence there does lead to some exciting complications in the action). The importance of the sub-plot varies from negligible to virtual equality with the main plot. Even though the plots generally stretch from the first act to the last, they can start anywhere and end anywhere. They do have to end, for a stable situation must be established before the final curtain; a "lady or the tiger?" ending is not permitted in a well-made play.

The dénouement must first of all be swift, often taking place in the last scene. There are several ways of bringing about the final reversal; by whatever means, it usually comes at the moment when all hope seems lost, when a solution seems either impossible or too late to prevent the catastrophe. The reversal must be unpredictable, and much of the art of the well-made play lies in the preparation of its elements in such a way that the audience will not be able to put them together before the right moment, but will quickly recognize the logic of the solution once it is presented to them.

While this summary of general tendencies, common practices, and even a few rules offers a kind of *portrait robot* of Scribe's plays, the many exceptions and variations emphasize their irreducibility, and the aesthetic choices implied by the characteristics cited indicate that the well-made play as developed by Scribe is as much a philosophy as it is a form. As Ferdinand

Brunetière pointed out, Scribe practices the theatrical equivalent of "l'art pour l'art," treating the theater as the Parnassians treated poetry.[6] Unlike them, however, a primary principle of his philosophy is a concern for pleasing his audience, which he saw as the general public, not an elite.

In the speech he delivered at his reception into the Académie Française, Scribe expressed a part of that philosophy:

> Vous courez au théâtre, non pour vous instruire ou vous corriger, mais pour vous distraire et vous divertir. Or, ce qui vous divertit le mieux, ce n'est pas la vÉité, c'est la fiction. Vous retracer ce que vous avez chaque jour sous les yeux n'est pas le moyen de vous plaire: mais ce qui ne se présente point à vous dans la vie habituelle, l'extraordinaire, le romanesque, voilà ce qui vous charme, c'est là ce qu'on s'empresse de vous offrir.[7]

Scribe's own plays show that this statement cannot be accepted literally, but with minor emendations it can be made to fit them with reasonable accuracy. It is apparent that he sought above all to entertain rather than to instruct or to correct his audience, which explains in large part the reaction against him by Dumas *fils* and the other writers of the *pièce à thèse*. Though there is a lesson in most of his plays, it is treated lightly and with good humor (*La Calomnie* is the exception among plays labeled "comédie"), so that the spectator has no sense of being preached to. There are also no lessons that his audience would not agree with, at least when applied to someone else. The primacy of entertainment is the root of Scribe's philosophy of the theater, from which grow the principles that he observed almost without exception. He himself indicated some of these principles in his preface to the *Théâtre de J.-F. Bayard:*

> C'était la gaieté, la verve, la rapidité, l'entrain dramatique! L'action une fois engagée ne languissait pas! Le spectateur, entraîné et pour ainsi dire emporté par ce mouvement de la scène, arrivait joyeusement et comme en chemin de fer, au but indiqué par l'auteur, sans qu'il lui fût permis de s'arrêter pour réfléchir ou pour critiquer. . . .
>
> Le faux et le larmoyant sont faciles; c'est avec cela que l'on fabrique du drame! voilà pourquoi nous en voyons tant! La vérité et la gaieté sont choses rares! La comédie en est faite! voilà pourquoi nous en voyons si peu!
>
> Peu d'auteurs ont possédé à un degré aussi élevé que lui, l'entente du théâtre, la connaissance de la scène et toutes les ressources de l'art dramatique! Sujet présenté et développé avec adresse, action serrée et rapide, péripéties soudaines, obstacles créés

Eugène Scribe

et franchis avec bonheur, dénoûment inattendu, quoique savamment préparé, tout ce que l'expérience et l'étude peuvent donner venait en aide chez lui à ce qui vient de Dieu seul et de la nature, l'inspiration, l'esprit, la verve et cette qualité la plus rare de toutes au théâtre: l'imagination, qui invente sans cesse du nouveau ou qui crée encore, même en imitant.[8]

Scribe was talking about Bayard, but the qualities he picks out and the values he reveals in expressing them represent as much a portrait of himself as a description of his colleague and collaborator. The first paragraph expresses the goal; the last indicates the means. Both are exemplified by Scribe's plays.

The reference to truth apparently contradicts the insistence on fiction in the passage cited earlier, but a careful reading of his plays clearly reveals that it is a certain combination of truth and fiction that is intended. Scribe's concept of truth is related to audience acceptance, or plausibility, a concern of most playwrights, but a special problem for Scribe, with his emphasis on the fictional, the extraordinary, and thus upon plot and the maintenance of suspense. This required characters that the audience can identify with and care about and, even more important, a basic situation and events that develop it and that are interesting. This means that they must be uncommon, for as Scribe pointed out in the passage quoted above, what one sees every day is not entertaining; but at the same time they must not be impossible, for then the spectator ceases to believe and loses interest. The same result follows a too-great consciousness of the fact that the playwright is in complete control, which can be caused by events that are too predictable or too capricious. The response to the danger of predictability leads Pierre Voltz to begin his definition of the "pièce bien faite" by calling it "une pièce où la part du hasard reste grande, puisque les événements passent au premier plan et doivent faire naître l'intérêt par leur imprévu."[9] The other extreme is avoided by the careful preparation that precedes the coincidences and other apparent interventions of chance, so that the audience accepts them as perfectly justified or even natural. Indeed it could be argued that the primary and most consistent characteristic of the well-made play is the thoroughness with which every action, every event, even every entrance and exit is prepared, explained, justified.

Another part of the solution is to imbue the fictions with an aura of reality, a process that leads Scribe to introduce a new degree of realism in the theater, and some critics, at least, have seen a definite resemblance between the world he portrays and contemporary France. Stendhal praises him for being "le seul homme de ce siècle qui ait eu l'audace de peindre, en esquisse il est vrai, les mœurs qu'il rencontre dans le monde."[10] The characters, the setting, the problems are all taken (except in his historical plays, and some would say even in them) from the society of his time. It is only the plot and certain situations that are manifestly fictional, and it is only there that one finds any substantial amount of "l'extraordinaire, le romanesque" of which Scribe spoke. Real life is not quite so full of happy endings, of coincidences, of elections—as Stendhal noted in the sequence of the passage quoted above—that are made in twenty-four hours, and not quite so many millions belong to unattached heiresses or handsome young men. The structure of Scribe's plays is thus totally artificial—while it may be flexible to fit the individual situation, it is still a kind of abstraction, imposed from the outset and designed to meet dramatic needs rather than to duplicate "real life." To hide this artificial skeleton, in addition to the measures described above and generally the suspense-building devices of which he makes such skillful use, he fleshes out his plays with many details chosen from reality; hence, the use of contemporary manners, life-style, and surroundings and the presence and especially the manipulation of an abundance of stage properties, which are, to all appearances, real, and whose significance in the action and variety of uses represent an important innovation in stagecraft. Even his much-criticized style, by corresponding closely to the actual spoken language of the day, is part of the reality he transfers to the stage to help maintain the plausibility of his plots and thus to permit him to hold the interest of the spectator.

To hold the interest of the spectator requires, of course, more than plausibility, and the study of Scribe's statements and plays shows us how he chose to go about it. He offered his audience involvement and excitement while they were in the theater and a sense of satisfaction to savor on the way home. Since audiences always love romance, every play has a love interest. Sometimes it is primary, but often it supports, by eliciting greater audience sympathy and involvement, a main plot that carries a social or moral message, or even, in a few plays, political commentary *(Bertrand et Raton, L'Ambitieux)*. He avoided ideas, events, or characters that would shock or displease and sought those with which the audience could most easily identify. In part because of that identification and also perhaps due to an innate gentleness and "gaieté," the comic elements in his plays arise from situation or language rather than from serious character flaws or farcical action. He enlivened his plays with a wide variety of characters, with amusing as well as admirable traits, but seldom is a character subject to ridicule. There are few real villains, and punishments for misdeeds are seldom cruel. The problems are real, or at least realistic, but the solutions are simpler than in real life, less painful, for the purpose is to distract the spectator from his problems, not to force him to confront them. The plot takes precedence over the message, and also over character development, a choice deplored by critics but apparently not regretted by audiences. Scribe kept them concentrating on the action, wondering how the play would end and how it would get there. He appreciated the visual as well as the verbal nature of drama, as can be seen in his emphasis on sets, on movements and stage business, and especially on the multiplicity of stage properties. His expositions are thorough, so that the action will be easy to follow and the motivations of the characters clear. He made the audience privy to most of the secrets, so that they would have a feeling of complicity with the author, but reserved some ingenious surprises, to avoid the boredom that would result from excessive predictability. The final surprise, of course, is the manner of producing the reversal that precipitates the dénouement that, in addition to being logical and credible, is complete, with no loose ends left dangling. It is also the ending the audience has come to desire, including the achievement of justice and the marriage of the two—or four—most sympathetic young people (exceptions: *Adrienne Lecouvreur* and the atypical melodrama *Les Frères invisibles,* which end in murder and suicide, respectively). Coincidences are frequent—often to simplify and expedite the development of the plot—but plausibly justified. Scribe scrupulously, even ruthlessly, eliminated non-essentials so that nothing slows down the action or diverts attention from it and exploited fully the dramatic potential of each situation and action. This extreme dramatic efficiency results in the use of the fewest possible characters: in a complex plot, they will often play multiple roles. Masham, for example, is the lover of

Abigail, the object of the rivalry between the queen and the duchess, and the killer (in a duel) of Bolingbroke's cousin *(Le Verre d'eau)*.

If these principles seem familiar—and they should—that is a measure of Scribe's success through the years, for they do not permit us to distinguish him from many of his successors, but they do differentiate him from his predecessors; though some followed a few of these principles, none adopted them all, and the new combination reveals his originality, as does his ability to use appropriately and imaginatively all the techniques, all the tricks and devices available to the playwright, impressive in their variety and their complexity. Attempts to reduce them to common factors only serve to emphasize this, as can be seen in the case of Michael Kaufmann,[11] whose long list of devices, situations, and actions that are repeated in Scribe's plays includes scarcely any items repeated more than a few times; and when one looks at the examples listed and at their contexts, it becomes apparent that the general circumstances, the significance, the importance, the types of characters involved, and often even the effect are so different that the various instances can be said to be repetitions only in the most superficial sense. Thus in the end Kaufmann brings new evidence of Scribe's ability to renew constantly the means at his disposal. He did not invent new ones, but as Gustave Larroumet said, "dès ses premières pièces, la façon dont le sujet est conçu, développé, conduit au dénouement, dénote un inventeur, et à un tel degré, que cette invention est du génie."[12] His philosophy of the theater led him to choose a form that was "dénué de poésie, de lyrisme, . . . de naturel," precisely because it resulted in a greater degree "de vérité, de naturel," according to his own definition and, apparently, that of his audience. It is not the mechanical application of a formula, but the deliberate choice of the elemental aspects of drama, developed with unusual imagination and skill, and a finely-honed sense of how to involve and satisfy an audience that constitute the well-made play of Eugène Scribe.

Notes

[1] *Théâtre complet* (Paris: Michel-Lévy, 1868), III, 206.

[2] *Histoire de l'art dramatique en France depuis vingt cinq ans* (Paris: Magnin, Blanchard, 1859), II, 234.

[3] Introduction to *Camille and Other Plays* (New York: Hill and Wang, 1957), pp. xii-xiii.

[4] *Œuvres complètes d' Eugène Scribe, 76* vols. (Paris: E. Dentu, 1874-1885), Vols. I-IX.

[5] Académie française, *Recueil des discours, rapports et pièces diverses lus dans les séances publiques et particulières de l'Académie française, 1860-1869, Première Partie* (Paris: Firmin Didot, 1866), p. 69.

[6] "Scribe et Musset," *Les Epoques du théâtre français* (1636-1850) (Conférences de l'Odéon) (Paris: Calmann-Lévy, 1899), p. 353.

[7] Académie française, *Recueil des discours, 1830-1839* (Paris: Firmin Didot, 1841), p. 325.

[8] *Théâtre de Jean-François Bayard précédé d'une notice par M. Eugène Scribe* (Paris: Hachette, 1855), I, vi, vii-viii.

[9] *La Comédie* (Paris: Armand Colin, 1964), p. 136.

[10] *Mémoires d'un touriste* (Paris: Honoré Champion, 1932), I, 449.

[11] *Zur Technik der Komödien von Eugène Scribe* (Hamburg: Lutke und Wulff, 1911).

[12] "Le Centenaire de Scribe," Pref., in Edouard Noël and Edmond Stoullig, *Les Annales du Théâtre et de la musique, 17e année* (Paris: Charpentier, 1891), p. vii.

THE INFLUENCE OF THE WELL-MADE PLAY

Donald Clive Stuart (essay date 1928)

SOURCE: "French Realistic Drama: The Problem Play," in *The Development of Dramatic Art,* D. Appleton and Company, 1928, pp. 514-41.

[*In the following chapter from* The Development of Dramatic Art, *Stuart traces the influence of Scribe and the well-made play on the development of the French realistic drama.*]

The *Mariage de Figaro* had combined a discussion of a social problem with an intricate plot handled with great dexterity. During the Revolution the theatre had been given over to propaganda. The characters were mere masks. The plots were often inartistically sacrificed for the sake of satire in comedy, and in order to voice republican sentiments in serious plays. Drama, like all other arts, was at low ebb. But, while the war over tragedy was being waged, comedy began a peaceful development which was to culminate in the work of Scribe and, through him, to exert a powerful influence on all European drama of the nineteenth century.

Picard, an actor-dramatist, was chiefly responsible for the reestablishment of true comedy on the stage. His *Médiocre et Rampant* (1797) was an artistic success in comparison to the plays of the *sans culottes* of the revolutionary period, although it was no novelty in comparison to the comedies of the Old Régime. In his *Entrée dans le Monde* (1799), Picard consciously sacrificed plot to a discussion of manners. He pointed out in his preface that he introduced episodic scenes and a large number of characters in order to show a part of the society of Paris in 1799, that he hurried events in an improbable manner, and that the dénouement does not spring either from the action or the characters. In 1801 he produced a study of the provincial manners entitled *La Petite Ville.* His point of departure was the theme of the unattractiveness of society in small towns. Realizing that there was no unified plot in the play, Picard called it an episodic comedy. He even deleted one of the acts without seriously harming what plot there was; but the element of plot, though insignificant in these two plays, was to become increasingly important in his work.

His *Duhautcours* (1801) was a step towards realistic comedy. Inspired by *Turcaret* and by Noland de Fatouville's *Banqueroutier,* Picard presents in this play a study of the world of high finance, which was to become the subject of countless plays in the new century. This comedy becomes a serious drama in the fourth act when Durville and his advisor, Duhautcours, try to effect a bankruptcy which will enrich them. They are finally foiled and exposed by Franval in a realistic scene which foreshadows many such episodes in modern drama in which, during a brilliant soirée, guests, creditors and lawyers assemble in the home of a captain of industry. The plot does not overshadow the study of high finance in 1801; but the question as to whether the would-be bankrupt can succeed in his nefarious plans is important enough to satisfy anyone who insists that every play must have a story. A secondary love story between the nephew of Durville and a young girl whose father is being ruined by the financier is loosely connected with the main action. Picard was still inclined to be episodic instead of neatly dovetailing the component parts of his action as Beaumarchais had done and as he himself was to do in a few years.

He said that his *Marionettes* (1806) was a play based on character and hence the plot was subordinate to the characters. However, his aim was to show that people are governed by events, not by will power or personal traits. In a word, we are all marionettes and when circumstance pulls the strings we dance accordingly. He developed this view of life still further in his *Ricochets* (1807). He says of the plot: "My little groom obeys his mistress. The son of the minister obeys his, the mistress obeys her own caprice; and the caprice, by which he is dominated, dominates and decides by a series of ricochets, the fate of all the personages. Finally, in destroying all hopes by the loss of a little dog, in causing them to be reborn, in realizing them, in bringing about marriages and getting positions by the gift of a canary bird, I prove that small causes often produced great results." That such a chain of cause and effect acts upon people that are marionettes was Picard's view of life. Scribe's method of constructing plays was to be based on this theory.

When Pascal remarked that if Cleopatra's nose had been shorter, the history of the world would have been different, he implied that small causes bring forth great effects; but the statement also embodies the idea that chance plays an important rôle in the drama of life. Fate and Chance are as far apart as the two poles and quite as similar in effect. The concepts expressed in these two words are diametrically opposed to each other, and yet, are so constantly interchanged, that they seem to the average man to be interchangeable. Is it Fate or Chance which rules the destiny of an Œdipus or a Romeo? The individual may answer the question according to the state of his digestion; but anyone who believes that small causes produce great results, that kingdoms are lost for want of a horse-shoe nail, that the upsetting of a glass of water may bring political upheavals, will allow the element of chance free play in his philosophy of life.

Many of Scribe's contemporaries believed that the destruction of class distinction by the Revolution had made the comedy of manners impossible. Scribe went much further and insisted that the stage never had been and never could be the mirror of society. Perhaps he was wearied of the solemn reiteration of the opposite view by the Academicians. It was his fate to mirror the larger part of contemporary society better than they did and better than the nervous romanticists who believed so ecstatically in missions and purposes of art. Holding these conceptions of life and of drama and becoming the master-builder of the well-made play, Scribe's influence on dramatic art in the nineteenth century was universally condemned by serious critics and dramatists. The critics were content to censure him. The dramatists criticized him consciously and imitated him unconsciously.

"You go to the theatre, not for instruction or correction, but for relaxation and amusement. Now what amuses you most is not truth, but fiction. To represent what is before your eyes every day is not the way to please you; but what does not come to you in your usual life, the extraordinary, the romantic, that is what charms you, that is what one is eager to offer you. . . . The theatre is then very rarely the expression of society; . . . it is very often the inverse expression."

Thus spoke Scribe to the Academicians in 1836. Not since Molière had a dramatist had the temerity to insist that the principal aim of the theatre is amusement. He began his career by writing *comédies-vaudevilles.* The *vaudeville* aims solely to entertain. It is a play in one to three acts in which songs are introduced. The plot is often based upon some curious, actual incident, and the *quiproquo* is constantly employed. A descendant of the farce, the vaudeville was often satirical. As Molière developed the farce into high comedy in the seventeenth century, so Scribe started with the *vaudeville*, and with the aid of the example of Picard, he gradually transformed the *vaudeville* into a comedy which actually deals with manners and society, but in which the plot is carefully stressed. Scribe's ability to build intricate situations and to extract from them the maximum amounts of surprise and suspense, has caused him to be considered usually as a playwright who sacrifices all to dramaturgic dexterity. The charge is true; but in spite of this sacrifice, some of his plays contain social problems.

His formula for constructing plays is simple. The variations of his method are many. As a rule, his point of departure is a plot. If he begins with a social problem, such as marriage, and money, or with the idea of showing how great results arise from small causes, or with a character, the plot assumes finally such importance that the problem, character or theme is overshadowed.

His point of attack is fairly close to his dénouement. Though his plots contain many incidents, he feels no need of the large framework of romantic drama. His *Bertrand et Raton* (1833), produced in the heyday of romanticism, is a compact historical comedy. When the curtain rises on any of his full length comedies, there is often much to be explained. Scribe is deliberate in his first act. He would be boring in some of his openings were it not for his wit. If a social problem is involved in the plot, he states it lucidly and discusses it clearly. If events of the past are to influence the present, he explains them and their effect on his characters. He does not avoid long speeches, asides or monologues, and does not mystify the spectator by keeping secrets.

By the end of the first act or in the first part of the second, all the important circumstances are clear. Then the fireworks begin. Letters miscarry. The *quiproquo* occurs at any moment. He weaves together the many threads of his plot and dexterously unties them at the end. It is the incidents which develop, not his characters.

An outstanding example of his dramatic juggling is his *Bataille de Dames* (1851). Henri de Flavigneul has been condemned to death for conspiracy and is hiding, disguised as a servant, in the home of the Countess d'Autreval. She is secretly in love with him. Her niece, Léonie, does not know who this valet is, but finds herself uncomfortably attracted by him. The juggling of the question: Will he be discovered? then begins. Henri is constantly on the point of revealing his identity by his gentlemanly manners and conduct. He confesses his identity to Léonie because she felt insulted at his attitude toward her after he rescued her from a bolting horse. Henri is in love

with Léonie, but he is in a very awkward position. The Countess loves him, and is saving him from death.

Montrichard is searching for Henri in order to capture him. Henri meets him, and pretends to aid him in his search. Léonie, questioned by Montrichard, practically betrays Henri through agitated answers. The Countess saves Henri by having an admirer of hers, De Grignan, dress as a servant and pose as Henri. Montrichard actually gives Henri a pass and a horse to carry a message. Henri escapes but learns that De Grignan has been taken. He returns. Montrichard discovers he has captured the wrong man. He returns. Henri conceals himself behind the broad skirts of the two ladies. Montrichard announces that Henri has been pardoned. Henri reveals himself. Montrichard immediately arrests him. His statement was a trick. He has won. The Countess is in consternation for a moment. Then she announces that Montrichard is joking; that his statement was true. Montrichard laughingly admits it. Henri is free. The Countess, however, is defeated. She must renounce Henri for the sake of Léonie; but she is partially consoled by accepting De Grignan.

Artificial as the plot is, it is deftly handled and enlivened by sparkling wit. The suspense, surprises and sudden appearances are mechanical; but the machinery runs so smoothly, so quietly, that one is not disturbed by it. Scribe sweeps gracefully to a climax while his contemporaries labored heavily to reach it. His theatrical effects may be meretricious, but they are never dull. Hugo piled up heavy complications and romantic drama cracked under them. Scribe wove complications into a piece of lace work—light and diaphanous.

The plausibility of the development of his situations has been a thorn in the flesh of his hostile critics. He was careful in his preparation. In *Adrienne Lecouvreur* his heroine dies through breathing a subtle poison. This event is not foreshadowed but is fully prepared in the first act. Scribe's characters always enter at the psychological moment; but their entrances are never improbable. Letters bring the dénouements of the *Mariage d'Argent* and of *Camaraderie;* but the spectator does not feel that the situation of the characters as the curtain falls is illogical. In *Bertrand et Raton* many suprising events take place, but he shows that those who actively conspire against a government, especially the bourgeois, are not the people who reap the benefits of a revolution. Much can be said for this idea. It is a sensible view; and common sense—meaning the point of view of the average man—dominates Scribe's plays. His popularity with the majority of theatre-goers and his unpopularity with the feverish romanticists were due partially to his common sense. The accusation that he was not a profound thinker is true; but he cannot be accused justly of being illogical. He had a sane outlook on life. He avoided sentimentality. He sacrificed the romantic to the reasonable. Even his theory of the small cause leading to great results has a certain plausible logic in it as he presents it in his developing actions.

His play *Une Chaine* is based upon the situation of a young musician who has succeeded in obtaining recognition through the efforts of a young married woman. They are lovers. He feels deep gratitude towards her; but when he falls in love with his cousin and wishes to marry her, his mistress becomes a chain. This idea is stated clearly three or four times during the play; but there is no study of the problem. The action develops through a series of events that is full of surprise, suspense, and Scribian tricks. The situation becomes complex to a high degree, but always remains clear. The play is more than well made; it is beautifully made. The interest lies in the plot, not in the problem. Yet the ending is logical and sensible although it is brought about by a trick. But the time was soon to come when Augier and the younger Dumas were to place much more emphasis on the problem and somewhat less on the plot. The well-made play, however, was to continue its vogue for many years. Scribe invented nothing. French playwrights for two centuries had shown great skill in construction. But Scribe used all the tricks of the trade all the time. Others used some of them some of the time. He excelled everyone in dramaturgic dexterity, and he taught the dramatists of the nineteenth century their art of playmaking. His greatest virtue was his greatest fault: he was too skilful. But as Sarcey says, "One must know Scribe. One must study, but not imitate him."

Augier and the younger Dumas owed much to Scribe; but, unlike him, they held that drama reflects contemporary society. Augier was content to treat problems impassively. Dumas sought to give the answer to the problem. He was militant, argumentative, presenting one side of the question with logic that seems, for the moment, irrefutable. Augier presented both sides of the problem with delicate balance. He concluded on the side of common sense like Scribe, like Molière; but the conclusion is unobtrusive. The final curtain of a play by the younger Dumas reminds one of the Q.E.D. of a geometrical problem. One has experienced a demonstration. The point has been hammered home.

The elder Dumas was the most romantic of all romantic playwrights. He was still producing great historical spectacles when the realistic problem play was evolving in the middle of the century. His *Antony* (1831) is an extravagant example of romanticism; yet it foreshadows the problem play as it was to be produced by his son. Vigny's *Chatterton* (1835) contains a romantic poet as a hero, but it is a conscious attempt to introduce that form of drama in which plot is relegated to the background and the idea or thought is the important element in the synthesis.

The curtain of *Antony* rises on the salon of Adèle d'Hervey. She receives a letter from Antony, who was in love with her before her marriage, but who has dropped out of her life for three years. He wishes to see her; but Adèle, the mother of a three-year-old child, fears to see him lest her former love for him revive. She arranges to go out in her carriage, leaving her sister Clara to interview Antony and dismiss him. Out of a window, Clara sees the horses take fright and a young man leap forward and save Adèle. It is Antony. He is badly injured. Adèle enters and is given a portfolio found on Antony. It contains her picture, her only letter to him—and a dagger. Antony is carried in. Adèle, feeling her love for him once more, says he may remain only if his life is in danger. He tears off the bandages and cries: "Now I can stay—can't I?"

The explanation of the situation is given in the second act. Antony is still at Adèle's home. The veils are withdrawn from the past. Antony left Adèle three years before, because a marriage was proposed between her and Colonel d'Hervey. Antony is a foundling without family, rank or occupation. He had asked for a space of two weeks in order to solve the secret of his birth. He was unsuccessful. Because of the prejudice of society against such men as he, Antony could not be the rival of Colonel d'Hervey. Adèle comes more and more under the spell of the pale, young romanticist as he talks of his life and love. Adèle confesses her love for him; but she has decided to seek the protection of her husband stationed in Strasbourg. Antony leaves her, knowing nothing of her decision which is to be communicated to him in a cold letter.

The third act is at an inn two leagues from Strasbourg. Antony arrives. He engages the two vacant rooms. He makes it impossible for any traveller to obtain fresh horses; but he tells the hostess he may give up the extra room if a guest arrives. He sends his servant to Strasbourg to watch Colonel d'Hervey. At the slightest sign of the Colonel's departure for Paris at any time, the servant is to inform Antony. In a passionate monologue, punctuated by driving his dagger into the table, he informs us that he has passed Adèle on the way. He is going to demand an explanation of her departure. He exits. Adèle arrives. The hostess gives her the extra room, since she cannot continue her journey. She hears a noise in the next room. She is beside herself with fear. Antony appears on the balcony, breaks the window and enters. Adèle screams. Antony takes her in his arms and, putting a handkerchief over her mouth, draws her into the other room as the curtain falls.

The fourth act passes some time later at a ball given by the Vicomtesse de Lacy. Adèle has ventured into society with Antony. Under the cloak of a discussion of literature, a Madame de Camps cites their case only too plainly. Left alone with Antony, Adèle is crushed by the impending scandal. Antony takes her in his arms, but the Vicomtesse enters too suddenly. Adèle rushes from the room. Antony's servant informs him that Colonel d'Hervey is nearing Paris.

The fifth act reveals a room in D'Hervey's house. Adèle has reached home. Antony arrives with the crushing news of her husband's arrival. They must fly. A pounding is heard at the door. The Colonel is outside. Nothing remains but death. Antony stabs Adèle. The door is broken down.

> ANTONY (*throwing the dagger at the* COLONEL'S *feet*)

> Yes. Dead. She resisted me and I killed her.

To the modern realist such a series of *coups de théâtre* so neatly dovetailed seems too melodramatic to represent life. The characters are too exceptional. Their psychological reactions seem as superannuated as the medicine practised by the doctor who bleeds Antony for an injury which has already caused a loss of blood. The passions displayed by Antony made him seem false to certain contemporaries. The element of chance in the action seems overworked, with the timely and untimely appearances of the personages and the remarkable succession of events of the past and present.

But Dumas was entirely conscious of what he was trying to do in constructing this *"drame d'exception,"* as he called it. The dialogue contains a running comment on his ideas. In the fourth act, Eugène, a dramatist, is asked why he does not write a play on a subject of modern society instead of the Middle Ages. "That is what I repeat to him every minute," says the Vicomtesse. "Do something of real life. Are we not much more interested in people of our own times, dressed like us, speaking the same language?" Beaumarchais and Diderot had asked the same question, years before, in regard to classical tragedy. It was pertinent to the new romantic historical drama. A baron replies for Eugène: "It is easier to take subjects from chronicles than from the imagination. One finds in them plays almost entirely written." Eugène—probably speaking for Dumas—says that comedy of manners is very difficult because the Revolution levelled all differences of rank. He continues:

> The drama of passion remains, and here another difficulty presents itself. History gives us facts, they belong to us by right of inheritance, they are incontestable, they belong to the poet. He revives the men of bygone times, clothes them in their costumes, agitates them with their passions which increase or diminish to the degree to which he desires to carry the dramatic. But if we tried, in the midst of our modern society, in our short-tailed, awkward coats, to lay bare the heart of man, one would not recognize it. The resemblance between the hero and the audience would be too great, the analogy too close. The spectator who follows, in the actor, the development of the passion will want to stop it where it would have stopped in his own heart. If it surpasses his own power of feeling or

expressing, he will not understand it any longer, he will say: "That is false; I do not feel thus; when the woman I love deceives me, I suffer without doubt . . . yes . . . for a time . . . but I don't stab her and die, and the proof is, here I am." Then the cries of exaggeration and melodrama, covering the applause of these few men, who, more happily or unhappily organized than the others, feel that passions are the same from the fifteenth to the nineteenth century.

This passage contains the indictment by the realists before they pronounced it upon romantic drama. Indeed, it is a common indictment of all drama. It implies the eternal question: Just how melodramatic can an art be which seems to represent real life actually before us? The point of melodramatic saturation depends entirely upon the views of contemporary society.

Dumas felt that in *Antony* he was writing something much more realistic than the romantic historical drama. Though some contemporaries called the hero false, he is the incarnation on the stage, not only of the romantic lovers in novels and poems of the time, but of the romanticists as they imagined themselves to be, as they were, in so far as was possible in an everyday world of reality. The success of the play would otherwise have been impossible.

Antony, the foundling of mysterious parentage, has descended from a long line of children, beginning with Euripides' Ion, who are lost for theatrical purposes in both tragedy and comedy. But Dumas' treatment of this idea of the foundling was both new and dramatic. The fact that Antony is an orphan of unknown parents is the determining factor in his character and raises the problem of the attitude of society towards foundlings. The play, therefore, not only foreshadows realistic drama because it deals with contemporary characters, but also because it raises a social problem. This question is the basis of the plot and is directly discussed in the second act in a manner resembling that of the later problem play. The unfaithful wife had appeared on the German stage in Kotzebue's *Menschenhass und Reue* in 1789; and his play had been given in French adaptations in 1792, 1799 and 1823. The grown-up, illegitimate child had been a source of sentimental emotion in European bourgeois drama from the time of Diderot's *Fils Naturel*. In *Antony,* however, the unfaithful wife and the illegitimate child are tragic characters. Their lives give rise to problems, rather than to sentimentality. The fallen woman on the stage can no longer always escape punishment by repentance and by living a life of charity and virtue. Thus *Antony* rightly belongs to the nineteenth century, while *Menschenhass und Reue* is clearly a product of the sentimental optimism of the eighteenth century.

Having struck this modern note in *Antony,* Dumas turned once more to romantic melodrama. It was easier for his active brain to construct plots than to study carefully problems of his society. But Alfred de Vigny, the most profound thinker of all the French romanticists, was deeply impressed by this drama. He insisted that it contained a dominating thought, that it was a moral satire against the atheism, materialism and egoism of the age. He denied that the play was too "talky." While the stage was ringing with the sonorous lyricism of Hugo and the spectators were being dazzled by theatrical surprises, Vigny revolted against the complicated mechanism of romantic drama. He said in his preface to *Chatterton* that the time had come for the "Drama of Thought." He proposed to show "the spiritual man stifled by a materialistic society." He chose the simplest possible plot: "the story of a man who has written a letter in the morning and who awaits the reply until evening; it comes and it kills him." Had there been a simpler plot, he would have chosen it, because in this play "the moral action is everything." The action is in the heart of Chatterton, the symbolic figure of the Poet; in the hearts of Kitty Bell and the Quaker.

In *Chatterton,* Vigny consciously produced a problem play before the expression itself was used as a term of dramatic criticism. Many dramatists before him had written eloquent prefaces to show how their plays taught morality by stripping vice of its mask and rewarding virtue. Social problems had been mirrored more or less consciously. But no dramatist had so clearly stated his problem, and deliberately reduced the plot to a bare skeleton in order to spend all the time on the "moral action." If dramatists had employed this method consciously, they had kept silent in regard to it. Diderot had advocated simplicity of plot and a study of family life, of profession and positions, such as *The Father,* instead of characters and characteristics such as *The Flatterer.* Sedaine, under the influence of Diderot, depicted a family in a charming manner and even introduced the problem of the duel in *Le Philosophe sans le Savoir.* But the bourgeois drama was not primarily a problem play as is *Chatterton* in which every character and every scene arise from the point of departure of "the spiritual man stifled by a materialistic society."

It is probable that Vigny was influenced by Sedaine rather than by Racine in re-introducing a simple plot into French drama. He admired Sedaine's *Philosophe sans le Savoir.* It was a beautiful work to him; and the result of careful study of human nature and art. The rarity of such plays was evidence of their extreme difficulty. He prophesied that this form of drama would gain in power as it treated graver and greater problems. The characters were "happy creations which time cannot wither." The simplicity of the dialogue, the gracious nobility of the scenes following each other with such ease and naturalness appealed to him. These words of high praise were written in 1841; but *Le Philosophe sans le Savoir* was constantly played and Vigny's knowledge and delight in this drama are certainly of earlier date.

The material action of *Chatterton* observes the unities strictly. It takes place in the house of John Bell, a gross materialist, in which Chatterton, the poet, has rented a room. He is starving. His brain refuses to work. He has pledged his body as security for a loan. He has written the Lord Mayor asking for a position. He has fallen in love with Bell's wife, Kitty; and she loves him, although both have locked their secret in their hearts. The Lord Mayor offers the poet a position as his valet. Chatterton drinks opium and dies. Kitty Bell's death follows symbolically and actually from his kiss.

The moral action is the clash of spirituality and materialism. The spiritual world is represented by Chatterton, Kitty Bell, her children, and the Quaker. John Bell is the successful industrialist, surrounded by young lords who live riotously and see in Kitty only a woman to seduce. The Lord Mayor is the personification of a thankless national government which sees in a poet only a worthless citizen.

Those who looked for a plot in the play saw only a justification of suicide; but fortunately the majority of the spectators caught the deeper meaning. The stupid keepers of their brother's morals are always with us in the theatre; but this time their vapid cry of immorality was soon drowned in applause. The *drame serieux* had returned to the French stage in the form of a problem play even while Hugo and Dumas were thundering forth their gorgeous melodramas and Eugène Scribe was playing his clever parlor tricks.

Throughout the period of romanticism, Scribe had preserved the compact classical form of drama. Augier was even more classical. The point of attack in his plays is almost as close to the dénouement as it is in the comedies of Molière or Regnard. The scene changes from one salon to another, but it does not wander from place to place as in romantic drama. The element of time is unimportant. One does not ask how many hours or days have elapsed between the acts. The epic and lyric elements of Hugo have disappeared. The striking settings, local color and the melodrama are things of the past so far as Augier is concerned.

His plots are complex but they are never imbroglios giving rise to surprising events. Mistaken identity and the *quiproquo* have no place in problem plays. When Augier employs a *coup de théâtre* or any technical device, it is not for the purpose of dazzling the spectator with his brilliant dexterity, but in order to show a new development of his plot. He holds a middle ground between Scribe and the later realists who would banish all the devices of the well-made play.

His situations are skilfully articulated. Just as he discusses both sides of the question, so he balances delicately both his characters and their fortunes. This equilibrium is beautifully exemplified in his *Gendre de M. Poirier,* which he wrote in collaboration with Landeau. In this comedy the clash between the ideals of the newly enriched bourgeois and the old nobility is depicted. Poirier, the rich bourgeois, has married his daughter, Antoinette, to Gaston, a young marquis riddled with debts. On both sides it is a marriage of convenience. Poirier wishes to become a peer of France. Gaston desires to live a life of idleness and luxury. They represent the extremists of their respective classes. Montmeyran personifies the more moderate wing of the nobility. He has accepted the fate of his class and become a soldier. Verdelet, Poirier's friend and Antoinette's godfather, is a bourgeois willing to remain a simple, solid citizen. Between the two parties stands Antoinette. Gaston, utterly egoistic, is not unconscious of the fact that she is attractive and charming; but he considers her merely the source of his income. He is carrying on an intrigue with a Madame de Montjay, more through force of habit than because he loves her. To have a mistress is a part of his scheme of life. The duel which he is to fight on her account is also a part of the code of his world. In spite of his faults, which are presented as those of his class, Gaston is a likeable character. Poirier also has grave faults, but the right is often enough on his side to make the audience sympathize with him at times.

The first three acts of the play deal with questions arising from the intermingling of the two classes. The attitudes of the nobleman and of the bourgeois in regard to honor, money, marriage, ambition, and usefulness to society are brilliantly set forth. The virtues and vices of each class are depicted with incisive wit. Neither side is entirely condemned or exonerated. Finally, the concrete question as to whether Gaston and Antoinette can continue to live together boils out of the social ferment. Gaston has learned to love her because she has shown true nobility of character, but will he give up his ideal of honor in order to prove his love for her, by refusing to fight the duel? Thus even the sentimental interest is the result of the clash of social ideas. Scribe sacrificed the study of a problem to the development of his plot; but it is the problem not the development of the story, which dominates the construction of this play from start to finish.

Social questions had formed the basis of many a play in past ages, but in the middle of the nineteenth century the problem play came into its own. So long as the rule of the separation of tragedy and comedy was observed, the canonical happy ending of comedy was often a false note, destroying the harmony of the developing action. Now, for practically the first time in France, the dramatist could observe social conditions and treat them on the stage with freedom from tradition or rules. The question as to whether comic scenes can be mingled with tragic situations is far less important than the question as to whether a dramatist is allowed to take a situation involving customs of contemporary society and develop it to its logical outcome, happy or bitter as the end may be. When dramatic art threw off the incubus of the rule of the separation of comedy and tragedy it scored a veritable triumph.

Looking back over the centuries of dramatic art one is impressed by the dearth of plays which deal with problems of men and women in their everyday life. Without detracting one iota from the tragedies and comedies of the Greeks, the Elizabethans, the French and the Germans, one feels that the human, personal touch is too often lacking, that a whole section of joys and sorrows of men and women has been left unrepresented. The dramatists depicted vice and virtue, true ideals and perverted ideals. But where was the picture of the normal man and woman laughing and weeping by turns in the comedy of life which ends with tragic tears? English, German and French domestic tragedy had attempted to supply such pictures of life; but they were often pictures and nothing more. The problem play, as the expression implies, deals with certain conditions in society which cause trouble. It seeks to analyze the opposition between social custom and the law, or between custom and justice. The dramatist does not consider the problem as merely ridiculous. He sees that there is right and wrong on both sides, although he concludes for or against one side of the question. This method is very different from the dramatic presentation of such vices as avarice, hypocrisy, affectation, etc., as ridiculous foibles of man. Molière could employ any means to end his play *Tartufe* after he had shown the effects of hypocrisy. The dénouement was unimportant, provided vice had been held up to ridicule. The portrait of the hypocrite was complete. In the problem play, each step must be logical. The dénouement becomes highly important for it contains the answer to the whole question. Thus the younger Dumas founded his whole scheme of dramaturgy on the basis of the problem. Social questions had been discussed in drama before his time; but he finally made the problem the point of departure.

His first drama, *La Dame aux Camélias* (1852), is a play which tells a story. He did not write it in order to discuss the question of a courtezan regenerated through love. His formula of play-making had not yet been devised. *Diane de Lys* (1853) likewise depends more upon its dramatic plot than upon the presentation of a problem of marital infidelity for its interest. However, the situations upon which these plays are based contain moral questions which only need to be discussed at length to turn the dramas into *pièces à thèse.* The problem of marital infidelity is inherent in the plot of *Antony;* but the rôle of the husband exists for purposes of plot and dénouement alone. What he thinks, what are his rights, are questions of vital importance in a *pièce à thèse;* but they are not raised by the elder

Dumas. In the final analysis, *Antony* is the portrayal of enthralling passion of the decade of the thirties, done in romantic style. In *Diane de Lys* the rôle of the husband is important. His situation, his rights are carefully set forth. The plot is still of greater interest than the discussion of the question of infidelity; but there is a marked development in the importance of the problem between *Antony* and *Diane de Lys*.

La Dame aux Camélias and *Diane de Lys* opened a long series of realistic plays which remains unbroken to the present day. The erring woman and her relation to society had been presented in the theatre sporadically; but from 1852 on she holds the centre of the stage. After three-quarters of a century of such plays and at a time when motion pictures rehabilitate the courtezan continuously every day from noon until midnight, it is difficult to imagine the younger Dumas' first play as being considered a rather shocking novelty when it was first produced. Its realism seems a bit sentimental. The pistol shot which brings down the curtain of *Diane de Lys* has become as banal as the arrival of the long-lost father or son with a fortune.

Scribe's *Dix Ans dans la Vie d'une Femme* (1832) was a realistic study of a woman who became a courtezan; but it was an isolated example without influence. These dramas of the younger Dumas ushered in a new development of dramatic art. When he wrote the *Demi-Monde,* the playwright turned still more to the study of a social problem. The plot is complicated; but on leaving the theatre one is not thinking merely of the fact that Suzanne, a member of the *demi-monde,* has not been able to rise out of it by marrying Raymond. Much less is one concerned with the marriage of Olivier to Marcelle by which she will escape from her surroundings. It is the whole social problem of the *demi-monde,* which is uppermost in one's thoughts. The spectator feels that a case has been tried and settled before him.

Hugo had used the five acts to present a complicated story embellished with long speeches resembling operatic arias. Scribe had taken advantage of the full length play to dazzle the spectators with kaleidoscopic developments of his plot. Dumas belongs to the Scribian school in that he usually devised a plot full of surprising turns; but he left plenty of time to argue his point and to paint his portraits fully. Especially impressive in this respect is the *Demi-Monde*. He presents several different types of people belonging to this society. Each one is clearly differentiated from the other. Little by little we learn of their past, their present, their ambitions, their habits, their incomes, and their previous relations with each other. He even succeeds in making a striking personality of Madame de Lornan who plays a part in the action, but who never appears on the stage. Likewise,

a Monsieur de Latour does not enter but is sketched into the picture as a type of the men who frequent this society.

The concrete question which forms the plot is: Can Suzanne, a woman with a past, rise out of the *demi-monde* by marrying Raymond? This causes the gradual disclosure, not only of her past, but that of all the other characters. The technique of developing the action by withdrawing veils from the past was employed by Dumas with great effectiveness. As each discovery takes place the action moves forward and the resultant phase of the moral problem is discussed.

While the audience is supposed to draw inferences from the development of the plot and especially from the dénouement in regard to the problem and its answer, much of the discussion is direct. It is a debate or argument, thinly disguised, in which each character presents his case. The whole drama is plainly a conflict of opposing forces, and the action works up to the point in which the opposing wills clash in an obligatory scene. One character is pre-eminent in leading the discussion and in presenting the author's views. In the *Demi-Monde,* Olivier de Jalin fills the rôle of the *raisonneur,* as it was called. This rôle has been compared to that of the chorus or the confidant in classical tragedy; but at least these characters are not mere moralizers. They are active and effective. They fight for a moral principle. They give their views; but they dominate the action to such an extent, that they resemble dangerously an exhibitor of marionettes as he moves the strings. Only Dumas' skill saves him from too apparently manipulating everything through the person of his *raisonneur.* While the rôle of the confidant persists in many modern dramas as a friend of the family or a kindly old uncle, the *raisonneur* is more than a mouthpiece for aphorisms. He may represent the crux of the whole action for the intellectuals in the audience; although he may not be the hero of the concrete story to the sentimentally inclined. Thouvenin, the *raisonneur* in *Denise,* harangues André for four and one-half minutes in order to prove to him that he should marry Marthe who is the mother of an illegitimate child. So far as the problem is concerned, this lecture, as Dumas called it, is the culmination of the drama.

Dumas believed that the *Demi-Monde* was more a portrayal of manners than a problem play; but in writing the *Fils Naturel* (1858) he reached the goal of the *pièce à thèse*. He said in the preface (1868): "For the first time, it is true, I was trying to develop a social thesis and to render, through the theatre, more than the depiction of manners, of characters, of ridiculous foibles and of passions. I hoped that the spectator would carry away from this spectacle something to think about a little." As Vigny's wish had been to introduce a theatre of "thought," so the younger Dumas dreamed of a "useful" and "legislative" theatre. "Through comedy, through tragedy, through drama, through buffoonery, in the form which fits us best, let us inaugurate the *useful* theatre, at the risk of hearing cry out the apostles of *art for art's sake*—four words absolutely empty of meaning."

The theatre was not the end but the means. Eleven years after writing this preface he admitted, in his preface to *L'Etrangère,* that people would not look to the theatre for the solution of great problems; but he was none the less sincere in his belief that the theatre should attempt to solve problems.

Sarcey held that the theatre never had reformed anyone and never will. He saw no reason, therefore, for treating Dumas' favorite theme: adultery. Sarcey was correct in his first contention. The theatre can only reform people indirectly, by showing life; but there is no reason why adultery or any other phase of society should not be represented on the stage, provided the portrayal is true. Innocence and ignorance were once practically synonymous terms when applied to women—especially young women. Even Dumas advocated veiling the dialogue so that certain passages could be understood only by men. The *jeune fille* had an influence on dramatic art far greater than that of the "tired business man." Happily both these innocents belong to the past.

Dumas considered drama as an art by itself and not as a mere branch of literature. When he said that drama ought always to be written as if it were only to be read, he meant that a play, in order to live, must contain ideas. He pointed out that the reader often does not find the emotion in the printed play which he did in the representation, because a word, a look, a gesture, a silence, a purely atmospheric combination had held him under its charm. The language of great writers would only teach the dramatist words and a number of these would have to be excluded because they lack "relief, vigor, almost the triviality necessary to put in action the true man on this false ground" (the stage). "The language of the theatre does not have to be grammatically correct. It must be clear, full of color, incisive." He cited the line by Racine: *"Je t'aimais inconstant: qu'aurai-je fait fidèle!"*—as an example of bad grammar but as an excellent line on the stage. The style of Scribe would be acceptable to Dumas if it contained a thought.

Such ideas are a bold challenge to the literary critic. They had been expressed, in part, by Diderot a century before. In the nineteenth century dialogue grew less and less stylistic, but Dumas' lines are by no means devoid of embellishment. In comparison with dialogue in our contemporary drama, his speeches are often rhetorical. In scenes of action he is clear and concise. The illuminating phrase came to him naturally. Not since Sedaine and Beaumarchais had a playwright

expressed his ideas so brilliantly, so tersely when brevity is demanded in the particular scene. His greatest fault was the constant use of aphorisms. It is easier for an author to be brilliant than to be life-like in dialogue. His use of the aside and the monologue is regrettable because he could be subtle, and subtlety is extinguished by the aside and the monologue used to explain facts obvious to the modern audience.

Dumas fought valiantly to set drama free to tell the truth about life. Whether he succeeded or not in always telling the truth is not now a vital question. He set up an ideal of sincerity in drama. He was never false to his conscience. He insisted upon the necessity of being a master in the art. He said in the preface to *Un Père Prodigue:* "A man without any value as a thinker, as a moralist, as a philosopher, as a writer, can be a man of the first order as a dramatic author. To be a master in this art, one must be clever in the business." He admired Scribe's ability as a technician, though he deplored his lack of depth and sincerity. If it were possible, he would think like Æschylus and write like Scribe. "The dramatic author who would know *man* like Balzac and the *theatre* like Scribe would be the greatest dramatic author that ever existed." He learned from Scribe to know the theatre. Indeed, at the close of his career, Dumas' plays were criticized for being too well made. Yet he never sacrificed what he felt was the logical demonstration of his thesis to a striking theatrical effect, although he devised *coups de théâtre* in order to prove his point. "The real in the foundation, the possible in the fact, the ingenious in the means, that is what can be demanded of us." But he never swerved from the belief that "the most indispensable quality is logic, which includes good sense and clearness."

"The truth (of a play)," he held, "can be absolute or relative according to the importance of the subject and the place that it occupies; the logic must be implacable between the starting point and the place of arrival, which it must never lose from view in the development of the idea or the fact." There must be "the mathematical, inexorable and fatal progression which multiplies scene by scene, event by event, act by act up to the dénouement which ought to be the total and the proof."

Thus the dénouement of a play assumed great importance. The desire of an audience for a happy ending, and the rule that comedy must end happily and tragedy unhappily went by the board. The whole construction of the play depended upon the ending. In the preface to *La Princesse Georges* Dumas said: "You can make mistakes in the details of execution; you have no right to be mistaken in the logic and in the linking of the sentiments and facts, still less in their conclusion. One ought never to modify a dénouement. One ought always to begin a play with the dénouement, that is, not begin the work until one has the scene, the movement and the word of the end." One cannot help wondering how much Molière would have changed the endings of his plays had he constructed them after this method.

Naturally a great deal of controversy arose over the dénouements of Dumas' plays. Were they logical? Were they moral? Were they practical solutions of the problems raised? He was accused of representing special cases and deducing general conclusions.

He did create situations which were extraordinary. He complicated his plots so much that the later naturalists dismissed them as improbable. It is very improbable that an illegitimate child could be brought up in affluence by its mother who had been poor; that the child as a young man should wish to marry his father's niece; that he would save France; that his father's brother would offer him a title; that his father would wish to recognize him in order to gain the title, etc. But that all happens in the *Fils Naturel.* Such a plot is not the result of observation of life, but is devised to present a thesis. His demonstration of his hypothesis may be perfectly logical, but the hypothesis is so far-fetched that he has not represented the usual, but an unusual problem of the illegitimate child. Dumas was quite correct in pointing out in his preface the advance he made in treating this subject. "It was agreed formerly, in the theatre, that an illegitimate child should groan, for five acts, at not having been recognized, and that at the end, after all kinds of trials, each more pathetic than the others, he would see his father repent and they would throw themselves in each other's arms crying: 'My father! My son!' to the applause of an audience in tears." This particular brand of sentimentality Dumas made ridiculous.

Scribe was a master technician who merely wished to amuse an audience. Dumas was a master technician who felt he had something to prove and wished to make an audience think. He finally constructed plays in which the plot was of secondary importance. In the *Question d'Argent* (1857), he was so intent upon presenting the various phases of the influence of money on contemporary society that the plot almost disappeared. The first and second acts are discussions of the thesis: money means success. By the end of the third act, Eliza, the daughter of an honorable but poverty-stricken nobleman, is going to marry Giraud, a man of the people, who has amassed a fortune by methods which are within the law but are questionable from the strict moral point of view. The audience knows that such a marriage spells tragedy; and Eliza finally repudiates her engagement. The interest of the play does not lie primarily in the story, but in the discussion of the whole money question and in the idea that one should win a fortune by esteem, not win esteem through a fortune.

As a rule, Dumas was careful to build up a gripping plot which unfolds with surprise and suspense. He insisted upon the "ingenious in the means." The ingeniousness appears somewhat overdone, now that the reaction against the *coup de théâtre* has put us on guard against the too cleverly devised scene. But if he forced events or characters it was in order to demonstrate his thesis. In *L'Ami des Femmes* he frankly used the legerdemain of Scribe throughout the play. De Ryons pulls the strings. He foretells what will happen. It seems as if what he prophesies is impossible. Then, presto, it comes to pass, but the thesis is proved. At the close of all his plays there is a surprising peripeteia. The unexpected happens. The last scenes form an exciting climax in which all the strings of the plot are gathered together and suddenly untied in an ingenious manner.

In *La Princesse Georges,* the husband of the heroine is apparently going to meet his certain death; but the bullet strikes another lover of Sylvanie. Césarine, in *La Femme de Claude,* seems on the verge of successfully betraying her husband and making good her escape. She has seduced his young assistant. The plans of the invention are in her grasp. Her confederate is just outside the window, and she is about to throw them to him when the sound of her husband's voice makes her stop involuntarily. Then the bullet strikes her. The climax of the *Demi-Monde* is produced when Olivier makes Suzanne—and the audience—believe he has killed Raymond. By this trick, he unmasks Suzanne, who declares her love for Olivier when she believes that Raymond is dead. Even in the *Question d'Argent,* the least exciting of his plays, Giraud's unexpected return, when everyone considers him an absconder, constitutes a surprising *coup de théâtre.*

Generally the last few minutes of Dumas' plays contain the psychological and dramatic climax. The curtain descends almost instantly after the line and event which bring the solution of the problem. The tension is not relaxed gradually with explanations or prophecies of the future, as in Shakespearean and Greek tragedy. The tension snaps. The knot is cut with one stroke. The spectator is left gasping with theatrical excitement. Dumas insisted that the dénouement should be unforeseen, but logical. This procedure was commonly followed by the realists. When Freytag was expounding his theory of the rise and fall of the dramatic action, the playwrights had ceased to represent the fall.

The objection was made, especially in regard to the pistol shot as a climax and dénouement, that social problems in real life were not solved by bullets. Alphonse Royer said in 1878: "This simple procedure which charges the arms manufacturer with the decision of questions that logic cannot solve has been the *pons asinorum* of the realistic school which has used and abused it as long as the public was willing to lend itself to this trickery against which it protests to-day." From the point of view that realism is a transcript of real life, the objection is sound. Dumas' attempt to answer such objections is found in the preface to *L'Étrangère.*

"When we attack a law on the stage, we can only do it by means of the theatre and most often without even mentioning the law. The public must draw the conclusions and say: 'Indeed, that is a case in which the law is wrong!' Our means are a certain combination of events drawn from the possible, laughter and tears, passion and interest, with an unforeseen dénouement, personal initiative, the intervention of a *deus ex machina,* mandatory of a Providence which does not always manifest itself so aptly in real life, and which, playing the rôle which the law should have undertaken, employs in the face of unsolvable situations, the great argument of the old theatre, the argument without reply—death."

To such arguments the naturalists replied: "That is not life, hence not truth." Dumas retorted: "That is logic, hence it is truth." He insisted that there is a vast difference between truth in life and truth in the theatre. Zola denied the existence of any such difference. The reason for this distinction, according to Dumas, was that audiences were governed by mob psychology, were enormous masses and had to be attracted and held by gross means. Truth had to make concessions; and he relied upon Goethe's prologue to *Faust* to show that "the public has been and always will be a child, both ignorant and wishing to learn nothing, curious and convinced that there are many things very natural, very true, of which the theatre should never speak, impressionable and heedless, sensitive and teasing . . . deaf to reasoning and always open to an emotion."

Such arguments voiced by a sincere man who had spent his life trying to reason even in his theatrical manner are depressing, far more depressing than if they came from Goethe, who was more of a poet-philosopher than a dramatist. This theory of the audience was widely accepted. But though an audience has some characteristics of a mob and though there are audiences of varying degrees of intelligence, people are enough the same in a theatre as outside of it to make it unnecessary to misrepresent life on the stage. A dramatist must write for an audience. He does not have to write down to an audience. He can tell the truth in the theatre, if he knows how to tell the truth in the theatre. Sooner or later popular success will be his. Where is the dramatist of ability who was faithful to the truth who failed to be recognized by the crowd as a great artist? At least, he has left no trace of his plays in written form.

When a subject fitted for dramatic representation and demonstration had occurred to Dumas, he studied it in all its ramifications. He knew the life history of all his characters. Thus in the preface to *Monsieur Alphonse* he gave a full biographical account of his principals up to the opening of the play. Such complete details cannot be presented in the play itself. The limit of time precludes that possibility. Yet such careful analysis of character and of the problem has its effect upon the drama. One may or may not agree with the author's conception of the development of the action; but one realizes that Dumas knew why his people are what they are and do what they do.

But they are what they are because of the problem; and they do what they do in order to prove his thesis. His characters impress one as his creations, not as people observed in life. In that period of naturalism when novel writers were striving to be impartial observers, Dumas sacrificed whatever power of objective observation he possessed to his thesis. His characters tend to become generalizations and in *La Femme de Claude,* allegorical abstractions. He admitted that he spoke through them. As Zola said, his characters are "colorless, stiff as arguments, which disappear from the mind as soon as the book is closed or the curtain falls. . . . All that he touches instead of becoming animate grows heavy and turns towards dissertation. . . . Balzac wants to paint and M. Dumas wants to prove." He was like a lawyer in court. He convinced his auditors by his arguments. But just as a lawyer may win a case by a clever array of facts which are not the real truth, so a dramatist writing a problem play is in danger of convincing an audience in a theatre only to have them question his conclusion on calmer consideration.

Evert Sprinchorn (essay date 1965)

SOURCE: Introduction to *20th-Century Plays in Synopsis,* edited by Evert Sprinchorn, Thomas Y. Crowell Company, 1965, pp. 1-13.

[*In the excerpt that follows, Sprinchorn discusses the dramatic legacy of the well-made play and its transformation under the naturalism and symbolism that influenced later realistic drama.*]

. . . Well-Made and Properly Motivated

By comparing plots, we can use them as cultural artifacts to tell us a great deal about changing mores. But in the present century even more enlightening than the change in audience response is a study of the playwright's attitude to the conception of plot itself. The classic view, as stated by Aristotle and maintained to the nineteenth century, held that plot was the most important element in a drama. By plot one meant the arrangement of incidents: the same story may be plotted in many different ways. When the Shakespearean theater disappeared and Paris became the cultural capital of Europe, Racine was recognized as the model playwright and the neoclassic drama as the ideal form. In the latter part of the eighteenth century the

Shakespearean influence finally made itself felt on the Continent as German writers began a literary revolution that threatened to hurl Racine from his throne. Some French dramatists now turned to writing romantic and poetic plays; others wrote pure melodramas that pleased the mob. But the playwrights who catered to the middle class steered a middle course. Remaining faithful to the neoclassic rules in principle, they allowed the social and political revolutions that followed 1789 to make deep inroads into the drama. Seizing on the empiricist and positivist philosophy, which had acquired a firm basis during the Enlightenment and which was used to buttress the logical structure of the neoclassic drama, and exploiting the popular emotionalism and colloquial flavor of the melodrama, a group of young French playwrights led by Eugène Scribe perfected a dramatic form that came to be known as *la pièce bien faite,* the well-made play.

From the Racinian model Scribe learned that a good play has a tight cluster of characters involved in a single action that builds steadily to a climax, which is followed by a quick resolution. From the melodrama he learned to hold an audience by cutting the long speeches or *tirades* that only bored the tired shopkeeper, by adding physical movement, and by appealing directly to class prejudices, patriotic ideals, and bourgeois moral standards. In all this there was nothing new. But Scribe borrowed from the field of science an idea that constituted the technical novelty in his method. He made each event in his plays seem realistic and convincing by anticipating the audience's how and why. Like a scientist he explained and justified what happened by giving every effect a cause and by making all the causes consistent with one another. Racine had taken a set of human relationships and examined the different alternatives; Scribe constructed a complicated clockwork machine that produced surprises at carefully timed intervals.

The opposite of the well-made play (a term that I am giving a wider application than it generally receives) was not a badly made play but the Shakespearean kind of drama in which the action seems as often as not to be improvised. Iago's motives are strangely inconsistent, and none of them is exploited in the course of the play. Scribe would have given one or two strong motives and made use of them to create certain dramatic situations—or else he would not have mentioned them at all. Shakespeare does not bother to explain why the ghost in *Hamlet* is visible to one person and not to another at the same time. A realistic dramatist writing well-made plays could not allow such an anomaly. Another example brings us to the essential difference between the two methods. Hamlet's skill at swordplay would have had to be introduced early in a well-made play to justify the final scene. Far from preparing us for Hamlet's skill, Shakespeare lets us know in Act Two that Hamlet has "forgone all custom of exercises."

On the other hand, Ibsen, the master builder of well-made plays, takes great pains to "plant" early in his drama the pistol with which Hedda Gabler shoots herself so that no one will be inclined to reply to Brack's curtain line, "People don't do such things!" with a skeptical "Of course not. Where did she get that pistol?" The fact that Ibsen was able to invest his "planted" properties with symbolic qualities shows how genius can make a virtue of necessity.

So important was this notion of explaining what happens in Act Three by referring to a minor point in Act One that drama was defined in the middle of the nineteenth century as the art of preparation. Like solid citizens and good students well-made plays were properly motivated. To Scribe a play was simply a machine designed to produce laughs, gasps, and tears. He regarded himself as a mere entertainer whose sole aim was to keep the *bourgeoisie* from yawning. The next generation of playwrights often had higher aspirations. They wrote with a reformer's zeal and sought to appropriate to the dramatist the functions of the journalist and the priest. Disdaining art for the sake of art, Dumas *fils* in 1868 called for a utilitarian theater serving social causes and wrote a series of plays dealing with women's rights and sexual morality. At about the same time the naturalist Zola ridiculed the cardboard characters and clockwork mechanism of the well-made play and urged dramatists to adopt the attitude of the scientist who dispassionately observes the world around him and ruthlessly draws his conclusions, regardless of what art and morality may dictate. In 1871 the Danish critic Brandes, swimming with the new intellectual currents, told his countrymen that in order to be significant modern literature must "submit current problems to debate."

It was under these pressures that Ibsen, who was living in Germany where it was impossible to escape the stimulus of the new ideas, and who had his poetic and national masterpieces *Brand* and *Peer Gynt* behind him, now turned to the realistic problem play and in so doing won international fame as the father of the modern drama. The young Ibsen had written plays that abounded in Scribean intrigue, in the plotting and counterplotting of hero against villain, but when he reached maturity, he banished these elements from his plays. Combining the German romantic conception of fate with nineteenth-century Darwinism and scientific determinism, he made the action of his plays consist in the working out of the forces of the past. The well-made play with its stress on preparation turned out to be perfectly suited to Ibsen's thought. Without radically changing the form of the well-made play, he revitalized it by cramming it with sociology, psychology, and symbolism. Not a borrower like Shakespeare, Ibsen with his extraordinary mythopoeic powers was able to invent stories that were capsule histories of his century. *Ghosts, The Wild Duck,* and *The Master Builder* became modern myths that could be subjected to a variety of interpretations and that have not lost their power to arouse the imagination and stir the intellect. While overhearing the subdued talk and suppressed whispers in Ibsen's Victorian parlors, one can hear the soft footsteps of history at one's back and the distant rumble of revolution on the horizon. Not only were whole lives compressed into Ibsen's plots; whole epochs passed in review.

No one believed a bourgeois entertainment could have such potential for transforming men's minds. Ibsen's triumph was so great that many critics were led to think that the whole history of dramaturgy had reached its culmination in *Hedda Gabler,* and the only way to preserve Shakespeare's greatness was to transform him, too, into an author of problem plays and psychological character studies. Playwriting manuals began to appear regularly, all based on the dramaturgy implicit in Ibsen's works. It seemed impossible to surpass the Norwegian genius; one could only imitate him or react against him.

Zola failed to accomplish his naturalistic reform of the stage because, though protesting against the artificialities of the well-made play (as everyone was doing after 1852 and the advent of Realism) and urging fidelity to nature as the only valid artistic principle, he worked within the structural pattern of the play form he despised. His own efforts in the drama were only badly made well-made plays. Strindberg, writing in the 1880's when Ibsen was bringing the well-made play to fulfillment, was the first to break the old plot pattern and create a new one. Instead of presenting three, four, or five acts forming exposition, rising action, climax, and denouement, Strindberg concentrated the action into one long, virtually uninterrupted act. *Miss Julie* and *Creditors,* both written in 1888, represented the first truly creative departure from the form of the well-made play.

But these one-act plays still had a great deal of action or story. A truly radical plotting innovation, the effects of which are being felt more strongly now than ever before, took place in the last decade of the century. Just as the realists had reduced the melodramatic intrigue of the well-made play to a minimum, so now action in general was reduced to a minimum. In the 1890s, the decade of symbolism, Maeterlinck came forward with the idea that the most deeply significant moments in life are precisely those in which nothing appears to happen. Protesting against the scenes of violence that authors inevitably make the focus of interest and reminding us that most lives are lived out without scenes of murder, poisoning, duels, and insane jealousy, Maeterlinck wished to put on stage the "tragedy of everyday life." The active life of the conventional hero of even the most realistic play inhibits the life of the spirit, said Maeterlinck. It is when the room is still and the body in repose that the mind blossoms and bends toward the source of silence to absorb the eternal forces and respond to the shy gods who play the major roles in our lives.

Although Maeterlinck's early plays were too unsubstantial to endure the coarseness and crudities of the stage, the theories he advocated have had an enormous influence on the modern drama. His most impressive efforts were in the area of the short one-act play. When he attempted full-length plays, he succumbed willy-nilly to the demons of plot and intrigue. Nothing much needs to happen in a twenty-minute sketch, but it is extremely difficult to hold an audience for two hours without having anything happen. Maeterlinck's solution was to follow Wagner into myth and legend for story material.

In 1898 Strindberg took the same course, up to a point. In *To Damascus* he created a drama in which he gave small events cosmic importance by drawing on the cultural storehouse of myths, legends, archetypes, and symbols. But there was a crucial difference between Strindberg's method and Maeterlinck's. When the latter resorted to legends to build a full-length play, he took them over whole, retelling them with new emphases here and there, a method followed by Giraudoux and a host of twentieth-century dramatists. Strindberg used them in bits and pieces and built his symbolic plays like mosaics, as he said, though it would be more meaningful nowadays to describe them as collages. Seeing his autobiographical protagonist as a hodgepodge of cultural potsherds, Strindberg was among the first, if not the very first, to give his antihero heroic significance by making him the sum of past and present history. Allusion replaced action in *To Damascus,* and thus the problem of how to hold the interest of the audience while avoiding intrigue and banal effects found one extremely fruitful solution.

Chekhov tried another approach. Though he is always classed among the realists, and rightly so, it should be remembered that his major plays were written from 1896 to 1903, when reaction against the naturalism of the 1880s had set in and the symbolist movement had spread throughout Europe. Chekhov distrusted conventional plot-making as much as Maeterlinck did. "In life," said Chekhov, "one dosen't fight duels, hang oneself, declare one's undying love, nor spout the most profound thoughts in one steady stream. No; more often than not, one eats, drinks, flirts, and says silly things. It is this that one should see on stage. A play should be written in which people come in, dine, talk about the rain or the good weather, and play whist, not because the author has willed it but because that is how things happen in real life."

Chekhov could admire Ibsen's craftsmanship but he felt oppressed by the Norwegian playwright's ever-present intellect shaping events. It has been remarked that the story of Madame Ranevsky's life, which she tosses off in a single speech in *The Cherry Orchard,* would suffice for a three-act play by Ibsen. But it is easy to tell that kind of story and insert it into a play. One can pick up a dozen like it in a single afternoon at a ladies' bridge party. The difficult thing is to plot such a story, that is, make a play of it; and it is infinitely more difficult to plot such a story and avoid all the stale situations that had been presented a thousand times on the nineteenth-century stage. Chekhov chose not to tell Ranevsky's story in the conventional way because in doing so he would have had to make the death of Ranevsky's little boy serve as a second-act climax and her abandonment by her lover and her subsequent attempt at suicide come as a fitting denouement. Her life would acquire a thrust and significance that Chekhov obviously felt it should not have. She was, in a word, not worth a play. Accordingly, Chekhov substitutes for action a number of excruciatingly banal situations, none of which is allowed to develop in the orthodox fashion. He has a number of people, all linked together in a daisy chain of triangular love affairs, drift on stage for a party or a homecoming and then drift off again. But the love affairs do not constitute the real plot or structure of *The Cherry Orchard* any more than do Gaev's imaginary billiard games. The plot of a Chekhov play shows how a sister-in-law usurps a house or how a beautiful ancestral estate is turned into a housing development. There is implicit in a Chekhov action ten times as much awkward intrigue as in an Ibsen play, but it is all off stage. Chekhov may say that fighting duels and killing oneself are not part of the ordinary day's routine, but his characters still do that sort of thing—off stage. The Greek tragedians kept on-stage violence to a minimum for technical production reasons (not for religious reasons, as one sometimes hears), but Chekhov banished it because he was tired of the conventional French boulevard drama that had overrun Europe and of everything associated with it: stereotyped acting, standard lines of business, interchangeable situations, cliché-ridden speeches, phony climaxes.

More important than these artistic reasons for his choice of technique was the fact that for him God did not exist, myths were mere superstitions, and at least part of him looked with skepticism on all programs and ideals, especially those of the middle class. It would have been dishonest of him, and temperamentally impossible, to cloak his plays with myths or adorn them with transcendental ideals. And he also knew that by shaping his plots like those of the well-made play he would be committing himself to the kind of thinking that created the form. Strindberg preferred to throw it out; Chekhov turned it inside out.

In less than a century the well-made play had undergone every vicissitude. As fresh and vivacious as an unspoiled ingenue at the beginning of the century, it looked by the end of the century like a tired character actor. Though the common man still liked his old favorite situations and asked for violence and intrigue in equally large doses, which the motion pictures were soon to give him, the intellectual vanguard looked for its aesthetic kicks in more ethereal realms. Or else made a shambles of the old-fashioned play by reducing it to the level of the comic strip, as Jarry did in *Ubu Roi,* staged in 1896—about the time, as a matter of fact, that the first comic strips did appear. . . .

FURTHER READING

Arvin, Neil Cole. *Eugène Scribe and the French Theatre, 1815-1860.* Cambridge: Harvard University Press, 1924, 268 p.

Studies Scribe's plays as social commentary on the mores of contemporary French culture and surveys the reaction of his contemporaries to his portrayal of the period.

Gillespie, Patti. "Plays: Well-Complicated." *Speech Monographs* 42, No. 1 (March 1975): 20-28

Defines some common characteristics of well-made plays through an examination of the ways in which Scribe establishes and resolves complication.

Habegger, Alfred. "*The Siege of London*: Henry James and the *Pièce Bien Faite.*" *Modern Fiction Studies* 15, No. 2 (Summer 1969): 219-30.

Explores the professed influence of Dumas and Augier on James's "The Siege of London," concluding that the work has little in common with the style of the well-made play.

Koon, Helene, and Richard Switzer. *Eugène Scribe.* Boston: Twayne, 1980, 174 p.

Critical biography of Scribe's life and times that explores the style of his social comedies and his history plays and their influence on later dramatists.

Lamm, Martin. "Scribe and Hebbel" and "French Drama of the Second Empire." In *Modern Drama,* translated by Karin Elliott, pp. 1-51. New York: Philosophical Library, 1953.

Describes the way in which the radically different styles of Scribe and Hebbel influenced modern drama through the realist drama of the Second Empire.

Legouvé, Ernest. "Eugène Scribe," translated by Albert D. Vandam. In *Papers on Playmaking,* edited by Brander Matthews, pp. 253-74. New York: Hill and Wang, 1957.

Short biographical sketch of Scribe's life, including an overview of the typical elements of the well-made play and a critical appraisal of Scribe's literary merits.

Matthews, Brander. "The Pleasant Land of Scribia." In *The Principles of Playmaking, and Other Discussions of the Drama,* pp. 133-46. New York: Charles Scribner's Sons, 1919.

Characterizes Scribe as the "chief" of the "story-tellers of the stage, content to be story-tellers only and satisfied to rely on the attraction of a sequence of ingenious situations artfully articulated."

Stanton, Stephen S. "Scribe's *Bertrand et Raton*: A Well-Made Play." *Tulane Drama Review* 2, No. 1 (Nov. 1957): 58-70.

Examines the first of Scribe's well-made plays to gain widespread popularity and attempts to identify political and social criticism within the formula of the well-made play.

——————. Introduction to *"Camille" and Other Plays,* edited by Stephen S. Stanton, pp. vii-xxxix. New York: Hill and Wang, 1957.

Surveys the characteristic elements of the well-made play, its influence on Dumas's *La Dame aux Camélias,* and the appearance of the well-made form in later British drama.

——————. "Shaw's Debt to Scribe." *Publications of the Modern Language Association of America* 76, No. 5 (Dec. 1961): 575-85.

Contends that, despite Shaw's well-known condemnation of Scribe and Sardou, he drew on many of the conventions of the well-made play in writing his own dramas.

Taylor, John Russell. "Tom Robertson and the 1870s." In *The Rise and Fall of the Well-Made Play,* pp. 19-34. London: Methuen & Co., 1967.

Discusses Scribe's influence on Tom Robertson, who initiated the realistic reform in English drama, and Robertson's later influence on his disciples.

Nineteenth-Century Literature Criticism

Topics Volume
Cumulative Indexes

Volumes 1-80

How to Use This Index

The main references

Calvino, Italo
1923–1985 .... CLC 5, 8, 11, 22, 33, 39,
73; SSC 3

list all author entries in the following Gale Literary Criticism series:

BLC = *Black Literature Criticism*
CLC = *Contemporary Literary Criticism*
CLR = *Children's Literature Review*
CMLC = *Classical and Medieval Literature Criticism*
DA = *DISCovering Authors*
DAB = *DISCovering Authors: British*
DAC = *DISCovering Authors: Canadian*
DAM = *DISCovering Authors: Modules*
    DRAM: Dramatists Module; *MST*: Most-Studied Authors Module;
    MULT: Multicultural Authors Module; *NOV*: Novelists Module;
    POET: Poets Module; *POP*: Popular Fiction and Genre Authors Module
DC = *Drama Criticism*
HLC = *Hispanic Literature Criticism*
LC = *Literature Criticism from 1400 to 1800*
NCLC = *Nineteenth-Century Literature Criticism*
PC = *Poetry Criticism*
SSC = *Short Story Criticism*
TCLC = *Twentieth-Century Literary Criticism*
WLC = *World Literature Criticism, 1500 to the Present*

The cross-references

See also CANR 23; CA 85-88;
obituary CA116

list all author entries in the following Gale biographical and literary sources:

AAYA = *Authors & Artists for Young Adults*
AITN = *Authors in the News*
BEST = *Bestsellers*
BW = *Black Writers*
CA = *Contemporary Authors*
CAAS = *Contemporary Authors Autobiography Series*
CABS = *Contemporary Authors Bibliographical Series*
CANR = *Contemporary Authors New Revision Series*
CAP = *Contemporary Authors Permanent Series*
CDALB = *Concise Dictionary of American Literary Biography*
CDBLB = *Concise Dictionary of British Literary Biography*
DLB = *Dictionary of Literary Biography*
DLBD = *Dictionary of Literary Biography Documentary Series*
DLBY = *Dictionary of Literary Biography Yearbook*
HW = *Hispanic Writers*
JRDA = *Junior DISCovering Authors*
MAICYA = *Major Authors and Illustrators for Children and Young Adults*
MTCW = *Major 20th-Century Writers*
NNAL = *Native North American Literature*
SAAS = *Something about the Author Autobiography Series*
SATA = *Something about the Author*
YABC = *Yesterday's Authors of Books for Children*

Literary Criticism Series
Cumulative Author Index

See also CA 85-88; CANR 81; DLB 108; HW
2

Albert the Great 1200(?)-1280   **CMLC 16**
See also DLB 115

Alcala-Galiano, Juan Valera y
See Valera y Alcala-Galiano, Juan

Alcott, Amos Bronson 1799-1888   **NCLC 1**
See also DLB 1

Alcott, Louisa May 1832-1888   **NCLC 6, 58;
DA; DAB; DAC; DAM MST, NOV; SSC
27; WLC**
See also AAYA 20; CDALB 1865-1917; CLR
1, 38; DLB 1, 42, 79; DLBD 14; JRDA;
MAICYA; SATA 100; YABC 1

Aldanov, M. A.
See Aldanov, Mark (Alexandrovich)

Aldanov, Mark (Alexandrovich) 1886(?)-1957
TCLC 23
See also CA 118

Aldington, Richard 1892-1962   **CLC 49**
See also CA 85-88; CANR 45; DLB 20, 36, 100,
149

Aldiss, Brian W(ilson) 1925-   **CLC 5, 14, 40;
DAM NOV**
See also CA 5-8R; CAAS 2; CANR 5, 28, 64;
DLB 14; MTCW 1, 2; SATA 34

Alegria, Claribel 1924-**CLC 75; DAM MULT;
HLCS 1; PC 26**
See also CA 131; CAAS 15; CANR 66; DLB
145; HW 1; MTCW 1

Alegria, Fernando 1918-   **CLC 57**
See also CA 9-12R; CANR 5, 32, 72; HW 1, 2

Aleichem, Sholom   **TCLC 1, 35; SSC 33**
See also Rabinovitch, Sholem

Aleixandre, Vicente 1898-1984
See also CANR 81; HLCS 1; HW 2

Alepoudelis, Odysseus
See Elytis, Odysseus

Aleshkovsky, Joseph 1929-
See Aleshkovsky, Yuz
See also CA 121; 128

Aleshkovsky, Yuz   **CLC 44**
See also Aleshkovsky, Joseph

Alexander, Lloyd (Chudley) 1924-   **CLC 35**
See also AAYA 1, 27; CA 1-4R; CANR 1, 24,
38, 55; CLR 1, 5, 48; DLB 52; JRDA;
MAICYA; MTCW 1; SAAS 19; SATA 3, 49,
81

Alexander, Meena 1951-   **CLC 121**
See also CA 115; CANR 38, 70

Alexander, Samuel 1859-1938   **TCLC 77**

Alexie, Sherman (Joseph, Jr.) 1966- **CLC 96;
DAM MULT**
See also AAYA 28; CA 138; CANR 65; DLB
175, 206; MTCW 1; NNAL

Alfau, Felipe 1902-   **CLC 66**
See also CA 137

Alger, Horatio, Jr. 1832-1899   **NCLC 8**
See also DLB 42; SATA 16

Algren, Nelson 1909-1981**CLC 4, 10, 33; SSC
33**
See also CA 13-16R; 103; CANR 20, 61;
CDALB 1941-1968; DLB 9; DLBY 81, 82;
MTCW 1, 2

Ali, Ahmed 1910-   **CLC 69**
See also CA 25-28R; CANR 15, 34

Alighieri, Dante
See Dante

Allan, John B.
See Westlake, Donald E(dwin)

Allan, Sidney
See Hartmann, Sadakichi

Allan, Sydney

See Hartmann, Sadakichi

Allen, Edward 1948-   **CLC 59**

Allen, Fred 1894-1956   **TCLC 87**

Allen, Paula Gunn 1939-**CLC 84;DAM MULT**
See also CA 112; 143; CANR 63; DLB 175;
MTCW 1; NNAL

Allen, Roland
See Ayckbourn, Alan

Allen, Sarah A.
See Hopkins, Pauline Elizabeth

Allen, Sidney H.
See Hartmann, Sadakichi

Allen, Woody 1935-   **CLC 16, 52; DAM POP**
See also AAYA 10; CA 33-36R; CANR 27, 38,
63; DLB 44; MTCW 1

Allende, Isabel 1942-   **CLC 39, 57, 97; DAM
MULT, NOV; HLC 1; WLCS**
See also AAYA 18; CA 125; 130; CANR 51,
74; DLB 145; HW 1, 2; INT 130; MTCW 1,
2

Alleyn, Ellen
See Rossetti, Christina (Georgina)

Allingham, Margery (Louise) 1904-1966**CLC
19**
See also CA 5-8R; 25-28R; CANR 4, 58; DLB
77; MTCW 1, 2

Allingham, William 1824-1889   **NCLC 25**
See also DLB 35

Allison, Dorothy E. 1949-   **CLC 78**
See also CA 140; CANR 66; MTCW 1

Allston, Washington 1779-1843   **NCLC 2**
See also DLB 1

Almedingen, E. M.   **CLC 12**
See also Almedingen, Martha Edith von
See also SATA 3

Almedingen, Martha Edith von 1898-1971
See Almedingen, E. M.
See also CA 1-4R; CANR 1

Almodovar, Pedro 1949(?)-**CLC 114; HLCS 1**
See also CA 133; CANR 72; HW 2

Almqvist, Carl Jonas Love 1793-1866 **N C L C
42**

Alonso, Damaso 1898-1990   **CLC 14**
See also CA 110; 131; 130; CANR 72; DLB
108; HW 1, 2

Alov
See Gogol, Nikolai (Vasilyevich)

Alta 1942-   **CLC 19**
See also CA 57-60

Alter, Robert B(ernard) 1935-   **CLC 34**
See also CA 49-52; CANR 1, 47

Alther, Lisa 1944-   **CLC 7, 41**
See also CA 65-68; CAAS 30; CANR 12, 30,
51; MTCW 1

Althusser, L.
See Althusser, Louis

Althusser, Louis 1918-1990   **CLC 106**
See also CA 131; 132

Altman, Robert 1925-   **CLC 16, 116**
See also CA 73-76; CANR 43

Alurista 1949-
See Urista, Alberto H.
See also DLB 82; HLCS 1

Alvarez, A(lfred) 1929-   **CLC 5, 13**
See also CA 1-4R; CANR 3, 33, 63; DLB 14,
40

Alvarez, Alejandro Rodriguez 1903-1965
See Casona, Alejandro
See also CA 131; 93-96; HW 1

Alvarez, Julia 1950-   **CLC 93;HLCS 1**
See also AAYA 25; CA 147; CANR 69; MTCW
1

Alvaro, Corrado 1896-1956   **TCLC 60**

See also CA 163

Amado, Jorge 1912- **CLC 13, 40, 106; DAM
MULT, NOV; HLC 1**
See also CA 77-80; CANR 35, 74; DLB 113;
HW 2; MTCW 1, 2

Ambler, Eric 1909-1998   **CLC 4, 6, 9**
See also CA 9-12R; 171; CANR 7, 38, 74; DLB
77; MTCW 1, 2

Amichai, Yehuda 1924-   **CLC 9, 22, 57, 116**
See also CA 85-88; CANR 46, 60; MTCW 1

Amichai, Yehudah
See Amichai, Yehuda

Amiel, Henri Frederic 1821-1881   **NCLC 4**

Amis, Kingsley (William) 1922-1995**CLC 1, 2,
3, 5, 8, 13, 40, 44; DA; DAB; DAC; DAM
MST, NOV**
See also AITN 2; CA 9-12R; 150; CANR 8, 28,
54; CDBLB 1945-1960; DLB 15, 27, 100,
139; DLBY 96; INT CANR-8; MTCW 1, 2

Amis, Martin (Louis) 1949- **CLC 4, 9, 38, 62,
101**
See also BEST 90:3; CA 65-68; CANR 8, 27,
54, 73; DLB 14, 194; INT CANR-27; MTCW
1

Ammons, A(rchie) R(andolph) 1926-**CLC 2, 3,
5, 8, 9, 25, 57, 108; DAM POET; PC 16**
See also AITN 1; CA 9-12R; CANR 6, 36, 51,
73; DLB 5, 165; MTCW 1, 2

Amo, Tauraatua i
See Adams, Henry (Brooks)

Amory, Thomas 1691(?)-1788   **LC 48**

Anand, Mulk Raj 1905-   **CLC 23, 93;DAM
NOV**
See also CA 65-68; CANR 32, 64; MTCW 1, 2

Anatol
See Schnitzler, Arthur

Anaximander c. 610B.C.-c. 546B.C.**CMLC 22**

Anaya, Rudolfo A(lfonso) 1937-   **CLC 23;
DAM MULT, NOV; HLC 1**
See also AAYA 20; CA 45-48; CAAS 4; CANR
1, 32, 51; DLB 82, 206; HW 1; MTCW 1, 2

Andersen, Hans Christian 1805-1875**NCLC 7,
79; DA; DAB; DAC; DAM MST, POP;
SSC 6; WLC**
See also CLR 6; MAICYA; SATA 100; YABC
1

Anderson, C. Farley
See Mencken, H(enry) L(ouis); Nathan, George
Jean

Anderson, Jessica (Margaret) Queale 1916-
CLC 37
See also CA 9-12R; CANR 4, 62

Anderson, Jon (Victor) 1940-   **CLC 9; DAM
POET**
See also CA 25-28R; CANR 20

Anderson, Lindsay (Gordon) 1923-1994**C L C
20**
See also CA 125; 128; 146; CANR 77

Anderson, Maxwell 1888-1959**TCLC 2; DAM
DRAM**
See also CA 105; 152; DLB 7; MTCW 2

Anderson, Poul (William) 1926-   **CLC 15**
See also AAYA 5; CA 1-4R; CAAS 2; CANR
2, 15, 34, 64; CLR 58; DLB 8; INT CANR-
15; MTCW 1, 2; SATA 90; SATA-Brief 39;
SATA-Essay 106

Anderson, Robert (Woodruff) 1917-**CLC 23;
DAM DRAM**
See also AITN 1; CA 21-24R; CANR 32; DLB
7

Anderson, Sherwood 1876-1941 **TCLC 1, 10,
24; DA; DAB; DAC; DAM MST, NOV;
SSC 1; WLC**

See also AAYA 30; CA 104; 121; CANR 61; CDALB 1917-1929; DLB 4, 9, 86; DLBD 1; MTCW 1, 2

Andier, Pierre
See Desnos, Robert

Andouard
See Giraudoux, (Hippolyte) Jean

Andrade, Carlos Drummond de   **CLC 18**
See also Drummond de Andrade, Carlos

Andrade, Mario de 1893-1945   **TCLC 43**

Andreae, Johann V(alentin) 1586-1654 **LC 32**
See also DLB 164

Andreas-Salome, Lou 1861-1937   **TCLC 56**
See also CA 178; DLB 66

Andress, Lesley
See Sanders, Lawrence

Andrewes, Lancelot 1555-1626   **LC 5**
See also DLB 151, 172

Andrews, Cicily Fairfield
See West, Rebecca

Andrews, Elton V.
See Pohl, Frederik

Andreyev, Leonid (Nikolaevich) 1871-1919
TCLC 3
See also CA 104

Andric, Ivo 1892-1975   **CLC 8**
See also CA 81-84; 57-60; CANR 43, 60; DLB 147; MTCW 1

Androvar
See Prado (Calvo), Pedro

Angelique, Pierre
See Bataille, Georges

Angell, Roger 1920-   **CLC 26**
See also CA 57-60; CANR 13, 44, 70; DLB 171, 185

Angelou, Maya 1928- **CLC 12, 35, 64, 77; BLC 1; DA; DAB; DAC; DAM MST, MULT, POET, POP; WLCS**
See also AAYA 7, 20; BW 2, 3; CA 65-68; CANR 19, 42, 65; CDALBS; CLR 53; DLB 38; MTCW 1, 2; SATA 49

Anna Comnena 1083-1153   **CMLC 25**

Annensky, Innokenty (Fyodorovich) 1856-1909
TCLC 14
See also CA 110; 155

Annunzio, Gabriele d'
See D'Annunzio, Gabriele

Anodos
See Coleridge, Mary E(lizabeth)

Anon, Charles Robert
See Pessoa, Fernando (Antonio Nogueira)

Anouilh, Jean (Marie Lucien Pierre) 1910-1987
CLC 1, 3, 8, 13, 40, 50; DAM DRAM; DC 8
See also CA 17-20R; 123; CANR 32; MTCW 1, 2

Anthony, Florence
See Ai

Anthony, John
See Ciardi, John (Anthony)

Anthony, Peter
See Shaffer, Anthony (Joshua); Shaffer, Peter (Levin)

Anthony, Piers 1934-   **CLC 35;DAM POP**
See also AAYA 11; CA 21-24R; CANR 28, 56, 73; DLB 8; MTCW 1, 2; SAAS 22; SATA 84

Anthony, Susan B(rownell) 1916-1991 **TCLC 84**
See also CA 89-92; 134

Antoine, Marc
See Proust, (Valentin-Louis-George-Eugene-) Marcel

Antoninus, Brother

See Everson, William (Oliver)

Antonioni, Michelangelo 1912-   **CLC 20**
See also CA 73-76; CANR 45, 77

Antschel, Paul 1920-1970
See Celan, Paul
See also CA 85-88; CANR 33, 61; MTCW 1

Anwar, Chairil 1922-1949   **TCLC 22**
See also CA 121

Anzaldua, Gloria 1942-
See also CA 175; DLB 122; HLCS 1

Apess, William 1798-1839(?) **NCLC 73; DAM MULT**
See also DLB 175; NNAL

Apollinaire, Guillaume 1880-1918 **TCLC 3, 8, 51; DAM POET; PC 7**
See also Kostrowitzki, Wilhelm Apollinaris de
See also CA 152; MTCW 1

Appelfeld, Aharon 1932-   **CLC 23, 47**
See also CA 112; 133

Apple, Max (Isaac) 1941-   **CLC 9, 33**
See also CA 81-84; CANR 19, 54; DLB 130

Appleman, Philip (Dean) 1926-   **CLC 51**
See also CA 13-16R; CAAS 18; CANR 6, 29, 56

Appleton, Lawrence
See Lovecraft, H(oward) P(hillips)

Apteryx
See Eliot, T(homas) S(tearns)

Apuleius, (Lucius Madaurensis) 125(?)-175(?)
CMLC 1
See also DLB 211

Aquin, Hubert 1929-1977   **CLC 15**
See also CA 105; DLB 53

Aquinas, Thomas 1224(?)-1274   **CMLC 33**
See also DLB 115

Aragon, Louis 1897-1982   **CLC 3, 22; DAM NOV, POET**
See also CA 69-72; 108; CANR 28, 71; DLB 72; MTCW 1, 2

Arany, Janos 1817-1882   **NCLC 34**

Aranyos, Kakay
See Mikszath, Kalman

Arbuthnot, John 1667-1735   **LC 1**
See also DLB 101

Archer, Herbert Winslow
See Mencken, H(enry) L(ouis)

Archer, Jeffrey (Howard) 1940-   **CLC 28; DAM POP**
See also AAYA 16; BEST 89:3; CA 77-80; CANR 22, 52; INT CANR-22

Archer, Jules 1915-   **CLC 12**
See also CA 9-12R; CANR 6, 69; SAAS 5; SATA 4, 85

Archer, Lee
See Ellison, Harlan (Jay)

Arden, John 1930- **CLC 6, 13, 15;DAM DRAM**
See also CA 13-16R; CAAS 4; CANR 31, 65, 67; DLB 13; MTCW 1

Arenas, Reinaldo 1943-1990   **CLC 41; DAM MULT; HLC 1**
See also CA 124; 128; 133; CANR 73; DLB 145; HW 1; MTCW 1

Arendt, Hannah 1906-1975   **CLC 66,98**
See also CA 17-20R; 61-64; CANR 26, 60; MTCW 1, 2

Aretino, Pietro 1492-1556   **LC 12**

Arghezi, Tudor 1880-1967   **CLC 80**
See also Theodorescu, Ion N.
See also CA 167

Arguedas, Jose Maria 1911-1969 **CLC 10, 18; HLCS 1**
See also CA 89-92; CANR 73; DLB 113; HW 1

Argueta, Manlio 1936-   **CLC 31**

See also CA 131; CANR 73; DLB 145; HW 1

Arias, Ron(ald Francis) 1941-
See also CA 131; CANR 81; DAM MULT; DLB 82; HLC 1; HW 1, 2; MTCW 2

Ariosto, Ludovico 1474-1533   **LC 6**

Aristides
See Epstein, Joseph

Aristophanes 450B.C.-385B.C. **CMLC 4; DA; DAB; DAC; DAM DRAM, MST; DC 2; WLCS**
See also DLB 176

Aristotle 384B.C.-322B.C.   **CMLC 31; DA; DAB; DAC; DAM MST; WLCS**
See also DLB 176

Arlt, Roberto (Godofredo Christophersen) 1900-1942 **TCLC 29; DAM MULT; HLC 1**
See also CA 123; 131; CANR 67; HW 1, 2

Armah, Ayi Kwei 1939-   **CLC 5, 33; BLC 1; DAM MULT, POET**
See also BW 1; CA 61-64; CANR 21, 64; DLB 117; MTCW 1

Armatrading, Joan 1950-   **CLC 17**
See also CA 114

Arnette, Robert
See Silverberg, Robert

Arnim, Achim von (Ludwig Joachim von Arnim) 1781-1831   **NCLC 5; SSC 29**
See also DLB 90

Arnim, Bettina von 1785-1859   **NCLC 38**
See also DLB 90

Arnold, Matthew 1822-1888 **NCLC 6, 29; DA; DAB; DAC; DAM MST, POET; PC 5; WLC**
See also CDBLB 1832-1890; DLB 32, 57

Arnold, Thomas 1795-1842   **NCLC 18**
See also DLB 55

Arnow, Harriette (Louisa) Simpson 1908-1986
CLC 2, 7, 18
See also CA 9-12R; 118; CANR 14; DLB 6; MTCW 1, 2; SATA 42; SATA-Obit 47

Arouet, Francois-Marie
See Voltaire

Arp, Hans
See Arp, Jean

Arp, Jean 1887-1966   **CLC 5**
See also CA 81-84; 25-28R; CANR 42, 77

Arrabal
See Arrabal, Fernando

Arrabal, Fernando 1932-   **CLC 2, 9, 18, 58**
See also CA 9-12R; CANR 15

Arreola, Juan Jose 1918-
See also CA 113; 131; CANR 81; DAM MULT; DLB 113; HLC 1; HW 1, 2

Arrick, Fran   **CLC 30**
See also Gaberman, Judie Angell

Artaud, Antonin (Marie Joseph) 1896-1948
TCLC 3, 36; DAM DRAM
See also CA 104; 149; MTCW 1

Arthur, Ruth M(abel) 1905-1979   **CLC 12**
See also CA 9-12R; 85-88; CANR 4; SATA 7, 26

Artsybashev, Mikhail (Petrovich) 1878-1927
TCLC 31
See also CA 170

Arundel, Honor (Morfydd) 1919-1973 **CLC 17**
See also CA 21-22; 41-44R; CAP 2; CLR 35; SATA 4; SATA-Obit 24

Arzner, Dorothy 1897-1979   **CLC 98**

Asch, Sholem 1880-1957   **TCLC 3**
See also CA 105

Ash, Shalom
See Asch, Sholem

Ashbery, John (Lawrence) 1927- **CLC 2, 3, 4,**

6, 9, 13, 15, 25, 41, 77; **DAM POET; PC 26**
See also CA 5-8R; CANR 9, 37, 66; DLB 5,
165; DLBY 81; INT CANR-9; MTCW 1, 2
Ashdown, Clifford
See Freeman, R(ichard) Austin
Ashe, Gordon
See Creasey, John
Ashton-Warner, Sylvia (Constance) 1908-1984
CLC 19
See also CA 69-72; 112; CANR 29; MTCW 1,
2
Asimov, Isaac 1920-1992 **CLC 1, 3, 9, 19, 26,
76, 92; DAM POP**
See also AAYA 13; BEST 90:2; CA 1-4R; 137;
CANR 2, 19, 36, 60; CLR 12; DLB 8; DLBY
92; INT CANR-19; JRDA; MAICYA;
MTCW 1, 2; SATA 1, 26, 74
Assis, Joaquim Maria Machado de
See Machado de Assis, Joaquim Maria
Astley, Thea (Beatrice May) 1925- **CLC 41**
See also CA 65-68; CANR 11, 43, 78
Aston, James
See White, T(erence) H(anbury)
Asturias, Miguel Angel 1899-1974 **CLC 3, 8,
13; DAM MULT, NOV; HLC 1**
See also CA 25-28; 49-52; CANR 32; CAP 2;
DLB 113; HW 1; MTCW 1, 2
Atares, Carlos Saura
See Saura (Atares), Carlos
Atheling, William
See Pound, Ezra (Weston Loomis)
Atheling, William, Jr.
See Blish, James (Benjamin)
Atherton, Gertrude (Franklin Horn) 1857-1948
TCLC 2
See also CA 104; 155; DLB 9, 78, 186
Atherton, Lucius
See Masters, Edgar Lee
Atkins, Jack
See Harris, Mark
Atkinson, Kate **CLC 99**
See also CA 166
Attaway, William (Alexander) 1911-1986**CLC
92; BLC 1; DAM MULT**
See also BW 2, 3; CA 143; CANR 82; DLB 76
Atticus
See Fleming, Ian (Lancaster); Wilson, (Thomas)
Woodrow
Atwood, Margaret (Eleanor) 1939-**CLC 2, 3,
4, 8, 13, 15, 25, 44, 84; DA; DAB; DAC;
DAM MST, NOV, POET; PC 8; SSC 2;
WLC**
See also AAYA 12; BEST 89:2; CA 49-52;
CANR 3, 24, 33, 59; DLB 53; INT CANR-
24; MTCW 1, 2; SATA 50
Aubigny, Pierre d'
See Mencken, H(enry) L(ouis)
Aubin, Penelope 1685-1731(?) **LC 9**
See also DLB 39
Auchincloss, Louis (Stanton) 1917-**CLC 4, 6,
9, 18, 45; DAM NOV; SSC 22**
See also CA 1-4R; CANR 6, 29, 55; DLB 2;
DLBY 80; INT CANR-29; MTCW 1
Auden, W(ystan) H(ugh) 1907-1973**CLC 1, 2,
3, 4, 6, 9, 11, 14, 43; DA; DAB; DAC; DAM
DRAM, MST, POET; PC 1;WLC**
See also AAYA 18; CA 9-12R; 45-48; CANR
5, 61; CDBLB 1914-1945; DLB 10, 20;
MTCW 1, 2
Audiberti, Jacques 1900-1965 **CLC 38; DAM
DRAM**
See also CA 25-28R
Audubon, John James 1785-1851 **NCLC 47**

Auel, Jean M(arie) 1936- **CLC 31, 107; DAM
POP**
See also AAYA 7; BEST 90:4; CA 103; CANR
21, 64; INT CANR-21; SATA 91
Auerbach, Erich 1892-1957 **TCLC 43**
See also CA 118; 155
Augier, Emile 1820-1889 **NCLC 31**
See also DLB 192
August, John
See De Voto, Bernard (Augustine)
Augustine 354-430**CMLC 6; DA; DAB; DAC;
DAM MST; WLCS**
See also DLB 115
Aurelius
See Bourne, Randolph S(illiman)
Aurobindo, Sri
See Ghose, Aurabinda
Austen, Jane 1775-1817 **NCLC 1, 13, 19, 33,
51; DA; DAB; DAC; DAM MST, NOV;
WLC**
See also AAYA 19; CDBLB 1789-1832; DLB
116
Auster, Paul 1947- **CLC 47**
See also CA 69-72; CANR 23, 52, 75; MTCW
1
Austin, Frank
See Faust, Frederick (Schiller)
Austin, Mary (Hunter) 1868-1934 **TCLC 25**
See also CA 109; 178; DLB 9, 78, 206
Autran Dourado, Waldomiro Freitas 1926-
See Dourado, (Waldomiro Freitas) Autran
See also CA 179
Averroes 1126-1198 **CMLC 7**
See also DLB 115
Avicenna 980-1037 **CMLC 16**
See also DLB 115
Avison, Margaret 1918- **CLC 2, 4, 97; DAC;
DAM POET**
See also CA 17-20R; DLB 53; MTCW 1
Axton, David
See Koontz, Dean R(ay)
Ayckbourn, Alan 1939- **CLC 5, 8, 18, 33, 74;
DAB; DAM DRAM**
See also CA 21-24R; CANR 31, 59; DLB 13;
MTCW 1, 2
Aydy, Catherine
See Tennant, Emma (Christina)
Ayme, Marcel (Andre) 1902-1967 **CLC 11**
See also CA 89-92; CANR 67; CLR 25; DLB
72; SATA 91
Ayrton, Michael 1921-1975 **CLC 7**
See also CA 5-8R; 61-64; CANR 9, 21
Azorin **CLC 11**
See also Martinez Ruiz, Jose
Azuela, Mariano 1873-1952 **TCLC 3; DAM
MULT; HLC 1**
See also CA 104; 131; CANR 81; HW 1, 2;
MTCW 1, 2
Baastad, Babbis Friis
See Friis-Baastad, Babbis Ellinor
Bab
See Gilbert, W(illiam) S(chwenck)
Babbis, Eleanor
See Friis-Baastad, Babbis Ellinor
Babel, Isaac
See Babel, Isaak (Emmanuilovich)
Babel, Isaak (Emmanuilovich) 1894-1941(?)
TCLC 2, 13; SSC 16
See also CA 104; 155; MTCW 1
Babits, Mihaly 1883-1941 **TCLC 14**
See also CA 114
Babur 1483-1530 **LC 18**
Baca, Jimmy Santiago 1952-

See also CA 131; CANR 81; DAM MULT; DLB
122; HLC 1; HW 1, 2
Bacchelli, Riccardo 1891-1985 **CLC 19**
See also CA 29-32R; 117
Bach, Richard (David) 1936- **CLC 14; DAM
NOV, POP**
See also AITN 1; BEST 89:2; CA 9-12R; CANR
18; MTCW 1; SATA 13
Bachman, Richard
See King, Stephen (Edwin)
Bachmann,Ingeborg 1926-1973 **CLC 69**
See also CA 93-96; 45-48; CANR 69; DLB 85
Bacon, Francis 1561-1626 **LC 18,32**
See also CDBLB Before 1660; DLB 151
Bacon, Roger 1214(?)-1292 **CMLC 14**
See also DLB 115
Bacovia, George **TCLC 24**
See also Vasiliu, Gheorghe
Badanes, Jerome 1937- **CLC 59**
Bagehot, Walter 1826-1877 **NCLC 10**
See also DLB 55
Bagnold, Enid 1889-1981 **CLC 25;DAM
DRAM**
See also CA 5-8R; 103; CANR 5, 40; DLB 13,
160, 191; MAICYA; SATA 1, 25
Bagritsky, Eduard 1895-1934 **TCLC 60**
Bagrjana, Elisaveta
See Belcheva, Elisaveta
Bagryana, Elisaveta 1893-1991 **CLC 10**
See also Belcheva, Elisaveta
See also CA 178; DLB 147
Bailey, Paul 1937- **CLC 45**
See also CA 21-24R; CANR 16, 62; DLB 14
Baillie, Joanna 1762-1851 **NCLC 71**
See also DLB 93
Bainbridge, Beryl (Margaret) 1933-**CLC 4, 5,
8, 10, 14, 18, 22, 62; DAM NOV**
See also CA 21-24R; CANR 24, 55, 75; DLB
14; MTCW 1, 2
Baker, Elliott 1922- **CLC 8**
See also CA 45-48; CANR 2, 63
Baker, Jean H. **TCLC 3, 10**
See also Russell, George William
Baker, Nicholson 1957- **CLC 61;DAM POP**
See also CA 135; CANR 63
Baker, Ray Stannard 1870-1946 **TCLC 47**
See also CA 118
Baker, Russell (Wayne) 1925- **CLC 31**
See also BEST 89:4; CA 57-60; CANR 11, 41,
59; MTCW 1, 2
Bakhtin, M.
See Bakhtin, Mikhail Mikhailovich
Bakhtin, M. M.
See Bakhtin, Mikhail Mikhailovich
Bakhtin, Mikhail
See Bakhtin, Mikhail Mikhailovich
Bakhtin, Mikhail Mikhailovich 1895-1975
CLC 83
See also CA 128; 113
Bakshi, Ralph 1938(?)- **CLC 26**
See also CA 112; 138
Bakunin, Mikhail (Alexandrovich) 1814-1876
NCLC 25, 58
Baldwin, James (Arthur) 1924-1987**CLC 1, 2,
3, 4, 5, 8, 13, 15, 17, 42, 50, 67, 90; BLC 1;
DA; DAB; DAC; DAM MST, MULT, NOV,
POP; DC 1; SSC 10, 33; WLC**
See also AAYA 4; BW 1; CA 1-4R; 124; CABS
1; CANR 3, 24; CDALB 1941-1968; DLB
2, 7, 33; DLBY 87; MTCW 1, 2; SATA 9;
SATA-Obit 54
Ballard, J(ames) G(raham) 1930-**CLC 3, 6, 14,
36; DAM NOV, POP; SSC 1**

See also AAYA 3; CA 5-8R; CANR 15, 39, 65; DLB 14, 207; MTCW 1, 2; SATA 93

Balmont, Konstantin (Dmitriyevich) 1867-1943 **TCLC 11**
See also CA 109; 155

Baltausis, Vincas
See Mikszath, Kalman

Balzac, Honore de 1799-1850 **NCLC 5, 35, 53; DA; DAB; DAC; DAM MST, NOV; SSC 5; WLC**
See also DLB 119

Bambara, Toni Cade 1939-1995 **CLC 19, 88; BLC 1; DA; DAC; DAM MST, MULT; SSC 35; WLCS**
See also AAYA 5; BW 2, 3; CA 29-32R; 150; CANR 24, 49, 81; CDALBS; DLB 38; MTCW 1, 2

Bamdad, A.
See Shamlu, Ahmad

Banat, D. R.
See Bradbury, Ray (Douglas)

Bancroft, Laura
See Baum, L(yman) Frank

Banim, John 1798-1842 **NCLC 13**
See also DLB 116, 158, 159

Banim, Michael 1796-1874 **NCLC 13**
See also DLB 158, 159

Banjo, The
See Paterson, A(ndrew) B(arton)

Banks, Iain
See Banks, Iain M(enzies)

Banks, Iain M(enzies) 1954- **CLC 34**
See also CA 123; 128; CANR 61; DLB 194; INT 128

Banks, Lynne Reid **CLC 23**
See also Reid Banks, Lynne
See also AAYA 6

Banks, Russell 1940- **CLC 37, 72**
See also CA 65-68; CAAS 15; CANR 19, 52, 73; DLB 130

Banville, John 1945- **CLC 46, 118**
See also CA 117; 128; DLB 14; INT 128

Banville, Theodore (Faullain) de 1832-1891 **NCLC 9**

Baraka, Amiri 1934- **CLC 1, 2, 3, 5, 10, 14, 33, 115; BLC 1; DA; DAC; DAM MST, MULT, POET, POP; DC 6; PC 4; WLCS**
See Jones, LeRoi
See also BW 2, 3; CA 21-24R; CABS 3; CANR 27, 38, 61; CDALB 1941-1968; DLB 5, 7, 16, 38; DLBD 8; MTCW 1, 2

Barbauld, Anna Laetitia 1743-1825 **NCLC 50**
See also DLB 107, 109, 142, 158

Barbellion, W. N. P. **TCLC 24**
See also Cummings, Bruce F(rederick)

Barbera, Jack (Vincent) 1945- **CLC 44**
See also CA 110; CANR 45

Barbey d'Aurevilly, Jules Amedee 1808-1889 **NCLC 1; SSC 17**
See also DLB 119

Barbour, John c. 1316-1395 **CMLC 33**
See also DLB 146

Barbusse, Henri 1873-1935 **TCLC 5**
See also CA 105; 154; DLB 65

Barclay, Bill
See Moorcock, Michael (John)

Barclay, William Ewert
See Moorcock, Michael (John)

Barea, Arturo 1897-1957 **TCLC 14**
See also CA 111

Barfoot, Joan 1946- **CLC 18**
See also CA 105

Barham, Richard Harris 1788-1845 **NCLC 77**

See also DLB 159

Baring, Maurice 1874-1945 **TCLC 8**
See also CA 105; 168; DLB 34

Baring-Gould, Sabine 1834-1924 **TCLC 88**
See also DLB 156, 190

Barker, Clive 1952- **CLC 52; DAM POP**
See also AAYA 10; BEST 90:3; CA 121; 129; CANR 71; INT 129; MTCW 1, 2

Barker, George Granville 1913-1991 **CLC 8, 48; DAM POET**
See also CA 9-12R; 135; CANR 7, 38; DLB 20; MTCW 1

Barker, Harley Granville
See Granville-Barker, Harley
See also DLB 10

Barker, Howard 1946- **CLC 37**
See also CA 102; DLB 13

Barker, Jane 1652-1732 **LC 42**

Barker, Pat(ricia) 1943- **CLC 32, 94**
See also CA 117; 122; CANR 50; INT 122

Barlach, Ernst 1870-1938 **TCLC 84**
See also CA 178; DLB 56, 118

Barlow, Joel 1754-1812 **NCLC 23**
See also DLB 37

Barnard, Mary (Ethel) 1909- **CLC 48**
See also CA 21-22; CAP 2

Barnes, Djuna 1892-1982 **CLC 3, 4, 8, 11, 29; SSC 3**
See also CA 9-12R; 107; CANR 16, 55; DLB 4, 9, 45; MTCW 1, 2

Barnes, Julian (Patrick) 1946- **CLC 42; DAB**
See also CA 102; CANR 19, 54; DLB 194; DLBY 93; MTCW 1

Barnes, Peter 1931- **CLC 5, 56**
See also CA 65-68; CAAS 12; CANR 33, 34, 64; DLB 13; MTCW 1

Barnes, William 1801-1886 **NCLC 75**
See also DLB 32

Baroja (y Nessi), Pio 1872-1956 **TCLC 8; HLC 1**
See also CA 104

Baron, David
See Pinter, Harold

Baron Corvo
See Rolfe, Frederick (William Serafino Austin Lewis Mary)

Barondess, Sue K(aufman) 1926-1977 **CLC 8**
See also Kaufman, Sue
See also CA 1-4R; 69-72; CANR 1

Baron de Teive
See Pessoa, Fernando (Antonio Nogueira)

Baroness Von S.
See Zangwill, Israel

Barres, (Auguste-) Maurice 1862-1923 **TCLC 47**
See also CA 164; DLB 123

Barreto, Afonso Henrique de Lima
See Lima Barreto, Afonso Henrique de

Barrett, (Roger) Syd 1946- **CLC 35**

Barrett, William (Christopher) 1913-1992 **CLC 27**
See also CA 13-16R; 139; CANR 11, 67; INT CANR-11

Barrie, J(ames) M(atthew) 1860-1937 **TCLC 2; DAB; DAM DRAM**
See also CA 104; 136; CANR 77; CDBLB 1890-1914; CLR 16; DLB 10, 141, 156; MAICYA; MTCW 1; SATA 100; YABC 1

Barrington, Michael
See Moorcock, Michael (John)

Barrol, Grady
See Bograd, Larry

Barry, Mike

See Malzberg, Barry N(athaniel)

Barry, Philip 1896-1949 **TCLC 11**
See also CA 109; DLB 7

Bart, Andre Schwarz
See Schwarz-Bart, Andre

Barth, John (Simmons) 1930- **CLC 1, 2, 3, 5, 7, 9, 10, 14, 27, 51, 89; DAM NOV; SSC 10**
See also AITN 1, 2; CA 1-4R; CABS 1; CANR 5, 23, 49, 64; DLB 2; MTCW 1

Barthelme, Donald 1931-1989 **CLC 1, 2, 3, 5, 6, 8, 13, 23, 46, 59, 115; DAM NOV; SSC 2**
See also CA 21-24R; 129; CANR 20, 58; DLB 2; DLBY 80, 89; MTCW 1, 2; SATA 7; SATA-Obit 62

Barthelme, Frederick 1943- **CLC 36, 117**
See also CA 114; 122; CANR 77; DLBY 85; INT 122

Barthes, Roland (Gerard) 1915-1980 **CLC 24, 83**
See also CA 130; 97-100; CANR 66; MTCW 1, 2

Barzun, Jacques (Martin) 1907- **CLC 51**
See also CA 61-64; CANR 22

Bashevis, Isaac
See Singer, Isaac Bashevis

Bashkirtseff, Marie 1859-1884 **NCLC 27**

Basho
See Matsuo Basho

Basil of Caesaria c. 330-379 **CMLC 35**

Bass, Kingsley B., Jr.
See Bullins, Ed

Bass, Rick 1958- **CLC 79**
See also CA 126; CANR 53; DLB 212

Bassani, Giorgio 1916- **CLC 9**
See also CA 65-68; CANR 33; DLB 128, 177; MTCW 1

Bastos, Augusto (Antonio) Roa
See Roa Bastos, Augusto (Antonio)

Bataille, Georges 1897-1962 **CLC 29**
See also CA 101; 89-92

Bates, H(erbert) E(rnest) 1905-1974 **CLC 46; DAB; DAM POP; SSC 10**
See also CA 93-96; 45-48; CANR 34; DLB 162, 191; MTCW 1, 2

Bauchart
See Camus, Albert

Baudelaire, Charles 1821-1867 **NCLC 6, 29, 55; DA; DAB; DAC; DAM MST, POET; PC 1; SSC 18; WLC**

Baudrillard, Jean 1929- **CLC 60**

Baum, L(yman) Frank 1856-1919 **TCLC 7**
See also CA 108; 133; CLR 15; DLB 22; JRDA; MAICYA; MTCW 1, 2; SATA 18, 100

Baum, Louis F.
See Baum, L(yman) Frank

Baumbach, Jonathan 1933- **CLC 6, 23**
See also CA 13-16R; CAAS 5; CANR 12, 66; DLBY 80; INT CANR-12; MTCW 1

Bausch, Richard (Carl) 1945- **CLC 51**
See also CA 101; CAAS 14; CANR 43, 61; DLB 130

Baxter, Charles (Morley) 1947- **CLC 45, 78; DAM POP**
See also CA 57-60; CANR 40, 64; DLB 130; MTCW 2

Baxter, George Owen
See Faust, Frederick (Schiller)

Baxter, James K(eir) 1926-1972 **CLC 14**
See also CA 77-80

Baxter, John
See Hunt, E(verette) Howard, (Jr.)

Bayer, Sylvia
See Glassco, John

Baynton, Barbara 1857-1929   **TCLC 57**
Beagle, Peter S(oyer) 1939-   **CLC 7,104**
   See also CA 9-12R; CANR 4, 51, 73; DLBY
   80; INT CANR-4; MTCW 1; SATA 60
Bean, Normal
   See Burroughs, Edgar Rice
Beard, Charles A(ustin) 1874-1948 **TCLC 15**
   See also CA 115; DLB 17; SATA 18
Beardsley, Aubrey 1872-1898   **NCLC 6**
Beattie, Ann 1947-**CLC 8, 13, 18, 40, 63; DAM**
   NOV, POP; SSC 11
   See also BEST 90:2; CA 81-84; CANR 53, 73;
   DLBY 82; MTCW 1, 2
Beattie, James 1735-1803   **NCLC 25**
   See also DLB 109
Beauchamp, Kathleen Mansfield 1888-1923
   See Mansfield, Katherine
   See also CA 104; 134; DA; DAC; DAM MST;
   MTCW 2
Beaumarchais, Pierre-Augustin Caronde 1732-
   1799   **DC 4**
   See also DAM DRAM
Beaumont, Francis 1584(?)-1616**LC 33; DC 6**
   See also CDBLB Before 1660; DLB 58, 121
Beauvoir, Simone (Lucie Ernestine Marie
   Bertrand) de 1908-1986**CLC 1, 2, 4, 8, 14,**
   31, 44, 50, 71; DA; DAB; DAC; DAM MST,
   NOV; SSC 35; WLC
   See also CA 9-12R; 118; CANR 28, 61; DLB
   72; DLBY 86; MTCW 1, 2
Becker, Carl (Lotus) 1873-1945   **TCLC 63**
   See also CA 157; DLB 17
Becker, Jurek 1937-1997   **CLC 7, 19**
   See also CA 85-88; 157; CANR 60; DLB 75
Becker, Walter 1950-   **CLC 26**
Beckett, Samuel (Barclay) 1906-1989 **CLC 1,**
   2, 3, 4, 6, 9, 10, 11, 14, 18, 29, 57, 59, 83;
   DA; DAB; DAC; DAM DRAM, MST,
   NOV; SSC 16; WLC
   See also CA 5-8R; 130; CANR 33, 61; CDBLB
   1945-1960; DLB 13, 15; DLBY 90; MTCW
   1, 2
Beckford, William 1760-1844   **NCLC 16**
   See also DLB 39
Beckman, Gunnel 1910-   **CLC 26**
   See also CA 33-36R; CANR 15; CLR 25;
   MAICYA; SAAS 9; SATA 6
Becque, Henri 1837-1899   **NCLC 3**
   See also DLB 192
Becquer, Gustavo Adolfo 1836-1870
   See also DAM MULT; HLCS 1
Beddoes, Thomas Lovell 1803-1849 **NCLC 3**
   See also DLB 96
Bede c. 673-735   **CMLC 20**
   See also DLB 146
Bedford, Donald F.
   See Fearing, Kenneth (Flexner)
Beecher, Catharine Esther 1800-1878 **N C L C**
   30
   See also DLB 1
Beecher, John 1904-1980   **CLC 6**
   See also AITN 1; CA 5-8R; 105; CANR 8
Beer, Johann 1655-1700   **LC 5**
   See also DLB 168
Beer, Patricia 1924-   **CLC 58**
   See also CA 61-64; CANR 13, 46; DLB 40
Beerbohm, Max
   See Beerbohm, (Henry) Max(imilian)
Beerbohm, (Henry) Max(imilian) 1872-1956
   TCLC 1, 24
   See also CA 104; 154; CANR 79; DLB 34, 100
Beer-Hofmann, Richard 1866-1945**TCLC 60**
   See also CA 160; DLB 81

Begiebing, Robert J(ohn) 1946-   **CLC 70**
   See also CA 122; CANR 40
Behan, Brendan 1923-1964 **CLC 1, 8, 11, 15,**
   79; DAM DRAM
   See also CA 73-76; CANR 33; CDBLB 1945-
   1960; DLB 13; MTCW 1, 2
Behn, Aphra 1640(?)-1689 **LC 1, 30, 42; DA;**
   DAB; DAC; DAM DRAM, MST, NOV,
   POET; DC 4; PC 13; WLC
   See also DLB 39, 80, 131
Behrman, S(amuel) N(athaniel) 1893-1973
   CLC 40
   See also CA 13-16; 45-48; CAP 1; DLB 7, 44
Belasco, David 1853-1931   **TCLC 3**
   See also CA 104; 168; DLB 7
Belcheva, Elisaveta 1893-   **CLC 10**
   See Bagryana, Elisaveta
Beldone, Phil "Cheech"
   See Ellison, Harlan (Jay)
Beleno
   See Azuela, Mariano
Belinski, Vissarion Grigoryevich 1811-1848
   NCLC 5
   See also DLB 198
Belitt, Ben 1911-   **CLC 22**
   See also CA 13-16R; CAAS 4; CANR 7, 77;
   DLB 5
Bell, Gertrude (Margaret Lowthian) 1868-1926
   TCLC 67
   See also CA 167; DLB 174
Bell, J. Freeman
   See Zangwill, Israel
Bell, James Madison 1826-1902   **TCLC 43;**
   BLC 1; DAM MULT
   See also BW 1; CA 122; 124; DLB 50
Bell, Madison Smartt 1957-   **CLC 41, 102**
   See also CA 111; CANR 28, 54, 73; MTCW 1
Bell, Marvin (Hartley) 1937-**CLC 8, 31; DAM**
   POET
   See also CA 21-24R; CAAS 14; CANR 59; DLB
   5; MTCW 1
Bell, W. L. D.
   See Mencken, H(enry) L(ouis)
Bellamy, Atwood C.
   See Mencken, H(enry) L(ouis)
Bellamy, Edward 1850-1898   **NCLC 4**
   See also DLB 12
Belli, Gioconda 1949-
   See also CA 152; HLCS 1
Bellin, Edward J.
   See Kuttner, Henry
Belloc, (Joseph) Hilaire (Pierre Sebastien Rene
   Swanton) 1870-1953 **TCLC 7, 18; DAM**
   POET; PC 24
   See also CA 106; 152; DLB 19, 100, 141, 174;
   MTCW 1; YABC 1
Belloc, Joseph Peter Rene Hilaire
   See Belloc, (Joseph) Hilaire (Pierre Sebastien
   Rene Swanton)
Belloc, Joseph Pierre Hilaire
   See Belloc, (Joseph) Hilaire (Pierre Sebastien
   Rene Swanton)
Belloc, M. A.
   See Lowndes, Marie Adelaide (Belloc)
Bellow, Saul 1915-**CLC 1, 2, 3, 6, 8, 10, 13, 15,**
   25, 33, 34, 63, 79; DA; DAB; DAC; DAM
   MST, NOV, POP; SSC 14; WLC
   See also AITN 2; BEST 89:3; CA 5-8R; CABS
   1; CANR 29, 53; CDALB 1941-1968; DLB
   2, 28; DLBD 3; DLBY 82; MTCW 1, 2
Belser, Reimond Karel Maria de 1929-
   See Ruyslinck, Ward
   See also CA 152

Bely, Andrey   **TCLC 7; PC 11**
   See also Bugayev, Boris Nikolayevich
   See also MTCW 1
Belyi, Andrei
   See Bugayev, Boris Nikolayevich
Benary, Margot
   See Benary-Isbert, Margot
Benary-Isbert, Margot 1889-1979   **CLC 12**
   See also CA 5-8R; 89-92; CANR 4, 72; CLR
   12; MAICYA; SATA 2; SATA-Obit 21
Benavente (y Martinez), Jacinto 1866-1954
   TCLC 3; DAM DRAM, MULT; HLCS 1
   See also CA 106; 131; CANR 81; HW 1, 2;
   MTCW 1, 2
Benchley, Peter (Bradford) 1940- **CLC 4, 8;**
   DAM NOV, POP
   See also AAYA 14; AITN 2; CA 17-20R; CANR
   12, 35, 66; MTCW 1, 2; SATA 3, 89
Benchley, Robert (Charles) 1889-1945**T C L C**
   1, 55
   See also CA 105; 153; DLB 11
Benda, Julien 1867-1956   **TCLC 60**
   See also CA 120; 154
Benedict, Ruth (Fulton) 1887-1948 **TCLC 60**
   See also CA 158
Benedict, Saint c. 480-c. 547   **CMLC 29**
Benedikt, Michael 1935-   **CLC 4, 14**
   See also CA 13-16R; CANR 7; DLB 5
Benet, Juan 1927-   **CLC 28**
   See also CA 143
Benet, Stephen Vincent 1898-1943 **TCLC 7;**
   DAM POET; SSC 10
   See also CA 104; 152; DLB 4, 48, 102; DLBY
   97; MTCW 1; YABC 1
Benet, William Rose 1886-1950   **TCLC 28;**
   DAM POET
   See also CA 118; 152; DLB 45
Benford, Gregory (Albert) 1941-   **CLC 52**
   See also CA 69-72; 175; CAAE 175; CAAS 27;
   CANR 12, 24, 49; DLBY 82
Bengtsson, Frans (Gunnar) 1894-1954**T C L C**
   48
   See also CA 170
Benjamin, David
   See Slavitt, David R(ytman)
Benjamin, Lois
   See Gould, Lois
Benjamin, Walter 1892-1940   **TCLC 39**
   See also CA 164
Benn, Gottfried 1886-1956   **TCLC 3**
   See also CA 106; 153; DLB 56
Bennett, Alan 1934-**CLC 45, 77; DAB; DAM**
   MST
   See also CA 103; CANR 35, 55; MTCW 1, 2
Bennett, (Enoch) Arnold 1867-1931 **TCLC 5,**
   20
   See also CA 106; 155; CDBLB 1890-1914;
   DLB 10, 34, 98, 135; MTCW 2
Bennett, Elizabeth
   See Mitchell, Margaret (Munnerlyn)
Bennett, George Harold 1930-
   See Bennett, Hal
   See also BW 1; CA 97-100
Bennett, Hal   **CLC 5**
   See also Bennett, George Harold
   See also DLB 33
Bennett, Jay 1912-   **CLC 35**
   See also AAYA 10; CA 69-72; CANR 11, 42,
   79; JRDA; SAAS 4; SATA 41, 87; SATA-
   Brief 27
Bennett, Louise (Simone) 1919 **CLC 28; BLC**
   1; DAM MULT
   See also BW 2, 3; CA 151; DLB 117

Benson, E(dward) F(rederic) 1867-1940
TCLC 27
See also CA 114; 157; DLB 135, 153

Benson, Jackson J. 1930- **CLC 34**
See also CA 25-28R; DLB 111

Benson, Sally 1900-1972 **CLC 17**
See also CA 19-20; 37-40R; CAP 1; SATA 1,
35; SATA-Obit 27

Benson, Stella 1892-1933 **TCLC 17**
See also CA 117; 155; DLB 36, 162

Bentham, Jeremy 1748-1832 **NCLC 38**
See also DLB 107, 158

Bentley, E(dmund) C(lerihew) 1875-1956
TCLC 12
See also CA 108; DLB 70

Bentley, Eric (Russell) 1916- **CLC 24**
See also CA 5-8R; CANR 6, 67; INT CANR-6

Beranger, Pierre Jean de 1780-1857 **NCLC 34**

Berdyaev, Nicolas
See Berdyaev, Nikolai (Aleksandrovich)

Berdyaev, Nikolai (Aleksandrovich) 1874-1948
TCLC 67
See also CA 120; 157

Berdyayev, Nikolai (Aleksandrovich)
See Berdyaev, Nikolai (Aleksandrovich)

Berendt, John (Lawrence) 1939- **CLC 86**
See also CA 146; CANR 75; MTCW 1

Beresford, J(ohn) D(avys) 1873-1947 **TCLC 81**
See also CA 112; 155; DLB 162, 178, 197

Bergelson, David 1884-1952 **TCLC 81**

Berger, Colonel
See Malraux, (Georges-)Andre

Berger, John (Peter) 1926- **CLC 2, 19**
See also CA 81-84; CANR 51, 78; DLB 14, 207

Berger, Melvin H. 1927- **CLC 12**
See also CA 5-8R; CANR 4; CLR 32; SAAS 2;
SATA 5, 88

Berger, Thomas (Louis) 1924- **CLC 3, 5, 8, 11,
18, 38; DAM NOV**
See also CA 1-4R; CANR 5, 28, 51; DLB 2;
DLBY 80; INT CANR-28; MTCW 1, 2

Bergman, (Ernst) Ingmar 1918- **CLC 16, 72**
See also CA 81-84; CANR 33, 70; MTCW 2

Bergson, Henri (-Louis) 1859-1941 **TCLC 32**
See also CA 164

Bergstein, Eleanor 1938- **CLC 4**
See also CA 53-56; CANR 5

Berkoff, Steven 1937- **CLC 56**
See also CA 104; CANR 72

Bermant, Chaim (Icyk) 1929- **CLC 40**
See also CA 57-60; CANR 6, 31, 57

Bern, Victoria
See Fisher, M(ary) F(rances) K(ennedy)

Bernanos, (Paul Louis) Georges 1888-1948
TCLC 3
See also CA 104; 130; DLB 72

Bernard, April 1956- **CLC 59**
See also CA 131

Berne, Victoria
See Fisher, M(ary) F(rances) K(ennedy)

Bernhard, Thomas 1931-1989 **CLC 3, 32, 61**
See also CA 85-88; 127; CANR 32, 57; DLB
85, 124; MTCW 1

Bernhardt, Sarah (Henriette Rosine) 1844-1923
TCLC 75
See also CA 157

Berriault, Gina 1926- **CLC 54, 109; SSC 30**
See also CA 116; 129; CANR 66; DLB 130

Berrigan, Daniel 1921- **CLC 4**
See also CA 33-36R; CAAS 1; CANR 11, 43,
78; DLB 5

Berrigan, Edmund Joseph Michael, Jr. 1934-
1983
See Berrigan, Ted
See also CA 61-64; 110; CANR 14

Berrigan, Ted **CLC 37**
See also Berrigan, Edmund Joseph Michael, Jr.
See also DLB 5, 169

Berry, Charles Edward Anderson 1931-
See Berry, Chuck
See also CA 115

Berry, Chuck **CLC 17**
See also Berry, Charles Edward Anderson

Berry, Jonas
See Ashbery, John (Lawrence)

Berry, Wendell (Erdman) 1934- **CLC 4, 6, 8,
27, 46; DAM POET**
See also AITN 1; CA 73-76; CANR 50, 73; DLB
5, 6; MTCW 1

Berryman, John 1914-1972 **CLC 1, 2, 3, 4, 6, 8,
10, 13, 25, 62; DAM POET**
See also CA 13-16; 33-36R; CABS 2; CANR
35; CAP 1; CDALB 1941-1968; DLB 48;
MTCW 1, 2

Bertolucci, Bernardo 1940- **CLC 16**
See also CA 106

Berton, Pierre (Francis Demarigny) 1920-
CLC 104
See also CA 1-4R; CANR 2, 56; DLB 68; SATA
99

Bertrand, Aloysius 1807-1841 **NCLC 31**

Bertran de Born c. 1140-1215 **CMLC 5**

Besant, Annie (Wood) 1847-1933 **TCLC 9**
See also CA 105

Bessie, Alvah 1904-1985 **CLC 23**
See also CA 5-8R; 116; CANR 2, 80; DLB 26

Bethlen, T. D.
See Silverberg, Robert

Beti, Mongo **CLC 27; BLC 1; DAM MULT**
See also Biyidi, Alexandre
See also CANR 79

Betjeman, John 1906-1984 **CLC 2, 6, 10, 34,
43; DAB; DAM MST, POET**
See also CA 9-12R; 112; CANR 33, 56; CDBLB
1945-1960; DLB 20; DLBY 84; MTCW 1,
2

Bettelheim, Bruno 1903-1990 **CLC 79**
See also CA 81-84; 131; CANR 23, 61; MTCW
1, 2

Betti, Ugo 1892-1953 **TCLC 5**
See also CA 104; 155

Betts, Doris (Waugh) 1932- **CLC 3, 6, 28**
See also CA 13-16R; CANR 9, 66, 77; DLBY
82; INT CANR-9

Bevan, Alistair
See Roberts, Keith (John Kingston)

Bey, Pilaff
See Douglas, (George) Norman

Bialik, Chaim Nachman 1873-1934 **TCLC 25**
See also CA 170

Bickerstaff, Isaac
See Swift, Jonathan

Bidart, Frank 1939- **CLC 33**
See also CA 140

Bienek, Horst 1930- **CLC 7, 11**
See also CA 73-76; DLB 75

Bierce, Ambrose (Gwinett) 1842-1914(?)
**TCLC 1, 7, 44; DA; DAC; DAM MST; SSC
9; WLC**
See also CA 104; 139; CANR 78; CDALB
1865-1917; DLB 11, 12, 23, 71, 74, 186

Biggers, Earl Derr 1884-1933 **TCLC 65**
See also CA 108; 153

Billings, Josh
See Shaw, Henry Wheeler

Billington, (Lady) Rachel (Mary) 1942- **CLC
43**
See also AITN 2; CA 33-36R; CANR 44

Binyon, T(imothy) J(ohn) 1936- **CLC 34**
See also CA 111; CANR 28

Bioy Casares, Adolfo 1914-1999 **CLC 4, 8, 13,
88; DAM MULT; HLC 1; SSC 17**
See also CA 29-32R; 177; CANR 19, 43, 66;
DLB 113; HW 1, 2; MTCW 1, 2

Bird, Cordwainer
See Ellison, Harlan (Jay)

Bird, Robert Montgomery 1806-1854 **NCLC 1**
See also DLB 202

Birkerts, Sven 1951- **CLC 116**
See also CA 128; 133; 176; CAAS 29; INT 133

Birney, (Alfred) Earle 1904-1995 **CLC 1, 4, 6,
11; DAC; DAM MST, POET**
See also CA 1-4R; CANR 5, 20; DLB 88;
MTCW 1

Biruni, al 973-1048(?) **CMLC 28**

Bishop, Elizabeth 1911-1979 **CLC 1, 4, 9, 13,
15, 32; DA; DAC; DAM MST, POET; PC
3**
See also CA 5-8R; 89-92; CABS 2; CANR 26,
61; CDALB 1968-1988; DLB 5, 169;
MTCW 1, 2; SATA-Obit 24

Bishop, John 1935- **CLC 10**
See also CA 105

Bissett, Bill 1939- **CLC 18; PC 14**
See also CA 69-72; CAAS 19; CANR 15; DLB
53; MTCW 1

Bissoondath, Neil (Devindra) 1955- **CLC 120;
DAC**
See also CA 136

Bitov, Andrei (Georgievich) 1937- **CLC 57**
See also CA 142

Biyidi, Alexandre 1932-
See Beti, Mongo
See also BW 1, 3; CA 114; 124; CANR 81;
MTCW 1, 2

Bjarme, Brynjolf
See Ibsen, Henrik (Johan)

Bjoernson, Bjoernstjerne (Martinius) 1832-
1910 **TCLC 7, 37**
See also CA 104

Black, Robert
See Holdstock, Robert P.

Blackburn, Paul 1926-1971 **CLC 9, 43**
See also CA 81-84; 33-36R; CANR 34; DLB
16; DLBY 81

Black Elk 1863-1950 **TCLC 33; DAM MULT**
See also CA 144; MTCW 1; NNAL

Black Hobart
See Sanders, (James) Ed(ward)

Blacklin, Malcolm
See Chambers, Aidan

Blackmore, R(ichard) D(oddridge) 1825-1900
TCLC 27
See also CA 120; DLB 18

Blackmur, R(ichard) P(almer) 1904-1965
CLC 2, 24
See also CA 11-12; 25-28R; CANR 71; CAP 1;
DLB 63

Black Tarantula
See Acker, Kathy

Blackwood, Algernon (Henry) 1869-1951
TCLC 5
See also CA 105; 150; DLB 153, 156, 178

Blackwood, Caroline 1931-1996 **CLC 6, 9, 100**
See also CA 85-88; 151; CANR 32, 61, 65; DLB
14, 207; MTCW 1

Blade, Alexander
See Hamilton, Edmond; Silverberg, Robert

Bowers, Edgar 1924-   **CLC 9**
See also CA 5-8R; CANR 24; DLB 5
Bowie, David   **CLC 17**
See also Jones, David Robert
Bowles, Jane (Sydney) 1917-1973 **CLC 3, 68**
See also CA 19-20; 41-44R; CAP 2
Bowles, Paul (Frederick) 1910- **CLC 1, 2, 19,
53; SSC 3**
See also CA 1-4R; CAAS 1; CANR 1, 19, 50,
75; DLB 5, 6; MTCW 1, 2
Box, Edgar
See Vidal, Gore
Boyd, Nancy
See Millay, Edna St. Vincent
Boyd, William 1952-   **CLC 28, 53, 70**
See also CA 114; 120; CANR 51, 71
Boyle, Kay 1902-1992 **CLC 1, 5, 19, 58, 121;
SSC 5**
See also CA 13-16R; 140; CAAS 1; CANR 29,
61; DLB 4, 9, 48, 86; DLBY 93; MTCW 1,
2
Boyle, Mark
See Kienzle, William X(avier)
Boyle, Patrick 1905-1982   **CLC 19**
See also CA 127
Boyle, T. C. 1948-
See Boyle, T(homas) Coraghessan
Boyle, T(homas) Coraghessan 1948- **CLC 36,
55, 90; DAM POP; SSC 16**
See also BEST 90:4; CA 120; CANR 44, 76;
DLBY 86; MTCW 2
Boz
See Dickens, Charles (John Huffam)
Brackenridge, Hugh Henry 1748-1816 **N C L C
7**
See also DLB 11, 37
Bradbury, Edward P.
See Moorcock, Michael (John)
See also MTCW 2
Bradbury, Malcolm (Stanley) 1932- **CLC 32,
61; DAM NOV**
See also CA 1-4R; CANR 1, 33; DLB 14, 207;
MTCW 1, 2
Bradbury, Ray (Douglas) 1920- **CLC 1, 3, 10,
15, 42, 98; DA; DAB; DAC; DAM MST,
NOV, POP; SSC 29; WLC**
See also AAYA 15; AITN 1, 2; CA 1-4R; CANR
2, 30, 75; CDALB 1968-1988; DLB 2, 8;
MTCW 1, 2; SATA 11, 64
Bradford, Gamaliel 1863-1932   **TCLC 36**
See also CA 160; DLB 17
Bradley, David (Henry), Jr. 1950-   **CLC 23,
118; BLC 1; DAM MULT**
See also BW 1, 3; CA 104; CANR 26, 81; DLB
33
Bradley, John Ed(mund, Jr.) 1958-   **CLC 55**
See also CA 139
Bradley, Marion Zimmer 1930- **CLC 30; DAM
POP**
See also AAYA 9; CA 57-60; CAAS 10; CANR
7, 31, 51, 75; DLB 8; MTCW 1, 2; SATA 90
Bradstreet, Anne 1612(?)-1672 **LC 4, 30; DA;
DAC; DAM MST, POET; PC 10**
See also CDALB 1640-1865; DLB 24
Brady, Joan 1939-   **CLC 86**
See also CA 141
Bragg, Melvyn 1939-   **CLC 10**
See also BEST 89:3; CA 57-60; CANR 10, 48;
DLB 14
Brahe, Tycho 1546-1601   **LC 45**
Braine, John (Gerard) 1922-1986 **CLC 1, 3, 41**
See also CA 1-4R; 120; CANR 1, 33; CDBLB
1945-1960; DLB 15; DLBY 86; MTCW 1

Bramah, Ernest 1868-1942   **TCLC 72**
See also CA 156; DLB 70
Brammer, William 1930(?)-1978   **CLC 31**
See also CA 77-80
Brancati, Vitaliano 1907-1954   **TCLC 12**
See also CA 109
Brancato, Robin F(idler) 1936-   **CLC 35**
See also AAYA 9; CA 69-72; CANR 11, 45;
CLR 32; JRDA; SAAS 9; SATA 97
Brand, Max
See Faust, Frederick (Schiller)
Brand, Millen 1906-1980   **CLC 7**
See also CA 21-24R; 97-100; CANR 72
Branden, Barbara   **CLC 44**
See also CA 148
Brandes, Georg (Morris Cohen) 1842-1927
TCLC 10
See also CA 105
Brandys, Kazimierz 1916-   **CLC 62**
Branley, Franklyn M(ansfield) 1915- **CLC 21**
See also CA 33-36R; CANR 14, 39; CLR 13;
MAICYA; SAAS 16; SATA 4, 68
Brathwaite, Edward (Kamau) 1930- **CLC 11;
BLCS; DAM POET**
See also BW 2, 3; CA 25-28R; CANR 11, 26,
47; DLB 125
Brautigan, Richard (Gary) 1935-1984 **CLC 1,
3, 5, 9, 12, 34, 42; DAM NOV**
See also CA 53-56; 113; CANR 34; DLB 2, 5,
206; DLBY 80, 84; MTCW 1; SATA 56
Brave Bird, Mary 1953-
See Crow Dog, Mary (Ellen)
See also NNAL
Braverman, Kate 1950-   **CLC 67**
See also CA 89-92
Brecht, (Eugen) Bertolt (Friedrich) 1898-1956
**TCLC 1, 6, 13, 35; DA; DAB; DAC; DAM
DRAM, MST; DC 3; WLC**
See also CA 104; 133; CANR 62; DLB 56, 124;
MTCW 1, 2
Brecht, Eugen Berthold Friedrich
See Brecht, (Eugen) Bertolt (Friedrich)
Bremer, Fredrika 1801-1865   **NCLC 11**
Brennan, Christopher John 1870-1932 **T C L C
17**
See also CA 117
Brennan, Maeve 1917-1993   **CLC 5**
See also CA 81-84; CANR 72
Brent, Linda
See Jacobs, Harriet A(nn)
Brentano, Clemens (Maria) 1778-1842 **N C L C
1**
See also DLB 90
Brent of Bin Bin
See Franklin, (Stella Maria Sarah) Miles
(Lampe)
Brenton, Howard 1942-   **CLC 31**
See also CA 69-72; CANR 33, 67; DLB 13;
MTCW 1
Breslin, James 1930-1996
See Breslin, Jimmy
See also CA 73-76; CANR 31, 75; DAM NOV;
MTCW 1, 2
Breslin, Jimmy   **CLC 4, 43**
See also Breslin, James
See also AITN 1; DLB 185; MTCW 2
Bresson, Robert 1901-   **CLC 16**
See also CA 110; CANR 49
Breton, Andre 1896-1966 **CLC 2, 9, 15, 54; PC
15**
See also CA 19-20; 25-28R; CANR 40, 60; CAP
2; DLB 65; MTCW 1, 2
Breytenbach, Breyten 1939(?)- **CLC 23, 37;**

DAM POET
See also CA 113; 129; CANR 61
Bridgers, Sue Ellen 1942-   **CLC 26**
See also AAYA 8; CA 65-68; CANR 11, 36;
CLR 18; DLB 52; JRDA; MAICYA; SAAS
1; SATA 22, 90; SATA-Essay 109
Bridges, Robert (Seymour) 1844-1930 **T C L C
1; DAM POET**
See also CA 104; 152; CDBLB 1890-1914;
DLB 19, 98
Bridie, James   **TCLC 3**
See also Mavor, Osborne Henry
See also DLB 10
Brin, David 1950-   **CLC 34**
See also AAYA 21; CA 102; CANR 24, 70; INT
CANR-24; SATA 65
Brink, Andre (Philippus) 1935- **CLC 18, 36,
106**
See also CA 104; CANR 39, 62; INT 103;
MTCW 1, 2
Brinsmead, H(esba) F(ay) 1922-   **CLC 21**
See also CA 21-24R; CANR 10; CLR 47;
MAICYA; SAAS 5; SATA 18, 78
Brittain, Vera (Mary) 1893(?)-1970   **CLC 23**
See also CA 13-16; 25-28R; CANR 58; CAP 1;
DLB 191; MTCW 1, 2
Broch, Hermann 1886-1951   **TCLC 20**
See also CA 117; DLB 85, 124
Brock, Rose
See Hansen, Joseph
Brodkey, Harold (Roy) 1930-1996   **CLC 56**
See also CA 111; 151; CANR 71; DLB 130
Brodskii, Iosif
See Brodsky, Joseph
Brodsky, Iosif Alexandrovich 1940-1996
See Brodsky, Joseph
See also AITN 1; CA 41-44R; 151; CANR 37;
DAM POET; MTCW 1, 2
Brodsky, Joseph 1940-1996 **CLC 4, 6, 13, 36,
100; PC 9**
See also Brodskii, Iosif; Brodsky, Iosif
Alexandrovich
See also MTCW 1
Brodsky, Michael (Mark) 1948-   **CLC 19**
See also CA 102; CANR 18, 41, 58
Bromell, Henry 1947-   **CLC 5**
See also CA 53-56; CANR 9
Bromfield, Louis (Brucker) 1896-1956 **T C L C
11**
See also CA 107; 155; DLB 4, 9, 86
Broner, E(sther) M(asserman) 1930- **CLC 19**
See also CA 17-20R; CANR 8, 25, 72; DLB 28
Bronk, William (M.) 1918-1999   **CLC 10**
See also CA 89-92; 177; CANR 23; DLB 165
Bronstein, Lev Davidovich
See Trotsky, Leon
Bronte, Anne 1820-1849   **NCLC 71**
See also DLB 21, 199
Bronte, Charlotte 1816-1855 **NCLC 3, 8, 33,
58; DA; DAB; DAC; DAM MST, NOV;
WLC**
See also AAYA 17; CDBLB 1832-1890; DLB
21, 159, 199
Bronte, Emily (Jane) 1818-1848 **NCLC 16, 35;
DA; DAB; DAC; DAM MST, NOV, POET;
PC 8; WLC**
See also AAYA 17; CDBLB 1832-1890; DLB
21, 32, 199
Brooke, Frances 1724-1789   **LC 6, 48**
See also DLB 39, 99
Brooke, Henry 1703(?)-1783   **LC 1**
See also DLB 39
Brooke, Rupert (Chawner) 1887-1915 **T C L C**

2, 7; DA; DAB; DAC; DAM MST, POET;
PC 24; WLC
See also CA 104; 132; CANR 61; CDBLB
1914-1945; DLB 19; MTCW 1, 2

Brooke-Haven, P.
See Wodehouse, P(elham) G(renville)

Brooke-Rose, Christine 1926(?)-   **CLC 40**
See also CA 13-16R; CANR 58; DLB 14

Brookner, Anita 1928- **CLC 32, 34, 51; DAB;
DAM POP**
See also CA 114; 120; CANR 37, 56; DLB 194;
DLBY 87; MTCW 1, 2

Brooks, Cleanth 1906-1994 **CLC 24, 86, 110**
See also CA 17-20R; 145; CANR 33, 35; DLB
63; DLBY 94; INT CANR-35; MTCW 1, 2

Brooks, George
See Baum, L(yman) Frank

Brooks, Gwendolyn 1917- **CLC 1, 2, 4, 5, 15,
49; BLC 1; DA; DAC; DAM MST, MULT,
POET; PC 7; WLC**
See also AAYA 20; AITN 1; BW 2, 3; CA 1-
4R; CANR 1, 27, 52, 75; CDALB 1941-
1968; CLR 27; DLB 5, 76, 165; MTCW 1,
2; SATA 6

Brooks, Mel   **CLC 12**
See also Kaminsky, Melvin
See also AAYA 13; DLB 26

Brooks, Peter 1938-   **CLC 34**
See also CA 45-48; CANR 1

Brooks, Van Wyck 1886-1963   **CLC 29**
See also CA 1-4R; CANR 6; DLB 45, 63, 103

Brophy, Brigid (Antonia) 1929-1995 **CLC 6,
11, 29, 105**
See also CA 5-8R; 149; CAAS 4; CANR 25,
53; DLB 14; MTCW 1, 2

Brosman, Catharine Savage 1934-   **CLC 9**
See also CA 61-64; CANR 21, 46

Brossard, Nicole 1943-   **CLC 115**
See also CA 122; CAAS 16; DLB 53

Brother Antoninus
See Everson, William (Oliver)

The Brothers Quay
See Quay, Stephen; Quay, Timothy

Broughton, T(homas) Alan 1936-   **CLC 19**
See also CA 45-48; CANR 2, 23, 48

Broumas, Olga 1949-   **CLC 10, 73**
See also CA 85-88; CANR 20, 69

Brown, Alan 1950-   **CLC 99**
See also CA 156

Brown, Charles Brockden 1771-1810 **N C L C
22, 74**
See also CDALB 1640-1865; DLB 37, 59, 73

Brown, Christy 1932-1981   **CLC 63**
See also CA 105; 104; CANR 72; DLB 14

Brown, Claude 1937- **CLC 30; BLC 1; DAM
MULT**
See also AAYA 7; BW 1, 3; CA 73-76; CANR
81

Brown, Dee (Alexander) 1908- **CLC 18, 47;
DAM POP**
See also AAYA 30; CA 13-16R; CAAS 6;
CANR 11, 45, 60; DLBY 80; MTCW 1, 2;
SATA 5

Brown, George
See Wertmueller, Lina

Brown, George Douglas 1869-1902 **TCLC 28**
See also CA 162

Brown, George Mackay 1921-1996 **CLC 5, 48,
100**
See also CA 21-24R; 151; CAAS 6; CANR 12,
37, 67; DLB 14, 27, 139; MTCW 1; SATA
35

Brown, (William) Larry 1951-   **CLC 73**

See also CA 130; 134; INT 133

Brown, Moses
See Barrett, William (Christopher)

Brown, Rita Mae 1944- **CLC 18, 43, 79; DAM
NOV, POP**
See also CA 45-48; CANR 2, 11, 35, 62; INT
CANR-11; MTCW 1, 2

Brown, Roderick (Langmere) Haig-
See Haig-Brown, Roderick (Langmere)

Brown, Rosellen 1939-   **CLC 32**
See also CA 77-80; CAAS 10; CANR 14, 44

Brown, Sterling Allen 1901-1989 **CLC 1, 23,
59; BLC 1; DAM MULT, POET**
See also BW 1, 3; CA 85-88; 127; CANR 26;
DLB 48, 51, 63; MTCW 1, 2

Brown, Will
See Ainsworth, William Harrison

Brown, William Wells 1813-1884   **NCLC 2;
BLC 1; DAM MULT; DC 1**
See also DLB 3, 50

Browne, (Clyde) Jackson 1948(?)-   **CLC 21**
See also CA 120

Browning, Elizabeth Barrett 1806-1861
**NCLC 1, 16, 61, 66; DA; DAB; DAC; DAM
MST, POET; PC 6; WLC**
See also CDBLB 1832-1890; DLB 32, 199

Browning, Robert 1812-1889   **NCLC 19, 79;
DA; DAB; DAC; DAM MST, POET; PC
2; WLCS**
See also CDBLB 1832-1890; DLB 32, 163;
YABC 1

Browning, Tod 1882-1962   **CLC 16**
See also CA 141; 117

Brownson, Orestes Augustus 1803-1876
NCLC 50
See also DLB 1, 59, 73

Bruccoli, Matthew J(oseph) 1931-   **CLC 34**
See also CA 9-12R; CANR 7; DLB 103

Bruce, Lenny   **CLC 21**
See also Schneider, Leonard Alfred

Bruin, John
See Brutus, Dennis

Brulard, Henri
See Stendhal

Brulls, Christian
See Simenon, Georges (Jacques Christian)

Brunner, John (Kilian Houston) 1934-1995
CLC 8, 10; DAM POP
See also CA 1-4R; 149; CAAS 8; CANR 2, 37;
MTCW 1, 2

Bruno, Giordano 1548-1600   **LC 27**

Brutus, Dennis 1924- **CLC 43; BLC 1; DAM
MULT, POET; PC 24**
See also BW 2, 3; CA 49-52; CAAS 14; CANR
2, 27, 42, 81; DLB 117

Bryan, C(ourtlandt) D(ixon) B(arnes) 1936-
CLC 29
See also CA 73-76; CANR 13, 68; DLB 185;
INT CANR-13

Bryan, Michael
See Moore, Brian

Bryant, William Cullen 1794-1878 **NCLC 6,
46; DA; DAB; DAC; DAM MST, POET;
PC 20**
See also CDALB 1640-1865; DLB 3, 43, 59,
189

Bryusov, Valery Yakovlevich 1873-1924
TCLC 10
See also CA 107; 155

Buchan, John 1875-1940   **TCLC 41; DAB;
DAM POP**
See also CA 108; 145; DLB 34, 70, 156; MTCW
1; YABC 2

Buchanan, George 1506-1582   **LC 4**
See also DLB 152

Buchheim, Lothar-Guenther 1918-   **CLC 6**
See also CA 85-88

Buchner, (Karl) Georg 1813-1837 **NCLC 26**

Buchwald, Art(hur) 1925-   **CLC 33**
See also AITN 1; CA 5-8R; CANR 21, 67;
MTCW 1, 2; SATA 10

Buck, Pearl S(ydenstricker) 1892-1973 **CLC 7,
11, 18; DA; DAB; DAC; DAM MST, NOV**
See also AITN 1; CA 1-4R; 41-44R; CANR 1,
34; CDALBS; DLB 9, 102; MTCW 1, 2;
SATA 1, 25

Buckler, Ernest 1908-1984   **CLC 13; DAC;
DAM MST**
See also CA 11-12; 114; CAP 1; DLB 68; SATA
47

Buckley, Vincent (Thomas) 1925-1988 **CLC 57**
See also CA 101

Buckley, William F(rank), Jr. 1925- **CLC 7, 18,
37; DAM POP**
See also AITN 1; CA 1-4R; CANR 1, 24, 53;
DLB 137; DLBY 80; INT CANR-24; MTCW
1, 2

Buechner, (Carl) Frederick 1926- **CLC 2, 4, 6,
9; DAM NOV**
See also CA 13-16R; CANR 11, 39, 64; DLBY
80; INT CANR-11; MTCW 1, 2

Buell, John (Edward) 1927-   **CLC 10**
See also CA 1-4R; CANR 71; DLB 53

Buero Vallejo, Antonio 1916-   **CLC 15, 46**
See also CA 106; CANR 24, 49, 75; HW 1;
MTCW 1, 2

Bufalino, Gesualdo 1920(?)-   **CLC 74**
See also DLB 196

Bugayev, Boris Nikolayevich 1880-1934
TCLC 7; PC 11
See also Bely, Andrey
See also CA 104; 165; MTCW 1

Bukowski, Charles 1920-1994 **CLC 2, 5, 9, 41,
82, 108; DAM NOV, POET; PC 18**
See also CA 17-20R; 144; CANR 40, 62; DLB
5, 130, 169; MTCW 1, 2

Bulgakov, Mikhail (Afanas'evich) 1891-1940
TCLC 2, 16; DAM DRAM, NOV; SSC 18
See also CA 105; 152

Bulgya, Alexander Alexandrovich 1901-1956
TCLC 53
See also Fadeyev, Alexander
See also CA 117

Bullins, Ed 1935- **CLC 1, 5, 7; BLC 1; DAM
DRAM, MULT; DC 6**
See also BW 2, 3; CA 49-52; CAAS 16; CANR
24, 46, 73; DLB 7, 38; MTCW 1, 2

Bulwer-Lytton, Edward (George Earle Lytton)
1803-1873   **NCLC 1, 45**
See also DLB 21

Bunin, Ivan Alexeyevich 1870-1953 **TCLC 6;
SSC 5**
See also CA 104

Bunting, Basil 1900-1985   **CLC 10, 39, 47;
DAM POET**
See also CA 53-56; 115; CANR 7; DLB 20

Bunuel, Luis 1900-1983   **CLC 16, 80; DAM
MULT; HLC 1**
See also CA 101; 110; CANR 32, 77; HW 1

Bunyan, John 1628-1688   **LC 4; DA; DAB;
DAC; DAM MST; WLC**
See also CDBLB 1660-1789; DLB 39

Burckhardt, Jacob (Christoph) 1818-1897
NCLC 49

Burford, Eleanor
See Hibbert, Eleanor Alice Burford

See Fisher, Dorothy (Frances) Canfield
Canin, Ethan 1960- **CLC 55**
See also CA 131; 135
Cannon, Curt
See Hunter, Evan
Cao, Lan 1961- **CLC 109**
See also CA 165
Cape, Judith
See Page, P(atricia) K(athleen)
Capek, Karel 1890-1938 **TCLC 6, 37; DA;
DAB; DAC; DAM DRAM, MST, NOV; DC
1; WLC**
See also CA 104; 140; MTCW 1
Capote, Truman 1924-1984**CLC 1, 3, 8, 13, 19,
34, 38, 58; DA; DAB; DAC; DAM MST,
NOV, POP; SSC 2; WLC**
See also CA 5-8R; 113; CANR 18, 62; CDALB
1941-1968; DLB 2, 185; DLBY 80, 84;
MTCW 1, 2; SATA 91
Capra, Frank 1897-1991 **CLC 16**
See also CA 61-64; 135
Caputo, Philip 1941- **CLC 32**
See also CA 73-76; CANR 40
Caragiale, Ion Luca 1852-1912 **TCLC 76**
See also CA 157
Card, Orson Scott 1951-**CLC 44, 47, 50; DAM
POP**
See also AAYA 11; CA 102; CANR 27, 47, 73;
INT CANR-27; MTCW 1, 2; SATA 83
Cardenal, Ernesto 1925- **CLC 31; DAM
MULT, POET; HLC 1; PC 22**
See also CA 49-52; CANR 2, 32, 66; HW 1, 2;
MTCW 1, 2
Cardozo, Benjamin N(athan) 1870-1938
TCLC 65
See also CA 117; 164
Carducci, Giosue (Alessandro Giuseppe) 1835-
1907 **TCLC 32**
See also CA 163
Carew, Thomas 1595(?)-1640 **LC 13**
See also DLB 126
Carey, Ernestine Gilbreth 1908- **CLC 17**
See also CA 5-8R; CANR 71; SATA 2
Carey, Peter 1943- **CLC 40, 55, 96**
See also CA 123; 127; CANR 53, 76; INT 127;
MTCW 1, 2; SATA 94
Carleton, William 1794-1869 **NCLC 3**
See also DLB 159
Carlisle, Henry (Coffin) 1926- **CLC 33**
See also CA 13-16R; CANR 15
Carlsen, Chris
See Holdstock, Robert P.
Carlson, Ron(ald F.) 1947- **CLC 54**
See also CA 105; CANR 27
Carlyle, Thomas 1795-1881 **NCLC 70; DA;
DAB; DAC; DAM MST**
See also CDBLB 1789-1832; DLB 55; 144
Carman, (William) Bliss 1861-1929 **TCLC 7;
DAC**
See also CA 104; 152; DLB 92
Carnegie, Dale 1888-1955 **TCLC 53**
Carossa, Hans 1878-1956 **TCLC 48**
See also CA 170; DLB 66
Carpenter, Don(ald Richard) 1931-1995**C L C
41**
See also CA 45-48; 149; CANR 1, 71
Carpenter, Edward 1844-1929 **TCLC 88**
See also CA 163
Carpentier (y Valmont), Alejo 1904-1980**CLC
8, 11, 38, 110; DAM MULT; HLC 1; SSC
35**
See also CA 65-68; 97-100; CANR 11, 70, DLB
113; HW 1, 2

Carr, Caleb 1955(?)- **CLC 86**
See also CA 147; CANR 73
Carr, Emily 1871-1945 **TCLC 32**
See also CA 159; DLB 68
Carr, John Dickson 1906-1977 **CLC 3**
See also Fairbairn, Roger
See also CA 49-52; 69-72; CANR 3, 33, 60;
MTCW 1, 2
Carr, Philippa
See Hibbert, Eleanor Alice Burford
Carr, Virginia Spencer 1929- **CLC 34**
See also CA 61-64; DLB 111
Carrere, Emmanuel 1957- **CLC 89**
Carrier, Roch 1937-**CLC 13, 78; DAC; DAM
MST**
See also CA 130; CANR 61; DLB 53; SATA
105
Carroll, James P. 1943(?)- **CLC 38**
See also CA 81-84; CANR 73; MTCW 1
Carroll, Jim 1951- **CLC 35**
See also AAYA 17; CA 45-48; CANR 42
Carroll, Lewis **NCLC 2, 53; PC 18; WLC**
See also Dodgson, Charles Lutwidge
See also CDBLB 1832-1890; CLR 2, 18; DLB
18, 163, 178; DLBY 98; JRDA
Carroll, Paul Vincent 1900-1968 **CLC 10**
See also CA 9-12R; 25-28R; DLB 10
Carruth, Hayden 1921- **CLC 4, 7, 10, 18, 84;
PC 10**
See also CA 9-12R; CANR 4, 38, 59; DLB 5,
165; INT CANR-4; MTCW 1, 2; SATA 47
Carson, Rachel Louise 1907-1964 **CLC 71;
DAM POP**
See also CA 77-80; CANR 35; MTCW 1, 2;
SATA 23
Carter, Angela (Olive) 1940-1992 **CLC 5, 41,
76; SSC 13**
See also CA 53-56; 136; CANR 12, 36, 61; DLB
14, 207; MTCW 1, 2; SATA 66; SATA-Obit
70
Carter, Nick
See Smith, Martin Cruz
Carver, Raymond 1938-1988 **CLC 22, 36, 53,
55; DAM NOV; SSC 8**
See also CA 33-36R; 126; CANR 17, 34, 61;
DLB 130; DLBY 84, 88; MTCW 1, 2
Cary, Elizabeth, Lady Falkland 1585-1639
LC 30
Cary, (Arthur) Joyce (Lunel) 1888-1957
TCLC 1, 29
See also CA 104; 164; CDBLB 1914-1945;
DLB 15, 100; MTCW 2
Casanova de Seingalt, Giovanni Jacopo 1725-
1798 **LC 13**
Casares, Adolfo Bioy
See Bioy Casares, Adolfo
Casely-Hayford, J(oseph) E(phraim) 1866-1930
TCLC 24; BLC 1; DAM MULT
See also BW 2; CA 123; 152
Casey, John (Dudley) 1939- **CLC 59**
See also BEST 90:2; CA 69-72; CANR 23
Casey, Michael 1947- **CLC 2**
See also CA 65-68; DLB 5
Casey, Patrick
See Thurman, Wallace (Henry)
Casey, Warren (Peter) 1935-1988 **CLC 12**
See also CA 101; 127; INT 101
Casona, Alejandro **CLC 49**
See also Alvarez, Alejandro Rodriguez
Cassavetes, John 1929-1989 **CLC 20**
See also CA 85-88; 127; CANR 82
Cassian, Nina 1924- **PC 17**
Cassill, R(onald) V(erlin) 1919- **CLC 4, 23**

See also CA 9-12R; CAAS 1; CANR 7, 45; DLB
6
Cassirer, Ernst 1874-1945 **TCLC 61**
See also CA 157
Cassity, (Allen) Turner 1929- **CLC 6, 42**
See also CA 17-20R; CAAS 8; CANR 11; DLB
105
Castaneda, Carlos (Cesar Aranha) 1931(?)-
1998 **CLC 12, 119**
See also CA 25-28R; CANR 32, 66; HW 1;
MTCW 1
Castedo, Elena 1937- **CLC 65**
See also CA 132
Castedo-Ellerman, Elena
See Castedo, Elena
Castellanos, Rosario 1925-1974**CLC 66; DAM
MULT; HLC 1**
See also CA 131; 53-56; CANR 58; DLB 113;
HW 1; MTCW 1
Castelvetro, Lodovico 1505-1571 **LC 12**
Castiglione, Baldassare 1478-1529 **LC 12**
Castle, Robert
See Hamilton, Edmond
Castro (Ruz), Fidel 1926(?)-
See also CA 110; 129; CANR 81; DAM MULT;
HLC 1; HW 2
Castro, Guillen de 1569-1631 **LC 19**
Castro, Rosalia de 1837-1885 **NCLC 3, 78;
DAM MULT**
Cather, Willa
See Cather, Willa Sibert
Cather, Willa Sibert 1873-1947 **TCLC 1, 11,
31; DA; DAB; DAC; DAM MST, NOV;
SSC 2; WLC**
See also AAYA 24; CA 104; 128; CDALB 1865-
1917; DLB 9, 54, 78; DLBD 1; MTCW 1, 2;
SATA 30
Catherine, Saint 1347-1380 **CMLC 27**
Cato, Marcus Porcius 234B.C.-149B.C.
CMLC 21
See also DLB 211
Catton, (Charles) Bruce 1899-1978 **CLC 35**
See also AITN 1; CA 5-8R; 81-84; CANR 7,
74; DLB 17; SATA 2; SATA-Obit 24
Catullus c. 84B.C.-c. 54B.C. **CMLC 18**
See also DLB 211
Cauldwell, Frank
See King, Francis (Henry)
Caunitz, William J. 1933-1996 **CLC 34**
See also BEST 89:3; CA 125; 130; 152; CANR
73; INT 130
Causley, Charles (Stanley) 1917- **CLC 7**
See also CA 9-12R; CANR 5, 35; CLR 30; DLB
27; MTCW 1; SATA 3, 66
Caute, (John) David 1936-**CLC 29;DAM NOV**
See also CA 1-4R; CAAS 4; CANR 1, 33, 64;
DLB 14
Cavafy, C(onstantine) P(eter) 1863-1933
TCLC 2, 7; DAM POET
See also Kavafis, Konstantinos Petrou
See also CA 148; MTCW 1
Cavallo, Evelyn
See Spark, Muriel (Sarah)
Cavanna, Betty **CLC 12**
See also Harrison, Elizabeth Cavanna
See also JRDA; MAICYA; SAAS 4; SATA 1,
30
Cavendish, Margaret Lucas 1623-1673**LC 30**
See also DLB 131
Caxton, William 1421(?)-1491(?) **LC 17**
See also DLB 170
Cayer, D. M.
See Duffy, Maureen

See Reed, Ishmael

Coleridge, M. E.
See Coleridge, Mary E(lizabeth)

Coleridge, Mary E(lizabeth) 1861-1907**TCLC 73**
See also CA 116; 166; DLB 19, 98

Coleridge, Samuel Taylor 1772-1834**NCLC 9, 54; DA; DAB; DAC; DAM MST, POET; PC 11; WLC**
See also CDBLB 1789-1832; DLB 93, 107

Coleridge, Sara 1802-1852 **NCLC 31**
See also DLB 199

Coles, Don 1928- **CLC 46**
See also CA 115; CANR 38

Coles, Robert (Martin) 1929- **CLC 108**
See also CA 45-48; CANR 3, 32, 66, 70; INT CANR-32; SATA 23

Colette, (Sidonie-Gabrielle) 1873-1954**TCLC 1, 5, 16; DAM NOV; SSC 10**
See also CA 104; 131; DLB 65; MTCW 1, 2

Collett, (Jacobine) Camilla (Wergeland) 1813-1895 **NCLC 22**

Collier, Christopher 1930- **CLC 30**
See also AAYA 13; CA 33-36R; CANR 13, 33; JRDA; MAICYA; SATA 16, 70

Collier, James L(incoln) 1928-**CLC 30; DAM POP**
See also AAYA 13; CA 9-12R; CANR 4, 33, 60; CLR 3; JRDA; MAICYA; SAAS 21; SATA 8, 70

Collier, Jeremy 1650-1726 **LC 6**

Collier, John 1901-1980 **SSC 19**
See also CA 65-68; 97-100; CANR 10; DLB 77

Collingwood, R(obin) G(eorge) 1889(?)-1943 **TCLC 67**
See also CA 117; 155

Collins, Hunt
See Hunter, Evan

Collins, Linda 1931- **CLC 44**
See also CA 125

Collins, (William) Wilkie 1824-1889**NCLC 1, 18**
See also CDBLB 1832-1890; DLB 18, 70, 159

Collins, William 1721-1759 **LC 4, 40; DAM POET**
See also DLB 109

Collodi, Carlo 1826-1890 **NCLC 54**
See also Lorenzini, Carlo
See also CLR 5

Colman, George 1732-1794
See Glassco, John

Colt, Winchester Remington
See Hubbard, L(afayette) Ron(ald)

Colter, Cyrus 1910- **CLC 58**
See also BW 1; CA 65-68; CANR 10, 66; DLB 33

Colton, James
See Hansen, Joseph

Colum, Padraic 1881-1972 **CLC 28**
See also CA 73-76; 33-36R; CANR 35; CLR 36; MAICYA; MTCW 1; SATA 15

Colvin, James
See Moorcock, Michael (John)

Colwin, Laurie (E.) 1944-1992**CLC 5, 13, 23, 84**
See also CA 89-92; 139; CANR 20, 46; DLBY 80; MTCW 1

Comfort, Alex(ander) 1920-**CLC 7;DAM POP**
See also CA 1-4R; CANR 1, 45; MTCW 1

Comfort, Montgomery
See Campbell, (John) Ramsey

Compton-Burnett, I(vy) 1884(?)-1969 **CLC 1,**

3, 10, 15, 34; DAM NOV
See also CA 1-4R; 25-28R; CANR 4; DLB 36; MTCW 1

Comstock, Anthony 1844-1915 **TCLC 13**
See also CA 110; 169

Comte, Auguste 1798-1857 **NCLC 54**

Conan Doyle, Arthur
See Doyle, Arthur Conan

Conde (Abellan), Carmen 1901-
See also CA 177; DLB 108; HLCS 1; HW 2

Conde, Maryse 1937- **CLC 52, 92; BLCS; DAM MULT**
See also Boucolon, Maryse
See also BW 2; MTCW 1

Condillac, Etienne Bonnot de 1714-1780 **LC 26**

Condon, Richard (Thomas) 1915-1996**CLC 4, 6, 8, 10, 45, 100; DAM NOV**
See also BEST 90:3; CA 1-4R; 151; CAAS 1; CANR 2, 23; INT CANR-23; MTCW 1, 2

Confucius 551B.C.-479B.C. **CMLC 19; DA; DAB; DAC; DAM MST; WLCS**

Congreve, William 1670-1729 **LC 5, 21; DA; DAB; DAC; DAM DRAM, MST, POET; DC 2; WLC**
See also CDBLB 1660-1789; DLB 39, 84

Connell, Evan S(helby), Jr. 1924-**CLC 4, 6, 45; DAM NOV**
See also AAYA 7; CA 1-4R; CAAS 2; CANR 2, 39, 76; DLB 2; DLBY 81; MTCW 1, 2

Connelly, Marc(us Cook) 1890-1980 **CLC 7**
See also CA 85-88; 102; CANR 30; DLB 7; DLBY 80; SATA-Obit 25

Connor, Ralph **TCLC 31**
See also Gordon, Charles William
See also DLB 92

Conrad, Joseph 1857-1924**TCLC 1, 6, 13, 25, 43, 57; DA; DAB; DAC; DAM MST, NOV; SSC 9; WLC**
See also AAYA 26; CA 104; 131; CANR 60; CDBLB 1890-1914; DLB 10, 34, 98, 156; MTCW 1, 2; SATA 27

Conrad, Robert Arnold
See Hart, Moss

Conroy, Pat
See Conroy, (Donald) Pat(rick)
See also MTCW 2

Conroy, (Donald) Pat(rick) 1945-**CLC 30, 74; DAM NOV, POP**
See also Conroy, Pat
See also AAYA 8; AITN 1; CA 85-88; CANR 24, 53; DLB 6; MTCW 1

Constant (de Rebecque), (Henri) Benjamin 1767-1830 **NCLC 6**
See also DLB 119

Conybeare, Charles Augustus
See Eliot, T(homas) S(tearns)

Cook, Michael 1933- **CLC 58**
See also CA 93-96; CANR 68; DLB 53

Cook, Robin 1940- **CLC 14;DAM POP**
See also BEST 90:2; CA 108; 111; CANR 41; INT 111

Cook, Roy
See Silverberg, Robert

Cooke, Elizabeth 1948- **CLC 55**
See also CA 129

Cooke, John Esten 1830-1886 **NCLC 5**
See also DLB 3

Cooke, John Estes
See Baum, L(yman) Frank

Cooke, M. E.
See Creasey, John

Cooke, Margaret

See Creasey, John

Cook-Lynn, Elizabeth 1930- **CLC 93;DAM MULT**
See also CA 133; DLB 175; NNAL

Cooney, Ray **CLC 62**

Cooper, Douglas 1960- **CLC 86**

Cooper, Henry St. John
See Creasey, John

Cooper, J(oan) California (?)-**CLC 56; DAM MULT**
See also AAYA 12; BW 1; CA 125; CANR 55; DLB 212

Cooper, James Fenimore 1789-1851**NCLC 1, 27, 54**
See also AAYA 22; CDALB 1640-1865; DLB 3; SATA 19

Coover, Robert (Lowell) 1932- **CLC 3, 7, 15, 32, 46, 87; DAM NOV; SSC 15**
See also CA 45-48; CANR 3, 37, 58; DLB 2; DLBY 81; MTCW 1, 2

Copeland, Stewart (Armstrong) 1952-**CLC 26**

Copernicus, Nicolaus 1473-1543 **LC 45**

Coppard, A(lfred) E(dgar) 1878-1957 **TCLC 5; SSC 21**
See also CA 114; 167; DLB 162; YABC 1

Coppee, Francois 1842-1908 **TCLC 25**
See also CA 170

Coppola, Francis Ford 1939- **CLC 16**
See also CA 77-80; CANR 40, 78; DLB 44

Corbiere, Tristan 1845-1875 **NCLC 43**

Corcoran, Barbara 1911- **CLC 17**
See also AAYA 14; CA 21-24R; CAAS 2; CANR 11, 28, 48; CLR 50; DLB 52; JRDA; SAAS 20; SATA 3, 77

Cordelier, Maurice
See Giraudoux, (Hippolyte) Jean

Corelli, Marie 1855-1924 **TCLC 51**
See also Mackay, Mary
See also DLB 34, 156

Corman, Cid 1924- **CLC 9**
See also Corman, Sidney
See also CAAS 2; DLB 5, 193

Corman, Sidney 1924-
See Corman, Cid
See also CA 85-88; CANR 44; DAM POET

Cormier, Robert (Edmund) 1925-**CLC 12, 30; DA; DAB; DAC; DAM MST, NOV**
See also AAYA 3, 19; CA 1-4R; CANR 5, 23, 76; CDALB 1968-1988; CLR 12, 55; DLB 52; INT CANR-23; JRDA; MAICYA; MTCW 1, 2; SATA 10, 45, 83

Corn, Alfred (DeWitt, III) 1943- **CLC 33**
See also CA 179; CAAE 179; CAAS 25; CANR 44; DLB 120; DLBY 80

Corneille, Pierre 1606-1684 **LC 28; DAB; DAM MST**

Cornwell, David (John Moore) 1931- **CLC 9, 15; DAM POP**
See also le Carre, John
See also CA 5-8R; CANR 13, 33, 59; MTCW 1, 2

Corso, (Nunzio) Gregory 1930- **CLC 1, 11**
See also CA 5-8R; CANR 41, 76; DLB 5, 16; MTCW 1, 2

Cortazar, Julio 1914-1984**CLC 2, 3, 5, 10, 13, 15, 33, 34, 92; DAM MULT, NOV; HLC 1; SSC 7**
See also CA 21-24R; CANR 12, 32, 81; DLB 113; HW 1, 2; MTCW 1, 2

Cortes, Hernan 1484-1547 **LC 31**

Corvinus, Jakob
See Raabe, Wilhelm (Karl)

Corwin, Cecil

Difusa, Pati
See Almodovar, Pedro
Dillard, Annie 1945- **CLC 9, 60, 115; DAM NOV**
See also AAYA 6; CA 49-52; CANR 3, 43, 62; DLBY 80; MTCW 1, 2; SATA 10
Dillard, R(ichard) H(enry) W(ilde) 1937- **CLC 5**
See also CA 21-24R; CAAS 7; CANR 10; DLB 5
Dillon, Eilis 1920-1994 **CLC 17**
See also CA 9-12R; 147; CAAS 3; CANR 4, 38, 78; CLR 26; MAICYA; SATA 2, 74; SATA-Essay 105; SATA-Obit 83
Dimont, Penelope
See Mortimer, Penelope (Ruth)
Dinesen, Isak **CLC 10, 29, 95; SSC 7**
See also Blixen, Karen (Christentze Dinesen)
See also MTCW 1
Ding Ling **CLC 68**
See also Chiang, Pin-chin
Diphusa, Patty
See Almodovar, Pedro
Disch, Thomas M(ichael) 1940- **CLC 7, 36**
See also AAYA 17; CA 21-24R; CAAS 4; CANR 17, 36, 54; CLR 18; DLB 8; MAICYA; MTCW 1, 2; SAAS 15; SATA 92
Disch, Tom
See Disch, Thomas M(ichael)
d'Isly, Georges
See Simenon, Georges (Jacques Christian)
Disraeli, Benjamin 1804-1881 **NCLC 2, 39, 79**
See also DLB 21, 55
Ditcum, Steve
See Crumb, R(obert)
Dixon, Paige
See Corcoran, Barbara
Dixon, Stephen 1936- **CLC 52; SSC 16**
See also CA 89-92; CANR 17, 40, 54; DLB 130
Doak, Annie
See Dillard, Annie
Dobell, Sydney Thompson 1824-1874 **NCLC 43**
See also DLB 32
Doblin, Alfred **TCLC 13**
See also Doeblin, Alfred
Dobrolyubov, Nikolai Alexandrovich 1836-1861 **NCLC 5**
Dobson, Austin 1840-1921 **TCLC 79**
See also DLB 35; 144
Dobyns, Stephen 1941- **CLC 37**
See also CA 45-48; CANR 2, 18
Doctorow, E(dgar) L(aurence) 1931- **CLC 6, 11, 15, 18, 37, 44, 65, 113; DAM NOV, POP**
See also AAYA 22; AITN 2; BEST 89:3; CA 45-48; CANR 2, 33, 51, 76; CDALB 1968-1988; DLB 2, 28, 173; DLBY 80; MTCW 1, 2
Dodgson, Charles Lutwidge 1832-1898
See Carroll, Lewis
See also CLR 2; DA; DAB; DAC; DAM MST, NOV, POET; MAICYA; SATA 100; YABC 2
Dodson, Owen (Vincent) 1914-1983 **CLC 79; BLC 1; DAM MULT**
See also BW 1; CA 65-68; 110; CANR 24; DLB 76
Doeblin, Alfred 1878-1957 **TCLC 13**
See also Doblin, Alfred
See also CA 110; 141; DLB 66
Doerr, Harriet 1910- **CLC 34**
See also CA 117; 122; CANR 47; INT 122
Domecq, H(onorio Bustos)
See Bioy Casares, Adolfo

Domecq, H(onorio) Bustos
See Bioy Casares, Adolfo; Borges, Jorge Luis
Domini, Rey
See Lorde, Audre (Geraldine)
Dominique
See Proust, (Valentin-Louis-George-Eugene-) Marcel
Don, A
See Stephen, Sir Leslie
Donaldson, Stephen R. 1947- **CLC 46; DAM POP**
See also CA 89-92; CANR 13, 55; INT CANR-13
Donleavy, J(ames) P(atrick) 1926- **CLC 1, 4, 6, 10, 45**
See also AITN 2; CA 9-12R; CANR 24, 49, 62, 80; DLB 6, 173; INT CANR-24; MTCW 1, 2
Donne, John 1572-1631 **LC 10, 24; DA; DAB; DAC; DAM MST, POET; PC 1; WLC**
See also CDBLB Before 1660; DLB 121, 151
Donnell, David 1939(?)- **CLC 34**
Donoghue, P. S.
See Hunt, E(verette) Howard, (Jr.)
Donoso (Yanez), Jose 1924-1996 **CLC 4, 8, 11, 32, 99; DAM MULT; HLC 1; SSC 34**
See also CA 81-84; 155; CANR 32, 73; DLB 113; HW 1, 2; MTCW 1, 2
Donovan, John 1928-1992 **CLC 35**
See also AAYA 20; CA 97-100; 137; CLR 3; MAICYA; SATA 72; SATA-Brief 29
Don Roberto
See Cunninghame Graham, R(obert) B(ontine)
Doolittle, Hilda 1886-1961 **CLC 3, 8, 14, 31, 34, 73; DA; DAC; DAM MST, POET; PC 5; WLC**
See also H. D.
See also CA 97-100; CANR 35; DLB 4, 45; MTCW 1, 2
Dorfman, Ariel 1942- **CLC 48, 77; DAM MULT; HLC 1**
See also CA 124; 130; CANR 67, 70; HW 1, 2; INT 130
Dorn, Edward (Merton) 1929- **CLC 10, 18**
See also CA 93-96; CANR 42, 79; DLB 5; INT 93-96
Dorris, Michael (Anthony) 1945-1997 **CLC 109; DAM MULT, NOV**
See also AAYA 20; BEST 90:1; CA 102; 157; CANR 19, 46, 75; CLR 58; DLB 175; MTCW 2; NNAL; SATA 75; SATA-Obit 94
Dorris, Michael A.
See Dorris, Michael (Anthony)
Dorsan, Luc
See Simenon, Georges (Jacques Christian)
Dorsange, Jean
See Simenon, Georges (Jacques Christian)
Dos Passos, John (Roderigo) 1896-1970 **CLC 1, 4, 8, 11, 15, 25, 34, 82; DA; DAB; DAC; DAM MST, NOV; WLC**
See also CA 1-4R; 29-32R; CANR 3; CDALB 1929-1941; DLB 4, 9; DLBD 1, 15; DLBY 96; MTCW 1, 2
Dossage, Jean
See Simenon, Georges (Jacques Christian)
Dostoevsky, Fedor Mikhailovich 1821-1881 **NCLC 2, 7, 21, 33, 43; DA; DAB; DAC; DAM MST, NOV; SSC 2, 33; WLC**
Doughty, Charles M(ontagu) 1843-1926 **TCLC 27**
See also CA 115; 178; DLB 19, 57, 174
Douglas, Ellen **CLC 73**
See also Haxton, Josephine Ayres; Williamson,

Ellen Douglas
Douglas, Gavin 1475(?)-1522 **LC 20**
See also DLB 132
Douglas, George
See Brown, George Douglas
Douglas, Keith (Castellain) 1920-1944 **TCLC 40**
See also CA 160; DLB 27
Douglas, Leonard
See Bradbury, Ray (Douglas)
Douglas, Michael
See Crichton, (John) Michael
Douglas, (George) Norman 1868-1952 **TCLC 68**
See also CA 119; 157; DLB 34, 195
Douglas, William
See Brown, George Douglas
Douglass, Frederick 1817(?)-1895 **NCLC 7, 55; BLC 1; DA; DAC; DAM MST, MULT; WLC**
See also CDALB 1640-1865; DLB 1, 43, 50, 79; SATA 29
Dourado, (Waldomiro Freitas) Autran 1926- **CLC 23, 60**
See also Autran Dourado, Waldomiro Freitas
See also CA 179; CANR 34, 81; DLB 145; HW 2
Dourado, Waldomiro Autran 1926-
See Dourado, (Waldomiro Freitas) Autran
See also CA 179
Dove, Rita (Frances) 1952- **CLC 50, 81; BLCS; DAM MULT, POET; PC 6**
See also BW 2; CA 109; CAAS 19; CANR 27, 42, 68, 76; CDALBS; DLB 120; MTCW 1
Doveglion
See Villa, Jose Garcia
Dowell, Coleman 1925-1985 **CLC 60**
See also CA 25-28R; 117; CANR 10; DLB 130
Dowson, Ernest (Christopher) 1867-1900 **TCLC 4**
See also CA 105; 150; DLB 19, 135
Doyle, A. Conan
See Doyle, Arthur Conan
Doyle, Arthur Conan 1859-1930 **TCLC 7; DA; DAB; DAC; DAM MST, NOV; SSC 12; WLC**
See also AAYA 14; CA 104; 122; CDBLB 1890-1914; DLB 18, 70, 156, 178; MTCW 1, 2; SATA 24
Doyle, Conan
See Doyle, Arthur Conan
Doyle, John
See Graves, Robert (von Ranke)
Doyle, Roddy 1958(?)- **CLC 81**
See also AAYA 14; CA 143; CANR 73; DLB 194
Doyle, Sir A. Conan
See Doyle, Arthur Conan
Doyle, Sir Arthur Conan
See Doyle, Arthur Conan
Dr. A
See Asimov, Isaac; Silverstein, Alvin
Drabble, Margaret 1939- **CLC 2, 3, 5, 8, 10, 22, 53; DAB; DAC; DAM MST, NOV, POP**
See also CA 13-16R; CANR 18, 35, 63; CDBLB 1960 to Present; DLB 14, 155; MTCW 1, 2; SATA 48
Drapier, M. B.
See Swift, Jonathan
Drayham, James
See Mencken, H(enry) L(ouis)
Drayton, Michael 1563-1631 **LC 8; DAM POET**

Feige, Hermann Albert Otto Maximilian
See Traven, B.

Feinberg, David B. 1956-1994   **CLC 59**
See also CA 135; 147

Feinstein, Elaine 1930-   **CLC 36**
See also CA 69-72; CAAS 1; CANR 31, 68;
DLB 14, 40; MTCW 1

Feldman, Irving (Mordecai) 1928-   **CLC 7**
See also CA 1-4R; CANR 1; DLB 169

Felix-Tchicaya, Gerald
See Tchicaya, Gerald Felix

Fellini, Federico 1920-1993   **CLC 16, 85**
See also CA 65-68; 143; CANR 33

Felsen, Henry Gregor 1916-   **CLC 17**
See also CA 1-4R; CANR 1; SAAS 2; SATA 1

Fenno, Jack
See Calisher, Hortense

Fenollosa, Ernest (Francisco) 1853-1908
TCLC 91

Fenton, James Martin 1949-   **CLC 32**
See also CA 102; DLB 40

Ferber, Edna 1887-1968   **CLC 18, 93**
See also AITN 1; CA 5-8R; 25-28R; CANR 68;
DLB 9, 28, 86; MTCW 1, 2; SATA 7

Ferguson, Helen
See Kavan, Anna

Ferguson, Samuel 1810-1886   **NCLC 33**
See also DLB 32

Fergusson, Robert 1750-1774   **LC 29**
See also DLB 109

Ferling, Lawrence
See Ferlinghetti, Lawrence (Monsanto)

Ferlinghetti, Lawrence (Monsanto) 1919(?)-
CLC 2, 6, 10, 27, 111; DAM POET; PC 1
See also CA 5-8R; CANR 3, 41, 73; CDALB
1941-1968; DLB 5, 16; MTCW 1, 2

Fernandez, Vicente Garcia Huidobro
See Huidobro Fernandez, Vicente Garcia

Ferre, Rosario 1942-
See also CA 131; CANR 55, 81; DLB 145;
HLCS 1; HW 1, 2; MTCW 1

Ferrer, Gabriel (Francisco Victor) Miro
See Miro (Ferrer), Gabriel (Francisco Victor)

Ferrier, Susan (Edmonstone) 1782-1854
NCLC 8
See also DLB 116

Ferrigno, Robert 1948(?)-   **CLC 65**
See also CA 140

Ferron, Jacques 1921-1985   **CLC 94; DAC**
See also CA 117; 129; DLB 60

Feuchtwanger, Lion 1884-1958   **TCLC 3**
See also CA 104; DLB 66

Feuillet, Octave 1821-1890   **NCLC 45**
See also DLB 192

Feydeau, Georges (Leon Jules Marie) 1862-
1921   **TCLC 22; DAM DRAM**
See also CA 113; 152; DLB 192

Fichte, Johann Gottlieb 1762-1814 **NCLC 62**
See also DLB 90

Ficino, Marsilio 1433-1499   **LC 12**

Fiedeler, Hans
See Doeblin, Alfred

Fiedler, Leslie A(aron) 1917-   **CLC 4, 13, 24**
See also CA 9-12R; CANR 7, 63; DLB 28, 67;
MTCW 1, 2

Field, Andrew 1938-   **CLC 44**
See also CA 97-100; CANR 25

Field, Eugene 1850-1895   **NCLC 3**
See also DLB 23, 42, 140; DLBD 13; MAICYA;
SATA 16

Field, Gans T.
See Wellman, Manly Wade

Field, Michael 1915-1971   **TCLC 43**

See also CA 29-32R

Field, Peter
See Hobson, Laura Z(ametkin)

Fielding, Henry 1707-1754   **LC 1, 46; DA;
DAB; DAC; DAM DRAM, MST, NOV;
WLC**
See also CDBLB 1660-1789; DLB 39, 84, 101

Fielding, Sarah 1710-1768   **LC 1, 44**
See also DLB 39

Fields, W. C. 1880-1946   **TCLC 80**
See also DLB 44

Fierstein, Harvey (Forbes) 1954-   **CLC 33;
DAM DRAM, POP**
See also CA 123; 129

Figes, Eva 1932-   **CLC 31**
See also CA 53-56; CANR 4, 44; DLB 14

Finch, Anne 1661-1720   **LC 3; PC 21**
See also DLB 95

Finch, Robert (Duer Claydon) 1900- **CLC 18**
See also CA 57-60; CANR 9, 24, 49; DLB 88

Findley, Timothy 1930-   **CLC 27, 102; DAC;
DAM MST**
See also CA 25-28R; CANR 12, 42, 69; DLB
53

Fink, William
See Mencken, H(enry) L(ouis)

Firbank, Louis 1942-
See Reed, Lou
See also CA 117

Firbank, (Arthur Annesley) Ronald 1886-1926
TCLC 1
See also CA 104; 177; DLB 36

Fisher, Dorothy (Frances) Canfield 1879-1958
TCLC 87
See also CA 114; 136; CANR 80; DLB 9, 102;
MAICYA; YABC 1

Fisher, M(ary) F(rances) K(ennedy) 1908-1992
CLC 76, 87
See also CA 77-80; 138; CANR 44; MTCW 1

Fisher, Roy 1930-   **CLC 25**
See also CA 81-84; CAAS 10; CANR 16; DLB
40

Fisher, Rudolph 1897-1934 **TCLC 11; BLC 2;
DAM MULT; SSC 25**
See also BW 1, 3; CA 107; 124; CANR 80; DLB
51, 102

Fisher, Vardis (Alvero) 1895-1968   **CLC 7**
See also CA 5-8R; 25-28R; CANR 68; DLB 9,
206

Fiske, Tarleton 1917-1994
See Bloch, Robert (Albert)
See also CA 179; CAAE 179

Fitch, Clarke
See Sinclair, Upton (Beall)

Fitch, John IV
See Cormier, Robert (Edmund)

Fitzgerald, Captain Hugh
See Baum, L(yman) Frank

FitzGerald, Edward 1809-1883   **NCLC 9**
See also DLB 32

Fitzgerald, F(rancis) Scott (Key) 1896-1940
**TCLC 1, 6, 14, 28, 55; DA; DAB; DAC;
DAM MST, NOV; SSC 6, 31; WLC**
See also AAYA 24; AITN 1; CA 110; 123;
CDALB 1917-1929; DLB 4, 9, 86; DLBD 1,
15, 16; DLBY 81, 96; MTCW 1, 2

Fitzgerald, Penelope 1916-   **CLC 19, 51, 61**
See also CA 85-88; CAAS 10; CANR 56; DLB
14, 194; MTCW 1

Fitzgerald, Robert (Stuart) 1910-1985 **CLC 39**
See also CA 1-4R; 114; CANR 1; DLBY 80

FitzGerald, Robert D(avid) 1902-1987 **CLC 19**
See also CA 17-20R

Fitzgerald, Zelda (Sayre) 1900-1948 **TCLC 52**
See also CA 117; 126; DLBY 84

Flanagan, Thomas (James Bonner) 1923-
CLC 25, 52
See also CA 108; CANR 55; DLBY 80; INT
108; MTCW 1

Flaubert, Gustave 1821-1880 **NCLC 2, 10, 19,
62, 66; DA; DAB; DAC; DAM MST, NOV;
SSC 11; WLC**
See also DLB 119

Flecker, Herman Elroy
See Flecker, (Herman) James Elroy

Flecker, (Herman) James Elroy 1884-1915
TCLC 43
See also CA 109; 150; DLB 10, 19

Fleming, Ian (Lancaster) 1908-1964   **CLC 3,
30; DAM POP**
See also AAYA 26; CA 5-8R; CANR
59; CDBLB 1945-1960; DLB 87, 201;
MTCW 1, 2; SATA 9

Fleming, Thomas (James) 1927-   **CLC 37**
See also CA 5-8R; CANR 10; INT CANR-10;
SATA 8

Fletcher, John 1579-1625   **LC 33; DC 6**
See also CDBLB Before 1660; DLB 58

Fletcher, John Gould 1886-1950   **TCLC 35**
See also CA 107; 167; DLB 4, 45

Fleur, Paul
See Pohl, Frederik

Flooglebuckle, Al
See Spiegelman, Art

Flying Officer X
See Bates, H(erbert) E(rnest)

Fo, Dario 1926-   **CLC 32, 109; DAM DRAM;
DC 10**
See also CA 116; 128; CANR 68; DLBY 97;
MTCW 1, 2

Fogarty, Jonathan Titulescu Esq.
See Farrell, James T(homas)

Folke, Will 1917-1994
See Bloch, Robert (Albert); Bloch, Robert
(Albert)
See also CA 179; CAAE 179

Follett, Ken(neth Martin) 1949-   **CLC 18;
DAM NOV, POP**
See also AAYA 6; BEST 89:4; CA 81-84; CANR
13, 33, 54; DLB 87; DLBY 81; INT CANR-
33; MTCW 1

Fontane, Theodor 1819-1898   **NCLC 26**
See also DLB 129

Foote, Horton 1916- **CLC 51, 91; DAM DRAM**
See also CA 73-76; CANR 34, 51; DLB 26; INT
CANR-34

Foote, Shelby 1916- **CLC 75; DAM NOV, POP**
See also CA 5-8R; CANR 3, 45, 74; DLB 2,
17; MTCW 2

Forbes, Esther 1891-1967   **CLC 12**
See also AAYA 17; CA 13-14; 25-28R; CAP 1;
CLR 27; DLB 22; JRDA; MAICYA; SATA
2, 100

Forche, Carolyn (Louise) 1950-   **CLC 25, 83,
86; DAM POET; PC 10**
See also CA 109; 117; CANR 50, 74; DLB 5,
193; INT 117; MTCW 1

Ford, Elbur
See Hibbert, Eleanor Alice Burford

Ford, Ford Madox 1873-1939 **TCLC 1, 15, 39,
57; DAM NOV**
See also CA 104; 132; CANR 74; CDBLB
1914-1945; DLB 162; MTCW 1, 2

Ford, Henry 1863-1947   **TCLC 73**
See also CA 115; 148

Ford, John 1586-(?)   **DC 8**

See also CDBLB Before 1660; DAM DRAM;
DLB 58

Ford, John 1895-1973 **CLC 16**
See also CA 45-48

Ford, Richard 1944- **CLC 46, 99**
See also CA 69-72; CANR 11, 47; MTCW 1

Ford, Webster
See Masters, Edgar Lee

Foreman, Richard 1937- **CLC 50**
See also CA 65-68; CANR 32, 63

Forester, C(ecil) S(cott) 1899-1966 **CLC 35**
See also CA 73-76; 25-28R; DLB 191; SATA
13

Forez
See Mauriac, Francois (Charles)

Forman, James Douglas 1932- **CLC 21**
See also AAYA 17; CA 9-12R; CANR 4, 19,
42; JRDA; MAICYA; SATA 8, 70

Fornes, Maria Irene 1930-**CLC 39, 61; DC 10;
HLCS 1**
See also CA 25-28R; CANR 28, 81; DLB 7;
HW 1, 2; INT CANR-28; MTCW 1

Forrest, Leon (Richard) 1937-1997 **CLC 4;
BLCS**
See also BW 2; CA 89-92; 162; CAAS 7; CANR
25, 52; DLB 33

Forster, E(dward) M(organ) 1879-1970 **C L C
1, 2, 3, 4, 9, 10, 13, 15, 22, 45, 77; DA; DAB;
DAC; DAM MST, NOV; SSC 27;WLC**
See also AAYA 2; CA 13-14; 25-28R; CANR
45; CAP 1; CDBLB 1914-1945; DLB 34, 98,
162, 178, 195; DLBD 10; MTCW 1, 2; SATA
57

Forster, John 1812-1876 **NCLC 11**
See also DLB 144, 184

Forsyth, Frederick 1938-**CLC 2, 5, 36; DAM
NOV, POP**
See also BEST 89:4; CA 85-88; CANR 38, 62;
DLB 87; MTCW 1, 2

Forten, Charlotte L. **TCLC 16; BLC 2**
See also Grimke, Charlotte L(ottie) Forten
See also DLB 50

Foscolo, Ugo 1778-1827 **NCLC 8**

Fosse, Bob **CLC 20**
See also Fosse, Robert Louis

Fosse, Robert Louis 1927-1987
See Fosse, Bob
See also CA 110; 123

Foster, Stephen Collins 1826-1864 **NCLC 26**

Foucault, Michel 1926-1984 **CLC 31, 34, 69**
See also CA 105; 113; CANR 34; MTCW 1, 2

Fouque, Friedrich (Heinrich Karl) de la Motte
1777-1843 **NCLC 2**
See also DLB 90

Fourier, Charles 1772-1837 **NCLC 51**

Fournier, Henri Alban 1886-1914
See Alain-Fournier
See also CA 104

Fournier, Pierre 1916- **CLC 11**
See also Gascar, Pierre
See also CA 89-92; CANR 16, 40

Fowles, John (Philip) 1926- **CLC 1, 2, 3, 4, 6,
9, 10, 15, 33, 87; DAB; DAC; DAM MST;
SSC 33**
See also CA 5-8R; CANR 25, 71; CDBLB 1960
to Present; DLB 14, 139, 207; MTCW 1, 2;
SATA 22

Fox, Paula 1923- **CLC 2, 8, 121**
See also AAYA 3; CA 73-76; CANR 20, 36,
62; CLR 1, 44; DLB 52; JRDA; MAICYA;
MTCW 1; SATA 17, 60

Fox, William Price (Jr.) 1926- **CLC 22**
See also CA 17-20R; CAAS 19; CANR 11; DLB

2; DLBY 81

Foxe, John 1516(?)-1587 **LC 14**
See also DLB 132

Frame, Janet 1924-**CLC 2, 3, 6, 22, 66, 96; SSC
29**
See also Clutha, Janet Paterson Frame

France, Anatole **TCLC 9**
See also Thibault, Jacques Anatole Francois
See also DLB 123; MTCW 1

Francis, Claude 19(?)- **CLC 50**

Francis, Dick 1920-**CLC 2, 22, 42, 102; DAM
POP**
See also AAYA 5, 21; BEST 89:3; CA 5-8R;
CANR 9, 42, 68; CDBLB 1960 to Present;
DLB 87; INT CANR-9; MTCW 1, 2

Francis, Robert (Churchill) 1901-1987 **C L C
15**
See also CA 1-4R; 123; CANR 1

Frank, Anne(lies Marie) 1929-1945**TCLC 17;
DA; DAB; DAC; DAM MST; WLC**
See also AAYA 12; CA 113; 133; CANR 68;
MTCW 1, 2; SATA 87; SATA-Brief 42

Frank, Bruno 1887-1945 **TCLC 81**
See also DLB 118

Frank, Elizabeth 1945- **CLC 39**
See also CA 121; 126; CANR 78; INT 126

Frankl, Viktor E(mil) 1905-1997 **CLC 93**
See also CA 65-68; 161

Franklin, Benjamin
See Hasek, Jaroslav (Matej Frantisek)

Franklin, Benjamin 1706-1790 **LC 25; DA;
DAB; DAC; DAM MST; WLCS**
See also CDALB 1640-1865; DLB 24, 43, 73

Franklin, (Stella Maria Sarah) Miles (Lampe)
1879-1954 **TCLC 7**
See also CA 104; 164

Fraser, (Lady) Antonia (Pakenham) 1932-
CLC 32, 107
See also CA 85-88; CANR 44, 65; MTCW 1,
2; SATA-Brief 32

Fraser, George MacDonald 1925- **CLC 7**
See also CA 45-48; CANR 2, 48, 74; MTCW 1

Fraser, Sylvia 1935- **CLC 64**
See also CA 45-48; CANR 1, 16, 60

Frayn, Michael 1933-**CLC 3, 7, 31, 47; DAM
DRAM, NOV**
See also CA 5-8R; CANR 30, 69; DLB 13, 14,
194; MTCW 1, 2

Fraze, Candida (Merrill) 1945- **CLC 50**
See also CA 126

Frazer, J(ames) G(eorge) 1854-1941**TCLC 32**
See also CA 118

Frazer, Robert Caine
See Creasey, John

Frazer, Sir James George
See Frazer, J(ames) G(eorge)

Frazier, Charles 1950- **CLC 109**
See also CA 161

Frazier, Ian 1951- **CLC 46**
See also CA 130; CANR 54

Frederic, Harold 1856-1898 **NCLC 10**
See also DLB 12, 23; DLBD 13

Frederick, John
See Faust, Frederick (Schiller)

Frederick the Great 1712-1786 **LC 14**

Fredro, Aleksander 1793-1876 **NCLC 8**

Freeling, Nicolas 1927- **CLC 38**
See also CA 49-52; CAAS 12; CANR 1, 17,
50; DLB 87

Freeman, Douglas Southall 1886-1953 **T C L C
11**
See also CA 109; DLB 17; DLBD 17

Freeman, Judith 1946- **CLC 55**

See also CA 148

Freeman, Mary Eleanor Wilkins 1852-1930
TCLC 9; SSC 1
See also CA 106; 177; DLB 12, 78

Freeman, R(ichard) Austin 1862-1943 **T C L C
21**
See also CA 113; DLB 70

French, Albert 1943- **CLC 86**
See also BW 3; CA 167

French, Marilyn 1929-**CLC 10, 18, 60; DAM
DRAM, NOV, POP**
See also CA 69-72; CANR 3, 31; INT CANR-
31; MTCW 1, 2

French, Paul
See Asimov, Isaac

Freneau, Philip Morin 1752-1832 **NCLC 1**
See also DLB 37, 43

Freud, Sigmund 1856-1939 **TCLC 52**
See also CA 115; 133; CANR 69; MTCW 1, 2

Friedan, Betty (Naomi) 1921- **CLC 74**
See also CA 65-68; CANR 18, 45, 74; MTCW
1, 2

Friedlander, Saul 1932- **CLC 90**
See also CA 117; 130; CANR 72

Friedman, B(ernard) H(arper) 1926- **CLC 7**
See also CA 1-4R; CANR 3, 48

Friedman, Bruce Jay 1930- **CLC 3, 5, 56**
See also CA 9-12R; CANR 25, 52; DLB 2, 28;
INT CANR-25

Friel, Brian 1929- **CLC 5, 42, 59, 115; DC 8**
See also CA 21-24R; CANR 33, 69; DLB 13;
MTCW 1

Friis-Baastad, Babbis Ellinor 1921-1970**C L C
12**
See also CA 17-20R; 134; SATA 7

Frisch, Max (Rudolf) 1911-1991**CLC 3, 9, 14,
18, 32, 44; DAM DRAM, NOV**
See also CA 85-88; 134; CANR 32, 74; DLB
69, 124; MTCW 1, 2

Fromentin, Eugene (Samuel Auguste) 1820-
1876 **NCLC 10**
See also DLB 123

Frost, Frederick
See Faust, Frederick (Schiller)

Frost, Robert (Lee) 1874-1963**CLC 1, 3, 4, 9,
10, 13, 15, 26, 34, 44; DA; DAB; DAC;
DAM MST, POET; PC 1; WLC**
See also AAYA 21; CA 89-92; CANR 33;
CDALB 1917-1929; DLB 54; DLBD 7;
MTCW 1, 2; SATA 14

Froude, James Anthony 1818-1894 **NCLC 43**
See also DLB 18, 57, 144

Froy, Herald
See Waterhouse, Keith (Spencer)

Fry, Christopher 1907- **CLC 2, 10, 14; DAM
DRAM**
See also CA 17-20R; CAAS 23; CANR 9, 30,
74; DLB 13; MTCW 1, 2; SATA 66

Frye, (Herman) Northrop 1912-1991**CLC 24,
70**
See also CA 5-8R; 133; CANR 8, 37; DLB 67,
68; MTCW 1, 2

Fuchs, Daniel 1909-1993 **CLC 8, 22**
See also CA 81-84; 142; CAAS 5; CANR 40;
DLB 9, 26, 28; DLBY 93

Fuchs, Daniel 1934- **CLC 34**
See also CA 37-40R; CANR 14, 48

Fuentes, Carlos 1928-**CLC 3, 8, 10, 13, 22, 41,
60, 113; DA; DAB; DAC; DAM MST,
MULT, NOV; HLC 1; SSC 24;WLC**
See also AAYA 4; AITN 2; CA 69-72; CANR
10, 32, 68; DLB 113; HW 1, 2; MTCW 1, 2

Fuentes, Gregorio Lopez y

MST; DC 1; SSC 4, 29; WLC
See also DLB 198

Goines, Donald 1937(?)-1974 **CLC 80; BLC 2; DAM MULT, POP**
See also AITN 1; BW 1, 3; CA 124; 114; CANR 82; DLB 33

Gold, Herbert 1924- **CLC 4, 7, 14, 42**
See also CA 9-12R; CANR 17, 45; DLB 2; DLBY 81

Goldbarth, Albert 1948- **CLC 5, 38**
See also CA 53-56; CANR 6, 40; DLB 120

Goldberg, Anatol 1910-1982 **CLC 34**
See also CA 131; 117

Goldemberg, Isaac 1945- **CLC 52**
See also CA 69-72; CAAS 12; CANR 11, 32; HW 1

Golding, William (Gerald) 1911-1993 **CLC 1, 2, 3, 8, 10, 17, 27, 58, 81; DA; DAB; DAC; DAM MST, NOV; WLC**
See also AAYA 5; CA 5-8R; 141; CANR 13, 33, 54; CDBLB 1945-1960; DLB 15, 100; MTCW 1, 2

Goldman, Emma 1869-1940 **TCLC 13**
See also CA 110; 150

Goldman, Francisco 1954- **CLC 76**
See also CA 162

Goldman, William (W.) 1931- **CLC 1,48**
See also CA 9-12R; CANR 29, 69; DLB 44

Goldmann, Lucien 1913-1970 **CLC 24**
See also CA 25-28; CAP 2

Goldoni, Carlo 1707-1793 **LC 4; DAM DRAM**

Goldsberry, Steven 1949- **CLC 34**
See also CA 131

Goldsmith, Oliver 1728-1774 **LC 2, 48; DA; DAB; DAC; DAM DRAM, MST, NOV, POET; DC 8; WLC**
See also CDBLB 1660-1789; DLB 39, 89, 104, 109, 142; SATA 26

Goldsmith, Peter
See Priestley, J(ohn) B(oynton)

Gombrowicz, Witold 1904-1969 **CLC 4, 7, 11, 49; DAM DRAM**
See also CA 19-20; 25-28R; CAP 2

Gomez de la Serna, Ramon 1888-1963 **CLC 9**
See also CA 153; 116; CANR 79; HW 1, 2

Goncharov, Ivan Alexandrovich 1812-1891 **NCLC 1, 63**

Goncourt, Edmond (Louis Antoine Huot) de 1822-1896 **NCLC 7**
See also DLB 123

Goncourt, Jules (Alfred Huot) de 1830-1870 **NCLC 7**
See also DLB 123

Gontier, Fernande 19(?)- **CLC 50**

Gonzalez Martinez, Enrique 1871-1952 **TCLC 72**
See also CA 166; CANR 81; HW 1, 2

Goodman, Paul 1911-1972 **CLC 1, 2, 4, 7**
See also CA 19-20; 37-40R; CANR 34; CAP 2; DLB 130; MTCW 1

Gordimer, Nadine 1923- **CLC 3, 5, 7, 10, 18, 33, 51, 70; DA; DAB; DAC; DAM MST, NOV; SSC 17; WLCS**
See also CA 5-8R; CANR 3, 28, 56; INT CANR-28; MTCW 1, 2

Gordon, Adam Lindsay 1833-1870 **NCLC 21**

Gordon, Caroline 1895-1981 **CLC 6, 13, 29, 83; SSC 15**
See also CA 11-12; 103; CANR 36; CAP 1; DLB 4, 9, 102; DLBD 17; DLBY 81; MTCW 1, 2

Gordon, Charles William 1860-1937
See Connor, Ralph

See also CA 109

Gordon, Mary (Catherine) 1949- **CLC 13, 22**
See also CA 102; CANR 44; DLB 6; DLBY 81; INT 102; MTCW 1

Gordon, N. J.
See Bosman, Herman Charles

Gordon, Sol 1923- **CLC 26**
See also CA 53-56; CANR 4; SATA 11

Gordone, Charles 1925-1995 **CLC 1, 4; DAM DRAM; DC 8**
See also BW 1, 3; CA 93-96; 150; CANR 55; DLB 7; INT 93-96; MTCW 1

Gore, Catherine 1800-1861 **NCLC 65**
See also DLB 116

Gorenko, Anna Andreevna
See Akhmatova, Anna

Gorky, Maxim 1868-1936 **TCLC 8; DAB; SSC 28; WLC**
See also Peshkov, Alexei Maximovich
See also MTCW 2

Goryan, Sirak
See Saroyan, William

Gosse, Edmund (William) 1849-1928 **TCLC 28**
See also CA 117; DLB 57, 144, 184

Gotlieb, Phyllis Fay (Bloom) 1926- **CLC 18**
See also CA 13-16R; CANR 7; DLB 88

Gottesman, S. D.
See Kornbluth, C(yril) M.; Pohl, Frederik

Gottfried von Strassburg fl. c.1210- **CMLC 10**
See also DLB 138

Gould, Lois **CLC 4, 10**
See also CA 77-80; CANR 29; MTCW 1

Gourmont, Remy (-Marie-Charles) de 1858-1915 **TCLC 17**
See also CA 109; 150; MTCW 2

Govier, Katherine 1948- **CLC 51**
See also CA 101; CANR 18, 40

Goyen, (Charles) William 1915-1983 **CLC 5, 8, 14, 40**
See also AITN 2; CA 5-8R; 110; CANR 6, 71; DLB 2; DLBY 83; INT CANR-6

Goytisolo, Juan 1931- **CLC 5, 10, 23; DAM MULT; HLC 1**
See also CA 85-88; CANR 32, 61; HW 1, 2; MTCW 1, 2

Gozzano, Guido 1883-1916 **PC 10**
See also CA 154; DLB 114

Gozzi, (Conte) Carlo 1720-1806 **NCLC 23**

Grabbe, Christian Dietrich 1801-1836 **NCLC 2**
See also DLB 133

Grace, Patricia Frances 1937- **CLC 56**
See also CA 176

Gracian y Morales, Baltasar 1601-1658 **LC 15**

Gracq, Julien **CLC 11, 48**
See also Poirier, Louis
See also DLB 83

Grade, Chaim 1910-1982 **CLC 10**
See also CA 93-96; 107

Graduate of Oxford, A
See Ruskin, John

Grafton, Garth
See Duncan, Sara Jeannette

Graham, John
See Phillips, David Graham

Graham, Jorie 1951- **CLC 48, 118**
See also CA 111; CANR 63; DLB 120

Graham, R(obert) B(ontine) Cunninghame
See Cunninghame Graham, R(obert) B(ontine)
See also DLB 98, 135, 174

Graham, Robert
See Haldeman, Joe (William)

Graham, Tom

See Lewis, (Harry) Sinclair

Graham, W(illiam) S(ydney) 1918-1986 **C L C 29**
See also CA 73-76; 118; DLB 20

Graham, Winston (Mawdsley) 1910- **CLC 23**
See also CA 49-52; CANR 2, 22, 45, 66; DLB 77

Grahame, Kenneth 1859-1932 **TCLC 64; DAB**
See also CA 108; 136; CANR 80; CLR 5; DLB 34, 141, 178; MAICYA; MTCW 2; SATA 100; YABC 1

Granovsky, Timofei Nikolaevich 1813-1855 **NCLC 75**
See also DLB 198

Grant, Skeeter
See Spiegelman, Art

Granville-Barker, Harley 1877-1946 **TCLC 2; DAM DRAM**
See also Barker, Harley Granville
See also CA 104

Grass, Guenter (Wilhelm) 1927- **CLC 1, 2, 4, 6, 11, 15, 22, 32, 49, 88; DA; DAB; DAC; DAM MST, NOV; WLC**
See also CA 13-16R; CANR 20, 75; DLB 75, 124; MTCW 1, 2

Gratton, Thomas
See Hulme, T(homas) E(rnest)

Grau, Shirley Ann 1929- **CLC 4, 9; SSC 15**
See also CA 89-92; CANR 22, 69; DLB 2; INT CANR-22; MTCW 1

Gravel, Fern
See Hall, James Norman

Graver, Elizabeth 1964- **CLC 70**
See also CA 135; CANR 71

Graves, Richard Perceval 1945- **CLC 44**
See also CA 65-68; CANR 9, 26, 51

Graves, Robert (von Ranke) 1895-1985 **C L C 1, 2, 6, 11, 39, 44, 45; DAB; DAC; DAM MST, POET; PC 6**
See also CA 5-8R; 117; CANR 5, 36; CDBLB 1914-1945; DLB 20, 100, 191; DLBD 18; DLBY 85; MTCW 1, 2; SATA 45

Graves, Valerie
See Bradley, Marion Zimmer

Gray,·Alasdair (James) 1934- **CLC 41**
See also CA 126; CANR 47, 69; DLB 194; INT 126; MTCW 1, 2

Gray, Amlin 1946- **CLC 29**
See also CA 138

Gray, Francine du Plessix 1930- **CLC 22; DAM NOV**
See also BEST 90:3; CA 61-64; CAAS 2; CANR 11, 33, 75, 81; INT CANR-11; MTCW 1, 2

Gray, John (Henry) 1866-1934 **TCLC 19**
See also CA 119; 162

Gray, Simon (James Holliday) 1936- **CLC 9, 14, 36**
See also AITN 1; CA 21-24R; CAAS 3; CANR 32, 69; DLB 13; MTCW 1

Gray, Spalding 1941- **CLC 49, 112; DAM POP; DC 7**
See also CA 128; CANR 74; MTCW 2

Gray, Thomas 1716-1771 **LC 4, 40; DA; DAB; DAC; DAM MST; PC 2; WLC**
See also CDBLB 1660-1789; DLB 109

Grayson, David
See Baker, Ray Stannard

Grayson, Richard (A.) 1951- **CLC 38**
See also CA 85-88; CANR 14, 31, 57

Greeley, Andrew M(oran) 1928- **CLC 28; DAM POP**
See also CA 5-8R; CAAS 7; CANR 7, 43, 69;

MTCW 1, 2

Green, Anna Katharine 1846-1935 **TCLC 63**
See also CA 112; 159; DLB 202

Green, Brian
See Card, Orson Scott

Green, Hannah
See Greenberg, Joanne (Goldenberg)

Green, Hannah 1927(?)-1996 **CLC 3**
See also CA 73-76; CANR 59

Green, Henry 1905-1973 **CLC 2, 13, 97**
See also Yorke, Henry Vincent
See also CA 175; DLB 15

Green, Julian (Hartridge) 1900-1998
See Green, Julien
See also CA 21-24R; 169; CANR 33; DLB 4,
72; MTCW 1

Green, Julien **CLC 3, 11, 77**
See also Green, Julian (Hartridge)
See also MTCW 2

Green, Paul (Eliot) 1894-1981 **CLC 25; DAM
DRAM**
See also AITN 1; CA 5-8R; 103; CANR 3; DLB
7, 9; DLBY 81

Greenberg, Ivan 1908-1973
See Rahv, Philip
See also CA 85-88

Greenberg, Joanne (Goldenberg) 1932- **C L C
7, 30**
See also AAYA 12; CA 5-8R; CANR 14, 32,
69; SATA 25

Greenberg, Richard 1959(?)- **CLC 57**
See also CA 138

Greene, Bette 1934- **CLC 30**
See also AAYA 7; CA 53-56; CANR 4; CLR 2;
JRDA; MAICYA; SAAS 16; SATA 8, 102

Greene, Gael **CLC 8**
See also CA 13-16R; CANR 10

Greene, Graham (Henry) 1904-1991 **CLC 1, 3,
6, 9, 14, 18, 27, 37, 70, 72; DA; DAB; DAC;
DAM MST, NOV; SSC 29; WLC**
See also AITN 2; CA 13-16R; 133; CANR 35,
61; CDBLB 1945-1960; DLB 13, 15, 77,
100, 162, 201, 204; DLBY 91; MTCW 1, 2;
SATA 20

Greene, Robert 1558-1592 **LC 41**
See also DLB 62, 167

Greer, Richard
See Silverberg, Robert

Gregor, Arthur 1923- **CLC 9**
See also CA 25-28R; CAAS 10; CANR 11;
SATA 36

Gregor, Lee
See Pohl, Frederik

Gregory, Isabella Augusta (Persse) 1852-1932
TCLC 1
See also CA 104; DLB 10

Gregory, J. Dennis
See Williams, John A(lfred)

Grendon, Stephen
See Derleth, August (William)

Grenville, Kate 1950- **CLC 61**
See also CA 118; CANR 53

Grenville, Pelham
See Wodehouse, P(elham) G(renville)

Greve, Felix Paul (Berthold Friedrich) 1879-
1948
See Grove, Frederick Philip
See also CA 104; 141, 175; CANR 79; DAC;
DAM MST

Grey, Zane 1872-1939 **TCLC 6;DAM POP**
See also CA 104; 132; DLB 212; MTCW 1, 2

Grieg, (Johan) Nordahl (Brun) 1902-1943
TCLC 10

See also CA 107

Grieve, C(hristopher) M(urray) 1892-1978
CLC 11, 19; DAM POET
See also MacDiarmid, Hugh; Pteleon
See also CA 5-8R; 85-88; CANR 33; MTCW 1

Griffin, Gerald 1803-1840 **NCLC 7**
See also DLB 159

Griffin, John Howard 1920-1980 **CLC 68**
See also AITN 1; CA 1-4R; 101; CANR 2

Griffin, Peter 1942- **CLC 39**
See also CA 136

Griffith, D(avid Lewelyn) W(ark) 1875(?)-1948
TCLC 68
See also CA 119; 150; CANR 80

Griffith, Lawrence
See Griffith, D(avid Lewelyn) W(ark)

Griffiths, Trevor 1935- **CLC 13, 52**
See also CA 97-100; CANR 45; DLB 13

Griggs, Sutton Elbert 1872-1930(?) **TCLC 77**
See also CA 123; DLB 50

Grigson, Geoffrey (Edward Harvey) 1905-1985
CLC 7, 39
See also CA 25-28R; 118; CANR 20, 33; DLB
27; MTCW 1, 2

Grillparzer, Franz 1791-1872 **NCLC 1**
See also DLB 133

Grimble, Reverend Charles James
See Eliot, T(homas) S(tearns)

Grimke, Charlotte L(ottie) Forten 1837(?)-1914
See Forten, Charlotte L.
See also BW 1; CA 117; 124; DAM MULT,
POET

Grimm, Jacob Ludwig Karl 1785-1863 **NCLC
3, 77**
See also DLB 90; MAICYA; SATA 22

Grimm, Wilhelm Karl 1786-1859 **NCLC 3, 77**
See also DLB 90; MAICYA; SATA 22

Grimmelshausen, Johann Jakob Christoffel von
1621-1676 **LC 6**
See also DLB 168

Grindel, Eugene 1895-1952
See Eluard, Paul
See also CA 104

Grisham, John 1955- **CLC 84;DAM POP**
See also AAYA 14; CA 138; CANR 47, 69;
MTCW 2

Grossman, David 1954- **CLC 67**
See also CA 138

Grossman, Vasily (Semenovich) 1905-1964
CLC 41
See also CA 124; 130; MTCW 1

Grove, Frederick Philip **TCLC 4**
See also Greve, Felix Paul (Berthold Friedrich)
See also DLB 92

Grubb
See Crumb, R(obert)

Grumbach, Doris (Isaac) 1918- **CLC 13, 22, 64**
See also CA 5-8R; CAAS 2; CANR 9, 42, 70;
INT CANR-9; MTCW 2

Grundtvig, Nicolai Frederik Severin 1783-1872
NCLC 1

Grunge
See Crumb, R(obert)

Grunwald, Lisa 1959- **CLC 44**
See also CA 120

Guare, John 1938- **CLC 8, 14, 29, 67; DAM
DRAM**
See also CA 73-76; CANR 21, 69; DLB 7;
MTCW 1, 2

Gudjonsson, Halldor Kiljan 1902-1998
See Laxness, Halldor
See also CA 103; 164

Guenter, Erich

See Eich, Guenter

Guest, Barbara 1920- **CLC 34**
See also CA 25-28R; CANR 11, 44; DLB 5,
193

Guest, Edgar A(lbert) 1881-1959 **TCLC 95**
See also CA 112; 168

Guest, Judith (Ann) 1936- **CLC 8, 30; DAM
NOV, POP**
See also AAYA 7; CA 77-80; CANR 15, 75;
INT CANR-15; MTCW 1, 2

Guevara, Che **CLC 87; HLC 1**
See also Guevara (Serna), Ernesto

Guevara (Serna), Ernesto 1928-1967 **CLC 87;
DAM MULT; HLC 1**
See also Guevara, Che
See also CA 127; 111; CANR 56; HW 1

Guicciardini, Francesco 1483-1540 **LC 49**

Guild, Nicholas M. 1944- **CLC 33**
See also CA 93-96

Guillemin, Jacques
See Sartre, Jean-Paul

Guillen, Jorge 1893-1984 **CLC 11; DAM
MULT, POET; HLCS 1**
See also CA 89-92; 112; DLB 108; HW 1

Guillen, Nicolas (Cristobal) 1902-1989 **C L C
48, 79; BLC 2; DAM MST, MULT, POET;
HLC 1; PC 23**
See also BW 2; CA 116; 125; 129; HW 1

Guillevic, (Eugene) 1907- **CLC 33**
See also CA 93-96

Guillois
See Desnos, Robert

Guillois, Valentin
See Desnos, Robert

Guimaraes Rosa, Joao 1908-1967
See also CA 175; HLCS 2

Guiney, Louise Imogen 1861-1920 **TCLC 41**
See also CA 160; DLB 54

Guiraldes, Ricardo (Guillermo) 1886-1927
TCLC 39
See also CA 131; HW 1; MTCW 1

Gumilev, Nikolai (Stepanovich) 1886-1921
TCLC 60
See also CA 165

Gunesekera, Romesh 1954- **CLC 91**
See also CA 159

Gunn, Bill **CLC 5**
See also Gunn, William Harrison
See also DLB 38

Gunn, Thom(son William) 1929- **CLC 3, 6, 18,
32, 81; DAM POET; PC 26**
See also CA 17-20R; CANR 9, 33; CDBLB
1960 to Present; DLB 27; INT CANR-33;
MTCW 1

Gunn, William Harrison 1934(?)-1989
See Gunn, Bill
See also AITN 1; BW 1, 3; CA 13-16R; 128;
CANR 12, 25, 76

Gunnars, Kristjana 1948- **CLC 69**
See also CA 113; DLB 60

Gurdjieff, G(eorgei) I(vanovich) 1877(?)-1949
TCLC 71
See also CA 157

Gurganus, Allan 1947- **CLC 70;DAM POP**
See also BEST 90:1; CA 135

Gurney, A(lbert) R(amsdell), Jr. 1930- **C L C
32, 50, 54; DAM DRAM**
See also CA 77-80; CANR 32, 64

Gurney, Ivor (Bertie) 1890-1937 **TCLC 33**
See also CA 167

Gurney, Peter
See Gurney, A(lbert) R(amsdell), Jr.

Guro, Elena 1877-1913 **TCLC 56**

Author Index

Gustafson, James M(oody) 1925-　**CLC 100**
See also CA 25-28R; CANR 37
Gustafson, Ralph (Barker) 1909-　**CLC 36**
See also CA 21-24R; CANR 8, 45; DLB 88
Gut, Gom
See Simenon, Georges (Jacques Christian)
Guterson, David 1956-　**CLC 91**
See also CA 132; CANR 73; MTCW 2
Guthrie, A(lfred) B(ertram), Jr. 1901-1991
　CLC 23
See also CA 57-60; 134; CANR 24; DLB 212;
SATA 62; SATA-Obit 67
Guthrie, Isobel
See Grieve, C(hristopher) M(urray)
Guthrie, Woodrow Wilson 1912-1967
See Guthrie, Woody
See also CA 113; 93-96
Guthrie, Woody　**CLC 35**
See also Guthrie, Woodrow Wilson
Gutierrez Najera, Manuel 1859-1895
See also HLCS 2
Guy, Rosa (Cuthbert) 1928-　**CLC 26**
See also AAYA 4; BW 2; CA 17-20R; CANR
14, 34; CLR 13; DLB 33; JRDA; MAICYA;
SATA 14, 62
Gwendolyn
See Bennett, (Enoch) Arnold
H. D.　**CLC 3, 8, 14, 31, 34, 73; PC 5**
See also Doolittle, Hilda
H. de V.
See Buchan, John
Haavikko, Paavo Juhani 1931-　**CLC 18, 34**
See also CA 106
Habbema, Koos
See Heijermans, Herman
Habermas, Juergen 1929-　**CLC 104**
See also CA 109
Habermas, Jurgen
See Habermas, Juergen
Hacker, Marilyn 1942-　**CLC 5, 9, 23, 72, 91;
DAM POET**
See also CA 77-80; CANR 68; DLB 120
Haeckel, Ernst Heinrich (Philipp August) 1834-
1919　**TCLC 83**
See also CA 157
Hafiz c. 1326-1389　**CMLC 34**
Hafiz c. 1326-1389(?)　**CMLC 34**
Haggard, H(enry) Rider 1856-1925 **TCLC 11**
See also CA 108; 148; DLB 70, 156, 174, 178;
MTCW 2; SATA 16
Hagiosy, L.
See Larbaud, Valery (Nicolas)
Hagiwara Sakutaro 1886-1942 **TCLC 60; PC
18**
Haig, Fenil
See Ford, Ford Madox
Haig-Brown, Roderick (Langmere) 1908-1976
　CLC 21
See also CA 5-8R; 69-72; CANR 4, 38; CLR
31; DLB 88; MAICYA; SATA 12
Hailey, Arthur 1920- **CLC 5; DAM NOV, POP**
See also AITN 2; BEST 90:3; CA 1-4R; CANR
2, 36, 75; DLB 88; DLBY 82; MTCW 1, 2
Hailey, Elizabeth Forsythe 1938-　**CLC 40**
See also CA 93-96; CAAS 1; CANR 15, 48;
INT CANR-15
Haines, John (Meade) 1924-　**CLC 58**
See also CA 17-20R; CANR 13, 34; DLB 212
Hakluyt, Richard 1552-1616　**LC 31**
Haldeman, Joe (William) 1943-　**CLC 61**
See also CA 53-56; CAAS 25; CANR 6, 70,
72; DLB 8; INT CANR-6
Hale, Sarah Josepha (Buell) 1788-1879 **NCLC**
75
See also DLB 1, 42, 73
Haley, Alex(ander Murray Palmer) 1921-1992
　**CLC 8, 12, 76; BLC 2; DA; DAB; DAC;
DAM MST, MULT, POP**
See also AAYA 26; BW 2, 3; CA 77-80; 136;
CANR 61; CDALBS; DLB 38; MTCW 1, 2
Haliburton, Thomas Chandler 1796-1865
　NCLC 15
See also DLB 11, 99
Hall, Donald (Andrew, Jr.) 1928- **CLC 1, 13,
37, 59; DAM POET**
See also CA 5-8R; CAAS 7; CANR 2, 44, 64;
DLB 5; MTCW 1; SATA 23, 97
Hall, Frederic Sauser
See Sauser-Hall, Frederic
Hall, James
See Kuttner, Henry
Hall, James Norman 1887-1951　**TCLC 23**
See also CA 123; 173; SATA 21
Hall, Radclyffe
See Hall, (Marguerite) Radclyffe
See also MTCW 2
Hall, (Marguerite) Radclyffe 1886-1943
　TCLC 12
See also CA 110; 150; DLB 191
Hall, Rodney 1935-　**CLC 51**
See also CA 109; CANR 69
Halleck, Fitz-Greene 1790-1867　**NCLC 47**
See also DLB 3
Halliday, Michael
See Creasey, John
Halpern, Daniel 1945-　**CLC 14**
See also CA 33-36R
Hamburger, Michael (Peter Leopold) 1924-
　CLC 5, 14
See also CA 5-8R; CAAS 4; CANR 2, 47; DLB
27
Hamill, Pete 1935-　**CLC 10**
See also CA 25-28R; CANR 18, 71
Hamilton, Alexander 1755(?)-1804 **NCLC 49**
See also DLB 37
Hamilton, Clive
See Lewis, C(live) S(taples)
Hamilton, Edmond 1904-1977　**CLC 1**
See also CA 1-4R; CANR 3; DLB 8
Hamilton, Eugene (Jacob) Lee
See Lee-Hamilton, Eugene (Jacob)
Hamilton, Franklin
See Silverberg, Robert
Hamilton, Gail
See Corcoran, Barbara
Hamilton, Mollie
See Kaye, M(ary) M(argaret)
Hamilton, (Anthony Walter) Patrick 1904-1962
　CLC 51
See also CA 176; 113; DLB 191
Hamilton, Virginia 1936-　**CLC 26; DAM
MULT**
See also AAYA 2, 21; BW 2, 3; CA 25-28R;
CANR 20, 37, 73; CLR 1, 11, 40; DLB 33,
52; INT CANR-20; JRDA; MAICYA;
MTCW 1, 2; SATA 4, 56, 79
Hammett, (Samuel) Dashiell 1894-1961 **C L C
3, 5, 10, 19, 47; SSC 17**
See also AITN 1; CA 81-84; CANR 42; CDALB
1929-1941; DLBD 6; DLBY 96; MTCW 1,
2
Hammon, Jupiter 1711(?)-1800(?)　**NCLC 5;
BLC 2; DAM MULT, POET; PC 16**
See also DLB 31, 50
Hammond, Keith
See Kuttner, Henry

Hamner, Earl (Henry), Jr. 1923-　**CLC 12**
See also AITN 2; CA 73-76; DLB 6
Hampton, Christopher (James) 1946- **CLC 4**
See also CA 25-28R; DLB 13; MTCW 1
Hamsun, Knut　**TCLC 2, 14, 49**
See also Pedersen, Knut
Handke, Peter 1942- **CLC 5, 8, 10, 15, 38; DAM
DRAM, NOV**
See also CA 77-80; CANR 33, 75; DLB 85, 124;
MTCW 1, 2
Hanley, James 1901-1985　**CLC 3, 5, 8, 13**
See also CA 73-76; 117; CANR 36; DLB 191;
MTCW 1
Hannah, Barry 1942-　**CLC 23, 38, 90**
See also CA 108; 110; CANR 43, 68; DLB 6;
INT 110; MTCW 1
Hannon, Ezra
See Hunter, Evan
Hansberry, Lorraine (Vivian) 1930-1965 **CLC
17, 62; BLC 2; DA; DAB; DAC; DAM
DRAM, MST, MULT; DC 2**
See also AAYA 25; BW 1, 3; CA 109; 25-28R;
CABS 3; CANR 58; CDALB 1941-1968;
DLB 7, 38; MTCW 1, 2
Hansen, Joseph 1923-　**CLC 38**
See also CA 29-32R; CAAS 17; CANR 16, 44,
66; INT CANR-16
Hansen, Martin A(lfred) 1909-1955 **TCLC 32**
See also CA 167
Hanson, Kenneth O(stlin) 1922-　**CLC 13**
See also CA 53-56; CANR 7
Hardwick, Elizabeth (Bruce) 1916- **CLC 13;
DAM NOV**
See also CA 5-8R; CANR 3, 32, 70; DLB 6;
MTCW 1, 2
Hardy, Thomas 1840-1928 **TCLC 4, 10, 18, 32,
48, 53, 72; DA; DAB; DAC; DAM MST,
NOV, POET; PC 8; SSC 2; WLC**
See also CA 104; 123; CDBLB 1890-1914;
DLB 18, 19, 135; MTCW 1, 2
Hare, David 1947-　**CLC 29, 58**
See also CA 97-100; CANR 39; DLB 13;
MTCW 1
Harewood, John
See Van Druten, John (William)
Harford, Henry
See Hudson, W(illiam) H(enry)
Hargrave, Leonie
See Disch, Thomas M(ichael)
Harjo, Joy 1951- **CLC 83; DAM MULT; PC 27**
See also CA 114; CANR 35, 67; DLB 120, 175;
MTCW 2; NNAL
Harlan, Louis R(udolph) 1922-　**CLC 34**
See also CA 21-24R; CANR 25, 55, 80
Harling, Robert 1951(?)-　**CLC 53**
See also CA 147
Harmon, William (Ruth) 1938-　**CLC 38**
See also CA 33-36R; CANR 14, 32, 35; SATA
65
Harper, F. E. W.
See Harper, Frances Ellen Watkins
Harper, Frances E. W.
See Harper, Frances Ellen Watkins
Harper, Frances E. Watkins
See Harper, Frances Ellen Watkins
Harper, Frances Ellen
See Harper, Frances Ellen Watkins
Harper, Frances Ellen Watkins 1825-1911
　**TCLC 14; BLC 2; DAM MULT, POET;
PC 21**
See also BW 1, 3; CA 111; 125; CANR 79; DLB
50
Harper, Michael S(teven) 1938-　**CLC 7, 22**

See also BW 1; CA 33-36R; CANR 24; DLB 41

Harper, Mrs. F. E. W.
See Harper, Frances Ellen Watkins

Harris, Christie (Lucy) Irwin 1907- **CLC 12**
See also CA 5-8R; CANR 6; CLR 47; DLB 88; JRDA; MAICYA; SAAS 10; SATA 6, 74

Harris, Frank 1856-1931 **TCLC 24**
See also CA 109; 150; CANR 80; DLB 156, 197

Harris, George Washington 1814-1869 **NCLC 23**
See also DLB 3, 11

Harris, Joel Chandler 1848-1908 **TCLC 2; SSC 19**
See also CA 104; 137; CANR 80; CLR 49; DLB 11, 23, 42, 78, 91; MAICYA; SATA 100; YABC 1

Harris, John (Wyndham Parkes Lucas) Beynon 1903-1969
See Wyndham, John
See also CA 102; 89-92

Harris, MacDonald **CLC 9**
See Heiney, Donald (William)

Harris, Mark 1922- **CLC 19**
See also CA 5-8R; CAAS 3; CANR 2, 55; DLB 2; DLBY 80

Harris, (Theodore) Wilson 1921- **CLC 25**
See also BW 2, 3; CA 65-68; CAAS 16; CANR 11, 27, 69; DLB 117; MTCW 1

Harrison, Elizabeth Cavanna 1909-
See Cavanna, Betty
See also CA 9-12R; CANR 6, 27

Harrison, Harry (Max) 1925- **CLC 42**
See also CA 1-4R; CANR 5, 21; DLB 8; SATA 4

Harrison, James (Thomas) 1937- **CLC 6, 14, 33, 66; SSC 19**
See also CA 13-16R; CANR 8, 51, 79; DLBY 82; INT CANR-8

Harrison, Jim
See Harrison, James (Thomas)

Harrison, Kathryn 1961- **CLC 70**
See also CA 144; CANR 68

Harrison, Tony 1937- **CLC 43**
See also CA 65-68; CANR 44; DLB 40; MTCW 1

Harriss, Will(ard Irvin) 1922- **CLC 34**
See also CA 111

Harson, Sley
See Ellison, Harlan (Jay)

Hart, Ellis
See Ellison, Harlan (Jay)

Hart, Josephine 1942(?)- **CLC 70; DAM POP**
See also CA 138; CANR 70

Hart, Moss 1904-1961 **CLC 66; DAM DRAM**
See also CA 109; 89-92; DLB 7

Harte, (Francis) Bret(t) 1836(?)-1902 **TCLC 1, 25; DA; DAC; DAM MST; SSC 8; WLC**
See also CA 104; 140; CANR 80; CDALB 1865-1917; DLB 12, 64, 74, 79, 186; SATA 26

Hartley, L(eslie) P(oles) 1895-1972 **CLC 2, 22**
See also CA 45-48; 37-40R; CANR 33; DLB 15, 139; MTCW 1, 2

Hartman, Geoffrey H. 1929- **CLC 27**
See also CA 117; 125; CANR 79; DLB 67

Hartmann, Sadakichi 1867-1944 **TCLC 73**
See also CA 157; DLB 54

Hartmann von Aue c. 1160-c.1205 **CMLC 15**
See also DLB 138

Hartmann von Aue 1170-1210 **CMLC 15**

Haruf, Kent 1943- **CLC 34**

See also CA 149

Harwood, Ronald 1934- **CLC 32; DAM DRAM, MST**
See also CA 1-4R; CANR 4, 55; DLB 13

Hasegawa Tatsunosuke
See Futabatei, Shimei

Hasek, Jaroslav (Matej Frantisek) 1883-1923 **TCLC 4**
See also CA 104; 129; MTCW 1, 2

Hass, Robert 1941- **CLC 18, 39, 99; PC 16**
See also CA 111; CANR 30, 50, 71; DLB 105, 206; SATA 94

Hastings, Hudson
See Kuttner, Henry

Hastings, Selina **CLC 44**

Hathorne, John 1641-1717 **LC 38**

Hatteras, Amelia
See Mencken, H(enry) L(ouis)

Hatteras, Owen **TCLC 18**
See also Mencken, H(enry) L(ouis); Nathan, George Jean

Hauptmann, Gerhart (Johann Robert) 1862-1946 **TCLC 4; DAM DRAM**
See also CA 104; 153; DLB 66, 118

Havel, Vaclav 1936- **CLC 25, 58, 65; DAM DRAM; DC 6**
See also CA 104; CANR 36, 63; MTCW 1, 2

Haviaras, Stratis **CLC 33**
See also Chaviaras, Strates

Hawes, Stephen 1475(?)-1523(?) **LC 17**
See also DLB 132

Hawkes, John (Clendennin Burne, Jr.) 1925-1998 **CLC 1, 2, 3, 4, 7, 9, 14, 15, 27, 49**
See also CA 1-4R; 167; CANR 2, 47, 64; DLB 2, 7; DLBY 80, 98; MTCW 1, 2

Hawking, S. W.
See Hawking, Stephen W(illiam)

Hawking, Stephen W(illiam) 1942- **CLC 63, 105**
See also AAYA 13; BEST 89:1; CA 126; 129; CANR 48; MTCW 2

Hawkins, Anthony Hope
See Hope, Anthony

Hawthorne, Julian 1846-1934 **TCLC 25**
See also CA 165

Hawthorne, Nathaniel 1804-1864 **NCLC 39; DA; DAB; DAC; DAM MST, NOV; SSC 3, 29; WLC**
See also AAYA 18; CDALB 1640-1865; DLB 1, 74; YABC 2

Haxton, Josephine Ayres 1921-
See Douglas, Ellen
See also CA 115; CANR 41

Hayaseca y Eizaguirre, Jorge
See Echegaray (y Eizaguirre), Jose (Maria Waldo)

Hayashi, Fumiko 1904-1951 **TCLC 27**
See also CA 161; DLB 180

Haycraft, Anna
See Ellis, Alice Thomas
See also CA 122; MTCW 2

Hayden, Robert E(arl) 1913-1980 **CLC 5, 9, 14, 37; BLC 2; DA; DAC; DAM MST, MULT, POET; PC 6**
See also BW 1, 3; CA 69-72; 97-100; CABS 2; CANR 24, 75, 82; CDALB 1941-1968; DLB 5, 76; MTCW 1, 2; SATA 19; SATA-Obit 26

Hayford, J(oseph) E(phraim) Casely
See Casely-Hayford, J(oseph) E(phraim)

Hayman, Ronald 1932- **CLC 44**
See also CA 25-28R; CANR 18, 50; DLB 155

Haywood, Eliza (Fowler) 1693(?)-1756 **LC 1, 44**

See also DLB 39

Hazlitt, William 1778-1830 **NCLC 29**
See also DLB 110, 158

Hazzard, Shirley 1931- **CLC 18**
See also CA 9-12R; CANR 4, 70; DLBY 82; MTCW 1

Head, Bessie 1937-1986 **CLC 25, 67; BLC 2; DAM MULT**
See also BW 2, 3; CA 29-32R; 119; CANR 25, 82; DLB 117; MTCW 1, 2

Headon, (Nicky) Topper 1956(?)- **CLC 30**

Heaney, Seamus (Justin) 1939- **CLC 5, 7, 14, 25, 37, 74, 91; DAB; DAM POET; PC 18; WLCS**
See also CA 85-88; CANR 25, 48, 75; CDBLB 1960 to Present; DLB 40; DLBY 95; MTCW 1, 2

Hearn, (Patricio) Lafcadio (Tessima Carlos) 1850-1904 **TCLC 9**
See also CA 105; 166; DLB 12, 78, 189

Hearne, Vicki 1946- **CLC 56**
See also CA 139

Hearon, Shelby 1931- **CLC 63**
See also AITN 2; CA 25-28R; CANR 18, 48

Heat-Moon, William Least **CLC 29**
See also Trogdon, William (Lewis)
See also AAYA 9

Hebbel, Friedrich 1813-1863 **NCLC 43; DAM DRAM**
See also DLB 129

Hebert, Anne 1916- **CLC 4, 13, 29; DAC; DAM MST, POET**
See also CA 85-88; CANR 69; DLB 68; MTCW 1, 2

Hecht, Anthony (Evan) 1923- **CLC 8, 13, 19; DAM POET**
See also CA 9-12R; CANR 6; DLB 5, 169

Hecht, Ben 1894-1964 **CLC 8**
See also CA 85-88; DLB 7, 9, 25, 26, 28, 86

Hedayat, Sadeq 1903-1951 **TCLC 21**
See also CA 120

Hegel, Georg Wilhelm Friedrich 1770-1831 **NCLC 46**
See also DLB 90

Heidegger, Martin 1889-1976 **CLC 24**
See also CA 81-84; 65-68; CANR 34; MTCW 1, 2

Heidenstam, (Carl Gustaf) Vernervon 1859-1940 **TCLC 5**
See also CA 104

Heifner, Jack 1946- **CLC 11**
See also CA 105; CANR 47

Heijermans, Herman 1864-1924 **TCLC 24**
See also CA 123

Heilbrun, Carolyn G(old) 1926- **CLC 25**
See also CA 45-48; CANR 1, 28, 58

Heine, Heinrich 1797-1856 **NCLC 4, 54; PC 25**
See also DLB 90

Heinemann, Larry (Curtiss) 1944- **CLC 50**
See also CA 110; CAAS 21; CANR 31, 81; DLBD 9; INT CANR-31

Heiney, Donald (William) 1921-1993
See Harris, MacDonald
See also CA 1-4R; 142; CANR 3, 58

Heinlein, Robert A(nson) 1907-1988 **CLC 1, 3, 8, 14, 26, 55; DAM POP**
See also AAYA 17; CA 1-4R; 125; CANR 1, 20, 53; DLB 8; JRDA; MAICYA; MTCW 1, 2; SATA 9, 69; SATA-Obit 56

Helforth, John
See Doolittle, Hilda

Hellenhofferu, Vojtech Kapristian z
See Hasek, Jaroslav (Matej Frantisek)

Heller, Joseph 1923-CLC **1, 3, 5, 8, 11, 36, 63; DA; DAB; DAC; DAM MST, NOV, POP; WLC**
See also AAYA 24; AITN 1; CA 5-8R; CABS 1; CANR 8, 42, 66; DLB 2, 28; DLBY 80; INT CANR-8; MTCW 1, 2

Hellman, Lillian (Florence) 1906-1984CLC **2, 4, 8, 14, 18, 34, 44, 52; DAM DRAM; DC 1**
See also AITN 1, 2; CA 13-16R; 112; CANR 33; DLB 7; DLBY 84; MTCW 1, 2

Helprin, Mark 1947-CLC **7, 10, 22, 32; DAM NOV, POP**
See also CA 81-84; CANR 47, 64; CDALBS; DLBY 85; MTCW 1, 2

Helvetius, Claude-Adrien 1715-1771 **LC 26**

Helyar, Jane Penelope Josephine 1933-
See Poole, Josephine
See also CA 21-24R; CANR 10, 26; SATA 82

Hemans, Felicia 1793-1835 **NCLC 71**
See also DLB 96

Hemingway, Ernest (Miller) 1899-1961 **C L C 1, 3, 6, 8, 10, 13, 19, 30, 34, 39, 41, 44, 50, 61, 80; DA; DAB; DAC; DAM MST, NOV; SSC 1, 25; WLC**
See also AAYA 19; CA 77-80; CANR 34; CDALB 1917-1929; DLB 4, 9, 102, 210; DLBD 1, 15, 16; DLBY 81, 87, 96, 98; MTCW 1, 2

Hempel, Amy 1951- **CLC 39**
See also CA 118; 137; CANR 70; MTCW 2

Henderson, F. C.
See Mencken, H(enry) L(ouis)

Henderson, Sylvia
See Ashton-Warner, Sylvia (Constance)

Henderson, Zenna (Chlarson) 1917-1983SSC 29
See also CA 1-4R; 133; CANR 1; DLB 8; SATA 5

Henkin, Joshua **CLC 119**
See also CA 161

Henley, Beth **CLC 23; DC 6**
See also Henley, Elizabeth Becker
See also CABS 3; DLBY 86

Henley, Elizabeth Becker 1952-
See Henley, Beth
See also CA 107; CANR 32, 73; DAM DRAM, MST; MTCW 1, 2

Henley, William Ernest 1849-1903 **TCLC 8**
See also CA 105; DLB 19

Hennissart, Martha
See Lathen, Emma
See also CA 85-88; CANR 64

Henry, O. **TCLC 1, 19; SSC 5; WLC**
See also Porter, William Sydney

Henry, Patrick 1736-1799 **LC 25**

Henryson, Robert 1430(?)-1506(?) **LC 20**
See also DLB 146

Henry VIII 1491-1547 **LC 10**
See also DLB 132

Henschke, Alfred
See Klabund

Hentoff, Nat(han Irving) 1925- **CLC 26**
See also AAYA 4; CA 1-4R; CAAS 6; CANR 5, 25, 77; CLR 1, 52; INT CANR-25; JRDA; MAICYA; SATA 42, 69; SATA-Brief 27

Heppenstall, (John) Rayner 1911-1981 **C L C 10**
See also CA 1-4R; 103; CANR 29

Heraclitus c. 540B.C.-c.450B.C. **CMLC 22**
See also DLB 176

Herbert, Frank (Patrick) 1920-1986 **CLC 12, 23, 35, 44, 85; DAM POP**
See also AAYA 21; CA 53-56; 118; CANR 5,

43; CDALBS; DLB 8; INT CANR-5; MTCW 1, 2; SATA 9, 37; SATA-Obit 47

Herbert, George 1593-1633 **LC 24; DAB; DAM POET; PC 4**
See also CDBLB Before 1660; DLB 126

Herbert, Zbigniew 1924-1998 **CLC 9, 43; DAM POET**
See also CA 89-92; 169; CANR 36, 74; MTCW 1

Herbst, Josephine (Frey) 1897-1969 **CLC 34**
See also CA 5-8R; 25-28R; DLB 9

Heredia, Jose Maria 1803-1839
See also HLCS 2

Hergesheimer, Joseph 1880-1954 **TCLC 11**
See also CA 109; DLB 102, 9

Herlihy, James Leo 1927-1993 **CLC 6**
See also CA 1-4R; 143; CANR 2

Hermogenes fl. c. 175- **CMLC 6**

Hernandez, Jose 1834-1886 **NCLC 17**

Herodotus c.484B.C.-429B.C. **CMLC 17**
See also DLB 176

Herrick, Robert 1591-1674LC **13; DA; DAB; DAC; DAM MST, POP; PC 9**
See also DLB 126

Herring, Guilles
See Somerville, Edith

Herriot, James 1916-1995CLC **12;DAM POP**
See also Wight, James Alfred
See also AAYA 1; CA 148; CANR 40; MTCW 2; SATA 86

Herrmann, Dorothy 1941- **CLC 44**
See also CA 107

Herrmann, Taffy
See Herrmann, Dorothy

Hersey, John (Richard) 1914-1993CLC **1, 2, 7, 9, 40, 81, 97; DAM POP**
See also AAYA 29; CA 17-20R; 140; CANR 33; CDALBS; DLB 6, 185; MTCW 1, 2; SATA 25; SATA-Obit 76

Herzen, Aleksandr Ivanovich 1812-1870 **NCLC 10, 61**

Herzl, Theodor 1860-1904 **TCLC 36**
See also CA 168

Herzog, Werner 1942- **CLC 16**
See also CA 89-92

Hesiod c. 8th cent. B.C.- **CMLC 5**
See also DLB 176

Hesse, Hermann 1877-1962CLC **1, 2, 3, 6, 11, 17, 25, 69; DA; DAB; DAC; DAM MST, NOV; SSC 9; WLC**
See also CA 17-18; CAP 2; DLB 66; MTCW 1, 2; SATA 50

Hewes, Cady
See De Voto, Bernard (Augustine)

Heyen, William 1940- **CLC 13, 18**
See also CA 33-36R; CAAS 9; DLB 5

Heyerdahl, Thor 1914- **CLC 26**
See also CA 5-8R; CANR 5, 22, 66, 73; MTCW 1, 2; SATA 2, 52

Heym, Georg (Theodor Franz Arthur) 1887-1912 **TCLC 9**
See also CA 106

Heym, Stefan 1913- **CLC 41**
See also CA 9-12R; CANR 4; DLB 69

Heyse, Paul (Johann Ludwig von) 1830-1914 **TCLC 8**
See also CA 104; DLB 129

Heyward, (Edwin) DuBose 1885-1940 **T C L C 59**
See also CA 108; 157; DLB 7, 9, 45; SATA 21

Hibbert, Eleanor Alice Burford 1906-1993 **CLC 7; DAM POP**
See also BEST 90:4; CA 17-20R; 140; CANR

9, 28, 59; MTCW 2; SATA 2; SATA-Obit 74

Hichens, Robert (Smythe) 1864-1950 **T C L C 64**
See also CA 162; DLB 153

Higgins, George V(incent) 1939-CLC **4, 7, 10, 18**
See also CA 77-80; CAAS 5; CANR 17, 51; DLB 2; DLBY 81, 98; INT CANR-17; MTCW 1

Higginson, Thomas Wentworth 1823-1911 **TCLC 36**
See also CA 162; DLB 1, 64

Highet, Helen
See MacInnes, Helen (Clark)

Highsmith, (Mary) Patricia 1921-1995CLC **2, 4, 14, 42, 102; DAM NOV, POP**
See also CA 1-4R; 147; CANR 1, 20, 48, 62; MTCW 1, 2

Highwater, Jamake (Mamake) 1942(?)- **C L C 12**
See also AAYA 7; CA 65-68; CAAS 7; CANR 10, 34; CLR 17; DLB 52; DLBY 85; JRDA; MAICYA; SATA 32, 69; SATA-Brief 30

Highway, Tomson 1951-CLC **92; DAC;DAM MULT**
See also CA 151; CANR 75; MTCW 2; NNAL

Higuchi, Ichiyo 1872-1896 **NCLC 49**

Hijuelos, Oscar 1951- CLC **65; DAM MULT, POP; HLC 1**
See also AAYA 25; BEST 90:1; CA 123; CANR 50, 75; DLB 145; HW 1, 2; MTCW 2

Hikmet, Nazim 1902(?)-1963 **CLC 40**
See also CA 141; 93-96

Hildegard von Bingen 1098-1179 **CMLC 20**
See also DLB 148

Hildesheimer, Wolfgang 1916-1991 **CLC 49**
See also CA 101; 135; DLB 69, 124

Hill, Geoffrey (William) 1932- CLC **5, 8, 18, 45; DAM POET**
See also CA 81-84; CANR 21; CDBLB 1960 to Present; DLB 40; MTCW 1

Hill, George Roy 1921- **CLC 26**
See also CA 110; 122

Hill, John
See Koontz, Dean R(ay)

Hill, Susan (Elizabeth) 1942- CLC **4, 113; DAB; DAM MST, NOV**
See also CA 33-36R; CANR 29, 69; DLB 14, 139; MTCW 1

Hillerman, Tony 1925- CLC **62;DAM POP**
See also AAYA 6; BEST 89:1; CA 29-32R; CANR 21, 42, 65; DLB 206; SATA 6

Hillesum, Etty 1914-1943 **TCLC 49**
See also CA 137

Hilliard, Noel (Harvey) 1929- **CLC 15**
See also CA 9-12R; CANR 7, 69

Hillis, Rick 1956- **CLC 66**
See also CA 134

Hilton, James 1900-1954 **TCLC 21**
See also CA 108; 169; DLB 34, 77; SATA 34

Himes, Chester (Bomar) 1909-1984CLC **2, 4, 7, 18, 58, 108; BLC 2; DAM MULT**
See also BW 2; CA 25-28R; 114; CANR 22; DLB 2, 76, 143; MTCW 1, 2

Hinde, Thomas **CLC 6, 11**
See also Chitty, Thomas Willes

Hindin, Nathan 1917-1994
See Bloch, Robert (Albert)
See also CA 179; CAAE 179

Hine, (William) Daryl 1936- **CLC 15**
See also CA 1-4R; CAAS 15; CANR 1, 20; DLB 60

Hinkson, Katharine Tynan

Ilf, Ilya   **TCLC 21**
See also Fainzilberg, Ilya Arnoldovich
Illyes, Gyula 1902-1983   **PC 16**
See also CA 114; 109
Immermann, Karl (Lebrecht) 1796-1840
   NCLC 4, 49
See also DLB 133
Ince, Thomas H. 1882-1924   **TCLC 89**
Inchbald, Elizabeth 1753-1821   **NCLC 62**
See also DLB 39, 89
Inclan, Ramon (Maria) del Valle
See Valle-Inclan, Ramon (Maria) del
Infante, G(uillermo) Cabrera
See Cabrera Infante, G(uillermo)
Ingalls, Rachel (Holmes) 1940-   **CLC 42**
See also CA 123; 127
Ingamells, Reginald Charles
See Ingamells, Rex
Ingamells, Rex 1913-1955   **TCLC 35**
See also CA 167
Inge, William (Motter) 1913-1973 **CLC 1, 8,**
   19; DAM DRAM
See also CA 9-12R; CDALB 1941-1968; DLB
   7; MTCW 1, 2
Ingelow, Jean 1820-1897   **NCLC 39**
See also DLB 35, 163; SATA 33
Ingram, Willis J.
See Harris, Mark
Innaurato, Albert (F.) 1948(?)-   **CLC 21, 60**
See also CA 115; 122; CANR 78; INT 122
Innes, Michael
See Stewart, J(ohn) I(nnes) M(ackintosh)
Innis, Harold Adams 1894-1952   **TCLC 77**
See also DLB 88
Ionesco, Eugene 1909-1994 **CLC 1, 4, 6, 9, 11,**
   15, 41, 86; DA; DAB; DAC; DAM DRAM,
   MST; WLC
See also CA 9-12R; 144; CANR 55; MTCW 1,
   2; SATA 7; SATA-Obit 79
Iqbal, Muhammad 1873-1938   **TCLC 28**
Ireland, Patrick
See O'Doherty, Brian
Iron, Ralph
See Schreiner, Olive (Emilie Albertina)
Irving, John (Winslow) 1942- **CLC 13, 23, 38,**
   112; DAM NOV, POP
See also AAYA 8; BEST 89:3; CA 25-28R;
   CANR 28, 73; DLB 6; DLBY 82; MTCW 1,
   2
Irving, Washington 1783-1859 **NCLC 2, 19;**
   DA; DAB; DAC; DAM MST; SSC 2; WLC
See also CDALB 1640-1865; DLB 3, 11, 30,
   59, 73, 74, 186; YABC 2
Irwin, P. K.
See Page, P(atricia) K(athleen)
Isaacs, Jorge Ricardo 1837-1895   **NCLC 70**
Isaacs, Susan 1943-   **CLC 32; DAM POP**
See also BEST 89:1; CA 89-92; CANR 20, 41,
   65; INT CANR-20; MTCW 1, 2
Isherwood, Christopher (William Bradshaw)
   1904-1986   **CLC 1, 9, 11, 14, 44; DAM**
   DRAM, NOV
See also CA 13-16R; 117; CANR 35; DLB 15,
   195; DLBY 86; MTCW 1, 2
Ishiguro, Kazuo 1954- **CLC 27, 56, 59, 110;**
   DAM NOV
See also BEST 90:2; CA 120; CANR 49; DLB
   194; MTCW 1, 2
Ishikawa, Hakuhin
See Ishikawa, Takuboku
Ishikawa, Takuboku 1886(?)-1912 **TCLC 15;**
   DAM POET; PC 10
See also CA 113; 153

Iskander, Fazil 1929-   **CLC 47**
See also CA 102
Isler, Alan (David) 1934-   **CLC 91**
See also CA 156
Ivan IV 1530-1584   **LC 17**
Ivanov, Vyacheslav Ivanovich 1866-1949
   TCLC 33
See also CA 122
Ivask, Ivar Vidrik 1927-1992   **CLC 14**
See also CA 37-40R; 139; CANR 24
Ives, Morgan
See Bradley, Marion Zimmer
Izumi Shikibu c. 973-c. 1034   **CMLC 33**
J. R. S.
See Gogarty, Oliver St. John
Jabran, Kahlil
See Gibran, Kahlil
Jabran, Khalil
See Gibran, Kahlil
Jackson, Daniel
See Wingrove, David (John)
Jackson, Jesse 1908-1983   **CLC 12**
See also BW 1; CA 25-28R; 109; CANR 27;
   CLR 28; MAICYA; SATA 2, 29; SATA-Obit
   48
Jackson, Laura (Riding) 1901-1991
See Riding, Laura
See also CA 65-68; 135; CANR 28; DLB 48
Jackson, Sam
See Trumbo, Dalton
Jackson, Sara
See Wingrove, David (John)
Jackson, Shirley 1919-1965   **CLC 11, 60, 87;**
   DA; DAC; DAM MST; SSC 9; WLC
See also AAYA 9; CA 1-4R; 25-28R; CANR 4,
   52; CDALB 1941-1968; DLB 6; MTCW 2;
   SATA 2
Jacob, (Cyprien-)Max 1876-1944   **TCLC 6**
See also CA 104
Jacobs, Harriet A(nn) 1813(?)-1897 **NCLC 67**
Jacobs, Jim 1942-   **CLC 12**
See also CA 97-100; INT 97-100
Jacobs, W(illiam) W(ymark) 1863-1943
   TCLC 22
See also CA 121; 167; DLB 135
Jacobsen, Jens Peter 1847-1885   **NCLC 34**
Jacobsen, Josephine 1908-   **CLC 48, 102**
See also CA 33-36R; CAAS 18; CANR 23, 48
Jacobson, Dan 1929-   **CLC 4, 14**
See also CA 1-4R; CANR 2, 25, 66; DLB 14,
   207; MTCW 1
Jacqueline
See Carpentier (y Valmont), Alejo
Jagger, Mick 1944-   **CLC 17**
Jahiz, al- c. 780-c. 869   **CMLC 25**
Jakes, John (William) 1932- **CLC 29; DAM**
   NOV, POP
See also BEST 89:4; CA 57-60; CANR 10, 43,
   66; DLBY 83; INT CANR-10; MTCW 1, 2;
   SATA 62
James, Andrew
See Kirkup, James
James, C(yril) L(ionel) R(obert) 1901-1989
   CLC 33; BLCS
See also BW 2; CA 117; 125; 128; CANR 62;
   DLB 125; MTCW 1
James, Daniel (Lewis) 1911-1988
See Santiago, Danny
See also CA 174; 125
James, Dynely
See Mayne, William (James Carter)
James, Henry Sr. 1811-1882   **NCLC 53**
James, Henry 1843-1916 **TCLC 2, 11, 24, 40,**

   47, 64; DA; DAB; DAC; DAM MST, NOV;
   SSC 8, 32; WLC
See also CA 104; 132; CDALB 1865-1917;
   DLB 12, 71, 74, 189; DLBD 13; MTCW 1,
   2
James, M. R.
See James, Montague (Rhodes)
See also DLB 156
James, Montague (Rhodes) 1862-1936 **TCLC**
   6; SSC 16
See also CA 104; DLB 201
James, P. D. 1920-   **CLC 18, 46, 122**
See also White, Phyllis Dorothy James
See also BEST 90:2; CDBLB 1960 to Present;
   DLB 87; DLBD 17
James, Philip
See Moorcock, Michael (John)
James, William 1842-1910   **TCLC 15, 32**
See also CA 109
James I 1394-1437   **LC 20**
Jameson, Anna 1794-1860   **NCLC 43**
See also DLB 99, 166
Jami, Nur al-Din 'Abd al-Rahman 1414-1492
   LC 9
Jammes, Francis 1868-1938   **TCLC 75**
Jandl, Ernst 1925-   **CLC 34**
Janowitz, Tama 1957-   **CLC 43; DAM POP**
See also CA 106; CANR 52
Japrisot, Sebastien 1931-   **CLC 90**
Jarrell, Randall 1914-1965 **CLC 1, 2, 6, 9, 13,**
   49; DAM POET
See also CA 5-8R; 25-28R; CABS 2; CANR 6,
   34; CDALB 1941-1968; CLR 6; DLB 48, 52;
   MAICYA; MTCW 1, 2; SATA 7
Jarry, Alfred 1873-1907   **TCLC 2, 14; DAM**
   DRAM; SSC 20
See also CA 104; 153; DLB 192
Jarvis, E. K.
See Bloch, Robert (Albert)
Jeake, Samuel, Jr.
See Aiken, Conrad (Potter)
Jean Paul 1763-1825   **NCLC 7**
Jefferies, (John) Richard 1848-1887 **NCLC 47**
See also DLB 98, 141; SATA 16
Jeffers, (John) Robinson 1887-1962 **CLC 2, 3,**
   11, 15, 54; DA; DAC; DAM MST, POET;
   PC 17; WLC
See also CA 85-88; CANR 35; CDALB 1917-
   1929; DLB 45, 212; MTCW 1, 2
Jefferson, Janet
See Mencken, H(enry) L(ouis)
Jefferson, Thomas 1743-1826   **NCLC 11**
See also CDALB 1640-1865; DLB 31
Jeffrey, Francis 1773-1850   **NCLC 33**
See also DLB 107
Jelakowitch, Ivan
See Heijermans, Herman
Jellicoe, (Patricia) Ann 1927-   **CLC 27**
See also CA 85-88; DLB 13
Jen, Gish   **CLC 70**
See also Jen, Lillian
Jen, Lillian 1956(?)-
See Jen, Gish
See also CA 135
Jenkins, (John) Robin 1912-   **CLC 52**
See also CA 1-4R; CANR 1; DLB 14
Jennings, Elizabeth (Joan) 1926- **CLC 5, 14**
See also CA 61-64; CAAS 5; CANR 8, 39, 66;
   DLB 27; MTCW 1; SATA 66
Jennings, Waylon 1937-   **CLC 21**
Jensen, Johannes V. 1873-1950   **TCLC 41**
See also CA 170

Jensen, Laura (Linnea) 1948-   CLC 37
  See also CA 103
Jerome, Jerome K(lapka) 1859-1927TCLC 23
  See also CA 119; 177; DLB 10, 34, 135
Jerrold, Douglas William 1803-1857 NCLC 2
  See also DLB 158, 159
Jewett, (Theodora) Sarah Orne 1849-1909
    TCLC 1, 22; SSC 6
  See also CA 108; 127; CANR 71; DLB 12, 74;
    SATA 15
Jewsbury, Geraldine (Endsor) 1812-1880
    NCLC 22
  See also DLB 21
Jhabvala, Ruth Prawer 1927-CLC 4, 8, 29, 94;
    DAB; DAM NOV
  See also CA 1-4R; CANR 2, 29, 51, 74; DLB
    139, 194; INT CANR-29; MTCW 1, 2
Jibran, Kahlil
  See Gibran, Kahlil
Jibran, Khalil
  See Gibran, Kahlil
Jiles, Paulette 1943-   CLC 13, 58
  See also CA 101; CANR 70
Jimenez (Mantecon), Juan Ramon 1881-1958
    TCLC 4; DAM MULT, POET; HLC 1; PC
    7
  See also CA 104; 131; CANR 74; DLB 134;
    HW 1; MTCW 1, 2
Jimenez, Ramon
  See Jimenez (Mantecon), Juan Ramon
Jimenez Mantecon, Juan
  See Jimenez (Mantecon), Juan Ramon
Jin, Ha 1956-   CLC 109
  See also CA 152
Joel, Billy   CLC 26
  See also Joel, William Martin
Joel, William Martin 1949-
  See Joel, Billy
  See also CA 108
John, Saint 7th cent. -   CMLC 27
John of the Cross, St. 1542-1591   LC 18
Johnson, B(ryan) S(tanley William) 1933-1973
    CLC 6, 9
  See also CA 9-12R; 53-56; CANR 9; DLB 14,
    40
Johnson, Benj. F. of Boo
  See Riley, James Whitcomb
Johnson, Benjamin F. of Boo
  See Riley, James Whitcomb
Johnson, Charles (Richard) 1948-CLC 7, 51,
    65; BLC 2; DAM MULT
  See also BW 2, 3; CA 116; CAAS 18; CANR
    42, 66, 82; DLB 33; MTCW 2
Johnson, Denis 1949-   CLC 52
  See also CA 117; 121; CANR 71; DLB 120
Johnson, Diane 1934-   CLC 5, 13, 48
  See also CA 41-44R; CANR 17, 40, 62; DLBY
    80; INT CANR-17; MTCW 1
Johnson, Eyvind (Olof Verner) 1900-1976
    CLC 14
  See also CA 73-76; 69-72; CANR 34
Johnson, J. R.
  See James, C(yril) L(ionel) R(obert)
Johnson, James Weldon 1871-1938 TCLC 3,
    19; BLC 2; DAM MULT, POET; PC 24
  See also BW 1, 3; CA 104; 125; CANR 82;
    CDALB 1917-1929; CLR 32; DLB 51;
    MTCW 1, 2; SATA 31
Johnson, Joyce 1935-   CLC 58
  See also CA 125; 129
Johnson, Judith (Emlyn) 1936-   CLC 7, 15
  See also CA 25-28R, 153; CANR 34
Johnson, Lionel (Pigot) 1867-1902 TCLC 19

  See also CA 117; DLB 19
Johnson, Marguerite (Annie)
  See Angelou, Maya
Johnson, Mel
  See Malzberg, Barry N(athaniel)
Johnson, Pamela Hansford 1912-1981CLC 1,
    7, 27
  See also CA 1-4R; 104; CANR 2, 28; DLB 15;
    MTCW 1, 2
Johnson, Robert 1911(?)-1938   TCLC 69
  See also BW 3; CA 174
Johnson, Samuel 1709-1784 LC 15, 52; DA;
    DAB; DAC; DAM MST; WLC
  See also CDBLB 1660-1789; DLB 39, 95, 104,
    142
Johnson, Uwe 1934-1984   CLC 5, 10, 15, 40
  See also CA 1-4R; 112; CANR 1, 39; DLB 75;
    MTCW 1
Johnston, George (Benson) 1913-   CLC 51
  See also CA 1-4R; CANR 5, 20; DLB 88
Johnston, Jennifer 1930-   CLC 7
  See also CA 85-88; DLB 14
Jolley, (Monica) Elizabeth 1923-CLC 46; SSC
    19
  See also CA 127; CAAS 13; CANR 59
Jones, Arthur Llewellyn 1863-1947
  See Machen, Arthur
  See also CA 104
Jones, D(ouglas) G(ordon) 1929-   CLC 10
  See also CA 29-32R; CANR 13; DLB 53
Jones, David (Michael) 1895-1974CLC 2, 4, 7,
    13, 42
  See also CA 9-12R; 53-56; CANR 28; CDBLB
    1945-1960; DLB 20, 100; MTCW 1
Jones, David Robert 1947-
  See Bowie, David
  See also CA 103
Jones, Diana Wynne 1934-   CLC 26
  See also AAYA 12; CA 49-52; CANR 4, 26,
    56; CLR 23; DLB 161; JRDA; MAICYA;
    SAAS 7; SATA 9, 70, 108
Jones, Edward P. 1950-   CLC 76
  See also BW 2, 3; CA 142; CANR 79
Jones, Gayl 1949-   CLC 6, 9; BLC 2; DAM
    MULT
  See also BW 2, 3; CA 77-80; CANR 27, 66;
    DLB 33; MTCW 1, 2
Jones, James 1921-1977   CLC 1, 3, 10, 39
  See also AITN 1, 2; CA 1-4R; 69-72; CANR 6;
    DLB 2, 143; DLBD 17; DLBY 98; MTCW 1
Jones, John J.
  See Lovecraft, H(oward) P(hillips)
Jones, LeRoi   CLC 1, 2, 3, 5, 10, 14
  See also Baraka, Amiri
  See also MTCW 2
Jones, Louis B. 1953-   CLC 65
  See also CA 141; CANR 73
Jones, Madison (Percy, Jr.) 1925-   CLC 4
  See also CA 13-16R; CAAS 11; CANR 7, 54;
    DLB 152
Jones, Mervyn 1922-   CLC 10, 52
  See also CA 45-48; CAAS 5; CANR 1; MTCW
    1
Jones, Mick 1956(?)-   CLC 30
Jones, Nettie (Pearl) 1941-   CLC 34
  See also BW 2; CA 137; CAAS 20
Jones, Preston 1936-1979   CLC 10
  See also CA 73-76; 89-92; DLB 7
Jones, Robert F(rancis) 1934-   CLC 7
  See also CA 49-52; CANR 2, 61
Jones, Rod 1953-   CLC 50
  See also CA 128
Jones, Terence Graham Parry 1942- CLC 21

  See also Jones, Terry; Monty Python
  See also CA 112; 116; CANR 35; INT 116
Jones, Terry
  See Jones, Terence Graham Parry
  See also SATA 67; SATA-Brief 51
Jones, Thom 1945(?)-   CLC 81
  See also CA 157
Jong, Erica 1942- CLC 4, 6, 8, 18, 83; DAM
    NOV, POP
  See also AITN 1; BEST 90:2; CA 73-76; CANR
    26, 52, 75; DLB 2, 5, 28, 152; INT CANR-
    26; MTCW 1, 2
Jonson, Ben(jamin) 1572(?)-1637 LC 6, 33;
    DA; DAB; DAC; DAM DRAM, MST,
    POET; DC 4; PC 17; WLC
  See also CDBLB Before 1660; DLB 62, 121
Jordan, June 1936-CLC 5, 11, 23, 114; BLCS;
    DAM MULT, POET
  See also AAYA 2; BW 2, 3; CA 33-36R; CANR
    25, 70; CLR 10; DLB 38; MAICYA; MTCW
    1; SATA 4
Jordan, Neil (Patrick) 1950-   CLC 110
  See also CA 124; 130; CANR 54; INT 130
Jordan, Pat(rick M.) 1941-   CLC 37
  See also CA 33-36R
Jorgensen, Ivar
  See Ellison, Harlan (Jay)
Jorgenson, Ivar
  See Silverberg, Robert
Josephus, Flavius c. 37-100   CMLC 13
Josipovici, Gabriel 1940-   CLC 6, 43
  See also CA 37-40R; CAAS 8; CANR 47; DLB
    14
Joubert, Joseph 1754-1824   NCLC 9
Jouve, Pierre Jean 1887-1976   CLC 47
  See also CA 65-68
Jovine, Francesco 1902-1950   TCLC 79
Joyce, James (Augustine Aloysius) 1882-1941
    TCLC 3, 8, 16, 35, 52; DA;DAB; DAC;
    DAM MST, NOV, POET; PC 22; SSC 3,
    26; WLC
  See also CA 104; 126; CDBLB 1914-1945;
    DLB 10, 19, 36, 162; MTCW 1, 2
Jozsef, Attila 1905-1937   TCLC 22
  See also CA 116
Juana Ines de la Cruz 1651(?)-1695   LC 5;
    HLCS 1; PC 24
Judd, Cyril
  See Kornbluth, C(yril) M.; Pohl, Frederik
Julian of Norwich 1342(?)-1416(?) LC 6, 52
  See also DLB 146
Junger, Sebastian 1962-   CLC 109
  See also AAYA 28; CA 165
Juniper, Alex
  See Hospital, Janette Turner
Junius
  See Luxemburg, Rosa
Just, Ward (Swift) 1935-   CLC 4, 27
  See also CA 25-28R; CANR 32; INT CANR-
    32
Justice, Donald (Rodney) 1925- CLC 6, 19,
    102; DAM POET
  See also CA 5-8R; CANR 26, 54, 74; DLBY
    83; INT CANR-26; MTCW 2
Juvenal c. 60-c. 13   CMLC 8
  See also Juvenalis, Decimus Junius
  See also DLB 211
Juvenalis, Decimus Junius 55(?)-c. 127(?)
  See Juvenal
Juvenis
  See Bourne, Randolph S(illiman)
Kacew, Romain 1914-1980
  See Gary, Romain

See also CA 108; 102
Kadare, Ismail 1936-   **CLC 52**
  See also CA 161
Kadohata, Cynthia   **CLC 59, 122**
  See also CA 140
Kafka, Franz 1883-1924**TCLC 2, 6, 13, 29, 47,**
  53; DA; DAB; DAC; DAM MST, NOV;
  SSC 5, 29, 35; WLC
  See also CA 105; 126; DLB 81; MTCW 1, 2
Kahanovitsch, Pinkhes
  See Der Nister
Kahn, Roger 1927-   **CLC 30**
  See also CA 25-28R; CANR 44, 69; DLB 171;
  SATA 37
Kain, Saul
  See Sassoon, Siegfried (Lorraine)
Kaiser, Georg 1878-1945   **TCLC 9**
  See also CA 106; DLB 124
Kaletski, Alexander 1946-   **CLC 39**
  See also CA 118; 143
Kalidasa fl. c. 400-   **CMLC 9; PC 22**
Kallman, Chester (Simon) 1921-1975 **CLC 2**
  See also CA 45-48; 53-56; CANR 3
Kaminsky, Melvin 1926-
  See Brooks, Mel
  See also CA 65-68; CANR 16
Kaminsky, Stuart M(elvin) 1934-   **CLC 59**
  See also CA 73-76; CANR 29, 53
Kandinsky, Wassily 1866-1944   **TCLC 92**
  See also CA 118; 155
Kane, Francis
  See Robbins, Harold
Kane, Paul
  See Simon, Paul (Frederick)
Kane, Wilson 1917-1994
  See Bloch, Robert (Albert)
  See also CA 179; CAAE 179
Kanin, Garson 1912-1999   **CLC 22**
  See also AITN 1; CA 5-8R; 177; CANR 7, 78;
  DLB 7
Kaniuk, Yoram 1930-   **CLC 19**
  See also CA 134
Kant, Immanuel 1724-1804   **NCLC 27, 67**
  See also DLB 94
Kantor, MacKinlay 1904-1977   **CLC 7**
  See also CA 61-64; 73-76; CANR 60, 63; DLB
  9, 102; MTCW 2
Kaplan, David Michael 1946-   **CLC 50**
Kaplan, James 1951-   **CLC 59**
  See also CA 135
Karageorge, Michael
  See Anderson, Poul (William)
Karamzin, Nikolai Mikhailovich 1766-1826
  NCLC 3
  See also DLB 150
Karapanou, Margarita 1946-   **CLC 13**
  See also CA 101
Karinthy, Frigyes 1887-1938   **TCLC 47**
  See also CA 170
Karl, Frederick R(obert) 1927-   **CLC 34**
  See also CA 5-8R; CANR 3, 44
Kastel, Warren
  See Silverberg, Robert
Kataev, Evgeny Petrovich 1903-1942
  See Petrov, Evgeny
  See also CA 120
Kataphusin
  See Ruskin, John
Katz, Steve 1935-   **CLC 47**
  See also CA 25-28R; CAAS 14, 64; CANR 12;
  DLBY 83
Kauffman, Janet 1945-   **CLC 42**
  See also CA 117; CANR 43; DLBY 86

Kaufman, Bob (Garnell) 1925-1986 **CLC 49**
  See also BW 1; CA 41-44R; 118; CANR 22;
  DLB 16, 41
Kaufman, George S. 1889-1961**CLC 38; DAM**
  DRAM
  See also CA 108; 93-96; DLB 7; INT 108;
  MTCW 2
Kaufman, Sue   **CLC 3, 8**
  See also Barondess, Sue K(aufman)
Kavafis, Konstantinos Petrou 1863-1933
  See Cavafy, C(onstantine) P(eter)
  See also CA 104
Kavan, Anna 1901-1968   **CLC 5, 13, 82**
  See also CA 5-8R; CANR 6, 57; MTCW 1
Kavanagh, Dan
  See Barnes, Julian (Patrick)
Kavanagh, Julie 1952-   **CLC 119**
  See also CA 163
Kavanagh, Patrick (Joseph) 1904-1967 **C L C**
  22
  See also CA 123; 25-28R; DLB 15, 20; MTCW
  1
Kawabata, Yasunari 1899-1972 **CLC 2, 5, 9,**
  18, 107; DAM MULT; SSC 17
  See also CA 93-96; 33-36R; DLB 180; MTCW
  2
Kaye, M(ary) M(argaret) 1909-   **CLC 28**
  See also CA 89-92; CANR 24, 60; MTCW 1,
  2; SATA 62
Kaye, Mollie
  See Kaye, M(ary) M(argaret)
Kaye-Smith, Sheila 1887-1956   **TCLC 20**
  See also CA 118; DLB 36
Kaymor, Patrice Maguilene
  See Senghor, Leopold Sedar
Kazan, Elia 1909-   **CLC 6, 16, 63**
  See also CA 21-24R; CANR 32, 78
Kazantzakis, Nikos 1883(?)-1957 **TCLC 2, 5,**
  33
  See also CA 105; 132; MTCW 1, 2
Kazin, Alfred 1915-1998   **CLC 34, 38, 119**
  See also CA 1-4R; CAAS 7; CANR 1, 45, 79;
  DLB 67
Keane, Mary Nesta (Skrine) 1904-1996
  See Keane, Molly
  See also CA 108; 114; 151
Keane, Molly   **CLC 31**
  See also Keane, Mary Nesta (Skrine)
  See also INT 114
Keates, Jonathan 1946(?)-   **CLC 34**
  See also CA 163
Keaton, Buster 1895-1966   **CLC 20**
Keats, John 1795-1821**NCLC 8, 73; DA; DAB;**
  DAC; DAM MST, POET; PC 1; WLC
  See also CDBLB 1789-1832; DLB 96, 110
Keene, Donald 1922-   **CLC 34**
  See also CA 1-4R; CANR 5
Keillor, Garrison   **CLC 40, 115**
  See also Keillor, Gary (Edward)
  See also AAYA 2; BEST 89:3; DLBY 87; SATA
  58
Keillor, Gary (Edward) 1942-
  See Keillor, Garrison
  See also CA 111; 117; CANR 36, 59; DAM
  POP; MTCW 1, 2
Keith, Michael
  See Hubbard, L(afayette) Ron(ald)
Keller, Gottfried 1819-1890 **NCLC 2; SSC 26**
  See also DLB 129
Keller, Nora Okja   **CLC 109**
Kellerman, Jonathan 1949-   **CLC 44; DAM**
  POP
  See also BEST 90:1; CA 106; CANR 29, 51;

INT CANR-29
Kelley, William Melvin 1937-   **CLC 22**
  See also BW 1; CA 77-80; CANR 27; DLB 33
Kellogg, Marjorie 1922-   **CLC 2**
  See also CA 81-84
Kellow, Kathleen
  See Hibbert, Eleanor Alice Burford
Kelly, M(ilton) T(erry) 1947-   **CLC 55**
  See also CA 97-100; CAAS 22; CANR 19, 43
Kelman, James 1946-   **CLC 58, 86**
  See also CA 148; DLB 194
Kemal, Yashar 1923-   **CLC 14, 29**
  See also CA 89-92; CANR 44
Kemble, Fanny 1809-1893   **NCLC 18**
  See also DLB 32
Kemelman, Harry 1908-1996   **CLC 2**
  See also AITN 1; CA 9-12R; 155; CANR 6, 71;
  DLB 28
Kempe, Margery 1373(?)-1440(?)   **LC 6**
  See also DLB 146
Kempis, Thomas a 1380-1471   **LC 11**
Kendall, Henry 1839-1882   **NCLC 12**
Keneally, Thomas (Michael) 1935- **CLC 5, 8,**
  10, 14, 19, 27, 43, 117; DAM NOV
  See also CA 85-88; CANR 10, 50, 74; MTCW
  1, 2
Kennedy, Adrienne (Lita) 1931-**CLC 66; BLC**
  2; DAM MULT; DC 5
  See also BW 2, 3; CA 103; CAAS 20; CABS 3;
  CANR 26, 53, 82; DLB 38
Kennedy, John Pendleton 1795-1870**NCLC 2**
  See also DLB 3
Kennedy, Joseph Charles 1929-
  See Kennedy, X. J.
  See also CA 1-4R; CANR 4, 30, 40; SATA 14,
  86
Kennedy, William 1928-   **CLC 6, 28, 34, 53;**
  DAM NOV
  See also AAYA 1; CA 85-88; CANR 14, 31,
  76; DLB 143; DLBY 85; INT CANR-31;
  MTCW 1, 2; SATA 57
Kennedy, X. J.   **CLC 8, 42**
  See also Kennedy, Joseph Charles
  See also CAAS 9; CLR 27; DLB 5; SAAS 22
Kenny, Maurice (Francis) 1929-   **CLC 87;**
  DAM MULT
  See also CA 144; CAAS 22; DLB 175; NNAL
Kent, Kelvin
  See Kuttner, Henry
Kenton, Maxwell
  See Southern, Terry
Kenyon, Robert O.
  See Kuttner, Henry
Kepler, Johannes 1571-1630   **LC 45**
Kerouac, Jack   **CLC 1, 2, 3, 5, 14, 29, 61**
  See also Kerouac, Jean-Louis Lebris de
  See also AAYA 25; CDALB 1941-1968; DLB
  2, 16; DLBD 3; DLBY 95; MTCW 2
Kerouac, Jean-Louis Lebris de 1922-1969
  See Kerouac, Jack
  See also AITN 1; CA 5-8R; 25-28R; CANR 26,
  54; DA; DAB; DAC; DAM MST, NOV,
  POET, POP; MTCW 1, 2; WLC
Kerr, Jean 1923-   **CLC 22**
  See also CA 5-8R; CANR 7; INT CANR-7
Kerr, M. E.   **CLC 12, 35**
  See also Meaker, Marijane (Agnes)
  See also AAYA 2, 23; CLR 29; SAAS 1
Kerr, Robert   **CLC 55**
Kerrigan, (Thomas) Anthony 1918-**CLC 4, 6**
  See also CA 49-52; CAAS 11; CANR 4
Kerry, Lois
  See Duncan, Lois

Kesey, Ken (Elton) 1935- CLC 1, 3, 6, 11, 46, 64; DA; DAB; DAC; DAM MST, NOV, POP; WLC
See also AAYA 25; CA 1-4R; CANR 22, 38, 66; CDALB 1968-1988; DLB 2, 16, 206; MTCW 1, 2; SATA 66

Kesselring, Joseph (Otto) 1902-1967CLC 45; DAM DRAM, MST
See also CA 150

Kessler, Jascha (Frederick) 1929- CLC 4
See also CA 17-20R; CANR 8, 48

Kettelkamp, Larry (Dale) 1933- CLC 12
See also CA 29-32R; CANR 16; SAAS 3; SATA 2

Key, Ellen 1849-1926 TCLC 65

Keyber, Conny
See Fielding, Henry

Keyes, Daniel 1927-CLC 80; DA; DAC; DAM MST, NOV
See also AAYA 23; CA 17-20R; CANR 10, 26, 54, 74; MTCW 2; SATA 37

Keynes, John Maynard 1883-1946 TCLC 64
See also CA 114; 162, 163; DLBD 10; MTCW 2

Khanshendel, Chiron
See Rose, Wendy

Khayyam, Omar 1048-1131 CMLC 11; DAM POET; PC 8

Kherdian, David 1931- CLC 6, 9
See also CA 21-24R; CAAS 2; CANR 39, 78; CLR 24; JRDA; MAICYA; SATA 16, 74

Khlebnikov, Velimir TCLC 20
See also Khlebnikov, Viktor Vladimirovich

Khlebnikov, Viktor Vladimirovich 1885-1922
See Khlebnikov, Velimir
See also CA 117

Khodasevich, Vladislav (Felitsianovich) 1886-1939 TCLC 15
See also CA 115

Kielland, Alexander Lange 1849-1906 T C L C 5
See also CA 104

Kiely, Benedict 1919- CLC 23, 43
See also CA 1-4R; CANR 2; DLB 15

Kienzle, William X(avier) 1928- CLC 25; DAM POP
See also CA 93-96; CAAS 1; CANR 9, 31, 59; INT CANR-31; MTCW 1, 2

Kierkegaard, Soren 1813-1855 NCLC 34, 78

Kieslowski, Krzysztof 1941-1996 CLC 120
See also CA 147; 151

Killens, John Oliver 1916-1987 CLC 10
See also BW 2; CA 77-80; 123; CAAS 2; CANR 26; DLB 33

Killigrew, Anne 1660-1685 LC 4
See also DLB 131

Kim
See Simenon, Georges (Jacques Christian)

Kincaid, Jamaica 1949- CLC 43, 68; BLC 2; DAM MULT, NOV
See also AAYA 13; BW 2, 3; CA 125; CANR 47, 59; CDALBS; DLB 157; MTCW 2

King, Francis (Henry) 1923-CLC 8, 53; DAM NOV
See also CA 1-4R; CANR 1, 33; DLB 15, 139; MTCW 1

King, Kennedy
See Brown, George Douglas

King, Martin Luther, Jr. 1929-1968 CLC 83; BLC 2; DA; DAB; DAC; DAM MST, MULT; WLCS
See also BW 2, 3; CA 25-28; CANR 27, 44; CAP 2; MTCW 1, 2; SATA 14

King, Stephen (Edwin) 1947-CLC 12, 26, 37, 61, 113; DAM NOV, POP; SSC 17
See also AAYA 1, 17; BEST 90:1; CA 61-64; CANR 1, 30, 52, 76; DLB 143; DLBY 80; JRDA; MTCW 1, 2; SATA 9, 55

King, Steve
See King, Stephen (Edwin)

King, Thomas 1943- CLC 89; DAC;DAM MULT
See also CA 144; DLB 175; NNAL; SATA 96

Kingman, Lee CLC 17
See also Natti, (Mary) Lee
See also SAAS 3; SATA 1, 67

Kingsley, Charles 1819-1875 NCLC 35
See also DLB 21, 32, 163, 190; YABC 2

Kingsley, Sidney 1906-1995 CLC 44
See also CA 85-88; 147; DLB 7

Kingsolver, Barbara 1955-CLC 55, 81; DAM POP
See also AAYA 15; CA 129; 134; CANR 60; CDALBS; DLB 206; INT 134; MTCW 2

Kingston, Maxine (Ting Ting) Hong 1940- CLC 12, 19, 58, 121; DAM MULT, NOV; WLCS
See also AAYA 8; CA 69-72; CANR 13, 38, 74; CDALBS; DLB 173, 212; DLBY 80; INT CANR-13; MTCW 1, 2; SATA 53

Kinnell, Galway 1927- CLC 1, 2, 3, 5, 13, 29; PC 26
See also CA 9-12R; CANR 10, 34, 66; DLB 5; DLBY 87; INT CANR-34; MTCW 1, 2

Kinsella, Thomas 1928- CLC 4, 19
See also CA 17-20R; CANR 15; DLB 27; MTCW 1, 2

Kinsella, W(illiam) P(atrick) 1935- CLC 27, 43; DAC; DAM NOV, POP
See also AAYA 7; CA 97-100; CAAS 7; CANR 21, 35, 66, 75; INT CANR-21; MTCW 1, 2

Kinsey, Alfred C(harles) 1894-1956TCLC 91
See also CA 115; 170; MTCW 2

Kipling, (Joseph) Rudyard 1865-1936 T C L C 8, 17; DA; DAB; DAC; DAM MST, POET; PC 3; SSC 5; WLC
See also CA 105; 120; CANR 33; CDBLB 1890-1914; CLR 39; DLB 19, 34, 141, 156; MAICYA; MTCW 1, 2; SATA 100; YABC 2

Kirkup, James 1918- CLC 1
See also CA 1-4R; CAAS 4; CANR 2; DLB 27; SATA 12

Kirkwood, James 1930(?)-1989 CLC 9
See also AITN 2; CA 1-4R; 128; CANR 6, 40

Kirshner, Sidney
See Kingsley, Sidney

Kis, Danilo 1935-1989 CLC 57
See also CA 109; 118; 129; CANR 61; DLB 181; MTCW 1

Kivi, Aleksis 1834-1872 NCLC 30

Kizer, Carolyn (Ashley) 1925-CLC 15, 39, 80; DAM POET
See also CA 65-68; CAAS 5; CANR 24, 70; DLB 5, 169; MTCW 2

Klabund 1890-1928 TCLC 44
See also CA 162; DLB 66

Klappert, Peter 1942- CLC 57
See also CA 33-36R; DLB 5

Klein, A(braham) M(oses) 1909-1972CLC 19; DAB; DAC; DAM MST
See also CA 101; 37-40R; DLB 68

Klein, Norma 1938-1989 CLC 30
See also AAYA 2; CA 41-44R; 128; CANR 15, 37; CLR 2, 19; INT CANR-15; JRDA; MAICYA; SAAS 1; SATA 7, 57

Klein, T(heodore) E(ibon) D(onald) 1947-

CLC 34
See also CA 119; CANR 44, 75

Kleist, Heinrich von 1777-1811 NCLC 2, 37; DAM DRAM; SSC 22
See also DLB 90

Klima, Ivan 1931- CLC 56;DAM NOV
See also CA 25-28R; CANR 17, 50

Klimentov, Andrei Platonovich 1899-1951
See Platonov, Andrei
See also CA 108

Klinger, Friedrich Maximilianvon 1752-1831 NCLC 1
See also DLB 94

Klingsor the Magician
See Hartmann, Sadakichi

Klopstock, Friedrich Gottlieb 1724-1803 NCLC 11
See also DLB 97

Knapp, Caroline 1959- CLC 99
See also CA 154

Knebel, Fletcher 1911-1993 CLC 14
See also AITN 1; CA 1-4R; 140; CAAS 3; CANR 1, 36; SATA 36; SATA-Obit 75

Knickerbocker, Diedrich
See Irving, Washington

Knight, Etheridge 1931-1991CLC 40; BLC 2; DAM POET; PC 14
See also BW 1, 3; CA 21-24R; 133; CANR 23, 82; DLB 41; MTCW 2

Knight, Sarah Kemble 1666-1727 LC 7
See also DLB 24, 200

Knister, Raymond 1899-1932 TCLC 56
See also DLB 68

Knowles, John 1926- CLC 1, 4, 10, 26; DA; DAC; DAM MST, NOV
See also AAYA 10; CA 17-20R; CANR 40, 74, 76; CDALB 1968-1988; DLB 6; MTCW 1, 2; SATA 8, 89

Knox, Calvin M.
See Silverberg, Robert

Knox, John c. 1505-1572 LC 37
See also DLB 132

Knye, Cassandra
See Disch, Thomas M(ichael)

Koch, C(hristopher) J(ohn) 1932- CLC 42
See also CA 127

Koch, Christopher
See Koch, C(hristopher) J(ohn)

Koch, Kenneth 1925- CLC 5, 8, 44;DAM POET
See also CA 1-4R; CANR 6, 36, 57; DLB 5; INT CANR-36; MTCW 2; SATA 65

Kochanowski, Jan 1530-1584 LC 10

Kock, Charles Paul de 1794-1871 NCLC 16

Koda Shigeyuki 1867-1947
See Rohan, Koda
See also CA 121

Koestler, Arthur 1905-1983CLC 1, 3, 6, 8, 15, 33
See also CA 1-4R; 109; CANR 1, 33; CDBLB 1945-1960; DLBY 83; MTCW 1, 2

Kogawa, Joy Nozomi 1935- CLC 78; DAC; DAM MST, MULT
See also CA 101; CANR 19, 62; MTCW 2; SATA 99

Kohout, Pavel 1928- CLC 13
See also CA 45-48; CANR 3

Koizumi, Yakumo
See Hearn, (Patricio) Lafcadio (Tessima Carlos)

Kolmar, Gertrud 1894-1943 TCLC 40
See also CA 167

Komunyakaa, Yusef 1947-CLC 86, 94; BLCS
See also CA 147; DLB 120

Lampman, Archibald 1861-1899 **NCLC 25**
See also DLB 92

Lancaster, Bruce 1896-1963 **CLC 36**
See also CA 9-10; CANR 70; CAP 1; SATA 9

Lanchester, John **CLC 99**

Landau, Mark Alexandrovich
See Aldanov, Mark (Alexandrovich)

Landau-Aldanov, Mark Alexandrovich
See Aldanov, Mark (Alexandrovich)

Landis, Jerry
See Simon, Paul (Frederick)

Landis, John 1950- **CLC 26**
See also CA 112; 122

Landolfi, Tommaso 1908-1979 **CLC 11, 49**
See also CA 127; 117; DLB 177

Landon, Letitia Elizabeth 1802-1838 **NCLC 15**
See also DLB 96

Landor, Walter Savage 1775-1864 **NCLC 14**
See also DLB 93, 107

Landwirth, Heinz 1927-
See Lind, Jakov
See also CA 9-12R; CANR 7

Lane, Patrick 1939- **CLC 25;DAM POET**
See also CA 97-100; CANR 54; DLB 53; INT 97-100

Lang, Andrew 1844-1912 **TCLC 16**
See also CA 114; 137; DLB 98, 141, 184; MAICYA; SATA 16

Lang, Fritz 1890-1976 **CLC 20, 103**
See also CA 77-80; 69-72; CANR 30

Lange, John
See Crichton, (John) Michael

Langer, Elinor 1939- **CLC 34**
See also CA 121

Langland, William 1330(?)-1400(?) **LC 19; DA; DAB; DAC; DAM MST, POET**
See also DLB 146

Langstaff, Launcelot
See Irving, Washington

Lanier, Sidney 1842-1881 **NCLC 6;DAM POET**
See also DLB 64; DLBD 13; MAICYA; SATA 18

Lanyer, Aemilia 1569-1645 **LC 10, 30**
See also DLB 121

Lao-Tzu
See Lao Tzu

Lao Tzu fl. 6th cent. B.C.- **CMLC 7**

Lapine, James (Elliot) 1949- **CLC 39**
See also CA 123; 130; CANR 54; INT 130

Larbaud, Valery (Nicolas) 1881-1957**TCLC 9**
See also CA 106; 152

Lardner, Ring
See Lardner, Ring(gold) W(ilmer)

Lardner, Ring W., Jr.
See Lardner, Ring(gold) W(ilmer)

Lardner, Ring(gold) W(ilmer) 1885-1933 **TCLC 2, 14; SSC 32**
See also CA 104; 131; CDALB 1917-1929; DLB 11, 25, 86; DLBD 16; MTCW 1, 2

Laredo, Betty
See Codrescu, Andrei

Larkin, Maia
See Wojciechowska, Maia (Teresa)

Larkin, Philip (Arthur) 1922-1985**CLC 3,5,8, 9, 13, 18, 33, 39, 64; DAB; DAM MST, POET; PC 21**
See also CA 5-8R; 117; CANR 24, 62; CDBLB 1960 to Present; DLB 27; MTCW 1, 2

Larra (y Sanchez de Castro), Mariano Josede 1809-1837 **NCLC 17**

Larsen, Eric 1941- **CLC 55**

See also CA 132

Larsen, Nella 1891-1964 **CLC 37; BLC 2; DAM MULT**
See also BW 1; CA 125; DLB 51

Larson, Charles R(aymond) 1938- **CLC 31**
See also CA 53-56; CANR 4

Larson, Jonathan 1961-1996 **CLC 99**
See also AAYA 28; CA 156

Las Casas, Bartolome de 1474-1566 **LC 31**

Lasch, Christopher 1932-1994 **CLC 102**
See also CA 73-76; 144; CANR 25; MTCW 1, 2

Lasker-Schueler, Else 1869-1945 **TCLC 57**
See also DLB 66, 124

Laski, Harold 1893-1950 **TCLC 79**

Latham, Jean Lee 1902-1995 **CLC 12**
See also AITN 1; CA 5-8R; CANR 7; CLR 50; MAICYA; SATA 2, 68

Latham, Mavis
See Clark, Mavis Thorpe

Lathen, Emma **CLC 2**
See also Hennissart, Martha; Latsis, Mary J(ane)

Lathrop, Francis
See Leiber, Fritz (Reuter, Jr.)

Latsis, Mary J(ane) 1927(?)-1997
See Lathen, Emma
See also CA 85-88; 162

Lattimore, Richmond (Alexander) 1906-1984 **CLC 3**
See also CA 1-4R; 112; CANR 1

Laughlin, James 1914-1997 **CLC 49**
See also CA 21-24R; 162; CAAS 22; CANR 9, 47; DLB 48; DLBY 96, 97

Laurence, (Jean) Margaret (Wemyss) 1926-1987 **CLC 3, 6, 13, 50, 62; DAC; DAM MST; SSC 7**
See also CA 5-8R; 121; CANR 33; DLB 53; MTCW 1, 2; SATA-Obit 50

Laurent, Antoine 1952- **CLC 50**

Lauscher, Hermann
See Hesse, Hermann

Lautreamont, Comte de 1846-1870**NCLC 12; SSC 14**

Laverty, Donald
See Blish, James (Benjamin)

Lavin, Mary 1912-1996**CLC 4, 18, 99; SSC 4**
See also CA 9-12R; 151; CANR 33; DLB 15; MTCW 1

Lavond, Paul Dennis
See Kornbluth, C(yril) M.; Pohl, Frederik

Lawler, Raymond Evenor 1922- **CLC 58**
See also CA 103

Lawrence, D(avid) H(erbert Richards) 1885-1930 **TCLC 2, 9, 16, 33, 48, 61, 93; DA; DAB; DAC; DAM MST, NOV, POET; SSC 4, 19; WLC**
See also CA 104; 121; CDBLB 1914-1945; DLB 10, 19, 36, 98, 162, 195; MTCW 1, 2

Lawrence, T(homas) E(dward) 1888-1935 **TCLC 18**
See also Dale, Colin
See also CA 115; 167; DLB 195

Lawrence of Arabia
See Lawrence, T(homas) E(dward)

Lawson, Henry (Archibald Hertzberg) 1867-1922 **TCLC 27; SSC 18**
See also CA 120

Lawton, Dennis
See Faust, Frederick (Schiller)

Laxness, Halldor **CLC 25**
See also Gudjonsson, Halldor Kiljan

Layamon fl. c. 1200- **CMLC 10**
See also DLB 146

Laye, Camara 1928-1980 **CLC 4, 38; BLC 2; DAM MULT**
See also BW 1; CA 85-88; 97-100; CANR 25; MTCW 1, 2

Layton, Irving (Peter) 1912-**CLC 2, 15; DAC; DAM MST, POET**
See also CA 1-4R; CANR 2, 33, 43, 66; DLB 88; MTCW 1, 2

Lazarus, Emma 1849-1887 **NCLC 8**

Lazarus, Felix
See Cable, George Washington

Lazarus, Henry
See Slavitt, David R(ytman)

Lea, Joan
See Neufeld, John (Arthur)

Leacock, Stephen (Butler) 1869-1944**TCLC 2; DAC; DAM MST**
See also CA 104; 141; CANR 80; DLB 92; MTCW 2

Lear, Edward 1812-1888 **NCLC 3**
See also CLR 1; DLB 32, 163, 166; MAICYA; SATA 18, 100

Lear, Norman (Milton) 1922- **CLC 12**
See also CA 73-76

Leautaud, Paul 1872-1956 **TCLC 83**
See also DLB 65

Leavis, F(rank) R(aymond) 1895-1978**CLC 24**
See also CA 21-24R; 77-80; CANR 44; MTCW 1, 2

Leavitt, David 1961- **CLC 34;DAM POP**
See also CA 116; 122; CANR 50, 62; DLB 130; INT 122; MTCW 2

Leblanc, Maurice (Marie Emile) 1864-1941 **TCLC 49**
See also CA 110

Lebowitz, Fran(ces Ann) 1951(?)-**CLC 11, 36**
See also CA 81-84; CANR 14, 60, 70; INT CANR-14; MTCW 1

Lebrecht, Peter
See Tieck, (Johann) Ludwig

le Carre, John **CLC 3, 5, 9, 15, 28**
See also Cornwell, David (John Moore)
See also BEST 89:4; CDBLB 1960 to Present; DLB 87; MTCW 2

Le Clezio, J(ean) M(arie) G(ustave) 1940- **CLC 31**
See also CA 116; 128; DLB 83

Leconte de Lisle, Charles-Marie-Rene 1818-1894 **NCLC 29**

Le Coq, Monsieur
See Simenon, Georges (Jacques Christian)

Leduc, Violette 1907-1972 **CLC 22**
See also CA 13-14; 33-36R; CANR 69; CAP 1

Ledwidge, Francis 1887(?)-1917 **TCLC 23**
See also CA 123; DLB 20

Lee, Andrea 1953- **CLC 36; BLC 2; DAM MULT**
See also BW 1, 3; CA 125; CANR 82

Lee, Andrew
See Auchincloss, Louis (Stanton)

Lee, Chang-rae 1965- **CLC 91**
See also CA 148

Lee, Don L. **CLC 2**
See also Madhubuti, Haki R.

Lee, George W(ashington) 1894-1976**CLC 52; BLC 2; DAM MULT**
See also BW 1; CA 125; DLB 51

Lee, (Nelle) Harper 1926- **CLC 12, 60; DA; DAB; DAC; DAM MST, NOV; WLC**
See also AAYA 13; CA 13-16R; CANR 51; CDALB 1941-1968; DLB 6; MTCW 1, 2; SATA 11

Lee, Helen Elaine 1959(?)- **CLC 86**

See also CA 148
Lee, Julian
See Latham, Jean Lee
Lee, Larry
See Lee, Lawrence
Lee, Laurie 1914-1997 **CLC 90; DAB; DAM POP**
See also CA 77-80; 158; CANR 33, 73; DLB 27; MTCW 1
Lee, Lawrence 1941-1990 **CLC 34**
See also CA 131; CANR 43
Lee, Li-Young 1957- **PC 24**
See also CA 153; DLB 165
Lee, Manfred B(ennington) 1905-1971 **CLC 11**
See also Queen, Ellery
See also CA 1-4R; 29-32R; CANR 2; DLB 137
Lee, Shelton Jackson 1957(?)- **CLC 105; BLCS; DAM MULT**
See also Lee, Spike
See also BW 2, 3; CA 125; CANR 42
Lee, Spike
See Lee, Shelton Jackson
See also AAYA 4, 29
Lee, Stan 1922- **CLC 17**
See also AAYA 5; CA 108; 111; INT 111
Lee, Tanith 1947- **CLC 46**
See also AAYA 15; CA 37-40R; CANR 53; SATA 8, 88
Lee, Vernon **TCLC 5; SSC 33**
See also Paget, Violet
See also DLB 57, 153, 156, 174, 178
Lee, William
See Burroughs, William S(eward)
Lee, Willy
See Burroughs, William S(eward)
Lee-Hamilton, Eugene (Jacob) 1845-1907 **TCLC 22**
See also CA 117
Leet, Judith 1935- **CLC 11**
Le Fanu, Joseph Sheridan 1814-1873 **NCLC 9, 58; DAM POP; SSC 14**
See also DLB 21, 70, 159, 178
Leffland, Ella 1931- **CLC 19**
See also CA 29-32R; CANR 35, 78, 82; DLBY 84; INT CANR-35; SATA 65
Leger, Alexis
See Leger, (Marie-Rene Auguste) Alexis Saint-Leger
Leger, (Marie-Rene Auguste) Alexis Saint-Leger 1887-1975 **CLC 4, 11, 46; DAM POET; PC 23**
See also CA 13-16R; 61-64; CANR 43; MTCW 1
Leger, Saintleger
See Leger, (Marie-Rene Auguste) Alexis Saint-Leger
Le Guin, Ursula K(roeber) 1929- **CLC 8, 13, 22, 45, 71; DAB; DAC; DAM MST, POP; SSC 12**
See also AAYA 9, 27; AITN 1; CA 21-24R; CANR 9, 32, 52, 74; CDALB 1968-1988; CLR 3, 28; DLB 8, 52; INT CANR-32; JRDA; MAICYA; MTCW 1, 2; SATA 4, 52, 99
Lehmann, Rosamond (Nina) 1901-1990 **CLC 5**
See also CA 77-80; 131; CANR 8, 73; DLB 15; MTCW 2
Leiber, Fritz (Reuter,Jr.) 1910-1992 **CLC 25**
See also CA 45-48; 139; CANR 2, 40; DLB 8; MTCW 1, 2; SATA 45; SATA-Obit 73
Leibniz, Gottfried Wilhelm von 1646-1716 **LC 35**
See also DLB 168

Leimbach, Martha 1963-
See Leimbach, Marti
See also CA 130
Leimbach, Marti **CLC 65**
See also Leimbach, Martha
Leino, Eino **TCLC 24**
See also Loennbohm, Armas Eino Leopold
Leiris, Michel (Julien) 1901-1990 **CLC 61**
See also CA 119; 128; 132
Leithauser, Brad 1953- **CLC 27**
See also CA 107; CANR 27, 81; DLB 120
Lelchuk, Alan 1938- **CLC 5**
See also CA 45-48; CAAS 20; CANR 1, 70
Lem, Stanislaw 1921- **CLC 8, 15, 40**
See also CA 105; CAAS 1; CANR 32; MTCW 1
Lemann, Nancy 1956- **CLC 39**
See also CA 118; 136
Lemonnier, (Antoine Louis) Camille 1844-1913 **TCLC 22**
See also CA 121
Lenau, Nikolaus 1802-1850 **NCLC 16**
L'Engle, Madeleine (Camp Franklin) 1918- **CLC 12; DAM POP**
See also AAYA 28; AITN 2; CA 1-4R; CANR 3, 21, 39, 66; CLR 1, 14, 57; DLB 52; JRDA; MAICYA; MTCW 1, 2; SAAS 15; SATA 1, 27, 75
Lengyel, Jozsef 1896-1975 **CLC 7**
See also CA 85-88; 57-60; CANR 71
Lenin 1870-1924
See Lenin, V. I.
See also CA 121; 168
Lenin, V. I. **TCLC 67**
See also Lenin
Lennon, John (Ono) 1940-1980 **CLC 12, 35**
See also CA 102
Lennox, Charlotte Ramsay 1729(?)-1804 **NCLC 23**
See also DLB 39
Lentricchia, Frank (Jr.) 1940- **CLC 34**
See also CA 25-28R; CANR 19
Lenz, Siegfried 1926- **CLC 27;SSC 33**
See also CA 89-92; CANR 80; DLB 75
Leonard, Elmore (John, Jr.) 1925- **CLC 28, 34, 71, 120; DAM POP**
See also AAYA 22; AITN 1; BEST 89:1, 90:4; CA 81-84; CANR 12, 28, 53, 76; DLB 173; INT CANR-28; MTCW 1, 2
Leonard, Hugh **CLC 19**
See also Byrne, John Keyes
See also DLB 13
Leonov, Leonid (Maximovich) 1899-1994 **CLC 92; DAM NOV**
See also CA 129; CANR 74, 76; MTCW 1, 2
Leopardi, (Conte) Giacomo 1798-1837 **NCLC 22**
Le Reveler
See Artaud, Antonin (Marie Joseph)
Lerman, Eleanor 1952- **CLC 9**
See also CA 85-88; CANR 69
Lerman, Rhoda 1936- **CLC 56**
See also CA 49-52; CANR 70
Lermontov, Mikhail Yuryevich 1814-1841 **NCLC 47; PC 18**
See also DLB 205
Leroux, Gaston 1868-1927 **TCLC 25**
See also CA 108; 136; CANR 69; SATA 65
Lesage, Alain-Rene 1668-1747 **LC 2, 28**
Leskov, Nikolai (Semyonovich) 1831-1895 **NCLC 25; SSC 34**
Lessing, Doris (May) 1919- **CLC 1, 2, 3, 6, 10, 15, 22, 40, 94; DA; DAB; DAC; DAM MST,**

NOV; SSC 6; WLCS
See also CA 9-12R; CAAS 14; CANR 33, 54, 76; CDBLB 1960 to Present; DLB 15, 139; DLBY 85; MTCW 1, 2
Lessing, Gotthold Ephraim 1729-1781 **LC 8**
See also DLB 97
Lester, Richard 1932- **CLC 20**
Lever, Charles (James) 1806-1872 **NCLC 23**
See also DLB 21
Leverson, Ada 1865(?)-1936(?) **TCLC 18**
See also Elaine
See also CA 117; DLB 153
Levertov, Denise 1923-1997 **CLC 1, 2, 3, 5, 8, 15, 28, 66; DAM POET; PC 11**
See also CA 1-4R, 178; 163; CAAE 178; CAAS 19; CANR 3, 29, 50; CDALBS; DLB 5, 165; INT CANR-29; MTCW 1, 2
Levi, Jonathan **CLC 76**
Levi, Peter (Chad Tigar) 1931- **CLC 41**
See also CA 5-8R; CANR 34, 80; DLB 40
Levi, Primo 1919-1987 **CLC 37, 50;SSC 12**
See also CA 13-16R; 122; CANR 12, 33, 61, 70; DLB 177; MTCW 1, 2
Levin, Ira 1929- **CLC 3, 6; DAM POP**
See also CA 21-24R; CANR 17, 44, 74; MTCW 1, 2; SATA 66
Levin, Meyer 1905-1981 **CLC 7; DAM POP**
See also AITN 1; CA 9-12R; 104; CANR 15; DLB 9, 28; DLBY 81; SATA 21; SATA-Obit 27
Levine, Norman 1924- **CLC 54**
See also CA 73-76; CAAS 23; CANR 14, 70; DLB 88
Levine, Philip 1928- **CLC 2, 4, 5, 9, 14, 33, 118; DAM POET; PC 22**
See also CA 9-12R; CANR 9, 37, 52; DLB 5
Levinson, Deirdre 1931- **CLC 49**
See also CA 73-76; CANR 70
Levi-Strauss, Claude 1908- **CLC 38**
See also CA 1-4R; CANR 6, 32, 57; MTCW 1, 2
Levitin, Sonia (Wolff) 1934- **CLC 17**
See also AAYA 13; CA 29-32R; CANR 14, 32, 79; CLR 53; JRDA; MAICYA; SAAS 2; SATA 4, 68
Levon, O. U.
See Kesey, Ken (Elton)
Levy, Amy 1861-1889 **NCLC 59**
See also DLB 156
Lewes, George Henry 1817-1878 **NCLC 25**
See also DLB 55, 144
Lewis, Alun 1915-1944 **TCLC 3**
See also CA 104; DLB 20, 162
Lewis, C. Day
See Day Lewis, C(ecil)
Lewis, C(live) S(taples) 1898-1963 **CLC 1, 3, 6, 14, 27; DA; DAB; DAC; DAM MST, NOV, POP; WLC**
See also AAYA 3; CA 81-84; CANR 33, 71; CDBLB 1945-1960; CLR 3, 27; DLB 15, 100, 160; JRDA; MAICYA; MTCW 1, 2; SATA 13, 100
Lewis, Janet 1899-1998 **CLC 41**
See also Winters, Janet Lewis
See also CA 9-12R; 172; CANR 29, 63; CAP 1; DLBY 87
Lewis, Matthew Gregory 1775-1818 **NCLC 11, 62**
See also DLB 39, 158, 178
Lewis, (Harry) Sinclair 1885-1951 **TCLC 4, 13, 23, 39; DA; DAB; DAC; DAM MST, NOV; WLC**
See also CA 104; 133; CDALB 1917-1929; DLB

9, 102; DLBD 1; MTCW 1, 2

Lewis, (Percy) Wyndham 1882(?)-1957**TCLC 2, 9; SSC 34**
See also CA 104; 157; DLB 15; MTCW 2

Lewisohn, Ludwig 1883-1955   **TCLC 19**
See also CA 107; DLB 4, 9, 28, 102

Lewton, Val 1904-1951   **TCLC 76**

Leyner, Mark 1956-   **CLC 92**
See also CA 110; CANR 28, 53; MTCW 2

Lezama Lima, Jose 1910-1976**CLC 4, 10, 101; DAM MULT; HLCS 2**
See also CA 77-80; CANR 71; DLB 113; HW 1, 2

L'Heureux, John (Clarke) 1934-   **CLC 52**
See also CA 13-16R; CANR 23, 45

Liddell, C. H.
See Kuttner, Henry

Lie, Jonas (Lauritz Idemil) 1833-1908(?)
TCLC 5
See also CA 115

Lieber, Joel 1937-1971   **CLC 6**
See also CA 73-76; 29-32R

Lieber, Stanley Martin
See Lee, Stan

Lieberman, Laurence (James) 1935- **CLC 4, 36**
See also CA 17-20R; CANR 8, 36

Lieh Tzu fl. 7th cent. B.C.-5th cent. B.C.
CMLC 27

Lieksman, Anders
See Haavikko, Paavo Juhani

Li Fei-kan 1904-
See Pa Chin
See also CA 105

Lifton, Robert Jay 1926-   **CLC 67**
See also CA 17-20R; CANR 27, 78; INT CANR-27; SATA 66

Lightfoot, Gordon 1938-   **CLC 26**
See also CA 109

Lightman, Alan P(aige) 1948-   **CLC 81**
See also CA 141; CANR 63

Ligotti, Thomas (Robert) 1953-**CLC 44; SSC 16**
See also CA 123; CANR 49

Li Ho 791-817   **PC 13**

Liliencron, (Friedrich Adolf Axel) Detlevvon 1844-1909   **TCLC 18**
See also CA 117

Lilly, William 1602-1681   **LC 27**

Lima, Jose Lezama
See Lezama Lima, Jose

Lima Barreto, Afonso Henriquede 1881-1922
TCLC 23
See also CA 117

Limonov, Edward 1944-   **CLC 67**
See also CA 137

Lin, Frank
See Atherton, Gertrude (Franklin Horn)

Lincoln, Abraham 1809-1865   **NCLC 18**

Lind, Jakov   **CLC 1, 2, 4, 27, 82**
See also Landwirth, Heinz
See also CAAS 4

Lindbergh, Anne (Spencer) Morrow 1906-
CLC 82; DAM NOV
See also CA 17-20R; CANR 16, 73; MTCW 1, 2; SATA 33

Lindsay, David 1878-1945   **TCLC 15**
See also CA 113

Lindsay, (Nicholas) Vachel 1879-1931 **TCLC 17; DA; DAC; DAM MST, POET; PC 23; WLC**
See also CA 114; 135; CANR 79; CDALB 1865-1917; DLB 54; SATA 40

Linke-Poot
See Doeblin, Alfred

Linney, Romulus 1930-   **CLC 51**
See also CA 1-4R; CANR 40, 44, 79

Linton, Eliza Lynn 1822-1898   **NCLC 41**
See also DLB 18

Li Po 701-763   **CMLC 2**

Lipsius, Justus 1547-1606   **LC 16**

Lipsyte, Robert (Michael) 1938-**CLC 21; DA; DAC; DAM MST, NOV**
See also AAYA 7; CA 17-20R; CANR 8, 57; CLR 23; JRDA; MAICYA; SATA 5, 68

Lish, Gordon (Jay) 1934-   **CLC 45;SSC 18**
See also CA 113; 117; CANR 79; DLB 130; INT 117

Lispector, Clarice 1925(?)-1977   **CLC 43; HLCS 2; SSC 34**
See also CA 139; 116; CANR 71; DLB 113; HW 2

Littell, Robert 1935(?)-   **CLC 42**
See also CA 109; 112; CANR 64

Little, Malcolm 1925-1965
See Malcolm X
See also BW 1, 3; CA 125; 111; CANR 82; DA; DAB; DAC; DAM MST, MULT; MTCW 1, 2

Littlewit, Humphrey Gent.
See Lovecraft, H(oward) P(hillips)

Litwos
See Sienkiewicz, Henryk (Adam Alexander Pius)

Liu, E 1857-1909   **TCLC 15**
See also CA 115

Lively, Penelope (Margaret) 1933- **CLC 32, 50; DAM NOV**
See also CA 41-44R; CANR 29, 67, 79; CLR 7; DLB 14, 161, 207; JRDA; MAICYA; MTCW 1, 2; SATA 7, 60, 101

Livesay, Dorothy (Kathleen) 1909-**CLC 4, 15, 79; DAC; DAM MST, POET**
See also AITN 2; CA 25-28R; CAAS 8; CANR 36, 67; DLB 68; MTCW 1

Livy c. 59B.C.-c. 17   **CMLC 11**
See also DLB 211

Lizardi, Jose Joaquin Fernandez de 1776-1827
NCLC 30

Llewellyn, Richard
See Llewellyn Lloyd, Richard Dafydd Vivian
See also DLB 15

Llewellyn Lloyd, Richard Dafydd Vivian 1906-1983   **CLC 7, 80**
See also Llewellyn, Richard
See also CA 53-56; 111; CANR 7, 71; SATA 11; SATA-Obit 37

Llosa, (Jorge) Mario (Pedro) Vargas
See Vargas Llosa, (Jorge) Mario (Pedro)

Lloyd, Manda
See Mander, (Mary) Jane

Lloyd Webber, Andrew 1948-
See Webber, Andrew Lloyd
See also AAYA 1; CA 116; 149; DAM DRAM; SATA 56

Llull, Ramon c. 1235-c. 1316   **CMLC 12**

Lobb, Ebenezer
See Upward, Allen

Locke, Alain (Le Roy) 1886-1954   **TCLC 43; BLCS**
See also BW 1, 3; CA 106; 124; CANR 79; DLB 51

Locke, John 1632-1704   **LC 7, 35**
See also DLB 101

Locke-Elliott, Sumner
See Elliott, Sumner Locke

Lockhart, John Gibson 1794-1854   **NCLC 6**
See also DLB 110, 116, 144

Lodge, David (John) 1935-**CLC 36;DAM POP**
See also BEST 90:1; CA 17-20R; CANR 19, 53; DLB 14, 194; INT CANR-19; MTCW 1, 2

Lodge, Thomas 1558-1625   **LC 41**

Lodge, Thomas 1558-1625   **LC 41**
See also DLB 172

Loennbohm, Armas Eino Leopold 1878-1926
See Leino, Eino
See also CA 123

Loewinsohn, Ron(ald William) 1937-**CLC 52**
See also CA 25-28R; CANR 71

Logan, Jake
See Smith, Martin Cruz

Logan, John (Burton) 1923-1987   **CLC 5**
See also CA 77-80; 124; CANR 45; DLB 5

Lo Kuan-chung 1330(?)-1400(?)   **LC 12**

Lombard, Nap
See Johnson, Pamela Hansford

London, Jack   **TCLC 9, 15, 39; SSC 4; WLC**
See also London, John Griffith
See also AAYA 13; AITN 2; CDALB 1865-1917; DLB 8, 12, 78, 212; SATA 18

London, John Griffith 1876-1916
See London, Jack
See also CA 110; 119; CANR 73; DA; DAB; DAC; DAM MST, NOV; JRDA; MAICYA; MTCW 1, 2

Long, Emmett
See Leonard, Elmore (John, Jr.)

Longbaugh, Harry
See Goldman, William (W.)

Longfellow, Henry Wadsworth 1807-1882
NCLC 2, 45; DA; DAB; DAC; DAM MST, POET; WLCS
See also CDALB 1640-1865; DLB 1, 59; SATA 19

Longinus c. 1st cent. -   **CMLC 27**
See also DLB 176

Longley, Michael 1939-   **CLC 29**
See also CA 102; DLB 40

Longus fl. c. 2nd cent. -   **CMLC 7**

Longway, A. Hugh
See Lang, Andrew

Lonnrot, Elias 1802-1884   **NCLC 53**

Lopate, Phillip 1943-   **CLC 29**
See also CA 97-100; DLBY 80; INT 97-100

Lopez Portillo (y Pacheco), Jose 1920-**CLC 46**
See also CA 129; HW 1

Lopez y Fuentes, Gregorio 1897(?)-1966**C L C 32**
See also CA 131; HW 1

Lorca, Federico Garcia
See Garcia Lorca, Federico

Lord, Bette Bao 1938-   **CLC 23**
See also BEST 90:3; CA 107; CANR 41, 79; INT 107; SATA 58

Lord Auch
See Bataille, Georges

Lord Byron
See Byron, George Gordon (Noel)

Lorde, Audre (Geraldine) 1934-1992**CLC 18, 71; BLC 2; DAM MULT, POET; PC 12**
See also BW 1, 3; CA 25-28R; 142; CANR 16, 26, 46, 82; DLB 41; MTCW 1, 2

Lord Houghton
See Milnes, Richard Monckton

Lord Jeffrey
See Jeffrey, Francis

Lorenzini, Carlo 1826-1890
See Collodi, Carlo

See also MAICYA; SATA 29, 100
Lorenzo, Heberto Padilla
  See Padilla (Lorenzo), Heberto
Loris
  See Hofmannsthal, Hugo von
Loti, Pierre   **TCLC 11**
  See also Viaud, (Louis Marie) Julien
  See also DLB 123
Lou, Henri
  See Andreas-Salome, Lou
Louie, David Wong 1954-   **CLC 70**
  See also CA 139
Louis, Father M.
  See Merton, Thomas
Lovecraft, H(oward) P(hillips) 1890-1937
    TCLC 4, 22; DAM POP; SSC 3
  See also AAYA 14; CA 104; 133; MTCW 1, 2
Lovelace, Earl 1935-   **CLC 51**
  See also BW 2; CA 77-80; CANR 41, 72; DLB
    125; MTCW 1
Lovelace, Richard 1618-1657   **LC 24**
  See also DLB 131
Lowell, Amy 1874-1925   **TCLC 1, 8; DAM
    POET; PC 13**
  See also CA 104; 151; DLB 54, 140; MTCW 2
Lowell, James Russell 1819-1891   **NCLC 2**
  See also CDALB 1640-1865; DLB 1, 11, 64,
    79, 189
Lowell, Robert (Traill Spence, Jr.) 1917-1977
    **CLC 1, 2, 3, 4, 5, 8, 9, 11, 15, 37; DA; DAB;
    DAC; DAM MST, NOV; PC 3;WLC**
  See also CA 9-12R; 73-76; CABS 2; CANR 26,
    60; CDALBS; DLB 5, 169;MTCW 1, 2
Lowenthal, Michael (Francis) 1969-**CLC 119**
  See also CA 150
Lowndes, Marie Adelaide (Belloc) 1868-1947
    TCLC 12
  See also CA 107; DLB 70
Lowry, (Clarence) Malcolm 1909-1957**TCLC
    6, 40; SSC 31**
  See also CA 105; 131; CANR 62; CDBLB
    1945-1960; DLB 15; MTCW 1, 2
Lowry, Mina Gertrude 1882-1966
  See Loy, Mina
  See also CA 113
Loxsmith, John
  See Brunner, John (Kilian Houston)
Loy, Mina   **CLC 28; DAM POET; PC 16**
  See also Lowry, Mina Gertrude
  See also DLB 4, 54
Loyson-Bridet
  See Schwob, Marcel (Mayer Andre)
Lucan 39-65   **CMLC 33**
  See also DLB 211
Lucas, Craig 1951-   **CLC 64**
  See also CA 137; CANR 71
Lucas, E(dward) V(errall) 1868-1938 **TCLC
    73**
  See also CA 176; DLB 98, 149, 153; SATA 20
Lucas, George 1944-   **CLC 16**
  See also AAYA 1, 23; CA 77-80; CANR 30;
    SATA 56
Lucas, Hans
  See Godard, Jean-Luc
Lucas, Victoria
  See Plath, Sylvia
Lucian c. 120-c. 180   **CMLC 32**
  See also DLB 176
Ludlam, Charles 1943-1987   **CLC 46,50**
  See also CA 85-88; 122; CANR 72
Ludlum, Robert 1927-**CLC 22, 43; DAM NOV,
    POP**
  See also AAYA 10; BEST 89:1, 90:3; CA 33-

36R; CANR 25, 41, 68; DLBY 82; MTCW
    1, 2
Ludwig, Ken   **CLC 60**
Ludwig, Otto 1813-1865   **NCLC 4**
  See also DLB 129
Lugones, Leopoldo 1874-1938   **TCLC 15;
    HLCS 2**
  See also CA 116; 131; HW 1
Lu Hsun 1881-1936   **TCLC 3; SSC 20**
  See also Shu-Jen, Chou
Lukacs, George   **CLC 24**
  See also Lukacs, Gyorgy (Szegeny von)
Lukacs, Gyorgy (Szegeny von) 1885-1971
  See Lukacs, George
  See also CA 101; 29-32R; CANR 62; MTCW 2
Luke, Peter (Ambrose Cyprian) 1919-1995
    CLC 38
  See also CA 81-84; 147; CANR 72; DLB 13
Lunar, Dennis
  See Mungo, Raymond
Lurie, Alison 1926-   **CLC 4, 5, 18, 39**
  See also CA 1-4R; CANR 2, 17, 50; DLB 2;
    MTCW 1; SATA 46
Lustig, Arnost 1926-   **CLC 56**
  See also AAYA 3; CA 69-72; CANR 47; SATA
    56
Luther, Martin 1483-1546   **LC 9, 37**
  See also DLB 179
Luxemburg, Rosa 1870(?)-1919   **TCLC 63**
  See also CA 118
Luzi, Mario 1914-   **CLC 13**
  See also CA 61-64; CANR 9, 70; DLB 128
Lyly, John 1554(?)-1606**LC 41; DAM DRAM;
    DC 7**
  See also DLB 62, 167
L'Ymagier
  See Gourmont, Remy (-Marie-Charles) de
Lynch, B. Suarez
  See Bioy Casares, Adolfo; Borges, Jorge Luis
Lynch, B. Suarez
  See Bioy Casares, Adolfo
Lynch, David (K.) 1946-   **CLC 66**
  See also CA 124; 129
Lynch, James
  See Andreyev, Leonid (Nikolaevich)
Lynch Davis, B.
  See Bioy Casares, Adolfo; Borges, Jorge Luis
Lyndsay, Sir David 1490-1555   **LC 20**
Lynn, Kenneth S(chuyler) 1923-   **CLC 50**
  See also CA 1-4R; CANR 3, 27, 65
Lynx
  See West, Rebecca
Lyons, Marcus
  See Blish, James (Benjamin)
Lyre, Pinchbeck
  See Sassoon, Siegfried (Lorraine)
Lytle, Andrew (Nelson) 1902-1995 **CLC 22**
  See also CA 9-12R; 150; CANR 70; DLB 6;
    DLBY 95
Lyttelton, George 1709-1773   **LC 10**
Maas, Peter 1929-   **CLC 29**
  See also CA 93-96; INT 93-96; MTCW 2
Macaulay, Rose 1881-1958   **TCLC 7, 44**
  See also CA 104; DLB 36
Macaulay, Thomas Babington 1800-1859
    NCLC 42
  See also CDBLB 1832-1890; DLB 32, 55
MacBeth, George (Mann) 1932-1992**CLC 2, 5,
    9**
  See also CA 25-28R; 136; CANR 61, 66; DLB
    40; MTCW 1; SATA 4; SATA-Obit 70
MacCaig, Norman (Alexander) 1910-**CLC 36;
    DAB; DAM POET**

See also CA 9-12R; CANR 3, 34; DLB 27
MacCarthy, Sir (Charles Otto) Desmond 1877-
    1952   **TCLC 36**
  See also CA 167
MacDiarmid, HughCLC 2, 4, 11, 19, 63; PC 9
  See also Grieve, C(hristopher) M(urray)
  See also CDBLB 1945-1960; DLB 20
MacDonald, Anson
  See Heinlein, Robert A(nson)
Macdonald, Cynthia 1928-   **CLC 13, 19**
  See also CA 49-52; CANR 4, 44; DLB 105
MacDonald, George 1824-1905   **TCLC 9**
  See also CA 106; 137; CANR 80; DLB 18, 163,
    178; MAICYA; SATA 33, 100
Macdonald, John
  See Millar, Kenneth
MacDonald, John D(ann) 1916-1986 **CLC 3,
    27, 44; DAM NOV, POP**
  See also CA 1-4R; 121; CANR 1, 19, 60; DLB
    8; DLBY 86; MTCW 1, 2
Macdonald, John Ross
  See Millar, Kenneth
Macdonald, Ross   **CLC 1, 2, 3, 14, 34, 41**
  See also Millar, Kenneth
  See also DLBD 6
MacDougal, John
  See Blish, James (Benjamin)
MacEwen, Gwendolyn (Margaret) 1941-1987
    CLC 13, 55
  See also CA 9-12R; 124; CANR 7, 22; DLB
    53; SATA 50; SATA-Obit 55
Macha, Karel Hynek 1810-1846   **NCLC 46**
Machado (y Ruiz), Antonio 1875-1939**T C L C
    3**
  See also CA 104; 174; DLB 108; HW 2
Machado de Assis, Joaquim Maria 1839-1908
    TCLC 10; BLC 2; HLCS 2; SSC 24
  See also CA 107; 153
Machen, Arthur   **TCLC 4; SSC 20**
  See also Jones, Arthur Llewellyn
  See also DLB 36, 156, 178
Machiavelli, Niccolo 1469-1527**LC 8, 36; DA;
    DAB; DAC; DAM MST; WLCS**
MacInnes, Colin 1914-1976   **CLC 4, 23**
  See also CA 69-72; 65-68; CANR 21; DLB 14;
    MTCW 1, 2
MacInnes, Helen (Clark) 1907-1985 **CLC 27,
    39; DAM POP**
  See also CA 1-4R; 117; CANR 1, 28, 58; DLB
    87; MTCW 1, 2; SATA 22; SATA-Obit 44
Mackenzie, Compton (Edward Montague)
    1883-1972   **CLC 18**
  See also CA 21-22; 37-40R; CAP 2; DLB 34,
    100
Mackenzie, Henry 1745-1831   **NCLC 41**
  See also DLB 39
Mackintosh, Elizabeth 1896(?)-1952
  See Tey, Josephine
  See also CA 110
MacLaren, James
  See Grieve, C(hristopher) M(urray)
Mac Laverty, Bernard 1942-   **CLC 31**
  See also CA 116; 118; CANR 43; INT 118
MacLean, Alistair (Stuart) 1922(?)-1987**C L C
    3, 13, 50, 63; DAM POP**
  See also CA 57-60; 121; CANR 28, 61; MTCW
    1; SATA 23; SATA-Obit 50
Maclean, Norman (Fitzroy) 1902-1990 **C L C
    78; DAM POP; SSC 13**
  See also CA 102; 132; CANR 49; DLB 206
MacLeish, Archibald 1892-1982**CLC 3, 8, 14,
    68; DAM POET**
  See also CA 9-12R; 106; CANR 33, 63;

CDALBS; DLB 4. 7, 45; DLBY 82; MTCW 1, 2

MacLennan, (John) Hugh 1907-1990 **CLC 2, 14, 92; DAC; DAM MST**
See also CA 5-8R; 142; CANR 33; DLB 68; MTCW 1, 2

MacLeod, Alistair 1936-**CLC 56; DAC; DAM MST**
See also CA 123; DLB 60; MTCW 2

Macleod, Fiona
See Sharp. William

MacNeice. (Frederick) Louis 1907-1963 **C L C 1, 4, 10. 53; DAB; DAM POET**
See also CA 85-88; CANR 61; DLB 10, 20; MTCW 1, 2

MacNeill. Dand
See Fraser, George MacDonald

Macpherson, James 1736-1796 **LC 29**
See also Ossian
See also DLB 109

Macpherson, (Jean) Jay 1931- **CLC 14**
See also CA 5-8R; DLB 53

MacShane, Frank 1927- **CLC 39**
See also CA 9-12R; CANR 3, 33; DLB 111

Macumber, Mari
See Sandoz, Mari(e Susette)

Madach, Imre 1823-1864 **NCLC 19**

Madden, (Jerry) David 1933- **CLC 5, 15**
See also CA 1-4R; CAAS 3; CANR 4, 45; DLB 6; MTCW 1

Maddern, Al(an)
See Ellison, Harlan (Jay)

Madhubuti, Haki R. 1942-**CLC 6, 73; BLC 2; DAM MULT, POET; PC 5**
See also Lee, Don L.
See also BW 2, 3; CA 73-76; CANR 24, 51, 73; DLB 5, 41; DLBD 8; MTCW 2

Maepenn, Hugh
See Kuttner, Henry

Maepenn, K. H.
See Kuttner, Henry

Maeterlinck, Maurice 1862-1949 **TCLC 3; DAM DRAM**
See also CA 104; 136; CANR 80; DLB 192; SATA 66

Maginn, William 1794-1842 **NCLC 8**
See also DLB 110, 159

Mahapatra, Jayanta 1928- **CLC 33;DAM MULT**
See also CA 73-76; CAAS 9; CANR 15, 33, 66

Mahfouz, Naguib (Abdel Aziz Al-Sabilgi) 1911(?)-
See Mahfuz, Najib
See also BEST 89:2; CA 128; CANR 55; DAM NOV; MTCW 1, 2

Mahfuz, Najib **CLC 52, 55**
See also Mahfouz, Naguib (Abdel Aziz Al-Sabilgi)
See also DLBY 88

Mahon, Derek 1941- **CLC 27**
See also CA 113; 128; DLB 40

Mailer, Norman 1923-**CLC 1, 2, 3, 4, 5, 8, 11, 14, 28, 39, 74, 111; DA; DAB; DAC; DAM MST, NOV, POP**
See also AITN 2; CA 9-12R; CABS 1; CANR 28, 74, 77; CDALB 1968-1988; DLB 2, 16, 28, 185; DLBD 3; DLBY 80, 83; MTCW 1, 2

Maillet, Antonine 1929- **CLC 54, 118; DAC**
See also CA 115; 120; CANR 46, 74, 77; DLB 60; INT 120; MTCW 2

Mais, Roger 1905-1955 **TCLC 8**
See also BW 1, 3; CA 105; 124; CANR 82; DLB

125; MTCW 1

Maistre, Joseph de 1753-1821 **NCLC 37**

Maitland, Frederic 1850-1906 **TCLC 65**

Maitland, Sara (Louise) 1950- **CLC 49**
See also CA 69-72; CANR 13, 59

Major, Clarence 1936-**CLC 3, 19, 48; BLC 2; DAM MULT**
See also BW 2, 3; CA 21-24R; CAAS 6; CANR 13, 25, 53, 82; DLB 33

Major, Kevin (Gerald) 1949- **CLC 26; DAC**
See also AAYA 16; CA 97-100; CANR 21, 38; CLR 11; DLB 60; INT CANR-21; JRDA; MAICYA; SATA 32, 82

Maki, James
See Ozu, Yasujiro

Malabaila, Damiano
See Levi, Primo

Malamud, Bernard 1914-1986**CLC 1, 2, 3, 5, 8, 9, 11, 18, 27, 44, 78, 85;DA; DAB; DAC; DAM MST, NOV, POP; SSC 15;WLC**
See also AAYA 16; CA 5-8R; 118; CABS 1; CANR 28, 62; CDALB 1941-1968; DLB 2, 28, 152; DLBY 80, 86; MTCW 1, 2

Malan, Herman
See Bosman, Herman Charles; Bosman, Herman Charles

Malaparte, Curzio 1898-1957 **TCLC 52**

Malcolm, Dan
See Silverberg, Robert

Malcolm X **CLC 82, 117; BLC 2; WLCS**
See also Little, Malcolm

Malherbe, Francois de 1555-1628 **LC 5**

Mallarme, Stephane 1842-1898 **NCLC 4, 41; DAM POET; PC 4**

Mallet-Joris, Francoise 1930- **CLC 11**
See also CA 65-68; CANR 17; DLB 83

Malley, Ern
See McAuley, James Phillip

Mallowan, Agatha Christie
See Christie, Agatha (Mary Clarissa)

Maloff, Saul 1922- **CLC 5**
See also CA 33-36R

Malone, Louis
See MacNeice, (Frederick) Louis

Malone, Michael (Christopher) 1942-**CLC 43**
See also CA 77-80; CANR 14, 32, 57

Malory, (Sir) Thomas 1410(?)-1471(?)**LC 11; DA; DAB; DAC; DAM MST; WLCS**
See also CDBLB Before 1660; DLB 146; SATA 59; SATA-Brief 33

Malouf, (George Joseph) David 1934-**CLC 28, 86**
See also CA 124; CANR 50, 76; MTCW 2

Malraux, (Georges-)Andre 1901-1976**CLC 1, 4, 9, 13, 15, 57; DAM NOV**
See also CA 21-22; 69-72; CANR 34, 58; CAP 2; DLB 72; MTCW 1, 2

Malzberg, Barry N(athaniel) 1939- **CLC 7**
See also CA 61-64; CAAS 4; CANR 16; DLB 8

Mamet, David (Alan) 1947-**CLC 9, 15, 34, 46, 91; DAM DRAM; DC 4**
See also AAYA 3; CA 81-84; CABS 3; CANR 15, 41, 67, 72; DLB 7; MTCW 1, 2

Mamoulian, Rouben (Zachary) 1897-1987 **CLC 16**
See also CA 25-28R; 124

Mandelstam, Osip (Emilievich) 1891(?)-1938(?) **TCLC 2, 6; PC 14**
See also CA 104; 150; MTCW 2

Mander, (Mary) Jane 1877-1949 **TCLC 31**
See also CA 162

Mandeville, John fl. 1350- **CMLC 19**
See also DLB 146

Mandiargues, Andre Pieyre de **CLC 41**
See also Pieyre de Mandiargues, Andre
See also DLB 83

Mandrake, Ethel Belle
See Thurman, Wallace (Henry)

Mangan, James Clarence 1803-1849**NCLC 27**

Maniere, J.-E.
See Giraudoux, (Hippolyte) Jean

Mankiewicz, Herman (Jacob) 1897-1953 **TCLC 85**
See also CA 120; 169; DLB 26

Manley, (Mary) Delariviere 1672(?)-1724 **L C 1, 42**
See also DLB 39, 80

Mann, Abel
See Creasey, John

Mann, Emily 1952- **DC 7**
See also CA 130; CANR 55

Mann, (Luiz) Heinrich 1871-1950 **TCLC 9**
See also CA 106; 164; DLB 66, 118

Mann, (Paul) Thomas 1875-1955 **TCLC 2, 8, 14, 21, 35, 44, 60; DA; DAB; DAC; DAM MST, NOV; SSC 5; WLC**
See also CA 104; 128; DLB 66; MTCW 1, 2

Mannheim, Karl 1893-1947 **TCLC 65**

Manning, David
See Faust, Frederick (Schiller)

Manning, Frederic 1887(?)-1935 **TCLC 25**
See also CA 124

Manning, Olivia 1915-1980 **CLC 5, 19**
See also CA 5-8R; 101; CANR 29; MTCW 1

Mano, D. Keith 1942- **CLC 2, 10**
See also CA 25-28R; CAAS 6; CANR 26, 57; DLB 6

Mansfield, KatherineTCLC 2, 8, 39; DAB; SSC 9, 23; WLC
See also Beauchamp, Kathleen Mansfield
See also DLB 162

Manso, Peter 1940- **CLC 39**
See also CA 29-32R; CANR 44

Mantecon, Juan Jimenez
See Jimenez (Mantecon), Juan Ramon

Manton, Peter
See Creasey, John

Man Without a Spleen, A
See Chekhov, Anton (Pavlovich)

Manzoni, Alessandro 1785-1873 **NCLC 29**

Map, Walter 1140-1209 **CMLC 32**

Mapu, Abraham (ben Jekutiel) 1808-1867 **NCLC 18**

Mara, Sally
See Queneau, Raymond

Marat, Jean Paul 1743-1793 **LC 10**

Marcel, Gabriel Honore 1889-1973 **CLC 15**
See also CA 102; 45-48; MTCW 1, 2

March, William 1893-1954 **TCLC 96**

Marchbanks, Samuel
See Davies, (William) Robertson

Marchi, Giacomo
See Bassani, Giorgio

Margulies, Donald **CLC 76**

Marie de France c. 12th cent. - **CMLC 8; PC 22**
See also DLB 208

Marie de l'Incarnation 1599-1672 **LC 10**

Marier, Captain Victor
See Griffith, D(avid Lewelyn) W(ark)

Mariner, Scott
See Pohl, Frederik

Marinetti, Filippo Tommaso 1876-1944**TCLC 10**
See also CA 107; DLB 114

Marivaux, Pierre Carlet de Chamblain de 1688-

See Bridie, James
See also CA 104

Maxwell, William (Keepers, Jr.) 1908-**CLC 19**
See also CA 93-96; CANR 54; DLBY 80; INT 93-96

May, Elaine 1932- **CLC 16**
See also CA 124; 142; DLB 44

Mayakovski, Vladimir (Vladimirovich) 1893-1930 **TCLC 4, 18**
See also CA 104; 158; MTCW 2

Mayhew, Henry 1812-1887 **NCLC 31**
See also DLB 18, 55, 190

Mayle, Peter 1939(?)- **CLC 89**
See also CA 139; CANR 64

Maynard, Joyce 1953- **CLC 23**
See also CA 111; 129; CANR 64

Mayne, William (James Carter) 1928-**CLC 12**
See also AAYA 20; CA 9-12R; CANR 37, 80; CLR 25; JRDA; MAICYA; SAAS 11; SATA 6, 68

Mayo, Jim
See L'Amour, Louis (Dearborn)

Maysles, Albert 1926- **CLC 16**
See also CA 29-32R

Maysles, David 1932- **CLC 16**

Mazer, Norma Fox 1931- **CLC 26**
See also AAYA 5; CA 69-72; CANR 12, 32, 66; CLR 23; JRDA; MAICYA; SAAS 1; SATA 24, 67, 105

Mazzini, Guiseppe 1805-1872 **NCLC 34**

McAuley, James Phillip 1917-1976 **CLC 45**
See also CA 97-100

McBain, Ed
See Hunter, Evan

McBrien, William Augustine 1930- **CLC 44**
See also CA 107

McCaffrey, Anne (Inez) 1926-**CLC 17; DAM NOV, POP**
See also AAYA 6; AITN 2; BEST 89:2; CA 25-28R; CANR 15, 35, 55; CLR 49; DLB 8; JRDA; MAICYA; MTCW 1, 2; SAAS 11; SATA 8, 70

McCall, Nathan 1955(?)- **CLC 86**
See also BW 3; CA 146

McCann, Arthur
See Campbell, John W(ood, Jr.)

McCann, Edson
See Pohl, Frederik

McCarthy, Charles, Jr. 1933-
See McCarthy, Cormac
See also CANR 42, 69; DAM POP; MTCW 2

McCarthy, Cormac 1933- **CLC 4, 57, 59, 101**
See also McCarthy, Charles, Jr.
See also DLB 6, 143; MTCW 2

McCarthy, Mary (Therese) 1912-1989**CLC 1, 3, 5, 14, 24, 39, 59; SSC 24**
See also CA 5-8R; 129; CANR 16, 50, 64; DLB 2; DLBY 81; INT CANR-16; MTCW 1, 2

McCartney, (James) Paul 1942- **CLC 12, 35**
See also CA 146

McCauley, Stephen (D.) 1955- **CLC 50**
See also CA 141

McClure, Michael (Thomas) 1932-**CLC 6, 10**
See also CA 21-24R; CANR 17, 46, 77; DLB 16

McCorkle, Jill (Collins) 1958- **CLC 51**
See also CA 121; DLBY 87

McCourt, Frank 1930- **CLC 109**
See also CA 157

McCourt, James 1941- **CLC 5**
See also CA 57-60

McCourt, Malachy 1932- **CLC 119**

McCoy, Horace(Stanley) 1897-1955**TCLC 28**

See also CA 108; 155; DLB 9

McCrae, John 1872-1918 **TCLC 12**
See also CA 109; DLB 92

McCreigh, James
See Pohl, Frederik

McCullers, (Lula) Carson (Smith) 1917-1967 **CLC 1, 4, 10, 12, 48, 100; DA; DAB; DAC; DAM MST, NOV; SSC 9, 24;WLC**
See also AAYA 21; CA 5-8R; 25-28R; CABS 1, 3; CANR 18; CDALB 1941-1968; DLB 2, 7, 173; MTCW 1, 2; SATA 27

McCulloch, John Tyler
See Burroughs, Edgar Rice

McCullough, Colleen 1938(?)- **CLC 27, 107; DAM NOV, POP**
See also CA 81-84; CANR 17, 46, 67; MTCW 1, 2

McDermott, Alice 1953- **CLC 90**
See also CA 109; CANR 40

McElroy, Joseph 1930- **CLC 5, 47**
See also CA 17-20R

McEwan, Ian (Russell) 1948- **CLC 13, 66; DAM NOV**
See also BEST 90:4; CA 61-64; CANR 14, 41, 69; DLB 14, 194; MTCW 1, 2

McFadden, David 1940- **CLC 48**
See also CA 104; DLB 60; INT 104

McFarland, Dennis 1950- **CLC 65**
See also CA 165

McGahern, John 1934- **CLC 5, 9, 48;SSC 17**
See also CA 17-20R; CANR 29, 68; DLB 14; MTCW 1

McGinley, Patrick (Anthony) 1937- **CLC 41**
See also CA 120; 127; CANR 56; INT 127

McGinley, Phyllis 1905-1978 **CLC 14**
See also CA 9-12R; 77-80; CANR 19; DLB 11, 48; SATA 2, 44; SATA-Obit 24

McGinniss, Joe 1942- **CLC 32**
See also AITN 2; BEST 89:2; CA 25-28R; CANR 26, 70; DLB 185; INT CANR-26

McGivern, Maureen Daly
See Daly, Maureen

McGrath, Patrick 1950- **CLC 55**
See also CA 136; CANR 65

McGrath, Thomas (Matthew) 1916-1990**CLC 28, 59; DAM POET**
See also CA 9-12R; 132; CANR 6, 33; MTCW 1; SATA 41; SATA-Obit 66

McGuane, Thomas (Francis III) 1939-**CLC 3, 7, 18, 45**
See also AITN 2; CA 49-52; CANR 5, 24, 49; DLB 2, 212; DLBY 80; INT CANR-24; MTCW 1

McGuckian, Medbh 1950- **CLC 48; DAM POET; PC 27**
See also CA 143; DLB 40

McHale, Tom 1942(?)-1982 **CLC 3, 5**
See also AITN 1; CA 77-80; 106

McIlvanney, William 1936- **CLC 42**
See also CA 25-28R; CANR 61; DLB 14, 207

McIlwraith, Maureen Mollie Hunter
See Hunter, Mollie
See also SATA 2

McInerney, Jay 1955-**CLC 34, 112;DAM POP**
See also AAYA 18; CA 116; 123; CANR 45, 68; INT 123; MTCW 2

McIntyre, Vonda N(eel) 1948- **CLC 18**
See also CA 81-84; CANR 17, 34, 69; MTCW 1

McKay, ClaudeTCLC 7, 41; BLC 3; DAB;PC 2**
See also McKay, Festus Claudius
See also DLB 4, 45, 51, 117

McKay, Festus Claudius 1889-1948
See McKay, Claude
See also BW 1, 3; CA 104; 124; CANR 73; DA; DAC; DAM MST, MULT, NOV, POET; MTCW 1, 2; WLC

McKuen, Rod 1933- **CLC 1, 3**
See also AITN 1; CA 41-44R; CANR 40

McLoughlin, R. B.
See Mencken, H(enry) L(ouis)

McLuhan, (Herbert) Marshall 1911-1980 **CLC 37, 83**
See also CA 9-12R; 102; CANR 12, 34, 61; DLB 88; INT CANR-12; MTCW 1, 2

McMillan, Terry (L.) 1951- **CLC 50, 61, 112; BLCS; DAM MULT, NOV, POP**
See also AAYA 21; BW 2, 3; CA 140; CANR 60; MTCW 2

McMurtry, Larry (Jeff) 1936-**CLC 2, 3, 7, 11, 27, 44; DAM NOV, POP**
See also AAYA 15; AITN 2; BEST 89:2; CA 5-8R; CANR 19, 43, 64; CDALB 1968-1988; DLB 2, 143; DLBY 80, 87; MTCW 1, 2

McNally, T. M. 1961- **CLC 82**

McNally, Terrence 1939- **CLC 4, 7, 41, 91; DAM DRAM**
See also CA 45-48; CANR 2, 56; DLB 7; MTCW 2

McNamer, Deirdre 1950- **CLC 70**

McNeal, Tom **CLC 119**

McNeile, Herman Cyril 1888-1937
See Sapper
See also DLB 77

McNickle, (William) D'Arcy 1904-1977 **C L C 89;DAM MULT**
See also CA 9-12R; 85-88; CANR 5, 45; DLB 175, 212; NNAL; SATA-Obit 22

McPhee, John (Angus) 1931- **CLC 36**
See also BEST 90:1; CA 65-68; CANR 20, 46, 64, 69; DLB 185; MTCW 1, 2

McPherson, James Alan 1943- **CLC 19, 77; BLCS**
See also BW 1, 3; CA 25-28R; CAAS 17; CANR 24, 74; DLB 38; MTCW 1, 2

McPherson, William (Alexander) 1933- **C L C 34**
See also CA 69-72; CANR 28; INT CANR-28

Mead, George Herbert 1873-1958 **TCLC 89**

Mead, Margaret 1901-1978 **CLC 37**
See also AITN 1; CA 1-4R; 81-84; CANR 4; MTCW 1, 2; SATA-Obit 20

Meaker, Marijane (Agnes) 1927-
See Kerr, M. E.
See also CA 107; CANR 37, 63; INT 107; JRDA; MAICYA; MTCW 1; SATA 20,61, 99

Medoff, Mark (Howard) 1940- **CLC 6, 23; DAM DRAM**
See also AITN 1; CA 53-56; CANR 5; DLB 7; INT CANR-5

Medvedev, P. N.
See Bakhtin, Mikhail Mikhailovich

Meged, Aharon
See Megged, Aharon

Meged, Aron
See Megged, Aharon

Megged, Aharon 1920- **CLC 9**
See also CA 49-52; CAAS 13; CANR 1

Mehta, Ved (Parkash) 1934- **CLC 37**
See also CA 1-4R; CANR 2, 23, 69; MTCW 1

Melanter
See Blackmore, R(ichard) D(oddridge)

Melies, Georges 1861-1938 **TCLC 81**

Melikow, Loris
See Hofmannsthal, Hugo von

Melmoth, Sebastian
 See Wilde, Oscar
Meltzer, Milton 1915-   **CLC 26**
 See also AAYA 8; CA 13-16R; CANR 38; CLR
 13; DLB 61; JRDA; MAICYA; SAAS 1;
 SATA 1, 50, 80
Melville, Herman 1819-1891 **NCLC 3, 12, 29,**
 45, 49; DA; DAB; DAC; DAM MST, NOV;
 SSC 1, 17; WLC
 See also AAYA 25; CDALB 1640-1865; DLB
 3, 74; SATA 59
Menander c. 342B.C.-c. 292B.C. **CMLC 9;**
 DAM DRAM; DC 3
 See also DLB 176
Menchu, Rigoberta 1959-
 See also HLCS 2
Menchu, Rigoberta 1959-
 See also CA 175; HLCS 2
Mencken, H(enry) L(ouis) 1880-1956 **TCLC**
 13
 See also CA 105; 125; CDALB 1917-1929;
 DLB 11, 29, 63, 137; MTCW 1, 2
Mendelsohn, Jane 1965(?)-   **CLC 99**
 See also CA 154
Mercer, David 1928-1980 **CLC 5; DAM DRAM**
 See also CA 9-12R; 102; CANR 23; DLB 13;
 MTCW 1
Merchant, Paul
 See Ellison, Harlan (Jay)
Meredith, George 1828-1909 **TCLC 17, 43;**
 DAM POET
 See also CA 117; 153; CANR 80; CDBLB 1832-
 1890; DLB 18, 35, 57, 159
Meredith, William (Morris) 1919- **CLC 4, 13,**
 22, 55; DAM POET
 See also CA 9-12R; CAAS 14; CANR 6, 40;
 DLB 5
Merezhkovsky, Dmitry Sergeyevich 1865-1941
 TCLC 29
 See also CA 169
Merimee, Prosper 1803-1870 **NCLC 6, 65; SSC**
 7
 See also DLB 119, 192
Merkin, Daphne 1954-   **CLC 44**
 See also CA 123
Merlin, Arthur
 See Blish, James (Benjamin)
Merrill, James (Ingram) 1926-1995 **CLC 2, 3,**
 6, 8, 13, 18, 34, 91; DAM POET
 See also CA 13-16R; 147; CANR 10, 49, 63;
 DLB 5, 165; DLBY 85; INT CANR-10;
 MTCW 1, 2
Merriman, Alex
 See Silverberg, Robert
Merriman, Brian 1747-1805   **NCLC 70**
Merritt, E. B.
 See Waddington, Miriam
Merton, Thomas 1915-1968 **CLC 1, 3, 11, 34,**
 83; PC 10
 See also CA 5-8R; 25-28R; CANR 22, 53; DLB
 48; DLBY 81; MTCW 1, 2
Merwin, W(illiam) S(tanley) 1927- **CLC 1, 2,**
 3, 5, 8, 13, 18, 45, 88; DAM POET
 See also CA 13-16R; CANR 15, 51; DLB 5,
 169; INT CANR-15; MTCW 1, 2
Metcalf, John 1938-   **CLC 37**
 See also CA 113; DLB 60
Metcalf, Suzanne
 See Baum, L(yman) Frank
Mew, Charlotte (Mary) 1870-1928 **TCLC 8**
 See also CA 105; DLB 19, 135
Mewshaw, Michael 1943-   **CLC 9**
 See also CA 53-56; CANR 7, 47; DLBY 80

Meyer, June
 See Jordan, June
Meyer, Lynn
 See Slavitt, David R(ytman)
Meyer-Meyrink, Gustav 1868-1932
 See Meyrink, Gustav
 See also CA 117
Meyers, Jeffrey 1939-   **CLC 39**
 See also CA 73-76; CANR 54; DLB 111
Meynell, Alice (Christina Gertrude Thompson)
 1847-1922   **TCLC 6**
 See also CA 104; 177; DLB 19, 98
Meyrink, Gustav   **TCLC 21**
 See also Meyer-Meyrink, Gustav
 See also DLB 81
Michaels, Leonard 1933- **CLC 6, 25; SSC 16**
 See also CA 61-64; CANR 21, 62; DLB 130;
 MTCW 1
Michaux, Henri 1899-1984   **CLC 8, 19**
 See also CA 85-88; 114
Micheaux, Oscar (Devereaux) 1884-1951
 TCLC 76
 See also BW 3; CA 174; DLB 50
Michelangelo 1475-1564   **LC 12**
Michelet, Jules 1798-1874   **NCLC 31**
Michels, Robert 1876-1936   **TCLC 88**
Michener, James A(lbert) 1907(?)-1997 **C L C**
 1, 5, 11, 29, 60, 109; DAM NOV, POP
 See also AAYA 27; AITN 1; BEST 90:1; CA 5-
 8R; 161; CANR 21, 45, 68; DLB 6; MTCW
 1, 2
Mickiewicz, Adam 1798-1855 **NCLC 3**
Middleton, Christopher 1926- **CLC 13**
 See also CA 13-16R; CANR 29, 54; DLB 40
Middleton, Richard (Barham) 1882-1911
 TCLC 56
 See also DLB 156
Middleton, Stanley 1919-   **CLC 7, 38**
 See also CA 25-28R; CAAS 23; CANR 21, 46,
 81; DLB 14
Middleton, Thomas 1580-1627 **LC 33; DAM**
 DRAM, MST; DC 5
 See also DLB 58
Migueis, Jose Rodrigues 1901- **CLC 10**
Mikszath, Kalman 1847-1910 **TCLC 31**
 See also CA 170
Miles, Jack   **CLC 100**
Miles, Josephine (Louise) 1911-1985 **CLC 1, 2,**
 14, 34, 39; DAM POET
 See also CA 1-4R; 116; CANR 2, 55; DLB 48
Militant
 See Sandburg, Carl (August)
Mill, John Stuart 1806-1873 **NCLC 11, 58**
 See also CDBLB 1832-1890; DLB 55, 190
Millar, Kenneth 1915-1983 **CLC 14; DAM POP**
 See also Macdonald, Ross
 See also CA 9-12R; 110; CANR 16, 63; DLB
 2; DLBD 6; DLBY 83; MTCW 1, 2
Millay, E. Vincent
 See Millay, Edna St. Vincent
Millay, Edna St. Vincent 1892-1950 **TCLC 4,**
 49; DA; DAB; DAC; DAM MST, POET;
 PC 6; WLCS
 See also CA 104; 130; CDALB 1917-1929;
 DLB 45, MTCW 1, 2
Miller, Arthur 1915- **CLC 1, 2, 6, 10, 15, 26, 47,**
 78; DA; DAB; DAC; DAM DRAM, MST;
 DC 1; WLC
 See also AAYA 15; AITN 1; CA 1-4R; CABS
 3; CANR 2, 30, 54, 76; CDALB 1941-1968;
 DLB 7; MTCW 1, 2
Miller, Henry (Valentine) 1891-1980 **CLC 1, 2,**
 4, 9, 14, 43, 84; DA; DAB; DAC; DAM

MST, NOV; WLC
 See also CA 9-12R; 97-100; CANR 33, 64;
 CDALB 1929-1941; DLB 4, 9; DLBY 80;
 MTCW 1, 2
Miller, Jason 1939(?)-   **CLC 2**
 See also AITN 1; CA 73-76; DLB 7
Miller, Sue 1943-   **CLC 44; DAM POP**
 See also BEST 90:3; CA 139; CANR 59; DLB
 143
Miller, Walter M(ichael, Jr.) 1923- **CLC 4, 30**
 See also CA 85-88; DLB 8
Millett, Kate 1934-   **CLC 67**
 See also AITN 1; CA 73-76; CANR 32, 53, 76;
 MTCW 1, 2
Millhauser, Steven (Lewis) 1943- **CLC 21, 54,**
 109
 See also CA 110; 111; CANR 63; DLB 2; INT
 111; MTCW 2
Millin, Sarah Gertrude 1889-1968 **CLC 49**
 See also CA 102; 93-96
Milne, A(lan) A(lexander) 1882-1956 **TCLC 6,**
 88; DAB; DAC; DAM MST
 See also CA 104; 133; CLR 1, 26; DLB 10, 77,
 100, 160; MAICYA; MTCW 1, 2; SATA 100;
 YABC 1
Milner, Ron(ald) 1938- **CLC 56; BLC 3; DAM**
 MULT
 See also AITN 1; BW 1; CA 73-76; CANR 24,
 81; DLB 38; MTCW 1
Milnes, Richard Monckton 1809-1885 **N C L C**
 61
 See also DLB 32, 184
Milosz, Czeslaw 1911- **CLC 5, 11, 22, 31, 56,**
 82; DAM MST, POET; PC 8; WLCS
 See also CA 81-84; CANR 23, 51; MTCW 1, 2
Milton, John 1608-1674 **LC 9, 43; DA; DAB;**
 DAC; DAM MST, POET; PC 19; WLC
 See also CDBLB 1660-1789; DLB 131, 151
Min, Anchee 1957-   **CLC 86**
 See also CA 146
Minehaha, Cornelius
 See Wedekind, (Benjamin) Frank(lin)
Miner, Valerie 1947-   **CLC 40**
 See also CA 97-100; CANR 59
Minimo, Duca
 See D'Annunzio, Gabriele
Minot, Susan 1956-   **CLC 44**
 See also CA 134
Minus, Ed 1938-   **CLC 39**
Miranda, Javier
 See Bioy Casares, Adolfo
Miranda, Javier
 See Bioy Casares, Adolfo
Mirbeau, Octave 1848-1917   **TCLC 55**
 See also DLB 123, 192
Miro (Ferrer), Gabriel (Francisco Victor) 1879-
 1930   **TCLC 5**
 See also CA 104
Mishima, Yukio 1925-1970 **CLC 2, 4, 6, 9, 27;**
 DC 1; SSC 4
 See also Hiraoka, Kimitake
 See also DLB 182; MTCW 2
Mistral, Frederic 1830-1914   **TCLC 51**
 See also CA 122
Mistral, Gabriela   **TCLC 2; HLC 2**
 See also Godoy Alcayaga, Lucila
 See also MTCW 2
Mistry, Rohinton 1952-   **CLC 71; DAC**
 See also CA 141
Mitchell, Clyde
 See Ellison, Harlan (Jay); Silverberg, Robert
Mitchell, James Leslie 1901-1935
 See Gibbon, Lewis Grassic

See also CA 104; DLB 15

Mitchell, Joni 1943-   **CLC 12**
  See also CA 112

Mitchell, Joseph (Quincy) 1908-1996**CLC 98**
  See also CA 77-80; 152; CANR 69; DLB 185;
  DLBY 96

Mitchell, Margaret (Munnerlyn) 1900-1949
  TCLC 11; DAM NOV, POP
  See also AAYA 23; CA 109; 125; CANR 55;
  CDALBS; DLB 9; MTCW 1, 2

Mitchell, Peggy
  See Mitchell, Margaret (Munnerlyn)

Mitchell, S(ilas) Weir 1829-1914   **TCLC 36**
  See also CA 165; DLB 202

Mitchell, W(illiam) O(rmond) 1914-1998**CLC
25; DAC; DAM MST**
  See also CA 77-80; 165; CANR 15, 43; DLB
  88

Mitchell, William 1879-1936   **TCLC 81**

Mitford, Mary Russell 1787-1855 **NCLC 4**
  See also DLB 110, 116

Mitford, Nancy 1904-1973   **CLC 44**
  See also CA 9-12R; DLB 191

Miyamoto, (Chujo) Yuriko 1899-1951 **T C L C
37**
  See also CA 170, 174; DLB 180

Miyazawa, Kenji 1896-1933   **TCLC 76**
  See also CA 157

Mizoguchi, Kenji 1898-1956   **TCLC 72**
  See also CA 167

Mo, Timothy (Peter) 1950(?)-   **CLC 46**
  See also CA 117; DLB 194; MTCW 1

Modarressi, Taghi (M.) 1931-   **CLC 44**
  See also CA 121; 134; INT 134

Modiano, Patrick (Jean) 1945-   **CLC 18**
  See also CA 85-88; CANR 17, 40; DLB 83

Moerck, Paal
  See Roelvaag, O(le) E(dvart)

Mofolo, Thomas (Mokopu) 1875(?)-1948
  TCLC 22; BLC 3; DAM MULT
  See also CA 121; 153; MTCW 2

Mohr, Nicholasa 1938-**CLC 12; DAM MULT;
HLC 2**
  See also AAYA 8; CA 49-52; CANR 1, 32, 64;
  CLR 22; DLB 145; HW 1, 2; JRDA; SAAS
  8; SATA 8, 97

Mojtabai, A(nn) G(race) 1938- **CLC 5, 9, 15,
29**
  See also CA 85-88

Moliere 1622-1673**LC 10, 28; DA; DAB; DAC;
DAM DRAM, MST; WLC**

Molin, Charles
  See Mayne, William (James Carter)

Molnar, Ferenc 1878-1952   **TCLC 20;DAM
DRAM**
  See also CA 109; 153

Momaday, N(avarre) Scott 1934- **CLC 2, 19,
85, 95; DA; DAB; DAC; DAM MST,
MULT, NOV, POP; PC 25; WLCS**
  See also AAYA 11; CA 25-28R; CANR 14, 34,
  68; CDALBS; DLB 143, 175; INT CANR-
  14; MTCW 1, 2; NNAL; SATA 48; SATA-
  Brief 30

Monette, Paul 1945-1995   **CLC 82**
  See also CA 139; 147

Monroe, Harriet 1860-1936   **TCLC 12**
  See also CA 109; DLB 54, 91

Monroe, Lyle
  See Heinlein, Robert A(nson)

Montagu, Elizabeth 1720-1800   **NCLC 7**

Montagu, Mary (Pierrepont) Wortley 1689-
1762   **LC 9; PC 16**
  See also DLB 95, 101

Montagu, W. H.
  See Coleridge, Samuel Taylor

Montague, John (Patrick) 1929- **CLC 13, 46**
  See also CA 9-12R; CANR 9, 69; DLB 40;
  MTCW 1

Montaigne, Michel (Eyquem) de 1533-1592
  LC 8; DA; DAB; DAC; DAM MST; WLC

Montale, Eugenio 1896-1981**CLC 7, 9, 18; PC
13**
  See also CA 17-20R; 104; CANR 30; DLB 114;
  MTCW 1

Montesquieu, Charles-Louis de Secondat 1689-
1755   **LC 7**

Montgomery, (Robert) Bruce 1921-1978
  See Crispin, Edmund
  See also CA 104

Montgomery, L(ucy) M(aud) 1874-1942
  TCLC 51; DAC; DAM MST
  See also AAYA 12; CA 108; 137; CLR 8; DLB
  92; DLBD 14; JRDA; MAICYA; MTCW 2;
  SATA 100; YABC 1

Montgomery, Marion H., Jr. 1925-   **CLC 7**
  See also AITN 1; CA 1-4R; CANR 3, 48; DLB
  6

Montgomery, Max
  See Davenport, Guy (Mattison, Jr.)

Montherlant, Henry (Milon) de 1896-1972
  CLC 8, 19; DAM DRAM
  See also CA 85-88; 37-40R; DLB 72; MTCW
  1

Monty Python
  See Chapman, Graham; Cleese, John
  (Marwood); Gilliam, Terry (Vance); Idle,
  Eric; Jones, Terence Graham Parry; Palin,
  Michael (Edward)
  See also AAYA 7

Moodie, Susanna (Strickland) 1803-1885
  NCLC 14
  See also DLB 99

Mooney, Edward 1951-
  See Mooney, Ted
  See also CA 130

Mooney, Ted   **CLC 25**
  See also Mooney, Edward

Moorcock, Michael (John) 1939-**CLC 5, 27, 58**
  See also Bradbury, Edward P.
  See also AAYA 26; CA 45-48; CAAS 5; CANR
  2, 17, 38, 64; DLB 14; MTCW 1, 2; SATA
  93

Moore, Brian 1921-1999**CLC 1, 3, 5, 7, 8, 19,
32, 90; DAB; DAC; DAM MST**
  See also CA 1-4R; 174; CANR 1, 25, 42, 63;
  MTCW 1, 2

Moore, Edward
  See Muir, Edwin

Moore, G. E. 1873-1958   **TCLC 89**

Moore, George Augustus 1852-1933**TCLC 7;
SSC 19**
  See also CA 104; 177; DLB 10, 18, 57, 135

Moore, Lorrie   **CLC 39, 45, 68**
  See also Moore, Marie Lorena

Moore, Marianne (Craig) 1887-1972**CLC 1, 2,
4, 8, 10, 13, 19, 47; DA; DAB; DAC; DAM
MST, POET; PC 4; WLCS**
  See also CA 1-4R; 33-36R; CANR 3, 61;
  CDALB 1929-1941; DLB 45; DLBD 7;
  MTCW 1, 2; SATA 20

Moore, Marie Lorena 1957-
  See Moore, Lorrie
  See also CA 116; CANR 39

Moore, Thomas 1779-1852   **NCLC 6**
  See also DLB 96, 144

Mora, Pat(ricia) 1942-

See also CA 129; CANR 57, 81; CLR 58; DAM
  MULT; DLB 209; HLC 2; HW 1, 2; SATA
  92

Morand, Paul 1888-1976   **CLC 41;SSC 22**
  See also CA 69-72; DLB 65

Morante, Elsa 1918-1985   **CLC 8, 47**
  See also CA 85-88; 117; CANR 35; DLB 177;
  MTCW 1, 2

Moravia, Alberto 1907-1990**CLC 2, 7, 11, 27,
46; SSC 26**
  See also Pincherle, Alberto
  See also DLB 177; MTCW 2

More, Hannah 1745-1833   **NCLC 27**
  See also DLB 107, 109, 116, 158

More, Henry 1614-1687   **LC 9**
  See also DLB 126

More, Sir Thomas 1478-1535   **LC 10, 32**

Moreas, Jean   **TCLC 18**
  See also Papadiamantopoulos, Johannes

Morgan, Berry 1919-   **CLC 6**
  See also CA 49-52; DLB 6

Morgan, Claire
  See Highsmith, (Mary) Patricia

Morgan, Edwin (George) 1920-   **CLC 31**
  See also CA 5-8R; CANR 3, 43; DLB 27

Morgan, (George) Frederick 1922- **CLC 23**
  See also CA 17-20R; CANR 21

Morgan, Harriet
  See Mencken, H(enry) L(ouis)

Morgan, Jane
  See Cooper, James Fenimore

Morgan, Janet 1945-   **CLC 39**
  See also CA 65-68

Morgan, Lady 1776(?)-1859   **NCLC 29**
  See also DLB 116, 158

Morgan, Robin (Evonne) 1941-   **CLC 2**
  See also CA 69-72; CANR 29, 68; MTCW 1;
  SATA 80

Morgan, Scott
  See Kuttner, Henry

Morgan, Seth 1949(?)-1990   **CLC 65**
  See also CA 132

Morgenstern, Christian 1871-1914 **TCLC 8**
  See also CA 105

Morgenstern, S.
  See Goldman, William (W.)

Moricz, Zsigmond 1879-1942   **TCLC 33**
  See also CA 165

Morike, Eduard (Friedrich) 1804-1875**NCLC
10**
  See also DLB 133

Moritz, Karl Philipp 1756-1793   **LC 2**
  See also DLB 94

Morland, Peter Henry
  See Faust, Frederick (Schiller)

Morley, Christopher (Darlington) 1890-1957
  TCLC 87
  See also CA 112; DLB 9

Morren, Theophil
  See Hofmannsthal, Hugo von

Morris, Bill 1952-   **CLC 76**

Morris, Julian
  See West, Morris L(anglo)

Morris, Steveland Judkins 1950(?)-
  See Wonder, Stevie
  See also CA 111

Morris, William 1834-1896   **NCLC 4**
  See also CDBLB 1832-1890; DLB 18, 35, 57,
  156, 178, 184

Morris, Wright 1910-1998**CLC 1, 3, 7, 18, 37**
  See also CA 9-12R; 167; CANR 21, 81; DLB
  2, 206; DLBY 81; MTCW 1, 2

Morrison, Arthur 1863-1945   **TCLC 72**

See also CA 120; 157; DLB 70, 135, 197

Morrison, Chloe Anthony Wofford
See Morrison, Toni

Morrison, James Douglas 1943-1971
See Morrison, Jim
See also CA 73-76; CANR 40

Morrison, Jim   **CLC 17**
See also Morrison, James Douglas

Morrison, Toni 1931-CLC **4, 10, 22, 55, 81, 87; BLC 3; DA; DAB; DAC; DAM MST, MULT, NOV, POP**
See also AAYA 1, 22; BW 2, 3; CA 29-32R; CANR 27, 42, 67; CDALB 1968-1988; DLB 6, 33, 143; DLBY 81; MTCW 1, 2; SATA 57

Morrison, Van 1945-   **CLC 21**
See also CA 116; 168

Morrissy, Mary 1958-   **CLC 99**

Mortimer, John (Clifford) 1923- CLC **28, 43; DAM DRAM, POP**
See also CA 13-16R; CANR 21, 69; CDBLB 1960 to Present; DLB 13; INT CANR-21; MTCW 1, 2

Mortimer, Penelope (Ruth) 1918-   **CLC 5**
See also CA 57-60; CANR 45

Morton, Anthony
See Creasey, John

Mosca, Gaetano 1858-1941   **TCLC 75**

Mosher, Howard Frank 1943-   **CLC 62**
See also CA 139; CANR 65

Mosley, Nicholas 1923-   **CLC 43, 70**
See also CA 69-72; CANR 41, 60; DLB 14, 207

Mosley, Walter 1952- CLC **97; BLCS; DAM MULT, POP**
See also AAYA 17; BW 2; CA 142; CANR 57; MTCW 2

Moss, Howard 1922-1987 CLC **7, 14, 45, 50; DAM POET**
See also CA 1-4R; 123; CANR 1, 44; DLB 5

Mossgiel, Rab
See Burns, Robert

Motion, Andrew (Peter) 1952-   **CLC 47**
See also CA 146; DLB 40

Motley, Willard (Francis) 1909-1965 CLC **18**
See also BW 1; CA 117; 106; DLB 76, 143

Motoori, Norinaga 1730-1801   **NCLC 45**

Mott, Michael (Charles Alston) 1930-CLC **15, 34**
See also CA 5-8R; CAAS 7; CANR 7, 29

Mountain Wolf Woman 1884-1960   **CLC 92**
See also CA 144; NNAL

Moure, Erin 1955-   **CLC 88**
See also CA 113; DLB 60

Mowat, Farley (McGill) 1921-CLC **26; DAC; DAM MST**
See also AAYA 1; CA 1-4R; CANR 4, 24, 42, 68; CLR 20; DLB 68; INT CANR-24; JRDA; MAICYA; MTCW 1, 2; SATA 3, 55

Mowatt, Anna Cora 1819-1870   **NCLC 74**

Moyers, Bill 1934-   **CLC 74**
See also AITN 2; CA 61-64; CANR 31, 52

Mphahlele, Es'kia
See Mphahlele, Ezekiel
See also DLB 125

Mphahlele, Ezekiel 1919-   CLC **25; BLC 3; DAM MULT**
See also Mphahlele, Es'kia
See also BW 2, 3; CA 81-84; CANR 26, 76; MTCW 2

Mqhayi, S(amuel) E(dward) K(rune Loliwe) 1875-1945TCLC **25; BLC 3;DAM MULT**
See also CA 153

Mrozek, Slawomir 1930-   **CLC 3, 13**
See also CA 13-16R; CAAS 10; CANR 29;

MTCW 1

Mrs. Belloc-Lowndes
See Lowndes, Marie Adelaide (Belloc)

Mtwa, Percy (?)-   **CLC 47**

Mueller, Lisel 1924-   **CLC 13, 51**
See also CA 93-96; DLB 105

Muir, Edwin 1887-1959   **TCLC 2, 87**
See also CA 104; DLB 20, 100, 191

Muir, John 1838-1914   **TCLC 28**
See also CA 165; DLB 186

Mujica Lainez, Manuel 1910-1984   **CLC 31**
See Lainez, Manuel Mujica
See also CA 81-84; 112; CANR 32; HW 1

Mukherjee, Bharati 1940-CLC **53, 115; DAM NOV**
See also BEST 89:2; CA 107; CANR 45, 72; DLB 60; MTCW 1, 2

Muldoon, Paul 1951-CLC **32, 72;DAM POET**
See also CA 113; 129; CANR 52; DLB 40; INT 129

Mulisch, Harry 1927-   **CLC 42**
See also CA 9-12R; CANR 6, 26, 56

Mull, Martin 1943-   **CLC 17**
See also CA 105

Muller, Wilhelm   **NCLC 73**

Mulock, Dinah Maria
See Craik, Dinah Maria (Mulock)

Munford, Robert 1737(?)-1783   **LC 5**
See also DLB 31

Mungo, Raymond 1946-   **CLC 72**
See also CA 49-52; CANR 2

Munro, Alice 1931-   CLC **6, 10, 19, 50, 95; DAC; DAM MST, NOV; SSC 3; WLCS**
See also AITN 2; CA 33-36R; CANR 33, 53, 75; DLB 53; MTCW 1, 2; SATA 29

Munro, H(ector) H(ugh) 1870-1916
See Saki
See also CA 104; 130; CDBLB 1890-1914; DA; DAB; DAC; DAM MST, NOV; DLB 34, 162; MTCW 1, 2; WLC

Murdoch, (Jean) Iris 1919-CLC **1, 2, 3, 4, 6, 8, 11, 15, 22, 31, 51; DAB; DAC; DAM MST, NOV**
See also CA 13-16R; CANR 8, 43, 68; CDBLB 1960 to Present; DLB 14, 194; INT CANR-8; MTCW 1, 2

Murfree, Mary Noailles 1850-1922   **SSC 22**
See also CA 122; 176; DLB 12, 74

Murnau, Friedrich Wilhelm
See Plumpe, Friedrich Wilhelm

Murphy, Richard 1927-   **CLC 41**
See also CA 29-32R; DLB 40

Murphy, Sylvia 1937-   **CLC 34**
See also CA 121

Murphy, Thomas (Bernard) 1935-   **CLC 51**
See also CA 101

Murray, Albert L. 1916-   **CLC 73**
See also BW 2; CA 49-52; CANR 26, 52, 78; DLB 38

Murray, Judith Sargent 1751-1820 NCLC **63**
See also DLB 37, 200

Murray, Les(lie) A(llan) 1938-CLC **40; DAM POET**
See also CA 21-24R; CANR 11, 27, 56

Murry, J. Middleton
See Murry, John Middleton

Murry, John Middleton 1889-1957 TCLC **16**
See also CA 118; DLB 149

Musgrave, Susan 1951-   **CLC 13, 54**
See also CA 69-72; CANR 45

Musil, Robert (Edler von) 1880-1942 T C L C **12, 68; SSC 18**
See also CA 109; CANR 55; DLB 81, 124;

MTCW 2

Muske, Carol 1945-   **CLC 90**
See also Muske-Dukes, Carol (Anne)

Muske-Dukes, Carol (Anne) 1945-
See Muske, Carol
See also CA 65-68; CANR 32, 70

Musset, (Louis Charles) Alfred de 1810-1857 **NCLC 7**
See also DLB 192

Mussolini, Benito (Amilcare Andrea) 1883-1945 **TCLC 96**
See also CA 116

My Brother's Brother
See Chekhov, Anton (Pavlovich)

Myers, L(eopold) H(amilton) 1881-1944 **TCLC 59**
See also CA 157; DLB 15

Myers, Walter Dean 1937- CLC **35; BLC 3; DAM MULT, NOV**
See also AAYA 4, 23; BW 2; CA 33-36R; CANR 20, 42, 67; CLR 4, 16, 35; DLB 33; INT CANR-20; JRDA; MAICYA; MTCW 2; SAAS 2; SATA 41, 71, 109; SATA-Brief 27

Myers, Walter M.
See Myers, Walter Dean

Myles, Symon
See Follett, Ken(neth Martin)

Nabokov, Vladimir (Vladimirovich) 1899-1977 CLC **1, 2, 3, 6, 8, 11, 15, 23, 44, 46, 64; DA; DAB; DAC; DAM MST, NOV; SSC 11; WLC**
See also CA 5-8R; 69-72; CANR 20; CDALB 1941-1968; DLB 2; DLBD 3; DLBY 80, 91; MTCW 1, 2

Nagai Kafu 1879-1959   **TCLC 51**
See also Nagai Sokichi
See also DLB 180

Nagai Sokichi 1879-1959
See Nagai Kafu
See also CA 117

Nagy, Laszlo 1925-1978   **CLC 7**
See also CA 129; 112

Naidu, Sarojini 1879-1943   **TCLC 80**

Naipaul, Shiva(dhar Srinivasa) 1945-1985 CLC **32, 39; DAM NOV**
See also CA 110; 112; 116; CANR 33; DLB 157; DLBY 85; MTCW 1, 2

Naipaul, V(idiadhar) S(urajprasad) 1932- CLC **4, 7, 9, 13, 18, 37, 105; DAB; DAC; DAM MST, NOV**
See also CA 1-4R; CANR 1, 33, 51; CDBLB 1960 to Present; DLB 125, 204, 206; DLBY 85; MTCW 1, 2

Nakos, Lilika 1899(?)-   **CLC 29**

Narayan, R(asipuram) K(rishnaswami) 1906- CLC **7, 28, 47, 121; DAM NOV; SSC 25**
See also CA 81-84; CANR 33, 61; MTCW 1, 2; SATA 62

Nash, (Frediric) Ogden 1902-1971 CLC **23; DAM POET; PC 21**
See also CA 13-14; 29-32R; CANR 34, 61; CAP 1; DLB 11; MAICYA; MTCW 1,2; SATA 2, 46

Nashe, Thomas 1567-1601(?)   **LC 41**
See also DLB 167

Nashe, Thomas 1567-1601   **LC 41**

Nathan, Daniel
See Dannay, Frederic

Nathan, George Jean 1882-1958   **TCLC 18**
See also Hatteras, Owen
See also CA 114; 169; DLB 137

Natsume, Kinnosuke 1867-1916
See Natsume, Soseki

See also CA 104

Natsume, Soseki 1867-1916   **TCLC 2, 10**
  See also Natsume, Kinnosuke
  See also DLB 180

Natti, (Mary) Lee 1919-
  See Kingman, Lee
  See also CA 5-8R; CANR 2

Naylor, Gloria 1950-**CLC 28, 52; BLC 3; DA; DAC; DAM MST, MULT, NOV, POP; WLCS**
  See also AAYA 6; BW 2, 3; CA 107; CANR 27, 51, 74; DLB 173; MTCW 1, 2

Neihardt, John Gneisenau 1881-1973**CLC 32**
  See also CA 13-14; CANR 65; CAP 1; DLB 9, 54

Nekrasov, Nikolai Alekseevich 1821-1878 **NCLC 11**

Nelligan, Emile 1879-1941   **TCLC 14**
  See also CA 114; DLB 92

Nelson, Willie 1933-   **CLC 17**
  See also CA 107

Nemerov, Howard (Stanley) 1920-1991**CLC 2, 6, 9, 36; DAM POET; PC 24**
  See also CA 1-4R; 134; CABS 2; CANR 1, 27, 53; DLB 5, 6; DLBY 83; INT CANR-27; MTCW 1, 2

Neruda, Pablo 1904-1973**CLC 1, 2, 5, 7, 9, 28, 62; DA; DAB; DAC; DAM MST, MULT, POET; HLC 2; PC 4; WLC**
  See also CA 19-20; 45-48; CAP 2; HW 1; MTCW 1, 2

Nerval, Gerard de 1808-1855**NCLC 1, 67; PC 13; SSC 18**

Nervo, (Jose) Amado (Ruiz de) 1870-1919 **TCLC 11; HLCS 2**
  See also CA 109; 131; HW 1

Nessi, Pio Baroja y
  See Baroja (y Nessi), Pio

Nestroy, Johann 1801-1862   **NCLC 42**
  See also DLB 133

Netterville, Luke
  See O'Grady, Standish (James)

Neufeld, John (Arthur) 1938-   **CLC 17**
  See also AAYA 11; CA 25-28R; CANR 11, 37, 56; CLR 52; MAICYA; SAAS 3; SATA 6, 81

Neville, Emily Cheney 1919-   **CLC 12**
  See also CA 5-8R; CANR 3, 37; JRDA; MAICYA; SAAS 2; SATA 1

Newbound, Bernard Slade 1930-
  See Slade, Bernard
  See also CA 81-84; CANR 49; DAM DRAM

Newby, P(ercy) H(oward) 1918-1997 **CLC 2, 13; DAM NOV**
  See also CA 5-8R; 161; CANR 32, 67; DLB 15; MTCW 1

Newlove, Donald 1928-   **CLC 6**
  See also CA 29-32R; CANR 25

Newlove, John (Herbert) 1938-   **CLC 14**
  See also CA 21-24R; CANR 9, 25

Newman, Charles 1938-   **CLC 2, 8**
  See also CA 21-24R

Newman, Edwin (Harold) 1919-   **CLC 14**
  See also AITN 1; CA 69-72; CANR 5

Newman, John Henry 1801-1890   **NCLC 38**
  See also DLB 18, 32, 55

Newton, (Sir)Isaac 1642-1727   **LC 35, 52**

Newton, Suzanne 1936-   **CLC 35**
  See also CA 41-44R; CANR 14; JRDA; SATA 5, 77

Nexo, Martin Andersen 1869-1954 **TCLC 43**

Nezval, Vitezslav 1900-1958   **TCLC 44**
  See also CA 123

Ng, Fae Myenne 1957(?)-   **CLC 81**
  See also CA 146

Ngema, Mbongeni 1955-   **CLC 57**
  See also BW 2; CA 143

Ngugi, James T(hiong'o)   **CLC 3, 7, 13**
  See also Ngugi wa Thiong'o

Ngugi wa Thiong'o 1938-   **CLC 36; BLC 3; DAM MULT, NOV**
  See also Ngugi, James T(hiong'o)
  See also BW 2; CA 81-84; CANR 27, 58; DLB 125; MTCW 1, 2

Nichol, B(arrie) P(hillip) 1944-1988 **CLC 18**
  See also CA 53-56; DLB 53; SATA 66

Nichols, John (Treadwell) 1940-   **CLC 38**
  See also CA 9-12R; CAAS 2; CANR 6, 70; DLBY 82

Nichols, Leigh
  See Koontz, Dean R(ay)

Nichols, Peter (Richard) 1927- **CLC 5, 36, 65**
  See also CA 104; CANR 33; DLB 13; MTCW 1

Nicolas, F. R. E.
  See Freeling, Nicolas

Niedecker, Lorine 1903-1970   **CLC 10, 42; DAM POET**
  See also CA 25-28; CAP 2; DLB 48

Nietzsche, Friedrich (Wilhelm) 1844-1900 **TCLC 10, 18, 55**
  See also CA 107; 121; DLB 129

Nievo, Ippolito 1831-1861   **NCLC 22**

Nightingale, Anne Redmon 1943-
  See Redmon, Anne
  See also CA 103

Nightingale, Florence 1820-1910   **TCLC 85**
  See also DLB 166

Nik. T. O.
  See Annensky, Innokenty (Fyodorovich)

Nin, Anais 1903-1977 **CLC 1, 4, 8, 11, 14, 60; DAM NOV, POP; SSC 10**
  See also AITN 2; CA 13-16R; 69-72; CANR 22, 53; DLB 2, 4, 152; MTCW 1, 2

Nishida, Kitaro 1870-1945   **TCLC 83**

Nishiwaki, Junzaburo 1894-1982   **PC 15**
  See also CA 107

Nissenson, Hugh 1933-   **CLC 4, 9**
  See also CA 17-20R; CANR 27; DLB 28

Niven, Larry   **CLC 8**
  See also Niven, Laurence Van Cott
  See also AAYA 27; DLB 8

Niven, Laurence Van Cott 1938-
  See Niven, Larry
  See also CA 21-24R; CAAS 12; CANR 14, 44, 66; DAM POP; MTCW 1, 2; SATA 95

Nixon, Agnes Eckhardt 1927-   **CLC 21**
  See also CA 110

Nizan, Paul 1905-1940   **TCLC 40**
  See also CA 161; DLB 72

Nkosi, Lewis 1936-   **CLC 45; BLC 3; DAM MULT**
  See also BW 1, 3; CA 65-68; CANR 27, 81; DLB 157

Nodier, (Jean) Charles (Emmanuel) 1780-1844 **NCLC 19**
  See also DLB 119

Noguchi, Yone 1875-1947   **TCLC 80**

Nolan, Christopher 1965-   **CLC 58**
  See also CA 111

Noon, Jeff 1957-   **CLC 91**
  See also CA 148

Norden, Charles
  See Durrell, Lawrence (George)

Nordhoff, Charles (Bernard) 1887-1947 **TCLC 23**

See also CA 108; DLB 9; SATA 23

Norfolk, Lawrence 1963-   **CLC 76**
  See also CA 144

Norman, Marsha 1947-**CLC 28; DAM DRAM; DC 8**
  See also CA 105; CABS 3; CANR 41; DLBY 84

Normyx
  See Douglas, (George) Norman

Norris, Frank 1870-1902   **SSC 28**
  See also Norris, (Benjamin) Frank(lin, Jr.)
  See also CDALB 1865-1917; DLB 12, 71, 186

Norris, (Benjamin) Frank(lin, Jr.) 1870-1902 **TCLC 24**
  See also Norris, Frank
  See also CA 110; 160

Norris, Leslie 1921-   **CLC 14**
  See also CA 11-12; CANR 14; CAP 1; DLB 27

North, Andrew
  See Norton, Andre

North, Anthony
  See Koontz, Dean R(ay)

North, Captain George
  See Stevenson, Robert Louis (Balfour)

North, Milou
  See Erdrich, Louise

Northrup, B. A.
  See Hubbard, L(afayette) Ron(ald)

North Staffs
  See Hulme, T(homas) E(rnest)

Norton, Alice Mary
  See Norton, Andre
  See also MAICYA; SATA 1, 43

Norton, Andre 1912-   **CLC 12**
  See also Norton, Alice Mary
  See also AAYA 14; CA 1-4R; CANR 68; CLR 50; DLB 8, 52; JRDA; MTCW 1; SATA 91

Norton, Caroline 1808-1877   **NCLC 47**
  See also DLB 21, 159, 199

Norway, Nevil Shute 1899-1960
  See Shute, Nevil
  See also CA 102; 93-96; MTCW 2

Norwid, Cyprian Kamil 1821-1883 **NCLC 17**

Nosille, Nabrah
  See Ellison, Harlan (Jay)

Nossack, Hans Erich 1901-1978   **CLC 6**
  See also CA 93-96; 85-88; DLB 69

Nostradamus 1503-1566   **LC 27**

Nosu, Chuji
  See Ozu, Yasujiro

Notenburg, Eleanora (Genrikhovna) von
  See Guro, Elena

Nova, Craig 1945-   **CLC 7, 31**
  See also CA 45-48; CANR 2, 53

Novak, Joseph
  See Kosinski, Jerzy (Nikodem)

Novalis 1772-1801   **NCLC 13**
  See also DLB 90

Novis, Emile
  See Weil, Simone (Adolphine)

Nowlan, Alden (Albert) 1933-1983 **CLC 15; DAC; DAM MST**
  See also CA 9-12R; CANR 5; DLB 53

Noyes, Alfred 1880-1958   **TCLC 7;PC 27**
  See also CA 104; DLB 20

Nunn, Kem   **CLC 34**
  See also CA 159

Nye, Robert 1939-   **CLC 13, 42;DAM NOV**
  See also CA 33-36R; CANR 29, 67; DLB 14; MTCW 1; SATA 6

Nyro, Laura 1947-   **CLC 17**

Oates, Joyce Carol 1938-**CLC 1, 2, 3, 6, 9, 11, 15, 19, 33, 52, 108; DA; DAB; DAC; DAM**

MST, NOV, POP; SSC 6;WLC
See also AAYA 15; AITN 1; BEST 89:2; CA 5-8R; CANR 25, 45, 74; CDALB 1968-1988; DLB 2, 5, 130; DLBY 81; INT CANR-25; MTCW 1, 2

O'Brien, Darcy 1939-1998   **CLC 11**
See also CA 21-24R; 167; CANR 8, 59

O'Brien, E. G.
See Clarke, Arthur C(harles)

O'Brien, Edna 1936-   **CLC 3, 5, 8, 13, 36, 65, 116; DAM NOV; SSC 10**
See also CA 1-4R; CANR 6, 41, 65; CDBLB 1960 to Present; DLB 14; MTCW 1, 2

O'Brien, Fitz-James 1828-1862   **NCLC 21**
See also DLB 74

O'Brien, Flann   **CLC 1, 4, 5, 7, 10, 47**
See also O Nuallain, Brian

O'Brien, Richard 1942-   **CLC 17**
See also CA 124

O'Brien, (William) Tim(othy) 1946-   **CLC 7, 19, 40, 103; DAM POP**
See also AAYA 16; CA 85-88; CANR 40, 58; CDALBS; DLB 152; DLBD 9; DLBY 80; MTCW 2

Obstfelder, Sigbjoern 1866-1900   **TCLC 23**
See also CA 123

O'Casey, Sean 1880-1964 CLC **1, 5, 9, 11, 15, 88; DAB; DAC; DAM DRAM, MST; WLCS**
See also CA 89-92; CANR 62;CDBLB 1914-1945; DLB 10; MTCW 1, 2

O'Cathasaigh, Sean
See O'Casey, Sean

Ochs, Phil 1940-1976   **CLC 17**
See also CA 65-68

O'Connor, Edwin (Greene) 1918-1968CLC **14**
See also CA 93-96; 25-28R

O'Connor, (Mary) Flannery 1925-1964   **C L C 1, 2, 3, 6, 10, 13, 15, 21, 66, 104; DA; DAB; DAC; DAM MST, NOV; SSC 1, 23;WLC**
See also AAYA 7; CA 1-4R; CANR 3, 41; CDALB 1941-1968; DLB 2, 152; DLBD 12; DLBY 80; MTCW 1, 2

O'Connor, Frank   **CLC 23; SSC 5**
See also O'Donovan, Michael John
See also DLB 162

O'Dell, Scott 1898-1989   **CLC 30**
See also AAYA 3; CA 61-64; 129; CANR 12, 30; CLR 1, 16; DLB 52; JRDA; MAICYA; SATA 12, 60

Odets, Clifford 1906-1963CLC **2, 28, 98; DAM DRAM; DC 6**
See also CA 85-88; CANR 62; DLB 7, 26; MTCW 1, 2

O'Doherty, Brian 1934-   **CLC 76**
See also CA 105

O'Donnell, K. M.
See Malzberg, Barry N(athaniel)

O'Donnell, Lawrence
See Kuttner, Henry

O'Donovan, Michael John 1903-1966CLC **14**
See also O'Connor, Frank
See also CA 93-96

Oe, Kenzaburo 1935-   **CLC 10, 36, 86; DAM NOV; SSC 20**
See also CA 97-100; CANR 36, 50, 74; DLB 182; DLBY 94; MTCW 1, 2

O'Faolain, Julia 1932-   **CLC 6, 19, 47, 108**
See also CA 81-84; CAAS 2; CANR 12, 61; DLB 14; MTCW 1

O'Faolain, Sean 1900-1991 CLC **1, 7, 14, 32, 70; SSC 13**
See also CA 61-64; 134; CANR 12, 66; DLB

15, 162; MTCW 1, 2
O'Flaherty, Liam 1896-1984CLC **5, 34; SSC 6**
See also CA 101; 113; CANR 35; DLB 36, 162; DLBY 84; MTCW 1, 2

Ogilvy, Gavin
See Barrie, J(ames) M(atthew)

O'Grady, Standish (James) 1846-1928 **T C L C 5**
See also CA 104; 157

O'Grady, Timothy 1951-   **CLC 59**
See also CA 138

O'Hara, Frank 1926-1966   **CLC 2, 5, 13, 78; DAM POET**
See also CA 9-12R; 25-28R; CANR 33; DLB 5, 16, 193; MTCW 1, 2

O'Hara, John (Henry) 1905-1970CLC **1, 2, 3, 6, 11, 42; DAM NOV; SSC 15**
See also CA 5-8R; 25-28R; CANR 31, 60; CDALB 1929-1941; DLB 9, 86; DLBD 2; MTCW 1, 2

O Hehir, Diana 1922-   **CLC 41**
See also CA 93-96

Ohiyesa 1858-1939
See Eastman, Charles A(lexander)
See also CA 179

Okigbo, Christopher (Ifenayichukwu) 1932-1967 **CLC 25, 84; BLC 3; DAM MULT, POET; PC 7**
See also BW 1, 3; CA 77-80; CANR 74; DLB 125; MTCW 1, 2

Okri, Ben 1959-   **CLC 87**
See also BW 2, 3; CA 130; 138; CANR 65; DLB 157; INT 138; MTCW 2

Olds, Sharon 1942-   **CLC 32, 39, 85; DAM POET; PC 22**
See also CA 101; CANR 18, 41, 66; DLB 120; MTCW 2

Oldstyle, Jonathan
See Irving, Washington

Olesha, Yuri (Karlovich) 1899-1960   **CLC 8**
See also CA 85-88

Oliphant, Laurence 1829(?)-1888   **NCLC 47**
See also DLB 18, 166

Oliphant, Margaret (Oliphant Wilson) 1828-1897   **NCLC 11, 61; SSC 25**
See also DLB 18, 159, 190

Oliver, Mary 1935-   **CLC 19, 34, 98**
See also CA 21-24R; CANR 9, 43; DLB 5, 193

Olivier, Laurence (Kerr) 1907-1989 **CLC 20**
See also CA 111; 150; 129

Olsen, Tillie 1912-CLC **4, 13, 114; DA; DAB; DAC; DAM MST; SSC 11**
See also CA 1-4R; CANR 1, 43, 74; CDALBS; DLB 28, 206; DLBY 80; MTCW 1, 2

Olson, Charles (John) 1910-1970CLC **1, 2, 5, 6, 9, 11, 29; DAM POET; PC 19**
See also CA 13-16; 25-28R; CABS 2; CANR 35, 61; CAP 1; DLB 5, 16, 193; MTCW 1, 2

Olson, Toby 1937-   **CLC 28**
See also CA 65-68; CANR 9, 31

Olyesha, Yuri
See Olesha, Yuri (Karlovich)

Ondaatje, (Philip) Michael 1943-CLC **14, 29, 51, 76; DAB; DAC; DAM MST**
See also CA 77-80; CANR 42, 74; DLB 60; MTCW 2

Oneal, Elizabeth 1934-
See Oneal, Zibby
See also CA 106; CANR 28; MAICYA; SATA 30, 82

Oneal, Zibby   **CLC 30**
See also Oneal, Elizabeth
See also AAYA 5; CLR 13; JRDA

O'Neill, Eugene (Gladstone) 1888-1953TCLC **1, 6, 27, 49; DA; DAB; DAC; DAM DRAM, MST; WLC**
See also AITN 1; CA 110; 132; CDALB 1929-1941; DLB 7; MTCW 1, 2

Onetti, Juan Carlos 1909-1994   **CLC 7, 10; DAM MULT, NOV; HLCS 2;SSC 23**
See also CA 85-88; 145; CANR 32, 63; DLB 113; HW 1, 2; MTCW 1, 2

O Nuallain, Brian 1911-1966
See O'Brien, Flann
See also CA 21-22; 25-28R; CAP 2

Ophuls, Max 1902-1957   **TCLC 79**
See also CA 113

Opie, Amelia 1769-1853   **NCLC 65**
See also DLB 116, 159

Oppen, George 1908-1984   **CLC 7, 13,34**
See also CA 13-16R; 113; CANR 8, 82; DLB 5, 165

Oppenheim, E(dward) Phillips 1866-1946 **TCLC 45**
See also CA 111; DLB 70

Opuls, Max
See Ophuls, Max

Origen c. 185-c. 254   **CMLC 19**

Orlovitz, Gil 1918-1973   **CLC 22**
See also CA 77-80; 45-48; DLB 2, 5

Orris
See Ingelow, Jean

Ortega y Gasset, Jose 1883-1955   **TCLC 9; DAM MULT; HLC 2**
See also CA 106; 130; HW 1, 2; MTCW 1, 2

Ortese, Anna Maria 1914-   **CLC 89**
See also DLB 177

Ortiz, Simon J(oseph) 1941-   **CLC 45; DAM MULT, POET; PC 17**
See also CA 134; CANR 69; DLB 120, 175; NNAL

Orton, Joe   **CLC 4, 13, 43; DC 3**
See also Orton, John Kingsley
See also CDBLB 1960 to Present; DLB 13; MTCW 2

Orton, John Kingsley 1933-1967
See Orton, Joe
See also CA 85-88; CANR 35, 66; DAM DRAM; MTCW 1, 2

Orwell, George   **TCLC 2, 6, 15, 31, 51; DAB; WLC**
See also Blair, Eric (Arthur)
See also CDBLB 1945-1960; DLB 15, 98, 195

Osborne, David
See Silverberg, Robert

Osborne, George
See Silverberg, Robert

Osborne, John (James) 1929-1994CLC **1, 2, 5, 11, 45; DA; DAB; DAC; DAM DRAM, MST; WLC**
See also CA 13-16R; 147; CANR 21, 56; CDBLB 1945-1960; DLB 13; MTCW 1, 2

Osborne, Lawrence 1958-   **CLC 50**

Osbourne, Lloyd 1868-1947   **TCLC 93**

Oshima, Nagisa 1932-   **CLC 20**
See also CA 116; 121; CANR 78

Oskison, John Milton 1874-1947   **TCLC 35; DAM MULT**
See also CA 144; DLB 175; NNAL

Ossian c. 3rd cent.   **CMLC 28**
See also Macpherson, James

Ossoli, Sarah Margaret (Fuller marchesa d') 1810-1850
See Fuller, Margaret
See also SATA 25

Ostrovsky, Alexander 1823-1886NCLC **30, 57**

Otero, Blas de 1916-1979 **CLC 11**
See also CA 89-92; DLB 134
Otto, Rudolf 1869-1937 **TCLC 85**
Otto, Whitney 1955- **CLC 70**
See also CA 140
Ouida **TCLC 43**
See also De La Ramee, (Marie) Louise
See also DLB 18, 156
Ousmane, Sembene 1923- **CLC 66; BLC 3**
See also BW 1, 3; CA 117; 125; CANR 81;
MTCW 1
Ovid 43B.C.-17 **CMLC 7; DAM POET; PC 2**
See also DLB 211
Owen, Hugh
See Faust, Frederick (Schiller)
Owen, Wilfred (Edward Salter) 1893-1918
TCLC 5, 27; DA; DAB; DAC; DAM MST,
POET; PC 19; WLC
See also CA 104; 141; CDBLB 1914-1945;
DLB 20; MTCW 2
Owens, Rochelle 1936- **CLC 8**
See also CA 17-20R; CAAS 2; CANR 39
Oz, Amos 1939-**CLC 5, 8, 11, 27, 33, 54; DAM**
NOV
See also CA 53-56; CANR 27, 47, 65; MTCW
1, 2
Ozick, Cynthia 1928- **CLC 3, 7, 28, 62; DAM**
NOV, POP; SSC 15
See also BEST 90:1; CA 17-20R; CANR 23,
58; DLB 28, 152; DLBY 82; INT CANR-
23; MTCW 1, 2
Ozu, Yasujiro 1903-1963 **CLC 16**
See also CA 112
Pacheco, C.
See Pessoa, Fernando (Antonio Nogueira)
Pacheco, Jose Emilio 1939-
See also CA 111; 131; CANR 65; DAM MULT;
HLC 2; HW 1, 2
Pa Chin **CLC 18**
See also Li Fei-kan
Pack, Robert 1929- **CLC 13**
See also CA 1-4R; CANR 3, 44, 82; DLB 5
Padgett, Lewis
See Kuttner, Henry
Padilla (Lorenzo), Heberto 1932- **CLC 38**
See also AITN 1; CA 123; 131; HW 1
Page, Jimmy 1944- **CLC 12**
Page, Louise 1955- **CLC 40**
See also CA 140; CANR 76
Page, P(atricia) K(athleen) 1916- **CLC 7, 18;**
DAC; DAM MST; PC 12
See also CA 53-56; CANR 4, 22, 65; DLB 68;
MTCW 1
Page, Thomas Nelson 1853-1922 **SSC 23**
See also CA 118; 177; DLB 12, 78; DLBD 13
Pagels, Elaine Hiesey 1943- **CLC 104**
See also CA 45-48; CANR 2, 24, 51
Paget, Violet 1856-1935
See Lee, Vernon
See also CA 104; 166
Paget-Lowe, Henry
See Lovecraft, H(oward) P(hillips)
Paglia, Camille (Anna) 1947- **CLC 68**
See also CA 140; CANR 72; MTCW 2
Paige, Richard
See Koontz, Dean R(ay)
Paine, Thomas 1737-1809 **NCLC 62**
See also CDALB 1640-1865; DLB 31, 43, 73,
158
Pakenham, Antonia
See Fraser, (Lady) Antonia (Pakenham)
Palamas, Kostes 1859-1943 **TCLC 5**
See also CA 105

Palazzeschi, Aldo 1885-1974 **CLC 11**
See also CA 89-92; 53-56; DLB 114
Pales Matos, Luis 1898-1959
See also HLCS 2; HW 1
Paley, Grace 1922- **CLC 4, 6, 37; DAM POP;**
SSC 8
See also CA 25-28R; CANR 13, 46, 74; DLB
28; INT CANR-13; MTCW 1, 2
Palin, Michael (Edward) 1943- **CLC 21**
See also Monty Python
See also CA 107; CANR 35; SATA 67
Palliser, Charles 1947- **CLC 65**
See also CA 136; CANR 76
Palma, Ricardo 1833-1919 **TCLC 29**
See also CA 168
Pancake, Breece Dexter 1952-1979
See Pancake, Breece D'J
See also CA 123; 109
Pancake, Breece D'J **CLC 29**
See also Pancake, Breece Dexter
See also DLB 130
Panko, Rudy
See Gogol, Nikolai (Vasilyevich)
Papadiamantis, Alexandros 1851-1911**TCLC**
29
See also CA 168
Papadiamantopoulos, Johannes 1856-1910
See Moreas, Jean
See also CA 117
Papini, Giovanni 1881-1956 **TCLC 22**
See also CA 121
Paracelsus 1493-1541 **LC 14**
See also DLB 179
Parasol, Peter
See Stevens, Wallace
Pardo Bazan, Emilia 1851-1921 **SSC 30**
Pareto, Vilfredo 1848-1923 **TCLC 69**
See also CA 175
Parfenie, Maria
See Codrescu, Andrei
Parini, Jay (Lee) 1948- **CLC 54**
See also CA 97-100; CAAS 16; CANR 32
Park, Jordan
See Kornbluth, C(yril) M.; Pohl, Frederik
Park, Robert E(zra) 1864-1944 **TCLC 73**
See also CA 122; 165
Parker, Bert
See Ellison, Harlan (Jay)
Parker, Dorothy (Rothschild) 1893-1967**CLC**
15, 68; DAM POET; SSC 2
See also CA 19-20; 25-28R; CAP 2; DLB 11,
45, 86; MTCW 1, 2
Parker, Robert B(rown) 1932-**CLC 27; DAM**
NOV, POP
See also AAYA 28; BEST 89:4; CA 49-52;
CANR 1, 26, 52; INT CANR-26; MTCW 1
Parkin, Frank 1940- **CLC 43**
See also CA 147
Parkman, Francis, Jr. 1823-1893 **NCLC 12**
See also DLB 1, 30, 186
Parks, Gordon (Alexander Buchanan) 1912-
CLC 1, 16; BLC 3; DAM MULT
See also AITN 2; BW 2, 3; CA 41-44R; CANR
26, 66; DLB 33; MTCW 2; SATA 8, 108
Parmenides c. 515B.C.-c.450B.C. **CMLC 22**
See also DLB 176
Parnell, Thomas 1679-1718 **LC 3**
See also DLB 94
Parra, Nicanor 1914- **CLC 2, 102; DAM**
MULT; HLC 2
See also CA 85-88; CANR 32; HW 1; MTCW
1
Parra Sanojo, Ana Teresa de la 1890-1936

See also HLCS 2
Parrish, Mary Frances
See Fisher, M(ary) F(rances) K(ennedy)
Parson
See Coleridge, Samuel Taylor
Parson Lot
See Kingsley, Charles
Partridge, Anthony
See Oppenheim, E(dward) Phillips
Pascal, Blaise 1623-1662 **LC 35**
Pascoli, Giovanni 1855-1912 **TCLC 45**
See also CA 170
Pasolini, Pier Paolo 1922-1975 **CLC 20, 37,**
106; PC 17
See also CA 93-96; 61-64; CANR 63; DLB 128,
177; MTCW 1
Pasquini
See Silone, Ignazio
Pastan, Linda (Olenik) 1932- **CLC 27; DAM**
POET
See also CA 61-64; CANR 18, 40, 61; DLB 5
Pasternak, Boris (Leonidovich) 1890-1960
CLC 7, 10, 18, 63; DA; DAB; DAC; DAM
MST, NOV, POET; PC 6; SSC 31;WLC
See also CA 127; 116; MTCW 1, 2
Patchen, Kenneth 1911-1972 **CLC 1, 2, 18;**
DAM POET
See also CA 1-4R; 33-36R; CANR 3, 35; DLB
16, 48; MTCW 1
Pater, Walter (Horatio) 1839-1894 **NCLC 7**
See also CDBLB 1832-1890; DLB 57, 156
Paterson, A(ndrew) B(arton) 1864-1941
TCLC 32
See also CA 155; SATA 97
Paterson, Katherine (Womeldorf) 1932-**CLC**
12, 30
See also AAYA 1; CA 21-24R; CANR 28, 59;
CLR 7, 50; DLB 52; JRDA; MAICYA;
MTCW 1; SATA 13, 53, 92
Patmore, Coventry Kersey Dighton 1823-1896
NCLC 9
See also DLB 35, 98
Paton, Alan (Stewart) 1903-1988 **CLC 4, 10,**
25, 55, 106; DA; DAB; DAC; DAM MST,
NOV; WLC
See also AAYA 26; CA 13-16; 125; CANR 22;
CAP 1; DLBD 17; MTCW 1, 2; SATA 11;
SATA-Obit 56
Paton Walsh, Gillian 1937-
See Walsh, Jill Paton
See also CANR 38; JRDA; MAICYA; SAAS 3;
SATA 4, 72, 109
Patton, George S. 1885-1945 **TCLC 79**
Paulding, James Kirke 1778-1860 **NCLC 2**
See also DLB 3, 59, 74
Paulin, Thomas Neilson 1949-
See Paulin, Tom
See also CA 123; 128
Paulin, Tom **CLC 37**
See also Paulin, Thomas Neilson
See also DLB 40
Paustovsky, Konstantin (Georgievich) 1892-
1968 **CLC 40**
See also CA 93-96; 25-28R
Pavese, Cesare 1908-1950 **TCLC 3; PC 13;**
SSC 19
See also CA 104; 169; DLB 128, 177
Pavic, Milorad 1929- **CLC 60**
See also CA 136; DLB 181
Pavlov, Ivan Petrovich 1849-1936 **TCLC 91**
See also CA 118
Payne, Alan
See Jakes, John (William)

Paz, Gil
See Lugones, Leopoldo
Paz, Octavio 1914-1998CLC **3, 4, 6, 10, 19, 51,**
65, 119; DA; DAB; DAC; DAM MST,
MULT, POET; HLC 2; PC 1;WLC
See also CA 73-76; 165; CANR 32, 65; DLBY
90, 98; HW 1, 2; MTCW 1, 2
p'Bitek, Okot 1931-1982   CLC **96; BLC 3;**
DAM MULT
See also BW 2, 3; CA 124; 107; CANR 82; DLB
125; MTCW 1, 2
Peacock, Molly 1947-   CLC **60**
See also CA 103; CAAS 21; CANR 52; DLB
120
Peacock, Thomas Love 1785-1866 NCLC **22**
See also DLB 96, 116
Peake, Mervyn 1911-1968   CLC **7, 54**
See also CA 5-8R; 25-28R; CANR 3; DLB 15,
160; MTCW 1; SATA 23
Pearce, Philippa   CLC **21**
See also Christie, (Ann) Philippa
See also CLR 9; DLB 161; MAICYA; SATA 1,
67
Pearl, Eric
See Elman, Richard (Martin)
Pearson, T(homas) R(eid) 1956-   CLC **39**
See also CA 120; 130; INT 130
Peck, Dale 1967-   CLC **81**
See also CA 146; CANR 72
Peck, John 1941-   CLC **3**
See also CA 49-52; CANR 3
Peck, Richard (Wayne) 1934-   CLC **21**
See also AAYA 1, 24; CA 85-88; CANR 19,
38; CLR 15; INT CANR-19; JRDA;
MAICYA; SAAS 2; SATA 18, 55, 97
Peck, Robert Newton 1928-   CLC **17; DA;**
DAC; DAM MST
See also AAYA 3; CA 81-84; CANR 31, 63;
CLR 45; JRDA; MAICYA; SAAS 1; SATA
21, 62; SATA-Essay 108
Peckinpah, (David) Sam(uel) 1925-1984 C L C
20
See also CA 109; 114; CANR 82
Pedersen, Knut 1859-1952
See Hamsun, Knut
See also CA 104; 119; CANR 63; MTCW 1, 2
Peeslake, Gaffer
See Durrell, Lawrence (George)
Peguy, Charles Pierre 1873-1914   TCLC **10**
See also CA 107
Peirce, Charles Sanders 1839-1914 TCLC **81**
Pellicer, Carlos 1900(?)-1977
See also CA 153; 69-72; HLCS 2; HW 1
Pena, Ramon del Valle y
See Valle-Inclan, Ramon (Maria) del
Pendennis, Arthur Esquir
See Thackeray, William Makepeace
Penn, William 1644-1718   CLC **25**
See also DLB 24
PEPECE
See Prado (Calvo), Pedro
Pepys, Samuel 1633-1703 LC **11; DA; DAB;**
DAC; DAM MST; WLC
See also CDBLB 1660-1789; DLB 101
Percy, Walker 1916-1990CLC **2, 3, 6, 8, 14, 18,**
47, 65; DAM NOV, POP
See also CA 1-4R; 131; CANR 1, 23, 64; DLB
2; DLBY 80, 90; MTCW 1, 2
Percy, William Alexander 1885-1942TCLC **84**
See also CA 163; MTCW 2
Perec, Georges 1936-1982   CLC **56, 116**
See also CA 141; DLB 83
Pereda (y Sanchez de Porrua), Jose Mariade

1833-1906   TCLC **16**
See also CA 117
Pereda y Porrua, Jose Maria de
See Pereda (y Sanchez de Porrua), Jose Maria
de
Peregoy, George Weems
See Mencken, H(enry) L(ouis)
Perelman, S(idney) J(oseph) 1904-1979 C L C
3, 5, 9, 15, 23, 44, 49; DAM DRAM; SSC
32
See also AITN 1, 2; CA 73-76; 89-92; CANR
18; DLB 11, 44; MTCW 1, 2
Peret, Benjamin 1899-1959   TCLC **20**
See also CA 117
Peretz, Isaac Loeb 1851(?)-1915   TCLC **16;**
SSC 26
See also CA 109
Peretz, Yitzkhok Leibush
See Peretz, Isaac Loeb
Perez Galdos, Benito 1843-1920   TCLC **27;**
HLCS 2
See also CA 125; 153; HW 1
Peri Rossi, Cristina 1941-
See also CA 131; CANR 59, 81; DLB 145;
HLCS 2; HW 1, 2
Perrault, Charles 1628-1703   LC **3, 52**
See also MAICYA; SATA 25
Perry, Brighton
See Sherwood, Robert E(mmet)
Perse, St.-John
See Leger, (Marie-Rene Auguste) Alexis Saint-
Leger
Perutz, Leo(pold) 1882-1957   TCLC **60**
See also CA 147; DLB 81
Peseenz, Tulio F.
See Lopez y Fuentes, Gregorio
Pesetsky, Bette 1932-   CLC **28**
See also CA 133; DLB 130
Peshkov, Alexei Maximovich 1868-1936
See Gorky, Maxim
See also CA 105; 141; DA; DAC; DAM DRAM,
MST, NOV; MTCW 2
Pessoa, Fernando (Antonio Nogueira) 1888-
1935TCLC **27; DAM MULT; HLC 2; PC**
20
See also CA 125
Peterkin, Julia Mood 1880-1961   CLC **31**
See also CA 102; DLB 9
Peters, Joan K(aren) 1945-   CLC **39**
See also CA 158
Peters, Robert L(ouis) 1924-   CLC **7**
See also CA 13-16R; CAAS 8; DLB 105
Petofi, Sandor 1823-1849   NCLC **21**
Petrakis, Harry Mark 1923-   CLC **3**
See also CA 9-12R; CANR 4, 30
Petrarch 1304-1374 CMLC **20; DAM POET;**
PC 8
Petronius c. 20-66   CMLC **34**
See also DLB 211
Petrov, Evgeny   TCLC **21**
See also Kataev, Evgeny Petrovich
Petry, Ann (Lane) 1908-1997   CLC **1, 7, 18**
See also BW 1, 3; CA 5-8R; 157; CAAS 6;
CANR 4, 46; CLR 12; DLB 76; JRDA;
MAICYA; MTCW 1; SATA 5; SATA-Obit 94
Petursson, Halligrimur 1614-1674   LC **8**
Peychinovich
See Vazov, Ivan (Minchov)
Phaedrus c. 18B.C.-c. 50   CMLC **25**
See also DLB 211
Philips, Katherine 1632-1664   LC **30**
See also DLB 131
Philipson, Morris H. 1926-   CLC **53**

See also CA 1-4R; CANR 4
Phillips, Caryl 1958-   CLC **96; BLCS; DAM**
MULT
See also BW 2; CA 141; CANR 63; DLB 157;
MTCW 2
Phillips, David Graham 1867-1911 TCLC **44**
See also CA 108; 176; DLB 9, 12
Phillips, Jack
See Sandburg, Carl (August)
Phillips, Jayne Anne 1952-CLC **15, 33; SSC 16**
See also CA 101; CANR 24, 50; DLBY 80; INT
CANR-24; MTCW 1, 2
Phillips, Richard
See Dick, Philip K(indred)
Phillips, Robert (Schaeffer) 1938-   CLC **28**
See also CA 17-20R; CAAS 13; CANR 8; DLB
105
Phillips, Ward
See Lovecraft, H(oward) P(hillips)
Piccolo, Lucio 1901-1969   CLC **13**
See also CA 97-100; DLB 114
Pickthall, Marjorie L(owry) C(hristie) 1883-
1922   TCLC **21**
See also CA 107; DLB 92
Pico della Mirandola, Giovanni 1463-1494LC
15
Piercy, Marge 1936- CLC **3, 6, 14, 18, 27, 62**
See also CA 21-24R; CAAS 1; CANR 13, 43,
66; DLB 120; MTCW 1, 2
Piers, Robert
See Anthony, Piers
Pieyre de Mandiargues, Andre 1909-1991
See Mandiargues, Andre Pieyre de
See also CA 103; 136; CANR 22, 82
Pilnyak, Boris   TCLC **23**
See also Vogau, Boris Andreyevich
Pincherle, Alberto 1907-1990   CLC **11, 18;**
DAM NOV
See also Moravia, Alberto
See also CA 25-28R; 132; CANR 33, 63;
MTCW 1
Pinckney, Darryl 1953-   CLC **76**
See also BW 2, 3; CA 143; CANR 79
Pindar 518B.C.-446B.C.   CMLC **12;PC 19**
See also DLB 176
Pineda, Cecile 1942-   CLC **39**
See also CA 118
Pinero, Arthur Wing 1855-1934   TCLC **32;**
DAM DRAM
See also CA 110; 153; DLB 10
Pinero, Miguel (Antonio Gomez) 1946-1988
CLC **4, 55**
See also CA 61-64; 125; CANR 29; HW 1
Pinget, Robert 1919-1997   CLC **7, 13, 37**
See also CA 85-88; 160; DLB 83
Pink Floyd
See Barrett, (Roger) Syd; Gilmour, David; Ma-
son, Nick; Waters, Roger; Wright, Rick
Pinkney, Edward 1802-1828   NCLC **31**
Pinkwater, Daniel Manus 1941-   CLC **35**
See also Pinkwater, Manus
See also AAYA 1; CA 29-32R; CANR 12, 38;
CLR 4; JRDA; MAICYA; SAAS 3; SATA 46,
76
Pinkwater, Manus
See Pinkwater, Daniel Manus
See also SATA 8
Pinsky, Robert 1940- CLC **9, 19, 38, 94, 121;**
DAM POET; PC 27
See also CA 29-32R; CAAS 4; CANR 58;
DLBY 82, 98; MTCW 2
Pinta, Harold
See Pinter, Harold

Price, (Edward) Reynolds 1933-CLC 3, 6, 13, 43, 50, 63; DAM NOV; SSC 22
See also CA 1-4R; CANR 1, 37, 57; DLB 2; INT CANR-37

Price, Richard 1949-   CLC 6, 12
See also CA 49-52; CANR 3; DLBY 81

Prichard, Katharine Susannah 1883-1969
CLC 46
See also CA 11-12; CANR 33; CAP 1; MTCW 1; SATA 66

Priestley, J(ohn) B(oynton) 1894-1984CLC 2, 5, 9, 34; DAM DRAM, NOV
See also CA 9-12R; 113; CANR 33;CDBLB 1914-1945; DLB 10, 34, 77, 100, 139; DLBY 84; MTCW 1, 2

Prince 1958(?)-   CLC 35

Prince, F(rank) T(empleton) 1912- CLC 22
See also CA 101; CANR 43, 79; DLB 20

Prince Kropotkin
See Kropotkin, Peter (Aleksieevich)

Prior, Matthew 1664-1721   LC 4
See also DLB 95

Prishvin, Mikhail 1873-1954   TCLC 75

Pritchard, William H(arrison) 1932- CLC 34
See also CA 65-68; CANR 23; DLB 111

Pritchett, V(ictor) S(awdon) 1900-1997 C L C 5, 13, 15, 41; DAM NOV; SSC 14
See also CA 61-64; 157; CANR 31, 63; DLB 15, 139; MTCW 1, 2

Private 19022
See Manning, Frederic

Probst, Mark 1925-   CLC 59
See also CA 130

Prokosch, Frederic 1908-1989   CLC 4, 48
See also CA 73-76; 128; CANR 82; DLB 48; MTCW 2

Propertius, Sextus c. 50B.C.-c.16B.C. C M L C 32
See also DLB 211

Prophet, The
See Dreiser, Theodore (Herman Albert)

Prose, Francine 1947-   CLC 45
See also CA 109; 112; CANR 46; SATA 101

Proudhon
See Cunha, Euclides (Rodrigues Pimenta) da

Proulx, Annie
See Proulx, E(dna) Annie

Proulx, E(dna) Annie 1935-   CLC 81;DAM POP
See also CA 145; CANR 65; MTCW 2

Proust, (Valentin-Louis-George-Eugene-) Marcel 1871-1922 TCLC 7, 13, 33; DA; DAB; DAC; DAM MST, NOV; WLC
See also CA 104; 120; DLB 65; MTCW 1, 2

Prowler, Harley
See Masters, Edgar Lee

Prus, Boleslaw 1845-1912   TCLC 48

Pryor, Richard (Franklin Lenox Thomas) 1940-
CLC 26
See also CA 122; 152

Przybyszewski, Stanislaw 1868-1927TCLC 36
See also CA 160; DLB 66

Pteleon
See Grieve, C(hristopher) M(urray)
See also DAM POET

Puckett, Lute
See Masters, Edgar Lee

Puig, Manuel 1932-1990CLC 3, 5, 10, 28, 65; DAM MULT; HLC 2
See also CA 45-48; CANR 2, 32, 63; DLB 113; HW 1, 2; MTCW 1, 2

Pulitzer, Joseph 1847-1911   TCLC 76
See also CA 114; DLB 23

Purdy, A(lfred) W(ellington) 1918- CLC 3, 6, 14, 50; DAC; DAM MST, POET
See also CA 81-84; CAAS 17; CANR 42, 66; DLB 88

Purdy, James (Amos) 1923-CLC 2, 4, 10, 28, 52
See also CA 33-36R; CAAS 1; CANR 19, 51; DLB 2; INT CANR-19; MTCW 1

Pure, Simon
See Swinnerton, Frank Arthur

Pushkin, Alexander (Sergeyevich) 1799-1837
NCLC 3, 27; DA; DAB; DAC; DAM DRAM, MST, POET; PC 10; SSC 27;WLC
See also DLB 205; SATA 61

P'u Sung-ling 1640-1715   LC 49; SSC 31

Putnam, Arthur Lee
See Alger, Horatio, Jr.

Puzo, Mario 1920-1999 CLC 1, 2, 6, 36, 107; DAM NOV, POP
See also CA 65-68; CANR 4, 42, 65; DLB 6; MTCW 1, 2

Pygge, Edward
See Barnes, Julian (Patrick)

Pyle, Ernest Taylor 1900-1945
See Pyle, Ernie
See also CA 115; 160

Pyle, Ernie 1900-1945   TCLC 75
See also Pyle, Ernest Taylor
See also DLB 29; MTCW 2

Pyle, Howard 1853-1911   TCLC 81
See also CA 109; 137; CLR 22; DLB 42, 188; DLBD 13; MAICYA; SATA 16, 100

Pym, Barbara (Mary Crampton) 1913-1980
CLC 13, 19, 37, 111
See also CA 13-14; 97-100; CANR 13, 34; CAP 1; DLB 14, 207; DLBY 87; MTCW 1, 2

Pynchon, Thomas (Ruggles, Jr.) 1937-CLC 2, 3, 6, 9, 11, 18, 33, 62, 72; DA; DAB; DAC; DAM MST, NOV, POP; SSC 14;WLC
See also BEST 90:2; CA 17-20R; CANR 22, 46, 73; DLB 2, 173; MTCW 1, 2

Pythagoras c. 570B.C.-c.500B.C.   CMLC 22
See also DLB 176

Q
See Quiller-Couch, SirArthur (Thomas)

Qian Zhongshu
See Ch'ien Chung-shu

Qroll
See Dagerman, Stig (Halvard)

Quarrington, Paul (Lewis) 1953-   CLC 65
See also CA 129; CANR 62

Quasimodo, Salvatore 1901-1968   CLC 10
See also CA 13-16; 25-28R; CAP 1; DLB 114; MTCW 1

Quay, Stephen 1947-   CLC 95
Quay, Timothy 1947-   CLC 95

Queen, Ellery   CLC 3, 11
See also Dannay, Frederic; Davidson, Avram (James); Lee, Manfred B(ennington); Marlowe, Stephen; Sturgeon, Theodore (Hamilton); Vance, John Holbrook

Queen, Ellery, Jr.
See Dannay, Frederic; Lee, Manfred B(ennington)

Queneau, Raymond 1903-1976 CLC 2, 5, 10, 42
See also CA 77-80; 69-72; CANR 32; DLB 72; MTCW 1, 2

Quevedo, Francisco de 1580-1645   LC 23

Quiller-Couch, Sir Arthur(Thomas) 1863-1944
TCLC 53
See also CA 118; 166; DLB 135, 153, 190

Quin, Ann (Marie) 1936-1973   CLC 6

See also CA 9-12R; 45-48; DLB 14

Quinn, Martin
See Smith, Martin Cruz

Quinn, Peter 1947-   CLC 91

Quinn, Simon
See Smith, Martin Cruz

Quintana, Leroy V. 1944-
See also CA 131; CANR 65; DAM MULT; DLB 82; HLC 2; HW 1, 2

Quiroga, Horacio (Sylvestre) 1878-1937
TCLC 20; DAM MULT; HLC 2
See also CA 117; 131; HW 1; MTCW 1

Quoirez, Francoise 1935-   CLC 9
See also Sagan, Francoise
See also CA 49-52; CANR 6, 39, 73; MTCW 1, 2

Raabe, Wilhelm (Karl) 1831-1910 TCLC 45
See also CA 167; DLB 129

Rabe, David (William) 1940-   CLC 4, 8, 33; DAM DRAM
See also CA 85-88; CABS 3; CANR 59; DLB 7

Rabelais, Francois 1483-1553LC 5; DA; DAB; DAC; DAM MST; WLC

Rabinovitch, Sholem 1859-1916
See Aleichem, Sholom
See also CA 104

Rabinyan, Dorit 1972-   CLC 119
See also CA 170

Rachilde 1860-1953   TCLC 67
See also DLB 123, 192

Racine, Jean 1639-1699 LC 28; DAB; DAM MST

Radcliffe, Ann (Ward) 1764-1823NCLC 6, 55
See also DLB 39, 178

Radiguet, Raymond 1903-1923   TCLC 29
See also CA 162; DLB 65

Radnoti, Miklos 1909-1944   TCLC 16
See also CA 118

Rado, James 1939-   CLC 17
See also CA 105

Radvanyi, Netty 1900-1983
See Seghers, Anna
See also CA 85-88; 110; CANR 82

Rae, Ben
See Griffiths, Trevor

Raeburn, John (Hay) 1941-   CLC 34
See also CA 57-60

Ragni, Gerome 1942-1991   CLC 17
See also CA 105; 134

Rahv, Philip 1908-1973   CLC 24
See also Greenberg, Ivan
See also DLB 137

Raimund, Ferdinand Jakob 1790-1836N C L C 69
See also DLB 90

Raine, Craig 1944-   CLC 32, 103
See also CA 108; CANR 29, 51; DLB 40

Raine, Kathleen (Jessie) 1908-   CLC 7, 45
See also CA 85-88; CANR 46; DLB 20; MTCW 1

Rainis, Janis 1865-1929   TCLC 29
See also CA 170

Rakosi, Carl 1903-   CLC 47
See also Rawley, Callman
See also CAAS 5; DLB 193

Raleigh, Richard
See Lovecraft, H(oward) P(hillips)

Raleigh, Sir Walter 1554(?)-1618 LC 31, 39
See also CDBLB Before 1660; DLB 172

Rallentando, H. P.
See Sayers, Dorothy L(eigh)

Ramal, Walter
See de la Mare, Walter (John)

Ramana Maharshi 1879-1950   **TCLC 84**
Ramoacn y Cajal, Santiago 1852-1934**T C L C 93**
Ramon, Juan
   See Jimenez (Mantecon), Juan Ramon
Ramos, Graciliano 1892-1953   **TCLC 32**
   See also CA 167; HW 2
Rampersad, Arnold 1941-   **CLC 44**
   See also BW 2, 3; CA 127; 133; CANR 81; DLB 111; INT 133
Rampling, Anne
   See Rice, Anne
Ramsay, Allan 1684(?)-1758   **LC 29**
   See also DLB 95
Ramuz, Charles-Ferdinand 1878-1947**T C L C 33**
   See also CA 165
Rand, Ayn 1905-1982 **CLC 3, 30, 44, 79; DA; DAC; DAM MST, NOV, POP; WLC**
   See also AAYA 10; CA 13-16R; 105; CANR 27, 73; CDALBS; MTCW 1, 2
Randall, Dudley (Felker) 1914-**CLC 1; BLC 3; DAM MULT**
   See also BW 1, 3; CA 25-28R; CANR 23, 82; DLB 41
Randall, Robert
   See Silverberg, Robert
Ranger, Ken
   See Creasey, John
Ransom, John Crowe 1888-1974 **CLC 2, 4, 5, 11, 24; DAM POET**
   See also CA 5-8R; 49-52; CANR 6, 34; CDALBS; DLB 45, 63; MTCW 1, 2
Rao, Raja 1909-   **CLC 25, 56;DAM NOV**
   See also CA 73-76; CANR 51; MTCW 1, 2
Raphael, Frederic (Michael) 1931-**CLC 2, 14**
   See also CA 1-4R; CANR 1; DLB 14
Ratcliffe, James P.
   See Mencken, H(enry) L(ouis)
Rathbone, Julian 1935-   **CLC 41**
   See also CA 101; CANR 34, 73
Rattigan, Terence (Mervyn) 1911-1977**CLC 7; DAM DRAM**
   See also CA 85-88; 73-76; CDBLB 1945-1960; DLB 13; MTCW 1, 2
Ratushinskaya, Irina 1954-   **CLC 54**
   See also CA 129; CANR 68
Raven, Simon (Arthur Noel) 1927-   **CLC 14**
   See also CA 81-84
Ravenna, Michael
   See Welty, Eudora
Rawley, Callman 1903-
   See Rakosi, Carl
   See also CA 21-24R; CANR 12, 32
Rawlings, Marjorie Kinnan 1896-1953**T C L C 4**
   See also AAYA 20; CA 104; 137; CANR 74; DLB 9, 22, 102; DLBD 17; JRDA; MAICYA; MTCW 2; SATA 100; YABC 1
Ray, Satyajit 1921-1992   **CLC 16, 76; DAM MULT**
   See also CA 114; 137
Read, Herbert Edward 1893-1968   **CLC 4**
   See also CA 85-88; 25-28R; DLB 20, 149
Read, Piers Paul 1941-   **CLC 4, 10, 25**
   See also CA 21-24R; CANR 38; DLB 14; SATA 21
Reade, Charles 1814-1884   **NCLC 2, 74**
   See also DLB 21
Reade, Hamish
   See Gray, Simon (James Holliday)
Reading, Peter 1946-   **CLC 47**
   See also CA 103; CANR 46; DLB 40

Reaney, James 1926-   **CLC 13; DAC;DAM MST**
   See also CA 41-44R; CAAS 15; CANR 42; DLB 68; SATA 43
Rebreanu, Liviu 1885-1944   **TCLC 28**
   See also CA 165
Rechy, John (Francisco) 1934- **CLC 1, 7, 14, 18, 107; DAM MULT; HLC 2**
   See also CA 5-8R; CAAS 4; CANR 6, 32, 64; DLB 122; DLBY 82; HW 1, 2; INT CANR-6
Redcam, Tom 1870-1933   **TCLC 25**
Reddin, Keith   **CLC 67**
Redgrove, Peter (William) 1932- **CLC 6, 41**
   See also CA 1-4R; CANR 3, 39, 77; DLB 40
Redmon, Anne   **CLC 22**
   See also Nightingale, Anne Redmon
   See also DLBY 86
Reed, Eliot
   See Ambler, Eric
Reed, Ishmael 1938-**CLC 2, 3, 5, 6, 13, 32, 60; BLC 3; DAM MULT**
   See also BW 2, 3; CA 21-24R; CANR 25, 48, 74; DLB 2, 5, 33, 169; DLBD 8; MTCW 1, 2
Reed, John (Silas) 1887-1920   **TCLC 9**
   See also CA 106
Reed, Lou   **CLC 21**
   See also Firbank, Louis
Reeve, Clara 1729-1807   **NCLC 19**
   See also DLB 39
Reich, Wilhelm 1897-1957   **TCLC 57**
Reid, Christopher (John) 1949-   **CLC 33**
   See also CA 140; DLB 40
Reid, Desmond
   See Moorcock, Michael (John)
Reid Banks, Lynne 1929-
   See Banks, Lynne Reid
   See also CA 1-4R; CANR 6, 22, 38; CLR 24; JRDA; MAICYA; SATA 22, 75
Reilly, William K.
   See Creasey, John
Reiner, Max
   See Caldwell, (Janet Miriam) Taylor (Holland)
Reis, Ricardo
   See Pessoa, Fernando (Antonio Nogueira)
Remarque, Erich Maria 1898-1970 **CLC 21; DA; DAB; DAC; DAM MST, NOV**
   See also AAYA 27; CA 77-80; 29-32R; DLB 56; MTCW 1, 2
Remington, Frederic 1861-1909   **TCLC 89**
   See also CA 108; 169; DLB 12, 186, 188; SATA 41
Remizov, A.
   See Remizov, Aleksei (Mikhailovich)
Remizov, A. M.
   See Remizov, Aleksei (Mikhailovich)
Remizov, Aleksei (Mikhailovich) 1877-1957 **TCLC 27**
   See also CA 125; 133
Renan, Joseph Ernest 1823-1892   **NCLC 26**
Renard, Jules 1864-1910   **TCLC 17**
   See also CA 117
Renault, Mary   **CLC 3, 11, 17**
   See also Challans, Mary
   See also DLBY 83; MTCW 2
Rendell, Ruth (Barbara) 1930- **CLC 28, 48; DAM POP**
   See also Vine, Barbara
   See also CA 109; CANR 32, 52, 74; DLB 87; INT CANR-32; MTCW 1, 2
Renoir, Jean 1894-1979   **CLC 20**
   See also CA 129; 85-88

Resnais, Alain 1922-   **CLC 16**
Reverdy, Pierre 1889-1960   **CLC 53**
   See also CA 97-100; 89-92
Rexroth, Kenneth 1905-1982 **CLC 1, 2, 6, 11, 22, 49, 112; DAM POET; PC 20**
   See also CA 5-8R; 107; CANR 14, 34, 63; CDALB 1941-1968; DLB 16, 48, 165, 212; DLBY 82; INT CANR-14; MTCW 1, 2
Reyes, Alfonso 1889-1959 **TCLC 33;HLCS 2**
   See also CA 131; HW 1
Reyes y Basoalto, Ricardo Eliecer Neftali
   See Neruda, Pablo
Reymont, Wladyslaw (Stanislaw) 1868(?)-1925 **TCLC 5**
   See also CA 104
Reynolds, Jonathan 1942-   **CLC 6, 38**
   See also CA 65-68; CANR 28
Reynolds, Joshua 1723-1792   **LC 15**
   See also DLB 104
Reynolds, Michael Shane 1937-   **CLC 44**
   See also CA 65-68; CANR 9
Reznikoff, Charles 1894-1976   **CLC 9**
   See also CA 33-36; 61-64; CAP 2; DLB 28, 45
Rezzori (d'Arezzo), Gregorvon 1914-1998 **CLC 25**
   See also CA 122; 136; 167
Rhine, Richard
   See Silverstein, Alvin
Rhodes, Eugene Manlove 1869-1934**TCLC 53**
Rhodius, Apollonius c. 3rd cent.B.C.- **C M L C 28**
   See also DLB 176
R'hoone
   See Balzac, Honore de
Rhys, Jean 1890(?)-1979 **CLC 2, 4, 6, 14, 19, 51; DAM NOV; SSC 21**
   See also CA 25-28R; 85-88; CANR 35, 62; CDBLB 1945-1960; DLB 36, 117, 162; MTCW 1, 2
Ribeiro, Darcy 1922-1997   **CLC 34**
   See also CA 33-36R; 156
Ribeiro, Joao Ubaldo (Osorio Pimentel) 1941- **CLC 10, 67**
   See also CA 81-84
Ribman, Ronald (Burt) 1932-   **CLC 7**
   See also CA 21-24R; CANR 46, 80
Ricci, Nino 1959-   **CLC 70**
   See also CA 137
Rice, Anne 1941-   **CLC 41;DAM POP**
   See also AAYA 9; BEST 89:2; CA 65-68; CANR 12, 36, 53, 74; MTCW 2
Rice, Elmer (Leopold) 1892-1967 **CLC 7, 49; DAM DRAM**
   See also CA 21-22; 25-28R; CAP 2; DLB 4, 7; MTCW 1, 2
Rice, Tim(othy Miles Bindon) 1944- **CLC 21**
   See also CA 103; CANR 46
Rich, Adrienne (Cecile) 1929-**CLC 3, 6, 7, 11, 18, 36, 73, 76; DAM POET; PC 5**
   See also CA 9-12R; CANR 20, 53, 74; CDALBS; DLB 5, 67; MTCW 1, 2
Rich, Barbara
   See Graves, Robert (von Ranke)
Rich, Robert
   See Trumbo, Dalton
Richard, Keith   **CLC 17**
   See also Richards, Keith
Richards, David Adams 1950- **CLC 59; DAC**
   See also CA 93-96; CANR 60; DLB 53
Richards, I(vor) A(rmstrong) 1893-1979**C L C 14, 24**
   See also CA 41-44R; 89-92; CANR 34, 74; DLB 27; MTCW 2

See also CA 61-64; 108; CANR 30; DLB 7
Sacks, Oliver (Wolf) 1933-   **CLC 67**
     See also CA 53-56; CANR 28, 50, 76; INT
       CANR-28; MTCW 1, 2
Sadakichi
     See Hartmann, Sadakichi
Sade, Donatien Alphonse Francois, Comte de
     1740-1814   **NCLC 47**
Sadoff, Ira 1945-   **CLC 9**
     See also CA 53-56; CANR 5, 21; DLB 120
Saetone
     See Camus, Albert
Safire, William 1929-   **CLC 10**
     See also CA 17-20R; CANR 31, 54
Sagan, Carl (Edward) 1934-1996 **CLC 30, 112**
     See also AAYA 2; CA 25-28R; 155; CANR 11,
       36, 74; MTCW 1, 2; SATA 58; SATA-Obit
       94
Sagan, Francoise   **CLC 3, 6, 9, 17, 36**
     See also Quoirez, Francoise
     See also DLB 83; MTCW 2
Sahgal, Nayantara (Pandit) 1927-   **CLC 41**
     See also CA 9-12R; CANR 11
Saint, H(arry) F. 1941-   **CLC 50**
     See also CA 127
St. Aubin de Teran, Lisa 1953-
     See Teran, Lisa St. Aubin de
     See also CA 118; 126; INT 126
Saint Birgitta of Sweden c. 1303-1373 **CMLC 24**
Sainte-Beuve, Charles Augustin 1804-1869
          NCLC 5
Saint-Exupery, Antoine (Jean Baptiste Marie
     Roger) de 1900-1944 **TCLC 2, 56; DAM**
     NOV;WLC
     See also CA 108; 132; CLR 10; DLB 72;
       MAICYA; MTCW 1, 2; SATA 20
St. John, David
     See Hunt, E(verette) Howard, (Jr.)
Saint-John Perse
     See Leger, (Marie-Rene Auguste) Alexis Saint-
       Leger
Saintsbury, George (Edward Bateman) 1845-
     1933   **TCLC 31**
     See also CA 160; DLB 57, 149
Sait Faik   **TCLC 23**
     See also Abasiyanik, Sait Faik
Saki   **TCLC 3; SSC 12**
     See also Munro, H(ector) H(ugh)
     See also MTCW 2
Sala, George Augustus   **NCLC 46**
Salama, Hannu 1936-   **CLC 18**
Salamanca, J(ack) R(ichard) 1922- **CLC 4, 15**
     See also CA 25-28R
Salas, Floyd Francis 1931-
     See also CA 119; CAAS 27; CANR 44, 75;
       DAM MULT; DLB 82; HLC 2; HW 1, 2;
       MTCW 2
Sale, J. Kirkpatrick
     See Sale, Kirkpatrick
Sale, Kirkpatrick 1937-   **CLC 68**
     See also CA 13-16R; CANR 10
Salinas, Luis Omar 1937-   **CLC 90; DAM**
     MULT; HLC 2
     See also CA 131; CANR 81; DLB 82; HW 1, 2
Salinas (y Serrano), Pedro 1891(?)-1951
     TCLC 17
     See also CA 117; DLB 134
Salinger, J(erome) D(avid) 1919- **CLC 1, 3, 8,**
     12, 55, 56; DA; DAB; DAC; DAM MST,
     NOV, POP; SSC 2, 28; WLC
     See also AAYA 2; CA 5-8R; CANR 39; CDALB
       1941-1968; CLR 18; DLB 2, 102, 173;

MAICYA; MTCW 1, 2; SATA 67
Salisbury, John
     See Caute, (John) David
Salter, James 1925-   **CLC 7, 52, 59**
     See also CA 73-76; DLB 130
Saltus, Edgar (Everton) 1855-1921 **TCLC 8**
     See also CA 105; DLB 202
Saltykov, Mikhail Evgrafovich 1826-1889
     NCLC 16
Samarakis, Antonis 1919-   **CLC 5**
     See also CA 25-28R; CAAS 16; CANR 36
Sanchez, Florencio 1875-1910   **TCLC 37**
     See also CA 153; HW 1
Sanchez, Luis Rafael 1936-   **CLC 23**
     See also CA 128; DLB 145; HW 1
Sanchez, Sonia 1934-   **CLC 5, 116; BLC 3;**
     DAM MULT; PC 9
     See also BW 2, 3; CA 33-36R; CANR 24, 49,
       74; CLR 18; DLB 41; DLBD 8;MAICYA;
       MTCW 1, 2; SATA 22
Sand, George 1804-1876NCLC **2, 42, 57; DA;**
     DAB; DAC; DAM MST, NOV; WLC
     See also DLB 119, 192
Sandburg, Carl (August) 1878-1967CLC **1, 4,**
     10, 15, 35; DA; DAB; DAC; DAM MST,
     POET; PC 2; WLC
     See also AAYA 24; CA 5-8R; 25-28R; CANR
       35; CDALB 1865-1917; DLB 17, 54;
       MAICYA; MTCW 1, 2; SATA 8
Sandburg, Charles
     See Sandburg, Carl (August)
Sandburg, Charles A.
     See Sandburg, Carl (August)
Sanders, (James) Ed(ward) 1939-   **CLC 53;**
     DAM POET
     See also CA 13-16R; CAAS 21; CANR 13, 44,
       78; DLB 16
Sanders, Lawrence 1920-1998CLC **41; DAM**
     POP
     See also BEST 89:4; CA 81-84; 165; CANR
       33, 62; MTCW 1
Sanders, Noah
     See Blount, Roy (Alton), Jr.
Sanders, Winston P.
     See Anderson, Poul (William)
Sandoz, Mari(e Susette) 1896-1966   **CLC 28**
     See also CA 1-4R; 25-28R; CANR 17, 64; DLB
       9, 212; MTCW 1, 2; SATA 5
Saner, Reg(inald Anthony) 1931-   **CLC 9**
     See also CA 65-68
Sankara 788-820   **CMLC 32**
Sannazaro, Jacopo 1456(?)-1530   **LC 8**
Sansom, William 1912-1976 **CLC 2, 6; DAM**
     NOV; SSC 21
     See also CA 5-8R; 65-68; CANR 42; DLB 139;
       MTCW 1
Santayana, George 1863-1952   **TCLC 40**
     See also CA 115; DLB 54, 71; DLBD 13
Santiago, Danny   **CLC 33**
     See also James, Daniel (Lewis)
     See also DLB 122
Santmyer, Helen Hoover 1895-1986 **CLC 33**
     See also CA 1-4R; 118; CANR 15, 33; DLBY
       84; MTCW 1
Santoka, Taneda 1882-1940   **TCLC 72**
Santos, Bienvenido N(uqui) 1911-1996   **C L C**
     22; DAM MULT
     See also CA 101; 151; CANR 19, 46
Sapper   **TCLC 44**
     See also McNeile, Herman Cyril
Sapphire
     See Sapphire, Brenda
Sapphire, Brenda 1950-   **CLC 99**

Sappho fl. 6th cent. B.C.-   **CMLC 3; DAM**
     POET; PC 5
     See also DLB 176
Saramago, Jose 1922-   **CLC 119;HLCS 1**
     See also CA 153
Sarduy, Severo 1937-1993CLC **6, 97; HLCS 1**
     See also CA 89-92; 142; CANR 58, 81; DLB
       113; HW 1, 2
Sargeson, Frank 1903-1982   **CLC 31**
     See also CA 25-28R; 106; CANR 38, 79
Sarmiento, Domingo Faustino 1811-1888
     See also HLCS 2
Sarmiento, Felix Ruben Garcia
     See Dario, Ruben
Saro-Wiwa, Ken(ule Beeson) 1941-1995 **C L C**
     114
     See also BW 2; CA 142; 150; CANR 60; DLB
       157
Saroyan, William 1908-1981CLC **1, 8, 10, 29,**
     34, 56; DA; DAB; DAC; DAM DRAM,
     MST, NOV; SSC 21; WLC
     See also CA 5-8R; 103; CANR 30; CDALBS;
       DLB 7, 9, 86; DLBY 81; MTCW 1, 2; SATA
       23; SATA-Obit 24
Sarraute, Nathalie 1900-CLC **1, 2, 4, 8, 10, 31,**
     80
     See also CA 9-12R; CANR 23, 66; DLB 83;
       MTCW 1, 2
Sarton, (Eleanor) May 1912-1995 **CLC 4, 14,**
     49, 91; DAM POET
     See also CA 1-4R; 149; CANR 1, 34, 55; DLB
       48; DLBY 81; INT CANR-34; MTCW 1, 2;
       SATA 36; SATA-Obit 86
Sartre, Jean-Paul 1905-1980CLC **1, 4, 7, 9, 13,**
     18, 24, 44, 50, 52; DA; DAB; DAC; DAM
     DRAM, MST, NOV; DC 3; SSC 32; WLC
     See also CA 9-12R; 97-100; CANR 21; DLB
       72; MTCW 1, 2
Sassoon, Siegfried (Lorraine) 1886-1967**C L C**
     36; DAB; DAM MST, NOV, POET; PC 12
     See also CA 104; 25-28R; CANR 36; DLB 20,
       191; DLBD 18; MTCW 1, 2
Satterfield, Charles
     See Pohl, Frederik
Saul, John (W. III) 1942-CLC **46; DAM NOV,**
     POP
     See also AAYA 10; BEST 90:4; CA 81-84;
       CANR 16, 40, 81; SATA 98
Saunders, Caleb
     See Heinlein, Robert A(nson)
Saura (Atares), Carlos 1932-   **CLC 20**
     See also CA 114; 131; CANR 79; HW 1
Sauser-Hall, Frederic 1887-1961   **CLC 18**
     See also Cendrars, Blaise
     See also CA 102; 93-96; CANR 36, 62; MTCW
       1
Saussure, Ferdinand de 1857-1913 **TCLC 49**
Savage, Catharine
     See Brosman, Catharine Savage
Savage, Thomas 1915-   **CLC 40**
     See also CA 126; 132; CAAS 15; INT 132
Savan, Glenn 19(?)-   **CLC 50**
Sayers, Dorothy L(eigh) 1893-1957 **TCLC 2,**
     15; DAM POP
     See also CA 104; 119; CANR 60; CDBLB 1914-
       1945; DLB 10, 36, 77, 100; MTCW 1, 2
Sayers, Valerie 1952-   **CLC 50, 122**
     See also CA 134; CANR 61
Sayles, John (Thomas) 1950-   **CLC 7, 10, 14**
     See also CA 57-60; CANR 41; DLB 44
Scammell, Michael 1935-   **CLC 34**
     See also CA 156
Scannell, Vernon 1922-   **CLC 49**

See also CA 5-8R; CANR 8, 24, 57; DLB 27;
SATA 59

Scarlett, Susan
See Streatfeild, (Mary) Noel

Scarron
See Mikszath, Kalman

Schaeffer, Susan Fromberg 1941- **CLC 6, 11, 22**
See also CA 49-52; CANR 18, 65; DLB 28;
MTCW 1, 2; SATA 22

Schary, Jill
See Robinson, Jill

Schell, Jonathan 1943- **CLC 35**
See also CA 73-76; CANR 12

Schelling, Friedrich Wilhelm Josephvon 1775-1854 **NCLC 30**
See also DLB 90

Schendel, Arthur van 1874-1946 **TCLC 56**

Scherer, Jean-Marie Maurice 1920-
See Rohmer, Eric
See also CA 110

Schevill, James (Erwin) 1920- **CLC 7**
See also CA 5-8R; CAAS 12

Schiller, Friedrich 1759-1805 **NCLC 39, 69; DAM DRAM**
See also DLB 94

Schisgal, Murray (Joseph) 1926- **CLC 6**
See also CA 21-24R; CANR 48

Schlee, Ann 1934- **CLC 35**
See also CA 101; CANR 29; SATA 44; SATA-Brief 36

Schlegel, August Wilhelmvon 1767-1845 **NCLC 15**
See also DLB 94

Schlegel, Friedrich 1772-1829 **NCLC 45**
See also DLB 90

Schlegel, Johann Elias (von) 1719(?)-1749 **L C 5**

Schlesinger, Arthur M(eier), Jr. 1917- **CLC 84**
See also AITN 1; CA 1-4R; CANR 1, 28, 58;
DLB 17; INT CANR-28; MTCW 1, 2; SATA 61

Schmidt, Arno (Otto) 1914-1979 **CLC 56**
See also CA 128; 109; DLB 69

Schmitz, Aron Hector 1861-1928
See Svevo, Italo
See also CA 104; 122; MTCW 1

Schnackenberg, Gjertrud 1953- **CLC 40**
See also CA 116; DLB 120

Schneider, Leonard Alfred 1925-1966
See Bruce, Lenny
See also CA 89-92

Schnitzler, Arthur 1862-1931 **TCLC 4; SSC 15**
See also CA 104; DLB 81, 118

Schoenberg, Arnold 1874-1951 **TCLC 75**
See also CA 109

Schonberg, Arnold
See Schoenberg, Arnold

Schopenhauer, Arthur 1788-1860 **NCLC 51**
See also DLB 90

Schor, Sandra (M.) 1932(?)-1990 **CLC 65**
See also CA 132

Schorer, Mark 1908-1977 **CLC 9**
See also CA 5-8R; 73-76; CANR 7; DLB 103

Schrader, Paul (Joseph) 1946- **CLC 26**
See also CA 37-40R; CANR 41; DLB 44

Schreiner, Olive (Emilie Albertina) 1855-1920 **TCLC 9**
See also CA 105; 154; DLB 18, 156, 190

Schulberg, Budd (Wilson) 1914- **CLC 7, 48**
See also CA 25-28R; CANR 19; DLB 6, 26, 28; DLBY 81

Schulz, Bruno 1892-1942 **TCLC 5, 51; SSC 13**

See also CA 115; 123; MTCW 2

Schulz, Charles M(onroe) 1922- **CLC 12**
See also CA 9-12R; CANR 6; INT CANR-6;
SATA 10

Schumacher, E(rnst) F(riedrich) 1911-1977 **CLC 80**
See also CA 81-84; 73-76; CANR 34

Schuyler, James Marcus 1923-1991 **CLC 5, 23; DAM POET**
See also CA 101; 134; DLB 5, 169; INT 101

Schwartz, Delmore (David) 1913-1966 **CLC 2, 4, 10, 45, 87; PC 8**
See also CA 17-18; 25-28R; CANR 35; CAP 2;
DLB 28, 48; MTCW 1, 2

Schwartz, Ernst
See Ozu, Yasujiro

Schwartz, John Burnham 1965- **CLC 59**
See also CA 132

Schwartz, Lynne Sharon 1939- **CLC 31**
See also CA 103; CANR 44; MTCW 2

Schwartz, Muriel A.
See Eliot, T(homas) S(tearns)

Schwarz-Bart, Andre 1928- **CLC 2, 4**
See also CA 89-92

Schwarz-Bart, Simone 1938- **CLC 7; BLCS**
See also BW 2; CA 97-100

Schwitters, Kurt (Hermann Edward Karl Julius) 1887-1948 **TCLC 95**
See also CA 158

Schwob, Marcel (Mayer Andre) 1867-1905 **TCLC 20**
See also CA 117; 168; DLB 123

Sciascia, Leonardo 1921-1989 **CLC 8, 9, 41**
See also CA 85-88; 130; CANR 35; DLB 177;
MTCW 1

Scoppettone, Sandra 1936- **CLC 26**
See also AAYA 11; CA 5-8R; CANR 41, 73;
SATA 9, 92

Scorsese, Martin 1942- **CLC 20, 89**
See also CA 110; 114; CANR 46

Scotland, Jay
See Jakes, John (William)

Scott, Duncan Campbell 1862-1947 **TCLC 6; DAC**
See also CA 104; 153; DLB 92

Scott, Evelyn 1893-1963 **CLC 43**
See also CA 104; 112; CANR 64; DLB 9, 48

Scott, F(rancis) R(eginald) 1899-1985 **CLC 22**
See also CA 101; 114; DLB 88; INT 101

Scott, Frank
See Scott, F(rancis) R(eginald)

Scott, Joanna 1960- **CLC 50**
See also CA 126; CANR 53

Scott, Paul (Mark) 1920-1978 **CLC 9, 60**
See also CA 81-84; 77-80; CANR 33; DLB 14, 207; MTCW 1

Scott, Sarah 1723-1795 **LC 44**
See also DLB 39

Scott, Walter 1771-1832 **NCLC 15, 69; DA; DAB; DAC; DAM MST, NOV, POET; PC 13; SSC 32; WLC**
See also AAYA 22; CDBLB 1789-1832; DLB 93, 107, 116, 144, 159; YABC 2

Scribe, (Augustin) Eugene 1791-1861 **NCLC 16; DAM DRAM; DC 5**
See also DLB 192

Scrum, R.
See Crumb, R(obert)

Scudery, Madeleine de 1607-1701 **LC 2**

Scum
See Crumb, R(obert)

Scumbag, Little Bobby
See Crumb, R(obert)

Seabrook, John
See Hubbard, L(afayette) Ron(ald)

Sealy, I. Allan 1951- **CLC 55**

Search, Alexander
See Pessoa, Fernando (Antonio Nogueira)

Sebastian, Lee
See Silverberg, Robert

Sebastian Owl
See Thompson, Hunter S(tockton)

Sebestyen, Ouida 1924- **CLC 30**
See also AAYA 8; CA 107; CANR 40; CLR 17;
JRDA; MAICYA; SAAS 10; SATA 39

Secundus, H. Scriblerus
See Fielding, Henry

Sedges, John
See Buck, Pearl S(ydenstricker)

Sedgwick, Catharine Maria 1789-1867 **NCLC 19**
See also DLB 1, 74

Seelye, John (Douglas) 1931- **CLC 7**
See also CA 97-100; CANR 70; INT 97-100

Seferiades, Giorgos Stylianou 1900-1971
See Seferis, George
See also CA 5-8R; 33-36R; CANR 5, 36;
MTCW 1

Seferis, George **CLC 5, 11**
See also Seferiades, Giorgos Stylianou

Segal, Erich (Wolf) 1937- **CLC 3, 10; DAM POP**
See also BEST 89:1; CA 25-28R, CANR 20, 36, 65; DLBY 86; INT CANR-20; MTCW 1

Seger, Bob 1945- **CLC 35**

Seghers, Anna **CLC 7**
See also Radvanyi, Netty
See also DLB 69

Seidel, Frederick (Lewis) 1936- **CLC 18**
See also CA 13-16R; CANR 8; DLBY 84

Seifert, Jaroslav 1901-1986 **CLC 34, 44, 93**
See also CA 127; MTCW 1, 2

Sei Shonagon c. 966-1017(?) **CMLC 6**

Sejour, Victor 1817-1874 **DC 10**
See also DLB 50

Sejour Marcou et Ferrand, Juan Victor
See Sejour, Victor

Selby, Hubert, Jr. 1928- **CLC 1, 2, 4, 8; SSC 20**
See also CA 13-16R; CANR 33; DLB 2

Selzer, Richard 1928- **CLC 74**
See also CA 65-68; CANR 14

Sembene, Ousmane
See Ousmane, Sembene

Senancour, Etienne Pivert de 1770-1846 **NCLC 16**
See also DLB 119

Sender, Ramon (Jose) 1902-1982 **CLC 8; DAM MULT; HLC 2**
See also CA 5-8R; 105; CANR 8; HW 1;
MTCW 1

Seneca, Lucius Annaeus c. 1-c. 65 **CMLC 6; DAM DRAM; DC 5**
See also DLB 211

Senghor, Leopold Sedar 1906- **CLC 54; BLC 3; DAM MULT, POET; PC 25**
See also BW 2; CA 116; 125; CANR 47, 74;
MTCW 1, 2

Senna, Danzy 1970- **CLC 119**
See also CA 169

Serling, (Edward) Rod(man) 1924-1975 **CLC 30**
See also AAYA 14; AITN 1; CA 162; 57-60;
DLB 26

Serna, Ramon Gomez de la
See Gomez de la Serna, Ramon

Serpieres

See Guillevic, (Eugene)

Service, Robert
See Service, Robert W(illiam)
See also DAB; DLB 92

Service, Robert W(illiam) 1874(?)-1958 **TCLC 15; DA; DAC; DAM MST, POET; WLC**
See also Service, Robert
See also CA 115; 140; SATA 20

Seth, Vikram 1952- CLC 43, 90; **DAM MULT**
See also CA 121; 127; CANR 50, 74; DLB 120; INT 127; MTCW 2

Seton, Cynthia Propper 1926-1982 **CLC 27**
See also CA 5-8R; 108; CANR 7

Seton, Ernest (Evan) Thompson 1860-1946 **TCLC 31**
See also CA 109; CLR 59; DLB 92; DLBD 13; JRDA; SATA 18

Seton-Thompson, Ernest
See Seton, Ernest (Evan) Thompson

Settle, Mary Lee 1918- **CLC 19, 61**
See also CA 89-92; CAAS 1; CANR 44; DLB 6; INT 89-92

Seuphor, Michel
See Arp, Jean

Sevigne, Marie (de Rabutin-Chantal) Marquise de 1626-1696 **LC 11**

Sewall, Samuel 1652-1730 **LC 38**
See also DLB 24

Sexton, Anne (Harvey) 1928-1974 **CLC 2, 4, 6, 8, 10, 15, 53; DA; DAB; DAC; DAM MST, POET; PC 2; WLC**
See also CA 1-4R; 53-56; CABS 2; CANR 3, 36; CDALB 1941-1968; DLB 5, 169; MTCW 1, 2; SATA 10

Shaara, Jeff 1952- **CLC 119**
See also CA 163

Shaara, Michael (Joseph, Jr.) 1929-1988 **CLC 15; DAM POP**
See also AITN 1; CA 102; 125; CANR 52; DLBY 83

Shackleton, C. C.
See Aldiss, Brian W(ilson)

Shacochis, Bob **CLC 39**
See also Shacochis, Robert G.

Shacochis, Robert G. 1951-
See Shacochis, Bob
See also CA 119; 124; INT 124

Shaffer, Anthony (Joshua) 1926- **CLC 19; DAM DRAM**
See also CA 110; 116; DLB 13

Shaffer, Peter (Levin) 1926- **CLC 5, 14, 18, 37, 60; DAB; DAM DRAM, MST; DC 7**
See also CA 25-28R; CANR 25, 47, 74; CDBLB 1960 to Present; DLB 13; MTCW 1, 2

Shakey, Bernard
See Young, Neil

Shalamov, Varlam (Tikhonovich) 1907(?)-1982 **CLC 18**
See also CA 129; 105

Shamlu, Ahmad 1925- **CLC 10**

Shammas, Anton 1951- **CLC 55**

Shange, Ntozake 1948- **CLC 8, 25, 38, 74; BLC 3; DAM DRAM, MULT; DC 3**
See also AAYA 9; BW 2; CA 85-88; CABS 3; CANR 27, 48, 74; DLB 38; MTCW 1, 2

Shanley, John Patrick 1950- **CLC 75**
See also CA 128; 133

Shapcott, Thomas W(illiam) 1935- **CLC 38**
See also CA 69-72; CANR 49

Shapiro, Jane **CLC 76**

Shapiro, Karl (Jay) 1913- **CLC 4, 8, 15, 53; PC 25**
See also CA 1-4R; CAAS 6; CANR 1, 36, 66;

DLB 48; MTCW 1, 2

Sharp, William 1855-1905 **TCLC 39**
See also CA 160; DLB 156

Sharpe, Thomas Ridley 1928-
See Sharpe, Tom
See also CA 114; 122; INT 122

Sharpe, Tom **CLC 36**
See Sharpe, Thomas Ridley
See also DLB 14

Shaw, Bernard **TCLC 45**
See also Shaw, George Bernard
See also BW 1; MTCW 2

Shaw, G. Bernard
See Shaw, George Bernard

Shaw, George Bernard 1856-1950 **TCLC 3, 9, 21; DA; DAB; DAC; DAM DRAM, MST; WLC**
See also Shaw, Bernard
See also CA 104; 128; CDBLB 1914-1945; DLB 10, 57, 190; MTCW 1, 2

Shaw, Henry Wheeler 1818-1885 **NCLC 15**
See also DLB 11

Shaw, Irwin 1913-1984 **CLC 7, 23, 34; DAM DRAM, POP**
See also AITN 1; CA 13-16R; 112; CANR 21; CDALB 1941-1968; DLB 6, 102; DLBY 84; MTCW 1, 21

Shaw, Robert 1927-1978 **CLC 5**
See also AITN 1; CA 1-4R; 81-84; CANR 4; DLB 13, 14

Shaw, T. E.
See Lawrence, T(homas) E(dward)

Shawn, Wallace 1943- **CLC 41**
See also CA 112

Shea, Lisa 1953- **CLC 86**
See also CA 147

Sheed, Wilfrid (John Joseph) 1930- **CLC 2, 4, 10, 53**
See also CA 65-68; CANR 30, 66; DLB 6; MTCW 1, 2

Sheldon, Alice Hastings Bradley 1915(?)-1987
See Tiptree, James, Jr.
See also CA 108; 122; CANR 34; INT 108; MTCW 1

Sheldon, John 1917-1994
See Bloch, Robert (Albert)
See also CA 179; CAAE 179

Shelley, Mary Wollstonecraft (Godwin) 1797-1851 **NCLC 14, 59; DA; DAB; DAC; DAM MST, NOV; WLC**
See also AAYA 20; CDBLB 1789-1832; DLB 110, 116, 159, 178; SATA 29

Shelley, Percy Bysshe 1792-1822 **NCLC 18; DA; DAB; DAC; DAM MST, POET; PC 14; WLC**
See also CDBLB 1789-1832; DLB 96, 110, 158

Shepard, Jim 1956- **CLC 36**
See also CA 137; CANR 59; SATA 90

Shepard, Lucius 1947- **CLC 34**
See also CA 128; 141; CANR 81

Shepard, Sam 1943- **CLC 4, 6, 17, 34, 41, 44; DAM DRAM; DC 5**
See also AAYA 1; CA 69-72; CABS 3; CANR 22; DLB 7, 212; MTCW 1, 2

Shepherd, Michael
See Ludlum, Robert

Sherburne, Zoa (Lillian Morin) 1912-1995 **CLC 30**
See also AAYA 13; CA 1-4R; 176; CANR 3, 37; MAICYA; SAAS 18; SATA 3

Sheridan, Frances 1724-1766 **LC 7**
See also DLB 39, 84

Sheridan, Richard Brinsley 1751-1816 **NCLC**

5; **DA; DAB; DAC; DAM DRAM, MST; DC 1; WLC**
See also CDBLB 1660-1789; DLB 89

Sherman, Jonathan Marc **CLC 55**

Sherman, Martin 1941(?)- **CLC 19**
See also CA 116; 123

Sherwin, Judith Johnson
See Johnson, Judith (Emlyn)

Sherwood, Frances 1940- **CLC 81**
See also CA 146

Sherwood, Robert E(mmet) 1896-1955 **TCLC 3; DAM DRAM**
See also CA 104; 153; DLB 7, 26

Shestov, Lev 1866-1938 **TCLC 56**

Shevchenko, Taras 1814-1861 **NCLC 54**

Shiel, M(atthew) P(hipps) 1865-1947 **TCLC 8**
See also Holmes, Gordon
See also CA 106; 160; DLB 153; MTCW 2

Shields, Carol 1935- **CLC 91, 113; DAC**
See also CA 81-84; CANR 51, 74; MTCW 2

Shields, David 1956- **CLC 97**
See also CA 124; CANR 48

Shiga, Naoya 1883-1971 **CLC 33; SSC 23**
See also CA 101; 33-36R; DLB 180

Shikibu, Murasaki c. 978-c. 1014 **CMLC 1**

Shilts, Randy 1951-1994 **CLC 85**
See also AAYA 19; CA 115; 127; 144; CANR 45; INT 127; MTCW 2

Shimazaki, Haruki 1872-1943
See Shimazaki Toson
See also CA 105; 134

Shimazaki Toson 1872-1943 **TCLC 5**
See also Shimazaki, Haruki
See also DLB 180

Sholokhov, Mikhail (Aleksandrovich) 1905-1984 **CLC 7, 15**
See also CA 101; 112; MTCW 1, 2; SATA-Obit 36

Shone, Patric
See Hanley, James

Shreve, Susan Richards 1939- **CLC 23**
See also CA 49-52; CAAS 5; CANR 5, 38, 69; MAICYA; SATA 46, 95; SATA-Brief 41

Shue, Larry 1946-1985 **CLC 52; DAM DRAM**
See also CA 145; 117

Shu-Jen, Chou 1881-1936
See Lu Hsun
See also CA 104

Shulman, Alix Kates 1932- **CLC 2, 10**
See also CA 29-32R; CANR 43; SATA 7

Shuster, Joe 1914- **CLC 21**

Shute, Nevil **CLC 30**
See also Norway, Nevil Shute
See also MTCW 2

Shuttle, Penelope (Diane) 1947- **CLC 7**
See also CA 93-96; CANR 39; DLB 14, 40

Sidney, Mary 1561-1621 **LC 19, 39**

Sidney, Sir Philip 1554-1586 **LC 19, 39; DA; DAB; DAC; DAM MST, POET**
See also CDBLB Before 1660; DLB 167

Siegel, Jerome 1914-1996 **CLC 21**
See also CA 116; 169; 151

Siegel, Jerry
See Siegel, Jerome

Sienkiewicz, Henryk (Adam Alexander Pius) 1846-1916 **TCLC 3**
See also CA 104; 134

Sierra, Gregorio Martinez
See Martinez Sierra, Gregorio

Sierra, Maria (de la O'LeJarraga) Martinez
See Martinez Sierra, Maria (de la O'LeJarraga)

Sigal, Clancy 1926- **CLC 7**
See also CA 1-4R

Sigourney, Lydia Howard (Huntley) 1791-1865
 NCLC 21
 See also DLB 1, 42, 73

Siguenza y Gongora, Carlos de 1645-1700 **L C 8; HLCS 2**

Sigurjonsson, Johann 1880-1919 **TCLC 27**
 See also CA 170

Sikelianos, Angelos 1884-1951 **TCLC 39**

Silkin, Jon 1930- **CLC 2, 6, 43**
 See also CA 5-8R; CAAS 5; DLB 27

Silko, Leslie (Marmon) 1948-**CLC 23, 74, 114;**
 DA; DAC; DAM MST, MULT, POP;
 WLCS
 See also AAYA 14; CA 115; 122; CANR 45,
 65; DLB 143, 175; MTCW 2; NNAL

Sillanpaa, Frans Eemil 1888-1964 **CLC 19**
 See also CA 129; 93-96; MTCW 1

Sillitoe, Alan 1928- **CLC 1, 3, 6, 10, 19, 57**
 See also AITN 1; CA 9-12R; CAAS 2; CANR
 8, 26, 55; CDBLB 1960 to Present; DLB 14,
 139; MTCW 1, 2; SATA 61

Silone, Ignazio 1900-1978 **CLC 4**
 See also CA 25-28; 81-84; CANR 34; CAP 2;
 MTCW 1

Silver, Joan Micklin 1935- **CLC 20**
 See also CA 114; 121; INT 121

Silver, Nicholas
 See Faust, Frederick (Schiller)

Silverberg, Robert 1935- **CLC 7;DAM POP**
 See also Jarvis, E. K.
 See also AAYA 24; CA 1-4R; CAAS 3; CANR
 1, 20, 36; CLR 59; DLB 8; INT CANR-20;
 MAICYA; MTCW 1, 2; SATA 13, 91; SATA-
 Essay 104

Silverstein, Alvin 1933- **CLC 17**
 See also CA 49-52; CANR 2; CLR 25; JRDA;
 MAICYA; SATA 8, 69

Silverstein, Virginia B(arbara Opshelor) 1937-
 CLC 17
 See also CA 49-52; CANR 2; CLR 25; JRDA;
 MAICYA; SATA 8, 69

Sim, Georges
 See Simenon, Georges (Jacques Christian)

Simak, Clifford D(onald) 1904-1988**CLC 1, 55**
 See also CA 1-4R; 125; CANR 1, 35; DLB 8;
 MTCW 1; SATA-Obit 56

Simenon, Georges (Jacques Christian) 1903-
 1989 **CLC 1, 2, 3, 8, 18, 47; DAM POP**
 See also CA 85-88; 129; CANR 35; DLB 72;
 DLBY 89; MTCW 1, 2

Simic, Charles 1938- **CLC 6, 9, 22, 49, 68;**
 DAM POET
 See also CA 29-32R; CAAS 4; CANR 12, 33,
 52, 61; DLB 105; MTCW 2

Simmel, Georg 1858-1918 **TCLC 64**
 See also CA 157

Simmons, Charles (Paul) 1924- **CLC 57**
 See also CA 89-92; INT 89-92

Simmons, Dan 1948- **CLC 44;DAM POP**
 See also AAYA 16; CA 138; CANR 53, 81

Simmons, James (Stewart Alexander) 1933-
 CLC 43
 See also CA 105; CAAS 21; DLB 40

Simms, William Gilmore 1806-1870 **NCLC 3**
 See also DLB 3, 30, 59, 73

Simon, Carly 1945- **CLC 26**
 See also CA 105

Simon, Claude 1913-1984 **CLC 4, 9, 15, 39;**
 DAM NOV
 See also CA 89-92; CANR 33; DLB 83; MTCW
 1

Simon, (Marvin) Neil 1927-**CLC 6, 11, 31, 39,**
 70; DAM DRAM

 See also AITN 1; CA 21-24R; CANR 26, 54;
 DLB 7; MTCW 1, 2

Simon, Paul (Frederick) 1941(?)- **CLC 17**
 See also CA 116; 153

Simonon, Paul 1956(?)- **CLC 30**

Simpson, Harriette
 See Arnow, Harriette (Louisa) Simpson

Simpson, Louis (Aston Marantz) 1923-**CLC 4,**
 7, 9, 32; DAM POET
 See also CA 1-4R; CAAS 4; CANR 1, 61; DLB
 5; MTCW 1, 2

Simpson, Mona (Elizabeth) 1957- **CLC 44**
 See also CA 122; 135; CANR 68

Simpson, N(orman) F(rederick) 1919-**CLC 29**
 See also CA 13-16R; DLB 13

Sinclair, Andrew (Annandale) 1935- **CLC 2,**
 14
 See also CA 9-12R; CAAS 5; CANR 14, 38;
 DLB 14; MTCW 1

Sinclair, Emil
 See Hesse, Hermann

Sinclair, Iain 1943- **CLC 76**
 See also CA 132; CANR 81

Sinclair, Iain MacGregor
 See Sinclair, Iain

Sinclair, Irene
 See Griffith, D(avid Lewelyn) W(ark)

Sinclair, Mary Amelia St. Clair 1865(?)-1946
 See Sinclair, May
 See also CA 104

Sinclair, May 1863-1946 **TCLC 3, 11**
 See also Sinclair, Mary Amelia St. Clair
 See also CA 166; DLB 36, 135

Sinclair, Roy
 See Griffith, D(avid Lewelyn) W(ark)

Sinclair, Upton (Beall) 1878-1968 **CLC 1, 11,**
 15, 63; DA; DAB; DAC; DAM MST, NOV;
 WLC
 See also CA 5-8R; 25-28R; CANR 7; CDALB
 1929-1941; DLB 9; INT CANR-7; MTCW
 1, 2; SATA 9

Singer, Isaac
 See Singer, Isaac Bashevis

Singer, Isaac Bashevis 1904-1991**CLC 1, 3, 6,**
 9, 11, 15, 23, 38, 69, 111; DA; DAB; DAC;
 DAM MST, NOV; SSC 3; WLC
 See also AITN 1, 2; CA 1-4R; 134; CANR 1,
 39; CDALB 1941-1968; CLR 1; DLB 6, 28,
 52; DLBY 91; JRDA; MAICYA; MTCW 1,
 2; SATA 3, 27; SATA-Obit 68

Singer, Israel Joshua 1893-1944 **TCLC 33**
 See also CA 169

Singh, Khushwant 1915- **CLC 11**
 See also CA 9-12R; CAAS 9; CANR 6

Singleton, Ann
 See Benedict, Ruth (Fulton)

Sinjohn, John
 See Galsworthy, John

Sinyavsky, Andrei (Donatevich) 1925-1997
 CLC 8
 See also CA 85-88; 159

Sirin, V.
 See Nabokov, Vladimir (Vladimirovich)

Sissman, L(ouis) E(dward) 1928-1976**CLC 9,**
 18
 See also CA 21-24R; 65-68; CANR 13; DLB 5

Sisson, C(harles) H(ubert) 1914- **CLC 8**
 See also CA 1-4R; CAAS 3; CANR 3, 48; DLB
 27

Sitwell, Dame Edith 1887-1964 **CLC 2, 9, 67;**
 DAM POET; PC 3
 See also CA 9-12R; CANR 35; CDBLB 1945-
 1960; DLB 20; MTCW 1, 2

Siwaarmill, H. P.
 See Sharp, William

Sjoewall, Maj 1935- **CLC 7**
 See also CA 65-68; CANR 73

Sjowall, Maj
 See Sjoewall, Maj

Skelton, John 1463-1529 **PC 25**

Skelton, Robin 1925-1997 **CLC 13**
 See also AITN 2; CA 5-8R; 160; CAAS 5;
 CANR 28; DLB 27, 53

Skolimowski, Jerzy 1938- **CLC 20**
 See also CA 128

Skram, Amalie (Bertha) 1847-1905 **TCLC 25**
 See also CA 165

Skvorecky, Josef (Vaclav) 1924- **CLC 15, 39,**
 69; DAC; DAM NOV
 See also CA 61-64; CAAS 1; CANR 10, 34,
 63; MTCW 1, 2

Slade, Bernard **CLC 11, 46**
 See also Newbound, Bernard Slade
 See also CAAS 9; DLB 53

Slaughter, Carolyn 1946- **CLC 56**
 See also CA 85-88

Slaughter, Frank G(ill) 1908- **CLC 29**
 See also AITN 2; CA 5-8R; CANR 5; INT
 CANR-5

Slavitt, David R(ytman) 1935- **CLC 5, 14**
 See also CA 21-24R; CAAS 3; CANR 41; DLB
 5, 6

Slesinger, Tess 1905-1945 **TCLC 10**
 See also CA 107; DLB 102

Slessor, Kenneth 1901-1971 **CLC 14**
 See also CA 102; 89-92

Slowacki, Juliusz 1809-1849 **NCLC 15**

Smart, Christopher 1722-1771 **LC 3; DAM**
 POET; PC 13
 See also DLB 109

Smart, Elizabeth 1913-1986 **CLC 54**
 See also CA 81-84; 118; DLB 88

Smiley, Jane (Graves) 1949-**CLC 53, 76; DAM**
 POP
 See also CA 104; CANR 30, 50, 74; INT CANR-
 30

Smith, A(rthur) J(ames) M(arshall) 1902-1980
 CLC 15; DAC
 See also CA 1-4R; 102; CANR 4; DLB 88

Smith, Adam 1723-1790 **LC 36**
 See also DLB 104

Smith, Alexander 1829-1867 **NCLC 59**
 See also DLB 32, 55

Smith, Anna Deavere 1950- **CLC 86**
 See also CA 133

Smith, Betty (Wehner) 1896-1972 **CLC 19**
 See also CA 5-8R; 33-36R; DLBY 82; SATA 6

Smith, Charlotte (Turner) 1749-1806 **N C L C**
 23
 See also DLB 39, 109

Smith, Clark Ashton 1893-1961 **CLC 43**
 See also CA 143; CANR 81; MTCW 2

Smith, Dave **CLC 22, 42**
 See also Smith, David (Jeddie)
 See also CAAS 7; DLB 5

Smith, David (Jeddie) 1942-
 See Smith, Dave
 See also CA 49-52; CANR 1, 59; DAM POET

Smith, Florence Margaret 1902-1971
 See Smith, Stevie
 See also CA 17-18; 29-32R; CANR 35; CAP 2;
 DAM POET; MTCW 1, 2

Smith, Iain Crichton 1928-1998 **CLC 64**
 See also CA 21-24R; 171; DLB 40, 139

Smith, John 1580(?)-1631 **LC 9**
 See also DLB 24, 30

Smith, Johnston
See Crane, Stephen (Townley)

Smith, Joseph, Jr. 1805-1844   NCLC 53

Smith, Lee 1944-   CLC 25, 73
See also CA 114; 119; CANR 46; DLB 143;
DLBY 83; INT 119

Smith, Martin
See Smith, Martin Cruz

Smith, Martin Cruz 1942-   CLC 25; DAM
MULT, POP
See also BEST 89:4; CA 85-88; CANR 6, 23,
43, 65; INT CANR-23; MTCW 2; NNAL

Smith, Mary-Ann Tirone 1944-   CLC 39
See also CA 118; 136

Smith, Patti 1946-   CLC 12
See also CA 93-96; CANR 63

Smith, Pauline (Urmson) 1882-1959TCLC 25

Smith, Rosamond
See Oates, Joyce Carol

Smith, Sheila Kaye
See Kaye-Smith, Sheila

Smith, Stevie   CLC 3, 8, 25, 44; PC 12
See also Smith, Florence Margaret
See also DLB 20; MTCW 2

Smith, Wilbur (Addison) 1933-   CLC 33
See also CA 13-16R; CANR 7, 46, 66; MTCW
1, 2

Smith, William Jay 1918-   CLC 6
See also CA 5-8R; CANR 44; DLB 5; MAICYA;
SAAS 22; SATA 2, 68

Smith, Woodrow Wilson
See Kuttner, Henry

Smolenskin, Peretz 1842-1885   NCLC 30

Smollett, Tobias (George) 1721-1771LC 2, 46
See also CDBLB 1660-1789; DLB 39, 104

Snodgrass, W(illiam) D(e Witt) 1926-CLC 2,
6, 10, 18, 68; DAM POET
See also CA 1-4R; CANR 6, 36, 65; DLB 5;
MTCW 1, 2

Snow, C(harles) P(ercy) 1905-1980 CLC 1, 4,
6, 9, 13, 19; DAM NOV
See also CA 5-8R; 101; CANR 28; CDBLB
1945-1960; DLB 15, 77; DLBD 17; MTCW
1, 2

Snow, Frances Compton
See Adams, Henry (Brooks)

Snyder, Gary (Sherman) 1930-CLC 1, 2, 5, 9,
32, 120; DAM POET; PC 21
See also CA 17-20R; CANR 30, 60; DLB 5,
16, 165, 212; MTCW 2

Snyder, Zilpha Keatley 1927-   CLC 17
See also AAYA 15; CA 9-12R; CANR 38; CLR
31; JRDA; MAICYA; SAAS 2; SATA 1, 28,
75

Soares, Bernardo
See Pessoa, Fernando (Antonio Nogueira)

Sobh, A.
See Shamlu, Ahmad

Sobol, Joshua   CLC 60

Socrates 469B.C.-399B.C.   CMLC 27

Soderberg, Hjalmar 1869-1941   TCLC 39

Sodergran, Edith (Irene)
See Soedergran, Edith (Irene)

Soedergran, Edith (Irene) 1892-1923 T C L C
31

Softly, Edgar
See Lovecraft, H(oward) P(hillips)

Softly, Edward
See Lovecraft, H(oward) P(hillips)

Sokolov, Raymond 1941-   CLC 7
See also CA 85-88

Solo, Jay
See Ellison, Harlan (Jay)

Sologub, Fyodor   TCLC 9
See also Teternikov, Fyodor Kuzmich

Solomons, Ikey Esquir
See Thackeray, William Makepeace

Solomos, Dionysios 1798-1857   NCLC 15

Solwoska, Mara
See French, Marilyn

Solzhenitsyn, Aleksandr I(sayevich) 1918-
CLC 1, 2, 4, 7, 9, 10, 18, 26, 34, 78; DA;
DAB; DAC; DAM MST, NOV; SSC
32;WLC
See also AITN 1; CA 69-72; CANR 40, 65;
MTCW 1, 2

Somers, Jane
See Lessing, Doris (May)

Somerville, Edith 1858-1949   TCLC 51
See also DLB 135

Somerville & Ross
See Martin, Violet Florence; Somerville, Edith

Sommer, Scott 1951-   CLC 25
See also CA 106

Sondheim, Stephen (Joshua) 1930- CLC 30,
39; DAM DRAM
See also AAYA 11; CA 103; CANR 47, 68

Song, Cathy 1955-   PC 21
See also CA 154; DLB 169

Sontag, Susan 1933-CLC 1, 2, 10, 13, 31, 105;
DAM POP
See also CA 17-20R; CANR 25, 51, 74; DLB
2, 67; MTCW 1, 2

Sophocles 496(?)B.C.-406(?)B.C.   CMLC 2;
DA; DAB; DAC; DAM DRAM, MST; DC
1; WLCS
See also DLB 176

Sordello 1189-1269   CMLC 15

Sorel, Georges 1847-1922   TCLC 91
See also CA 118

Sorel, Julia
See Drexler, Rosalyn

Sorrentino, Gilbert 1929-CLC 3, 7, 14, 22, 40
See also CA 77-80; CANR 14, 33; DLB 5, 173;
DLBY 80; INT CANR-14

Soto, Gary 1952- CLC 32, 80; DAM MULT;
HLC 2
See also AAYA 10; CA 119; 125; CANR 50,
74; CLR 38; DLB 82; HW 1, 2; INT 125;
JRDA; MTCW 2; SATA 80

Soupault, Philippe 1897-1990   CLC 68
See also CA 116; 147; 131

Souster, (Holmes) Raymond 1921-CLC 5, 14;
DAC; DAM POET
See also CA 13-16R; CAAS 14; CANR 13, 29,
53; DLB 88; SATA 63

Southern, Terry 1924(?)-1995   CLC 7
See also CA 1-4R; 150; CANR 1, 55; DLB 2

Southey, Robert 1774-1843   NCLC 8
See also DLB 93, 107, 142; SATA 54

Southworth, Emma Dorothy Eliza Nevitte
1819-1899   NCLC 26

Souza, Ernest
See Scott, Evelyn

Soyinka, Wole 1934-CLC 3, 5, 14, 36, 44; BLC
3; DA; DAB; DAC; DAM DRAM, MST,
MULT; DC 2; WLC
See also BW 2, 3; CA 13-16R; CANR 27, 39,
82; DLB 125; MTCW 1, 2

Spackman, W(illiam) M(ode) 1905-1990C L C
46
See also CA 81-84; 132

Spacks, Barry (Bernard) 1931-   CLC 14
See also CA 154; CANR 33; DLB 105

Spanidou, Irini 1946-   CLC 44

Spark, Muriel (Sarah) 1918-CLC 2, 3, 5, 8, 13,
18, 40, 94; DAB; DAC; DAM MST, NOV;
SSC 10
See also CA 5-8R; CANR 12, 36, 76; CDBLB
1945-1960; DLB 15, 139; INT CANR-12;
MTCW 1, 2

Spaulding, Douglas
See Bradbury, Ray (Douglas)

Spaulding, Leonard
See Bradbury, Ray (Douglas)

Spence, J. A. D.
See Eliot, T(homas) S(tearns)

Spencer, Elizabeth 1921-   CLC 22
See also CA 13-16R; CANR 32, 65; DLB 6;
MTCW 1; SATA 14

Spencer, Leonard G.
See Silverberg, Robert

Spencer, Scott 1945-   CLC 30
See also CA 113; CANR 51; DLBY 86

Spender, Stephen (Harold) 1909-1995CLC 1,
2, 5, 10, 41, 91; DAM POET
See also CA 9-12R; 149; CANR 31, 54; CDBLB
1945-1960; DLB 20; MTCW 1, 2

Spengler, Oswald (Arnold Gottfried) 1880-1936
TCLC 25
See also CA 118

Spenser, Edmund 1552(?)-1599LC 5, 39; DA;
DAB; DAC; DAM MST, POET; PC 8;
WLC
See also CDBLB Before 1660; DLB 167

Spicer, Jack 1925-1965 CLC 8, 18, 72; DAM
POET
See also CA 85-88; DLB 5, 16, 193

Spiegelman, Art 1948-   CLC 76
See also AAYA 10; CA 125; CANR 41, 55, 74;
MTCW 2; SATA 109

Spielberg, Peter 1929-   CLC 6
See also CA 5-8R; CANR 4, 48; DLBY 81

Spielberg, Steven 1947-   CLC 20
See also AAYA 8, 24; CA 77-80; CANR 32;
SATA 32

Spillane, Frank Morrison 1918-
See Spillane, Mickey
See also CA 25-28R; CANR 28, 63; MTCW 1,
2; SATA 66

Spillane, Mickey   CLC 3, 13
See also Spillane, Frank Morrison
See also MTCW 2

Spinoza, Benedictus de 1632-1677   LC 9

Spinrad, Norman (Richard) 1940-   CLC 46
See also CA 37-40R; CAAS 19; CANR 20; DLB
8; INT CANR-20

Spitteler, Carl (Friedrich Georg) 1845-1924
TCLC 12
See also CA 109; DLB 129

Spivack, Kathleen (Romola Drucker) 1938-
CLC 6
See also CA 49-52

Spoto, Donald 1941-   CLC 39
See also CA 65-68; CANR 11, 57

Springsteen, Bruce (F.) 1949-   CLC 17
See also CA 111

Spurling, Hilary 1940-   CLC 34
See also CA 104; CANR 25, 52

Spyker, John Howland
See Elman, Richard (Martin)

Squires, (James) Radcliffe 1917-1993CLC 51
See also CA 1-4R; 140; CANR 6, 21

Srivastava, Dhanpat Rai 1880(?)-1936
See Premchand
See also CA 118

Stacy, Donald
See Pohl, Frederik

Stael, Germaine de 1766-1817

See Stael-Holstein, Anne Louise Germaine Necker Baronn
See also DLB 119

Stael-Holstein, Anne Louise Germaine Necker Baronn 1766-1817   **NCLC 3**
See also Stael, Germaine de
See also DLB 192

Stafford, Jean 1915-1979**CLC 4, 7, 19, 68; SSC 26**
See also CA 1-4R; 85-88; CANR 3, 65; DLB 2, 173; MTCW 1, 2; SATA-Obit 22

Stafford, William (Edgar) 1914-1993 **CLC 4, 7, 29; DAM POET**
See also CA 5-8R; 142; CAAS 3; CANR 5, 22; DLB 5, 206; INT CANR-22

Stagnelius, Eric Johan 1793-1823 **NCLC 61**

Staines, Trevor
See Brunner, John (Kilian Houston)

Stairs, Gordon
See Austin, Mary (Hunter)

Stairs, Gordon
See Austin, Mary (Hunter)

Stalin, Joseph 1879-1953   **TCLC 92**

Stannard, Martin 1947-   **CLC 44**
See also CA 142; DLB 155

Stanton, Elizabeth Cady 1815-1902**TCLC 73**
See also CA 171; DLB 79

Stanton, Maura 1946-   **CLC 9**
See also CA 89-92; CANR 15; DLB 120

Stanton, Schuyler
See Baum, L(yman) Frank

Stapledon, (William) Olaf 1886-1950 **TCLC 22**
See also CA 111; 162; DLB 15

Starbuck, George (Edwin) 1931-1996**CLC 53; DAM POET**
See also CA 21-24R; 153; CANR 23

Stark, Richard
See Westlake, Donald E(dwin)

Staunton, Schuyler
See Baum, L(yman) Frank

Stead, Christina (Ellen) 1902-1983 **CLC 2, 5, 8, 32, 80**
See also CA 13-16R; 109; CANR 33, 40; MTCW 1, 2

Stead, William Thomas 1849-1912 **TCLC 48**
See also CA 167

Steele, Richard 1672-1729   **LC 18**
See also CDBLB 1660-1789; DLB 84, 101

Steele, Timothy (Reid) 1948-   **CLC 45**
See also CA 93-96; CANR 16, 50; DLB 120

Steffens, (Joseph) Lincoln 1866-1936 **TCLC 20**
See also CA 117

Stegner, Wallace (Earle) 1909-1993**CLC 9, 49, 81; DAM NOV; SSC 27**
See also AITN 1; BEST 90:3; CA 1-4R; 141; CAAS 9; CANR 1, 21, 46; DLB 9, 206; DLBY 93; MTCW 1, 2

Stein, Gertrude 1874-1946**TCLC 1, 6, 28, 48; DA; DAB; DAC; DAM MST, NOV, POET; PC 18; WLC**
See also CA 104; 132; CDALB 1917-1929; DLB 4, 54, 86; DLBD 15; MTCW 1, 2

Steinbeck, John (Ernst) 1902-1968**CLC 1, 5, 9, 13, 21, 34, 45, 75; DA; DAB; DAC; DAM DRAM, MST, NOV; SSC 11;WLC**
See also AAYA 12; CA 1-4R; 25-28R; CANR 1, 35; CDALB 1929-1941; DLB 7, 9, 212; DLBD 2; MTCW 1, 2; SATA 9

Steinem, Gloria 1934-   **CLC 63**
See also CA 53-56; CANR 28, 51; MTCW 1, 2

Steiner, George 1929-   **CLC 24;DAM NOV**

See also CA 73-76; CANR 31, 67; DLB 67; MTCW 1, 2; SATA 62

Steiner, K. Leslie
See Delany, Samuel R(ay, Jr.)

Steiner, Rudolf 1861-1925   **TCLC 13**
See also CA 107

Stendhal 1783-1842**NCLC 23, 46; DA; DAB; DAC; DAM MST, NOV; SSC 27; WLC**
See also DLB 119

Stephen, Adeline Virginia
See Woolf, (Adeline) Virginia

Stephen, Sir Leslie 1832-1904   **TCLC 23**
See also CA 123; DLB 57, 144, 190

Stephen, Sir Leslie
See Stephen, SirLeslie

Stephen, Virginia
See Woolf, (Adeline) Virginia

Stephens, James 1882(?)-1950   **TCLC 4**
See also CA 104; DLB 19, 153, 162

Stephens, Reed
See Donaldson, Stephen R.

Steptoe, Lydia
See Barnes, Djuna

Sterchi, Beat 1949-   **CLC 65**

Sterling, Brett
See Bradbury, Ray (Douglas); Hamilton, Edmond

Sterling, Bruce 1954-   **CLC 72**
See also CA 119; CANR 44

Sterling, George 1869-1926   **TCLC 20**
See also CA 117; 165; DLB 54

Stern, Gerald 1925-   **CLC 40, 100**
See also CA 81-84; CANR 28; DLB 105

Stern, Richard (Gustave) 1928-   **CLC 4, 39**
See also CA 1-4R; CANR 1, 25, 52; DLBY 87; INT CANR-25

Sternberg, Josefvon 1894-1969   **CLC 20**
See also CA 81-84

Sterne, Laurence 1713-1768   **LC 2, 48; DA; DAB; DAC; DAM MST, NOV; WLC**
See also CDBLB 1660-1789; DLB 39

Sternheim, (William Adolf) Carl 1878-1942 **TCLC 8**
See also CA 105; DLB 56, 118

Stevens, Mark 1951-   **CLC 34**
See also CA 122

Stevens, Wallace 1879-1955 **TCLC 3, 12, 45; DA; DAB; DAC; DAM MST, POET; PC 6; WLC**
See also CA 104; 124; CDALB 1929-1941; DLB 54; MTCW 1, 2

Stevenson, Anne (Katharine) 1933-**CLC 7, 33**
See also CA 17-20R; CAAS 9; CANR 9, 33; DLB 40; MTCW 1

Stevenson, Robert Louis (Balfour) 1850-1894 **NCLC 5, 14, 63; DA; DAB; DAC; DAM MST, NOV; SSC 11; WLC**
See also AAYA 24; CDBLB 1890-1914; CLR 10, 11; DLB 18, 57, 141, 156, 174; DLBD 13; JRDA; MAICYA; SATA 100; YABC 2

Stewart, J(ohn) I(nnes) M(ackintosh) 1906-1994   **CLC 7, 14, 32**
See also CA 85-88; 147; CAAS 3; CANR 47; MTCW 1, 2

Stewart, Mary (Florence Elinor) 1916-**CLC 7, 35, 117; DAB**
See also AAYA 29; CA 1-4R; CANR 1, 59; SATA 12

Stewart, Mary Rainbow
See Stewart, Mary (Florence Elinor)

Stifle, June
See Campbell, Maria

Stifter, Adalbert 1805-1868**NCLC 41; SSC 28**

See also DLB 133

Still, James 1906-   **CLC 49**
See also CA 65-68; CAAS 17; CANR 10, 26; DLB 9; SATA 29

Sting 1951-
See Sumner, Gordon Matthew
See also CA 167

Stirling, Arthur
See Sinclair, Upton (Beall)

Stitt, Milan 1941-   **CLC 29**
See also CA 69-72

Stockton, Francis Richard 1834-1902
See Stockton, Frank R.
See also CA 108; 137; MAICYA; SATA 44

Stockton, Frank R.   **TCLC 47**
See also Stockton, Francis Richard
See also DLB 42, 74; DLBD 13; SATA-Brief 32

Stoddard, Charles
See Kuttner, Henry

Stoker, Abraham 1847-1912
See Stoker, Bram
See also CA 105; 150; DA; DAC; DAM MST, NOV; SATA 29

Stoker, Bram 1847-1912**TCLC 8; DAB; WLC**
See also Stoker, Abraham
See also AAYA 23; CDBLB 1890-1914; DLB 36, 70, 178

Stolz, Mary (Slattery) 1920-   **CLC 12**
See also AAYA 8; AITN 1; CA 5-8R; CANR 13, 41; JRDA; MAICYA; SAAS 3; SATA 10, 71

Stone, Irving 1903-1989   **CLC 7;DAM POP**
See also AITN 1; CA 1-4R; 129; CAAS 3; CANR 1, 23; INT CANR-23; MTCW 1, 2; SATA 3; SATA-Obit 64

Stone, Oliver (William) 1946-   **CLC 73**
See also AAYA 15; CA 110; CANR 55

Stone, Robert (Anthony) 1937-**CLC 5, 23, 42**
See also CA 85-88; CANR 23, 66; DLB 152; INT CANR-23; MTCW 1

Stone, Zachary
See Follett, Ken(neth Martin)

Stoppard, Tom 1937-**CLC 1, 3, 4, 5, 8, 15, 29, 34, 63, 91; DA; DAB; DAC; DAM DRAM, MST; DC 6; WLC**
See also CA 81-84; CANR 39, 67; CDBLB 1960 to Present; DLB 13; DLBY 85; MTCW 1, 2

Storey, David (Malcolm) 1933-**CLC 2, 4, 5, 8; DAM DRAM**
See also CA 81-84; CANR 36; DLB 13, 14, 207; MTCW 1

Storm, Hyemeyohsts 1935-   **CLC 3;DAM MULT**
See also CA 81-84; CANR 45; NNAL

Storm, Theodor 1817-1888   **SSC 27**

Storm, (Hans) Theodor (Woldsen) 1817-1888 **NCLC 1; SSC 27**
See also DLB 129

Storni, Alfonsina 1892-1938 **TCLC 5; DAM MULT; HLC 2**
See also CA 104; 131; HW 1

Stoughton, William 1631-1701   **LC 38**
See also DLB 24

Stout, Rex (Todhunter) 1886-1975   **CLC 3**
See also AITN 2; CA 61-64; CANR 71

Stow, (Julian) Randolph 1935-   **CLC 23, 48**
See also CA 13-16R; CANR 33; MTCW 1

Stowe, Harriet (Elizabeth) Beecher 1811-1896 **NCLC 3, 50; DA; DAB; DAC; DAM MST, NOV; WLC**
See also CDALB 1865-1917; DLB 1, 12, 42,

74, 189; JRDA; MAICYA; YABC 1

Strachey, (Giles) Lytton 1880-1932 **TCLC 12**
See also CA 110; 178; DLB 149; DLBD 10;
MTCW 2

Strand, Mark 1934- **CLC 6, 18, 41, 71; DAM POET**
See also CA 21-24R; CANR 40, 65; DLB 5;
SATA 41

Straub, Peter (Francis) 1943- **CLC 28, 107; DAM POP**
See also BEST 89:1; CA 85-88; CANR 28, 65;
DLBY 84; MTCW 1, 2

Strauss, Botho 1944- **CLC 22**
See also CA 157; DLB 124

Streatfeild, (Mary) Noel 1895(?)-1986 **CLC 21**
See also CA 81-84; 120; CANR 31; CLR 17;
DLB 160; MAICYA; SATA 20; SATA-Obit
48

Stribling, T(homas) S(igismund) 1881-1965
CLC 23
See also CA 107; DLB 9

Strindberg, (Johan) August 1849-1912 **TCLC 1, 8, 21, 47; DA; DAB; DAC; DAM DRAM, MST; WLC**
See also CA 104; 135; MTCW 2

Stringer, Arthur 1874-1950 **TCLC 37**
See also CA 161; DLB 92

Stringer, David
See Roberts, Keith (John Kingston)

Stroheim, Erich von 1885-1957 **TCLC 71**

Strugatskii, Arkadii (Natanovich) 1925-1991
CLC 27
See also CA 106; 135

Strugatskii, Boris (Natanovich) 1933-**CLC 27**
See also CA 106

Strummer, Joe 1953(?)- **CLC 30**

Strunk, William, Jr. 1869-1946 **TCLC 92**
See also CA 118; 164

Stryk, Lucien 1924- **PC 27**
See also CA 13-16R; CANR 10, 28, 55

Stuart, Don A.
See Campbell, John W(ood, Jr.)

Stuart, Ian
See MacLean, Alistair (Stuart)

Stuart, Jesse (Hilton) 1906-1984 **CLC 1, 8, 11, 14, 34; SSC 31**
See also CA 5-8R; 112; CANR 31; DLB 9, 48,
102; DLBY 84; SATA 2; SATA-Obit 36

Sturgeon, Theodore (Hamilton) 1918-1985
CLC 22, 39
See also Queen, Ellery
See also CA 81-84; 116; CANR 32; DLB 8;
DLBY 85; MTCW 1, 2

Sturges, Preston 1898-1959 **TCLC 48**
See also CA 114; 149; DLB 26

Styron, William 1925-**CLC 1, 3, 5, 11, 15, 60; DAM NOV, POP; SSC 25**
See also BEST 90:4; CA 5-8R; CANR 6, 33,
74; CDALB 1968-1988; DLB 2, 143; DLBY
80; INT CANR-6; MTCW 1, 2

Su, Chien 1884-1918
See Su Man-shu
See also CA 123

Suarez Lynch, B.
See Bioy Casares, Adolfo; Borges, Jorge Luis

Suassuna, Ariano Vilar 1927-
See also CA 178; HLCS 1; HW 2

Suckow, Ruth 1892-1960 **SSC 18**
See also CA 113; DLB 9, 102

Sudermann, Hermann 1857-1928 **TCLC 15**
See also CA 107; DLB 118

Sue, Eugene 1804-1857 **NCLC 1**
See also DLB 119

Sueskind, Patrick 1949- **CLC 44**
See also Suskind, Patrick

Sukenick, Ronald 1932- **CLC 3, 4, 6, 48**
See also CA 25-28R; CAAS 8; CANR 32; DLB
173; DLBY 81

Suknaski, Andrew 1942- **CLC 19**
See also CA 101; DLB 53

Sullivan, Vernon
See Vian, Boris

Sully Prudhomme 1839-1907 **TCLC 31**

Su Man-shu **TCLC 24**
See also Su, Chien

Summerforest, Ivy B.
See Kirkup, James

Summers, Andrew James 1942- **CLC 26**

Summers, Andy
See Summers, Andrew James

Summers, Hollis (Spurgeon, Jr.) 1916-**CLC 10**
See also CA 5-8R; CANR 3; DLB 6

**Summers, (Alphonsus Joseph-Mary Augustus)
Montague** 1880-1948 **TCLC 16**
See also CA 118; 163

Sumner, Gordon Matthew **CLC 26**
See also Sting

Surtees, Robert Smith 1803-1864 **NCLC 14**
See also DLB 21

Susann, Jacqueline 1921-1974 **CLC 3**
See also AITN 1; CA 65-68; 53-56; MTCW 1,
2

Su Shih 1036-1101 **CMLC 15**

Suskind, Patrick
See Sueskind, Patrick
See also CA 145

Sutcliff, Rosemary 1920-1992 **CLC 26; DAB; DAC; DAM MST, POP**
See also AAYA 10; CA 5-8R; 139; CANR 37;
CLR 1, 37; JRDA; MAICYA; SATA 6, 44,
78; SATA-Obit 73

Sutro, Alfred 1863-1933 **TCLC 6**
See also CA 105; DLB 10

Sutton, Henry
See Slavitt, David R(ytman)

Svevo, Italo 1861-1928 **TCLC 2, 35;SSC 25**
See also Schmitz, Aron Hector

Swados, Elizabeth (A.) 1951- **CLC 12**
See also CA 97-100; CANR 49; INT 97-100

Swados, Harvey 1920-1972 **CLC 5**
See also CA 5-8R; 37-40R; CANR 6; DLB 2

Swan, Gladys 1934- **CLC 69**
See also CA 101; CANR 17, 39

Swarthout, Glendon (Fred) 1918-1992**CLC 35**
See also CA 1-4R; 139; CANR 1, 47; SATA 26

Sweet, Sarah C.
See Jewett, (Theodora) Sarah Orne

Swenson, May 1919-1989**CLC 4, 14, 61, 106; DA; DAB; DAC; DAM MST, POET; PC 14**
See also CA 5-8R; 130; CANR 36, 61; DLB 5;
MTCW 1, 2; SATA 15

Swift, Augustus
See Lovecraft, H(oward) P(hillips)

Swift, Graham (Colin) 1949- **CLC 41, 88**
See also CA 117; 122; CANR 46, 71; DLB 194;
MTCW 2

Swift, Jonathan 1667-1745 **LC 1, 42; DA; DAB; DAC; DAM MST, NOV, POET; PC 9; WLC**
See also CDBLB 1660-1789; CLR 53; DLB 39,
95, 101; SATA 19

Swinburne, Algernon Charles 1837-1909
TCLC 8, 36; DA; DAB; DAC; DAM MST, POET; PC 24; WLC
See also CA 105; 140; CDBLB 1832-1890;
DLB 35, 57

Swinfen, Ann **CLC 34**

Swinnerton, Frank Arthur 1884-1982**CLC 31**
See also CA 108; DLB 34

Swithen, John
See King, Stephen (Edwin)

Sylvia
See Ashton-Warner, Sylvia (Constance)

Symmes, Robert Edward
See Duncan, Robert (Edward)

Symonds, John Addington 1840-1893 **NCLC 34**
See also DLB 57, 144

Symons, Arthur 1865-1945 **TCLC 11**
See also CA 107; DLB 19, 57, 149

Symons, Julian (Gustave) 1912-1994 **CLC 2, 14, 32**
See also CA 49-52; 147; CAAS 3; CANR 3,
33, 59; DLB 87, 155; DLBY 92; MTCW 1

Synge, (Edmund) J(ohn) M(illington) 1871-
1909 **TCLC 6, 37; DAM DRAM; DC 2**
See also CA 104; 141; CDBLB 1890-1914;
DLB 10, 19

Syruc, J.
See Milosz, Czeslaw

Szirtes, George 1948- **CLC 46**
See also CA 109; CANR 27, 61

Szymborska, Wislawa 1923- **CLC 99**
See also CA 154; DLBY 96; MTCW 2

T. O., Nik
See Annensky, Innokenty (Fyodorovich)

Tabori, George 1914- **CLC 19**
See also CA 49-52; CANR 4, 69

Tagore, Rabindranath 1861-1941**TCLC 3, 53; DAM DRAM, POET; PC 8**
See also CA 104; 120; MTCW 1, 2

Taine, Hippolyte Adolphe 1828-1893 **NCLC 15**

Talese, Gay 1932- **CLC 37**
See also AITN 1; CA 1-4R; CANR 9, 58; DLB
185; INT CANR-9; MTCW 1, 2

Tallent, Elizabeth (Ann) 1954- **CLC 45**
See also CA 117; CANR 72; DLB 130

Tally, Ted 1952- **CLC 42**
See also CA 120; 124; INT 124

Talvik, Heiti 1904-1947 **TCLC 87**

Tamayo y Baus, Manuel 1829-1898 **NCLC 1**

Tammsaare, A(nton) H(ansen) 1878-1940
TCLC 27
See also CA 164

Tam'si, Tchicaya U
See Tchicaya, Gerald Felix

Tan, Amy (Ruth) 1952- **CLC 59, 120; DAM MULT, NOV, POP**
See also AAYA 9; BEST 89:3; CA 136; CANR
54; CDALBS; DLB 173; MTCW 2; SATA
75

Tandem, Felix
See Spitteler, Carl (Friedrich Georg)

Tanizaki, Jun'ichiro 1886-1965**CLC 8, 14, 28; SSC 21**
See also CA 93-96; 25-28R; DLB 180; MTCW
2

Tanner, William
See Amis, Kingsley (William)

Tao Lao
See Storni, Alfonsina

Tarassoff, Lev
See Troyat, Henri

Tarbell, Ida M(inerva) 1857-1944 **TCLC 40**
See also CA 122; DLB 47

Tarkington, (Newton) Booth 1869-1946**TCLC 9**

See also CA 110; 143; DLB 9, 102; MTCW 2; SATA 17

Tarkovsky, Andrei (Arsenyevich) 1932-1986
     CLC 75
     See also CA 127

Tartt, Donna 1964(?)-   **CLC 76**
     See also CA 142

Tasso, Torquato 1544-1595   **LC 5**

Tate, (John Orley) Allen 1899-1979**CLC 2, 4, 6, 9, 11, 14, 24**
     See also CA 5-8R; 85-88; CANR 32; DLB 4, 45, 63; DLBD 17; MTCW 1, 2

Tate, Ellalice
     See Hibbert, Eleanor Alice Burford

Tate, James (Vincent) 1943-   **CLC 2, 6, 25**
     See also CA 21-24R; CANR 29, 57; DLB 5, 169

Tavel, Ronald 1940-   **CLC 6**
     See also CA 21-24R; CANR 33

Taylor, C(ecil) P(hilip) 1929-1981   **CLC 27**
     See also CA 25-28R; 105; CANR 47

Taylor, Edward 1642(?)-1729   **LC 11; DA; DAB; DAC; DAM MST, POET**
     See also DLB 24

Taylor, Eleanor Ross 1920-   **CLC 5**
     See also CA 81-84; CANR 70

Taylor, Elizabeth 1912-1975   **CLC 2, 4, 29**
     See also CA 13-16R; CANR 9, 70; DLB 139; MTCW 1; SATA 13

Taylor, Frederick Winslow 1856-1915 **T C L C 76**

Taylor, Henry (Splawn) 1942-   **CLC 44**
     See also CA 33-36R; CAAS 7; CANR 31; DLB 5

Taylor, Kamala (Purnaiya) 1924-
     See Markandaya, Kamala
     See also CA 77-80

Taylor, Mildred D.   **CLC 21**
     See also AAYA 10; BW 1; CA 85-88; CANR 25; CLR 9, 59; DLB 52; JRDA; MAICYA; SAAS 5; SATA 15, 70

Taylor, Peter (Hillsman) 1917-1994**CLC 1, 4, 18, 37, 44, 50, 71; SSC 10**
     See also CA 13-16R; 147; CANR 9, 50; DLBY 81, 94; INT CANR-9; MTCW 1, 2

Taylor, Robert Lewis 1912-1998   **CLC 14**
     See also CA 1-4R; 170; CANR 3, 64; SATA 10

Tchekhov, Anton
     See Chekhov, Anton (Pavlovich)

Tchicaya, Gerald Felix 1931-1988   **CLC 101**
     See also CA 129; 125; CANR 81

Tchicaya U Tam'si
     See Tchicaya, Gerald Felix

Teasdale, Sara 1884-1933   **TCLC 4**
     See also CA 104; 163; DLB 45; SATA 32

Tegner, Esaias 1782-1846   **NCLC 2**

Teilhard de Chardin, (Marie Joseph) Pierre 1881-1955   **TCLC 9**
     See also CA 105

Temple, Ann
     See Mortimer, Penelope (Ruth)

Tennant, Emma (Christina) 1937-**CLC 13, 52**
     See also CA 65-68; CAAS 9; CANR 10, 38, 59; DLB 14

Tenneshaw, S. M.
     See Silverberg, Robert

Tennyson, Alfred 1809-1892   **NCLC 30, 65; DA; DAB; DAC; DAM MST, POET; PC 6; WLC**
     See also CDBLB 1832-1890; DLB 32

Teran, Lisa St. Aubin de   **CLC 36**
     See also St. Aubin de Teran, Lisa

Terence c. 184B.C.-c. 159B.C.**CMLC 14; DC 7**

See also DLB 211

Teresa de Jesus, St. 1515-1582   **LC 18**

Terkel, Louis 1912-
     See Terkel, Studs
     See also CA 57-60; CANR 18, 45, 67; MTCW 1, 2

Terkel, Studs   **CLC 38**
     See also Terkel, Louis
     See also AITN 1; MTCW 2

Terry, C. V.
     See Slaughter, Frank G(ill)

Terry, Megan 1932-   **CLC 19**
     See also CA 77-80; CABS 3; CANR 43; DLB 7

Tertullian c. 155-c. 245   **CMLC 29**

Tertz, Abram
     See Sinyavsky, Andrei (Donatevich)

Tesich, Steve 1943(?)-1996   **CLC 40, 69**
     See also CA 105; 152; DLBY 83

Tesla, Nikola 1856-1943   **TCLC 88**

Teternikov, Fyodor Kuzmich 1863-1927
     See Sologub, Fyodor
     See also CA 104

Tevis, Walter 1928-1984   **CLC 42**
     See also CA 113

Tey, Josephine   **TCLC 14**
     See also Mackintosh,Elizabeth
     See also DLB 77

Thackeray, William Makepeace 1811-1863
     NCLC 5, 14, 22, 43; DA; DAB; DAC; DAM MST, NOV; WLC
     See also CDBLB 1832-1890; DLB 21, 55, 159, 163; SATA 23

Thakura, Ravindranatha
     See Tagore, Rabindranath

Tharoor, Shashi 1956-   **CLC 70**
     See also CA 141

Thelwell, Michael Miles 1939-   **CLC 22**
     See also BW 2; CA 101

Theobald, Lewis, Jr.
     See Lovecraft, H(oward) P(hillips)

Theodorescu, Ion N. 1880-1967
     See Arghezi, Tudor
     See also CA 116

Theriault, Yves 1915-1983   **CLC 79; DAC; DAM MST**
     See also CA 102; DLB 88

Theroux, Alexander (Louis) 1939- **CLC 2, 25**
     See also CA 85-88; CANR 20, 63

Theroux, Paul (Edward) 1941- **CLC 5, 8, 11, 15, 28, 46; DAM POP**
     See also AAYA 28; BEST 89:4; CA 33-36R; CANR 20, 45, 74; CDALBS; DLB 2; MTCW 1, 2; SATA 44, 109

Thesen, Sharon 1946-   **CLC 56**
     See also CA 163

Thevenin, Denis
     See Duhamel, Georges

Thibault, Jacques Anatole Francois 1844-1924
     See France, Anatole
     See also CA 106; 127; DAM NOV; MTCW 1, 2

Thiele, Colin (Milton) 1920-   **CLC 17**
     See also CA 29-32R; CANR 12, 28, 53; CLR 27; MAICYA; SAAS 2; SATA 14, 72

Thomas, Audrey (Callahan) 1935-**CLC 7, 13, 37, 107; SSC 20**
     See also AITN 2; CA 21-24R; CAAS 19; CANR 36, 58; DLB 60; MTCW 1

Thomas, D(onald) M(ichael) 1935- **CLC 13, 22, 31**
     See also CA 61-64; CAAS 11; CANR 17, 45, 75; CDBLB 1960 to Present; DLB 40, 207; INT CANR-17; MTCW 1, 2

Thomas, Dylan (Marlais) 1914-1953**TCLC 1, 8, 45; DA; DAB; DAC; DAM DRAM, MST, POET; PC 2; SSC 3; WLC**
     See also CA 104; 120; CANR 65; CDBLB 1945-1960; DLB 13, 20, 139; MTCW 1, 2; SATA 60

Thomas, (Philip) Edward 1878-1917   **T C L C 10; DAM POET**
     See also CA 106; 153; DLB 98

Thomas, Joyce Carol 1938-   **CLC 35**
     See also AAYA 12; BW 2, 3; CA 113; 116; CANR 48; CLR 19; DLB 33; INT 116; JRDA; MAICYA; MTCW 1, 2; SAAS 7; SATA 40, 78

Thomas, Lewis 1913-1993   **CLC 35**
     See also CA 85-88; 143; CANR 38, 60; MTCW 1, 2

Thomas, M. Carey 1857-1935   **TCLC 89**

Thomas, Paul
     See Mann, (Paul) Thomas

Thomas, Piri 1928-   **CLC 17;HLCS 2**
     See also CA 73-76; HW 1

Thomas, R(onald) S(tuart) 1913- **CLC 6, 13, 48; DAB; DAM POET**
     See also CA 89-92; CAAS 4; CANR 30; CDBLB 1960 to Present; DLB 27; MTCW 1

Thomas, Ross (Elmore) 1926-1995   **CLC 39**
     See also CA 33-36R; 150; CANR 22, 63

Thompson, Francis Clegg
     See Mencken, H(enry) L(ouis)

Thompson, Francis Joseph 1859-1907**TCLC 4**
     See also CA 104; CDBLB 1890-1914; DLB 19

Thompson, Hunter S(tockton) 1939- **CLC 9, 17, 40, 104; DAM POP**
     See also BEST 89:1; CA 17-20R; CANR 23, 46, 74, 77; DLB 185; MTCW 1, 2

Thompson, James Myers
     See Thompson, Jim (Myers)

Thompson, Jim(Myers) 1906-1977(?)**CLC 69**
     See also CA 140

Thompson, Judith   **CLC 39**

Thomson, James 1700-1748   **LC 16, 29, 40; DAM POET**
     See also DLB 95

Thomson, James 1834-1882   **NCLC 18;DAM POET**
     See also DLB 35

Thoreau, Henry David 1817-1862**NCLC 7, 21, 61; DA; DAB; DAC; DAM MST; WLC**
     See also CDALB 1640-1865; DLB 1

Thornton, Hall
     See Silverberg, Robert

Thucydides c.455B.C.-399B.C.   **CMLC 17**
     See also DLB 176

Thurber, James (Grover) 1894-1961 **CLC 5, 11, 25; DA; DAB; DAC; DAM DRAM, MST, NOV; SSC 1**
     See also CA 73-76; CANR 17, 39; CDALB 1929-1941; DLB 4, 11, 22, 102; MAICYA; MTCW 1, 2; SATA 13

Thurman, Wallace (Henry) 1902-1934**T C L C 6; BLC 3; DAM MULT**
     See also BW 1, 3; CA 104; 124; CANR 81; DLB 51

Ticheburn, Cheviot
     See Ainsworth, William Harrison

Tieck, (Johann) Ludwig 1773-1853 **NCLC 5, 46; SSC 31**
     See also DLB 90

Tiger, Derry
     See Ellison, Harlan (Jay)

Tilghman, Christopher 1948(?)-   **CLC 65**
     See also CA 159

Tillinghast, Richard(Williford) 1940-CLC 29
See also CA 29-32R; CAAS 23; CANR 26, 51

Timrod, Henry 1828-1867   NCLC 25
See also DLB 3

Tindall, Gillian(Elizabeth) 1938-   CLC 7
See also CA 21-24R; CANR 11, 65

Tiptree, James, Jr.   CLC 48, 50
See also Sheldon, Alice Hastings Bradley
See also DLB 8

Titmarsh, Michael Angelo
See Thackeray, William Makepeace

**Tocqueville, Alexis (Charles Henri Maurice
   Clerel, Comte) de 1805-1859
                                              NCLC 7, 63**

**Tolkien, J(ohn) R(onald) R(euel) 1892-1973
   CLC 1, 2, 3, 8, 12, 38; DA; DAB; DAC;
   DAM MST, NOV, POP; WLC**
See also AAYA 10; AITN 1; CA 17-18; 45-48;
   CANR 36; CAP 2; CDBLB 1914-1945; CLR
   56; DLB 15, 160; JRDA; MAICYA; MTCW
   1, 2; SATA 2, 32, 100; SATA-Obit 24

Toller, Ernst 1893-1939   TCLC 10
See also CA 107; DLB 124

Tolson, M. B.
See Tolson, Melvin B(eaunorus)

**Tolson, Melvin B(eaunorus) 1898(?)-1966
   CLC 36, 105; BLC 3; DAM MULT, POET**
See also BW 1, 3; CA 124; 89-92; CANR 80;
   DLB 48, 76

Tolstoi, Aleksei Nikolaevich
See Tolstoy, Alexey Nikolaevich

**Tolstoy, Alexey Nikolaevich 1882-1945TCLC
   18**
See also CA 107; 158

Tolstoy, Count Leo
See Tolstoy, Leo (Nikolaevich)

**Tolstoy, Leo (Nikolaevich) 1828-1910TCLC 4,
   11, 17, 28, 44, 79; DA; DAB; DAC; DAM
   MST, NOV; SSC 9, 30; WLC**
See also CA 104; 123; SATA 26

Tomasi di Lampedusa, Giuseppe 1896-1957
See Lampedusa, Giuseppe (Tomasi) di
See also CA 111

Tomlin, Lily   CLC 17
See also Tomlin, Mary Jean

Tomlin, Mary Jean 1939(?)-
See Tomlin, Lily
See also CA 117

**Tomlinson, (Alfred) Charles 1927-CLC 2, 4, 6,
   13, 45; DAM POET; PC 17**
See also CA 5-8R; CANR 33; DLB 40

**Tomlinson, H(enry) M(ajor) 1873-1958TCLC
   71**
See also CA 118; 161; DLB 36, 100, 195

Tonson, Jacob
See Bennett, (Enoch) Arnold

Toole, John Kennedy 1937-1969 CLC 19, 64
See also CA 104; DLBY 81; MTCW 1

**Toomer, Jean 1894-1967CLC 1, 4, 13, 22; BLC
   3; DAM MULT; PC 7; SSC 1; WLCS**
See also BW 1; CA 85-88; CDALB 1917-1929;
   DLB 45, 51; MTCW 1, 2

Torley, Luke
See Blish, James (Benjamin)

Tornimparte, Alessandra
See Ginzburg, Natalia

Torre, Raoul della
See Mencken, H(enry) L(ouis)

Torrey, E(dwin) Fuller 1937-   CLC 34
See also CA 119; CANR 71

Torsvan, Ben Traven
See Traven, B.

Torsvan, Benno Traven

See Traven, B.

Torsvan, Berick Traven
See Traven, B.

Torsvan, Berwick Traven
See Traven, B.

Torsvan, Bruno Traven
See Traven, B.

Torsvan, Traven
See Traven, B.

**Tournier, Michel (Edouard) 1924-CLC 6, 23,
   36, 95**
See also CA 49-52; CANR 3, 36, 74; DLB 83;
   MTCW 1, 2; SATA 23

Tournimparte, Alessandra
See Ginzburg, Natalia

Towers, Ivar
See Kornbluth, C(yril) M.

Towne, Robert (Burton) 1936(?)-   CLC 87
See also CA 108; DLB 44

Townsend, Sue   CLC 61
See also Townsend, Susan Elaine
See also AAYA 28; SATA 55, 93; SATA-Brief
   48

Townsend, Susan Elaine 1946-
See Townsend, Sue
See also CA 119; 127; CANR 65; DAB; DAC;
   DAM MST

**Townshend, Peter (Dennis Blandford) 1945-
   CLC 17, 42**
See also CA 107

Tozzi, Federigo 1883-1920   TCLC 31
See also CA 160

Traill, Catharine Parr 1802-1899   NCLC 31
See also DLB 99

Trakl, Georg 1887-1914   TCLC 5;PC 20
See also CA 104; 165; MTCW 2

**Transtroemer, Tomas (Goesta) 1931-CLC 52,
   65; DAM POET**
See also CA 117; 129; CAAS 17

Transtromer, Tomas Gosta
See Transtroemer, Tomas (Goesta)

Traven, B. (?)-1969   CLC 8, 11
See also CA 19-20; 25-28R; CAP 2; DLB 9,
   56; MTCW 1

Treitel, Jonathan 1959-   CLC 70

Tremain, Rose 1943-   CLC 42
See also CA 97-100; CANR 44; DLB 14

**Tremblay, Michel 1942- CLC 29, 102; DAC;
   DAM MST**
See also CA 116; 128; DLB 60; MTCW 1, 2

Trevanian   CLC 29
See also Whitaker, Rod(ney)

Trevor, Glen
See Hilton, James

**Trevor, William 1928-CLC 7, 9, 14, 25, 71, 116;
   SSC 21**
See also Cox, William Trevor
See also DLB 14, 139; MTCW 2

**Trifonov, Yuri (Valentinovich) 1925-1981
   CLC 45**
See also CA 126; 103; MTCW 1

Trilling, Lionel 1905-1975   CLC 9, 11, 24
See also CA 9-12R; 61-64; CANR 10; DLB 28,
   63; INT CANR-10; MTCW 1, 2

Trimball, W. H.
See Mencken, H(enry) L(ouis)

Tristan
See Gomez de la Serna, Ramon

Tristram
See Housman, A(lfred) E(dward)

Trogdon, William (Lewis) 1939-
See Heat-Moon, William Least
See also CA 115; 119; CANR 47; INT 119

**Trollope, Anthony 1815-1882NCLC 6, 33; DA;
   DAB; DAC; DAM MST, NOV; SSC 28;
   WLC**
See also CDBLB 1832-1890; DLB 21, 57, 159;
   SATA 22

Trollope, Frances 1779-1863   NCLC 30
See also DLB 21, 166

Trotsky, Leon 1879-1940   TCLC 22
See also CA 118; 167

**Trotter (Cockburn), Catharine 1679-1749L C
   8**
See also DLB 84

Trout, Kilgore
See Farmer, Philip Jose

Trow, George W. S. 1943-   CLC 52
See also CA 126

Troyat, Henri 1911-   CLC 23
See also CA 45-48; CANR 2, 33, 67; MTCW 1

Trudeau, G(arretson) B(eekman) 1948-
See Trudeau, Garry B.
See also CA 81-84; CANR 31; SATA 35

Trudeau, Garry B.   CLC 12
See also Trudeau, G(arretson) B(eekman)
See also AAYA 10; AITN 2

Truffaut, Francois 1932-1984   CLC 20, 101
See also CA 81-84; 113; CANR 34

Trumbo, Dalton 1905-1976   CLC 19
See also CA 21-24R; 69-72; CANR 10; DLB
   26

Trumbull, John 1750-1831   NCLC 30
See also DLB 31

Trundlett, Helen B.
See Eliot, T(homas) S(tearns)

**Tryon, Thomas 1926-1991   CLC 3, 11;DAM
   POP**
See also AITN 1; CA 29-32R; 135; CANR 32,
   77; MTCW 1

Tryon, Tom
See Tryon, Thomas

Ts'ao Hsueh-ch'in 1715(?)-1763   LC 1

Tsushima, Shuji 1909-1948
See Dazai Osamu
See also CA 107

**Tsvetaeva (Efron), Marina (Ivanovna) 1892-
   1941   TCLC 7, 35; PC 14**
See also CA 104; 128; CANR 73; MTCW 1, 2

Tuck, Lily 1938-   CLC 70
See also CA 139

Tu Fu 712-770   PC 9
See also DAM MULT

Tunis, John R(oberts) 1889-1975   CLC 12
See also CA 61-64; CANR 62; DLB 22, 171;
   JRDA; MAICYA; SATA 37; SATA-Brief 30

Tuohy, Frank   CLC 37
See also Tuohy, John Francis
See also DLB 14, 139

Tuohy, John Francis 1925-1999
See Tuohy, Frank
See also CA 5-8R; 178; CANR 3, 47

Turco, Lewis (Putnam) 1934-   CLC 11, 63
See also CA 13-16R; CAAS 22; CANR 24, 51;
   DLBY 84

**Turgenev, Ivan 1818-1883   NCLC 21; DA;
   DAB; DAC; DAM MST, NOV; DC 7; SSC
   7; WLC**

**Turgot, Anne-Robert-Jacques 1727-1781 L C
   26**

Turner, Frederick 1943-   CLC 48
See also CA 73-76; CAAS 10; CANR 12, 30,
   56; DLB 40

**Tutu, Desmond M(pilo) 1931-CLC 80; BLC 3;
   DAM MULT**
See also BW 1, 3; CA 125; CANR 67, 81

Tutuola, Amos 1920-1997**CLC 5, 14, 29; BLC 3; DAM MULT**
See also BW 2, 3; CA 9-12R; 159; CANR 27, 66; DLB 125; MTCW 1, 2

Twain, Mark **TCLC 6, 12, 19, 36, 48, 59; SSC 34; WLC**
See also Clemens, Samuel Langhorne
See also AAYA 20; CLR 58; DLB 11, 12, 23, 64, 74

Tyler, Anne 1941- **CLC 7, 11, 18, 28, 44, 59, 103; DAM NOV, POP**
See also AAYA 18; BEST 89:1; CA 9-12R; CANR 11, 33, 53; CDALBS; DLB 6, 143; DLBY 82; MTCW 1, 2; SATA 7, 90

Tyler, Royall 1757-1826 **NCLC 3**
See also DLB 37

Tynan, Katharine 1861-1931 **TCLC 3**
See also CA 104; 167; DLB 153

Tyutchev, Fyodor 1803-1873 **NCLC 34**

Tzara, Tristan 1896-1963 **CLC 47; DAM POET; PC 27**
See also CA 153; 89-92; MTCW 2

Uhry, Alfred 1936- **CLC 55; DAM DRAM, POP**
See also CA 127; 133; INT 133

Ulf, Haerved
See Strindberg, (Johan) August

Ulf, Harved
See Strindberg, (Johan) August

Ulibarri, Sabine R(eyes) 1919-**CLC 83; DAM MULT; HLCS 2**
See also CA 131; CANR 81; DLB 82; HW 1, 2

Unamuno (y Jugo), Miguel de 1864-1936 **TCLC 2, 9; DAM MULT, NOV; HLC 2; SSC 11**
See also CA 104; 131; CANR 81; DLB 108; HW 1, 2; MTCW 1, 2

Undercliffe, Errol
See Campbell, (John) Ramsey

Underwood, Miles
See Glassco, John

Undset, Sigrid 1882-1949**TCLC 3; DA; DAB; DAC; DAM MST, NOV; WLC**
See also CA 104; 129; MTCW 1, 2

Ungaretti, Giuseppe 1888-1970**CLC 7, 11, 15**
See also CA 19-20; 25-28R; CAP 2; DLB 114

Unger, Douglas 1952- **CLC 34**
See also CA 130

Unsworth, Barry (Forster) 1930- **CLC 76**
See also CA 25-28R; CANR 30, 54; DLB 194

Updike, John (Hoyer) 1932-**CLC 1, 2, 3, 5, 7, 9, 13, 15, 23, 34, 43, 70; DA; DAB; DAC; DAM MST, NOV, POET, POP; SSC 13, 27; WLC**
See also CA 1-4R; CABS 1; CANR 4, 33, 51; CDALB 1968-1988; DLB 2, 5, 143; DLBD 3; DLBY 80, 82, 97; MTCW 1, 2

Upshaw, Margaret Mitchell
See Mitchell, Margaret (Munnerlyn)

Upton, Mark
See Sanders, Lawrence

Upward, Allen 1863-1926 **TCLC 85**
See also CA 117; DLB 36

Urdang, Constance (Henriette) 1922-**CLC 47**
See also CA 21-24R; CANR 9, 24

Uriel, Henry
See Faust, Frederick (Schiller)

Uris, Leon (Marcus) 1924- **CLC 7, 32; DAM NOV, POP**
See also AITN 1, 2; BEST 89:2; CA 1-4R; CANR 1, 40, 65; MTCW 1, 2; SATA 49

Urista, Alberto H. 1947-
See Alurista

See also CA 45-48; CANR 2, 32; HLCS 1; HW 1

Urmuz
See Codrescu, Andrei

Urquhart, Jane 1949- **CLC 90; DAC**
See also CA 113; CANR 32, 68

Usigli, Rodolfo 1905-1979
See also CA 131; HLCS 1; HW 1

Ustinov, Peter (Alexander) 1921- **CLC 1**
See also AITN 1; CA 13-16R; CANR 25, 51; DLB 13; MTCW 2

U Tam'si, Gerald Felix Tchicaya
See Tchicaya, Gerald Felix

U Tam'si, Tchicaya
See Tchicaya, Gerald Felix

Vachss, Andrew (Henry) 1942- **CLC 106**
See also CA 118; CANR 44

Vachss, Andrew H.
See Vachss, Andrew (Henry)

Vaculik, Ludvik 1926- **CLC 7**
See also CA 53-56; CANR 72

Vaihinger, Hans 1852-1933 **TCLC 71**
See also CA 116; 166

Valdez, Luis (Miguel) 1940- **CLC 84; DAM MULT; DC 10; HLC 2**
See also CA 101; CANR 32, 81; DLB 122; HW 1

Valenzuela, Luisa 1938- **CLC 31, 104; DAM MULT; HLCS 2; SSC 14**
See also CA 101; CANR 32, 65; DLB 113; HW 1, 2

Valera y Alcala-Galiano, Juan 1824-1905 **TCLC 10**
See also CA 106

Valery, (Ambroise) Paul (Toussaint Jules) 1871-1945 **TCLC 4, 15; DAM POET; PC 9**
See also CA 104; 122; MTCW 1, 2

Valle-Inclan, Ramon (Maria) del 1866-1936 **TCLC 5; DAM MULT; HLC 2**
See also CA 106; 153; CANR 80; DLB 134; HW 2

Vallejo, Antonio Buero
See Buero Vallejo, Antonio

Vallejo, Cesar (Abraham) 1892-1938**TCLC 3, 56; DAM MULT; HLC 2**
See also CA 105; 153; HW 1

Valles, Jules 1832-1885 **NCLC 71**
See also DLB 123

Vallette, Marguerite Eymery
See Rachilde

Valle Y Pena, Ramon del
See Valle-Inclan, Ramon (Maria) del

Van Ash, Cay 1918- **CLC 34**

Vanbrugh, Sir John 1664-1726 **LC 21; DAM DRAM**
See also DLB 80

Van Campen, Karl
See Campbell, John W(ood, Jr.)

Vance, Gerald
See Silverberg, Robert

Vance, Jack **CLC 35**
See also Kuttner, Henry; Vance, John Holbrook
See also DLB 8

Vance, John Holbrook 1916-
See Queen, Ellery; Vance, Jack
See also CA 29-32R; CANR 17, 65; MTCW 1

Van Den Bogarde, Derek Jules Gaspard Ulric Niven 1921-1999
See Bogarde, Dirk
See also CA 77-80; 179

Vandenburgh, Jane **CLC 59**
See also CA 168

Vanderhaeghe, Guy 1951- **CLC 41**

See also CA 113; CANR 72

van der Post, Laurens (Jan) 1906-1996**CLC 5**
See also CA 5-8R; 155; CANR 35; DLB 204

van de Wetering, Janwillem 1931- **CLC 47**
See also CA 49-52; CANR 4, 62

Van Dine, S. S. **TCLC 23**
See also Wright, Willard Huntington

Van Doren, Carl (Clinton) 1885-1950 **TCLC 18**
See also CA 111; 168

Van Doren, Mark 1894-1972 **CLC 6, 10**
See also CA 1-4R; 37-40R; CANR 3; DLB 45; MTCW 1, 2

Van Druten, John (William) 1901-1957**TCLC 2**
See also CA 104; 161; DLB 10

Van Duyn, Mona (Jane) 1921- **CLC 3, 7, 63, 116; DAM POET**
See also CA 9-12R; CANR 7, 38, 60; DLB 5

Van Dyne, Edith
See Baum, L(yman) Frank

van Itallie, Jean-Claude 1936- **CLC 3**
See also CA 45-48; CAAS 2; CANR 1, 48; DLB 7

van Ostaijen, Paul 1896-1928 **TCLC 33**
See also CA 163

Van Peebles, Melvin 1932- **CLC 2, 20; DAM MULT**
See also BW 2, 3; CA 85-88; CANR 27, 67, 82

Vansittart, Peter 1920- **CLC 42**
See also CA 1-4R; CANR 3, 49

Van Vechten, Carl 1880-1964 **CLC 33**
See also CA 89-92; DLB 4, 9, 51

Van Vogt, A(lfred) E(lton) 1912- **CLC 1**
See also CA 21-24R; CANR 28; DLB 8; SATA 14

Varda, Agnes 1928- **CLC 16**
See also CA 116; 122

Vargas Llosa, (Jorge) Mario (Pedro) 1936- **CLC 3, 6, 9, 10, 15, 31, 42, 85; DA; DAB; DAC; DAM MST, MULT, NOV;HLC 2**
See also CA 73-76; CANR 18, 32, 42, 67; DLB 145; HW 1, 2; MTCW 1, 2

Vasiliu, Gheorghe 1881-1957
See Bacovia, George
See also CA 123

Vassa, Gustavus
See Equiano, Olaudah

Vassilikos, Vassilis 1933- **CLC 4, 8**
See also CA 81-84; CANR 75

Vaughan, Henry 1621-1695 **LC 27**
See also DLB 131

Vaughn, Stephanie **CLC 62**

Vazov, Ivan (Minchov) 1850-1921 **TCLC 25**
See also CA 121; 167; DLB 147

Veblen, Thorstein B(unde) 1857-1929 **TCLC 31**
See also CA 115; 165

Vega, Lope de 1562-1635 **LC 23; HLCS 2**

Venison, Alfred
See Pound, Ezra (Weston Loomis)

Verdi, Marie de
See Mencken, H(enry) L(ouis)

Verdu, Matilde
See Cela, Camilo Jose

Verga, Giovanni (Carmelo) 1840-1922 **TCLC 3; SSC 21**
See also CA 104; 123

Vergil 70B.C.-19B.C. **CMLC 9; DA; DAB; DAC; DAM MST, POET; PC 12; WLCS**
See also Virgil

Verhaeren, Emile (Adolphe Gustave) 1855-1916 **TCLC 12**

See also CA 109

Verlaine, Paul (Marie) 1844-1896 **NCLC 2, 51;**
DAM POET; PC 2

Verne, Jules (Gabriel) 1828-1905 **TCLC 6, 52**
See also AAYA 16; CA 110; 131; DLB 123;
JRDA; MAICYA; SATA 21

Very, Jones 1813-1880 **NCLC 9**
See also DLB 1

Vesaas, Tarjei 1897-1970 **CLC 48**
See also CA 29-32R

Vialis, Gaston
See Simenon, Georges (Jacques Christian)

Vian, Boris 1920-1959 **TCLC 9**
See also CA 106; 164; DLB 72; MTCW 2

Viaud, (Louis Marie) Julien 1850-1923
See Loti, Pierre
See also CA 107

Vicar, Henry
See Felsen, Henry Gregor

Vicker, Angus
See Felsen, Henry Gregor

Vidal, Gore 1925- **CLC 2, 4, 6, 8, 10, 22, 33, 72;**
DAM NOV, POP
See also AITN 1; BEST 90:2; CA 5-8R; CANR
13, 45, 65; CDALBS; DLB 6, 152; INT
CANR-13; MTCW 1, 2

Viereck, Peter (Robert Edwin) 1916- **CLC 4;**
PC 27
See also CA 1-4R; CANR 1, 47; DLB 5

Vigny, Alfred (Victor) de 1797-1863 **NCLC 7;**
DAM POET; PC 26
See also DLB 119, 192

Vilakazi, Benedict Wallet 1906-1947 **TCLC 37**
See also CA 168

Villa, Jose Garcia 1904-1997 **PC 22**
See also CA 25-28R; CANR 12

Villarreal, Jose Antonio 1924-
See also CA 133; DAM MULT; DLB 82; HLC
2; HW 1

Villaurrutia, Xavier 1903-1950 **TCLC 80**
See also HW 1

Villiers de l'Isle Adam, Jean Marie Mathias
Philippe Auguste, Comte de 1838-1889
NCLC 3; SSC 14
See also DLB 123

Villon, Francois 1431-1463(?) **PC 13**
See also DLB 208

Vinci, Leonardo da 1452-1519 **LC 12**

Vine, Barbara **CLC 50**
See also Rendell, Ruth(Barbara)
See also BEST 90:4

Vinge, Joan (Carol) D(ennison) 1948- **CLC 30;**
SSC 24
See also CA 93-96; CANR 72; SATA 36

Violis, G.
See Simenon, Georges (Jacques Christian)

Viramontes, Helena Maria 1954-
See also CA 159; DLB 122; HLCS 2; HW 2

Virgil 70B.C.-19B.C.
See Vergil
See also DLB 211

Visconti, Luchino 1906-1976 **CLC 16**
See also CA 81-84; 65-68; CANR 39

Vittorini, Elio 1908-1966 **CLC 6, 9, 14**
See also CA 133; 25-28R

Vivekananda, Swami 1863-1902 **TCLC 88**

Vizenor, Gerald Robert 1934- **CLC 103; DAM**
MULT
See also CA 13-16R; CAAS 22; CANR 5, 21,
44, 67; DLB 175; MTCW 2; NNAL

Vizinczey, Stephen 1933- **CLC 40**
See also CA 128; INT 128

Vliet, R(ussell) G(ordon) 1929-1984 **CLC 22**

See also CA 37-40R; 112; CANR 18

Vogau, Boris Andreyevich 1894-1937(?)
See Pilnyak, Boris
See also CA 123

Vogel, Paula A(nne) 1951- **CLC 76**
See also CA 108

Voigt, Cynthia 1942- **CLC 30**
See also AAYA 3, 30; CA 106; CANR 18, 37,
40; CLR 13, 48; INT CANR-18; JRDA;
MAICYA; SATA 48, 79; SATA-Brief 33

Voigt, Ellen Bryant 1943- **CLC 54**
See also CA 69-72; CANR 11, 29, 55; DLB 120

Voinovich, Vladimir (Nikolaevich) 1932- **CLC**
10, 49
See also CA 81-84; CAAS 12; CANR 33, 67;
MTCW 1

Vollmann, William T. 1959- **CLC 89; DAM**
NOV, POP
See also CA 134; CANR 67; MTCW 2

Voloshinov, V. N.
See Bakhtin, Mikhail Mikhailovich

Voltaire 1694-1778 **LC 14; DA; DAB; DAC;**
DAM DRAM, MST; SSC 12; WLC

von Aschendrof, Baron Ignatz
See Ford, Ford Madox

von Daeniken, Erich 1935- **CLC 30**
See also AITN 1; CA 37-40R; CANR 17, 44

von Daniken, Erich
See von Daeniken, Erich

von Heidenstam, (Carl Gustaf) Verner
See Heidenstam, (Carl Gustaf) Verner von

von Heyse, Paul (Johann Ludwig)
See Heyse, Paul (Johann Ludwig von)

von Hofmannsthal, Hugo
See Hofmannsthal, Hugo von

von Horvath, Odon
See Horvath, Oedoen von

von Horvath, Oedoen
See Horvath, Oedoen von

von Liliencron, (Friedrich Adolf Axel) Detlev
See Liliencron, (Friedrich Adolf Axel) Detlev
von

Vonnegut, Kurt, Jr. 1922- **CLC 1, 2, 3, 4, 5, 8,**
12, 22, 40, 60, 111; DA; DAB; DAC; DAM
MST, NOV, POP; SSC 8; WLC
See also AAYA 6; AITN 1; BEST 90:4; CA 1-
4R; CANR 1, 25, 49, 75; CDALB 1968-
1988; DLB 2, 8, 152; DLBD 3; DLBY 80;
MTCW 1, 2

Von Rachen, Kurt
See Hubbard, L(afayette) Ron(ald)

von Rezzori (d'Arezzo), Gregor
See Rezzori (d'Arezzo), Gregor von

von Sternberg, Josef
See Sternberg, Josef von

Vorster, Gordon 1924- **CLC 34**
See also CA 133

Vosce, Trudie
See Ozick, Cynthia

Voznesensky, Andrei (Andreievich) 1933-
CLC 1, 15, 57; DAM POET
See also CA 89-92; CANR 37; MTCW 1

Waddington, Miriam 1917- **CLC 28**
See also CA 21-24R; CANR 12, 30; DLB 68

Wagman, Fredrica 1937- **CLC 7**
See also CA 97-100; INT 97-100

Wagner, Linda W.
See Wagner-Martin, Linda (C.)

Wagner, Linda Welshimer
See Wagner-Martin, Linda (C.)

Wagner, Richard 1813-1883 **NCLC 9**
See also DLB 129

Wagner-Martin, Linda (C.) 1936- **CLC 50**

See also CA 159

Wagoner, David (Russell) 1926- **CLC 3, 5, 15**
See also CA 1-4R; CAAS 3; CANR 2, 71; DLB
5; SATA 14

Wah, Fred(erick James) 1939- **CLC 44**
See also CA 107; 141; DLB 60

Wahloo, Per 1926-1975 **CLC 7**
See also CA 61-64; CANR 73

Wahloo, Peter
See Wahloo, Per

Wain, John (Barrington) 1925-1994 **CLC 2,**
11, 15, 46
See also CA 5-8R; 145; CAAS 4; CANR 23,
54; CDBLB 1960 to Present; DLB 15, 27,
139, 155; MTCW 1, 2

Wajda, Andrzej 1926- **CLC 16**
See also CA 102

Wakefield, Dan 1932- **CLC 7**
See also CA 21-24R; CAAS 7

Wakoski, Diane 1937- **CLC 2, 4, 7, 9, 11, 40;**
DAM POET; PC 15
See also CA 13-16R; CAAS 1; CANR 9, 60;
DLB 5; INT CANR-9; MTCW 2

Wakoski-Sherbell, Diane
See Wakoski, Diane

Walcott, Derek (Alton) 1930- **CLC 2, 4, 9, 14,**
25, 42, 67, 76; BLC 3; DAB; DAC; DAM
MST, MULT, POET; DC 7
See also BW 2; CA 89-92; CANR 26, 47, 75,
80; DLB 117; DLBY 81; MTCW 1, 2

Waldman, Anne (Lesley) 1945- **CLC 7**
See also CA 37-40R; CAAS 17; CANR 34, 69;
DLB 16

Waldo, E. Hunter
See Sturgeon, Theodore (Hamilton)

Waldo, Edward Hamilton
See Sturgeon, Theodore (Hamilton)

Walker, Alice (Malsenior) 1944- **CLC 5, 6, 9,**
19, 27, 46, 58, 103; BLC 3; DA; DAB;
DAC; DAM MST, MULT, NOV, POET,
POP; SSC 5; WLCS
See also AAYA 3; BEST 89:4; BW 2, 3; CA
37-40R; CANR 9, 27, 49, 66, 82; CDALB
1968-1988; DLB 6, 33, 143; INT CANR-27;
MTCW 1, 2; SATA 31

Walker, David Harry 1911-1992 **CLC 14**
See also CA 1-4R; 137; CANR 1; SATA 8;
SATA-Obit 71

Walker, Edward Joseph 1934-
See Walker, Ted
See also CA 21-24R; CANR 12, 28, 53

Walker, George F. 1947- **CLC 44, 61; DAB;**
DAC; DAM MST
See also CA 103; CANR 21, 43, 59; DLB 60

Walker, Joseph A. 1935- **CLC 19; DAM**
DRAM, MST
See also BW 1, 3; CA 89-92; CANR 26; DLB
38

Walker, Margaret (Abigail) 1915-1998 **CLC 1,**
6; BLC; DAM MULT; PC 20
See also BW 2, 3; CA 73-76; 172; CANR 26,
54, 76; DLB 76, 152; MTCW 1, 2

Walker, Ted **CLC 13**
See also Walker, Edward Joseph
See also DLB 40

Wallace, David Foster 1962- **CLC 50, 114**
See also CA 132; CANR 59; MTCW 2

Wallace, Dexter
See Masters, Edgar Lee

Wallace, (Richard Horatio) Edgar 1875-1932
TCLC 57
See also CA 115; DLB 70

Wallace, Irving 1916-1990 **CLC 7, 13; DAM**

Wells, Rosemary 1943-   **CLC 12**
    See also AAYA 13; CA 85-88; CANR 48; CLR
    16; MAICYA; SAAS 1; SATA 18, 69
Welty, Eudora 1909-   **CLC 1, 2, 5, 14, 22, 33,**
    105; DA; DAB; DAC; DAM MST, NOV;
    SSC 1, 27; WLC
    See also CA 9-12R; CABS 1; CANR 32, 65;
    CDALB 1941-1968; DLB 2, 102, 143;
    DLBD 12; DLBY 87; MTCW 1, 2
Wen I-to 1899-1946   **TCLC 28**
Wentworth, Robert
    See Hamilton, Edmond
Werfel, Franz (Viktor) 1890-1945   **TCLC 8**
    See also CA 104; 161; DLB 81, 124
Wergeland, Henrik Arnold 1808-1845 **N C L C**
    5
Wersba, Barbara 1932-   **CLC 30**
    See also AAYA 2, 30; CA 29-32R; CANR 16,
    38; CLR 3; DLB 52; JRDA; MAICYA; SAAS
    2; SATA 1, 58; SATA-Essay 103
Wertmueller, Lina 1928-   **CLC 16**
    See also CA 97-100; CANR 39, 78
Wescott, Glenway 1901-1987 **CLC 13;SSC 35**
    See also CA 13-16R; 121; CANR 23, 70; DLB
    4, 9, 102
Wesker, Arnold 1932-   **CLC 3, 5, 42; DAB;**
    DAM DRAM
    See also CA 1-4R; CAAS 7; CANR 1, 33;
    CDBLB 1960 to Present; DLB 13; MTCW 1
Wesley, Richard (Errol) 1945-   **CLC 7**
    See also BW 1; CA 57-60; CANR 27; DLB 38
Wessel, Johan Herman 1742-1785   **LC 7**
West, Anthony (Panther) 1914-1987 **CLC 50**
    See also CA 45-48; 124; CANR 3, 19; DLB 15
West, C. P.
    See Wodehouse, P(elham) G(renville)
West, (Mary) Jessamyn 1902-1984 **CLC 7, 17**
    See also CA 9-12R; 112; CANR 27; DLB 6;
    DLBY 84; MTCW 1, 2; SATA-Obit 37
West, Morris L(anglo) 1916-   **CLC 6, 33**
    See also CA 5-8R; CANR 24, 49, 64; MTCW
    1, 2
West, Nathanael 1903-1940   **TCLC 1, 14, 44;**
    SSC 16
    See also CA 104; 125; CDALB 1929-1941;
    DLB 4, 9, 28; MTCW 1, 2
West, Owen
    See Koontz, Dean R(ay)
West, Paul 1930-   **CLC 7, 14, 96**
    See also CA 13-16R; CAAS 7; CANR 22, 53,
    76; DLB 14; INT CANR-22; MTCW 2
West, Rebecca 1892-1983   **CLC 7, 9, 31, 50**
    See also CA 5-8R; 109; CANR 19; DLB 36;
    DLBY 83; MTCW 1, 2
Westall, Robert (Atkinson) 1929-1993 **CLC 17**
    See also AAYA 12; CA 69-72; 141; CANR 18,
    68; CLR 13; JRDA; MAICYA; SAAS 2;
    SATA 23, 69; SATA-Obit 75
Westermarck, Edward 1862-1939 **TCLC 87**
Westlake, Donald E(dwin) 1933-   **CLC 7, 33;**
    DAM POP
    See also CA 17-20R; CAAS 13; CANR 16, 44,
    65; INT CANR-16; MTCW 2
Westmacott, Mary
    See Christie, Agatha (Mary Clarissa)
Weston, Allen
    See Norton, Andre
Wetcheek, J. L.
    See Feuchtwanger, Lion
Wetering, Janwillem van de
    See van de Wetering, Janwillem
Wetherald, Agnes Ethelwyn 1857-1940 **T C L C**
    81

See also DLB 99
Wetherell, Elizabeth
    See Warner, Susan (Bogert)
Whale, James 1889-1957   **TCLC 63**
Whalen, Philip 1923-   **CLC 6, 29**
    See also CA 9-12R; CANR 5, 39; DLB 16
Wharton, Edith (Newbold Jones) 1862-1937
    TCLC 3, 9, 27, 53; DA; DAB; DAC; DAM
    MST, NOV; SSC 6; WLC
    See also AAYA 25; CA 104; 132; CDALB 1865-
    1917; DLB 4, 9, 12, 78, 189; DLBD 13;
    MTCW 1, 2
Wharton, James
    See Mencken, H(enry) L(ouis)
Wharton, William (a pseudonym) **CLC 18, 37**
    See also CA 93-96; DLBY 80; INT 93-96
Wheatley (Peters), Phillis 1754(?)-1784 **L C 3,**
    50; BLC 3; DA; DAC; DAMMST, MULT,
    POET; PC 3; WLC
    See also CDALB 1640-1865; DLB 31, 50
Wheelock, John Hall 1886-1978   **CLC 14**
    See also CA 13-16R; 77-80; CANR 14; DLB
    45
White, E(lwyn) B(rooks) 1899-1985 **CLC 10,**
    34, 39; DAM POP
    See also AITN 2; CA 13-16R; 116; CANR 16,
    37; CDALBS; CLR 1, 21; DLB 11, 22;
    MAICYA; MTCW 1, 2; SATA 2, 29, 100;
    SATA-Obit 44
White, Edmund (Valentine III) 1940- **CLC 27,**
    110; DAM POP
    See also AAYA 7; CA 45-48; CANR 3, 19, 36,
    62; MTCW 1, 2
White, Patrick (Victor Martindale) 1912-1990
    CLC 3, 4, 5, 7, 9, 18, 65, 69
    See also CA 81-84; 132; CANR 43; MTCW 1
White, Phyllis Dorothy James 1920-
    See James, P. D.
    See also CA 21-24R; CANR 17, 43, 65; DAM
    POP; MTCW 1, 2
White, T(erence)H(anbury) 1906-1964   **C L C**
    30
    See also AAYA 22; CA 73-76; CANR 37; DLB
    160; JRDA; MAICYA; SATA 12
White, Terence deVere 1912-1994   **CLC 49**
    See also CA 49-52; 145; CANR 3
White, Walter
    See White, Walter F(rancis)
    See also BLC; DAM MULT
White, Walter F(rancis) 1893-1955 **TCLC 15**
    See also White, Walter
    See also BW 1; CA 115; 124; DLB 51
White, William Hale 1831-1913
    See Rutherford, Mark
    See also CA 121
Whitehead, E(dward) A(nthony) 1933- **CLC 5**
    See also CA 65-68; CANR 58
Whitemore, Hugh (John) 1936-   **CLC 37**
    See also CA 132; CANR 77; INT 132
Whitman, Sarah Helen (Power) 1803-1878
    NCLC 19
    See also DLB 1
Whitman, Walt(er) 1819-1892   **NCLC 4, 31;**
    DA; DAB; DAC; DAM MST, POET; PC
    3; WLC
    See also CDALB 1640-1865; DLB 3, 64; SATA
    20
Whitney, Phyllis A(yame) 1903-   **CLC 42;**
    DAM POP
    See also AITN 2; BEST 90:3; CA 1-4R; CANR
    3, 25, 38, 60; CLR 59; JRDA; MAICYA;
    MTCW 2; SATA 1, 30
Whittemore, (Edward) Reed (Jr.) 1919- **CLC 4**

See also CA 9-12R; CAAS 8; CANR 4; DLB 5
Whittier, John Greenleaf 1807-1892 **NCLC 8,**
    59
    See also DLB 1
Whittlebot, Hernia
    See Coward, Noel (Peirce)
Wicker, Thomas Grey 1926-
    See Wicker, Tom
    See also CA 65-68; CANR 21, 46
Wicker, Tom   **CLC 7**
    See also Wicker, Thomas Grey
Wideman, John Edgar 1941- **CLC 5, 34, 36, 67,**
    122; BLC 3; DAM MULT
    See also BW 2, 3; CA 85-88; CANR 14, 42,
    67; DLB 33, 143; MTCW 2
Wiebe, Rudy (Henry) 1934-   **CLC 6, 11, 14;**
    DAC; DAM MST
    See also CA 37-40R; CANR 42, 67; DLB 60
Wieland, Christoph Martin 1733-1813 **N C L C**
    17
    See also DLB 97
Wiene, Robert 1881-1938   **TCLC 56**
Wieners, John 1934-   **CLC 7**
    See also CA 13-16R; DLB 16
Wiesel, Elie(zer) 1928- **CLC 3, 5, 11, 37; DA;**
    DAB; DAC; DAM MST, NOV; WLCS
    See also AAYA 7; AITN 1; CA 5-8R; CAAS 4;
    CANR 8, 40, 65; CDALBS; DLB 83; DLBY
    87; INT CANR-8; MTCW 1, 2; SATA 56
Wiggins, Marianne 1947-   **CLC 57**
    See also BEST 89:3; CA 130; CANR 60
Wight, James Alfred 1916-1995
    See Herriot, James
    See also CA 77-80; SATA 55; SATA-Brief 44
Wilbur, Richard (Purdy) 1921- **CLC 3, 6, 9, 14,**
    53, 110; DA; DAB; DAC; DAM MST,
    POET
    See also CA 1-4R; CABS 2; CANR 2, 29, 76;
    CDALBS; DLB 5, 169; INT CANR-29;
    MTCW 1, 2; SATA 9, 108
Wild, Peter 1940-   **CLC 14**
    See also CA 37-40R; DLB 5
Wilde, Oscar 1854(?)-1900 **TCLC 1, 8, 23, 41;**
    DA; DAB; DAC; DAM DRAM, MST,
    NOV; SSC 11; WLC
    See also CA 104; 119; CDBLB 1890-1914;
    DLB 10, 19, 34, 57, 141, 156, 190; SATA 24
Wilder, Billy   **CLC 20**
    See also Wilder, Samuel
    See also DLB 26
Wilder, Samuel 1906-
    See Wilder, Billy
    See also CA 89-92
Wilder, Thornton (Niven) 1897-1975 **CLC 1, 5,**
    6, 10, 15, 35, 82; DA; DAB; DAC; DAM
    DRAM, MST, NOV; DC 1; WLC
    See also AAYA 29; AITN 2; CA 13-16R; 61-
    64; CANR 40; CDALBS; DLB 4, 7, 9; DLBY
    97; MTCW 1, 2
Wilding, Michael 1942-   **CLC 73**
    See also CA 104; CANR 24, 49
Wiley, Richard 1944-   **CLC 44**
    See also CA 121; 129; CANR 71
Wilhelm, Kate   **CLC 7**
    See also Wilhelm, KatieGertrude
    See also AAYA 20; CAAS 5; DLB 8; INT
    CANR-17
Wilhelm, Katie Gertrude 1928-
    See Wilhelm, Kate
    See also CA 37-40R; CANR 17, 36, 60; MTCW
    1
Wilkins, Mary
    See Freeman, Mary Eleanor Wilkins

Willard, Nancy 1936-   **CLC 7, 37**
See also CA 89-92; CANR 10, 39, 68; CLR 5;
DLB 5, 52; MAICYA; MTCW 1; SATA 37,
71; SATA-Brief 30

William of Ockham 1285-1347   **CMLC 32**

Williams, Ben Ames 1889-1953   **TCLC 89**
See also DLB 102

Williams, C(harles) K(enneth) 1936-**CLC 33,
56; DAM POET**
See also CA 37-40R; CAAS 26; CANR 57; DLB
5

Williams, Charles
See Collier, James L(incoln)

Williams, Charles (Walter Stansby) 1886-1945
TCLC 1, 11
See also CA 104; 163; DLB 100, 153

Williams, (George) Emlyn 1905-1987**CLC 15;
DAM DRAM**
See also CA 104; 123; CANR 36; DLB 10, 77;
MTCW 1

Williams, Hank 1923-1953   **TCLC 81**

Williams, Hugo 1942-   **CLC 42**
See also CA 17-20R; CANR 45; DLB 40

Williams, J. Walker
See Wodehouse, P(elham) G(renville)

Williams, John A(lfred) 1925-**CLC 5, 13; BLC
3; DAM MULT**
See also BW 2, 3; CA 53-56; CAAS 3; CANR
6, 26, 51; DLB 2, 33; INT CANR-6

Williams, Jonathan (Chamberlain) 1929-
CLC 13
See also CA 9-12R; CAAS 12; CANR 8; DLB
5

Williams, Joy 1944-   **CLC 31**
See also CA 41-44R; CANR 22, 48

Williams, Norman 1952-   **CLC 39**
See also CA 118

Williams, Sherley Anne 1944-**CLC 89; BLC 3;
DAM MULT, POET**
See also BW 2, 3; CA 73-76; CANR 25, 82;
DLB 41; INT CANR-25; SATA 78

Williams, Shirley
See Williams, Sherley Anne

Williams, Tennessee 1911-1983**CLC 1, 2, 5, 7,
8, 11, 15, 19, 30, 39, 45, 71, 111; DA; DAB;
DAC; DAM DRAM, MST; DC 4;WLC**
See also AITN 1, 2; CA 5-8R; 108; CABS 3;
CANR 31; CDALB 1941-1968; DLB7;
DLBD 4; DLBY 83; MTCW 1, 2

Williams, Thomas (Alonzo) 1926-1990**CLC 14**
See also CA 1-4R; 132; CANR 2

Williams, William C.
See Williams, William Carlos

Williams, William Carlos 1883-1963**CLC 1, 2,
5, 9, 13, 22, 42, 67; DA; DAB; DAC; DAM
MST, POET; PC 7; SSC 31**
See also CA 89-92; CANR 34; CDALB 1917-
1929; DLB 4, 16, 54, 86; MTCW 1, 2

Williamson, David (Keith) 1942-   **CLC 56**
See also CA 103; CANR 41

Williamson, Ellen Douglas 1905-1984
See Douglas, Ellen
See also CA 17-20R; 114; CANR 39

Williamson, Jack   **CLC 29**
See also Williamson, John Stewart
See also CAAS 8; DLB 8

Williamson, John Stewart 1908-
See Williamson, Jack
See also CA 17-20R; CANR 23, 70

Willie, Frederick
See Lovecraft, H(oward) P(hillips)

Willingham, Calder (Baynard, Jr.) 1922-1995
CLC 5, 51

See also CA 5-8R; 147; CANR 3; DLB 2, 44;
MTCW 1

Willis, Charles
See Clarke, Arthur C(harles)

Willis, Fingal O'Flahertie
See Wilde, Oscar

Willy
See Colette, (Sidonie-Gabrielle)

Willy, Colette
See Colette, (Sidonie-Gabrielle)

Wilson, A(ndrew) N(orman) 1950-   **CLC 33**
See also CA 112; 122; DLB 14, 155, 194;
MTCW 2

Wilson, Angus (Frank Johnstone) 1913-1991
CLC 2, 3, 5, 25, 34; SSC 21
See also CA 5-8R; 134; CANR 21; DLB 15,
139, 155; MTCW 1, 2

Wilson, August 1945-   **CLC 39, 50, 63, 118;
BLC 3; DA; DAB; DAC; DAM DRAM,
MST, MULT; DC 2; WLCS**
See also AAYA 16; BW 2, 3; CA 115; 122;
CANR 42, 54, 76; MTCW 1, 2

Wilson, Brian 1942-   **CLC 12**

Wilson, Colin 1931-   **CLC 3, 14**
See also CA 1-4R; CAAS 5; CANR 1, 22, 33,
77; DLB 14, 194; MTCW 1

Wilson, Dirk
See Pohl, Frederik

Wilson, Edmund 1895-1972**CLC 1, 2, 3, 8, 24**
See also CA 1-4R; 37-40R; CANR 1, 46; DLB
63; MTCW 1, 2

Wilson, Ethel Davis (Bryant) 1888(?)-1980
CLC 13; DAC; DAM POET
See also CA 102; DLB 68; MTCW 1

Wilson, John 1785-1854   **NCLC 5**

Wilson, John (Anthony) Burgess 1917-1993
See Burgess, Anthony
See also CA 1-4R; 143; CANR 2, 46; DAC;
DAM NOV; MTCW 1, 2

Wilson, Lanford 1937- **CLC 7, 14, 36; DAM
DRAM**
See also CA 17-20R; CABS 3; CANR 45; DLB
7

Wilson, Robert M. 1944-   **CLC 7, 9**
See also CA 49-52; CANR 2, 41; MTCW 1

Wilson, Robert McLiam 1964-   **CLC 59**
See also CA 132

Wilson, Sloan 1920-   **CLC 32**
See also CA 1-4R; CANR 1, 44

Wilson, Snoo 1948-   **CLC 33**
See also CA 69-72

Wilson, William S(mith) 1932-   **CLC 49**
See also CA 81-84

Wilson, (Thomas)Woodrow 1856-1924**T C L C
79**
See also CA 166; DLB 47

Winchilsea, Anne (Kingsmill) Finch Counte
1661-1720
See Finch, Anne

Windham, Basil
See Wodehouse, P(elham) G(renville)

Wingrove, David (John) 1954-   **CLC 68**
See also CA 133

Winnemucca, Sarah 1844-1891   **NCLC 79**

Winstanley, Gerrard 1609-1676   **LC 52**

Wintergreen, Jane
See Duncan, Sara Jeannette

Winters, Janet Lewis   **CLC 41**
See also Lewis, Janet
See also DLBY 87

Winters, (Arthur) Yvor 1900-1968 **CLC 4, 8,
32**
See also CA 11-12; 25-28R; CAP 1; DLB 48;

MTCW 1

Winterson, Jeanette 1959-**CLC 64;DAM POP**
See also CA 136; CANR 58; DLB 207; MTCW
2

Winthrop, John 1588-1649   **LC 31**
See also DLB 24, 30

Wirth, Louis 1897-1952   **TCLC 92**

Wiseman, Frederick 1930-   **CLC 20**
See also CA 159

Wister, Owen 1860-1938   **TCLC 21**
See also CA 108; 162; DLB 9, 78, 186; SATA
62

Witkacy
See Witkiewicz, Stanislaw Ignacy

Witkiewicz, Stanislaw Ignacy 1885-1939
TCLC 8
See also CA 105; 162

Wittgenstein, Ludwig (Josef Johann) 1889-1951
TCLC 59
See also CA 113; 164; MTCW 2

Wittig, Monique 1935(?)-   **CLC 22**
See also CA 116; 135; DLB 83

Wittlin, Jozef 1896-1976   **CLC 25**
See also CA 49-52; 65-68; CANR 3

Wodehouse, P(elham) G(renville) 1881-1975
**CLC 1, 2, 5, 10, 22; DAB; DAC; DAM
NOV; SSC 2**
See also AITN 2; CA 45-48; 57-60; CANR 3,
33; CDBLB 1914-1945; DLB 34, 162;
MTCW 1, 2; SATA 22

Woiwode, L.
See Woiwode, Larry (Alfred)

Woiwode, Larry (Alfred) 1941-   **CLC 6, 10**
See also CA 73-76; CANR 16; DLB 6; INT
CANR-16

Wojciechowska, Maia (Teresa) 1927-**CLC 26**
See also AAYA 8; CA 9-12R; CANR 4, 41; CLR
1; JRDA; MAICYA; SAAS 1; SATA 1, 28,
83; SATA-Essay 104

Wolf, Christa 1929-   **CLC 14, 29, 58**
See also CA 85-88; CANR 45; DLB 75; MTCW
1

Wolfe, Gene (Rodman) 1931- **CLC 25;DAM
POP**
See also CA 57-60; CAAS 9; CANR 6, 32, 60;
DLB 8; MTCW 2

Wolfe, George C. 1954-   **CLC 49; BLCS**
See also CA 149

Wolfe, Thomas (Clayton) 1900-1938**TCLC 4,
13, 29, 61; DA; DAB; DAC; DAM MST,
NOV; SSC 33; WLC**
See also CA 104; 132; CDALB 1929-1941;
DLB 9, 102; DLBD 2, 16; DLBY 85, 97;
MTCW 1, 2

Wolfe, Thomas Kennerly, Jr. 1930-
See Wolfe, Tom
See also CA 13-16R; CANR 9, 33, 70; DAM
POP; DLB 185; INT CANR-9; MTCW 1, 2

Wolfe, Tom   **CLC 1, 2, 9, 15, 35, 51**
See also Wolfe, Thomas Kennerly, Jr.
See also AAYA 8; AITN 2; BEST 89:1; DLB
152

Wolff, Geoffrey (Ansell) 1937-   **CLC 41**
See also CA 29-32R; CANR 29, 43, 78

Wolff, Sonia
See Levitin, Sonia (Wolff)

Wolff, Tobias (Jonathan Ansell) 1945- **C L C
39, 64**
See also AAYA 16; BEST 90:2; CA 114; 117;
CAAS 22; CANR 54, 76; DLB 130; INT 117;
MTCW 2

Wolfram von Eschenbach c. 1170-c. 1220
CMLC 5

See also DLB 138

Wolitzer, Hilma 1930-   **CLC 17**
See also CA 65-68; CANR 18, 40; INT CANR-
18; SATA 31

Wollstonecraft, Mary 1759-1797   **LC 5, 50**
See also CDBLB 1789-1832; DLB 39, 104, 158

Wonder, Stevie   **CLC 12**
See also Morris, Steveland Judkins

Wong, Jade Snow 1922-   **CLC 17**
See also CA 109

Woodberry, George Edward 1855-1930
TCLC 73
See also CA 165; DLB 71, 103

Woodcott, Keith
See Brunner, John (Kilian Houston)

Woodruff, Robert W.
See Mencken, H(enry) L(ouis)

Woolf, (Adeline) Virginia 1882-1941**TCLC 1,
5, 20, 43, 56; DA; DAB; DAC; DAM MST,
NOV; SSC 7; WLC**
See also Woolf, Virginia Adeline
See also CA 104; 130; CANR 64; CDBLB
1914-1945; DLB 36, 100, 162; DLBD 10;
MTCW 1

Woolf, Virginia Adeline
See Woolf, (Adeline) Virginia
See also MTCW 2

Woollcott, Alexander (Humphreys) 1887-1943
TCLC 5
See also CA 105; 161; DLB 29

Woolrich, Cornell 1903-1968   **CLC 77**
See also Hopley-Woolrich, Cornell George

Wordsworth, Dorothy 1771-1855   **NCLC 25**
See also DLB 107

Wordsworth, William 1770-1850 **NCLC 12,
38; DA; DAB; DAC; DAM MST, POET;
PC 4; WLC**
See also CDBLB 1789-1832; DLB 93, 107

Wouk, Herman 1915-**CLC 1, 9, 38; DAM NOV,
POP**
See also CA 5-8R; CANR 6, 33, 67; CDALBS;
DLBY 82; INT CANR-6; MTCW 1, 2

Wright, Charles (Penzel, Jr.) 1935-**CLC 6, 13,
28, 119**
See also CA 29-32R; CAAS 7; CANR 23, 36,
62; DLB 165; DLBY 82; MTCW 1, 2

Wright, Charles Stevenson 1932-   **CLC 49;
BLC 3; DAM MULT, POET**
See also BW 1; CA 9-12R; CANR 26; DLB 33

Wright, Frances 1795-1852   **NCLC 74**
See also DLB 73

Wright, Frank Lloyd 1867-1959   **TCLC 95**
See also CA 174

Wright, Jack R.
See Harris, Mark

Wright, James (Arlington) 1927-1980**CLC 3,
5, 10, 28; DAM POET**
See also AITN 2; CA 49-52; 97-100; CANR 4,
34, 64; CDALBS; DLB 5, 169; MTCW 1, 2

Wright, Judith (Arandell) 1915- **CLC 11, 53;
PC 14**
See also CA 13-16R; CANR 31, 76; MTCW 1,
2; SATA 14

Wright, L(aurali) R. 1939-   **CLC 44**
See also CA 138

Wright, Richard (Nathaniel) 1908-1960 **C L C
1, 3, 4, 9, 14, 21, 48, 74; BLC 3; DA; DAB;
DAC; DAM MST, MULT, NOV; SSC 2;
WLC**
See also AAYA 5; BW 1; CA 108; CANR
64;CDALB 1929-1941; DLB 76, 102; DLBD
2; MTCW 1, 2

Wright, Richard B(ruce) 1937-   **CLC 6**

See also CA 85-88; DLB 53

Wright, Rick 1945-   **CLC 35**

Wright, Rowland
See Wells, Carolyn

Wright, Stephen 1946-   **CLC 33**

Wright, Willard Huntington 1888-1939
See Van Dine, S. S.
See also CA 115; DLBD 16

Wright, William 1930-   **CLC 44**
See also CA 53-56; CANR 7, 23

Wroth, Lady Mary 1587-1653(?)   **LC 30**
See also DLB 121

Wu Ch'eng-en 1500(?)-1582(?)   **LC 7**

Wu Ching-tzu 1701-1754   **LC 2**

Wurlitzer, Rudolph 1938(?)-   **CLC 2, 4, 15**
See also CA 85-88; DLB 173

Wyatt, Thomas c. 1503-1542   **PC 27**
See also DLB 132

Wycherley, William 1641-1715**LC 8, 21; DAM
DRAM**
See also CDBLB 1660-1789; DLB 80

Wylie, Elinor (Morton Hoyt) 1885-1928
TCLC 8; PC 23
See also CA 105; 162; DLB 9, 45

Wylie, Philip (Gordon) 1902-1971   **CLC 43**
See also CA 21-22; 33-36R; CAP 2; DLB 9

Wyndham, John   **CLC 19**
See also Harris, John (Wyndham Parkes Lucas)
Beynon

Wyss, Johann David Von 1743-1818**NCLC 10**
See also JRDA; MAICYA; SATA 29; SATA-
Brief 27

Xenophon c. 430B.C.-c.354B.C.   **CMLC 17**
See also DLB 176

Yakumo Koizumi
See Hearn, (Patricio) Lafcadio (Tessima Carlos)

Yamamoto, Hisaye 1921-**SSC 34; DAM MULT**

Yanez, Jose Donoso
See Donoso (Yanez), Jose

Yanovsky, Basile S.
See Yanovsky, V(assily) S(emenovich)

Yanovsky, V(assily) S(emenovich) 1906-1989
CLC 2, 18
See also CA 97-100; 129

Yates, Richard 1926-1992   **CLC 7, 8, 23**
See also CA 5-8R; 139; CANR 10, 43; DLB 2;
DLBY 81, 92; INT CANR-10

Yeats, W. B.
See Yeats, William Butler

Yeats, William Butler 1865-1939**TCLC 1, 11,
18, 31, 93; DA; DAB; DAC; DAM DRAM,
MST, POET; PC 20; WLC**
See also CA 104; 127; CANR 45; CDBLB
1890-1914; DLB 10, 19, 98, 156; MTCW 1,
2

Yehoshua, A(braham) B. 1936-   **CLC 13, 31**
See also CA 33-36R; CANR 43

Yep, Laurence Michael 1948-   **CLC 35**
See also AAYA 5; CA 49-52; CANR 1, 46; CLR
3, 17, 54; DLB 52; JRDA; MAICYA; SATA
7, 69

Yerby, Frank G(arvin) 1916-1991   **CLC 1, 7,
22; BLC 3; DAM MULT**
See also BW 1, 3; CA 9-12R; 136; CANR 16,
52; DLB 76; INT CANR-16; MTCW 1

Yesenin, Sergei Alexandrovich
See Esenin, Sergei (Alexandrovich)

Yevtushenko, Yevgeny (Alexandrovich) 1933-
CLC 1, 3, 13, 26, 51; DAM POET
See also CA 81-84; CANR 33, 54; MTCW 1

Yezierska, Anzia 1885(?)-1970   **CLC 46**
See also CA 126; 89-92; DLB 28; MTCW 1

Yglesias, Helen 1915-   **CLC 7, 22**

See also CA 37-40R; CAAS 20; CANR 15, 65;
INT CANR-15; MTCW 1

Yokomitsu Riichi 1898-1947   **TCLC 47**
See also CA 170

Yonge, Charlotte(Mary) 1823-1901**TCLC 48**
See also CA 109; 163; DLB 18, 163; SATA 17

York, Jeremy
See Creasey, John

York, Simon
See Heinlein, Robert A(nson)

Yorke, Henry Vincent 1905-1974   **CLC 13**
See also Green, Henry
See also CA 85-88; 49-52

Yosano Akiko 1878-1942   **TCLC 59;PC 11**
See also CA 161

Yoshimoto, Banana   **CLC 84**
See also Yoshimoto, Mahoko

Yoshimoto, Mahoko 1964-
See Yoshimoto, Banana
See also CA 144

Young, Al(bert James) 1939-**CLC 19; BLC 3;
DAM MULT**
See also BW 2, 3; CA 29-32R; CANR 26, 65;
DLB 33

Young, Andrew(John) 1885-1971   **CLC 5**
See also CA 5-8R; CANR 7, 29

Young, Collier 1917-1994
See Bloch, Robert (Albert)
See also CA 179; CAAE 179

Young, Edward 1683-1765   **LC 3, 40**
See also DLB 95

Young, Marguerite(Vivian) 1909-1995**CLC 82**
See also CA 13-16; 150; CAP 1

Young, Neil 1945-   **CLC 17**
See also CA 110

Young Bear, Ray A. 1950-   **CLC 94;DAM
MULT**
See also CA 146; DLB 175; NNAL

Yourcenar, Marguerite 1903-1987**CLC 19, 38,
50, 87; DAM NOV**
See also CA 69-72; CANR 23, 60; DLB 72;
DLBY 88; MTCW 1, 2

Yurick, Sol 1925-   **CLC 6**
See also CA 13-16R; CANR 25

Zabolotsky, NikolaiAlekseevich 1903-1958
TCLC 52
See also CA 116; 164

Zagajewski, Adam   **PC 27**

Zamiatin, Yevgenii
See Zamyatin, Evgeny Ivanovich

Zamora, Bernice (B. Ortiz) 1938-   **CLC 89;
DAM MULT; HLC 2**
See also CA 151; CANR 80; DLB 82; HW 1, 2

Zamyatin, Evgeny Ivanovich 1884-1937
TCLC 8, 37
See also CA 105; 166

Zangwill, Israel 1864-1926   **TCLC 16**
See also CA 109; 167; DLB 10, 135, 197

Zappa, Francis Vincent, Jr. 1940-1993
See Zappa, Frank
See also CA 108; 143; CANR 57

Zappa, Frank   **CLC 17**
See also Zappa, Francis Vincent, Jr.

Zaturenska, Marya 1902-1982   **CLC 6,11**
See also CA 13-16R; 105; CANR 22

Zeami 1363-1443   **DC 7**

Zelazny, Roger(Joseph) 1937-1995   **CLC 21**
See also AAYA 7; CA 21-24R; 148; CANR 26,
60; DLB 8; MTCW 1, 2; SATA57; SATA-
Brief 39

Zhdanov, AndreiAlexandrovich 1896-1948
TCLC 18
See also CA 117; 167

Zhukovsky, Vasily(Andreevich) 1783-1852
    NCLC 35
  See also DLB 205
Ziegenhagen, Eric   **CLC 55**
Zimmer, Jill Schary
  See Robinson, Jill
Zimmerman, Robert
  See Dylan, Bob
Zindel, Paul 1936-**CLC 6, 26; DA; DAB; DAC;**
    DAM DRAM, MST, NOV; DC 5
  See also AAYA 2; CA 73-76; CANR 31, 65;
    CDALBS; CLR 3, 45; DLB 7, 52; JRDA;
    MAICYA; MTCW 1, 2; SATA 16, 58, 102
Zinov'Ev, A. A.
  See Zinoviev, Alexander (Aleksandrovich)
Zinoviev, Alexander(Aleksandrovich) 1922-
    CLC 19
  See also CA 116; 133; CAAS 10
Zoilus
  See Lovecraft, H(oward) P(hillips)
Zola, Emile (Edouard Charles Antoine) 1840-
    1902**TCLC 1, 6, 21, 41; DA; DAB; DAC;**
    DAM MST, NOV; WLC
  See also CA 104; 138; DLB 123
Zoline, Pamela 1941-   **CLC 62**
  See also CA 161
Zorrilla y Moral, Jose 1817-1893   **NCLC 6**
Zoshchenko, Mikhail (Mikhailovich) 1895-1958
    TCLC 15; SSC 15
  See also CA 115; 160
Zuckmayer, Carl 1896-1977   **CLC 18**
  See also CA 69-72; DLB 56, 124
Zuk, Georges
  See Skelton, Robin
Zukofsky, Louis 1904-1978**CLC 1, 2, 4, 7, 11,**
    18; DAM POET; PC 11
  See also CA 9-12R; 77-80; CANR 39; DLB 5,
    165; MTCW 1
Zweig, Paul 1935-1984   **CLC 34, 42**
  See also CA 85-88; 113
Zweig, Stefan 1881-1942   **TCLC 17**
  See also CA 112; 170; DLB 81, 118
Zwingli, Huldreich 1484-1531   **LC 37**
  See also DLB 179

Literary Criticism Series
Cumulative Topic Index

This index lists all topic entries in Gale's *Classical and Medieval Literature Criticism, Contemporary Literary Criticism, Literature Criticism from 1400 to 1800, Nineteenth-Century Literature Criticism,* and *Twentieth-Century Literary Criticism.*

Topic Index

Topic Index

Topic Index

Young Playwrights Festival
1988—CLC 55: 376-81
1989—CLC 59: 398-403
1990—CLC 65: 444-8

NCLC Cumulative Nationality Index

Nationality Index

ISBN 0-7876-3151-5